MARKETING MANAGEMENT

MARKETING MANAGEMENT

RICHARD P. BAGOZZI
University of Michigan

JOSÉ ANTONIO ROSA
University of Illinois–Urbana

KIRTI SAWHNEY CELLY
University of California–Irvine

FRANCISCO CORONEL
Hampton University

Prentice Hall
Upper Saddle River, New Jersey 07458

Acquisitions Editor: Whitney Blake
Developmental Editor: Trish Taylor
Assistant Editor: John Larkin
Editorial Assistant: Rachel Falk
Vice-President/Editorial Director: James Boyd
Director of Development: Stephen Deitmer
Marketing Manager: John Chillingworth
Production Editor: Aileen Mason
Production Coordinator: Carol Samet
Managing Editor: Dee Josephson
Associate Managing Editor: Linda DeLorenzo
Manufacturing Supervisor: Arnold Vila
Manufacturing Manager: Vincent Scelta
Design Manager: Pat Smythe
Interior Design: Siren Design
Cover Design: Cheryl Asherman
Illustrator (Interior): Siren Design
Production/Composition: Carlisle Communications, Ltd.
Cover Art: Matsu

Credits and acknowledgements for materials borrowed from other sources and reproduced, with permission, in this textbook appear on page C-1.

 Copyright © 1998 by Prentice-Hall, Inc.
A Simon & Schuster Company
Upper Saddle River, New Jersey 07458

Library of Congress Cataloging-in-Publication Data
Marketing management / Richard P. Bagozzi . . . [et al.].
    p.   cm.
  Includes bibliographical references and index.
  ISBN 0-02-305162-0
   1. Marketing—Management.   I. Bagozzi, Richard P.
  HF5415.13.M35223   1998
  658.8—dc21   97-36484
                                      CIP

Prentice-Hall International (UK) Limited, London
Prentice-Hall of Australia Pty. Limited, Sydney
Prentice-Hall Canada, Inc., Toronto
Prentice-Hall Hispanoamericaña, S.A., Mexico
Prentice-Hall of India Private Limited, New Delhi
Prentice-Hall of Japan, Inc., Tokyo
Simon & Schuster Asia Pte. Ltd., Singapore
Editora Prentice-Hall do Brasil, Ltda., Rio de Janeiro

Printed in the United States of America

10 9 8 7 6 5 4 3 2 1

For our families, teachers, and students.

BRIEF CONTENTS

CONTENTS

PREFACE

This book aims to bridge the gap between the science of marketing—marketing research, consumer psychology, economics, management science, strategic management—and the art of marketing—practitioners' struggle to make sound decisions in all areas of the marketing mix in the face of uncertainty and volatility. We present how and why marketing is practiced as it is, and issues managers should consider as they practice marketing in the future.

Our book is directed at traditional full-time M.B.A. programs with students who wish to pursue either practitioner or academic careers; at executive M.B.A. programs in which students generally face decisions about various areas of the marketing mix every day, and at Junior–Senior level undergraduate capstone courses that many business schools use to integrate their programs. We have special empathy with those students who take the course to gain practical knowledge, because two of us earned our M.B.A.s while working in industry. We wanted to strongly emphasize the practical applications of marketing theory so that students could see how our discussions relate directly to their business experiences. With this broader audience, our present-day students will be able to make more grounded decisions by knowing how decisions in all functional areas can benefit from marketing principles and research. The beginning of each chapter covers basic concepts and history of the discipline, either schematically or in the discussion, especially appropriate for those students who may be anxious about their relative lack of background in marketing. The end of each chapter builds to more detailed accounts of current marketing issues or dilemmas that should challenge students with a broader academic or practical background.

We all began our careers not in academia, but as practicing managers in various marketing functions and in different parts of the world. Our experiences in the business world range from product engineering at General Motors to advertising consultancy with J. Walter Thompson to management consultancy at A.F. Ferguson in India to economist at the Chicago Board of Trade to marketing and purchasing roles at General Motors. These diverse backgrounds and experiences shaped our knowledge and outlooks about marketing and set the stage for our subsequent career moves into the university.

Each of us is deeply committed to marketing education, as evidenced by our numerous teaching and research awards. Rick Bagozzi received teaching awards from the University of California at Berkeley and the University of Michigan as well as the Richard D. Irwin Distinguished Educator award, in addition to his research awards from the Association for Consumer Research and the American Marketing Association and the Maynard award for best contribution to marketing theory. Jose Rosa was recognized with the University of Illinois at Urbana-Champaign College of Commerce Weinstein Excellence Award for undergraduate teaching and development as well as the UIUC MBA Association MBA Professor of the Year. Kirti Celly teaches popular international marketing and business classes at the University of California at Irvine, and Francisco Coronel is a renowned teacher of marketing and marketing research throughout South America and Europe. All four of us have taught numerous courses in the discipline, and continue to take an active role in undergraduate and graduate teaching at our respective universities.

We quickly reached a consensus about three overarching goals as we began this project: to impart valid knowledge to students based on actual research and practitioner experience, to instill enthusiasm for the subject matter, and to build respect for the marketing function among both marketing majors and the roughly

80 percent of non-marketing majors who take this course as their only exposure to marketing topics.

This book resembles other texts in that it treats the core concepts of the marketing mix directly along the traditional lines set out by marketing scholars such as Professor Philip Kotler, to whom we owe a debt of gratitude. We do not try to create an entirely new paradigm and then force the data to fit that paradigm, as some recent textbooks are wont to do. We present these core concepts directly and in practitioners' terms, so that students can apply what they are learning directly to their business experiences. When we introduce new terms, we do so according to how contemporary discourse in the marketing discipline uses those terms, and then define and illustrate each term to facilitate learning.

In other ways, this book differs substantially from other authors' treatments of marketing as a discipline:

1. The book does not focus solely on a strategic management or quasi-economics perspective, but rather integrates the strategic approach and economic concerns with other behavioral science and business disciplines to explain the "so what" rather than merely the "what" of marketing. We include discussions about product management (chapters 7 and 8), pricing (chapter 12), advertising and promotion (chapters 9 and 10), consumer behavior and psychology (chapter 4), distribution concerns (chapters 13 and 14), and strategy and its execution (chapters 2, 16, and 17).

2. Our book creates a sense of how marketing practices and research have evolved over time, and how they are likely to change in the future.

3. Our book provides a stable learning environment that allows professors to capture the best of both traditional lecture courses and a quasi-case approach. Many instructors face a quandary in teaching this course in that they seem to have to choose between covering the theory or devoting class time to case discussions. This text allows them to address both issues, blending lectures with short class discussions about examples that illustrate concepts from the lectures. Expanded Marketing Anecdotes in each chapter tell stories of decisions that real companies and individual managers face every day, and that impact various aspects of the marketing mix. Because these illustrations integrate material from various chapters, they can act as a catalyst for detailed class discussions of the issues at hand. At the same time, our book provides structure in terms of the theoretical underpinnings of those issues in student-friendly parlance. Additional mini-cases appear in the *Instructors' Manual*.

   Look, for example, at the opening vignettes in chapters 2, 6, and 15. These integrative stories show how marketers must address current business environment issues and the strategic challenges that attend those issues. Reviewers have especially liked chapters 13 and 14 as well, as they illustrate distribution issues not only from a producer's perspective, but also from channel members' points of view. The three illustrations that open chapter 4 illustrate aspects of consumer behavior and build on these examples to present a comprehensive model that traces consumers' complex buying decision processes both internally and externally. Reviewers have been quite complimentary about this ground-breaking integration of psychological and market forces.

4. Reviewers have also praised the way the book integrates international marketing throughout the book. Not only does chapter 15 present a concise yet complete discussion of the trade-offs involved in international expansion paths, but individual chapters also address international issues involved in each area of the marketing mix.

5. Throughout the book, we emphasize research in many fields such as business environments, psychology, institutional behavior, logistics, international relations and traditional marketing research methods. The products of such research can reduce uncertainty and volatility as managers seek to make informed decisions in all marketing mix and functional areas. But we also integrate the current research with existing business practices, so that students can see how the research applies directly to business decisions.

Comment on the Book and Auxiliary Materials

Our experience shows that students consistently rate their interest in and usefulness of assigned textbooks lower than their satisfaction with the course and instructor. Through reviews, we think that many instructors would agree with this assessment. We also think that students will like our textbook better than many competitors'. Why? Because the book is student oriented. It describes and explains the subject matter thoroughly. Each chapter provides fundamental frameworks for thinking about the central ideas in that chapter. We then interweave our many examples with our presentation of basic and more advanced principles, and we integrate visual aids, anecdotes, and illustrations with the content. The ancillary package for instructors provides chapter and topic summaries, lecture outlines, syllabi, and suggestions for individual and group exercises, as well as hints for further discussions. Together with PHLIP, these materials and the text provide a rich, comprehensive learning experience that will make the course enjoyable for student and instructor alike.

Acknowledgments

We would first like to express our gratitude to the people at Prentice-Hall. Dave Borkowsky was our initial Acquisitions Editor and provided us with much support, feedback, and encouragement. Whitney Blake, our current Editor, helped us better focus the book, was a champion within Prentice Hall for the project, and in general managed our efforts with considerable skill and sensitivity. Aileen Mason, our Production Editor, made everything flow seamlessly and helped produce a first-rate presentation. We appreciate as well various suggestions made over time by John Chillingworth, Steve Deitmer, Sheila Lynch, and Sandy Steiner. To these and others we have dealt with at Prentice Hall, we are most appreciative. We also express our sincere thanks to the anonymous reviewers for their efforts and excellent recommendations, and to the focus group participants who gave us valuable positioning insights in the early stages. Finally, we would like to thank the many business people who have shared their experiences with us, allowing us to illuminate the book with many first-hand examples.

Our special thanks and kudos to Trish Taylor from Colorado State University, our Development Editor. She provided detailed editing, made many structural and pedagogical recommendations, ensured that our writing styles meshed, helped with examples and visual presentations, suggested numerous substantive changes, and in general managed the whole process with enthusiasm, skill, and insight. Her dedication to the project made a significant and irreplaceable contribution.

We are most appreciative to the authors of the *Instructors' Manual* and test bank, Anne Gogela and John Weiss (both also at Colorado State University), who have done an outstanding job capturing the essence of the text and communicating pedagogical ideas to prospective adopters. Dana Weiss prepared an excellent set of transparencies to help instructors present the material. Trish Taylor also directed and developed the ancillary package.

Finally, we wish to thank Carolyn Maguire for preparation of early drafts and the final manuscript. Carolyn worked tirelessly, discovered a number of inconsistencies and problems, and made many editorial and other suggestions. Her value system and approach to life were simply inspirational, and we feel fortunate having worked with her over the years.

Richard P. Bagozzi
José Antonio Rosa
Kirti Sawhney Celly
Francisco Coronel

CHAPTER 1

MARKETING MANAGEMENT: INTRODUCTION AND OVERVIEW

CHAPTER OBJECTIVES

When you are done with this chapter, you should have achieved the following:

- A thorough understanding of how marketing is rooted in social exchange
- Familiarity with the book's primary theme: how managers use marketing principles to make sound decisions

CHAPTER OUTLINE

Russia

After much effort and searching, an owner of a small shop that sells clothing purchased a large container of new socks from a distributor. Unfortunately, all pairs of socks were of a single size. No problem. The shopowner merely stretched them to fit five different sizes, and customers purchased all pairs in short order.

Indonesia

Economic growth has mushroomed as U.S., Japanese, and Korean firms have transferred production to this mammoth (200 million people), low-wage labor market. Government planners, however, debate the best way to achieve a market economy and ensure the long-run viability of the country after oil production declines. Some want to continue to encourage multinational companies to invest in manufacturing and thereby help the country move from a lesser developed to an industrialized society. The recent evolutions experienced by Taiwan and Korea are cited as role models.

Retailers of every size and description have to decide how to make their wares attractive to customers—that is, how to market their products. This Russian "department store" is no exception.

Others believe that Indonesia can leapfrog this state of development and instead move to an economy based on high technology, such as that found in electronics and transportation equipment. Marketing will play an essential role no matter which option is chosen.

The United States

In 1992, the International Business Machines (IBM) Corporation had worldwide sales of $57 billion, an amount about the same as the gross national product of Hungary! But soon thereafter IBM fell on hard times and had an operating loss of $5 billion. Even shedding more than 100,000 employees over a five-year period has failed to stem the losses. Industry watchers put the blame on bad marketing. IBM failed to anticipate the demand for personal computers. When they finally did respond to the market, the competition reacted even quicker. And IBM's machines were priced 40 to 50 percent more than the competition.

As these vignettes suggest, marketing occurs at many levels all over the world. Marketing is obviously a part of small business. The shopkeeper must know what customers want and must make goods or buy them from suppliers at a cost that will be both affordable and attractive to customers, yet provide a profit to the shopkeeper.

Marketing also occurs at the national level. Government planners and regulators have a profound effect on the vitality of an economy, and the economy in turn affects the lives of every person or institution in the country. Indeed, the health of the market within a country has spillover effects on surrounding countries and even on the world economy at large. Witness the awakening of marketing within China. In 1992, while many economies were stagnant or even shrinking, China experienced a 12 percent growth rate, exported $85 billion in goods, and received $37 billion in foreign investment. All this occurred on the heels of an average annual growth rate of about 14.5 percent over the previous decade, the fastest rate among the 50 largest economies in the world. As recently as 1996, China's economy grew 9.7 percent, with only 6 percent inflation. The effects of this growth are felt well beyond Asia.

Between the scales of small businesses and nation-states, firms of varied sizes struggle or thrive on the power of their marketing programs. Let us return to the case of IBM. In 1990, IBM sold its printer, typewriter, keyboard, and related replacement supply businesses to an investment firm, Lexmark. Under IBM, new product development took an average of three years, and eight layers of management existed between top management and the assembly line. Today, Lexmark International sells more than $2 billion a year, takes only 18 months to develop new products, and has only four layers of management from top to bottom. Its line of laser printers, first introduced in spring 1993, has been a huge success and helped make the company profitable in a way not possible under IBM. Management and independent observers credit much of the success to changes made in marketing. Recently IBM has cut its losses and even introduced new products, such as its Aptiva S Series personal computers and the 390 Parallel Enterprise server. Sales in 1995 reached $72 billion, with more than $4 billion in profits.

In this text we introduce you to the concepts and tools needed to design, implement, and control effective marketing programs. We have two goals in this chapter. First, we introduce the *concept of marketing* by focusing on its centrality to the firm and describing two guiding principles behind marketing: customer analysis and competitor analysis. The idea is that successful marketing begins with the needs of customers and provides a better offering than the competition. Of course, these objectives must be accomplished subject to the service and financial goals of the organization. Finally, the chapter closes with an overview of *marketing implementation*. The heart of any implementation resides in planning the marketing effort and in product, communication, pricing, and distribution decisions. This chapter provides a capsule summary of the rest of the text. You may want to return to it periodically as you read the text to gain overall perspective on the field.

MARKETING DEFINED

The American Marketing Association (AMA), an international organization of practitioners and academicians, defines marketing as follows:

> Marketing is the process of planning and executing the conception, pricing, promotion, and distribution of ideas, goods, and services to create exchanges that satisfy individual and organizational objectives.[1]

Let us look at this definition in greater detail.

We begin with what is marketed. Notice that marketing can be applied to ideas, goods, and services. We normally think of marketing in terms of the selling of such physical products as clothing, food, automobiles, and electronic wares. Indeed, marketing is an essential activity for all who sell such goods. At the same time, it is important to realize that marketing can be applied to the promotion of ideas. Heads of religious bodies or political parties, environmentalists, and educators are all engaged in the marketing of ideas. Finally, marketing is a central, perhaps *the* central, activity for services. Whether one sells dry cleaning, maintenance contracts, or banking services, marketing is likely to be a key part of the business.

This definition of marketing emphasizes one compound goal or objective for marketing: the creation of exchanges that satisfy needs. The notion of exchange might even be called the sine qua non of marketing. By exchange, we mean the transfer of things of value between two or more parties. The parties are typically labeled buyer and seller, and the things of value entail not only physical items such as money or goods but also psychological currency such as information, praise, emotional support, shame, and guilt. Further, marketing exchanges entail more than economic arrangements, and involve social elements such as friendship, intimacy, obligations, reciprocity, and even power and conflict. As we shall see later in the chapter, the idea of social relationships is central to modern conceptualizations of marketing exchanges. Marketing may on occasion involve unanticipated, one-shot, or infrequent encounters between buyer and seller, but the aims of both parties in an exchange often entail lasting relationships of mutual benefit. Moreover, any exchange is typically embedded within a network of complex social relationships. Marketing must be concerned with the broader social relationships surrounding an exchange and not merely with the narrow exchange itself, if it is to be successful.

But what constitutes a successful marketing exchange? We said earlier that the compound goal of marketing is to create exchanges that satisfy needs. But whose needs are to be served by the creation of exchanges? The answer to this depends on the personal value systems of the parties to an exchange, as well as the larger political and cultural system within which the parties operate. This is not the place to give a definitive answer to these complex questions, for individual, corporate, and societal value systems articulate in diverse ways around the world, and our purpose here is to focus on marketing management. Nevertheless, we can say generally that a successful exchange is one in which all parties to the exchange achieve mutual satisfaction and at the same time the rules and norms of the society in which the exchange takes place are fulfilled. At points throughout the text, we will consider psychological, economic, social, and legal forces that bear upon the issues of satisfaction of needs and how the conduct of marketing relates to these. For now it can be stated that the most obvious needs consist of customer desires, firm survival and profitability, and the protection of the environment and other people and organizations in society.

The final component of the definition of marketing previously presented concerns the "how" of marketing. Need-satisfying exchanges are created by identifying unfulfilled needs, designing products and services to meet these needs, pricing the offerings in an optimal way, communicating the terms of trade, and getting the offerings to customers when and where they need them. All this must be done in a way that not only meets customer needs, but also fulfills firm objectives and beats the competition. This book focuses primarily on the "how" of marketing, yet it is mindful of the "why" and other broader concerns introduced throughout.

THE EVOLUTION OF MARKETING

The relative emphasis of business functions ebbs and flows with changes in the business cycle and economic development. In lesser developed economies, fiscal policy and employment take center stage, and marketing receives relatively less attention. Nevertheless, issues related to the distribution of goods and services, a subarea of marketing, are very important in such economies.

As economies mature, marketing becomes indispensable. Yet economic conditions shape the relative importance of marketing and all business functions.

The 1970s and early 1980s saw considerable instability in world markets. Most countries experienced rampant inflation and shortages of key goods. Perhaps for the first time, people in the so-called developed countries realized that their welfare depended intimately on global economic forces and the ability of their own businesses and government institutions to adjust to the new world order. Under these conditions, financial matters and production achieved greatest priority, as did such select marketing activities as procurement and pricing.

Beginning in the mid-1980s and continuing until the mid-1990s, business in many parts of the world was marked by mergers and acquisitions, downsizing, and other efforts at cost-cutting. A case in point is the experience in Britain in which the top 12 companies cut their workforces by an average of 44 percent between 1990 and 1995.[2] Even businesses in Japan were forced to focus on costs throughout the early part of the 1990s, as the real estate market collapsed and international markets for their goods stagnated or became more competitive. Although the media frequently gave the impression that investment and financial matters dominated world business during this decade, it is important to realize that marketing activities— pricing, new product development, brand management, distribution, personal selling, advertising, promotion, and publicity—acquired renewed impetus because of their demand-stimulating properties and their use as tools in combating competitive inroads. Marketing may not have gotten the publicity that financial crises received, but it constituted a central role in the planning and implementation functions of every business.

Today we are witnessing a new maturation in business institutions in general and marketing in particular. Consider first the evolution of businesses in recent years. Most firms begin as small operations and focus their activities on circumscribed geographical markets, typically those surrounding their main operations. After a while, sales of any product or service are likely to slow or even decline. The firms' responses are generally some combination of finding new markets or finding ways to take market share away from existing competitors in the established markets. In the former case, distribution, entry pricing strategies, and communication (e.g., advertising, personal selling) are key marketing activities for success. In the latter, brand management, defensive pricing strategies, market segmentation, and product repositioning are the primary marketing activities needed. New product development will be required in both cases to sustain growth. Soon firms reach national distribution or at least compete in the most promising markets countrywide.

At some point, opportunities are recognized abroad. Typically, the first action in this regard is to attempt to sell existing products or services to selected countries adjacent to the firm's base of operations or farther afield. Here key marketing functions are distribution, finding and providing incentives to foreign partners, and communicating the firm's offerings to customers. This is often a hit-or-miss strategy, and successful firms soon learn that it is necessary to respond to particular cultural, political, and economic exigencies in each market they desire to enter. Hence formal analyses of customers and the competition, product design, advertising copy, pricing, and other marketing activities must be tailored to local conditions in international markets. Even such giants as Coca-Cola, who find near universal appeal for their products, discover that peculiarities in distribution, media habits, language, and other factors require adjustments from country to country.

The evolution of business does not end with a progression in orientation from domestic to export to local responsiveness in international markets. The most successful firms nowadays strive to achieve a truly global orientation in which national responsiveness in worldwide markets is integrated with all functions of the firm and decentralized in a coordinated way in multiple countries.[3] This means that product design, production, and other key business decisions are made not in a "home office" located in one country but rather in a decentralized manner as dictated by company resources, competitive pressures, and customer needs. More and more firms are expanding multiple facets of their operations worldwide.

A case in point is Minnesota Mining and Manufacturing (3M). The 3M company began in the United States but now has four primary world regions in which it does business. Indeed, more than 50 percent of its business now originates outside the United States. Its early international strategy involved the use of country affiliates and locally adapting, producing, and marketing products based on core technologies developed at home. But recently 3M implemented a new strategy to distribute global and world regional production and marketing leadership mandates among countries in which its markets are located. The company has created a new balance among international coordination, integration, and responsiveness throughout its businesses, and management promotion and compensation are directly tied to such a global outlook.

Today more than ever, firms realize that their activities must be performed on a worldwide basis if they are to succeed. Of course, it is important to realize that these global trends happened primarily for medium- to large-sized organizations. Entrepreneurs and small businesses thrive at the margins in niche markets and may be affected by global conditions only indirectly.

Marketing, too, has undergone an evolution parallel to that seen in multinational corporations. Three quite new trends are worth briefly mentioning.

The first concerns the cohesive role marketing performs within modern firms. As individual firms grow, functions multiply and problems of coordination of activities inevitably demand attention. If action is not taken, a firm might evolve to a state resembling the existence of quasi-independent fiefdoms within its borders. So many things go on at once that short run goals fall by the wayside or become obsolete and long-term objectives become thwarted. Complexity may become so great and communication so poor that no one knows fully how bad things really are. Hence pressures build for reorganization or restructuring where integration and coordination receive new impetuses.

Marketing often acts as the integrative glue that holds together the inner workings of the organization. Marketing in modern firms coordinates manufacturing and production with demand estimation and forecasting, new product development, and distribution. The mission of the firm and strategic planning influence and are influenced by marketing strategy and implementation decisions. The impact of changing customer needs, government regulation, economic conditions, and competitive threats are first felt and responded to by marketing functions within the firm. Certain accounting practices and financial decisions are integrated by marketing through policies and decisions concerning pricing, product design, sales growth, and profitability. These decisions feed back to manufacturing and corporate planning. Customer service, too, is coordinated by marketing, as it affects other operations and functions within the firm.

Perhaps the best way to view the integrative role of marketing within the firm is through the emerging philosophy advocated by corporate chief executive officers (CEOs) and leading consultants and commentators on the business scene. In the words of Regis McKenna, marketing consultant and guru:

> Marketing is not a new ad campaign or this month's promotion. Marketing has to be all-pervasive, part of everyone's job description, from the receptionists to the board of directors. Its job is neither to fool the customer nor to falsify the company's image. It is to integrate the customer into the design of the product and to design a systematic process for interaction that will create substance in the relationship.[4]

New Holland, born in 1991 through the merger of Fiat Geotech and Ford New Holland, is one of the world's leaders in agricultural equipment. Following the 1991 merger, in response to a structural decline in worldwide demand for agricultural equipment during the 1980s, the company substantially restructured its operations to rationalize its production facilities and distribution networks. The restructuring process led to a substantial turnaround in operating results, from a net loss of $449 million in 1991 to net income of $324 million in 1996.

After the merger, the new top management team established new headquarters in London, reducing the headquarters staff from 1,500 people (including both the Fiat Geotech Headquarters in Modena, Italy, and the Ford New Holland Headquarters in New Holland, Pa.) to only 50 people. This was the first very important symbol to shape the strategy and the culture of the new company. In this restructuring period, no manufacturing plants were closed, but New Holland employment level decreased from about 30,000 to 18,000 people. Nevertheless, this process, which was believed necessary for company survival, was coordinated with special emphasis on care for human resources; in fact, the new corporate strategy relied on human competence and motivation as central themes throughout its operations.

New Holland is one of the most geographically diversified manufacturers and distributors of agricultural equipment in the industry and a world leader (in unit volume) among sales of agricultural tractor and combine harvester manufacturers. To capitalize on strong customer loyalty and high brand awareness, New Holland initially marketed certain of its product lines under the established brand names of its predecessors, including FiatAgri, Ford, and FiatAllis. In 1996, with the goal of increasing exposure and awareness of New Holland as a unified global brand, the company introduced the New Holland brand name and blue leaf logo as the primary brand name on all of its agricultural equipment.

To facilitate the sales of its products, New Holland's Financial Services operations offer wholesaler financing to its dealers and retail financing to qualified end-users in its major North American and European markets. New Holland's mission is to be a customer-driven organization: flexible, agile and innovative, with its people, dealers, suppliers, and partners working together to be the best globally positioned company in the agricultural and industrial equipment businesses.

To achieve these goals, New Holland's strategy concentrates on the following points:

- focus on the customer
- global market coverage
- product line expansion
- global product development
- dealer network development
- cost-containment and efficiency
- empowered motivated staff.

In 1997 second quarter New Holland reported substantial earnings growth, bringing first-half earnings per share (EPS) up 68 percent over the same period in 1996.

Source: Massimo Bergami, Management Consultant and Professor, University of Bologna, Italy.

An example of this can be seen in the corporate philosophy of Nissan, called *Kaizen*, which advocates a system for continuous improvement through teamwork.

This brings us to a second trend that has transformed the practice of marketing. At one time—and to a certain extent in contemporary economic theory—consumers and firms were regarded as distinct entities who acted in isolation and came into contact in an impersonal way and only intermittently. Consumers and firms alike were treated as homogenous objects, and except for the commodities changing hands, no real connection tied them together. Indeed, the one-shot transaction was the model of marketing exchanges until quite recently.

Today, marketing is conceived as a process of building marketing exchanges in a social sense. Emphasis is on the relationship between customer and the firm.[5] Sometimes this is practiced to the point of creating a partnership between buyer and seller. The goal is to form long-term relationships of mutual benefit between customers and marketer. Exactly how this is done is not easy to specify and accomplish. In this book we consider many actions and practices organizations can implement for building marketing relationships.

The third and final trend in marketing is happening right at this moment in progressive firms around the globe. The old, formal distinctions among business functions are slowly, and in some cases dramatically, breaking down. Marketing, finance, accounting, and other traditional departments are giving way to a redefinition of businesses around the organization of processes. A good example of this is the case of the New Holland corporation, a firm making tractors and other equipment used in farming and construction.

FORCES BEHIND THE EVOLUTION OF MARKETING

Before we describe the emerging role of marketing and the new forms it is taking, let us briefly sketch the forces producing the changes. The forces are phenomena with which you are familiar, but you probably have not realized just how far reaching their effects have been.

Perhaps the most important changes concern the *customer*. At the micro level, individual tastes are becoming more numerous, more refined, and more fickle. The result has been a proliferation of distinct market segments that demand unique products and services and new ways to reach them. At the same time, there has been a continual shift in aggregate markets. Some emerge overnight. Some persist a long time and either experience a rebirth or die. Others grow slowly. Still others expand by leaps and bounds. Obviously, if it is to satisfy market segments and profitably reap the rewards of volatile markets, a firm must adjust and readjust its marketing programs on an ever more frequent basis. Before it can do this it needs to identify promising markets. This, in turn, means developing knowledge of the micro side of consumption (e.g., customer needs, shopping behavior, customer satisfaction and dissatisfaction, information processing) as well as the macro (e.g., overall short- and long-run demand, market segments, trends, product life cycles).

The adjustment process also becomes a new imperative because of a second factor: the *competitor*. In recent years, more aggressive and more sophisticated rivals have been vying for the same markets as those served by existing brands. Advances in product and production technologies, market monitoring techniques, and strategic managerial know-how have raised the level of competition to a new plane. To compound matters, legal and regulatory bodies, which have always been procompetition, now seem to push free enterprise with an evangelistic fervor. Yet barriers to competition exist in different degrees around the world. Increased competition puts new burdens on marketing, because it is primarily through product design, pricing, promotion, advertising, and distribution that competitive effects are mitigated or overcome.

A third force influencing the nature and importance of marketing is the *world economy* and variations from region to region and country to country. Except during deep recessions or depressions, which tended to be few and far between, heretofore managers could count on a growing population, ever-increasing disposable incomes, low credit terms, tax incentives, and in general a favorable business climate. But mild recessions have occurred more frequently, thus increasing competitive pressures and putting new strains on marketing. Even in inflationary times, marketing must be pursued with a new urgency as people feel the impulse to spend in new ways and marketers scramble to uncover the ever-budding market segments. Changes in economic conditions across markets and economies are both constraints and opportunities for marketers that must be monitored and anticipated as best as possible. No longer can managers expect prosperity to continue unabated. Rather, we seem to face a never-ending alternation of turmoil and calm for indeterminate periods of time. Marketing tools are an essential means to adapt to, and even influence, these fluctuations.

As the consumer, the competitor, and the economic environments change, marketers increasingly realize that it is not enough merely to respond to the forces around them. New advances in marketing strategy and tactics make it possible to influence consumer choices, the competitive climate, and economic conditions to a certain extent.

TWO GUIDING PRINCIPLES

In much the same way that individual behavior is driven by one's fundamental values or goals and social behavior is governed by norms and laws, marketing efforts are—or should be—motivated by two principles. Specifically, marketing strives to (1) meet customer needs and (2) provide a product or service superior to those offered by competitors. Both of these goals must be achieved subject to such organizational goals as profitability, market share, employee welfare, and environmental responsibility.

As simple as these principles might seem, they are difficult to sustain in practice, and each year the failures regularly outnumber the successes. Let us examine some of these failures and successes to gain a perspective before we turn to an examination of the key functional areas of marketing.

Customer Analysis

To meet customer needs, firms spend a lot of time and money on research. A common strategy is to concentrate on new product development. The rationale is that consumers are satisfied through products, so it behooves one to begin here. Consider the case of Frost 8/80 in Marketing Anecdote 1.2.

As we explore in more depth later in this chapter, one objective of customer research is to first discover which product attributes are important to consumers, and only then to design a product to meet consumers' needs. Following a more or less armchair approach, Brown-Forman turned the process on its head by assuming that a white whiskey would meet needs similar to those filled by the traditional clear liquors. They began with a product and then hoped to prove that a need existed.

Brown-Forman Distillers introduced a "dry white" whiskey named Frost 8/80 a number of years ago. After much fanfare and a reported $20 million investment, Brown-Forman withdrew the brand from the market less than two years after its introduction. The reason given was that sales were simply too low. Estimates of the losses extend beyond the $6 million mark.

The Frost 8/80 case is noteworthy because Brown-Forman appeared to have done all the right things prior to launch. The brand was targeted at a unique niche in the market. Management thought that a large enough segment of consumers would welcome a clear whiskey, just as many buyers had earlier accepted the concept of a light whiskey. But unlike the latter, which was amber in color and was considered a less strong-tasting whiskey intended to be consumed straight or with water, Frost 8/80 was positioned as a versatile mixer. The product seemed destined for success, given industry statistics showing a shift in drinking preferences from the harsher bourbons and whiskeys toward the softer liquors such as vodka, gin, or scotch. Moreover, women and young people increasingly were turning to sweeter, less alcoholic mixed drinks. Because Frost 8/80 was basically a filtered whiskey, Brown-Forman hoped that sufficient sales here would forestall the effects of the slow growth and eventual decline in demand for its traditional whiskey brands.

Before deciding to market Frost 8/80, Brown-Forman performed a series of activities quite typical of modern companies. First, a concept study was conducted to get an idea of public receptivity to a dry, white whiskey. Favorable reactions led to interviews and surveys to discover how people might consume the product and what their feelings were toward it. A third step was a taste test, which tended to show that people liked the product. Fourth, outside experts were consulted in the choosing of a name, bottle, and label. Consumer panels were utilized to obtain still more information in a fifth step. The final stage consisted of heavy advertising to inform the public of the brand and its uses.

With such a textbook program, why did Frost 8/80 fail? Industry watchers offered many reasons, including an insufficient market base, neglect to test market, and a reluctance of management to stick it out until a customer franchise could be built. The most likely explanations, however, lay in Brown-Forman's failure to perform a proper customer analysis. Essentially, the company did not carry its research deep enough into how consumers make choices and how they would respond to Frost 8/80.

Some of the facts of this Marketing Anecdote are drawn from Frederick C. Klein, "How a New Product Was Brought to Market Only to Flop Miserably," Wall Street Journal, *January 5, 1973, pp. 1, 19. The dollar figures given here have been converted from those in the article into estimates of current value.*

More important, the research performed by Brown-Forman did not get to the heart of customer decision making, rather it revealed only surface symptoms of consumer behavior. Contemporary research over a wide range of products and services shows that key activities in the decision process concern how consumers make inferences as to product attributes, how they then organize the information so gleaned, and how finally the structure of information in memory influences consumer choices. The process proceeds in the following manner:

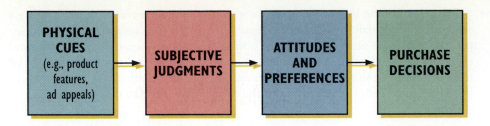

That is, objective information communicated through actual physical product attributes or ads is perceived by the consumer who, in turn, makes abstractions from the "hard" information to form subjective judgments. The inferred data need not be directly related to the physical cues but can be connected to other thoughts and feelings, which may even be at odds with the intended communication. Next, the subjective information is integrated into an attitude, which then influences one's decision to make a purchase.

Consider how the process works for a hypothetical consumer, Tom R. Tom R. bought a bottle of Frost 8/80 at the suggestion of the retail clerk at his local liquor store. A dealer promotion made the purchase attractive in that it was a full dollar below the regular price and two dollars below the price of existing liquor brands. At home, Tom R. poured a small amount of Frost 8/80 in a glass, just to see how it tasted. But Tom R. could not decide whether he liked Frost 8/80. The physical cues—the clear liquid, the lack of a strong odor, the advertising—suggested to him that the product would be tasteless. But when he tried it, he found something quite different: a strong whiskey taste. In effect, his expectations were violated, and the dissonance produced confusion. Had he tried first to mix Frost 8/80 with 7-Up or Coke, he may never have had such an ambivalent reaction. But the initial, undiluted taste created a first impression that remained with him and generated uncertainties. His doubts were raised as to the purity of Frost 8/80 as well. After all, vodka is colorless and supposedly made of "pure" potatoes. But Tom R. wondered what exactly was the new taste. Perhaps artificial ingredients were added to make the drink a synthetic concoction. Equally disconcerting was the thought that other people would have a similar reaction. The safe decision would be not to risk social embarrassment and to forgo serving it to guests. As a consequence of such reactions, repeat sales never reached desirable levels in the market.

It is easy to see how such negative inferences, both conscious and nonconscious, could arise in response to the physical cues. In addition, such negative attributions can easily lead to unfavorable attitudes and a decision not to buy the brand again. If decision making is construed as an attempt to gain knowledge and confidence about the world around us, then the uncertainty engendered by Frost 8/80 was an impediment to the process of consumer choice. Note, too, that Brown-Forman compounded the uncertainty by switching ad agencies during the first year. The resulting change in themes led to even more confusion. This would be expected to affect the rate of first-time, as well as repeat, purchasing. What consumers needed was a way to "learn" about the product under favorable circumstances. Free tastings of mixed drinks in stores (where legal) or taverns, where the seller could control the consumer's initial introduction to the product, advertising that prepared prospective customers for what they would experience when they tried the product, and other tactics might have been more fruitful. But even more basic than this, Brown-Forman never demonstrated that Frost 8/80 satisfied a genuine need and that a sufficiently large market existed.

The point of the Frost 8/80 example is to stress the importance of performing a sound customer analysis. This means discovering what consumers' needs are; which product attributes satisfy these needs; how customers will search for, evaluate, and consume the product; and how the tools under the control of the marketer can be used to facilitate the customer decision-making process. Some firms never seem to learn, as recent disappointments with the soft drink Clear Tab demonstrate.[6]

Competitive Analysis

Even if one has developed a product that meets consumers' needs, success may not be forthcoming if competitors get the upper hand. Therefore, analysis of the competition is as important as study of the consumer. The goal is to meet customer needs with a product or service that achieves a differential advantage over the competition. The differential advantage might be superior product quality, lower price, greater availability, more favorable credit terms, better service, unique brand image, and so on.

Typically, to overcome competitive threats, one of three broad approaches can be taken: product differentiation, overall cost leadership, or special market focus.[7] Let us consider each approach through an illustration.

Product Differentiation: The Case of 7-Up

7-Up was introduced in 1929 and quickly established itself as a popular drink, despite the presence of literally hundreds of competitors that tasted much the same. Nevertheless, its market share was small, and most people purchased it as either a good mixer (especially with bootlegged whiskey in those Prohibition years) or a remedy for headache and other minor ills. Indeed, a key promotion advocated 7-Up "for home and hospital use." In 1942, the J. Walter Thompson ad agency took over the account and stressed the product's fresh taste along with the image of "you like it, it likes you." Although it eventually became the third leading soft drink behind Coca-Cola and Pepsi, it lagged far behind the two leaders. Moreover, sales growth in the mid-1960s was considerably below the industry average, and four new competitors were threatening 7-Up: Coca-Cola's Sprite, PepsiCo's Teem, Canada Dry's Wink, and Royal Crown's Upper-10.

Something had to be done, and the first step was consumer research. The findings were surprising. Management had believed that consumers thought of 7-Up as one of a number of soft drinks. Therefore, they had also believed that the brand would at least enter the set of possible thirst-quenching alternatives when consumers needed to choose a drink. But what they found was quite different. When asked to list what they thought of when the words "soft drink" came to mind, most people listed Coke, Pepsi, Dr. Pepper, or another cola. In the minds of most consumers, "soft drink" was equated with "cola." 7-Up either never entered their thoughts or tended to be considered only as a mixer or health aid. So when consumers made up a shopping list, went to a restaurant, or were offered a soft drink at the home of a friend, most of them never really considered 7-Up.

The problem could thus be seen as one of brand image, consumer knowledge, and the strength and entrenchment of the competition. Yet the solution was not straightforward. One might think that the expenditure of more money on advertising or promotion was called for; but, nevertheless, examination of the competition suggested a caution. In 1967, Pepsi spent approximately $55 million on advertising, and Coke about $44 million. This was about four times as much as 7-Up's $12 million. To make matters worse, Sprite and Teem spent $10 million and $9 million, respectively, on advertising. Clearly, more advertising dollars would be expensive and problematic in its effect. 7-Up had to get many cola-drinking consumers to try 7-Up—and it had to do so without raising costs excessively or initiating a price/advertising/promotion war with the leaders, who had greater resources.

The solution pursued was the now famous "uncola" campaign by the J. Walter Thompson ad agency. 7-Up changed its advertising to introduce 7-Up as an alternative to cola drinks. Some ads emphasized that 7-Up has a "fresh, clean taste," and is "wet . . . wild, never too sweet . . . (with) no aftertaste." Other ads called attention to the occasions one might want a 7-Up: at a restaurant, with a hamburger, on a picnic, with snacks, and so forth. Still other ads made direct comparisons to colas, stressing, for example, the "fresh, clean," and "alive" ingredients of 7-Up (i.e., lemons and limes) versus the dark, shriveled, and dead-looking contents of colas (i.e., cola nuts). Promotions included free 7-Up glasses in the shape of the famous Coca-Cola glass, but upside down. In short, consumers were forced to consider 7-Up uniquely and in a new comparative light.

The campaign worked. In the three years following introduction of the uncola campaign, 7-Up's sales increased an average of nearly 20 percent per year, compared with only about 14 percent for the industry. This contrasted well with the three prior years, which, had shown a 3 percent per year average gain for 7-Up and a 10 percent yearly average for the industry.[8]

The 7-Up case is a classic example of a (pure) product differentiation competitive strategy. The firm's brand was positioned relative to the competition, and consumers perceived it in a unique way. This campaign was done on a marketwide basis, in contrast to the alternative strategy of product differentiation for specific segments, which is a special case of the market focus strategy that we will consider shortly. Product differentiation creates a distinctive image for a brand, and, if done properly, meets a genuine need and increases the loyalty of customers. It can make consumers less price-sensitive and less vulnerable to the offerings of competitors. Although 7-Up created differentiation primarily through its new advertising and secondarily through its product formulation, product differentiation can also be produced by pricing, distribution, packaging, auxiliary services, or other marketing tactics. Product differentiation must be based on perceptions by the consumer as real benefits or repeat sales will not materialize. Also, differentiated products can be expensive to create, and can be imitated by the competitors in the long run. Therefore, more than other strategies, differentiation demands constant injections of new ideas—and money.

Overall Cost Leadership: From Computers to Chain Saws

The goal in overall cost leadership is to keep manufacturing, material, and/or other costs to a minimum and in so doing increase demand through the expected effect that a relatively low industry price will have. The increased volume, in turn, leads to absolute economies of scale and experience curve effects (discussed later), which then feed back lowering costs still further. The hoped-for ultimate effect, as with product differentiation, is a large market share. Indeed, cost leadership seems to work best for firms that already have a high relative market share. Furthermore, overall cost leadership entails a never-ending vigil of stringent cost and overhead control and the weeding out of marginal customers and product variations. Like the (pure) product differentiation strategy, overall cost leadership is a marketwide competitive strategy.

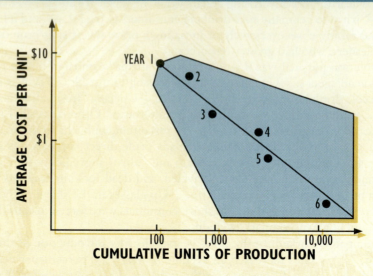

The line plotted through the data points is typical; the shaded area indicates that the slopes of actual experience curves vary considerably according to the nature of the product and other variables.

A number of firms follow an overall cost leadership approach. This is perhaps most obvious in the home computer industry. Let us briefly focus on Texas Instruments. Its president, J. Fred Bucy, identified four strategic components as central to the company's success.[9] The first is the *experience curve* concept.[10] As shown in Figure 1.1, the average cost per unit of an item typically decreases as cumulative output increases. In fact, the Boston Consulting Group asserts that the costs of most items will decline about 20 to 30 percent for each doubling of cumulative production. Why? Because with the passage of time, labor becomes more efficient, innovations arise in manufacturing, products are redesigned to take advantage of material and other savings, and other learning occurs. This is especially so within the solid-state electronics industry, where it is not uncommon to experience a doubling and even redoubling of cumulative production in the first two or three years. Obviously, firms that ride the crest of the experience curve phenomenon, such as Texas Instruments, can charge relatively lower prices and capture larger market shares. Notice, too, that experience curve effects are not limited to production costs but may apply to marketing costs as well.

A second component of Texas Instruments' overall cost leadership approach is the *importance of being first* to develop a new market. Although not a necessary component for success, being first typically permits an early capitalization on the experience curve, leads to a favorable brand image and the building of a customer base, and results in higher profit margins. Being first can be risky, however, if market acceptance is slower than expected and competitors wait in the wings to take advantage of the learning and primary demand investment of the market pioneer. In the case of Texas Instruments, being first was a decided advantage.

Accumulated units of production with products related to a focal product is a third component of Texas Instruments' strategy and is termed *shared experience*. Thus, Texas Instruments finds similar uses for its semiconductors in hand calculators, minicomputers, digital watches, and computer terminals. This permits a reduction in costs by parceling them out among products, and the shared experience then enhances the overall cost leadership of individual products still further.

Finally, Texas Instruments follows a philosophy of *design to cost*. In Bucy's words, "This involves deciding today what the selling price and performance of a given product must be years in the future and designing the product and the equipment for producing it to meet both cost performance goals."[11] Primary emphasis is thus placed on cost; the secondary objective is "to avoid designing into a product more performance than the market is willing to buy."[12]

Overall cost leadership is thus at odds with the product differentiation strategy. It is not so much that firms such as Texas Instruments do not differentiate their products. Indeed, they do this to some extent through product design, advertising, market segmentation, and distribution policies. Nevertheless, low costs are given the highest priority, and product differentiation is emphasized to a lesser extent than it is by firms that pursue a (pure) product differentiation posture. Similarly, the product differentiator is not unconcerned with costs. Rather, goals for superior product quality, brand image, or other factors are met first. This generally entails spending more; hence the inherent trade-off. In rare instances (for example, the components businesses), it is, in fact, possible to find both high product quality and overall cost leadership.[13] But this is the exception rather than the rule.

Overall cost leadership is a powerful strategy, but it can be dangerous in the long run. We have already mentioned the possibility of slow consumer adoption of the product. Another potential problem is that price competition, the primary demand stimulation tool, is easily copied by others. Still another threat is the possibility that competitors will develop new technologies and modify the product significantly to advantage or even create a substitute. Then, too, even if consumers are initially enthusiastic, tastes may change, and the firm will be left with an unfulfilled recovery of its investment.

For Texas Instruments, the home computer market proved damaging in the long run. The introduction of its Model 99/4A in 1979 led to a market share of 26 percent by 1982. However, competition, based primarily on price, by Commodore, Radio Shack, Atari, and Timex forced Texas Instruments to lower its price from a high of $1,000 in 1979 to less than $250 in 1982. Further intensification of competition in 1983 saw the price of Model 99/4A plummet to less than $89 with a rebate. Market share slipped to 19 percent in 1983 as well. Although the overall size of the market doubled between 1982 and 1983, Texas Instruments could not profitably compete in the home computer market and therefore withdrew. Not only the price wars but also shifts in consumer tastes took their toll as buyers became more sophisticated and demanded value and certain benefits as the primary product attributes. Price became relatively less important. Such is the pitfall of relying too heavily on an overall cost leadership strategy over time. Today successful competitors in the personal computer market emphasize costs so as to keep prices low, yet at the same time are forced to provide the same innovative features as competitors.

As a final comment on the overall cost leadership strategy, we note that each industry typically witnesses a variety of strategies, and one or more firms frequently find overall cost leadership viable. In the chain saw industry, for example, during the early years of growth in sales to households, we see that one market leader, McCulloch (with 27 percent of the market), pursued an overall cost leadership approach, whereas the other market leader, Homelite (with 28 percent of the market), followed a product differentiation strategy based on high quality and a network of servicing dealers.[14] These firms and the industry as a whole tended to sell large, high-priced chain saws, most of which were bought by

Whereas the product differentiation and overall cost leadership strategies strive to dominate—or at least survive in—entire markets, the market focus strategy aims at a particular segment or small number of segments of a larger market. Once such a segment is found, the firm employs either a product differentiation or overall cost leadership approach to attack it. In this sense, special market focus can be considered a subset of the previous two strategies.

A good example of a market focus strategy is the case of Lipton Herbal Teas. Prior to 1980, the market for herbal teas in the United States was minuscule, perhaps only 2 or 3 percent of the entire black tea market. In Germany and other parts of Europe, in contrast, herbal teas were thought to account for 40 to 45 percent of the entire market for tea. Therefore, it was thought the United States might well represent a large, untapped market. (Note that herbal teas are not teas, strictly speaking, and are caffeine-free.)

In 1979 and 1980, Lipton launched its entries into the herbal tea market, which at that time was pursued primarily by Celestial Seasonings and Bigelow. Its alleged goal was sales of at least 5 percent of the black tea market in the first year or so. Lipton hoped also to achieve economies of scale in production and reduce overhead, since it was already making regular tea. This would give Lipton a cost advantage over its smaller competitors, including Celestial Seasonings. Nevertheless, its principal strategy was one of product differentiation, for reasons we will mention shortly.

The target audience was defined as women aged 25 to 49, with middle to upper incomes, and who were average to heavy black tea drinkers. Herbal tea drinkers were, of course, also sought. In addition, the psychographic profile of the target consumer was "an independent woman, with strong convictions, and who feels comfortable making decisions."[15] As a consequence, a very specific and relatively small market segment was sought.

Differentiation from regular tea was accomplished through a variety of tactics. The product was made with high-quality, natural ingredients, and, as noted, no caffeine. Originally,

professional woodsmen and farmers. Soon Beaird-Poulan began marketing very low priced, smaller chain saws for casual users. Its market share then was about 8 percent. With other firms soon following suit, the market exploded as a consequence of the new mass appeal of chain saws. By 1977, the market shares of Homelite, Beaird-Poulan, and McCulloch were approximately 23 percent, 22 percent, and 20 percent, respectively, and the market for casual users increased from about 430,000 units in 1972 to 1,750,000 in 1977. The casual user segment was now about 70 percent of a $1.15 billion market.

Notice that the market leaders employed the two generic strategies we have discussed. Notice also that, contrary to Texas Instruments' experience, price rivalry had not harmed the position of the original cost leader, McCulloch. And further, notice the dramatic rise of Beaird-Poulan, the other practitioner of overall cost leadership. The chain saw industry also illustrates the possibility of other strategic approaches. For example, the German company, Stihl, uses a product differentiation strategy but directs its brand to a particular market segment: professional users. Its product is of even higher quality (and price) than Homelite's, and it finds that a place exists for it in the market, too. In fact, it consistently

five flavors were offered: orange, spice, chamomile, hibiscus, and almond. Later a sixth was added: citrus sunset, which contains the davana herb from India. Print ads stressed "naturally delicious" and "no caffeine." They contained colorful pictures of the tea boxes and very little copy. A cents-off coupon worth as much as 25 cents on a box of 16 bags was often part of the ad. One television ad emphasized the quality of life, another natural settings. The theme of romance was discernible in most ads as well. Dealer promotions such as "2 free with 10" and "no payment for 6 months" were tried to gain retail acceptance. Finally, although the familiar rectangular box was used, the packaging was made more exotic, feminine, and flowery than traditional styles. Further, the rectangular box was designed so that the largest side caught the eye of the consumer, rather than the end, as is usually the case. This not only provided a larger shelf facing, but it minimized overhead, since more boxes could be stacked advantageously to reduce space.

Lipton thus pursued a small segment of the market and used a product differentiation strategy. It explicitly strove to create "maximum differentiation" from its regular and flavored teas. This was done in order not to cannibalize sales. Also, Lipton was concerned that a "no caffeine" selling point might backfire on its other, high-caffeine, products, which, with sales in the hundreds of millions of dollars, could be hurt if the same consumers were pursued. Finally, Lipton's marketing people believed that many U.S. consumers would find the cost of herbal tea excessive (about 10 cents more per box), the idea of drinking "flowers" repugnant, the image of an herbal tea drinker as too hip or exotic and not in keeping with the regular tea-drinker's self-image, or drinking herbal tea dangerous (some people believe that herbs are upsetting or potentially toxic). Hence, product differentiation was called for to protect Lipton's existing products and to reach the proper market segment.

maintained a market share of 7 or 8 percent for well over a decade. Other firms in the industry with no or ill-defined competitive strategies (for example Remington or Roper) have fared less well.

Special Market Focus: Lipton Herbal Teas

The market focus strategy is applied not only by giants such as Lipton. As a matter of fact, many small- and medium-sized firms find the strategy the only way to survive against their larger rivals. In other words, they find it essential to go after market niches. We see the market focus strategy being applied with increasing frequency, too, as a consequence of the ever-greater splintering of consumer markets. In certain ways, a market focus orientation even requires more marketing than other strategies. Segments are difficult to find and reach. They must be of a sufficient size and/or the product and a marketing campaign must be altered to make a profit. Also, they are more sensitive to competition and changes in consumer tastes, thereby requiring closer monitoring and more frequent changes in marketing programs.

This completes our discussion of the two guiding principles of modern marketing: customer analysis and competitive analysis. Implicit in the presentation was a third activity: analysis of the constraints, power, and liabilities of the firm. This, in turn, implies taking into account the firm's goals, its financial and human resources, its production capabilities, its organization structure, the economic environment, and the social–political–legal environment, as well as other factors. Each of these must be considered from a marketing perspective. By way of summary, we might say that marketing strives to "orient all business actions around one integrating objective: superior value-delivery at a cost allowing acceptable profit."[16] We turn now to the marketing tools that managers have at their disposal to respond to or influence their markets.

IMPLEMENTING THE MARKETING EFFORT

Market Selection

The choice of what market(s) to serve is perhaps the most crucial decision faced by a firm because not only do all other marketing decisions follow from this choice, but the ultimate success of the firm depends on the acceptance of its products. It is not enough to assume that a market exists, or that once a product is made marketing can invariably sell it. Rather, one must begin with an assessment of customer needs. Given that the product fills a need and (it is hoped) achieves a competitive advantage, one can then evaluate the size of the market and begin to plan and carry through the tactical activities needed to reach it in a profitable way.

Consumer Behavior

A key activity in market selection is the analysis of customer behavior. Earlier we presented a simplified model and said that the consumer decision process begins by exposure to physical cues. The consumer then perceives these as subjective attributes, benefits, and so forth, and somehow organizes them in memory to form an attitude toward the product offering. Finally, attitude is thought to influence the decision process one way or the other.

In reality, of course, the decision process is much more complex than this. As a matter of fact, marketers have developed a number of theories that break down the process into many psychological components. It is beyond the scope of this chapter to consider these theories here (the details are presented in chapter 4). We, however, briefly describe the central elements that cut across many of the theories and indicate how these are used in practice.

Thinking Processes

The dominant consideration in virtually all theories of consumer choice is how consumers process information. One way to represent information processing is in terms of the beliefs consumers have and the organization of these beliefs in their memory. Beliefs are subjective judgments as to the attributes of a product (e.g., its weight, durability, or cost) and how much of each attribute the product possesses (e.g., heavy, highly durable, or moderately expensive). A belief might consist also of a judgment about the consequences of purchase or product use (e.g., "Brand X will keep my floors clean for two weeks"). Beliefs are used by consumers to make choices among alternative brands or among broad consumption options.

Marketers have developed many models to depict how beliefs are formed, grouped, and used in decision making. Obviously, from a managerial perspective, if we know what beliefs a consumer has toward our brand, we can better decide how to communicate its attributes; change, add, or remove attributes; influence beliefs and decision making; and so on. In addition, we can see how consumers view our brand and the competitors' brands in order to discover our relative advantage or disadvantage and help determine what, if anything, we must do to further improve the situation. Thinking processes constitute the more or less rational side of consumption decisions. They dominate industrial buying and play an important role in everyday consumer choice as well.

Feeling Processes

It is also important to understand the emotional reactions of consumers to our products. These reactions harbor needs and motives for buying, as well as evaluations of the utility or importance of specific product attributes. Together with beliefs, our feelings determine our attitudes and thus indirectly influence choice. A firm's knowledge of the feelings of consumers about its products (and the products of its competitors) contributes to the design of its products, packages, persuasive communications, promotions, and deals; to its pricing; and even to its distribution decisions. Like beliefs, feelings toward our brand and rival brands need to be considered in order to assess the strength of our competitive position. Emotional considerations obviously pervade everyday consumer decision making, yet they can be salient factors in industrial buying, too, despite efforts to focus on economic and other supposedly rational criteria.

Social Processes

Buying is not strictly a psychological process. Social processes shape consumption, too. This takes many forms, such as the influence of norms, peer pressure, family decision-making activities, organizational buying processes, and bargaining and negotiation, among others. Knowledge of the role of social factors in choice is especially helpful in the design of advertising and other marketing communications.

A Model

To gain insight into how consumers make choices, marketers have developed representations, or models, of the processes. These imperfect models represent the causes of decisions, processes in decision making, and their relationship to actual choice outcomes. Sometimes this modeling is done in laboratory experiments; at other times naturalistic surveys are employed. One model that has proved useful in forecasting as well as in product design and advertising is the attitude model. In simplified form, this model can be written as:

$$P \text{ or } I = f(B, F, S)$$

That is, actual purchase behaviors (P) or intentions to buy (I) are hypothesized to be a function of one's beliefs (B), feelings (F), and social pressures (S). More complicated models are used to represent choices among alternative brands and to account for the full range of psychological and social determinants. The literature is filled with specific examples. Although most of these models employ quantitative methods, qualitative research serves as an essential complement in most real-world applications.

Market Segmentation

Customer analysis is primarily an activity directed at the study of consumers as individuals. It thus focuses on microphenomena. Although this helps in product design and other tactical decisions, it does not provide information on the size and

Supermarkets use point-of-purchase displays and pricing techniques to take maximum advantage of consumer behavior patterns. Impulse purchases like candy appeal to the younger set.

composition of markets or how groups of consumers will respond to product offerings. Knowledge of the macro side of consumption is essential because for most firms it is impossible to make and deliver a unique product to each and every consumer. Trade-offs must be made between the ideal of fully satisfying everyone's needs and the capabilities of firms to meet these needs. In practice, well-defined markets or market segments must be identified so that the firm can take advantage of some standardization and accompanying efficiencies. The process for doing so has come to be known as *market segmentation.*

Market segmentation identifies subgroups of the population as potential customers. Segmentation should yield a group of people with favorable attitudes toward—and, it is to be hoped, intentions to buy—one's product. In addition, the segment should be reachable, not overly competitive, and of a sufficient size to warrant pursuit. The following criteria represent typical bases for market segmentation in that tastes of people classified into each category vary and represent different opportunities for marketing that must be assessed:

- *Demographic:* age, sex, income, occupation, family size, education, religious affiliation, marital status, race.
- *Geographic:* section of country, such as urban, rural, or suburban.
- *Psychological:* personality, attitudes, lifestyle.
- *Social:* social class, group affiliation.
- *Behavioral:* benefits sought, typical consumption amount, end use, consumption status (e.g., nonuser, first time, repeat).

One of the most fruitful means of segmentation is known as *benefit segmentation.* Consumers are grouped according to the product attributes they desire most or the consequences of product use they value most highly. Notice that this procedure begins with criteria that are clearly related to consumer needs. Indeed, the objective is to discover relatively homogeneous clusters of buyers with similar needs. After consumers have been grouped in this way, correlates of people within segments are sought. For instance, key demographic and psychological attributes of people are often recorded, as are actual behaviors (previous purchases,

For years, Xerox owned the copy machine market. Its marketing was based on products that used a dry toner and parts unique to each model of machine. Xerox manufactured and assembled most of its components. This permitted the manufacture of a high-quality, durable machine suitable for customers who wanted high-quality, high-volume production. Of course, the price of the machine was high. The company had its own sales force and service personnel, and customers leased the machines from Xerox. Its high-quality machines regularly captured 70 percent or more of the market.

Enter the competition. Savin saw an opportunity to go after the low-price, infrequent-user market. To do this, it used the cheaper liquid toner technology and employed interchangeable parts across its line of machines. Although the speed and quality of its copies could not match those of Xerox, the target market accepted this trade-off to get a much lower price. A side benefit was somewhat better reliability. To reach the more fragmented market, Savin used a dealer system and sold its machines rather than leasing them. This was not only necessary but cheaper. Service was provided by the dealers; a simpler machine made this possible, and Savin provided support to the dealer. Finally, Savin purchased all of its parts, and assembled them in Japan; this gave the company further cost advantage. The result was that Savin succeeded in finding an unfulfilled market segment and providing a product that would satisfy consumers in that segment. Today, many competitors pursue the low and high end of the copy machine market, and Xerox has been forced to actively segment and alter its marketing tactics to meet this competition.

statements of preferences, activities, and so on). This gives management a picture of the key benefits people seek in the product it offers, how many people prefer each benefit, and what characteristics describe the people in each benefit segment. Such information can be used in decisions about product design, advertising, pricing, and distribution. Table 1.1 provides an example applied to the market for bank services. Notice that five distinct groups of consumers emerge, each varying in size and benefits sought. Notice further how the consumers differ by segment and how they perceive the various banks. A particular bank could use these data to see if it is serving who it thinks it is and determine if an untapped market exists. The picture thus provided could also help the bank in tailoring services and communicating with customers.

Market segmentation can be a useful strategic tool. Consider the case of the copy machine business (see Marketing Anecdote 1.4).[17]

Market Monitoring and Decision Support Systems

A key factor in market selection, as well as in the management of the entire marketing program, is the collection, analysis, and use of information. Modern marketing organizations are increasingly establishing separate departments for this function, which goes by such names as *management information systems* or *decision support systems*. Just as frequently, firms perform the information function through closer coordination of their many separate departments. Discussion of this important topic is beyond the scope of this chapter, but we cover it in some detail in chapter 5. At the risk of understatement,

TABLE 1.1 AN EXAMPLE OF BENEFIT SEGMENTATION

	1 FRONT RUNNERS	2 LOAN SEEKERS	3 REPRESENTATIVE SUBGROUP	4 VALUE SEEKERS	5 ONE-STOP BANKERS
Principal benefits sought	Large Bank for all Good advertising	Good reputation Loans easily available Low loan interest	No differences (about average on all benefits sought)	High savings interest Quick service Low loan interest Plenty of parking	Wide variety of services Convenient hours Quick service Encourage financial responsibility Convenient branch
Banks favored	Commercial A	Commercial B Savings X	Commercial A Commercial B	Savings Y Savings Z	Commercial A Commercial B
Demographic	Young Rent home	More transient More blue collar		Tend to save more	Older
Lifestyle characteristics[a]	High ability to manage money	Liberal about use of credit Positive about bank loans		Conservative overall lifestyle Conservative about use of credit Low propensity toward risk taking	Conservative about use of credit Positive toward checking account
Size (n)	8 (2%)	51 (15%)	118 (34%)	89 (26%)	78 (23%)

[a]*Dimensions represent factor scores of all 196 general and banking-specific lifestyle items.*

Source: Roger J. Calatone and Alan G. Sawyer, "The Stability of Benefit Segments," Journal of Marketing Research 15 (August 1978): 400. Reprinted with the permission of the American Marketing Association.

we simply note that special attention must be given to consumer research; data analysis and storage (for example, collection of scanner data, statistical modeling, establishment of an archive); normative support systems (such as mathematical models and interactive computer support programs); and new ways of disseminating and using the information. We turn now to the tactical and operational side of marketing. These encompass product decisions, communication decisions, price decisions, and distribution decisions.

Product Decisions

New-Product Development

Changing consumer tastes and evolving economic and competitive conditions make product innovation a necessity for maintaining a healthy business. Today's leading companies no longer leave things to chance or the inventive genius of a founder; they rely on a purposive program of new product development. To be sure, the program is part art and part science. But the large expenditures involved, together with the sobering realization that failure rates are high, make it imperative that efforts be made to meld art and science and do so well before the product is launched. It is estimated that the cost of designing, developing, and introducing a new industrial product averages more than $5 million, and expenditures for a new consumer product average about $15 million. The chance for success at the design stage is given as about 30 percent for industrial and 20 percent for consumer goods.[18]

Many activities must be coordinated to bring a product successfully to market. The most important fall within the following five stages:

creative phase → design and development phase → testing phase → product launch → ongoing management

In the *creative phase*, new ideas are generated. These may arise from secondary sources, consumer research (for example, interviews), the research and development (R&D) department, feedback from salespeople, consumer suggestions or complaints, employee contributions, and even the competition. Some firms use separate creative groups or executive brainstorming sessions. Brand managers generally provide important input here. Occasionally, outside agencies or individuals are consulted. Once a new idea is generated, its utility must be assessed. This is usually done by means of subjective judgments, perhaps aided by rules of thumb and ranking or rating methods. Criteria considered at this early stage include estimates of the cost of development, potential receptivity of consumers, ease and cost of manufacture and marketing, profitability, degree of probable competition, and likelihood of success at each of the remaining four stages of the new-product development process.

The *design and development phase* is in many ways the most crucial. It is here that the product takes shape conceptually and physically, that marketing plans are first formulated, and that a realistic assessment of costs and expected sales and profits is made. A particularly critical activity is customer analysis and market segmentation. This is done, in part, through a technique termed *perceptual mapping*, which we will describe in a moment. At the same time, the new product must be analyzed vis-à-vis the competition. This also can be done, in part, through perceptual mapping in a process termed *product positioning*. Finally, in the case of most consumer goods, the design will be given its toughest evaluation through mock pretests, in which consumers evaluate both the product and ads and express their preferences in simulated purchase environments. Various models and rules of thumb have been developed to aid in the interpretation of the data thus obtained. The Assessor model or BBDO Worldwide's NEWS model are two leading examples.[19] The goal is to get feedback on the attractiveness of product attributes and communication tactics and to estimate trial and repeat purchasing. The design and development phase is a particularly sensitive one, as managers have vested interests, and the firm wants to avoid rejecting potentially fruitful products or approving losers. Yet considerable uncertainty persists at this stage.

The third stage, the *testing phase*, is designed to reduce uncertainty and provide more feedback. Typically, the product is given to one or a few users if it is an industrial product, or introduced into one or a few cities if it is a consumer good. Test marketing is expensive, generally costing $4 million to $6 million. However, the information it provides for the fine-tuning of the entire marketing effort is more valid than that supplied by most pretests because testing is done under more naturalistic conditions and with larger, more representative samples. The information sought includes awareness of the brand, knowledge of product attributes, attitudes and preferences, intentions to try the product, and actual trial and repeat purchase rates. In addition, panel diaries of consumers are sometimes used, as are store audits, consumer intercepts at the time of purchase, and posttrial interviews. Demographic, psychographic, lifestyle, and media exposure data may also be monitored. As with pretest data, the information gained from test marketing may be used in formal models to forecast trial and repeat purchasing behaviors after the product is put on the market. The drawbacks of test marketing, in addition to its high cost, are that rollout and national introduction may be delayed. This permits the competition to learn at the firm's expense and to catch up. Some companies even sabotage the test marketing of their competitors by changing their own pricing, advertising, and promotion programs in the public test market. For these reasons, many firms bypass test marketing, despite the loss in information that entails. Some companies, such as manufacturers of durable goods or industrial goods, find it impractical to test market in any event.

Product launch is the fourth new-product development step. Here the product is introduced to the public, either nationwide or on a market-by-market basis to coordinate with production or other constraints. Special care is given to the monitoring of consumer adoptions, reactions by competitors, and problems in distribution. Invariably there are bugs in coordinating the entire marketing effort, and these require immediate attention. Planning, monitoring, and a resilient, fast-acting management control system are essential at this stage.

Finally, the new-product development process "ends" with *ongoing management*. We discuss this transition in chapters 7 and 8 as we consider managing the product through its life cycle.

Perceptual Maps and Product Positioning

Most products and services have many physical and intangible attributes with varied consequences for a would-be purchaser. An automobile is not merely "an automobile." Rather, for a consumer, it is a bundle of objective and subjective characteristics (size, color, ease of handling, roominess, comfort, price, and so on) and consequences (such as feelings of pride, power, or prestige). The marketer's task is the difficult one of deciding how many attributes to build into the product, how much quality to include in each attribute, and how to put the attributes together to gain a competitive advantage. Fortunately, due largely to implicit coping strategies employed by consumers in everyday decision making, only a few product attributes are important in any actual choice process. Indeed, two or three key attributes are often sufficient to predict consumer choices. As products become more complex and consumers become more sophisticated, however, marketers must build more attributes into the product. Note, too, that key attributes vary by market segment and therefore the marketing effort must change accordingly.

The conjunction of key product attributes and consumer perceptions (or beliefs) can be fruitfully represented in a perceptual map. Figure 1.2 presents one consumer's perception of beers for sale in northern California. Perceptual maps can also be prepared for groups of consumers and market segments. The dots show the perceived positions of different beers (disregard the circles for the moment). The two most common methodologies used to produce perceptual maps are multidimensional scaling and factor analysis, discussed in chapter 5.

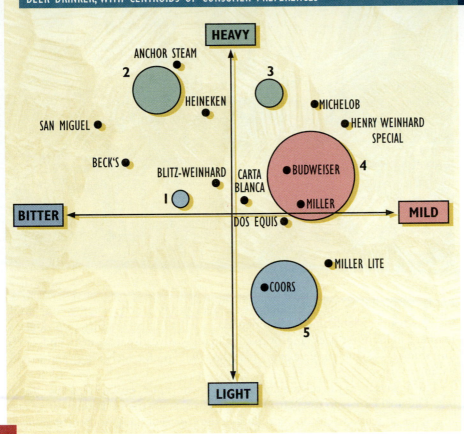

FIGURE 1.2

PERCEPTUAL MAP OF THE BEER MARKET IN NORTHERN CALIFORNIA ACCORDING TO ONE BEER DRINKER, WITH CENTROIDS OF CONSUMER PREFERENCES

Notice first in Figure 1.2 that this consumer uses two attributes to describe beers: heavy or light and bitter or mild. Some people employ more attributes and different ones (for instance, gaseousness and calorie content), but the two in the figure are quite common across the population. Notice further that the brands cover much of the map. This indicates that the consumer believes that brands differ on the two dimensions to a considerable degree. San Miguel is perceived as a rather heavy, bitter beer, for example, whereas Miller Lite is seen as a very mild, moderately light beer.

What can one learn from perceptual maps? First, they indicate the most important attributes in consumer decision making. These attributes then can become the focal points in product design and advertising decisions. Second, perceptual maps show where a firm's own brand and competing brands score in the minds of consumers on each salient attribute. Management thus obtains an indication of where it is strong or weak and who its primary rivals are. Third, perceptual maps suggest possible opportunities in the market. In Figure 1.2, for example, we see that no beer is perceived by this particular consumer to be both bitter and light. This suggests a potential entry point for a new product or an alternative strategy for a beer on the

These are only a few of the many beers offered in the Northern California market, where beer drinkers evaluate their choices as if they were fine wines.

border of the bitter–light quadrant (e.g., Beck's). Of course, whether this unfilled niche is really a viable market will depend on (1) the firm's ability to produce and market a light, bitter beer (and/or to convincingly advertise it as such), and—of first importance—(2) the number of people who would prefer such a beer and would be willing to try it.

This brings us to the related and important concept of *product (or brand) positioning.* The goal here is to use perceptual maps to suggest the best competitive tactics to pursue in market selection, product design (or redesign), and communication, pricing, and distribution decisions. Study of a product's position relative to that of its competitors on a perceptual map serves as a starting point for exploring competitive moves and their implications.

To take an example, let us assume the perspective of Carta Blanca. Figure 1.2 presents estimates of the sizes of consumer groups preferring various combinations of heavy–light and bitter–mild attributes in a beer. The circles represent centroids of consumer preferences; the size of the circle indicates the number of people (or share of the market) preferring the respective combinations of heavy–light and bitter–mild beer attributes. For purposes of discussion, we will assume that the perceptions of everyone surveyed can be represented as shown. We will further assume that Carta Blanca is losing market share and feels a need to respond accordingly.

Carta Blanca has three options. First, it can compete with Blitz-Weinhard and go after preference group 1. To do this, it might use advertising to stress that its product is neither too heavy nor too light, too bitter nor too mild, and rather, it is "the best balanced beer." Comparative ads with Blitz-Weinhard might be considered as well. In addition, a reformulation of the brewing process or ingredients might be called for to make Carta Blanca somewhat more bitter. Consumer research would show if this is necessary. Whether pursuit of preference group 1 is viable depends on the number of people in this group, their current brand preferences, the cost of going after these people, and the attractiveness of the remaining two preference group options.

Carta Blanca's second option is to take on Budweiser and Miller, who "own" preference group 4, the largest market segment. This probably is not viable, given that Carta Blanca is an imported beer that appeals to small numbers of beer drinkers, whereas Budweiser and Miller are domestic products with well-entrenched popular images. Budweiser and Miller also have cost advantages and greater marketing resources.

Carta Blanca's third option would be to go after preference group 5. This large segment desires a mild, light beer and currently has only three competitors. Here, Carta Blanca must consider the costs of changing its image, the costs of reformulating its product, and the size and receptivity of the preference group.

Whatever option is chosen, it is important to consider also the likely responses of competitors, as we show in chapter 2 on strategic planning. For example, Blitz-Weinhard would be likely to counter any threat by Carta Blanca. It could do this by cutting its price (not difficult because it has a distribution advantage), by advertising, or by doing both. A long-shot option for Carta Blanca might be to create a new market and pursue a slightly bitter, slightly light position in the hope of changing people's taste preferences or winning new adherents in the empty quadrant. Many other competitive issues are suggested by perceptual maps, but we will not examine them here.

Before we consider the ongoing management of products, we should mention a recently developed tool that is proving to be especially useful in the design phase. *Conjoint analysis* is an analytical technique that permits management to compare alternative product or service designs on the basis of consumer reactions. The procedure provides measures of consumer utility for attributes of products and enables management to select product versions with maximum appeal.

Managing the Product through Its Life Cycle

As we discuss in chapters 7 and 8, all products pass through life cycles. An ideal sequence of sales might be represented as follows:

product introduction → rapid growth → slow growth → leveling off → decline

Of course, some products never make it past introduction, others skip a stage or two, and still others continue on indefinitely as if renewed from time to time. Whatever the pattern of sales, management must orchestrate the application of marketing tactics throughout the life cycle of a product. In this sense, the product life cycle is at least partially controllable by management. Each stage in the life cycle of a product will require a different balance among marketing tactics. Resources must be allocated to advertising, promotions, personal selling, distribution, and pricing in a way that meets the goals of the firm. During the *product introduction* phase, profits are nonexistent and the objective typically is to increase consumers' product awareness and trial purchases (and stimulate a healthy repurchase rate in the case of frequently purchased products). Advertising will be heavy to inform people. Promotions will be used to motivate dealers and consumers. The sales force will concentrate its efforts on building distribution. The price may be set low to take advantage of experience curve effects and forestall competition. Or it may be set high to reap early rewards (more on this shortly).

During periods of *rapid growth*, adjustments must be made. These should, in turn, be guided by market research, including so-called tracking studies of awareness, attitudes, intentions, trial purchase rates, and repeat purchase rates. Market share may become a critical barometer, too. Fine-tuning and shifts in emphasis from one marketing tactic to another invariably take place. Normative managerial models and simulations may be used to aid in decision making here also. Advertising will shift from informative presentations to persuasion and may be reduced somewhat from initially high introductory levels. Promotion, too, will be reduced and shifted from trial-inducing tactics, such as sampling, to repeat purchase teasers, such as coupons or cents-off deals. The sales force will work to cement dealer relationships and ensure that deliveries, product quality, and so forth will be fulfilled. Prices may be lowered somewhat to meet the competition.

Slow growth and leveling off periods demand still other responses. Here the firm must assess its own growth in relation to market growth as well as take into account its market share. A change in product design may be required to meet the demanding tastes of people slow to try the product or to compete effectively with a new entrant. Advertising and promotion may have to be changed again to combat wearout (i.e., a decline in ad effectiveness over time) or meet the competition. Prices may have to be lowered still further. Market segmentation takes on a special urgency as a means of survival and furthering of the goals of the firm.

As the *decline* phase approaches, the firm faces difficult decisions, as discussed in chapters 2 and 8. Should the firm harvest, disinvest, or reinvest? Again, growth and market share must be weighed against goals and capabilities of the firm and the nature of the market and competition. An outcome to avoid is the self-fulfilling prophecy whereby an "apparent" decline is accelerated by a withdrawal of marketing support, and a potentially viable product is brought to a premature end. If the firm decides to harvest, then most expenditures on marketing will be reduced, and the product will be left to die on its own. If the firm chooses instead to reinvest, it may have to do so across the board, with major product design innovations, repositioning, and renewed expenditures on advertising, promotion, selling, and distribution.

A final set of product decisions concern *product-line planning*. The firm must decide whether to have a product line and, if so, what its composition should be. Consumer needs, the location of market segments, competition, market growth, market share, cannibalization, and profitability are important inputs to the decision process. Creating a well-designed product line entails looking not only at the health of each brand but also at the synergy among brands. The image and profitability of brands may be enhanced by careful design of the entire line, as cross-fertilization often occurs. The role of the product line also changes over time, with the leveling-off phase of the product life cycle revealing the product line's maximum contribution. The product portfolio and strategic group frameworks are especially useful in product line decisions, as we discuss in upcoming chapters. Given the decision to employ product lines, the marketer's task must be viewed as allocating marketing expenditures to the support of tactics that will best meet the firm's goals for profitability, market share, and growth. Enhancing brand equity and capitalizing on it through line extensions demands special attention.[20] We cover these topics in chapter 5 and again in chapter 8.

Communication Decisions

A Communication Model

Communication tactics are one of the most important and flexible links between an organization and its markets. Unlike product, price, and distribution tactics, which are more difficult to change and which remain relatively stable over time, communication is often the first and most effective lever an organization has to respond to or influence its markets. The range of communication tactics includes advertising, promotion, publicity, and personal selling. The goal of communication is to inform, educate, persuade, and/or influence behavior directly.

In simplified form, the communication process is as follows:

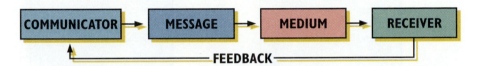

That is, a communicator sends a message through some medium to a receiver who processes the message and responds with feedback. Of course, communicator and receiver often change roles in rapid succession, and instead of a one-way sequence, the process is very much one of mutual exchanges. Nevertheless, in analyzing and designing communication tactics, it is useful to consider the process of communication as just depicted.

Figure 1.3 outlines the main variables and processes underlying communication in marketing, which we cover in more detail in chapter 9. Let us begin with a description of the processes going on within the consumer (i.e., receiver) after receipt of a message (see bottom of figure). Exposure to an ad, sales pitch, or other marketing communication leads first to perceptual processes. These may occur at the level of awareness or involve conscious allocation of attention. In any case, perceived information may have one or both of two effects (see *a* and *b* in Fig. 1.3). One is to influence the consumer's needs or motives and induce affective responses (path *a*). For example, physiological responses might be stimulated, along with felt positive emotions, and the desire for a product actuated. This, in turn, might lead to thoughts about the brand, how to acquire it, and so forth (*c*). Alternatively, perceived information might lead directly (*b*) to message comprehension and further cognitive responses (for example, generation of support for or counterarguments against the core selling point). The resulting "information processing" might stimulate feelings about the message, spokesperson, brand, and so forth as well (*d*). Information (*e*) and affective reactions (*f*) then are organized and integrated, and an attitude toward the brand and/or communication is formed (*g*). The output of this stage serves as input to mental decision-making activities, in which the consumer activates old preferences or develops new ones. This may lead further (*h*) to intentions to buy and, eventually, to actual purchase. Postpurchase experiences finally result in satisfaction/dissatisfaction and feedback upon the consumer's needs, motives, and feelings (*i*) and/or knowledge (*j*).

The value of examining how consumers process messages lies in the use of this information in the design of communications, discussed in chapter 9. Each stage shown in the bottom of Figure 1.3 will be affected differently by different communication tactics. For instance, humorous ads can be effective in stimulating attention, creating desired emotional responses, and at times inducing yielding to a persuasive appeal. But they are less useful in conveying information and aiding directly in decision making. Rational appeals, in contrast, excel in developing understanding, promoting effective information integration, and generally enhancing decision making. But they are less effective in influencing emotions. One goal in the study of how consumers process messages is to select the most appropriate communication tactic, given the product, consumer characteristics, competition, and stage of the product in its life cycle. Notice also that the ultimate choice to buy will be a

FIGURE 1.3 | COMMUNICATION PROCESSES IN MARKETING

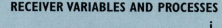

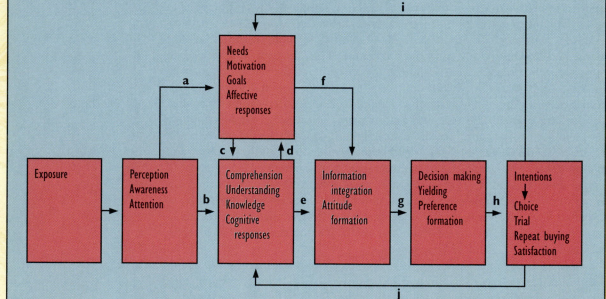

COMMUNICATOR VARIABLES

Credibility (expertise, trustworthiness)
Attractiveness
Mediator of rewards and/or punishments

MESSAGE VARIABLES

MESSAGE CONTENT
Product attributes
Consequences of use
Emotional appeals
Positive or negative moods
Humor
Fear
Extraneous factors
Use of a foil
Distraction

MESSAGE STRUCTURE
One-sided versus two-sided appeals
Order of presentation of arguments
Amount of information
Repetition

MEDIA VARIABLES

PERSONAL MEDIA
Face-to-face
Phone

NONPERSONAL MEDIA
Advertising (television, magazines, billboards, etc.)
Promotion
Publicity
Mail

RECEIVER VARIABLES AND PROCESSES

Needs
Motivation
Goals
Affective responses

Exposure

Perception
Awareness
Attention

Comprehension
Understanding
Knowledge
Cognitive responses

Information integration
Attitude formation

Decision making
Yielding
Preference formation

Intentions
Choice
Trial
Repeat buying
Satisfaction

differential function of the nature of communications and how they are processed at various stages leading up to choice. Only by considering the differential mental and emotional effects of messages at each stage can managers select the best communication options. This, in turn, requires that consumer research be performed along with the design of communication programs.

The top of Figure 1.3 presents the three primary levers that managers have to influence the communication process: communicator variables, message variables, and media variables. The options noted for each, individually and in combination, compose the communication mix. Let us briefly consider these.

The effect of a message can be augmented through the choice of characteristics of the *communicator*. To the extent that a spokesperson is perceived as being more expert, trustworthy, or attractive, the message will be believed to a stronger degree. Similarly, the more that a communicator is perceived to directly or indirectly provide a message receiver with rewards (monetary, psychic, or social outcomes), the greater the likelihood that a communication will have its intended effect. Note that communicator variables are separate elements under the control of management and work along with other determinants to influence consumers. Skillful choice of a communicator can lead to the development of a unique brand image (Elizabeth Taylor for Passion cosmetics, for example) and can influence special target markets (such as Michael Jordan for Nike basketball shoes).

Perhaps the most effective means of influence lie in the *message* itself (see Fig. 1.3). Here managers must give special attention to what is said (message content) and how it is said (message structure).

Two basic choices underlie the *message content* decision. Should rational or emotional appeals be used? A product with distinct attributes and benefits for a consumer or one that has utilitarian overtones lends itself to a rational approach. Ads for drain cleaners, motor oil, and investments generally follow this approach. Products whose appeal lies in psychic or social consequences or brands that differ only slightly from the competition find emotional appeals more effective. We see this in cosmetics, soft drink, and clothing advertisements. Of course, sometimes rational arguments and mood or other nonrational stimulants are combined into a single message. Witness Mercedes-Benz ads, which stress engineering yet also appeal to desires for luxury, status, and even excitement. Although difficult to execute, such dual tactics can be quite effective. In addition, seemingly extraneous content will be included occasionally along with the primary message. For example, small levels of distraction will be used to temporarily inhibit counterargumentation by an audience until the focal selling point can be made. Many ploys common to novels, plays, or the opera are employed: the use of a foil, fantasy, drama, comedy, slice-of-life, testimonials, satire, suspense, or storytelling, to name a few.

Equally critical is the organization of message content, which we term *message structure* in Figure 1.3. Here decisions must be made as to the use of one-sided versus two-sided appeals (i.e., presentation of only positive or of positive and negative information), order of presentation of arguments (i.e., whether to place the strongest argument first, in the middle, or at the end of a message), the amount of information to convey in any one message, and the scheduling of messages over time.

A third lever in the communication mix is *media selection*. This is an important problem area, not only because of its obvious role in reaching customers and in market selection, but because different media are more persuasive than others, depending on the needs of consumers and the characteristics of the focal product and the competition. Personal media (i.e., salespeople) are particularly effective for presenting expensive products, prolonged negotiations, custom designing of the product, influencing intermediaries, and closing sales. Nonpersonal media such as advertising, promotion, publicity, or catalog and mail marketing have the advantages of extensive reach capabilities, low cost per prospect reached, and the ability to stimulate trial use or purchase, remind people about availability, and reinforce other modes of selling (e.g., advertising can prepare and soften up a prospect before the encounter with a retailer or salesperson). We return to these topics in chapters 10 and 11.

Advertising

Three special concerns of advertising include repetition, message execution, and operations management.

Repetition. What is the optimal number of exposures of an ad? One industry researcher claims that three exposures are all that are needed to achieve the desired effects of advertising.[21] The argument is as follows. The first exposure to an ad is needed to attract attention. The consumer reacts with a "What is it?" response. A later, second exposure has two effects. One is a recognition reaction (i.e., "Ah ha, I've seen this before!"), whereas the second is an evaluative response (i.e., "What of it?"). Beyond this point, no deeper information processing occurs. The third and each succeeding exposure are simply reminder ads calling up from memory that which is already known (or believed). According to this argument, more than three exposures is not only wasteful but leads to disengagement of audience interest. This is the so-called wearout phenomenon.

One operational objective of advertising, then, might be to produce as many repetitions as are needed to achieve three exposures for as many people in a target audience as is feasible. Inevitably, some people will become overexposed, and as time passes the message will have less and less effectiveness. This might be indicated by a leveling off in awareness measures or even sales. What can be done to overcome wearout? One solution is to change the content or structure of the message. New communicators (spokespersons) or new humorous executions might be tried, for instance. Or new media might be explored in an effort to reach previously inaccessible consumers. Still another tactic is to introduce new product attributes not advertised before.

Message execution. How should one design and implement an advertisement? At least three issues must be addressed here. One is *media involvement*. Each medium has its own characteristics, which are more or less interesting to a target customer. For example, television is generally considered a low-involvement medium in that viewers tend to sit passively, let their minds drift, or even tune out commercials. Magazines, on the other hand, are more involving and permit exposure to ads to occur at more active and deeper levels. Obviously, every advertiser attempts to make its ads alluring, whatever the medium chosen. However, product characteristics, consumer media habits, and other considerations suggest that the marketer should carefully match his or her offering to the advertising medium and the target audience. Different media pose different problems and offer different opportunities.

A related issue is *product involvement*. Just as consumers are involved to different degrees with different media, so too do they find products to be important in varying degrees. For products of lesser salience to a consumer, information processing may occur in a shallow way, encompass few product attributes, and proceed quickly. Habit and impulse frequently play roles as well. More salient products encourage deeper information processing and over a wider spectrum of attributes, with much comparison among brands. Television ads for Panasonic video cameras convey about a dozen product attributes, whereas Trident gum ads seldom stress more than one or two. This, too, will affect the choice of media, the type of messages constructed, the scheduling of repetitions, and so on. Note also that *brand involvement* can be a factor. People are attached to or identify with brands to different degrees.

Finally, message execution should take into account how consumers will react to a message and the processes they will go through as they react. Marketers have found that the following sequences occur most frequently in real-world decision making.[22]

1. learn → feel → do
2. feel → learn → do
3. do → learn → feel
4. do → feel → learn

By "learn" we mean the comprehension, information integration, and decision-making activities shown in Figure 1.3. "Feel" refers to needs, motives, affective responses, attitudes, and preference formation. "Do" stands for actual trial or repeat buying activities or other behaviors: shopping, examination of independent consumer reports, talking to a salesperson, making a purchase, and so on.

Sequence 1 applies when products are complex, risky, expensive, and/or are considered important by the consumer. Here considerable information is first scrutinized and weighed before feelings develop and a decision whether to act is made. The purchase of a home computer would be an example. Sequence 2 also occurs in instances where consumers find the product to be important to them, but where the nature of the product or message is such as to first induce affective reactions. These reactions, in turn, generate thinking processes that lead to action. The purchase of clothing often fits this pattern. Sequence 3 figures in the purchase of everyday items such as dishwashing detergent, coffee, or milk. Either through habit or impulse, or because a product is so simple or uninvolving, it is purchased with little or no forethought. Its subsequent use or contemplation, however, leads to thoughts about the brand ("For small loads of dishes, I'll try half a capful") and, finally, affective reactions ("I really like brand X detergent"). Sequence 4 is similar to sequence 3, but here feelings follow action directly and then lead to thoughts. For instance, at midmorning, a vaguely perceived hunger pang might stimulate purchase of a candy bar from a vending machine. Biting into the bar triggers pleasurable feelings and elicits such thoughts as "This is a good buy" and "I think I'll get another."

If advertisers have sound information about how consumers react to messages and the processes they go through in decision making, they can create more effective ads. For example, products falling within sequence 1 typically require a demonstration of the product's use and benefits and detailed information—which requires considerable ad copy or personal selling efforts (chapter 11). More involving media, such as magazines or direct mail, may dominate. Products in sequence 2 require emotional appeals to involve an audience and make use of appeals to the ego or to self-esteem. Magazine ads and strong television executions may be needed here. Those products that elicit sequence 3 demand executions that induce trial purchases or remind consumers of an offering. Radio or television spots might work well; so might magazine ads with coupons. Sequence 4 products suggest ads that arouse emotions. Magazine or strong television commercials are a possibility. Point-of-purchase displays are options for products in sequences 3 and 4 as well.

These considerations are, of course, only rough guidelines. In the final analysis, any ad will reflect the particular philosophy, history, and style of the ad agency that creates it. Thus marketers must not only know their own products, customers, and competitors well but must also carefully evaluate alternative agencies and ad executions to arrive at a proper fit. These are largely subjective decisions.

Operations management. Finally, the advertising effort must be well managed. Two critical concerns here are copy testing and advertising budgeting. *Copy testing* refers to measurement of the effectiveness of advertising. Although statistical and mathematical modeling can be used to establish the relationship between advertising expenditures and sales (or market share), more frequently the effects of ads are determined by gauging their impact on intermediate variables, such as consumers' awareness, knowledge, recall, or recognition of the ad; their beliefs about the product's attributes; their interest in the product; and their intentions to buy or not to buy. Such indirect measurement is employed because it is easier, cheaper, and yet thought to be reasonably valid. Many independent companies offer copy testing services to advertisers.

Advertising budgets are set in a variety of ways. Sometimes a budget is made on the basis of subjective judgments by executives. A second method is simply to peg the budget to that of the competition: to meet the competitor's ad budget, exceed it, or fall below it by some percentage. Usually, however, budgets are set as a percentage of sales (e.g., last quarter's or this quarter's expectations). Unfortunately, each of the aforementioned tactics tends to be a hit-or-miss affair. A better way is to set ad budgets at levels needed to achieve some desired goal. The *objective and task method* attempts to do just this. The organization first defines a specific goal to be achieved—say, "60 percent awareness of our new brand in market Y by next year." Next, the tasks—number of repetitions, media selection, spokesperson, and so forth—are designed to reach the goal. The budget is then set on the basis of the tasks needed to reach the goal. Experimentation, statistical modeling, normative models, and market monitoring may be used in trying to meet the goal.

Promotion

Promotions are incentives directed at consumers or dealers to get them to buy a specific brand. Whereas advertising is most often designed to induce a psychological response prior to action or reinforce a previous exposure to an ad or previous purchase, promotions are attempts to stimulate actions directly. The most common consumer promotions are coupons, free samples, premiums, cents-off deals, contests, games, and prizes. *Speciality advertising* is really a type of promotion whereby free gifts in the form of a pen, calendar, coffee mug, or other item are given to a consumer. The gift serves as a reward for performing the desired action (patronizing dry cleaner X, buying magazine Y) and usually bears the name and telephone number of the sponsor as a constant reminder. Typical dealer promotions include point-of-purchase (POP) displays, cash allowances, credits, gifts, bonuses, "2 for 1" deals, contests, prizes, and free advice or information.

An important point to stress is that the communication mix tactics are interdependent and sometimes mutually reinforcing. This is nowhere more evident than with advertising and promotion. One study, for example, showed that advertising and promotion work together to produce a multiplier effect such that sales were much greater when both were used than when either one was employed alone. This study found, for example, that sales of coffee were 0.6 purchases per 100 shoppers when no ads or POP displays were used, 2.5 purchases per 100 when only POP displays were used, 1.9 per 100 with only ads, but 8.1 per 100 when *both* ads and POP displays were used.[23] Note, too, that many promotions reach consumers only through ads.

The question faced by management, then, is not so much whether to promote or to advertise but rather what proportion of each to employ. In practice, a wide range of advertising-to-promotion budget ratios are used. One consumer product firm, for example, sets its ratio at 70:30, which means it spends $7 for advertising for every $3 it spends in dealer and consumer promotions such as displays or coupons. What factors govern the balance? One is buyer behavior. If, for example, most prospective purchasers of a certain product decide to buy (or not) before they enter the store, then the ratio should be more heavily in favor of advertising. But if most prospects make up their minds at the shelf, then the ratio should favor promotion—specifically, POP promotion. Competition is a second factor. A small competitor cannot hope to emulate a large one, but it may gain a competitive edge by using a vastly different advertising-to-promotion ratio than the competition uses. Still another consideration is the stage of a product in its life cycle. Introduction, growth, leveling off, and decline require different tactics. Many other considerations, including market share, strategic group position, and firm constraints, may enter the picture.

Personal Selling

Face-to-face communication, although expensive, is the most compelling medium available to most sellers, especially for industrial products, as discussed in chapter 6. Personal contact permits a dynamic adjustment of needs and offerings on the part of both buyer and seller, and it facilitates the gaining of a commitment. Moreover, salespeople smooth out problems subsequent to the sale (e.g., late delivery), provide feedback about the market, and generate new business. In an age where everything and everyone seems to get lost in the crowd, personal selling lets the firm tailor its offerings, reach the right customer, communicate complex benefits and terms, and push control deeper into the channel of distribution. Although more expensive on a per customer basis than advertising, personal selling frequently costs less in absolute terms when the number of customers is small, the items are high-priced, or both.

For decades, researchers and practitioners have searched in vain for the magical profile of the "ideal" salesperson. At one time or another, salespeople were thought to need money more than achievement, to have high ego strength, empathy, verbal skills, aggressiveness, an aloof attitude, unusual levels of drive, or to be loved, and so on. Eventually, the ideal salesperson could be described by any and all attributes, and no one—or everyone—could fit the bill.

There is no such thing as the ideal salesperson. But within the past few years, research has identified a small number of fundamental attributes or abilities common to most successful outside salespeople. First and foremost, they must be motivated. Salespeople must value the intrinsic and extrinsic rewards associated with selling and believe that working hard will earn them these rewards. Second, leading salespeople tend to have high levels of self-confidence and self-esteem, especially in relation to the specific job at hand. To the extent that attaining high levels of sales is consistent with their task-specific self-image, salespeople are motivated to work hard to achieve at a level in concert with that self-image. Third, the ability to learn from feedback and supervision is crucial, especially as it serves to promote and reinforce job satisfaction. Fourth, successful salespeople generally cope better with ambiguity on the job. (Ambiguity arises from lack of certainty as to what the supervisor, customer, and others expect.) Fifth, salespeople must be able to deal with conflict, tension, and strain. These aspects of the job are consequences of organizational boundary-spanning activities and differences in interests, points of view, and job pressures. Finally, effective selling requires an ability to analyze customer needs and plan and adjust one's activities and communication tactics to advantage. In personal selling, interpersonal skills reign supreme.

The management of a company's personal selling effort entails several key decisions. As we discuss in chapter 11, after goals for sales and profitability are set, one of the manager's first tasks is to determine the size of the sales force. This might be done by estimating the desired productivity of salespeople and taking into account the number of total customers (actual plus potential) as well as geographic, economic, and other considerations. At the same time, the manager must decide how to organize the sales force (by geographic territory, customer type, product category, brand, or whatever). This done, the manager can determine the size of each territory or the number of accounts and/or products that each salesperson will have. These decisions should, if possible, be based at least partly on target sales or profit figures. A recruitment, selection, and training program must be designed as well. Finally, supervision, compensation, work standards (e.g., call norms), and general planning, management, and control mechanisms must be set in place. Many of these issues can be approached through various normative models that have been proposed by marketers to aid in planning and decision making. Job design, leadership, and career development principles are important, too.

Just as advertising and promotion are mutually reinforcing activities, so too may personal selling interact with other modes in the communication mix to more effectively generate sales. A key decision is whether to pursue a push, a pull, or a push–pull strategy. That is, should the firm place major emphasis on selling to intermediaries (the push strategy), to final customers (the pull strategy), or both? The push strategy requires a vigorous sales force, dealer promotions, and relatively high margin pricing. The pull strategy rests largely on advertising with perhaps some consumer promotions. Most firms use a push–pull strategy; industrial goods sellers rely relatively more on a push mode, whereas the strategies of consumer goods sellers are more balanced or lean toward a pull mode. The choice of balance between push and pull depends on how and where consumers make decisions, the size of the market, what consumer media habits are, the nature and complexity of the product, the competition, market growth, market share, and so forth.

Price Decisions

Goals and Constraints in Pricing

Long gone are the days when prices were set haphazardly as an automatic and more or less fixed markup over costs. Today, price is viewed in an active and not merely reactive sense as one way to stimulate demand, compete effectively, or both. As a tactical tool, price offers a number of benefits to the firm. First, unlike most communication, product, or distribution tactics that entail up-front costs as well as involved plans and procedures for their implementation, price moves do not require costly expenditures and can be instituted relatively easily. Second, consumers find appeals based on price easier to understand and respond to than the more indirect and abstract effects of advertising, product attribute, and distribution-based (e.g., location) appeals. Finally, even when other tactics such as personal selling or image advertising are the primary concern, price can be a valuable and readily applied adjunct, reinforcing the effects of other marketing tools. On the other hand, price cutting can be perceived as a threat by competitors and lead to price wars, in which all companies suffer. Also, price cuts can lead to negative inferences about product quality.

The pricing process begins with the goals of the firm and the objectives for the brand in question. Common options are to view price as a means to achieve or maintain market share, stimulate primary and secondary demand, increase short- or long-run profitability, signal competitors that one will respond aggressively to threats or alternatively wishes to avoid a price war, discourage new entrants, strengthen and reward intermediaries (e.g., by providing them with healthy margins), communicate value to consumers, stay within the law, or simply act in a socially responsible way. Most of these ends require that the firm conduct research to determine the relationship between price and sales. This may mean conducting experiments, running statistical analyses of data, performing simulations, or employing normative models based on managerial judgments and other data.[24] In many countries, sellers of like products set prices in collusive or coordinated ways. In a few countries, among them the United States, price collusion is forbidden by law.

With rare exceptions, prices are constrained to fall within a relatively narrow range. At the bottom end, costs provide a floor below which the firm cannot survive for long. At the top end, prices are constrained by competitive undercutting or by a ceiling on what consumers can afford or what they feel gives them value. In between lie the degrees of freedom open to a firm.

Taking a proactive stance, we can think of the pricing problem as one of maximizing profits or some other goal. For example, we know that profits (z) can be written as a function of price (p), costs (c), and quantity sold (q), $z = (p - c)q$. Our objective is to arrive at the highest level of z through an optimal choice of p. However, p is constrained by consumer preferences, the competition, and government regulations. Further, profits can be influenced by keeping costs low, which, in turn, depends on the quantity sold, experience curve effects, and shared experience and costs with other products (see earlier discussion on overall cost leadership and learning curve effects). Moreover, q, itself, is at least partially influenceable through p and the remaining marketing mix tools. Thus, z can be increased indirectly by stimulating demand. We find, therefore, that the maximization of z is a complex endeavor. Nevertheless, once we have an idea of the determinants of constraints for p, c, and q, we can use calculus or simulations to arrive at a maximum z. The task thus depends on arriving at realistic functions for p, c, and q. It is beyond the scope of this chapter to cover the many recent developments in this area.[25] We, however, briefly sketch here some of the qualitative considerations. We explore price relationships further in chapter 12 on pricing.

Consider first the constraints on price and the implications of setting various price levels. To satisfy consumer needs, price should reflect, and be set on the basis of, perceived benefits to consumers. But how can this be done? One way is to use conjoint analysis and treat price as a product attribute along with other attributes. In a survey, the consumer then must choose a product with a bundle of attributes producing that consumer's highest utility. Conjoint analysis yields the consumer's judged disutility of specific price options and shows the trade-offs between various prices and product attributes. The price suggested by a conjoint analysis is, of course, constrained further by what competitors are offering and what is legally permissible. Product differentiation and careful market selection can lessen the impact of these constraints, however. A last point to note is that price elasticities—especially those that are a function of product life cycle stage—must be taken into account in planning.

The determinants of costs must also be scrutinized. Fixed costs that are large relative to variable costs often dictate low pricing in order to increase capacity utilization. On the other hand, large variable costs relative to fixed costs sometimes force the price up. In either case, however, efforts will be made to drive down both fixed and variable costs. Economies of scale, experience curves, shared learning, and product line considerations play roles here. Moreover, overall strategic goals must be taken into account. An overall cost leadership orientation will result in lower prices than will a product differentiation approach, for example.

Pricing must be coordinated with all the tactics used in implementing the marketing mix. This is so not only because the various tactics interact and can thwart or augment each other but also because profits and other goals are proportional to the magnitude of marketing mix expenditures that stimulate demand, as suggested by the profit formula discussed earlier. Therefore, the effects on demand of *all* of the marketing tactics including price must be ascertained when determining price.

Pricing Tactics

Prices come in various forms; they are not limited to a single "purchase price." Quantity discounts, "2 for 1" deals, promotion allowances, coupons, and other gambits widen the scope of pricing tactics. Let us explore the options open to a marketer.

For a new product, either a price skimming or penetration pricing tactic is warranted. With *price skimming*, a high price is set. The hope is that there are enough customers who will be willing to pay a premium for the brand. As this market dries up, prices will be reduced gradually to draw in other customers. Price skimming is used when one wants to create an image of high product quality, when rivals will be slow to enter the market, when buyers value the product highly and demand is inelastic, or when fixed and variable costs either benefit little from experience curve effects or fail to achieve significant economies of scale. Hewlett-Packard, Polaroid, and DuPont have been known to practice price skimming.

Penetration pricing is the tactic of introducing a product at a low price, perhaps in anticipation of future cost declines and a burgeoning market. Over time, the price may be raised, but not necessarily. Penetration pricing is frequently employed as part of a market share strategy, as well as a means to generate primary demand. Unlike skimming, penetration pricing tends to discourage new entrants in that it signals strong price competition and relatively low profits. Penetration pricing works best when production and distribution channels are in place, consumers are price sensitive, either the adoption process is fast or the product is a frequently purchased good, and sufficient economies of scale and experience curve effects are forthcoming. Texas Instruments, Japanese automakers, and Beaird-Poulan have used this approach, for example.

The prices of industrial goods are strongly influenced by costs and competition, as we discuss in chapter 6. Indeed, many such goods are sold through competitive bidding arrangements. Alternatively, contracts are employed that focus on cost-plus or target-incentive considerations. Functionality and value are, of course, central concerns. In the selling of industrial goods, there is much negotiating of terms and tailoring of the product to the individual customer. This tends to make price not so much a decision variable, set independently by the seller and presented to the buyer in a take-it-or-leave-it fashion, as it is a mutually constructed accommodation that is constrained by factors that face both seller and buyer.

By contrast, pricing of consumer goods necessarily is done much more on the basis of company needs and before presentation to the consumer. Although market research is performed, so many buyers are involved, with different tastes and resources, that an "average" price must be set. In addition, the manufacturer must often take wholesalers and retailers into account when setting prices. Intermediaries require incentives and compensation for their efforts. This complicates the price-setting task and introduces an additional set of constraints. Industrial goods sold through distributors or manufacturers' representatives exhibit similar problems.

Pricing decisions must be made throughout the life cycle of a product. Price elasticities typically decline as the product moves from the introduction phase, through the growth phase, to the leveling-off phase. They increase, however, in the decline phase. Moreover, increases in competition throughout the product life cycle drive prices downward. At the same time, variations in growth, market share, and profitability across brands in a product line interact complexly with price decisions and must be watched carefully.

Distribution Decisions

Designing the Channel

The *channel of distribution* is the system of institutions used to deliver goods to the final consumer, as discussed in more detail in chapters 13 and 14. The intermediaries who make up a given channel might include brokers, manufacturers' representatives, distributors, wholesalers, and retailers. Some or all might be wholly owned by the manufacturer or even by one of the intermediaries. Alternatively, the system might consist of independent businesses that buy and sell the goods of producers or act as the producers' agents through contractual agreements. Still another possibility is that a manufacturer might sell directly to its customers without going through intermediaries. For instance, direct mail, a sales force coupled with delivery through common carriers, or mobile company stores might be used. With greater sophistication in communication, market research, operations, and delivery, firms are frequently turning to direct marketing to reach customers. No matter what system is employed to bring the goods to market, certain functions must be fulfilled: transportation, storage, transfer of title, provision of credit or other special services, assortment, selling, delivery, receipt of funds, and so on.

Channel decisions must be considered carefully for several reasons. First, and most obvious, the channel of distribution is an essential link, a gatekeeper to the market. Shelf space in the supermarket or an account with an aggressive distributor is not only a necessity but tends to function as a self-fulfilling prophecy. That is, the channel stimulates demand, just as advertising, product design, and price cuts do. Second, it is very expensive and time consuming to set up and maintain a distribution channel. The commitment risks are great, and there is little room for error. Moreover, it is difficult to make changes in a channel once the channel has been set in place. Third, the channel of distribution may provide the competitive edge over rivals. This edge may be a unique location, efficient delivery and inventory practices, special selling skills, market monitoring services, or some other advantage. Finally, the selection of a channel will constrain or facilitate the choice and implementation of other marketing tactics. For example, retailers often require assistance from manufacturers in the form of promotions and business advice and at the same time expect the manufacturer to conduct advertising and other demand-stimulating activities. Different channel options imply different balances of power, influence, and control between manufacturer and intermediary as well.

The design of the channel depends on how consumers make decisions about the particular product, the number and dispersion of consumers, the amount of goods to be sold and their value, the costs of various channel options, the tasks that must be performed (e.g., service, credit provision, market research), and competitive practices. For example, when purchasing clothing, most people like to compare many styles, colors, and brands, try on alternatives, receive a certain amount of help from salespeople, and make use of tailoring services. These factors, in turn, make clothing stores or store departments the dominant form of distribution. Nevertheless, for a few people who have neither the time nor the inclination to shop, catalog shopping is attractive, despite the uncertainties of fit and the absence of service. L.L. Bean and Lands' End, for example, achieve worldwide distribution for busy consumers.

We can view the *channel design* process as follows. First, the firm must decide whether to sell direct or to work through intermediaries. This decision, in turn, depends upon (1) how well each channel option can perform the aforementioned distribution functions for the firm, (2) the costs of reaching consumers, and (3) the degree of control the firm desires in managing the distribution of its goods. Selling direct provides the maximum control but is more expensive and less flexible in providing certain functions. Management must, therefore, weigh the gains against the costs to determine what is best in its own particular situation. Most consumer goods manufacturers find that it is easier and cheaper to go through independent wholesalers or distributors than it is to sell to retailers. But there are exceptions. Gallo Wine, for example, is large enough to do much of its own distribution directly to retailers. Industrial goods firms sometimes sell through distributors, yet in many cases they find direct selling possible.

If management decides to sell through intermediaries, then it must choose the *breadth of coverage* needed to reach consumers. Three possibilities exist. One is an *intensive distribution* system, in which the producer seeks as many outlets for its wares as possible in a market area. This option is most appropriate for selling to the mass market, particularly by producers of convenience consumer goods (e.g., breakfast cereal or paper napkins) or undifferentiated industrial goods (e.g., nuts and bolts). Buyers of these goods do little shopping around, purchase with a minimal amount of deliberation, and value convenience more than anything else. Intensive distribution also lends itself to products whose costs per unit to store, display, or sell are low. Pepsi Cola, Johnson's Wax, and Kellogg's Raisin Bran employ intensive distribution.

A second breadth of coverage option is *exclusive distribution*. This is the polar opposite of intensive distribution in that only a single outlet per market area is utilized. The producer hopes to create a unique image for its product, to obtain more vigorous selling efforts, and to extend its control over certain practices of the distributor or retailer (for instance in pricing, quality control, or market monitoring). In exchange, the intermediary receives the right to be the sole seller for the producer's goods and thereby gains special services and a competitive advantage in the market area. Most automotive companies, some manufacturers of expensive china, and certain appliance makers use exclusive distribution arrangements.

Selective distribution is the third option for achieving breadth of coverage. Here the firm seeks more than one, but considerably fewer than all, outlets in a market in the hope of obtaining many of the advantages of exclusive distribution while at the same time reaching further into the market. However, being a compromise tactic, it shares some disadvantages of both polar extremes. Selective distribution is especially appropriate for medium to moderately high priced shopping, specialty, or industrial goods where personal selling is required. For example, Calvin Klein clothes, Hartmann Luggage, and Pioneer Electronics use what is essentially a selective distribution approach.

In addition to choosing a breadth of coverage option, the user of intermediaries also must decide upon the vertical *length of the channel system*. Here, too, at least three possibilities exist: corporate, contractual, or independent (also termed conventional or administered) systems.

The *corporate marketing channel* is one in which all stages from manufacture through distribution come under single ownership. Leading examples include Goodyear tires, Sherwin-Williams paints, and Shell oil and gas services. The advantages of a corporate system include lower costs (through standardization and other economies of scale) and greater control than with the other options. In particular, a firm can achieve more influence over hiring, pricing, promotion and selling, provision of service, and even product quality with a corporate system than it can with a contractual or an independent system. On the other hand, corporate systems require very large capital investments, are risky both financially and legally (i.e., they may invite antitrust actions), and tend to be less adaptive to changing market and competitive conditions. It should be noted that some firms employ a modified corporate channel system by vertically integrating partway into distribution.

Contractual channel systems consist of collections of more or less independent companies bound by legal agreements akin to exclusive distribution, yet going even further. The most common contractual systems are franchises, but retail cooperatives and voluntary chains organized by wholesalers are also examples. Here we focus on franchising, which accounts for about one third of all retail sales in the United States and is a growing approach in other parts of the world.

Under franchising, the franchisor provides the franchisee with materials, a product, financial know-how, and other services. An exclusive right to sell the franchisor's product or service in a market area is also provided. The franchisee, in turn, agrees to abide by certain requirements and procedures dealing with selling, product or service quality, and other marketing functions, and perhaps also to pay a fee and/or percentage of revenues. Soft drink producers such as Coca-Cola, for example, sell the right to use their names and market their products in a market area and provide syrup concentrate to bottlers (i.e., franchised wholesalers) in exchange for finished production and marketing services. Another type of franchise operation is exemplified by Burger King, which provides land, equipment, supplies, technical and managerial advice, marketing plans, advertising support, and other services to a franchisee, who pays an up-front investment fee, makes periodic royalty payments, and manages the business.

Franchising has pros and cons for franchisor and franchisee alike. On the plus side, franchisors obtain capital, a highly motivated distributor/retailer, and some economies of scale through purchases of supplies, manufacture, advertising, and promotion. Moreover, although franchising affords less control than does a corporate channel system, a strong degree of influence over marketing practice is still possible. Franchisees benefit in that they receive considerable amounts of money and support to get started in their own business, "instant" brand recognition and reputation, and ongoing managerial advice. On the negative side, however, the franchisor loses some control over, and is even dependent on, the franchisees. Uneven quality control by one or a few franchisees can hurt the industrywide image of the franchisor's business, and legal encounters sometimes mar ongoing relationships with franchisees as well. Further, franchisees occasionally find that their freedom is restricted and that they must purchase supplies or services they do not want or which they could procure at less cost elsewhere. The initial investment for a franchise can be heavy, too, reaching into the hundreds of thousands of dollars or more.

Independent channel systems—the third vertical option—consist of loose associations of separate private enterprises that cooperate with each other for mutual gain. Typically, an independent wholesaler or distributor handles the goods for many producers and manufacturers. The services that independent intermediaries provide include such functions as storage and inventory control, delivery to retailers, provision of credit to buyers, a sales force, transfer of title, and information gathering on the marketplace. The intermediary usually buys goods from a manufacturer at a discount and resells them to retailers at a profit. Consignment selling and the right to return unsold merchandise are also frequent practices.

Independent channel systems offer producers the advantage of obtaining marketing services at a cost less than they would incur themselves. Moreover, with an independent system the producer gains more flexibility and incurs less risk than it would with a corporate or contractual system. One may more easily switch to other independent intermediaries or set up an entirely new system in response to a changing market or competitive threats. Still another benefit is the expertise and market-monitoring services provided. Unlike a contractual or franchise system, independents deal with competitors and sometimes are closer to the market. On the negative side, producers lose considerable control and at times pay higher margins. Procter & Gamble and General Electric are two well-known users of independent channels of distribution.

Managing Channel Relationships

Distribution decisions do not end with the design and establishment of the channel. Rather, choices must be made continuously with regard to channel modifications and ongoing management. Consumer tastes and purchase habits change, competitors invent new products and ways of marketing, and intermediaries' loyalties and levels of performance shift over time. The firm must evaluate the effectiveness of its current channel relations and alter them as necessary. This might mean adding or deleting wholesalers or retailers to change the breadth of coverage. More fundamentally, it might even mean introducing or bypassing a level in the length of the channel or exploring entirely new ways of bringing goods to the market. Which of these options is chosen will depend on the discovery of new markets or evolutions in old ones, competitive moves by rivals, or inadequacies in the existing arrangements.

Ongoing management of channel relationships, which may well constitute the producer's largest commitment in time and energy, can be the key to achievement of a competitive edge. A central concern here is motivation. The success of a firm rests, in part, on the productivity of individuals over whom it may have limited control. Healthy margins, attractive compensation, credit, contests, promotional allowances, point-of-purchase displays, various services, and other facets of the terms of trade can boost individual efforts to the producer's advantage. In addition, the intangible side of management—leadership and the everyday human contact—deserve attention. Formal and informal lines of communication facilitate the implementation of influence and accommodations that must be made in both directions if the channel is to compete effectively.

Also important is the management of conflict among channel members. Misunderstandings, conflicts of interest, and tension and strain are endemic to interpersonal and interfirm relationships. To cope with these, an attempt must be made to reduce ambiguity in expectations, rights, and responsibilities. A climate of cooperation and fairness must be fostered. These can be accomplished, in part, by establishing clear rules and procedures, making communications explicit, and engaging in joint decision making where appropriate.

Finally, a firm must establish managerial controls over channel operations. This means formulating appropriate goals, monitoring performance, administering rewards or corrective actions, and adjusting the functions of the channel to the other marketing tools.

MARKETING MANAGEMENT: AN OVERVIEW

The marketing management process can be viewed as an integrated sequence of five steps with feedback (Fig. 1.4). In abbreviated form, the process can be written as:

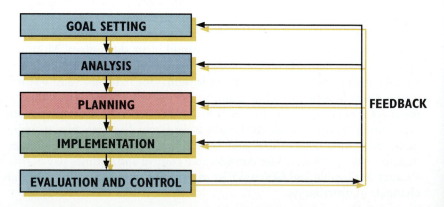

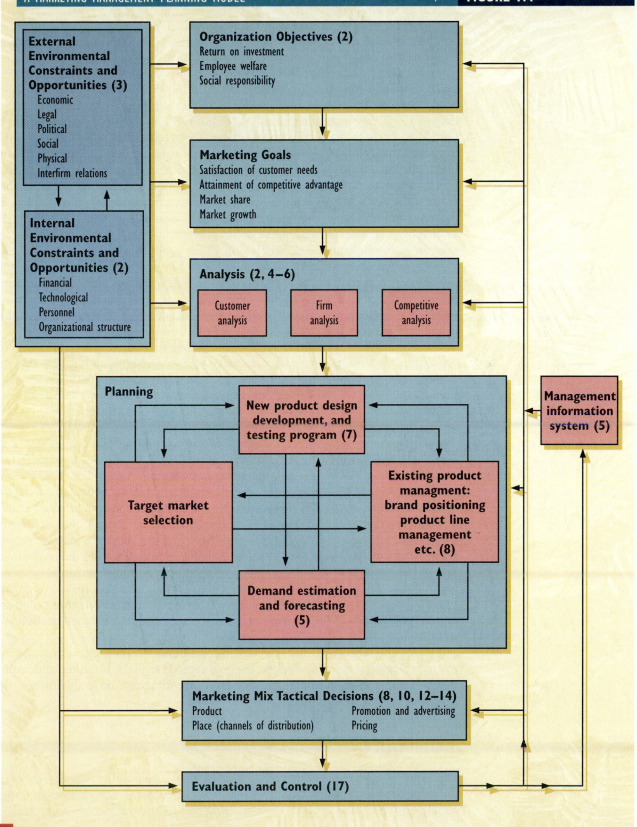

A MARKETING MANAGEMENT PLANNING MODEL   **FIGURE 1.4**

External Environmental Constraints and Opportunities (3)
Economic
Legal
Political
Social
Physical
Interfirm relations

Internal Environmental Constraints and Opportunities (2)
Financial
Technological
Personnel
Organizational structure

Organization Objectives (2)
Return on investment
Employee welfare
Social responsibility

Marketing Goals
Satisfaction of customer needs
Attainment of competitive advantage
Market share
Market growth

Analysis (2, 4–6)
Customer analysis
Firm analysis
Competitive analysis

Planning
New product design development, and testing program (7)
Target market selection
Existing product managment: brand positioning product line management etc. (8)
Demand estimation and forecasting (5)

Management information system (5)

Marketing Mix Tactical Decisions (8, 10, 12–14)
Product
Place (channels of distribution)
Promotion and advertising
Pricing

Evaluation and Control (17)

Let us outline the steps here as a prelude to the full development and description contained in subsequent chapters.

The marketing management process begins with *goal setting*. Management sets goals that serve as intermediate steps in the pursuit of the organization's mission. Marketing goals also function as measures of the firm's performance. The goals then become operational standards guiding the analysis, planning, implementation, and evaluation and control activities of the organization.

Analysis constitutes an important early step in the process. *Customer analysis* addresses the needs of consumers, and determines which current products satisfy or fail to satisfy those needs, why those products succeed or fail, what kinds of products might be required to satisfy those needs, how consumers go about satisfying needs and making decisions, and what the overall consumer market(s) looks like. *Firm analysis* considers the ability of the organization to meet the needs of consumers. This entails assessment of the firm's current products, the potential for developing new products, the financial and production capabilities of the firm, the availability of needed inputs, public policy considerations, and the opportunity for effective communication and distribution of the product. *Competitive analysis* constitutes an assessment of existing or potential rivalry among firms selling the same product, the power dependence relations of the firm with customers and others, and the role of alternative sources of satisfaction as a competitive threat. All three forms of analysis—customer, firm, and competitive—are performed through research and managerial decision making, topics we consider throughout this book.

Following analysis, four *planning* processes come to the fore. The first, *new product design, development, and testing*, is a crucial activity for the firm. It is here that the organization generates innovations and translates them into need-satisfying products. Most firms have special departments and people who perform these new product functions, and we devote two chapters in this book to their description. A second, related planning process is *existing product management*. Obviously, after a new product becomes established, the need for sound management does not end. Decisions must be made about the brand's current position, the need to add new features or models, and the need to eliminate some features or models. *Demand estimation and forecasting* comprise still a third essential planning activity. Indeed, the livelihood of the firm itself depends on how well it predicts demand. Finally, because it is both impractical and inefficient to capture all markets, strategic choices must be made in *target market selection*. These four planning processes are interactive, not static. For example, one cannot estimate demand without knowing the target market, and the selection of the target market depends on potential demand.

The strategic plans must next be *implemented*. This is accomplished through tactical choices among the marketing mix. Different levels and combinations of products, channels of distribution, promotion, and prices are the tools used to stimulate and meet demand.

Finally, the marketing management process ends, temporarily, with *evaluation and control* programs and *feedback* on the goal setting, analysis, planning, and implementation processes. Throughout this book, we elaborate on and illustrate the processes previously outlined.

SUMMARY

Marketing is both the glue that binds the functional areas of the firm together and the bridge to the outer environment that leads to consumer satisfaction and, ultimately, to the firm's survival. It is marketing and its many functions that produce true synergy within a firm and make exchanges with customers mutually satisfactory. Marketing helps to make the whole truly more than the sum of its parts. Now that we have provided an overview of marketing and marketing management, we turn to detailed consideration of its parts.

QUESTIONS FOR DISCUSSION

1. Ralph Waldo Emerson is credited with saying, "If a man . . . makes a better mousetrap . . . the world will beat a path to his door." What do you think he meant by this statement? In what sense does it relate to marketing management? In what sense is it shortsighted?

2. Pick an organization you know or one in which you are interested. What is its main mission? Who are its customers? What are the features or attributes of its brands or services, and what needs do these serve? How does it communicate to the market, and how are its products or services delivered? What strategy does it follow in its pricing?

3. Postal systems are often criticized by the public and business managers. What do you think the postal service could do to improve its image and services?

4. A few years ago, 7-Up met with considerable success when it turned to its uncola campaign. But after a while, sales fell again to disappointing levels. Why do you think 7-Up is so far behind the market leaders, Coca-Cola and Pepsi? What does 7-Up have to do to achieve success?

5. After two decades of decline, the U.S. auto industry has shown signs of reversing the trend. What lessons do the experiences of General Motors, Ford, and Chrysler have for marketing managers?

NOTES FOR FURTHER READING

1. American Marketing Association, 1985.

2. Arnold Kransdorff, "History Sacrificed on the Altar of Downsizing," *The European*, September 19–25, 1996, p. 24.

3. See C. A. Bartlett and S. Ghoshal, *Managing Across Borders: The Transnational Solution* (Boston: Harvard Business School Press, 1989); Y. L. Doz and C. K. Prahalad, "Managing DMNCs: A Search for a New Paradigm," *Strategic Management Journal* 12 (1991): 145–164; C. K. Prahalad and Y. L. Doz, *The Multinational Mission: Balancing Local Demands and Global Vision* (New York: Free Press, 1987).

4. Regis McKenna, "Marketing Is Everything," *Harvard Business Review*, January–February 1991, pp. 65–79.

5. Regis McKenna, *Relationship Marketing* (Reading, Mass.: Addison-Wesley, 1991); Jagdish N. Sheth and A. Parvatiyar, "The Evolution of Relationship Marketing" (Paper presented at the conference on Historical Thought in Marketing, Atlanta, Ga., June 1993). Christian Grönroos, "The Rebirth of Modern Marketing—Six Propositions about Relationship Marketing" (Swedish School of Economics and Business Administration, Helsinki, Finland, 1995).

6. David Lavinsky, "When Novelty Wears Off, Soft Drinks Clearly Will Fail," *Marketing News*, March 15, 1993, p. 4.

7. The three approaches are described in Michael E. Porter, *Competitive Strategy: Techniques for Analyzing Industries and Competitors* (New York: The Free Press, 1980). See also William K. Hall, "Survival Strategies in a Hostile Environment," *Harvard Business Review* 58 (September–October, 1980): 75–85.

8. In later years, after the 1978 acquisition of 7-Up by Philip Morris and the switch in ad agencies to N W Ayer, and into the 1980s, 7-Up lost some of its earlier hard-won successes. It is still far behind the market leaders—Coke and Pepsi—and after being sold by Philip Morris and acquired by an investment group, the new Dr. Pepper/7-Up Companies have reached a steady rate of 4.2 percent market share for all of 7-Up brands (Patricia Winters, "7-Up Logs 'Un'-usual Gains in Market Share," *Advertising Age*, November 16, 1992, p. 43). Perhaps 7-Up has reached a watershed in consumer acceptance, or perhaps the competition is too powerful to overcome, particularly in terms of distribution. Interestingly, 7-Up's new ad agency, Leo Burnett, has revived the uncola campaign.

9. J. Fred Bucy, "Marketing in a Goal-Oriented Organization: The Texas Instruments Approach," in J. Backman and J. Czepiel, eds., *Changing Marketing Strategy in a New Economy* (Indianapolis, Ind.: Bobbs Merrill, 1977).

10. "Note on the Use of Experience Curves in Competitive Decision Making" (Boston: Harvard Business School, Intercollegiate Case Clearing House, 9-175-174, 1975).

11. Bucy, "Marketing in a Goal-Oriented Organization."

12. Ibid.

13. Lynn W. Phillips, Dae R. Chang, and Robert D. Buzzell, "Product Quality, Cost Position and Business Performance: A Test of Some Key Hypotheses," *Journal of Marketing* 47 (Spring 1983): 26–43.

14. The data quoted for the firms in the chain saw industry came from personal communication with Harvard Business School professor Michael E. Porter, as well as two cases he wrote: "The Chain Saw Industry in 1974" (Boston: Harvard Business School, Intercollegiate Case Clearing House, 9-379-157, 1975); and "The Chain Saw Industry in 1978" (Boston: Harvard Business School, Intercollegiate Case Clearing House, 9-379-176, 1979).

15. Much of the information presented here on Lipton Herbal Teas is drawn from a presentation by, and subsequent personal communications with, John W. Sullivan, who at the time of the case was president of Kelly, Nason, the ad agency for Lipton Herbal Teas.

16. Michael Lanning and Lynn Phillips, "Strategy Shifts Up a Gear," *Marketing*, October 1991, p. 9.

17. This example is taken from a presentation by Elliot B. Ross of McKinsey and Company to an MBA class at Stanford University.

18. The estimated costs and failure rates are derived from Glen L. Urban and John R. Hauser, *Design and Marketing of New Products* (Upper Saddle River, N.J.: Prentice-Hall, 1980), ch. 2. We have made adjustments to their figures to account for inflation.

19. Alvin J. Silk and Glen L. Urban, "Pre-test Market Evaluation of New Packaged Goods: A Model and Measurement Methodology," *Journal of Marketing Research* 15 (May 1978): 171–191. See also Thomas D. Kuczmarski, *Managing New Products: The Power of Innovation*, 2nd ed. (Upper Saddle River, N.J.: Prentice-Hall, 1992).

20. David A. Aaker, *Managing Brand Equity* (New York: Free Press, 1991).

21. Herbert E. Krugman, "Why Three Exposures May Be Enough," *Journal of Advertising Research* 12 (December 1972): 11–14.

22. Richard Vaughn, "How Advertising Works: A Planning Model," *Journal of Advertising Research* 20 (1980): 27–33; Richard Vaughn, "How Advertising Works: A Planning Model Revisited," *Journal of Advertising Research* 26 (1986): 57–66.

23. Point-of-Purchase Advertising Institute, 1978, quoted in D. I. Hawkins, R. J. Best, and K. A. Coney, *Consumer Behavior: Implications for Marketing Strategy* (Plano, Tex.: Business Publications, 1983), p. 563.

24. Kent B. Monroe and Albert J. Della Bitta, "Models for Pricing Decisions," *Journal of Marketing Research* 15 (August 1978): 413–428. Kent B. Monroe, *Pricing: Making Profitable Decisions* (New York: McGraw-Hill, 1990).

25. See, for example, Robert J. Dolan and Abel P. Jeuland, "Experience Curves and Dynamic Demand Models: Implications for Optimal Pricing Strategies," *Journal of Marketing* 18 (Winter 1981): 52–73; C. D. Fogg and K. H. Kohnken, "Price-Cost Planning," *Journal of Marketing* 15 (April 1978): 97–106; Hermann Simon, "Dynamics of Price Elasticity and Brand Life Cycles: An Empirical Study," *Journal of Marketing Research* 16 (November 1979): 439–452; Frank M. Bass and Alain V. Bultez, "A Note on Optimal Strategic Pricing of Technological Innovations," *Marketing Science* 1 (Fall 1982): 371–378; B. Robinson and C. Lakhani, "Dynamic Price Models for New-Product Planning," *Management Science* 21 (1975): 1113–1122.

CHAPTER

2

STRATEGIC PLANNING AND MARKETING ORIENTATION

CHAPTER OBJECTIVES

When you are done with this chapter, you should have achieved the following:

- A thorough grasp of the importance of marketing as a philosophy of doing business and a marketing orientation being widely disseminated throughout a company.

- A basic understanding of the strategic management process and how it cuts across structural and organizational thinking levels.

- A basic understanding of fundamental aspects of strategic management and how marketing influences their development.

- A basic understanding of portfolio techniques for evaluating strategies, their application in line with marketing principles across multiple structural levels of the company, and some of their limitations.

- A basic understanding of the role of marketing in the successful implementation of strategic initiatives throughout a company.

CHAPTER OUTLINE

Dedicated to being the world's best at bringing people together anywhere, anytime—this is the essence of AT&T's mission statement. It summarizes the guiding vision for the company into the information-rich twenty-first century. From being the world's largest regulated monopoly throughout most of its history, AT&T is transforming itself into a firm that can take advantage of the convergence of voice, data, and video digital communications, and can offer bundled communication services to consumers around the world. The strategic planning and management required for this transformation is a good example of the importance of marketing as a business philosophy in modern organizations.

After the breakup of the American Telephone & Telegraph monopoly in the early 1980s, AT&T was left with a long-distance network and telephone hardware manufacturing facilities, but was barred from offering local phone services. The company struggled initially. It recognized the potential for growth in the digital telecommunications industry, as consumers demanded increasingly versatile, reliable, and fast communications. AT&T attempted to bridge the gap between digital applications and its communications network through strategic partnerships with companies such as Olivetti, Sun Microsystems, and other hardware and software producers. These partners' entrepreneurial cultures differed from AT&T's own more bureaucratic style, however, and the alliances were not fruitful. At the same time, because of being busy

Companies, like people, must move boldly into the future. AT&T was one of the first companies to offer their own credit cards.

trying to make its alliances work, AT&T overlooked the emerging cellular communications business, which was captured by independent companies and several of the "Baby Bells" (e.g., Ameritech, BellSouth). Throughout the 1980s, many industry experts expressed doubts over AT&T's ability to compete in fast-paced markets, and compared the company to a lumbering dinosaur doomed to extinction.

AT&T, however, believes that dinosaurs can survive and thrive in fast-paced environments. Through its setbacks in strategic alliances, and later in its 1991 acquisition of the large computer manufacturer NCR, AT&T learned much about the integration of digital-based communications media and about how to make it work over its long-distance network. More recently, AT&T has assembled an impressive array of strategic business units with which to compete in this market. A consistent factor in AT&T's strategic efforts is its use of marketing expertise to collect market and industry information, which are the basis of the company's strategic initiatives for the late 1990s and beyond.

AT&T's strategic transformation has involved selective expansion and downsizing. Based on its core long-distance business, AT&T has been able to generate funds to invest in other businesses. One expansion move was to enter the credit-card market with the very successful Universal Card. Even in diversifying into the credit-card market, however,

AT&T built on its strengths, as managing a credit-card operation made use of AT&T's cash management and billing expertise from years of handling long-distance billing for millions of individuals and companies. In addition, the AT&T Universal Card was designed for use in charging long-distance telephone calls around the world. Universal Card's many subscribers have contributed to higher call volumes on AT&T's long-distance network. Another expansion move was AT&T's acquisition of McCaw Cellular Communications, now renamed AT&T Wireless. When McCaw was acquired in 1993, it was the world's largest cellular telephone company with 2.2 million subscribers, and it had unmatched cellular installation expertise. Since then McCaw has grown to well over 6 million subscribers and maintained its industry leadership. This makes up for AT&T's early oversight of the cellular market and positions the company to capture part of the growing global market for cellular communications.

In addition to these large investments, AT&T has made smaller but significant investments in other areas. It has selectively invested in companies with path-breaking technologies, such as General Magic, a software company that develops information search agents for World Wide Web applications. It has launched new services, such as World-Net, an Internet-access service, which became the number two provider of Internet access in the United States in less than a year. It has expanded its service array to include both local and long-distance service in many markets. Lastly, it has established joint ventures with telecommunications companies around the world, including WorldPartners, a loose federation of sixteen companies in Asia and Europe.

AT&T's strategic moves have also included divestitures in various areas. Its two biggest changes involved spinning off its computer and telephone hardware manufacturing operations into separate businesses. AT&T acquired NCR in 1991 and merged it with its existing computer operations. By 1995, however, it became clear that the computer hardware business was too far away from AT&T's core competencies for the company to manage it effectively. In a move that was initially criticized but that ultimately proved successful, AT&T Global Information Systems was sold to shareholders. At the same time, AT&T also divested itself, through a similar financial arrangement, of its AT&T Network Equipment operations, which were renamed Lucent Technologies.

Through these strategic changes, AT&T has transformed itself into a digital communications company that can compete effectively across the spectrum of consumer-driven services. These strategic moves have allowed the company to remain a significant player in the U.S. market for bundled communications. They have also allowed AT&T to make more efficient use of its long-distance global network, and to provide digital communications services to emerging markets in Eastern Europe and Asia ahead of its competitors. Although the market for digital communications services is likely to remain very competitive, there is little doubt that AT&T will be a leader in the industry for the foreseeable future.

Sources: "AT&T's Three-way Split," *The Economist*, September 23, 1995, pp. 51–52.

Alan Brew, "Putting the Marketplace Ahead of the Ego," *Brandweek*, January 22, 1996, p. 13.

Andrew Kupfer, "AT&T: Ready to Run, Nowhere to Hide," *Fortune*, April 29, 1996, pp. 116–118.

Jonathan E. Levine, "For Emerging Countries, Cellular Is No Luxury," *Business Week*, April 5, 1993, p. 60.

Susan Pulliam, "Buy McCaw and Put It On Hold," *Wall Street Journal*, June 9, 1994, p. C2.

EXEMPLIFYING MARKET ORIENTATION

While many other companies are still talking about their plans for the information age, AT&T is making its plans a reality through marketing-oriented strategic management of its resources. Like many other market-driven companies, AT&T develops both long- and short-term strategies that are sensitive to customer needs and have high profit potential, and it looks for ways to make these strategic initiatives complement one another. Commercial and nonprofit organizations around the world are adopting marketing as a philosophy of doing business (a marketing orientation), and are incorporating marketing concepts and perspectives into practically every functional area of their businesses. This trend has been termed the "new role of marketing."[1]

A look at AT&T's investment and divestiture strategy reveals a serious long-term commitment to being at the forefront of the digital communications industry through new communications services (e.g., integrated audio and video communications), and the enhancement of existing ones (e.g., bundling cellular, Internet access, and regular telephone services), all while remaining a profitable publicly traded company. A commitment to meeting customers' current and future needs profitably is at the root of AT&T's current strategies. As a successful company, AT&T is a good example of a company integrating a marketing orientation into management decisions at all levels of the business, from the mission of the company, to the strategies and objectives of its business units, to the product, pricing, promotion, and distribution tactics of its many divisions.

MARKETING'S TRANSITION FROM FUNCTION TO PHILOSOPHY

Except for some visionary companies such as IBM, Procter & Gamble, and Quaker Oats, the notion of customer orientation articulated in the 1950s was treated by most companies as academically interesting but not very practical.[2] The claims that product, promotion, pricing, and distribution decisions should be integrated and focused on customer satisfaction seldom found their way into the day-to-day practices of most organizations. In a typical organization, the marketing area was responsible for promotional efforts such as sales and advertising, and it competed for resources and management attention with other functional areas such as accounting, manufacturing, and personnel. Fundamental shifts in global competition and consumer demands, however, made old ways of doing business obsolete and demanded a marketing orientation. The transition of marketing from function to philosophy is exemplified by the changes at Ford Motor Company during the 1980s (see Marketing Anecdote 2.1).

At Ford Motor Company, the transformation led to the sincere belief that "Quality is Job 1." This is more than a catchy slogan. It captures the attitude of Ford employees, from the assembly line to the corner office. Through its competitive struggles in the 1970s, Ford discovered a deeper level of the marketing concept, and adopted it as a way of life for all company members. A similar pattern of behavior can be seen in many other organizations in the United States, Canada, and Europe, by companies that suffered serious setbacks at the hands of competitors who were more in tune with customer needs. They had to transform their organizations or risk going out of business. Although they may have achieved success without a marketing orientation in the past, the changes in consumer attitudes and global competition in the 1970s and 1980s necessitated such an orientation. Even companies that had been held up as examples of "good marketing" in the 1950s and 1960s

At Ford Motor Company, staff groups performed many of the tasks associated with the marketing mix (product, price, promotion, and distribution) for many years with little marketing guidance, and these groups often did not work together well. Engineering and design groups developed new products, routinely ignoring input from marketing research. The financial organization controlled pricing based on cost and profit objectives for the model year, and the materials management organization handled distribution. None of these groups considered consumer attitudes in their decisions. The marketing area did control promotional efforts to a greater extent, but even here advertising agencies did much of the work, limiting the marketing area's role to setting general guidelines and overseeing agency efforts. Selling, of course, fell to independent dealers using different sales strategies that were only partially controlled by the marketing group. Most of Ford's relations with dealers focused on making sure dealers had adequate inventory, convincing them to participate in sales-promotion programs, and responding to customer-service problems.

At the same time, Ford's strategic managers focused primarily on financial factors. Sales and revenue projections, break-even analysis, return on investment, and other financial measures dominated senior management's thinking and were seen as the most important determinants of company strategy. In the stable automotive markets of the 1950s and 1960s, future performance was easily forecast from past trends, and the occasional exception was seldom significant enough to cause permanent changes in the company's standards and procedures. Even large failures such as the Edsel were relatively short lived. They were typically offset within a few years by great successes such as the Mustang and did not produce significant changes in the strategic management process.

The role of marketing at Ford began to change in the 1970s, as the company's market share eroded and the strategies typically used to generate consumer demand did not work. By the late 1970s, no successes had offset product failures such as the Mustang II and Granada, and the company's product reputation suffered permanent and seemingly irreparable damage. Japanese automobile manufacturers, with a stronger focus on product quality, customer satisfaction and aggressive pricing, made substantial gains in market share around the world and redefined the criteria used by U.S. car buyers in choosing a vehicle. Ford management's assumptions that styling was the most important factor considered by the car-buying public—and that reliability, fit-and-finish quality, and customer service were secondary—were no longer true, and strategies based on this belief system, which had worked in the past, could not counteract the company's decline.

Understanding the customer's new attitudes and desires, however, was not simply a matter of conducting superficial market research studies. Customer changes touched many more areas of their lives than car purchases. Ford discovered that younger customers had a fundamentally different perspective on the world, different aspirations, and higher standards of acceptable quality and performance in all consumption areas in the 1980s than this age group had in the 1950s, 1960s, and 1970s. Market research also revealed that customers' standards were constantly escalating. It is difficult to ascertain whether Japanese automobile manufacturers were consciously better at marketing than U.S. manufacturers, or whether Honda, Nissan, and others simply had a philosophy of doing business that was more appropriate for the times. But as market share and profits continued to decline, the answer quickly became irrelevant. What mattered was that customers had changed, competition had increased, and past practices and perspectives no longer worked.

As a matter of survival, Ford was forced to abandon its traditional procedures and attitudes toward marketing. Managers and employees alike had to dispense with outdated traditions and values. Starting with the development teams for the Taurus and Sable car lines in the mid-1980s, marketing principles and a sincere commitment to customer satisfaction have been slowly integrated into all aspects of Ford's management process. Greater integration has been the primary motivation behind the Ford 2000 reorganization initiative, and is evident in world-class products such as the Windstar minivan and completely remodeled F-150 pickup truck. The Taurus/Sable, Windstar, and F-150 all entered the market with world-class quality and performance levels, and they met with almost immediate success. The impact of a strong marketing orientation on the success of these products has motivated other parts of the Ford organization to adopt this new philosophy of doing business, and it accelerated the integration of marketing principles into all areas of the business. One example is the area of supplier relationships, where concerns about customer satisfaction and profitability have led to greater cooperation between Ford and its suppliers, and longer-lasting relationships. Today Ford is often mentioned as a success story and cited as an example of a marketing-driven company. This image, however, is a relatively recent phenomenon.

Sources: Kirk Cheifits, "Can Ford Put It Back Together?" *Monthly Detroit*, April 1980, pp. 43–48.

Rebecca Fannan, "The Road Warriors," *Marketing and Media Decisions* 22 (March 1987): 60–66.

"Ford After Henry II," *Business Week*, April 30, 1979, pp. 62–65.

Kathy Jackson, "Strategy at Ford: Develop Cars Fast," *Automotive News*, November 16, 1992, p. 1.

Kathleen Kerwin and Larry Armstrong, "Red Hot, Red Ink," *Business Week*, January 11, 1993, pp. 26–27.

Mary Machacek (director of purchasing for Ford's Commercial Truck Division), speech delivered at the Automotive News World Congress, January 10, 1995.

Russell Mitchell, "How Ford Hit the Bull's Eye with Taurus," *Business Week*, June 30, 1986, pp. 69–70.

Keith Naughton, "How Ford's F-150 Lapped the Competition," *Business Week*, July 29, 1996, pp. 74–76.

Allan Nervins and Frank Ernest Hill, *Ford: Decline and Rebirth, 1933–1962* (New York: Scribner's, 1962).

found that they had to become even more focused on understanding consumers and meeting their needs.

The pervasiveness across industries of management choosing consciously to adopt a marketing orientation has led to the widespread adoption of marketing as a philosophy, rather than simply a functional area. Factors such as global competitiveness, customer diversity, just-in-time inventory management, and a focus on quality have become increasingly important over a long time, and these same factors will likely remain important for the foreseeable future. Consequently, the trend toward greater emphasis on marketing will probably not be reversed any time soon. The environment calls for a new role for marketing in organizational management.

Starting with the premise that market-oriented companies seek to meet the needs of customers profitably, this chapter discusses the marketing role at three related structural levels: *corporate*, *business unit*, and *product market*. It also looks at the role of marketing at three levels of organizational thinking: *culture*, *strategies*, and *tactics*. Putting together these structural and conceptual levels provides a more in-depth understanding of how a marketing orientation flourishes throughout the organization, and serves as a basis for discussing elements of strategic management and their execution. We examine:

- mission statements
- goals and objectives
- strategies for growth and consolidation
- organizational and industry factors that affect the adoption of different strategies
- portfolio techniques for evaluating alternatives.

The chapter also shows how managers across different organizational levels implement plans based on marketing principles.

Adopting a marketing orientation throughout an organization does not imply that conflicts will not occur; misunderstandings and personal differences are always possible in human interaction. However, with such a marketing concept, conflicts are likely to be less severe and easier to resolve because all members of the organization share a mind-set and consequently employ concepts and ideas in their problem solving that are easily understood by others. *Mind-sets* are the beliefs, attitudes, and values people use to make sense of their environment and to take action. Carefully managed mind-sets shared by an organization's members can be a major competitive advantage.[3] The marketing concept should serve as the core around which corporate mind-sets can be established. Consequently, combining marketing and strategic management should result in more responsive, flexible, and competitively strong organizations.

MARKETING ACROSS LEVELS OF ORGANIZATIONAL STRUCTURE

Conventional thinking in strategic management suggests that organizations develop strategies at three structural levels.[4] At the *corporate* or most senior level, managers coordinate the company's activities to achieve corporate objectives and to comply with the performance standards set by the organization's constituencies (e.g., stockholders, employees, customers, suppliers). Corporate management deals with questions such as, "In what business or businesses should we be involved?" and "How should we allocate resources among different business areas to achieve our general objectives?" For example, AT&T's corporate management decided that the company needed to be a major player in the telecommunications industry and allocated resources to areas such as large-capacity Internet-access servers, personal communications technology, and improving the performance of its long-distance network. Marketing's role at the corporate level is to make sure that management considers important external factors, such as unmet customer needs and competitors' strategic moves, in its decisions.

Corporate management typically focuses its attention on hiring competent people and securing sufficient resources to maintain a competitive advantage in at least some business areas. It also looks for ways to build operational linkages between business areas that will enhance the organization's competitive advantage. Such linkages often involve areas such as technology, manufacturing, and human resources. AT&T, for example, built its resource base through acquisitions, such as McCaw Cellular Communication, and promoted performance-enhancing linkages by instituting a management structure that broke down divisional barriers, such as different financial reporting standards and computer platforms between McCaw and other areas of the company. McCaw and other AT&T areas that impinged on the cellular communications business became an autonomous division named

AT&T Wireless, eliminating bureaucratic hurdles and helping the company move aggressively into the cellular communications market.[5] Performance can also improve by sharing manufacturing facilities, sales personnel, distribution channels, or corporate staff support.

At the business-unit level, management is more focused on the industry in which the unit competes than on the general business climate.[6] *Business unit* refers to an organization that manages several related products and technologies in a broadly defined market. At AT&T, for example, a unit responsible for providing wireless communications services (cellular telephones, personal digital communications services, satellite-based conferencing) to other organizations is a business unit.

At the business-unit level, marketing provides a detailed understanding of market needs and the various means by which other organizations in the industry are responding to those needs. Business units seek to capitalize on what they do best to secure and maintain a competitive advantage. Companies with a technological advantage, for example, build on this strength by offering outstanding products and services and by reinvesting the profits to retain their technological edge. George Lucas followed this approach when he established his Industrial Light and Magic special-effects company. When Lucas produced the first *Star Wars* movie in 1977, he used better and more sophisticated special effects than any seen in motion pictures before. Instead of limiting these technologies to his own motion pictures, however, Lucas formed a company to provide special-effects production to other motion picture and television studios. Almost overnight, Industrial Light and Magic became a multimillion dollar business and one of the dominant companies in the special-effects industry. It has sustained its competitive advantage by investing in new technologies as they emerge, such as the powerful workstations developed by Silicon Graphics and used in the production of motion pictures such as *Jurassic Park*.[7] Companies may also pursue competitive advantage through access to low-cost raw materials or supplies, highly efficient manufacturing facilities, or highly skilled workforces. Finding these sources of competitive advantage is not always easy, however, because it requires business unit management to understand both the business and its environment very well. Management can apply market research techniques to gather information and assist the business unit achieve its goals. Companies that discipline themselves to search for hidden value are in better positions to compete over the long term.[8]

Product-market management focuses on the "four P's" of marketing (product, price, promotion, and place) as they relate to specific products in specific markets. The management of cellular telephone services in Malaysia is an example of a product market. Another example is the creation of the Value Point line of computers by IBM.[9] Prior to the creation of the Value Point line in 1992, IBM's PS/2 models had been losing market share in the personal computer business to the ProLineas and Conturas that Compaq marketed to value-minded customers. The Value Point line was introduced to compete directly with Compaq's products for entry-level and budget-minded computer buyers. The product features and performance of Value Point models matched those of the Compaq line, and the price was competitive. In addition, the Value Point line had the advantage of being sold by both PS/2 dealers and IBM's direct response unit in Atlanta. Although the Value Point line has since been replaced by the Aptiva line, its mixed distribution strategy, excellent performance, and competitive price helped IBM retain market share in a very competitive market. As this example illustrates, product-market level managers deploy the right combinations of resources to achieve detailed objectives.

A marketing orientation can influence behavior at different levels of management, and sharing a market orientation across levels can help to integrate marketing activities. It can be argued, for example, that because the AT&T Wireless senior managers and cellular service product managers throughout Asia are all striving to meet customer needs profitably, they are able to agree on how corporate-level goals translate into performance standards for Asian sales efforts, and how sales results in Asia impinge on future corporate decisions. The compatibility that exists between the actions of senior managers and product managers, however, depends on more than marketing orientation being shared across structural levels. It also depends on members of the AT&T organization understanding one another well enough to share a common vision and a sense of how to achieve it. In other words, compatibility also requires a marketing orientation across levels of organizational thinking.

MARKETING ACROSS LEVELS OF ORGANIZATIONAL THINKING

Marketing concerns differ in content across the various structural levels of organizations, but all levels share some aspects of organizational thinking. This is not to suggest that organizations have a mind of their own, but that the people in organizations share knowledge and beliefs about the business at different levels of abstraction, and that marketing should play a role in shaping their thinking at every level. The levels of shared thinking that marketing should influence are culture, strategies, and tactics, each of which should in some way reflect a commitment to meeting customer needs profitably.

The most abstract level of managerial thinking is that of culture. *Culture* is defined as a set of fundamental assumptions, values, and behavioral norms shared by organization members. Culture influences how organization members see themselves, how well they work together, and the direction in which they move the organization. Organizational culture has been discussed extensively in management and marketing circles, and has been identified as a strong influence on an organization's strategic management.[10] For example, a company in which all members see themselves as independent contractors, responsible only for their specific assignments and expected to "mind their own business," will have a very different culture than a company in which people see themselves as "members of a family" who need to support one another. This difference in culture will affect how people feel about their jobs and the organization, as well as the company's ability to respond to major challenges or opportunities. In the telecommunications industry, culture has been an important factor in the success or failure of collaboration attempts, such as WorldPartners and the merger of British Telecomm and MCI.[11] Companies that have widely divergent cultures may have all the right technological and structural components in place, and yet fail to achieve the market orientation required to serve customers profitably.

Marketing affects culture by increasing the organization's sensitivity to customer needs at multiple levels, and by putting top priority on meeting those needs profitably. When marketing affects an organization's culture, its members see themselves as personally involved in meeting customer needs and contributing to the bottom line, and this view influences every aspect of their work. At Ford, for example, "Quality is Job 1" has become part of the value structure for most employees. It provides a guiding principle to the accountant processing financial information, to the college recruiter screening potential candidates, and to the line worker putting the finishing touches on a new car or truck.

Strategies are also sets of beliefs shared by members of the organization, but they are beliefs about how to achieve a specific set of company objectives. Strategy can be thought of as the "plan of attack" by which a company deploys resources to achieve objectives such as increasing profits, improving customer satisfaction, or stopping market-share erosion. A plan of attack should be detailed in terms of location, resources, direction, and timing. Seeing strategy as a plan of attack uses "war" as a metaphor for business, which is a popular way to approach marketing problems around the world.[12]

Within an organization, shared strategic beliefs are not as widespread as organizational culture beliefs, because people seldom need to know how to achieve objectives for which they are not responsible. Thus, at AT&T we would expect the culture to be shared even though the strategies are different across divisions, such as AT&T Transmission Systems and AT&T Universal Card. Such was the case when these two divisions won Malcolm Baldrige National Quality Awards in 1992.[13] The Malcolm Baldrige National Award competition, sponsored by the U.S. Department of Commerce, gives awards annually to companies that meet very demanding quality standards in all areas of their business. Winning two awards in one year is a feat that has not been repeated by any other company in the United States.

The two AT&T divisions that won Baldrige Awards followed different strategies to achieve their high levels of quality, but both were focused on customers needs and profitability. The Universal Card division focused on showing enthusiasm when dealing with individual customers and finding innovative solutions to their problems quickly, be they lost cards, incorrect billings, or disagreements with retailers. The Transmission Systems division, in contrast, adopted a strategy for solving customer problems that involved people at many levels finding the "right" technical solution. This division's customers are other companies who are building telephone exchange systems, of which the division's products are important components. Large-scale installations such as telephone exchange systems typically suffer complex problems, and such customers are willing to wait if it means that problems will be fixed right the first time.

Marketing influenced the strategies of these two divisions by providing information about customers and competitors that was used to develop their detailed plans. Marketing also provided information about the organization's strengths and weaknesses and how they affect its ability to meet external demands. In addition, marketing ideas and concepts are often used to determine the proper time horizon for strategies, for defining meaningful objectives, and for setting those objectives at challenging but achievable levels.

Tactics embody the most concrete thinking level in organizations. These are the specific solutions that are developed on an almost continual basis in response to changes in the environment. Marketing's effect on tactics is obvious, since many of the tactics involve marketing functions like new products, advertising, pricing, distribution, and sales. In 1993, for example, USAir started offering free domestic flights to funeral directors for every 30 corpses that were shipped with the airline. The air shipment of corpses has become increasingly popular in the United States as highly mobile people still want to be buried close to their roots. USAir's program resulted in a 30 percent increase in corpse shipments in the first four months of 1993, and was considered very successful. It has since been copied by other airlines.

Even when tactical moves involve other functional areas, marketing has an effect. Occasional problems with truck engine shortages at Ford, for example, typically involve production and materials management for resolution. They also include efforts by the sales organization, however, to minimize adverse dealer and customer reactions to not being able to get the engines they want in their new trucks. Salespeople often implement programs that encourage dealers and customers to use alternative engine-truck configurations until the shortages are alleviated.

	CORPORATE	BUSINESS UNIT	PRODUCT MARKET
CULTURE	CULTURE-SHAPING VALUES	Values emphasized that make sense for specific markets	General perspective or world view
STRATEGIES	Evaluation of mergers, acquisitions, and strategic alliances in terms of synergy to meet customer needs	STRATEGIC PLANS FOR TARGET MARKETS AND INDUSTRY	How to aggregate tactics into a coherent approach to the market
TACTICS	Specific tactics for guiding, developing, and motivating key members of the organization	Specific tactics for developing important technological or manufacturing resources	TACTICS FOR PRODUCT, PRICE, PROMOTION, AND DISTRIBUTION

The effects of marketing on all three levels of organizational structure and thinking can be combined to create the summary matrix in Figure 2.1. This matrix highlights the most important areas affected by marketing at each level. Corporate management must shape the *culture* of the organization. Sensitivity to customer needs and profitability concerns should be part of the mind-set of all members of the organization as they respond to the environment, and such beliefs need to be disseminated through the actions and words of senior management. Top AT&T and Ford managers, for example, seem to have disseminated cultural values very well, given their success.

Culture is further articulated by business-unit managers relative to their specific markets. For some business units, the culture might be one focused on achieving high profit levels without jeopardizing customer goodwill, whereas in other units winning customer confidence may be the most important goal. Although these different cultural orientations suggest different priorities for their respective business units, both are shaped by marketing. In the personal computer industry, for example, companies such as Compaq and Hewlett-Packard are involved in both the home personal computer market and the high-end business workstation market. While retaining their unique cultures, both of these companies emphasize efficiency and cost reduction in the home personal computer market, given its thin margins, and emphasize customer service in the more profitable business workstation market. Both companies are also expanding into the computer peripheral market, and are developing strategies to service customers and encourage additional purchases.[14]

At the product-market level we expect that cultural values will affect the perceptual screens or lenses that managers apply to make sense of day-to-day activities. Managers at a Ford assembly plant, for example, will see each vehicle as a means of enhancing customer satisfaction with the company, in addition to seeing it as a complex collection of components that the company must assemble efficiently.

Detailed *strategic* plans are most important at the business-unit level. Business units need coherent and well-developed strategic plans. They need plans for offsetting competitors' strengths, for identifying and reaching target customers, and for positioning products or services to maximize their impact on performance. Detailed strategic plans can also be developed at the corporate level for some functional areas, such as human resource development strategies to staff senior management positions. However, such detailed strategic plans at the corporate level are not common.

Product-market managers must develop *tactics*. Although tactics can also be employed to achieve very specific objectives at the corporate and business-unit levels, tactical plans are implemented, evaluated, and adjusted at the product-market level on a daily basis. The level of specificity at which tactical plans must be drawn and their very narrow scope of application require a lot of attention and quick reaction. Timing is a critical issue in executing tactical plans, since many of the problems that emerge at this level require a quick response. The announcement that two AT&T divisions won the Baldrige Award, for example, triggered a flurry of promotional activity as the firm developed advertising to capitalize on this unprecedented achievement. Sales tactics across other divisions of AT&T were likely also changed to capitalize on the successes of their sister divisions.

When companies have adopted marketing as a business philosophy to cut across structural and organizational thinking levels, it should be evident in different aspects of the companies' overall strategic management, from the mission statement to the techniques used to evaluate different investment opportunities.

Mission Statement

Whether the organization is a large corporation or a small nonprofit agency, its mission statement articulates its strategic scope clearly. The mission statement should answer fundamental questions such as, "What is our business?" "Who are our constituencies?" "What value do we provide customers, employees, suppliers, and other constituent groups?" and "What should our business be in the future?" Senior management in all businesses needs to answer such questions, and it is safe to conclude that the largest share of responsibility for developing and articulating a mission statement is at the corporate level.[15]

Mission statements should be driven by three factors: *heritage*, *resources*, and *environment*. The organization's *heritage* is its history—where it has been, what it has done well, and what it has done poorly. A good mission statement cannot ignore previous events and how they shaped the organization. It also must be sensitive to the organization's image in the minds of its constituencies. Past successes should be extended, past failures avoided, and the organization's current image must be addressed realistically. For example, for a machine tool manufacturing company to adopt a mission statement such as "to be a world leader in information technology in five years" will be perceived as unrealistic by customers, employees, and shareholders. Such a mission statement is likely to elicit more skepticism than support.

Resources refer to everything the organization can manage, such as cash reserves, recognized brands, unique technologies, and talented employees. Resources can also include borrowing power, existing relationships with distributors, and excess plant capacity. A good mission statement notes the organization's resources and sets paths that are compatible with what the organization has at its disposal. As in the case of heritage, mission statements that are out of touch with the organization's resources elicit skepticism and can do more harm than good. If a regional beverage brand such as Faygo were to include "penetrating Asian markets" in its mission statement, it would be met with substantial skepticism, given the overwhelming obstacles to international distribution that even giants such as Coca-Cola have encountered.[16]

The *environment* is everything happening currently that affects the company's ability to achieve objectives or implement strategies, both inside and outside the organization. Some environmental factors are temporary, such as a hurricane in Florida or a bumper soybean crop in Illinois. Most temporary factors are too short lived to be considered in a mission statement. Other factors, however, such as changes in the political system of the Russian Republic or the rise of Islamic fundamentalism, have a longer life and should be considered in the mission statement if they affect the organization's ability to survive and prosper.

At the corporate level, the mission statement defines the organization's business and reflects fundamental beliefs about its strengths and weaknesses, as well as its environment. The mission statement of a large corporation, for example, General Electric, must encompass its diverse interests in areas such as aerospace, electrical systems, and financial services. It must also address the organization's responsibilities to customers, employees, shareholders, suppliers, and the government. General Electric's corporate mission focuses on enhancing overall competitiveness by eliminating the "boundaries" that separate its business units, customers, suppliers, and employees, and thus improving the company's responsiveness to the environment.[17] Most recently, the pursuit of this "boundary-less" state in an information-rich, efficiency-driven, and service-quality–committed environment has led the company to expand the service component of its operations across the many industries in which it competes.[18]

Corporate mission statements can vary in length, but should always communicate a clear sense of the organization's purpose and be specific enough to be useful in developing goals and objectives. Typically, mission statements focus on meeting customer needs and providing value to its shareholders. In addition, they often include judgments about the most promising directions for organizations, implying that directions not listed are not as promising and should be given lower priority or ignored altogether.

Marriott Corporation's 1988 mission statement (Fig. 2.2), for example, focuses on being the best provider of food and lodging services in the world.[19] It seems safe to assume Marriott would consider real estate speculation a low priority, even though its global real estate investments give it considerable expertise in this area. Mission statements usually define a relatively narrow scope for their companies, based on the current environment and the organization's capabilities, and the statement can change as the environment or the organization changes. This suggests that mission statements need periodic revision.

Much of our discussion about mission statements has been at the corporate level, but mission statements are not developed solely at that level. In fact, sometimes they must be developed at the level of the business unit in order to make sense. This happens most often at large organizations with diverse business interests. One example is General Motors. Although primarily identified with automobile and truck marketing, General Motors is also involved in the financial services industry through its General Motors Acceptance Corporation subsidiary, in the insurance industry through its Motors Insurance Corporation, and in the entertainment and digital communications business through its GM–Hughes subsidiary. In addition, General Motors runs one of the largest basic R&D centers in the world, and it plays an important role in safety and environment-related research. As a diversified company and responsible corporate citizen, the General Motors mission statement is stated primarily in terms of deploying corporate resources and fulfilling its corporate responsibility to numerous

Source: Marriott Corporation, 1988 Annual Report.

> We are committed to being the best lodging and food service company in the world, by treating employees in ways that create extraordinary customer service and shareholder value.
>
> Marriott International, Inc.

constituencies, leaving the development of mission statements that address external markets to its different divisions and subsidiaries. At General Motors, divisional and subsidiary mission statements represent their individual heritage, resources, and competitive environment, and can be different from one to the other.[20]

Not all organizations have mission statements, and not all mission statements meet the ideal standards described here. Developing a company mission statement that provides long-term vision and guidance in developing goals and objectives can be difficult. Writing an effective mission statement requires senior managers to struggle with the questions listed earlier—questions that sound simple but can be tough issues for an organization to address. The increasing visibility and importance of marketing as a philosophy for doing business, however, forces many organizations to tackle the task of defining their corporate mission. At the same time, an emphasis on marketing also helps organizations ensure that meeting customer needs profitably lies at the center of any mission statement.

Strategic Objectives

Strategic management also requires that firms set *strategic objectives*—specific and measurable performance standards for strategically important areas. Whereas a mission statement may set broad goals, such as "being the best food service company in the world," strategic objectives must specify what it means to be "best." Management must define criteria it will use to assess performance and then specify a desired level of achievement for each criterion.

Strategic objectives can be stated in terms of different criteria, such as dollar sales, market share, or return on investment, or they can be stated in absolute or relative terms. For example, Michigan National Corporation, a banking and financial services company, set itself the objective of ranking in the top 10 percent of like-sized banking and financial services firms in profitability, as measured by return on equity. This objective appears in relative terms because it refers to position compared with peer banks. The peer banks for Michigan National are superregional banks of roughly the same size that compete primarily by offering consumer banking services and commercial banking services to midsized companies. An objective in absolute terms would specify a value, such as 18 percent return on equity. In the banking and financial services industry, absolute-term objectives are not found often, given the dramatic effect that fiscal monetary policy has on interest rates and investment returns, which banks do not control.

The criteria used for stating objectives must be compatible with a company's mission and long-term goals. At AT&T, for example, the essence of its corporate mission is to "bring people together anytime, anywhere," and its long-term goals are to be a major player in the digital telecommunications industry. Although these statements are visionary and provide overall guidance, AT&T business-unit managers need specific guidelines for making the hundreds of decisions they face, and those guidelines should be articulated in ways that make sense for the company. For long-distance services, the objectives may be stated in terms of total market share and revenue increases for the U.S. market. AT&T dominates this large, mature, and highly competitive market, which provides much of the financial support for the company's other businesses. For the AT&T Wireless business, however, more relevant criteria may be total number of new subscribers and increases in customer satisfaction with new products relative to satisfaction with older and competing products. Such objectives would reflect the high rate of growth and technological development in mobile communications, as well as its competitive volatility.

Another characteristic of strategic objectives is that they are most often too specific to be applied at the corporate level. To be effective, objectives must be specific and concrete in terms of:

- the *performance dimension* being measured
- the *measures* most appropriate for the performance dimension
- the *target value* for each measure
- the *time* by which the target should be achieved

Typically, these items can be specified only within the context of a single industry or product market. The Michigan National objective has three of these components, and implies the fourth. The performance dimension is profitability, the specific measure is return on equity, and the target is the top 10 percent of peer banks. The time horizon of a year can be inferred from the context in which the objective was presented—the company's annual report. Note that industry and product market limits are set by return on equity—a measure used primarily by the banking industry—and by using peer banks as the point of reference for achieving a top 10 percent rank.

For companies that operate primarily in a single industry, as in the case of Michigan National, business objectives can also act as corporate objectives. If Michigan National were owned by a larger diversified corporation, however, these would be business-level objectives; and if Michigan National covered only the Detroit metropolitan area, the objectives might be relevant for only a narrow product market. For organizations involved in numerous business areas, objectives must often be stated at the business unit and/or product market levels, and corporate objectives are typically composites of the lower-level objectives. General Motors car and truck divisions, for example, may state their objectives in terms of target market share in their specific product markets (e.g., 12 percent of the U.S. luxury car market, 20 percent of U.S. and Canada new automobile financing), whereas the company may state its objectives in terms of percent gains in market share (e.g., 5 percent improvement in aggregate market share from last year).

The emphasis given each component of the organization's objectives, and the level at which measures and the time horizon are set, can vary at different organizational levels. At the corporate level, profit and growth objectives might be most important and the time horizon might be set in five-year increments. At a business-unit level, however, cash flow and cost reductions may be most important in declining markets, and market share gains in emerging markets. Likewise, the time horizon might be shorter than five years for business units because a new technology will render current operations obsolete, or it might be longer because market acceptance is slow. The characteristics of business units and their immediate environment should primarily determine strategic objectives, provided that the objectives do not violate the organization's mission. The objectives should also be compatible with the culture unless the business unit is soon to be divested.

Strategic objectives at different organizational levels can sometimes conflict. One example would be if AT&T were to set growth objectives at the corporate level at the same time that its long-distance business unit was setting objectives for minimizing market share losses to new competitors. Conflict can also arise between the different levels of organizational thinking. An organization might set objectives pertaining to a desired culture that conflict with its more specific objectives for staff development. Consider, for example, a mission statement that states as a goal providing opportunities for employee personal development at the same time that the company claims to value teamwork. Maximizing individual employee development can undermine teamwork if the primary means of development is to promote high performers quickly. Such a company has conflicting objectives, even if they are implicit and not easily recognized.

Managers must establish strategic objectives with great care. Strategic objectives must be articulated at every level of the organization at which it makes sense to have objectives. They must be expressed in terms that are easily understood by the people who are required to achieve them, they must be measurable and specific, and they must be set at achievable levels. Setting objectives at attainable yet challenging levels is important, because research has shown that for complex issues, such as marketing strategies, objectives set at easy levels lead to substandard performance, whereas objectives set at unattainable levels can lead to dysfunctional strategies.[21]

It should be clear that strategic objectives must be compatible with the organization's mission; at the same time they may conflict over what are relevant evaluation criteria, performance measures, and time horizons. Conflict between strategic objectives must be resolved through compromise, and it is senior management's job to reconcile these differences within the broad framework of having a market-oriented philosophy of doing business.

Generic Strategies for Growth and Downsizing

Another aspect of strategic management is the development of specific strategies for achieving company objectives. Strategies must respond to the environment and provide specific guidelines for decision making. Because organizations face unique combinations of internal and external factors, the strategies developed by any one organization are unlikely to be entirely adaptable to any other organization. At a more general level, however, it is possible to discern recurring patterns in the strategies adopted by organizations. These recurring patterns are called *generic strategies*. One way to think of generic strategies is as combinations of variables that focus the organization on different facets of its business and the environment. Some of the most widely used generic strategies are captured by two-dimensional matrices, with market potential along one dimension and technological capabilities along the other. Two matrices are created: one that assumes the organization is growing and one that assumes the organization is downsizing. The matrices and the strategies associated with each quadrant are illustrated in Figure 2.3.

Strategies for Growth

The upper two-by-two grid in Figure 2.3 illustrates common strategies for companies that are expanding their market presence. Organizations seeking to grow by gaining a larger market share in their current industry or market (upper left quad-

FIGURE 2.3

EXPANSION STRATEGIES

	Current Markets	Additional Markets
Current Products	Market or Industry Penetration	Market or Industry Development
Additional Products	Product or Technology Development	Diversification

DOWNSIZING STRATEGIES

	Current Markets	Abandon Markets
Current Products	Harvesting	Retrenchment
Abandon Products	Pruning	Divestment

Source: Adapted from H. Igor Ansoff, Corporate Strategy: An Analytical Approach to Business Policy for Growth and Expansion (New York: McGraw-Hill, 1965), p. 109.

rant) follow a *penetration* strategy. Penetration strategies can be very successful when the company has a technological or production advantage that allows it to take market share away from competitors while still operating profitably. Such strategies can be very costly, however, if they rely primarily on setting prices below those of competing products. In its defense of the long-distance market, AT&T has primarily followed a very costly penetration strategy in the United States, in which financial incentives and cut-rate pricing have been used extensively by AT&T and its competitors. Procter & Gamble (P&G) has also followed a market penetration strategy in many of its consumer-products markets.[22] An interesting aspect of P&G's strategy, however, is that it sought to improve both market share and profitability by reducing prices, which on the surface seems counterintuitive. The key to P&G's achieving both aims was to slash promotional spending in the U.S. market. Procter & Gamble and other consumer products manufacturers had for years been caught in a market share war focused almost exclusively on consumer and trade financial incentives (e.g., coupons, quantity discounts, and so forth)—a market-share war that had become very expensive. Procter & Gamble was actually able to reduce prices, gain market share, and improve profits by eliminating many of its promotional incentives and reducing others. The primary objectives in P&G's strategy were improved profits in the U.S. market with which to finance expansion in the emerging markets of Asia and Europe.

Organizations can also remain within their established industries or markets and seek expansion (lower left quadrant) by introducing new products or services. This is a called a *product* or *technology development* strategy. Such a strategy has been followed by Acer, a producer of personal computers, peripherals, and other consumer electronics, which is headquartered in Taipei, Taiwan.[23] After establishing a strong global presence in the personal computer and peripherals markets, Acer embarked on a growth strategy focused on developing and marketing other intelligent consumer products, such as Internet-appliances, high-end video games, and video telephones, for its existing markets. To accomplish this, Acer has built more than 30 assembly facilities around the world, and has invested heavily to expand its engineering and product development operations, from which come the company's proprietary designs.

Product development strategies are in peril if competitors can easily copy the new products being introduced by using lower manufacturing or delivery costs. They can also be at risk if the products are not different enough from existing products to inspire demand. Acer protects itself against both of these threats by seeking low-cost manufacturing capability around the world, and by trying to obsolete its products with new technological breakthroughs before anyone else does. Rendering one's own designs obsolete ahead of competitors is a strategy also followed by Hewlett-Packard in the laser and ink-jet printer markets.

When an organization retains the same products but seeks new markets (upper right quadrant of expansion matrix in Fig. 2.3), it is following a *market* or *industry development* strategy. This is the strategy being followed by Procter & Gamble and Colgate-Palmolive as they aggressively invest in the growing markets of Asia and Eastern Europe. It is also exemplified by the large investments made by Coca-Cola in China, as that market has become increasingly open to companies based in non-communist economies.[24] Another example of market development is Harley-Davidson's success in the Japanese and European markets (see Marketing Anecdote 2.2). Harley-Davidson has kept its product technology basically unchanged and has used other elements of the marketing mix to gain market share in the international market.

Pursuing a growth strategy by introducing new products or technologies in new markets or industries (lower right quadrant of expansion matrix in Fig. 2.3) is called *diversification*. This term is frequently associated with expansion into areas unrelated to the company's current operations in order to offset cyclical downturns in one area with cyclical growth in other areas. Diversification was popular with many large companies in the 1970s and gave rise to legendary conglomerates such as Gulf-Western and Litton Industries. However, managing greatly diversified holdings proved to be a difficult task. Today the preferred diversification strategy is to expand into areas that build on the organization's core competencies and in which the company can capitalize on past learning. AT&T's selective acquisitions in cellular telephones and Internet-based software and services are good examples of strategic diversification, because they all use digital communications technology and build on its long-distance network.

Another example of diversification is provided by Timex Corporation. Timex management realized that consumer use of watches has evolved from a primarily functional focus to one that combines function and fashion utility. It has also realized that successful manufacturers need numerous brands and product lines to compete in what has become a widely fragmented market. Timex used its size and purchasing power to expand into several areas. First, it acquired several upscale brands, such as Guess, Nautica, and Monet, in order to gain a presence in department and jewelry stores. Second, it licensed its name to a line of wall and table clocks, and it established strategic business units to focus on three markets: sports, high-fashion, and traditional watches. Third, it invested in a patented technology for luminescent watches that did not require exposure to an external light source, which it has marketed under the Indiglo label. By following a diversification strategy within the broad confines of the watch and clock market, Timex expanded its product line and overall market share while the rest of the industry remained relatively flat.[25]

From the crowded streets of Tokyo and Mexico City, to the forests and fields of Europe, to the sometimes primal savanna of Africa, increasing numbers of motorcycle riders are spending big money for what they consider a unique experience: riding a Harley-Davidson motorcycle. Priced in excess of $25,000 in many international markets, Harleys can hardly be called a poor man's treat. In spite of the high price tag, however, international sales account for more than 30 percent of the company's $1.3 billion sales in 1996 and continue to escalate.

Harley-Davidson has not always been this successful in international markets. Throughout much of the 1970s and 1980s, Harley virtually ignored all international markets, as it fought for survival in the United States. After dominating the U.S. market for many years, however, Harley suffered serious setbacks at the hands of more efficient and better-quality Japanese motorcycles. Japanese manufacturers, led by Honda, were already the only competitors in the small- and medium-sized motorcycle market and moved decisively into the heavyweight segment (machines with engines larger than 850 cubic centimeters) as the market started growing. Other non-Japanese manufacturers, such as Ducati and Moto-Guzzi, practically disappeared from the U.S. market during this time period also, and Harley went from a 40 percent market share in 1970 to a 23 percent share by 1983.

The company did not quit, however. It worked hard to address serious quality problems, such as oil leaks and vibrations, and to offset the price advantage of Japanese motorcycles by lobbying for import tariffs on large displacement machines. It also sought to revive the Harley aura associated with James Dean and the 1950s, just as consumers in their 30s, 40s, and 50s with plenty of disposable income,

sought to recapture some of their youth. The result was that by 1990, Harley had regained more than 60 percent of the large-bike market in the United States, and was ready to reenter the international markets decisively.

As Harley's strategy has unfolded, a key element has been to extend the Harley experience beyond the technological aspects of the machine. Instead of following the Japanese lead toward increasingly sophisticated engines and transmissions, Harley retained a reliable and relatively simple two-cylinder engine and manual transmission design, to which it made hundreds of small improvements. At the same time, however, its marketing efforts created the idea of a "Harley lifestyle," sustained through related products and activities. In addition to motorcycles, Harley-Davidson licenses a wide array of clothing and accessories that bear the Harley logo and are sold by Harley dealers around the world. Wearing Harley accessories and clothing is as much a part of the Harley lifestyle as is driving the motorcycle. Harley also sponsors rallies and other activities for the famous Harley Owners' Groups (HOGs). Company-sponsored HOG rallies around the world, culminating with the annual anniversary weekend bash at Harley headquarters in Milwaukee, are big events in the lives of Harley owners, and go a long way to keep the Harley image alive.

Harley turned its attention to overseas markets at the same time that levels of affluence in many countries were increasing and disposable income could be used for luxuries such as large motorcycles. In going overseas, the company maintained its practice of making relatively small changes to its products, but it internationalized its advertising and promotional programs to fit the different markets. In Japan, for example, advertising was turned over to a

Japanese advertising company familiar with the unique taste of Japanese consumers. The agency took advantage of the popularity of U.S. icons such as Harley-Davidson without offending Japanese sensitivities. In Europe, advertising was also changed by avoiding some of the "lonesome biker" images popular in the United States but misunderstood in Europe. In addition, the format of company-sponsored HOG rallies was changed to fit European tastes for very late night partying.

Harley realizes that international interest in one aspect of the U.S. lifestyle does not mean that foreign cultures are ready to embrace all aspects of the U.S. value system. Consequently, the company is constantly trying to find new ways of fitting into different cultures without losing its unique identity. This strategy is working very well and promises more growth for Harley-Davidson as new Asian, African, and European markets continue to open.

Sources: Lore Croghan, "Customers for Life: How to Hang on to Your Core Market the Harley-Davidson Way," *Financial World* 164 (September 26, 1995), pp. 26–31.

Bob Filipczak, "The Soul of the Hog: Harley-Davidson's Corporate Values," *Training* 33 (February 1996), pp. 38–42.

Steve Gelsi, "Harley Revs Up Parts, Licensed Stuff," *Brandweek* 36 (October 16, 1995), p. 9.

Kevin Kelly and Karen Lowry Miller, "The Rumble Heard Around the World: Harleys," *Business Week*, May 24, 1993, p. 58.

Duff-J. McDonald, "Cashing in on the Best New Multinationals," *Money* 25 (May 1996), pp. 136–137.

Richard Melcher, "Tune-Up Time for Harley," *Business Week*, April 8, 1996, pp. 90–94.

Strategies for Downsizing

Organizations experience decline as well as growth. A downsizing organization needs generic strategies for reducing the size of the business, and some have been developed that use the same dimensions of market potential and technological capabilities as expansion strategies. These are illustrated by the bottom grid in Figure 2.3.

When organizations reduce their involvement in terms of products and markets (upper left quadrant), they pursue a *harvesting* strategy. In this situation, the company reduces its investment in all areas of the marketing mix and seeks to maximize profits or minimize losses; even sales volumes are allowed to decline. Harvesting strategies are often used by automobile manufacturers on established product lines (e.g., rear-wheel-drive full-size passenger vehicles) that will soon be replaced by more advanced vehicles, but which still retain a loyal customer group. Auto companies seldom advertise these products heavily or make expensive product improvements, but they keep prices high. The end result is high profitability for a one- to two-year period before the volume drops below a level that can be produced profitably.

When companies retain their product line but abandon some markets (upper right quadrant), they pursue a *retrenchment* strategy. Organizations can abandon markets for different reasons. Some companies are unable to sustain a presence in highly competitive markets and choose instead to focus on other markets in which their chances for success are greater. Such was the case for Peugeot, a French automobile manufacturer, which left the highly competitive North American market in the late 1980s to focus on the European market and on emerging markets in Asia.[26] Organizations can also abandon markets because they are no longer strategically sustainable, even if they are still profitable. When Coca-Cola abandoned the market in India in the mid-1970s, it was still a profitable market. However, changes in foreign investment regulation enacted by the Indian government, as well as acrimonious relationships with its local bottlers, increased the probability that Coke's secret formula would be revealed. The company chose to abandon a lucrative market to protect its global interests. Changes in the competitive and legislative environment have recently motivated Coca-Cola to reenter the Indian market.[27]

Some companies choose to remain involved in their traditional markets but to reduce the product line or technologies in which they are involved (lower left quadrant). This approach is known as *pruning* and appears in Harley-Davidson's product strategy during its recovery in the early 1980s (see Marketing Anecdote 2.2). During the mid-1970s, Harley tried to compete with Japanese manufacturers in the small motorcycle market and had a diverse product line. After getting into financial trouble, however, the company pruned its product line by eliminating light- and middleweight motorcycles, and it focused solely on the heavyweight motorcycle segment. Another example of pruning is the case of Subaru of America. Subaru started selling automobiles in the United States in the 1970s, and had a strong reputation in both the all-wheel drive and front-wheel drive automobile markets by the early 1980s. During the highly competitive auto market of the late 1980s, however, Subaru lost its competitive edge, and started losing both sales and profits. At one time the company dealers had more than a 300-day supply of autos—this in an industry in which a 90-day supply is considered high. Subaru management recognized that it could not compete with Toyota, Honda, and domestic manufacturers in the front-wheel drive automobile market, but that it remained strong in the all-wheel drive category. Subaru therefore eliminated all front-wheel drive products from its lineup, and focused its attention solely on improving sales of its all-wheel drive vehicles. This pruning and refocusing of its product line coincided with the increase in popularity of sport-utility vehicles, giving Subaru a much-needed boost in sales and profits. Having made a commitment to remain in the all-wheel drive market, the company added highly successful models such as the Outback, which was engineered as an all-wheel drive passenger car but styled to look like a sport-utility vehicle. By the mid-1990s, Subaru had returned to record sales and profits in the U.S. market.[28]

Divestment occurs when an organization abandons a product or technology area and its related markets, either by selling its interests or by closing down operations. One example of divestment is the departure of Texas Instruments from the personal computer market in the mid-1980s. The company did not sell the business to another company but simply liquidated its operations and sold or reassigned its manufacturing capacity. Texas Instruments was not only divesting itself of a product line, it was also abandoning the personal computer market altogether. Divestment frequently occurs when companies find specific businesses unprofitable. It can also occur if companies recognize that remaining in an industry is detrimental to other parts of their business, even if such ventures are profitable.

One example of such diversification is the sale by Sears, Roebuck and Company of its Dean Witter and Company, Discover, and Coldwell Banker Real Estate subsidiaries.[29] Although all three ventures were profitable in 1993, Sears recognized that being involved in the financial services and real estate marketing businesses was drawing managerial resources away from its troubled retail operations. All three subsidiaries were spun off to investors, and Sears used the cash generated by the divestment to upgrade and expand retail operations. Some funds were used to refurbish existing department stores, and other funds were used to finance the opening of new single-line hardware stores in small towns and shopping strips.

Characteristics of Generic Strategies

Some characteristics of generic strategies must be noted. First, strategies can be implemented at different levels in the organization. This is seen in the case of Sears, in which the divestment of profitable business units was a corporate-level strategy, and its decision to refurbish retail stores and open new ones, equivalent to a market-penetration strategy, was a business-unit–level strategy. Multilevel strategies are also seen in IBM's strategic initiatives during the early 1990s. At the corporate level, the declining mainframe business was initially harvested and later pruned. At the business-unit level, however, whereas older mainframe designs were being harvested, mainframes designed around multiple microprocessor technology were being successfully introduced in what amounted to a product-development strategy.[30]

The IBM and Sears examples also illustrate that several strategies can also be pursued concurrently. Sears implemented its divestment and market-penetration strategies concurrently, and IBM implemented its harvesting and product-development strategies at the same time. Finally, several strategies can be implemented simultaneously at the same organizational level. Computer manufacturers such as IBM and Hewlett-Packard often harvest some product lines at the same time that they launch new product lines or develop new markets. In the case of automobile manufacturers, established car lines are typically harvested at the same time that more advanced lines are being introduced.

The Influence of Marketing in Developing Generic Strategies

Marketing plays two important roles in developing a company's strategies. First, marketing personnel gather and interpret information that can help companies make correct decisions. Although at one time strategic decisions were made primarily on the basis of financial projections and economic models, such an approach was predicated on assumptions about market efficiencies and information flows that have proved untenable, leading most companies to abandon sole reliance on such methods. Financial information and projections still play an important role, but now they are supplemented with substantial amounts of market and internal information. Financial projections are one of several factors used in evaluating proposed strategies, along with information about consumer and employee attitudes, cultural values, political-legal trends, and other market information.

One example is the redesigned Chrysler minivan introduced in 1996, which may be one of the best researched automobile concepts in recent history.[31] Chrysler based its product design and content decision not only on the traditional measures of piece cost and market segment projections used by the auto industry, but also on substantial amounts of consumer attitude and behavior data on optional features such as the driver's-side rear door. Sales results for the new Chrysler minivan, and for the driver's-side rear door option in particular, have been outstanding since their introduction. Marketing managers in most companies have the attention of senior management, and marketing's ideas about how consumers will respond to different alternatives are greatly valued.

Second, marketing professionals enhance organizational learning by giving advance warning about opportunities and threats. Because marketing personnel interact with many people outside the company, they can see indications of market shifts and trends long before such changes become evident to other members of the organization. New technologies that affect product performance or manufacturing costs, political changes that hamper the organization's ability to function in different markets, and changes in consumer values that may alter the demand for products and services may be evident to marketing managers before they become firmly established, and can help companies adopt strategies to take advantage of the changes. A classic example is the case of Electronic Data Systems (EDS) prior to the revolution in Iran in 1979. The marketing staff in contact with government and private business gave EDS management advanced warning of the impending revolution, and enabled the company to move many of its assets and personnel out of Iran prior to that government's collapse.[32]

Organizational and Industry Assessment

In addition to focusing on market attractiveness and product development, organizations need to conduct systematic analyses of their positions relative to competitors and to use this information to choose generic strategies. A theoretical framework that many organizations apply focuses on two dimensions: the organization's distinctive advantage and its overall business scope.[33] A *distinctive advantage* can be either a cost advantage or a technological advantage. By *cost advantage* we mean that the organization can produce goods or services at a lower cost than competitors and can therefore charge lower prices or achieve higher profit margins. Texas Instruments and Casio, for example, have a cost advantage in integrated circuit manufacturing because of their manufacturing expertise and proprietary designs, and can produce advanced calculators at a lower cost than practically any other competitor. In the service sector, Electronic Data Systems has a cost advantage over competitors because of its highly integrated centralized processing facilities, and can typically set prices below those of competitors when offering its services to banks and other financial institutions.

A *technological advantage* means that the organization can do something (e.g., manufacture more efficiently or at higher quality levels, manage material flows more efficiently, produce products of unmatched performance) different and better than competitors, and consequently can demand higher prices for those products. In the pharmaceutical industry, for example, companies such as Genentech often have products that cannot be matched by any other company. Such an example is an enzyme-based remedy for cystic fibrosis symptoms called DNase, or Pulmozyme (see Marketing Anecdote 2.3).

Business scope refers to how broadly or narrowly an organization defines the markets in which it competes. Organizations that define their scope broadly consider all market segments for a particular product or service relevant to their strategic mission, and they develop marketing plans for each one. Texas Instruments, for example, defines its business scope for portable calculators broadly, producing a large array of models for business and scientific use as well as simpler ones for office and home use. Panasonic, in contrast, defines its scope in the calculator market more narrowly, marketing only simple machines for office and home use. Other examples of broad and narrow scope can be found in the oil industry. Companies such as Exxon are involved in all aspects of the business from exploration to retail sales, whereas other companies are primarily involved in only one or two aspects. Managers decide on the scope of an organization based on many factors, but the decision is typically most affected by the resources the organization can devote to the business. Exxon, for example, has ample resources with which to expand retail operations and oil transportation operations at the same time and can consequently be a participant in both areas, but a small oil exploration company with limited resources may choose to remain focused on exploration and not expand into other areas of the oil industry.

In August 1993, the Food and Drug Administration (FDA) recommended the drug DNase (or Pulmozyme), produced by Genentech, as a treatment for cystic fibrosis. Cystic fibrosis is a hereditary disease in which a flawed strand of DNA causes cells to produce a defective protein, which leads to mucus buildup in the bronchial passages. The mucus cannot be expelled naturally, and the buildup causes repeated lung infections and severely restricts breathing capacity, often leading to death at an early age.

Until DNase became available, the most effective treatment for removing the mucus lining was "percussion therapy," daily chest and back pounding that loosens the mucus so it can be expelled. DNase, based on a bovine enzyme, liquefies the mucus in cystic fibrosis patients, and makes percussion therapy more effective and in some cases unnecessary. The cost of DNase to the typical cystic fibrosis patient runs between $10,000 and $15,000 per year. Although it is expensive, the drug reduces the need for antibiotics and hospital visits, which can cost up to $50,000 per year. Thus, DNase can represent substantial savings to patients and the health-care system.

DNase gave Genentech a competitive advantage, since the gene-splicing technology required to produce DNase is patented and demand for the drug is relatively stable, at least in the short term. The company uses the proceeds from DNase to fund research and development of drug treatments for other ailments and to search for a permanent cure for cystic fibrosis. Genentech's search for a permanent cure has been in progress for several years, and recent breakthroughs suggest that the most successful treatment will be to find a way of replacing the defective genes that cause the disorder. This will cause cells to produce the correct protein and eliminate the mucus buildup. If Genentech is able to also market the permanent cure for cystic fibrosis, it will have several additional competitive advantages. One obvious advantage is replacing the profit stream from DNase with that of the permanent cystic fibrosis cure. A second and perhaps more important advantage is preserving Genentech's technological position in the genetically engineered drug industry, against such giants as Schering-Plough, Eli Lilly, and Amgen. This is very important for Genentech, which has built a reputation with consumers and stockholders for being at the cutting edge in this area. The development and marketing of DNase was in itself a significant gamble by the company. It moved the drug from conceptual development to production in 4 years instead of the typical 10 to 12, and made investments in manufacturing equipment long before the testing was completed. If the FDA had turned down DNase, the losses to Genentech would have been substantial.

Sources: Gene Bylinsky, "Got a Winner? Back It Big," *Fortune*, March 21, 1994, pp. 69–70.

Jim Carlton, "Genentech Inc. Receives FDA Approval for Breakthrough Cystic Fibrosis Drug," *Wall Street Journal*, December 31, 1993, p. 10.

Marilyn Chase, "Genentech to Post Strong 1st Quarter: Drug Test Reported," *Wall Street Journal*, April 5, 1994, p. B6.

Joan O. C. Hamilton, "A Star Drug is Born," *Business Week*, August 23, 1993, pp. 66–68.

Strategic Orientations Based on Distinctive Advantage and Business Scope

Combining the dimensions of distinctive advantage and business scope in a matrix results in the strategic orientation typology illustrated in Figure 2.4. A *cost leadership* orientation suggests that the company will try to be the low-cost producer in the markets and industries in which it competes, as in the case of Texas Instruments. A

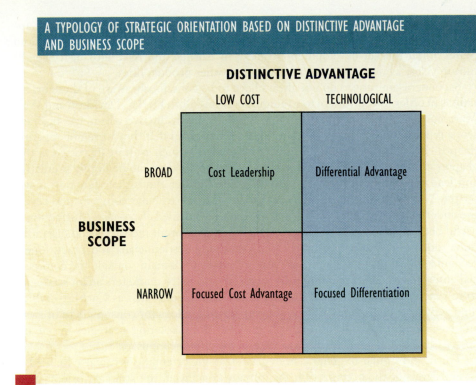

DISTINCTIVE ADVANTAGE

	LOW COST	TECHNOLOGICAL
BROAD	Cost Leadership	Differential Advantage
NARROW	Focused Cost Advantage	Focused Differentiation

BUSINESS SCOPE

Source: Adapted with the permission of The Free Press, a division of Simon & Schuster, from Michael E. Porter, Competitive Advantage: Creating and Sustaining Superior Performance (New York: Free Press, 1985), p. 12. Copyright © 1985 by Michael E. Porter.

differential advantage orientation occurs when the organization focuses on staying ahead of its competitors in the technological and performance aspects of its operations. Hewlett-Packard adopted this strategic orientation when the market for handheld calculators was in the early stages. Hewlett-Packard calculators were more expensive than Texas Instruments products, but their technology and performance were superior. In recent years Texas Instrument matched the performance and technological features of Hewlett-Packard calculators while retaining its cost leadership, forcing Hewlett-Packard to reduce its prices.

Focused cost advantage and *focused differentiation* are similar to the broader strategies, but have limited target markets. An organization with a focused cost orientation seeks to be the low-cost producer in only one product line or in a limited geographic market. Wal-Mart initially followed a focused cost strategy, seeking to be the low-cost retailer in small cities and towns that were overlooked by other discounters. As it grew, Wal-Mart was able to adopt the more broadly defined cost leadership position it holds today. Focused differentiation can also be seen in Harley-Davidson's decision to stay in the heavyweight motorcycle segment, where it had distinctive styling.

Characteristics of Strategic Orientations

Some of our examples illustrate several characteristics of strategic orientations based on distinctive advantage and business scope. The first and most important is the fact that these strategic orientations complement the generic strategies for growth and downsizing discussed earlier. For example, we discussed Harley-Davidson in the context of the market development and pruning strategies. But before the company could institute these strategies, it needed to evaluate its resources and distinctive competitive advantages. Looking at organizational factors helped the company determine that it was best prepared to adopt a focused differentiation approach, which in turn led it to adopt a market-penetration strategy in the United States and a market-development strategy in Europe and Asia with heavyweight motorcycles, while at the same time pruning other product lines.

Second, organizations do not always have to be consciously aware of these orientations in order to apply them to strategic decisions. Both Harley-Davidson and Wal-Mart started their strategic development before the distinctive advantage–business scope typology was popularized, but this does not mean that they were not applying the principles captured by it. Theoretical frameworks such as those discussed in this chapter can serve more than one purpose. Sometimes they can be highly predictive and lead companies in radically new directions. Other times their function is descriptive, to strip away all the details pertaining to a particular company and reveal the underlying forces at work. This stripping away is called *abstraction*. Abstraction is useful because it allows knowledge transfer across different industries and organizational domains. Abstraction has helped marketing academicians and practitioners recognize the applicability of marketing principles to domains outside the commercial enterprise, such as the nonprofit sector. It also helps marketers adapt strategies from one industry to another. Popular used-car retailers, such as CarMax—which hold very large inventories, offer computer-based catalogs for consumers to browse, and have fixed price policies—show how successful marketing strategies in one industry (discount appliance sales) can be used by another industry.[34]

Third, and similar to generic strategies, strategic orientations can also be held at several levels of the organization. As initially conceived, the strategic orientations were developed at the business-unit level, and this is still the level at which strategies based on these orientations are most often discussed. In some circumstances, however, they can be used to develop strategy at the corporate level or at a product level. At the corporate level, for example, Wal-Mart uses its electronic data processing and telecommunications capabilities to achieve cost leadership in every geographic market area and retail industry in which it competes. Although its warehouse clubs are a separate business unit from its discount and convenience stores, all of these businesses share the same system in communicating with suppliers, and all are cost leaders in their respective industries.

At the product level, the Chevrolet Motor Division of General Motors (GM) is an example of a business unit that applies different strategic orientations at the product level. Chevrolet has historically produced and sold GM's least expensive product line and has applied what is best characterized as a cost-leadership orientation. Since 1953, however, it has also sold the Corvette, a high performance, two-seater sports car that seeks a differential advantage through features such as composite plastic suspension parts, fiberglass body panels, sophisticated six-speed transmissions, and high-powered engines. The Corvette is redesigned from the ground up at Chevrolet every ten to twelve years, and serves as a test bed for advanced automotive technology. Thus Chevrolet has followed a differentiation approach with the Corvette, while pursuing an overall cost-leadership strategy with the rest of its product lines.

Note that this typology, along with the generic strategies discussed earlier, are frameworks that managers can use to make sense of organizations and their environments. In doing so, managers should not be constrained by tradition or by the context in which these frameworks were initially developed. All marketing-oriented managers should strive to apply different frameworks and theories creatively, yet with healthy skepticism about any single theory's assumptions. The assumptions underlying a theory or framework are often implicit. For example, Wal-Mart's pursuit of cost leadership across all business areas is based on the assumptions that (1) the factors affecting supplier relationships are the same across all areas of retailing in which the company is involved, (2) these factors can be addressed with the same technological solutions, and (3) these factors will result in similar cost advantages across business units. Wal-Mart's senior management should periodically reexamine such assumptions.

The Influence of Marketing in Adopting Strategic Orientations

The ways in which marketing influences the adoption of a strategic orientation are similar to its roles in the development and implementation of generic strategies. Marketing helps the organization make sense of its environment by providing and interpreting information. Marketing frequently provides information about competitors that helps organizations determine whether they have a distinctive advantage. Marketing also provides advanced warning about possible changes in the organization's position in the industry. In the case of Genentech, for example, sales personnel might be able to gain early intelligence about other potential uses for DNase that could have significant implications for Genentech. Salespeople can also be the first to learn about competing treatments or therapies that would hurt the market potential of DNase.

PORTFOLIO TECHNIQUES FOR EVALUATING STRATEGIES

Portfolio techniques help marketing managers evaluate alternative strategies and allocate resources across a number of businesses and markets. Based on techniques used by investment analysts to manage stock and bond portfolios, these techniques treat businesses and product markets as if they are financial assets. An underlying assumption of these methods is that organizations are looking for ways to reduce overall risk through diversification. Portfolio techniques help managers evaluate the attractiveness of widely different strategic options relative to one another and the company's ideal standards by focusing attention on factors that are common to all the strategic options. Exxon, for example, may use portfolio techniques to evaluate and compare exploration opportunities in Southeast Asia, transportation opportunities in the Middle East, and retail opportunities in North America. These three strategic options are very different in terms of the markets they serve, their operational constraints, and the revenue involved. They can be compared on attributes such as market share and growth rate, however, which can be calculated for each alternative and for most other alternatives Exxon may be considering. Most companies that engage in strategic management use some variation of portfolio techniques.[35]

In this section we discuss two of the more popular portfolio techniques: the growth-share model and the directional-policy (DP) model. Many other portfolio techniques currently in use are variations of these two models. Our discussion differs from more traditional treatments of these models in that we argue that they can be applied across organizational levels (corporate, business unit, and product market) with minor variations. As initially developed, these techniques were recommended for corporate-level managers to evaluate different strategic business units of the company. However, they can be used to evaluate strategic alternatives across different levels of the organization if managers change the factors they consider.

The Growth-Share Model

One of the oldest—and probably the best known—portfolio techniques, the growth-share model was developed in the late 1960s by the Boston Consulting Group, and its assumptions and critical variables reflect much of the strategic

FIGURE 2.5

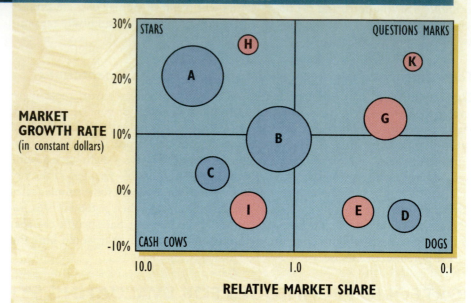

BOSTON CONSULTING GROUP GROWTH-SHARE MODEL

Adapted from Long Range Planning (February), B. Heldey, "Strategy and the Business Portfolio," 1–17, 1997, with kind permission from Elsevier Science, Ltd. The Boulevard, Langford Lane, Kidlington, OX5 1GB, UK.

Sample calculations of relative market share:

Assume circle A represents Harley-Davidson's heavyweight motorcycle business unit with a market share of 60 percent. When it is compared with Honda's 10 percent market share, as its next closest competitor, Harley-Davidson's relative market share would be 60 percent divided by 10 percent, or 6. Thus, the center of circle A would be located at 6 along the horizontal axis.

Now assume that circle G represents Cellular One, a cellular phone company that competes with AT&T Wireless, the market leader. If AT&T Wireless has 25 percent of the cellular phone market in the United States, and Cellular One has 12.5 percent, the position of Cellular One along the horizontal axis would be calculated by dividing 12.5 percent by 25 percent, which is equal to 0.5.

management thinking of the period. The late 1960s were the heyday of the widely diversified conglomerate—large corporations comprising unrelated businesses that were managed autonomously except for the tight financial controls exercised by senior management. Senior management considered primarily what each unrelated business (seen as an investment alternative) could contribute to the corporation's profitability or cash flow both now and in the future. The dimensions of the growth-share matrix reflect these priorities.

Figure 2.5 illustrates a typical application of the growth-share model. The horizontal axis represents the relative market share of the different business units, calculated by comparing the market share of each business to that of the leading competitor in the industry. (Note that we cover methods for calculating market share and other relevant data in chapters 5 and 16.) If the business being evaluated is the industry leader, the point of reference should be the next closest competitor and the relative market share is calculated by dividing the industry leader's market share by that of its closest competitor. Thus, the relative market share for an industry leader should always have a value of one or greater than one.

If the business unit being evaluated is not the industry leader, its market share should be compared to that of the industry leader, and calculated by dividing its market share by that of the industry leader. Thus, the relative market share of an industry participant other than the leader should have a value of one or less than one. Sample calculations for relative market share are illustrated in Figure 2.5. In the figure, businesses A, B, C, H, and I are industry leaders, and E, D, G, and K are not industry leaders.

The vertical axis represents the rate of market share growth in constant dollars, which can range from negative numbers in declining industries to high positive rates in high-growth industries. In Figure 2.5, D, E, and I are in declining industries; B, C, and G are in slow-growth industries; and A, H, and K are in high-growth industries. Another dimension captured in Figure 2.5 is the proportion of total market sales volume captured by each business, which is represented by the size of the circles. Large circles, such as A and B, represent business units that capture large total market sales in their industries, whereas small circles (e.g., E and K) capture small amounts of total sales in their industries. The scale used to determine the size of the circles varies by company application of the growth-share model.

The theory behind the growth-share model makes specific assumptions about market growth rate and relative market share. Market growth rate is assumed to indicate market maturity. High market growth indicates emerging markets with a promising future, low market growth indicates mature markets with limited future potential, and negative growth indicates declining markets. Relative market share is assumed to indicate competitive strength. Businesses with high relative market share are considered strong competitors, and businesses with low relative market share are considered weak competitors.

The theory behind the growth-share model also assumes that an organization must generate cash flows from businesses with a strong competitive position in mature markets and invest these funds in businesses with high future potential, captured by the value-laden labels used for each quadrant. *Stars* are highly desirable businesses because they have a high market growth rate and high relative market share. But because they are in highly competitive industries (assuming high market growth attracts competitors), however, they require large investments to sustain their position, and consequently they produce little profit. *Dogs* are low market share, low-growth businesses that drain capital and produce little or zero profit; the organization should consider liquidating or divesting such businesses. *Cash cows* are dominant businesses in low-growth industries that require little investment to maintain their market share and consequently produce substantial profits. Because they are no longer growing, these businesses should be "milked" for funds to invest in stars and question marks. Cash cows are expected eventually to decline along with their industry. *Question marks* are businesses in industries that are doing well, but where the specific business unit is not doing as well as the industry. They are called question marks because they are an unknown for management. In general, the theory suggests that, given the proper investment in product development, plant capacity, and marketing, these businesses can gain market share and become stars, but without proper investment the businesses eventually go into decline and become dogs. The level of proper investment for each business, however, is industry and business specific, and the growth-share model is not helpful at that level of decision making.

The Directional-Policy Model

The directional-policy model shares some historical aspects and the use of external market and internal business dimensions with the growth-share model. The dimensions of the directional-policy model, however, are composed of many external and internal factors, which can include the market growth and relative market share factors from the growth-share matrix, but are not limited to those factors. Thus, the growth-share model is a special case of the directional-policy model.

The initial application of the directional-policy model is most often attributed to General Electric, but it has also been used by consulting firms such as McKinsey and Company, large companies such as Royal Dutch Shell, and others. When the directional-policy model was first developed, General Electric was managing a widely diversified portfolio of businesses ranging from manufacturing small electrical appliances, lighting products, and nuclear power plants to financial services. The company needed tools for comparing investments in very different industries and business areas, but it realized that focusing only on financial dimensions would overlook other important factors. To address this problem, General Electric and other companies came up with the idea of two general dimensions—market attractiveness and business strength—and identified a large number of factors that composed these dimensions, but which could vary in importance depending on the particular industry. This approach gave managers flexibility in terms of which factors to consider and how much weight to assign to each.

Figure 2.6 illustrates an imaginary application of the directional-policy model, which model consists of a nine-section matrix, with each section associated with a general investment recommendation: investment and growth for the upper left-hand section, selective investment to maintain relative position for the diagonal from upper right to lower left, and disinvestment leading to harvesting or divestment for the lower right-hand section. In Figure 2.6, business units A and B have high potential and should receive financial and organizational resources to promote their growth at a rate faster than that of the industry. Business units C, D, E, and G also require investment and attention, but less than A and B. These businesses are relatively stable, and the organization needs to protect them but not necessarily seek to expand them. Business units F and H are no longer attractive. They require attention only to protect cash flow, leading eventually to divestment with minimal effects on the rest of the organization. In this matrix, the size of the circle is also proportional to the overall sales contribution of each business.

The main difference between the directional-policy model and the growth-share model lies in how managers develop the dimensional scores. In the growth-share model, dimensional scores are relative market share and market share growth, as discussed earlier. For the directional-policy model, in contrast, dimensional scores are composites of scores on multiple factors with each component factor being weighted for importance, and each business receiving a rating on each individual factor. Market attractiveness, for example, may depend primarily on overall market size and industry profit margins, with market size being more important that profit margins for a particular business unit. For a different business unit, the components of market attractiveness may be market growth rate and technological sophistication, with each having equal importance weights.

The inclusion of different factors with different importance weights in the dimensional scores for various businesses makes application of the directional-policy model more complex than the growth-share model. It requires management to determine the relevant factors for each dimension for every business unit, set a weight or importance rating for each factor, and rate each business or investment area on each dimension. These judgments are very time consuming, and typically senior managers make them with the help of industry and company experts.

The calculation of market attractiveness and business strength dimensional scores based on factor weights and ratings is illustrated in Table 2.1 on page 78.

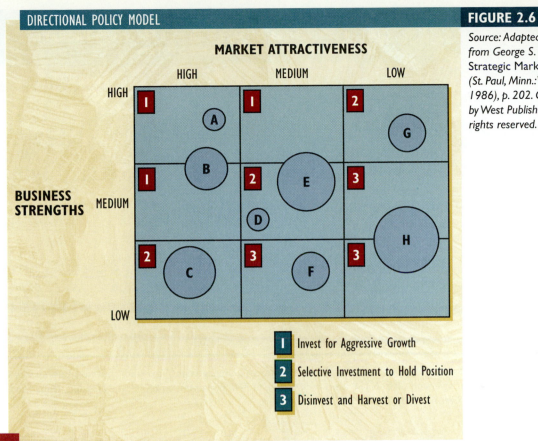

DIRECTIONAL POLICY MODEL

FIGURE 2.6

MARKET ATTRACTIVENESS

HIGH   MEDIUM   LOW

BUSINESS STRENGTHS

HIGH

MEDIUM

LOW

1 Invest for Aggressive Growth

2 Selective Investment to Hold Position

3 Disinvest and Harvest or Divest

The factor scores and ratings are for a fictitious product from Hewlett-Packard called the Digital Image Management System: a powerful graphical supercomputer that competes with the Silicon Graphics workstations used for special-effects development by Industrial Light and Magic. Potential customers for this product are special-effects producers and large advertising agencies that do their own ad production work. The composite score calculations in Table 2.1 use a small number of factors for each dimension. Note that each factor is weighed on the basis of its hypothesized importance to Hewlett-Packard at the time of the analysis, with all weights being between 0 and 1, and the sum of all factor weights for a dimension being one. Each factor is then rated on a scale of one to seven, with one being low and seven being high. The use of a 1 to 7 scale is arbitrary in this example. Companies can use whatever rating scale is most meaningful to them, provided that the same scale is used for all factors under the same dimension, and that the same rating scale's low and high end points be used as low and high end points for the overall dimension. The low and high end points for market attractiveness and business strengths in this example, for instance, must also be 1 and 7, respectively. A factor value is calculated for each factor (e.g., market size, competition, market share) by multiplying the rating (between 1 and 7) by its weight (between 0 and 1), and all factor values are added together to arrive at a composite dimensional score for the business being evaluated. According to the results in Table 2.1, the Digital Image Management System has a dimensional score of 5.65 on market attractiveness and 6.35 on business strength.

TABLE 2.1 A HYPOTHETICAL BUSINESS STRENGTHS–MARKET ATTRACTIVENESS ANALYSIS OF THE HEWLETT-PACKARD DIGITAL IMAGE MANAGEMENT SYSTEM

	Weight	Rating (1–7)	Value
Market Attractiveness Factors			
Market Size	0.20	3	0.60
Market Growth Rate	0.30	6	1.80
Competition	0.10	6	1.50
Technology Involved	0.15	5	0.75
Profit Margin	0.25	4	1.00
Overall Market Attractiveness Rating	1.00		5.65
Business Strengths Factors			
Market Share	0.20	4	0.80
Product Quality	0.30	6	2.40
Productive Capacity	0.15	6	0.90
Brand Reputation	0.10	5	0.50
Distinct Features	0.25	7	1.75
Overall Business Strengths Rating	1.00		6.35

Source: Adapted from LaRue T. Hosmer, Strategic Management: Text and Cases on Business Policy (Englewood Cliffs, N.J.: Prentice-Hall, 1984), p. 310. By permission of Prentice-Hall, Inc., Upper Saddle River, N.J. Copyright © 1984.

Dimensional scores are then used to position businesses on the directional policy matrix, where the boundaries between sectors are based on the scale used for rating the factors. In the case of the hypothetical Hewlett-Packard example, the boundary between low and medium would be set at 2.5 and that between medium and high would be set at 5.0, since a scale of 1 to 7 was used. If a directional-policy matrix were drawn for this example, the Digital Image Management System would be positioned in the upper left-hand corner and considered a high-potential business.

As mentioned earlier, the directional-policy model requires senior management to make decisions on which factors to include in each dimension, their weights, and the scores of each business being evaluated. Proper use of the directional-policy model is a complex task. The insight it provides management, however, is very rich and is considered worthwhile by many firms. From a marketing perspective, the most important step is the choice of factor components for market attractiveness and business strength, and their weights. It is in these decisions that a marketing orientation can make a significant difference. Having market-oriented senior management helps ensure that both profitability and customer needs are considered in the choice of factor components and weights.

Applying Portfolio Techniques to Product Markets and Product Lines

As mentioned earlier, the growth-share and directional-policy models were initially conceived as tools for use in evaluating highly diversified business opportunities. However, sometimes product markets and even individual product lines can be large enough to constitute stand-alone businesses, so large companies can use these techniques to evaluate product-market opportunities, and business units managing individual product markets can use them to evaluate single product lines.

For example, IBM product-market managers could have used such techniques to evaluate the purchase of Lotus Corporation for its Notes groupware: software, which allows coworkers to share information easily and collaborate on computer-based projects. Lotus had developed Notes in the early 1990s and had made substantial inroads with corporate clients when IBM considered acquiring the company.[36] Groupware as a product category, however, was facing increasing competition from Internet-based applications and the product market's future was uncertain. At the time that IBM acquired Lotus, the groupware product market would have most likely been a question mark in the growth-share model. On the directional-policy model, it would have been categorized as a selective investment alternative. Even as the groupware market leader, Notes would require a large investment to be fully Internet compatible, and there was uncertainty as to its long-term potential against low-cost applications on the World Wide Web (WWW). Nevertheless, in 1995 IBM Corporation acquired Lotus for $3.5 billion, primarily for the Notes groupware technology and customer base.[37] Since 1995, IBM has invested millions of dollars to make Notes compatible with its own software as well as competitor's software, and to offer secure and versatile Notes-based communications for companies using the web. As the operational importance of networking across the WWW has grown for large corporate clients, IBM has been better positioned than any other groupware supplier to gain market share. It could be said that Notes has gone from being a question mark to being a star, or high-performance investment, for IBM, at least with large corporate customers.

At the product-line level, we can also use IBM as an example of how portfolio techniques may be applied. In 1993, as IBM continued to lose market share in the U.S. and European personal computer markets, it launched the Ambra product line. The Ambra line relied on outsourcing for a much larger percentage of its components than the PS/2 and APTIVA lines, also offered by IBM, and it was designed to be sold through mass discounters and mail order. It was priced to compete with the products of other low-end producers such as Dell, Gateway 2000, and Packard Bell.[38] Sudden shifts in microprocessor technology, however, rendered the Ambra and competing designs built on 386- and 486-microprocessors obsolete shortly after introduction, turning what would have been classified as a question mark (low market share in a high-growth segment) on the growth-share model into a dog (low market share and low growth). A year after its introduction, the Ambra line was eliminated by IBM, as it consolidated its personal computer operations.[39] It is not public knowledge if IBM product managers used the growth-share or directional-policy models to evaluate their investment, but their actions were compatible with the recommendations of these techniques.

Limitations of Portfolio Techniques in Strategic and Marketing Management

The context in which the growth-share model, the directional-policy model, and other portfolio techniques were initially developed, and their almost exclusive treatment of investments as financial assets, suggest some limitations of these techniques in making strategic decisions. If managers rely on factors that are easily quantifiable, they may overlook other factors that are equally important but cannot be made to fit within a financial accounting framework. Issues such as organizational culture and climate, employee morale, and the emotional aspects and implications of consumer attitudes can be very difficult to objectify in financial accounting terms, but can nevertheless be key determinants of the success or failure of different marketing initiatives.

Portfolio techniques also tend to ignore interaction or synergy between the different business opportunities being evaluated. If Hewlett-Packard were to consider only the factors presented in Table 2.1 when evaluating advanced products such as the Digital Image Management System, it might ignore how the company's commitment to risky ventures affects the morale and productivity of project teams at other divisions, or how the technological achievements involved in this product can be incorporated into other divisions' products.

Further, these techniques are limited because they rely on imperfect measures and estimates. Even with relatively simple dimensions such as relative market share and market growth, the actual estimation of these factors for each alternative being evaluated must rely on incomplete and sometimes incorrect historical information, and on estimates by experts whose "crystal balls" may be cloudy. Pessimistic projections can cause companies to ignore high-potential products, and overly optimistic projections can lead companies to make large investments in ventures that are doomed to fail. Such might have been the case with IBM's original investment in the Ambra line.

A final limitation of these techniques is that business units, product markets, and product lines are not perfectly equivalent to stock and bond securities. This makes any application of portfolio techniques to these business decisions inherently imperfect. Managers and analysts must remember that portfolio techniques are tools for making sense of the environment. Although users can adapt the techniques to different sets of circumstances and different levels of product and organizational focus, the adaptations must be made carefully. Not all of the assumptions underlying these models carry across different levels of the organization, and some of the steps in implementing these techniques can be more or less difficult depending on the level at which they are used. It can be much more difficult, for example, to ascertain the growth rate or profitability of an individual product line than of a strategic business unit.

Portfolio techniques are attractive to managers for several reasons. First, the techniques make it possible to compare widely diverse alternatives by using the same factors in a relatively consistent manner. They also allow managers to simplify very complex problems to more manageable levels by eliminating hundreds of details. Reducing the information processing load of decision makers enables them to understand problems better and to project into the future with more confidence and accuracy. In short, portfolio techniques make the evaluation of strategic alternatives simpler and more manageable, and for those reasons alone they are valuable.

THE INFLUENCE OF MARKETING ON STRATEGY IMPLEMENTATION

Just as marketing as a philosophy of doing business—or what can also be called a *marketing orientation*—should permeate the development of a company's strategy, it should also be involved in the implementation of the strategy. A marketing orientation at the strategic level helps make strategic initiatives more compatible. A marketing orientation at the implementation level helps make the actions of the company more efficient and effective.

Information dissemination is an area critical to strategy implementation that is affected by a marketing orientation in various ways. First, having a marketing orientation encourages members to share information with one another, making it more likely that rich, consistent, and up-to-date information is the basis for strategic activities across all levels. Second, a marketing orientation enhances feedback and control mechanisms, so that the necessary adjustments during strategy implementation can be made quickly and efficiently. No strategic plan is accurate enough to be implemented without adjustments. When marketing as a philosophy of doing business permeates the organization, however, more of the people involved in implementation are sensitive to how the unfolding strategy may miss achieving the desired levels of customer satisfaction and profitability, and may motivate them to make adjustments as required. Finally, a shared marketing orientation involves a greater number of employees in the interpretation of data from focus groups, surveys, and observations, and may help to better identify hindrances to the implementation process that must be eliminated, or opportunities that should be capitalized.

Another implementation area influenced by a shared marketing orientation is the communication of important ideas and ideals, so that they are relevant to managers and employees at all levels. Culture, for example, is an important contributor to successful strategy implementation. It makes automatic thinking through hundreds of details that make for consistent interpretation and support of strategic objectives and initiatives throughout the organization. When culture is not shared, for example, business units may apply different criteria when using portfolio techniques, and arrive at different conclusions regarding what are desirable or undesirable investments. If culture were not shared in a multidivisional company, it would be possible for one division to pursue disjointed and high-risk ventures because of an entrepreneurial culture, while another division remains entrenched in only one product market because of a bureaucratic culture. Neither approach may be optimal for the company as a whole.

Marketing can be used to disseminate cultural values throughout an organization. Promotional techniques such as advertising, personal sales, and sales promotional programs, for example, can be used to communicate values, mission statements, and strategies throughout the company, and to facilitate their adoption at all levels. In addition, managers can use marketing to make new strategic initiatives known, and to make sure that the objectives behind such strategic initiatives are clear and accepted by employees and customers.

Finally, a shared marketing orientation plays an important role in the implementation and execution of strategic initiatives at the business and product market levels. Many such strategies involve changes to the elements of the company's marketing mix (product, price, promotion, and distribution), which are controlled by marketing managers. Marketing personnel such as salespeople, price analysts, and advertising specialists are the ones who work out the hundreds of details involved in the successful execution of these strategies. Overlooking the importance of a shared marketing orientation at this level can be a serious mistake. A good strategy can fail miserably if the people responsible for its implementation are not fully cognizant of its implications for the company and committed to its success. The importance of having a marketing orientation in the execution of many marketing functions will be revisited and expanded upon throughout the rest of this book.[40]

SUMMARY

The role of marketing in organizations has changed over the last several years. The marketing concept and marketing principles have gone from being applied primarily in functional areas such as advertising, sales, and sales promotion to being incorporated into every aspect of organizational management. In most organizations, marketing is as much a philosophy of doing business as a set of functional concerns.

Marketing is incorporated into strategic management at three structural levels:

- The corporate level is concerned with managing organizational resources for the benefit of the company's constituencies. A marketing orientation at this level ensures that customer satisfaction and profitability are primary concerns and that the company has an adequate understanding of the concerns of all constituencies.

- The business-unit level is concerned with managing the organization's activities in one or more related industries. Marketing influences business units by highlighting the customers' most important needs and how they are met by all industry participants. Marketing also provides insight into emerging market opportunities.

- The product-market level is concerned with marketing a product or line of products in a target market. Marketing influences product-market management by providing guidance in the areas of product, promotion, pricing, and distribution.

Marketing is also incorporated into three levels of organizational thinking:

- Culture involves the assumptions, values, and behavioral norms shared by all members of the organization. A marketing orientation affects culture by making "customer orientation" and "profitability" fundamental values of the organization and "contributing to profitable customer satisfaction" a behavioral norm.

- Strategies focus organizational thinking on achieving specific objectives in a specific business area. Marketing influences strategy by providing principles and techniques that help the organization achieve its objectives while maintaining a customer orientation.

- Tactics involve the decisions the organization makes each day. Because marketing influences functional decisions related to product, promotion, pricing, and distribution, it affects tactics.

Strategic management has several aspects. One aspect is the mission statement, which should address fundamental questions such as "What is our business?" and "What value do we provide our constituencies?" Mission statements are most commonly developed at the corporate level, but also can be developed for business units and product markets. A second aspect are strategies. Strategies are developed around objectives—measurable and specific statements of what the organization wants to accomplish. Strategies can be aimed at growth or downsizing, and can be focused on existing products and markets or on adding or abandoning products and markets.

When developing strategies, the organization must analyze its internal and external environment to identify its distinctive advantage and business scope.

- Distinctive advantage can be based either on technology or operating costs. Technological advantages allow companies to offer products or services that are different from those of competitors and can command a premium price. Cost advantages allow companies to offer prices below those of competitors while remaining profitable.

- Business scope refers to how broadly or narrowly the organization defines the markets in which it competes. Organizations must choose strategies that are compatible with the organization's current position relative to its competitors and its target market.

Marketing has numerous roles throughout the strategic management process:

- It provides information to the organization about itself and its environment.
- It provides information used in assessing the organization's distinctive advantage and business scope.
- It provides guidance as to which areas of the marketing mix should most concern the organization.

The last element in the strategic management process is implementing strategies in a consistent and coherent manner. Marketing influences implementation of strategies in various ways:

- It encourages members to share up-to-date information with one another as a basis for strategic activities.
- It enhances feedback and control mechanisms for quick and efficient adjustments during strategy implementation.
- It involves employees in identifying hindrances to the implementation process that must be eliminated or opportunities that should be capitalized.
- It helps communicate cultural values throughout the organization and facilitates their adoption.
- It helps ensure that strategic initiatives are properly implemented at the business-unit and product-market levels.

QUESTIONS FOR DISCUSSION

1. Summarize and evaluate how marketing is applied to strategic management at AT&T across all three levels of organizational structure (corporate, business unit, product market). Explain why you think AT&T is doing a good or bad job and what you would do differently.

2. If you were a senior manager at Ford Motor Company in charge of advanced product development, which level of organizational thinking would be your biggest concern? Why? If you were the product manager in charge of the Ford F-150, which level of organizational thinking would be your biggest concern? Why?

3. Develop a hypothetical mission statement for Harley-Davidson based on what you know about the company and its strategy.

4. Develop a set of objectives for the Harley-Davidson subsidiary in charge of developing eastern European markets. What should be the subsidiary's biggest concerns?

5. Your university is facing declining enrollment in its undergraduate and professional schools, except in programs for its nontraditional students. At the same time, state tax revenue has declined and state funds for the university have been reduced. Apply generic strategies to develop a plan for the university. Consider the following:
   a. Your university has an excellent reputation overseas.
   b. Your university has been approached by the state government to help train its workforce.

c. Your university already has the highest tuition rates in the state. Don't forget to consider marketing issues in your answer.

6. What do you think are the major distinctive advantages of Exxon, Minnesota Mining and Manufacturing (3M), and Time Warner?

7. Gateway 2000 Corporation has limited its distribution to mail order and sells computers designed for home and office use only (as opposed to use in factories or warehouses). How would you characterize Gateway's business scope? Explain your answer.

8. Assume that a single company owns businesses A through H represented in the accompanying diagram. Use the market attractiveness–business strengths parameters to develop recommendations for the parent company. What generic strategies do you recommend for each business unit?

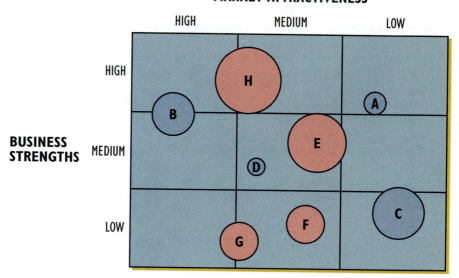

9. Draw the growth-share matrix and position the businesses from question 6 where you think they would fit in the model. Justify your positioning.

NOTES FOR FURTHER READING

1. Frederick E. Webster, "The Changing Role of Marketing in the Corporation," *Journal of Marketing*, 56 (October 1992): 1–17.

2. For some early discussion of these concepts, see the following: Peter Drucker, *The Practice of Management* (New York: Harper & Row, 1954); and John B. McKitterick, "What is the Marketing Management Concept," in Frank M. Bass, ed., *The Frontiers of Marketing Thought and Action* (Chicago: American Marketing Association, 1957), pp. 71–82.

3. Dave Ulrich and Dale Lake, "Organizational Capability: Creating Competitive Advantage," *Academy of Management Executive*, 5 (February 1991), pp. 77–92.

4. Charles W. Hofer and Dan Schendel, *Strategy Formulation: Analytical Concepts* (St. Paul, Minn.: West Publishing, 1978), pp. 27–29.

5. For more information, see Catherine Arnst and Peter Coy, "AT&T: Will the Bad News Ever End," *Business Week*, October 7, 1996, pp. 122–130.

6. Donald C. Hambrick, "Operationalizing the Concept of Business-Level Strategy," *Academy of Management Review*, 5 (1980): 567–575.

7. For more information, see Michael Karol, "It Came From Inside a Computer," *Graphic Arts Monthly* 65 (October 1993), pp. 62–63; and Gregory E. David, "Silicon Graphics: No

Time Like Tomorrow," *Financial World* 162 (November 23, 1993), pp. 21–22.

8. Matthew J. Kiernan, "The New Strategic Architecture: Learning to Compete in the Twenty-First Century," *Academy of Management Executive* 7 (February 1993), pp. 7–21.

9. For more information, see Catherine Arnst, "Big Blue Has a Clone of Its Own," *Business Week*, November 2, 1992, p. 152.

10. For more information on the role of culture in management, see Edgar H. Schein, *Organizational Culture and Leadership* (San Francisco: Jossey-Bass, 1985). References to the importance of culture are pervasive throughout the strategic management literature. Some examples are: Michael A. Hitt, Robert E. Hoskisson, and Jeffrey S. Harrison, "Strategic Competitiveness in the 1990s: Challenges and Opportunities for U.S. Executives," *Academy of Management Executive* 5 (May 1991), pp. 7–22; Stuart L. Hart, "An Integrative Framework for the Strategy-Making Process," *Academy of Management Review* 17 (April 1992), pp. 327–357; and Roger A. Kerin, Vijay Mahajan, and P. Rajan Varadarajan, *Contemporary Perspectives on Strategic Planning* (Boston: Allyn & Bacon, 1990).

11. Julia Flynn, Stanley Reed, and Amy Barrett, "Worldphone Inc.?" *Business Week*, November 18, 1996, pp. 54–55.

12. For an in-depth study of the relationship between war and business, see Wee Chow Hou, Lee Khai Sheang, and Bambang Walujo Hidajat, *Sun Tzu: War and Management* (Singapore: Addison-Wesley, 1991).

13. For more information, see Peter Coy, "AT&T Smacks a Double," *Business Week*, October 26, 1992, p. 37.

14. For more information, see Peter Burrows, "Why Bother Making Home PCs," *Business Week*, September 30, 1996, pp. 72–74; and R. Lee Sullivan, "Compaq's Barbie-Doll Strategy," *Forbes*, November 4, 1996, p. 352.

15. For more discussion on the role of management in the design of mission statements and their importance to organizations, see Peter Drucker, *Management Tasks, Responsibilities, and Practices* (New York: Harper & Row, 1973), ch. 7; and David A. Aaker, *Strategic Market Management* (New York: Wiley, 1988), ch. 3.

16. For more information, see Mark L. Clifford, Nicole Harris, Dexter Roberts, and Manjeet Kripalani, "Coke Pours into Asia," *Business Week*, October 28, 1996, p. 72.

17. Lewis S. Edelheit, "Renewing the Corporate R&D Laboratory," *Research Technology Management* 38 (November/December 1995), pp. 14–18.

18. For more information, see Tim Smart, "Jack Welch's Encore," *Business Week*, October 28, 1996, pp. 155–160.

19. Marriott Corporation Annual Report (1988).

20. Companies the size of General Motors often do not have short mission statements, but publish summaries of their positions at different levels. To capture General Motors mission, it is necessary to combine statements from its annual reports, its public interest reports, and published summaries of the positioning statements developed by its subsidiaries in the United States and overseas.

21. Amelia A. Chesney and Edwin A. Locke, "Relationship Among Goal Difficulty, Business Strategies, and Performance on a Complex Management Simulation Task," *Academy of Management Journal* 34 (June 1991), pp. 400–424.

22. For more information, see Zachary Schiller, "Procter & Gamble Hits Back," *Business Week*, July 19, 1993, pp. 20–22; and Zachary Schiller, Greg Burns, and Karen Lowry Miller, "Making It Simple," *Business Week*, September 9, 1996, pp. 96–104.

23. For more information, see Pete Engardio and Peter Burrows, "Acer: A Global Powerhouse," *Business Week*, July 1, 1996, pp. 94–96.

24. For more information, see Havis Dawson, "It's Coke Time," *Beverage World* 114 (September 1995), p. 98; and Clifford, "Coke Pours into Asia."

25. For more information, see Chris Roush, "At Timex, They're Positively Glowing," *Business Week*, July 12, 1993, p. 141.

26. For more information, see Stewart Toy, David Woodruff, Ian Katz, and David Lindorff, "Peugeot Picks Up Speed Far from Home," *Business Week*, June 17, 1996, pp. 84–86.

27. For more information, see Clifford et al., "Coke Pours Into Asia."

28. For more information, see Larry Armstrong, "Subaru Goes Far by Going Back," *Business Week*, November 4, 1996, pp. 170–172.

29. For more information, see Kevin Kelly, "The Big Store is on a Big Roll," *Business Week*, August 30, 1993, pp. 82–84.

30. For more information, see Ira Seger and Amy Cortese, "IBM: Why the Good News Isn't Good Enough," *Business Week*, January 23, 1995, pp. 72–73; Ira Seger, "IBM's Parallel Power Rangers," *Business Week*, January 30, 1995, pp. 81–82; and Ira Seger, "How IBM Became a Growth Company Again," *Business Week*, December 9, 1996, pp. 154–162.

31. Brock Yates, *The Critical Path: Inventing an Automobile and Reinventing a Corporation* (Boston, Mass.: Little, Brown, 1996).

32. For more information about this incident, see Ken Follett, *On Wings of Eagles* (New York: New American Library, 1983).

33. Adapted from Michael E. Porter, *Competitive Advantage: Creating and Sustaining Superior Performance* (New York: Free Press, 1985).

34. For more information, see Kathleen Kerwin, Thane Peterson, Keith Naughton, Bill Vlasic, and Gail De George, "Used-Car Fever," *Business Week*, January 22, 1996.

35. George Day, *Analysis for Strategic Market Decisions* (St. Paul, Minn.: West Publishing, 1986).

36. For more information, see Gary McWilliams, "Lotus 'Notes' Get a Lot of Notice," *Business Week*, March 29, 1993, pp. 84–85; and Gary McWilliams, "Software's Comeback Kid," *Business Week*, August 16, 1993, pp. 101–102.

37. For more information, see Amy Cortese and Ira Sager, "Gerstner at the Gates," *Business Week*, June 19, 1995, pp. 36–38.

38. For more information, see Michael Miller, "IBM to Launch Two PC Units in New Markets," *Wall Street Journal*, July 1, 1993, p. B1.

39. For more information, see Glenn Rifkin, "Cuts and Relocations for IBM's PC Unit," *New York Times*, July 30, 1994, p. 35.

40. For a detailed discussion of the importance of implementation, see Thomas V. Bonoma, *The Marketing Edge* (New York: Free Press, 1985).

CHAPTER

3

THE MARKETING ENVIRONMENT

CHAPTER OBJECTIVES

When you are done with this chapter, you should have achieved the following:

- A thorough grasp of how important it is for managers to understand, respond to, and sometimes change the environment.

- A basic understanding of the interdependence among different functional areas of the organization in serving the customer, and of the importance of the organizational environment to marketing success.

- A basic understanding of what constitutes the microenvironment for most companies, how marketing functions are affected by changes in areas of the microenvironment, and how marketing managers should approach understanding, responding to, and managing the microenvironment.

- A basic understanding of what constitutes the macroenvironment, how marketing strategies and tactics are influenced by changes in areas of the macroenvironment, and how marketing managers should approach understanding, responding to, and managing the macroenvironment.

- A basic understanding of how beliefs about the environment held by marketing managers can help them find and use market information, their preferred approach to solving marketing problems, and their strategic orientation.

CHAPTER OUTLINE

(continued)

The Environment as Analyzable
The Environment as Malleable
Interpretation Modes
SUMMARY

QUESTIONS FOR DISCUSSION

NOTES FOR FURTHER READING

Defense Contractors Respond to the End of the Cold War

In the aftermath of the Cold War—as the Soviet Union disintegrated, China changed its stance on global commerce, and Europe moved toward economic unity—the market for defense-related products changed dramatically. In areas as diverse as fighter aircraft and defense electronics, there were drops in demand and significant environmental threats to the companies involved in such markets. In the United States alone, Pentagon spending declined by almost 50 percent between 1987 and 1996. Although not as dramatic, the industry also saw cuts in Europe and Asia—cuts that were not offset by the well-publicized increases in defense spending of some Middle Eastern and African countries.

These "mothballed" airfleets reflect major shifts in the defense industry since the late 1980s. Defense contractors have had to redefine themselves as a result.

As traditional marketing opportunities dwindled, defense contractors in the United States and Europe needed to change their marketing strategies in order to survive. Defense contractors such as McDonnell Douglas, Raytheon, and Hughes Electronics all responded to these environmental changes successfully but in different ways, betraying some of their differences in past practices and business orientations. The paths these companies followed to meet customer needs profitably differed, but their commitments to marketing were very similar.

In the mid-1980s and prior to its merger with Boeing, McDonnell Douglas supplied most military fighter and cargo airplanes around the world and was widely recognized for its sophisticated and reliable products. Its reputation was a competitive strength that the company did not want to abandon, so McDonnell Douglas management adjusted its marketing response to the traditional markets' decline accordingly. Following a market diversification strategy (defined in chapter 2), McDonnell Douglas diverted some of its marketing efforts away from the U.S. market, and concentrated on countries in the Middle East and Asia that were still concerned with national security. The company used its superior product quality reputation to gain large contracts for its F-15 fighter aircraft with countries such as Israel and Saudi Arabia, and thus retained its leadership in the military aircraft market.

Whereas McDonnell Douglas used global market intelligence to find new markets for its traditional products, Raytheon used similar information to shift its product mix. Raytheon, an already diversified company in the mid-1980s, had historically served commercial markets such as environmental services, commercial aircraft, and home appliances in addition to the defense market. During much of the 1970s and 1980s, however, its primary revenue came from weapons systems such as the Patriot missile, for which demand declined substantially as defense spending dropped. Raytheon's response was to shift resources and marketing emphasis to its nondefense businesses, to make up for lost defense revenues through increased sales in those areas. One example is the home appliance market, where the company sought to increase sales by 60 percent. Raytheon owned the Amana, Caloric, and Speed Queen lines, all of which were recognized brands in the U.S. market. Based on research information on demographic and technological trends, Raytheon consolidated and upgraded its appliance manufacturing facilities and product lines, and increased its promotional spending, resulting in market share gains throughout the 1990s against larger competitors such as General Electric and Whirlpool.

To offset its losses in the defense business, Hughes Electronics capitalized on the growing importance of entertainment and mobile communications to consumers worldwide. Building on its expertise in defense satellite technology,

Hughes developed its Spaceway global satellite network, which in turn served as the backbone for services such as DirecTV satellite broadcasting and DirecPC satellite-based Internet hookups, as well as a global array of wireless and cellular telephone networks. Hughes sales revenue grew to more than $15 billion by 1995 as a result of these changes, and the company is today a recognized leader in consumer and defense electronics.

McDonnell Douglas, Raytheon, and Hughes Electronics all responded to reduced defense spending by paying close attention to their environment and capitalizing on unexplored market opportunities.

Sources: Jeff Cole, "McDonnell Gets Israeli Jet Order for $2 Billion," *Wall Street Journal*, January 28, 1994, p. A3.

James E. Ellis and Richard S. Dunham, "McDonnell Douglas: Unfasten the Seat Belts," *Business Week*, February 14, 1994, p. 36.

Richard Jaccoma, "In with the Wash," *Dealerscope Merchandising* 35 (February 1993): 92–94.

Reinhardt Krause, "AT&T Dials Up Hughes for DBS Stake," *Electronic News*, January 29, 1996, p. 21.

"Raytheon Regroups," *Dealerscope Merchandising* 35 (August 1993): 85–86.

Eric Shine, Larry Armstrong, and Kathleen Kerwin, "Liftoff," *Business Week*, April 22, 1996, pp. 136–147.

Geoffrey Smith, "Raytheon's Strategy: Guns and Lots More Butter," *Business Week*, November 16, 1992, p. 96.

THE IMPORTANCE OF UNDERSTANDING, RESPONDING TO, AND MANAGING THE ENVIRONMENT

The responses of Raytheon, McDonnell Douglas, and Hughes Electronics to defense-spending cuts are good examples of how companies benefit from understanding, responding to, and sometimes managing their marketing environments. All three companies monitored international military developments and anticipated some of the resulting changes. Lobbying activities in Washington, D.C., and elsewhere also kept them abreast of proposed government actions and gave them opportunities to influence those actions. Because of their efforts to understand, respond to, and manage the environment, the company managers foresaw U.S. and

European defense-spending declines. Such efforts also allowed them to assess their competitive positions in other market segments, identify and help shape new opportunities, and prepare for likely competitive responses in those markets.[1]

In chapter 1, we saw that marketing is based on exchange relationships, with exchange taking place both inside companies and with outside constituencies. All organizational members share responsibility for exchange relationships within a company. The formal responsibility for exchange relationships outside the company, however, falls primarily on departments and functional areas called boundary spanners—areas in organizations that operate at their boundaries, and that have contact with outside companies and individuals. Purchasing, shipping, and accounts receivable all span boundaries in important ways, but marketing is perhaps the most important boundary-spanning function.

The marketing function facilitates exchange with customers as it negotiates the purchase of the company's outputs at profitable price levels. Without successful marketing, the company cannot sustain any other area in the organization very long, because they all depend on profits to facilitate their activities. Marketing managers, therefore, must understand their customers' attitudes and behaviors, and help to guide the efforts of other areas of the company in meeting those needs. In addition, marketing managers must be concerned with other constituencies, such as competitors, intermediaries, and suppliers, who can affect the company's ability to market its products successfully, and they must pay close attention to broad-scale forces that affect those constituencies.[2] In other words, marketing managers must understand, respond to, and manage their environments if they are to be market oriented.[3]

The fundamental premise of this chapter is that understanding, responding to, and managing the environment can result in successful marketing initiatives, in terms of meeting customer needs and profitability. We show how companies understand, respond to, and manage microlevel factors—such as customer needs, attitudes, and behaviors; supplier and intermediary demands; and competitors' actions—as well as the macrolevel factors—such as economic, political and legal, demographic, sociocultural and technological developments. We begin, however, with how marketing managers understand, respond to, and manage the environment within their own organizations.

THE ORGANIZATIONAL ENVIRONMENT

Three areas of the environment that concern marketing managers are illustrated in Figure 3.1. The organizational environment encompasses all areas of the company outside of marketing that can affect marketing strategy execution, such as accounting, purchasing, engineering, manufacturing, and finance. At Raytheon's Amana division, for example, marketing arranges direct sales to major buyers of appliances, such as retailers and real estate developers, whereas the accounts-receivable department typically handles invoicing. However, customers seldom see the same pronounced distinctions between those areas as Raytheon's employees do, and unsatisfactory performance by one department can easily affect the customer's attitude toward the company as a whole. Because Amana's marketing managers facilitate exchange with customers, they need to be concerned with all possible factors that can affect the customer relationship, including the accounts receivable area. If accounts receivable wants to change its billing practices and reduce the amount of time allowed for payment, for example, marketing should be concerned because the change will increase the net cost of products to the customer.

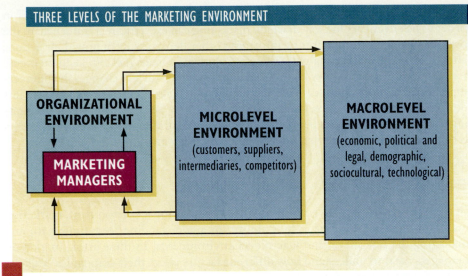

ORGANIZATIONAL ENVIRONMENT

MARKETING MANAGERS

MICROLEVEL ENVIRONMENT (customers, suppliers, intermediaries, competitors)

MACROLEVEL ENVIRONMENT (economic, political and legal, demographic, sociocultural, technological)

Marketers should likewise remain abreast of trends in other areas of the organization, not only to identify problems, but also to recognize marketing opportunities that may otherwise go unnoticed. Engineers at Amana, for example, may develop smaller and simpler electric appliance motors as a way to reduce warranty expense and costs, but overlook the fact that smaller motors reduce required cabinet size that would make it possible to offer a line of downsized appliances aimed at apartment dwellers. By being informed of such developments, marketing can help bring about a new and profitable product line for Amana. Effective marketing managers, therefore, try to be aware of activities throughout the organization and how they can affect marketing efforts and customer satisfaction. They make it their job to understand, respond to, and sometimes manage such activities, as depicted by the arrows in Figure 3.1.

Managing the Environment

Marketing managers can influence their environment only to a limited extent. Within the organizational environment, for example, the actual management of activities remains the responsibility of senior management. Even if an organization has a strong marketing orientation, and senior managers are acquainted with the concerns and objectives of the marketing area, they cannot focus solely on marketing area demands. Marketing personnel at McDonnell Douglas, for example, may have wanted to accelerate the DC-10 production schedule in response to labor problems at Boeing hindering its ability to ship product. It was up to senior managers, however, to balance marketing's demands with the needs of manufacturing for stable production schedules, and they made the final decision.

In spite of the limited ability of marketers to manage the environment, overlooking opportunities in this area can impose unnecessary limitations on marketing activity. In some situations, a small amount of social influence is all that is needed to achieve marketing objectives, such as when Bombardier—a diversified manufacturer of railcars, subway trains and other transportation-related products—in helping to manage China's largest passenger-rail factory, removed hindrances to purchases of its rail-car components, and gave the company a significant presence in the Chinese market.[4] In addition, not all management of the environment needs to be direct in order to be effective. One way in which marketing can exert indirect influence on the organizational environment is by informing other departments of how their actions affect customers and profitability. Effective marketing managers also keep their customers informed about relevant internal developments, such as changes in engineering standards, production schedules, or payment policies. Regardless of whether it is done through the salesforce, public relations, or other forms of promotion, facilitating the flow of information between different areas of the company and its customers is one way in which marketing helps shape the environment.

THE MICROLEVEL ENVIRONMENT

In contrast to their limited control over the organizational environment, marketing managers bear more direct responsibility for understanding, responding to, and managing the microlevel and macrolevel environments. In these areas, marketing managers need to understand how different factors affect their companies' abilities to meet customer needs and take action to offset emerging threats and capitalize on opportunities.

The microlevel environment is composed of groups and organizations in four broad categories—customers, suppliers, intermediaries, and competitors—with which a company is directly involved and which can have an immediate effect on its ability to market products or services. Most of a company's daily activities take place in the microlevel environment. On a day-to-day basis, companies deal with customers, suppliers, and intermediaries, and are affected by the actions of competitors. Microlevel factors consume much of the marketing manager's time and effort. Understanding, responding to, and managing these factors is critical to the success of any marketing effort.

Customers

Marketers need information about customer needs and to "hear the voice of the market."[5] Some companies develop very sophisticated systems to understand and respond to customers, by keeping track of customer purchase behavior, and by using such information to guide current marketing efforts and plan future marketing campaigns. Kraft USA, for example, combines consumer purchase information logged by register scanners at retail stores with customer profiles from census-like surveys to develop typical-customer profiles by store. Such profiles are used to identify the Kraft products that sell best at each store location, and to manage the product line inventory at each store accordingly. At stores within a single metropolitan area such as New York City, Kraft provides retailers with store-specific inventory combinations of products such as Philadelphia cream cheese, Kraft Singles, and Velveeta cheese, designed to enhance demand. Kraft also provides store-specific shelf placement recommendations based on its knowledge of consumers. Another example of understanding and responding to the customer environment comes from Whirlpool, which collects and analyzes customer service information by individual customer and product line. The company uses this information to identify and correct design problems, and sometimes to renegotiate warranty terms with suppliers if the suppliers' components are defective. It also uses such information to guide future product programs.[6]

Effective marketers are also involved in managing the customer environment. The notion of managing customers sometimes elicits sinister visions of Machiavellian behavior and "big brother" intervention. Such management has been mentioned as a danger in media-dependent societies such as the United States, Japan, Canada, and much of Western Europe. Although some of these concerns might be justified, it is a mistake to consider all attempts to manage consumer perceptions and behaviors as evil.

Customers often do not know they need a good or service until a marketer leads them to consider the product and their own situations carefully. In the 1980s, this was true with minivans, personal computers, and health maintenance organizations, all of which are established members of the consumer products landscape today. It can also be true of consumable products. When 3M Corporation introduced its Post-It brand of notes, customers were not aware that they "needed" these self-adhering slips of paper. The company managed the customers' understanding and interest in the product by giving away free samples and letting customers experience the convenience and greater productivity that comes from this simple product. The end result, of course, was that the product became a staple in most office environments, and a great success for 3M.

In fact, customers occasionally insist that marketers manage their purchase behavior, and they hold marketers accountable for incorrect judgments. In the financial services area, customers rely heavily on the advise of stockbrokers and financial-planning consultants, and often hold brokers liable for losses incurred from following their advice. Because stockbrokers and financial-planning consultants earn their income from sales commissions, they are, in effect, marketers who manage their customers' purchases. Cosmetics consultants are another example of marketers who are entrusted with their customers' decisions on skin care and beauty products, and who must make sure that recommended products are compatible with each customer's complexion.

In marketing industrial products, managing customer knowledge and behaviors can be even more important, as was illustrated by the actions of Bombardier in securing contracts from the Chinese government. Another example is that of the British royal family. One of the British royal family's responsibilities is to help British companies manage relationships with countries and companies that are potential customers. On a visit to South Korea, for example, Prince Charles helped bring the chairmen of Hyundai, Samsung Shipbuilding, and Daewoo Telecom together for a roundtable discussion on ecological issues, which ultimately resulted in business for several British firms such as Nedstrom Ltd., the world leader in the ecology management industry. In this situation, Prince Charles was neither a manipulator nor a politician, but an accomplished statesman who facilitated good works (the preservation of the environment) in Asia and advanced British commercial interests in the process. Prince Charles has also been involved in similar roles in Africa and eastern Europe.[7]

Suppliers

As marketing managers monitor their industries and markets, they watch suppliers, defined as all of the outside firms and individuals that provide goods and services that companies need to operate. Raytheon's Amana division, for example, depends on suppliers for many of its appliance components, ranging from the injection-molded panels that line refrigerator interiors to the integrated circuit controls used in electric ranges. Amana also depends on service suppliers, such as trucking companies that carry finished product to retailers, as well as companies that service copiers, personal computers, and large data-processing systems. Not all of these suppliers may be directly involved with the final product, but they can have an impact on the firm's ability to meet customer needs because of functional integration. In most modern organizations, functions such as accounting, materials management, and manufacturing are highly integrated with each other, and the failure of a supplier in one functional area (e.g., trucking companies affecting the inflow of components) can have serious implications for the company's ability to build and ship products. Understanding, responding to, and managing suppliers, therefore, can be very important in a company's ability to execute marketing programs effectively and profitably.

High levels of functional integration in companies also suggests that indirect as well as direct suppliers' actions may have serious consequences for marketing efforts, making it sometimes necessary to monitor companies that render goods and services to the direct suppliers as well. In fact, companies selling to direct suppliers can be just as important as the direct suppliers themselves. Consider the case of Amana's refrigerator liners. There are probably many suppliers of injection-molded panels in the United States, but practically all must buy thermoplastic resins and compounds from the same source, as this is a highly concentrated industry dominated by companies such as DuPont and General Electric. Problems with one supplier of thermoplastic resins and compounds, therefore, can have global implications, not only for Amana but also for the hundreds of other companies that use injection-molded plastics in their products. Raytheon marketing managers monitor both their direct suppliers of injection-molded panels and the companies that supply important raw and manufactured materials to those direct suppliers, and they develop contingency strategies in case of supply problems in either industry.

Another example of the need for supplier monitoring is the case of Amway Japan, and its highly successful home-use water-treatment system. This water-treatment system was designed by Amway specifically for small Japanese kitchens and is the only product on the market that uses both ultraviolet light and conventional activated-charcoal filters.[8] Amway Japan, however, does not produce the units, making it dependent on the unit's manufacturer and on the suppliers of conventional filters and ultraviolet lamps. Because the sales of these units produce millions of dollars in revenue to Amway Japan, the company monitors both its direct supplier and the suppliers of these key components. Trouble with either set of suppliers can seriously curtail Amway's progress in the Japanese market.

Supplier Industry Factors: Growth and Decline

In addition to monitoring individual direct and indirect suppliers, marketing managers responsible for longer-range strategic planning also pay attention to supplier industry developments. Managers pay close attention to growth and decline trends in supplier industries. Much of the concern over supplier industry trends is due to the distribution of scarce resources in competitive markets.

Supplier industries that are growing in terms of sales revenues and profits are healthy, and are most likely also growing in terms of economic power and their ability to expand into other markets. Effective marketers make it their business to understand the causes of growth in supplier industries, and to identify which of the suppliers' current sources of business can represent future threats to them as either customers or competitors. Unless the supplier industry's growth is a direct result of the marketer's own company's growth, supplier industry growth suggests there is demand from other companies, demand that might eventually curtail the marketer's access to important components and raw materials. For example, if the injection-molded panels industry started growing quickly because of demand from Japanese appliance manufacturers, Raytheon may face future supply shortages or significant increases in refrigerator panel costs, which would affect its competitive position, and for which it must develop contingency plans.

Extraordinary declines in supplier industries should also be monitored by marketing managers, because they might indicate changes in competitors' practices. A drop in a major supplier's reported sales or advanced orders, for example, should be investigated if the company supplies similar products and services to competitors, because the drop may be caused by a competitor's move to more advantageous sources of raw materials or more advanced technologies, or by a competitor struggling, or by suppliers adopting a retrenchment strategy in anticipation of declining demand for their products. For example, in the highly fragmented personal computer industry, the actions of microprocessor manufacturer Intel are closely watched by competing personal computer manufacturers who find it difficult to monitor one another directly. If Intel were to stop construction on microprocessor plants already in progress, or cancel plans for additional manufacturing capacity, personal computer manufacturers would monitor the situation closely because it may indicate a major shift in the marketing strategies of large computer manufacturers such as IBM, Compaq, or Hewlett-Packard.

Supplier Industry Factors: Consolidation and Fragmentation

Supplier industry consolidation or fragmentation trends are also important because they have a direct bearing on the supplier industry's financial health and the balance of power in the supplier chain. Consolidation—a reduction in the total number of suppliers—can give remaining suppliers more economic and negotiating power, and ultimately result in tighter supplies and higher prices. Industry consolidation is often caused by mergers and acquisitions between supplier companies, or by some suppliers abandoning the industry. Fragmentation—a proliferation of suppliers—can eventually lead to more competition and lower prices, but also greater supplier industry instability. Fragmentation is often caused by the entry of small manufacturers, as technological and legal barriers to entry are eliminated.

As an example, consider the case if patent protection were to expire for the electronic controls Raytheon purchases for its ranges, and suppliers with lower manufacturing costs were able to offer the same products. In such a situation, competition among suppliers would most likely result in lower prices for Raytheon. If at the same time, however, the injection-molded panels industry consolidated so that only two viable suppliers remained, Raytheon would probably see stable or increasing prices for plastic panels. An industry that is consolidating is also likely to result in more powerful suppliers, who force changes in manufacturing and delivery practices in addition to higher prices. Other examples of supplier consolidation can be found in the automotive components industry, where companies such as Dana Corporation have been acquiring many small producers in the United States and Europe. Dana Corporation's consolidation strategy is motivated by several factors, such as avoiding the cyclical fluctuations in the U.S. automobile market and wanting to be closer to its global customers. In addition, consolidation in the automotive component industry also reduces the power of auto manufacturers to demand large cost reductions from their suppliers.[9]

Marketing managers often show interest in suppliers, such as Dana Corporation, who can change industry practice or demand large concessions from their customers. Understanding the implications of supplier actions can help marketers anticipate change and take action that protects their ability to meet customer demands. Some companies address this need by becoming more involved in the management decisions of suppliers, and letting suppliers have direct input into their own operations. We discuss this trend toward "relationship marketing" in the chapters on organizational buyer behavior (chapter 6) and distribution management (chapter 13). For now, note that traditional arm's-length buyer-seller relationships are giving away to cooperative partnerships in many industries.

Innovative Suppliers

Marketing managers also benefit from monitoring companies who compete with current suppliers and who may overtake current suppliers in important areas, such as manufacturing costs, quality standards, or product performance. This kind of monitoring helps marketing managers identify innovative suppliers, who may help manufacturers establish or enhance their competitive advantage. Automotive manufacturers have monitored innovative leaders in supplier industries for several years, as illustrated in Marketing Anecdote 3.1, and this monitoring has contributed to U.S. auto manufacturers' competitiveness and improved quality. In the early 1990s, U.S. automobile manufacturers noted Plumley's performance improvements and sought it as a supplier. Plumley's high quality standards and consistent performance ultimately resulted in lower warranty costs and higher customer satisfaction, which benefited U.S. auto producers. It is interesting to note that Japanese auto producers in the United States were also monitoring the supplier environment and noticed Plumley's outstanding performance as well. Japanese auto producers, who typically relied on Japan-based component manufacturers due to the comparatively poorer quality of U.S. component producers, ultimately adopted Plumley as a supplier for both its U.S.- and Japan-based factories. By monitoring the supplier environment and adopting innovative suppliers, the Japanese auto manufacturers were able to partially neutralize some of the gains being made by their U.S. competitors in the 1990s.

Intermediaries

Intermediaries—companies and individuals who help marketers distribute goods and services to the final customer—are very important to most companies. Not all customers can be served by the marketing company directly, so most are serviced by intermediaries. Some intermediaries distribute goods and services directly, such as wholesalers and retailers who purchase Amana appliances for resale. Other intermediaries influence distribution indirectly by providing important services. Trucking companies such as Roadway and Consolidated Freightway, for example, transport appliances and many other products from manufacturing facilities to retail stores, and help insure a steady and adequate supply of products, whereas finance companies, such as GE Capital, facilitate profitable transactions by providing consumers with the necessary credit and payment arrangements. Different types of intermediaries and the functions they serve are discussed in more detail in the chapters on distribution management and the marketing concerns of intermediaries (chapters 13 and 14). The importance of intermediaries to marketing managers depends on the marketing company's size and internal resources, but few companies can market their products without relying on intermediaries for at least some aspects of marketing. Thus, understanding, responding to, and managing the intermediary environment is important to practically all companies.

Growth and Decline Trends among Intermediaries

Marketers seek to understand, respond to, and manage intermediaries just as they do suppliers. Intermediary industry growth and decline trends are important to marketers because of the implications for their ability to distribute goods and ser-

Plumley Company, based in Paris, Tennessee, is a manufacturer of sealants, gaskets, and rubber products for the automotive industry. In the early 1980s, the company was in trouble, as General Motors and other U.S.-based automobile manufacturers dropped it as a supplier because of poor quality. Instead of quitting, however, Plumley fought back by fixing its in-house problems. The company did an internal assessment and found it needed to improve in two areas: employee training and manufacturing equipment.

Plumley found that many of its workers had substandard reading and math skills, and had trouble operating modern equipment and applying statistical process-control methods. It corrected the problem by investing in employee education. At a minimum, Plumley sought to provide all employees with high-school–level reading skills, establishing a common level at which all employees could process written information. In addition, it provided college-level education for all employees responsible for complex processes and customer interface.

As employee reading and math skills improved, another problem surfaced: Plumley's manufacturing equipment could not consistently produce products that matched the close tolerances required by modern automotive design. Plumley resolved this problem by investing millions of dollars in new equipment. Almost immediately, Plumley saw a dramatic improvement in quality and consistency.

Plumley's improvements were quickly noted by automotive manufacturers who were monitoring nonsuppliers, and the company was reinstated as a supplier by several companies. Eventually, Plumley's performance led to quality awards from General Motors, Nissan, and Ford. It also led to Plumley being one of the few U.S.-based automotive component manufacturers to become a permanent supplier to Japanese auto plants, in both the United States and Japan. Plumley's success ultimately led Dana Corporation to acquire it in 1995, as automotive suppliers sought greater economies of scale and competitiveness through consolidation.

Sources: Gary Burrows, "Plumley Feasts on Japanese Business: Paris, Tenn.–based Automotive Parts Company Supplies Japanese Auto Plants in U.S. and Japan," *American Shipper*, October 1993, pp. 79–80.

Lindsay Chappell, "Rural Firms Face Challenge of Under-Educated Workers," *Automotive News*, June 12, 1989, p. 24.

Tim Keenan, "Spanning the Globe," *Ward's Auto World*, July 1996, pp. 37–38.

James B. Treece, "A Little Bit of Smarts, A Lot of Hard Work," *Business Week*, November 30, 1992, pp. 70–71.

vices. An intermediary industry that is experiencing healthy growth can be a boon for marketers if the growth opens new markets or enhances the marketer's competitive position in other ways. If retailers that sell Amana appliances in the United States and Canada are adding stores in Latin America, for example, it improves Raytheon's market reach as long as its brands retain their position in the retailer's offerings.

Intermediaries also grow in ways that benefit marketers when they devote more resources to automation and other innovations that improve their efficiency and service level. Large trucking companies, for example, invest in electronic data interchange facilities, making it easier to track shipments and reduce transit times. This benefits Raytheon by enhancing its responsiveness to retailer and consumer alike. In contrast, intermediary industries in decline can be a serious threat to manufacturers. After the U.S. government deregulated the trucking industry in the early 1980s, many small trucking companies found they could not compete with larger and more efficient carriers. Unable to meet delivery schedules with their regular carriers, many manufacturers had to seek alternative carriers, such as United Parcel Service and Federal Express, and pay higher prices to insure timely and accurate deliveries.

Consolidation and Fragmentation Trends among Intermediaries

Consolidation and fragmentation among intermediaries are of concern to marketing managers because such trends can affect the balance of power in the channel and the ability of intermediaries to perform distribution functions adequately. Unless the whole intermediary industry is in decline, such as the railroad industry in the 1950s or mass merchandising in the 1970s, a reduction in the total number of intermediaries in an industry suggests that those remaining will be larger companies with greater control of critical resources, as well as a greater ability to dictate prices and terms. As intermediary power and control of resources increases relative to that of manufacturers, marketers are often less able to control pricing, promotion, and other aspects of the marketing mix.

In the 1950s and 1960s, for example, appliances were sold primarily by independent retailers who closely followed manufacturers' pricing and sales recommendations. In the 1970s, however, large discounters started making inroads into the appliance retailing industry, and by the 1990s a relative small number of powerful discounters, such as Circuit City and Best Buy, dominated appliance sales and controlled nationwide distribution. Appliance discounters often formulate their own pricing and promotion tactics and force manufacturers to comply. In some cases, these retailers even set performance parameters for the brand products they will sell, and some retailers force manufacturers to develop special product lines sold only through their outlets. Many appliance manufacturers have responded to the rising power of retailers by developing different product lines for different intermediary types, while concurrently helping to preserve independent retailers as viable intermediaries. Both Amana and General Electric, for example, still sell some of their more sophisticated product lines exclusively through independent retailers, to whom they also offer special financing and promotional assistance. Note that consolidation can occur in different sectors of the retailing and wholesaling industries, and in most circumstances it upsets the established balance of power in the channel.

Fragmentation—the proliferation of small intermediaries because of dislocations in industry structure—affects marketers by changing the functions that intermediaries can perform. If, instead of consolidating, the appliance retail industry were to become more fragmented, Raytheon might regain some of its lost power, but it would also need to invest in support services for small retailers who cannot respond to the company's distribution needs. Transportation costs might increase because small retailers would not be able to accept the truckload-sized shipments that large discounters accept, and Raytheon would have to rely more on costly less-than-truckload shipping. In order to have a full array of products on display at retailers, Raytheon might also have to finance dealer inventories or offer more generous floor-model discount policies.

Customer service is an area hurt often by fragmentation among intermediaries, and to which marketers must respond. One example is retail distribution of personal computer software. In the early years of the personal computer industry, most software was sold through authorized dealers, who were responsible for customer service as well. In the current environment, however, software is sold through a wide array of retailers, ranging from specialty stores in malls to high-volume catalog sales operations, to cyber-boutiques accessible only through the World Wide Web.[10] Software retailing is a highly fragmented industry, and the customer-service capabilities of these various retailers are as varied as their means of contacting customers. In such an environment, software manufacturers such as Microsoft, Lotus, and Corel cannot rely on retailers to offer customer support, and in turn must maintain customer service operations accessible via toll-free numbers, file-transfer-protocol, fax servers, and the Web.

Indirect Intermediaries

Some marketers also consider growth, decline, consolidation, and fragmentation trends among their indirect intermediaries, because of their potential influence on marketing success. For example, credit suppliers such as finance companies, banks, credit unions, and even some national credit card companies have competed since the 1980s for lucrative consumer financing of large purchases such as homes, automobiles, appliances, furniture, and expensive vacations, and for commercial financing of new construction, capital equipment, and corporate vehicle fleets. Not only is there a growth trend in the lending business, it has also become more fragmented, as large conglomerates such as General Motors and General Electric have added the consumer financing market to their traditionally strong commercial lending business, large companies such as AT&T have introduced their own consumer financing services, and traditional lenders such as commercial banks, credit unions, and credit card companies have become very aggressive.

Because many consumers base their purchase decision on credit terms (e.g., size of payment, interest rate) as well as product attributes and performance, marketing managers monitor the credit industry carefully, and they respond in different ways. In times of tight credit availability, for example, some marketers intervene by setting up their own financing subsidiaries, as is the case with Whirlpool in the appliance industry and General Motors in the automobile market. Other marketers seek close working relationships with existing credit suppliers to ensure a stable credit supply for their customers. Marketing managers adjust their actions to complement or offset those of financing providers and other indirect intermediaries to meet customer needs.

New Intermediary Types

Marketers need to understand, respond to, and possibly manage new intermediary types because of their potential for adverse effects on existing intermediaries as well as to create new opportunities to reach new customers. New intermediary types can emerge from unlikely sources and are not always immediately recognized, making monitoring in this area particularly important.

In the commercial aircraft industry, for example, the emergence of limited partnerships as a source of capital in the 1970s gave airlines a new way of financing aircraft purchases, and resulted in an overall increase in the size of the aircraft market. Commercial aircraft manufacturers such as Boeing and McDonnell Douglas, who were attentive to the intermediary financing market, identified this new financing early and capitalized on it by guiding some customers to this type of financing.

A medium in which new and diverse intermediary types are emerging in great numbers is the World Wide Web. Almost daily, new commercial ventures and intermediary applications emerge, ranging in scope from retailing books and software, to offering financial services (e.g., life insurance), to third-party brokering of product information, to facilitating electronic data interchange between corporate giants and even the smallest suppliers and customers. Consumers and businesses can use the web to purchase hundreds of different types of products or services, from Swiss bank accounts to gourmet coffee, and they can do it from practically anywhere in the world where they can establish a WWW connection.

The marketing implications of the World Wide Web are very broad. Some will be discussed later in this and other chapters. Of immediate importance is the fact that the web extends the possibilities for remote shopping by many consumers, and it is likely to affect thousands of product categories in the future. It is already possible, for example, to do at least preliminary shopping for automobiles and car financing on the web, resulting in consumers being much more educated when they enter the dealer showroom. It is also possible to shop from large retailers, such as Sears and Wal-Mart, from specialty stores such as Eddie Bauer, and from web-only cyberstores such as Fire Fly. Shopping via the web and other cyber-venues is changing retailing practices for practically all consumer products. Marketers of such products will benefit from understanding, responding to, and managing this emerging medium and the intermediary possibilities it creates.

Competitors

As we discussed in chapter 2, companies need to understand and respond to direct competitors if they are to command consumers' attention and purchasing power. In the overcrowded painkiller markets, for example, the 1994 entry of Aleve as a joint venture of Roche Holding and Procter & Gamble commanded the attention of industry giants such as Johnson & Johnson (Tylenol), Bristol-Myers Squibb (Excedrin, Nuprin), and Bayer AG (Bayer Aspirin). Aleve was the first truly new painkiller to enter the market in ten years, and, considering P&G's marketing expertise, it represented a significant threat to competitors.[11]

Even more significant, however, was P&G's selling out of the Aleve joint venture two years later. After spending $100 million to introduce Aleve in the United States, P&G sold out its 50 percent interest in the brand as part of a product line simplification initiative that caught the consumer products industry by surprise. Other long-standing P&G brands that were sold are Lava Soap and Lestoil.[12] Such moves by P&G had significant implications for competitors across the spectrum of consumer products, since they signaled a significant strategic shift by Procter & Gamble. Needless to say, P&G's subsequent actions are being carefully scrutinized and responded to by its competitors.

Often marketing managers do not go far enough when it comes to understanding and responding to competitors. A common mistake is to include only similar products in the competitive set, and thus overlook products and strategies that serve the same function but use different technology. When marketers fail to look at the broader competitive environment, they often miss competitive threats and opportunities until it is too late to respond adequately.

The notion of a broader competitive environment is illustrated in Figure 3.2, which focuses on the competitive environment for McDonnell Douglas's defense products. The McDonnell Douglas F-15 fighter, one of the most advanced fighter aircraft in the world in terms of speed and versatility, competes often with the Russian-built MIG-21, which is not as advanced but considerably less costly, and the French-built Mirage F1-C, which has performance and cost roughly matching those of the F-15. A McDonnell Douglas marketing manager who adopts a narrow perspective might monitor solely the manufacturers of these fighter aircraft. To customers, however, fighter aircraft are only one of many defense options available. A

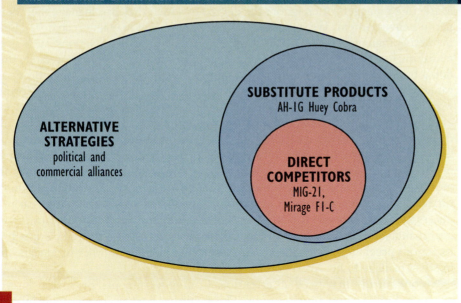

country that institutes a proactive and independent defense program, for example, can replace fighter aircraft with missile equipped helicopter gunships such as the AH-1G Huey Cobra. Helicopter gunships are not as fast as the F-15, but they are more maneuverable and can match fighter aircraft defense capabilities in many situations. In addition, countries may choose not to spend resources on defense directly, but to spend them instead on developing cooperative agreements with powerful military allies, for example, by providing support to allied military operations (e.g., land for military bases) in exchange for protection.

The tendency to define the competitive field too narrowly was recognized as a problem more than 30 years ago by marketing guru Theodore Levitt, who named the phenomenon "marketing myopia."[13] Levitt used the shortsightedness of railroads in the 1950s to illustrate his point; Railroad managers defined their competitive set as only other railroads and failed to see the threat that interstate trucking companies posed until the railroad industry was already in crisis. Although recognized as a significant problem, marketing myopia has not disappeared from the list of mistakes made by marketing managers. Because most noticeable day-to-day problems arise from direct competitors' actions, managers typically focus only on their most salient problems. They should not ignore the broader competitive environment, however, because competitive threats emerging from other sectors can often be more significant and more difficult to offset. In the mid-1980s, for example, the front-wheel–drive Chrysler minivans made substantial inroads into the family sedan market dominated by General Motors and Ford, but the trend went unrecognized for several years. By the time General Motors and Ford recognized this and engineered their own front-wheel–drive minivans, Chrysler had established a firm hold on the segment, and it has remained the dominant minivan producer in the world. Marketing personnel need to monitor more than just other producers of similar products. They also need to monitor the producers of alternative product categories that can meet the same customer needs, and even emerging technologies and practices that can eliminate the customers' needs altogether.

Managing the Competitive Environment

Marketing managers often ignore the degree to which they can manage their competitive environment. We suggest at least three ways that managers can do so. First, marketing managers may look for ways to restrict competitors' actions, such as establishing long-term alliances with customers and suppliers that may preclude their doing business with a competitor or, at a minimum, neutralize the competitor's advantage. After Microsoft's late start on Internet software, for example, it formed working alliances with suppliers such as Sun Microsystems, creator of the Java programming language.[14] Such cooperation with suppliers helped Microsoft close the competitive gap between itself and Netscape Communications Corporation, the acknowledged Internet pioneer. Strategic alliances are also possible for small pioneering firms in danger of their products being copied and marketed by larger and more powerful competitors. For example, One Xcel, developer of a line of nondistorting sports visors, established marketing agreements with large sports gear producers such as Karhu and Riddel shortly after product introduction. Because sports gear manufacturers were some of One Xcel's most powerful potential competitors, its actions precluded the entry into the sport visor market of other producers, and in effect managed One Xcel's competitors.[15]

Second, firms may seek intervention from governments or special-interest groups to limit a competitor's options. This tactic has been used repeatedly by commercial aircraft manufacturers such as Boeing, McDonnell Douglas, and Airbus Industries. All three companies have at some point sought protection from their home governments (United States and France) against the marketing attempts of their competitors, citing reasons such as national security interests and unfair subsidies as justification for government intervention.

Third, marketing managers may try to force competitors into wasteful actions or premature competitive moves. Large companies, such as Ford in automobiles, Boeing in commercial aircraft, and Microsoft in computer software, have often been accused by competitors of issuing a new product announcement long before the product was ready for the market. The alleged intent in most situations was to discourage competitors from developing their own versions of the products, or to force competitors to introduce their products ahead of schedule and before all engineering, production, or marketing problems had been worked out.

Actions that restrict or in other ways force competitors to take unnecessary action can sometimes be found to restrict trade excessively and be declared illegal by agencies such as the Federal Trade Commission (FTC) or the U.S. Justice Department. Adverse government rulings can, at a minimum, force companies to cease and desist from such practices. They can also result in companies having to make reparations to competitors. The possibility of government intervention makes it important that marketing managers exercise care in their attempts to manage competitors. The threat of legal action, however, should not result in marketers ignoring the possibility of managing competitors as part of their overall marketing strategy.

THE MACROLEVEL ENVIRONMENT

All marketing organizations exist in broad environments composed of dynamic and static forces, which act and interact in diverse and sometimes unpredictable ways to create opportunities and pose threats for industries and companies. The broad, or macrolevel, environment includes five domains in which changes occur that are typically outside the company's control, but which can have both immediate and long-term implications for a company's ability to market its product or services.

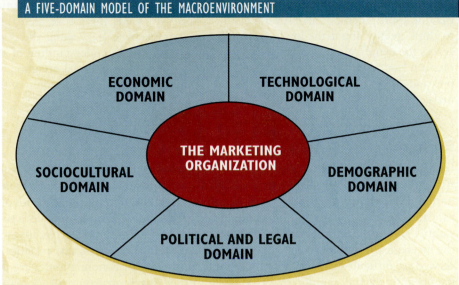

These five domains are economic, political and legal, demographic, sociocultural, and technological, as illustrated in Figure 3.3. Macrolevel forces are multidimensional, however, and can be addressed in more than one domain simultaneously. Worldwide interest-rate fluctuations, for example, can influence demand for McDonnell Douglas's fighter aircraft through both the political and legal domain and economic domain. Consequently, any static model of the macroenvironment, be it five-dimensional or otherwise, is not an exact representation, nor should such models be taken to imply that macrolevel forces are easy to classify and manage. In fact, practically all attempts at modeling the environment are flawed, either because they miss some aspects in their attempt to be simple, or because their accuracy makes the models too complex to be useful. The value of modeling the macroenvironment is in forcing marketing managers to adopt a broad and systematic perspective when considering the factors that can affect their companies' marketing strategies.

Managers who systematically monitor the macroenvironment benefit in two ways. First, they have greater confidence in proposed tactics and strategies, because they have looked at a greater number of factors than have managers who simply react to late breaking news or other more limited information sources. In other words, their proposed solutions and strategies are less likely to cause problems to other functional areas because they used an environmental checklist to insure that all critical areas are covered.

Second, managers who monitor these domains usually take a multidimensional and multilevel perspective on problems and situations, which leads to more complex representations of problems and to more thorough plans of action. Since most macrolevel forces affect multiple domains, marketing managers who systematically monitor the environment across domains will revisit some issues several times from different perspectives, and thus gain a greater overall understanding of how the company will be affected.

The distinction between these benefits can be made more clear if we consider environmental research on a marketing problem as analogous to studying an apple.

Systematic monitoring of all environmental domains leads the researcher to notice that the apple is composed of several distinct parts (skin, seeds, meal, core, stem) and to think deeply about the apple from different perspectives (e.g., along the core, across the center, along the surface). Just as a more thorough understanding of apples can lead to better decisions about their consumption (some apples are good for pies and others for apple sauce, for example), a more thorough understanding of the marketing environment can lead to better marketing strategy.

Economic

Global and local economic factors are critically important to marketing managers. Economic activity has been systematically studied and modeled for more than a hundred years, and in the 1990s is constantly analyzed and summarized by both private and public institutions. The amount of economic information available is substantial, but in spite of the high level of attention given to economic forces, many of the mechanisms by which such factors affect the demand for a particular product or service are difficult to ascertain precisely and consistently. Economic forces are dynamic and change rapidly in response to other macroenvironment domains. Marketing managers must consequently monitor the economic environment regularly and use new economic evidence to reexamine past assumptions about how economic factors affect the company's performance. Precise econometric models and their market demand forecasts are accurate only as long as the relationships among economic variables remain relatively stable. Major structural shifts may make existing economic models obsolete, requiring researchers to develop new models or recalibrate old ones. The oil embargoes of 1974 and 1979, for example, permanently altered assumptions about the cost and availability of energy that were embedded in many industrial econometric models. The predictive power of such models was consequently nullified, until they were updated with new energy cost and availability assumptions and new links between energy costs and other sectors.

Several economic variables have a direct effect on the demand for products and services, and marketing managers should focus most of their attention on these variables.

Income

Income levels and fluctuations are important because of their direct influence on consumer demand for products and services. Marketers focus on real income and disposable income most often. Real income is personal income adjusted for inflation. When real income levels rise, consumers can afford to purchase previously inaccessible items, and conditions become more favorable for introducing new products as well as increasing existing product sales. Real income gains are particularly important for companies that sell expensive products such as automobiles and appliances, because rising real income empowers consumers to purchase more expensive models than in the past. When real income levels stagnate or decline, the demand for new products and more sophisticated versions of existing products also falls off.

The demand for many consumer products also depends on the overall level of disposable income—the money that consumers have left over after paying fixed obligations such as taxes and house payments. Rising disposable income means that consumers have more money available for purchasing goods and services than before, which will likely generate increased demand. Tax rate reductions, for example, give consumers more money to spend, even if their total income remains the same. Changes in credit policies that reduce the size of credit payments or extend repayment periods can also result in disposable income increases. Obviously, tax rate increases or tighter credit policies reduce disposable income if total income levels remain stable.

Real and disposable income fluctuations influence not only final consumer purchase behavior, but also the demands of organizational customers for goods and services. Growing industrial customers typically experience real income gains and are much more likely to upgrade plant and equipment or expand their productive capacity. Growing companies are also more likely to spend on improving employee working conditions, which also involves capital improvements. Increases in disposable income can also generate additional industrial buyer demands for products and services. Such increases are often caused by business income tax rate reductions or by restructuring debt to reduce payment size.

In contrast, organizations in decline typically experience a drop in real income and accompanying expenditures. They may still represent an opportunity for marketers whose products can be used to reduce the customer's operating costs and improve profit margins. Industries or companies in decline usually represent less promising prospects for most marketing organizations. Likewise, decreases in industrial buyer disposable income caused by tax rate increases or other factors are almost always accompanied by reduced demand for discretionary products and services, and in an overall negative environment for companies that market to such customers.

Other Variables Affecting Income Levels

Credit repayment policies, inflation, and income taxes all affect real and disposable income levels for final consumers and organizations, and as such are economic variables that marketing managers monitor. Since the income-level effects of changes in these variables can take days, weeks, or months to be realized, marketing managers who monitor these variables can readily anticipate income fluctuations and possible demand shifts, and take action to maximize gains when demand is high or to minimize losses when demand is low.

Other economic variables that affect income levels include employment levels in different sectors of the economy and interest rate changes. When employment levels rise, more people have money to spend, and if high-wage industries such as steel manufacturing and white-collar professions show employment gains, the increases in spending are likely to be even higher. In contrast, decreased employment reduces spending in two ways. First, some consumers disappear from the market because they have no income. Second, other consumers become worried even if they are still employed, and they conserve on spending. Either way, reduced spending represents fewer opportunities for marketers and often require adjustments to marketing strategies.

Interest rates also affect consumer spending in two ways. When interest rates rise, payment levels on credit purchases tend to rise also (unless repayment periods are extended), so people cannot afford to borrow as much. In effect, disposable income decreases. In addition, rising interest rates may motivate consumers to increase their savings at favorable rates, and as people save more they spend less on products.

Aggregate Economic Indicators

Income, employment levels, interest rates, inflation, and consumer confidence all tend to move together due to their high level of interdependence, and they are often aggregated into general indices of economic expansion and recession. In expansion periods, income levels rise as interest rates and unemployment drop, which leads to higher levels of consumer confidence and an overall more positive marketing environment. Inflation also tends to rise during expansion periods, although it lags income and consequently does not affect current consumer confidence adversely. Under these conditions, the demand for products and services rises and marketers sell more goods. In recession periods, unemployment and interest rates rise as income levels and consumer confidence declines, and demand for goods and services also drops. Such drops are particularly pronounced for high-priced consumer durable goods, such as automobiles, appliances, and home entertainment equipment.

Some marketing managers monitor the economic environment using aggregate indices instead of the more focused measures, such as disposable income, discussed earlier. Such aggregate indices, however, can lead managers to misjudge the market. During the 1990–1992 recession cycle, for example, the demand for some discretionary items, such as automobiles and fancy vacations, decreased as expected. Surprisingly though, demand for televisions, VCRs, and other electronic items actually increased. Two causes for the increased demand were obscured in aggregate indices of the economic environment. First, the price of electronic goods actually dropped significantly relative to inflation, making the goods less costly as a percentage of total income. Second, customers who were forced to stay at home because of the recession were better able to justify home entertainment expenditures. Lower prices and being forced to stay home combined to produce a boom market for electronic products in an otherwise dismal economic environment.[16] Thus, although monitoring aggregate measures of economic conditions can be useful, marketing managers also benefit from monitoring more specific economic measures, ones that relate closely to customer demand for the goods and services they sell.

International Currency Exchange Rates

Currency exchange rates between the host countries of marketing managers and their major trading partners are also important. As discussed in chapter 1, many companies today do business in global markets, exporting products into many different countries from a single manufacturing country, or importing components from several countries for local assembly. For these companies, exchange-rate fluctuations can cause fast and dramatic differences in the prices for which they sell their products in different markets and large dislocations in manufacturing costs. One example is the price of automobiles exported by Japan to the United States. In the early 1990s, a highly valued yen caused the price of Japanese vehicles to rise more than 15 percent in spite of stable manufacturing costs in the home market, and gave domestic auto manufacturers a competitive advantage. More recently, however, the value of the yen has declined relative to major Western currencies, at the same time that Japanese producers have achieved significant manufacturing cost reductions. The end result is that automobile producers such as Toyota are able to increase the performance and standard content of products such as the Camry while lowering the price, and are once again threatening to take market share from U.S. producers.[17] Marketing managers involved in transnational trade must monitor exchange rates carefully, and adopt marketing strategies flexible enough to deal with sudden and dramatic shifts in costs and revenue.

Political and Legal

Some aspects of the political and legal environment relate directly to the economic domain, such as fiscal policy changes designed to manage interest rates and either stimulate or curtail demand for goods and services. But government action can affect companies' marketing efforts in other ways also. Marketing managers benefit from understanding the historical political and legal factors that have shaped their marketing environment, and current trends that might produce additional changes. The political and legal domain breaks down into roughly two areas: legislative activity and regulatory activity.

Legislation

In the United States and some other countries, governments enact legislation that sets limits on what companies can and cannot do in the marketplace. The amount of legislation around the world is extensive and beyond the scope of our discussion. The major U.S. federal legislation enacted in the 100 years from 1890 to 1990, summarized in Table 3.1, illustrates the diversity of governmental concerns and the proliferation of recent legislation. Adding to this extensive legislation, many state and provincial governments have enacted laws that complement or extend federal ones.

Some legislation intends to preserve competition in markets that would otherwise be dominated by one or two major companies, such as the Sherman Antitrust Act of 1890 and the Robinson-Patman Act of 1936. Federal antitrust action is still evident today. This is exemplified by recent Justice Department investigations of Intel Corporation and other semiconductor manufacturers for alleged irregularities in the granting of technology licenses, and investigations of Microsoft Corporation for alleged unfair practices in the bundling of Internet access software with its Windows 95 operating system.[18] Sometimes, however, legislation is enacted to protect and restrict monopolistic arrangements that are important to national interests. Such was the case with the old American Telephone & Telegraph Company, the precursor of modern-day AT&T and the "Baby Bells." Although not officially protected by an act of Congress, from the 1920s to the 1970s federal and state legislation restricted the activities of AT&T's competitors in the United States, while at the same time placing limits on AT&T's allowable businesses and on the prices it could charge for services. The U.S. government protected AT&T because of concern that a proliferation of incompatible communications systems would endanger national security. Other countries have had similar concerns since the invention of the telephone, and they responded by establishing government-owned telephone companies, such as Nippon Telephone and Telegraph in Japan and British Telecomm in the United Kingdom. It is interesting that both of these companies were privatized in the 1980s, concurrent with the breakup of American Telephone and Telegraph.

Concerns over national security still motivate legislative and judicial action in the telecommunications industry, even in the wake of deregulation and mergers that cross national boundaries, such as that of British Telecomm and MCI.[19] In the modern digital world, system compatibility is no longer the issue, but unauthorized access and information terrorism are. In the United States and around the world, much of the industrial, entertainment, military, and energy distribution infrastructures are interconnected through a global network of computers accessible to millions of people through thousands of entry points. Such interconnectedness contributes greatly to the quality of life enjoyed by millions of consumers, and to the efficiency and profitability of thousands of companies. It also renders vast sectors in the industrialized world susceptible to computer-initiated terrorism, which would be difficult to track down, and which could be perpetrated from anywhere in the world. The electric power grids in the United States, Canada, and throughout much of Europe, for example, are controlled via computers hooked up to this global network, and can be

TABLE 3.1 U.S. LEGISLATION AFFECTING MARKETING

SHERMAN ANTITRUST ACT (1890). Prohibits monopolies or attempts to monopolize; bars contracts, combinations, or conspiracies in restraint of trade in interstate and foreign commerce.

FEDERAL FOOD AND DRUG ACT (1906). Forbids the manufacture, sale, or transport of adulterated or fraudulently labeled foods and drugs in interstate commerce. This was replaced by the Food, Drug, and Cosmetics Act of 1938, which was later amended by the Food Additives Amendment of 1958 and the Kefauver-Harris Amendment of 1962. The 1962 amendment addresses the issues of pretesting drugs for safety and effectiveness before they are introduced and generic drug labeling.

MEAT INSPECTION ACT (1906). Mandates sanitary regulations in the meat-packing industry and promotes federal inspection of companies selling meat in interstate commerce.

FEDERAL TRADE COMMISSION ACT (1914). Establishes a group of specialists as a commission with broad authority to investigate and restrict unfair methods of competition in commerce.

CLAYTON ACT (1914). Extends the Sherman Antitrust Act by prohibiting specific practices that may substantially lessen competition or tend to cause a monopoly in any line of commerce. Specifically prohibits some types of price discrimination, tying clauses, intercorporate stockholdings, and interlocking directorates.

ROBINSON-PATMAN ACT (1936). Amended the Clayton Act to place greater restrictions on quantity discounts, brokerage allowances, promotional allowances, and services provided unless they are made available to all customers on proportionately equal terms. This Act gave the FTC jurisdiction over pricing issues and declared price discrimination unlawful.

MILLER-TYDINGS ACT (1937). Amends Sherman Antitrust Act to exempt fair trade agreements from antitrust prosecution.

WHEELER-LEA ACT (1938). Prohibits unfair and deceptive practices and acts even if the competition is not affected adversely. This Act also places food and drug advertising under FTC jurisdiction.

ANTIMERGER ACT (1950). Amends the Clayton Act by broadening the power to prevent inter-corporate acquisitions that may have a substantial negative effect on competition.

AUTOMOBILE INFORMATION DISCLOSURE ACT (1958). Prohibits car dealers from inflating factory prices on new cars.

NATIONAL TRAFFIC AND SAFETY ACT (1958). Creates compulsory safety standards for automobiles and tires.

FAIR PACKAGING AND LABELING ACT (1966). Permits FTC regulation of consumer goods packaging and labeling. Places requirements on manufacturers to disclose package contents, who made the contents, and how much the package contains by volume.

---

turned off remotely. Theoretically, terrorists could shut down power grids and endanger the lives of people in northern Europe, Canada, or the United States for several days during the winter, or to cause industry-paralyzing outages at any time. Although such terrorism requires very high computer skill levels, it remains a possibility against which governments must guard. Therefore, international mergers such as that of British Telecomm and MCI, and technology transfers such as the global distribution of Netscape via the World Wide Web, receive substantial government scrutiny. Legislation has also been enacted to curtail the transfer of encryption and other computer network security technologies. Although the reinstatement of broad legislative controls over the telecommunications industry seems unlikely at this time, it remains a possibility in more hostile environments.

Table 3.1 shows a shift in legislative focus from protecting businesses in 1945 to protecting consumers in 1990. Other countries displayed similar shifts toward consumer protection, with some social democratic governments such as those of Sweden and Denmark becoming very restrictive in all areas of product marketing. Some of this legislative activity was motivated by company excesses, such as the Child Protection Act passed in 1966 to protect children from increasingly dangerous products marketed by the highly competitive toy industry.

Some of the shift is also in response to consumerist values that have become popular since the 1960s. Consumerism is the organized movement of individuals and

TABLE 3.1 U.S. LEGISLATION AFFECTING MARKETING—CONTINUED

CHILD PROTECTION ACT (1966). Prohibits the sale of hazardous toys and apparel. Amended in 1969 to include articles that pose electrical, mechanical, and thermal danger.

FEDERAL CIGARETTE LABELING AND ADVERTISING ACT (1967). Requires that cigarette packages warn consumers about the health dangers of cigarette smoking as determined by the surgeon general.

TRUTH-IN-LENDING ACT (1968). Requires credit providers to reveal the true costs of credit transactions. Also outlaws the use of actual or threatened violence in collecting loans and restricts the dollar amount of garnishments. Established the National Commission on Consumer Finance.

NATIONAL ENVIRONMENTAL POLICY ACT (1969). Sets a national policy on the environment and establishes the Council on Environmental Quality. Amended in 1970 to establish the Environmental Protection Agency (EPA).

FAIR CREDIT REPORTING ACT (1970). Mandates that consumer credit reports contain only accurate, relevant, and recent information, and that they are kept confidential, accessible only by appropriate parties for legitimate purposes.

CONSUMER PRODUCT SAFETY ACT (1972). Establishes the Consumer Products Safety Commission to set safety standards for consumer products and specific penalties for failure to meet standards.

CONSUMER GOODS PRICING ACT (1975). Prohibits price maintenance agreements between manufacturers and retailers engaged in interstate commerce.

MAGNUSON-MOSS WARRANTY/FTC IMPROVEMENT ACT (1975). Authorizes the FTC to set rules on consumer warranties and provides means of redress for consumers. Expands FTC jurisdiction over unfair or deceptive practices.

EQUAL CREDIT OPPORTUNITY ACT (1975). Prohibits discrimination in credit transactions because of sex, marital status, race, national origin, religion, age, or receipt of public assistance.

FAIR DEBT COLLECTION PRACTICES ACT (1978). Makes it illegal for collectors to harass or abuse any person, make false statements, or use other unfair methods of collection.

FTC IMPROVEMENT ACT (1980). Provides the House of Representatives jointly with veto power over FTC trade regulation rules. Enacted to limit FTC regulation of "unfairness" issues.

TOY SAFETY ACT (1984). Gives government the power to recall toys quickly when they are found to be dangerous.

NUTRITION LABELING AND EDUCATION ACT (1990). Requires that food product labels provide detailed nutritional information in standardized format.

their government representatives to protect buyers' rights against sellers' interests. Consumerist concerns have ebbed and flowed for many years, and in varying degrees from country to country. Overall, however, marketers around the world have come to expect increased scrutiny over how their activities affect final consumers, and to expect the government to take action whenever consumers appear to be exploited or misled by marketers. One recent example of consumerist activity in the United States is the public outcry against the targeting of high school– and college-age young people by the smokeless tobacco companies.[20] Another more pointed example was the crusade against the distribution of "gangsta rap" led by the National Political Congress of Black Women. Gangsta rap music often features lyrics that have high levels of pornographic and violent imagery. The National Political Congress of Black Women called for entertainment industry giants such as Time Warner to curtail the distribution of gangsta rap recordings, and for consumers to boycott such companies until they complied.[21]

More recent legislative and administrative actions have promoted competitive and healthy industries, and in particular supported quality improvements across all industries. A leader in this area has been the Japanese government, which since the 1950s has sponsored the Deming Quality Award Competition for domestic and foreign companies that show a significant commitment to offering quality products and services. The United States has an equivalent to the Deming Award in the Malcolm Baldrige National Quality Award, which, since its inception in 1987, has generated hundreds of entries. The Baldrige Award has also motivated many states to establish quality programs of their own.[22]

The Swedish government has also promoted quality, but in social democratic fashion has taken a more national-level approach. Since 1990, the Swedish government has invested millions of dollars in developing and implementing a national customer satisfaction barometer, which measures customer satisfaction in more than thirty industries and one hundred corporations.[23] The index has provided valuable information to participating companies and represents a major effort by Swedish legislators to improve their country's competitiveness in world markets. The success of the program has motivated consideration of similar indices by the governments of the United States, Japan, Norway, and Singapore.

Regulation

Marketing managers also monitor regulation at multiple levels of government. Regulation differs from legislation in that it involves more specific and detailed instructions from the government on what a company must or must not do. The Food, Drug, and Cosmetics Act of 1938, for example, provides broad guidelines in marketing those product categories. Regulations related to this act are the responsibility of the Food and Drug Administration, which oversees the industries involved in marketing food and drug products. The level of regulation of various industries, interpretations of the act in different situations, and the aggressiveness with which regulations are enforced all depend on the regulation side of the political and legal environment. Recent moves by the Food and Drug Administration to extend its regulatory powers over the tobacco industry, for example, represent an interpretation of its mandate to regulate the sale and distribution of health-affecting substances that is more aggressive in the 1990s than in prior years.

Other regulatory agencies that have a significant effect on marketing include the following:

- *Environmental Protection Agency*, which regulates the design of products to make them environmentally safe. Some product areas affected by the EPA are automobile emissions and the use of ozone-depleting chlorofluorocarbons in refrigerators and air conditioners.

- *Federal Communications Commission*, which regulates media such as radio and television for content and invasive practices. An example of an invasive practice is the broadcasting of advertising at a higher volume than regular shows.

- *Federal Trade Commission*, which regulates many aspects of interstate commerce, such as transportation costs and procedures that can influence availability and price of goods.

- *National Transportation Safety Board*, which is concerned with the safety of passenger transportation through public and private means. This board, for example, oversees safety practices in the airline industry and the mandatory installation of safety devices such as airbags and side-impact protection in automobiles.

Regulatory intensity can shift with or without legislative changes, depending on political factors such as national security concerns, economic stability, and the mood of the voting public. For example, during the 1973 oil embargo, large oil companies were allowed to collaborate in gasoline rationing, a practice that in any other circumstances would have been seen as collusion. In contrast, oil industry profits four years later were at an all-time high and the regulatory attitude was more belligerent, leading to very tight scrutiny of oil pricing and industry communications, and allegations of price fixing. Although price fixing was never substantiated, the scrutiny and visibility motivated the adoption of high income tax rates on oil industry windfall profit gains.

Differences in the legislative and regulatory tone, both between government administrations within one country and between the governments of different countries, can be a source of frustration for marketers. For example, countries that seek to protect their markets while giving the appearance of being open to free trade often enact legislation that sounds open but may be ambiguous, and then use regulatory loopholes to keep foreign marketers at a competitive disadvantage. In France, for example, concerns over French sovereignty have guided protectionist regulatory activity for decades, creating what appear to be contradictions between the French legislative embrace of the European Union and the continuing regulatory support of large state-owned companies. Similar restrictive trade practices have been a major source of controversy between Japan and the United States throughout the 1980s and 1990s. Although Japanese legislation has repeatedly affirmed its commitment to free trade and open markets, the immense Japanese bureaucracy continues to hamstring the efforts of U.S. and European companies to penetrate the Japanese home market.

Even within a single market, companies can find themselves implementing changes in their products and marketing practices under one regulatory climate, only to reverse course when the winds of public sentiment change direction and a new government assumes power. In the United States, for example, a shift in government from Democratic to Republican in the early 1980s brought about an easing of automobile emissions, safety, and fuel economy regulations that had been enacted and enforced during the 1970s under Democratic leadership. The 1992 election of a Democratic administration, and its 1996 reelection, however, empowered regulatory agencies to once more be aggressive in their demands for safety, clean air, and fuel economy advancements from the automobile industry. The shift in regulatory tone from Republican to Democratic is also evident in the reversal of probusiness policies in areas such as antitrust enforcement. Industries such as computer software and pharmaceuticals, which had experienced substantial freedom in the 1980s, have come under increased scrutiny from the Justice Department due to allegations of restraint of competition and excessive prices for protected products.[24]

Although in most democratic countries a change in government does not produce the radical changes in the economic climate that changes in totalitarian governments can bring about, it is important for marketing managers to pay attention to changes in the legislative and regulatory climate, because they can have significant marketing implications. Marketing managers should be particularly attentive to existing and pending legislation and to the manner in which various regulatory agencies implement legislation, as well as to the underlying motivations and attitudes behind such actions.

Technological

Technological developments clearly influence companies and consumers in everyday life. Seldom does a week pass without the announcement of a discovery or invention that can potentially change some aspect of our lives. In some industries, such as computer manufacturing, the rate of change has been extraordinary, and keeping up with those changes seems an almost impossible task. In most industries, however, technological change is not as rapid, and companies can take advantage of new technologies, provided they detect changes early.[25] Marketing managers cannot neglect to monitor the technological environment because of the significant long-term impact that new technologies can have on a company's marketing strategy.

Technology and Market Boundaries

One area new technologies influence is the definition of competitive markets, both by opening new markets and eliminating existing ones. Some experts have proposed that market boundaries and rivalries are often a function of the beliefs that managers within an industry hold about different technologies active in the industry and their implications for what is produced.[26] As new technologies emerge, managerial belief structures are often undermined and boundaries become fuzzy, creating opportunities for new entries and threats from existing competitors. One example is the reach into global markets achieved by cable-television entertainment companies such as Home Box Office (HBO), and the redefinition of market boundaries they have generated.

Modern communications satellites and digital information exchange protocols make it possible to meet transmission standards for different countries while maintaining a centralized broadcast location, and thus to have what amounts to global TV networks. HBO and other cable broadcasters compete very effectively with local TV networks (government and privately owned) around the world for advertising dollars, and have ended local TV networks' monopoly over consumer entertainment. In response, local TV networks have been forced to redefine their competitive boundaries and change many of their programming and pricing practices in order to be competitive. Commercial television, for example, has finally been allowed in Denmark, Sweden, and Belgium, due in part to pressure from global cable-TV competition.

A related example is the redefinition of competitive boundaries within the cable-TV industry itself, in response to advances in computer technology and the World Wide Web. Even as the cable-TV industry has sought to establish a global presence, it has been threatened by the entry of software and hardware producers such as Microsoft and Intel into the family entertainment business through ventures such as The Microsoft Network and Intel Architecture Labs.[27] The Microsoft Network provides varied educational and entertainment programming through the WWW. Intel is working with Hollywood studios on high-level (e.g., three-dimensional picture and sound) interactive programming. The advantage of entertainment, such as what Microsoft and Intel are producing, is that it is available on demand—whenever and wherever the customer wants it—as compared to the structured transmission schedule followed by cable-TV companies and networks. Thus, a new venue for family entertainment is being created, and the boundaries of the market are being redefined. In both of these examples, it is technology (e.g., telecommunications, information processing) that has caused changes in market boundaries.

Technology and the Marketing Mix

Technological change also affects execution in all areas of the marketing mix. U.S. automobile producers, for example, use information and telecommunications technology to increase automation in assembly plants and reduce the need for large in-process inventories, which has resulted in reduced costs and improved quality, and has therefore made manufacturers more price competitive. Technology has also changed the way in which automobiles are distributed. On-line expert systems have helped automobile dealers respond more fully to customer questions and demands in their sales and service departments, resulting in improved customer satisfaction and higher potential for repeat business. Even promotional strategies have been affected, as the effectiveness of advertising can be taken to higher levels than in the past, while at the same allowing for low-cost targeting of sales promotions to select groups.

Improvements in automation, market reach, and managing consumer responses have been realized in many other industries in addition to automobile manufacturing, such as apparel and home appliance manufacturing, and services. Improvements have also been realized in many industrial markets, ranging from marketing raw materials to office supplies. In every one of these industries, the tasks associated with managing marketing functions has changed, and marketers are called on to adopt new technology-driven methods and tactics or lose some of their competitive edge. Marketing managers, therefore, cannot afford to ignore how technological changes influence marketing on a day-to-day basis.

Technology and New Products and Services

The most obvious and direct way in which technology affects companies is by creating opportunities for new products and services, and by reducing or eliminating the need for existing ones. New technologies, for example, were exploited by Japanese automobile manufacturers to raise the industry standard of product performance during the 1980s, not only by adding features such as electronic transmissions and sophisticated sound systems to their products, but also by improving fuel efficiency and passenger safety, reducing harmful emissions, and making autos less susceptible to collision damage, more durable, and quieter. U.S. auto manufacturers have adopted—and in some instances improved on—Japanese applications of technology in automotive engineering as they have sought to regain market share and a quality image throughout the 1990s.

History is full of examples of new product ideas and the existing products that suffered because of advances in technology: kerosene lamps were replaced by electric light bulbs, the mainframe computer market declined as personal computers became more powerful. Interestingly, history is also full of examples of companies that failed to exploit new technologies that threatened their existing products, only to be threatened later by new companies that used the new technology. A classic example is Eastman Kodak, which ignored xerographic technology and permitted the Haloid Company (later Xerox) to market it successfully. Another example is IBM's failure to see the potential for selling computer processing capacity to small businesses. Ross Perot proposed this idea to IBM when he still worked for the company. When IBM did not respond, Perot quit his job and founded Electronic Data Systems, which today is a multibillion dollar computer services company.

Sources of Technological Innovation

All marketing managers should monitor the technological environment. Although many companies rely on internal research and development for technological improvement of their products and services, the quantity and diversity of research around the world makes it necessary for marketers to also monitor the external environment for potentially valuable ideas.

Marketing managers benefit from paying attention to technological developments in other companies. They can also gain good ideas by monitoring government-funded research. Government-funded research, typically carried out at universities and research laboratories, focused primarily on basic science from 1940 to

1980. Many breakthroughs in this type of research were later developed into products used today, such as Plexiglas, instant breakfast beverages, freeze-dried foods, and water-filtering systems. During the 1980s, in response to declines in U.S. competitiveness and economic forces, government sponsorship of research was reduced, and much of what remained was focused on applied technologies. Although these applied technologies increased commercial innovations throughout the 1980s and 1990s, a void in basic research advances by the United States may result, which will be filled by other countries in the twenty-first century.[28] Marketing managers would do well to monitor not only the short-term increase in commercially viable technologies, but also the more long-term potential for basic achievements by countries such as Japan, Germany, Canada, and the United Kingdom, as well as by the United States. Different countries have emerged as leaders in different industries and fields of study, and marketing managers can no longer look only to U.S.-based research. Some areas of technological development to monitor carefully in the next several years are biotechnology and genetic engineering in the United Kingdom, ecological management controls and practices in Japan, information processing and telecommunications in the United States, agriculture in Germany, and energy conservation and alternative sources in Canada. Leadership in these and other fields of study is hotly contested around the world, and the scope of technology monitoring must be global.

Demographic

The demographic environment refers to changes and trends in the development of the market populations, based on several factors, such as age, household structure, labor, and mobility.

Age Distribution

The age distribution in the market population has important marketing implications. The United States, for example, has a bimodal age distribution, split between the large number of people born between 1945 and 1960 (the "baby boomers") and their children, born in the 1970s and 1980s. In other markets, however, age distributions are significantly different. In Mexico, the average age of the population has dropped dramatically in the last thirty years, to less than twenty-five years old in the mid 1990s. Modern Mexico is a country of young people with high aspirations, and it is likely to remain that way for the next two to three decades. Several countries in the Pacific Rim, including China and Thailand, have also experienced a drop in the average age, although at a slower rate than Mexico. In fact, demographic trends suggest that, over the next 50 years, the areas with highest population growth potential are Latin America and Asia, with Europe, North America, and Africa lagging behind. The long-term outlook, however, is for a global slowdown in population growth as more countries implement population planning programs.[29]

Trends in a population's age distribution provide good long-term indicators of product demand. In spite of the recent dislocations caused by overcapacity in the health-care sector and changes in government funding of health-care programs in the United States, the outlook for health-care services remains positive over the long term, because as baby boomers age they will require substantial amounts of medication and treatment. At the same time, a growing and diverse teenage population, which has grown up in a high technology environment, will likely demand higher performance from computer-based automation and telecommunications services than any prior generations, and will spur producers in this sector to more creative uses of information technology than ever before achieved. The teenage market in the United States and its implications for other areas are discussed in Marketing Anecdote 3.2.

In Mexico and China and similar developing countries, markets for entertainment devices, home appliances, and automobiles are very promising. The populations of these countries are quickly adopting the conveniences and lifestyles of more developed nations, spurring very high demand for products in these and similar categories. In some product areas, developing societies may even leapfrog developed nations where existing infrastructure restrains the adoption of new technology. Cellular and personal communications systems, for example, are likely to enjoy higher penetration in developing countries than in developed countries because these new markets do not have existing hard-wire networks to compete with the new technologies. Because the installation of cellular networks is less costly than that of copper-wire networks, countries now developing their communications infrastructure will probably never adopt the hard-wire networks and instead go directly to digital cellular systems.

Household Structure and Labor Distribution

Demographically, changes in the typical household structure in markets also affect marketing strategies. In the United States and Europe, which have long traditions of independent nuclear family units, single-adult households are on the rise relative to the number of two-adult households. In countries such as China and India, it is the dissolution of multigenerational households that holds more critical implications for marketers. Both trends suggest that the total number of established homesteads will grow faster than the population as a whole, representing opportunities for construction-related industries, as well as for manufacturers of household goods. Furthermore, in the United States many of the single-adult households have children, creating high demand for child-care services; and as these children grow older and become more capable of caring for themselves, they often also become responsible for household management tasks, and assume substantial control over the household budget. For marketers, this suggests that products historically purchased by, and marketed to, female heads-of-household will be purchased in increasing numbers by teenagers, and that the marketing mix should be redesigned with these new buyers in mind.

The distribution of labor within the household also holds marketing implications. Households in which all able-bodied adults work to generate income are nothing new; they persist today in many agrarian and developing economies where income levels are low. Even young children are forced to work in many of these societies. The ideal in the industrial world for many years, however, was for advancement of one person in the household (typically the male) to the point where his or her income would be sufficient to meet household needs, and for other adults and children to not work outside the home. Traditionally, once some comfortable standard of living was achieved, family expectations were adjusted to live within the means provided by the income earner.

This single-earner ideal has lost favor in many industrialized countries, and households that would have been considered affluent under the old single-earner standard persist on having multiple members involved in the workforce and aspire to ever higher levels of affluence. Households that contain multiple income generators represent opportunities for marketers because they generally have greater purchasing power. They are also a bigger challenge, however, because multiple income generators within a household exercise more spending autonomy. These

In the late 1960s and early 1970s, teenagers as a market segment exploded into the consciousness of U.S. marketers. The post–World War II baby boomer bulge was reaching adolescence, and it was a group unlike any that U.S. marketers had encountered. A large group (close to 30 million at its peak in 1975), it had substantial purchasing power, fueled by family allowances and teenage employment earnings with few fixed obligations. Having grown up in an age of prosperity, these well-educated baby-boomer teenagers were demanding and were unwilling to go along with the example their parents set as consumers. Teenagers nearly dictated the fashions in food and apparel during the early 1970s, and they have continued to affect every other major consumer products industry in the United States.

"Mallrats" have become a specific demographic segment for marketers.

The baby boomers have now reached middle age, and they represent the single largest concentration of purchasing power in the U.S. market. But close behind are their children, now reaching adolescence, who display some of the same demographic characteristics their parents did twenty years ago. Teenagers in this generation are even more numerous, expected to go over the 30 million mark by the year 2010. They

also have high disposable incomes, fueled at least in part by overindulgent parents who both work outside the home and must delegate purchasing responsibilities to their children. In the United States in 1993, the average thirteen-year-old spent twenty dollars per week, and the average eighteen-year-old spent eighty. In addition, most of these purchases were discretionary, because teenagers still have few fixed obligations. Industries that benefit most from teenage spending produce athletic shoes, apparel, health and beauty aids, and food.

In other aspects, teenagers of the 1990s differ from the teenagers of the 1960s, creating a new marketing challenge. One difference is their diversity. More than 30 percent of the teenagers today are black, Latino, or Asian. These young people have grown up with cultural diversity and resist superficial stereotypes. They do not react well to the superficial treatment that some marketers give to racial and ethnic differences in their marketing strategies, and they will demand a more genuine and in-depth treatment of these differences in the future. For example, advertising that tries to be all-encompassing by including token African Americans and Latinos is seen as shallow and naive by these young

household arrangements require marketers to devise ways of assessing the needs of diverse consumers within them, and the best ways of communicating with them. For example, traditional wisdom was that in single-income households, major purchases (e.g., appliances, automobiles) were a joint decision of husband and wife, with minimal input from children. Advertising, therefore, could be developed for delivery through family-used media such as television and general-purpose publications. In multiple-income households, however, each income earner may make such large purchases individually, even though they live in the same household and share many of the same media habits. In multiple-income households, shared me-

people, who may think of the advertising sponsors as shallow and naive as well.

Another difference is the independence of these teenagers from parental guidance and influence. The teenagers of the 1960s rebelled against controlling parents. Many teenagers in the 1990s have grown up without parental involvement, however, and would sometimes welcome a little more parental guidance than what they are receiving. Having grown up as latchkey children in single-parent households, many of these teenagers have been forced to assume adult consumer responsibilities early. They are consequently discriminating consumers on a broader range of product categories, going beyond fashion apparel and entertainment to include household supplies, major appliances, a broad range of food items, and other household product categories. They also are cynical about most advertising claims, leading some marketers to move away from puffery in their advertising to a harsher representation of the product and the consumption environment. The famous "Obey Your Thirst" campaign by Sprite is a case in point. Shunning extraordinary claims that drinking soft drinks makes one more popular or capable, the Sprite campaign focuses on thirst quenching as the only reason to drink soft drinks, and Sprite as a good choice to fulfill this need. Teenagers today are demanding consumers and likely to remain that way.

One additional difference in today's teenagers is in their thoughts about the future. Whereas teenagers in the 1960s were primarily concerned with issues such as social justice and world peace, teenagers in the 1990s, who share some of those concerns, are also distracted by personal worries that the earlier generation did not share. When asked about their biggest worries, today's teenagers respond with issues such as not being able to get into college, not getting good jobs as adults, contracting AIDS, impending global economic collapse, and having to suffer through divorce. These young people are worried about their own futures, and sometimes have little time to worry about issues that seem distant from their everyday lives. Marketers who try to reach these consumers have to appeal to them at a more personal level, and to use images to suggest that the company cares about consumers as people. This is made difficult, however, by the cynical attitude most teenagers take toward advertising and other marketing activities.

Sources: Paul Koenigsberg and Jennifer Koen, "The New Marketing Darling—the Teenager," *Discount Merchandiser,* November 1994, p. 32.

Don Pettit, "Brand Building among Teens," *Drug & Cosmetic Industry* 158 (June 1996), pp. 62–64.

Howard Schlossberg, "What Teenagers Find Hot Today Will Be Cold Tomorrow," *Marketing News,* December 6, 1993, p. 7.

Laura Zinn, Jonathan Berry, Kate Murphy, Sandra Jones, Marti Benedetti, and Alice Z. Cuneo, "Teens: Here Comes the Biggest Wave Yet," *Business Week,* April 11, 1994, pp. 76–86.

dia must serve as the conduit for messages aimed at husbands, wives, and children, leading to a higher overall number of advertising messages being required, and possibly to more media clutter.

Population Mobility

A third demographic factor affecting marketing efforts is increased population mobility around the world. This phenomenon has been evident in three ways. First, the frequency with which people move has increased dramatically in the post–World War II period. In the United States, frequent moves have created markets for rental trucks and moving equipment, storage facilities, and the unbundling of moving services (e.g., hire a moving company for transportation but not for packing). In other parts of the world, such as Taiwan and Korea, higher mobility has given rise to a household moving industry where none had existed previously.

Second, the population has shifted from some geographic areas to others. In the United States, the moves have been primarily to the south and west, mostly due to improved climate control technology, communications, transportation systems, and the promise of a more leisurely lifestyle. There has also been a nationwide trend away from major urban centers, such as New York, Washington, D.C., and San Francisco, and toward scores of small cities and towns—a population shift due largely to some of the advances in telecommunications and computer technology discussed earlier.[30] In other parts of the world, the moves have been motivated by employment opportunities and falling international economic barriers (e.g., the population shifts between members and aspiring members of the European Union). Regardless of the cause, large population shifts create many new opportunities for the wholesale and retail trade in growing areas, while at the same time threatening businesses in declining areas.

Third, there has been an influx of immigrants from developing countries into industrialized nations. In the United States, immigration has been primarily from Latin America and some near-Asian countries such as Indonesia and Vietnam, whereas in the Middle East and Europe the influx has been more from eastern Europe, central Asia, and various parts of Africa. A typical result from having large immigrant communities is that in some geographic markets, ethnic groups become the predominant consumers, and they force changes in the array of products and services that can be marketed. Such a phenomenon was observed in the early 1900s in the markets of New York and Boston, as thousands of immigrants came from Italy, Ireland, Germany, and other parts of Europe. The phenomenon is being observed once again in cities such as Los Angeles, London, Toronto, and Paris. Many southern California retailers, for example, have changed their decor and product offerings to fit Hispanic and Asian tastes, and some retailers in Paris have adjusted to their predominant Muslim customer base, which has immigrated from northern Africa.

Over the foreseeable future, increased mobility worldwide will likely continue to present marketers with significant opportunities and threats. In Europe, the breakup of the Soviet Union, the opening of eastern European markets, and the economic disparity between East and West all have created mobile populations. Ethnic and religious conflicts in the former Yugoslavia and some parts of Africa have also mobilized many people, and created population displacements not seen since the 1920s. Workers from countries such as Romania, Bulgaria, and Poland, for example, have joined the already large migrant worker populations of Turkey and Greece in seeking employment in France and Germany, and have created markets in such host countries for housing and amenities compatible with their own cultural values. Similar population shifts are also occurring in China, Indonesia, and other Asian countries, as commercial borders are opened and transportation becomes more accessible.

Countries and geographic areas experiencing an immigrant influx face ample marketing opportunities, not only to sell products and services, but also to establish manufacturing operations that can be staffed with relatively inexpensive labor, because immigrants are often willing to do work that local residents find distasteful or unacceptable. At the same time, countries and geographic areas experiencing population declines face serious threats to established businesses and marketing practices, because the remaining population may not be large enough to sustain businesses and marketing practices that worked in the past. Countries and areas with declining populations however, also represent opportunities for innovative marketers to meet the needs of the consumers that remain. In China, for example, millions of workers have left small farms in the interior of the country in favor of large metropolitan areas such as Shanghai and Beijing. Those cities have enjoyed many new opportunities for wholesale and retail growth, whereas stores in small villages have lost business. In such small villages, however, there is still a need to farm the land, and a growing need to package food for transportation to the cities. This has created opportunities for producers of agricultural and food-processing equipment, which have invested in land cultivation training and food-processing facilities, and have created jobs for a new generation of Chinese farmers. It is only a matter of time before Chinese farmers achieve income levels high enough to support new retail and wholesale ventures, and thus create new marketing opportunities.

Sociocultural

The social conditions in which people grow up shape their belief systems and behaviors for the rest of their lives. Values and attitudes acquired early in life are difficult, if not impossible, to change, and they inform purchase decisions in many ways—not only those of final consumers, but also those of organizations. As we discuss in chapter 6, organizations can some times develop cultures under the long-term leadership of a single manager, or because of protracted sets of circumstances that can affect the process and speed with which they make purchase decisions. Sociocultural environments change very slowly, and if marketing managers were to manage them, it would require considerable effort over long periods of time. Most marketers focus primarily on understanding and responding to sociocultural trends in both consumer and industrial markets, recognizing such efforts as being critical to long-term marketing success.

A list of sociocultural values and how they shape marketing opportunities globally would take up several volumes and is beyond the scope of this book. It is possible, however, to mention some sociocultural factors that have significant marketing implications, and which generalize across many major markets around the world. They are changes in family and sex-based roles, nationalism, and concerns about ecology and social justice.

Change in Family and Sex-Based Roles

Some changes in roles have already been discussed briefly in the context of demographic influences on family structure, the most important being adolescents assuming of responsibility for many family purchases. Another change in family roles stems from the growing number of women in the professional workforce, which suggests that women's traditional caretaking role has expanded to include career management and income-generation characteristics, whereas men's roles have added domestic duties such as cooking and caring for children. It must be noted that since the 1970s, the combination of these two trends has severely undermined traditional family roles based on sex and age, and has created new consumer types to which marketers are responding. In addition, it is also important that these trends are found not only in the United States, but in other industrialized and developing countries as well, suggesting that the challenges to marketers are global in scope.

Japan, for example, also exhibits both of these trends. The expanding role of women in Japan has been hinted at by educated Japanese women refusing to marry, mostly because they do not accept traditional Japanese female roles. It was dramatically affirmed in choosing a Harvard-educated, professional woman to be the next empress of Japan. Japan's imperial house has for centuries been the showcase in Japanese society of all that is good about their culture. The dramatic change that has occurred in the traditional background and behavior of the Japanese empress is a clear indication to the country and the world of the changing values in that society. The changes in young people's roles in Japan are not as profoundly evident as they are in the United States, because Japanese teenagers have not assumed household purchase responsibilities in large numbers. Changes have been noted by retailers, however, who find Japanese consumers between the ages of eighteen and twenty-one much more demanding than those of the previous generation, and more emphatic about being able to express themselves through their attire and other purchases.[31]

Similar changes in the professional involvement of women, increased sharing of household roles by various members, and greater independence and responsibility being assumed by young people are also evident in countries throughout Europe and Latin America, many of which follow the example of the United States. Such changing social roles have implications for different aspects of the marketing mix. Product design in many sectors, such as automobiles, kitchen appliances, home furnishings, office furniture, and computer equipment, need to take into account the ergonomic characteristics of both sexes if their use is to be shared by men and women.

Changing social roles also hold great implications for promotional activity. Because both men and women are actively involved in household management, for example, promotional messages must now appeal to both sexes, and must be shown through media used by both men and women. For some manufacturers, this means shifting advertising from daytime television to the evening hours. For others, it may mean reducing reliance on a single medium such as television, in favor of a more eclectic media strategy that includes radio and print ads as well. Promotion must also adjust to the emerging role of children in household management. Advertising that targets children as shoppers, and not just as consumers, of household products is likely to become increasingly common.

Changing marketing practices in the automotive industry, as discussed in Marketing Anecdote 3.3, exemplify how product design and promotional strategies are being adjusted in response to changing sex-based roles. It is interesting to note that in order to better respond to its large female customer base, the auto industry has had to give women a significant voice in its own marketing management structure, perhaps based on the idea that good marketing decisions are best made by managers who understand their customers well. Similar gains by women executives are also evident at marketing-oriented companies such as Nike, Reebok, Microsoft, JCPenney, and Avon.[32]

Nationalism

Nationalism is devotion to the interests, unity, and independence of one's own country. A natural set of values, nationalism has affected marketing activities for centuries. Nationalistic fervor ebbs and flows, however, and its level can have a significant effect on a marketer's ability to succeed in any particular market. In the United States, for example, concerns over jobs being lost and the national image being tarnished motivated some automobile buyers to choose U.S.-built automobiles over comparable imported vehicles. The influence of nationalism was particularly pronounced among blue-collar members of large labor unions throughout the country, who mounted "Buy American" campaigns. Although not its sole determinant, the influence of nationalism on automobile buyers in the mid-1980s con-

The importance of women as a growing market segment has not been lost on automobile manufacturers, and most make some allowances for female customers in their advertising. Ford, Cadillac, and Mazda go further, however, by putting women in charge of other marketing strategy decisions, and seeking to make all areas of their marketing mix sensitive to female customers.

At Ford and Cadillac, women have been put in charge of product development efforts, in order to enhance the appeal of some of their products to women. One example was Mimi Vandermolen, chief designer for the 1993 Ford Probe, whose task with the Probe was to make her predominantly male product-engineering staff address issues such as entry and exit, seat positioning, and instrument panel control placement from a woman's

The Mazda Miata appeals especially to urban and suburban professional women, reflecting a new segment of consumers that car manufacturers defined in the 1980s.

perspective. She approached the task by forcing male designers to suffer with some of the troubles that women experience first-hand. Vandermolen also forced designers to consider the fifth-percentile—a primarily female group that represents the lowest 20 percent of the population in terms of height and weight. As a result of her efforts, the Probe was designed so that shorter people could easily reach the controls, and it requires less physical effort in functions such as steering, braking, and shifting than other Ford products. The efforts of Vandermolen and her staff made the Probe a vehicle with considerable cross-gender appeal.

At Cadillac, a team of women product developers were put in charge of most design, engineering, and marketing decisions for the new Cadillac Catera. From its inception, the Catera was aimed at upscale women buyers, a market segment that Cadillac had ignored and that was controlled by BMW, Mercedes, and Lexus. To maximize Catera's market appeal, Cadillac brought the "voice of the target customer" into the everyday decisions of automotive design, starting with appointing Karen Licari as Catera's brand manager. Similar to Vandermolen at Ford, the women in Catera's product team sought ways to help male engineers experience products as women experience them. In one of several product test clinics, for example, male product engineers were asked to place paper clips on their fingertips to simulate long fingernails as they tested different knob and control configurations. In addition, Cadillac conducted extensive focus group research with women drivers. At one of those sessions, concerns over automatic lock mechanisms that unlock every door of the vehicle when activated, and are considered unsafe by many women, got considerable attention. The discussions led to the Catera having programmable automatic locks that can unlock only the driver's door if desired. It is on the strength of its female marketing managers that Cadillac expects the Catera to be successful.

At Mazda, it was Jan Thompson, as vice-president of advertising, who made a difference. Thompson had a long history in automotive sales and marketing when she joined Mazda in 1988, and it was her input that helped reposition Mazda as a brand for people outside the mainstream. Her approach was straightforward—avoid the macho image favored by many auto manufacturers and adopt a more personal and warm message. She introduced the "It Just Feels Right" campaign and changed advertising to show more caring people—even if they were not all women. Thompson also helped develop the nostalgic introductory theme for the successful Miata coupe. Although Mazda has struggled in the Japanese and U.S. markets recently for other reasons, its advertising remains memorable, and the brand's appeal to women buyers remains higher than that of most other automotive brands, due in part to Thompson's ability to reach female customers.

Sources: Larry Armstrong, "Women Power at Mazda," *Business Week*, September 21, 1992, p. 84.

Greg Bowens, "Mimi Vandermolen: Women Drivers Have a Friend at Ford," *Business Week*, November 16, 1992, p. 66.

Maria Mallory, Dan McGraw, Jill Jordan Sieder, and David Fischer, "Women on the Fast Track," *U.S. News & World Report*, November 6, 1995, pp. 60–72.

tributed to the first registered drop in the import auto market share after almost twenty years of continuous increases. At the same time, Japanese nationalism is in part responsible for Japan's resistance to imported products from almost all other countries. Many Japanese consumers sincerely believe that no other country can produce products for the Japanese market as well as Japanese companies. This belief has created conflicts between Japan and the other countries over agricultural products, technology transfers, and other areas of trade.

When nationalism is high, domestic marketers should expect more favorable markets for many of their goods, even if they are of inferior quality, and foreign marketers of comparable products should expect less favorable demand. Furthermore, demand for imported products can decrease even when the products category is not produced by the host country, if consumers believe that any patronage of foreign companies is threatening to national interests. Thus, for example, farmers in China may refuse to purchase Japanese-made farm equipment, even if it does not compete directly with equipment made in China, simply because they believe that any Japanese advancement threatens China's national interests.

Although nationalism is a sociocultural factor, it can interact with political and legal factors. This is true in markets where consumers are already predisposed to see the patronage of foreign producers as threatening, because any political or legal actions that exacerbate the differences between the importing and exporting countries can have an adverse effect on marketing efforts. McDonnell Douglas, for example, could see a decrease in demand for its F-15 fighter from nationalistic Moslem countries such as Saudi Arabia and Kuwait if the United States were to take an active pro-Israel stance in any international dispute, even if the dispute does not involve the countries directly. During the 1980s, political differences between South Africa and virtually all its trading partners led to trade sanctions being imposed against that country. Many South African consumers did not complain, however, instead altering their consumption patterns to fit with what was available in their country, and seeking to protect what they believed was their nation's right to self-determination.

Nationalism is a relatively permanent phenomenon, and marketers can use this force to their own advantage. Appeals to nationalistic pride have been used in many countries (e.g., soft drinks producers in India and fast food retailers in the

Philippines) to win market support for local products, and by savvy foreign marketers who position themselves as fighting along with the host country against a common enemy. Fiat, for example, plays on nationalism by positioning its cars in Italy and other European markets as alternatives to Japanese and U.S. imports. Nationalism can also be devastating to an otherwise good marketing strategy, however, as U.S. farmers have discovered in their efforts to export rice to Japan. Marketers seeking to enter foreign markets, or already involved in foreign markets where national competitors exist, need to monitor the level of nationalistic pride and activism and adjust either their marketing positioning or the timing of marketing actions accordingly.

Concerns about Ecology

Consumers in the 1990s care more about the natural environment—and about the inherent flaws in government and organizational systems that permit ecological damage—than at any other time throughout the twentieth century. Many consumers make their purchase decisions to force companies to correct what they perceive to be serious problems, such as air and water pollution, overflowing landfills, and energy waste. Environmentally conscious consumers create opportunities and threats for marketers. For example, in spite of cyclical fluctuations and its high cost, the demand for recycled paper is expected to grow across many categories of paper products over the long term. Even in the highly lucrative office stationery market, consumer preferences have moved toward recycled buff or off-white paper and away from pure white linen paper, due in part to environmental concerns.[33] Consequently, paper manufacturers who do not respond to this trend by investing in recycling capacity are at risk of losing out on future business.

The 1980s and 1990s saw a dramatic increase in the number of products claiming to be ecologically sensitive, and many of these claims were substantiated by the products' performance. Industries as diverse as textiles and apparel, food processing, steel and rubber manufacturing, and household appliance manufacturing changed their products and processes to reduce emissions, conserve energy, and increase product safety. Although there is still room for improvement, consumers and marketers have succeeded in improving the natural environment around the world.

In France, Germany, and the United Kingdom, air and water quality have been dramatically improved, largely as a result of consumer demands for a more active stance on these issues by government and industry. The United States and Canada have also seen substantial progress, although it has been marred by false environmental claims by some companies and the need for more stringent policing of advertising and packaging. Some plastics producers, for example, have claimed their garbage bags are biodegradable without explaining to their customers that they are biodegradable only under very specific conditions that hardly ever exist in landfills. False claims by plastics producers have forced investigations of the garbage-bag market by the FTC and state agencies concerned with truth in advertising.

There remain opportunities for companies to improve their ecological record and to make innovative contributions toward a safer and cleaner environment. In the toy industry, for example, many battery-powered products could be designed to replace disposable batteries with rechargeable batteries and electrical adapters. Disposable batteries cause serious water contamination in landfills, and companies should explore alternatives to them. The toy industry is also guilty of creating products that are not repairable and must be thrown away when they fail. Toys and other mechanical and electronic products that are engineered to be thrown away might be less expensive to produce, but they are also wasteful.

Consumer and commercial markets are increasingly demanding products that can be repaired or recycled, and companies that respond to this demand can have a substantial advantage over their competitors.

In addition, there are many opportunities for products and services that help resolve problems created by ecological carelessness. Disposing of solid and hazardous waste in North and South America, Asia, and Europe; cleaning polluted rivers and lakes around the world; improving air quality in eastern Europe and Asia; and preserving natural resources such as the rain forests of South America and Indonesia are all problems that still need solutions. They represent marketing opportunities for companies with research and development resources—opportunities to develop products for consumers and industry that make a contribution, such as recycled paper in saving natural forests, and for which customers have already shown a willingness to pay a premium price.

ORGANIZATIONAL CAPABILITIES AND RESPONSE TO THE ENVIRONMENT

Thus far, our discussion about how marketing managers understand, respond to, and manage their environments has taken a somewhat idealistic view of marketing organizations—a view in which companies and their managers are logical and proactive in their analysis of, and reaction to, environmental factors, and in which there is a clear "best strategy" to be pursued. Not all marketing organizations approach their environment this way, however, and seldom is an optimal strategy obvious. Differences in environmental stability and organizational history between companies cause them to vary significantly in terms of what constitutes a successful approach to any one set of environmental circumstances.

Organizational theorists have developed a model, presented in Figure 3.4, that helps to explain how organizations can interpret and respond to their environments differently.[34] To better appreciate the model we need some assumptions and definitions. We begin with the assumption that marketing-oriented organizations are open social systems that scan their environments, and they process and respond to information from these environments. This is a reasonable assumption for marketing managers because it is very compatible with being market oriented (e.g., understanding and reacting to customer needs profitably).[35] Scanning refers to the process by which organizations search the external environment to identify important events or issues that might affect them. Organizations differ in their scanning in terms of the data sources and methods of acquisition they use. To process information means to collect and interpret data, and interpretation means to organize information into conceptual structures or frameworks that are meaningful to members of the organization.[36] Thus, we assume that all companies gather, interpret, and respond to information from their environments. We do not assume, however, that all companies gather, interpret, and respond in the same ways. A group of companies may all gather sales and customer data on the same industry, organize it into market segments, and develop marketing strategies for those segments, but not all segment structures or strategies need be the same.

The model depicted in Figure 3.4 uses two dimensions to partially explain how companies gather, interpret, and respond to environmental information differently: (1) a company's beliefs about how much the environment can be analyzed, and (2) its beliefs about how much the environment can be shaped or molded.

FIGURE 3.4

A MODEL OF ORGANIZATIONAL INTERPRETATION MODES AND RELATED ORGANIZATIONAL PROCESSES

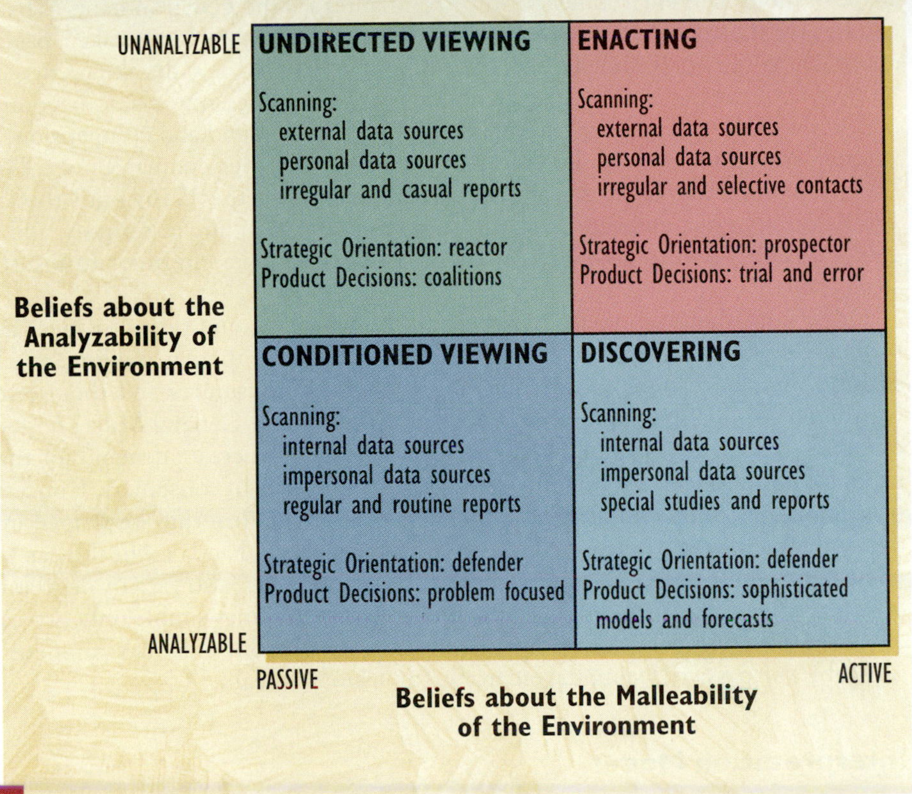

Source: Adapted from Richard L. Daft and Karl E. Weick, "Toward a Model of Organizations as Interpretation Systems," Academy of Management Review 9 (March 1984): 284–295.

UNANALYZABLE

Beliefs about the Analyzability of the Environment

UNDIRECTED VIEWING

Scanning:
external data sources
personal data sources
irregular and casual reports

Strategic Orientation: reactor
Product Decisions: coalitions

ENACTING

Scanning:
external data sources
personal data sources
irregular and selective contacts

Strategic Orientation: prospector
Product Decisions: trial and error

CONDITIONED VIEWING

Scanning:
internal data sources
impersonal data sources
regular and routine reports

Strategic Orientation: defender
Product Decisions: problem focused

DISCOVERING

Scanning:
internal data sources
impersonal data sources
special studies and reports

Strategic Orientation: defender
Product Decisions: sophisticated models and forecasts

ANALYZABLE

PASSIVE   ACTIVE

Beliefs about the Malleability of the Environment

The Environment as Analyzable

Companies can hold different assumptions about how easily and thoroughly their environment can be analyzed. Some companies see their environments as inherently analyzable and predictable, as orderly arrangements of cause and effect relationships that may be complex but can be deciphered and understood. For these companies, their environment is deterministic and correct solutions are believed to exist. Such a view of the environment is common among long-lived companies that have existed in stable environments and for whom past performance is the best predictor of future performance. Steel firms competing in the United States throughout the 1950s and 1960s, for example, could have developed this view of the environment because they enjoyed stable and steady growth in market demand during most of that period.

Other companies, however, see their environments as unpredictable and difficult to understand. For these companies, many possible interpretations of observed phenomena are plausible. This view of environments is most common among companies in emerging or fast-changing industries, where competitors rise and fall rapidly, and where past performance seldom, if ever, correlates directly with what is happening currently or with future expectations. Personal computer companies in the 1990s could easily adopt this perspective. Companies can vary by degrees in how analyzable they see their environments, but for simplicity, we have only two categories in the model: seeing the environment as analyzable and not analyzable.

The Environment as Malleable

The second dimension captures how much companies believe they can actively shape or mold their environments. Some companies see their environments as fixed, and believe they must adjust to current conditions. These companies take a passive approach to the environment, changing themselves to fit new developments and "rolling with the punches." This passive approach is most common among companies in markets where either external factors control demand and competition, or where a strong industry leader sets the pattern for all other companies to follow. Defense contractors lived in such an environment from the 1950s until the late 1980s, as the Pentagon protected national interests by spending generously, and by giving business on key weapon systems to multiple suppliers in order to insure a steady supply.

Other companies see their environments as malleable, and they test ideas and products on the market regularly. These companies see their marketing role as shaping their environments advantageously for both consumers and themselves. Consumer products firms such as Procter & Gamble and General Mills are good examples of such companies. These firms believe they can create demand for their products out of the often ambiguous desires and concerns of consumers. Concerns over family nutrition and little time for meal preparation can thus be shaped into demand for a new line of frozen entrees, or fears over dental and oral health can become demand for tartar-control toothpaste. Companies can also vary by degrees in how malleable they see their environments, but to keep things simple only two categories are used: organizational intrusiveness as active (seeing the environment as malleable) or passive (seeing the environment as not malleable).

Interpretation Modes

The two dimensions are used to identify four interpretation modes that companies can adopt: undirected viewing, enacting, conditioned viewing, and discovering. The four interpretation modes are based on companies' beliefs about their environments; they have implications for how companies might best scan their environments, for making new product decisions, and for their strategic orientation. Strategic orientation refers to a company's predominant product strategy. Table 3.2 summarizes the four broad strategic orientations that have been identified.[37]

Undirected Viewing

The undirected viewing mode is most typical of companies in environments that are difficult to understand and change, and it is best associated with the reactor strategic orientation. It can be a difficult mode in which to succeed over the long term, because it calls for reacting to environmental changes that are not always readily evident or interpretable, thus putting companies in constant danger of misreading environmental cues and making costly strategic mistakes. For some companies, however, it may be the only interpretation mode possible, and it can be successful if companies develop strategic coalitions with important constituencies that can help guide its decision making. In the computer industry, for example, small Taiwanese companies such as Twinhead and Compal may have a difficult time understanding the intricacies of the market or having a substantial influence on its development. They survive and prosper, however, by establishing coalitions with large companies such as IBM, Apple, and Dell, and letting those coalitions determine their marketing strategies.[38] Following a similar strategy, companies such as Acer have grown to become significant and influential competitors in the computer industry.

TABLE 3.2 STRATEGIC ORIENTATIONS PROPOSED BY MILES AND SNOW

Prospector: Operates within a broad product-market domain that is redefined periodically, but not predictably. The organization puts value on being the "first mover" in its market areas, regardless of the final profitability of the effort. The company responds quickly to early signals of the emergence of new markets or of changes in existing markets, and competes primarily by introducing new products and exploiting new opportunities, not by controlling existing product markets and technologies.

Analyzer: Makes decisions deliberately and at a slower pace than the prospector, focusing on a relatively narrow range of products and services. The company tries to compete in some sectors with innovative designs, and in other sectors through manufacturing efficiencies and being the low-cost producer. The organization avoids being the first mover. The typical approach is to monitor closely the results achieved by the first mover, and either enter the market with a better or lower-cost product, or avoid the market altogether.

Defender: Tries to maintain a secure position in a relatively stable market or product sector. The company offers a limited array of products and is resistant to ventures into unproved or relatively new product markets. Decisions are slow and deliberate and tend to be focused on operational issues, as the company seeks to protect its position by offering lower-cost or better-quality goods and services than the competition. Not a likely candidate for implementing new technologies in the product or manufacturing areas.

Reactor: Does not have a fixed set of products or services on which it focuses. The company responds primarily when forced by the actions of competitors. The company seeks to emulate, or respond to the lead of, competitors or other strong constituent groups. Decisions can be quick, but seldom are based on a systematic analysis of the situation.

Source: Robert E. Miles and Charles C. Snow, Organizational Strategy, Structure, and Process (New York: McGraw-Hill, 1978).

Enacting

The enacting mode works best for companies in unstable environments that can be shaped by the organization's actions. New and fragmented markets, such as telecommunications, provide suitable environments for the enacting mode. Under this interpretation mode, marketing managers want scanning to be done constantly and by many members of the organization through their informal and personal contacts. Company scientists at a conference and campus recruiters on a college visit, along with market researchers, are all likely sources for new product ideas. Once new product ideas emerge, the enacting view suggests that they be introduced quickly to the marketplace, without formal prototypes or market testing. New product decisions are based on trial and error. Because the company uses the market instead of formal research programs to test ideas, its strategic orientation is most like that of a prospector. Such an informal and opportunistic marketing approach has been shown to result in good performance when companies operate in turbulent and fast-changing environments.[39]

Conditioned Viewing

Companies in stable markets and rigid environments, where there is little chance of changing the market in perceptible ways, are often better off adopting a conditioned viewing mode. Small companies in the beverage industry, for example, seldom have the resources to influence their markets, and must instead follow the lead of industry giants. Thus Shasta, a California-based regional brand, must constantly respond to the moves of companies such as Coca-Cola and PepsiCo in order to remain viable. For Shasta, the actions of major competitors determine what it is most likely to sell in the near future and what types of products it needs to develop to compete successfully. Scanning at Shasta consists of routinely studying the moves of industry leaders, and product decisions are typically in response to problems caused by those moves. Companies that adopt a conditioned viewing mode of interpretation are most like defender organizations. Their scanning is done routinely and their decision processes are methodical and problem focused. These organizations are often successful by using a traditional strategic management approach (analyzing, planning, implementing, and controlling).[40]

Discovering

The discovering mode is more suitable for companies in stable but malleable environments—environments where change is possible but not easy. In such markets, not all companies can take a discovering approach, but it is an option for companies with enough resources to scan the environment in depth and to take forceful action. In contrast to small companies such as Subaru, large auto manufacturers such as Toyota and Chrysler can spend large sums to study their environment, relying on special studies, impersonal sources, and formal market research for practically all of their information. They can also afford to develop systematic product plans for select product markets, and to test their products before introduction. Such large companies, therefore, scan through market research and analysis, and base their new product decisions on sophisticated models and forecasting.[41] Discovering organizations most often adopt an analyzer strategic orientation, and allocate considerable resources to making sense of the environment. It has been found that for some companies systematic and formal scanning can produce very positive results. In a study of existing companies, systematic and formal scanning led to environmental factors being seen more as opportunities than as threats and therefore as more controllable, which in turn led to a more proactive stance being adopted by the company and thus better performance.[42] Sophisticated scanning, however, is costly and not an option for all companies

Strategic Orientations versus Interpretation Modes

When the Miles and Snow typology was first proposed, marketers evaluated the different strategic orientations normatively, and some orientations were seen as better than others. Marketers typically presented the prospector orientation as the most desirable, due to the widely held belief that being the market pioneer is a strong determinant of market success. In this line of thinking, the reactor orientation was seen as analogous to the "stuck-in-the-middle" strategy, which Porter argued is highly undesirable.[43] Consequently, companies were advised to become prospectors and avoid the reactor orientation at all costs.

In our discussion of interpretation modes, however, we have presented strategic orientation as being dependent on the company's interpretation mode, which is in turn determined by the company's immediate circumstances. In so doing, we have argued that any strategic orientation can be a good or poor choice, depending on the circumstances and the organization's capabilities. A reactor orientation may actually be the best option for companies in fast-changing and hard-to-affect environments, whereas a prospector orientation may be a poor choice for companies in stable and rigid markets with little opportunity for market pioneering ventures. Rather than trying to adopt a particular strategic orientation, companies may be better off adopting the strategic orientation for which they are best suited, and deploying their resources into the corresponding types of scanning and decision-making processes.

Marketing managers responsible for understanding, responding to, and managing their environments can help their organizations choose appropriate interpretation modes. They can also help their companies assess the compatibility of their adopted interpretation mode with environmental conditions, and make adjustments accordingly. Few marketing organizations will ever match perfectly the characteristics implied by the interpretation modes in our model or by the different strategic orientations. To the degree that managers are guided by these theories in their adjustments to the environment, however, the theories are valuable.

SUMMARY

Understanding, responding to, and managing the marketing environment is an integral part of what it means to have a market orientation. Marketing managers are boundary spanners concerned with managing exchange relationships with outside constituencies, and they benefit from giving close attention to the actors and forces involved in making exchange possible.

The marketing environment consists of three dimensions: the organizational environment, the microlevel environment, and the macrolevel environment.

The organizational environment is all individuals and groups within the marketer's organization.

- Managing the organizational environment is the responsibility of senior management.
- Marketers contribute to the organization's success by understanding and responding to the needs and actions of other members of the organization.

The microlevel environment is the realm in which most daily activities of a company take place, and it consists of customers, suppliers, intermediaries, and competitors.

- Managers can understand, respond to, and manage their customers in many ways. The degree to which customers are managed varies by product and customer type.
- Marketers benefit from monitoring direct and indirect suppliers. Marketing managers pay close attention to supplier growth and decline trends, and to tendencies toward consolidation or fragmentation in the supplier industry.
- Marketing managers also benefit from monitoring growth or decline trends and consolidation or fragmentation tendencies in their intermediaries. Intermediaries include companies and individuals that affect the exchange process.
- Competitors constitute an important area of the microlevel environment. In defining competitors, marketing managers need to take the customer's perspective to insure that all types of competition are considered. Competitors can be understood, responded to, and managed, but in managing competitors, marketers must be careful to not violate the law.

The macrolevel environment consists of five major domains: economic, political and legal, technological, demographic, and sociocultural.

- The economic domain is the most volatile and often responds to changes in other domains.

- Economic activity is monitored by many public and private institutions, and can be modeled successfully.

- Several economic factors have a direct effect on demand for goods and services and need close attention: real and disposable income, interest rates, credit policies, employment levels, inflation, and income taxes.

- The political and legal domain involves three major areas: legislation, regulation, and the political agenda of the current administration.

- Marketing managers benefit from monitoring technological advances that create new product and service opportunities, that open or close different market segments, and that affect ways of executing marketing strategies. Marketers need to monitor internal and external research and development efforts on a global basis.

- The demographic domain includes factors such as age, income level, education, household structure, and population mobility.

- The size and composition of age groups (e.g., teenagers, retired adults) varies among national markets and has significant implications for the marketing mix.

- The downsizing of the typical household and increased mobility in the United States, Europe, and Asia are also important trends for marketers to monitor.

- The sociocultural domain is the most stable domain. In this domain, several factors that marketers should research at a general level are changes in family and sex-based roles, rising nationalism, and concerns about the ecology.

Organizations differ in their beliefs about the analyzability of market environments and about how much they can shape or mold the market environment.

- These two dimensions—analyzability and malleability—can be used to identify four interpretation modes that can be successfully adopted by organizations: enacting, discovering, conditioned viewing, and undirected viewing.

- These four interpretation modes vary in their sources and methods of acquiring information, and have implications for the company's strategic orientation and decision-making processes.

QUESTIONS FOR DISCUSSION

1. Assume war breaks out along the Sino-Russian border and China invades India to avert the possibility of a surprise attack from Russia's long-time ally. What implications would these actions have for the defense business of McDonnell Douglas and Raytheon? Consider all microlevel and macrolevel domains in your assessment.

2. A major competitor has been anxiously awaiting the expiration of patent protection on a medication you currently market. The patent expires in twelve months. What actions can you take without violating the law to manage your competitor's actions and gain a competitive advantage?

3. List in order of priority the macrolevel domains of greatest concern to (a) Burger King, a subsidiary of Metropolitan PLC, and (b) to United Waste Systems, a waste management company.

4. Consumer products companies such as Procter & Gamble are watching closely the population shift in China from the rural interior to coastal cities. What are

possible reasons why the people are moving to the cities? Does this situation create realistic opportunities for consumer products companies in the urban markets? In the rural markets?

5. As marketing manager for Whirlpool's Kitchen Aid division in North America, what would you do to facilitate communications between your customers and your engineering staff? Why is this communication necessary?

6. Prince Charles serves an important function for British business by facilitating conversation and cooperation between foreign governments and British companies. Can Prince Charles fulfill this role with all major trading partners of the United Kingdom? What macrolevel factors facilitate or hinder his effectiveness?

7. What are the primary concerns of the pharmaceutical industry in the supplier environment? In the intermediate environment? At the macrolevel, pharmaceutical companies have been very concerned with developments in the political and legal domain. What factors in other domains also have implications for the industry?

8. The average age of an automobile being used in the United States during the 1960s was about three years. In the 1990s the average age is about five years. What factors do you think account for this change in average age of cars? Consider all microlevel and macrolevel domains in formulating your response.

9. The Malcolm Baldrige National Quality Award competition has generated high participation and effort by U.S. companies. What are the implications of this level of participation on macrolevel domains other than the political and legal domain?

10. Home Box Office and other cable entertainment channels are available via satellite to many parts of the world in addition to the United States. Almost all the programming on these channels, however, is produced in the United States and depicts U.S. lifestyles and values. What opportunities and threats does this phenomenon represent for U.S. consumer goods companies? For U.S. industrial goods companies?

11. Raytheon's appliance division controls about 5 percent of the appliance market in the United States, compared to Whirlpool's 30 percent, and the company has virtually no overseas business. What interpretation mode do you think Raytheon is most likely to adopt? Why?

12. Many farmers in the United States are independent businesspeople who rely on cooperatives and buyers of agricultural commodities for guidance on what to grow and in what quantities. What macrolevel domains are most likely to be important to farmers? What microlevel domains? Can the interpretation mode model be applied to farmers, and if so, what mode do you think is applicable to most?

NOTES FOR FURTHER READING

1. According to George S. Day and Robin Wensley, "Marketing Theory with a Strategic Orientation," *Journal of Marketing* 47 (Fall 1983), pp. 79–89, an important part of any company's market orientation is to gather and interpret information from multiple sources on all aspects of the environment, an activity called *intelligence generation*. The Raytheon, McDonnell Douglas, and Hughes Electronics examples illustrate that the gathering of relevant intelligence can be an important determinant of a company's long-term success.

2. For a detailed discussion of the relationship between market orientation and profitability, and the importance of understanding, responding to, and managing the environment, see John C. Narver and Stanley F. Slater, "The Effect

of Market Orientation on Profitability," *Journal of Marketing* 54 (October 1990), pp. 20–35.

3. Ajay K. Kohli and Bernard J. Jaworski, "Market Orientation: The Construct, Research Propositions, and Managerial Implications," *Journal of Marketing* 54 (April 1990), pp. 1–18.

4. For more information, see William C. Symonds, Farah Nayeri, Geri Smith, and Ted Plafker, "Bombardier's Blitz," *Business Week*, February 6, 1996, pp. 62–66.

5. Vincent P. Barabba and Gerald Zaltman, *Hearing the Voice of the Market: Competitive Advantage through Creative Use of Market Information* (Boston: Harvard Business School Press, 1991).

6. For more information, see John W. Verity, "The Gold Mine of Data in Customer Service," *Business Week*, March 21, 1994, pp. 113–114.

7. For more details on the importance of the royal family to British business, see Paula Dwyer, "Who Needs the Monarchy? Great Britain PLC," *Business Week*, December 25, 1992, p. 53; and Richard A. Melcher, "Put Away the Ponies, Jeeves, and Send in the PR Chap," *Business Week*, May 24, 1993, p. 52.

8. For more information, see Neil Weinberg, "Garlic and Licorice, Anyone?" *Forbes*, November 18, 1996, pp. 47–48.

9. For more information, see Tim Keenan, "Spanning the Globe," *Ward's Auto World*, July 1996, pp. 37–38.

10. For more information, see I. Jeanne Dugan, "The Internet Is the Great Equalizer," *Business Week*, October 21, 1996, p. E10.

11. For more information, see Joseph Webber and Zachary Schiller, "Painkillers Are about to O.D.," *Business Week*, April 11, 1994, pp. 54–55.

12. For more information, see Zachary Schiller, Greg Burns, and Karen Lowry Miller, "Make It Simple," *Business Week*, September 9, 1996, pp. 96–104.

13. Theodore Levitt, "Marketing Myopia," *Harvard Business Review*, July–August 1960, pp. 45–56.

14. For more information on some of the tactics used by Microsoft to make gains in the Internet software market, see Kathy Rebello, "Inside Microsoft," *Business Week*, July 15, 1996, pp. 56–67.

15. For more information, see Neil Gross and Greg Greenberg, "A New Vision for Athletes," *Business Week*, July 8, 1996, p. 40.

16. For more detailed information, see Lois Therrien, "Recession, Hell—Let's Buy Another TV," *Business Week*, October 19, 1992, p. 35.

17. For more information, see Larry Armstrong and Keith Naughton, "The New Camry's One-Two Punch, *Business Week*, September 16, 1996, pp. 82–84.

18. For more information, see Catherine Yang, "Trustbusters Go Gunning for High Tech," *Business Week*, March 7, 1994, pp. 64–66; and Steve Lohr, "Justice Dept. in New Inquiry into Microsoft: Marketing of Products for Internet is at Issue," *New York Times*, September 20 1996, p. D1.

19. For more information, see Julia Flynn, Stanley Reed, and Amy Barrett, "Worldphone Inc.?" *Business Week*, November 18, 1996, pp. 54–55.

20. For more information, see Tim Smart and Ed Brown, "No Smoke, but Plenty of Heat," *Business Week*, January 6, 1996, p. 35.

21. For more detailed information, see Richard S. Dunham and Michael Oneal, "Gunning for the Gangstas," *Business Week*, June 19, 1995, p. 41.

22. For more information, see Kevin Kelly, "How the States Are Playing Midwife to Baby Baldriges," *Business Week*, November 30, 1992, p. 69.

23. Claes Fornell, "A National Customer Satisfaction Barometer; The Swedish Experience," *Journal of Marketing* 56 (January 1992): 6–21.

24. For more information, see Catherine Yang, "Annie Gets Her Antitrust Gun," *Business Week*, August 23, 1993, p. 23.

25. For a more detailed discussion of how some companies have responded to new technologies, see Arnold C. Cooper and Clayton Smith, "How Established Firms Respond to Threatening Technologies," *Academy of Management Executive* 6 (May 1992), pp. 55–70.

26. Joseph F. Porac and Howard Thomas, "Taxonomic Mental Models in Competitor Definition," *Academy of Management Review* 15 (March 1990), pp. 224–240; Joseph F. Porac, Howard Thomas, Fiona Wilson, Douglas Paton, and Alaina Kanfer, "Rivalry and the Industry Model of Scottish Knitwear Producers," *Administrative Science Quarterly* 40 (June 1995), pp. 203–227.

27. For more information, see Kathy Rebello, "Honey, What's On Microsoft?" *Business Week*, October 21, 1996, pp. 134–136; and Andy Reinhardt, "Intel Inside the Net?" *Business Week*, November 18, 1996, pp. 166–174.

28. For more information, see John Carey, Robert D. Huff, Emily T. Smith, Peter Burrows, and Resa King, "Could America Afford the Transistor Today?" *Business Week*, March 7, 1994, pp. 80–84.

29. For more information, see Emily T. Smith, "The Baby Boom That Has to End," *Business Week*, April 11, 1994, p. 73.

30. For more information, see David Greising and Kate Murphy, "The Boonies Are Booming," *Business Week*, October 9, 1995, pp. 104–112.

31. For more information, see Karen Lowry Miller, "You Just Can't Talk to These Kids," *Business Week*, April 19, 1993, pp. 104–106.

32. See, for example, Maria Mallory, Dan McGraw, Jill Jordan Sieder, and David Fischer, "Women on the Fast Track," *U.S. News & World Report*, November 6, 1995, pp. 60–72; Stephanie Anderson Forest, "JCPenney's Fashion Statement," *Business Week*, October 14, 1996, pp. 66–67; and Dyan Machan, "The Makeover," *Fortune*, December 2, 1996, pp. 135–140.

33. For more information, see Mary Beth Regan, "How Much 'Green' in Green Paper?" *Business Week*, November 1, 1992, pp. 60–61.

34. Richard L. Daft and Karl E. Weick, "Toward a Model of Organizations as Interpretation Systems," *Academy of Management Review* 9 (March 1984): 284–295.

35. Kohli and Jaworski, "Market Orientation."

36. For a more in-depth discussion of interpretation in a marketing context, see Rashi Glazer, "Marketing in an Information-Intensive Environment: Strategic Implications of Knowledge as an Asset," *Journal of Marketing* 55 (October 1991): 1–19.

37. Based on the strategic orientation typology proposed by Robert E. Miles and Charles C. Snow, *Organizational Strategy, Structure, and Process* (New York: McGraw-Hill, 1978). The Miles and Snow typology is one of several strategic orientation classifications proposed in the management literature, all of which are helpful to managers trying to interpret their environment. It is used here because it is compatible with the Daft and Weick model of interpretation systems (Figure 3.4).

38. For more information, see Pete Engardio, George Wehrfritz, Neil Gross, and Peter Burrows, "Taiwan: The Arms Dealer of the Computer Wars," *Business Week*, June 29, 1993, pp. 51–54.

39. Rashi Glazer and Allen M. Weiss, "Marketing in Turbulent Environments: Decision Processes and the Time-Sensitivity of Information," *Journal of Marketing Research* 30 (November 1993): 501–521.

40. For a more in-depth discussion of formal planning, see D. Sinha, "The Contribution of Formal Planning to Decisions," *Strategic Management Journal* 11 (1990): 479–492.

41. For more information, see William Spindle, Larry Armstrong, and James B. Treece, "Toyota Retooled," *Business Week*, April 4, 1994, pp. 54–57.

42. James B. Thomas, Shawn M. Clark, and Dennis A. Gioia, "Strategic Sensemaking and Organizational Performance: Linkages Among Scanning, Interpretation, Action, and Outcomes," *Academy of Management Journal* 36 (April 1993): 239–270.

43. Michael E. Porter, *Competitive Strategy* (New York: Free Press, 1980), pp. 41–44.

CHAPTER 4

INDIVIDUAL CONSUMER'S BEHAVIOR IN THE MARKETPLACE

CHAPTER OBJECTIVES

When you are done with this chapter, you should have achieved the following:

- An understanding of the three types of consumption: impulse purchases, habitual buying, and more complex and involved decisions known as consumption problem solving
- Familiarity with the general model of consumer decision making based upon information processing and volitional and affective processes
- A basic understanding of how consumers implement decisions
- A basic understanding of the contextual determinants of consumption

CHAPTER OUTLINE

A battle is raging between a U.S. company and the government. On one side is the Kellogg Company. On the other is the federal government and the governments of the states of California, Florida, Iowa, Minnesota, Texas, and Wisconsin. The sale and advertising of certain breakfast cereals are at issue.

Case number 1: Heartwise cereal. Kellogg promoted Heartwise cereal for its health benefits, namely, its alleged ability to reduce serum cholesterol, an ingredient in blood linked to heart disease. Kellogg bases this claim on the effects of psyllium, a high-fiber plant product found in Heartwise cereal.

Sometimes it's hard to decide just how healthy cereals are—and the FDA wants cereal manufacturers to clarify and substantiate their claims.

The U.S. Food and Drug Administration so far has refused to recognize that psyllium is a safe and effective agent for the reduction of serum cholesterol. Herein lies the dispute. Based on Kellogg's claim that Heartwise is more than a cereal and in fact is an unapproved drug, plus the assertion that it poses hazards to those consuming it, the attorney general and the Department of Health of Texas placed an embargo on Heartwise cereal, preventing it from being marketed. The alleged health risks primarily center on the possibility of severe allergic reactions. Kellogg denies any problems with the product and stands behind the claims made in its ads.

Case number 2: Frosted Flakes and Special K. Iowa, with support from the states named above, has challenged Kellogg's claims that Frosted Flakes is superior to certain fruits and that Special K prevents muscle loss. The states

claim that the alleged benefits are false and/or that negative attributes (e.g., high sugar content) outweigh the benefits. Again Kellogg stands by its products and advertising.

The battle dates back to 1988 with little sign of resolution a decade later. Meanwhile, considerable name calling and general mean-spiritedness has transpired among all parties. In addition, there have been drawn-out court battles.

The many issues to be resolved between the disputants are special cases of broader issues: the rights of the public to know what is in the products it buys and to be protected from harmful foods; the rights of companies to engage in commercial free speech; the determination of what is false or deceptive advertising; and the right for a hearing to air grievances and, if necessary, seek a speedy resolution of disputes.

What seems to have been lost in all the uproar between Kellogg and the government is the consumer. Both parties owe their existence to consumers, but neither seems to be basing its arguments on *how* consumers process information and make decisions. Businesses need to know this in order to design (1) products that will best meet consumer needs in a competitive environment; (2) communication programs (advertising, personal selling, publicity) that will reach, inform, and convince consumers to try the product and buy it again; and (3) distribution programs that will match how consumers go about acquiring the products they desire. The government needs to know how consumers process information and make decisions in order to ascertain how best to protect the consumer and in general ensure a safe and effective marketplace.

Legal battles are important societal happenings, but they represent only a small part of the everyday activities of business and the government regulation of business. More central to the proper functioning of business in society is how the behavior of consumers is understood and taken into account in business decisions. Take the purchase of breakfast cereal as a case in point.

To win the competitive battle in the supermarket and make a profit, companies such as Kellogg need to know what attributes consumers desire in a cereal, how consumers perceive brands to deliver these attributes, how consumers weigh and integrate judgments of attributes and brand perceptions, and so on. Government regulators also need to know similar things. For example, how many consumers read the nutritional information on packages? What information do they need? How do they evaluate, integrate, and use this information in decision making? Are consumers vulnerable to health and nutritional claims, which may be false or misleading?

This chapter provides a basis for answering these questions. It examines the forces that drive consumption from the consumer's point of view. In later chapters, we reverse the perspective and more explicitly discuss the marketer and government perspectives.

The heart of consumer behavior resides, of course, in the psychological processes that comprise decision making. We devote much attention to the details of these processes, for they provide the bulk of input to marketing decision making. The chapter closes with more contextual concerns: namely, the situational, social, personality, and cultural factors that shape decision making.

THREE FUNDAMENTAL KINDS OF CONSUMPTION ACTIVITIES

Before we look in detail at consumer decision making and the many forces shaping consumption, we consider three basic categories of consumer behavior cutting across all consumption activities. These are impulse buying, habitual purchase behavior, and consumption problem solving.

Impulse Buying

We are all familiar with the impulse-buying situation, but probably have not thought much about what actually goes on within the mind of the consumer. Let us consider first the outward, easily observed manifestations of impulse buying.

Frank Bollo, a husband with traditional sex-role values, is forced to do the weekly family shopping for food. Normally his wife does this, but this week she is recovering from a bout with the flu. Although Frank is not very familiar with the layout of the supermarket, his shopping proceeds uneventfully, largely due to the detailed list of groceries his wife has provided for him. Indeed, the entire process goes very smoothly, albeit at a slower than normal

That little impulse—a marketer's dream.

pace, and within forty-five minutes Frank has successfully obtained every item on the list. As he approaches the checkout counter with his cart of groceries, however, something unusual and unplanned occurs. His eye catches a large, colorful display of wines, cheeses, and crackers located strategically a few steps from the cash registers. Frank is generally a beer drinker, but for some reason he can't resist the imported bottles of Valpolicella. Quickly, and apparently without thought, he grabs a bottle with his free hand and pushes the cart up to an open register.

Why did Frank purchase the wine and how did he make the decision? If we asked Frank directly, he might simply answer, "I don't know," or "It looked good, so I thought I might try it." We know from the scenario that wine was not on his shopping list and that he normally did not drink wine. So this gives us some evidence to rule out both prior planning and habit as causes. Most likely, Frank was not aware of the reasons for his behavior at the time. We might say that he purchased the wine "on impulse." But what does this mean in terms of specific causes of the action? Surely, some mental activities took place, however hidden these may be to Frank and to us as observers.

Consumers who make impulse purchases do employ some mental and emotional processes. If we had an insider's view of Frank's mental activities, the processes might appear something like the following. As Frank passed the display, the bright colors, size of the display, and cheese odors were initial external stimuli picked up by perceptual and sensing processes (see Figure 4.1, stage 1). The olfactory responses to the cheese odors then stimulated early food-related reactions, such as salivation and gastric juice production in the stomach. Similarly, the colors in the display and its physical size and shape created an orientation reaction consisting of visual sensing processes, resulting in turning of the head and related motor responses.

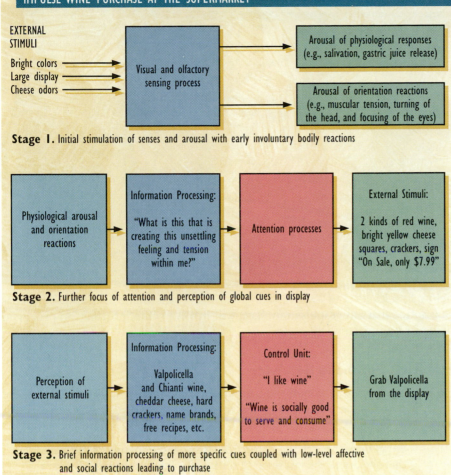

EXTERNAL STIMULI

Bright colors
Large display
Cheese odors
→ Visual and olfactory sensing process →

Arousal of physiological responses (e.g., salivation, gastric juice release)

Arousal of orientation reactions (e.g., muscular tension, turning of the head, and focusing of the eyes)

Stage 1. Initial stimulation of senses and arousal with early involuntary bodily reactions

Physiological arousal and orientation reactions →

Information Processing: "What is this that is creating this unsettling feeling and tension within me?" →

Attention processes →

External Stimuli: 2 kinds of red wine, bright yellow cheese squares, crackers, sign "On Sale, only $7.99"

Stage 2. Further focus of attention and perception of global cues in display

Perception of external stimuli →

Information Processing: Valpolicella and Chianti wine, cheddar cheese, hard crackers, name brands, free recipes, etc. →

Control Unit: "I like wine" "Wine is socially good to serve and consume" →

Grab Valpolicella from the display

Stage 3. Brief information processing of more specific cues coupled with low-level affective and social reactions leading to purchase

Next, in stage 2, the physiological and orientation reactions lead to very brief, and probably unconscious, information processing. The motivation for the information processing might be merely to find out what is causing the physiological disequilibrium and psychological tension. Thus, attention might be allocated to global stimuli in the display such as the two types of wine (red and white), the presence of cheese, and a sign indicating, "On Sale, only $7.99."

In stage 3, information processing of the stimuli might proceed somewhat further to the extent that Frank noticed two kinds of red wine, cheddar cheese, hard crackers, "name brands," and free recipes. More detailed information processing might then come into play. Even though Frank is not a regular wine drinker, he is a second-generation Italian American, and his experiences while growing up had instilled a positive feeling for wine as well as the realization that wine is a symbol of friendship and family ties. The former functions as affect, whereas the latter is a type of goal or value related to the unconscious pull of tradition. In any case, the processing up to this point was sufficient to lead Frank to reach for the bottle of wine. Most of the processes outlined in Figure 4.1 probably occurred

below Frank's level of awareness at the time. Frank made an impulse purchase. But notice that any impulse purchase will involve some information processing, however minimal.

Habitual Purchase Behavior

Perhaps even more common than impulse purchases are so-called purchases by habit. The following scenario is typical of many of these instances of consumer behavior (see Fig. 4.2).

> Sonja Bender is driving home from work and remembers suddenly that she drank the last drop of milk earlier this morning. Her first decision is to search for a supermarket because it has greater variety and lower prices. If she finds a supermarket, she then looks for one-quart sizes because she lives alone and any larger container tends to spoil. Her decision sequence from this point on in the supermarket is to determine whether her favorite brand is available, the price is reasonable, and the milk is fresh (as indicated by the date stamped on the container). If one-quart sizes are not available and/or any one of the other criteria is not satisfied, then she considers a half-gallon size. Her logic is that, should an acceptable half-gallon container be available, it is probably cheaper in the long run to purchase it rather than waste time and gasoline driving to another store, and possibly pay a higher price. On the other hand, if half-gallon sizes are not available in the supermarket (or no supermarkets are found nearby), then she will consider a specialty or "mom-and-pop" store. If one of these is handy, then she applies the same ordered criteria as employed in the supermarket. If no stores are available, then she decides to wait until tomorrow when her regular shopping for the week is scheduled.

Habitual purchase behaviors exhibit a number of features that deserve mention. First, the process begins with the stimulation of a need. Sonja recalled her need, thus the need resulted in this case from internal forces. It would have been possible, of

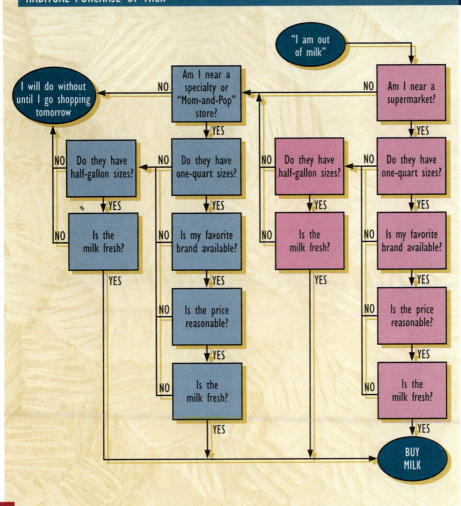

course, for her need to have arisen also as a function of an external stimulus such as a billboard advertisement for milk. In either case, the perceived need then leads to a well-structured process. Second, notice that a specific set of criteria was employed: supermarket availability, size of container, favorite brand, price, and so on. Presumably, these have been learned through (1) many previous experiences in shopping and consumption; and (2) the development of decision rules reflective of Sonja's biological needs, feelings, thoughts, and goals. Third, notice that the criteria were applied in a particular order. This, too, is most likely a consequence of prior learning, and the order of attribute consideration is probably one of decreasing importance. A fourth point to stress is that the criteria are simple in structure and content. Rather than applying many finely coded criteria, Sonja applied a small number of binary requirements. The price was reasonable or not, the milk was fresh or not, and so on. It is just not feasible or worth one's while to do an elaborate cost-benefit analysis for so inexpensive and readily available a product. In many habitual purchase situations, consumers will employ only one or two decision criteria. In fact, one's "favorite brand" is the only requirement needed for some consumption decisions. In others, the consumer uses favorite brand as the most important cue in a lexicographic ordering (i.e., as the first most important criterion, followed by the second, and so on), but may accept other brand names or dealer brands if the favorite brand is unavailable or too expensive.

In summary, consumers generally make habitual purchase decisions purposefully but with little thought. Memory, affect, and goals play a dominant role, whereas information processing is shallow and brief. In one sense, consumers have "worked out" the decision in the past and stored it in their memories. It is reactivated each time a need for the product is triggered, as when Sonja remembered she was out of milk. Researchers refer to such automatic-type decision rules and processes as scripts. Even the purchase of an automobile can resemble habitual purchase behavior for some people. A recent survey of Hispanic business executives showed that 99 percent of the owners of the Cadillac Seville planned to purchase another the next time they are in the market.

Consumption Problem Solving

Many consumer choice situations are neither impulsive nor habitual. Rather, they involve complex decisions that require extensive information processing. Consider one person's decision to purchase an automobile.

Carl Sanchez, a recent university graduate, has decided to buy a new car. Although he has bought used cars before, the cost of a new one is so great and the options to consider are so numerous that he decides to be systematic in his decision making. Carl begins by thumbing through magazines, looking for attractive ads, in order to get some idea of the styles and range of options available. He also hopes to narrow his search down to two or three manufacturers because he plans to visit only a few dealers. Carl's preliminary search indicates that he wants a somewhat sporty, but economical car. The three makes he will consider are Toyota, Honda, and Ford. Because he can spend about $20,000 to $22,000, the most attractive models for him are the Camry, Accord LX, and Taurus SHO.

Carl intends to get price quotes from at least two dealers of each brand, but before he does this he believes that more information from disinterested sources would reduce the risk of too hasty a purchase. He remembers that Ted Stern, a colleague at work, owns a Taurus SHO, and he makes a point to plan to talk to Ted tomorrow at lunch. In the meantime, Carl decides to go to the local library to study what *Consumer Reports*—an independent magazine that rates cars and other products—has to say. This turns out to be an eye-opener, for *Consumer Reports* evaluated each of the three cars on many product attributes. For example, the magazine presented a helpful summary table comparing the cars on such criteria as fuel economy, fuel tank capacity, ease of maintenance, costs of repair, ride and handling, passenger and luggage room, and overall comfort. Although Carl still feels he is far from a final decision, the information in *Consumer Reports* leads him to remove the Camry from his list of considerations (his "evoked set") because the luggage capacity and rear seat are too small for his needs. His study of the information in the magazine also suggests that he

You never forget that feeling you get when you buy your first new car, especially if you really do your homework first.

should consider ease of maintenance and frequency of breakdowns as decision criteria, in addition to the ones he already believes to be important (i.e., styling, fuel economy, ride and handling, and roominess for passengers and luggage).

The activities of the next day add still further information and help Carl crystallize his decision. His conversation with Ted reinforces his prior judgments about, and attraction for, the Taurus SHO. Similarly, his "once-over" of an Accord LX parked in the employee parking lot confirms his beliefs about, and liking for, this car. He feels ready to examine new cars at the dealers and take test rides. Later that day and on each of the following two evenings, Carl carefully appraises the cars on each of his decision criteria. He records this information on a note pad along with price quotes from the salespeople.

On the fourth day, and after considerable stewing and pressure from the salespeople, Carl summarizes his thoughts and feelings before making a final decision. He constructs a table to represent his beliefs as to how each car scored on scales from 1 to 10 for the product attributes he was considering.

Product Attributes						
Model	Styling	Economy	Ride and Handling	Roominess	Ease of Maintenance	Frequency of Breakdowns
Accord LX	9	9	6	8	7	6
Taurus SHO	8	7	8	9	5	8

Carl has no particular weighting or order of importance among the criteria. Moreover, his construction of the table represents the extent of his formal decision-making activities. Rather than consciously applying some decision rule, Carl simply internalizes the information and subjectively selects one of the two cars. The only other major determinant in the process is his belief that whatever choice he makes should "feel right." Carl decides to purchase the Accord LX and somewhat nervously proceeds to the dealer offering the lowest price.

Carl Sanchez's decision to buy the Accord LX is an example of *consumption problem solving* (CPS). Several features of CPS differentiate it from impulse buying and habitual purchase behavior. First, it is obvious that CPS is a lengthy process. For some products, it may take days to make a decision, with the time spent to gather and evaluate information and discover what one really wants. Second, CPS usually concerns products that are important to a person and/or are expensive. The elements of personal and financial risk are typically factors. Third, the process is made up of both conscious and unconscious activities. Carl Sanchez's decision making, for example, involved a number of planned, purposive acts as well as subjective evaluations, many of which he was largely unaware. A fourth point to note is that CPS generally proceeds in stages marked by initial searches of information in memory or externally, followed by information integration and evaluation, followed by further information gathering, then evaluation, and so on. Fifth, CPS typically begins with a need and its arousing effects. Although perhaps not apparent from the above scenario, Carl Sanchez's motivation for the new car was a complex mix of transportation, personality, and social needs. Further, the needs are typically of a higher magnitude than those associated with impulse and habitual purchases. Finally, CPS is invariably a complex activity: Many product attributes must be assessed, the attributes often occur as shades of fine gradation, many brands may enter consideration; and the interactions of affect and goals with information processing can be quite intricate.

In sum, CPS is an important class of decision making. We might view it as a continuum of consumption instances varying from relatively simple problem solving, such as found in the purchase of a winter coat, to more involved decision making, such as is exemplified in the purchase of a new home. Along with impulse and habitual purchasing, CPS covers most of the real-world cases of buying.

Furthermore, marketers often try in their campaigns to convert CPS decisions at one point in time to habitual choices at a later point in time, which is termed "brand loyalty" or simply "repeat purchasing." Marketers also try to convert impulse purchases into either subsequent CPS or habitual purchases. Thus it can be seen that the understanding of CPS is a key aspect of marketing. We turn now to a detailed model of CPS. A simple way to remember CPS is to think of it in the following terms: need recognition → information search → evaluation → decision → purchase → post purchase reaction (e.g., satisfaction or dissatisfaction).

A GENERAL MODEL OF CONSUMER BEHAVIOR

Introduction to the Model

Consumer decision-making processes are quite complex and are influenced by many forces both within and external to the individual. Yet, if we are to understand why and how people make choices, and if managers are to effectively adjust their offerings in order to respond to and stimulate the demand for goods by consumers, then we must attempt to represent the dynamics of those consumer actions.

Fortunately, we can identify a relatively small number of elements common to most everyday consumption decisions. Figure 4.3 is one example. Notice that consumer behavior is represented as a stimulus → organism → response system, with

FIGURE 4.3

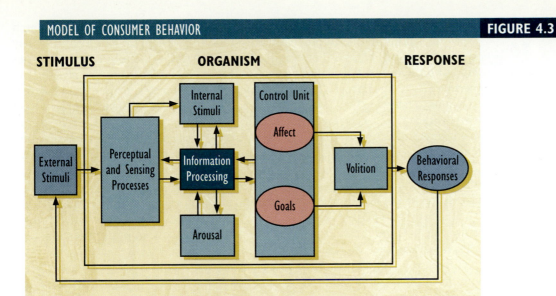

MODEL OF CONSUMER BEHAVIOR

special emphasis placed on the internal structures and processes occurring within the organism (i.e., the person). The elements of the model (e.g., arousal, information processing, and so forth) represent functions (some psychological, others physiological) within the person. We do not actually "see" the functions. Rather, we infer their existence by observing and measuring people's thoughts, feelings, bodily states, and overt actions. For example, when asked, "What would be the better buy, two pounds of hamburger for $7.20 or one pound for $3.80?," a consumer might answer, "Two pounds for $7.20." If so, we might infer that the consumer computed a per-pound cost of $3.60 for the first option and compared this to the $3.80 per-pound cost for the second option. In other words, the consumer went through the information-processing stage of decision making.

The functions of this model are interconnected in many ways. For now, it should be noted that the model in Figure 4.3 represents a compromise between the many atomistic frameworks in the literature that explain very specific acts with highly specialized theories and the grand approaches that, through complex flow diagrams, attempt to capture the entirety of consumption in all its complexity. As such, it attempts to point out a few of the more fundamental aspects of consumer decision making.

As we look more closely at the model and its functioning, we begin with an overview of its parts and their relationships. The consumption process appears to begin with an external stimulus striking the consumer's perceptual and sensing processes. In reality, at least three different triggers can initiate consumption: (1) the consumer detects an external stimulus (e.g., an advertisement) and acts upon it, (2) a physiological agitation within the consumer presses for equilibrium, or (3) a psychological imbalance strives for resolution.

External stimuli refer to any changes in the environment that consumers can potentially perceive or sense. Changes in the physical attributes of products, package design, price, advertisements, promotion tactics, or persuasive sales appeals represent common marketing examples. A whole science has grown around the strategic use of stimuli in marketing; we will elaborate further on these tactics in upcoming chapters on product design, communication, advertising, personal selling, and channels of distribution.

Although exposure to an advertisement, an appealing package, or a sales pitch will often motivate one to purchase a product, the actual purchase behavior may spring from *internal forces*. For example, if Cindy has not eaten for an extended period of time, this will produce chemical and hormonal imbalances that she will experience as hunger pangs. This physiological tension may function as an internal stimulus to heighten Cindy's perceptual readiness to detect a restaurant or fast-food store while driving a car, say. Thus, the direction of the motivation to purchase goes from internal stimuli to perceptual and sensing processes. If the hunger is strong enough, a person might even actively search for a restaurant, in which case the force of the motivation might continue from perceptual and sensing processing to pursuit of external stimuli (see Fig. 4.3).

Although the need for food, water, warmth, and sex are powerful and pervasive factors shaping our actions, physiological changes are not the only internal stimuli. Our thoughts and feelings also give rise to consumption-related activities, often without external stimulation. For instance, a desire for novelty, intellectual stimulation, or solitude can lead one to patronize an amusement park, purchase a best-selling nonfiction book, or rent a cottage in the wild. These and other similar consumption activities often have their roots in psychological tensions within us.

Perceptual and Sensing Processes

The role of *perceptual and sensing processes* is an important one, for it serves as our conduit to the outside world (see Fig. 4.3). We experience the world through one of the five senses: seeing, hearing, touching, smelling, and tasting. These senses are at the periphery of our autonomic nervous system (ANS). They pick up information from our immediate environment and transfer it, via nerves, to various mental and/or physiological centers in the body. Sometimes sensations activate arousal mechanisms in the subcortex (i.e., the lower reaches of the brain such as the limbic system, where some of our emotional and sexual responses are believed to be housed). At other times, they will stimulate a particular neural response that is ultimately connected to a gland or other organ deep in the ANS. The direction of stimulation for the latter is from perceptual and sensing processes to internal stimuli, whereas the former is from perceptual and sensing processes to arousal (see Fig. 4.3). More often than not, we act upon our perceptions cognitively in an activity called *information processing*. For example, an alluring end-of-aisle display for cheese and paté in a supermarket might stimulate thoughts about new ways to prepare hors d'oeuvres.

Perceptual and sensing processes can be further broken down into their component parts, as shown in Figure 4.4. External stimuli are initially monitored by perceptual and sensing processes in a stage termed the *sensory register* (also called a *buffer*). Its function is to briefly hold information from the external environment until it can be processed further. The sensory register is believed to store information in veridical form, that is, as it is represented physically as a visual, auditory, or other stimulus. Later, this veridical information may be transformed and recoded to a form more easily stored and manipulated by other parts of the mind that are, in turn, housed in the information-processing stage (see bottom of Figure 4.4). Information from stimuli are stored very briefly in the sensory register. For example, visual information is thought to be stored in the sensory register for less than one second. In fact, much of it may have decayed or been erased after

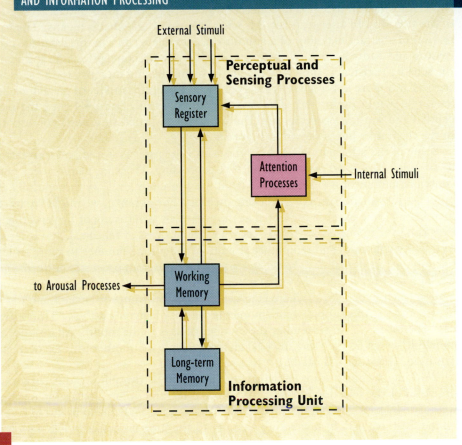

about 0.3 second or so. The short life of information storage in our sensory register actually serves an important purpose. We are continually bombarded by so much external stimulation at any one point in time that it would be physically and psychologically overwhelming to cope with all of it at once. Only so much information can be monitored; hence, the rapid decay in the sensory register prevents a bottleneck and overload from occurring. In a sense, it also serves to prevent new information from overlapping with the old. As stimuli impinge on the sensory register, some is transferred to other stages for further processing (or for long-term storage), and some is merely erased or forgotten. This permits one to be able to accept new information on an ongoing basis.

A couple of other points need to be stressed about the sensory register. Although psychologists are not absolutely certain, it is believed that there may be not one but many sensory registers. That is, we may all have a sensory register for visual stimuli, one for auditory, one for olfactory, and so on. Finally, for purposes of analysis, the term "sensory register" refers only to our monitoring and storing stimuli for very short times. These processes are basically preattentive and precategorical. The sensory register is preattentive in the sense that we are not consciously aware of information it receives and stores. Rather, awareness occurs in other stages (e.g., through attention processes and in working memory).

The sensory register is also precategorical: it neither stores specific information nor performs operations on the meaning of stimuli for the person. Rather, it stores information in a global, concrete way based on the physical characteristics of the stimulus. In a sense, it records what *is*, rather than what it means. The formation of abstract meaning of a stimulus occurs deeper in the information-processing and control units. However, note that our preconceptions do influence the sensory register, as shown by the arrow from working memory to the sensory register in Figure 4.4. Figure 4.4 is a subset of the entire model of consumer behavior shown in Figure 4.3. The two dashed boxes in Figure 4.4 (i.e., the perceptual and sensing processes and the information processing unit) correspond to the respective boxes shown in Figure 4.3.

Some of the information reaching the sensory register is stored and transferred to *working (short-term) memory* for further processing. Working memory has both conscious and unconscious aspects to it. At the conscious level, we thoughtfully act upon the information entering working memory. For example, we might try to remember a phone number presented at the end of an advertisement by repeating it over and over to ourselves. This is known as the process of rehearsal, and it serves to transfer conscious and temporary storage of the phone number to more or less unconscious *permanent (long-term) memory*. Other conscious processes performed in working memory include the use of mnemonics and other tactics to organize information (such as chunking, where facts are grouped in clumps to make them easier to remember). An example of mnemonics is the use of rhymes such as "Thirty days has September . . ." to remember the number of days in the month. An instance of chunking would be the grouping of digits in a telephone number for ease of memorization: 1-800-CLUB MED.

Working memory also encompasses conscious activation of our attention processes or the selection of pertinent information, and occurs, for example, when we hurriedly pass through the supermarket looking for a particular brand of cereal on the shelf (see path from working memory to attention processes in Fig. 4.4). It is not clear whether working memory can unconsciously act upon information. If it does, unconscious processing in working memory might be limited to comparisons or matching of information from the sensory register to stored representations from long-term memory. For example, Brendan glances at the nutritional information on a package while passing a shelf in the supermarket, he might unconsciously compare the information to a preconceived set of important purchasing criteria: low sugar, low fat, and high protein. Although Brendan would be consciously aware of seeing most of the nutritional information on the package, an integration of the thinking and motor reactions required to stop and grab the package might not be triggered until the cues of low sugar, low fat, and high protein have been unconsciously interpreted and compared to personal requirements stored in his long-term memory. Of course, the whole process often occurs for some people entirely at a conscious level, as when a health-food connoisseur meticulously examines product labels to find a satisfactory offering.

Working memory is also characterized by the amount of information it can handle, the length of time it can store information, and how it can store information. Generally, a person's short-term memory can process only about 7 pieces of information at any one point in time. The sensory register, on the other hand, is believed to be capable of handling 15 or more items of information. Working memory stores the information for longer periods of time than does the sensory register, however. Depending on whether one looks at visual or auditory information, researchers believe that working memory lasts about 15 to 30 seconds, as opposed to less than one second for the sensory register. Information can be retained indefinitely in working memory only through rehearsal. Finally, working memory apparently stores information in recoded form, as opposed to the veridical storage of the sensory register. The exact nature of this new code is little understood except that it is abstract and can entail verbal and visual images as well as semantic meaning.

The final component of perceptual and sensing processes is called *attention processes* (see Fig. 4.4). Attention is the conscious allocation of mental processing capacity to information in the sensory register. Whether one will attend to information depends on (1) the number and strength of environmental stimuli competing with the attended input for attention, (2) internal stimuli, and (3) certain inputs from memory. The first constraint operates as follows. Whenever one or more pieces of information in the sensory register become objects of attention, the quality and amount of the input attended to (as well as transferred to working memory) will be affected by background noise (distraction). The attention processes allocate the limited amount of human capacity for monitoring information; but background noise continually disrupts this process if it breaks through a threshold level. Ads use repetition, novelty, and vividness, for example, to counteract people's tendency to not pay attention to them. Internal stimuli influence the process, too—physiological and psychological imbalances and needs stimulate people's attention to seek a means of correcting those imbalances and satisfying needs. All of us pay particular attention to sources of satisfaction when we are needy or deprived. Similarly, stored information in memory—such as learned categories, intentions, and goals—influences how we allocate our attention. For example, regular moviegoers learn to tune out or tune in to particular critics: they tend to ignore evaluations by disliked critics, while they watch for reviews by liked critics. As we discuss in chapter 10, marketers design advertisements to exploit these aspects of human attention processes. One example of this is the rule of thumb practiced by some advertisers that a television commercial must mention and show the product and brand name within the first 10 seconds of an ad to attract attention and have the desired effect on brand remembrance. Mentioning a brand name too late in an ad typically results in fewer people remembering it when tested at a later time. If they cannot remember the brand name, they will be less likely to buy it.

Information Processing

An important stage of consumer behavior is information processing. As indicated in Figure 4.4, information processing occurs in two components: working memory and long-term memory. From the viewpoint of marketing, information processing can be described in three classes of phenomena: (1) memory or storage, (2) judgment processes, and (3) control processes and volition (see Fig. 4.5).

All that we know or experience is stored in our brain as coded information in a *memory bank*, or long-term memory. Declarative knowledge consists of factual information about a product, service, person, place, or object.[1] This knowledge may be about specific concepts and their concrete attributes or characteristics. For example, the brand name Scope mouthwash and its attributes—sugarless, minty taste, and contains fluoride—are all instances of concrete declarative knowledge. By the same token, declarative knowledge can reflect abstract constructs. For example, Pontiac automotive's metaphoric slogan, "We are driving excitement," or Thomasville's recent print ads for its Elysée furniture collection, where the attributes "beautiful, serene, and romantic" are highlighted, are instances of abstract declarative knowledge.

FIGURE 4.5   COMPONENTS OF INFORMATION PROCESSING

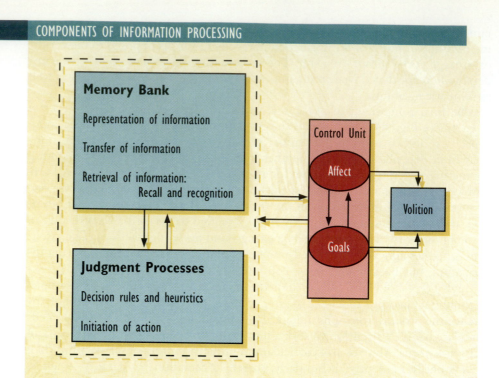

The second kind of information in long-term memory is procedural knowledge. Procedural knowledge entails production rules, which are "if-then" types of propositions connecting particular concepts in memory. For example, a decision maker may have the following set of interconnected inferences in reaction to ads for low-fat potato chips: low-fat chips → I will not gain weight, and heart and arteries will be healthier → I will be attractive to others and I will live longer.

The actual representation of information in memory differs for declarative and procedural knowledge. Figure 4.6 represents one way that a consumer's declarative knowledge may be manifest in the concept *coffee*. Notice that coffee is associated with many attributes (e.g., expensive, bitter) and is a subset or superset of other concepts (e.g., a drink, brand A). Actually, we have included elements of procedural knowledge in the mental structure represented by Figure 4.6: coffee can have caffeine, which a consumer may conclude makes him or her nervous; likewise coffee often quenches one's need to alleviate thirst impulses.

A more elaborated example of procedural knowledge can be seen in Figure 4.7, which depicts a cognitive schema held by people strongly favorable toward U.S. President Clinton. This schema is actually a fragment from a larger mental network found in a survey of the public prior to the fall 1996 presidential election.[2] Let us inspect the schema, for it illustrates properties common to many representations in memory. Keep in mind that this example covers only a portion of positive reactions to the president; many other positive and negative reactions were found, but are omitted for purposes of simplicity.

The concepts shown in Figure 4.7 can be thought of as values, which are beliefs with motivational or goal-directed implications. For instance, enhances quality of life, improves society, and cares about people are values the public perceived in President Clinton. Notice that the values are arranged along a continuum of ab-

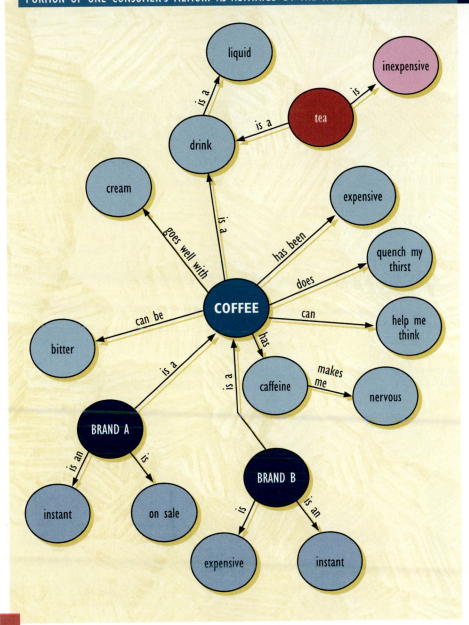

stractness, from the concrete to the highly abstract. Seven concrete values (in this case attributes or actions taken by President Clinton) are shown. Three deal with policies the president supported—health care, broad economic, and specific budgetary policies; three are subjective judgments that he is doing a good job, holds similar beliefs to oneself, and tries hard; and one sees him in a relative sense as being better than the alternatives, the Republicans.

The concrete, lower-level values lead to values higher in the hierarchy. At the top of the hierarchy are the most general, enduring values or motivational concerns. Enhances the quality of life, improves society, the country runs well, and fair to all reflect abstract moral virtues or ends in this sense. "Helps me" refers to personal, business, or family gain and also is at the highest level of abstraction for those individuals in the sample strongly favorable toward President Clinton. For the cognitive schema of President Clinton held by people only somewhat favorable toward him, the value "helps me" was relatively more concrete. Apparently those individuals who are strongly favorable toward Clinton depersonalize the self-gain and treat it as more of an abstraction, perhaps selfishly, than others less favorable. Of course, helps me was not a value for people unfavorable toward President Clinton but such value judgments as lacks integrity, does not stand up for his beliefs, and cannot be trusted were frequent for those unfavorable toward Clinton.

Between the most abstract and concrete values in Figure 4.7 are five values at intermediate levels of abstractness. These can serve as ends in and of themselves (economy improves) or as means to this or other more abstract values (controlling the deficit, cares about people, deals with issues better than do Republicans, and affordable health care).

Cares about people, an intermediate value, functions in a central manner by channeling the effects of a number of concrete values onto the values at the top of the hierarchy. Values such as this are termed basic-level values and often serve as prototypes for deciding whether President Clinton is to be labeled in a strongly favorable way. Basic-level values also often function as effective ways to activate schemas in the minds of people. Clinton's fall 1996 advertising campaign frequently

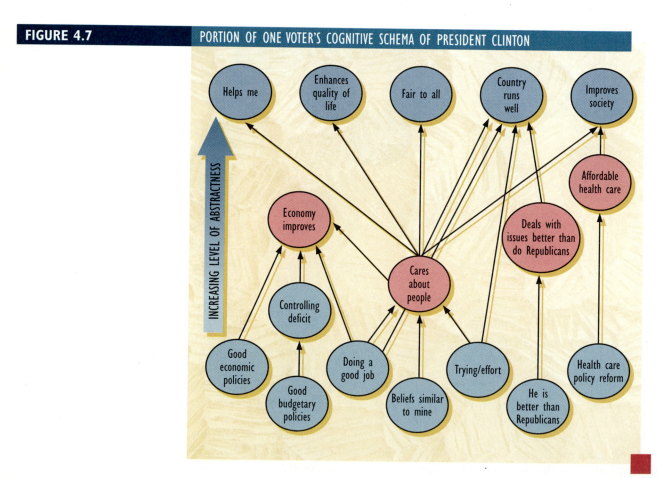

FIGURE 4.7 PORTION OF ONE VOTER'S COGNITIVE SCHEMA OF PRESIDENT CLINTON

focused on this value to remind people already favorable toward him why they should vote for him. Research shows that when people process and communicate information, basic-level knowledge functions as the primary vehicle. More abstract (superordinate) and less abstract (subordinate) categories of knowledge generally require greater mental effort for processing.

Mental or cognitive schemas play a central role in marketing research and inform the decisions made by marketers in product/service design, advertising, pricing, and distribution. Before we leave the topic of schemas, it is important therefore to point out a few more of their properties.[3] Cognitive schemas are knowledge structures of ideas or values that one holds as well as the connections among these ideas or values. They are learned through experience, and new information to which we are exposed to is interpreted and integrated through existing categories in the schemas. Thus, when communicating the attributes of their products to consumers, marketers must take into account the knowledge structure already learned by consumers. Continuing our example of political actor schemas, we note that the most effective values leading to the public's attitude formation and intentions to vote for President Clinton were cares about people, easy to relate to, doing a good job, and protects future; the key inferential linkages (i.e., procedural knowledge) in this regard were doing a good job → cares about people, cares about people → protects future, and easy to relate to → cares about people. The above findings applied to those initially favorable toward Clinton. For those initially unfavorable, the public's attitude formation and intentions not to vote for him were driven by such value judgments as lack of trust, broken promises, and bad budgetary policy, and such inferences as bad budgetary policy → economy suffers, broken promises → lack of trust, and fighting with Congress → doing a poor job.

Attitude change is difficult to bring about when one already holds a schema toward a product or politician, because people tend to encode information that is consistent with it. Moreover, people tend to make schema-consistent inferences. Finally experience or involvement is related to attitude change. It has been found, for example, that experts (i.e., those with considerable knowledge in a domain) take into account schema-inconsistent information when making inferences more than do novices with respect to both products and politicians.[4] We discuss how schemas can be influenced in later chapters on communication, advertising, and personal selling.

If it is to be useful, information must be transferred from the memory bank to other stages shown in the model. This is a little understood and very difficult process to study, but two phenomena, recall and recognition, have been thoroughly studied and are very important to a basic understanding of consumer behavior. Indeed, advertisers rely heavily on data on how well consumers recall and recognize ads in order to measure the effectiveness of the ads. We say more about this later in chapter 10 on advertising. For now, it should be noted that recall involves producing information from memory with no or few cues. Recognition entails comparing a cue to a representation in memory and indicating whether one has seen or heard a particular stimulus. For instance, if a consumer were asked if he or she had seen an advertisement for radial tires on the television within the past two days and, if so, to identify its sponsor and major selling point, then this would require the (aided) recall of information. On the other hand, if a person were shown a television commercial with all brand name identification eliminated and asked to identify the brand, he or she would be engaged in a (masked) recognition activity. This entails matching the just-viewed commercial to information in memory and noting whether one had seen it before or not. Unaided recall and nonmasked recognition methods are used in research as well.

TABLE 4.1 SUBJECTIVE JUDGMENTS OF A CONSUMER ON FOUR CRITERIA APPLIED TO FIVE BRANDS OF CEREAL

Brand	Price	Nutrition	Texture	Taste
A	5	10	6	5
B	8	6	6	8
C	7	6	8	9
D	7	7	8	7
E	6	8	7	4

Note: The higher the number, the better the respective brand scores on the criterion.

Information Integration

Information is mentally acted upon in the information-processing stage through *judgment processes* (Fig. 4.5). To be useful in decision making, the coded information in memory must be combined into a more condensed and meaningful (from the consumer's standpoint) representation. This might include an ordering and/or weighting scheme applied to the information. Imagine, for example, that a consumer uses information about price, nutrition, texture, and taste to select a breakfast cereal. How is the consumer to assess many brands on these criteria and use the information? Table 4.1 lists five brands of cereal that the consumer is considering and how each brand scores on the criteria. The numbers in the table represent the consumer's subjective beliefs about how each brand scores on each criterion on a scale from one to ten, with the higher numbers indicating that the respective brand scores well on the corresponding criterion. For example, brand A scores better than any other brand on nutrition but worse than any other brand on price. Given the information in the table, how can we predict which brand the consumer will purchase? Clearly, we need to know how the consumer uses and weighs the information.

Psychologists and consumer researchers have discovered that people use one or more of a number of decision rules to make choices when confronted with a task such as choosing a brand of cereal, as depicted in Table 4.1. For example, some consumers might simply add up the judgments of each brand on all criteria (attributes) to arrive at a single overall rating. Thus, for the consumer's responses in Table 4.1, the overall ratings for brands A through E might be the following:

$$R_{1A} = 26, R_{1B} = 28, R_{1C} = 30, R_{1D} = 29, \text{ and } R_{1E} = 25$$

where R_{ij} is person i's rating of brand j. Presumably, if the consumer follows this simple adding rule, then brand C should be selected. We can write this rule in general form as

$$R_{ij} = \sum_{k=1}^{n} B_{ijk} \qquad 4.1$$

where B_{ijk} is consumer i's belief as to how well brand j scores on criterion k, and n is number of criteria. In Table 4.1, $i = 1$ because it reflects one person's judgments; $j = 1, 2, 3, 4, 5$ for the five brands A through E, respectively; and $n = 4$ for the four criteria. Equation 4.1 is really a special case of a somewhat more general rule called the *linear compensatory model* (LCM), which can be expressed as follows:

$$LCM_{ij} = \sum_{k=1}^{n} B_{ijk} V_{ik} \qquad\qquad 4.2$$

where V_{ik} is person i's value (or importance) of criterion k and the remaining symbols are defined as for equation 4.1. In other words, the linear compensatory model implies that a consumer (1) forms beliefs about how each brand in the decision set scores on each of a set of criteria, (2) weighs those beliefs by the personal value or importance of the criteria, and (3) arrives at an overall attitude or judgment, LCM_{ij}.

Notice that the model of equation 4.1, R_{ij}, assumes that each criterion is equally valued or equally important. The weight of unity is implicitly assigned to each criterion (i.e., $V_{ij} = 1$, for all i and k in equation 4.1). In equation 4.2, one's beliefs are in a sense weighted by one's values or importances for the criteria.

As an example of the linear compensatory model applied to the data of Table 4.1, imagine that the consumer's importances for the criteria are expressed as follows:

	Very Unimportant								Very Important	
	1	2	3	4	5	6	7	8	9	10
Price		✔								
Nutrition									✔	
Texture							✔			
Taste			✔							

This might be a typical profile for certain health-conscious consumers who at the same time are less concerned with price and taste. With the above importances, we can now compute the linear compensatory model judgment:

$$LCM_{11} = 5(2) + 10(9) + 6(7) + 5(3) = 157$$
$$LCM_{12} = 8(2) + 6(9) + 6(7) + 8(3) = 136$$
$$LCM_{13} = 7(2) + 6(9) + 8(7) + 9(3) = 151$$
$$LCM_{14} = 7(2) + 7(9) + 8(7) + 7(3) = 154$$
$$LCM_{15} = 6(2) + 8(9) + 7(7) + 4(3) = 145$$

As a consequence, by the linear compensatory model, the consumer prefers brand A ($j = 1$). Note that, instead of importances, evaluations of attributes might constitute the appropriate value weights.

Many other rules can, of course, be followed in decision making. Some of the more common include affect referral, general information integration, conjunctive, disjunctive, lexicographic, sequential elimination, elimination by aspects, satisficing, lexicographic semi-order, and additive difference rules.[5] We briefly describe only one of these rules here: the lexicographic rule. Under a lexicographic judgment rule, a consumer first ranks criteria or attributes in order of importance. Next, all brand or choice alternatives are compared on the most important criterion. If one brand scores higher on the most important criterion than any other brand, then it is chosen. If not (for example, suppose it is tied with two others), then the inferior brands are eliminated and comparisons are made among the tied brands using the second most important criterion. The procedure is continued until a final superior brand remains to be chosen or until no further brands can be eliminated. For example, suppose the consumer whose beliefs are listed in Table 4.1 ranks the criteria in the following order of importance (from highest to lowest): texture, price, nutrition, and taste. Given this ordering and the data of Table 4.1, which cereal brand would that consumer choose, if any? If the consumer followed the lexicographic rule, brand D would be chosen. The logic is as follows: Brands C and D are tied on the most important criterion, texture, so brands A, B, and E can be eliminated. But brands C and D are also tied on the second most important criterion, price. Hence, we must examine the third most important criterion, nutrition. Because brand D is higher than brand C on nutrition, the consumer chooses it as the most preferred cereal (according to the lexicographic rule). Notice that in this particular example the lexicographic rule results in a different choice than either the linear compensatory model or its equal weighted version.

Several assumptions underlying human judgment by rules deserve mention. First, most people are not consciously aware of the particular rule that they may be employing in any decision-making situation. Our mental processes occur too rapidly and below the threshold of awareness for this to happen. Of course, some people might purposely decide to use a linear compensatory or other model before shopping and then gather information and place the numbers representing their beliefs and values into the formula. However, this is the exception, not the rule. Rather, we as consumers generally take in a wealth of information and then later make a decision without knowing exactly how it was made, per se.

A second point to note is that the various decision rules that researchers investigate are not necessarily meant to correspond perfectly to the rules actually used by the consumers under study. Rather, the rules are models or simplified representations of complex, unobservable processes, and we hope that they will capture enough of actual consumer decision making to yield accurate predictions in the marketplace.

Third, it should be stressed that the rules mentioned above probably represent only a portion of the rules that people implicitly follow. Indeed, even the small number of rules that have been investigated to date are not employed by everyone. Furthermore, it may be possible that some rules are context-specific or are a function of the mental capacities, learning experiences, or personalities of individual people. An example of the context-specific nature of rules can be seen in decision situations for which time pressures exist. Here people may use expedient or "fuzzy" rules to simplify their decision problems. For instance, a consumer with an upset stomach might go to a pharmacy and purchase the first brand that is perceived to be adequate to relieve the discomfort. An extended comparison of the prices and features of each competing brand would be unnecessary and prolong the agony. It should be noted, too, that sequences or combinations of rules are sometimes applied.

A fourth assumption to note with respect to the use of decision rules by consumers is that people are presumed to see product and brand alternatives as multi-attribute offerings. To the consumer, a car is not merely a "car." Rather, it is a bundle of benefits consisting of styling, handling, purchase price, miles per gallon (or kilometers per liter), aesthetic appeal, feelings of pride, and so on. Similarly, a trip on an airplane is not merely "transportation," but rather a collection of experiences and feelings related to safety, departure and arrival times, convenience, price, and amenities. People make decisions based on a combination of the attributes associated with a product or service and the implications these attributes have for them. Marketers sometimes refer to this combination simply as "benefits."

Finally, it should be noted that decision rules are but one of a number of factors determining consumers' choices. Internal feelings, fears, and hopes, for example, sometimes override or interact with the rational evaluations that people make; and external forces such as social pressure constrain choices as well.

TABLE 4.2 AFFECT AND COGNITIONS: TWO FUNDAMENTAL CONCEPTS IN CONSUMER DECISION MAKING

	Affect	Cognitions
Common synonyms	Feelings, emotions, tastes, utility	Beliefs, thoughts, subjective probabilities, expectancies
Definition	The feeling or emotional component of psychological reactions toward products	Factual mental images about the attributes of a product and/or what they can lead to for the person
	Usually entails a physiological response (e.g., increased heart rate)	Can be proven true or false in principle and do not necessarily imply an action on the part of the person holding them
	Has a polarity and intensity associated with it	Are what is commonly termed "thoughts"
	Generally implies an action on the part of the person holding it, all else being equal	Are the principal content of information-processing activities

The Elements of the Control Unit and Their Impact on Behavior

Whether a favorable evaluation of information will result in an intention, decision, or plan to purchase will often depend on further mental activities related to one's affect toward a product or brand and one's goals (see the control unit in Figs. 4.3 and 4.5). Consider first affect and its role in decision making.

Affect refers to the emotional, or "feeling," component of a consumer's psychological reactions. Generally, five aspects of affect differentiate it from cognitions or beliefs, which, in turn, are the basic units of thought in information processing (see Tab. 4.2). First, affect possesses a polarity. One may feel positively or negatively toward a product or service, for example. Cognitions do not have a polarity in this sense. Second, affect may vary in intensity in that one experiences positive or negative feelings, attraction or repulsion, like or dislike, and so forth, as a matter of degree. We may like or dislike a brand a small amount, a moderate amount, or very much, for instance. In contrast, although our confidence in beliefs may vary, the beliefs themselves do not have an intensity associated with them. Third, affect is typically a relational concept connecting a person to another person, product, or thing. We do not see affect, per se, but rather infer it from the behavior of a consumer or our own behavior in relation to a product or service. Cognitions, in contrast, are property concepts referring not to the relationship between a person and a product but rather to either a believed factual aspect of the product (e.g., "this wallpaper is washable") or to what consequences a product can lead (e.g., "if I buy this wallpaper, it will brighten the drab dining room in our house considerably and lead to a faster sale of the house when we put it on the market"). Fourth, an affective reaction toward a product implies a felt urge to act on the part of the person holding the feeling. All things constant, if a person feels positive toward a particular brand of cereal and has the need and means to acquire it, then that person will do so.[6] Cognitions do not necessarily imply an action on the part of the person holding one and are said to be action-neutral. Finally, affect is relatively more person-centered and subjective, whereas cognitions are relatively more product-centered and objective. Our beliefs, for example, can be proven true or false in principle because they refer to matters of fact. Affect does not have this property and is neither true nor false. Rather, our emotions toward products are experiences we have and, while influenced by factual content to a certain extent, are not based upon them by definition.

Affect influences decision making in a number of ways. One is that our feelings can lead us to weight product characteristics according to the meaning or implications of those characteristics for us. When the expressed importances or values of a consumer are used as weights in the linear compensatory model, they, in effect, serve as proxies for the consumer's evaluative (e.g., good–bad) or affective (e.g., pleasant–unpleasant) reactions toward product attributes. A second way affect might enter the decision process is as a direct constraint or influence on the judgments one makes. For instance, our feelings or mood can cause us to overlook some product attributes or misperceive others. Still another way that affect can influence decision making is as a parallel cause of actual choices, along with rational evaluations in information processing. In this sense, judgments and feelings do not interact, but have independent impacts on choice. Finally, some marketers believe that the most common sequence in consumer behavior is judgments or beliefs → affect → purchase behavior. Thus, they maintain that cognitive judgments of a brand are formed first, which leads, in turn, to emotional reactions toward the brand, and then actual choice behavior follows. On occasion, however, the sequence between beliefs and affect is reversed such that affect forms first and colors one's beliefs. This is known as the "halo effect" and suggests that it is not always fruitful to assume consumers make decisions based on product attributes.[7] Instead, judgments of product attributes in some real-world contexts are functions of attitudes or preferences. This seems to have happened in the U.S. presidential campaign in 1996. People who knew little factual information about Clinton nevertheless developed positive emotional responses based on his personality, speaking ability, and tendency to hug voters (as presented on television), and these positive emotions later served as a filter when the media portrayed negative information (i.e., the public discounted the negative information). Ronald Reagan enjoyed the same phenomenon in the 1980s, coming to be known as "The Teflon President" because voters did not attach any bad news to Reagan's popularity.

A final word needs to be said with regard to affect. For simplicity, we discussed affect as if it were a unidimensional entity. In fact, affect exists in discrete, although sometimes overlapping or intercorrelated, states. Basic research in psychology, which is only now being applied in marketing, finds that at least four positive and five negative emotional reactions underlie people's affect in everyday situations.[8] The positive emotions are love, joy, hope, and pride; the negative emotions are anger, sadness, fear, guilt or shame, and disgust. Most descriptors of emotions—and there more than 500 words in the English language that describe emotions—fall within the nine discrete categories listed above. For example, anxiety and worry are subtle forms of fear; elation, happiness, satisfaction, and gladness are variants of joy; and liking, attraction, and affection are subclasses of love.

Each of the discrete emotions is produced by a unique set of appraisals performed by a consumer, and each leads to well-defined coping responses. To take a goal situation as an example, sadness results under the appraisal conditions in which (1) external circumstances are perceived to influence one's goal attainment, (2) one's personal motive is the hope of a rewarding goal, (3) the overall situation is consistent with one's motives, (4) the probability of achieving the goal is low, and (5) personal power is low. A single change in one of the above five appraisals illustrated for sadness can change the emotion. Thus, if all the appraisals noted above remain the same, except motivation—which is altered to be the avoidance of an aversive outcome instead of hope of a reward—the emotion changes subtlety to distress, a form of fear. All emotions can be seen to be a function of different combinations of agency (self-caused, other-caused, circumstance-caused), outcome (aversive or appetitive), motive (consistent or inconsistent with one's goals), probability (attainment uncertain or certain), and power (weak or strong).[9] Finally, each emotion can be seen to relate to a set of action tendencies or coping responses.[10] Thus, when one is angry, the response may be to lash out or hurt; when one is frightened, the response may be to freeze, flee, or even fight; and when one is sad, the reaction may be to do nothing or to seek comfort and support, depending on the circumstances.

The fine-grained specification of emotional behavior is useful not only in seeing consumers' reactions to product attributes and advertising appeals to inform product and ad design decisions, respectively, but it can also help us better understand consumer dissatisfaction. For example, marketers need to know when a product or service failure leads to disappointment and subsequently to a decision to buy a competitor's brand, or when failure leads to anger and the urge to bad-mouth the product and complain.

The second major part of the control unit involves the goals one has (see Fig. 4.3). *Goals* are desired end states in relation to which an individual seeks information, evaluates alternative courses of action, and makes choices. They are largely cognitive in content and operate at the both conscious and unconscious levels of awareness. Indeed, we can conceive of goals along a continuum. At one end are the relatively subconscious goals people use to organize their actions. These include norms, values, and other internalized guidelines derived from socialization processes or the expectations of specific individuals, groups, or society-at-large. At this end of the spectrum, the goals function largely automatically with little or no forethought or awareness. Some forms of conspicuous consumption fall within this category, as when people buy "to keep up with the Joneses." Similarly, purchases made in response to social or peer pressure or as a function of tradition often stem from the influence of unconscious goals. At the other extreme are well-developed plans, rules, and procedures that one consciously follows. These may be internally developed through considerable effort and even years of trial and error. They may also be externally imposed, such as is done in the use of checklists prescribed for buyers within an organization. More often than not, goals are socially negotiated and represent a joint decision between two or more people. For example, some husbands and wives construct elaborate budgets to manage their consumption. Overall, goals serve as a means for the self-regulation of one's behavior (see Marketing Anecdote 4.1).

Goals interact with affect and judgment processes to influence choices in a variety of ways. For instance, goals may determine what information is to be gathered and how it is to be evaluated. Or we may develop feelings toward a product, brand, or its features as a function of how well it promises to fulfill our goals. Alternatively, goals may serve as independent determinants of choice in some situations, along with affect and rational judgment processes.

Volitions

The final component of the general model of consumer behavior is *volitions*. The term, "volition" is an umbrella label for a set of mental processes that transform attitudes, preferences, or goals, on the one hand, into action or goal attainment, on

A good example of how one marketer takes advantage of consumer goals is General Motors Corporation's strategy, Brandscape. General Motors first identifies what consumers strive for and then creates a car and supporting communication to help consumers achieve their goals in a car. For example, the following brands have very specific consumers in mind:

Pontiac Grand Prix: for those who are "youthful . . . energetic . . . expressive"

Oldsmobile Intrigue: for those who are "detail driven . . . educated . . . upscale"

Buick Century: for those who are "sensible . . . solid . . . dignified"

Chevrolet Malibu: for those who are "proud . . . prudent . . . American"

As Richard Wagoner, president of GM's North American operations, puts it, "The advantage we have at GM that we really haven't used in the past is rather than having all of our products shooting for the middle of the market, we can have products which go for the sporty buyer, the traditional buyer, the value buyer, the refined buyer."*

The task for GM is to convince consumers that their goals can be fulfilled by purchasing the right GM automobile. Of course, competitors also market cars that fulfill customer needs, and consumers can fulfill their goals through consumption of completely different products or even through nonconsumption activities.

---

*Quoted in Matt Nauman, "GM Aims for Brand Identity to Cut Inside Competition," *San Jose Mercury News,* January 4, 1996.*

---

the other. Before we describe volitions, we should acknowledge that all consumer actions are not necessarily preceded by volitions. Sometimes consumers act automatically or mindlessly with no volitional input, per se. This might happen when an intense emotion causes one to act without forethought, such as when a parent is in a hurry in the supermarket and pressure from a noisy toddler causes one to "agree" to purchase candy. Or mindless behaviors happen now and then when people act habitually, especially when the action is simple, not costly, and frequently enacted, such as brushing our teeth in the morning.

Most actions are not mindless; they do involve forethought. Once consumers have processed information about a set of brands, they may make decisions about which brand to buy. An intention to buy a particular brand may lead to a further decision process concerning how to buy the brand. Plans may be made in this regard and then later initiated, sustained, and implemented en route to purchase. The activities that go on between the point in time when one processes information and has a desire to make a purchase and the point in time when one actually makes the purchase or fails along the way are termed volitions. Volitions involve decisions, choices, intentions, plans, initiation of instrumental acts, monitoring of progress and adjustments, resistance of temptations taking one away from goal pursuit, maintaining motivation and effort, and making the purchase. These obviously are very important processes for marketers to understand but surprisingly have received little research to date. Instead, the vast majority of research has focused upon information processing, and secondarily on perceptual processes, memory, and affect. Volitions and their close companions, goals, are the next frontier in consumer research.

PUTTING THE PIECES TOGETHER: HOW MARKETING MANAGERS USE MODELS OF CONSUMER BEHAVIOR

The two most common ways marketers use models of consumer behavior are the following. First, based on the general model in Figure 4.3, marketers examine how potential customers process information about the attributes of a product or service. Different combinations of attributes, each at alternative levels, are presented to consumers, and consumers are asked to make judgments and state their preferences. Usually marketers present one or more competitors' brands in the study as well, and consumers make choices as to their preferred brand(s). One type of study in this regard examines how consumers incorporate product and service benefits in their decision making and how their judgments of, and preferences for, benefits of products and services determine the choice of a particular brand. This is especially useful in the design of new products and updating or changing of existing products. The information learned also provides guidance in such advertising decisions as what product features to stress in ads and when and where to place ads. We consider examples of the use of consumer models in the above senses in upcoming chapters. Laboratory and field experiments, as well as surveys, are the primary means of research for addressing the above managerial problems.

A second major way marketers use models of consumer behavior is to link the consumers' psychological reactions to products or services (such as represented in the variables presented in Fig. 4.3) to the processes or steps people go through to plan and shop for, acquire, use, and dispose of or disengage from products or services. Researchers typically use surveys to reveal these steps. Samples of representative consumers are asked to describe their needs and shopping behaviors and to react to products and services and their attributes by expressing their beliefs, judgments, affective responses, and intentions, among other responses. The variables and processes measured in real-world studies of this sort are many and complex, so it helps to organize them in a model to make the research manageable.

Let us describe a comprehensive framework in this regard.[11] Figure 4.8 presents a contemporary model for identifying key variables and steps in consumer goal pursuit. Just about any consumption activity—from purchasing a magazine at a newsstand to buying a home video and sound system—can be described as a goal-directed activity. We are not conscious of all the processes that go on when we make consumption decisions or when we watch others do so, but research demonstrates that they indeed do occur.

It is useful to conceive of decision making in two broad senses. Some decisions are made with the certainty that they will be carried out and that no internal impediments (e.g., lack of will power or unconscious habits) or external impediments (e.g., changing economic conditions or likely competitive responses) will occur. A few everyday decisions fit these types of decisions, such as deciding to replenish one's toothpaste or to pick up one's dry cleaning after work or school. Other decisions, however, are regarded by a decision maker as more or less problematic as to their outcome or success. In such cases, the decision maker approaches the task as one of *trying* to achieve a goal. Making decisions in which the outcome is problematic differs fundamentally from making decisions under certainty. Under the former, the decision maker takes into account the possibilities of success and failure, and action must be understood as a complex process of judgment, planning, striving, and personal control. The need for control is particularly pressing after one has made a decision to pursue a goal.

For nonproblematic contexts, once a decision to act has been made, the steps to act begin either immediately or after a delay, but proceed largely under their own momentum and in an automatic—even mindless—way. Buying a candy bar from a

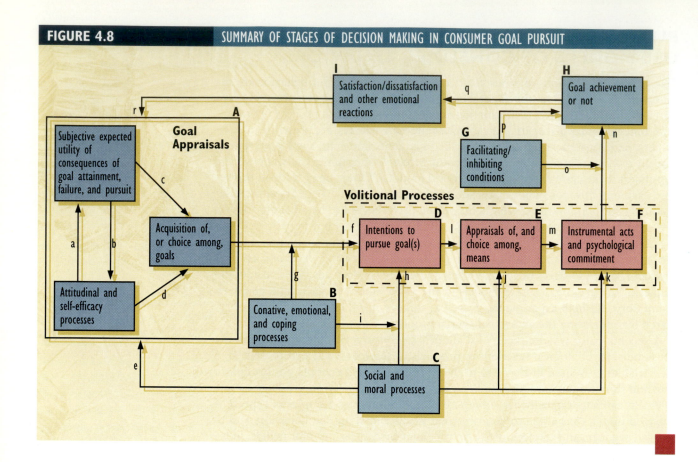

machine or vendor in response to pangs of hunger is an example. Self-regulation in nonproblematic situations does not come into play much unless an unexpected event intervenes to thwart consummation of an act. However, most consumption behaviors are problematic goals in the minds of decision makers, although people may not always be conscious of the processes.

An initial question to address in problematic goal situations is how goals arise in the first place. In general, three origins of goals can be identified. First, goals can be forced upon us, either through coercion or more subtly by virtue of our position in an organization, family, or other social unit, whereby we are obligated to work toward predefined ends. A newly hired brand manager is expected to strive for profitability or market share. The birth of a child opens up new imperatives for parents. Second, we often simply "have" a goal in the sense that it arises nonconsciously because of biological, emotional, moral, or normative forces. When we feel ill, our goal is to get better. When we experience an unexpected reward, we seek to share the good news; or with personal losses we search for support. We often accept moral duties without question. Socialization and enculturation also lead to the uncritical following of certain ends. Finally, we form goals, or at least consider them as possibilities, as a function of reasoned reactions to external stimuli (e.g., the presentation of a new product, an alluring package, a provocative advertisement, a persuasive appeal by a salesperson) or internal stimuli (e.g., a conclusion drawn at the end of problem solving or the mere thought that one has a need). Exposure to possible goals in these latter senses leads to evaluations of their personal relevance.

Being aware of and attracted by a goal are, of course, not sufficient impetuses for goal pursuit in most situations. Self-regulation is needed and begins with the processes shown in box A in Figure 4.8, which might be termed, broadly, goal appraisals. The first reactions one generally has to exposure to goal possibilities are appraisals of either (1) the consequences of goal attainment, failure, and pursuit, per se; or (2) the overall goal itself. The former entails judgments of the likelihoods of consequences and their personal relevance in a hedonic or utilitarian sense. These are commonly labeled expected-value or expectancy-value reactions. For instance, an advertisement for a new health club might lead to a judgment that the club is convenient, low priced, uncrowded, and contains the latest equipment, which for the particular perceiver are very attractive attributes. The latter involve global evaluations or emotional reactions to the overall goal object or action. They are sometimes referred to as preferences or attitudes. For example, a person deciding to join a health club might summarize his or her attitude by being "excited," or alternatively "turned-off," by the prospective of joining.

Notice that expectancy-value reactions and attitudes are hypothesized to be interdependent in a reciprocal causation sense (see paths a and b in Fig. 4.8). Marketers have usually assumed that the flow of causality is unidirectional, from expectancy-value reactions to attitudes (path a). This is implied, for example, in the well-known "attitude model":

$$A_{\text{act}} = \sum_{i=1}^{n} b_i e_i$$

where A_{act} is one's attitude toward a specific action, b_i is one's belief or assessment that the action will lead to consequence i, e_i is one's evaluation of affective response to consequence i, and n is the number of consequences one considers in a particular decision to act. Despite the logic of the $\Sigma b_i e_i \rightarrow A_{\text{act}}$ sequence, and despite the empirical findings that support it, it is possible in certain situations for feedback to occur such that beliefs and/or evaluations are affected by one's global attitudes (path b in Fig. 4.8). For example, people sometimes retrieve an existing attitude from memory or have a preference or prejudice toward a person, product, or action, and this, in turn, shapes or colors their later judgments about the attributes or properties of the person, product, or action. This is another example of the halo effect.

With respect to consideration of possible goals, it is important to stress that whether one acquires a goal, or alternatively the particular goal(s) one chooses, can be a function of either expectancy-value reactions (path c in Fig. 4.8), which are based on detailed assessments of the pros and cons of the goals, or attitudinal and self-efficacy processes (path d), which are based on overall, summary evaluations of the goals. Recent research shows that consumer choices are determined by a comparison of either expectancy-value judgments or attitudes, depending on the circumstance.[12] In any particular product or service context, marketers must ascertain what factors govern which process—molecular (path c) or molar (path d)—operates.

Intentions to pursue a goal (box D in Fig. 4.8) can thus be seen to depend on goal appraisals (path f). But such appraisals do not inevitably or automatically stimulate intentions. Rather, self-regulatory processes moderate the goal appraisal to intention relation (see box B and path g in Fig. 4.8). The self-regulatory processes encompass conative, emotional, and coping responses.[13] Intentions also are shown in Figure 4.8 to be influenced by social and moral forces (box C and path h). However, these too are modulated by the self-regulatory processes displayed in box B (see path i). Significantly, social and moral forces constrain goal appraisals (path e) and each of the three volitional stages shown in Figure 4.8 (paths h, j, and k).

The intention to pursue a goal can be thought of as a psychological mechanism translating the reasons for acting (which result from goal appraisals) into a decision or plan to act. Once a person forms an intention to pursue a goal, he or she is faced with the question of how to go about achieving it. Intentions to try to reach a goal thus lead (path l) to appraisals of, and choices among, means (box E). These, in turn, initiate (path m) instrumental acts and result in enhanced psychological commitment to goal pursuit (box F).

Whether efforts to pursue a goal will lead to achievement (box H) depends not only on the person (path n) but also on facilitating and inhibiting factors in the goal context (box G). Indeed, forces beyond one's control sometimes even produce goal attainment independent of our agency (path p), although the more common outcome is for external forces to retard or multiply our endeavors (path o).

Whether we achieve our goals, the outcomes (path q) have immediate psychological and delayed economic implications for us. The most common reactions are satisfaction or dissatisfaction, but we can identify other emotional and coping responses as well.[14] These reactions, summarized in box I in Figure 4.8, feed back (path r) upon perceived likelihoods and evaluations of the consequences of goal attainment, failure, and pursuit and upon attitudes and self-efficacy. To the extent that success or failure matches our desires, the conative, emotional, and coping processes noted in box B trigger self-regulatory activities, which determine whether we seek the same goal again (e.g., repeat purchase) or abandon it, whether we strive for a new goal (e.g., brand switching), or whether we suspend, temporarily at least, all consideration of goals (e.g., withdrawal from the market).

Each of the variables shown in Figure 4.8—or more likely the subsets of them—can be measured and used to predict consumption behaviors. Parts of the model have been tested in the prediction of the use of coupons in everyday supermarket shopping and in decision making with regard to exercising, dieting, and weight control.[15] The model has even been adapted to predict the behavior of industrial salespeople.[16]

CONTEXTUAL DETERMINANTS OF CONSUMPTION

The processes highlighted in Figure 4.3 do not occur in a vacuum. The impetus for consumption may sometimes originate internally as a function of cognitive processes and motivational forces, but more often than not the external context is the instigator. Of course, the meaning of the context is typically filtered through self-interpretive processes. Yet sometimes the mental processes are ineffable and the context seemingly influences our consumption responses in a direct way. In any case, we do need to understand the forces in the context of consumption. Indeed, marketers attempt to control, create, and anticipate naturally occurring forces.

What are the contextual elements of consumption? The most obvious one is the *environment*. By environment we mean the physical cues (e.g., brand names and logos, point-of-sale stimuli, competitive responses, background music), social cues (e.g., salespeople, peer pressure), temporal cues (e.g., holidays, hours of store opening), and regulatory cues (e.g., self- and other-rules that specify contingencies, institutional and government constraints).[17]

Let us look at some examples. When a consumer shops in the supermarket, many environmental forces shape that customer's actions.[18] Sellers have learned that something as subtle as the height of a product on the shelf affects sales. Research shows that 51 to 53 inches (1.30 to 1.35 meters) high is the optimum. At least this is often the height at which people first focus, and therefore products placed at or just above or below this level will have the best chances to be noticed.

One study showed that sales for toothbrushes increased 8 percent when displayed at eye level.

With so many brands of products available from which to choose, how should they be organized on the supermarket shelf? Sellers have found, for example, that placement by brand (e.g., Kellogg cereals in one group, General Mills cereals in another) works better than organization by type (e.g., oat, bran, corn, high sugar versus low). In one experiment, sales fell 5 percent when cereal was placed by type instead of by brand.[19] Likewise, music can have a profound effect. Sales increased by about 38 percent when the tempo of ambient music was slowed from 108 to 60 beats per second in one instance.[20]

Typically, the control of physical cues is done simply to take advantage of natural perceptual processes. Unconditioned responses to the brightness of light and color, loudness of sounds, strength of odors, pleasantness of tastes, and feel of tactile sensations are taken into account in the design of marketing stimuli. Here basic physiological urges become the target, such as the needs for food, water, comfort, or sex. This is carried a step further when marketers hook into our conditioned responses for particular foods, sexual content, aesthetic experiences, and even prejudices. Many of our everyday emotions—love, interpersonal attraction, happiness, joy, pride, anger, disgust, sadness, shame, and anxiety—are aroused through conditioned associations learned early in life. Leveraging conditioned responses have come to be known as classical conditioning, or Pavlovian learning. We only have to look at nudity in ads, violence in movies, or fear appeals by politicians to recognize the use of conditioned stimuli. Innate biological responses become transformed into consumption wants through years of socialization and repeated exposure to persuasive appeals and modeling activities in advertisements.

Yet another environmental force that shapes behavior is instrumental learning or operant conditioning (sometimes termed *Skinnerian learning* after one of its pioneering researchers, B. F. Skinner). Some of our behavior is guided by the consequences of our actions and not so much by the direct influence of stimuli, per se. We all have a tendency to act now and then in an unplanned, mindless way and to experience a reward or punishment after the fact. Researchers have found that, by the strategic application of such positive (or negative) reinforcers, people will have a tendency to perform (or refrain from performing) the same action again, compared to the case where no reinforcer was present. Of course, much of the reinforcement occurs in the formative years of life when one's habits and tastes are developing. Yet some reinforcement occurs throughout life, guiding our behavior. A good example of instrumental learning occurs in everyday consumption. After we make a purchase and consume a product, a coupon in a package, a follow-up call from a salesperson, or even praise from a friend or family member may serve as reinforcements, which enhance the likelihood that we will buy that product again.

We should stress that classical and operant conditioning are not the only determinants of consumption. The processes summarized in Figure 4.3 probably capture many of the important forces that mediate the effects of conditioning on behavior. Yet it is important to realize that not all consumption can be explained through the general information processing approach. Classical and operant conditioning offer practical—if not completely satisfactory—explanations of and suggestions for influencing consumption.

A second broad contextual variable that deserves mention is *culture*, which might be considered a special case or elaboration of environmental forces. By culture we mean the shared knowledge, values, beliefs, rules, laws, and customs of a group of people that lead them to act in distinctive ways. In a sense, culture bridges or integrates the environment with the people in or exposed to it. A culture can be huge, encompassing

The marketing of services in a modern economy can take unusual turns. Consider recent practices in Japan. It can be very expensive under any circumstances to put on a wedding, but economic stagnation in recent years has made cost cutting even more of a necessity.

Party rooms and catering at a hotel must be paid for. Friends and relatives incur travel, food, and lodging expenses, as well as lost income from their jobs to attend a wedding. What can be done to reduce the costs borne by all parties? Well, brides and grooms are increasingly turning to the services of "convenience agencies," who provide surrogate guests for weddings. This not only saves money but, equally important, it saves face in the sense that the newlyweds and their parents avoid looking cheap and guests who know the bride and groom go away believing that all is well in the social milieu in which the newlyweds function. People can avoid a similar loss of face at funerals, when enough guests are hired to create a public image that the deceased had many friends and relatives.

The role of the public self-image in Japan can be seen in still another service provided by convenience agencies. Japan is a society in which the elderly depend on their children for emotional support and general care. But the demands of work seemingly provide too little time for such pursuits, and as the population has increased and jobs and housing have become scarce, older parents and their working children have been forced to live far apart. These forces have made it difficult for children, especially sons, to visit their parents regularly. The solution? Surrogate sons are hired to check in on parents. This avoids public embarrassment for parents and sons and maintains the fiction that traditional responsibilities are being met by sons. Notice that the need for such services in Japan is driven more by social norms than personal values, per se. Shame plays a role in the use of such services in an interdependent-based culture. In the West, where independent-based cultures predominate, social pressures for such services are weaker and personal motives such as guilt take precedence. Both cultures obviously exhibit similar emotions of love binding child to parent, but they differ in the way that certain social emotions drive consumption.

nearly everyone in a particular country (e.g., Japanese; see Marketing Anecdote 4.2). Or it can represent a relatively small group of people within or across geographical areas (e.g., the Cantonese ethnic community in San Francisco, California). Consumption practices typically vary dramatically from one culture to another.

Specifically, culture functions in one of two ways to influence consumption. First, culture can have a direct effect on behavior. Researchers term this a main effect. For example, in many interdependent or group-based cultures, such as China and Korea, decisions are made not so much as a function of personal desires or attitudes as they are determined by a need to fit in with one's group (e.g., family, clan, work group, friendship group) or express one's solidarity with the group or one's larger membership in a group category or country. In such societies, consumption choices are frequently made in a way so as not to be different or stand out from others. Thus people tend to watch what others in their group do before acting, and brand loyalty tends to be high.[21]

Contrast the above with some independent cultures, such as Italy and Canada, where consumers make a special effort to purchase goods that are conspicuous in their distinctiveness and that express one's uniqueness and individuality. Whereas the choice in the interdependent culture is more a function of group norms or expectations, which have an effect relatively independent from personal tastes, the choice in an independent-based culture is more a result of individual, as opposed to shared, preferences. Culture in the former case often "swamps" or overrides individual factors in decision making. Culture in the latter tends to be a parallel force along with individual tastes or desires, and in a sense is traded-off with them in any particular consumption context.

A second way that culture works is to condition or temper the effects of personal factors on consumption. Researchers term this a moderating effect. Many consumption decisions are determined by judgments consumers make and motives they have, no matter what their culture. But the relative influence of beliefs, attitudes, personal needs, and so forth will vary across cultures. That is, culture can be thought to regulate how, when, and to what degree individual characteristics, desires, attitudes, and so forth influence consumption.

Consider the role of brands in consumer decision making. Even within Europe, a relatively independent-based culture, differences exist between countries on how much credence is placed on brand names as guarantors of quality. Fully 77 percent of Spaniards believe that brand names are a good basis for judging product quality, whereas only 43 percent of Dutch people believe so.[22]

A final contextual force is *individual difference variables.* For example, level of *expertise* has been found to influence how people process information about the attributes of products. Research shows that experts tend to examine and integrate many individual attributes, whereas novices look at things in global, stereotype-like senses when making product decisions.[23] The former is an instance of piecemeal-based processing, whereas the latter represents category-based processing. This finding has been demonstrated with regard to the purchase of cameras, and likely applies to a wide range of products that have at least a moderate degree of complexity or personal relevance.

More generally, *personality* operates to influence consumption in a variety of ways. By personality we mean unique aspects of the way a person interprets his or her own self and interacts with others. As compared to situational forces and one's responses to them, which vary from time to time and place to place, personality is relatively stable and enduring. Moreover, we think of personality as determined by characteristics or processes within the person. Despite being idiosyncratic to any one individual person, however, personality tends to exist or be expressed through a relatively small number of categories or patterns, when we look across people. This makes the marketer's task easier when searching for and summarizing personality constraints on consumption behavior.

Recent research has found a number of personality variables that influence consumption. People differ in their attention to social comparison information (ATSCI). Research shows that some people have a predisposition to act more than others in response to how they perceive the expectations or evaluations of people around them. People scoring high on the trait of ATSCI have been found to consume particular products as a consequence of social cues more than those scoring low on ATSCI.[24]

Action versus state orientation also affects consumer behavior. An action-oriented person is one who tends to enact behavior under high self-regulatory control. Such a person has a firm grasp of his or her own attitudes and behaves without excessive deliberation. The state-oriented person tends to be low in self-regulatory control and in the extreme deliberates in an obsessive or dysfunctional way; deliberation focuses more on identifying what others expect one to do and acting accordingly than on what one's own attitudes are. When a person acts on the basis of his or her attitudes (i.e., under action control), the response is automatic, or at least faster than action under deliberative control (i.e., under state orientation). The influence of action versus state orientation has been shown in a study of the determinants of coupon usage. Researchers found that coupon usage is driven by attitudes toward coupons for those high in action control and by subjective normative pressure (i.e., peer pressure) for those high in state control.[25]

An important personality variable that captures differences in decision-making styles, particularly for interdependent- versus independent-based cultures, is self-consciousness. Self-consciousness comprises three parts: private self-consciousness, public self-consciousness, and social anxiety. People from interdependent-based cultures tend to score high on social anxiety (i.e., shame associated with violation of others' expectations is felt strongly), whereas people in independent-based cultures score high in private self-consciousness. Surprisingly, both cultures score equally high on public self-consciousness.[26] The latter finding is a consequence of different motivations toward others. Those in interdependent-based cultures attune themselves to others and maintain a public self so as to coordinate actions with them and generally fit in. Those in independent-based cultures see maintenance of the public self as a means to express one's individuality.

Still another individual difference variable is the level of effort required to perform an action or achieve a goal. By effort, we mean the amount of mental energy (e.g., detailed planning) and physical energy needed to acquire a product or service. When effort required is great, attitudes influence intentions and intentions affect behavior. In other words, behavior is guided by volitions. When effort required is low, attitudes directly influence behavior and volitions play no or a limited role. In essence, affect or emotions initiate actions.[27]

Consumer researchers have been giving increasing emphasis to the study of personality and individual difference variables in recent years. In addition to those previously mentioned, some of the variables under study are self-monitoring, self-esteem, need for cognition, and need for evaluation. Rather than main effects, these variables seem to function most powerfully as moderators of particular stages in decision making.

SUMMARY

This chapter describes the psychological and contextual processes that govern consumption. Consumption can be thought of as a stimulus → organism → response process. In this chapter, we especially emphasize the "organism" by focusing on the psychological mechanisms shaping consumer behavior.

Most acts of consumption fall under one of three categories: *impulse buying, habitual purchase behavior,* or *consumption problem solving.*

- Impulse buying generally occurs because an external (e.g., advertisement) or internal (e.g., deprivation) stimulus has caught the consumer's attention, and the product is easy to acquire. Very little thought occurs; rather, emotional or motivational processes are primarily at work. These, however, may occur below the level of self-awareness.

- Under habitual purchase behavior, prior learning is crucial. Although needs usually initiate the purchase in such instances, cognitive processes predominate and include the execution of action sequences and the evaluation of limited decision criteria.

- Consumption problem solving involves extensive search, processing of information, and integration with one's needs. Cognitive processes and affective responses play important roles in consumption problem solving.

The central variables in the stimulus-organism-response model are perceptual processes, internal and external stimuli, arousal, information processing (e.g., abstraction, schema formation, integration, and evaluation), affect and goal setting, volition, and behavior.

An important aspect of consumption that has only recently been studied is the process that goes on between the point in time when a decision has been made and a behavior is finally performed. This process involves volition and goal pursuit. Once a decision has been made to acquire a product, a series of steps must be performed to achieve this goal. Various means to the end are considered, and one or more are chosen. Plans are made, means initiated, and progress en route monitored. Obstacles must be overcome, temptations resisted, and motivation maintained. Goal attainment or failure is determined by these self-regulatory efforts in conjunction with facilitating or inhibiting forces in the environment. The goal-pursuit process "ends" with satisfaction or dissatisfaction and other emotions feeding back upon the decision-making process.

Various contextual forces shape consumption. Physical and other cues from the environment are important factors in this regard. The personality of the consumer is another variable influencing decision making. Finally, culture provides subtle input to any consumption decision.

QUESTIONS FOR DISCUSSION

1. Three key components of the general stimulus-organism-response model of consumer behavior (Fig. 4.3) are (a) perceptual and sensing processes, (b) information processing, and (c) the control unit (i.e., affect and goals). Briefly describe the parts and functions of these components.

2. How do decision rules operate in consumer information processing and choice?

3. Three broad classes of consumption include impulse buying, habitual purchase behavior, and consumption problem solving. Compare and contrast these and give an example of each.

4. Describe the process you went through for your last decision to go to the cinema. Do the same for your last purchase of an expensive product.

5. What are volitions? Discuss the various processes that make up volitional decision making.

6. Pick a consumption goal that you recently had or now have. Describe what the goal is, why you have it, and how it arose. How did you decide to achieve the goal? What means did you consider; which one(s) did you choose? Why? Which of the processes outlined in Figure 4.8 came into play? Describe these. How did you feel after you achieved the goal or failed to achieve it? What did you do after you achieved or failed to achieve the goal?

7. What is culture? How does it influence consumption? Give an example of cultural influences on consumption in your country or ethnic group and in another country or ethnic group.

8. Personality influences consumption. Find a print advertisement that tries to take advantage of or influence personality responses. Describe the personality addressed, what is going on in the ad, and what the marketer's assumptions and goals seem to be.

NOTES FOR FURTHER READING

1. John R. Anderson, *The Architecture of Cognition* (Cambridge, Mass.: Harvard University Press, 1983).

2. Richard P. Bagozzi and Pratibha A. Dabholkar, "Structure and Function of Political Person Perceptions: The Public's View of President Clinton," Unpublished manuscript, The University of Michigan. 1997.

3. Valerie S. Folkes and Tina Kiesler, "Social Cognition: Consumers' Inferences about the Self and Others," in Thomas S. Robertson and Harold H. Kassarjian, eds., *Handbook of Consumer Behavior* (Upper Saddle River, N.J.: Prentice-Hall, 1991), pp. 281–315; Susan T. Fiske and Shelley E. Taylor, *Social Cognition*, 2nd ed. (New York: McGraw-Hill, 1991).

4. Susan T. Fiske, Richard R. Lau, and Richard A. Smith, "On the Varieties and Utilities of Political Expertise," *Social Cognition* 8,1 (1990): 31–48; Mita Sujan, "Consumer Knowledge: Effects on Evaluation Strategies Mediating Consumer Judgments," *Journal of Consumer Research* 12 (June 1985): 31–46.

5. James R. Bettman, *An Information Processing Theory of Consumer Choice* (Reading, Mass.: Addison-Wesley, 1979), pp. 176–203. Bettman terms these decision rules, "heuristics," and discusses their measurement and limitations. See also James R. Bettman, Eric J. Johnson, and John W. Payne, "Consumer Decision Making," in Robertson and Kassarjian, *Handbook of Consumer Behavior*, pp. 50–84.

6. Sometimes theorists maintain that a desire is required for action. See Richard P. Bagozzi, "The Self-Regulation of Attitudes, Intentions, and Behavior," *Social Psychology Quarterly* 55 (1992): 178–204.

7. Richard P. Bagozzi, "The Role of Arousal in the Creation and Control of the Halo Effect in Attitude Models," *Psychology & Marketing* 13 (1996): 235–264.

8. Richard S. Lazarus. *Emotion and Adaptation* (New York: Oxford University Press, 1991).

9. Ira J. Roseman. "Appraisal Determinants of Discrete Emotions," *Cognition and Emotion* 5,3 (1991): 161–200.

10. Nico H. Frijda, Peter Kuipers, and Elisabeth ter Schure, "Relations Among Emotion, Appraisal, and Emotional Action Readiness," *Journal of Personality and Social Psychology* 57,2 (1989): 212–228.

11. See Richard P. Bagozzi, "The Role of Emotion and Volition in the Regulation of Economic Behavior," in Lennart Sjöberg, Richard P. Bagozzi, and David Ingvar, eds., *Will and Economic Behavior* (Stockholm: Economic Research Institute, 1996).

12. Pratibha Dabholkar, "Introducing Choice Criteria into Attitude Models: A Comparative Analysis," *Journal of Consumer Research* 20 (1994): 100–118.

13. Bagozzi, "Self-Regulation of Attitudes, Intentions, and Behavior."

14. Ibid.

15. Richard P. Bagozzi, Hans Baumgartner, and Youjae Yi, "Appraisal Processes in the Enactment of Intentions to Use Coupons," *Psychology of Marketing* 9 (November/December 1992): 469–486; Richard P. Bagozzi, Hans Baumgartner, and Youjae Yi, "State Versus Action Orientation and the Theory of Reasoned Action: An Application to Coupon Usage," *Journal of Consumer Research* 18 (March 1992): 505–518; Richard P. Bagozzi and Elizabeth A. Edwards, "Goal Setting and Goal Pursuit in the Regulation of Body Weight," *Psychology & Health* n.d.; Richard P. Bagozzi, Hans Baumgartner, and Rick Pieters, "Goal-directed Emotions," *Cognition & Emotions*, 1997, 11.

16. Stephen P. Brown, W. L. Cron, and J. W. Slocum, Jr., "Effects of Goal-directed Emotions on Salesperson Volitions, Behavior, and Performance: A Longitudinal Study," *Journal of Marketing* 61 (1997).

17. Gordon R. Foxall, *Consumer in Context: The BPM Research Program* (London: Routledge, 1996); Gordon R. Foxall, *Consumer Choice and Marketing Response* (London: Macmillan, 1997).

18. Jack Hitt, "The Theory of Supermarkets," *New York Times Magazine*, March 10, 1996, pp. 56–61, 94, 98.

19. Ibid.

20. Ibid.

21. Chris Robinson, "Asian Culture: The Marketing Consequences," *Journal of the Market Research Society* 38,1 (1996): 55–62.

22. Henley Centre/Research International, 1991/2, cited in Marieke de Mooij, *Advertising Worldwide*, 2nd ed. (New York: Prentice-Hall, 1994), p. 93.

23. Sujan, "Consumer Knowledge."

24. William O. Bearden and Randall L. Rose, "Attention to Social Comparison Information: An Individual Difference Factor Affecting Consumer Conformity," *Journal of Consumer Research* 16 (March 1990): 461–471.

25. Bagozzi, Baumgartner, and Yi, "State Versus Action Orientation." See also Bagozzi, Baumgartner, and Yi, "Appraisal Processes."

26. Shuzo Abe, Richard P. Bagozzi, and Pradip Sadarangani, "An Investigation of Construct Validity and Generalizability of the Self-concept: Self-consciousness in Japan and the United States," *Journal of International Consumer Marketing* 9 (1996).

27. Richard P. Bagozzi, Youjae Yi, and Johann Baumgartner, "The Level of Effort Required for Behaviour as a Moderator of the Attitude-Behaviour Relation," *European Journal of Social Psychology* 20 (1990): 45–59. Richard P. Bagozzi and Youjae Yi, "The Degree of Intention Formation as a Moderator of the Attitude-Behavior Relation," *Social Psychology Quarterly* 52 (December 1989): 266–279.

CHAPTER 5

MARKET SEGMENTATION, ANALYSIS, TARGETING, AND POSITIONING

CHAPTER OBJECTIVES

When you are done with this chapter, you should have achieved the following:

- A recognition of the difference between mass marketing and individualized marketing.
- A basic understanding of the principles of market segmentation, targeting, and positioning.
- A basic understanding of the broad uses of marketing research, the marketing research process, and characteristics of good research.
- Familiarity with how firms use research to analyze markets into segments and position their products.

CHAPTER OUTLINE

"Just Say[ing] No" Is Not Enough!

The Partnership for a Drug-Free America (PDFA) opened shop with seed money from the American Association of Advertising Agencies in 1986 at a time when illegal drug use was widespread in the United States and national concern about the drug problem was high. A mammoth coalition of social entrepreneurs, PDFA successfully developed, through the voluntary efforts of individuals, ad agencies, public relations firms, media organizations, and production companies, one of the largest public service ad campaigns in history in an attempt to reduce demand for illegal drugs. The premise: A social marketing program using professional selling and marketing communications techniques aimed at changing individual and social attitudes about the risks and benefits of drug use would lead to lasting changes in drug consumption behavior.

PDFA faced a twofold marketing challenge. First, the only data available were government drug usage studies. The kind of data needed for designing an effective marketing campaign just did not exist. To his amazement, Tom Hedrick, an experienced advertising account manager who had signed up with PDFA, found that he could learn more about Wrigley's chewing gum in a day than he could about the drug problem in a year.

Second, the Partnership had to decide between a single, focused theme, such as the Reagan administration's antidrug slogan, "Just Say No," and a multifocus campaign. Identifying a versatile slogan for the former, which would involve variations of that single slogan for all markets (such as Kids, Just Say No to the drug pusher, Parents, help your children to Just Say No, and so forth), would be a challenge. It would, however, be simpler to explain to volunteers and to execute, and have the benefit of potentially large impact. The diversified campaign would, on the other hand, lend itself to greater creative freedom, a message tailored to the dominant concerns of each target group, and a better fit with each media outlet. The decision would be informed by the research results, specifically the number of diverse market segments, and the number that PDFA would target.

After examining all available data, PDFA conducted more than 400 hours of focus groups to understand how people—ex-addicts who worked as informants, addicts, pushers, kids, experts—felt about drugs. This qualitative research was complemented by an annual survey of drug-use–related attitudes, the Partnership Attitude Tracking Survey (PATS), designed with the voluntary assistance of the research firm Gordon S. Black Corporation. Administered nationally through volunteer field service organizations, the objective was to obtain periodic cross-sectional data from a representative national sample on drug use during the previ-

The PDFA employs many marketing research techniques to reach its target audiences—in this case, parents and grandparents of school-age children.

ous 12 months and likely use over the next 12 months, as well as a host of questions on attitudes, beliefs, risks, benefits, peers, availability, and reasons for not using drugs. Continuous qualitative research in all settings where drugs were exchanged and used or drug education conducted supplemented Black's formal research to obtain a deep understanding of the strongest social and emotional aspects underlying drug-related attitudes and usage.

PDFA decided that a diversified communications strategy was most appropriate, given that there "were just too many different groups of people using drugs for too many different sets of reasons and too many different sets of attitudes." They segmented the illegal drug market by drug usage into addicts, heavy users, occasional users, and nonusers. Research suggested that the aggregate market be segmented into primary targets and influencers. The primary target was further segmented using age, and included preteens, 12- to 17-year-olds, 18- to 25-year-olds, and 26- to 34-year-olds. PDFA further segmented influencers according to their strength of influence into parents, peer groups, top managers, and health-care professionals. Other segmentation criteria included gender and type of drug (marijuana, cocaine, crack).

PDFA's segmentation scheme evolved over time. Sequential waves of consumer research suggested that narrower segments be defined using age, race and geography. Thus, PDFA identified inner cities as critical segments and targeted them with a campaign in 1992. This was done not only for the primary targets, but also for the influencers. For example, one segment of influencers—parents—were subsegmented into parents of 6- to 8-year-olds, parents of preteens, and parents of teenagers, because the key issues each group faced were different, warranting distinctive advertising messages and media.

Consistent with their objective of achieving maximum impact through mass media, PDFA decided to focus on prevention rather than intervention. So they excluded addicts and heavy users from their targets. Also consistent with this objective, younger segments were regarded as priority targets.

The results: In less than a year, 30 television, 64 print media, and 14 radio messages targeted at various segments had been produced for PDFA. The three television networks—ABC, CBS, and NBC—13 cable networks, 13 radio networks, and various print media had donated space. Their visibility earned PDFA the 18th rank among the 25 most popular TV ads in 1987. As of 1992, PDFA had generated $1.5 billion in total donated media placements or about $360 million per year, and more than $50 million worth of creative production. As a brand, PDFA had five times Coca-Cola's advertising support and ranked second only to McDonald's.

Sources: Jon Berry, "Against All Odds," *Brandweek*, September 28, 1992, pp. 16–21.

Cynthia Cotts, "Condoning the Legal Stuff? Hard Sell in the Drug War," *Nation*, March 9, 1992, pp. 300–303.

Joshua Levine, "Don't Fry Your Brain," *Forbes*, February 4, 1991, pp. 116–117.

Diana Chapman Walsh, Barbara Moeykens, and Rima Rudd, "The Partnership for a Drug-Free America (A)," Harvard Business School Case 9-594-028, 1993.

Sandra A. Waddock and James E. Post, "Catalytic Alliances for Social Problem Solving," *Human Relations*, 48, August 1995: 951–973.

FROM MASS TO INDIVIDUALIZED MARKETING

Mass Marketing

As the PDFA story illustrates, marketers often need to abandon a broad brush approach to their markets in favor of marketing programs that are finely tuned to the needs of individual market segments. In the *mass marketing* approach, a single product is mass produced and sold using a single marketing approach to the whole market or "to all who we can persuade to buy it."

The organization may leverage the lower costs of this "one size fits all" approach—derived from economies of scale at every stage of the process—into higher margins or lower prices. However, the starting point for this approach is generally the product or production process and the underlying, somewhat naïve, assumption that all buyers have similar wants, motivations, and preferences. Mass marketers are prone to getting caught in a market-share mentality where they view customers as a means of gaining share. Thus, they may fail to pay sufficient attention to actual consumer differences in the market.

Emerging Market Realities and Individualized Marketing

The reality is that most markets have changed so that

> economies of scale will never again be as important as they are today. Having the size necessary to produce, advertise, and distribute vast quantities of standardized products won't be a precondition for success. Instead, products will be increasingly tailored to individual tastes, electronic media will be inexpensively addressed to individual consumers, and many products ordered over the phone will be delivered to the home in eight hours or less.[1]

Remember the all-black instrument that Bell Telephone (and many national telephone monopolies worldwide) placed in so many homes in the early twentieth century? It is almost a part of history, with telephones now available in a maddening variety of colors, shapes, sizes, and combinations of functions! Recall (if you can) a world in which you had to make a trip to the local store to buy everything you needed (except perhaps your milk and newspaper, which were delivered to your doorstep). Today, not only do you have a multitude of product choices, but you can buy almost anything via a channel of your choice, even without leaving your home.

There are two major driving forces behind this trend away from mass marketing. The first is technology. The proliferation of marketing channels made possible by technological advances allows customers to express their choice of preferred channel. Technology has simultaneously made it possible for organizations to customize marketing offerings down to the level of the individual customer—mass customization—and to collect and manage the information required to do so—database marketing.[2] For example, the National Bicycle Industrial Company in Kokubu, Japan, can deliver a made-to-order bicycle, off an assembly line within two weeks, at a price only 10 percent higher than ready-made models. In order to cater to different customer preferences for waiting and delivery, most mail-order companies accept mailed, telephoned (toll-free), and faxed orders, and offer regular mail and overnight delivery options. Pottery Barn customers, who opt for the in-home, white-glove delivery option for large furniture, get services such as unpacking, inspection, and setup. Increasingly, such companies are offering fax response numbers to rapidly communicate additional information on any item featured in their catalogs to customers who would rather not wait for a service representative.

The second force is a paradigm shift in the way many organizations conceive of their markets. From merely chasing market share by increasing their customer base, many organizations now are attempting to increase share by building deeper relationships with customers in order to secure a greater share of each customer's business. This emphasis on relationship marketing is reflected in many aspects of organizations' marketing: dialogues between marketer and customer, designated account managers for each customer or customer group, frequency marketing programs, and brand-loyalty programs.

New parents across the United States receive offers to become customers for reusable, cloth diaper services. These services deliver a preferred number of hygienic, clean diapers each week, with larger sizes as your infant grows, to your doorstep, with a pick up of soiled diapers at the same time. In addition, they provide an entire system to conveniently and odorlessly store used diapers. Airlines have long offered frequent flier programs to reward their loyal customers. At the same time, they collect information on these customers, and attempt to increase their share of these customers' lifetime air travel expenditures. Companies in many industries—greeting cards, food retailing, automobile servicing, cafés and restaurants—have their own customer loyalty programs fashioned after the airlines' programs, offering membership cards (which allow them to track customer purchase patterns), cumulative volume purchase incentives, and information (such as reminders on important occasions when customers might purchase their products and services, and new product announcements).

THREE BUILDING BLOCKS OF MARKETING

Mass marketing and individualized marketing are at two ends of the marketing strategy spectrum. The former is efficient; the latter can be very expensive because the marketing approach is developed and executed for each customer. With the dual objectives of achieving customer satisfaction and achieving competitive advantage in mind, marketing managers search for efficient and effective ways to execute their programs. Consumer heterogeneity—differences in consumers' attitudes, beliefs, motivations, and purchase and usage patterns—makes this a challenging task.

Managers therefore attempt to *segment* the market, that is, to identify groups of consumers that are internally homogeneous, but distinct from each other. Very small groups of customers identified through the segmentation process are called niche markets. Managers then select one or more market segments and niches to *target* with their marketing programs. For each target market, they need to make decisions on how to *position* their products in order to differentiate themselves from the competition and to create a unique spot in customers' minds. Figure 5.1 describes the process of segmentation, targeting, and positioning (STP).

The implicit goal of all STP is to improve marketing performance over what it would be without this process. Thus, an organization may aim to use STP to increase customer satisfaction, competitive differentiation, and/or profitability. The STP process offers additional benefits when used properly. It greatly increases marketers' ability to develop a thorough understanding of the needs of their well-defined customer segments, and it improves their ability to respond to changing segment needs. Marketing efficiency is improved as resources are targeted at segments that offer the most potential for the organization. Because the marketing program is better matched with segment requirements, effectiveness of the marketing

0. Market Definition
1. Define market.

I. Segmentation
1. Group consumers/markets/organizations into internally homogeneous clusters according to the basis selected (e.g., attitudes, purchase propensities, usage, media habits, etc.).
2. Describe/profile segment characteristics.

II. Targeting
1. Evaluate segments according to normative criteria such as organizational goals and resources, and the environmental and competitive forces.
2. Rank all segments according to fit with these criteria.
3. Select one or more segments to target.

III. Positioning
1. Identify positioning alternatives for each segment, given consumer needs and competitor's positions.
2. Select desirable positioning in the context of overall organizational goals.

IV. Design and Implement Marketing Program
1. Design all elements of the marketing program consistent with the positioning strategy.
2. Implement marketing program.

approach is enhanced. Specifically, STP analyses help marketing managers design a product line to meet market demand, determine advertising messages that will have most appeal, select media that will have maximum impact for each segment, and time product and advertising launches to capitalize on market responsiveness.[3]

Prior to conducting STP analyses, managers should define the purpose and scope of segmentation, including their marketing objectives, whether the purpose is to explore new segments or better serve existing ones, whether existing data will be used or money will be invested in market research, and the level of detail they need from the STP exercise. These choices help focus the segmentation effort on the most important issues for the organization. For example, when the purpose is to better serve current segments, researchers need to pay greater attention to profiling these segments. On the other hand, if the purpose is to identify new segments, researchers will pay greater attention to grouping customers, identifying the number of segments, and profiling new segments.

Segmentation

Market *segmentation* is the classification of consumers and markets into groups on the basis of one or more of their characteristics. Managers generally use the term to refer to the grouping of consumers with similar needs, but also occasionally to describe the classification of products into homogeneous groups.[4] Thus, segmentation is the descriptive process managers use to discover the distribution of consumers in the market, the number of consumer segments, and segment characteristics. Simply, it is the art and science of identifying distinctive groups that exhibit relatively homogeneous needs.

The purpose of market segmentation is to identify critical dimensions along which consumers vary, and to provide firms with profiles of the identified group(s). Coupled with an understanding of organizational goals and resources, as well as competitive analysis, managers may use this information to select the market segment(s) in which the firm wishes to compete, and to design appropriate marketing program(s).

Market Definition: An Essential Precursor to Segmentation[5]

Market definition is critical because it is the starting point for all marketing strategy formulation, including estimation of market size and growth rates, as well as market segmentation. Good market segmentation is contingent on precise market definition, which helps the organization exclude groups that would not use their product, regardless of the benefits it offers. A market is a group of consumers that want a product or service, and have the ability, income, and authority to buy it. Broad market definition stems from the organization's overall mission. The mission of PDFA was to prevent drug use, so its broad market definition excluded drug addicts. Firms and strategic business units often compete in more than one market, so managers must conduct the STP process for each market.

Defining markets is challenging because the market may range from a single buyer to billions of buyers, concentrated or spread out worldwide. When there is more than one buyer for a product, it is unlikely that buyers will have identical needs. Managers may use a number of different approaches, depending on the theoretical perspective and the purpose of the market definition exercise, but no clear-cut normative criteria exist for selecting a particular approach for market definition. In general, the market definition process attempts to balance *focus* (so that the served market needs are met well) with *breadth* (to ensure that the analysis identifies both competitive threats and new product opportunities).

In practice, organizations define markets using one or more of four dimensions: products, types of customers, geography, and stages in the production-distribution system.

- *Products*. Firms may choose a broad or narrow market definition. For example, wood furniture manufacturers may define their market narrowly to include only wood furniture, more broadly to include wood and particle board furniture, or even more broadly to include all furniture. Further, the definition may be based on product functions and uses, and/or on technology. When using products as the basis for market definition, an organization must recognize that, as a result of historical and cumulative marketing efforts, consumers may have well-developed perceptions of the functionality and substitutability of technology. Managers must pay attention to these perceptions as well as actual, physical criteria when defining their markets. Thus, conventional wood furniture may not have the same functionality as rattan or tubular steel furniture, which are also based on different manufacturing technology (so the wood furniture manufacturer may exclude the latter from their defined market). When products are used as the basis for market definition, marketers have to be mindful of the basic needs they are satisfying so as not to fall prey to marketing myopia, discussed in chapter 2.[6] Myopic market definitions result in underestimating the threat from new substitutes and technologies that meet the same consumer needs.

- *Types of customers*. Organizations may define their markets by type of customer. Furniture manufacturers may define their markets according to whether they cater to consumer or business furnishing needs. They may define their business markets using industries such as restaurants, architects, builders [based on the Standard Industrial Classification (SIC) code]. They may also define their markets according to the class of customer served—end-user, retailers (or retailer subcategory), builders, and so forth.

- *Geography.* Organizations such as restaurants and gasoline stations (service industries), or small produce growers and egg farmers (perishable products), may compete only in limited geographic areas. Such organizations often define their markets using a geographic basis.

- *Stages in the production-distribution system.* Raw material producers (e.g., mango growers, aluminum manufacturers) may limit their market to downstream manufacturers who add value, or they may also choose to add value themselves (e.g., manufacture canned mango pulp, aluminum cans). When they produce raw materials as well as add value, they need to define their markets to include two levels in the value chain, because they compete not only in the intermediate market, but also in the final market. Indian tea estates historically defined their market as the corporations and foreign government buyers to whom they sold bulk tea. Increasingly, these tea estates are packaging and branding their tea in order to capture additional revenue from the sales of such value-added tea. Thus, they have extended their market definition to include tea drinkers directly.

Segmentation Bases: Consumer and Organizational Markets

Once marketers have defined their markets in broad terms, they should identify the variables they will use to group buyers within these markets into segments. They may need to use more than one variable to arrive at segments for whom it is meaningful to differentiate their offering. The best variables for segmenting a market are those that predict purchase and use probabilities for the product concerned. Usually marketers depend on one or two variables for segmenting their market, and the remaining variables are used to build comprehensive descriptions of the derived segments.

Industries and companies differ in terms of segmentation sophistication. Consumer goods companies have long used segmentation as an intrinsic part of their marketing strategy formulation. As their markets mature, consumer goods manufacturers look for new opportunities for differentiation, which require continuous market segmentation looking for niches and even microniches—narrow segments that they may serve with precisely differentiated and customized products and/or communications. Similarly, performance chemical manufacturers segment their customers very precisely based on specific applications. In contrast, many industrial companies segment simply by customer size or do not segment at all, as we discuss in chapter 6. Or they may segment their markets once, and fail to reevaluate whether their bases of segmentation are still valid as their markets mature.

Broadly speaking, the major bases for segmenting consumer and organizational markets are similar: demographic, geographic, psychographic, and behavioral variables. The first three categories reflect consumer *background characteristics*; the last category reflects *market history*, or consumer behavior in the product category. There are differences both in the common terms used by consumer and business marketers to label these variables and in the actual variables that are used. We will therefore discuss the segmentation variables for these two broad markets sequentially.

Segmenting Consumer Markets. Table 5.1 provides a listing of common variables used for segmenting consumer markets. *Demographic segmentation* uses one or more population characteristics to distinguish consumer groups. Demographics are

TABLE 5.1 COMMON VARIABLES FOR SEGMENTING CONSUMER MARKETS

Segmentation Variable	Example
DEMOGRAPHIC	
Population size	Less than 20,000; 20,000–99,999; 100,000–249,999; More than 250,000
Age	Under 18; 18–22; 23–30; 31–35; 36–44; 45–54; Over 55
Gender	Female; Male
Marital status	Never married; Married; Separated; Divorced; Widowed
Household size	1; 2; 3–4; More than 4
Monthly income	Less than $1,000; $1,000–2,499; $2,500–4,999; More than $5,000
Occupation	Unemployed; Full-time job; Student; Retired
Education	High school graduate; College graduate; Professional degree
Religion	None; Catholic; Hindu; Jewish; Moslem; Protestant
Race	Asian American; Other
Nationality	People's Republic of China; Taiwan; Singapore; Malaysia
Property ownership	Renter; Condominium owner; Single-family home owner
GEOGRAPHIC	
Country	Canada; Mexico; United States
Region	New England; Mid-Atlantic; Central; Southeast; Southwest; West; Pacific Northwest
State	California; Nevada; Arizona
County	Los Angeles; Orange; San Bernadino; Ventura
City, metropolitan area	Costa Mesa; Irvine; Laguna Niguel; Newport Beach
Neighborhood	University housing; Other
Climate	Tropical; Subtropical; Temperate
PSYCHOGRAPHIC	
Lifestyles	Attitudes: Conservative; Liberal
	Activities and Interests
	Opinions toward work, leisure, consumption
Personality	Introvert; Extrovert
Motivation or need level	Orientation toward safety, family, self-esteem, self-actualization
BEHAVIORAL	
User status	Nonuser, never tried; Nonuser, tried;
	Current first-time user; Current regular user
Buyer readiness stage	Unaware; Informed—aware, with trial intention;
	Interested—aware, with no intention to try;
	Trial, no repeat; Trial, repeat occasionally; Trial, repeat frequently
Usage rate	Light; Moderate; Heavy
Loyalty status	Switcher, random; Switcher, variety-seeker;
	Brand loyal; Producer loyal; Store loyal
Benefit sought	Economy; Performance; Service; Prestige

popular bases of segmentation because these data are standard and readily available. Further, marketers may believe that consumer preferences and behaviors are highly correlated with demographic variables. For example, higher income groups are more likely to be interested in luxury automobiles and expensive vacations, consistent with Maslow's hierarchy. In developing countries, income-based segmentation is useful because consumer demand follows a predictable pattern. As incomes rise, demand for—and pattern of purchase of—luxury goods varies with percentage spending on basic needs, and income elasticity of demand is high. Similarly, international marketers may use population age distributions and family size to assess demand in countries. Spending patterns are different for countries with large youthful populations versus countries with large aging populations, or those with a large number of small, nuclear families versus those with many large, joint families.

Even where demographic variables are not used to group customers, they are inevitably used to describe segments derived using other variables. This profiling helps marketers make many decisions, such as selecting the media, advertising spokespeople, and salespeople that are most likely to impact targeted segments.

Despite the relative ease of using demographic variables, they offer no *direct* information about consumer motivations and preferences. In the mid-1960s, marketing research pioneer Daniel Yankelovich likened using demographic data alone for segmentation to trying to win a national election by relying purely on census data. Census data—like demographic data—do not identify crucial issues, habits, attitudes, and values that drive decision making.[7] With reference to multibrand companies such as American Tobacco, Procter & Gamble, and General Motors, Yankelovich pointed to the need for nondemographic bases of segmentation:

> These companies sell to the whole market, not by offering one brand that appeals to all people, but by covering the different segments with multiple brands. How can they prevent these brands from cannibalizing each other? How can they avoid surrendering opportunities to competitors by failing to provide brands that appeal to all important segments? In neither automobiles, soaps, nor cigarettes do demographic analyses reveal to the manufacturer what products to make or what products to sell to what segments of the market. Obviously, some modes of segmentation other than demographic are needed to explain why brands which differ so little nevertheless find their own niches in the market, each one appealing to a different segment.[8]

In fact, the premise that buyer behavior correlates with demographics may not be true, or segments identified using other variables may be identical demographically. "Are Grace Slick and Tricia Nixon Cox the same person?" asked an academic article in 1973.[9] Grace Slick, lead singer of Jefferson Airplane, was demographically indistinguishable from Tricia Nixon Cox, Richard Nixon's daughter. They were both in the 25- to 35-year age group, and both were urban, working women with similar income levels and one child. Like Yankelovich's research, this article by the then-president of advertising company Foote, Cone and Belding pointed to the need for nondemographic data in segmentation.

Yankelovich described seven modes of segmentation: value, susceptibility to change, purpose of use, aesthetic concepts, attitudes, individualized needs, and self-confidence in decision making. Further, he suggested that no one particular segmentation approach is always best. Rather, managers should consider all means of segmentation, and then choose the one with the most significant action implications.

Identical twins? Well, demographically, perhaps.

Geographic segmentation is the oldest form of market segmentation. Marketers recognize that many differences in consumer behavior correlate with geographic differences. Simply, demand for parkas is greater in polar and mountainous areas, whereas demand for cool, refreshing beverages is greater in hot, tropical climates. Many small businesses, such as automobile dealers and fast-food franchises, define their market in terms of the local areas in which they operate. As we discuss in chapter 15, large international marketers often use country and regional borders as the bases for segmenting their markets. Increasingly, though, national and international marketers are paying closer attention to regional market segments within countries.

As with demographic segmentation, geographic segmentation alone provides marketers with limited information about *real* differences in customer preferences, values, and attitudes. Nevertheless, geographic segmentation is easy to conduct, and is often combined with demographic segmentation to arrive at well-defined segments. One example of this geodemographic segmentation, or geoclustering, is marketing research firm Claritas's Potential Rating Index by Zip Markets (PRIZM), which identifies 62 demographically similar clusters in the United States.[10]

Psychographic segmentation groups people according to psychological variables. The most common psychographic segmentation approach is lifestyle segmentation. Marketers who employ this approach generally use a number of variables such as activities, attitudes, interests, and opinions, which help them understand consumer motivations, or *why* consumers do what they do. Thus, psychographic segmentation provides additional, valuable information on how consumers think and feel, which demographic and geographic segmentation do not.

Marketers may use psychographic segmentation to guide marketing strategy within the United States as well as internationally. The most common method used for psychographic segmentation is the syndicated research survey conducted by Simmons Market Research Bureau and other companies. VALS 2 (Values and Lifestyles)[11] classifies U.S. adults using this method of segmentation, and Global Scan[12] by advertising agency Backer Spielvogel Bates Worldwide, is an international psychographic segmentation scheme. Within Europe, many psychographic, pan-European segmentation studies have been conducted by a variety of research and advertising agencies in France, Germany, and the United Kingdom. Similarly, country-specific lifestyle research has been conducted in Hong Kong, Japan, Singapore, Malaysia, Taiwan, and Thailand.[13]

The original VALS typology introduced in 1978 by Stanford Research Institute was a pioneering effort to describe how U.S. consumers' personalities shaped their buying decisions. It divided the U.S. population into four personality groups and further divided these groups into nine lifestyles, according to Maslow's hierarchy of needs. VALS had limited marketing use because it did not relate consumer motivations to their purchasing power. VALS 2, introduced in 1989 to correct this shortcoming, uses the concept of self-orientation to divide consumers into three groups—principle-oriented, status-oriented, or action-oriented people—and subdivide these into eight segments according to buying ability.

Psychographic segmentation has several limitations. One danger of using standardized, "off the shelf" segmentation schemes is that they divide the market into segments without regard to a specific product or service. Even though the segments they identify are often interesting (and metaphorically labeled!) and support creative work at advertising agencies, they provide little value to marketers seeking to understand the differential responses of individuals in the various segments to their marketing programs, and the profitability of various segments, for two reasons. First, these segmentation schemes rely on interviews and long surveys with large, representative national (and cross-national) samples on a wide variety of product categories, brands, activities, attitudes, and opinions. High nonresponse rates and/or lengthy survey questionnaires make it very difficult to obtain the large unbiased databases required for further statistical analyses. Second, statistical summaries of various segments are themselves of limited use, because they attempt to predict consumer behavior from self-reported attitudes and intentions. As we have suggested in chapter 4, attitudes and intentions tell only an incomplete (and sometimes unreliable) story about future consumer behavior. In fact, an article in *Fortune* magazine with the startling title "Ignore Your Customer"[14] suggests that managers should ignore what their customers *say* they will do, and focus on what they *actually do*.

Behavioral segmentation, the most successful approach for market segmentation, classifies consumers according to actual product-class and brand-related preferences and behavior patterns. Common behavioral segmentation bases are user status, buyer readiness stage, usage rate, loyalty status, and benefit sought. Segmenting by *user status* helps marketers understand why some people never buy a product or brand, others who may have bought it before never buy again, and why those who continue to buy do so. Perhaps those in the first segment are simply unaware of the product or brand or do not know where it is available. Those in the second segment may have been disappointed by particular product or service features, or they prefer a competitor's offering. And current users may buy simply because they lack alternatives, or because they actually prefer the product to available alternatives.

Similarly, segmenting by *buyer readiness stage* may provide marketers with an understanding of how effective the present marketing efforts have been, as well as suggest what further needs to be done. This information can help marketers seek ways to increase message reach, to design communication messages, or to improve product availability. For example, if the segment that is unaware of the product is large, informational and educational advertising can suggest possible uses for the product. If the group that is unaware of the product is small, but the segment unaware of the particular brand is large, brand awareness advertising may be required, or direct comparison advertising to show buyers how that brand compares with competing brands in the product category.

Usage rate segmentation, based on "heavy half theory," suggests that heavy users represent a numerically small share of the overall market for a product, but a large share of the consumption volume. Such segmentation allows marketers to distinguish between nonusers and light, medium, and heavy users, as well as to identify usage occasions and opportunities to increase consumption.

Thus, volume segmentation is based on the simple reality that for companies in a wide range of industries, a majority of their business (sales, revenues, profits) comes from a minority of their customers. The principle underlying this reality was articulated in 1896 by Italian economist and sociologist Vilfredo Pareto, when he discovered that income and wealth were distributed unevenly, with a few people accounting for the greatest shares. In marketing, this is commonly called the "20:80" rule (20 percent of the customers of a brand or product category account for 80 percent of the volume and, other things being constant, 80 percent of the profits). The actual percentages, of course, vary across industries, product categories, and brands.[15] However, the principle underlying this segmentation basis is that some customers are more valuable than others in terms of their contribution to sales and profitability. In order to design marketing strategy appropriately, it is important to know which customers these are.

Loyalty status can segment markets when managers track actual brand purchase behavior over time. Marketers recognize that the value of their loyal and heavy-half customers is many times that of other customers. For example, loyal customers outspend others by ratios of 16:1 in retailing, 13:1 in the restaurant business, 12:1 in airlines, and 5:1 in the hotel and motel industry.[16] Hence, tracking purchase information over time, and segmentation by loyalty status, provides marketers with a means of differentiating between their most valuable customers and others.

Thus, marketers design frequency and loyalty programs (see Marketing Anecdote 5.1) to provide them with information on customers' purchase patterns and preferences, to reward customers for frequent use, and to build loyalty. Examples of programs abound: Hallmark's Gold Crown program, Northwest Airlines WorldPerks, Pavilions Supermarkets' ValuePlus Club. Members contribute to marketers' databases by using their cards or membership numbers each time they make a purchase, as well as responding to interviews and surveys and to special promotional privileges. Within the airlines' programs, the most loyal (and largest in terms of usage volume, frequency, and value) customers are given special privileges (e.g., Northwest's WorldPerks Preferred), including the use of special reservation lines, airport lounges, personalized baggage tags, priority baggage handling, and preferential upgrades.

Marketers define six categories of loyalty. Random switchers are buyers who select a brand within the product class randomly. These buyers are not motivated by specific brand attributes or marketing communications. Variety seekers are motivated by a need for variety. Market stimulus switchers switch brands in response to marketing stimuli such as promotional deals or product launches. Brand loyals tend to purchase only the preferred brand or brands, unless they are unavailable. Producer loyals are motivated by particular manufacturers, and would buy any of a particular manufacturer's brands. Distinguishing between brand and producer loyals helps a marketer introduce new products and make branding decisions when stretching product lines (as discussed in chapters 7 and 8, respectively). When appealing to producer loyals, it may make sense to use a corporate umbrella for branding new products. Finally, store loyals consistently patronize particular stores.

Benefit segmentation groups consumers according to specific benefit(s) they seek from a product. These benefits could be directly related to product attributes and functions, or could relate to overall image and prestige associated with product ownership and/or use. Marketers may use this information to target specific segments with products and communications designed specifically with their preferred benefits in mind.

Loyalty programs are probably as old as selling itself. They have evolved from the Egyptian merchant who handed his customer an extra roll of papyrus as a token of appreciation for the scribe's business, to Sperry & Hutchinson's Green Stamps in the 1950s and American Airlines AAdvantage Program in the 1980s. Such programs give more to customers who buy more.

With the onset of the information age, marketers can easily identify their important customers, communicate with them, and provide them with substantial monetary rewards. The AAdvantage Program laid the foundation for many programs that followed with hotel, car rental, and telephone companies: the rewards offered to "loyal" customers were critical for encouraging repurchase. These rewards, effectively volume discounts, had, and can have, a huge impact on a company's customer base, especially for early adopters. Consider the tremendous success of MCI's Friends & Family program. MCI not only motivated high-volume, high-profit customers to identify others, but also to recruit them to switch long-distance telephone companies to MCI.

But is a customer who repeat purchases necessarily a loyal customer? Apparently not. As various markets matured, "discount wars" and direct comparative price advertising revealed that so-called loyal customers were in reality quite fickle, ready to switch to the product with the best price. This discovery, as well as the realization that special treatment and perks (such as being greeted by name, upgrades, and early boarding) offered to a frequent flier could be as important as free tickets, led to the development of brand loyalty programs at a variety of companies in product categories where the economics did not allow large monetary rewards.

The distinction between frequent buyer programs and brand loyalty programs is fine. The former create a sort of transaction loyalty (for example, you travel on American Airlines until you accumulate enough miles for a free ticket, then switch). The latter attempt to build real loyalty by developing relationships. A classic example of an early brand loyalty program was the one developed by Ogilvy & Mather Direct for Kimberly-Clark in 1983. It was the first nontransactional, nonreward-based brand loyalty program. It revolved around a series of newsletters called *The Beginning Years* sent four times a year to new parents. The newsletters provided useful child-rearing information that was very relevant to the target audience. The only monetary "rewards" included were coupons for Huggies purchases, but customers loved the unexpected recognition and information. The loyalty program was very successful: results of a year-long panel test led to a national program roll-out in 1985, steady growth in Huggies market share, and eventual adoption of similar programs by arch-rival Procter & Gamble's Pampers, as well as infant formula and baby food marketers.

Source: This example is based on Garth Hallberg, *All Consumers Are Not Created Equal: The Differential Marketing Strategy for Brand Loyalty and Profits* (New York: Wiley, 1995).

In a seminal 1968 *Journal of Marketing* article Russell Haley (research director at Grey Advertising, founder of AHF Research, and then professor of marketing at the University of New Hampshire) suggested that segmenting by consumer needs was superior and laid the foundation for benefit segmentation.[17] The results of his classic example of benefit segmentation of the toothpaste market are described in Table 5.2. Four benefit segments are labeled to capture the essence of the main benefit

TABLE 5.2 BENEFIT SEGMENTATION: AN ILLUSTRATION OF THE TOOTHPASTE MARKET

	Segment Name			
	THE SENSORY SEGMENT	**THE SOCIABLES**	**THE WORRIERS**	**THE INDEPENDENT SEGMENT**
Principal Benefit Sought	Flavor, product appearance	Brightness of teeth	Decay prevention	Price
Demographic Strengths	Children	Teens, young people	Large families	Men
Special Behavior Characteristics	Users of spearmint-flavored toothpaste	Smokers	Heavy users	Heavy users
Brands Disproportionately Favored	Colgate, Stripe	Macleans, Plus White, Ultra Brite	Crest	Brands on sale
Personality Characteristics	High self-involvement	High sociability	High hypochondriasis	High autonomy
Lifestyle Characteristics	Hedonistic	Active	Conservative	Value oriented

Source: Russell I. Haley, "Benefit Segmentation: A Decision-oriented Research Tool," Journal of Marketing 21 (July 1968), p. 33.

sought in toothpaste by each group. The sensory segment seeks good taste, sociables seek cosmetic appearance of their teeth, worriers seek the medicinal benefit of decay prevention, and the independent segment seeks economy or low price. These segments are also distinguishable demographically (sociables are young people, worriers are made up of large families), by personality (the sensory segment exhibits high self-involvement, the independents are autonomous), lifestyle (worriers are conservative, sociables active), brand preferences (the sensory segment prefers Colgate and Stripe, the independents prefer brands on sale), and usage (worriers and independents are heavy users).

Market researchers in a wide range of product categories such as airline travel, credit cards, office equipment, soft drinks, and telecommunications conduct benefit segmentation using a procedure similar to the one used by Haley. They ask a large cross section of buyers to rate many different (but closely related) benefits (e.g., prevents halitosis) and attributes (e.g., fresh flavor) of a product in terms of their importance. They may then use a classification procedure such as cluster analysis to group people looking for the same benefits into segments, each segment looking for different benefits.

It is important to recognize that benefits sought by consumers are related to product-market evolution and the marketing efforts of all competitors in a product category. Often, marketers may lead consumers by suggesting (or discovering) benefits that were hitherto latent. For example, until Minolta and Canon introduced several automated functions in sophisticated cameras, the market for such cameras was segmented by price and performance. Ease-of-use subsequently became a key benefit (and therefore a key segmentation criterion) in the high-end camera market.[18]

Segmenting Organizational Markets. Table 5.3 lists the major segmentation variables for organizational markets. As with consumer market segmentation, organizational market segmentation is a process in which several bases are sequentially applied to arrive at final segments. Behavioral segmentation is recognized as

TABLE 5.3 COMMON VARIABLES FOR SEGMENTING ORGANIZATIONAL MARKETS

Segmentation Variable	Example
DEMOGRAPHIC	
Industry	Banking; Medical services; Government Standard Industrial Classification (SIC) codes
Company size	Small business; Medium; Fortune 500
GEOGRAPHIC	
Company location	Americas; Europe; Asia
BEHAVIORAL	
Product Application	
Customer technologies	
Buyer Decision-Making Style	
Purchasing function	Centralized; Decentralized
Power structure	Engineering; Finance; Production; Marketing
General purchasing policies	Systems purchase; Sealed bidding; Transactional; Relational
Buying Behavior	
User status	Nonuser; Current customer; Competitor's customer National accounts; Field accounts; Dealer accounts
Usage status	Large; Medium; Small Frequent; Intermittent; Sporadic
Order size	Large; Medium; Small
Order frequency	Frequent; Intermittent, regular; Infrequent
Buying Situation	Capital; Parts; Service; Materials Routine purchase; Nonroutine purchase
CUSTOMER BENEFITS SOUGHT	
Purchasing criteria	Price; Delivery; Service; Quality

superior to traditional industry type, customer size (demographic), or customer location (geographic) segmentation.

For example, DuPont segmented its market for Kevlar by three customer benefits. Kevlar's lightness offered fuel savings, greater fish-carrying capacity, and speed—benefits that appealed to fishing-boat owners. Its high strength-to-weight ratio appealed to aircraft manufacturers, and its inert nature appealed to plant managers looking for asbestos substitutes.

When segmenting organizational markets, managers usually pay close attention to various behavioral characteristics of the buyers, including the nature of the buying group or decision-making unit, buying situation, and buying decision-making style and process (see chapter 6), as well as previous purchase history such as user and usage status, order size, and frequency. Because organizational purchasing is generally structured and guided by formal policies, understanding these factors can help the selling firm develop its sales force and selling strategy. Segmenting organizational markets based on buyer decision-making processes is desirable because it groups organizations according to the actual purchase determinants. However, it requires detailed information on buyers and prospects, which is difficult to obtain.

Choffray and Lilien's four-step procedure for segmenting organizational markets based on decision-making processes illustrates both the sequential nature of organizational segmentation and the intensity of data required.[19] First, measure the pattern of involvement in the purchasing process for all concerned firms in each macrosegment identified on the basis of demographics or other variables. This may be done by asking senior managers to name all those involved with organizational purchasing decisions, and then asking all involved to report on the nature and extent of their involvement at every stage of the purchasing process. Next, construct an index of similarity in the involvement patterns. Third, identify organizational segments with similar purchasing processes. Finally, describe these microsegments in terms of the involvement patterns and other characteristics that are meaningful for designing distribution, sales, communications, and pricing strategies.

Organizational marketers face a growing challenge when segmenting mature markets. Product attributes may not provide useful segmentation bases in mature markets because most customers are knowledgeable about the features, benefits, and functionalities of a variety of products, and no longer want such information. Competing offerings become closely related and less differentiable along such attributes as the product-market matures. Consequently, markets may best be segmented by two customer benefits sought: service and price.

Signode Corporation, the market leader in the mature steel strapping (for packaging) category,[20] used this segmentation approach. This study again illustrates the detailed data requirements for segmenting industrial markets based on customer benefits sought, and also the tremendous value of such an approach for evaluating the implications of alternative marketing approaches for sales and profitability. Signode segmented its market using customer size (small, medium, large, and national accounts) and SIC code (industry within each size segment). This segmentation study used in-house data on price and quality (relative to other customer segments), account size (annual purchases), and market share (Signode's share in total dollar purchases in the product category) to further segment the national account macrosegment using customer benefits. It complemented this data with judgmental data on sales elasticities from sales representatives and national account managers, and used a hierarchical clustering procedure to reveal four customer microsegments.

- Programmed buyers had the least price and service sensitivity. Additionally, they were small buyers with low annual purchases, and Signode's market share was small relative to its share of other segments. These buyers had routinized purchase procedures and split purchases across two or more suppliers without explicitly evaluating the product or price-service trade-offs.

- Relationship buyers paid relatively high prices for low service. They were small buyers, cared about the product, and were informed about competitive offerings. Signode accounted for a larger share of their purchases, and they were less prone to negotiating price or service, and to switching suppliers.

- Transaction buyers paid somewhat lower prices for better service, and were very sensitive to service and product. They were double the size of their counterparts in the relationship segment, very knowledgeable about competitive offerings, and prone to switching.

- Bargain hunters received the largest discounts and highest service. They were large-volume customers, most sensitive to price and service, and most likely to switch suppliers.

Using the results of this segmentation analysis, Signode was able to assess the implications of reducing or increasing price or service for each of these segments.

Specifically, it realized that despite pressure from its national accounts to reduce prices, price reductions would be unprofitable in all microsegments because of low demand elasticity to price reductions. The biggest advantage of this type of segmentation is that it provides managers with the detailed segment-specific knowledge they need to evaluate the profitability of their current and proposed marketing mixes.

Assessing the Usefulness of Segmentation

Markets may be segmented using one or more of a multitude of segmentation alternatives. However, appropriate segmentation bases for any market are those that differentiate or discriminate consumers along dimensions that are meaningful for further marketing program development and execution. For example, many firms use geography to segment their markets. When consumer buying behavior really differs across countries and regions, this approach is useful. In general, though, bases that exert a substantial influence on purchasing and usage behavior, and benefits sought, are more important.

Segments derived from any segmentation exercise are useful to marketers when the following characteristics apply.

- A reliable and objective analytic segmentation procedure is used. Each of the statistical procedures that can be used in the segmentation exercise has its advantages and disadvantages. Marketing researchers and marketing managers should be aware of the implications of using a particular segmentation technique. We discuss some of these techniques later in this chapter.

- Careful thought is given to the appropriate bases of segmentation. Managers need to understand the theoretical rationale for their final choice of segmentation variables. Usually, hybrid segmentation approaches with multiple bases are needed. Further, where multiple bases are used, the order in which these are applied is important.

- Segments derived using this procedure are internally homogeneous (similar) and distinct from each other, so that the marketing program designed for a particular segment can be used uniformly within that segment, and it is worthwhile to design separate marketing programs for each segment.

- Segments are well described in terms of their characteristics as well as sales and profit potential. A complete segment description requires three dimensions—the customer groups who buy the product, the functions that the product performs for these customers, and the form that the product takes.[21] Further, marketers should be able to reliably determine to which segments individuals belong.

- Segments should also be substantial enough to serve. Marketers must be able to reach identified segments with their communications and distribution, and serve them profitably.

- Segment differences in response to marketing programs are real and actionable, warranting customized marketing approaches. Existing differences among individuals along demographic, geographic, psychographic, and behavioral dimensions should be used as bases for segmentation only when marketers expect consumer responses to differ along those lines. For example, unless women and men react differently to a marketer's brand, there is no point in using gender to segment the market.

- Marketers recognize the dynamic nature of markets. The entire market may evolve, or change dramatically, segments may change, and buyer attitudes and behavior within segments also change. These changes stem from the interplay between external factors (such as changes in target-customer lifestyles) and factors internal to the product market (such as product life cycle and technological changes). Segmentation should therefore be an ongoing effort, and segments should be reassessed as new market data become available.

Putting Market Segmentation into Practice

According to Derek Abell at the International Institute for Management Development in Switzerland, market definition and segmentation should begin with creative brainstorming and speculation about the market.[22] This process generates hypotheses that marketers can then test by formal market research. The types of questions managers should ask at this stage include:

- *What* do customers seek? What influences customers? What risks do they perceive?
- *How* do customers buy? How long does the buying process last? How much do they buy?
- *Where* is the decision to buy made? Where do customers seek information? Where do they buy?
- *When* is the first purchase made? When are repurchases made?
- *Why* do customers buy? Why do they choose one brand over others?
- *Who* buys our products? Who buys competitors' products? Why?

Top managers must assume responsibility for critical strategic areas such as market definition and segmentation. However, the segmentation process should involve all organizational levels to capture the fine-grained nature of customer needs and motivations. Simply put, people closer to the markets can better focus on and reflect market details. The segmentation exercise should deliberately look at several different levels of aggregation and assess which level is most meaningful for the organization. Finally, market segmentation is an eclectic and creative process that organizations use to create competitive advantage. Managers must recognize this creative, eclectic nature and distinguish between segmentation (or creating a road map of the market), and targeting and positioning (or choosing in which parts of the market they will operate).

Targeting: Market Evaluation and Selection

Once an organization has discovered and described its market segments, it has to evaluate them to determine which ones offer the best opportunities; decide on which segments and how many to target; and select these for further analyses, product positioning, and program development. This is a challenging task, because there are usually a large number of market segments to evaluate and from which to select.

Segment Attractiveness and Segment Fit

When evaluating market segments, managers need to assess both segment attractiveness and segment fit. Managers use multiple criteria to evaluate market segments, including:

- Size/sales potential: Sales volume and value.
- Growth potential: Sales volume and value, number of customers, potential for increasing breadth and depth of customer relationships.

- Profitability.
- Competitors' strengths and weaknesses in each segment.
- Organizational strengths and weaknesses relative to each segment.
- Fit of specific segment opportunities with organizational goals.
- Resource requirements for segment development and resource availability.

Keeping in mind that one goal of segmentation is to improve profitability, managers must explicitly evaluate the profit potential of various segments, rather than select targets based on face validity (for example, "this target makes sense," "the best target has the heaviest users," or "these people are looking for product benefits our client's brand can deliver"[23]) of particular segments.[24] Marketers have become keenly aware of the need to track the profitability of their programs. As such, profit segmentation and targeting recognizes that all consumers are not equal. Thus, marketers must assess the profit potential of each consumer, and group consumers according to their potential.[25]

Product Focus, Market Focus, and Market Dominance

In selecting target markets, managers decide on the number of segments they will serve as well as their approach to serving the selected segments. In addition to target market selection choices, firms must also make product differentiation decisions. These choices, illustrated in Figure 5.2, are discussed next.

Single-segment focus. An organization (such as firm A catering to segment 1 with product 1 in Figure 5.2) may sell a single, undifferentiated product to a single market segment. Thus, a janitorial services company catering to the daily cleaning needs of the banking segment would be an example of an undifferentiated offering to a single segment.

Product focus. An organization (such as firm B) may choose to specialize in a particular product, which it sells to several market segments. Thus, the janitorial services company may offer regular cleaning to the banking industry, bulk chemical manufacturers, and trade show organizer market segments. Organizations that enjoy monopolies or operate in developing country markets where demand far exceeds supply often offer a single, undifferentiated offering for a number of market segments.

Market focus. Organizations may focus on meeting the needs of a particular market segment (e.g., firm C serves market segment 3 with three products) with a differentiated offering. For example, the janitorial services company may offer several janitorial services packages, such as regular daily cleaning, special weekend cleaning, and special events cleaning, or it may expand its offering to include indoor plant maintenance and flower arrangements for the banking industry. The objective would be to increase the overall share of segment business with differentiated offerings that meet as many of the segment's needs as possible.

Market dominance. Organizations may select all market segments to target (firm D targets each of the three market segments with all three products). For example, the janitorial services company may offer daily cleaning services, indoor plant maintenance, and flower arranging to the banking industry, bulk chemical manufacturers, and trade show organizers. Alternately, it could choose to differentiate its product offering by examining the needs of each target market, and offering it only those services that it needs. Thus, it may offer end-of-day cleaning to the banking segment, end-of-production-run cleaning to the bulk chemical segment, and end-of-event disassembly, disposal, and cleaning to trade show organizers.

This strategy of product differentiation combined with market dominance may be a long-term market strategy for those organizations that often have to evolve

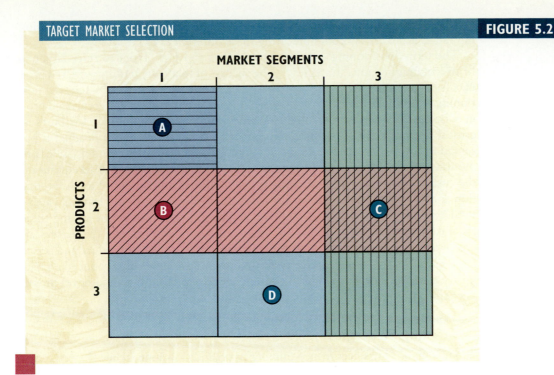

MARKET SEGMENTS

through the various other stages before they can build the expertise to differentially cater to multiple segment needs. For example, Toyota entered the U.S. market with a single, large automobile model, which it had to pull out. It then targeted (also with a single car model) the low-income segment that large U.S. automobile manufacturers had ignored. As its scale of operations grew, it developed product offerings for every segment of the car market, including luxury cars and, most recently, sport-utility vehicles under the Lexus brand for the high-income group.

Positioning

Once an organization has selected its target markets, it needs to further analyze each target market relative to customer needs and competitive offerings. Such analyses aim to develop positioning strategies for offerings within each segment that successfully differentiate them from competitors' offerings. The term *positioning* refers to the company's choice of marketing mix—including its desired image, product attributes, communications message, distribution, and pricing—to achieve its intended position in target customers' minds. It also refers to the achieved position of the brand, that is, how target customers view the company's offering along attributes important to them and relative to competing offerings.

Therefore, an organization's positioning strategy, used to achieve its intended position, represents an important starting point toward the actual position it occupies in target customers' minds. In addition, every aspect of program implementation, as well as competitors' actions, influence achieved position.

Positioning aims to emphasize points of sustainable competitive advantage by identifying and serving customer segments and niches with distinct needs via a particular differentiated strategy. Marketers may achieve distinctive positioning by differentiating their products and services along attributes that are distinctive, difficult to imitate, and important to their target customers. At least as important, positioning requires effectively communicating these differences to customers.

The term "positioning" was used by Al Ries and Jack Trout to refer largely to firms' communications strategies.[26] The success of relatively undifferentiated products (such as Coke and Pepsi) depends on clear communication of a selected positioning strategy. However, clear positioning also benefits more differentiated products because it helps customers understand which of many product attributes are critical determinants of overall brand quality. Certainly, the way a product is presented to customers—its marketing communications including branding, sales promotion, and advertising—alone may be sufficient to create a sharp differentiation in the customer's mind. But positioning usually follows from real product differentiation and/or differentiating along service dimensions the customer expects (such as service, support, and delivery), and then augmenting the product by adding things the customer does not expect.[27] In fact, competitors differentiate themselves and create unique positions by the degree of attention they pay to product and service features. In the automobile industry, for example, Lexus not only produced a superb luxury car, but distinguished itself through its excellent, unique, and novel presale, sale, and postsale service offerings.

Positioning Strategies

Organizations may select from a number of positioning approaches.[28]

- **Product attributes and benefits.** An organization emphasizes one or more specific product attributes and the related benefits they provide for the target segment. To be effective, these attributes should be both important to target consumers and distinctive. One example is Crest toothpaste, which introduced fluoride (containing fluoride is an attribute) with decay-prevention properties (a benefit). Other attributes and benefits include price and quality.

- **Usage occasions or functions.** An organization emphasizes that its brand is appropriate for particular applications. Arm and Hammer baking soda is positioned as suitable both for cooking and for use as a refrigerator deodorant. To increase winter sales, Coke is positioned as "The Only Real Holiday Refreshment."

- **User category.** An organization, product, or brand may be positioned for particular user groups. Many restaurants have separate "light" menus for people concerned about dietary fat.

- **Advantage relative to competitors.** The competitor may be named explicitly (such as in direct comparison advertising), when the objective is to take customers from the competitor by emphasizing some point of advantage. For example, in the United States, Kia, the Korean automobile company, positioned itself directly against Honda, stating that it provided the same quality for a lower price. Or the competitor may be unnamed, and only suggested in the positioning. Or a company may position its product against the market leader. Many store-brand products position themselves as offering better value against the branded market leader. Their choice of packaging and shelf position is closely associated with the brand against which they are positioning themselves. Sometimes, a marketer may choose to simultaneously associate with and distance itself from the market leader and the entire product category in an attempt to create a new positioning basis in the customers' minds. A classic example of this is 7-Up's very successful "uncola" marketing campaign in the 1970s. Thus, 7-Up succeeded in establishing itself as a distinctive soft drink. Until then, the two cola brands Coke and Pepsi were so dominant that they constituted the soft drink category in consumers' minds; 7-Up had been perceived as a special occasions drink.

Another choice that confronts marketers is the number of bases for positioning. Should the marketer use a *single* unique selling proposition (USP) for each brand—a concept popularized by advertising professional Rosser Reeves—or multiple bases? This decision must be guided by an understanding of the benefits that target customers seek, the firm's overall objectives, and desired positioning, and an understanding that as the number of bases for positioning increases, it becomes more challenging to clearly communicate the selected position, as discussed in chapter 9. When communicating a brand's USP, positioning is often a single word, thought, attribute, or benefit. For example, Clorox bleach—brightening; Mercedes-Benz—engineering; and Pepsi-Cola—youth. Or the positioning idea could be longer. For example, Apple computers—easy to use; BMW—the ultimate driving machine; and Visa—accepted at places that don't accept American Express. Products, product classes, and product categories may also be positioned. For example, diamonds are "forever," and pork is "the other white meat."

When Swatch, the Swiss watch, was introduced in the early 1980s, the company's choice of positioning was guided by two important corporate objectives. First, volume was critical. They needed to sell a large number of watches to become profitable. Two, Swatch was to be the Swiss watch industry's savior, competing directly with low-priced competition from Asia. Having defined its market segment as fashion-conscious youths, Swatch chose a fashion and price positioning. This careful customer-benefit based positioning allowed Swatch to sell large numbers of watches (they were affordable; Swatch constantly introduced dramatic, new styles; and Swatch made it chic to wear an armful of watches) and surpass its own original performance expectations. Swatch's segmentation and positioning guided all aspects of its marketing program. It sold through a variety of nontraditional channels (not jewelry stores), and subsequently extended its offering to include "Eyes" sunglasses with interchangeable lenses and even a car, the "Swatchmobile"!

Perceptual Mapping: A Marketing Research Tool for Positioning

Marketers have developed an analytic procedure for measuring and plotting consumers' reactions to important attributes and benefits of a set of competing products: *perceptual mapping.* Conceptually, a perceptual map is a multidimensional image of the perceived similarities and differences among products and brands. The number of dimensions reflects the number of important customer attributes. Perceptual maps may be derived from data on consumer perceptions of similarities between brands using a statistical procedure called multidimensional scaling.[29]

Plotting a perceptual map allows marketers to visually illustrate the following attributes and benefits.

- Attributes that are most important in consumer decision making. These attributes form the axes (and the axis anchors) of the perceptual map. Note that it is possible (although unlikely) that consumers use only one dimension to evaluate products, and to have a single axis perceptual "map."

- Product strengths and weaknesses relative to competing products along important attributes. This is revealed by the positions of the marketer's brand and competing brands along the axes.

- Market opportunities. These are revealed by empty spaces in the perceptual map, which need to be examined together with the preferred combinations of

Volvo, the Swedish automobile marketer, plans to reposition itself in the U.S. market. Their goal is to expand market coverage beyond their current target market, thirty-nine-year-olds with families. Volvo's historical "safety" positioning has huge appeal for their target customers. According to Bob Austin, marketing communications director at Volvo of North America, 85 percent of Volvo owners are married with children.

But one of the factors limiting Volvo's growth in the competitive and evolving U.S. automobile market is its demographic market definition. People buy many cars before they are age 39, and many after their children are grown. For these markets, Volvo's single-minded safety message has little appeal.

Following Mercedes' successful repositioning, Volvo and its U.S. ad agency, Messner Vetere Berger McNamee Schmetterer/Euro RSCG, are trying to reach younger buyers and empty nesters through lifestyle positioning. The platform: fun! In order not to disenfranchise their core customers, the new advertisements will continue to emphasize Volvo's core safety theme, while adding emotional aspects.

But is a "fun" positioning credible, given Volvo's large, staid, boxy cars? To address this, the new positioning is to be colaunched with the new C70, Volvo's first convertible in 40 years. Consistent with the fun theme, the new car line is to be livelier and less boxy. The C70 made its debut at the Detroit auto show in January 1997, and in March appeared in *The Saint*, a $10 million movie tie-in with Paramount Pictures.

Source: Jean Halliday, "Volvo Looks to Pair Fun with Usual Safety Theme," *Advertising Age*, January 20, 1997, p. 4.

attributes that each segment reveals. Consumers will likely select brands that are closest to their preferred combination or ideal points. Thus, overlaying a map of consumers' perceptions of the existing market with their ideal points will reveal potential for new brands and opportunities for repositioning existing brands. Marketing Anecdote 5.2 discusses Volvo's repositioning efforts.

- Market evolution. Tracking customer perceptions over time, and comparing perceptual maps developed at each point in time, can reveal how the market is changing. First, ideal points may shift as new offerings enter the market and as markets mature. For example, as product and process quality programs diffused through industry, consumers' ideal points are likely to have shifted to reflect higher quality expectations, as well as to reflect closer positions of competing offerings along the quality dimension. Second, the most important attributes may change as a result of environmental changes and the creative positioning of new entrants. Prior to the 1970s, fuel efficiency was not likely to emerge as a dominant automobile attribute in the United States. After the fuel crisis of 1973, and with Japanese competitors' fuel-efficient offerings, fuel efficiency became an important attribute. Thus, perceptual maps may be used to document where the market has been in the past, currently is, and where customers think it is going in the future.

Managers may use perceptual maps at a variety of levels, such as for brand, product, and corporate positioning. Perceptual maps of brands may be used to assess opportunities for new brands, as well as for repositioning existing brands. Figure 5.3

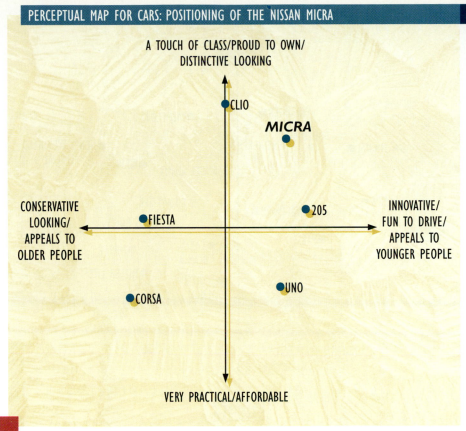

Source: Marieke de Mooij,
Advertising Worldwide, 2nd ed.
(Hertfordshire, London: Prentice
Hall International [UK] Ltd., 1994),
p. 559.

A TOUCH OF CLASS/PROUD TO OWN/
DISTINCTIVE LOOKING

CLIO

MICRA

CONSERVATIVE
LOOKING/
APPEALS TO
OLDER PEOPLE

FIESTA

205

INNOVATIVE/
FUN TO DRIVE/
APPEALS TO
YOUNGER PEOPLE

UNO

CORSA

VERY PRACTICAL/AFFORDABLE

provides one example of a perceptual map for the Nissan Micra, a car designed for the European market and manufactured in the United Kingdom. Figure 5.4 provides an example of a perceptual map for beer.

Product perceptual maps may be used to examine the competition between generic substitutes such as all beverages, and may help identify new, unexpected ways in which customer needs may be met. Corporate perceptual maps could provide useful information on how to position a company in relation to its competitors, an area that is growing in importance as organizations realize that building corporate image is necessary for long-term success.[30]

Perceptual maps generally work in conjunction with market segmentation information. When researchers develop perceptual maps for each segment, managers can develop a fine-grained description of the market and competition in each segment. Further, perceptual maps may combine with consumer attitudinal and preference data to explore how well each brand meets consumer preferences. Alternatively, perceptual mapping may be the input for segmentation. Once maps are drawn, market researchers may use clustering procedures to group similar brands, products, or companies.

Customer perceptual maps can also validate managers' own market maps. Managers' conceptions of how their products are differentiated in the marketplace may not accurately reflect consumers' perceptions. Comparing perceptual maps derived from managerial and customer data would highlight areas in which the marketing program needs to change. In fact, even though positioning is critical to the success of many products and brands, results of research from national cross sections of buyers in various product categories suggest that few customers can accurately associate brands with

FIGURE 5.4   PERCEPTUAL MAP FOR BEER

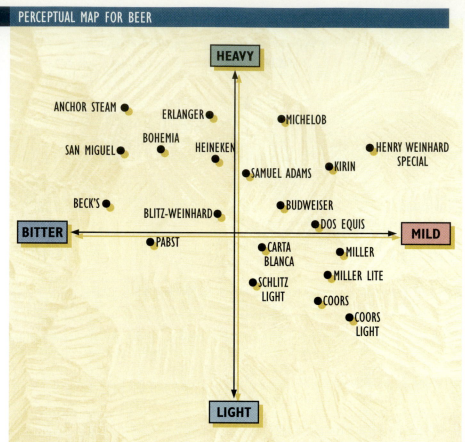

Source: Richard P. Bagozzi,
Principles of Marketing
Management (Chicago: Science
Research Associates, 1986), p. 245.

their intended positioning. Unaided awareness of positioning—in which customers are asked what each of the five leading brands in a category represent—ranges from 8 percent (overall) to 12 percent (for advertising-intensive categories such as automobiles and beer, and in categories with few dominant brands). Aided awareness—in which customers are asked to associate particular slogans and positioning strategies with brands—is only 16 percent. Average, fully prompted, recall—in which customers are asked whether they recall brand X stating position/slogan Y—for most categories is less than 30 percent.[31]

Several reasons may limit firms' success in creating a unique position in customers' minds:

- The company did not carefully define its target segment.
- The company did not develop a clear positioning strategy in conjunction with its advertising agency.
- Marketing communications, including product, packaging, advertising, promotion, pricing, and distribution did not clearly articulate or communicate its positioning strategy.
- The media selected were improper, and did not reach or impact the target market.

Creating a unique positioning is a challenging but necessary step for marketers because the positioning strategy guides decisions about all aspects of the marketing program.

MARKETING RESEARCH AND MARKET ANALYSIS

The Purpose of Marketing Research

Marketing research is the "function that links the consumer, customer, and public to the marketer through marketing information."[32] Managers use marketing research for several purposes:

- To analyze their markets—customer needs, expectations, and responses, as well as competitors' offerings and strategies, as is illustrated in our discussion of perceptual mapping.
- To identify market opportunities in terms of aggregate demand and potential, as well as the types of products and services they should offer, also previously illustrated.
- To design marketing programs, including informing new product development decisions, as is discussed in chapter 7.
- To facilitate program implementation, as is discussed in chapters 15 and 16.
- To evaluate marketing program performance, as is discussed in chapter 17.

Broadly, then, managers use research to reduce uncertainty. Research provides them with a structured approach that can complement judgmental decision making, based on accumulated experience. Decisions on product positioning, distribution, pricing, and promotion should all be based on carefully conducted marketing research. Because markets and competitive environments are dynamic, there is no substitute for good, timely, and ongoing research. The cost of making a mistake can be fatal, as the Lockheed example in Marketing Anecdote 5.3 illustrates.

Organizations may conduct their own marketing research, as many large corporations do, or they may use commercial marketing research services. Typically, marketing research is conducted through coordinating a number of internal and external entities such as the marketing manager, senior corporate managers, marketing information systems (MIS) and marketing decision support systems (MDSS) managers, marketing researchers, R&D managers, research suppliers, and advertising agencies. In addition, the primary research organization may subcontract components of the marketing research process—such as field data collection or data analysis—to specialized, independent organizations. Marketing research organizations such as Nielsen and Information Resources, Inc. provide a variety of research products and services for their clients. These include syndicated research services based on common pools of data such as diary- and scanner-panel-based studies; standardized research services conducted using the same research design for different customers; and customized services designed to meet client-specific research needs.

Given the variety of marketing research options, marketing managers must have a working understanding of the purposes that marketing research can serve, the marketing research process, and the characteristics of good research. Figure 5.5 provides an overview of the types of research studies that managers can use to inform marketing decisions made at various stages of the product life cycle. Marketing research needs evolve over the product life cycle. Prelaunch research activities like concept testing, product, package, and name testing facilitate new product development. Test marketing facilitates demand estimation and product launch. In the introductory and growth stages of the product life cycle, the purpose of marketing research studies such as market tracking and positioning studies is primarily to provide information on consumer attitudes, preferences, and purchase patterns, as well as the competitive

In early 1968, Lockheed, in an attempt to reduce its reliance on the military market, made a huge commitment to a new wide-body (two passenger aisles) jet. They had identified a gap in the commercial airplane market. Boeing offered the large four-engine 747, but there was no small plane on the market. Using technology Lockheed had developed for a transport plane, they elected to build a three-engine trijet, rather than a twin-jet.

Less than three months into the project, when Lockheed had committed less than 2 percent of the billion dollar-plus development costs for the TriStar, it became clear from the pattern of early orders and McDonnell Douglas's announcement of the directly competing DC-10 that their demand forecasts should be revised downward. Not only would they have to split the market with the DC-10, but McDonnell Douglas had a differential advantage stemming from their cumulative experience in selling commercial aircraft. Despite the DC-10's close positioning, Lockheed's senior managers were confident in their ability to meet their sales target of more than 300 planes, based largely on their own perceptions of the technical superiority of the TriStar. They assumed the TriStar's superior design and its Rolls-Royce engines would automatically give it an advantage over the DC-10.

Unfortunately, Lockheed took a rather narrow view of buyer benefits. Major commercial airlines, their market, made their buying decisions on price, reputation, and supplier nationality considerations. Thus, they were unwilling to pay more for the design-related features of the TriStar. McDonnell Douglas's reputation won them orders from United and American, the two largest domestic carriers. These airlines just did not trust the British Rolls-Royce, which had been locked out of the U.S. market. In fact, they viewed McDonnell Douglas as the only credible competitor to Boeing—which had a monopoly—and therefore the one to back.

Had Lockheed carefully reevaluated its target market potential, its positioning relative to its competitor from the point of view of *buyer benefits* and trade-offs, and its choice of product offering, it may have considered the broader market and potential for the twin-jet. In fact, the European Airbus consortium later attacked the market with the twin-jet and succeeded. Lockheed lost more than $2.5 billion on the TriStar project, nearly went bankrupt, and eventually terminated the project in 1983.

Source: Pankaj Ghemawat, *Commitment: The Dynamic of Strategy* (New York: Free Press, 1991), pp. 53–80.

structure of the market. Finally, segmentation and repositioning studies may be used to understand changing customer service requirements, assess price elasticities, and make decisions on pricing changes and cost reduction opportunities.

The Marketing Research Process

Information Management

Marketing research relies on information. Such information is necessary to support organization decision making, as we have previously outlined. Organizations use a variety of information-handling systems:

FIGURE 5.5

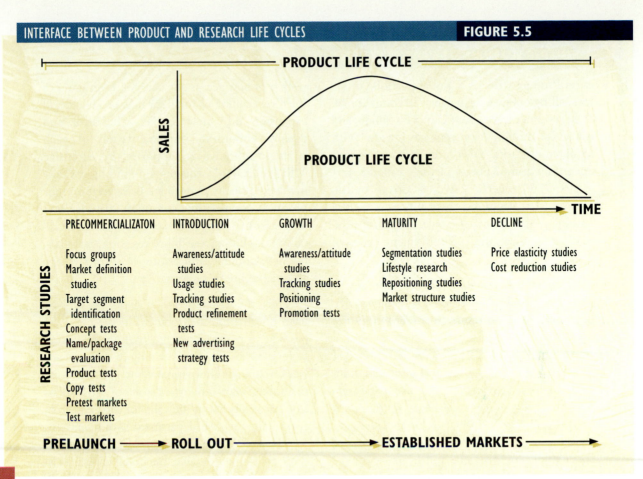

Source: Marketing Research in a Marketing Environment, William R. Dillon, Thomas J. Madden, Neil H. Firtle, ed. 3 (Burr Ridge, Ill. : Irwin, 1994), p. 20.

- MIS are organized processes for collecting, storing, analyzing and reporting marketing data. To be useful, MIS must make information available to marketing decision makers in a form that they are able to use.

- Marketing databases comprise extensive, organized data on products, customers, new markets, industry sales, competitors, and environmental trends. Organizations rely on their own databases as well as those maintained by publishers, government authorities, and research suppliers.

- MDSS are systems, tools, techniques, and statistical models that allow marketers to analyze their marketing data to support a variety of marketing decisions.

MDSS may be designed to help managers answer specific questions like "what are our quarterly sales by product line?," "how do our year-to-date marketing expenses compare with our budgets?," and "how do each of our segments react (in terms of volume sales, brand switching, and store switching) to a 5 percent price increase?" Well-designed MDSS provide flexible and systematic, computerized approaches for collecting, analyzing, and modeling data to provide useful information on customer and competitive responses. They thereby offer specific benefits in the form of enhanced efficiency, greater understanding of, and heightened ability to respond to, market dynamics, and the ability to conduct "what-if" sensitivity analyses.

Avon Products, Inc. is a global portfolio of direct selling operations in over 130 countries. Its 1996 revenues were about U.S. $4.8 billion, and it had 2.3 million Avon reps worldwide. With 65 percent of total sales coming from overseas operations and 62 percent from cosmetics, fragrances, and toiletries, Avon is driven by the mission articulated by their CEO to be the "company that best *understands and satisfies* the product, service, and self-fulfillment needs of women, globally."

To achieve their stated mission, Avon recognizes the critical role of *marketing research* (MR). Beginning in 1984, the company began to hire professional marketing researchers to staff a corporate MR group. At the time, MR provided the company with basic tactical information on the U.S. market. Most MR initiatives were *reactive*, and many were undertaken to address a specific problem. In 1989, MR became *proactive*, focusing on strategic issues such as image and positioning, competition, and business expansion. Avon also began to look at worldwide markets. By 1995, MR at Avon had evolved to an extent that it was totally integrated with Avon's strategic planning. By this time much of its focus was on strategy implementation in the areas of global marketing, new market entry, new category, and new business identification.

MR identifies issues and opportunities that are crucial in strategy formulation at Avon. For example, MR identified that Avon needed to enhance its image with consumers, improve customer access to the company, and provide new products for existing customers. This led to a global branding strategy, development and testing of new access alternatives, leveraging of the direct selling channel for new products, and expansion into new markets. In turn, and equally important, implementation of each strategic initiative is supported by extensive MR. For example, the global branding strategy involved globally coordinated research on new products, competition, consumer attitudes, and usage. Similarly, new markets are selected based on MR including feasibility research, positioning development, and testing of entry strategy and marketing mix alternatives.

Thus, the MR function at Avon has evolved from information management in the pre-1984 period and performance feedback in the period from 1984 to 1988, to providing insight and advice on strategic alternatives in the 1990s. In part, the increasingly important role of MR stems from Avon's belief in the value of such research. Avon staffed its MR department with quality researchers. This established the MR function as a center of unquestionable functional expertise. In turn, the researchers started small, focused only on the most critical strategic issues, delivered results, and developed strong and broad knowledge of Avon's business across all functions and countries, thereby developing credibility throughout the Avon organization. MR has therefore made a huge difference at Avon.

Source: Joseph V. Faranda, vice-president, Global Strategic Planning/Marketing Research, Avon Products, Inc. "Creating Growth: Why Research Makes a Difference at Avon," address at Marketing Science Institute Conference, Use and Usability: Business-Focused Market Research, Boston, September 12–13, 1996. Used with permission.

Companies and industries vary in how sophisticated they are in collecting and using marketing data, as well as the extent to which they rely on formal and informal approaches to marketing decision making. Often, firms evolve through several stages from having no marketing research function to a stage where marketing research is an integral part of marketing strategy formulation and execution.

Marketing Anecdote 5.4 illustrates how marketing research has evolved at the Avon Products, Inc.

Stages in the Research Process

The marketing research process has several steps:

1. Recognizing the need for research. The marketing research process begins with a recognition of the need for research. Marketing research may be required to answer specific questions about program performance, such as the tracking attitudes toward a brand. Or its scope could be broad, such as to assess market opportunities.

2. Defining the problem. At this stage, marketing managers and researchers need to jointly define the purpose for which marketing research will be conducted, including the types of questions that the research must answer, the types of information already available, additional information wanted, and the use to which research results will be put. *Exploratory* research at this stage helps clarify what the problem really is and generate ideas on alternate research approaches.

3. Designing the research, setting the research budget, and identifying data sources. The researcher must identify how much is already known about the research question, including the data, models, and analytic techniques available. Further, she needs to identify whether the research is *descriptive* (i.e., attempting to describe a marketing phenomenon, such as how consumers shop) or *causal* (i.e., attempting to predict cause-effect relationships, such as sales changes when a product package change is introduced). The type of data required and the manner in which it is collected are driven by the research design. For example, qualitative data may be sufficient for descriptive research, but experiments or quasi experiments may be necessary for causal research. When identifying data sources, the researcher must answer questions such as who the target population is, whether a sample is required, and if so, what sampling frame will be used, what type of sample will be drawn, how it will be drawn, and how large it will be.

4. Collecting data. Decisions at this stage include who will collect the data, the timeframe for data collection, required supervision, and the methods that will be used to ensure data quality and comparability across samples and studies. Data can be collected in a variety of ways. At the initial, exploratory stage of the research process, including problem definition and hypotheses generation, managers may collect information informally by "walking around." Discussions with colleagues, field marketing personnel, distributors, customers, and noncustomers can provide valuable information (see chapter 15 on how Japanese firms conduct research). Additional data may be collected from secondary sources (published sources, syndicated studies) and through primary research, which includes a variety of research methods such as interviews, surveys, focus groups, observation, and experiments. Table 5.4 lists the types of data and data collection methods and provides brief descriptions of key uses of each.

5. Analyzing the data and interpreting the results. Marketing researchers rely on both qualitative and quantitative research analyses to analyze their data. The analytic procedures to be used are generally selected prior to data collection, so that the data collection procedures used are appropriate. Decisions at this stage relate to data coding, tabulations, and analytic techniques. When interpreting and communicating the research results, marketing researchers need to keep in mind who the target audience for their report is, and ensure that the results are communicated so as to ensure that the managerial recommendations are apparent.[33]

TABLE 5.4 Types of Data, Data Collection Methods, and Key Uses

Type of Data/Data Collection Method	Description	Use
Secondary data	Already exist as a result of routine company record keeping and previous research, or external sources of published data (e.g., sales and shipment reports, MIS data, supermarket scanner data)	Good starting point for most research because data are readily available and relatively low cost (e.g., analysis of sales and shipment data may be used to forecast demand, identify usage segments, plan logistics, develop channels).
Primary data	Collected specifically as part of the research process; may be demographic, socioeconomic, psychological, or relate to attitudes, opinions, knowledge, purchase intentions, or behavior	Key use where secondary data are unavailable or unreliable (e.g., address a large number of research questions such as what consumer attitudes and preferences are, how they shop, and how they consume).
Observational data	Collected via observation of natural or contrived market settings; variety of techniques include personal and mechanical observation	Useful to gain understanding of actual consumer behavior, particularly when the researcher believes that the consumers are unable or unwilling to articulate their motivations and preferences.
Focus group data	Collected from observation of small groups of people brought together to discuss a subject of interest; discussion moderated to ensure that all individuals participate	Useful for generating hypotheses for further testing; collecting information to help structure interview and survey questionnaires; obtaining overall consumer reaction to new concepts.
Interview data	Collected from personal or telephone interviews with one or more participants on subjects of interest	Useful to gain in-depth knowledge of the areas of interest, especially where focus groups may interfere with candid responses (e.g., doing research on competitors, sensitive and personal topics for which privacy is essential).
Survey data	Collected from mail, telephone, fax, and electronic mail interviews of a sample of respondents from the population of interest. Questionnaires may be self-administered or interviewer administered, and include a number of different types of response formats including fixed alternative, open-ended, and projective questions.	Useful where a larger sample is required, so impersonal survey methods offer benefits. Also useful where the purpose of the research is descriptive and the researcher needs a lot of information on the population of interest (e.g., segmentation studies).
Experimental data	Collected in carefully controlled conditions where the researcher can manipulate variables of interest and examine their effects on other variables	Useful for causal research where hypotheses generated at other stages of the research process are tested (e.g., test marketing).

Characteristics of Good Research

Because all marketing research aims to provide information that facilitates and supports marketing decision making, it must be reliable. To produce results that are reliable, generalizable, and meaningful, marketing researchers use the scientific method. The scientific method is characterized by a well-documented process of observation, hypotheses generation, data collection, analysis, and interpretation. Researchers often use multiple methods to collect and analyze data, and test several different models to examine which one makes the most sense in the context of the data. Marketing research must address issues that are important to the marketing function, produce timely results, and communicate convincingly (read how Avon's marketing research group adds value to the company in Marketing Anecdote 5.4).

Some Techniques for Market Analysis[34]

The range of marketing research tools and models, as well as the issues involved in designing and conducting such research, are far beyond the scope of our discussion. However, to appreciate the potential of marketing research, and to understand how it is used, we have provided a list and description of key marketing research techniques with examples of the questions they help answer in Table 5.5. In addition, we briefly discuss a few statistical techniques researchers use for market analysis. We concentrate on describing how the techniques are used to segment markets and position products and services.

Cluster Analysis, Factor Analysis, and Discriminant Analysis

Cluster analysis[35] is a set of techniques used to identify groups of similar variables and objects based on their characteristics. In market segmentation applications, cluster analysis uses predetermined criteria (segmentation bases) to group individuals or organizations into clusters that are internally homogeneous and externally heterogeneous. The three sequential steps required for such analysis are partitioning, interpretation, and profiling. In addition to the many statistical issues involved in the first stage, the researcher has to decide how many clusters or market segments should be formed. This decision is in part based on a thorough understanding of the market, including how many segments are manageable.

Consider for example, a simple attempt to segment the beer market. If the researcher believes that attitudes toward consumption of light and regular beer may be used to classify beer consumers into groups, cluster analysis can be used for this grouping. A survey questionnaire with a number of attitudinal statements, as well as questions on demographics, alcohol, and beer consumption may be used. Consumers may be asked to indicate the extent to which they agree or disagree (on a seven-point scale) with each attitudinal statement. Examples include, "Regular beer has a full-bodied taste," "Light beer tastes smoother," and "Light beer is healthy." If, as is usual, a very large number of such statements is used, factor analysis may be used to attempt to reduce the number of attitudinal statements by combining them into a smaller number of composite dimensions.

Factor analysis is a set of techniques that explores the interdependence among variables in order to explain them in terms of their underlying dimensions. These techniques are primarily used for data reduction and summarization. Conducting a factor analysis with the beer attitude responses may lead to the discovery of a taste factor, a health factor, and so on. If appropriate, these composite factors may be used as the clustering variables.

A clustering procedure may then be used to group individuals based on their responses to all the attitudinal statements. Let us assume that three distinct clusters are discovered. The attitude patterns of the resulting segments, if any, can be interpreted, and the segments labeled descriptively. This interpretation involves examining the average cluster scores for each attitudinal statement used in the clustering. The procedure usually used to examine average group scores is called discriminant analysis.

Discriminant analysis attempts to find the combination of independent variables that best discriminates between two or more predefined clusters or groups. It is the appropriate statistical technique used when the dependent variable is categorical (e.g., cluster membership) and the predictor variables are metric. In our beer example, we may find two clusters with positive attitudes toward light beers, one of which is also positive to regular beers, and one cluster with a negative attitude toward light

TABLE 5.5 LEADING MARKETING RESEARCH TECHNIQUES

Technique Name	Description	Use	Example Questions Addressed
Factor analysis	Statistical procedure for reducing a set of measures to a smaller number of underlying variables, termed factors	To build scales from items and test for unidimensionality in questionnaire development To identify valid measures for variables to be used, in turn, as independent and dependent variables in other hypothesis testing or predictive contexts To construct perceptual maps based on consumer reactions to product attributes	What are the underlying attribute dimensions governing consumer perceptions of a brand? How do different brands score on the key attributes of a product class? Do the measures of a scale validly indicate the underlying construct they are purported to measure?
Correlation or bivariate contingency table analyses	Statistical procedure for ascertaining the strength of association between two variables	To determine the correlates of a focal variable with other variables To discover patterns of association among a set of variables	Does market share correlate with profitability? What is the association between advertising expenditures and sales? Are attitudes toward a brand positively correlated with intentions to try it?
Multiple regression	Statistical technique for determining the degree of dependence that a dependent variable has on two or more independent variables	To identify valid causes of a dependent variable of interest and compare their relative effect To predict the values of a dependent variable as a function of independent variables	Which perceived attributes of a brand contribute to consumer intentions to purchase it? What is the relative contribution of pricing and promotion, advertising, and distribution expenditures on sales of a product? For a given level of couponing, free sampling advertising, and other marketing expenditures planned, what will the level of sales be?
Discriminant analysis	Statistical technique where membership in a group is related to a set of independent variables (where the latter are typically measured at the interval level)	To determine on what bases two groups differ To predict the classification of an object (e.g., person) to one of two groups on the basis of a set of predictors	Do two market segments differ in terms of the attitudes, opinions, and life styles of consumers? Based on personal characteristics and one's past behavior, what is the likelihood that a given customer applying for a loan will be a credit risk? Do users and nonusers of a brand differ in terms of their judgments of product attributes?
Multidimensional scaling (MDS)	Procedure for representing perceptions spatially, typically in two or three dimensions	To reveal the dimensions underlying consumer perceptions of brand attributes. To locate one's own and competitors' brands on the dimensional space of attributes.	What are the underlying attribute dimensions governing consumer perceptions of a brand? How do consumer preferences correspond to existing perceptions of brands in the attribute space?

TABLE 5.5 LEADING MARKETING RESEARCH TECHNIQUES—CONTINUED

Technique Name	Description	Use	Example Questions Addressed
		To identify opportunities for positioning a new brand or repositioning an old one.	Which attributes should a new brand stress? How should an existing brand change its attributes or consumer perceptions of its attributes?
Conjoint analysis	Method for measuring consumer utilities for levels of product attributes	To ascertain the relative importance of product attributes To aid in the decision of the optimum level of product attributes To estimate market share for a new product	Which attributes of a brand are most salient for consumers? How much of each attribute and which features should a brand incorporate to maximize consumer satisfaction while minimizing costs? What level of sales and market share will be achieved for alternative attribute levels?
Analysis of variance (ANOVA)	Statistical procedure for analyzing the effects of one or more categorical independent variables, which are typically manipulated in a controlled experiment, on the means of a dependent variable measured at least intervally	To determine main and interaction effects of independent variables on a dependent variable (ANOVA) or on multiple dependent variables (multivariate ANOVA) To determine the effects of independent variables on a dependent variable, while controlling for the effects of one or more intervally scaled variables (analysis of covariance)	How do consumer attitudes, preferences, and intentions to purchase vary as a function of exposure to rational, emotional, or humorous advertising executions? To what extent does consumption vary as a function of different market segments? Do sales vary as a consequence of low versus moderate price changes?
Cluster analysis	Method for classifying things into relatively homogeneous groups (i.e., "clusters")	To group customers on the basis of common characteristics To categorize products on the basis of like competitive attributes To cluster markets on the basis of common properties	What groups of customers exist in a market as defined by the unique benefits they seek in a product? Which brands in a market share like attributes and constitute competitive groups with rivalry primarily within clusters? Can homogeneous markets be defined on the basis of geography or other factors?
Path analysis and structural equation modeling	Technique for relating independent and dependent variables in complex chains and patterns	To discover if one or more variables mediate the effects of a set of independent variables on a set of dependent variables To model complex sequences of effects, feedback, and reciprocal causation	Do intentions translate preferences and normative pressure into action? Do attitudes influence choices or do choices determine attitudes? How do attitudes toward a brand, attitudes toward an ad, brand loyalty, and background factors affect decisions and actual purchase behaviors?

beers, all of whom also had negative attitudes toward regular beers. The first cluster, which likes only light beer, may be called "Health Conscious"; the second, which likes both light and regular beers, may be called "Guzzlers"; and the third, which likes neither light nor regular beer, may be called "Wine Drinkers." Note that the cluster labels may be given after the profiling, as in our case.

The next step involves profiling the clusters to reveal similarities and differences in other variables (those not already used in the clustering), such as demographics, lifestyles, alcohol and beer consumption, and purchase behavior. In our example, the profiling might reveal that the health conscious group is younger and more physically active than the other two segments, that the guzzlers drink the most beer, and that the wine drinkers drink the least beer, are concentrated in California, and prefer wine to other alcoholic beverages.

Multidimensional Scaling

Multidimensional scaling (MDS)[36] is a large group of techniques that help marketing researchers to understand a number of factors:

- What dimensions consumers use to evaluate products, advertisements, companies, and so forth.
- How many dimensions they use in their evaluations.
- The relative importance of each dimension in their evaluations.
- How the products are related perceptually, in order to determine which are directly competitive (similar in the consumers' judgments).
- How the consumers are grouped into market segments based on similarities in their preference judgments.

MDS helps researchers draw pictures of data so that they can visualize and communicate the relationships in complicated data that may be obscure when viewing just the numbers. Researchers recognize two important issues. First, consumers may use perceptual dimensions to evaluate the product, which may not overlap with or share anything in common with the objective attributes of the product. Second, consumers' perceptions, even when they are the same as the objective dimensions the marketer uses, may not always be consistent. Continuing our beer example, consumers may use their perceptions of how filling the beer is to make judgments about the beer's calorie content. But these judgments may not accurately reflect the actual calorie content.

These procedures are complicated by the reality that each consumer is different. Consumers may not all use the same dimensions in their evaluations. Even when they do, they may not all attach the same level of importance to the dimensions. And they may change both the dimensions and the importance of each over time, and as they are exposed to marketing stimuli. For example, one consumer may use perceived calorie content as a dimension, whereas another may not use calorie content at all, instead using price, packaging, and availability on deal. The first consumer may not consider price at all important, while it may be extremely important to the second. The first consumer, when exposed to constant sales, may at a later time increase the importance of price.

Input data to MDS could be preference data. In this case, we could simply ask our beer consumers to directly rank the beers from most to least preferred. Or we could ask them to rate each beer on a multipoint scale from "strongly prefer" to "hardly prefer," or "very suitable for the Superbowl" to "not at all suitable for the Superbowl." Or similarity data could be used. In the simplest case, we could ask the beer consumers to rank all possible pairs of beers from those that are most similar to those that are most dissimilar.

Once the data are collected and sorted, they may be analyzed using one of a number of MDS approaches to arrive at a map. As with cluster analysis, in addition to some objective statistics, researcher judgment is required to decide on the appropriate number of dimensions. The dimensions may actually be labeled by asking respondents or experts to interpret the maps subjectively. Or they may be identified in terms of objective attributes. In terms of our beer example, the MDS of similarity data we collect might give us a map that looks like the perceptual map in Figure 5.4. This map can be used in a variety of ways, as we have discussed earlier in this chapter in the section on perceptual mapping.

Conjoint Analysis

As we discuss in chapter 7, any brand, product, advertisement or company may be evaluated by consumers as a bundle of attributes. For example, one might think of a new beer as a combination of various levels of a number of attributes, including brand, number of ounces in container, container type (bottle, can, tap), price, calories, and so forth. Each consumer will have an individual rule for combining the values associated with each attribute into an overall choice. This rule may be explicit, but more often is implicit, and unknown to both consumer and researcher.

Conjoint analysis[37] is a technique that relates independent variables and their levels to a response variable such as a consumer's relative brand preference using a particular rule for combining the attributes. This technique has many managerial uses, including the following:

- New product design: selecting the optimum combination of features.
- Determining the relative importance of each feature in choice.
- Estimating potential market shares of products with different combinations of features.
- Grouping potential customers into segments, based on the similarity in the relative importance of various features to the choice process.
- Assessing segment potential.
- Determining the opportunity for new product feature combinations.

Again, consider our simple beer example. As brand managers, we may wish to select the final characteristics of a new beer. For this, we need to determine the combination of attributes that leads to brand choice in the beer market. Let us assume that we have three attributes: brand name (Dark versus Lite), bottle size (16 ounces versus 32 ounces), and calories (high versus low). We could ask each consumer to evaluate the eight possible combinations of attributes by ranking them. These data are then used to estimate how much each attribute level contributes to overall choice, given our assumption about the model consumers are using to make their choices.

Across all consumers, the results may suggest that brand name has the greatest relative importance, whereas bottle size is least important. Or, if we conduct the conjoint analysis within each segment we have determined, we may find that relative importance varies by segment, with brand name having the greatest relative importance for Wine Drinkers, bottle size for Guzzlers, and calories for the Health Conscious. Thus, conjoint analysis may be combined with cluster analysis to determine benefit segments that have similar patterns of relative importance within a segment, but differ across segments. Results of this kind may be used to make new product decisions, as well as to assess the need and basis for product differentiation required to serve various market segments.

SUMMARY

Driven by the realization that building customer relationships is important, marketers have moved away from a mass-marketing approach to individualized marketing. The process of segmentation, targeting, and positioning (STP) is critical for marketers as they attempt to serve customers well and to be competitive. The goal of STP is to improve marketing performance.

- *Segmentation* is the process of describing the market in terms of the number of distinct groups of similar consumers that exist and their characteristics. Before segmenting their markets, managers must define their markets on the basis of product functions and technology, type of customer, geography, or stage in the production-distribution system. The segmentation process involves selecting variables that best differentiate between consumers, and using those variables in a segmentation procedure to group consumers. Consumer and organizational marketers use demographic, geographic, psychographic, and behavioral variables as segmentation bases.

- Geographic and demographic segmentations are relatively easy to perform, but do not provide information on consumer attitudes, motivations, preferences and behavior.

- Psychographic segmentation attempts to address this issue by collecting lifestyle data from large samples of consumers, and using these as segmentation variables. However, this method attempts to make predictions about consumer purchases based on their attitudes.

- Behavioral segmentation uses actual past behavior in the product category and consumer benefits sought for segmentation. Thus, it has been the most successful of the segmentation approaches.

To be useful for market targeting and positioning, segmentation should be reliable, use bases of segmentation that differentiate between segments, identify distinct segments, and describe them well. Further markets are dynamic, so segmentation should be an ongoing process.

- *Targeting* refers to evaluating identified segments and selecting segments to be served. In identifying the best segment opportunities, marketers evaluate segment attractiveness—size, growth potential, profitability, competitor profiles—and fit with organizational objectives and resources. When selecting segments, marketers also decide between concentrating their efforts on one segment or serving many segments. When concentrating on one segment, they may offer the single segment an undifferentiated offering (a single-segment focus) or a differentiated offering (a market focus). When multiple segments are selected, the firm may choose a product focus—offering a single product to all segments—or differentiate its offering in an attempt to provide each segment with a customized product—a market dominance approach.

- *Positioning* strategy refers to the approach a firm uses to achieve a desired and distinct position in the customer's mind. In addition to real product differences, distinctive positioning stems from good communication. Managers must decide how to position—attributes, benefits, usage occasions, user categories, and competitors—as well as how many aspects to include when positioning. A unique selling proposition with one clear basis for positioning is easy to communicate. Perceptual mapping is a useful and widely used analytic technique that aids positioning decisions and has a number of other important marketing uses.

Marketing research provides information for marketing decisions such as segmentation, targeting, and positioning; program design and implementation; and measuring program performance. The information is managed using marketing information systems, databases, and decision support systems. Good research uses the scientific method, proceeds through a series of stages from problem definition and research design, to data collection, analysis, and implementation. It also addresses important issues and provides timely results.

A variety of techniques are available to help marketing managers answer their research questions. Of the large variety of tools and techniques available to marketing researchers, cluster, factor, and discriminant analyses are useful in market segmentation. Multidimensional scaling is used extensively in positioning, and conjoint analysis is used to aid new product decisions as well as for segmentation.

QUESTIONS FOR DISCUSSION

1. What is targeting? How is it different from segmentation?

2. You have been appointed as brand manager in a medium-sized mail-order company. The company has historically used demographic segmentation. Develop a convincing plan for adopting behavioral segmentation.

3. As a frequent business flier on American Airlines (AA), what aspects of the AAdvantage program do you most appreciate? How is your response likely to differ from that of a leisure traveler? How might AA collect and use this information?

4. With reference to the above, what criteria would you use to evaluate the effectiveness of AA segmentation?

5. Think about the local car wash service. How might the car wash apply the concepts of segmentation, targeting, and positioning to improve its profitability?

6. Snapple iced tea was a great success. However, the product has recently lost sales to competing products. When it was launched, how was Snapple positioned? Why was a clear positioning important for its success? Why might it have been difficult to achieve? Should Snapple attempt to reposition itself?

7. What marketing research tools are available for assisting positioning decisions? segmenting decision? new product decisions? How are they useful?

8. For the local car wash in question 5, design a research study to help improve customer satisfaction and repurchase. What questions would you ask? Whom? Where?

NOTES FOR FURTHER READING

1. Don Peppers and Martha Rogers, *The One to One Future: Building Relationships One Customer at a Time* (New York: Doubleday, 1993), p. 5.

2. B. Joseph Pine II, Don Peppers, and Martha Rogers, "Do You Want to Keep Your Customers Forever?" *Harvard Business Review*, March–April 1995, pp. 103–114.

3. Daniel Yankelovich, "New Criteria for Market Segmentation," *Harvard Business Review*, March–April 1964, pp. 83–90.

4. See Louis P. Bucklin, "Retail Strategy and the Classification of Consumer Goods," *Journal of Marketing* 27 (January 1963), pp. 50–55; and Richard H. Holton,

"The Distinction between Convenience Goods, Shopping Goods, and Specialty Goods," *Journal of Marketing* 22 (July 1958), pp. 53–56.

5. Much of this section is based on Robert D. Buzzell, "Note on Market Definition and Segmentation," *Harvard Business School Note #579-083.*

6. Theodore Levitt, "Marketing Myopia," *Harvard Business Review*, 1960, reprinted as an HBR Classic in *Harvard Business Review*, September–October 1975, pp. 26–48.

7. Yankelovich, "New Criteria for Market Segmentation," pp. 83–90.

8. Ibid., p. 84.

9. This example is taken from Peppers and Rogers, *The One to One Future*, p. 97–99.

10. "PRIZM Lifestyle Segmentation," *Claritas Brochure*, 1995.

11. For more information on VALS and VALS 2, see Kevin J. Clancy and Robert S. Shulman, "The Marketing Revolution," (New York: Harper Business, 1993), pp. 61–63; and Marieke De Mooij, *Advertising Worldwide*, 2nd ed. (Hertfordshire, London: Prentice-Hall International (UK), 1994), pp. 163–165.

12. Salah S. Hassan and Roger D. Blackwell, *Global Marketing: Perspectives and Cases* (Fort Worth, Tex.: Dryden Press, 1994); and De Mooij, *Advertising Worldwide.*

13. See De Mooij, *Advertising Worldwide*, for excellent descriptions of several such studies.

14. Justine Martin, "Ignore your Customer," *Fortune*, May 1, 1995.

15. Dick Warren Twedt, "How Important to Marketing Strategy Is the 'Heavy'? *Journal of Marketing* 28 (January 1964).

16. James Vander Putten, quoted in Peppers and Rogers, *The One to One Future*, p. 108.

17. Russell I. Haley, "Benefit Segmentation: A Decision-oriented Research Tool," *Journal of Marketing* 21 (July 1968).

18. Jean-Philippe Deschamps and P. Ranganath Nayak, *Product Juggernauts* (Cambridge, Mass.: Harvard Business School Press, 1995), ch. 3.

19. Jean-Marie Choffray and Gary L. Lilien, *Market Planning for New Industrial Products* (New York: Ronald Press, 1980).

20. V. Kasturi Rangan, Rowland Moriarty, and Gordon Swartz, "Segmenting Customers in Mature Industrial Markets," *Journal of Marketing* 56 (1992): 72–82.

21. Derek F. Abell, *Defining the Business: The Starting Point of Strategic Planning* (Upper Saddle River, N.J.: Prentice-Hall, 1980).

22. Derek F. Abell, *Managing with Dual Strategies: Mastering the Present, Preempting the Future* (New York: Free Press, 1993). For information on market segmentation, see also Clancy and Shulman, *The Marketing Revolution*, pp. 54–83.

23. Kevin J. Clancy and Robert S. Shulman, *Marketing Myths that Are Killing Business*, (New York: McGraw-Hill, 1994), p. 116.

24. See Clancy and Shulman, *The Marketing Revolution*, pp. 54–83, for an excellent treatment of the issues, process, and example of selecting a profitable target market.

25. Alan W. H. Grant and Leonard A. Schlesinger, "Realize Your Customers' Full Profit Potential," *Harvard Business Review*, September–October 1995, pp. 59–72. For an excellent book on marketing for profitability, see Garth Hallberg, *All Consumers Are Not Created Equal: The Differential Marketing Strategy for Brand Loyalty and Profits* (New York: Wiley, 1995).

26. Al Ries and Jack Trout, *Positioning: The Battle for Your Mind* (New York: Warner Books, 1982).

27. Theodore Levitt, "Marketing Success Through Differentiation—of Anything," *Harvard Business Review*, January–February 1980, pp. 83–91.

28. Yoram J. Wind, *Product Policy: Concepts, Methods, and Strategy* (Reading, Mass.: Addison-Wesley, 1982), pp. 79–81.

29. Paul E. Green and Donald S. Tull, *Research for Marketing Decisions* (Upper Saddle River, N.J.: Prentice-Hall, 1978).

30. James R. Gregory, *Marketing Corporate Image: The Company as Your Number One Product* (Chicago: NTC Business Books, 1993).

31. Clancy and Shulman, *Marketing Myths that Are Killing Business*, p. 116.

32. "AMA Board Approves New Marketing Definition," *Marketing News*, March 1, 1985, pp. 1, 14.

33. For more details on marketing research, see a good standard textbook such as Gilbert A. Churchill, Jr., *Marketing Research: Methodological Foundations*, 6th ed. (Fort Worth, Tex.: Dryden Press, 1995).

34. See Richard P. Bagozzi, *Principles of Marketing Management;* Joseph F. Hair, Jr., Rolph E. Anderson, and Ronald L. Tatham, *Multivariate Data Analysis*, 2nd ed. (New York: Macmillan, 1987). We build on a beer example in this book.

35. Girish Punj and David W. Stewart, "Cluster Analysis in Marketing Research: Review and Suggestions for Application," *Journal of Marketing Research* (May 1983): 134–148.

36. Yoram Wind and Patrick J. Robinson, "Product Positioning: An Application of Multidimensional Scaling," *Attitude Research in Transition* (Chicago: American Marketing Association, 1972), pp. 155–175.

37. Paul E. Green, Stephen M. Goldberg, and Mila Montemayor, "A Hybrid Utility Estimation Model for Conjoint Analysis," *Journal of Marketing* (Winter 1981): 33–41.

CHAPTER OBJECTIVES

When you are done with this chapter you should have achieved the following:

- A thorough understanding of similarities and differences between organizational customers and individual consumers.
- An appreciation of how socially complex the organizational buyers' decision-making processes are relative to those of individual consumers.
- Familiarity with some of the ways in which vendors can segment organizational buyers to improve their product positioning and selling efforts
- An appreciation of the importance of segmenting organizational customers.

CHAPTER OUTLINE

DIFFERENTIATING ORGANIZATIONAL BUYERS

Size and Concentration
Multiple Decision Makers and Complex Decisions
Close and Intricate Relationships
Professional Buyers

CATEGORIZING ORGANIZATIONAL BUYERS

Objective-based Categories of Organizational Buyers
Output-based Categories of Organizational Buyers

TYPES OF BUYING SITUATIONS

Straight Rebuy
Modified Rebuy
New-Task Buying

STAGES IN THE ORGANIZATIONAL BUYING PROCESS

Modeling the Organizational Buying Process

Diffusion of Innovation and the Order of Stages in the Buying Process

TYPES OF PRODUCTS AND SERVICES PURCHASED BY ORGANIZATIONS

Raw Materials
Components and Partially Processed Materials
Capital Goods
Ancillary Equipment
Supplies
Services

DERIVED AND FLUCTUATING DEMAND

COMPLEX DECISION PROCESSES IN ORGANIZATIONAL PURCHASES

External Influences on Organizational Buying Behavior
Internal Influences on Organizational Buying Behavior

(continued)

The Fall and Rise of the Automobile Components Industry in the United States

Delphi–Engine Management Systems, a division of General Motors Corporation, produces many components that manage fuel and exhaust flow in automobiles. Its products range from fuel tanks and fuel pumps to catalytic converters, as well as the well-known AC spark plugs. For more than 70 years, Delphi–EMS has developed products that help General Motors meet government standards for fuel economy and emissions, but many people at Delphi–EMS say their toughest challenge has been the continuing crusade begun in the 1980s to reduce costs and improve efficiency in order to stay in business. For more than 50 years, Delphi–EMS enjoyed a straight rebuy relationship with GM assembly divisions, such as Chevrolet and Buick, because it was also part of the corporation. Initially, favoring Delphi–EMS created a competitive advantage for GM because the close relationship gave assembly divisions increased control over supply and costs. Starting in the midseventies, however, the division be-

Many companies sell components to manufacturers of final consumer goods: AC Delco manufactures electrical components for GM.

came a net liability to GM because of its rising manufacturing costs in the face of increasing global competition.

After reorganizing in 1985, General Motors began reducing the privileged status enjoyed by Delphi–EMS. Today Delphi–EMS competes on the same terms as all non-GM sources in what amounts to modified-rebuy relationships. If Delphi–EMS cannot provide superior products in terms of cost, quality, and just-in-time delivery, it will not get the business. In addition, the division has been forced to market its products aggressively to non-GM customers such as Ford and Chrysler.

Delphi––EMS is the only GM division in this type of relationship. Virtually all of GM's component divisions in the United States receive the same treatment from the parent company. They must compete on an equal basis with all other suppliers, and they must therefore seek business outside GM. In this new strategy, GM's domestic component divisions are following their European counterparts, which since 1992 have seen dramatic increases in sales and profits, and currently sell more than 40 percent of their output to non-GM carmakers such as Peugeot and Honda. Although the current outlook for those divisions is very positive, such has not always been the case. Historically, the European automobile market has been more competitive than the U.S. domestic market, and margins have been narrower. In the 1980s, profits of GM's vehicle divisions in Europe fell more dramatically than those of domestic divisions, and the European vehicle divisions started pressuring component suppliers to reduce costs. The result was a crisis for parts suppliers, who had to lower prices and improve performance or risk going out of business. GM's European component divisions responded by consolidating their operations into a single large division and using engineering, manufacturing, and marketing resources more efficiently. This enabled the component divisions to meet GM's aggressive pricing demands and to address customer needs for integrated manufacturing and materials management. Domestic divisions of GM are now making similar changes.

Similar competitive pressures have affected other domestic automobile component manufacturers, who are working with the same determination as Delphi–EMS and other GM divisions on both sides of the Atlantic. For example, when Japanese automobile manufacturers started establishing assembly operations in North America, they found U.S. suppliers unable to meet their high standards. In addition, Japanese carmakers were used to being as influential in the internal affairs of suppliers as they were in their own operations. Japanese buyers expected to make suggestions about ways to improve supplier operations and to share in the savings produced by their suggestions. This was in sharp contrast to the arm's length relationships common in the United States. The differ-ent expectations resulted in strained business and interpersonal relationships.

U.S. domestic suppliers initially reacted with a take-it-or-leave-it attitude that offended Japanese manufacturers, who responded by importing all of their components from outside the United States and inviting their Japanese suppliers to establish operations on the North American continent. Later, as Japanese automakers captured a large percentage of the U.S. car market, and domestic automakers suffered losses, domestic suppliers suffered substantial losses as well. Domestic suppliers were hurt further when some U.S.-based automakers also started buying components from Japanese suppliers, such as when GM assembly divisions bought instrument clusters from Nippodenso instead of Delco Electronics. The loss of business forced domestic manufacturers to reconsider their approach to Japanese customers; they improved the quality of their components and efficiency of their delivery systems, and they adopted more cooperative attitudes. Crisis has fostered a fundamental change in how automobile-component manufacturers approach continuous improvement, and they have become their own most demanding critics.

Sources: Personal interviews with Delphi–EMS personnel.

Merrill Goozner, "U.S. Auto Parts Firms Idling in Japan," *Chicago Tribune*, November 24, 1991, p. 7:3.

Kevin Kelly, Neil Gross, and James B. Treece, "Besting Japan," *Business Week*, June 7, 1993, pp. 26–28.

Stewart Toy and David Woodruff, "For GM, the Word from Europe is Parts," *Business Week*, January 18, 1993, pp. 53–54.

James B. Treece, Karen Lowry Miller, Zachary Schiller, and Kevin Kelly, "U.S. Part Makers Get More Mileage Out of Japan," *Business Week*, April 12, 1993, p. 74.

Joseph B. White, "U.S. Car-Parts Firms Form Japanese Ties," *Wall Street Journal*, April 12, 1988, p. 6.

Delphi–EMS and other automobile-component manufacturers in North America sell billions of dollars worth of products every year, although virtually none of them sell products directly to consumers. They are thus seldom concerned with understanding consumers in the same way that General Foods or Kellogg must. They sell to companies that manufacture automobiles, such as General Motors, Honda, and Ford, and to businesses that service vehicles or sell parts to do-it-yourself mechanics, such as Western Auto and Sears Roebuck. Thus, they are part of the large group of businesses that market to organizations. *Organizational buying* (sometimes also called *industrial* or *institutional buying*) is the decision-making process by which formal organizations establish the need for purchased products and services, and identify, evaluate, and choose among alternative brands and suppliers, and it is the primary concern of companies such as Delphi–EMS.[1]

Formal organizations include different types of businesses, as well as government agencies that range in size from country stores to the Pentagon. In the case of automobile-component manufacturers, both buyers and sellers are formal organizations. In some cases the company supplying goods to an organization may also buy products from that company or its competitors. Delphi–EMS, for example, buys steel from Inland Steel, computer services from Electronic Data Systems, and automobiles for its executives from GM assembly divisions. In total, purchases of products and services by organizational buyers in the United States added up to about $3.5 trillion in 1995, or about 50 percent of total U.S. sales of goods and services.

Around the world, literally millions of organizations purchase goods and services, and these customers must be approached with marketing programs that are as well developed as those used for final consumers. Many processes involved in marketing to organizations resemble those involved in selling to individual consumers, because both involve convincing entities to exchange one set of resources for another. Organizations are complex social entities, however, and their purchasing-decision processes can differ substantially and in important ways from those of individual consumers.

Marketing managers in industrial products or service industries must keep in mind that individual consumers and organizational buyers purchase goods and services for different reasons. Some organizational purchases are directly aimed at improving company welfare, such as when GM assembly divisions started buying instrument clusters from Nippodenso to reduce costs and improve quality. In this respect, organizational buyers are motivated by self-interests similar to those individual consumers exhibit.

Organizations purchase other goods and services, however, to benefit employees and customers or to meet moral and legal obligations that individual consumers do not face. Some examples are the purchase of employee health insurance by companies such as General Motors, FMC Corporation, and Hewlett-Packard, or environmental waste cleanup by companies such as US Steel and ALCOA. In addition, even when they purchase out of self-interest, organizations must balance the interests of a larger number of constituencies (e.g., employees, shareholders, customers, communities) and must consider the implications of their actions over a longer time horizon. General Motors assembly divisions decided to purchase instrument panels from non-GM component suppliers only after a multiyear study of the impact of such a decision on GM employees' welfare and on the investment returns to GM stockholders.

If companies want to reach organizational buyers, they need to recognize these differences in purchase objectives and time horizons, and to design marketing strategies to communicate and persuade organizational buyers more effectively.

They must also keep in mind other differences between individual and organizational customers, such as differences in

- overall size (e.g., financial resources, number of employees)
- formality of relationships
- categories of buyers
- kinds of goods and services organizational customers purchase and the complexity of their decision-making processes
- the product and service attributes such customers consider most important.

These topics are considered throughout this chapter.

We begin by discussing some common organizational buyer characteristics, such as their size and geographic concentration. We discuss objectives-based and output-based categories of buyers, and the types of purchasing arrangements each is likely to use. Next we look at the stages in the organization's decision-making process and the types of products and services most organizations purchase. After that we discuss factors that make organizational decision making complex—factors that vendors must understand to be successful. These include external factors, such as the economy and interpersonal relations, and factors internal to individual decision makers. We also discuss how social context and roles influence the behavior of buying-center members and the decision outcomes themselves. We conclude the chapter by discussing some general trends in how vendors market to different types of organizational buyers and the importance of segmentation in marketing to organizations.

DIFFERENTIATING ORGANIZATIONAL BUYERS

Organizational buyers differ from individual consumers, and these differences have implications for how vendors develop and implement their marketing strategies. Table 6.1 summarizes and gives examples of the major characteristics of organizational buyers.

Size and Concentration

Two obvious differences between individual consumers and organizational buyers are their size and number. Organizational buyers usually represent a relatively small number of large entities that have substantial resources and influence on their markets compared to those of the millions of individual customers for consumer products. Some automobile-tire manufacturers, for example, may sell to fewer than 20 organizational customers in the United States, but each one of those customers is a multimillion dollar operation. Vendors can seldom afford to ignore even a single customer. In contrast, companies marketing to individual consumers often ignore single individuals—and sometimes even large groups of customers—without seriously threatening their business. In addition, because organizational customers represent a small, demanding, and highly competitive group, vendors must adjust to each customer's proprietary technologies without accidentally revealing those technologies to the customer's competitors who buy similar equipment. A supplier of production control equipment who targets the tire industry, for example, must match its hardware and software to that used by Goodyear and Firestone without revealing to either customer how the other one controls its production flow.

Even though having a small number of large customers makes it easier for vendors to reach customers individually and cater to their needs more accurately, the disadvantage is that customers expect a higher level of attention because of their

TABLE 6.1 CHARACTERISTICS OF ORGANIZATIONAL BUYERS

Characteristic	Example
Organizational buyers are usually larger than individual consumers in terms of resources and the amount of their purchases.	Apparel retailers such as Kmart purchase hundreds of the same shirt or blouse, whereas individual consumers purchase only one.
Organizational buyers are fewer in number than individual consumers.	The output from most steel mills in the United States is sold directly to less than 50 Fortune 500 firms.
Organizational buyers in different industries tend to be geographically concentrated.	Most automobile manufacturing in the United States takes place in Michigan, Ohio, and California.
Relationships between organizational buyers and their suppliers tend to be close in terms of shared tasks and mutual influence.	Multiyear buy-sell agreements are the norm between Japanese manufacturers and their suppliers.
Organizational buying decisions are often managed by purchasing professionals and involve decision groups composed of representatives from different areas.	The purchase of engineering workstations at General Electric involves personnel from finance, information systems, engineering, manufacturing, materials management, plant engineering, and senior management.

greater purchase volume. Expectations for more attention often surface as demands for customized delivery schedules, discounts, and changes to the product design, among other things.

One additional factor related to the small number of buyers is that they tend to be more geographically concentrated than individual consumers. Automobile-tire manufacturers, for example, have historically located primarily in Ohio and Indiana, and oil exploration companies are headquartered mainly in Texas, Oklahoma, and California. Geographic concentration is an advantage because it reduces direct sales costs and permits more precise and focused monitoring of industry trends. Tracking the oil exploration industry, for example, requires monitoring the news media in only a relatively few markets.

Multiple Decision Makers and Complex Decisions

Organizational buyers also differ from individual customers in that organizational purchases often involve multiple decision makers from different areas of the organization acting together as a decision-making unit. The size of the decision unit depends on the type of purchase. In marketing, decision-making units are traditionally called *buying centers*—individuals and groups who participate in purchase decision processes and share common goals and risks arising from the decision.[2] In organizations in which members function more autonomously and share many job responsibilities, decision-making units have also been called *buying networks*.[3] Regardless of which term is used, decision units in organizations are unique in that their members often apply different criteria to the same buying decisions. A manufacturing engineer at Toyota who is considering the use of Delphi–EMS catalytic converters, for example, may base her decision primarily on ease of assembly, whereas the quality-control manager at the same plant may be more concerned with reliability. Vendors may not know initially who the decision makers are or what criteria they use, and thus they must be careful to gain the approval of all key decision makers before finalizing the terms of sale.

Many organizational buyers also follow formal policies and procedures in making purchases. At Chevrolet or Ford, for example, having Delphi–EMS as a supplier was discussed by a committee over a period of months before a final decision was made, and committees continue to review Delphi's performance on a regular basis. We discuss the influence of social context and roles on group purchase decisions later in this chapter.

Another set of differences between organizational and individual customers arises from the greater complexity of organizational decision processes relative to those of individual consumers. Although the fundamentals of adoption and diffusion, as discussed in chapter 5, are the same for all consumers—individuals as well as organizations—the actual processes by which organizations make decisions and what they demand of sellers may differ substantially from that of individuals. It follows, therefore, that buying decisions in organizations typically take longer and involve more attention to detail than individual-level purchases.

Close and Intricate Relationships

Relationships between buyers and sellers in organizational markets tend to be closer and more intricate than relationships between consumer-products companies and their individual customers, partly because only a small number of large customers are involved. Such relationships also arise from the complex nature of the products and services purchased. Quite often, vendors adapt their products and services to the needs of buyers in terms of technology, lot sizes, delivery schedules, and other factors, in order to satisfy concerns from different areas of the buyer's business.[4] Adaptation requires that buyers and sellers cooperate extensively throughout the transaction process and seek to build trust. Personnel at multiple levels of both buyer and seller organizations form extended networks during the development process, through which they try to understand one another, and commit to one another's success beyond what is typical in practically all buyer-seller dyads at the individual consumer level.[5] For example, vendors of the machinery used to mold automobile tires must work closely with engineers, financial analysts, and quality-control personnel from tire manufacturers, and they treat purchases as episodes in their ongoing relationships.

Industrial buying decisions may also involve other organizations, such as labor unions affected by the proposed changes, other suppliers, or government officials who must approve changes to a manufacturing facility. Even citizen groups concerned with tax implications or the environmental impact of a proposed product or service may get involved in such decisions. Some organizational purchases require consultation between the vendor and each affected party, and it may take months or even years for a final decision.

The 1980s and 1990s have seen an important trend in buyer-seller relationships: the emergence of *partner relationships*. In these arrangements, buyers and sellers display genuine interest in each other's welfare. They share detailed information about products, costs, and manufacturing operations, and they look for ways to integrate their efforts to everyone's benefit. Vendors benefit from partner relationships because they lower the costs of selling and administration below those typical of transaction-based relationships.[6] We discuss the implications and demands that partner relationships impose in greater detail in chapter 11 on sales and sales management and chapter 13 on distribution concerns from the producer's perspective. Marketing Anecdote 6.1 demonstrates how this trend has become standard practice in some industries.

Professional Buyers

The relationship that sellers have with organizational buyers also differs from that with consumers because organizations often have professional buyers who manage the buying process. In small buying organizations, the owner often handles

In 1993, Forrest Knox was an engine-mount buyer for Chrysler Corporation. But for a few days that year, he served as a member of a GROWTH team at the Freudenberg-NOK Rubber Products factory in Ligonier, Indiana. GROWTH stands for Get Rid Of Waste Through Team Harmony, and it is the Freudenberg-NOK version of *kaizen*, or continuous improvement. Starting in 1992, Freudenberg-NOK has been sending such teams into its various factories to identify ways to reduce costs and improve quality.

Kaizen teams are used by many companies across industries. Typically composed of hourly workers, engineers, customer representatives, and personnel from other areas as needed, these teams usually work for only short periods of time and focus their attention on a specific area of the factory, such as sheet-metal presses or component assembly. Teams are also given specific goals, such as a 20 percent capacity im-

provement, and are typically allowed to experiment with different techniques that companies can implement quickly. In most companies, kaizen teams receive cooperation from workers in the focal operation, largely because management has adopted a policy of protecting jobs in spite of efficiency improvements. Without the threat of losing their jobs, most plant workers feel free to contribute to company attempts to improve quality and reduce cost.

In the case of Freudenberg-NOK's plant in Ligonier, for example, teams were charged with improving the capacity of the engine-mount operations by 20 percent without adding equipment. This was part of the company's effort to meet the 6 percent annual price cut demanded by Chrysler and Ford. The teams' approach in almost all cases at Freudenberg-NOK plants is simple: observe how operations are done, identify inefficiencies and bottlenecks, and find ways to fix them. A key requirement is that solutions be

purchasing and makes primary decisions. For example, the purchase of a new oven by a family-owned restaurant is typically handled by the owner with some input from the kitchen staff. These situations are relatively straightforward and not much different from the sale of durable products or real estate to individual consumers. In medium-sized and large organizations, however, professional buyers often oversee and coordinate the actual buying processes and negotiate the best prices and terms from vendors. If the Bob Evans restaurant chain were to purchase new ovens, for example, a professional buyer would probably handle the transaction for all stores, with some input from others in the company. Vendors must work closely with professional buyers and gain access to all functional areas that can influence the buying decision.

CATEGORIZING ORGANIZATIONAL BUYERS

Our discussion thus far has treated organizational buyers as a homogeneous group. Marketers benefit, however, from distinguishing between types of organizational buyers, if they do so based on characteristics that are relevant to their marketing strategies. In this section, we categorize organizational buyers at two levels. First, we categorize them by their objectives and discuss how each category requires a slightly different marketing approach. Second, we categorize them based on their output or economic activity, and discuss how SIC code classifications can help marketers.

quick and cheap. This means that proposals requiring capital expenditures, such as robotics and automation, are eliminated right away. Teams must also talk with workers, listen to their concerns, and find ways to improve their efficiency and welfare. Companies realize that continuous improvement depends, at least in part, on committed and satisfied workers.

Whenever GROWTH teams are active at Freudenberg-NOK, they observe all operating shifts. At the Ligonier plant, the team observed three shifts and identified and implemented many small changes. Examples include changing the way natural rubber was fed into a press to reduce downtime and installing a shield to protect workers from rubber shavings. On average, the "quick and dirty" changes implemented by GROWTH teams achieve work-in-process reductions of more than 30 percent the first time they review an operation, and can improve productivity between 10 and 20 percent. GROWTH-team efforts also help to identify major causes of capacity constraints, which can-

not be fixed easily but can be addressed through careful engineering.

Management at Freudenberg-NOK and other companies often comment, however, that the longest lasting and most important benefit produced by GROWTH teams is collaboration among different functional areas within the company and with their customers. People that participate in GROWTH teams leave with a better understanding of the challenges and opportunities in other areas of the business and are better equipped to sustain a marketing orientation in their own jobs.

Sources: Al Fleming, "Lean and Happy: Freudenberg-NOK Finds Principles Fattens Bottom Line," *Automotive News*, May 31, 1993, supp. Insight, p. 16i.

Kathy Jackson, *"Chrysler Execs Help Look for Gains on O-Ring Line,"* Automotive News, December 19, 1994, p. 45.

James B. Treece, "Improving the Soul of an Old Machine," *Business Week*, October 25, 1993. pp. 134–136.

Objective-based Categories of Organizational Buyers

Although at some level of detail every organization is uniquely different from every other organization, organizational buyers can be grouped on the basis of their primary objectives. Table 6.2 summarizes three objective-based categories of organizational customers: industrial buyers, resellers, and institutional buyers.

Industrial Buyers

Industrial buyers are the largest group of organizational buyers in terms of dollar sales, and they buy the most diverse set of products and services. The approximately 680,000 industrial buyers in the United States—buy $3.2 trillion worth of products each year.[7] Industrial buyers produce goods and services for resale—goods that range in complexity from aircraft carriers to facial tissue and from hostile takeovers to lawn maintenance services. Industrial buyers buy goods and services as components of their products or to make producing such goods easier and more efficient.

Industrial buyers are normally independent, for-profit businesses, so they need to ensure that the value that purchased products add to their output exceeds the cost of such purchases. State-owned industries in more socialist leaning countries such

TABLE 6.2 CATEGORIES OF ORGANIZATIONAL BUYERS AND THEIR DISTINGUISHING CHARACTERISTICS

Characteristics	Industrial Buyers	Resellers	Institutional Buyers
Primary Motivation	Profitability	Profitability	Serving constituencies
Primary Use of Purchased Goods	Inclusion or consumption in the production of goods and services	Reselling to individual consumers and/or other organizations	Inclusion or consumption in the production of goods and services
Primary Concerns	Cost, delivery schedules, quality, reliability, adequate supplies	Cost, promotional discounts, depth of assortment	Quality, performance that meets specification
Typical Decision-making Unit	Group representing all affected functional areas	Single buyer responsible for the product category	Group representing all affected areas
Most Commonly Purchased Goods	Raw materials, components, manufacturing facilities, and machinery	Finished goods and supplies, retail space, and fixtures	Finished goods and supplies, capital goods, and installations
Biggest Challenges to Marketers	Technological innovations that preserve differentiation	Private label sourcing and low loyalty to suppliers	Shifting priorities with changing political administrations
Examples	Kellogg purchasing new equipment for making cereal	Major grocery store choosing which types of cereals to carry	The Pentagon purchasing cold cereals for its overseas troops

as France and Sweden are an exception to this rule, because most state-owned companies aim not so much for profit as for social welfare, and low cost might not be as important as full employment to these companies. A steel manufacturer in Indonesia, for example, may be more interested in generating jobs in the economy than in producing steel profitably.

Industrial buyers also seek purchases that help them differentiate their products. Most industrial buyers compete with other companies that produce similar goods, and they are interested in technological aspects of products that help to differentiate their own products and services from those of competitors. Industrial buyers will frequently pay a premium for goods and services that help differentiate their products in the consumer marketplace.

Resellers

Although they do not buy as much in terms of volume as industrial buyers, resellers represent the largest market in terms of the number of companies involved, with more than 1.4 million in the United States buying goods worth in excess of $3 trillion.[8] As the name implies, resellers purchase products and services for resale. They also purchase products and services, such as advertising, packaging, and supplies, that help them in the resale of other goods. Most often, resellers purchase finished products ready for distribution. Like industrial buyers, resellers are concerned with profits and are sensitive to costs.

Resellers vary in the types of products and services they sell, and consequently in the variety of products they purchase. Department stores such as Bloomingdale's, mass discounters such as Kmart, and broad-line wholesalers such as Associated Grocers carry a large assortment of products but a limited selection within each product category. Specialty retailers such as GAP, in contrast, normally carry a narrower product assortment but offer more variety within their limited product categories. Resellers usually buy from more suppliers than do industrial or institutional buyers, and they tend to exhibit less loyalty to any one supplier. Resellers are most loyal to suppliers who offer unique products or beneficial services. Levi Straus, for example, is a sportswear manufacturer to whom many apparel resellers are loyal because of its strong brand name, quality products, and sophisticated inventory management systems. The different types of resellers and their strategies are discussed in more detail in chapter 14.

Institutional Buyers

Institutional buyers—organizations that provide services to society at large—include federal, state, and local governments; charitable health-care organizations; colleges and universities; and other nonprofit organizations. In the United States alone, more than 86,000 government units spend more than $1.1 trillion annually, and more than 6 million additional institutional buyers spend more than $250 billion annually.[9] Institutional buyers purchase close to 25 percent of all sales in the United States alone, and an even higher proportion in countries with more centralized governments.

Institutional buyers differ from industrial buyers and resellers in that they seldom work toward profit, even though they can be sensitive to costs. In addition, institutional buyers are often held accountable by numerous constituencies (e.g., voters, patients, clients, other institutions), who frequently make irreconcilable demands. Hospitals, for example, face pressure to reduce costs from government and insurance providers at the same time that patients demand better quality care and physicians demand access to advanced medical equipment. Trying to improve health-care quality and simultaneously reduce costs has been difficult for many community hospitals, and some have been forced to close down.

Institutional buyers purchase a wide range of products and services. Some buyers, such as the Pentagon, buy highly sophisticated goods and place great emphasis on technological advances and confidentiality. Most other institutional buyers, however, purchase standard-grade goods that meet rigid performance specifications and pay fair prices for them. The prospect of fair profits for quality products makes institutional buyers attractive to many vendors.

Output-based Categories of Organizational Buyers

Another useful organizational buyer categorization scheme is one based on the Standard Industrial Classification system. The SIC system, developed by the U.S. Census Bureau, classifies U.S. businesses at multiple levels of aggregation based on economic output. Figure 6.1 illustrates the system's primary and subordinate levels of classification. The highest, most general level is the *division*, represented by a range of two-digit codes. Companies whose primary economic activity is manufacturing, for example, are in the 20 to 39 range, and retailers are in the 52 to 59 range. More narrowly defined groupings of businesses within a division are represented by distinct two-digit codes. Thus, the manufacturing division breaks down into 20 *major groups* based on product output, such as transportation (group 37) and food and kindred products (group 20). Each major group, in turn, contains several *subgroups* that are more specific and are represented by three-digit codes, such as meat products (subgroup 201) and beverages (subgroup 208). Subgroups are further segmented into even more specific clusters of *industries* represented by four-digit codes, such as wines and brandy (industry 2084) and bottled soft drinks (industry 2086). Notice that as we move down the levels, starting with the divisions, each subsequent level is more specific as to what the company produces, and that the levels are linked

Principal Divisions in SIC	Major Group Number	Subgroup Number	Industry Number
01–09 Agriculture, Forestry, & Fishing 10–14 Mining 15–17 Construction 20–39 Manufacturing 40–49 Transportation, Communications, Electric, Gas, & Sanitary Services 50–51 Wholesale Trade 52–59 Retail Trade 60–67 Finance, Insurance, & Real Estate 70–89 Services 91–97 Public Administration 99 Nonclassifiable Establishments	20 Food and Kindred Products 21 Tobacco Manufacturers 22 Textile Mill Products 23 Apparel Products 24 Lumber and Wood Products, except Furniture 25 Furniture and Fixtures 26 Paper and Allied Products 27 Printing, Publishing, and Allied Industries 28 Chemicals and Allied Products 29 Petroleum Refining and Allied Industries 30 Rubber & Miscellaneous Plastic Products 31 Leather & Leather Products 32 Stone, Clay, Glass, & Concrete Products 33 Primary Metal Industries 34 Fabricated Metal Products, except Machinery & Transportation 35 Machinery, except Electrical 36 Electrical and Electronic 37 Transportation 38 Measuring, Photographic, Medical, Optical, Watches, etc. 39 Miscellaneous Manufacturing Industries	201 Meat Products 202 Dairy Products 203 Canned and Preserved Fruits and Vegetables 204 Grain Mill Products 205 Bakery Products 206 Sugar & Confectionery Products 207 Fats and Oils 208 Beverages 209 Miscellaneous Food Preparation and Kindred Products	2082 Malt Beverages 2083 Malt 2084 Wines, Brandy, and Brandy Spirits 2085 Distilled, Rectified, and Blended Liquors 2086 Bottled and Canned Soft Drinks and Carbonated Water 2087 Flavoring Extracts and Flavoring Syrups, Not Elsewhere Classified

Source: Standard Industrial Classification Manual (Washington D.C.: Office of Management and Budget, 1987).

by code to the parent level. Thus, for the soft drinks industry (2086), the 20 refers to the manufacturing group, the 8 to the beverage subgroup, and the 6 to soft drinks. In total the Census Bureau uses SIC codes of seven digits to classify companies all the way to the specific product (e.g., pliers are SIC code 3423111). For marketing to organizations, the first four levels are the most useful. Starting on January 1, 1997, SIC codes are to be replaced by North American Industry Classification System (NAICS) codes, to be used by all members of the North American Free Trade Agreement (NAFTA). The adoption of NAICS codes will take some time.

One obvious advantage of categorizing buyers by NAICS or SIC code is that it provides vendors with an indication of the buyers' line of business, and by implication, what these firms are most likely to seek from vendors. For vendors who sell products across many industries, these highly informative classification schemes facilitate many procedures, such as collecting and managing market research information through surveys and literature studies, and allocating marketing resources (e.g., salespeople, advertising) on the basis of industry outlook.

Vendors also use such codes to estimate market potential and to forecast sales by market segment. Using codes to collect and segregate market information can produce the highly detailed and accurate market projections necessary to manage a business. For example, assume process-controller manufacturer Allen Bradley is trying to sell its product to beverage manufacturers. Process controllers are programmable computers that help integrate the activities of automated manufacturing equipment. Around the world, beverage production is becoming increasingly automated, as complex machinery moves product from the mixing of raw ingredients to the shipping dock. Such automation levels require the reliable and versatile process controllers produced by Allen Bradley. Having a good product, however, is not enough to ensure that Allen Bradley will be successful.

For Allen Bradley to sell its product to beverage producers, the company needs to deploy its marketing resources carefully, assign advertising dollars judiciously, and make sure its salespeople are calling on the right companies and preparing for their sales calls with the proper expectations. In addition, it needs to anticipate sales accurately enough to have adequate manufacturing capacity, and to plan the flow of material into its factories and its production schedules to give customers on-time delivery while keeping in-process and finished goods inventories at low levels. Accurate sales forecasts are necessary for Allen Bradley, and by basing forecasts on industry classifications, Allen Bradley can achieve its aims.

To use the SIC system, for example, Allen Bradley would first identify the four-digit SIC codes for beverage types that use highly automated production processes, because those producers are good candidates for process controllers. In this example, we assume that SIC codes 2082 (malt beverages) and 2086 (bottled and canned soft drinks and carbonated water) are the most automated and consequently the most likely to need process controllers. Allen Bradley managers can judge which SIC codes are the best targets by looking at the SIC codes of existing customers, by consulting industry experts, and by surveying a large number of companies chosen from the more general beverages subgroup (SIC code 208).

Once it identifies the appropriate four-digit SIC codes, Allen Bradley must estimate the number of process controllers each manufacturing location would require. The basis for such estimates can be as specific as the number of production machines per manufacturing location or as general as sales revenue. The choice of a basis must balance accuracy with the availability of information. Highly detailed information about items such as automated machines is seldom available from public sources, and most vendors must rely on using more general measures such as sales revenue, output capacity, or amount of material processed. If we assume that output capacity in cases per day is the best basis for the beverage industry, Allen Bradley would ask existing and potential customers in the target SIC codes about the optimal number of process controllers for every thousand cases of output capacity. Allen Bradley would then collect information on output capacity for its target customers and arrive at market potential estimates for the malt and soft drink beverage industry sectors. If in the United States, for example, malt beverage manufacturers had 125 facilities with average output of 10,000 cases per day per facility, and a process controller was required for every 4,100 cases of capacity, national potential in the malt beverage industry would be calculated as follows:

$$\frac{(125 \text{ facilities} \times 10,000 \text{ cases per facility})}{4,100 \text{ cases per controller}} = 305 \text{ controllers}$$

Estimating industrywide market potential would be useful to Allen Bradley for planning advertising campaigns or planning capacity. For allocating sales personnel, however, Allen Bradley may need to break down the number of facilities by geographic area or some other means of assigning sales territories. Calculating the market potential for each territory, however, would be the same as for the national market. By combining SIC codes with sales territories, Allen Bradley can segment the malt beverage industry in managerially useful ways. We discuss the importance of segmentation later in this chapter.

The main point of this example is to illustrate the level of precision achievable by using industry codes, both because of their varying levels of aggregation and the availability of information by codes from multiple sources. Because they are maintained by the Census Bureau, SIC or NAICS codes are used by many government agencies to report economic and demographic data. In addition, many industry and trade groups have adopted such codes as a means of categorizing much of their own information. The widespread use of code systems has resulted in substantial amounts of information being classified by codes, and has made it easier and more efficient for organizational vendors to gather, analyze, and use information.

TYPES OF BUYING SITUATIONS

Earlier in our discussion of organizational buyers, we mentioned that buying decisions can vary substantially in terms of the number of people involved or the amount of effort required. Some organizational purchases require only a telephone call or electronic message and are transacted in a manner of minutes or seconds. Other purchases may require many presentations or negotiation sessions over several months or years before the buyer makes a decision. Different buying situations require vendors to adopt different strategies in terms of the resources they deploy and the intensity of their marketing efforts. Consequently, vendors often categorize buying situations and develop generalized approaches for each type of situation.

Marketing scholars Robinson, Farris, and Wind proposed a useful descriptive framework for categorizing organizational buying situations.[10] They identified three situations for organizational buying: *straight rebuy*, *modified rebuy*, and *new task*.

Straight Rebuy

In *straight-rebuy* situations, organizations simply reorder products they have purchased before. Reorders are typically routine and automatic, and buyers expend very little effort. For example, if the sales department at Citibank needed more computers and ordered them to match equipment currently in use, the steps in the process would simply be those illustrated in Figure 6.2.

Straight rebuys normally involve only a purchasing professional, and they represent a large portion of all organizational buying. Other examples of straight rebuys might include Procter & Gamble ordering glass containers for its Folger's brand coffee or the U.S. Treasury buying special paper stock for printing savings bonds.

| FIGURE 6.2 | STAGES IN STRAIGHT-REBUY SITUATION |

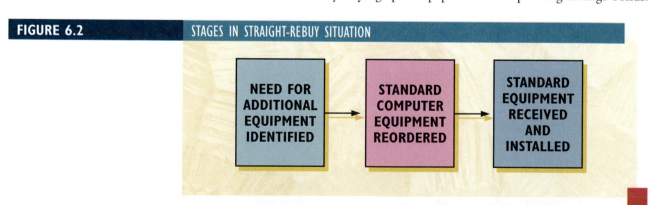

NEED FOR ADDITIONAL EQUIPMENT IDENTIFIED → STANDARD COMPUTER EQUIPMENT REORDERED → STANDARD EQUIPMENT RECEIVED AND INSTALLED

Straight rebuys typically involve ordering from suppliers on an "approved" list. Suppliers not on the list rarely get any business, so vendors need to protect their positions. This is done most often by maintaining or improving their product quality and service. Vendors also protect their positions by setting up automatic reorder systems and electronic data exchanges to make repurchases easier.

New vendors typically find it difficult to break into a straight-rebuy relationship. New suppliers often try to get small orders by offering reduced prices, hoping that buyers will be satisfied and expand the size of subsequent purchases. This is similar to the use of loss leaders by consumer marketers to build foot traffic and encourage other purchases. Vendors also try to capitalize on buyer dissatisfaction with current suppliers. This strategy can backfire, though, if the criticism of established suppliers implies that the buyer made a poor initial choice.

Modified Rebuy

In *modified-rebuy* situations, existing products or terms are no longer satisfactory and must be adapted to new conditions. Such situations usually involve changes to attributes of the product or service, or to related aspects such as delivery schedules, return policies, financing arrangements, or price. For example, if Citibank were buying computer workstations for the public relations department instead of for the sales department, and public relations' demands differed from those of sales, the process would be as illustrated in Figure 6.3.

Buyers who modify rebuy relationships often want additional information and implement new decision criteria, which frequently involve multiple decision makers such as purchasing professionals, financial analysts, and materials management personnel. Other examples of modified rebuy situations are Ford Motor Company deciding on the headlamp supplier for its restyled minivan, or the Mayo Clinic deciding on a supplier of hospital beds for a refurbished hospital wing.

In modified-rebuy situations, established suppliers enjoy a competitive edge because of their previous relationship with the buying organization, but they are at risk of losing the business if they do not respond to the customer's changing demands. Current suppliers need to approach modified-rebuy situations with the same intensity with which they approach new business opportunities because decision units in modified-rebuy situations are often instructed to consider all potential suppliers equally. Needless to say, modified rebuys present good opportunities for new suppliers.

Modified rebuys have become the norm in many industries as competitive pressures increase. The philosophy of *kaizen*, or continuous improvement, has

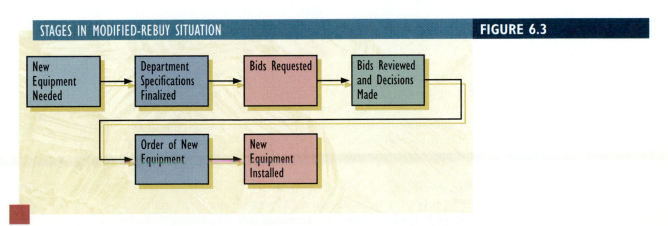

STAGES IN MODIFIED-REBUY SITUATION　　　　　　　　　　　**FIGURE 6.3**

In 1992, as General Motors continued to lose market share and profits in the U.S. market, it sought to reduce the cost of its purchased components. To achieve this, the company enlisted J. Ignacio Lopez de Arriortua as director of purchasing for all of General Motors. Lopez had served in a similar capacity for GM's European operations and was credited with greatly improving the profitability and efficiency of all European divisions.

Lopez employed an aggressive new approach in his relationship with suppliers. Shortly after taking over, he announced that GM would renegotiate practically all contracts with suppliers. He also demanded that his staff have access to all supplier facilities and instituted investigative teams to evaluate supplier operations. The teams inspected supplier facilities, identified areas of inefficiency, suggested improvements, and demanded price reductions commensurate with the savings expected from these improvements. Suppliers were forced to comply with Lopez's demands or risk losing lucrative GM business.

Lopez also instituted changes at GM headquarters in Detroit. He demanded that all members of his staff follow a "warrior diet" of fruit and low-fat foods and that all of them wear their watches on their right wrists until GM achieved cost reductions of at least 20 percent. Late-night meetings and quick decisions became the norm for the purchasing staff as

Lopez led the company through the most radical restructuring of supplier relationships in automobile industry history.

Lopez left General Motors during the summer of 1993 to accept a similar position with Volkswagen in Europe. Although his departure from GM was tainted with allegations of espionage, and some of his methods were retrospectively denounced as heavy handed and detrimental to quality, Lopez left his mark on GM North American operations. Versions of the supplier evaluation teams he instituted continue to work within GM to reduce costs in all supplier operations, and his sense of urgency about the future of the company has become firmly entrenched in the GM culture. Complacent General Motors suppliers are a thing of the past.

Sources: Audrey Choi and Monica Houston-Waesch, "Germany Approves U.S. Plea for Help in GM's Espionage Dispute," *Wall Street Journal*, August 12, 1994, p. A4.

Kevin Kelly and Kathleen Kerwin, "There's Another Side to the Lopez Saga," *Business Week*, August 23, 1993, p. 26.

David C. Smith, "Inside GM's Global Purchasing," *Ward's Auto World* 31 (April, 1995), p. 45ff.

John K. Teahen, Jr., "J. Ignacio Lopez Takes the Cake" (Year in Review), *Automotive News*, December 27, 1993, pp. 2–3ff..

John Templeman, Stewart Toy, and Paula Dwyer, "How Many Parts Makers Can Stomach the Lopez Diet?" *Business Week*, June 28, 1993, pp. 45–46.

put increased pressure on buyers and vendors to constantly reconsider and improve established products and arrangements. This means that companies revise product specifications, scrutinize delivery and payment schedules, and do not commit to ongoing business with established vendors who merely meet the initial purchase standards. Many organizational buyers establish moving targets for quality, performance, and price that suppliers must meet in order to remain on "approved lists." In effect, some industries feature suppliers in perpetual modified-rebuy situations. General Motors adopted this approach under the leadership of J. Ignacio Lopez de Arriortua (see Marketing Anecdote 6.2).

New-Task Buying

In *new-task buying* situations, organizational buyers face problems or demands with which they have little or no experience. These are inherently risky situations for buyers so they place greater emphasis on information gathering and evaluation of alternatives than they do in other buying situations. Thus, the decision process for new-task buying is longer and usually involves more people. If Citibank wanted to replace its standard mainframe computer with a massively parallel supercomputer, for example, the process would be as illustrated in Figure 6.4.

New-task buying frequently involves representatives from every functional area of the organization and sometimes requires senior management input and approval. New-task situations often arise when organizations must make large capital investments or design new products. For example, there was much new-task buying involved in building the English Channel tunnel, which links England to the European continent. Opened in 1994, the project involved new technologies in building, paving, and electric power transfer and created many opportunities for new product development. Another example comes from the fertilizer and pest-control industries, where environmental concerns have put great pressure on companies to design products that are less harmful to the water supply and wildlife. These companies, in turn, have created opportunities for companies that sell the specialty chemicals and processing equipment required to manufacture environmentally safe fertilizer and pest-control products.

New-task buying provides vendors great opportunities as well as great challenges. In new-task situations, all suppliers have a chance to get at least a portion of the business and to influence product specifications in their favor. Quite often, buyers who face new-task buying are not knowledgeable enough to develop a complete set of detailed specifications and must rely on suppliers for assistance. These situations give astute vendors opportunities to educate customers in ways that put their products and services in the best possible light.

Categorizing buying situations as straight rebuys, modified rebuys, or new-task buying can help marketers improve their strategies and make the best use of limited resources in reaching multiple customers. Obviously, the complexity of the purchase situation and the demands on the vendor for problem-solving and communication

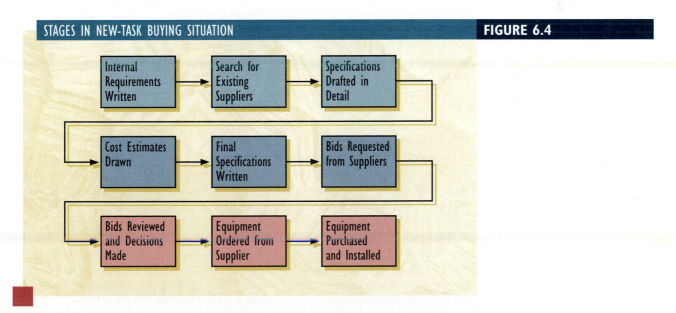

STAGES IN NEW-TASK BUYING SITUATION — **FIGURE 6.4**

skills will vary in each situation. We must therefore be careful in the use of these labels. Like most classification schemes, this one is a simplified representation of reality. Organizational buying situations cover a spectrum of complexity in which some instances are well represented by these stereotypical categories and others are better characterized as combinations of them. In a single sales call, for example, a vendor of hospital bed supplies may handle the straight rebuy of sheets and pillowcases, discuss a modified rebuy of footstools after a minor engineering change, and present a proposal for new hospital beds designed to reduce nursing staff muscle strain injuries when moving overweight patients. This vendor needs to balance expedient response to some customer demands with flexibility to the customer's other concerns, and do it on the spot. Vendors therefore should try to anticipate the specific characteristics of each buying situation and their implications, and develop appropriate strategies.

STAGES IN THE ORGANIZATIONAL BUYING PROCESS

To anticipate what will happen in buying situations, vendors should recognize the tasks or stages typically involved in the organizational buying process, and the influence of social and environmental forces on how this process works.

Modeling the Organizational Buying Process

Cyert, Simon, and Trow's early classification scheme in the 1950s identified three types of processes involved in organizational buying.[11] *Common processes* are routines that pervade one or more stages of decision making, such as completing requisition forms and conducting credit checks on suppliers. To the extent that vendors can automate such common processes, they offer a valuable service. *Communication processes* involve the transfer and flow of formal and informal information among people and groups. These are important processes for vendors to master, given the importance and complexity of organizational buying decisions. *Problem-solving processes* involve searching for and evaluating alternative solutions. Problem solving is what motivates organizational buyers to initiate the buying process, and only the vendors that contribute potential solutions will remain in the consideration set. Vendors need to see themselves as solution providers.

Distinguishing among process types can be useful to vendors because the processes are roughly linked to the type of purchase decision. Straight-rebuy situations, for example, primarily involve common processes that ensure accuracy and adequate response time to customer demands. New-task situations, in contrast, primarily involve problem-solving and communication processes on the part of both vendor and buyer as they seek to define problems and solutions.

Webster extended the Cyert et al. framework by adding a time element and suggesting that buyers move between stages, with each stage emphasizing some processes more than others.[12] The Webster framework, illustrated in Figure 6.5, proposes that organizational buying involves four activities: (1) problem recognition, (2) assignment of responsibilities for purchase tasks, (3) search for and evaluation of alternative products and suppliers, and (4) choosing among alternatives. According to this view of the buying process, different processes receive more or less emphasis at different stages, and vendors can rely on cues about a buyer's current stage to ascertain which processes are most important. Webster acknowledged, however, that these stages are seldom perfectly linear. The assignment of purchase task responsibilities, for example, may introduce to the buying process people whose insight causes the problem to be redefined. The potentially iterative nature of this process is captured by the dotted lines in Figure 6.5.

Source: Adapted from Frederick E. Webster Jr., "Modeling the Industrial Buying Process," Journal of Marketing Research 2 (November 1965): 370–376.

A problem with both of the above frameworks is that they are not specific enough for precise planning by vendors. A more comprehensive model that addresses this weakness and is often used in business settings is the BUYGRID model proposed by Robinson, Farris, and Wind.[13] This model identifies eight stages in organizational buying decisions and links these stages to the types of buying situations in which they are most likely to be encountered. Their framework is summarized in Table 6.3.

The buying process always begins when someone in the organization recognizes a problem that can be solved by a purchased product or service. Sometimes the "problem" is nothing more than the company running out of regularly purchased items, in which case the purchasing professional determines the quantity needed and reorders the product or service. This would be a straight-rebuy situation. *Recognizing the problem* (stage 1), *determining the product and quantity* (stage 3), and *evaluating the performance of the product or service* (stage 8), are found in all three types of buying situations. Therefore, a minimum of three stages are found in all organizational purchases.

Buying organizations must sometimes make a concerted effort to *elaborate the attributes* (stage 2) required to meet an identified need, either in new-task buying situations or in modified-rebuy situations calling for a reevaluation of past

TABLE 6.3 STAGES IN ORGANIZATIONAL BUYING DECISION MAKING AND CORRESPONDING BUYING SITUATIONS

Stages	New Task	Modified Rebuy	Straight Rebuy
1. Anticipation and recognition of a problem and general solution	Always	Always	Always
2. Elaboration of the desired attributes of the product or service that potentially solves the problem	Always	Sometimes	Never
3. Determination of the product or service desired and quantities needed	Always	Always	Always
4. Search for potential suppliers and preliminary evaluation of their suitability	Always	Sometimes	Never
5. Acquisition and initial analysis of offerings (samples) from suppliers	Always	Sometimes	Never
6. Evaluation of offerings and selection of supplier(s)	Always	Sometimes	Never
7. Selection of an order routine	Always	Sometimes	Never
8. Performance feedback and evaluation	Always	Always	Always

Source: Adapted from Patrick J. Robinson, Charles W. Farris, and Yoram Wind, Industrial Buying and Creative Marketing (Boston: Allyn & Bacon, 1967).

practices. For example, in 1990, National Steel Corporation decided to subcontract its corporate mail operations to an outside vendor, and it hired Ameriscribe Corporation.[14] Going to an outside vendor, however, forced National Steel to specify the required corporate mail services in great detail, including security and confidentiality factors that it had taken for granted when it managed its mail internally. The process also involved reevaluating the initial specifications and estimates of the volume of mail involved as the *search for suitable vendors* (stage 4) highlighted factors that the company had overlooked initially. One overlooked area was the need to maintain audit-quality records on all packages handled by the mail room. Such records had been unnecessary under the internally managed system.

Buying mail services was a *new task*, and hence National Steel had to determine and evaluate required attributes. These steps also appear in *modified rebuy* situations when changes are extensive. When Motorola started the process of reducing its supplier base from 10,000 to 3,000 in the late 1980s, for example, selected suppliers were given exclusive contracts and additional business, contingent on performance factors such as zero defect delivery and applying for the Malcolm Baldrige National Quality Award. Motorola expended a lot of time and effort to determine which performance factors were most essential. In addition, some of their suppliers, such as American Micro Products, decided that the cost of meeting Motorola standards was too high and resigned their contracts, forcing Motorola to also search for new suppliers.[15]

Searching for and evaluating new suppliers also involves *evaluating vendor specific offerings* (stage 6) before making a final selection. When products are involved, vendors must often submit prototypes or small batches of production-grade goods for extended testing by the buyer. In the case of services, buyers find extended testing more difficult; some companies have suppliers provide services for only a portion of the organization during a testing period. Companies in the computer services area, such as Andersen Consulting and Electronic Data Systems, often serve only a portion of a customer organization, one or two divisions or departments, during a trial period. At the end of the testing period—usually six to twelve months—clients evaluate the supplier's performance and either make a longer-term commitment or dismiss the vendor.

The *selection of an order routine* (stage 7) almost always occurs in new-task situations and sometimes occurs in modified-rebuy situations. The only exceptions occur when the purchased product will not be consumed during the production of goods and services or when its consumption is so irregular that reorder frequency becomes unpredictable. The federal government, for example, will establish a reorder routine for ground-to-air missiles or fatigue uniforms because the military consumes these items regularly. It would not set up a reorder routine for computer systems or for heavy equipment used in flood control, however, because such products are not used regularly. Thus, for capital and ancillary goods, vendors can expect organizations to follow stages 1 through 6 (see Table 6.3) and to evaluate the acquisition over time.

The eight-stage BUYGRID framework is only one of several descriptions of organizational buying that researchers have proposed. Although the BUYGRID framework provides by far the most popular description of organizational buying, it is not necessarily the most accurate in all situations. Marketing scholars Backhaus and Gunter proposed a 12-stage model that represents complex multiproduct and multisource buying situations more realistically.[16] Their model becomes excessively intricate, however, for describing the more mundane situations that most vendors encounter. Remember that all models of organizational buying are abstract and simplified representations of how organizations make decisions. These models can serve as tools for making sense of interactions with buyers, but vendors should recognize deviations from the models and respond appropriately.

Diffusion of Innovation and the Order of Stages in the Buying Process

Two additional factors arise when we use models of organizational buying. The first is that organizational buyers do not always follow the sequence of steps presented by BUYGRID and similar models. The second is that buying decisions are not always initiated or controlled by purchasing professionals. Organizations are made up of individuals, who may be subject to emotional and irrational influences, and sometimes take actions that are neither logical nor profitable.[17] Most organizations have made unnecessary purchases or overlooked new products and services that would give them a competitive advantage at some point in their histories.

Some of these unnecessary purchases and omissions are understandable in light of how diffusion of innovations takes place.[18] *Diffusion of innovation* has been an important area of sociological research for many years, used to explain the adoption of concepts such as hygiene and birth control as well as the purchase of commercial goods. In its simplest form, the theory suggests that decision makers follow this sequence in adopting innovations:

awareness → interest → evaluation → trial → adoption

Consumers or buyers become aware of the product, develop sufficient interest to collect information, evaluate the product or products based on this information, try using the product, and adopt it if it is found satisfactory. Although on the surface these steps are similar to those of the BUYGRID model, the diffusion model does not assume that decision makers move rationally and consciously between stages. The diffusion model allows instead for innovations to be adopted for reasons other than rational business needs, such as psychological, sociocultural, or peer group pressures. For example, a company may adopt personal workstations or sophisticated software because the technology fits with its image, because its competitors have adopted them, or simply because its CEO likes to brag about the company's use of automation, even if it does not add to productivity. Some analysts suggest, in fact, that much of the computer hardware and software purchased during the 1980s failed to produce significant productivity gains until organizations started transforming their structures and processes to match the new tools' capabilities.[19] In these cases, organizations became aware of and interested in computer innovations long before they could articulate their preferences, and they adopted the innovations on the basis of factors unrelated to business requirements.

Marketers need to remember that organizations are made up of individuals, and not all decision-making units are rational about their purchase decisions. Vendors have an obligation to present their products with integrity and not take advantage of buyers even when the diffusion process makes it possible to sell products that are unnecessary or for which the return on investment is substandard. Marketer self-restraint makes both moral and business sense. An organization that gets into financial trouble by buying unnecessary products and services can affect the lives of thousands or even millions of people, and can result in higher overall social costs. In addition, customers remember poor investments and often blame overly eager vendors for their own mistakes. In either case, risk to the marketer can be higher and longer lasting than the short-term benefit from increased sales.

TYPES OF PRODUCTS AND SERVICES PURCHASED BY ORGANIZATIONS

Organizations purchase many types of products and services that differ from what individual consumers buy. Even when they purchase the same products, organizations purchase them for different reasons than individuals do. These differences have important implications for marketing to organizational buyers. Table 6.4 summarizes the major types of products and services purchased by organizations. This section discusses each of these goods and services as well as the primary reasons organizations buy them.

Raw Materials

Raw materials, by definition, receive little or no processing before they are sold. The rock salt used in water softeners, for example, receives little more processing than being ground to the size required for home use and placed into 50-pound bags. Raw materials are purchased by manufacturers as primary inputs to the production of other goods and services, and are often the most important products sold by developing countries (e.g., Brazil's coffee exports). Industrialized countries with large agricultural or natural resource sectors also produce raw materials: the United States and Canada have well-developed industrial bases and also produce and export farm products such as wheat, corn, and soybeans, and Russia exports large amounts of petroleum and natural gas.

In recent years, some raw materials have become scarce, affording sellers a greater influence on prices. These advantages can be relatively short-lived, however, if prices rise so much that competitors enter the market or develop alterna-

TABLE 6.4 PRODUCTS AND SERVICES PURCHASED BY ORGANIZATIONAL BUYERS

Product or Service	Description	Demand	Examples
Raw Materials	Unprocessed or slightly processed goods that become part of the final product	Demand is very price sensitive and vendor switching is common	Farm products, steel, copper
Components and Partially Processed Materials	Become part of the final product, but have value added from manufacturing when purchased	Demand is price sensitive and vendor switching is common	Parts for complex products, powdered milk used in processed foods
Capital Goods	Buildings and major pieces of equipment used to produce the final product or to house the means of production	Demand is not price sensitive, but vendor choice is influenced by price differences	Steel mills, printing presses, warehousing facilities
Ancillary Equipment	Finished goods that facilitate the production of final products or services	Demand is not price sensitive, but vendor choice is influenced by price differences	Fork-lift trucks, hand tools, office equipment
Supplies	Expendable goods used to support production or reselling operations	Demand is price sensitive and vendor switching is common	Office and janitorial supplies
Services	Specialized functions that can be purchased without hampering core operations	Demand is sensitive to the level of effectiveness and support provided	Advertising, payroll processing, pension management

tive products. Petroleum price fluctuations since the early 1970s are a good illustration of this point. After the initial OPEC agreement to limit production and raise prices in 1973, the price-per-barrel of petroleum more than tripled, and oil producers made large profits. Sustained high prices, however, provided economic incentives for oil exploration, alternative fuel development, and fuel conservation programs. As a result, by the early 1990s petroleum markets were glutted and prices dropped to the point that some oil exploration and pumping operations became unprofitable.

Components and Partially Processed Materials

Manufacturers may purchase components and partially processed materials as inputs for other products and services. Some organizations, in fact, purchase materials and components to produce goods that are themselves components for other manufacturers. For example, Delphi–EMS produces most of its products from components, and in turn sells its products to automobile manufacturers as components for cars and trucks. Components and partially processed materials sold by one supplier can sometimes be differentiated from those sold by other suppliers, but such technological differentiation is difficult to sustain. Recently, suppliers have gained competitive advantages by providing special services, such as managing joint vendor–buyer design teams, on-time delivery, and consistently meeting stringent quality standards. "Just-in-time" materials management, for example, is important in the automotive industry and until recently placed Delphi–EMS at a disadvantage relative to Japanese suppliers. With just-in-time materials management, the materials arrive *where* they are needed *when* they are needed. Working under a just-in-time philosophy reduces in-plant inventories and quality problems, but places greater demands on suppliers. The just-in-time philosophy and its implications for marketing management are discussed in greater detail in chapter 13.

Capital Goods

Most large organizational buyers purchase capital goods—the buildings and major equipment that organizations use to carry out their business. Capital goods can include factories and manufacturing equipment, warehouse facilities, and office space. Marketing capital goods is a specialized task because most buildings and machinery require customized design and represent substantial investments for buyers. They are also long-lived assets (30 to 50 years for some types of facilities) with long-term implications for the buyer's business. The actual decision to build a new plant or refurbish existing operations, therefore, can take many months and involve a large investment of time and effort by the vendor before the buyer makes a decision. Suppliers of capital goods often have only a few direct competitors, but each competing firm represents a significant threat.

Whereas 30 years ago firms usually contacted local or national contractors to meet their capital needs, the marketing of capital goods has evolved into a global industry as companies from the United States, Canada, Japan, France, Germany, and other developed countries compete for major projects around the world. Companies that market capital goods need to know their target customers and develop innovative ways to meet their demands. In addition, vendors of capital goods need to be comfortable dealing with customers and suppliers from different cultures and to be adept at communicating and negotiating on a global basis. Vendors of telecommunications hardware such as AT&T and Northern Telecom, for example, need to understand how business transactions differ in Japan, India, Hungary, and Russia if they are to compete effectively in the growing global market.

Ancillary Equipment

Ancillary equipment is also necessary to produce goods and services. Ancillary goods have shorter life expectancies and require lower initial investments than capital goods. Purchasing decisions for ancillary equipment can be just as long and complex as those for capital goods, however, and the competition can be just as fierce. Ancillary equipment markets are very competitive, in part because the goods are highly standardized and consequently difficult to differentiate; another reason is that although initial purchases are not as large as for capital goods, buying cycles are shorter and the potential for replacement or expanded sales is higher. A company that purchases personal computers from a supplier, for example, is more likely to purchase replacement computers or additional computers from the same supplier if it is satisfied with the initial purchase. Being the initial supplier, therefore, represents a significant competitive advantage. Markets for ancillary equipment are global in scope—in the personal computer industry, for example, companies from the United States, Asia, and Europe compete in all major global markets. The companies best positioned to market personal computers as ancillary equipment produce goods that meet consumer needs at attractive prices and maintain good working relationships with customers after the initial sale.

Supplies

Supplies, such as pens, typewriter ribbons, and envelopes, do not become part of the buyers' products or services, and consequently seldom qualify as strategic purchases. For many organizations, in fact, supply purchases are considered nuisances and given little attention. Routinely purchased supplies normally represent a small portion of an organization's total operating costs. Vendors of supplies find it difficult to differentiate themselves on technological or cost bases. At the same time, however, they can easily capture and retain business from large customers by meeting their needs consistently. Vendors of supplies to medium and large organizations are quite likely to retain their business as long as they service customers well and respond to customers' evolving demands. Because supplies tend to be standardized, competitors may not be able to capture customer attention except through lower prices. Low prices, however, come at the expense of reduced margins and/or services. New competitors trying to sell supplies may have to offer lower prices, at least initially, and then differentiate themselves from competitors by providing enhanced services such as money-back guarantees, expedited delivery, and retail showrooms. Office Depot, a vendor of office supplies, has made substantial inroads with organizational buyers by providing low prices and convenient order and delivery services. Office Depot customers can place orders via phone, fax, or e-mail and enjoy expedited delivery, or they can place orders in person and take the product back to the office from the store.

Services

Organizations have purchased legal and financial advice, consulting, advertising, market research, security and janitorial services, landscaping and maintenance, transportation and other specialized services for a long time. Service industries represent an area of growth because many companies worldwide are downsizing and eliminating internal operations that they do not see as strategically important. In the 1960s and 1970s, the model of a successful organization was a large and self-sufficient enterprise, but today that is no longer the case. Today's successful firms have fewer employees and layers of management, and they staff only those functional areas that they see as directly relevant to the company's main objectives. These firms contract for many nonstrategic support functions with specialized companies that can deliver the services more efficiently and at a lower cost than could be provided internally. Services tend to be less price sensitive than other products because of their specialized nature, although rising competition in some areas has decreased this differentiation and brought about more price competition. Services are also intangible and difficult to evaluate objectively, so suppliers must respond quickly and correctly to customer preferences and demands in order to gain and retain an organization's business. Vendors often achieve quick and accurate responses through partnering relationships, such as those that information-systems consulting companies such as Andersen Consulting and Electronic Data Systems establish with their clients—relationships in which the vendor becomes an integral part of the customer's management team.

DERIVED AND FLUCTUATING DEMAND

The primary motivations behind the demand generated from organizational buyers differ significantly from those from individual consumers of products and services, and in important ways. As discussed in chapter 4, consumers purchase products and services primarily for personal or family consumption, and in that sense their demand for goods and services is motivated directly by their own perceived needs. Organizational buyers, in contrast, exist primarily to better meet the needs and preferences of their constituencies, and purchase the products or services that help them achieve those goals. Organizational buyers' demands for raw materials, capital goods, services, and other types of purchased goods, therefore, can be said to *derive* from market demand for their own products and services. Some of the derived demand can be linked directly to consumer purchases of the organization's output, such as Mattel's demand for moldable skin-colored plastic being determined by sales of Barbie dolls, and Mars' demand for peanuts being determined by sales of peanut M&Ms and Snickers. But even demand for products and services not directly involved in production, such as staples and pencils, is considered as derived because these products and services perform functions that help the company serve its constituents. Understanding derived demand is important to marketers because it provides insight into the buying behavior of different organizational buyers in the same way that understanding cultural background gives insight into the buying behavior of consumers.

Derived demand and the complex way in which many products and services are produced contribute to another difference between organizational buyers and individual consumers: organizational buyers tend to be less sensitive than consumers in their total *demand* to price fluctuations. Consumers, for example, may respond to small fluctuations in the price of milk by moderating their daily consumption. A producer of milk chocolate, however, may find it difficult to change its consumption of milk in small increments in response to price variations. One reason is that consumer demand for milk chocolate does not fluctuate in synchrony with the price of milk. A second reason is that production and materials management systems are often geared for handling purchased products in set lot sizes that cannot be changed easily.

Most organizational buyers have substantial investments in plant and equipment and a trained workforce that must be kept working to achieve a positive return on investment. Most companies with large investments and high fixed costs find it economically better to pay whatever price is necessary for the goods and services they need to keep output at steady levels than to change output levels. This is particularly true when the product or service being purchased represents a small portion of the finished product's total cost. When market demand for apparel is high, for example, clothing manufacturers will purchase zippers regardless of the price (i.e., overall demand for zippers is price inelastic).

The fact that organizational buyers do not adjust their purchase volume in response to price fluctuations in the same way as consumers do, however, does not mean that organizational buyers are less price sensitive than consumers. Organizational buyers, in fact, can show greater willingness than individual consumers to switch suppliers in response to price differences. Whereas a consumer may keep buying the same brand of milk even if it is priced five cents per gallon higher than a competing brand, a milk-chocolate producer would probably switch between comparable milk vendors for a price difference of one to two cents per gallon. The reason for this high price sensitivity is that small differences in per unit price can add up to substantial differences in overall profit for high-volume items. Supplier loyalty tends to be lower for organizational buyers than for final consumers.

Finally, organizational demand tends to fluctuate in larger increments than individual consumer demand. That is to say, changes in total demand tend to be more dramatic for organizational buyers than for individual consumers. These swings are also tied to the complex way in which many products and services are produced. Consider the demand for paper clips by individual consumers versus that of Delphi–EMS. Consumers adjust their paper clip consumption almost continually, in response to the number of situations that require paper clips. Within some bounds, Delphi–EMS adjusts its consumption of paper clips in the same way, but its demand schedule also includes some discontinuous shifts. Imagine that the Delphi–EMS catalytic converter plant produces four to five million catalytic converters per year and that demand for next year will go to 6.2 million converters. To meet this increased demand, Delphi–EMS will have to increase its manufacturing capacity by building another plant. The addition of this plant will require adding new employees, some of whom will need paper clips, thus producing a dramatic increase in Delphi–EMS's total demand for paper clips. In contrast, if demand for catalytic converters dropped below four million converters, Delphi–EMS might have to close a plant and lay off workers, some of whom were paper-clip users. The end result, of course, would be a dramatic decrease in Delphi–EMS's demand for paper clips.

Differences between individual consumers and organizational buyers in the types of products they purchase and the reasons why they purchase them can result in radically different marketing strategies being required for each group. Vendors can better tailor their approach to organizational buyers by paying attention to how the customer intends to use the products or services being purchased, and to how derived demand and the complexity of the production process can affect the customer's buying behavior.

COMPLEX DECISION PROCESSES IN ORGANIZATIONAL PURCHASES

Throughout this chapter we have made several references to the complexity of the decision process for organizational buyers. We have not discussed in detail, however, the factors that make the decision process complex. Individual members of decision units are influenced by what is happening around them, both in the environment and within their organization. They are also affected by what is happening within them, in terms of how they view the world and what they feel is expected of them. Vendors need to take into account both external and internal factors that influence members of decision units and to determine how these factors will influence their likely decisions.

External Influences on Organizational Buying Behavior

Earlier in this chapter we discussed structural factors that affect organizational buying behavior, such as derived demand and production processes. Other external factors affect organizational buyers as well. Marketing scholars Webster and Wind provide a thorough and systematic description of forces that influence organizational buying, summarized in Figure 6.6.[20] They developed a framework of four major determinants of buyer behavior. We treat three of these—environmental factors, organizational factors, and interpersonal factors—as external to organizational buyers. The fourth category is individual factors, which we treat as internal factors and discuss in the next section.

Environmental Factors

Organizational buyers are influenced by forces in their environment such as aggregate demand, inflation, interest rates, and economic outlook. When inflation rates are high, for example, organizations may stockpile large purchases of raw materials and components to avoid future price hikes. If interest rates are also high, however, companies may curtail their stockpiling because the cost of carrying inventory yields a lower return relative to other investments. This was a factor, for example, during the oil crisis of the early 1980s. Although the cost of petroleum was rising dramatically and made stockpiling advisable, the rate of return on short-term investments was also very high and made holding large cash reserves attractive. Some oil companies

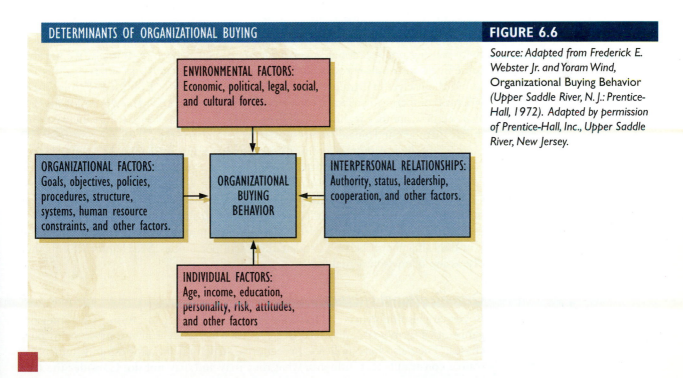

DETERMINANTS OF ORGANIZATIONAL BUYING

FIGURE 6.6

ENVIRONMENTAL FACTORS:
Economic, political, legal, social, and cultural forces.

ORGANIZATIONAL FACTORS:
Goals, objectives, policies, procedures, structure, systems, human resource constraints, and other factors.

ORGANIZATIONAL BUYING BEHAVIOR

INTERPERSONAL RELATIONSHIPS:
Authority, status, leadership, cooperation, and other factors.

INDIVIDUAL FACTORS:
Age, income, education, personality, risk, attitudes, and other factors

Source: Adapted from Frederick E. Webster Jr. and Yoram Wind, Organizational Buying Behavior (Upper Saddle River, N. J.: Prentice-Hall, 1972). Adapted by permission of Prentice-Hall, Inc., Upper Saddle River, New Jersey.

Imagine the number of components that NASA had to procure from outside vendors to build the space shuttle.

followed a highly criticized strategy of placing excess cash in short-term investments, continuing to buy oil in the volatile spot market, and passing the higher costs onto consumers. This strategy tarnished the oil industry's image and created dissatisfied customers. High inflation and interest rates can also cause organizations to curtail plans for purchasing capital goods as they anticipate higher prices and lower demand for their products.

Other environmental factors that affect organizational buyers are technological advancements, social and cultural changes, legal considerations, competitors' actions, and political interests. Recent developments in the retail compact disc (CD) market exemplify how some of these forces influence organizational buyers (see Marketing Anecdote 6.3). In this example, we see shifts in technology and consumer price sensitivity causing organizational buyers to change their behaviors. Initially, we see that some music distributors responded punitively to their retailer customers' actions and found themselves constrained by legal considerations (the Robinson–Patman Act), whereas competing distributors cooperated with retailers and gained their loyalty. We also see how another technological factor and partnering relationships between industry members and outside interests may have rendered the debate over the used CD market obsolete. Although political interests were not immediately involved, they could be if the new technology were seen as a way of reducing tensions over the issue of clandestine copies of CDs being exported to the United States from Mexico and China. In that case, government interests could influence tax and regulatory policies on the new technology to favor its quick adoption. It should be clear that marketers—in this case distributors of recorded music—have to monitor environmental forces and how they affect buyer behavior and marketing opportunities. See chapter 3 for further discussion of environmental factors.

Organizational Factors

Buyers are also influenced by factors within their own organizations. Customer organizations form goals and objectives against which they evaluate most major purchases. They also have policies, procedures, structural limitations, and human resource constraints that influence what they may and may not do. Consider the case

Compact discs use laser technology to read digitally recorded material and produce higher fidelity sound than magnetic tape. They were introduced commercially as a medium for recorded music in the early 1980s, and in just a few years dominated the recorded music industry. Two recent developments, however, are changing CD marketing in the United States: the used disc market and in-store high-speed CD duplicating equipment.

Since CD players transmit information with a beam of light instead of the mechanically produced magnetic waves used by tape, nothing actually contacts the CD surface. Thus users may play a disc hundreds or thousands of times without changing the sound quality or in any way wearing it out. Consequently, used compact discs sound just as good as new ones, and are attractive to value-conscious consumers. The market for used discs started soon after CD technology was introduced, primarily through hobbyist and small music shops. As long as used compact discs were sold by only a few stores, music distribution companies such as Sony, Warner Music, Capitol–EMI, and MCA had no problem. As the sale of used discs has become a significant factor in the total business of large music retailers, however, it has also become a concern to major distributors of new compact discs.

Some distributors have responded to used disc sales with negative tactics, such as withholding cooperative advertising payments, which provide compensation to retailers for local promotion and are used by retailers to offset revenue losses from discounting popular CD titles. Other distributors have responded by reducing new CD prices and by working with retailers to increase the sales of both new and used recordings. Retailers have also responded in different ways—some by halting the sale of used CDs, and others by selling more used disks and accusing distributors of illegal price discrimination. The problem continues, but may soon be overshadowed by the prospect of point-of-sale CD production.

Blockbuster Entertainment, IBM, and some music distributors are working on hardware and software technology that will allow the high-speed duplication of CDs in the store. The proposed system would be connected to a repository of hundreds or thousands of CD masters, which customers can preview using headphones. Once the customer has made a selection, the system will copy the music onto a blank disc, charging the customer the retail price and sending royalty payments to the record company. CD labels and storage boxes will be printed using color printers, for in-store "manufacture" of a product that matches what music distributors normally ship. A significant advantage of this technology is that it reduces in-store inventory and space requirements relative to conventional music stores. With this technology, a 12-foot x 12-foot kiosk can carry just as many selections as a large store. The technology may also result in lower consumer prices, as retailers can pass on the savings from reduced transportation costs. High-speed on-demand duplication of CDs may help defuse the used-CD market in two ways. First, it may narrow the price differential between new and used CDs to the point that consumers are unwilling to risk purchasing used CDs. Second, it may reduce the overall supply of used CDs available for sale because retailers will be less likely to sell overstocked new CDs at discounted prices, only to see them reenter the market as used discs.

Sources: Larry Armstrong, "What's Wrong with Selling Used CD's?" *Business Week*, July 26, 1993. p. 38.

Ed Christman, "Can Retail's Shaky Health Be Cured?" *Billboard*, December 23, 1995.

Kevin Maney, "Revolution in Store for Record Shops," *USA Today*, May 17, 1996.

of Delphi–EMS, now as a customer of goods and services. In order to compete with Japanese suppliers, Delphi–EMS had to improve its productivity by reducing supervisory staff, changing work rules to give workers more flexibility, and training supervisory and hourly personnel in new inventory management and manufacturing practices. Delphi–EMS, however, faced adversarial relationships with its unionized hourly workers, and had to work around several labor-contract–imposed restrictions. As Delphi–EMS sought to make itself more competitive through internal change, its suppliers also had to change their own products and services, and take into account its labor problems and other internal factors. One example involves the trucking companies serving Delphi–EMS, who were forced to adjust their pick-up and delivery procedures several times as Delphi–EMS and the United Auto Workers negotiated the implementation of just-in-time systems over a two-year period.

Other organizational factors that industrial vendors must consider are long-term contracts, single-supplier sourcing, consolidated purchasing for multidivisional companies, monitoring supplier quality on multiple dimensions (e.g., delivery, reliability), electronic data interchange of order and inventory levels, and automatic reordering. Vendors also need to monitor emerging ideas and trends among existing customers and anticipate what demands these factors will generate. Organizational researchers have described the 1990s as the decade of transformation. To remain viable, vendors need to transform their strategies and tactics to meet their customers' transformations.

Interpersonal Relationships

When decision units have more than one member, vendors must consider interpersonal relationships and their effects on buyer behavior. Members of typical decision units differ in their interests, their authority within the company, their knowledge of the products and services being considered, and their persuasive abilities.

Vendors who deal with multimember decision units need to observe interpersonal relationships during joint meetings and pay attention to any indication that interpersonal alliances or conflicts may arise in the decision process. In the best of situations, interpersonal relationships in a decision unit are positive and focused on common goals, and respect for others puts restraints on the use of power. In some situations, however, decision units may have negative and problematic interpersonal relationships that prevent the group from reaching agreement. Under these circumstances, the vendor can either try to bypass some decision unit members or withdraw from actively marketing to that customer.

Internal Influences on Organizational Buying Behavior

Webster and Wind suggested that as vendors prepare their marketing strategies they need to consider buyers' predispositions.[21] Buying decisions, after all, are made by people who are affected by what has happened to them, by their personality traits, and even by their gender. Webster and Wind's suggestions have been enriched by research on the frames of reference that buyers bring to decisions and the social expectations imposed on them, both by their jobs and by their involvement in the decision process. In this section, we discuss individual factors, frames of reference, social context influences, and roles imposed by functional responsibility.

Individual Factors

In the final analysis, individuals make all organizational buying decisions. Each individual has personal interests, opinions, fears, and perceptual biases that can affect purchase decisions. Vendors need to keep these individual-level factors in

Lyn St. James is the only woman race-car driver in the Indy circuit. She won the Rookie of the Year award at the 1992 Indianapolis 500. In addition, she is a writer, served as president of the Women's Sports Foundation, has been a guest at the White House on numerous occasions, and is an accomplished pianist. She has also served as a consultant to automobile companies on several product programs, and owned an auto-parts company for several years. By most measures, St. James is a talented and successful woman and a welcome business associate. Nevertheless, until very recently she had remained an outsider to the inner circle of automobile racing and had a difficult time getting sponsors.

The problem was her gender. In the male-dominated world of auto racing, St. James had difficulty being taken seriously, and could not get the attention or support of major sponsors despite her winning record. After years of trying to get sponsorships from traditional sources, St. James has gained the support of companies with a high proportion of women customers and interest in women's issues. In 1992, when word of the trouble St. James was having getting sponsors reached the chairman and CEO of JCPenney, he arranged for her to make a marketing presentation to three female executives at their Dallas headquarters. These executives were impressed with St. James's

credentials and not distracted by her gender. They admired her determination in the face of substantial odds and also saw the potential returns to JCPenney from advertising to a racing audience that is more than 30 percent female, and from the special appeal that supporting the leading female in a predominantly male sport would have for sympathetic women customers, even if they were not racing fans.

Because they connected with St. James as an individual, the JCPenney executives recommended a $250,000 investment in the race team for 1992, for which JCPenney received an estimated $2 million of promotional benefit. For 1993, JCPenney invested even more in the St. James Indy car campaigns, and invited producers of other products sold through the company to sponsor the team as well. As a result, companies such as Jantzen, Nike, and Revlon joined the investor group as well. Sponsoring the St. James team was a good business decision for JCPenney and others, but it did not happen until St. James presented her ideas to buyers who could relate to her at an individual level.

Sources: Matthew Grimm, "Sports Marketing: Heart Like a Wheel and a Nose for a Deal," *Brandweek,* April 12, 1993, p. 9.

Jill Lieber, "A Road Less Taken," *Sports Illustrated,* May 3, 1993, pp. 52–55.

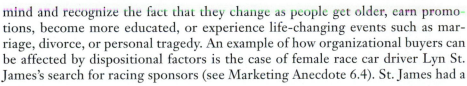

mind and recognize the fact that they change as people get older, earn promotions, become more educated, or experience life-changing events such as marriage, divorce, or personal tragedy. An example of how organizational buyers can be affected by dispositional factors is the case of female race car driver Lyn St. James's search for racing sponsors (see Marketing Anecdote 6.4). St. James had a

difficult time attracting business sponsors for her racing team in spite of having a winning record, largely because of long-standing biases against the success of women in automobile racing and against aggressive women in general. Her gender and personality, both individual-level factors, were opposed by organizational and interpersonal factors at most of the traditional sponsoring organizations. These same individual-level factors, however, helped St. James convince JCPenney's managers of the high potential returns they could gain from sponsoring her highly visible team.

Another example of the potential effect of individual factors can be found in the story of Sheri Poe and Ryka Inc.[22] In 1986, Poe combined social activism with business management to launch Ryka Inc. as a producer of athletic shoes designed especially for women. Ryka competed against larger companies such as Reebok and Nike, but had a vision that was compelling to many customers. Poe, a rape survivor, emerged from the experience committed to improving the lives of women victims of violence. What every vendor dealing with Ryka needed to consider was the close link that existed between Ryka's business decisions and Poe's personal values. Under Poe's direction, Ryka set aside a portion of its profits to aid women who had been victims of violent crime, and it favored hiring women and giving business to companies run by women. For Poe, the actions of Ryka needed to be motivated by social responsibility as well as profitability. Most vendors approaching Ryka, therefore, should have expected to be asked about their views on the problem of violence against women and about their broad human rights and social-action track record. This was one situation in which a buyer's personal experiences and values influenced practically all decisions of the business, including purchase decisions.

Vendors who focus excessively on individual-level factors, however, may err on the side of interpreting all decision-maker motivations at a personal rather than a business level. Salespeople need to observe and try to make sense of buyers' behaviors based on available information, but they must not read too much psychological meaning into their decisions, or probe indiscreetly into their customers' lives. The best approach for vendors is empathy—trying to envision themselves in each decision-maker's position in order to understand their customers better.

Frames of Reference

The Webster and Wind framework does not address frames of reference, but cognition-focused research has revealed that organizational buying can be affected by its decision-unit members' frames of reference. Frames of reference are mental models that guide people's decision processes in terms of what attributes they consider important and the steps they follow in making decisions. People develop mental models through experience. Consequently, models can vary between individuals and between organizations. In a study of companies making major capital expenditures, management researchers Shrivastava and Mitroff found four different frames of reference, which they labeled *entrepreneurial, bureaucratic, professional,* and *political*.[23] These frames of reference and their distinguishing characteristics are summarized in Table 6.5.

Frames of reference include organizational, interpersonal, and individual elements, and members of an organization use such frames to make sense of problem situations and determine which factors are most important. Influential and experienced people, for example, often adopt an entrepreneurial frame of reference, which relies on personal experiences and intuition to evaluate new products and services, and focuses on the specific demands the product meets. In contrast, people who serve as technical experts, and who do not have any major influential role, are more

TABLE 6.5 FRAMES OF REFERENCE AND THEIR DISTINGUISHING CHARACTERISTICS

Frames of Reference	Information Sources	Means of Analysis	Means for Testing	Breadth of Perspective	Examples
Entrepreneurial	Subjective information	Judgmental intuitive analysis	Self-experience	Problem specific	An independent building contractor chooses a vendor of roofing shingles based on past experiences and job-specific pricing.
Bureaucratic	Objective information	Computational analysis	Rules and procedures	Departmental	A purchasing clerk for a large construction company chooses a vendor of roofing shingles from an approved list.
Professional	Intersubjective information	Planning and computational analysis	Empirical and experimental proofs	Organizational	An architect specifies a brand of roofing shingles based on performance ratings published by a professional association.
Political	Objective and subjective information	Bargaining and negotiation	Popular wisdom	Organizational and regional	A contractor chooses a vendor of roofing shingles based on promises of future business and favors owed.

Source: Adapted from Paul Shrivastava and Ian Mitroff, "Frames of Reference Managers Use," in Robert Lamb, ed., Advances in Strategic Management, *vol. 1 (Greenwich, Conn: JAI Press, 1983, pp. 161–182.*

likely to adopt a professional frame of reference, which relies more on objective information and testing procedures, and takes the broader organizational implications of the new product or service into account.

Frames of reference provide useful templates for understanding the behaviors and responses of organizational buyers. Vendors who successfully identify the various frames of reference (e.g., entrepreneurial, professional) in a decision unit can vary the information sources and approach they use for different members (e.g., image considerations, adherence to professional standards), and thereby encourage each member to approve the proposed product or service, even if for different reasons.

The Influence of Social Context and Role on the Behavior of Buyers

In the field of social psychology, role theory explains some ways in which individuals relate to specific social groups and to society at large. Its main premise is simple: individuals are influenced by two forces, (1) the broad social context in which they live and work and (2) the particular role or roles in which they function. Thus, human action can be seen as a response to social forces.[24]

To better understand social context and particular roles, as well as their effects, consider the example of an accounting analyst purchasing office supplies directly, as diagrammed in Figure 6.7. The analyst is influenced by the social context of his organization, and this perceived context is probably dominated by the accounting department's culture. We assume that at this company the culture includes preferences for conservative attire, detailed specifications, and low-cost alternatives, so behavior

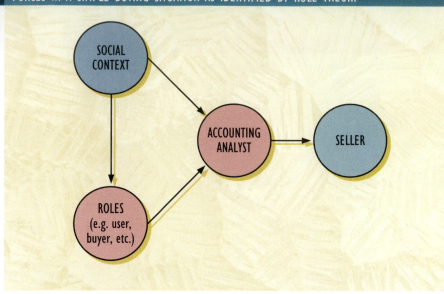

that complies with these preferences is favored. To the extent that our analyst identifies with the organization, he has adopted these preferences, and they are likely to influence his buying behavior. It is reasonable to expect that, all other things being equal, the accounting analyst will buy from someone who dresses conservatively, and thus we have the social context influencing the buying decision.

The analyst is also affected, however, by the task-related role of acting as a buyer for his company, which may adhere to or conflict with the social context. The buyer role consists of a set of expectations initiated by the purchasing area and shared by members of the organization who are empowered to purchase goods from outside suppliers. "Expectations" mean rules about conducting business, such as always soliciting bids from multiple suppliers and observing equal-opportunity guidelines for minority-owned sources. Expectations may be codified into procedures followed by all departments, or they may be communicated informally by a purchasing professional to the accounting analyst. In either case, the analyst is influenced by these expectations, and he must balance their influence with those of the broader social context. In our example, it may be possible that the analyst preferred buying from a conservatively dressed salesperson, but the buying role demands that he ask for bids from multiple suppliers, review the bids carefully, and choose the vendor that is best qualified according to company standards. If the best-qualified vendor is a minority-owned supplier whose salesperson dressed in vibrant colors, the accounting analyst will put aside his preference for conservative dress in awarding the business. In this situation the analyst would set aside the social context expectation's in favor of the buyer role demands. It can also happen, however, that task-related roles are set aside in favor of social context recommended behaviors.

Note that, according to role theory, the social context also affects the expectations associated with a role (note the arrow from social context to roles in Fig. 6.7.), so that task-related roles can vary from one social context to another. For example, a vendor may find that buyers have more autonomy in their purchases in organizations that emphasize creativity and entrepreneurship as part of their culture. In con-

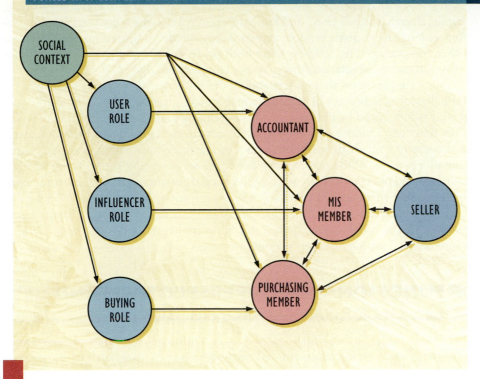

trast, buyers may be more constrained and conservative in organizations where the culture punishes mistakes more severely than it rewards achievements.

The interplay between roles and social context becomes even clearer if we change the example situation to one of buying computer workstations and add a purchasing professional and an information systems engineer to the decision unit. This situation is diagrammed in Figure 6.8 Here the accounting analyst no longer acts as a buyer representing the company; instead, the analyst is a user giving input to the buyer. In this situation, the analyst will likely focus more on the accounting area's preferences and delegate concerns about compatibility, cost, and supplier characteristics to the information systems and purchasing members of the decision unit.

The information systems engineer will most likely act as an influencer concerned with workstation compatibility to other information systems and with the performance standards set for all computer equipment. The purchasing professional will assume the role of buyer, responsible for choosing a vendor and representing the company in the same way as the accounting analyst did in the first example. Purchasing areas usually maintain preferred suppliers lists for computer equipment as well as size and financial stability standards that they apply to all suppliers. If several possible suppliers want the business, the purchasing professional will make the final choice of a supplier and negotiate delivery and installation arrangements.

Note in Figure 6.8 that the corporate culture aspect of social context is shared by the three members of the decision unit. This suggests that in some areas all three members will behave in similar ways because of their shared values and beliefs. Notice also that the decision-unit members influence one another, illustrated in the figure by the dashed lines. For example, a powerful systems engineer will have a strong direct effect on the decision and will also affect how accounting and purchasing professionals fulfill their roles.

One additional aspect that can also influence the purchase decision (not shown in Fig. 6.8) is that decision-unit members also belong to other social contexts (e.g., family, church, softball team) and fulfill different roles in these contexts (parent, sibling, elder, player). Some vendors may socialize with decision-unit members in these other contexts, getting to know them both professionally and personally, and may rely on these social relationships to gain a competitive edge.

Our examples show that understanding the influence of roles and social context on behavior is important in organizational buying situations. A decision-unit's behavior is influenced by the roles its members fulfill and the social context in which they function. Vendors who become familiar with the culture of customer organizations prior to their first official contact can have a competitive advantage during the sales process. Marketers can also benefit from observing the behavior of decision-unit members to identify which roles they are assuming, as well as from learning about the members' roles outside the organization. In the next section we discuss the characteristics of functional areas and buying-center roles found across most organizations as a foundation that industrial marketers can use to develop more detailed analyses of their various customers.

THE INFLUENCE OF FUNCTIONAL-AREA PERSPECTIVES AND BUYING-CENTER ROLES ON ORGANIZATIONAL BUYING

In organizational buying situations, two sources influence the behavior of decision-unit members. One is the functional area in which they work, such as accounting, marketing, or manufacturing. Each functional area develops unique aspects of professional culture that inform the members' perspectives and influence how they behave in buying situations. The second influence comes from the different roles involved in all buying decisions, which are typically assumed by different decision-unit members. Being sensitive to both sources of influence can help marketers improve their marketing approaches.

Functional Areas and Their Influence on Buying Behavior

Organizations in Western countries frequently divide themselves into functional areas. For example, although the Internal Revenue Service and CBS Broadcasting engage in radically different businesses (government revenue collection versus entertainment), both have auditing departments that protect their organization's financial integrity. The importance of functional areas for vendors is that they often differ in their perspectives on purchases, and consequently demand a slightly different marketing approach. Table 6.6 describes six functional areas found in most organizations and their perspectives on purchasing.

The Financial Function

Most organizations in industrialized societies feature a financial function because of the prevalence of monetary value as the way to represent and manage businesses in the open market. Monetary equivalents give managers a common basis by which to compare the different goods and services that companies produce, the types of assets they own, and the diverse activities in which they are involved. Without monetary equivalents, organizations could not easily exchange goods and services. Virtually all organizations use monetary equivalents to manage their assets and represent their net worth, from the Roman Catholic Church to the New York Yankees baseball team.

TABLE 6.6 FUNCTIONAL AREAS COMMON TO ORGANIZATIONAL BUYERS

Area	Description of Function	Typical Perspective on Purchases
Financial	Manages cash flow and reports on the operation of the company from a monetary perspective	Compares the cost of products and services being considered to the value of outputs generated and to alternatives
Marketing	Responds to the demands of external constituencies and translates them into recommendations for action by other areas of the organization	Evaluates the proposed purchase in terms of its influence on the company's ability to meet current customer demands
Production	Transforms purchased inputs into desirable outputs by managing the organization's productive assets	Evaluates the immediate effects of the proposed purchase on productive capacity and ability
Planning	Designs the organization's outputs and how to produce them in ways that meet external and internal demands	Adopts and integrates the perspective of various functional areas to anticipate short- and long-term potential challenges and opportunities
Materials Management	Schedules and manages the flow of input to and within the organization, and the flow of output from the organization	Recommends delivery schedules and ordering practices that reduce in-transit and in-house inventory; also concerned with packaging
Human Resource Management	Assists other functional areas in the selection, development, and management of the workforce	Makes recommendations when proposed purchase can affect employee welfare

Using monetary equivalents, for example, a financial professional working for both the Church and the Yankees can evaluate the cost of janitorial service, and can offset it with the monetary equivalent of income received from people attending their events, whether Sunday morning mass or a Sunday afternoon double-header.

In most organizational buying, the financial professionals are part of the buying center, and are responsible for evaluating the products and services being considered in terms of their cost and the benefits they produce. One way that vendors must respond to the influence of the financial function is by converting the benefits of their products or services into monetary terms, and providing some monetary basis for comparing alternative products. To sell replacement personal computers to Inland Steel, for example, IBM must provide dollar estimates of how much the new equipment will save over the products offered by IBM competitors, and expect these estimates will be reviewed by financial professionals at Inland. IBM sales personnel must also be ready to answer questions expressed in financial terms. In many organizations the monetary dimension is considered more objective and believable than most other dimensions, and "bottom-line" considerations take precedence in most purchasing decisions. If vendors cannot provide information in monetary terms, their proposals will probably not be considered very seriously.

This overreliance on the financial perspective has some problems, however. Whenever organizations reduce complex products and services to a single dimension (i.e., dollar value), they will almost always fail to consider all aspects of the decision equally because not all aspects can be converted to monetary terms with equal accuracy or confidence. Consider, for example, a furniture manufacturer considering staples instead of screws for final assembly. The benefit of using staples is a 50 percent reduction in assembly time, and the drawback is a consumers' perceptions of lower quality. In this situation, the dollar value of labor savings is easy to quantify objectively, but the lower quality image is not easily quantified, and it is possible that the "hard numbers" will have more influence on the decision than the "soft concerns." This could be a mistake, of course, if the lower quality image ultimately results in lost sales.

The financial function provides a powerful social context because many unit members put more importance on numerical analyses and financial estimates than on other aspects of the product or service being offered. To the degree that an organization's senior management has a financial background, this influence may extend to areas of the company beyond accounting and finance. In practically all organizational buying situations, vendors should expect demands for some financial analysis and be ready to provide it. Vendors should also be sensitive to instances of buyer overreliance on financial information, and point out the important aspects of the product that are lost in a purely financial perspective.

The Marketing Function

The marketing function is also commonly represented in organizational buying groups. Marketing in this context refers to the areas responsible for responding to the organization's constituencies, be they customers or other constituent types. All organizations have marketing functions, even if that label is not used. A church, for example, may not have a marketing department, but it has committees for membership visitation and new convert outreach that respond to different constituencies. A visitation minister or committee is just as concerned with meeting church members' demands as a Delphi–EMS salesperson is with meeting the demands of automobile manufacturers. Both entities bring a similar perspective to buying decisions, even though their "products" are vastly different. Given that most organizations exist primarily to exchange something of value (e.g., ideas, services, products) with other entities (e.g., customers, members, voters), they are all concerned with marketing, and the marketing perspective will influence most of their complex buying decisions.

Marketing professionals measure performance in terms of customer goodwill and positive attitudes, in addition to sales revenue and profits. In a decision-making unit, marketers will have a strong customer orientation and will typically ask how the vendor's product or service will improve customer satisfaction. People adopting this perspective show little interest in products and services that only indirectly affect the organization's outputs and customer welfare, such as office equipment or energy-efficient lighting. Marketing professionals also tend to protect products and processes that have proven track records of customer satisfaction. Therefore, they tend to resist changes that improve efficiency or reduce costs if such changes will also change the appearance or performance of their currently successful products.

Vendors must be ready to respond to marketing concerns by emphasizing how proposed products or services will enhance customer satisfaction and the organization's overall ability to meet its constituents' demands. For example, a salesperson for Xerox might encounter resistance to a new copier from a bookstore's sales personnel, and must point out that the new equipment will improve the quality of the bookstore's publications and present a better image to its customers. Likewise, a Delphi–EMS salesperson might face resistance from an automaker's marketing organization to a more reliable fuel pump because it raises car prices. The Delphi–EMS vendor must convince the automaker's sales organization that the more expensive fuel pump will result in fewer automobile breakdowns and higher customer satisfaction in the long run.

The marketing function provides a different social context from other functional areas, one that emphasizes current customer satisfaction, and resists changes that threaten current performance levels. In practically all buying situations, vendors will find some members of the buying center that subscribe to this perspective, and they must be ready to address the demands of these members. Vendors may find it useful to study the customer's current marketing strategies and be familiar with its areas of competitive advantage. Positioning the proposed product and service as a new and better way to meet constituencies' demands is a good way of gaining the support of the marketing members of the buying center. At the least, the vendor must minimize the customer's marketing professionals' perceptions that the proposed product or service will affect their own marketing efforts adversely.

The Production Function

Production generates the product or service that organizations exchange with other entities. The IRS, for example, produces three things on which it focuses most of its resources: processed tax returns and refunds for taxpayers, timely and accurate revenue reports for the federal government, and audits of companies and individuals suspected of not paying their taxes. These IRS outputs are among its primary management concerns. Production personnel focus mainly on the "here and now," because they are concerned with meeting known and quantifiable demands within a specified period of time. Due to this preoccupation with short-term results, people adopting a production perspective are seldom willing to speculate about the future and may find it difficult to get excited about products and services with long-term payoffs.

Knowing what motivates production-oriented members of the buying center is important to vendors for two reasons. First, vendors must be ready to address objections to purchases that change the organization's inputs, processes, or outputs. For example, if a new fuel filter offered by Delphi–EMS changes the way automobiles are assembled, production personnel are likely to object to its adoption. Vendors must anticipate the concerns of production personnel and have workable and beneficial solutions; for example, that time study information shows the new fuel filter requires the same amount of time and effort to install as the old one. Second, vendors must ensure that the production perspective has not been excluded from the buying process. Vendors sometimes need to take the initiative to include production personnel in the decision process even if the members from other functional areas have not considered it.

In fact, vendors can often avoid costly changes late in the sales process by making sure that production concerns are addressed early in the decision process. As an example, again consider the Xerox salesperson, who this time is trying to sell a new copier to a social services agency. The copier salesperson must make sure that all therapy and administrative personnel who use the copier and will be affected by changes are involved in the decision process, and the vendor must explore their needs before finalizing the specifications for new equipment. This might involve distributing a questionnaire to all regular users and conducting in-depth interviews with managers. Knowing all user demands and incorporating them into initial specifications will help to ensure better acceptance of the proposed product.

The buying-center members who come from a production perspective tend to have a very short term perspective on new products and services, and to resist anything that changes how they produce the organization's outputs. Knowing production's concerns helps vendors develop more accurate specifications for the product being sold, which in turn results in better execution of the vendor's own production process and a smoother implementation at the time of delivery.

The Planning Function

Most organizations undertake short-term and long-term planning, and that function can be fulfilled by different organization members. Planners combine and coordinate the organization's resources to produce desirable outputs. In small and midsized companies, senior management undertakes planning. In larger organizations it may be done by technical specialists. A manufacturing company, for example, may ask some of the engineers responsible for designing products and manufacturing equipment to work on plans, whereas new tax initiatives at the IRS involve senior-level agents and auditors. Planners are typically responsible for evaluating new ideas in terms of how they fit with their organization's mission and objectives. They often try to reconcile the conflicting demands of other functional areas to arrive at workable solutions, which suggests that the best planners are broad minded and capable of adopting other functional area perspectives. Planners also tend to be firmly anchored in pragmatic solutions, and are sometimes unwilling to adopt innovative ideas that require major changes. They tend to prefer incremental improvements over radical changes.

Planners in organizational buying units tend to be concerned with technical aspects of products and services, and with their integration into current practices. They often ask some of the most challenging questions and are seldom satisfied with superficial responses. Not all organizational buying decisions will require heavy involvement by planning personnel because not all new products and services demand changes to the organization's current products and processes. In fact, planning involvement is related to the complexity of the buying decision; new-task buying involves the most planning and straight rebuys involve the least. When the goods being offered involve change, however, vendors must anticipate planners' concerns. In some situations, it is advisable for vendors to consult planners during the development of products and services that they will offer to other functional areas. Delphi–EMS, for example, involves product planners from its major customers (e.g., GM, Ford, Honda) as it estimates performance parameters and sales volume for fuel delivery systems that are still on the drawing boards.

Planners work in a social context that demands expansive thinking as they consider the implications of new products and services, ask tough critical questions, and integrate other functional area concerns into their own evaluations. Vendors need to be ready for planners' preference for incremental improvement over radical changes, and for their ability to see problems where different functional areas converge. The best way for a vendor to be ready for planners is to know the customer's business well, and to involve the planners early in the process of developing new products and services, even if they are intended to benefit other functional areas.

The Materials Management Function

Like the planning function, this function is not independently represented in many organizations, particularly in small and midsized organizations where senior managers participate in day-to-day operations. In a hair-styling salon, for example, a vendor will probably not find one person whose sole job is to purchase supplies and equipment, unless it is a very large operation. In most large organizations, a group of purchasing and inventory management professionals serve this function.

Materials management professionals coordinate the movement of materials in and out of the facility, and operate under the same time constraints as production function personnel. If Delphi–EMS must assemble lots of 100,000 fuel pumps per week, materials management personnel must ensure that all required inputs are available when production begins, and that the pumps are shipped to customers as they are completed. This preoccupation with movement means that materials management professionals will be interested in how new products or services are likely to affect the flow of goods. In a firm that manufactures personal computers and practices just-in-time inventory management, for example, materials management personnel will be most concerned with delivery schedules and product reliability, and will ask for terms that minimize material inventory held on the production floor. They may also be interested in recyclable and durable packaging that reduces waste and deters damage or theft.

This smooth and efficient flow of inputs and outputs is vital for all organizations for which time is an important competitive advantage, making it necessary for vendors to give heed to materials management concerns. Vendors are best prepared for the concerns of materials managers in the buying center when they can offer production and delivery schedules, packaging, and transportation arrangements that meet customer demands.

The Human Resource Management Function

Human resource professionals select, train, develop, and manage employees at all organizational levels. In most medium-sized and large companies, human resources is a separate functional area that participates whenever employee welfare or deployment is affected. For example, a company decision to use raw materials that increase the risk of toxic contamination will involve human resource managers who must enforce OSHA standards. Capital expenditures, such as new buildings or production equipment, will also involve human resource personnel concerned with employee safety and quality of work life.

Vendors whose products or services have human resource implications should become familiar with buyers' human resource management practices, and should anticipate their concerns. Some vendors target human resource departments because their products are specifically designed to help companies manage employees. This is true, for example, of vendors of employee benefit services, testing and training services, and employee development seminars. But even vendors of other products need to be concerned with human resource demands. Producers of raw materials and components, for example, must often train customer employees in the safe handling of their products, and producers of machinery must instruct customer employees in the safe operation of the equipment. Cincinnati Milacron, a manufacturer of multispindle lathes, includes specially designed operator shields to meet a particular customer's safety requirements and trains operators in proper shield maintenance as part of their product package. Human resource–oriented members of the buying center will be most concerned with the welfare of the employees affected by the product or service being offered, and vendors are wise to show empathy and sensitivity to the human element as they present their products.

Different Roles in the Buying Center

A second perspective that helps vendors understand organizational buyers is the set of six roles proposed by Webster and Wind.[25] The roles, summarized in Table 6.7, describe the behavior of buying-center members' decision processes, as opposed to their primary functional responsibilities. Although buying-center members naturally tend to adopt roles that are compatible with their functional backgrounds, nothing restrains them from adopting other roles, given different circumstances.

Users

Users are the people who use or will use the product or service being purchased, such as an engineer purchasing a new workstation or a manufacturing manager purchasing a new conveyor. They can come from any functional area or subarea, and

TABLE 6.7 ROLES COMMON TO ORGANIZATIONAL BUYERS

Role	Description	Contribution to the Purchase
Users	People who use the product or service being purchased	Provide functional specifications, initiate the purchasing process
Gatekeepers	People who control access to members of the decision unit	Provide initial screening of vendors and product information
Influencers	People who influence the buying decision because of their expertise or authority	Apply high levels of expertise to ensure that functional and nonfunctional specifications are complete and accurate
Deciders	People who make the final decision on product requirements or the final choice among alternative suppliers	Approve purchases that make good use of firm resources from a top management perspective
Approvers	People who authorize the recommendations of deciders after considering the concerns of influencers and users	Review proposed purchases for proper procedures being followed and match organizational objectives
Buyers	People responsible for final supplier selection and purchase arrangements	Manage early selection of potential vendors and details of the final purchase agreement

Source: Adapted from Frederick E. Webster, Jr. and Yoram Wind, Organizational Buying Behavior *(Upper Saddle River, N. J.: Prentice-Hall, 1972), pp. 78–80. Adapted by permission of Prentice-Hall, Inc., Upper Saddle River, N. J.*

from any level of the organization. Users often initiate purchases by requesting a purchase approval from the appropriations committee, asking the purchasing department for information, or asking a vendor to make a presentation. Users often compile the functional specifications for the product or service being purchased. In small organizations or with small purchases, users may be completely in charge of the buying process.

Gatekeepers

Gatekeepers limit vendor access to other members of the buying center. Medium-sized and large companies frequently receive many unsolicited sales presentations and attempts to influence purchase decisions from outside organizations. Gatekeepers protect their decision-making units from such solicitations by screening incoming information and proposals, and allowing only relevant proposals to reach other departments. Gatekeepers provide a very important service when a company makes important or expensive purchases, and when the number of unsolicited, and often unqualified contacts can impede the decision. Gatekeepers can come from any functional area, but are often from the materials management or financial areas.

Influencers

Influencers have a legitimate effect on the organization's buying decisions and may be directly or indirectly affected by the purchase. Influencers can come from any of the functional areas, and can affect the purchase decision in varying degrees. As discussed in the last section, for example, human resource personnel frequently influence purchases that affect employee welfare or the company's ability to manage personnel issues, and materials management personnel may influence purchases that affect material flow in and out of the plant. Influencers are not always easy to identify in the initial stages of the buying process, but can become highly visible if they oppose a purchase decision. To avoid last-minute objections, vendors should learn about the organization in advance and try to involve all potential influencers early.

Deciders

Deciders make final decisions on purchases, often after considering recommendations from other members of the buying center. Deciders may take completely separate roles within the buying center, particularly in medium-sized and large organizations where expenditures are approved at higher management levels than those at which operational decisions are made. For example, an engineer may manage the purchase of a CAD workstation until the final choice of vendor is required, at which point the vice-president of operations makes the decision. Deciders are important to vendors, often becoming the focal point of marketing efforts late in the buying process. Whenever deciders are separate from other roles, marketers must identify them early and address their concerns.

Approvers

Approvers play separate roles only in medium-sized and large organizations that have relatively strict divisions of responsibility. Some organizations separate the approval function in order to force their members to justify all purchases consistently and adequately. Approvers in some companies are high-level executives, charged with overseeing the organization as a whole and ensuring that all purchases meet organizational objectives. Planners often adopt the approver role in companies that have a planning function, but the role can also be filled by managers from other functional areas. Approvers may also play separate roles only for certain kinds or sizes of purchases, such as the purchase of toxic chemicals, or expenditures of more than $100,000. In such situations, approvers will most often come from a functional area related to the determining parameter; for example, members of the financial department approve purchases of more than $100,000, and production engineers approve the purchase of toxic chemicals. Vendors often do not become aware of any separate approver role until late in the buying process, particularly when dealing with new customers.

Buyers

Buyers, if they have separate roles, can be found early in the buying process and again as arrangements are being finalized. This is the only role that is closely linked to a functional area because it is often filled by purchasing professionals. Sometimes, however, the buyer role may be separate and not linked to purchasing, as in the case of an administrative assistant charged with managing the purchase of office supplies specified by other organization members. Buyers select which vendors make sales presentations to the buying center. They are charged with knowing technological trends in their industry sector, and with having at least a general idea of the vendor industry structure (e.g., names and reputations of key suppliers and their areas of expertise). Late in the process, buyers may also select final suppliers and finalize purchasing arrangements. Buyers negotiate financial terms, make arrangements for delivery or payment, and distribute large orders between multiple vendors when necessary. They also monitor and maintain relationships with suppliers. For vendors, relationships with buyers are often the most important ones throughout the buying process, and worth cultivating if repeat business is possible. Buyers determine if vendors are included in the consideration set for future purchases, and they can best help vendors make sense of the demands or objections of other buying-center members.

Although some connections exist between functional areas and the roles of the buying-center members, it is important to recognize that these roles are interchangeable among members of the buying center, depending on the product or service being purchased and on the managerial practices of the customer organization. When buying scientific equipment at a large company such as Texas Instruments, for example, financial professionals will probably act as the approvers of expenditures recommended by the research and development manager, who acts as the decider. When the product is payroll management services, however, the financial department assumes the decider role, whereas the research and development staff might act as influencers. And the purchase of both scientific equipment and payroll management services by a small computer hardware manufacturer may have the head of research and development as the decider and the president as approver.

Because there are similarities between organizations in the same industry or companies of similar size, we can develop rules of thumb linking functional areas to roles, such as that purchasing professionals are often gatekeepers and buyers, planners are often influencers, and financial professionals are often approvers for large expenditures. Vendors should use these rules of thumb, however, only in the initial planning of the marketing effort. As the sales process progresses, vendors should test all assumptions about roles and functional areas early, by asking buying-center members about their concerns, and listening carefully to ascertain what perspectives members bring to the decision.

Note also that the roles are present in every buying situation, regardless of the number of people involved in the decision process. The simplest buying decision involves only a seller and a user, but even here all the roles are present and assumed by the user. Such simple buying situations arise most often when organizations are purchasing items of such low value that no other functional area needs to be involved, or in straight rebuys of regularly used products. In such cases the user also sets the specifications (influencer), screens the suppliers (gatekeeper), makes the final decision (decider and approver), and actually makes the purchase (buyer).

Although a two-person exchange is relatively simple in its interpersonal demands, role theory suggests that the decision process is no less complex or important than if many people were involved. The vendor, consequently, needs to keep in mind the potential influences that the various roles may have on the decision even if they are all embodied in a single person. Vendors who discipline themselves to consider and respond to the different roles in every buying situation, regardless of the number of people that comprise the buying center, will be consistently better prepared to deal with customer demands, able to handle increasingly complex situations, and less disturbed when they encounter unanticipated participants in the buying process.

MARKETING TO DIFFERENT TYPES OF ORGANIZATIONS: CURRENT TRENDS

Earlier in this chapter, we discussed three types of organizations encountered by marketers: industrial buyers, resellers, and institutional buyers. The demands of these organization types and the best marketing strategies for reaching them can change, based on economic and sociocultural trends. Current trends as to what these types of buyers expect from vendors and the most successful ways to reach them can be generalized, however.

Industrial Buyers

For most industrial buyers, purchase decisions are made by a buying center representing the functional areas that use the goods and those charged with managing organizational resources. Some exceptions are single-owner production operations such as farms, small construction companies, and machine shops, in which owners make all purchasing decisions. Multimember decision groups usually share organizational goals (e.g., customer satisfaction and profits), even if members don't agree on the means to achieve them. Industrial buyers vary in terms of their bureaucracy and political tendencies, however, and marketers have to adjust their approach to those differences.

Recent trends among industrial buyers include greater emphasis on just-in-time inventory management to reduce inventory financing costs and increase quality. Companies pressure suppliers to improve quality control and manufacturing processes. Industrial buyers also want suppliers to adopt integrated manufacturing processes that allow quick adjustments to what is being produced and the rate of output. Industrial buyers usually reward suppliers who comply with these demands with long-term contracts at reasonable profit levels. One additional trend is toward reducing prices to match those of foreign competitors. This has become a global trend as developing countries take advantage of their labor surplus to invade profitable markets.

Resellers

Both retail and wholesale businesses have become increasingly competitive around the world as transportation and communications advantages allow resellers to invade foreign markets and capture larger shares of their local markets. Increased competition has narrowed profit margins in practically all categories of resellers, however, making them very receptive to vendor services that reduce costs. Among the more popular tools used by vendors to attract resellers are:

- trade allowances and discounts that reduce the net cost of the product
- advertising and promotional programs in which vendors assume some advertising costs
- generous return and exchange policies that reduce the risk of inventories with zero value
- automatic order and billing management that reduces operational costs and inventory.

Current reseller demands include electronic data interchange, more sophisticated shelf space management, and increased use of private labels. In the United States, Canada, Japan, and much of Western Europe, resellers have become increasingly powerful as consumer spending becomes a greater percentage of total economic activity. In addition, many resellers have instituted data collection systems that give them more extensive information about their customers than what is available to vendors. Resellers have automated their operations, improved their customer service, and raised their expectations of vendors. They have also used their marketing influence to gain customer approval of private-label products, which are better values to consumers and more profitable to resellers, but hurt the sales of name brand products.

Institutional Buyers

To meet the conflicting demands of increasingly powerful and vocal constituencies such as government and medical professionals, institutional buyers tend to be more loosely coupled than for-profit organizations, and they require different marketing practices. Loose coupling means that the different functional areas work independently and autonomously to meet conflicting demands. Unfortunately, it also means that communication among areas can be inefficient or nonexistent. Loosely coupled buying-decision units are often fragmented and show little or no motivation to make consistent or efficient decisions. Such organizations present a challenge to vendors, who must identify the needs and demands of all parties involved and appeal to those needs individually, or figure out ways to keep resistant parties out of the decision process.

Global political and economic instabilities also affect how vendors respond to institutional buyers whose resources are directly or indirectly linked to government allocations (e.g., defense, social services, state universities). Demand for the products and services purchased by these institutions, their performance standards for suppliers, and even the individuals involved in the purchase decision can vary dramatically whenever a new government is voted into power or economic conditions change. In Europe, the shift from socialist to more market-oriented economies in many countries has greatly altered the role of institutional buyers, the types of products they purchased, and the procedures involved. Producers of steel products, for example, no longer have to meet local content regulations in many countries or show proof that they are responsible social citizens. They must be highly competitive in price, however, and can be very creative in their negotiations. A vendor may find that steel producers want to barter, that is, to pay in product (e.g., steel bars) instead of hard currency, and the vendor must be willing to help sell the customer's products in foreign markets before a deal can be finalized.

Political pressure also affects institutional buyers' responses to environmental issues. Constituents of institutional buyers throughout the world are concerned with the environment and are pressuring institutional buyers to add environmental responsibility to their vendor evaluation standards. In some countries, such as the United States and Canada, the human rights record has also been added to the supplier evaluation list. Focusing attention on the vendor's performance in areas of social responsibility unrelated to the products or services being offered is a relatively new factor in dealing with institutional buyers, and one to which vendors are still learning to respond.

SEGMENTING ORGANIZATIONAL BUYERS: IMPLICATIONS FOR MARKETING STRATEGY

Throughout this chapter we have discussed a number of categorization schemes used to distinguish organizational buyers, ranging from size and geographic location to SIC codes, types of products purchased, and the objectives of the organization. We have also suggested that categorizing organizational buyers based on these and other characteristics is useful in developing marketing strategies.

We discussed the importance of categorizing or segmenting customers in chapter 5; such categories are no less important to vendors who market to organizational buyers than to markets reaching individual consumers. Segmentation helps marketers identify new opportunities, design effective marketing programs, and improve their overall strategic use of resources. The need to segment organizational buyers has been widely recognized in marketing, and experts have recommended

TABLE 6.8 SEGMENTATION VARIABLES FOR ORGANIZATIONAL BUYERS

Major Segment	Major Subsegment	Examples of Categories	Examples of Business Relevance
DEMOGRAPHIC			
	Company size	Fortune 500, middle market	Larger orders, more stringent demands
	Industry	Steel, autos, textiles	Industry and demand growth rate
	Geographic location	Northeast, Midwest	Reduces cost of salesperson travel
OPERATIONAL			
	Technological base	Electric motor or gas engine	Established or emerging, risk levels
	In-house capabilities	Programming, assembly, storage	Bundle of individual services
	User/nonuser status	Heavy user, light user	Quantity discounts, size of order
BUYING APPROACH			
	Purchasing structure	Centralized, decentralized	Responsiveness to users
	Purchasing policies	Leasing, sealed bids	Different costs of doing business
	Purchasing criteria	Low price, quality	Compatibility with vendor strengths
	Dominant perspective	Financial, engineering, marketing	Main focus of marketing efforts
	Existing relationship	Trust, arm's length	Ability to access decision makers
SITUATION FACTORS			
	Size of order	Large, small	Effects of production scheduling
	Purchase timing	Expedited or regular delivery	Sensitivity to price, trust relationship
	Application	Widespread or single-site use	Sales volume, access to other users
PERSONAL TRAITS			
	Loyalty to vendors	Loyal, not loyal	Willingness to favor buyer over others
	Attitudes toward risk	Risk taker, risk avoider	Attributes of product to emphasize
	Similarity	Similar, dissimilar	Ease of communication, complementarity

Source: Adapted from Thomas V. Bonoma and Benson P. Shapiro, Segmenting the Industrial Market (Lexington, Mass.: Lexington Books, 1983).

many methods to develop segmentation schemes.[26] As an example, Table 6.8 illustrates a list of factors by which organizational buyers can be segmented, arranged in decreasing order of information accessibility and interpretability. Thus, vendors can access and interpret size information easier than information about their customers' dominant perspective. Note that many of the factors listed in Table 6.8, such as size and dominant perspective, are analogous to characteristics discussed throughout this chapter.

Marketers often find it relatively easy to segment on some of the variables listed on Table 6.8, such as demographic characteristics, and to use assumptions about the different segments to develop marketing tactics. For example, it is relatively easy to get size information on buyers from various sources. Furthermore, most people agree that buying professionals in large organizations specialize by type of product and base more of their purchase decisions on price than do buying professionals in small organizations, who purchase a wider array of products and place more emphasis on trust and past vendor performance. By combining size information with assumptions about how buyers behave in different-sized organizations therefore, vendors can develop marketing tactics and manage the marketing effort. Such a segmentation scheme, for instance, might lead Delphi–EMS to focus on highly detailed cost and profitability estimates when they present products to General Motors buyers, but focus on trust building with the owner-operator of an auto parts store in Smalltown U.S.A. Segmenting on the basis on industry, geographic location, or other demographic variables can be equally useful and easy to implement. A drawback of segmenting on the basis of easy-to-use criteria, however, is that any competitive advantage gained from the segmentation scheme can be lost quickly because competitors can implement the same segmentation scheme just as easily.

Segmentation on the basis of other characteristics listed on Table 6.8 may be useful and strategically more defensible, but it is more difficult to implement because data collection and interpretation become more difficult. Vendors often assess organizational buyers' dominant perspectives or purchasing criteria, for example, on the basis of salespeople's perceptions and interpretations of the buyer's behavior. Collecting such data is difficult and costly, and interpreting the data's implications for marketing strategy often requires subjective judgments that may be wrong.

For example, to segment organizational buyers by dominant perspective (i.e., financial, marketing), a vendor might collect information from multiple sources, such as current and potential customers, industry experts, and in-depth interviews of its own sales force. It must then reconcile and integrate this information into a description of each major customer and prospect, and then it must update the information frequently, given the dynamic industry environments in which mergers and acquisitions occur often. Even if the vendor could collect the data and segment the market on the basis of characteristics such as dominant functional perspective, it may not be able to translate that knowledge into workable strategies and to see the relevance of the segments to the operational decisions its marketing managers make. The vendor who uses dominant functional area still has to answer difficult questions such as, "Do we target companies whose dominant functional area matches ours because it makes communication easier? Or do we target companies whose dominant functional area complements ours?" before they can develop a strategy.

Because of this trade-off between ease of segmentation scheme implementation and strategic defensibility, most strategists suggest that the best use of segmentation variables for organizational buyers is to combine them in ways that are strategically and tactically relevant to the task being performed, and to vary segmentation schemes as necessary.[27] When developing their product strategy, for example, Delphi–EMS may segment organizational buyers based on their SIC codes *and* dominant perspectives to arrive at the strategic decision to make three grades of fuel pumps: low grade for low-price resellers, medium grade for quality-minded automobile manufacturers and upscale retailers, and high grade for luxury-car manufacturers and racing applications. To manage its advertising and sales efforts, however, Delphi–EMS may segment based only on size and purchasing structure. The company may decide to reach General Motors through orchestrated advertising and personal sales campaigns aimed at GM's centralized purchasing organization, whereas it may try to reach stock car racing teams through advertising in racing journals and informal meetings with their mechanics and drivers.

The number of segmentation-variable combinations vendors can use is as large as the number of possible strategies they can adopt. The guiding principles for segmenting organizational buyers, however, are relatively few. As mentioned, segmentation variables should be *strategically and tactically relevant:* vendors' choices of variables are predicated by whatever decision they are trying to make. Including segmentation variables that are neither strategically nor tactically relevant adds complexity to the segmentation scheme without adding value. In addition, vendors must choose *measurable* variables for segmentation, using measurement methodologies that are as objectively quantifiable as possible (e.g., surveys, structured interviews). Although vendors must rely to some extent on subjective judgments, sole reliance on opinions is not wise. Finally, the variables used for segmentation should result in segments that are *actionable*—segments for which vendors can formulate and implement plans and measure results. Segments that are conceptually feasible but cannot be reached effectively through the promotional and distribution methods available are nothing more than conceptually interesting phenomena.

Following these principles, vendors choose variables on which to base their segmentation schemes. Once they develop the segments and profiles, they can match current and prospective customers to the segments they fit best. Then vendors can develop marketing strategies for each market segment and implement them across the organization. Although vendors may need to slightly vary strategy executions on a customer-by-customer basis, their consistent application of an overarching strategy across customers should lead to resources being used more efficiently and results being more predictable than if a totally custom-tailored strategy were used for each buyer.

SUMMARY

Organizational buyers represent a major market opportunity. They differ from individual consumers in important ways:

- Organizational buyers are usually large entities with substantial resources and influence.
- Organizational buyers tend to be concentrated in terms of their total number and geographic location.
- Organizational buyers tend to be more precise in their demands, and are more powerful members of the exchange relationship.
- Organizational buyers often include input from numerous people in their decisions.
- Organizational buyers expect the supplier to develop a more intimate and complex relationship with them.
- Organizational buyers place more professionally stringent demands on vendors than do individual consumers.

Organizational buyers can be categorized by their objectives as industrial buyers, resellers, and institutional buyers.

- Industrial buyers are typically for-profit organizations, use their purchases to produce other goods and services, are price sensitive and demanding of quality, exhibit flexible manufacturing practices, and use just-in-time delivery.
- Resellers buy goods and services for resale, typically operate with narrow profit margins, are highly competitive and sensitive to price, and are responsive to support services such as promotional discounts and cooperative advertising.
- Institutional buyers are primarily nonprofit organizations and government agencies, vary in the types of products they purchase, demand consistent performance, and are preoccupied with the social and environmental track record of potential suppliers.

Organizational buyers can also be categorized based on their economic output, using the North American Industry Classification System or the Standard Industrial Classification system. These systems, maintained by the national governments, are highly detailed and facilitate the development of highly specific forecasts and market potential estimates.

Organizations face three types of buying situations:

- Straight rebuy
- Modified rebuy
- New-task buying

Understanding the types of buying situations and how the decision process varies among them helps vendors allocate their time and resources wisely. In straight-rebuy situations it is very difficult for a new supplier to make a sale unless the current supplier offers substandard products or services. Modified-rebuy and new-task situations have higher potential but require more extensive negotiations.

The buying process consists of several stages, which have been described in many ways. The popular BUYGRID model proposes eight stages:

- Problem recognition
- General attribute description
- Elaboration of product and quantity needed
- Search for potential suppliers
- Proposal solicitation
- Supplier evaluation
- Order routine specification
- Performance review

Not all stages are involved in every buying task. The minimum number of stages is three: problem recognition, elaboration of product and quantity needed, and performance review. Organizational buyers do not always make rational buying decisions. They participate in the diffusion of innovation process and are susceptible to social and cultural factors

Organizations purchase different products: raw materials, components and partially processed materials, capital goods, ancillary equipment, supplies, and professional services. Organizational buyers' demand for goods is primarily derived from the demand for their own products and services, as against their plans for direct consumption. Derived demand and production constraints make organizational buyers less price elastic than individual consumers, and less loyal to any single supplier.

Organizational buying processes are very complex for several reasons. One is that organizations must respond to multiple external and internal factors in their decisions.

- External factors: environmental forces, organizational practices and constraints, and the interpersonal relationship between buyer and seller representatives
- Internal factors: individual-level predispositions, the frames of reference buyers can adopt, and social context and roles imposed on the buyer.

In some situations, marketers can focus on the organizational buyer's frame of reference as the integration of the organizational, interpersonal, and individual influences.

Organizational buyers encompass different functional areas that are often involved in the decision process. There are six broad functional areas found in most organizations that influence buying decisions:

- Financial
- Promotion
- Production

- Planning
- Materials management
- Human resource management

The decision units of organizations normally include representatives from some or all of these functional areas, and each one brings to the unit a specialized perspective and set of demands. The members of the decision unit also assume one or more of the following roles:

- User
- Gatekeeper
- Influencer
- Decider
- Approver
- Buyer

By combining knowledge about functional areas and roles, marketers can create an accurate profile of the decision unit and use it to anticipate the concerns and reactions of different members.

Industrial buyers, resellers, and institutional buyers differ in their current demands on vendors:

- Industrial buyers focus on expediting transactions and improved quality through means such as just-in-time materials management and integrated manufacturing.
- Resellers demand higher margins and more control over shelf space, and have access to valuable data with which they exercise greater influence on vendors.
- Institutional buyers are concerned with social, political, and environmental issues, as well as advancing their national interests in highly competitive markets.

Organizational buyers can be segmented along many of the different categorization schemes presented in the chapter. Vendors must trade off the ease of applying a segmentation scheme with its ability to provide a competitive advantage. All segmentation schemes used for organizational buyers should be based on variables that:

- Are strategically and tactically relevant to the vendor's objectives.
- Are accurately and objectively measurable.
- Yield segments on which the company can take action and achieve results.

QUESTIONS FOR DISCUSSION

1. Why has the auto industry in the United States, Japan, and Europe been so important in the development of organizational buying practices and their impact on marketing? Are there other industries that can be expected to be as influential in the future?

2. Name the functional areas of the organization that are likely to be involved in the following buying situations:
   a. The purchase of rubber stock for the manufacture of tennis balls by Slazenger.
   b. The purchase of an injection molding machine for the manufacture of pen shells by Parker Pen Co.

c. The purchase of two computers to serve as servers by a Social Security Administration office.

d. The purchase of a building in Beijing for the manufacture of razor blades by Gillette.

3. What buying center roles would you expect to be involved in each of the situations described in question 2?

4. Use role theory to analyze a buying situation in which a purchasing agent, the comptroller, and the president of a small university are replacing the school's fleet of maintenance vehicles. What roles are involved? What social context factors does the marketer need to monitor? What personal factors might affect the decision?

5. Describe a strategy for the following situations in which you are the established or dominant supplier:

a. The repurchase of fasteners (screws and nuts) by a manufacturer of metal furniture for which you are already the established supplier.

b. The purchase of metal stampings as components for a new line of furniture by a company for which you already supply components for other lines of furniture.

c. The purchase of robotics equipment, for which you are the industry leader, by a metal furniture manufacturer.

6. Describe a strategy for the following situations in which you are a small and relatively unknown supplier:

a. The repurchase of fasteners (screws and nuts) by a manufacturer of metal furniture for which you are a new supplier.

b. The purchase of metal stampings as components for a new line of furniture by a company you have never supplied with components.

c. The purchase of robotics equipment, for which you are a newcomer to the industry, by a metal furniture manufacturer.

7. What are some of the environmental factors that Boeing must consider when marketing airplanes for foreign governments and carriers? Make sure to consider all five areas of the environment from chapter 3.

8. Use the frame of reference model to anticipate the most likely perspective and responses for the following situations:

a. Marketing a new cash register to an independent retailer of guns and ammunition.

b. Marketing cleaning services to a biotechnology start-up company with about fifteen employees.

c. Marketing fleet replacement vehicles to the Federal Bureau of Investigation (FBI).

NOTES FOR FURTHER READING

1. Frederick E. Webster Jr. and Yoram Wind, *Organizational Buying Behavior* (Upper Saddle River, N. J.: Prentice-Hall, 1972).

2. Ibid., p. 6.

3. Julia M. Bristor and Michael J. Ryan, "The Buying Center is Dead: Long Live the Buying Center," in *Advances in Consumer Research* 1987), pp. 225–258.

4. Lars Hallen, Jan Johanson, and Nazeem Seyed-Mohamed, "Interfirm Adaptation in Business Relationships", *Journal of Marketing* 55 (April 1991): 29–37.

5. Lars-Erik Gadde and Lars-Gunnar Mattson, "Stability and Change in Network Relationships," *International Journal of Research in Marketing* 4(1987): 29–41.

6. Manohar U. Kalwani and Narakesari Narayandas, "Long-Term Manufacturer-Supplier Relationships: Do They Pay Off for Supplier Firms" *Journal of Marketing* 59 (January 1995): 1–16.

7. *Statistical Abstract of the United States* (1992): The National Data Book, 112th ed., United States Bureau of the Census, Washington, D.C.: G.P.O.

8. Ibid.

9. The number of government units comes from the *Statistical Abstract of the United States* (1992). The amount of government purchases comes from the *Economic Report of the President* (Washington D.C.: U.S. Government Printing Office, 1993) The size and volume of the non-government institutional market is from Larry C. Giunipers, William Crittenden, and Vicky Crittenden, "Industrial Marketing in Non-Profit Organizations," *Industrial Marketing Management* 19 (1990): p. 279.

10. Patrick J. Robinson, Charles W. Faris, and Yoram Wind, *Industrial Buying and Creative Marketing* (Boston: Allyn & Bacon, 1967).

11. Richard M. Cyert, Herbert A. Simon, and Donald B. Trow "Observation of a Business Decision," *Journal of Business* 29 (October 1956): 237–248.

12. Frederick E. Webster Jr., "Modeling the Industrial Buying Process," *Journal of Marketing Research* 2 (November 1965): 370–376.

13. Robinson et al., *Industrial Buying and Creative Marketing*.

14. For more information, see Michael Selz, "Small Companies Thrive by Taking Over Some Specialized Tasks for Big Concerns, *Wall Street Journal*, September 11, 1991, p. B1.

15. For more information, see John R. Emshwiller, "Suppliers Struggle to Improve Quality as Big Firms Slash Their Vendor Rolls," *Wall Street Journal*, August 16, 1991, B1.

16. K. Backhaus and B. Gunter, "A Phase-Differentiated Interaction Approach to Industrial Marketing Decisions," *Industrial Marketing Management* 5 (October 1976): 255–270.

17. H. Lazo "Emotional Aspects of Industrial Buying," in R. S. Hancock, ed., *Dynamic Marketing for a Changing World* (Chicago: American Marketing Association, 1960), pp. 258–265, Robert F. Shoaf, ed., *Emotional Factors Underlying Industrial Purchasing* (Cleveland: Penton Publications, 1959).

18. Everett M. Rogers, "New Product Adoption and Diffusion," *Journal of Consumer Research* 2 (March 1976): 290–301, Everett M. Rogers, *Diffusion of Innovations* (New York: Free Press, 1983).

19. For more information, see Howard Gleckman, John Carey, Russell Mitchell, Tim Smart, and Chris Rousch, "The Technology Payoff," *Business Week*, June 14, 1993, pp. 56–68.

20. Webster and Wind, *Organizational Buying Behavior.*

21. Ibid.

22. For more information, see Ron Stodghill II, "What Makes Ryka Run? Sheri Poe and Her Story." *Business Week*, June 14, 1993, pp. 82–84.

23. Paul Shrivastava and Ian Mitroff, "Frames of Reference Managers Use," in Robert Lamb, ed., *Advances in Strategic Management*, vol. 1 (Greenwich, Conn.: JAI Press, 1983), pp. 161–182.

24. Bruce I. Biddle and Edwin J. Thomas, eds., *Role Theory: Concepts and Research* (Huntington, N.Y.: R. E. Krieger Publishing Co., 1979).

25. Webster and Wind, *Organizational Buying Behavior,* pp. 78–80.

26. Thomas V. Bonoma and Benson P. Shapiro, *Segmenting the Industrial Market* (Lexington Mass.: Lexington Books, 1983).

27. Ibid.

CHAPTER 7

NEW PRODUCT DEVELOPMENT

CHAPTER OBJECTIVES

When you are done with this chapter, you should have achieved the following:

- An understanding of how managers use the terms "new" and "product."
- A recognition of the importance of new products and problems that arise in their development.
- Consideration of how new product development is evaluated.
- The ability to show how managers develop and introduce new products.

CHAPTER OUTLINE

New products spur economic growth as essential competitive tools in most enterprises. The number of new products introduced each year is mind boggling. In the United States, for example, companies introduce more than 15,000 new products each year into supermarkets alone.

What differentiates new product successes from failures? Sometimes the first evidence of success is seen in the effect a new product launch has on a firm's stocks. Throughout 1989 and the first nine months of 1990, stock prices for Apple Computer stagnated at about $34 per share. In October 1990, the company introduced the Mac Classic, a low-price ($1,000) version of its Macintosh, and two new models in the $3,000 to $4,000 price range, the MacLC and IIsi. The market responded quickly, and by April 1991, six months later, the price of Apple stock had soared to $66

Toy manufacturers never know which new products might catch on. Each Christmas there seem to be a few winners.

per share. Computer companies, like many other firms, cannot survive without a constant stream of new products. A case in point is Compaq Computer Corporation, where fully 50 percent of revenues each year comes from products introduced in the previous year.

Yet new products can also fail spectacularly and threaten a firm's livelihood. A few years ago, Federal Express lost nearly $200 million on its ill-fated Zap Mail venture. RJR Nabisco lost even more—over $250 million—on its failed smokeless cigarette, Premier.

Sources: "Another 15,000 New Products Expected for U.S. Supermarkets," *Marketing News*, June 10, 1991, p. 8.

"Federal Express Will Scuttle Zap Mail, Take $190 Million Write-off," *Wall Street Journal*, September 30, 1986, p. 2.

Howard Schlossberg, "Experts Share Formulas for Innovative Success," *Marketing News*, June 10, 1991, p. 8.

Clearly, new products create huge risks and potentially huge rewards for organizations. The purpose of this chapter is to study the new product management process and consider how its functions should be conducted. The following chapter addresses the companion topic of managing products throughout their life cycles.

WHAT IS A PRODUCT AND WHAT DO WE MEAN BY NEW?

Definition of a Product

What is a product? The answer to this question may seem obvious. After all, can't any product be described with some combination of the five senses? We can see, hear, touch, smell, or taste most products. So why bother to define a product? Is there really anything more to identify?

Actually, if managers focus only on their products' physical aspects, as intuitive as this may seem, they may entirely miss the subtleties that make people want to buy their brand instead of a competing brand. Marketplace success requires that managers come to see their offering not so much as a physical entity, but rather as *means* for consumers to fulfill their utilitarian or experiential needs. Aside from the physical aspects, products have rational, moral, and emotional meanings for consumers.

Figure 7.1 presents a more fruitful way to think about products than the commonly assumed physical interpretation. Managers must think about products in terms of what it takes to satisfy consumer needs and wants. The brand manager controls the features or attributes built into the product, which consumers then mentally process and interpret in terms of their personal goals. These goals represent the value that consumers anticipate. In turn, consumers use perceived values to estimate their likely satisfaction arising from purchase. After purchase and use, consumers' actual satisfaction or dissatisfaction feeds back and either confirms or negates the value assessment. This leads to decisions to repurchase or not, good or bad word-of-mouth communication, and other actions in relation to a product or company.

With Figure 7.1 as a starting point, let us explore in more depth what products really are. A product is, of course, an entity, or total offering represented in some way in the consumer's and seller's minds. This total offering comprises both a whole and a sum of various parts or attributes, which can be adjusted further by marketing mix factors such as promotional activities, distribution alternatives, and pricing options. The whole is the total effect that the product has on customers. People often desire products that do useful things. Products accomplish objectives, such as keeping food cool and fresh, removing dirt and grease from clothes, or linking families to information. Products may save time or money. People also want products for the intellectual and emotional experiences the products bring to their lives. Thus products may create happiness, express pride or love, or contribute to a whole host of other personal experiences. Of course, many products represent combinations of utilitarian and experiential benefits. A fancy new car serves a transportation function but may also, depending on the person, provide feelings of prestige, power, pride, or even affection.

The effects of a product as a whole are produced through their composite parts. Marketers typically term these parts *product attributes*. Many products deliver only two or three basic attributes—the product's salient characteristics that consumers recognize in deciding whether or not to buy the product. Thus, laundry detergents emphasize "effectiveness" and "mildness" as their key selling points. Computer consumers look for machines that will be "useful," "easy to use," and "fun."

It is important to realize, however, that each of the basic attributes of any product can be thought of as bundles of more or less similar subattributes. Consider

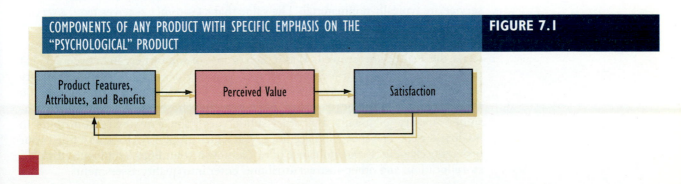

COMPONENTS OF ANY PRODUCT WITH SPECIFIC EMPHASIS ON THE "PSYCHOLOGICAL" PRODUCT

FIGURE 7.1

Product Features, Attributes, and Benefits → Perceived Value → Satisfaction

laundry detergents. "Effectiveness," an abstract basic attribute, summarizes such concrete subattributes as power, grease stain removal, color brightening, whitening, dirt or grass removal, and so forth. "Mildness" translates into safety for lingerie, color fastness, appropriateness for synthetic fabrics, and softening ability. Notice that we purposefully frame product attributes in terms of their *benefits to consumers*. Manufacturers of laundry detergents must combine cleaning agents and other chemicals to most effectively and efficiently produce these benefits. The physical features of laundry detergents have meaning for consumers only in terms of their eventual subjective benefits—for example, clean, "fresh-smelling," undamaged clothing.

It is important to realize that the boundary for any product goes beyond its physical form or even its characteristics. We should think of any product in terms of its psychological boundary, which encompasses information added to physical products to create *brand images*. The whole is indeed more than the sum of its parts. To produce subjective product attributes and the benefits associated with them, managers begin with their own brands, and add *psychological value* to the products' physical characteristics through information about price, availability, and especially communication cues, noting tangible and intangible benefits for the customer.

Figure 7.1 contains a summary term, *perceived value*, which captures the essence of how customers process and judge product features and attributes. Perceived value has two main parts: the *quality* the customer perceives in a product or service, and the *cost* the customer anticipates in acquiring that product or service. When the quality, or gain, is greater than the cost, customers will consider the product to have positive value. Of course, customers generally prefer the brand with the greatest positive value in comparison to other brands.

Quality represents a global evaluative judgment of a product by the customer. Marketing researchers sometimes measure quality evaluations through questionnaires that record customer attitudes. Consumer preferences are built into their quality assessments. Quality can be good or bad, perceptually differing among products and among consumers as a matter of degree. We prefer higher to lower "quality" in terms of our own personal standards for goodness. At the same time, customers' overall quality judgments reside in secondary judgments of quality. These secondary judgments refer to dimensions of the product (e.g., durability) as well as its consequences (e.g., saves time) and special meaning for us (e.g., a favorite restaurant). The secondary qualities are in part a function of the customer's needs and standards and in part a function of what the marketer does in terms of product design, distribution, advertising, and so on.

To make these ideas more concrete, let us consider a customer service. Although relatively intangible, services are in certain senses products. Instead of tangible attributes, however, such as the durability of a pair of blue jeans, the properties of a service are typically nonmaterial. The value that a customer receives from a service is a complex bundle of subjective and abstract benefits.

Recall your most recent trip to a fast-food restaurant. How would you characterize the quality you received? Was it high or low, or somewhere in between? What things contribute to your judgment of overall quality or contribute to its summary level? Obviously, your reactions to the food itself forms a large part of your opinion about quality. The tastiness, texture, and nutritious value of the food affect any consumer's quality judgments. But other subtle cues related to service contribute to quality as well. The speed and accuracy with which employees took and filled your order, the cleanliness and ambiance of restaurant surroundings, employee attitudes, store location, and other abstract attributes enter into quality assessments.

Across a wide assortment of services from banking, to retailing, to repair businesses, researchers have identified five fundamental dimensions that dictate service quality:

Tangibles: Physical facilities, equipment, and appearance of personnel

Reliability: Ability to perform the promised service dependably and accurately

Responsiveness: Willingness to help customers and provide prompt service

Assurance: Employees' knowledge and courtesy and their ability to inspire trust and confidence

Empathy: Caring employees' individualized attention to customers.[1]

Each of these contributes to a customer's judgment of overall service quality and indirectly influences satisfaction.

The quality customers perceive in physical products is often easier to assess than service quality because the linkages between material aspects of a product and its meanings for the customer are more direct than the linkages between nonmaterial aspects of a service and its meanings for the customer. For instance, it is easier and more accurate to measure consumers' evaluative responses to a new taco dip (e.g., "tasty–tasteless," "exciting–dull," "strong–weak") than their evaluative responses to a new department store lobby (e.g., "pleasant–unpleasant," "cheerful–depressing," "surprising–predictable"). But managers also can find product quality more difficult to assess than service quality because basic quality dimensions vary considerably from physical product to physical product, whereas the five service-quality dimensions mentioned above generalize across most services.[2]

To see this diversity in subdimensions of quality for physical products, consider the research results from two consumer products: a new seasoned dry sausage[3] in the Netherlands and a new nonprescription analgesic containing naproxen in the United States (older analgesics contain either ibuprofen, acetaminophen, or aspirin). For the dry sausage product, which was intended as a snack or sandwich ingredient, three quality dimensions were relevant: sensory quality (e.g., tastiness, tenderness, juiciness, and freshness), healthiness (with respect to fat, coloring agents, salt, and calories), and freshness.

For the new analgesic, quite different quality dimensions arose: efficacy (e.g., effectiveness of relief for sports-related aches and pains as well as arthritis pain), gentleness (e.g., lack of side effects such as upset stomach or drowsiness), convenience (e.g., cap removal ease for arthritic or elderly users), safety (especially for users with children), and length of dosage intervals (e.g., once every 8 to 12 hours compared to the once every 4 to 8 hours typical of the competition). These five dimensions provide a common set of general factors that underlie service quality judgments.

Managers of services must identify what activities and benefits peculiar to their business produce the basic service quality dimensions for their particular clients. The number and nature of quality dimensions are idiosyncratic to the kind of physical product under scrutiny, so managers must identify both the fundamental product quality dimensions and the unique product attributes to produce high scores on these specific quality dimensions. Distribution, packaging, and communication cues add to the service or product features to generate overall quality. Quality relates to the utilitarian, intellectual, and/or emotional benefits customers seek, so brand managers must orchestrate these *psychological benefits* to produce customer satisfaction.

In addition to quality concerns, customers also consider *costs*. In general, customers incur four kinds of costs, which offset products' quality dimensions: financial, physical temporal, psychological, and social. Financial costs are the monetary expenses necessary to acquire a product, including the product price as well as travel, storage, delivery,

Aleve, a division of Procter & Gamble, stresses "cost per 24 hours of pain relief" in its ads in order to obtain an advantage over competitors. For 24 hours of pain relief, one must take three Aleve pills at a total cost of $0.31. Compare this to Advil's $0.63 (6 pills), Extra Strength Tylenol's $0.94 (12 pills) and there emerges a clear value advantage for Aleve.

This Lands' End ad for a classic blazer also illustrates this idea of life-cycle costs: Lands' End's well-made blazer uses the finest materials and classic tailoring so that the customer will only have to buy one blazer

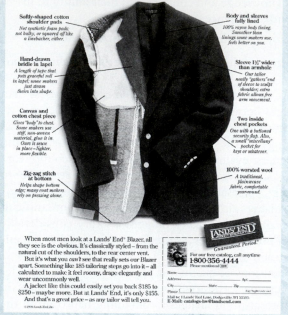

that will remain in style over several seasons rather than replacing a cheaper, more trendy blazer each season. Further, they use fabrics that work year round, so the customer can wear their Lands' End blazer anytime.

When prorated over a 4-year period, the purchase of a Lands' End blazer actually saves the customer money (and time) compared to the purchase of two competitor's blazers over the same period.

Source: Aleve advertisement, *Newsweek*, July 17, 1995, p. 53.

and other expenses incurred when consumers purchase and take possession of the product. Thus financial costs associated with an automobile purchase include the price paid for transportation to and from the dealership, dealer preparation charges, license fees, and taxes in addition to the sticker price. Financial costs also include the savings consumers could have gained had they purchased an alternative brand or product that met their needs at a lower cost. For an example of "life-cycle" cost and its relation to value and the competition, see Marketing Anecdote 7.1.

Physical costs include the effort consumers exert to acquire a product, and temporal costs include an account of the time they spend acquiring the product. Psychological costs often accompany a purchase, too. Guilt, shame, anxiety, anger, disappointment, and regret are common psychological losses attached to purchases. Finally, social costs sometimes arise. Buyers sometimes face contempt or ridicule from others if they make certain purchases—this happens, for example, when a person buys a foreign-made car and is criticized for not purchasing a domestic-made automobile. People risk ridicule if they overspend, purchase a product that fails, or looks foolish in some other way. Many a transaction must overcome social pressure of one form or another if a sale is to be consummated. Of course, social pressure can also push one to make a purchase even if other costs are perceived to be high.

Figure 7.1 reveals that perceived value lies at the heart of what we mean by the psychological product. Consumers calculate value by offsetting their quality and cost judgments. We know little about the exact mechanisms behind this psychological integration. Metaphorically speaking, we might think of "value = (quality − costs)." But researchers find it difficult to pin down this mental algebra. Some consumers seem to value certain products based on a ratio of quality to costs or costs to quality rather than a difference between the two. Quality and cost may also influence each other at times. For example, consumers often infer better quality on the basis of higher prices. "You get what you pay for," is a common refrain of consumers and sellers alike, often encouraging customers to invest in more expensive products to ensure quality. However, research in the Netherlands finds that the association between quality and price in the marketplace explains less than 9 percent of the variation in quality.[4] Thus, price is not always a very informative cue for product quality. This is a consequence, in part, of the wide variability in quality at any given price level in competitive markets.

What Is a New Product?

Firms and customers typically define "new" differently. New York consulting firm Booz, Allen & Hamilton surveyed corporate executives and product managers at more than 700 Fortune 1000 companies to find out what these experts considered to be "new" products.[5] These managers identified a total of 13,311 "new" products, although their viewpoints about what constitutes a "new" product were less clear.

As shown in Figure 7.2, the survey found at least six categories of "newness." The newest of the new was termed, "new-to-the-world" products to signify novel products

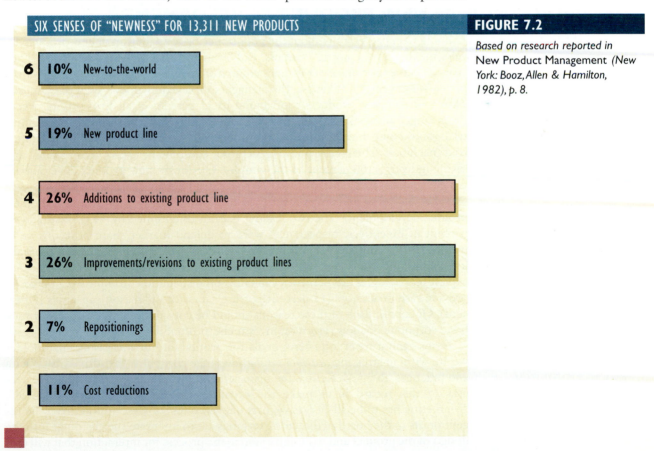

SIX SENSES OF "NEWNESS" FOR 13,311 NEW PRODUCTS

FIGURE 7.2

Based on research reported in New Product Management *(New York: Booz, Allen & Hamilton, 1982), p. 8.*

6 10% New-to-the-world

5 19% New product line

4 26% Additions to existing product line

3 26% Improvements/revisions to existing product lines

2 7% Repositionings

1 11% Cost reductions

that created a new market. Of all new product introductions conducted by more than 700 firms, 10 percent were new-to-the-world. A second category consisted of "new product lines," which include products already in the marketplace that the company had not marketed before. About 19 percent of all new product introductions fell into this category. Next, 26 percent of new products were "additions to existing product lines," or line extensions. A fourth category was named "improvements in/revisions to existing product lines," designed to improve performance or increase perceived value. This category also accounted for 26 percent of all new products. Fifth, existing products that were targeted at new markets or new market segments were termed, "repositionings." Only 7 percent of new products fit this designation. Finally, the remaining 11 percent of "new" products were simply "cost reductions." Booz, Allen & Hamilton further found that many new product programs mixed the six categories.

See if you can identify the category of newness for each of the following six products at the time they were launched: Procter & Gamble's Aleve brand of pain reliever, Wilson's "wide-body" Profile tennis racquet, Fuji's Color Quick Snap disposable camera, Miller's Genuine Draft beer, Marlboro cigarettes, and the Macintosh Classic computer. Did you guess new product line, improvement in/revision to existing product, new-to-the-world, addition to existing product line, repositioning (from a so-called women's to a man's cigarette), and cost reduction, respectively? In the final analysis, "newness" rests with customer perceptions. Buyers value "newness" and seem predisposed to try new products, yet they approach seller claims about newness with skepticism. Thus marketers must convince buyers of product novelty.

THE IMPORTANCE OF NEW PRODUCT DEVELOPMENT

Echoing Compaq's claims about the importance or contribution of new product development toward company success, Rubbermaid's chairman recently said, "Each year, 30 percent or more of our sales come from new products introduced over the previous five years."6 Likewise, the managers surveyed by Booz, Allen & Hamilton estimated that new products contributed to 32 percent of all firm profits. These firms ranged from consumer goods companies (40 percent of the sample) to industrial goods companies in information processing, instrument and controls, industrial machinery, chemicals, power-generating equipment, OEM components, and textile industries (60 percent of the sample). Obviously, new product development is a continuous, long-term proposition that must be managed properly.

What did these executives identify as the specific reasons for emphasizing new product development? The two leading reasons (mentioned by 44 percent and 46 percent of executives, respectively) were to defend market share positions or to maintain firm reputation as product innovators. Other reasons given were to establish footholds in new markets (38 percent), preempt market segments (33 percent), exploit technologies (28 percent), capitalize on distribution strengths (25 percent), provide cash generators (13 percent), or use excess or off-season capacities (7 percent). Of course, each of these reasons should be considered in the context of such basic corporate goals as return on investment, profitability, and sales growth.

Firms cannot meet long-term goals for profitability or increasing shareholder wealth without stressing *customer satisfaction* as the core value that drives its policies and practices. Regis McKenna, the management guru, believes that the key to success in this regard is to make the organization more "marketing oriented": "Marketing has to be all-pervasive, part of everyone's job description, from the receptionists to the board of directors. Its job is . . . to integrate the customer into the design of the product and to design a systematic process for interaction that will create substance in the relationship."[7] Because customer needs change and firms compete fiercely, innovative product offerings are necessary for success.

We might say that new product development begins with customer needs and ends with customer satisfaction. But should a firm put customers at the center of its mission in general and new product development in particular? The answer to this is both yes and no. Designing products to meet customer needs, measuring post-purchase satisfaction, and acting accordingly are indispensable activities, to be sure. But at the same time, firms must meet these consumer needs while still meeting company needs and operating under company constraints and market realities. Sometimes this means balancing customer needs with the firm's technological know-how. Raychem CEO Paul Cook cautions that an overemphasis on the customer can work against a company. He points out an alternative:

> Too many American companies are only immersed in their markets. They bring along whatever technology they think is necessary to satisfy a market need. Then they fall flat on their faces because the technology they deliver isn't sophisticated enough or because they don't know what alternatives the competition can deliver. We think of our business differently. Raychem's mission is to creatively interpret our core technologies to serve the marketplace. That means we don't want to be innovators in all technologies. We restrict our charter . . . to niches that can sponsor huge growth over a long period of time and in which we can be pioneers, the first and best in the world. Then we draw on those core technologies to proliferate thousands of products in which we have a powerful competitive advantage and for which our customers are willing to pay us lots of money.[8]

A customer focus by itself is not sufficient. And obviously a product or technological focus by itself is not enough. Whether a firm starts with the customer or with its core technology and resources, it must end up with a marriage of the two that creates a competitive advantage. New product development is a key step in this process.

PITFALLS IN NEW PRODUCT DEVELOPMENT

Although new product development is important to virtually any organization's success, this development process also has a downside. Consider General Foods Corporation's experience as an illustration of the gauntlet faced by modern firms.[9] Over a 10-year period, General Foods screened and analyzed 600 new product ideas. Of these, 118 were deemed worthy for further development. After 31 of these were eliminated for various reasons, General Foods eventually test-marketed 87. But 47 of these ideas ultimately failed, leaving 40 of the original 600 ideas fit for commercialization. Over time, 10 of the 40 products failed and were abandoned. Thus, less than 7 percent of all new product concepts succeeded. Since General Foods is a leader in new product innovations and uses the best in management practice to generate and evaluate new ideas, we can see how difficult and expensive it is for modern corporations to keep up with the competition. The total investment by General Foods for the 10-year period was in excess of $1 billion in today's terms.

New product development is expensive, time consuming, and risky. Prior to launch in 1990, Gillette spent more than $310 million to develop its Sensor razor.[10] How does this compare with other firms and other products? The costs for developing a new airplane are obviously much more than this, whereas the costs for developing a new shampoo, say, are generally much less. Some experts estimate that the average

The ideal situation for firms is to sell the same product in as many markets worldwide as possible. This provides economies of scale, reduces costs, and capitalizes on learning-curve effects in manufacturing, marketing, and other functions of the firm. Thus, the formula for Coca-Cola is constant worldwide, Rice Krispies breakfast cereal is the same in the United States and Europe, and Häagen-Dazs ice cream remains unchanged across its international markets, although the demand for one flavor or another varies.

Subtle and not so subtle differences in consumer tastes and cultural practices make it necessary, in more cases than not, to change products accordingly. McDonald's Big Macs and fries may be found wherever one goes, but local variations can be seen in many locations. For example, patrons in Germany can have a beer with their Big Mac, burgers in Norway and India feature salmon and mutton, respectively, instead of beef, and teriyaki burgers are the norm in McDonald's Japanese restaurants.

Sometimes product changes are dictated by legal constraints. Laws regarding color additives, artificial sweeteners, preservatives, and other ingredients lead to different product formulations.

If U.S. tourists were to try the seemingly familiar brand of Heinz 57 sauce in Europe, for example, they would find a very different tasting product.

The major factor forcing marketers to adjust their products from market to market is variation in tastes. Kellogg has tailored its cereals in many ways to capture market share. The U.S. brand Cocoa Krispies has been renamed Choco Pops and formulated with a different chocolate for the European palate. Raisin Bran in Europe is made from a different wheat and uses unsugared golden raisins instead of the brown frosted ones popular in the United States. Even something as seemingly minor as removing the green loops from Froot Loops has been found necessary to adapt to consumer demands in certain countries.

International marketing often begins with an attempt to find markets where one's current products will be accepted and ends with the need to change the product to meet unique needs of different markets.

Source: Some of the examples used here are drawn from Sara Hope Franks, "Overseas, It's What's Inside That Sells," *Washington Post National Edition*, December 5–11, 1994, p. 21.

---

cost for developing a consumer packaged good is about $13 million and that for industrial chemicals it is $5 million.[11] These development costs can reach $100 million and $15 million, or more, respectively. Costs are extremely difficult to estimate accurately, and most firms recognize that budgets must accommodate short- and long-range resources for new product development (see Marketing Anecdote 7.2).

Timing a new product investment can be equally unpredictable. Some products can be brought from concept to market in a few years. Ban roll-on deodorant took six years, for example, and Purina Dog Chow took only four.[12] Other products take longer: Maxim freeze-dried instant coffee took 10 years, and the Polaroid color camera was in the works for more than 15 years.[13] Of course, companies must also factor in a pay-back period after a product is successfully launched, so the new product is indeed a long-term proposition. To give a sense of the length of time involved for typical products, experts estimate that the average total elapsed time from idea generation to product launch is 51 months for chemicals, machinery, and electronics; 60 months for pharmaceuticals; and 27 months for consumer goods.[14] Specific products' time frames may vary widely from these averages.

A number of researchers have estimated new product development risks. For new industrial products, the overall probability of success is about one in four,[15] based on the likelihood of the following sequence of outcomes: the design reaches test-market, test-market is successful, and market is successful, given commercialization. When factors preceding design are taken into account (i.e., idea generation and screening plus business analysis), the overall probability of success is perhaps one in five or six.

For new consumer goods, the overall likelihood of success has been estimated at approximately one in five.[16] However, as with the forecasts for industrial products, this estimate fails to take predesign steps such as idea generation, screening, and business analysis into account. Hence, the probability of success for a new consumer good is most likely somewhere in the one in six to seven range.

Over time—as managerial expertise and new product development technology and testing have improved—success ratios have improved dramatically. Booz, Allen & Hamilton conducted a study about these increasing odds, which is summarized in Figure 7.3. The number of ideas surviving at each of the stages in new product development (screening, business analysis, development, test marketing,

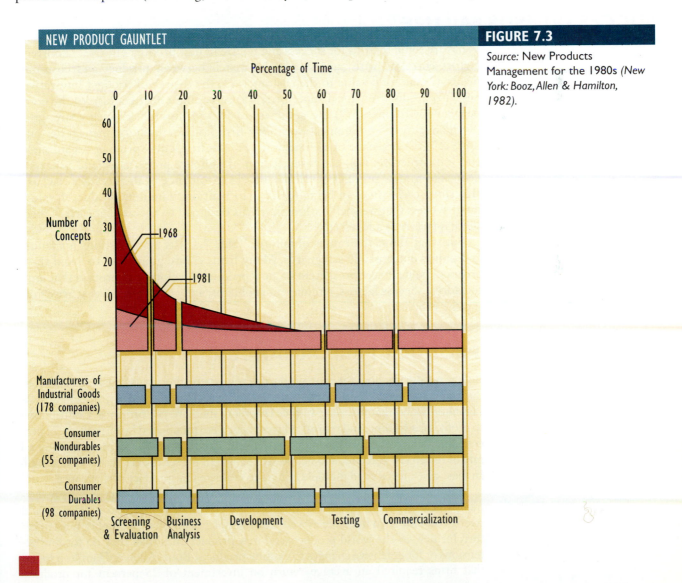

FIGURE 7.3

Source: New Products Management for the 1980s *(New York: Booz, Allen & Hamilton, 1982).*

commercialization) is depicted on the vertical axis. The horizontal axis shows cumulative time from idea generation to commercialization. The figure shows a rapid falloff from many ideas to one remaining for commercialization. In 1968, Booz, Allen & Hamilton found that out of an average 58 ideas generated by 51 companies, only one successful idea came to the market. Forty-six of the 58 ideas fell out after initial screening, and six more were pruned out through business analyses examining potential revenues and costs. About three or four ideas failed to make it through the development process itself (i.e., product engineering, consumer response measurement, and so forth). Product testing eliminated another one or two ideas. So only one made it through the gauntlet to commercialization. By the early 1980s, the picture had changed radically but still revealed considerable risk. Now seven new ideas must be generated for every successful idea. When we combine this brutal pruning process prior to commercialization with increasing competition from other firms after introduction, it is little wonder that business is such a risky endeavor.

SUCCESS VERSUS FAILURE

What are some reasons for success and failure in new product efforts?[17] Fourteen factors correlate with success: (1) the match between product and customer needs; (2) the total value to the customer; (3) the degree of product innovativeness; (4) product technical superiority; (5) screening effectiveness; (6) the competitive environment; (7) the goodness-of-fit with internal company strengths; (8) the quality of communication among firm functions; (9) top managerial support; (10) the presence of a champion; (11) the firm's new product organization and infrastructure; (12) the instantiation of policies, procedures, and processes dedicated to new product development; (13) avoidance of unnecessary risk; and (14) short cycle times in bringing ideas to fruition. The new product development process that we shall outline shortly is designed to ensure that each of these success factors is addressed.

But what about the causes of failure? Table 7.1 lists many reasons for failure and points out possible safeguards. Many firms create guidelines to avoid these errors. The next section sketches a new product development process that aims to address success factors, circumvent problems, and correct losses that arise during the process.

MEASURING NEW PRODUCT PERFORMANCE

Before we discuss how the new product development process is organized and conducted, it is important to briefly consider its goals. In their survey, Booz, Allen & Hamilton found that firms use various criteria to measure performance. Contribution to profit, sales volume, and return on investment were mentioned by 80 percent, 72 percent, and 72 percent of companies, respectively. Payback period (55 percent), internal rate of return (30 percent), and net present value (18 percent) were mentioned as well. In most cases, firms cited multiple criteria to evaluate new product performance.

Companies usually set different standards or levels of these criteria because investment levels vary from product to product, and customer behavior, competition, and strengths of the firm fluctuate as well. For example, firms often set higher rates of return for new-to-the world products and new product lines than they do for line extensions or for defensive changes to existing products. Booz, Allen & Hamilton found that firms required an average return on investment of 25 percent for products

TABLE 7.1 NEW PRODUCT FAILURES: REASONS AND SAFEGUARDS

Failure Reason	Elaboration	Suggested Safeguard
Market too small	There is insufficient demand for this type of product.	Market is defined and rough potential estimated in opportunity identification. Perform demand forecasts in design and in testing.
Poor match for the company	Company capabilities do not match the requirements for producing and marketing the product.	In opportunity identification the company's capabilities are matched to the strategic plan. This is then tested in prelaunch, pretest, and test-markets.
Not new or not different	This is a poor idea that really offers nothing new to the customer. The technology may be new, but the benefit to consumers is not evident.	Institute creative and systematic idea generation in opportunity identification. Design product with a focus on the customer. Test product and position before launch.
No real benefit	Product does not offer better performance vis-à-vis customer needs. There is underinvestment in core technologies.	In design, a strategic benefit position is identified and the product is engineered to deliver these benefits. R&D designs real product performance improvements. Product tests with customers assure adequate benefit delivery.
Poor positioning versus competition	Perceived benefits from the product are dominated by a mix of competitive products. Product is of low value.	The use of perceptual mapping, value mapping, and preference analysis identifies gaps in the market relative to competitive products.
Inadequate support from the channel of distribution	Product fails to generate expected channel support. Demonstrations are not provided if needed. Product is not available to customers. After-purchase service is not available.	The channel is considered in opportunity identification. Service delivery is part of the product design. The channel reaction is monitored in testing and in launch.
Forecasting error	Excess production occurs due to overestimation of sales. Opportunities are lost because of underestimation of sales and low production and marketing.	Systematic methods in design, pretest, and testing phases of the process improve earlier forecasts as the product and marketing strategy near completion.
Poor timing	Product is entered too late in the market. The cycle time is too long. Product misses window of technology or market opportunity.	Design process to get to market fast. Monitor changes. Trade off risks of go or delay.
Competitive response	Competitors respond quickly before the product can achieve a success in the market. Price and promotion. Competitors copy design and improve it.	Institute strategic positioning vis-à-vis competition. Consider competitive response in design, pricing, and marketing plans. "Consider what-if" scenarios. Monitor tests and launch. Move aggressively to establish product first in market advantages.
Major shifts in technology	Product is "blind-sided" by radical change in technology. Stay with old technology too long.	Monitor new technologies. Look for new benefits they can produce. Provide continuing education for R&D. Have a contingency plan for shifts.
Changes in customers' tastes	A substantial shift occurs in customer preference before product achieves market penetration.	Ensure frequent monitoring and updating of customer preferences in the design, testing, and launch phases.
Changes in environmental constraints	Drastic change occurs in some key factor such as economic conditions or material costs.	Perform analysis of environmental constraints in opportunity identification, monitoring in testing and launch, and adaptability in design.

TABLE 7.1 NEW PRODUCT FAILURES: REASONS AND SAFEGUARDS—CONTINUED

Failure Reason	Elaboration	Suggested Safeguard
Poor repeat purchase or no diffusion of sales	Customers buy the product in the beginning, but sales never reach potential.	Perform trial and repeat, and diffusion measured in design phase and monitored in testing and launch. Be sure product is designed to deliver real benefits, advertising is matched to product's benefits delivery.
Poor after-sales service	Product complex or not reliable and service not delivered.	Have service considered as an explicit designed-in benefit, and monitored in testing and launch.
Insufficient return on investment	There is poor profit relative to investment (e.g., poor sales or excessive costs).	Ensure careful selection of markets, forecasting of demand, design of product for low-cost production. Value maps facilitate profit maximization.
Lack of coordination in functions	R&D develops a product that does not meet customer needs. Marketing identifies benefits that cannot be delivered. Design changes make production difficult.	New-product process is used to coordinate marketing, R&D, engineering, and production. Input from the customer drives the design.
Organizational problems	Conflicts exist among marketing, R&D, and production. There is inadequate communication of key aspects of design and marketing.	Pay careful attention to communication and explicit programs to coordinate with quality design programs. Provide management involvement and review at various stages of the process. Make careful go/no go decisions with objective criteria.

Source: Glen L. Urban and John R. Hauser, Design and Marketing of New Products, 2nd ed. (Upper Saddle River, N.J.: Prentice-Hall, 1993), pp. 55–57.

designed to enter new geographic markets but only 15 percent for products designed to increase shelf space at retail stores. Firms thus set higher benchmarks for risky and costly ventures than for "new" products that require only minor modifications.

THE NEW PRODUCT DEVELOPMENT PROCESS

Because developing new products is so risky and expensive, firms have identified six distinct tasks or stages to maximize the chances for new product success. Each stage requires specific details and management decisions. Figure 7.4 presents the stages, which can be summarized as follows:

Idea generation → Analysis of opportunities → Design → Development → Testing → Commercialization

As you read each description, remember that managers evaluate the product's chances at each stage based on current information, so each stage also includes evaluation, as shown in Figure 7.4.

Idea Generation

Managers must undertake two interrelated tasks in the first stage: they must *define the market* and *create concepts* that potentially translate into innovations that will satisfy consumers.

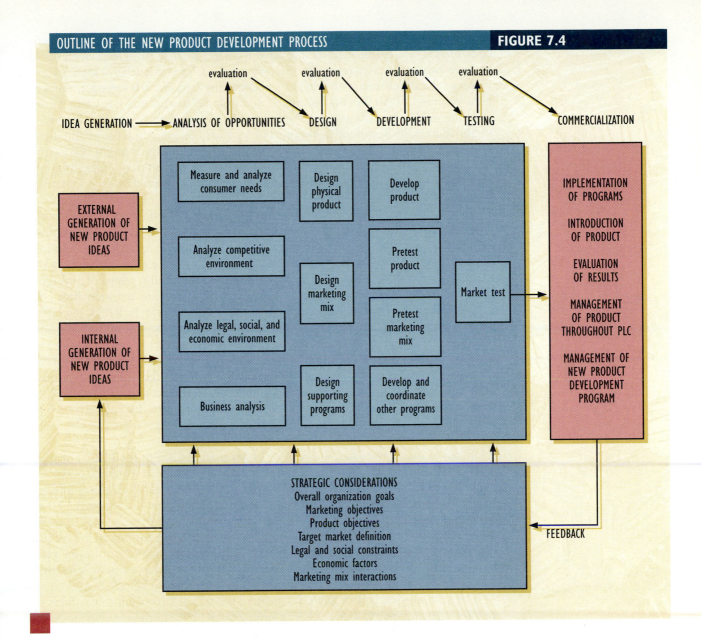

OUTLINE OF THE NEW PRODUCT DEVELOPMENT PROCESS — **FIGURE 7.4**

Market Definition

As we noted in chapter 5 on market segmentation, there are many ways to define market opportunities. All definitions identify one or more desirable features of a market, such as total expected sales volume, rate of sales growth, market share, stage in product life cycle, order of entry into the market, experience curve characteristics, profits and other rewards anticipated, avoidance of excessive risk, and synergy with the organization. Very early on, managers must appraise a potential market with regard to the aforementioned characteristics. Typically, managers develop a matrix of characteristics for each new product possibility that weights desirable market attributes according to firm strategy.

For example, imagine that you are the brand manager for a food company and are asked to choose between two new product concepts and recommend one for further product development: a new high-energy, nutritious snack bar targeted at the exerciser market or a frozen cannoli mix for the dessert market. To select which of the two new product ideas to pursue further, you must analyze their relative merits. First, you set relevant criteria with which to evaluate the options. For example, the left-hand column of Table 7.2 lists the criteria noted above. In a full analysis, each of these criteria would have many associated subdimensions. For instance, the risk dimension might address the likelihood of existing competitors lowering their prices and introducing counter advertising, possibilities that needed input supply might become inadequate or costly, the chance that consumer tastes or consumption patterns might change for the worse, or the probability that government regulation could interfere with plans.

So as a manager you must evaluate how well each potential new product innovation scores on each of the market criteria listed in Table 7.2. The ratings shown summarize your best judgments. These might be based on a consensus, a simple average of the managers performing the ratings, a formal procedure such as the Delphi technique, or other rules set by management. Typically, teams of managers from various functional areas provide the ratings. The members might include personnel from the brand management group, marketing research, R&D, manufacturing, engineering, accounting, and finance, among others. Through discussion, decision makers agree on a weighting scheme for each criterion and then agree on importance weights for each product innovation. The relative importance of the nine criteria in our example are shown in Table 7.2. Given the ratings and relative weights of various criteria, managers compute a weighted evaluation score. They then add the weighted evaluation scores to achieve total scores for each alternative. Although crude, these scores usually represent managers' best judgments about opportunities in the early stages of new product development.

In our example, the cannoli mix fares better than the health food bar. The cannoli mix shows better potential in terms of sales growth, market share potential, stage in product life cycle, and order of market entry. Because the cannoli mix is a new-to-the market product and the health food bar is new only to the company (i.e., no cannoli mixes exist at present but many other companies currently market health food bars), the aforementioned criteria make the cannoli mix more attractive. Although such evaluation schemes suggest direction, they constitute only one input to managerial decision making. The final word lies with top management, who must weigh other opportunities and constraints on the corporation as well.

The scheme sketched in Table 7.2 presumes we have two or more products or markets to compare and wish to choose among them. The alternative offerings were taken as a given. Now let us step back a moment and consider how the offerings were derived to begin with.

Idea Generation Process

Organizations and people tend to become set in their ways. The status quo often thwarts efforts to change. Organization functions, rules, and procedures tend to solidify, and individuals become accustomed to the immediate world as it exists around them. Groups, managers, and employees develop vested interests. In short, change is often seen as a threat, or at least managers become numb to certain changes. In some respects, this is a natural outcome. People cannot hope to deal with all the stimuli impinging on them at one time, so they develop ways of coping with change. Similarly, organization members selectively focus on those activities they deem most important.

However, too much selectivity and a resistance to change weakens an organization's ability to adjust and survive. Indeed, one way for firms to break out of this hu-

TABLE 7.2 EVALUATION OF NEW PRODUCT INNOVATIONS IN TERMS OF MARKET POTENTIAL: EXAMPLE OF A NEW HEALTH FOOD BAR VERSUS A NEW CANNOLI MIX

Criteria	Rating on Criteria		Relative Importance Rating	Weighted Evaluation on Criteria	
	HEALTH FOOD BAR	CANNOLI MIX		HEALTH FOOD BAR	CANNOLI MIX
Sales Volume	6	5	5	30	25
Sales Growth	4	6	8	32	48
Market Share	2	5	7	14	35
Stage in Product Life Cycle	3	7	6	18	42
Order of Market Entry	1	8	3	3	24
Experience Curve Effects	6	4	4	24	16
Profitability and Other Rewards	8	6	9	72	54
Risk	1	4	2	2	8
Synergy with Firm's Core Competencies	8	6	1	8	6
			Total:	203	258

man tendency to resist change is to maintain a healthy *variation-seeking system*. This means that organizations must foster the flow of new ideas from within. The greater the ability of the firm to acquire and produce new ideas, the greater the probability that evaluation processes will produce a winner, all things being equal. Organizations need to encourage exploration and change or they will stagnate and become vulnerable to erosive forces in the marketplace.

Successful firms employ a number of approaches to generate new ideas. They regularly monitor and consult sources outside the organization. For example, they use ongoing panels, surveys, or focus groups to track consumer reactions and discover changes in tastes. In fact, one study shows that 74 percent of all new ideas for technological products come from customers.[18] The actions of competitors, especially with respect to new product designs or improvements, are followed closely. Managers attend trade shows to pick up new ideas and tidbits of things to come. They study governmental publications, the popular press, and academic and professional journals, and they consult professional services, such as those provided by marketing research firms, ad agencies, and new product consultants. Occasionally, new ideas come from universities, through licensing arrangements with other firms, as a result of unsolicited proposals by inventors, or simply through library searches or browsing the World Wide Web. A firm's *marketing information system* provides a primary conduit to these outside sources of information. The MIS personnel collect data, analyze it, store it, interpret it, and disseminate new ideas, thus performing an important role in research, forecasting, and advising.

Sources inside the organization also generate important new ideas. Brand managers, for instance, are knowledgeable about consumer needs, competitive offerings, and new developments, so their views are regularly sought by decision makers at many levels of the organization. Salespeople, too, often provide ideas because they are in direct contact with customers and marketplace trends. Managers participate actively in producing new ideas either as individuals or as members of committees or new venture teams. Employees-at-large are frequently contacted by brand managers and researchers for their ideas, and some companies have formal programs to encourage and reward suggestions made by workers who are seemingly removed from product management. Finally, groups and departments within the firm are assigned special responsibility for generating new ideas. Product engineering, R&D departments, marketing research, or various other groups often generate ideas and spearhead new product development.

Top managers often provide strategic and product guidelines that influence the idea-generation process. Strategies provide focus and structure, guiding the search and formulation of ideas. For example, Gillette rejects ideas from outsiders unless they are already patented, presumably to avoid legal complications.[19] Many firms define their overall business mission, target market, or product forms narrowly to hold the number of new ideas to manageable levels. Still other companies face potential antitrust actions if they enter a new market, or risk competitive retaliation or public resistance if they enter another. Firms with extensive product lines face cannibalization issues if new products adversely "eat into" sales for established ones. Thus, they are wary of devoting too many resources to develop products that overall might be counterproductive. In short, many strategic issues often influence where and how firms go about generating new product ideas.

Firms face a danger of imposing too much control on the idea-generation process. Too restrictive a search and brainstorming process may eliminate potentially good ideas prematurely. Perhaps less obvious is the functional linkage between idea generation and subsequent new product development implementation processes. The selection process depends directly on the input of ideas because the number or quality of new ideas affects the outcome of selection to a great extent. If not enough new ideas are generated and/or the selection process is too discriminating, for example, then the firm may miss opportunities. On the other hand, too many ideas and/or too loose a selection process can drain resources and allow poor products to reach the market. This possibility is less likely in practice, however, because there rarely are too many good ideas. Because new product development processes naturally function best when they are thorough, their success will be enhanced still further by providing as many ideas as possible. Hence, companies should avoid exerting too much control at this point through strategic and other considerations because these tend to reduce variation (i.e., the number of good and bad ideas) and introduce preevaluation biases.

Analysis of Opportunities

Idea generation is but the first step in new product development. As shown in Figure 7.4, the second step is the analysis of opportunities. Here managers must conduct at least four activities: measuring and analyzing customer needs; assessing the competitive environment; appraising the legal, social, and economic environment; and evaluating the idea via a hard-nosed business (especially financial) analysis.

Consider first the *measurement and analysis of customer needs*. This is the first time product developers scrutinize customer tastes, preferences, and willingness to buy. Typically, depending on the product or service, they use a combination of approaches such as qualitative depth interviews and focus groups with small numbers of existing or potential customers to identify basic needs, values, and motives related to the new product or service. Managers may perform crude surveys on larger, more representative samples, once key characteristics of buyers and promising product and/or service attributes have been identified. More refined and comprehensive surveys may occur in the design and development stages of new product development (see Fig. 7.4). Initial surveys might ask customers to rate existing brands on various attributes or to compare brands. Managers use this information to construct perceptual maps that reveal a small number of fundamental product attributes, to see how well existing brands meet customer needs on these attributes, to determine how much competition exists at the product attribute level, and to reveal any unmet needs and opportunities for designing the new product or service. New product developers evaluate all of the above information, at least qualitatively, to ascertain the strength of demand for the new product.

Second, managers must assess *the competitive environment*. This analysis, of course, should integrate the evolving definition of the market with the model of customer decision making tentatively formulated under measurement and analysis of customer needs. To do so, managers interpret preliminary perceptual maps and carefully analyze key competitive conditions, such as those detailed under Harvard professor Michael Porter's framework.[20] For example, they must consider substitute availability, the bargaining power of suppliers, the bargaining power of customers (both final and intermediary), the threat of new entrants, and the rivalry among firms within the industry in question.

Marketers can bring together competitive environment analysis with knowledge about the market and customer behavior through *hierarchical market definition* diagrams. Figure 7.5 illustrates such a diagram. Imagine that you are a brand manager for Hills Brothers Coffee, which sells ground coffee and wishes to consider other

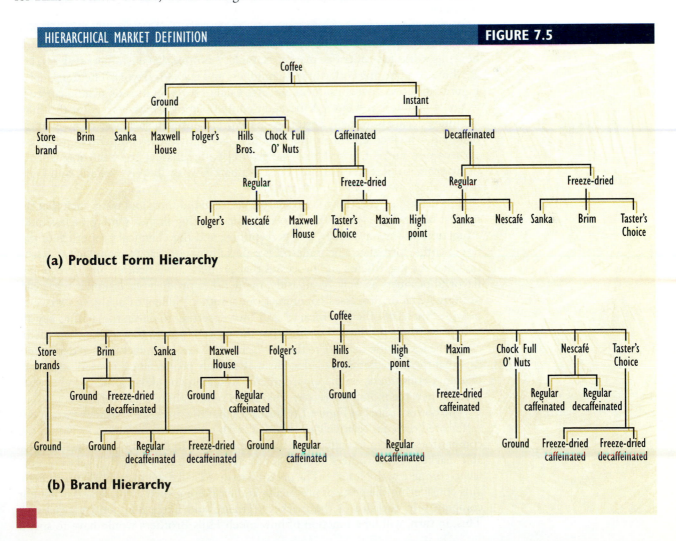

HIERARCHICAL MARKET DEFINITION   **FIGURE 7.5**

(a) Product Form Hierarchy

(b) Brand Hierarchy

opportunities in the coffee market. Where should you begin your analysis of market opportunity? Notice that Figure 7.5 shows the coffee market in two forms: one organized by product form, where the brands under each form are displayed as branches in a tree-like structure, and a second organized by brand, with different forms displayed under each brand. As a manager, you need to create a mental model of how people buy coffee—how many consumers consider product form versus brand first—before you can assess market opportunities.

The product form hierarchy shows that Hills Brothers competes in only the ground coffee market. As a Hills Brothers brand manager, you need to evaluate the size of the instant coffee market, whether Hills Brothers can efficiently produce and market one or more instant formulas, and the strength of competition before deciding to enter the instant market. On the other hand, considering the brand hierarchy (see bottom of Figure 7.5), Hills Brothers must decide whether marketing an instant brand would seriously cannibalize its established ground coffee sales.

Thus, any market and competitive analysis should consider how customers actually make decisions and how many consumers make decisions the same way. Hierarchical market definitions suggest low switching between branches and high switching within branches. Researchers use surveys and consumer panels to gather data for such analyses, applying cluster analysis and other techniques to construct the trees.

As a brand manager you can carry the analysis one step further by introducing perceptual maps into any hierarchical market definition. Figure 7.6 demonstrates how this works for our coffee market example.[21] Notice that customers seek two key attributes in choosing coffee brands: mildness and taste (or flavor). The top panel of Figure 7.6 shows how consumers perceive each of seven brands of ground coffee in terms of mildness and taste. A marketer contemplating whether to enter this market must decide how many customers have preferences in each area of the perceptual map, which competitors offer products, and how those competitors might react to a new entrant. The home-use ground coffee market has been stagnant for many years, so potential entrants must evaluate how easily their brands could take market share away from competitors.

To a certain extent, there is a trade-off between mildness and taste, such that the mildest brands have less taste, whereas the best-tasting brands tend to be less mild: a function of our physiology, our perceptions, and the chemical properties of different coffee formulas. The trade-off is especially of concern to manufacturers who find that the ingredients and processes that produce a mild coffee often create less flavorful products as well. As an aside, many other products face similar trade-offs as ingredients or processes counteract one another. Sellers of analgesics strive to provide "speed of relief," "efficacy," and "not upsetting to one's stomach" as key attributes of their products, but find that the more effective they make their medicines, the less gentle they are to the stomach. Likewise, manufacturers of detergents find that the ingredients needed to clean effectively produce negative side effects to clothing, consumers, or the environment. Research and development and investment in new technologies are ways that firms reduce these trade-offs.

The bottom panel of Figure 7.6 illustrates that the market for regular instant decaffeinated coffee is relatively uncrowded, with only three competitors. Two of the competitors offer mild coffees scoring relatively low in taste. In searching for a viable market, Hills Brothers might want to consider selling a flavorful, yet mild, coffee to compete with Nescafé. The decision to do so will depend on likely profit margins considering the costs of producing and marketing such a coffee and pricing it competitively, the size of the market segment, and likely competitive reactions. This, in turn, will be a function of how much Hills Brothers would have to spend

FIGURE 7.6

PERCEPTUAL MAPS EMBEDDED IN A PRODUCT FORM HIERARCHICAL
MARKET DEFINITION OF THE COFFEE MARKET

Source: Glen L. Urban and John R. Hauser, Design and Marketing of New Products, 2nd ed. (Upper Saddle River, N.J.: Prentice-Hall, 1993), p. 108.

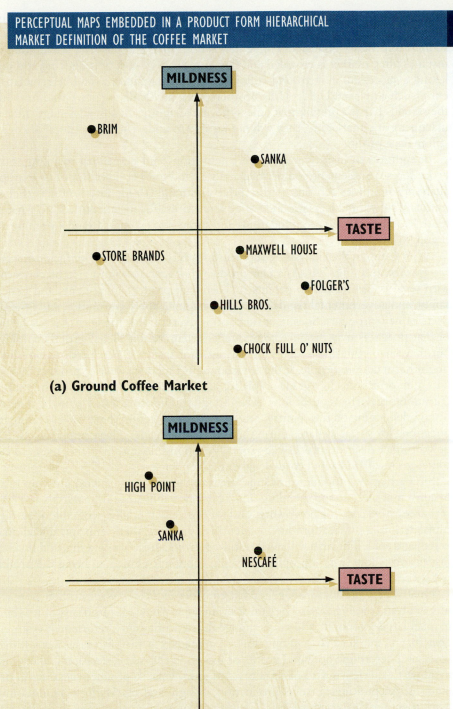

(a) Ground Coffee Market

(b) Regular Instant Decaffeinated Market

on the marketing mix: advertising, packaging, and promotions to trade and final customers. A key issue, too, is whether Hills Brothers has the wherewithal and resources to produce an instant coffee that is both mild and flavorful. Given that the instant coffee market is crowded and flat, and the high cost of producing and marketing a successful new ground coffee, most manufacturers would be reluctant to enter such a market. Unless Hills Brothers has a highly distinctive brand for which they could charge a premium or unless they have significant cost advantages in manufacturing and marketing, they will not be able to undercut competitors' prices and still make a profit.

In addition to hierarchical market definitions and perceptual mapping, other procedures complement competitive analysis and market definition. For example, analysts sometimes scrutinize cross price elasticities to identify products that are mutually substitutable: is ground coffee a substitute for instant coffee? To what extent? Researchers also use simulations and surveys to estimate brand switching and brand loyalty.

A third step in the analysis of opportunities is to evaluate the *legal/social/economic environment* (see Fig. 7.4). As a new product manager, you must also be concerned with legal issues related to patents or licensing; product ingredients and general safety; and governmental regulations on packaging, labels, warranties, and other aspects of new products. Social considerations overlap with the legal, but go further in that products may produce consequences that are not illegal, strictly speaking, but may have ethical or social implications. For instance, products or ingredients might harm certain people or the environment. Full disclosure of product ingredients, unit prices, product grade or quality, and open dating of perishables might help consumers make better decisions, even though this information may not be required by law, depending on the country. Any organization's actions have wide-ranging implications for social welfare; a firm that formally considers these implications in its new product decision processes is socially responsible and may also increase customer goodwill and avoid costly legal entanglements.

Similarly, new product teams must analyze the economic environment in terms of consumer income and spending trends, the availability of raw materials and labor resources, the costs of borrowing, and so on. A potentially profitable idea must translate into a physical product or identifiable service that can be produced, marketed, and sold. The firm will need resources from a host of economic and financial institutions, along with a hospitable overall economic climate to bring the product out successfully.

Finally, new product managers must consider *business analysis* in their opportunity analysis (see Fig. 7.4). They must evaluate any new idea in terms of its ability to meet larger corporate and marketing goals for profitability, return on investment, growth, and market share, among others. So managers must forecast sales, estimate costs, and determine potential profits or losses. In this stage, decision makers must meld past experience with uncertainty and guesswork to produce meaningful predictions. Accounting, finance, production, design, and marketing personnel must work together to accomplish this. Chapter 12 on pricing elaborates and illustrates typical business analyses.

The analytical outputs noted in Figure 7.4 are evaluated according to rules and standards set by management. For example, perceptions and attitudes of consumers must reach certain levels of favorability early on to justify a positive evaluation and further consideration in the new product development process. Potential sales and profits of minimal levels must be forthcoming to warrant further consideration. As one example of how evaluations might be quantified, consider Table 7.3. The firm assesses new product concepts and evaluates each on market performance, competitive ad-

Table 7.3 Example of a New Product Evaluation Form

Criterion	1	2	3	4	5	6	7	8	9	10	Importance of Criterion	Rating	Subtotal
MARKET PERFORMANCE CRITERIA													
Overall Sales Level					✔						0.20	1.00	
Growth Potential			✔								0.30	0.90	
Market Share						✔					0.30	1.80	
Profitability							✔				0.20	1.40	5.10
COMPETITIVE ADVANTAGES													
Product Quality								✔			0.20	1.60	
Price		✔									0.30	0.60	
Advertising					✔						0.20	1.00	
Sales Force			✔								0.05	0.15	
Promotion							✔				0.05	0.35	
Distribution									✔		0.20	1.80	5.50
INTERNAL OPERATIONS													
Supply Considerations	✔										0.30	0.30	
Financial Issues			✔								0.30	0.90	
Production Issues								✔			0.25	2.00	
Personnel				✔							0.10	0.40	
Shipping					✔						0.05	0.25	3.85
												Total	14.45

vantages related to the product and the potential marketing mix programs, and internal operations. Each new product alternative is evaluated on each criterion on a scale of 1 to 10. A 1 indicates "product concept is very poor on the criterion," a 10 indicates "product concept is very good on the criterion," and a 5 or 6 indicates "neither poor nor good (i.e., neutral)." The persons doing the ratings might be a committee of managers from R&D, marketing research, product management, and so forth.

Table 7.3 shows scores for one hypothetical product. Managers assign scores to products based on their subjective judgments, and they may also assign weights to the criteria based on their relative importance. Managers then compute a new product rating by multiplying the subjective evaluation score by the importance weight. Importance weights might be set according to company norms and from discussion among the key managers in the firm. Depending on the product, many other criteria might be applied, or the scoring of products on the criteria may differ, as may the formula used to weight and combine weighted scores into a total overall index. But whatever rule is used, each new product alternative can be compared to any others to choose the one with the highest score and presumably the greatest chance for success.

Design

If a new product idea passes criteria in the idea generation and the analysis of opportunities stages, it will next move on to the design phase. As indicated in Figure 7.4, three design activities are crucial: design of the physical product (or service), design of the marketing mix, and design of supporting programs within the organization. We briefly consider these below.

As they *design the physical product or service*, managers must translate the new product idea into a form that can be manufactured and delivered efficiently and that will satisfy consumer needs, gain differential advantages over the competition, and earn a profit. Somehow managers must find a compromise between the ideal and the possible. They might well start the design phase by examining research about consumer needs and perceptions. If the firm can realize product attributes that genuinely satisfy needs, the product will have overcome a fundamental obstacle to success. And if the firm can either improve old attributes or introduce new attributes that satisfy needs but are not fielded by the competition, it will gain an edge over rivals. Many technological, engineering, and stylistic design decisions must be made, and most organizations rely on specialists in each area. Physical product design is part science and part art. Designers, given more or less abstract ideas and incomplete information, must fashion a concrete product early in the process so the firm can evaluate the product's potential market reception. From an organizational standpoint, prototype development requires coordination of creative personnel and activities with technical and pragmatic concerns. Such coordination is very much one that sociologists term "the social construction of reality." It is a rational, political, and fortuitous process of interpersonal negotiation.

For example, one of the authors recently performed research for a food-service company in Italy. For proprietary reasons, we shall call this company "Gustoso." The company was considering entering a geographical market currently dominated by three other food-service companies. The questions it needed to answer concerned what key service attributes it should stress and how it stacked up relative to the competition on these attributes. Qualitative research based on interviews with managers at all levels of the organization generated a total of 33 service attributes to serve as a starting point. A survey of 382 people then rated the three existing companies on each attribute on an 11-point scale (0 = does not describe company at all to 10 = describes company completely). This survey included responses from final customers as well as decision makers in target organizations who made the final food-service choice. A factor analysis of the data with a standard statistical package revealed four key dimensions to summarize the service attributes. The four dimensions explained 83.1 percent of variance in responses, with the first two dimensions accounting for 89 percent of this variance.

Dimension 1, the "core service," summarized such attributes as freshness, taste, quality, and variety of food; healthiness of food (in terms of low in fat or cholesterol, high in vitamins and minerals); convenience (with regard to location and time); value; and fast service. Dimension 2, the "peripheral service" attributes, referred to cleanliness of tables, floors, toilet facilities, and employees, and the perception that the food served was prepared in a hygienic way. The third dimension, the "personableness of the service," captured how pleasant, helpful, and efficient the consumers perceived service providers to be. Finally, dimension 4, "service atmosphere," concerned the perceived comfort, "look," and climate (e.g., air temperature, air quality) in the food-service setting (see Marketing Anecdote 7.3).

Figure 7.7 on page 290 shows a perceptual map for the three competitors (X, Y, and Z) currently in the market (a province in central Italy). We show only the first two dimensions—"core service" and "peripheral service" attributes—for simplicity. Notice that all three companies received mediocre scores on the core service attributes. A detailed inspection of the individual questionnaire items concerned with core service revealed that competitors were noticeably lacking in terms of variety and taste of the food, speed of service, and value (i.e., people felt that the ra-

If you're running a restaurant, you want lots of red. But for other types of businesses, there's no one correct answer.

"Red tends to be a color that makes people eat more—and be willing to pay more for what they're eating," says Ellen Olsen, a color expert at Colorado Institute of Art. It also makes us feel that time is passing quickly, thereby discouraging lingering over coffee. Red gets customers in and out more quickly.

Olsen says the rods and cones of the eye are most sensitized by red, the color with the longest wavelength in the spectrum. The eye sends a message to the brain, which alerts the pituitary gland, which releases epinephrine, which triggers hunger. It also causes the heart to beat faster and the body temperature to rise.

If you're packaging food to be sold in a grocery store, conventional wisdom says to put it in a red container, since red is the first color we notice. But green is quickly surmounting red as the color of choice on food packaging.

"Green is now being used to promote low-fat items," says Samuelle Easton, a New York

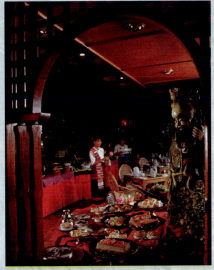

Gustoso had to choose how to present its new product, including the restaurant's color and ambiance.

color psychologist. "It's the greening of America, the idea that vegetables have no fat."

Green is also the No. 1 color choice for cars today, Easton says. The reason: These are environmentally conscious times, and green speaks to the whole eco-friendly movement.

Americans view black as indicating precision and quality. That's why most of our electronic equipment is black. Not so in Japan, where most electronic equipment is green, Easton says.

The successful marketer will consider what product is being sold and its potential audience when choosing color schemes, Easton says.

"Lighter colors are perceived as being friendly, approachable, more feminine. Darker colors are more authoritative, more masculine," she says. "Brighter colors are fun and enthusiastic, muted colors are more casual, shy. Warm colors are earthy and friendly, cool colors are authoritative and refined."

Source: Rebecca Jones, *The Rocky Mountain News*, March 21, 1997. p. 2D.

---

tio of quality to price paid was too low). With respect to the peripheral service, company Y scored quite well, but companies X and Z were perceived as somewhat dingy, dirty places to eat.

From the perceptual map, management of Gustoso learned that customers were most concerned with attributes defining the core service and peripheral service. If Gustoso were to enter this market and wanted to attract and hold customers, it would have to score reasonably high on these attributes. Indeed, based on its performance in other markets, top management felt confident that it could achieve satisfactory levels on these key attributes.

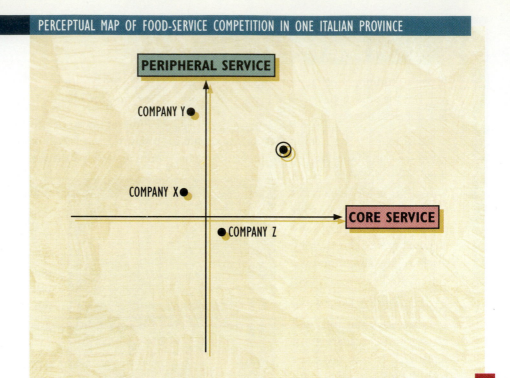

Another conclusion from the research summarized in Figure 7.7 was that little competition appeared to exist in the upper right-hand quadrant. To the extent that Gustoso could deliver high levels of core and peripheral services, it should achieve a competitive advantage.

Now that Gustoso had a picture of the market in terms of customer needs and the competitive situation, it had to address a number of further issues before proceeding. Ideally, Gustoso preferred to enter the market with its services perceived by customers to score in the vicinity of the bull's-eye (◉) shown in Figure 7.7. What issues must the company further consider and what decisions must management make before they continued with the next stage in its new service development process?

First, Gustoso needed to determine the total market size. Because Gustoso provides food services to businesses and government agencies, it counted the number of manufacturers, service organizations, hospitals, schools, and federal and provincial offices in the province. Next, it estimated the sizes of the companies and agencies and identified which ones purchased from one of the three existing food-service companies and which ones represented undeveloped potential. With this picture of the market, Gustoso management ascertained that there were enough customers to warrant further evaluation. Gustoso felt that enough undeveloped business existed in the province that they would not have to take business away from existing companies to make a profit. This undeveloped business consisted of institutions that either provided their own food services or contracted with small local operators to supplement in-house services. Smaller local operators often offered narrow, inefficient services with inconsistent quality.

Second, management needed to ascertain the costs involved to enter the market in the vicinity of the bull's-eye. Clearly, if costs are too high, profits will not result.

What are the costs? Gustoso knew that food quality (e.g., freshness), dependable suppliers, efficient preparation methods, and well-trained and managed employees were critical. Although top management was confident that Gustoso could deliver high levels on the core and peripheral services, middle managers were wary. In particular, middle managers believed that in order to achieve and maintain high levels of cleanliness in all phases of the business, they would not only have to devote more time to these activities than the competition did, thereby increasing labor costs, but they would also need special equipment and cleaning chemicals and supplies. Customer demands and the excellence already achieved by competitor company Y in the market set the standard. Moreover, Gustoso had to develop new sources of supply for some of its fruits, vegetables, and meats; in some cases, it had to ship supplies farther than other food service firms in the existing market. This, too, threatened to raise costs. After some give and take, all managers acknowledged that they were uncertain about the firm's ability to achieve the bull's-eye. Managers were worried, too, whether the competing firms would react by improving their offerings and service. Acknowledging these concerns, top management decided to wait until after the product was fully developed before fully committing to the project. The food-service concept needed more work on design and evaluation.

Gustoso then turned to various product and service design issues. Regional areas in Italy differ considerably in their food preferences, so the company had to develop the right combination of pastas, entrees, and side dishes, and the style of preparation was also crucial. This necessitated quite a bit of experimentation by the chefs and cooks and many taste tests on local residents to achieve the right local flair and flavor.

In most established markets, Gustoso relies primarily on personal contact and word of mouth to sell its service. Advertising is limited generally to a few institutional ads in magazines and small billboards. Trade fairs and festivals also complement its marketing efforts. This works fine in markets where the company already has a presence. But to enter this new market, Gustoso needed something more.

Prior to this venture, Gustoso had entered new markets by either acquisition or by expansion into areas geographically adjacent to existing businesses. To enter a province relatively removed from its main markets, Gustoso recognized that they had to give special effort to designing a new marketing mix. Further, their efforts had to be coordinated to prepare the market, stimulate interest and trial, and convey a general image of a quality provider of food services at a reasonable, although perhaps premium, price.

In some cities, Gustoso has restaurants open to the general public, which serve a broader communication function as well as providing profitable business in their own right. Gustoso considered opening a restaurant in a central city in an Italian province before aggressively pursuing its main business activities. Once established, this central restaurant would help communicate the desired quality image and give the company some name recognition. In the early stages of marketing, Gustoso used "events" to introduce the public to their services, including sponsorship of sporting and cultural events, as well as fairs and food festivals. At the same time, the company pursued possible clients through personal selling to switch food services or try one for the first time. It advertised in high-visibility trade and popular magazines to reinforce the corporate name and image. Gustoso middle managers began preliminary discussions with suppliers (farmers, manufacturers, distributors) in the areas, and prepared plans and cost analyses for needed facilities and shipping arrangements.

Even as physical models are being designed, managers must make early decisions about the *marketing mix* (i.e., promotion, product, place (physical distribution), and price). Firms can design the best physical product in the world but if they fail to make it available to the public through retailers, or to inform consumers of the offering and persuade them to try it, or to price it attractively and competitively, the product will likely fail. The marketing mix is so intimately intertwined with the product and its meaning for the consumer that effective marketing demands coordinated processes, especially between the design and development teams. Once the development team decides on a product concept and perhaps designs a picture, mockup, or prototype, they can begin to develop a core selling proposition, a brand name, copy design for advertisements, promotional materials, sales presentations, and alternative distribution plans. These activities often take so much time to coordinate that they must be begun well before market introduction. At any point in the development process, management might decide to scrap the product because new information makes it less than promising. All of that development money will then be wasted—but such are the risks associated with any business venture.

Finally, the design team must *design supporting programs* within the firm. Production must begin planning for a potential new product by retooling equipment. Financial specialists must arrange the needed investment and operating capital. The personnel department must anticipate and provide labor needs. These topics are better treated in specialized management texts but deserve mention because all of a firm's activities must be integrated in order to bring a product successfully to market.

Development

As companies *develop new products*, they must design the product or service and develop models that are as close to the final version as possible. Automotive companies build prototypes largely by hand and put the prototypes through extensive road and consumer testing. Convenience-food makers go through hundreds of combinations of ingredients and preparation techniques before achieving a promising formulation. Video-game developers meld together intuition with trial and error to produce products that challenge and entertain. All of these efforts require considerable developmental activities.

Once a firm has developed a physical product and built a prototype, it is ready for *pretesting*. Actually, firms often construct and test several design variations as they seek the right product to market. One commonly used procedure for pretesting—especially for products with strong personal and subjective dimensions—is expert judgment. For example, producers of beer, soft drinks, snack foods, and prepared desserts rely heavily on expert tasters' opinions. These experts, through years of apprenticeship and trial and error, are quite sensitive to product ingredients and can identify subtle variations and effects.

A second pretesting method uses employee evaluations. Manufacturers of soaps and detergents, for instance, regularly provide free products to their employees and ask them for their assessments. Producers of snacks, beverages, and other foods often maintain kitchens and testing rooms on their premises to obtain employee and guest feedback. Although employee evaluations pose disadvantages, such as biased responses or nonrepresentative samples relative to final market, the benefits of this early testing frequently outweigh the limitations. Some companies combine expert judgments and employee evaluations. Procter & Gamble, for instance, gives employees its mouthwash and deodorant products and then allegedly monitors their effectiveness through professional breath and armpit sniffers as employees arrive at work!

A third pretesting method is laboratory testing, which is particularly suited to testing product or component reliability and durability. Governments and independent institutions, such as Consumer's Union and Underwriter's Laboratories, do similar testing after products reach the market. Laboratory tests offer the advantage of providing accurate, controllable simulations of product usage. Such tests are often performed during the design stage to simulate usage under heavy and even extreme conditions. A disadvantage of this approach is that laboratories cannot always simulate all usage conditions. People use products differently, and many dimensions of product usage are subjective and difficult to measure or forecast.

To provide more realistic usage conditions, firms go through considerable effort to duplicate consumer usage as closely as possible through field testing. A good example is afforded by the automotive industry. Cars are pretested under realistic conditions ranging from highway and backroad conditions to mountain and desert driving. Most auto firms also maintain elaborate "proving grounds" with cement, asphalt, brick, and dirt roads. This realistic testing combines with numerous laboratory tests of individual components, systems of components (e.g., radio, engine), and the entire car itself. Sometimes car manufacturers use police forces and taxi companies as testing grounds. All of these pretesting procedures precede market testing.

New product managers also conduct *marketing mix pretests* to gain preliminary indications of mix effectiveness. Experts scrutinize advertising copy, personal selling presentations, promotion deals, and distribution alternatives and evaluate these elements using mathematical and simulation models. Some of these tests are conducted by specialists in the home company, some by personnel in advertising agencies, and some by private consultants outside the firm.

The final area for development is the *development and coordination of other programs* of the firm. To bring a new product idea and design to fruition requires, as we noted above, orchestrated production, quality control, purchasing, finance, shipping, legal, and other functions, along with marketing operations. Not only must each functional area of the firm design and plan ahead for the activities required by new product development, it must also operationalize its ideas and plans in concert with the evolving product. Most companies work out this complex, ever-changing process using critical path scheduling and setting a whole host of procedures and operations in motion, then pretesting and refining them. This, too, is an evolutionary process that management must continually monitor, evaluate, and control (more about implementation and control in chapters 16 and 17).

For many consumer goods manufacturers, pre-test market forecasting is a key to coordinating programs throughout the firm.[22] Such forecasting integrates many of the activities noted in Figure 7.4 under development. For example, a large company was considering entering the laundry detergent market.[23] After determining that a market existed for an improved laundry powder and that the firm could produce and market such a product, it developed a prototype and tested it in the lab and through employees. At this stage, the firm took a series of research steps, culminating in the application of the Assessor model, a leading pretest evaluation procedure that combines real data with managerial judgment in a statistical and simulation model.

Qualitative research identified 21 attributes that consumers thought important in a laundry detergent. Some of these included dirt removal, grass stain removal, gets dirt out, removes grass stains, gets whites really clean, gentleness to natural fabrics, color safety, and lingerie and synthetic fabric appropriateness. The researchers asked a sample of consumers to rate each of eight leading brands on these attributes and then factor-analyzed the data. Two dimensions resulted, and the brands were plotted on a perceptual map.

The results revealed that customers evaluated both mildness and effectiveness when choosing a laundry detergent, and that no existing brand scored highly on both these attributes, thereby identifying a marketing opportunity. The nature of chemical cleaning agents, however, tends to produce one of those trade-offs: the greater the cleaning power, the harsher the detergent is on clothes. So the company invested time and money to develop new technologies that sufficiently combined mildness and effectiveness. Existing firms tended to score high on mildness (Cheer), or high on effectiveness (Ajax), or in the middle for both (Tide).

Next the firm asked about the relative importance of mildness and effectiveness to consumers. This answer was important for at least two reasons. First, with limited resources, advertising campaigns needed to focus on attributes most important to the consumer. The firm needed to determine central product attributes early on and use this information to design advertising copy and develop an ad campaign. Second, and most crucial at this stage in developing a new product, management needed to discover attributes most valued by customers in order to design the product optimally. The company in question could pursue options with very different costs for the chemicals and processes that would produce different degrees of mildness and effectiveness. As it turned out in this particular example, their survey research with real consumers showed that mildness and effectiveness were equally important, so the firm had to focus on both. Sometimes different market niches can be found for certain products in which one attribute dominates all others, and a firm can focus primarily on that attribute for the segments in question. For example, some industrial customers may essentially care only about effectiveness.

Management then researched the optimal product composition in terms of physical product cues that consumers would perceive. They tested three different formulations: color (green, blue, or white), texture (coarse or fine), and overall composition (all one color or white with added colored particles). Researchers applied a statistical procedure called conjoint analysis to a new survey of potential users to determine consumers' preferences (i.e., "utilities") for each combination of color, texture, and overall composition, with perceived mildness and efficacy as the dependent variables in the analysis. The results showed that a white, fine powder with added blue particles produced consumers' highest-utility perceptions of both effectiveness and gentleness.

Researchers next estimated the probability of product trial and performed a market share forecast for the new laundry detergent by use of a logit regression model. The simulation found the best mix of advertising, price, free sampling, and distribution levels to yield the market share forecast (i.e., the predicted percentage of the market for each firm). After obtaining estimates of costs, management then computed profits for their expected market share. They fine-tuned the marketing mix elements to confirm their model and eventually decided to launch the product. In the meantime, brand managers and researchers were testing different packaging, promotions, and brand names and finalizing the overall marketing plan.

How are the data for pretest market forecasts obtained? Let us consider consumer goods here because industrial goods are more difficult to test in the marketplace this early in the process. For consumer goods, researchers use a multi-step procedure. Researchers might set up a pretest in a trailer near a supermarket and sample consumers as they come out of the store. Respondents are screened by initial criteria (e.g., confirming that they use the product class, are a regular user or light user, and so forth) and then asked to identify the brands they consider, rate each brand on a set of attributes via a questionnaire, and reveal their relative preferences for existing brands. After filling out the questionnaire, respondents are typically shown ads for established brands as well as for the new brand. Researchers record consumer reactions to the ads via open-ended and closed-ended questions.

Respondents are then exposed to a simulated shopping environment near the end of the trailer, where existing brands and the new brand are displayed in addition to other products. Respondents are given a small sum of money to keep or to spend on whatever they wish for their own use. By giving respondents money and the chance to keep or spend it, researchers simulate an actual purchase situation.

After several weeks, after consumers have had sufficient time to use the product, respondents are recontacted and asked about their consumption experiences, intentions to purchase the brand, and other information. The data so gleaned are then used in computer simulations and in pretest market forecast models, such as previously described for the laundry detergent example.

Pretest market models, such as Assessor, provide marketers with good forecasts of success or failure before they invest heavily in tooling, facilities, labor, and marketing. Pretest market forecasting costs approximately $100,000, and has been shown to be reasonably accurate, predicting long-run sales within 25 percent either way about 75 percent of the time.[24] In practice, for consumer goods firms, brand managers recommend a "go" decision when the predicted market share is more than two points above the minimum required by the company in its decisions in order to have a 75 percent probability of success.[25]

Testing

Pretest market forecasts are not as accurate as actual *market tests* performed under realistic conditions before launching the product (see Fig. 7.4). Market tests come closer to representing all the competitive, economic, social, and psychological forces at work in the marketplace. But market testing is more expensive than pretest market forecasting (typically 10 to 30 times more expensive) and more time-consuming, requiring lead times of a few months to many months, depending on the product. Therefore, all firms do not necessarily perform market tests in every situation.

Firms typically use at least two criteria to decide whether to test market. First, they examine and evaluate estimated test marketing costs relative to the expected gains and losses from the product. Test markets for frequently purchased consumer goods found in supermarkets, for example, can cost from $2 million to $3 million for each city in which the product is tested. Companies must make reasonably sure that product revenues and profits after introduction will recoup the test market costs in addition to normal production and marketing costs. Every firm will have a different expected payback period, but large firms seldom support a losing proposition for more than two to four years. Small firms, of course, have shorter time horizons.

A second criterion that managers apply to test marketing decisions is competitors' likely reactions. Test marketing can provide information to rivals about product innovations, planned market strategies, communication tactics, and so on. In some situations, firms might be prudent to forgo a market test to avoid giving competitors the extra time to learn from their new ideas. Because test markets often take from six months to a year to complete, rivals can gain valuable time to respond to potential competitive threats. By skipping test marketing, firms can maintain an element of surprise that gives them a crucial head start.

In addition, test marketing may be vulnerable to sabotage by the competition. Through their pricing, promotion, and advertising policies, competitors sometimes influence test market results of a potential new rival product. If they feel that a new rival might eventually eat into their sales, competitors might drop their prices, increase advertising, introduce a new deal, or employ other strategies to hamper a firm's test market sales. Even if competitors do not necessarily fear a new product entry, they might raise their prices or reduce their promotion support to inflate a new product's test performance artificially. That is, if competitors believe the rival firm's new product is inferior, they may encourage the product's introduction so that the firm subsequently incurs a loss to the benefit of the competition. Instead of systematic tactics, firms also have been alleged to randomly change marketing mix variables to disrupt the test market results of rivals. Some unscrupulous marketers have even damaged competitor's goods or interfered with test marketing in other illegal ways. Fortunately, however, from the new product marketer's standpoint, the gains from test marketing often outweigh the losses.

If managers decide to go ahead with market tests, they must choose a test market strategy. Researchers typically practice one or more of three options: representative introductions, natural field experiments, or controlled field experiments. Marketers may choose one or more cities as *representative introductions*. For example, some U.S. firms choose Peoria, Fresno, or Syracuse, because these cities represent the entire country in terms of sociodemographic characteristics, yet the cities are not so large that they make a test cost prohibitive. Of course, "representativeness" is a relative term; these cities may not appropriately represent the firm's target market. Syracuse might be representative of the target market if a firm is testing a new toothpaste for the "average" consumer, but it might be a poor choice if the firm is testing a new "Tex-Mex"–style food product. Denver, Phoenix, or Austin might be more representative test markets for the latter.

Representative introductions attempt to test a product under realistic conditions. Firms hold product characteristics constant (i.e., the new product is tested as designed), and conduct no unusual changes in levels of advertising, promotion, or other factors. Nor do marketers vary these factors much across cities during the tests. They might set advertising as a simple percentage of planned total advertising for the city size under test. Firms monitor sales at key points in time throughout the test market period, as well as at the end of the test period. This might be done by recording the sales in each store, the amount shipped from the home firm to retailers and wholesalers, or the amount shipped from wholesalers to retailers. Depending on the firm, only one of these types of data may be available or reliable.

In a *natural field experiment*, firms attempt to measure consumer responses to different prices, advertising levels, promotions, and so on. However, rather than setting these factors before the test, firms offer one product at one uniform price and promotion schedule to retailers who, in turn, set their own prices, decide whether to adopt promotions, control shelf space allocated to the new product, and so on. Researchers may have to visit stores to find out what was done. The firm then studies sales as a function of the naturally varying in-store stimuli. The advantage of the approach is that it allows a deeper analysis than does the representative introduction (i.e., rather than looking at only total sales, firms can examine the response of sales to variations in the marketing mix). A disadvantage is that firms impose little or no control on the marketing mix variations, thus making analysis difficult and preventing a full examination of ranges of effects.

Using *controlled field experiments*, firms can manipulate product design, prices, advertising, and other stimuli in different markets to ascertain the optimal marketing mixes and to gauge overall product receptivity. Researchers using this method can more validly infer connections between each change in product design, price level, and so on, on the one hand, and actual sales, on the other. However, this wealth of information costs more because coordination and measurement procedures are complex. Moreover, these experiments are difficult to design and can be contaminated by competitors' actions and unknown changes in consumers or the marketplace.

For many consumer goods, marketers use formal test marketing models to evaluate market test results. The Sprinter model, one of the best known of these models, combines information from test market data and subjective managerial judgment in mathematical and statistical formulas.[26] The main goal is to forecast national sales before product introduction. Using a consumer behavior model, Sprinter represents different product flow rates for various consumer categories (e.g., first-time triers, repeat purchasers, switchers) based on their trial and repeat purchase patterns. Sprinter tracks availability of the product and awareness, intent, and purchases of consumers periodically over the test period, and makes or updates market share forecasts. The model not only gives an indication of overall product acceptability, but it splits sales into trial and repeat components so that managers can spot problems, make adjustments in the marketing mix, and perform better forecasts. For example, sometimes new product sales increase dramatically in the early weeks and even months of a test market, exceeding sales goals. But after a while, total sales might drop to unacceptably low levels. The early success might result from very high consumer interest in the product, subsequent trial, and then disappointing repeat sales. Instead of waiting for an entire year or more to discover a product's final acceptance or determine causes of consumer discontent, these early data can be used to accurately foretell trial and repeat rates, and hence later sales. Poor repeat sales early on should signal the marketing group to discover the cause, which might result from distribution problems, high relative prices, packaging deficiencies, inferior product ingredients, low awareness levels due to suboptimal advertising, or other shortcomings with the product or in the marketing mix.

Commercialization

The final step in the new product development process is commercialization, or launching the product, probably one of the most exciting and anxiety-provoking times in any business's day-to-day operations. The costs and risks can be considerable. When Miller began marketing its Lite beer in the southern United States in the early 1980s, it spent about $250 million for a new plant in Georgia. Advertising and promotion expenditures for Gillette's launch of its new Sensor razor in the early 1990s were greater than $50 million. Obviously, firms have a lot at stake when they introduce a new product into the marketplace.

To effectively launch a new product, brand managers must conduct three activities: planning the introduction, monitoring its progress, and making changes as needed. The marketing team must plan many simultaneous activities. Table 7.4 illustrates the critical steps involved in the launch of a new home word processor. Notice that production, distribution, sales, advertising, service, market research, R&D, and global activities each involve a series of tasks, and management must coordinate among them. Firms sometimes use a critical path diagram such as shown in Figure 7.8 on page 299 for a frequently purchased consumer good. Here we see the advertising, promotions, personal selling, and manufacturing activities that must be carried out to achieve launch by a particular date. Because of the expenses incurred, the limited capacity of production facilities, and/or the desire to reduce risk, firms frequently use a phased roll-out strategy to introduce new products. Thus

TABLE 7.4 LAUNCH ACTIVITIES FOR HOME WORD PROCESSOR

Activities	1990				1991											
	SEP	OCT	NOV	DEC	JAN	FEB	MAR	APR	MAY	JUN	JUL	AUG	SEP	OCT	NOV	DEC
Production		Set up line and suppliers				Production test		Ship product								
Distribution		Recruit retailers and distributors					Train retail sales staff/ institute promotion plan				Point-of-purchase Install				Monitor	
Sales		Sell channel					Aid in training and dealer advertising						Support dealers			
Advertising		Final TV copy and print ads		Test ads and buy media							Revise and finalize copy		National advertising and promotion			
Service		Write service manual				Train dealers					Stock parts	Correct any defects				
Market research		Monitor market					Ad copy test				Set up UPC sample		Telephone survey			
R&D		Work on YWP-2000		Monitor technology												
Global		Global strategy meeting	Tactical plans by country				Review tactics		Coordinate ad and training materials				Share learning		Strategy review	

Source: Glen L. Urban and Steven H. Star, Advanced Marketing Strategy: Phenomena Analysis and Decisions (Upper Saddle River, N.J.: Prentice-Hall, 1991), p. 503.

they may introduce a product in a few cities at a time or by geographical area, taking a year or more to distribute the product nationwide. Export, foreign licensing, and even foreign production may be considered at this time as well.

As a new product is being launched, the brand manager must monitor its progress. The brand manager must track sales to see if trial and repeat buying are progressing as planned. Yet these are only the tip of the iceberg, so to speak. Sales are the final outcome of marketing efforts, but the brand manager must follow developments of factors that cause or predict sales. Thus special efforts must be made to measure (1) how well and how fast products are entering the distribution channel and stores, (2) whether word of mouth communication is positive or negative and how much word of mouth communication is occurring, (3) how fast customer awareness of the new product and its availability are growing, (4) consumer attitudes, intentions, and satisfaction, (5) competitor responses, (6) economic conditions, (7) political and legal developments, and (8) any other forces in the marketplace that could affect sales. The above information will typically be gathered through surveys and commercial data sources. As the data are collected, the brand manager will compare actual results to expectations and forecasts.

If actual sales and other monitored criteria deviate from expectations, the brand manager must make appropriate changes. Poor initial sales could result from many factors. Maybe retailers fail to stock the firm's product to the extent the firm desires. The brand manager then needs to investigate why their product lacks acceptance by retailers. Perhaps margins are too low; perhaps a misunderstanding exists with respect to deals and promotions; maybe the product's packaging is prone to damage in shipping or during stocking; or perhaps retailers do not know the best way to market the product. The brand manager must address these problems quickly. Or maybe the product gets into stores, but cus-

FIGURE 7.8

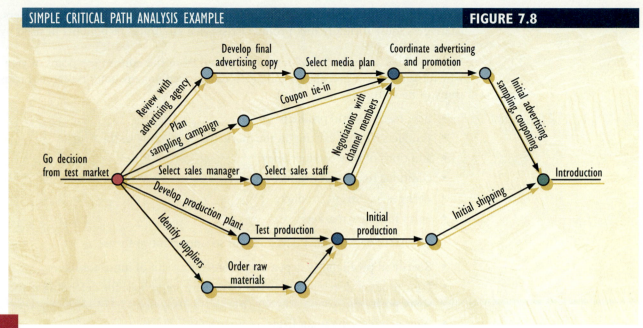

Source: Glen L. Urban and John R. Hauser, Design and Marketing of New Products, 2nd ed. (Upper Saddle River, N.J.: Prentice-Hall, 1993), p. 538.

tomers are not willing to try it as much as the firm had hoped. Is the price too high? Have competitors countered the firm's introduction? Is product quality a problem? The brand manager must rectify any problems found. A formal management information system, coupled with marketing research, will be invaluable during launch.

Invariably, marketers find that their original marketing mix needs to be fine-tuned. Some changes may be made piecemeal, in response to specific problems found with one or more parts of the whole marketing program. A brand manager will find it useful to take an adaptive perspective, trying to learn from errors or marketplace changes. Firms should not merely react, but also must act to influence the market as they can. Brand managers should experiment to discover market response functions and, in turn, learn what specific levels of the marketing mix variables to aim for. For example, a firm might try different levels of advertising, promotions, prices, and even aspects of the product, if feasible, across a number of its submarkets to see how sales respond. Of course, these trial levels should be tested systematically and according to principles of experimental design standards. The results need then to be integrated with models and interpreted accordingly.

In the next chapter, we cover what managers do to foster the product through its life cycle.

SUMMARY

What is a product and what makes it new? A product is, of course, the physical entity that is perceived by the senses, but it is important also to think of it in terms of its psychological meaning for consumers. Products have attributes and supply benefits for consumers. These aspects, along with the bundle of marketing mix elements needed to sell the product, provide perceived value, which in turn are reflected in the overall quality and cost judgments made by consumers. Managers must formally link product or service attributes to benefits desired by consumers.

In the final analysis, "new" must be defined from the consumer's point of view, which is a matter of perception and needs to be based on consumer research. Firms think of new products in terms of

- new-to-the-world products
- products already existing in the marketplace yet new to the firm
- additions of new product lines
- additions to current product lines
- changes in current products
- entry into new markets

What makes new product development so important to firms?

- Sustained profitability depends on a steady stream of innovations
- New product development is an essential strategic tool for defending market share positions
- New products maintain firms' reputations
- Firms can enter new markets

New products represent many potential pitfalls. New product development is expensive, time consuming, and risky. Table 7.1 lists many reasons for new product failures and suggested general safeguards.

The new product development process consists of six main steps:

Idea generation → Analysis of opportunities → Design → Development → Testing → Commercialization

Figure 7.4 summarizes the central activities that must be performed in each step.

- Idea generation: managers focus on market definition and the processes needed to produce, evaluate, and select new product ideas.
- Analysis of opportunities: carries the process a step further and concerns four activities:
  - measurement and analysis of customer needs
  - analysis of the competitive environment
  - appraisal of the legal, social, and economic environment
  - a business (especially financial) analysis
- Design: encompasses design of the physical product, marketing mix, and supporting programs. Special effort is needed to coordinate these activities.
- Development
  - continues the guided evolution of the product
  - introduces pretesting of the product and marketing mix
  - refines coordination of marketing with production, personnel, and other functions in the firm
- Testing: a market test may be instituted prior to commercialization.
- Commercialization: an on-going managerial activity that guides the product through the competitive environment.

QUESTIONS FOR DISCUSSION

1. What is a product? Discuss its meaning from the perspective of the buyer and from that of the seller.

2. How do product attributes produce benefits, perceived quality, and value? What must managers do to create a positive psychological product and ultimately enhance customer satisfaction?

3. Compare and contrast product pretesting and market testing. What are their advantages and disadvantages?

4. How might new product development differ between consumer products, industrial products, and high-tech products?

5. What are different ways to define market opportunities? Discuss their pros and cons. How can market definitions be related to consumer behavior?

6. Discuss the various methods used in pretesting of new products. Describe how you would pretest a new high-definition television set. How would you pretest a new bleaching procedure for whitening teeth?

7. What are common problems in new product rollout and commercialization? What should managers do to ensure success?

8. What makes a successful soft drink from the point of view of consumers' tastes? What does a brand manager need to consider when developing a new soft drink?

NOTES FOR FURTHER READING

1. A. Parasuraman, Valerie A. Zeithaml, and Leonard L. Berry, "SERVQUAL: A Multi Item Scale for Measuring Consumer Perception of Service Quality," *Journal of Retailing* 64 (Spring 1988): 12–40. See also A. Parasuraman, Valerie A. Zeithaml, and Leonard L. Berry, "Reassessment of Expectations as a Comparison Standard in Measuring Service Quality: Implications for Future Research," *Journal of Marketing* 58 (January 1994): 111–124; J. Joseph Cronin Jr. and Steven A. Taylor, "SERVPERF versus SERVQUAL: Reconciling Performance-Based and Perceptions-Minus-Expectations Measurement of Service Quality," *Journal of Marketing* 58 (January 1994): 125–131; and R. Kenneth Teas, "Expectations as a Comparison Standard in Measuring Service Quality: An Assessment of a Reassessment," *Journal of Marketing* 58 (January 1994): 132–139.

2. David A. Garvin, "Quality on the Line," *Harvard Business Review* 61 (September 1983): 65–75; Chr. Hjorth-Anderson, "The Concept of Quality and the Efficiency of Markets for Consumer Products," *Journal of Consumer Research* 11 (September 1984): 708–718; David A. Garvin, "What Does 'Product Quality' Really Mean?" *Sloan Management Review* (1, 1984): 25–43.

3. Jan-Benedict E.M. Steenkamp, *Product Quality* (Assen/Maastricht, Netherlands: van Gorcum, 1989).

4. Ibid., 231.

5. *New Products Management for the 1980s* (New York: Booz, Allen & Hamilton, 1982).

6. Quoted in Thomas D. Kuczmarski, *Managing New Products: The Power of Innovation* (Upper Saddle River, N.J.: Prentice-Hall, 1992), p. 2.

7. Regis McKenna, "Marketing Is Everything," *Harvard Business Review* (January–February 1991): 65–79.

8. William Taylor, "The Business of Innovation: An Interview with Paul Cook," *Harvard Business Review* (March–April 1990): 97–106.

9. See *Business Week*, August 25, 1973, p. 50.

10. The $310 million amount is from Glen L. Urban and John R. Hauser, *Design and Marketing of New Products*, 2nd ed. (Upper Saddle River, N.J.: Prentice-Hall, 1993), p. 61. Of the total expenditure, $75 million was for R&D, $125 million for capital investment, and $110 million for advertising and promotion.

11. Ibid., p. 60.

12. L. Adler, "Time Lag in New Product Development," *Journal of Marketing Research* 3 (January 1996): 18–20.

13. Ibid.

14. See E. Mansfield, J. Schnee, S. Wagner, and M. Hamberger, *Research and Innovation in the Model Corporation* (New York: W. W. Norton, 1971). See also Urban and Hauser, *Design and Marketing of New Products* (1993), p. 62.

15. T. Elrod and A. P. Kelman, "Reliability of New Product Evaluation as of 1968 and 1981," unpublished working paper, Owen Graduate School of Management, Vanderbilt

University, 1987; E. Mansfield and S. Wagner, "Organizational and Strategic Factors Associated with Probabilities of Success in Industrial R&D," *Journal of Business* (April 1975).

16. Glen L. Urban and John R. Hauser, *Design and Marketing of New Products* (Upper Saddle River, N.J.: Prentice-Hall, 1980), pp. 46–59.

17. See *New Products Management for the 1980s*; R. G. Cooper and E. J. Kleinschmidt, "An Investigation into the New Product Process—Steps, Deficiencies, and Impact," *Journal of Product Innovation* 3 (1986): 71–85; R. G. Cooper, "New Products: What Separates Winners from Losers?" *Journal of Product Innovation Management* 4 (1987): 169–184; M. G. Duerr, *The Commercial Development of New Products* (New York: Conference Board, 1986); U. DeBrentani, "Success and Failure in New Industrial Services, *Journal of Product Innovation* 6 (1989): 239–258; and Hauser and Urban, *Design and Marketing of New Products* (1993), pp. 51–57.

18. Eric von Hippel, "Has a Customer Already Developed Your Next Product?" *Sloan Management Review* 18 (Winter 1977): 63.

19. Urban and Hauser, *Design and Marketing of New Products* (1980), p. 125.

20. Professor Porter's framework for analyzing competive markets can be found in Michael E. Porter, *Competitive Strategy: Techniques for Analyzing Industries and Competitors* (New York: Free Press, 1980); Michael E. Porter, *Competitive Advantage: Creating and Sustaining Superior Performance* (New York: Free Press, 1985). See also C. K. Prahalad and Gary Hamel, "The Core Competence of the Corporation," *Harvard Business Review* (May–June 1990): 79–91.

21. Urban and Hauser, *Design and Marketing of New Products* (1993), pp. 107–108.

22. For a quantitative, managerial-based model of pretesting, see Alvin J. Silk and Glenn L. Urban, "Pretest Market Evaluation of New Packaged Goods: A Model and Measurement Methodology," *Journal of Marketing Research* 15 (May 1978): 171–191. See also Urban and Hauser, *Design and Marketing of New Products* (1993), ch. 16.

23. A fuller description of this example can be found in Urban and Hauser, *Design and Marketing of New Products* (1980).

24. Urban and Hauser, *Design and Marketing of New Products* (1993), p. 450.

25. Ibid.

26. Glen L. Urban, "Sprinter Mod III: A Model for the Analysis of New Frequently Purchased Consumer Products," *Operations Research*, 18 (September–October 1970): 805–853. Another market test model is NEWS: L. G. Pringle, R. D. Wilson, and E. I. Brody, "NEWS: A Decision-Oriented Model for New Product Analysis and Forecasting," *Marketing Science* 1 (Winter 1982): 1–30. For discussions of these and additional ideas, see Urban and Hauser, *Design and Marketing of New Products* (1993), ch. 17.

CHAPTER 8

MANAGING PRODUCT LIFE CYCLES

CHAPTER OBJECTIVES

When you are done with this chapter, you should have achieved the following:

- An understanding of the meaning of product life cycle and of how product life cycles work.

- An appreciation of the importance of product brands and brand management.

- The ability to show how managers can use the concept of the product life cycle to help make sound marketing decisions.

CHAPTER OUTLINE

Ricoh, the Japanese office automation firm, recently celebrated 25 years of operating in Europe. Sales in 1996 topped $1.3 billion.

Ricoh's success can be traced to its ongoing introduction of new products over the years and the globalizing of its businesses. The company introduced the first plain-paper facsimile machine (1983), the first digital facsimile machine (1989), and the fastest digital full-color plain-paper copier (1990). Although not the first producer for many technologies, Ricoh has followed a policy of introducing products new to the company every few years since operations began in Europe in

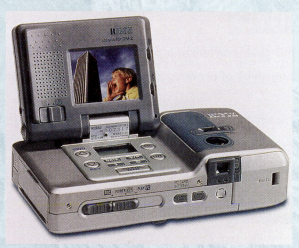

Office equipment has become increasingly compact and sophisticated to accommodate telecommuters. Ricoh is ready to accommodate this new segment by "reinventing" existing technology.

1971. Ricoh's milestones include its first office computer (1971); dry-electrostatic-transfer plain-paper copier (1972); liquid plain-paper machine, which eventually became the highest-selling copier worldwide (1975); dry toner plain-paper copier (1982); laser printer (1983); analogue color copier (1985); multifunctional digital image-processing system (1991); and multimedia digital camera (1995). The company is obviously a marketing and technology leader, yet it finds time to develop innovative recycling programs, for which it has won awards and public recognition.

It is important to think of Ricoh as a company that continually renews itself. To sustain overall sales growth and avoid stagnation in individual products, Ricoh invests heavily in R&D (nearly 9 percent of sales annually), moves production and other decision-making functions to multiple overseas locations, and aggressively manages new product introductions. The goal is to forestall or even overcome the all too frequent life cycle of introduction, growth, leveling off, and decline characteristic of most products, firms, and industries.

In 1996, Ricoh took perhaps its boldest initiative by introducing the Aficio, a digital copier based on a modular design. Aficio is especially designed with the decentralized or remote office concept in mind, where firms need multiple functions but do not want to buy a product with all functions, especially those they do not need, bundled together. Instead, Aficio permits buyers to add the modules they need for faxing, laser printing, copying, or connecting to personal computers. This means that some buyers can avoid purchasing three or four different machines and save office space; others can use existing machines and purchase only the functions they need at the moment, later replacing the existing machines when they become obsolete. Further, Aficio's functions can be upgraded as needed over the years. At the same time, Aficio's digital technology yields higher-quality images and permits easier manipulation of images than current technologies.

Ricoh's objective is to provide the so-called "virtual office." Its new product development and ongoing product management programs are key to its success.

As important as new products are to companies, they are just the beginning. Successful products require management attention throughout their life cycles. In this chapter, we discuss the product life cycle (PLC)[1] and its significance and limitations for aiding managers' decisions for effective management. We also build on the decisions of strategic marketing, discussed in chapter 2, to apply these strategic principles to managing specific products and product lines.

STAGES IN THE PRODUCT LIFE CYCLE

An Early Definition

Drawing upon an analogy from biology (i.e., birth → growth → decline → death), marketing researchers suggest that products also pass through well-defined stages from their inception until their withdrawal from the marketplace. Figure 8.1 shows a common representation of the PLC concept, which plots dollar sales and profits against time in years. Sales increase slowly in the *introduction* stage; that is, the curve is relatively flat. Many people are not aware of the product, and even those consumers who are aware of it might resist purchasing an untried entity. In this stage, marketers must build consumer awareness and confidence through promotion and advertising, gain acceptance by retailers, and gear up production to meet anticipated demand.

Once consumers evaluate a product favorably and try it, initial and perhaps repeat sales increase more rapidly. Thus, the *growth* stage shows a relatively steep slope. Here, marketers adjust production, distribution, advertising, and pricing to meet demand and stave off potential competitors. To keep competitors from cutting into their markets, firms might have to further expand production, reach out to new markets, maintain relatively high advertising levels, or lower prices somewhat. Competition can be intense at this stage, as competing firms produce their own versions of successful introductions.

After a while, the market gets saturated and/or competitors make large inroads. Sales increase more slowly, and perhaps even flatten out. This stage is termed *maturity*.

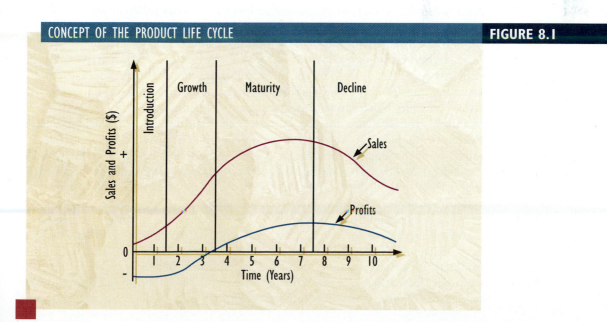

CONCEPT OF THE PRODUCT LIFE CYCLE   **FIGURE 8.1**

Competition among firms for sales reaches its peak during this stage. Firms may take defensive positions by cutting costs, searching for new markets, or making promotional deals with retailers. Other firms assume aggressive postures by increasing advertising, improving their products, and decreasing prices. Occasionally firms adopt marketing strategies that use both defensive and offensive tactics during the maturity stage.

In the final stage, *decline*, sales begin a downward trend. Sometimes this descent is gradual, occurring over many years. At other times, consumer tastes change quickly and/or competitors gain dramatically so that sales dip abruptly. The end result is often removal of the product from the marketplace. If the demise of the product is irreversible, then marketers will typically lower their advertising and promotion budgets to reduce expenses, stop R&D work on the product, and curtail overall marketing support.

The traditional PLC concept shown in Figure 8.1 shows that profits also tend to follow a regular pattern of growth, saturation, and decline. Profits lag sales at the beginning point of rapid growth stages, or firms may well suffer losses in the beginning of the growth stage, with profits emerging only years after product introduction. Profits usually peak at the end of the growth stage or the beginning of maturity.

Personal computers (PCs) provide a good example of the PLC. The 286 processor PC lasted only a few years before it was replaced by 386 and then 486 processors. The 486 also was short lived, after the Pentium processors arrived. With each succeeding generation of PCs, production of the old soon ceased. Manufacturers of PCs have been able to sustain sales by developing ever faster processors. Some buyers delay first purchase until the advent of a "satisfactory" new machine; current users find their existing machines "obsolete" at some point in time and purchase the latest innovation. Meanwhile, the life cycle of the PC goes on.

Refinements in the PLC Concept

As seen in Figure 8.1, the length of each stage in the PLC varies. The introduction stage is the shortest, growth is somewhat longer, maturity is longer yet, and decline is about as long as maturity. In reality, the stages can be shorter or longer than shown in the figure, depending on market conditions and the actions of the firm. This raises an interesting question: How do we know when any product arrives at a particular stage of its PLC? Managers may find these stages difficult to ascertain, because the transition from one stage to another is not necessarily inevitable, nor is it always possible to determine the causes of any transition.

Indeed, the evidence for the existence of PLCs in the real world is mixed. Researchers Dhalla and Yuspeh, for example, could not find any products that definitely went through the four stages.[2] On the other hand, others have found some products that roughly follow the PLC curve.[3] But even for products that appear to follow the PLC, the duration of stages varies widely so the overall PLC shapes deviate from the neat S-shaped curve shown in Figure 8.1. For example, in one study of instant coffee and frozen orange juice, the time from the beginning of growth to maturity for each was about 12 years.[4] In contrast, another study found that the growth stage for five industrial goods examined varied from 3 to 10 years.[5] Other products' PLC curves do not exhibit the S-shape at all but show rising, falling, flat, or widely fluctuating patterns.[6] One or more of the stages shown in Figure 8.1 may not exist in reality, depending on the product.

Sales Definition and Measurement

At least five issues impact the validity of PLC curves. The first concerns the *definition* and *measurement* of sales.[7] Companies measure sales variously as units sold, total dollar value, total dollar value corrected for inflation or seasonality, sales in regions or territories, sales by customer groupings, sales per unit of time, and so on. No foolproof rule indicates that one measure is more accurate or better than another in every situation. Yet, measurement methods obviously influence the shape of the PLC curve. Until a sound rationale and research reveal the best measure or measures, one might examine a number of alternatives to see the implications. Previous failures to observe PLC curves for some products may have stemmed from improper or fallible measures. Any measurement will depend on the specific goals and situation at hand.

Second, PLC curves can be drawn based on various product *aggregation levels*. Table 8.1 shows some possibilities. Researchers can model the life cycles of products for generic product classes, product classes, product forms, or for individual brands embedded within those classes. For example, we might plot sales of alcoholic or nonalcoholic beverages over time to see how consumption patterns of these two *generic product classes* have changed. In one sense, all beverages compete with one another because they satisfy people's thirst or act as social props.

At the next level of specificity, we can examine the sales of a *homogeneous product class* within the generic category. A homogeneous product class includes products that act more or less as direct substitutes for one another. Some homogeneous product classes under the category of beverages might be coffee, tea, soft drinks, mineral water, or juices. Loosely speaking, each of these competes with the others when people are thirsty, so we could plot a PLC for each.

Homogeneous product classes, in turn, can be subdivided into *product forms*, variations of a homogeneous product that satisfy the same general needs plus more specific subneeds. For instance, the need for coffee is stimulated in part by the general thirst drive plus a consumer's specific preference or craving for coffee because of personal habits, physiological dependence on caffeine, or flavors inherent in coffee. Product forms for coffee include ground caffeinated, instant, and instant decaffeinated. We could graph a PLC for each. The curves might suggest trends and turning points in consumption and add to information in decision making. In some parts of the world, as people become more health conscious, the demand for decaffeinated coffees has risen dramatically, putting the corresponding curve in the growth phase, and telling managers how attractive the new demand is.

TABLE 8.1 LEVELS OF AGGREGATION OF SALES FOR THE PRODUCT LIFE CYCLE

Phenomenon to be Represented			
GENERIC PRODUCT CLASS	HOMOGENEOUS PRODUCT CLASS	PRODUCT FORM	BRAND
Beverages	Coffee	Instant coffee	Brim Instant
Transportation	Automobiles	Sports car	Porsche
Educational and Entertainment Activities	Museums	Art museums	The Louvre

Finally, each product form consists of *competing brands*. Among ground coffees in the United States, for example, Maxwell House, Folger's, Hills Brothers, Chock Full O'Nuts, and numerous store brands vie for the consumer's dollar. Table 8.1 lists Brim Instant, a freeze-dried decaffeinated instant coffee, as an example of one brand. The PLC concept applies to individual brands as well as to aggregate product categories. In fact, we might even examine the PLC for subgroupings of individual brands such as sales of Brim Instant in the midwestern United States or purchases of Brim Instant by particular ethnic groups. Table 8.1 presents two other examples: transportation and educational and entertainment activities. Brand managers might use such subgroupings to evaluate a new market segment or redefine their existing markets.

Table 8.1 suggests that the PLC concept applies at many levels of aggregation. But to which, if any, does the PLC concept apply in reality? Although research continues in this area, product forms seem to fit a PLC most closely. Individual brands fluctuate greatly and their PLC curves frequently deviate from the ideal shape. Similarly, homogeneous and generic product classes often follow longer time frames and are subject to more forces, making analysis difficult. At the present, it seems that the PLC reflects mostly industry sales of product forms. For example, it would apply better to sales of electric lawn mowers than to all lawn mower types or to a Sears Craftsman Electric Mower in particular. As researchers look deeper into PLCs in the future and learn more about measuring the dynamics involved, they may well discover that the PLC works at both broader and more specific levels of analysis.[8]

PLC Timing

Still another issue that impacts the PLC concept is *timing*. How long is each stage? How can we define the specific dimensions of a stage? What accounts for variations in the length of a stage over time and across products? One way to determine the length of stages is to plot changes over time and then, when a transition occurs, call it the end of one stage and the beginning of another. Although this is a subjective procedure, it may yield satisfactory results if the data are well behaved and roughly follow an S-shape. Alternatively, researchers have set norms that generalize to at least a relatively broad class of products. For example, some researchers have specified the transition from introduction to growth and from growth to maturity for 37 selected household appliances as follows: The beginning of the growth stage is defined as the first two successive years of sales growth rate of 5 percent or greater following introduction, and the end of the growth stage into maturity is signaled by a yearly rate of growth (percentage change in sales) equal to or less than the growth rate in consumer expenditures for all household products.[9] These norms offer advantages in that they are explicit, exhibit some face validity, and allow testing and replication. However, any rule of thumb is somewhat arbitrary. Individual products and product classes may still vary widely, depending on circumstances. For example, researchers found that PLC periods for 37 household appliances varied from 0 to 18 years as introduction stages and from 3 to 44 years as growth stages.[10] If even similar types of products vary so widely, no wonder generalizations and predictions from PLC theory are difficult to make. Yet another problem exists: Researchers have trouble setting realistic norms for the transition from maturity to decline because sales sometimes decrease, then increase, and then decrease before they reach a constant pattern.

Research continues into the study of PLC timing issues. Some evidence suggests that introduction and growth stages have shortened for new product entrants over the years.

Product Groups	Introductory Stage Duration (years)	Growth Stage Duration (years)
12 Household Appliances Introduced 1922–1942	12.5	33.8
16 Household Appliances Introduced 1945–1964	7.0	19.5
9 Household Appliances Introduced 1965–1979	2.0	6.8

As Table 8.2 shows, the length of time from introduction to maturity has shortened from an average 46.3 years for household appliances introduced from 1922 to 1942, to 26.5 years for the period 1945 to 1964, to less than 9 years for the period 1965 to 1979.[11] Today, the PLCs for some appliances, such as VHS tape players remain the same, whereas for others, such as home video games, the PLCs have shortened dramatically. The truncation of the PLC is most likely due to an acceleration in technological change, competition, and the increased education and sophistication of consumers.

Consumer Purchase Patterns

The overall *pattern of consumer purchases* with respect to first-time sales, repeat sales, and total sales also affect PLC shapes. Some products, such as toothpaste or office supplies, have relatively short lives, so the same consumers make many repeat purchases. If we were to plot only total sales, we could miss important dynamics of consumer behavior that reflect how the public is receiving the product. Figure 8.2 shows two PLC curves for similar products in which total sales for each are roughly equal. However, notice that case A shows total sales composed of trial plus repeat sales, where trial sales rise quickly, then stagnate and decline, and repeat sales begin a somewhat similar ascent and then also level off and then decline. In contrast, case B produces similar total sales, yet trial and repeat purchase levels differ considerably. Although trial sales for case B are quite good, reaching higher levels than for case A, very poor repeat sales keep case B from surpassing case A sales.

If managers focus only on total sales, they would conclude that products A and B are identical. Yet, as the curves reveal, case A has not achieved ideal initial market acceptance, perhaps because advertising is inferior or insufficient, or distribution is inadequate. Case B, although generating amazing first-time purchases, fails to satisfy consumers sufficiently to generate acceptable repeat purchases, perhaps because the product fails to meet expectations established by advertising, or because competitors have created products with differential advantages discovered later. The point is that managers can gain a better understanding of PLC behavior by examining the components of total sales. Notice that total sales for cases A and B and trial sales for case A tend to follow the classic S-shaped PLC curve, whereas repeat sales for case B do not show the expected form. The forms for the curves can be represented through equations and used to explain and forecast sales. Finally, note that trial and repeat curves can cross each other over time.

PLC Curve Determinants

PLC concepts describe sales only with respect to time; they do not take the *determinants of the curve* (e.g., the causes of sales) into account. This omission can create

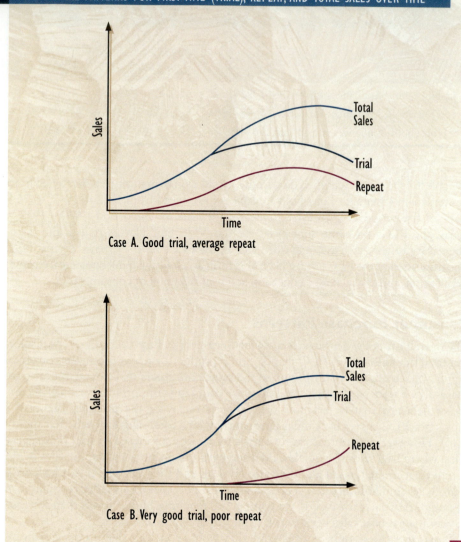

Case A. Good trial, average repeat

Case B. Very good trial, poor repeat

a false impression that sales growth and decline are inevitable regardless of the actions taken by managers. The PLC concept fails to note that many factors influence sales and these factors, in turn, can be influenced by management decisions.

A classic example of this is Procter & Gamble's detergent, Tide.[12] Tide was introduced in 1947 and has not followed the classic PLC curve at all. In fact, Tide still might be considered in its growth stage. It has not reached maturity in more than five decades. What accounts for this unusual longevity and vitality and Tide's implied profitability? P&G has incorporated no fewer than 55 major improvements into the product over the years. Presumably, these improvements have stimulated consumer demand in terms of first-time purchases, repeat purchases, and brand switching. Procter & Gamble's managers have successfully won the detergent battle. In short, P&G has been able to circumvent the forces that tend to produce a full PLC from birth to death through close attention to consumer segments and appropriate demand stimulation changes in the marketing mix.

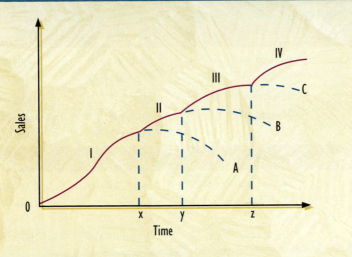

Theodore Levitt, a marketing guru, termed this phenomenon an exploitation, or extension, of the PLC by the firm.[13] The idea is shown graphically in Figure 8.3. At time zero, the firm introduces the product, which grows along a PLC curve (I) until it reaches point x in time. If managers make few changes in the marketing mix, sales might well flatten out and begin a decline toward point A. The curve from 0 to A represents the expected PLC path under "normal" marketing expenditures and competitive pressures. However, if at time x the firm finds a new geographical market, a new use for the product, or stimulates sales in some other way (e.g., through a major redesign of the product, more advertising, a price drop, and so on), then the "life" of the product might be renewed along curve II. At point y in time, a potential decline, toward B, is again possible. Managers can once again avoid such a decline by developing new markets or marketing programs, creating an increase in sales along curve III, and so on. Thus, the rise and fall of products are not certain events, at least in the short- or midterm, and management can influence the shape of the PLC for its products.

By now, it should be obvious that the PLC concept is an oversimplification. Nevertheless, it harbors enough truth to serve as a guide in many firms for strategic planning and implementation of the marketing mix, and therefore it deserves our scrutiny. Instead of the idealistic shape and sequences represented in Figure 8.3, managers should develop models allowing more complex patterns and stages to come closer to reality. Marketing researchers may yield enough information about the causes of the PLC to develop a small number of fundamental forms. One direction for research is to develop contingency theories. That is, the shape and sequences might depend on particular consumer groups, product technologies or functions, geographical or other segments, and so on.

PLC AS A MANAGEMENT TOOL

Table 8.3 summarizes the most common implications of the PLC and appropriate managerial responses. These situations exemplify the norm across a wide spectrum of products. Each stage in the PLC characterizes typical sales, profits, cash flow, customer targets, and competitive environments. The maturity stage, for instance, indicates slow

TABLE 8.3 TYPICAL OUTCOMES THROUGHOUT THE STAGES OF THE PLC AND MANAGERIAL RESPONSES

Characteristics	Introduction	Growth	Maturity	Decline
Sales	Low	Fast growth	Slow growth	Decline
Profits	Negligible	Peak levels	Declining	Low or zero
Cash Flow	Negative	Moderate	High	Low
Customers	Innovative	Mass market	Mass market	Laggards
Competitors	Few	Growing	Many rivals	Declining number

Responses	Introduction	Growth	Maturity	Decline
Strategic Focus	Expand market	Market penetration	Defend share	Productivity
Marketing Expenditures	High	High (declining %)	Falling	Low
Marketing Emphasis	Product awareness	Brand preference	Brand loyalty	Selective
Distribution	Patchy	Intensive	Intensive	Selective
Price	High	Lowest	Lowest	Rising
Product	Basic	Differentiated	Differentiated	Rationalized

Source: Peter Doyle, "The Realities of the Product Life Cycle," Quarterly Review of Marketing 2 (Summer 1976): 5. Reprinted with the permission of the publisher.

or nonexistent sales growth, declining profits, high cash flow, orientation to the mass market or at least an expanded market, and intensive interfirm rivalry. The table also shows typical managerial responses to each outcome in each stage of the PLC. Managers must tailor strategic focus, marketing expenditures, marketing emphasis, distribution, pricing, and product decisions to each stage. For example, in the growth stage, management's main strategy is to penetrate the market and generate sales. Thus successful marketing in this stage requires high marketing expenditures (although perhaps less than those needed to launch the product) to build brand preferences and stimulate brand loyalty. Depending on the product and customers, this stage also may demand intensive distribution to as many outlets as possible. Managers may lower the price to induce trial by those not easily enticed by new products. Firms may refine products themselves to improve quality.

As an illustration of the concept of the management of a product throughout its life cycle, Table 8.4 shows how managers change the marketing mix throughout the life cycle of a brand of toothpaste. In the introduction stage (called "entry" in this case), the firm tries to establish a foothold in the market by emphasizing product quality and real advantages over the competition. Advertising and promotion programs strive to build awareness first and then induce trial. The sales force makes special efforts to persuade retailers to stock the brand and give it maximum shelf space. Managers set price based on costs plus a sought-after margin, which depends, perhaps, on expected sales and a particular target return-on-investment norm.

As the market grows and competitors develop their own market entries, managers shift their efforts from penetrating markets to maintaining market share (the "maintenance" stage in Tab. 8.4). Research efforts identify product weaknesses, and firms make necessary changes. Advertising stresses product benefits to build brand loyalty. Salespeople build rapport with retailers, perhaps through providing more service. Prices are set competitively.

TABLE 8.4 PRODUCT LIFE CYCLE STRATEGIES FOR A BRAND OF TOOTHPASTE

| STRATEGY CONSIDERATION | Product Life Cycle Stage | | | |
	ENTRY	MAINTENANCE	PROLIFERATION	EXIT/DECLINE
Objective	Establish market position	Stabilize market share	Secure new market segments	Prepare for re-entry
Product Design	Assure high quality	Identify weaknesses	Adjust size, color, package, and flavor	Modify weak features
Promotion	Build brand awareness	Stress favorable evaluation	Communicate new features	Educate on re-entry features
Distribution	Build distribution network	Solidify channel relationships	Deliver all versions	Smooth re-entry features
Pricing	Use cost-plus	Price with competition	Use price deals	Reduce price to clear stock

Source: Ben M. Enis, Raymond La Grace, and Arthur E. Prell, "Extending the Product Life Cycle," Business Horizons 20 (June 1977): 53. Reprinted with the permission of the publisher.

In the proliferation stage (i.e., maturity), sales stagnate. The firm responds by searching for new geographical markets or new unserved segments. But new markets are usually not enough. Firms recognize the need to change the product and introduce an "improved" version. Brand managers might change ingredients, packaging, sizes, and so on. Advertising copy adjusts accordingly, and salespeople must inform and persuade retailers to stock new product versions through price and promotion deals.

Finally, the decline arrives, and managers must decide whether to modify the product as a "new improved" offering or to introduce a new toothpaste entirely. Procter & Gamble, for example, has modified earlier Crest and Gleem brands, which became Crest Plus and Gleem II. Over the years, Procter & Gamble has also introduced new flavors and new ingredients to combat tartar, plaque, and gingivitis.

Sellers may be tempted to work products out of the decline stage by making cosmetic product changes and increasing advertising and/or promotion. For example, although introduced as a dandruff shampoo, consumers quickly accepted Procter & Gamble's Head & Shoulders, and it eventually became the best selling shampoo in the United States. However, after a while, Johnson's Baby Shampoo and other brands made competitive inroads and took leadership away from Head & Shoulders. The relative decline of Head & Shoulders was also related to consumer perceptions that the product was harsh on hair, particularly because most people used it every day to fit "the dry look" of the day. Procter & Gamble's research showed that their product was not significantly harsher than other shampoos, so they attempted to counter such "false" attributions with a change in advertising. In effect, their ads stressed the idea that Head & Shoulders left people's hair soft and manageable even after frequent washings. The campaign failed to return the product to its prior leadership role, so Procter & Gamble conducted further consumer research. This round of research showed that, despite advertising claims to the contrary, people still perceived the product as too harsh on hair because of the product's medicinal fragrance. Consumers' perceptions equated harshness (often subconsciously) with the fragrance, so many people would not buy the shampoo.

To counteract this trend, Procter & Gamble changed the fragrance and advertised a new, improved product. The subsequent success of the product over the years can be attributed, in part, to this change. The moral of this story is that marketers must often consider physical changes in their products rather than relying solely on advertising to make claims. The example also shows the role and value of consumer research. It illustrates again that people buy products not so much based on so-called objective criteria but rather based on subjective evaluations and judgments. A successful marketer of new products must study and understand the psychology of the consumer and how it relates to the product, the competition, and other socioeconomic forces (see chapter 4).

PRODUCT STRATEGY AND THE LARGER PICTURE

Now that we have described how firms develop new products and manage products throughout their life cycles, we step back and consider the overall role of product marketing decisions and specific product strategies that guide the whole process from beginning to end. Figure 8.4 shows how product decisions fit in with the whole marketing management process. Notice first that product decisions begin with the *overall organization goals*. Top management sets these ultimate ends and objectives necessary for the survival of the firm and the effective implementation of its mission. They typically formulate goals as targets related to profitability, return on investment, meeting customer needs, being socially responsible in terms of employment and pollution practices, and so on. Managers throughout the organization then plan resource use, including production, personnel, marketing, R&D, financial, accounting, and other programs to meet the firm's overall goals. As we see in chapters 2 and 16, each functional area has its own subgoals, which we term objectives.

Only *marketing objectives* appear in Figure 8.4, but, of course, the objectives of other functional areas interact with those of marketing. Marketing objectives reflect goals for sales, market share, market growth, product-line interactions, profitability, brand image, and so on. Although there is a fine line between marketing goals and the goals of the firm, marketing goals are usually derived from the firm's overall mission, but are typically more specific. Marketing objectives directly constrain and even determine *product objectives* and indirectly shape *product tactics*, the means to achieve those ends (see Fig. 8.4). Product objectives are even more specific and focused than marketing objectives. Along with objectives from other marketing areas, they typically serve as subgoals needed to achieve the broader marketing objectives.

Recall from chapter 2 that there are four different types of growth decisions faced by any firm: market penetration (existing products in existing markets), market expansion (existing products in new markets), narrowly construed new product development (new products in existing markets), and diversification (new products in new markets). Each strategy involves different, although sometimes overlapping, product decisions. Let us focus on the primary strategic product decisions facing most firms.

Product-Line Decisions

Managers must decide whether to market a single product, a full line of products, or a limited line of products. They consider many factors, such as the sizes of markets, consumer tastes, competition, profit forecasts, and the ability of the firm to manage the offerings, as they decide how many different products and how many brands of each product they should sell.

Large firms offer many product lines with multiple brands under each line and variations under each brand. For example, Procter & Gamble's major divisions include

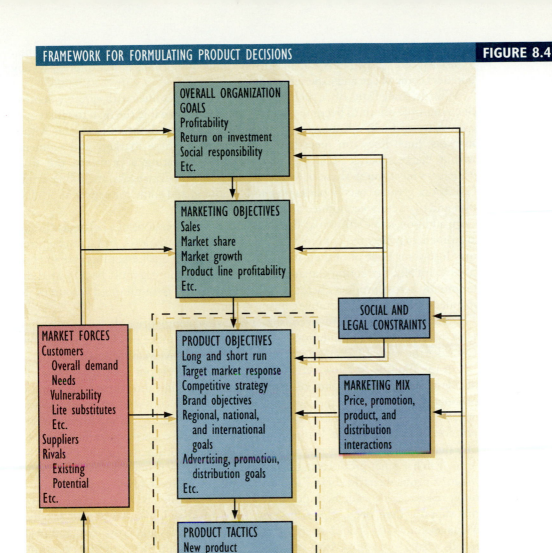

laundry and cleaning items, personal care, and traditional foods. Tide, Joy, and Comet are well-known brands under the first division. Ivory soap, Crest toothpaste, Scope mouthwash, and Prell and Head & Shoulders shampoos are leading brands under the second. Crisco oil, Duncan Hines cake mix, and Folger's coffee fall under the third. A *product line* classifies a group of brands under a product class. Thus P&G sells eight brands under the detergent line—Bold, Bonus, Cheer, Dash, Duz, Gain, Oxydol, and Tide—so the *length* of this product line is eight. *Width* refers to the number of different product lines a firm sells. Michelin sells maps, tires, and restaurant-rating services, and thus has a width of three. *Depth* refers to the number of variations of a typical brand. For example, Crest toothpaste comes in original flavor, mint gel, or mint paste in both tartar control and cavity protection formulas. In addition to traditional tubes, a "neat squeeze" dispenser is available. Even a gingivitis formula is now offered, as baby boomers come of age and experience gum problems.

Why do some firms offer such wide and long product lines with variable depths? Such multiple offerings become competitive tools that enable the firm to satisfy specific tastes and take advantage of different markets and different segments within markets. Such lines can meet customers' needs in these markets and segments within markets better than the competition, generating a profit to the firm. Managers must weigh these benefits against potential drawbacks, including cannibalization, greater costs in packaging and handling, and some reduction in production and marketing economies of scale.

In addition, some stores may decide not to stock all versions of a particular brand; customers may become confused by the many brand variations, and manufacturers may lose some control of their many products as their businesses increase in complexity. Finally, marketing expenditures and other resources must be allocated differentially across products because a firm seldom has the unlimited resources demanded by the different strategic business units.

Brand managers must weigh consumer tastes and competitive environments along with the capacities and limitations of a firm when they make product line decisions. Consider the case of Cuisinart and its food processors (Marketing Anecdote 8.1).

On the flip side of line-stretching and widening decisions, managers must also decide when to delete brands or product lines. Although they must take brand or product-line profitability into account, managers must consider other, less obvious criteria as well. One of these is the product's stage in its life cycle and management's best forecast for the future. Increasing competition and costs or dwindling numbers of potential new customers may support a decision to prune the product. Likewise, if the firm has other products in the growth stage or new product ideas that promise a better profit scenario, brand managers may prune their lines. If production or other resources are stretched too far and more profitable products cannot be given the support they need, the firm may have to abandon a less-viable product. Managers must pay special attention to product revenues and costs, cost and profit trends, changes in competitive responses, the health of the firm's product portfolio, resources in and outside of marketing, and consumer tastes.

Brand Decisions

Closely related to product-line decisions, managers must decide first whether to use brand names for its products or to sell them unbranded. Brand names offer definite advantages. For consumers, brand names can make shopping faster, because consumers may use brand names as cues to avoid wasteful searches and comparisons. Shopping can be less risky if brand names serve as symbols of quality, value, or some other sought-after asset. Sellers can use brand names to influence consumer behavior: consumers who have not tried a new product may try it because of their prior experiences with that particular brand. Manufacturers' reputations generalize or "rub off" on all of their brands. Consumers who have purchased the brand often may continue to do so without much deliberation and with essentially no comparisons to other offerings. Consumers do so because of habitual behavior and their tendency to mentally associate a frequently purchased brand with their needs and decision rules more strongly than other brands. Hence, from a firm's viewpoint, a brand can be both a promotional device and a competitive lever.

However, brands sometimes pose costs. Consumers can become too habitual when they automatically purchase a product without considering cheaper or better-quality

Cuisinart marketed a top-of-the-line food processor, which achieved a market niche among more affluent consumers. However, many buyers found the product too complex to clean and maintain, so they often left the product sitting in the cupboard. Enter Sunbeam. Sunbeam saw the need for a food processor that was less expensive, easier to use, and easier to clean and maintain. Hence the birth of Oskar. This is an example of one firm expanding or filling its product line in an existing market by positioning a new entry against the competition.

Should Cuisinart have offered a deeper product line? Possibly. By doing so it might have captured customers who either could not afford the top of the line or who did not want the hassle of a sophisticated product. In addition, a low-priced brand of Cuisinart might have "cultivated" the market: less affluent buyers may have learned to appreciate food processors more after using a simpler version, and later may have traded up to the top of the line. Moreover, younger buyers needed a less expensive alternative. When their income increases and they develop more sophisticated tastes, these early users become prime targets for better models.

On the other hand, Cuisinart had to weigh any damage done to its quality image by giving its name to lesser-priced models. Also, managers had to consider how much lower-line models might cannibalize their top brand's sales. Perhaps they could use a different brand name and/or design clearly different brands in terms of price and quality to avoid these problems. The new brand could be marketed through different retailers so as not to alienate current retailers. All these factors, such as whether to deepen a line and, if so, how to brand it, must be weighed in any product-line decisions. The issue here is sometimes termed a "line-stretching strategy." Should a firm attempt to market both high- and low-quality offerings of the same product? If so, how?

As it turned out, Cuisinart went bankrupt and was acquired by Conair in the early 1990s. Lee Rizzuto, the chairman of Conair, attributed Cuisinart's problems to the failure to add new products to its existing lines of processors and cookware.

Source: Some of the information here is from "Conair Head Planning Strategy for Cuisinarts," *New York Times,* January 2, 1989.

alternatives. For the seller, branding incurs expenses for special packages, promotion, and advertising. Also, the firm is especially vulnerable if the brand should, rightly or wrongly, get a bad name. Firestone tires, for example, experienced serious safety and legal problems with one of its lines of tires some time ago. The publicity was so negative that people avoided Firestone brands, and sales of the entire company suffered. Among other measures to correct this negative image, the company ran an expensive television advertising campaign with the late actor James Stewart as their spokesperson. A brand image is a fickle, yet important and powerful, asset for any firm.

Private or Dealer Brands

The alternative to branding is to sell *private* or *dealer brands.* The manufacturer can market similar products by putting retailer labels on them. Most supermarket chains, for instance, have their own private-label brands, which they sell along with the well-known brands. Manufacturers find dealer brands a chance to sell more volume than they might be able to sell strictly through their regular branded marketing. They can thus schedule more efficient production, capture economies of scale, and enjoy higher total sales. Consumers sometimes prefer private brands because they are cheaper and offer at least adequate quality. However, profit margins on private brands are typically lower. In addition, sales tend to fluctuate more, and the seller is relatively more vulnerable because sellers compete more fiercely with price with the relatively more standardized private brand. Private brands also pose somewhat more uncertainty and shopping effort for consumers relative to well-known brands. The manufacturer of branded goods is motivated more to maintain product quality. Sellers of national brands often assert, however, that their offerings are more reliable or higher in quality, convenience, or other desirable attributes.

Brand Strategy Issues

If a firm decides to employ a brand strategy, managers must address additional issues, such as whether to use individual brands for each product or a *family brand* (i.e., a single brand name across products). For example, General Foods creates individual brands for its products. More people are aware of Jell-O, Maxwell House coffee, Log Cabin syrup, and Sanka coffee than they are of the manufacturer, General Foods. In contrast, Kellogg and General Mills employ the family-brand strategy by attaching their name as an umbrella for each brand they sell (e.g., Kellogg's Rice Krispies, Kellogg's Frosted Flakes). Managers must also decide on what particular brand name to use. We have already discussed the effect of brand names on consumers. Sellers must select new brand names with forceful symbolic impacts and/or use existing names. Occasionally, new spin-offs of an old name are used: General Foods did so with Maxim freeze-dried coffee, suggesting a connection to its long-standing Maxwell House brand, as well as implying good quality or value.

A third brand-related issue concerns where to market (e.g., what market segment to pursue, whether to market internationally), and a fourth relates to marketing mix interactions—price, advertising, distribution, and so on.

Brand Equity

Figure 8.5 presents a useful framework for thinking about brand decisions. *Brand equity*, the focal point of brand decisions, is defined as "a set of brand assets and liabilities linked to a brand, its name and symbol, that add to or subtract from the value provided by a product or service to a firm and/or to that firm's customers."[14] A brand's value to a firm is manifest in brand loyalty, greater profitability, and leverage with the trade, among others.

To customers, brand equity facilitates information processing, leads to greater confidence in decision making, and, marketers hope, creates enhanced satisfaction. Underlying brand equity are five broad "assets": brand loyalty, brand awareness, perceived quality, brand associations, and other proprietary brand assets.

Brand loyalty encourages customers to buy a particular brand time after time and remain insensitive to competitors' offerings. Brand loyalty varies by product class. For example, nearly two thirds of all consumers of mayonnaise are loyal to a single brand, whereas only about one in four buyers are loyal to a particular brand of athletic shoes. Some buyers may become brand loyal because a particular brand

FIGURE 8.5

Source: David A. Aaker, Managing Brand Equity: Capitalizing on the Value of a Brand Name *(New York: Free Press, 1991), inside cover. Reprinted with permission.*

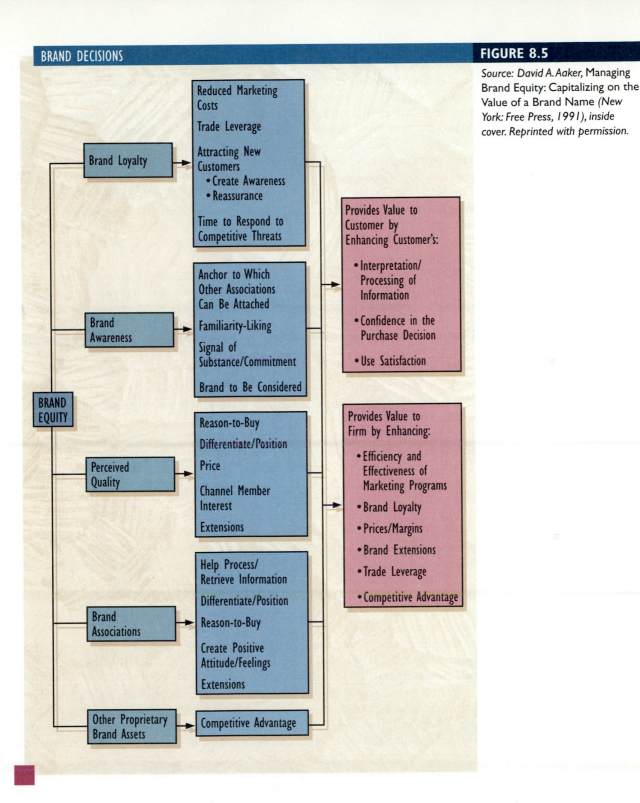

satisfices (i.e., "is good enough"), and they do not find product or price differentials worthwhile to change brands. Frequently purchased, relatively low-priced items such as toothpaste, dry cleaning services, and soft drinks often fit this picture; in economic terms, demand for these items is price inelastic. Sellers frequently go to great lengths to advertise, price, and promote such products to get people to switch brands because they can just charge higher prices to loyal customers.

Other consumers become brand loyal for deeper reasons. Consumers start to see a particular brand as part of their personality or social identity to such an extent that loyalty develops. This happens most obviously when people adopt certain brands of cosmetics, automobiles, and clothing. But it can be a factor as well with their choice of restaurants, hair-care establishments, and even such everyday products as candy bars. In England, preferences for the all purpose sauce, HP, has reached near cult-like proportions because it is such a distinctive product and people identify with it.

Another aspect of brand equity is known simply as *brand awareness*. Brand names attract attention, convey images of familiarity, serve as cues in classical conditioning or reinforcements in instrumental learning, or initiate information processing. Brand names go only so far, however. Life Savers candies have a loyal following, but when the manufacturer tried to extend the brand name to Life Savers gum, consumers did not accept transfer of the brand image to the new product and the product flopped.

Brand names can be abstract symbols for the *quality* of the product or service they represent. Marriott Hotel's "Marriott Margins" name suggests superb quality, whereas its Fairfield Inn subsidiary conveys lower-quality ("economy"). The quality imagery of a brand can be maintained or coopted by competitors who wish to enhance their own product's images and lower their competitor's perceived value. Consider the following headline from a classic print ad for fine china: "Royal Doulton. The China of Stoke-on-Trent, England" versus "Lenox. The China of Pomona, New Jersey." What does this convey to consumers?

Brand associations refer to ideas, values, and other information linked to a focal brand. Sellers attempt to connect as many positively valued thoughts to a brand as possible because managers believe that consumers' attitudes toward, and preferences for, brands are formed via such associations. Recent research has demonstrated how brand names, brand attitudes, and information associated with a brand are acquired, stored, and used in memory for decision making. This research provides guidance on how to communicate more effectively with consumers, and can be found in recent volumes of the *Journal of Consumer Research*, among other journals.

Other proprietary brand assets include patents, trademarks, and marketing channel relationships. Each of these protects the integrity of the brand name and ensures that competitors will find inroads into the market difficult.

In sum, brand equity provides value to customers by enhancing efficient information processing and shopping, building confidence in decision making, reinforcing buying, and contributing to self-esteem. Brand equity helps sellers increase marketing efficiency and effectiveness, build brand loyalty, improve profit margins, gain leverage over retailers, and achieve distinctiveness over the competition.

Managers must make many specific decisions concerning a brand. One of these is the brand name itself. Typically, firms turn to professionals to find a name for their products. The overall goal is to create a memorable, compatible name that conveys desirable images. More specifically, researchers have identified at least five characteristics of a successful brand name: ideally a brand name should (1) be distinctive (e.g., Microsoft, Fidelity Investments, Prodigy); (2) be easy to pronounce, recognize, recall, and store in memory (e.g., Coca-Cola, Jeep); (3) suggest something about the product's benefits (e.g., Acuvue disposable contact lenses); (4) suggest the attributes of the product (e.g., Compaq); and (5) avoid misleading, nontranslatable, or potentially dysfunctional associations. Some firms have been known to use the same brand name or a literal translation of the brand name when marketing internationally. The potential problems with the following require no comment: Green Pile (a Japanese lawn dressing), Creap (a Japanese coffee creamer), Super Piss (a Finnish aid for unfreezing car locks), and Bum (a Spanish brand of potato crisps or chips).[15]

Beyond naming a brand, managers face another decision. Any brand, once established, will produce images in customers' minds. Typically, the image will relate to the brand's scores on two or three salient product attributes. For example, Excedrin is perceived to be one of the most effective analgesics, but harsh on the stomach; Tylenol is perceived to be somewhat less effective than Excedrin, but gentler to the stomach. If consumers perceive a firm's brand at a disadvantage vis-à-vis the competition, or if the brand appeals to a narrow, unprofitable segment of the market, management may have to reposition the product. Should it change consumer's perceptions via advertising, change the physical product, or both? A lot depends on the target "repositioning" of the brand. Does the technology exist for achieving the new position? For instance, can Excedrin change its formula to increase gentleness to the stomach without decreasing its effectiveness? If so, how much will this cost and will enough consumers value the change? How much will it cost to change the image of the product? Will the competition counter by challenging the new claims or by improving its own product? Such are decisions faced by brand managers. Marketing Anecdote 8.2 points out how the roles of brand managers are changing.

As a final comment, note that brand managers should pay heed to the meanings of their brands to consumers. We can think of consumers' brand knowledge in two senses: brand awareness and brand image associations.[16] Brand awareness pays dividends in two ways. First, top of the mind awareness aids in the recall of the brand name when consumers self-initiate their decision-making activities. Sellers of soft drinks, fast-food services, and magazines invest in brand name management because they want customers to immediately think of their brands when they are thirsty, hungry, or in need of reading materials at the airport. Second, awareness in the sense of brand recognition helps sellers stimulate sales when consumers are not actively engaged in decision making, or even when they are. The sight of a new Gucci purse may rekindle a desire to acquire this luxury good; or when considering the purchase of a stereo system for the first time, a young consumer might be swayed by recognition of the name Bang & Olufsen.

Brand knowledge also resides in brand image associations in which beliefs about a brand are interconnected in memory in distinctive ways. Brand image associations occur with respect to at least three areas. First, product and service attributes cluster together by brand in consumers' minds. Some of these are, of course, product related, such as the sweetness and carbonation of a soft drink. Some are non–product related such as the price, packaging, user imagery, and usage imagery connected to a product. Designer beers, for example, are high priced, come in fancy bottles and packages, and convey images of sophisticated drinkers and exclusive restaurants.

Second, benefits of products and services pattern themselves in systematic ways in consumers' memories. Generally, knowledge of benefits organize by functional, experiential, or symbolic associations. Cuisinart's Deluxe Pasta Machine, a top-of-the-line kitchen appliance, makes well-formed, uniform shapes; provides a sense of accomplishment, pride, and recognition; and links some consumers symbolically to their ancestors and Italy.

As we will discuss more fully in chapter 16, brand management involves two key parts: designing and implementing tactics to influence sales. To take packaged goods as an example, a brand manager's task involves specifying the nature and amount of couponing and in-store promotions, advising the advertising account manager and media planners about key product attributes to stress and sociodemographic and psychometric profiles of customers, working with financial planners on pricing, coordinating new package designs with production, reporting to strategic planners on trends in sales and competitor inroads, informing distributors of changes in packaging, and researching the impact of contemplated line extensions. In short, brand managers act as generalists, filling their time with many varied activities.

As central as these activities are, firms have exhibited a trend recently toward more integrated marketing within the firm and improving relationships with final and intermediate customers outside the firm. The trend is generally known as *information-driven marketing and relationship marketing*, a variant of so-called "relationship marketing."

Procter & Gamble is a leader in this movement, which they term efficient consumer response (ECR). Under ECR, P&G and retailers work together to optimize sales and profits. Stores track with scanners, and P&G and retailers evaluate sales in response to pricing, couponing, advertising, and other changes in the marketing mix and environment. For the retailer, the information provides guidance on shelf-space allocation, the number of national and dealer brands to stock, and product pricing, among other areas. For P&G, the information can improve distribution, pricing, deals and promotion, and advertising decisions. In addition, point-of-sale information can guide brand addition or deletion decisions.

In the long run, information-driven marketing can match customer needs with product offerings and thereby increase profits and lower prices. However, retailers will likely offer less variety, and consumers may come to see brands as exhibiting few real differences. Thus, the role of brand image in particular and brand equity in general could be reduced. Likewise, P&G and large retailers might develop stronger partnerships, with uncertain effects on consumers. P&G might even have to rethink its broader strategies. Up until now,

---

Third, brand attitudes and emotions also group together in structural relationships. A favorite resort in Cancun, for example, might conjure up complex feelings of excitement, affection, and thrill seeking.

Brand image associations vary in their favorability, strength, and uniqueness. Managers try to create brand images that convey benefits, attitudes, and emotions that are not only satisfying in their own right but are distinctive from competitors. Publicity related to brand image can take unusual turns, as illustrated by Marketing Anecdote 8.3 on page 324.

QUALITY MANAGEMENT

Brand managers need to view their jobs as managing the total quality of their products or services. Quality function deployment (QFD) is one way of thinking about bridging the gap between product concepts and actual realization of physical products meeting customers' and firms' goals.[17] QFD is a procedure for allocating in-

P&G has striven to be a market leader. Indeed, it sells the leading brand in about half of the 40 or so categories in which it competes and is among the top three brands in nearly 35 of the 40 categories. But as the ECR system becomes fine-tuned, P&G may have to consider abandoning some geographical markets and discontinuing national brands in some instances. This will inevitably threaten P&G's market share dominance in some categories. On the other hand, its profitability in these categories should increase.

Consider the recent marketing changes P&G made in the dishwashing liquid detergent market. Following its success with concentrated laundry detergents in the early 1990s, P&G decided to introduce concentrated dishwashing liquids for its Dawn, Ivory, and Joy brands. This was a dangerous strategy for P&G, since over the years it has controlled nearly half of the $700 million light-duty dishwashing liquid market. Would consumers value a concentrated dishwashing detergent? Unlike laundry detergents, where a similar change resulted in significant space savings, liquid dishwasher containers are not all that big to begin with. Moreover, unless consumers perceive cost savings by using a concentrate, they are not likely to see a real benefit in the new product form. Thus, advertising had its work cut out for it if it was to educate and convince the consumer of the benefits of a concentrate. P&G has historically been patient in waiting for new products to become successes: Pringles took many years to reach profit goals. But the ECR campaign may not be so forgiving for the new concentrates. And the competition may play on the uncertainty and confusion among consumers. Should P&G market a concentrate in a container smaller than the 22-ounce standard? If it does, competitors could point out the seemingly greater value offered by its larger, nonconcentrated versions. If P&G opts for a smaller container, they will need to take special effort to persuade consumers that they will reap savings.

There are two further problems for P&G. A change to smaller bottles for concentrated liquid dishwashing detergents forces retailers to alter shelf layouts, rethink the marketing of dealer brands, and/or separate the new concentrates from the dealer brands. Second, as consumers eat out more in restaurants or use more convenience foods with disposable containers, the demand for liquid dishwashing detergents could decline in general.

puts in the form of costs, quality, reliability, technology, and other factors so that the final attributes of a product are created and put together in a manner meeting consumer needs.[18]

Figure 8.6 on page 325 presents a QFD matrix for personal computers. To perform QFD, managers must determine the benefits consumers seek, the importance consumers assign to these benefits, specifications of the product potentially linked to the benefits, consumer perceptions of where each competing brand scores on each benefit, and objective scores of competitors on specifications.

To keep the illustration simple, Figure 8.6 lists only three consumer benefits sought: ease of use, usefulness, and fun. However, not only will most products have more than three benefits, each benefit may be described at different levels of abstraction and specificity, and each benefit may have subaspects under it. Thus, for example, usefulness might be expressed with regard to the scope of analyses that can be performed on the computer; ease of use might be broken down into convenience of controls, number and placement of icons, quality of presentation of help menus

Kenny Rogers Roasters fast-food chain, a rotisserie-chicken restaurant, had 258 outlets worldwide at last count. But its outlet on Broadway between 71st and 72nd Streets in New York City had an unexpected antagonist in 1996. A lawyer working upstairs and upwind from the restaurant could no longer take the never-ending aroma of roasted chicken and hung a sign out of his window with the words, "Bad chicken," and an arrow, "↓", pointing directly down to the restaurant below. Needless to say, the media attention given to this incident was disconcerting to management.

Where's Kramer? His taste for Kenny Rogers Roasters boosted sales nationwide.

The company, however, experienced an unusual turn of events. Writers for the popular television comedy, *Seinfeld*, heard of the incident and turned it into a humorous episode. The character, Kramer, the disgruntled citizen, this time protesting the effect of the neon "Roasters" sign on his sleep habits. The episode ends with Kramer admitting, "I'm hooked on [Kenny Rogers'] chicken." Sales across the country reputedly increased by as much as 18 percent as a result of the episode's showing. With advertising costing about $1 million on *Seinfeld* and other popular shows, the free publicity of many minutes on the show was certainly a welcome event.

and manuals, and so on. Likewise we have listed only nine product specifications (e.g., motherboard, processor, RAM, and so on), but we could have included others and elaborated upon each.

Near the right of the top matrix in Figure 8.6 appear consumer perceptions of where three computers—a focal firm's brand and two competitors—score on each of the three benefits. Notice that competitor B is perceived to be the easiest to use, competitor A the most difficult to use, and the focal brand in between. The importance ratings reveal that the segment of buyers represented in this example give usefulness high priority and are less interested in ease of use and fun. The feature comparisons in the middle matrix contrast the three computer brands on product specifications, which, unlike the subjective judgments reflected in consumer perceptions, are objective assessments. The top matrix of Figure 8.6 shows the relationship or correlation between consumer benefits and product specifications, where H indicates a high correlation, L a low correlation, and no entry the absence of any association. For example, usefulness is highly correlated with the motherboard, RAM, and processor, but has a low correlation with the hard drive, and is not correlated with the other specifications.

Managers provide the entries in the QFD matrix based on research (e.g., surveys, experimentation), experience, and intuition. A team of managers across functions

EXAMPLE OF QUALITY FUNCTIONAL DEPLOYMENT FOR PERSONAL COMPUTERS — FIGURE 8.6

PRODUCT SPECIFICATIONS

Consumer Benefits	Motherboard	Hard drive	RAM	Floppy drive	Processor	CD-ROM	Video card	Sound card	Footprint	etc.	Consumer perceptions 1 2 3 4 5	Importance ratings
Ease of use		L		H					L		A F B	3
Usefulness	H	L	H		H						A,B F	5
Fun						H	H	H			F A B	2
etc.												

FEATURE COMPARISONS

	Motherboard	Hard drive	RAM	Floppy drive	Processor	CD-ROM	Video card	Sound card	Footprint
Firm's brand	5	3	5	4	5	3	3	3	2
Competitor A	3	3	4	1	3	3	3	2	3
Competitor B	3	3	3	5	3	4	4	4	4
etc.									

F = Firm's brand
A = Competitor A
B = Competitor B
H = High correlation
L = Low correlation

	Motherboard	Hard drive	RAM	Floppy drive	Processor	CD-ROM	Video card	Sound card	Footprint
Target specifications	5	4	5	5	5	4	4	4	3
Cost to achieve	5	3	4	2	5	4	3	3	4

Note all ratings are on 5-point scales, 1=lowest; 5=highest

(e.g., brand managers, design engineers, production managers, R&D personnel) typically computes the matrix through consensus.

Managers use the QFD matrix to identify linkages between benefits perceived by consumers and specifications under managers' control. The matrix might suggest which existing specifications are already key determinants of customer satisfaction and which ones might be improved. Use of the matrix could also kindle a need to search for new specifications correlated with consumer benefits.

To continue our example, we see in Figure 8.6 that the focal computer brand scores worse than competitor B on ease of use, which is regarded as a moderately important benefit by consumers. Notice also that the type of floppy drive is the specification most influential, and the hard drive and footprint are less influential regarding ease of use. However, as shown under feature comparisons, the focal brand scores the lowest of all on footprint, somewhat below competitor B on floppy drive, and the same as both competitors on hard drive. To improve its competitive position, the focal computer brand may have to improve its footprint and floppy drive. The bottom of Figure 8.6 presents the target specifications, according to managers, that are needed to produce benefits equal to or better than the competition. Of course, whether the Focal Firm will make the changes will depend on the costs and anticipated gains in revenue.

The final point we wish to make with respect to QFD analyses is that these must be applied and integrated with all relevant areas of the firm. For example, managers' decisions to upgrade or add to specifications of a personal computer must be evaluated by and coordinated with procurement, manufacturing, distribution, and other functions. Then, too, quality decisions are not limited to the physical product. Managers must also focus on service quality by considering gaps between expected and perceived service outcomes by consumers, gaps between actual service delivery and communication of service delivery to consumers, gaps between intended and actual service delivery quality, and gaps between intended service delivery and consumer expectations.[19]

SUMMARY

Sales of products pass through stages of growth and decline, but it is difficult to predict which specific stages they will pass through and when transitions will occur. The idealized S-shaped curve in Figure 8.1 approximates the evolution of many products in their life cycles. The pattern is demarcated into phases of introduction, growth, maturity, and decline.

The important precept for managers to realize is that any progression along a life cycle is neither inevitable nor beyond their control. Indeed, managers can influence the timing, duration, and level of the life cycle to a certain extent by:

- periodically making strategic changes to the product
- strategically applying marketing mix tactics in support of the product.

Table 8.3 lists common tactics that can be employed to manage the product throughout its life cycle.

Product decisions interface with decisions in other areas of marketing and the firm. Figure 8.4 summarizes the important points here. Specific product decisions include product line decisions, brand decisions, the decision to use private or dealer brands, and brand strategy decisions. Brand equity was covered in Fig. 8.5.

In considering quality management, quality function deployment (QFD) is a procedure for allocating inputs in product design in a manner producing consumer benefits and achieving a competitive advantage.

QUESTIONS FOR DISCUSSION

1. What is the concept of a product life cycle? What problems does it pose? What implications does the PLC have for management?

2. Define brand equity and discuss its implications for management and how it can be created and controlled.

3. What are the major choices involved in product-line decisions? When should each be implemented?

4. What are the pros and cons of branding? When should dealer brands be considered?

5. What is the purpose of quality function deployment? Discuss how it is applied.

NOTES FOR FURTHER READING

1. For a recent review of the literature on the PLC concept, see David R. Rink and John E. Swan, "Product Life Cycle Research: A Literature Review," *Journal of Business Research* 7 (September 1979): 219–242. See also Yoram Wind, *Product Policy: Concepts, Methods, and Strategy* (Reading, Mass.: Addison-Wesley, 1982); and George S. Day, "The Product Life Cycle: Analysis and Applications Issues," *Journal of Marketing* 45 (Fall 1981): 60–67.

2. Nariman K. Dhalla and Sonia Yuspeh, "Forget the Product Life Cycle Concept!" *Harvard Business Review*, (January–February 1976), pp. 102–112.

3. Robert D. Buzzell, "Competitive Behavior and Product Life Cycle," in J. S. Wright and J. L. Goldstucker, eds., *New Ideas for Successful Marketing* (Chicago: American Marketing Association, 1966), pp. 46–48; William E. Cox, Jr., "Product Life Cycles as Marketing Models," *Journal of*

Business 40 (October 1967): 375–84; Rolando Polli and Victor Cook, "Validity of the Product Life Cycle," *Journal of Business* 42 (October 1962): 385–400; and Frank M. Bass, "A New Product Growth Model for Consumer Durables," *Management Science* 15 (January 1969): 215–217.

4. Buzzell, "Competitive Behavior and Product Life Cycles."

5. M. T. Cummingham, "The Application of Product Life Cycles to Corporate Strategy: Some Research Findings," *British Journal of Marketing* 33 (Spring 1969): 32–44.

6. Cox, "Product Life Cycles as Marketing Models"; Buzzell, "Competitive Behavior and Product Life Cycles"; Rink and Swan, "Product Life Cycle Research."

7. See Wind, *Product Policy*, for a discussion of some of these issues.

8. One new direction of research in this regard concerns work across firms in industrial, consumer, and other industries. Preliminary work with Profit Impact of Market Strategy (PIMS) data shows that the PLC concept has wide generalizability and interacts in predictable ways with market structure, performance, and strategic marketing decision variables. See, for example, Hans B. Thorelli and Stephen C. Burnett, "The Nature of Product Life Cycles for Industrial Goods Businesses," *Journal of Marketing* 45 (Fall 1981): 76–80.

9. William Qualls, Richard W. Olshavsky, and Ronald E. Michaels, "Shortening of the PLC—An Empirical Test," *Journal of Marketing* 45 (Fall 1981): 76–80.

10. Qualls, Olshavsky, and Michaels, "Shortening of the PLC."

11. Adapted from data appearing in ibid.

12. For a discussion of the Tide situation, see David S. Hopkins, *Business Strategies for Problem Products* (New York: Conference Board, 1977).

13. Theodore Levitt, "Exploit the Product Life Cycle," *Harvard Business Review*, November–December 1965, pp. 81–94.

14. David A. Aaker, *Managing Brand Equity: Capitalizing on the Value of a Brand Name* (New York: Free Press, 1991), p. 15.

15. Kim Robertson, "Strategically Desirable Brand Name Characteristics," *Journal of Consumer Marketing* (Fall 1989): 61–70.

16. Kevin Lane Keller, "Conceptualizing, Measuring, and Managing Customer-Based Brand Equity," *Journal of Marketing* 57 (January 1993): 1–22.

17. John R. Hauser and Don Clausing, "The House of Quality," *Harvard Business Review*, May–June 1988, pp. 63–73; John R. Hartley, *Concurrent Engineering* (Cambridge, Mass.: Productivity Press, 1992).

18. Vincent P. Barabba and Gerald Zaltman, *Hearing the Voice of the Market* (Cambridge, Mass.: Harvard Business School Press, 1991).

19. Valerie A. Zeithaml, A. Parasuraman, and Leonard L. Berry, "A Conceptual Model of Service Quality and Its Implications for Future Research," *Journal of Marketing* 49 (Fall 1985): 41–50.

CHAPTER 9

MARKETING COMMUNICATION

CHAPTER OBJECTIVES

When you are done with this chapter, you should have achieved the following:

- A basic familiarity with the various models and concepts that describe and explain communication's importance to a marketing effort.
- A grasp of elements of the promotion mix.
- A familiarity with the elaboration likelihood model and the emotion and adaptation model.
- A basic understanding of how managers make communication decisions.

CHAPTER OUTLINE

Communication Is More Than Meets the Eye (or Ear)

What do you think the following have in common: Lay's potato chips, Fritos, Cheetos, Tostitos, Rold Gold pretzels, Doritos, Smartfood popcorn, Ruffles potato chips, and Sunchips? If you guessed "salty snacks," you are correct. What you may not know, however, is that these are all brands from Frito-Lay, a division of PepsiCo. Frito-Lay, a master marketer of salty snacks, captures 42 percent of what is estimated to be a $13.4 billion market in the United States each year.

Most firms rely on communication as their main mechanism for stimulating sales. It is also the glue that binds together the many pieces of the marketing mix. What are Frito-Lay's communication tactics? Probably what comes to mind first is advertising. In 1991 Frito-Lay spent $14.6 million to advertise its new Sunchips brand; it spent about $13.8 million each to advertise its Frito and Dorito snacks. But Frito-Lay's communication program goes far beyond advertising.

To learn about what consumers desire, Frito-Lay asks them directly. In a typical year it conducts hundreds of taste tests as well as 500,000 interviews with consumers. It spends $20 million on research and development alone. The information gained in these ways is used to guide new-product development, advertising and promotion strategies, pricing, and distribution decisions. For instance, the company emphasizes quality control in order to produce snacks with the thickness, texture, and taste desired by consumers. Consumers are not all alike, however, so different product formulations are targeted to different regions of the country. People in the northern states, for example, prefer chips that are fried longer. (Perhaps you have noticed that potato chips sold in the North are darker than those sold in the South.)

Communication informs all decisions at Frito-Lay—even the shades of blue and gold used on the packaging for Ruffles potato chips, which were chosen on the basis of information gained from consumer focus groups. Using demographic data and other facts about consumers, the company adjusts the brands and amounts of products it sells to supermarkets throughout the nation so that customers in different regions, cities, and even neighborhoods can buy the snacks they prefer. Using handheld computers, its 10,000 salespeople, or "communication specialists," keep track of competitors' activities and the amounts of its brands on store shelves and notify headquarters immediately about important developments. Through these and other forms of communication, Frito-Lay maintains its dominant position in the marketplace.

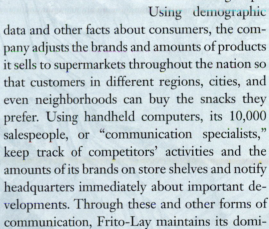

Snack food manufacturers need to communicate their products' salient features to differentiate their offerings from lots of other alternatives.

Sources: Advertising Age, September 23, 1992, p. 51.

Robert Johnson, "In the Chips—At Frito-Lay, the Consumer Is an Obsession," *Wall Street Journal,* March 22, 1991, Sec. B, p. 1.

Jennifer Lawrence, "Frito's Micro Move," *Advertising Age,* February 12, 1990, p. 44.

From a marketing management perspective, communication has two main goals: to inform and to influence another party. By *inform*, we mean to provide information so that decision makers can make up their own minds. For example, when an advertiser conveys a list of product attributes, the price of its brand, or the place where it may be purchased, it informs the public about its offerings. The goal is primarily to create awareness or remind consumers about a brand. By *influence*, we mean to stimulate desire, change attitudes, shape decisions, or cause an action. When advertisers use emotional appeals, retailers offer a rebate, or salespeople make a concession, they are trying to influence consumers. Note that the line between informing and influencing is often blurred. Marketing communications try to achieve both goals.

A CLASSIC MODEL OF COMMUNICATION

Figure 9.1 presents an outline of the source-message-media-receiver (SMMR) model of communication, whose origins can be traced at least as far back as Aristotle. In this chapter we provide an updated version of this model, because in many ways it is still valid and can serve to organize the study of marketing communication.[1]

Before we examine the parts of the SMMR model, let us briefly describe it in global terms. Beginning at the left side of Figure 9.1, we see that a *sender or communicator* desires to make contact with a potential receiver. This is done by preparing a *message*, a set of symbols used to express meaning. As we shall discover, the decisions of what to say (message content) and how to say it (message structure) are complex, with many parts and options. The message itself must then be conveyed in some way, and this involves the choice of one or more *media*. Messages may be conveyed through either personal (face-to-face) or nonpersonal (mass media) channels. Each of these alternatives can take a variety of forms, which we describe later in this chapter and in the next chapter. The communication process "ends" with a *receiver* decoding, processing, and interpreting the message and reacting in some way. If the sender monitors and picks up a reaction on the part of the receiver, we say that *feedback* has occurred. All of the processes outlined in Figure 9.1 occur within an environment in which interference or distortion (i.e., "noise") can thwart communication.

We are now in a position to discuss the SMMR model in greater detail, beginning with the sender. In the discussion that follows, keep in mind that each element represents a unique determinant of receiver's behavior. Whether a person will engage in that behavior (e.g., purchase brand X) depends on the sender's characteristics, the nature of the message, the power of the media, and the receiver's attributes.

The Sender

Potential buyers pay the most attention to three specific characteristics of the sender: credibility, attractiveness, and mediation of rewards and punishments.

Source Credibility

Imagine that the advertiser of a pain remedy had two options for a television spot. One consisted of an unknown elderly announcer describing a new ingredient and explaining why arthritis sufferers should try the brand that contains it. The second employed exactly the same message but used Robert Young to deliver it. Young, a familiar actor to millions of elderly Americans, played the title role in the 1970s TV series, *Marcus Welby, M.D.* The advertiser, of course, wanted to achieve the

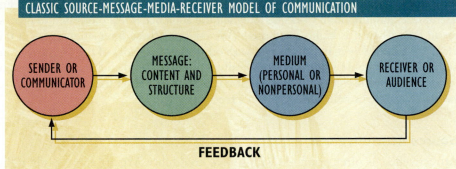

SENDER OR COMMUNICATOR

MESSAGE: CONTENT AND STRUCTURE

MEDIUM (PERSONAL OR NONPERSONAL)

RECEIVER OR AUDIENCE

FEEDBACK

most effective advertising at the lowest possible cost. We know that an ad using Robert Young as spokesperson would have been more expensive, but would it have been more effective? Intuitively, you might guess that the ad with Robert Young was perceived as more credible than the ad with an unknown announcer. And indeed, research indicates that source credibility often increases attitude change, persuasion, and even desired behaviors. But what exactly is a credible source? Would the ad have been even more "credible" with a Nobel Prize–winning medical researcher as the spokesperson? To answer these questions, let us look at the meaning of credibility in greater depth.[2]

Buyers assess a source's credibility based on the source's expertise and trustworthiness. Consumers will perceive sources as expert if they are believed to be highly educated, to have considerable first-hand experience, or to be particularly competent. We tend to believe the persuasive appeals of experts more than those of nonexperts, and this is especially true when the education, experience, and/or competence of the speaker is strongly related to the issue at hand. If we have car trouble, for example, we are likely to place more credence in the master mechanic's assessment than a local pharmacist's opinion. But the master mechanic's opinion on the best medication for a skin problem would be less valued than the pharmacist's. Source expertise may also be related to status (i.e., the higher the status, the higher the perceived expertise).[3] Thus advertisers sometimes enhance the effects of their messages by using high-status spokespersons.

Source trustworthiness refers to the audience's perception that the sources are honest and sincere in their intentions.[4] We generally attribute greater trustworthiness to speakers who do not appear to have a vested interest in the behavior being advocated. This partly explains why advertisements and personal selling are not always effective: We usually perceive advertisers and sellers as standing to gain from a sale, so we tend to discount their messages. The trick is to use a credible source who does not appear to be acting solely out of self-interest.

Another aspect of trustworthiness is consistency. Sources who exhibit the same behavior and advocate the same arguments over time are more likely to be perceived as trustworthy. Spokespeople who switch positions too often or do so for insufficient or self-serving reasons are seen as less trustworthy. During his two terms in office, President Clinton was often perceived as flip-flopping on such issues as welfare and medical care, and this hurt his public image.

Source credibility—that is, perceived expertise and trustworthiness—affects an audience in several ways. Clearly, a spokesperson's credibility rubs off on the message content and makes the receiver more likely to view it as valid. In addition, credibility interacts in complex ways with characteristics of the message, media, and receiver. For example, credibility often works better when the audience is less motivated to process an ad than when it is highly motivated. (We consider these interactions later in this chapter.) Credibility may also interact with other characteristics of the source. For instance, most credible sources are physically attractive, command unusual respect or sympathy, or exude charisma. Often those characteristics, rather than credibility per se, produce attitude or behavior change in a receiver.

Source Attractiveness

Attractiveness is often confused with source credibility. We are more easily influenced by people to whom we are attracted.[5] Why is this so? One reason might be that we feel more comfortable and less threatened by someone we like or with whom we are familiar. Another reason might be that attraction itself, through emotional processes, produces attitude change and behavioral compliance. Still another reason is that the receiver feels a need to identify with an attractive source. This is similar to the notion of referent power.[6] A more cognitive explanation is that an attractive source (relative to an unattractive one) causes a receiver to inflate the utility of a message from that source.[7] For example, research shows that people believe the promises of an attractive source more than they do the promises of an unattractive one, whereas audiences believe the threats from an unattractive source more than those same threats from an attractive one.

These findings suggest that communication and influence will be enhanced when spokespersons or salespeople are physically or socially attractive. However, advertisers do not want the attraction to be so strong that it detracts from the content of the message and the ability of the audience to evaluate a brand, develop a positive attitude, and decide to buy the brand. One study indicates that even low levels of attraction (similarity, in this case) between salesperson and customer may be sufficient to produce a sale.[8]

Mediation of Rewards and Punishments

Another way in which a source can influence receivers is through mediation of rewards and punishments.[9] Two factors need to be considered: capability and intentionality. Capability means that the source can control rewarding and/or punishing stimuli and communicate this ability to the receiver. However, it is not sufficient to merely possess the ability to control rewards or punishments. The source must also be willing to use this capability, and the receiver must understand that the source can and will do so under the appropriate conditions.

The potential to mediate rewards and/or punishments affects the communication process. Perhaps the most obvious effect is the use of extreme amounts of reward or punishment as the sole means of influence. The compliance of the receiver is obtained through the pleasure-seeking power of a reward or the pain-avoidance power of a punishment, rather than through rational choice, per se. An example of this sometimes occurs during negotiations between buyers and sellers of homes when one party or the other threatens in exasperation to withdraw from negotiating. More common in marketing is the administration of a small reward or punishment as an auxiliary to an exchange between a buyer and seller. For example, in addition to exchanging a product for money, manufacturers may offer small gifts, provide entertainment, promise additional services, give cash discounts for prompt payment, and so forth as part of transactions with an industrial or retail buyer. Many other physical, psychological, and social rewards

TABLE 9.1 SUMMARY OF SOURCE CHARACTERISTICS IN THE COMMUNICATION PROCESS	
Source Characteristic	**Description**
Credibility	*Source expertise:* Buyers perceive competence, education, experience, and other expertise of source.
	Source trustworthiness: Buyers perceive honesty, sincerity, accommodation, nonbias, and consistency of source.
Attractiveness	Buyers perceive similarity, familiarity, liking, and other attributes of source.
Mediator of Rewards or and/or Punishments	Buyers perceive that source is capable of providing rewards or punishments and is willing to administer them.

and punishments sometimes accompany formal exchanges. An example of an implied punishment is the seller's warning that after a future date the price for the advertised product will increase.

Final Comments on the Sender

As a summary, Table 9.1 presents the source variables that are common in most communication situations. Again, note that these represent only some of the possible determinants of receiver behavior. As shown in Figure 9.1, characteristics of the message, media, and receiver also influence receiver behavior.

Note that source characteristics and other determinants influence receiver behavior in two ways. First, each cause has a direct effect on the receiver, independent of any other cause. This type of influence is known as a *main effect.* For example, source credibility can influence the purchase intentions of a receiver regardless of the nature of the message and the personality of the receiver. A second way in which the variables shown in Figure 9.1 influence the receiver is by interacting with other variables; such effects are termed *interaction effects.* For instance, research shows that appeals to fear only work, or work best, when the source is highly credible. When the source has very little credibility, appeals to fear in a persuasive argument usually lack impact.[10]

The Message

Communicators must consider both message content and message structure options to reach an audience effectively. Table 9.2 lists the major options available when deciding on the content and structure of a message. Note that the art of communication reflects an optimal combination of message content and structure. In chapter 10 we describe how advertisers strategically combine content and structure. It turns out that each advertising agency tends to have its own unique approach—its own personality—which is reflected in the way message content and structure are executed. We term this the agency's "creative style." Message content and structure go hand in hand, and we separate them in Table 9.2 only for purposes of discussion.

Rational Appeals

In a message with rational appeal, a set of facts is presented, perhaps with a conclusion, and an appeal made to the receiver's ability to reason. The communicator presents the content dispassionately and logically. Marketers typically apply rational appeals by

TABLE 9.2 KEY MESSAGE VARIABLES IN THE COMMUNICATION PROCESS: WHAT TO SAY (MESSAGE CONTENT) AND HOW TO SAY IT (MESSAGE STRUCTURE)

Message Content	Message Structure
Rational Appeals	One-sided versus Two-sided Appeals
Product attributes	
Consequences of use	Order of Presentation of Arguments
Emotional Appeals	Amount of Information
Positive or negative mood	
Humor	Repetition
Fear	
Extraneous Factors	
Distraction and counterargumentation	
Use of foil	

describing specific product attributes to suggest benefits of using or owning the product. Such consequences might be utilitarian, physical, psychological, or social. The objective is to speak to the receivers' thought processes.

Rational appeals are probably used most often by salespeople selling industrial products or consumer durable goods. Nevertheless, we often see rational appeals in ads for everyday products such as floor cleaners, detergents, and lawn-care products. Rational appeals are especially useful when products have functional characteristics, are used to accomplish some goal, and/or result in saving time or money. A good example: ads for Mobil 1 oil. Among other benefits, the ads stress increased mileage (up to 10 miles, or 15 kilometers, per tankful), longer intervals between oil changes, reduced engine wear, and easier starting in very hot and very cold conditions. These are very much rational appeals.

Communicators must decide whether to include a definite conclusion in a message based on rational appeals. Research indicates that messages that draw conclusions are more persuasive than those that do not.[11] On the other hand, a definite conclusion may insult or turn off the receiver.[12] For instance, a communication that draws a conclusion too strongly or dogmatically can backfire by inducing counterarguments, disparaging thoughts, and other negative reactions in the receiver. Intelligent consumers do not like to be talked down to, and may raise doubts out of spite.

Rational appeals influence us in a particular way: They function as sources of information used to form beliefs. Those beliefs, in turn, become integrated with our stored knowledge, values, and emotions and eventually influence our attitudes. If their effect is strong enough, they may ultimately instigate actual behaviorial changes (e.g., product trial). Rational appeals tend to have a special status in our minds because of their noncoercive and relatively nonevaluative content. We are likely to attribute any resulting attitude change to our own decision making rather than to the external influence—at least when compared to other, more overt forms of influence such as rewards or coercion. We attribute our attitude to free choice, with the implicit thought that "I drew the conclusion myself without external compulsion, so I must really believe what was said, and it has valid meaning for me."

Emotional Appeals

Whereas rational appeals work through our thought processes, emotional appeals play on our feelings. They are based on the idea that feelings are motivational conduits to action.

Emotional messages typically work toward one of two goals. On the one hand, emotional appeals might strive to put the audience in a particular mood that will enhance attention, facilitate rational content processing, and/or transfer to the product or brand in the sense of making the audience like it. On the other hand, emotional appeals might be so compelling that they, in and of themselves, stimulate us to act without necessarily processing and evaluating rational content. In marketing, emotional appeals usually use one of three basic tactics: positive or negative mood, humor, or fear.

Positive or Negative Mood. Some communications, particularly radio and television advertisements but also in print ads on occasion, attempt to place the audience in a positive or negative mood.[13] They do so with music, words, pictures, and images designed to either conjure up emotionally tinged memories or induce new feelings. Communicators hope that these feelings will create an internal tension or dissonance, and that this, in turn, will encourage coping behaviors such as information seeking or product trial.

Positive moods result from pleasant music, attractive scenes or spokespersons, reminders of fondly remembered events or places, and other pleasing stimuli. Usually, direct tie-ins to the senses are made through unusual or familiar tastes, aromas, sights, sounds, and physical sensations. Appeals to involuntary responses, biological and otherwise, work, too. Examples include pictures of babies, animals, human nudity, food, and the like.[14] Such positive stimuli arouse basic and learned needs. They also make the audience more alert and motivated and thus enhance information processing. At the same time, feelings of well-being and elation are believed to transfer to the brand itself. If we feel fine and even euphoric, this might lead to a positive evaluation of brand X. For example, ads for soft drinks or beer often attempt to create joyous, novel social scenes so that audiences will be in positive moods and associate the advertised brand and its consumption with the positive moods.

Negative moods may also enhance communication and influence at times. How often have you been annoyed by unpleasant, abrasive ads addressing such issues as bad breath, clogged sinuses, excruciating headaches, loose dentures, or ring around the collar? Advertisers believe such ads not only attract attention but also help people confront "problems" that are normally denied or repressed. Of course, for people who do not recognize or accept these issues as problems, such ads miss the mark and may even create ill will. Nevertheless, advertisers believe that some people will be reached, if only because these people see the ad as a sympathetic and public acknowledgment that their "problems" are real and worth addressing. Advertisers seldom address whether such attempts at persuasion "create" problems that do not really exist or play on people's vulnerabilities. Most ads probably do not go that far, but the line between persuasion and manipulation is a fine one.

Ads that induce negative moods may have another effect as well. Intuitively, we all know that our memory for facts, places, and ads decays over time. But some memories decay more quickly than others, and some do not decay much or do so very slowly. Imagine what happens when we watch the seemingly silly ad for Charmin toilet tissue with the equally abrasive Mr. Whipple, a wimpish elderly man with a squeaky voice, as spokesperson. Immediately after viewing the ad, we might remember "Charmin toilet tissue," "soft," and our general distaste for Mr. Whipple and the ad. However, as time passes, we might disassociate Mr. Whipple and his accompanying negative effect from "soft Charmin toilet tissue." Later, as we pass the shelf of toilet tissue in the supermarket, our unconscious memory that Charmin is soft might be the trigger needed to induce us to reach for Charmin instead of another brand. To the extent that our negative images dissipate quicker than our remembrance of the brand name and its attributes, the attention-getting and dissonance-arousing aspects of the ad might be beneficial. A related phenomenon is the "sleeper effect," in which liking a brand actually increases over time as a function of exposure to an ad.[15]

Humor. The role of humor[16] in communication is a hotly debated topic among advertising experts. Some advertisers explicitly avoid humor because they believe that (1) it is often too subtle and will not be appreciated or understood by everyone; (2) it takes too long to develop in 30- or 60-second ads and therefore uses up too much valuable time; (3) it can distract attention away from the brand and its attributes; (4) it is too ephemeral and will not be remembered as well as factual information; (5) it is too expensive to produce; and/or (6) it is out of character with the brand or company image. As a consequence, many advertisers prefer rational appeals.

On the other hand, some advertisers employ humor in nearly all or many of their ads. These advertisers believe that humorous ads (1) attract and hold attention; (2) involve the audience with the ad and the product in deeper cognitive and affective ways than rational ads; (3) reward the audience and create a positive mood, thereby increasing liking for the brand; (4) communicate more effectively to all levels of social and intellectual development (because situations that are difficult to put into words are more easily expressed in funny skits); (5) are almost the only way to advertise painful, sensitive, and embarrassing topics; and/or (6) are remembered better than factual ads.

Although research to date has yielded few clear conclusions about using humor, we suggest that the following tentative conclusions are warranted:

1. Humorous messages attract attention.
2. Humorous messages may detrimentally affect comprehension of selling points.
3. Humor may distract the audience long enough to inhibit counterargumentation.
4. Humorous messages are persuasive but not necessarily more so than serious appeals.
5. Humor tends to enhance source credibility.
6. Audience effects may confound the effect of humor (e.g., the values or background of audience might interfere with humor).
7. A humorous context may increase liking for the source and in turn enhance persuasive effect of the rational part of the message.
8. Humor can function as a positive reinforcer and enhance the message.[17]

Clearly, the role of humor in communication is important and is frequently used in practice. One study found that 15 percent of television ads use humor.[18] We say more about humor when we discuss other models of communication later in this chapter and when we consider agency styles in chapter 10.

Fear. Marketers occasionally employ messages designed to arouse anxiety or fear in an audience.[19] At least two kinds of fear appeals have been used in this way. One type features the threat of *negative physical consequences*. For example, a communicator might stress the harm that would befall a person who does not adopt a certain practice (e.g., "You may get cavities and toothaches if you don't brush your teeth with brand X") or refrain from a certain practice (e.g., "You may get lung cancer, emphysema, or heart disease if you don't stop smoking").

The second type of fear appeal dramatizes the threat of *social disapproval*. Here the communicator suggests that the receiver runs the risk of being shunned, disparaged, ridiculed, or in some other sense belittled as a person. For example, ads for mouthwashes, antiperspirants, deodorant soaps, car waxes, and lawn fertilizers often imply that if consumers do not use the appropriate product, other people will surely develop a negative image of them. This type of appeal targets people's need for approval from others and the anxiety created by possible shame, guilt, or embarrassment. Closely related to this are ads implying that consumers will not be loved unless they behave in a particular way. Advertisements have been known to not-so-subtly imply that if a "housewife" does not cook with brand Y, her husband and children will reject her, or if a husband does not buy his wife diamonds, his wife will withhold love and affection.

Exactly how does an appeal to fear produce its effects? An obvious explanation is that the arousal of fear threatens the well-being of the individual and causes emotional and cognitive dissonance (e.g., "If I do not buy life insurance, my family may suffer"). To resolve the dissonance, the receiver can either reject the message, repress having seen it, or act to relieve the tension (e.g., by purchasing insurance from firm Z).

From a marketing standpoint, two questions need to be asked: Should fear be used, and if so, how strong should the appeal be? An answer to the first question involves value judgments. Fear appeals appear to be appropriate for insurance, medical, and personal-care products. However, marketers must weigh ethical issues and the possibility that people may feel that advertisers are taking advantage by manipulating the audience. An answer to the second question is a practical concern and needs to be based on experience and research. Given that an appeal to fear is deemed appropriate, it might be thought that the greater the fear aroused in a communication, the greater the persuasion. This has been found to be true in some cases, but in others persuasion was found to decrease as the level of fear rose.[20]

The main conclusion that can be drawn from current research is that the relationship between fear and persuasion is curvilinear (see Fig. 9.2). With low levels of fear, persuasion increases as fear rises. Soon, however, fear becomes overwhelming; after reaching a peak, persuasion actually declines as fear increases beyond a certain point. Why? One possibility is that fear has two opposing mental effects—arousal and emotional blocking—that cancel each other out at low and high levels of fear.[21] When the level of fear is low, both arousal and the tendency to block the message from awareness are minimal. Hence, persuasion is low. As the level of fear rises, arousal tends to accentuate the importance of the message, but emotional blocking does not increase as quickly; the net effect is an increase in persuasion. However, further increases in arousal produce a greater tendency to block the message from conscious awareness, resulting in a slower increase in perception of the salience of the message. Thus, when the stronger tendency to block is combined with the relatively weaker salience of the message, persuasion declines. Over the full range of possible levels of fear, the relation to persuasion is curvilinear, as seen in Figure 9.2.

Extraneous Factors

A common reaction to arguments and statements of fact is skepticism. We are especially likely to question a statement if we perceive that the speaker will benefit in some way from our acceptance of the message. Moreover, people typically counter-

FIGURE 9.2 CURVILINEAR RELATIONSHIP BETWEEN FEAR AND PERSUASION

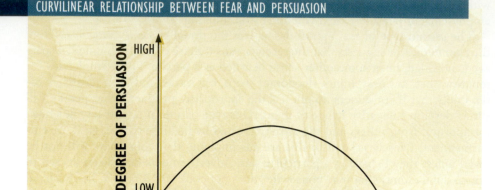

argue (usually silently) against attempts to change their attitudes or persuade them to do something. What can marketers do to overcome this natural reaction by the receiver?

Counterargumentation might have one or both of two effects. First, it competes with the argument for mental processing time. Second, it enters the decision and evaluation process as negatively weighted information. In either case, counterarguments have the effect of diminishing persuasion. Strange as it may seem, it has been found that persuasion can sometimes be enhanced if *distracting elements* are included in a communication.[22] Distracters are believed to inhibit counterargumentation on the part of the audiences, thereby increasing persuasion. The danger is that the distracters might also interfere with the arguments in the message. The trick is to target distracters at counterargumentation and/or to make sure they are not so strong that they prevent the argument from getting through.

How is this done? Normally, distracters consist of audio or visual elements that are incidental to the main content and point of a communication. For example, background music or extraneous noises are sometimes used in radio and television ads. Similarly, busy colors are used in print ads, or quick movements peripheral to the primary action appear in television ads. Humor is also used as a subtle distracter.

Still another extraneous message content factor is borrowed from drama and literature. Authors and playwrights have long known that if they hope to "educate" their audiences, they should not directly "lecture" to them. Rather, writers use a *foil*, a character in the story or play who is educated by another character. The foil then becomes a vehicle for learning by the audience. The use of a foil avoids the teacher-pupil, master-servant, or parent-child connotations that frequently arise in audiences when people attempt to teach them something. In effect, the use of a foil cuts down on counterargumentation. The audience learns vicariously or through observational learning processes.

Some findings of psychological research support the occurrence of greater persuasion under conditions in which the audience overhears a person attempting to persuade another person than when the audience is confronted directly.[23] Marketing professionals apply this idea in television ads that show "secret" viewings of conversations (called "slice-of-life" commercials) in which one or both parties extol the virtues of a product. Seemingly unplanned testimonials or "blind" supermarket tests surreptitiously monitored by a camera fall within this category as well. Perhaps viewers believe such overheard messages because the participants seemingly have no ulterior motives. As we noted earlier in our discussion of the sender of communications, messages communicated by paid spokespersons are often discounted or given less credibility.

One-Sided versus Two-Sided Appeals

Among the decisions a communicator must make is how to structure a persuasive argument.[24] Should the appeal mention only positive attributes of a product, or should it also acknowledge negative attributes? Should it present only favorable arguments for purchasing one's product, or should unfavorable arguments also be included? There are no clear answers to these questions.

Classic research by Hovland et al. established the following generalizations:[25] (1) A one-sided approach tends to work better when the audience is already favorable to one's arguments or issue and/or will not hear opposing arguments. Presumably, for these people use of a two-sided appeal would raise needless doubts and produce less persuasion. (2) A two-sided approach tends to work better when the audience is unfavorable to one's arguments, is better educated, or is likely to hear counterarguments.

What accounts for the superiority of two-sided arguments in the conditions just noted? One possibility is that mention of negative factors "inoculates" the audience against potential counterclaims.[26] That is, if an ad acknowledges certain negative points about a product and then refutes or at least mitigates them, the audience will not be surprised by competitors' subsequent counterarguments. In fact, the receiver might well refute the counterarguments and thereby develop resistance to competitive threats.

Another reason two-sided appeals might be more effective is that they enhance the credibility of the source and/or the message.[27] People are more likely to respect and believe a speaker who presents both sides of an issue; and whatever side of the issue they decide upon, they are likely to hold to it more firmly because they feel that they arrived at it themselves. Some research also shows that two-sided appeals induce more supporting arguments and fewer derogations of the source than one-sided appeals.[28]

How might two-sided appeals be implemented most effectively? One option is to state a drawback as a minor one and emphasize the advantages to be gained from the product's positive attributes. For example, oil- and latex-based paints compete with each other for use in exterior house painting. An advertiser of oil-based paints might say, "Sure, our oil-based paint is a little more difficult to apply than latex paints, but it looks better, allows the wood to breathe, and will last longer." This approach has been called a *refutational appeal* in the literature on the subject.

One-sided arguments often work well in *comparison advertising*,[29] defined as explicitly naming and comparing one or more competitors in an ad. The advertiser almost always asserts that its brand is superior, either as a whole or in one or more important attributes. As one might expect, consumers typically doubt the truthfulness of comparison ads.[30] Advertisers therefore often use "independent research firms" to make test comparisons, stating the test results to build credibility. Comparison advertising is particularly effective for positioning a brand in relation to competitors. Presumably, it will work best to the extent that there are clear differences between the brands.

Evidence regarding the effectiveness of comparison advertising is mixed. One researcher discovered that viewers seem to have greater recall of the message content of comparison ads versus noncomparison ads.[31] Another study found that comparison ads did not produce significantly higher believability, credibility, or purchase intentions than noncomparison ads.[32] Still other researchers have found that comparison messages that mention the competition by name were more effective than noncomparison messages but less effective than comparison messages that mention only "brand X" designations.[33] Although comparative ads generally induce more counterargumentation than noncomparative ads, favorable attitude change is greater when two sides are presented than when only one side is presented.[34] There is even some circumstantial evidence suggesting that ads comparing Bayer and Anacin pain remedies with Tylenol actually helped the competition (i.e., Tylenol) more than the advertisers.[35]

A final issue regarding one-sided versus two-sided messages is the use of *corrective advertising*.[36] In corrective advertising, certain product attributes or possible consequences of product use are explicitly disclosed. This form of advertising was instituted by the Federal Trade Commission in order to remedy the effects of deceptive or false advertising. The warnings placed on cigarette packages and in cigarette ads are a good example. Another is a corrective television commercial in which the seller of bottled juices, Ocean Spray, acknowledged that the phrase "food energy" in earlier ads for cranberry juice was simply referring to calories. Corrective advertising is designed to benefit the public by presenting "the facts." In a sense, it represents a two-sided message when viewed in the context of the sponsor's communications history. Because they have been seldom used and little research exists, corrective ads remain a little understood topic.

Order of Presentation of Arguments

An important decision regarding message structure concerns the order of presentations. Two issues must be considered. The first is *within-message order effects*. Given that the advertiser has numerous arguments or product features to stress, in what order should it present the information? Should it place the most forceful arguments first, last, or in the middle of the message? Second, within a medium such as magazines or television, where should the message be placed? This question deals with *across-message order effects*. Will communication be more effective in the beginning, end, or center of a magazine, television program, or sequence of ads? Because research on these issues is sparse,[37] we provide only some tentative conclusions and guidelines.

Research on human memory indicates that, given a series of things to remember, we generally remember the items presented first and last better than those presented in the middle. As a result, one might conclude that the best arguments and the most salient product attributes should be presented early or late in a communication but not buried in the center. Memory research also tends to show that material presented last is remembered somewhat better than material presented first. On the other hand, we sometimes learn important material better if it is presented early. Hence, a trade-off exists, and advertisers should use experimentation to determine which option (first or last) is best in any particular instance.

The preceding comments apply to the effects of order of presentation on memory. However, the audience's memory is not the only criterion for assessing the effectiveness of a message. With respect to receptivity, putting the most important or forceful content first appears to have the best chance of attracting attention and motivating the receiver to consider all of the ensuing arguments. But if one desires to leave the audience in as positive a frame of mind as possible, putting the best arguments at the end might be more effective, because progressing from weak arguments to strong ones could build to a climax.

If pros and cons are to be presented in a message, putting the favorable information first might create a positive attitude, causing the subsequent negative information to have less of an impact than it might have if it were presented first. On the other hand, if a person has greater memory for later content, the resulting attitude might be more negative than it would have been if the negative information had been presented first.

We thus see that the issue of order of presentation is far from clear. For short communications, such as 30-second television commercials, the position of arguments within the message might not be as crucial as other factors such as source, message content, or media effects. For longer communications, such as salesperson-customer interactions, which can go on for an hour or more, the order of arguments is more important. However, there are no research findings that indicate which order is the most effective.

Similarly, we know little about the optimal order of messages within a medium. Magazines charge more for ads in the centerfold, on the back, or on the inside covers because they are presumably viewed more often. Television ads tend to be viewed most when they occur in the center of a program and least when they occur at the beginning or end of a program. But these conclusions are largely hearsay, and no definitive research exists on the issue.

Amount of Information

Decisions about how much information to place in a single communication involve both content and structure.[38] We intuitively know that at any one point in time we can attend to and process only a limited amount of information. As the amount of information increases, we reach a point at which our ability to handle it diminishes. Information "overload" results in slower, less accurate, inefficient processing and may produce feelings of confusion and frustration. Moreover, the transmission of too much information may cause receivers to focus on unimportant or misleading information. As a result, audiences may develop a false sense of confidence in their evaluation of the message, believing that they have received "full information."

As indicated in chapter 4, we know that decision makers cope with abundant information by applying simplifying rules. But the conditions under which this approach becomes dysfunctional are not well understood. Recent research has focused on the design of information environments[39] and on consumer characteristics related to information processing and overload,[40] but these topics are beyond the scope of this text.

Various rules of thumb have been developed over the years with respect to the optimum number of product attributes or arguments to include in marketing communications. For short messages, such as 30-second or 60-second television ads, received wisdom suggests that consumers cannot absorb more than three selling points. Indeed, some advertisers believe that an ad should contain only one major selling point, given the low involvement of audiences, the relative unimportance of products, and the short time available for processing. In other contexts, such as longer television advertisements (e.g., 90-second ads), magazine ads, and customer-seller interactions, the magic rule of "7 plus or minus 2" is sometimes invoked.[41] That is, the receiver can cope with only about seven pieces of information in a message.

A final comment related to amount of information is that some research has been done on the type of information needed to make effective shopping decisions in a supermarket. That research has focused on open dating (i.e., printing the perishable date on products),[42] unit pricing (i.e., presentation of the price per unit quantity of a good),[43] and nutritional labeling.[44]

Repetition

The final message structure variable that we will consider is the role of repetition.[45] Here we discuss the role of repetition in learning; in chapter 10 we consider the effects of repetition on information processing and other psychological processes.

Repetition occurs in two ways. Within a message, a brand name or product attribute can be repeated; such repeated exposures are said to have *intrastimulus effects*. In addition, the same message can be repeated on numerous occasions, leading to *interstimulus effects*.

Repetition affects audiences in a number of ways. First, some research suggests that audiences develop positive feelings toward something solely through repeated exposure to it. This has been called the *mere exposure effect*, and it is believed to occur without awareness or learning.[46] Second, and more typically, repetition increases learning.[47] According to learning theory, the probability of learning is increased by the pairing of a neutral with a rewarding stimulus, by a response-reward sequence, or by the presentation of stimuli that may become associated in the mind of the observer. For example, repeated exposure to a "neutral" stimulus (such as an ad, product, or brand name) associated with a reward (such as pleasant sights, sounds, tastes, or other rewarding stimuli) can result in the development of an emotional reaction to the originally neutral stimulus. This is termed *classical conditioning*. *Instrumental learning* (also termed operant conditioning) occurs when a behavioral response to a stimulus is subsequently rewarded (reinforced) sufficiently and frequently enough. *Cognitive learning* occurs through observation of associations or inferred causal connections.

What does research reveal? One study found that repetition enhances recall (i.e., learning).[48] As the number of repetitions in ads rose, recall increased, but with diminishing returns. Higher levels of repetition increased recall, but at relatively smaller rates than lower levels. Repetition had little or no discernible effect on attitudes, intentions, or behavior. In addition, the research showed that repetition works best with convenience goods as opposed to shopping goods. Apparently, because of consumers' low interest in and involvement with convenience goods, repetition is required to build awareness, whereas shopping goods are salient enough so that people seek information on their own without the need for much advertising.

In analyzing repetition effects, we should keep in mind that communication occurs at two levels: the micro, or individual, level and the macro, or aggregate, level. At the microlevel, individuals need repetition to become aware of products and their features. Because an ad often contains a number of ideas, people need to be exposed to it a number of times to pick up all the information in the message. Each exposure results in new information being transmitted. Also, people tend to forget what they have learned or become preoccupied with other matters. Repetition increases memory, reduces forgetting, and keeps the memories of brands and product attributes in the receiver's mind closer to the time of actual decision making. Finally, to the extent that the content in repetitive messages is positively reinforcing, repetition tends to build or at least maintain liking for those stimuli. A point might be reached at which the message becomes too familiar and the receiver begins to tune it out, pay less attention, or counterargue.

At the macrolevel, repetition is needed to reach larger and larger numbers of consumers who are unaware of the product or its attributes. In addition, competitors continually woo away portions of the market that must be regained. This would seem to call for more repetition. However, given the relatively fixed size of any market and the fact that repetition reaches some people who are already aware of the product, one might expect diminishing returns to scale at the macrolevel. (We discuss the topic of advertising "wearout" in chapter 10.)

The Medium

Up to this point, we have maintained that effective communication depends on the characteristics of the *source* (i.e., credibility, attractiveness, ability to mediate rewards and punishments) and the *message* (i.e., what is said and how it is said). Now we will explore still another variable influencing communication: the *medium* (see Fig. 9.1).

Personal and Nonpersonal Media

Between any source and receiver, we can identify two types of media: personal and nonpersonal. With *personal media*, the "distance" between source and receiver is small. Both parties are in relatively direct contact, and verbal and nonverbal communication plays an important role. The source and receiver are aware of each other's identity. Feedback is instantaneous, and interactions occur in a readily identifiable sequence. Face-to-face contact between a salesperson and a customer is perhaps the most common example of a personal medium, but telephone calls and letters can also serve as personal media.

Nonpersonal media, in contrast, put more distance between the source and the receiver. Contact is indirect and occurs through one or more channels; feedback, if it occurs at all, is delayed; and the communication "process" occurs largely in only one direction, from source to receiver. In addition, the source and receiver are generally unknown to each other as individuals. The source views the receiver as a largely impersonal audience, whereas the receiver views the source as an impersonal institution or perhaps an agent for the institution. Radio, television, magazines, newspapers, flyers, and billboards are the most frequently used nonpersonal media. Nonpersonal media are sometimes referred to simply as *mass media*.

We limit our discussion of media here to consideration of the two-step flow model of communication, which represents a combination of personal and nonpersonal media and explains part of the process of social influence. We explore other aspects of media in later chapters.

The Two-Step Flow Model

Exactly how do mass communications influence the public? A classic study was performed more than 50 years ago to answer such key questions and issues.[49] In particular, the researchers were concerned with why people vote the way they do. Radio and print media were thought to influence voting, but no one seemed to know ex-

FIGURE 9.3 CLASSIC TWO-STEP FLOW MODEL OF COMMUNICATION

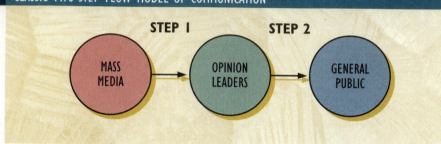

actly how. The results of the study were surprising. Mass media were found to have a negligible impact on voting. That is, the mass media did not influence the public directly, but rather, the influence was found to be indirect. As represented in Figure 9.3, mass media had the greatest impact on a small number of individuals, termed *opinion leaders*, and these people, in turn, influenced the general public. Step 1 in the model represents nonpersonal contact, whereas step 2 constitutes direct, interpersonal contact. In sum, the mass media were found to work largely through intermediaries. Opinion leaders might include scientists, doctors, religious leaders, respected politicians, outstanding professionals, or simply trusted friends.

The two-step model was an important revelation in the political arena as well as in marketing. It showed that mass media had a smaller direct effect than was commonly believed. After the discovery of the two-step flow of influence, the practice of communication changed drastically. Advertising spokespersons were chosen from the ranks of opinion leaders. Messages were designed to reach opinion leaders more directly, and media were selected on the basis of which outlets were watched or read more by opinion leaders. Professionals in advertising agencies have become experts in each of these phases of communication.

Research into the dynamics of communication continued, with a number of new findings coming to light during the decades following the seminal study just described.[50] Although the sequence of events shown in Figure 9.3 was often corroborated by later studies, other sequences were found to occur as well. In particular, as shown in Figure 9.4, three additional effects (drawn as solid lines) were identified. Researchers observed that the general public did not always wait for opinion leaders to make pronouncements, and often sought them out for information and advice. Hence, in Figure 9.4 an arrow is drawn from the general public to opinion leaders.

A second finding was that mass media often have a direct impact on other receivers in addition to opinion leaders. Specifically, we can identify innovators and reference group members as people who are not necessarily opinion leaders and are sometimes reached directly by mass media. Solid arrows are drawn from the mass media to innovators and reference group members in Figure 9.4 to reflect this influence.

Third, and very important, researchers discovered that *word-of-mouth communication* is a powerful means of influence among peers, family members, coworkers, and others of the general public.[51] Social comparison and other processes play important roles as well. The solid arrows from innovators and reference group members to the general public in Figure 9.4 represent these effects.

A number of other, less influential flows are shown as dashed lines in Figure 9.4. Notice that the mass media directly affect the general public and that opinion leaders directly affect innovators and reference group members, too.

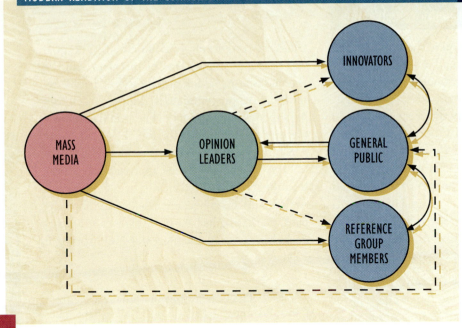

Researchers have also attempted to identify the types of individuals who are likely to be opinion leaders[52] and how they influence others.[53] There are also numerous ways of measuring opinion leadership.[54] We will not discuss this research here because of space limitations.

Applications of the Model

Communication strategies have attempted to reach, stimulate, and even create opinion leaders. Opinion leaders might be reached through personal contact, phone calls, personalized mail, or strategic selection of effective media. Research is needed to identify the reading and viewing habits of opinion leaders; to find key mailing lists; to identify leaders in the community; and to understand the lifestyles, psychographics (e.g., opinions, attitudes, values, goals, personalities), and activities of opinion leaders. Opinion leadership can sometimes be stimulated by hiring influential people to use a product or simply by giving the product to highly visible people. The Blitz-Weinhard Brewing Company once paid selected beer drinkers to drink and advertise their beer in taverns. Sporting goods companies provide free equipment bearing their logo to professional athletes in the hope of stimulating sales to amateurs. Opinion leaders also can be created by selecting highly visible, respected, and influential people in groups or communities and educating them, increasing their enthusiasm for a product, and so on.[55] Pharmaceutical companies pay selected, well-known doctors to do presentations at national meetings of pharmacists or doctors, in part with the aim of taking advantage of them as opinion leaders.

Another strategy building on recent research is to increase word-of-mouth communication. Advertisements, packages, slogans, and even products can be designed to stimulate word-of-mouth conversations. A recent Chex cereal television commercial showed a family eating Chex; they then passed the box to another family, presumably next door. This was followed by the second family trying the cereal,

After years of consolidation in the beer industry and dominance by a small number of giant firms, microbreweries are finding a niche in the marketplace for consumers who desire high-quality beers with distinctive tastes. Much of the lure of these specialty beers goes beyond taste and owes its success to image. A problem faced by small breweries is how to attract customers when marketing budgets are small and competitors dominate the media. How can microbrewers communicate their distinctive tastes and images most efficiently?

New Amsterdam Beer is a classic example. Faced with no resources for advertising, this New York City brewery decided to take a novel approach and use word-of-mouth communication. It began in 1982 by targeting sales to the trendiest restaurants in Manhattan. The goal was to reach trendsetters, people who lead the way in fashion, values, and lifestyles. To the extent that people (emulators) desire, consciously or subconsciously, to be like trendsetters or identify with the kind of life they lead, New Amsterdam Beer thought it could ride the wave of "free advertising." The approach was an extraordinary success. Within five years, New Amsterdam Beer became a $4.5 million company, marketing its beer in 1400 restaurants, supermarkets, and delis in greater New York and 22 states.

Source: The facts for this illustration come from Eileen Prescott, "Talk is Cheap," *Success,* September 1987, pp. 18, 20.

---

passing it on, and so forth. The power of word-of-mouth communication can be phenomenal, and it is free (see Marketing Anecdote 9.1).

However, sometimes word-of-mouth communication can hurt a product. For years McDonald's has had to fight rumors that it uses digestible plastics in its shakes and red worm meat in its hamburgers. The latter rumor alone is alleged to have lowered sales by as much as 30 percent in areas where the rumor was rampant.[56] Similarly, for many years Procter & Gamble tried to counteract rumors that its logo resembles a fiendish symbol of Satan, but in 1985 it gave up and changed the logo. Thus, ads that implore us to "tell your neighbor" or "pass it on" may constitute a double-edged sword. A rough rule of thumb is that customers are likely to tell what they dislike about a brand to twice as many people as they would tell what they like about it. Thus marketers place special emphasis on building customer satisfaction and avoiding negative word of mouth.

The Receiver

In addition to the source, message, and medium, certain *characteristics of the receiver* determine the outcome of a marketing communication attempt. In this section we describe research on how those characteristics influence communication; in later sections, we elaborate on the cognitive processes and affective responses of receivers.

Some research suggests that the personality of a receiver affects the communication process. For example, people with low self-esteem are more easily persuaded than people with high self-esteem.[57] However, when a communication contains rewards or punishments, high self-esteem leads to greater compliance.[58] Presumably, people with high self-esteem are less anxious and better able to assess the meaning of the communication for them. Similarly, some research has indicated that people who tend to trust others are more easily persuaded.[59] Like people with high self-esteem, they tend to view messages as more believable and attribute higher credibility to the source than do people with low trust or low self-esteem.

Audiences also differ in education, intelligence, patience, values, and attitudes. The same source, message, or medium will have different effects, depending on the receiver's abilities, inclinations, prejudices, orientations, cognitive styles, and learning histories. However, probably the most important factors affecting the outcome of communication attempts are emotional and cognitive processes, which we discuss next.

AN INFORMATION-PROCESSING PERSPECTIVE ON COMMUNICATION

The classic SMMR model of communication is an important one, but it tends to emphasize the sender's actions and to underemphasize what the receiver does when confronted by a persuasive appeal. That is, it fails to consider how receivers *process* information. In recent years considerable research has focused on these processes.

Consumers respond to persuasive communications in either of two ways: rationally or emotionally. Actually, rational and emotional responses can occur together; however, one or the other tends to dominate in any particular situation. Moreover, any product or service can be characterized either by its utilitarian, or functional, nature or by its expressive, or hedonic, character. This, in turn, determines whether the communication strategy should take a rational or an emotional approach. Two theories have evolved to explain the reactions of people to persuasive communications. One is the elaboration likelihood model (ELM); the other is the emotion and adaptation model (EAM).

The Elaboration Likelihood Model

The ELM model[60] is portrayed in Figure 9.5. In this model, a persuasive communication (e.g., an appeal in an ad or a pitch by a salesperson) is first reacted to globally in terms of its personal relevance. In a sense, the audience asks itself, "Am I motivated to process this communication?" Consumers will feel highly motivated to the extent that the communication is perceived to have personal meaning, intrinsic importance, or significant consequences. Motivation is also related to the receiver's ego involvement with the communication and/or their vested interest or involvement with the topic or product. The ELM assumes that as personal relevance increases, motivation to process the communication also increases. Other factors, such as need for cognition or perceived responsibility to pay attention to messages, may also contribute to motivation.

However, having the motivation is not sufficient for an audience to engage in further information processing. The audience must also have the ability to do so. There are a number of forces that either enhance or reduce ability to process a communication. One of these is distraction. Distraction in a message or medium makes processing more difficult in most cases. Repetition, on the other hand, increases the chances that a communication will be processed, provided the receiver does not become bored or irritated. Prior knowledge of or familiarity with the content of a message also strengthens the ability to process a communication. Finally, time pressure, the clarity of the communication, and mood affect an audience's ability to process a message.

FIGURE 9.5 BASIC STAGES IN THE ELABORATION LIKELIHOOD MODEL

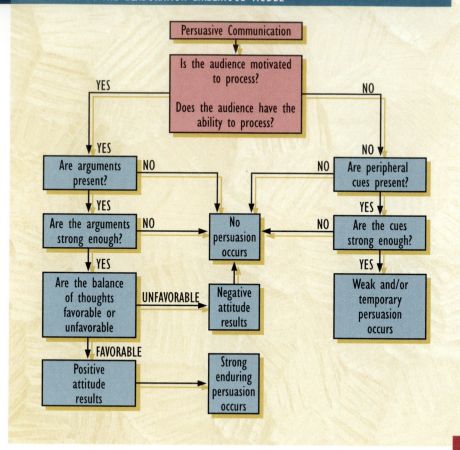

Degree of motivation and ability to process a communication set the stage for one of two "routes" to persuasion: the central route (outlined in the left-hand column of Fig. 9.5) and the peripheral route (shown at the right of Fig. 9.5). Let us consider the peripheral route first. When an audience has neither sufficient motivation nor the ability to process a communication, it fails to consider its content. Obviously, the rational content in the communication, if any, cannot be effective if it is not processed. Moreover, if no indirect information is conveyed, the communication will fail to persuade. On occasion, however, persuasive communications contain cues in the form of indirect information, which has the potential to influence audiences—hence the term *peripheral cues*. The perceived credibility and attractiveness of spokespersons are two important peripheral cues. Likewise, the amount of information conveyed in a communication and the medium (e.g., audio versus video) can serve as peripheral cues.

One way in which peripheral cues induce persuasion is by operating as a heuristic.[61] Exposure to a strong peripheral cue activates a stored decision rule in the mind of a recipient. For example, an expert spokesperson might stimulate the heuristic, "Experts can be trusted." Presentation of many facts or product attributes, even if one fails to attend to their details, might lead to the inference, "The more features a brand has, the better it must be." Or the use of a celebrity in an ad might take advantage of the implicit heuristic, "People generally agree with persons they like and admire." Similarly, an expensive-looking ad might lead to the inference,

"Companies that spend a lot on advertising must have a high-quality product to generate the revenues needed to pay for the ads." Heuristics like these have been shown to lead to persuasion.

Persuasion occurring via the peripheral route, however, tends to be weak and temporary. This is because little or no cognitive content results from such communications and therefore there is little opportunity for storage of conclusions or development of strong convictions.

The strongest cases of persuasion occur via the central route, which is initiated by high motivation and ability to process a communication (see Fig. 9.5). We can think of this motivation and ability as influencing the extent or intensity of processing. But, obviously, *what* is processed is important, too. When the central route is followed, message content, such as arguments or reasons for purchasing a product, becomes a crucial determinant of persuasion. Thus, the valence of information (i.e., pro or con arguments and their mix) in a communication combines with intensity to produce persuasion.

How does it do this? If the arguments in a message are compelling enough, they will stimulate *cognitive responses* in the audience. Cognitive responses are thoughts, ideas, inferences, or conclusions drawn as a result of processing a persuasive communication. They may be either conscious or subconscious. The heuristics described earlier are one class of cognitive responses commonly generated by consumers exposed to ads and other communications.

Four other basic cognitive responses include counterarguments, support arguments, source derogations, and source bolsterings.[62] A *counterargument* is a mental statement contradicting, disputing, or refuting a point made in a communication. For example, a person might see a television ad asserting that regular use of drain cleaner Y will keep one's drains unclogged for "up to four weeks." The viewer, however, might react by thinking (or saying), "I used that drain cleaner before and it didn't keep my drain clean for even a week." A *support argument* is a mental assertion upholding, corroborating, or backing a point made in a communication. Another viewer of the drain cleaner ad might think, "It seems to me I remember my neighbor saying that drain cleaner Y performed well for him, especially in the kitchen sink." In *source derogation* the spokesperson or message is viewed as inferior, evaluated negatively, or otherwise disparaged in the mind of the receiver. Yet another viewer of the drain cleaner ad might feel that it is stupid and insulting or that the spokesperson is not credible and is delivering the message only because she was paid to do so. Finally, *source bolstering* (sometimes called execution bolstering) is a mental reaction positively evaluating the spokesperson or message: "The person in the ad was really sincere," or "I really think the ad was clever."

The main idea behind the central route to persuasion is that the cognitive responses generated by a receiver are combined or integrated to form an overall attitude toward a product or the communication (see Fig. 9.5). Cognitive responses are either favorable or unfavorable. A mental integration of these responses that is unfavorable leads to a negative attitude and, therefore, to failure to persuade. An integration that is favorable leads to a positive attitude and to successful persuasion.

In a classic experiment showing how the ELM explains reactions to ads, the researchers desired to see the effects of three independent variables: argument quality, attractiveness of endorser, and involvement of the audience.[63] To do this they created print ads for "Edge Razor," a fictitious brand of disposable razor. The experiment manipulated the independent variables in different versions of the ad to see their effects on attitude change as a function of viewing the ads.

The argument quality was either strong (e.g., the razor gives twice as close a shave as its nearest competitor, is scientifically designed, eliminates nicks and cuts)

Source: Results are from an experiment cited in Richard E. Petty, John T. Cacioppo, and David Schumann, "Central and Peripheral Routes to Advertising Effectiveness: The Moderating Role of Involvement," Journal of Consumer Research 10 (September 1983): 134–148.

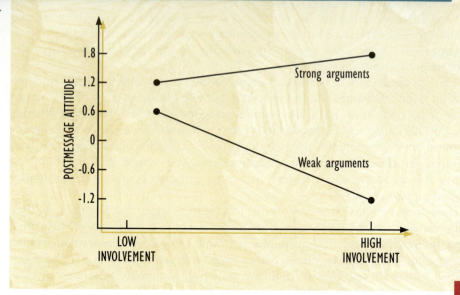

or weak (e.g., the razor floats, can be used only once but the shave will be memorable). The effectiveness of arguments depends on the receiver's level of involvement. Under the ELM, low involvement means that the audience is not highly motivated to process the arguments, whether weak or strong. Therefore, we would expect that attitude change would not be statistically different in subjects exposed to strong and weak arguments when both exposures occur under conditions of low involvement. But under conditions of high involvement, people are motivated to process the arguments. If the arguments are strong, a person should develop a relatively positive attitude. If they are weak, a person should react with a relatively negative attitude. Figure 9.6 shows the results of this part of the experiment. Statisticians term the pattern shown in the figure an "interaction effect"—involvement and the quality of arguments interact to produce attitude change.

Next consider the effect of attractiveness on attitude change. The researchers manipulated source attractiveness by using professional golfer Jack Nicklaus and tennis player Tracy Austin in one condition (famous celebrity endorser) and "average looking people who were unfamiliar to the subjects" in another condition (nonfamous endorser). Again, the results showed that the effects of spokesperson attractiveness depend on the level of involvement of the audience. In fact, the impact of source attractiveness is greater when audience involvement is low. Why is this so? Under high involvement, the audience is motivated to process the arguments in the message whether the spokesperson is attractive or not. Therefore, attitude change, which results from processing the arguments, should be equal for attractive and unattractive spokespersons. But an audience that is not very involved is not motivated to process the arguments; under these conditions, peripheral cues become more significant. The attractiveness of the endorser therefore influences attitude change. Figure 9.7 presents the findings of this experiment.

The ELM is primarily a rational model of information processing. Emotion enters the model only tangentially, through motivation, involvement, peripheral cues such as source attractiveness, and the effect implied by attitude formation. Some re-

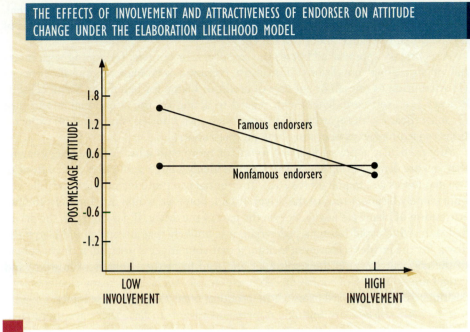

Source: Results are from an experiment cited in Richard E. Petty, John T. Cacioppo, and David Schumann, "Central and Peripheral Routes to Advertising Effectiveness: The Moderating Role of Involvement," Journal of Consumer Research 10 (September 1983): 134–148.

FIGURE 9.7

THE EFFECTS OF INVOLVEMENT AND ATTRACTIVENESS OF ENDORSER ON ATTITUDE CHANGE UNDER THE ELABORATION LIKELIHOOD MODEL

cent research has attempted to introduce more emotional content, but this has been limited to the effects of mood on information processing.[64] Because emotions sometimes have a more dominant role in persuasion than the ELM can accommodate, there is a need for another model, one that can account for emotional reactions to real-world communications.

The Emotion and Adaptation Model

The emotion and adaptation model (EAM)[65] is useful in assessing emotional reactions that are not accommodated by the ELM. In skeleton form, the EAM hypothesizes that people react to persuasive communications by first performing an appraisal of internal psychological and external situational conditions. This appraisal leads to a specific emotional response. Finally, the receiver copes with his or her emotional response in ways that may fulfill the intent of the communicator. Thus, the EAM proposes the following sequence of psychological processes in response to persuasive communications: appraisal → emotional response → coping.

Appraisals consist of an evaluation of the significance of a communication in terms of one's own well-being. Appraisals occur more or less automatically and usually below the level of self-awareness. Psychologists distinguish between *primary* and *secondary* appraisals. In a primary appraisal, one assesses (1) the motivational relevance of the conditions leading to the appraisal (i.e., their importance in terms of one's own goals); (2) the motivational congruence, or the extent to which the conditions thwart or facilitate achievement of one's goals; and (3) one's ego involvement. In a sense, primary appraisals are similar to the first stage in the ELM, but instead of processing message arguments or peripheral cues, as under the ELM, the recipient processes the significance of outcomes received in the past or anticipated in the future. The information processed under the EAM can be verbal, but it typically has a strong nonverbal component (e.g., one achieves a long-sought goal, or fails to do so, or longs for a positive outcome, or dreads an unpleasant engagement).

Thus, primary appraisals under the EAM are characteristically stronger, less verbal, more quickly processed, and less subject to conscious awareness than assessment of motivational relevance under the ELM.

A secondary appraisal addresses the resources, or options, for coping with internal or situational conditions. The most common secondary appraisals concern (1) attribution to oneself or another of credit or blame for benefit or harm; (2) self-efficacy (i.e., self-confidence) with regard to acting on the situational conditions; (3) self-efficacy with regard to regulating one's own internal states; and (4) expectations regarding forces operating beyond one's control.

Any particular appraisal will lead to one or more emotions. For example, imagine that you are driving along a highway when suddenly a large semitrailer cuts in front of you and forces you to pull off the road. Your initial panic and terror might be followed immediately by anger toward the driver. Anger, however, would develop only after an attribution of blame for negligence on the part of the driver. If, for example, the driver had swerved to avoid hitting a pedestrian, it is unlikely that anyone would blame the driver for the incident. However, assuming that your anger is justified, it might spread to the company owning the semitrailer and lead to further feelings of hostility and vengefulness. This is, of course, an extreme example. Yet it shares many elements with customer reactions toward firms whose products break down or cause injury.

Emotional responses are highly complex and varied. In fact, there are more than 550 terms in the English language that describe subtle variations in emotionality.[66] Nearly all emotions can be classified according to the positive and negative categories shown in Table 9.3.[67] A skillful communicator must know not only which category of emotions to target but also which subtype(s) to pursue (e.g., elation or joy; affection or caring; sadness or distress). To these categories of emotion, we need to add another aspect of emotionality: *affect intensity*. Any emotion experienced by a person, whether positive or negative, will vary in its strength or magnitude, and any individual is likely to experience emotions in a characteristic way.[68]

Advertisers try to stimulate emotions as a way of getting customers to respond favorably to their offerings. Consumers' coping behavior provides the key link between emotion and purchase-related responses. Any emotional reaction, if strong enough, will require some sort of coping on the part of the person experiencing it. Two broad coping responses are possible: problem-focused coping and emotion-focused coping. *Problem-focused coping* consists of efforts to overcome or reduce the effects of an undesirable situation or to maintain or increase the effects of a desirable situation. Such a response might entail, for example, changing the physical situation, breaking off a relationship, or persuading someone to do something to remove an external threat or to facilitate an opportunity. *Emotion-focused coping* refers to mental strategies to master, reduce, or tolerate an undesirable situation or to enhance a desirable one. Such strategies might entail denial, avoiding thinking about an appraisal, reconceptualizing the source of dissonance or its meaning, or building up the courage to act. Each emotion and the conditions under which it occurs can be shown to imply a set of specific coping alternatives.[69] Word-of-mouth communication, complaint behaviors, brand loyalty, brand switching, and new product trial are examples of coping responses.

To make the EAM more understandable, we close this chapter with an examination of a real-world situation.

Application of the EAM to Anti-child-abuse Advertisements

Child abuse is a widespread social problem. In 1992 about 3 million cases of child abuse were reported to public-service agencies in the United States, an increase of 132 percent over annual rates for the previous decade. Public-service personnel in

TABLE 9.3 BASIC CATEGORIES OF EMOTIONAL REACTIONS

Category	Examples
Positive Emotions	
Joy	Happiness, enjoyment, elation, pride, cheerfulness, pleasure, satisfaction
Love	Affection, attraction, caring, compassion, liking, fondness
Negative Emotions	
Anger	Frustration, rage, hostility, hate, disgust, loathing
Sadness	Sorrow, suffering, anguish, disappointment, depression, dismay, loneliness
Guilt or shame	Regret, remorse, self-disgust, blameworthy
Fear	Panic, worry, terror, nervousness, anxiety, fright, tenseness

ad agencies throughout the world have developed advertisements aimed at reducing child abuse.[70] Many of the ads ask for help in the form of financial or personal support. The typical ad plays upon the audience's negative emotions, with appeals to fear being the most common tactic.

Unfortunately, many of these efforts are misguided and wasteful because the ads are designed with little idea of what will optimally motivate people to help. The ads seem to be based on the notion that fear or shock will cause the receiver to want to help. But the designers of the ads have given little thought to how shock works, and therefore the ads are not as effective as they might be.

Recently researchers have proposed a theory based on the EAM. The idea is that for an anti-child-abuse ad to be effective under normal viewing conditions it must first stimulate intense negative emotions; these must then engender empathy for victims of child abuse; and this in turn must be followed by a decision to help. Figure 9.8 presents the theory. After reviewing this diagram, take a moment to read the description of the television commercial reviewed in Marketing Anecdote 9.2 on page 355. This ad had very little verbal content but relied on action and the emotional reactions of the main character, a young boy.

The theory shown in Figure 9.8 is fine as far as it goes. But what negative emotions should one aim for and what kind of empathic responses work best? After an exhaustive search of the research literature and numerous pretests, the researchers chose four negative emotions: anger, sadness, fear, and tension.

Anger was chosen because it is the classic reaction to a threat to one's ego identity and has been found to emerge vicariously in response to societal dangers. Psychologists have demonstrated that people get increasingly angry if they consider a situation arbitrary, inconsiderate, and/or malevolent—common emotions in situations of child abuse.

Sadness was chosen because it represents a feeling of loss and helplessness, with overtones of anguish, sorrow, and despair. The feeling of loss experienced when one is made aware of child abuse involves a threat to one's ego ideal, moral values, and image of other persons and their well-being. Helplessness arises with respect to perceptions of past cases of child abuse or present cases over which one has no control. Anti-child-abuse ads can be designed to reinforce this feeling. It is likely that initial feelings of helplessness with respect to child abuse (such as viewed in an ad) lead quickly to feelings of anger toward the perpetrator. Indeed, sadness is not an isolated emotion: "When we experience a loss, we rarely feel a single

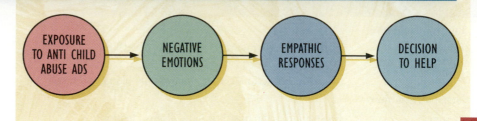

emotion such as sadness. We grieve, are angry, anxious, guilty, envious, even hopeful, and defensive."[71]

The *fear* engendered as individuals become aware of child abuse is likely to have two parts. People become anxious, responding with worry or apprehension. Ambiguity or uncertainty increases this anxiety. Anti-child-abuse ads are constructed to reinforce this reaction. A second part of fear is fright in response to "concrete and sudden danger of imminent physical harm."[72]

Finally, *tension* is a generalized feeling of uneasiness and distress. The ad described in Marketing Anecdote 9.2 was especially effective in creating tension.

The four negative emotions—anger, sadness, fear, and tension—create threatening conditions with which the audience must cope. One way people cope is to respond empathetically to the victim of child abuse. Such empathetic responses often include four specific reactions to anti-child-abuse ads: perspective taking, compassion or pity, protection motivation, and fantasy elaboration.[73] *Perspective taking* is the tendency to adopt the point of view of a person in need. *Compassion or pity* refers to other-oriented feelings such as concern. *Protection motivation* is the desire to shield the person in need or to intervene on his or her behalf. *Fantasy elaboration* is the propensity to go beyond the information provided about a person in need to develop feelings of identification and other emotional attachments. To design an effective anti-child-abuse ad, advertisers must stimulate all four reactions.

Figure 9.9 summarizes the key variables and processes governing the decision to help in response to emotion-laden anti-child-abuse ads. The paths from negative emotions to empathic responses and from empathy to the decision to help are based on the role of empathy in coping with the threatening conditions aroused by the emotions. The experience of negative affect leads to a need to feel better, and help-

Anti-child-abuse ads appeal especially to their audience's empathy.

ing others is one way to achieve this. Helping others is viewed as rewarding either because it is seen as a way to receive social recognition or because it is intrinsically rewarding (for example, when based on internalized moral norms).

Two experiments were designed to test the hypotheses implied by Figure 9.9.[74] In the first experiment, subjects viewed either an emotional ad or a rational ad appealing for help to reduce child abuse. The ads were embedded in the television program *Jeopardy* to create a realistic setting. As predicted, negative emotions and empathy mediated the effects of the ads on the decision to help. The emotional ad stimulated negative emotions (anger, sadness, fear, tension); these led to enhanced empathy (protection motivation, perspective taking, compassion or pity, fantasy

ELABORATION OF NEGATIVE EMOTIONS AND EMPATHY AS MEDIATORS OF THE EFFECTS OF ANTI-CHILD-ABUSE ADS ON THE DECISION TO HELP   FIGURE 9.9

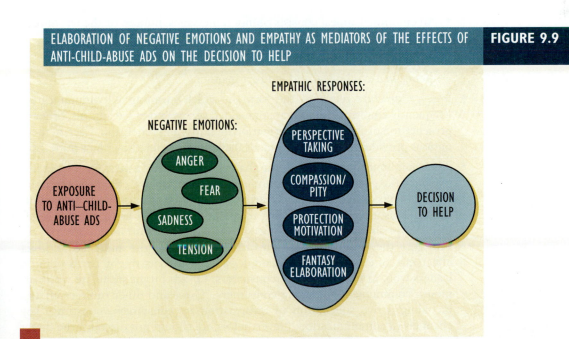

elaborations), and these, in turn, led to a decision to help. In the second experiment, two ads were patterned after the one described in Marketing Anecdote 9.2. One group of subjects saw a weak version of the ad (the whimpering of the boy was masked and the one-second piercing scream deleted); another group saw the strong version. Again the ads were embedded in the show *Jeopardy*. The prediction was that the greater the felt emotionality, the greater the empathy. This prediction was borne out. Unlike the rational information processing found in the ELM, the responses of the audience were driven by emotional and empathic reactions.

SUMMARY

Organizations cannot function well or for long if they do not develop effective communication programs. Communication is needed not only to inform customers but also to convince them of the best brands to consider. As with all of the marketing mix tools, communication is an essential tactic for meeting consumer needs and achieving a competitive edge.

The classic *source-message-medium-receiver model* stipulates that whether a communication will produce its intended effect depends on who says what, in which channel, and to whom. That is, influence depends on source characteristics, message content and structure, media selection, and receiver characteristics.

- The key *source characteristics* are credibility (i.e., expertise, trustworthiness), attractiveness, and the ability and intention to mediate rewards or punishments. Each of these can be thought of as an independent variable influencing consumer behavior, over and above the other communication variables.

- *Message content* includes rational appeals, emotional appeals, distraction, and use of a foil. Message content variables serve to convey meaning to a receiver.

  - A rational appeal stresses beneficial product attributes or consequences of product use.

  - An emotional appeal consists of mood messages, humor, or the use of fear.

  - Distraction in a message is employed to prevent counterargumentation.

  - A foil included in a communication is a dialogue designed to educate an audience in a symbolical and indirect manner.

- *Message structure* refers to the form in which meaning is communicated. Frequently employed options are one-sided versus two-sided appeals, order of presentation of arguments, information quantity, and repetition. Each of these options provides managers with tactical alternatives but also entails trade-offs.

- The communication *medium* is the channel used to send a message. Generally, personal (i.e., face-to-face) or nonpersonal (i.e., mass) channels are used. Media effects can be analyzed in terms of the *two-step flow model* of communication. This model maintains that mass communication has a number of effects. Surprisingly, the most important of those effects do not necessarily result from the direct transmission of the message to the audience. Indirect effects are often crucial. For example, advertisements might reach opinion leaders who, in turn, influence consumers. Or ads might stimulate word-of-mouth communication among consumers. These and other indirect effects, including active solicitation of information by consumers, constitute key channels of communication. Nevertheless, we should not discount the direct impact of mass communication efforts.

- The final variable in the SMMR model is the *receiver*. Key characteristics of receivers are self-esteem, demographic and life characteristics, personality traits, and past learning experiences. Because communication effects are dependent on receiver characteristics, one must take these into account in designing a persuasive campaign.

Two fundamental approaches to communication are the elaboration likelihood model (ELM) and the emotion and adaptation model (EAM).

- The ELM conceives of consumers as information processors.
  - The primary or "central" route to persuasion under the ELM is through motivated processing of arguments in a message. Persuasion depends on the balance of favorable and unfavorable thoughts that the recipient generates in response to the message. If favorable thoughts outweigh unfavorable ones, a positive attitude results. If not, no change in attitude results.
  - The secondary or "peripheral" route to persuasion in the ELM occurs when the audience is not motivated to process the arguments in a message but nevertheless is influenced by cues attached to the spokesperson or other aspects of the message. Perceived expertise, trustworthiness, or attractiveness of the spokesperson are important cues in this sense. The cues stimulate stored rules or heuristics in the mind of a message recipient. For instance, an attractive spokesperson might trigger the heuristic, "People generally agree with people they like and admire." Persuasion via the peripheral route happens through the influence afforded by information that is tangential to the main arguments in a message. Such variables as audience involvement interact with argument quality and source characteristics to produce complex effects on persuasion.
- The EAM is a fundamentally different approach to communication that places more emphasis on emotions than the ELM. In the EAM, the receiver is thought first to react to a persuasive message by making an appraisal of its relevance or significance, as well as the receiver's ability to cope with the consequences of the message. Depending on the nature of the appraisal, one or more discrete emotional responses are evoked (e.g., anger, sadness, fear, guilt, love, joy). Each emotion then leads to specific coping responses designed to satisfy a desire or avoid a negative outcome.

Marketing communication is considered further in subsequent chapters. Chapter 10 addresses advertising, publicity, and promotion. Chapter 11 considers face-to-face communication, particularly from the perspective of the sales force.

QUESTIONS FOR DISCUSSION

1. What is meant by communication? Compare and contrast communication and social influence.
2. Figure 9.1 presents the classic source-message-medium-receiver model of communication. Why is this model important and how can it be used in the design and execution of marketing communications?
3. Many people believe that marketing communication should be limited to providing factual information. What is your position on this issue? What consequences might ensue if an organization's communication were limited to providing factual information?

4. Three characteristics of the sender of a message to influence audiences are source credibility, attractiveness, and mediation of rewards and punishments. Briefly describe each characteristic and how it functions.

5. A basic decision in any communication program is whether to use rational or emotional appeals. Discuss the pros and cons of each type of appeal.

6. What is counterargumentation and how might it be reduced or overcome? What is meant by the use of a foil in persuasive communications?

7. Discuss the central issues and choices concerning the design of message structures.

8. What is the two-step flow model of communication and why is it important?

9. How would you design a communication program to attract blood donors?

10. How would you design a communication program for a chain of health-food stores to market tofu-based ice-cream cones and packaged ice cream?

11. Compare and contrast the elaboration likelihood model with the emotion and adaptation model. Find print advertisements and indicate how they fit each model.

NOTES FOR FURTHER READING

1. An early synthesis of the classic view of communication can be found in Harold D. Lasswell, *Power and Personality* (New York: W. W. Norton, 1948), pp. 37–51, 178–190. For an introduction to communication theory, see S. Littlejohn, *Theories of Human Communication* (Columbus, Ohio: Charles Merrill, 1978). Comprehensive, modern treatments from a marketing perspective can be found in Michael L. Ray, *Advertising and Communication Management* (Upper Saddle River, N.J.: Prentice-Hall, 1982); John R. Rossiter and Larry Percy, *Advertising and Promotion Management* (New York: McGraw-Hill, 1987); Terence A. Shimp, *Promotion Management and Marketing Communication*, 3rd ed. (Fort Worth, Texas: Dryden, 1993).

2. Representative research on source credibility can be found in C. Hovland and W. Weiss, "The Influence of Source Credibility on Communication Effectiveness," *Public Opinion Quarterly* 15 (Winter 1951): 635–650. See also G. Miller and J. Baseheart, "Source Trustworthiness, Opinionated Statements, and Response to Persuasive Communication," *Speech Monographs* 36 (1969): 1–7. In marketing, see Robert B. Settle and Linda L. Golden, "Attribution Theory and Advertiser Credibility," *Journal of Marketing Research* 11 (May 1974): 181–185. A new perspective can be found in Ruby R. Dholakia and Brian Sternthal, "Highly Credible Sources: Persuasive Facilitators or Persuasive Liabilities?" *Journal of Consumer Research* 3 (March 1977): 223–232.

3. L. S. Harms, "Listener Judgments of Status Cues in Speech," *Quarterly Journal of Speech* 47 (April 1961): 164–168.

4. C. I. Hovland, I. L. Janis, and H. H. Kelley, *Communication and Persuasion* (New Haven, Conn.: Yale University Press, 1953).

5. Classic treatments of attraction can be found in T. M. Newcomb, "The Prediction of Interpersonal Attraction," *American Psychologist* 11 (1956): 575–586; C. W. Backman and P. F. Secord, "The Effect of Liking on Interpersonal Attraction," *Human Relations* 12 (1959): 379–384; T. M. Newcomb, "Varieties of Interpersonal Attraction," in D. Cartwright and A. Zander, eds., *Group Dynamics*, 2nd ed. (New York: Harper & Row, 1960); and D. Byrne, *The Attraction Paradigm* (New York: Academic Press, 1971). More recent discussions include E. Berscheid, "Interpersonal Attraction," in G. Lindzey and E. Aronson, eds., *Handbook of Social Psychology*, 3rd ed., vol. 2 (New York: Random House, 1985), 413–484; Lynn R. Kahle and Pamela M. Homer, "Physical Attractiveness of the Celebrity Endorser: A Social Adaptation Perspective," *Journal of Consumer Research* 11 (March 1985): 954–961; Roobina Ohanian, "Construction and Validation of a Scale to Measure Celebrity Endorsers' Perceived Expertise, Trustworthiness, and Attractiveness," *Journal of Advertising* 19, 3 (1990): 39–52; Jessica Severn, George E. Belch, and Michael A. Belch, "The Effects of Sexual and Non-sexual Advertising Appeals and Information Level on Cognitive Processing and Communication Effectiveness," *Journal of Advertising* 19, 1 (1990): 14–22; and Michael J. Baker and Gilbert A. Churchill, Jr., "The Impact of Physically Attractive Models on Advertising Evaluation," *Journal of Marketing Research* 14 (November 1977): 538–555.

6. J. R. P. French, Jr., and B. Raven, "The Bases of Social Power," in D. Cartwright, ed., *Studies in Social Power* (Ann Arbor, Mich.: Institute of Social Research, 1959), pp. 150–167.

7. James T. Tedeschi, Barry R. Schlenker, and Thomas V. Bonoma, *Conflict, Power, and Games* (Chicago: Aldine, 1973), pp. 66–69.

8. T. C. Brock, "Communicator-Recipient Similarity and Decision Change," *Journal of Personality and Social Psychology* 1 (1965): 640–654.

9. See French and Raven, "The Bases of Social Power"; Tedeschi, Schlenker, and Bonoma, *Conflict, Power, and Games;* J. D. Singer, "Interpersonal Influence: A Formal Model," *American Political Science Review* 57 (1963): 420–430; and J. Z. Rubin and B. R. Brown, *The Social Psychology of Bargaining and Negotiation* (New York: Academic Press, 1975).

10. Brian Sternthal and C. Samuel Craig, "Fear Appeals: Revisited," *Journal of Consumer Research* 1 (December 1974): 22–34.

11. C. Hovland and W. Mandell, "An Experimental Comparison of Conclusion-Drawing by the Communicator and by the Audience," *Journal of Abnormal and Social Psychology* 47 (1952): 581–588; B. Fine, "Conclusion-Drawing, Communicator Credibility and Anxiety as Factors in Opinion Change," *Journal of Abnormal and Social Psychology* 54 (1957): 369–374.

12. See Jack W. Brehm, *A Theory for Psychological Reactance* (New York: Academic Press, 1966), especially chapter 6; and R. A. Wright, "Attitude Change as a Function of Threat to Attitudinal Freedom and Extent of Agreement with a Communicator," *European Journal of Social Psychology* 16 (1986): 43–50.

13. N. Schwarz, H. Bless, and G. Bohner, "Mood and Persuasion: Affective States Influence the Processing of Persuasive Communications," in M. P. Zanna, ed., *Advances in Experimental Social Psychology*, vol. 24 (San Diego: Academic Press, 1991), pp. 161–199.

14. Michael S. LaTour, Robert E. Pitts, and David C. Snook-Luther, "Female Nudity, Arousal, and Ad Response: An Experimental Investigation," *Journal of Advertising* 19, 4 (1990): 51–62.

15. See Noel Capon and James Hulbert, "The Sleeper Effect—An Awakening," *Public Opinion Quarterly* 37 (Fall 1973): 322–358; A. R. Pratkanis, A. G. Greenwald, M. R. Leippe, and M. H. Baumgardner, "In Search of Reliable Persuasion Effects: III. The Sleeper Effect Is Dead. Long Live the Sleeper Effect," *Journal of Personality and Social Psychology*, 54 (1988): 203–218; and Darlene B. Hannah and Brian Sternthal, "Detecting and Explaining the Sleeper Effect," *Journal of Consumer Research* 11 (September 1984): 632–642.

16. For basic research into humor, see A. J. Chapman and H. C. Foot, eds., *Humor and Laughter: Theory, Research, and Applications* (London: Wiley, 1976); A. J. Chapman and H. C. Foot, eds., *It's a Funny Thing, Humour* (Oxford: Pergamon, 1977); P. McGhee, *Humor: Its Origin and Development* (San Francisco: Freeman Press, 1979); and Karen O'Quin and Joel Aronoff, "Humor as a Technique of Social Influence," *Social Psychology Quarterly* 44 (December 1981): 349–357. For humor in marketing, see Brian Sternthal and C. Samuel Craig, "Humor in Advertising," *Journal of Marketing* 37 (October 1973): 12–18; J. Patrick Kelly and Paul J. Solomon, "Humor in Television Advertising," *Journal of Advertising* 4 (Summer 1975): 31–35; and Mervin D. Lynch and Richard C. Hartman, "Dimensions of Humor in Advertising," *Journal of Advertising Research* 8 (December 1968): 39–45.

17. Sternthal and Craig, "Humor in Advertising," p. 17.

18. Kelly and Solomon, "Humor in Television Advertising."

19. The classic study investigating the effects of fear arousal was conducted by Irving L. Janis and Seymour Feshbach, "Effects of Fear-Arousing Communication," *Journal of Abnormal and Social Psychology* 48 (January 1953): 78–92. For a psychological perspective, see Harold Leventhal, "Findings and Theory in the Study of Fear Communications," in L. Berkowitz, ed., *Advances in Experimental Social Psychology*, vol. 5 (New York: Academic Press, 1970), pp. 119–186. For marketing viewpoints, see Michael L. Ray and William Wilkie, "Fear: The Potential of an Appeal Neglected by Marketing," *Journal of Marketing* 34 (January 1970): 54–62; Brian Sternthal and C. Samuel Craig, "Fear Appeals: Revisited and Revised," *Journal of Consumer Research* 1 (December 1974): 22–34; John F. Tanner, Jr., B. Hunt, and David R. Eppright, "The Protection Motivation Model: A Normative Model of Fear Appeals," *Journal of Marketing* 55 (July 1991): 36–45; and Richard P. Bagozzi and David J. Moore, "Public Service Advertisements: Emotions and Empathy Guide Prosocial Behavior," *Journal of Marketing* 58 (January 1994): 56–70.

20. See, for example, Leventhal, "Findings and Theory in the Study of Fear Communications"; Irving L. Janis, *The Contour of Fear* (New York: Wiley, 1968); and Sternthal and Craig, "Fear Appeals: Revisited and Revised."

21. William J. McGuire, "An Information-Processing Model of Advertising Effectiveness," unpublished working paper, Department of Psychology, Yale University, 1969.

22. J. Allyn and Leon Festinger, "The Effectiveness of Unanticipated Persuasive Communications," *Journal of Abnormal and Social Psychology* 62 (February 1961): 35–40; Leon Festinger and Nathan Maccoby, "On Resistance to Persuasive Communication," *Journal of Abnormal and Social Psychology* 68 (November 1964): 359–366; J.L. Freedman and D. O. Sears, "Warning, Distraction, and Resistance to Influence," *Journal of Personality and Social Psychology* 1 (1965): 262–266; Robert A. Osterhouse and Timothy C. Brock, "Distraction Increases Yielding to Propaganda by Inhibiting Counterarguing," *Journal of Personality and Social Psychology* 15 (August 1970): 344–358; David M. Gardner, "The Distraction Hypothesis in Marketing," *Journal of Advertising Research* 10 (December 1970): 25–30; M. Venkatesan and Gordon A. Haaland, "Divided Attention and Television Commercials: An Experimental Study," *Journal of Marketing Research* 5 (May 1968): 203–205; Stewart W. Bither, "Comments on Venkatesan and Haaland's Test of the Festinger–Maccoby

Divided Attention Hypothesis," *Journal of Marketing Research* 6 (May 1969): 237–238.

23. Elaine Walster and Leon Festinger, "The Effectiveness of 'Overhead' Persuasive Communications," *Journal of Abnormal and Social Psychology* 65 (1962): 395–402.

24. One-sided versus two-sided appeals are addressed by Carl I. Hovland, Arthur A. Lumsdaine, and Fred D. Sheffield, *Experiments on Mass Communication* (New York: Wiley, 1949); Carl I. Hovland, *The Order of Presentation in Persuasion* (New Haven, Conn.: Yale University Press, 1957); and E. W. Faison, "Effectiveness of One-Sided and Two-Sided Mass Communications in Advertising," *Public Opinion Quarterly* 25 (1961): 468–469. The use of two-sided appeals (i.e., acknowledging competitor claims) is also known as refutational advertising.

25. Hovland et al., *Experiments on Mass Communication*.

26. William J. McGuire, "Inducing Resistance to Persuasion: Some Contemporary Approaches," in L. Berkowitz, ed., *Advances in Experimental Social Psychology*, vol. 1 (New York: Academic Press, 1964), pp. 191–229; George J. Szbillo and Richard Heslin, "Resistance to Persuasion: Inoculation Theory in a Marketing Concept," *Journal of Marketing Research* 10 (November 1973): 396–403.

27. E. Walster, E. Aronson, and D. Abrahams, "On Increasing the Persuasiveness of a Low Prestige Communicator," *Journal of Experimental Social Psychology* 2 (1966): 325–342; Settle and Golden, "Attribution Theory and Advertiser Credibility."

28. Michael A. Kamins and Henry Assael, "Two-Sided Versus One-Sided Appeals: A Cognitive Perspective on Argumentation, Source Derogation, and the Effect of Disconfirming Trial on Belief Change," *Journal of Marketing Research* 24 (February 1987): 29–39.

29. Stanley M. Ulanoff, *Comparative Advertising: A Historical Perspective* (Cambridge, MA: Marketing Science Institute, 1975); Linda L. Golden, "Consumer Reactions to Explicit Brand Comparisons in Advertisements," *Journal of Marketing Research* 16 (November 1979): 517–532; Stephen Goodwin and Michael Etgar, "An Experimental Investigation of Comparative Advertising: Impact of Message Appeal, Information Load, and Utility of Product Class," *Journal of Marketing Research* 17 (May 1980): 187–202; Mita Sujan and Christine Dekleva, "Product Categorization and Inference Making: Some Implications for Comparative Advertising," *Journal of Consumer Research* 14 (December 1987): 372–378; Gerald J. Gorn and Charles B. Weinberg, "The Impact of Comparative Advertising on Perception and Attitude: Some Positive Findings," *Journal of Consumer Research* 11 (September 1984): 719–727; Darrell D. Muehling, Donald E. Stern, Jr., and Peter Raven, "Comparative Advertising: Views from Advertisers, Agencies, Media, and Policy Makers," *Journal of Advertising Research* 29 (October/November 1989): 38–48.

30. Thomas Barry and Roger Tremblay, "Comparative Advertising: Perspectives and Issues," *Journal of Advertising* 4 (Winter 1975): 15–20. In addition to discovering the perception of lack of truthfulness, these authors found that the consumers surveyed did not particularly like comparative ads. However, because the practice of comparison advertising was new at the time of the study, people may not have thought deeply about the issues.

31. Kanti V. Prasad, "Communications Effects of Comparative Advertising: A Laboratory Analysis," *Journal of Marketing Research* 13 (May 1976), pp. 128–137.

32. Golden, "Consumer Reactions to Explicit Brand Comparisons."

33. Goodwin and Etgar, "An Experimental Investigation of Comparative Advertising."

34. William R. Swinyard, "The Interaction between Comparative Advertising and Copy Claim Variation," *Journal of Marketing Research* 18 (May 1981): 175–186.

35. "A Pained Bayer Cries 'Foul,'" *Business Week*, July 25, 1977, p. 142.

36. Michael B. Mazis and Janice E. Adkinson, "An Experimental Evaluation of a Proposed Corrective Advertising Remedy," *Journal of Marketing Research* 13 (May 1976): 178–183; William L. Wilkie, Dennis L. McNeill, and Michael B. Mazis, "Marketing's 'Scarlet Letter': The Theory and Practice of Corrective Advertising," *Journal of Marketing* 48 (Spring 1984): 11–31.

37. H. Gilkinson, S. Paulson, and D. Sikkink, "Effects of Order and Authority in an Argumentative Speech," *Quarterly Journal of Speech* 40 (1954): 183–192; Hovland, *The Order of Presentation in Persuasion*.

38. Jacob Jacoby, Donald Speller, and Carol Kohn, "Brand Choice Behavior as a Function of Information Load," *Journal of Marketing Research* 11 (February 1974): 63–69; Jacob Jacoby, Donald Speller, and Carol Kohn Berning, "Brand Choice Behavior as a Function of Information Load: Replication and Extension," *Journal of Consumer Research* 1 (June 1974): 33–42; J. Edward Russo, "More Information Is Better: A Reevaluation of Jacoby, Speller, and Kohn," *Journal of Consumer Research* 1 (December 1974): 68–72; Jacob Jacoby, "Information Load and Decision Quality: Some Contested Issues," *Journal of Marketing Research* 14 (November 1977): 569–573; John O. Summers, "Less Information Is Better?" *Journal of Marketing Research* 11 (November 1974): 467–468; William L. Wilkie, "Analysis of Effects of Information Load," *Journal of Marketing Research* 11 (November 1974): 462–466.

39. James R. Bettman, "Issues in Designing Consumer Information Environments," *Journal of Consumer Research* 2 (December 1975): 169–177; James R. Bettman and Pradeep Kakkar, "Effects of Information Presentation Format on Consumer Information Strategies," *Journal of Consumer Research* 3 (March 1977): 233–240; Valerie A. Zeithaml, "Consumer Response to In-store Price Information Environments," *Journal of Consumer Research* 8 (March 1982): 357–369.

40. Lawrence A. Crosby and James R. Taylor, "Effects of Consumer Information and Education on Cognition and Choice," *Journal of Consumer Research* 8 (June 1981): 43–56.

41. George A. Miller, "The Magical Number Seven, Plus or Minus Two: Some Limits on Our Capacity for Processing Information," *Psychological Review* 63 (1956): 81–97.

42. Prabhaker Nayak and Larry J. Rosenberg, "Does Open Dating of Food Products Benefit the Consumer?" *Journal of Retailing* 51 (Summer 1975): 10–20.

43. J. Edward Russo, "The Value of Unit Price Information," *Journal of Marketing Research* 14 (May 1977): 193–202; James M. Carman, "A Summary of Unit Pricing in Supermarkets," *Journal of Retailing* 48 (Winter 1972–1973): 63–71; Zeithaml, "Consumer Response to In-store Price Information Environments."

44. Edward H. Asam and Louis P. Bucklin, "Nutrition Labeling for Canned Goods: A Study of Consumer Response," *Journal of Marketing* 37 (April 1973): 32–37; Warren A. French and Hiram C. Barksdale, "Food Labeling Regulations: Efforts toward Full Disclosure," *Journal of Marketing* 38 (July 1974): 14–19.

45. Alan G. Sawyer, "The Effects of Repetition: Conclusions and Suggestions about Experimental Laboratory Research," in G. David Hughes and Michael L. Ray, eds., *Buyer/Consumer Information Processing* (Chapel Hill: University of North Carolina Press, 1974), pp. 190–219; Alan G. Sawyer, "Repetition and Affect: Recent Empirical and Theoretical Developments," in A. G. Woodside, J. N. Sheth, and P. D. Bennett, eds., *Consumer and Industrial Buying Behavior* (New York: North-Holland, 1977); Alan G. Sawyer, "Repetition, Cognitive Responses, and Persuasion," in R. E. Petty, T. M. Ostrom, and T. C Brock, eds., *Cognitive Responses to Persuasion* (Hillsdale, N.J.: Erlbaum, 1981).

46. Robert B. Zajonc, "Attitudinal Effects of Mere Exposure," *Journal of Personality and Social Psychology Monograph* 9 (1968): 1–28; William R. Wilson, "Feeling More than We Can Know: Exposure Effects without Learning," *Journal of Personality and Social Psychology* 37 (1979): 811–821.

47. Steuart Henderson Britt, "Applying Learning Principles to Marketing," *MSU Business Topics* 23 (Spring 1975): 5–12; Michael L. Ray, "Psychological Theories and Interpretations of Learning," in S. Ward and T. S. Robertson, eds., *Consumer Behavior: Theoretical Sources* (Upper Saddle River, N.J.: Prentice-Hall, 1973), pp. 45–117.

48. Michael L. Ray and Alan G. Sawyer, "Repetition in Media Models: A Laboratory Technique," *Journal of Marketing Research* 8 (February 1971): 20–29.

49. Paul F. Lazarsfeld, Bernard Berelson, and Hazel Gaudet, *The People's Choice*, 2nd ed. (New York: Columbia University Press, 1948).

50. Elihu Katz, "The Two-Step Flow of Communication: An Up-to-date Report on a Hypothesis," *Public Opinion Quarterly* 21 (Spring 1957): 61–78; Elihu Katz and Paul F. Lazarsfeld, *Personal Influence* (New York: Free Press, 1955); Bernard Berelson and Gary A. Steiner, *Human Behavior: An Inventory of Scientific Findings* (New York: Harcourt, Brace & World, 1964); Kenny K. Chan and Shekhar Misra, "Characteristics of the Opinion Leader: A New Dimension," *Journal of Advertising* 19, 3 (1990): 53–60.

51. William H. Whyte, Jr., "The Web of Word-of-Mouth," in L. H. Clark, ed., *The Life Cycle and Consumer Behavior* (New York: New York University Press, 1955), pp. 113–122; Ernest Dichter, "How Word of Mouth Advertising Works," *Harvard Business Review*, November–December 1966, pp. 147–166; Jagdish N. Sheth, "Word-of-Mouth in Low-Risk Innovations," *Journal of Advertising Research* 11 (June 1971): 15–18; Johan Arndt, "Selective Processes in Word-of-Mouth," *Journal of Advertising Research* 8 (June 1968): 19–22; James F. Engel, Robert J. Kegerreis, and Roger D. Blackwell, "Word-of-Mouth Communication by the Innovator," *Journal of Marketing* 33 (July 1969): 15–19; Paul M. Herr, Frank R. Kardes, and John Kim, "Effects of Word-of-Mouth and Product-Attribute Information on Persuasion: An Accessibility-Diagnosticity Perspective," *Journal of Consumer Research* 17 (March 1991), 454–462.

52. Thomas S. Robertson and James H. Myers, "Personality Correlates of Opinion Leadership and Innovative Buying Behavior," *Journal of Marketing Research* 6 (May 1969): 164–168; Lawrence G. Corey, "People Who Claim to Be Opinion Leaders: Identifying Their Characteristics by Self-Report," *Journal of Marketing* 35 (October 1971): 48–53; James H. Myers and Thomas S. Robertson, "Dimensions of Opinion Leadership," *Journal of Marketing Research* 9 (February 1972): 41–46; William R. Darden and Fred D. Reynolds, "Predicting Opinion Leadership for Men's Apparel Fashions," *Journal of Marketing Research* 9 (August 1972): 324–328; John O. Summers, "The Identity of Women's Clothing Fashion Opinion Leaders," *Journal of Marketing Research* 7 (May 1970): 178–185; Stephen A. Baumgarten, "The Innovative Communicator in the Diffusion Process," *Journal of Marketing Research* 12 (February 1975): 12–18; Chan and Misra, "Characteristics of the Opinion Leader."

53. Katz and Lazarsfeld, *Personal Influence*; Alvin J. Silk, "Overlap across Self-designated Opinion Leaders: A Study of Selected Dental Products and Services," *Journal of Marketing Research* 3 (August 1966): 253–259; John G. Myers, "Patterns of Interpersonal Influence in the Adoption of New Products," in R. M. Haas, ed., *Proceedings of the American Marketing Association Educator's Conference* (Chicago: American Marketing Association, 1966), pp. 750–757; David B. Montgomery and Alvin J. Silk, "Clusters of Consumer Interests and Opinion Leaders' Spheres of Influence," *Journal of Marketing Research* 8 (August 1971): 317–321; Johan Arndt, "Role of Product-related Conversations in the Diffusion of a New Product," *Journal of Marketing Research* 4 (August 1967): 291–295; Baumgarten, "The Innovative Communicator in the Diffusion Process"; Fred D. Reynolds and William R. Darden, "Mutually Adaptive Effects of

Interpersonal Communication," *Journal of Marketing Research* 8 (November 1971): 449–454.

54. Everett M. Rogers and F. Floyd Shoemaker, *Communication of Innovations*, (New York: Free Press, 1971); Michael J. Houston, "An Evaluation of Measures of Opinion Leadership," in K. L. Bernhardt, ed., *Marketing 1776–1976 and Beyond* (Chicago: American Marketing Association, 1976), pp. 564–571; Silk, "Overlap across Self-designated Opinion Leaders"; Arndt, "Role of Product-related Conversations"; Myers, "Patterns of Interpersonal Influence in Adoption of New Products"; Summers, "Identity of Women's Clothing Fashion Opinion Leaders"; Reynolds and Darden, "Mutually Adaptive Effects of Interpersonal Communication."

55. Joseph R. Mancuso, "Why Not Create Opinion Leaders for New Product Introductions?" *Journal of Marketing* 33 (July 1969): 20–25.

56. Alice M. Tybout, Bobby J. Calder, and Brian Sternthal, "Using Information Processing Theory to Design Marketing Strategies," *Journal of Marketing Research* 18 (February 1981): 73–79.

57. I. L. Janis and P. B. Field, "A Behavior Assessment of Consistency of Individual Differences," in C. I. Hovland and I. L. Janis, eds., *Personality and Persuasibility* (New Haven, Conn.: Yale University Press, 1959): 29–54.

58. S. Lindskold and J. T. Tedeschi, "Self-Esteem and Sex as Factors Affecting Influenceability," *British Journal of Social and Clinical Psychology* 10 (1971): 114–122.

59. Tedeschi, Schlenker, and Bonoma, *Conflict, Power, and Games.*

60. Richard E. Petty and John T. Cacioppo, *Communication and Persuasion: Central and Peripheral Routes to Attitude Change* (New York: Springer-Verlag, 1986). For a similar approach, see Shelly Chaiken, "The Heuristic Model of Persuasion," in M. P. Zanna, J. M. Olson, and C. P. Herman (eds.), *Social Influence: The Ontario Symposium*, vol. 5 (Hillsdale, N.J.: Erlbaum, 1987), pp. 3–39.

61. Chaiken, "The Heuristic Model of Persuasion."

62. D. F. Roberts and N. Maccoby, "Information Processing and Persuasion: Counterarguing Behavior," in P. Clarke, ed., *New Models for Communication Research* (Beverly Hills, Calif.: Russell Sage Foundation, 1973); Peter Wright, "The Cognitive Processes Mediating Acceptance of Advertising," *Journal of Marketing Research* 10 (February 1973): 53–62; Peter Wright, "Consumer Choice Strategies: Simplifying vs. Optimizing," *Journal of Marketing Research* 12 (February 1975): 60–67; Peter Wright, "Cognitive Responses to Mass Media Advocacy," in R. E. Petty, T. M. Ostrom, and T. C. Brock, eds., *Cognitive Responses to Persuasion* (Hillsdale, N.J.: Erlbaum, 1981); James R. Bettman, *An Information Processing Theory of Consumer Choice* (Reading, MA: Addison-Wesley, 1979).

63. Richard E. Petty, John T. Cacioppo, and David Schumann, "Central and Peripheral Routes to Advertising Effectiveness: The Moderating Role of Involvement," *Journal of Consumer Research* 10 (September 1983): 134–148.

64. Richard E. Petty, David W. Schumann, Steven A. Richman, and Alan J. Strathman, "Positive Mood and Persuasion: Different Roles for Affect Under High- and Low-Elaboration Conditions," *Journal of Personality and Social Psychology*, 64, 1 (1993): 5–20; Richard E. Petty, John T. Cacioppo, and Jeff A. Kasmer, "The Role of Affect in the Elaboration Likelihood Model of Persuasion," in L. Donohew, H. E. Sypher, and E. T. Higgins, eds., *Communication, Social Cognition, and Affect* (Hillsdale, N.J.: Erlbaum, 1988), pp. 117–146; Richard E. Petty, Rao H. Unnava, and Alan J. Strathman, "Theories of Attitude Change," in T. S. Robertson and H. H. Kassarjian, eds., *Handbook of Consumer Behavior* (Upper Saddle River, N.J.: Prentice-Hall, 1991), pp. 241–280. Some research shows, for example, that positive moods sometimes lead to less processing of message arguments than neutral moods, when people are moderately motivated to process a message. When people are more highly motivated, mood may bias information processing in the sense of increasing (positive mood) or decreasing (negative mood) the effects of the information.

65. Richard S. Lazarus, *Emotion and Adaptation* (New York: Oxford University Press, 1991); Richard P. Bagozzi, "The Self-Regulation of Attitudes, Intentions, and Behavior," *Social Psychology Quarterly* 55, 2 (1992): 178–204; Ira J. Roseman, "Appraisal Determinants of Discrete Emotions," *Cognition and Emotion* 5, 3 (1991): 161–200; Bagozzi and Moore, "Public Service Advertisements."

66. A list of 558 emotions can be found in J. R. Averill, "A Semantic Atlas of Emotional Concepts," *JSAS: Catalog of Selected Documents in Psychology* 5, ms no. 421 (1975).

67. Phillip Shaver, Judith Schwartz, Donald Kirson, and Gary O'Connor, "Emotion Knowledge: Further Exploration of a Prototype Approach," *Journal of Personality and Social Psychology* 52, 6 (1987): 1061–1086; David Watson, Lee Anna Clark, and Auke Tellegen, "Development and Validation of Brief Measures of Positive and Negative Affect: The PANAS Scales," *Journal of Personality and Social Psychology* 54, 6 (1988): 1063–1070.

68. Randy J. Larsen and Ed Diener, "Affect Intensity as an Individual Difference Characteristic: A Review," *Journal of Research in Personality* 21 (1987): 1–39.

69. Bagozzi, "Self-Regulation of Attitudes, Intentions, and Behavior."

70. Bagozzi and Moore, "Public Service Advertisements."

71. Lazarus, *Emotion and Adaptation*, p. 250.

72. Ibid., p. 235.

73. M. H. Davis, "Measuring Individual Differences in Empathy: Evidence for a Multidimensional Approach," *Journal of Personality and Social Psychology* 44 (1983): 113–126; Randy J. Larsen, Ed Diener, and Russell S. Cropanzano, "Cognitive Operations Associated with Individual Differences in Affect Intensity," *Journal of Personality and Social Psychology* 53 (1987): 767–774.

74. Bagozzi and Moore, "Public Service Advertisements."

CHAPTER 10

ADVERTISING, SALES PROMOTION, AND PUBLICITY

CHAPTER OBJECTIVES

When you are done with this chapter, you should have achieved the following:

- A familiarity with the purpose, scope, and players in modern advertising
- A general overview of the art and science of advertising
- An understanding of how advertising effectiveness is measured
- A general framework for advertising management
- Ability to discuss social and legal aspects of advertising

CHAPTER OUTLINE

Is Advertising Necessary?

Many people equate advertising with the marketing function and do not understand the purpose of advertising. The general public often regards advertising as unnecessary, even wasteful. Why is it, they ask, that 60 cents of the price of a box of cereal goes to advertising? Managers, too, frequently question the value of advertising. Indeed, Southwest Airlines founder, Rollin King, once said, "In my opinion, most advertising is a waste of money."

Is advertising wasteful? Do managers really believe that the money they spend on advertising is unnecessary? Are they correct in their beliefs?

Let us look first at advertising in the ready-to-eat cereal industry. More than 150 brands compete for sales in an $8 billion market. Without advertising, any particular com-

Breakfast cereal manufacturers rely on advertising to differentiate their products, and they advertise during different time periods to reach their customers.

pany would have difficulty doing business. To attract new customers and hold on to existing ones, firms must advertise. But granting the necessity of firms advertising in order to compete and survive, do consumers receive value for the money they spend? R. Craig Shulstad of General Mills answers this way: "Where else are you going to get convenience, taste, and nutrition for between fifteen cents and nineteen cents a serving?"

Top managers sometimes think that the only reason they advertise is that their competitors do. But deep down they have little confidence in advertising's ability to generate sales, and they allocate advertising funds begrudgingly. Intuitively, we know that there is more to advertising than folly. After all, why is $128 billion, half the worldwide total, spent each year on

In chapter 9, we introduced a communication model for the marketplace that focused on the psychological and social mechanisms underlying communication. Here we consider communication from the point of view of the firm with particular emphasis placed upon how managers make particular decisions. Figure 10.1 indicates five broad communication options the firm may choose, and Table 10.1 on page 367 provides definitions of each option. In this chapter we concentrate primarily on advertising, with some brief coverage of promotion and publicity. We cover personal selling in chapter 11 and promotion in chapters 11, 12, and 13.

Before we begin consideration of advertising, promotion, and publicity, we should point out two caveats. Although we discuss elements of the communication mix separately, we do so for presentation reasons only. Managers must consider when each tool is appropriate and what combination of tools is most desirable in any overall marketing program. Furthermore, communication or promotion-mix decisions represent only one area under the control of management; product, price, and distribution programs must be integrated with communication options in any overall marketing effort.

advertising in the United States alone? Is advertising effective? That is a more difficult question to answer with certainty.

A recent study provides one indication of the value of advertising from the perspective of the firm. The study compared results for firms that cut back their advertising during two recession years versus firms that did not, after normalizing to make the comparisons meaningful. Firms that did not cut back advertising sold approximately 50 percent more than firms that did cut back during the recession, and about 60 percent more in the two years following the recession. Indeed, net income was nearly 50 percent greater both during the two recessionary years and two years afterward for firms that did not cut back advertising compared to those who did. No single study is definitive or without limitations. But these findings illustrate the essential role that advertising plays for the success of individual firms.

Why advertise? Chewing gum magnate Wrigley summed it up: "On a train journey to California, a friend asked Mr. Wrigley why, with the lion's share of the market, he continued to advertise his chewing gum. 'How fast do you think this train is going?' asked Wrigley. 'I would say about ninety miles an hour.' 'Well,' said Wrigley, 'do you suggest we unhitch the engine?' "

Sources: The 60-cent figure for cereal advertising is an estimate based on a long-run industry estimate that 15 percent of sales goes to advertising from Paul D. Scanlon, "Oligopoly and 'Deceptive' Advertising: The Cereal Industry Affair," *Antitrust Law & Economics Review* 3 (Spring 1970): 99–110.

King's quote is from a question-and-answer session following discussion of a Southwest Airlines case and videotaped by one of the authors.

Shulstad's quote is from Veronica Byrd, "High-Priced Cereals Crunch Food Budgets," *Detroit Free Press*, August 11, 1992, pp. 1E–2E.

The Wrigley quote is from David Ogilvy, *Ogilvy on Advertising* (New York: Crown Publishers, 1983), pp. 171–172.

Other sources include:

David A. Aaker, Rajeev Batra, and John G. Myers, *Advertising Management*, 4th ed. (Upper Saddle River, N.J.: Prentice-Hall, 1992), pp. 549–582.

"The Advertising Fact Book," *Advertising Age*, January 4, 1993, p. 20.

INTRODUCTION TO ADVERTISING

Purpose and Scope of Advertising

Without question, advertising represents one of the most pervasive and least costly modes of communication available to a manager. We cannot escape exposure to ads. Indeed, estimates indicate that the average family sees or hears more than a thousand ads in a normal day,[1] yet *People* magazine charges only $10.84 per thousand people reached.[2] Radio, television, newspapers, and other media ads can be equally inexpensive based on cost per thousand people reached.

Purpose

In general, advertising and other elements of the communication mix try to increase sales in one or more of five ways:

1. Recruit new users who have never tried the product class.
2. Encourage former users to renew purchases.

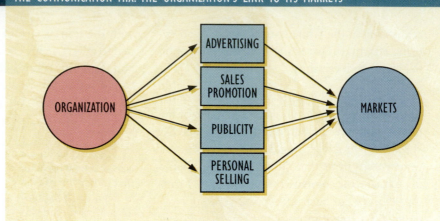

3. Encourage users of competing brands to switch.

4. Recruit switchers who are not loyal to any brand.

5. Increase consumption by current users.

Any one of these methods will increase sales, but the objectives and effects of advertising are actually more complex than the five ways noted above. Sometimes managers focus advertising at very specific groups within the above categories such as "elderly purchasers of competitor brand X," based on market segmentation strategies as we discussed in chapter 5. At other times, a market segment will cut across categories such as "all women aged 25 to 35, married with at least one child." Then, too, increased sales are not always the primary or immediate goal of an advertising campaign. For example, the objective may be merely to increase awareness of one's brand in market Y from 10 percent to 35 percent. Indeed, any one or more of the psychological stages audiences pass through when exposed to ads may be a goal in a specific ad campaign. Advertising may lack any particular objective relative to a target audience, instead aiming merely to build a positive company image in employees and the public at large or, occasionally, to serve simply as an advertiser's expression of pride with no particular utilitarian goal in mind.

In this chapter, we emphasize the purposeful or utilitarian side of advertising. Typically, marketers attempt to influence either consumers' psychological states or their behavior. Psychological variables include, among others, brand awareness, knowledge of product attributes, beliefs about the consequences of product use, emotional reactions toward a brand (e.g., interest, liking), and intentions to purchase. Behavioral variables encompass, among others, trial purchase, brand loyalty, increased usage, switching, and overall sales.

Scope of Advertising

With more than $128 billion spent on advertising in the United States, advertising is obviously big business. About 2.3 percent of the U.S. gross national product—about $512 per person per year—is spent on advertising. To place this in perspective, Table 10.2 shows how 12 other countries around the world compare to the United States. All told, the United States currently accounts for just under half of the free world's expenditures on advertising.[3] Even socialist countries advertise extensively, although we know little about their actual expenditures.[4]

TABLE 10.1 DEFINITIONS AND EXAMPLES OF THE PRIMARY TOOLS IN THE COMMUNICATION MIX

Communication Tool	Definition	Examples
Advertising	Any paid form of nonpersonal presentation of ideas, goods, and services by an identified sponsor.[1]	Television, radio, newspaper, magazine, direct mail, outdoor (e.g., billboard), specialty (e.g., embossed pens, calendars), and transit (e.g., bus and subway signs).
Sales Promotion	Short-term incentives by an identified sponsor directed at final customers or intermediaries with the purpose of encouraging purchase or adoption of a product, practice, or activity.	Coupons, free samples, price-off packages, contests, bonus packs, premiums, rebates, point-of-purchase materials, store demonstrations, trade shows and exhibits, trade allowances, and consumer education services.
Publicity	Any form of nonpaid, commercially significant news or editorial comment about ideas, products, or institutions.[2]	Conferences, press releases, newsletters, feature articles, photos, films, slides, tapes, annual reports, fund raising, special events, and public affairs.
Personal Selling	Oral presentation of ideas, goods, or services by a paid spokesperson directly to a prospective buyer or adopter.	Industrial salespeople, sales engineers, missionary salespeople, clerical salespeople, door-to-door salespeople, telephone sales, and team selling.

[1] Ralph S. Alexander and the Committee on Definitions, *Marketing Definitions* (Chicago: American Marketing Association, 1963), p. 9.

[2] *Marketing Definitions: A Glossary of Marketing Terms* (Chicago: American Marketing Association, 1960). *See also Peter D. Bennett, Dictionary of Marketing Terms (Chicago: American Marketing Association, 1988).*

TABLE 10.2 COMPARISON OF ADVERTISING EXPENDITURES IN THE UNITED STATES AND TWELVE OTHER COUNTRIES

Country	Percentage of Gross National Product (1990)	Per Capita Expenditures in U.S. Dollars (1990)
Spain	2.4	263
United States	2.4	512
Switzerland	1.9	613
United Kingdom	1.7	275
Bolivia	1.4	9
Sweden	1.3	319
Australia	1.3	226
Japan	1.2	311
Colombia	1.2	15
Mexico	1.0	26
Belgium	0.8	128
Italy	0.6	99
India	0.3	1

Source: World Advertising Expenditures *(Mamaroneck, N.Y.: Starch INRA Hooper, 1992), pp. 16–19. Reproduced with permission.*

TABLE 10.3 TOP FIFTEEN ADVERTISING AGENCIES IN THE WORLD IN 1996

Agency	Capitalized Volume (in millions of U.S. $)	Gross Income (in millions of U.S. $)
1. Dentsu Inc.	14,047.9	1,929.9
2. McCann-Erickson Worldwide	9,232.5	1,299.0
3. J. Walter Thompson Co.	7,288.0	1,073.0
4. BBDO Worldwide	7,456.1	925.2
5. Hakuhodo	6,677.0	897.7
6. Leo Burnett Co.	5,821.1	866.3
7. DDB Needham Worldwide	6,629.2	848.3
8. Grey Advertising	5,621.9	841.8
9. Euro RSCG	6,064.5	823.8
10. Ogilvy & Mather Worldwide	6,937.6	793.0
11. Foote, Cone & Belding	6,190.2	767.9
12. Young & Rubicam	7,348.9	707.3
13. Saatchi & Saatchi Advertising	5,710.2	685.2
14. Publicis Communication	4,617.7	676.8
15. Bates Worldwide	5,084.4	611.0

Source: Advertising Age, *April 21, 1997, p. A24. Reproduced with permission.*

More than 10,000 advertising agencies do business worldwide. Table 10.3 lists the top 15 in terms of capitalized volume or world billings (i.e., total amount of money charged to clients for media, production, and other services) and gross income (i.e., revenues). Notice that all the companies listed are billion-dollar operations; their percentages of business based in the United States varies from about 36 percent to 73 percent per firm. Table 10.4 presents the top 25 national advertisers. Procter & Gamble is the leading single advertiser with nearly $2.7 billion spent per year.

Overall, more than 17,000 companies in the United States advertise to sell their wares,[5] although less than 100 account for about 30 percent of all expenditures on national advertising.[6]

Advertising in Early Times

Throughout history, sellers have used some form of advertising to reach buyers. Primitive traders simply hung an animal carcass on a pole to announce their offerings. The Phoenicians painted messages on boulders and mountainsides along trade routes to inform and lure buyers. Craftsmen from Roman times and throughout the Middle Ages used special markings on their products and on the sides of their buildings to advertise their skills and wares.

Of course, the growth of advertising has closely paralleled the development of new technologies in communication. With the advent of the printing press, for example, advertising leaflets and newspapers began in the early 1500s. Indeed, advertising quickly became so widespread that in 1759, English philosopher Dr. Samuel Johnson noted, perhaps prematurely, "The trade of advertising is now so near perfection, it is not easy to propose any improvement."[7] But improve it did. As telephones, radios, and television emerged, so too did new forms of advertising.

TABLE 10.4 TWENTY-FIVE LEADING U.S. ADVERTISERS IN 1994

Company	Advertising Expenditures (in millions of U.S. $)
1. Procter & Gamble Co.	2,689.8
2. Philip Morris Cos.	2,413.3
3. General Motors Corp.	1,929.4
4. Ford Motor Co.	1,186.0
5. Sears, Roebuck & Co.	1,134.1
6. AT&T Corp.	1,102.7
7. PepsiCo	1,097.8
8. Chrysler Corp.	971.6
9. Walt Disney Co.	934.8
10. Johnson & Johnson	933.7
11. Nestle SA	894.2
12. Time Warner	860.0
13. Warner-Lambert Co.	831.2
14. Toyota Motor Corp.	766.1
15. Grand Metropolitan	764.3
16. McDonald's Corp.	763.7
17. Kellogg Co.	732.9
18. Unilever NV	654.7
19. JCPenney Co.	621.7
20. Federated Dept. Stores	614.0
21. American Home Products	572.7
22. General Mills	520.9
23. Sony Corp.	518.6
24. Anheuser-Busch Cos.	511.5
25. Honda Motor Co.	494.2

Source: Advertising Age, *September 27, 1995, p. 16. Reproduced with permission.*

New developments in computers and other electronic wonders will stimulate ever-refined and creative ways to reach others. For example, L.L. Bean and other vendors provide on-line computer catalogs for their products—a form of home-shopping networks.

Advertising and Modern Institutional Relationships

Today, we can characterize advertising through the increasingly specialized organizations that have evolved to create and produce the messages: the institutions that pay for the messages and media organizations that promulgate the messages and communicate it. Figure 10.2 presents a simple schematic of these key actors. Advertisers, of course, are the sponsoring firms that wish to reach the public with a message. Advertising agencies are specialized firms that design, produce, and distribute the advertising messages. Media organizations (e.g., newspaper, magazine,

FIGURE 10.2   PRIMARY ACTORS IN ADVERTISING

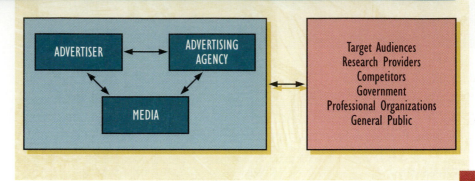

television, and radio companies) actually communicate these messages. On the right side of Figure 10.2 we list people and institutions who interact with advertisers, agencies, and media. Let us take a closer look at the key actors.

The Advertiser

A wide assortment of institutions sponsor advertisements. Most consumer and industrial goods manufacturers advertise, as do the majority of retail establishments. The governments of most countries also advertise heavily. In 1989, for example, the U.S. federal government spent $310 million for advertising, including $100 million for military recruiting, and $45 million by the U.S. Postal Service.[8] Nonprofit organizations also find advertising indispensable; the Red Cross, March of Dimes, and churches, among others, run frequent ad campaigns. Dentists, doctors, and lawyers have even joined the ranks of advertisers, although belatedly and with some controversy.

Nearly every organization sponsors special functional areas to handle communication tasks. Private companies typically have the most elaborate communication systems. Usually, communication tasks fall under the leadership of an advertising director, the vice president of marketing, the head of public relations, or, on occasion, the vice president of sales. But companies employ different frameworks to accomplish this and other goals. Most firms are organized under either a functional or a brand management system.[9] Figure 10.3 illustrates a typical functional hierarchy. Notice the five central business functions shown directly below the chief executive officer. One of these is marketing, and marketing itself is divided into five subfunctions: sales, advertising, marketing research, new product development, and distribution. For the example shown in Figure 10.3, the advertising director carries the responsibility for all forms of communication: promotion planning, media planning, and advertising account management. A functional marketing organization holds no one person or group responsible for the entire design, development, and management of a specific product or brand. Rather, this organizational structure parcels out the tasks required to market brands to specialized subgroups under the vice president of marketing. Thus, the advertising subgroup handles communication issues for all brands but has no responsibility for selling, marketing research, product development, or distribution of those brands. Separate groups address such tasks under a functional organization.

On the other hand, Figure 10.4 demonstrates a brand management organization of marketing tasks. Although some functional specialization exists for basic marketing tasks, most general marketing responsibilities fall to brand managers. In Figure 10.4

EXAMPLE OF A FUNCTIONAL ORGANIZATIONAL HIERARCHY (PARTIAL RENDITION) FIGURE 10.3

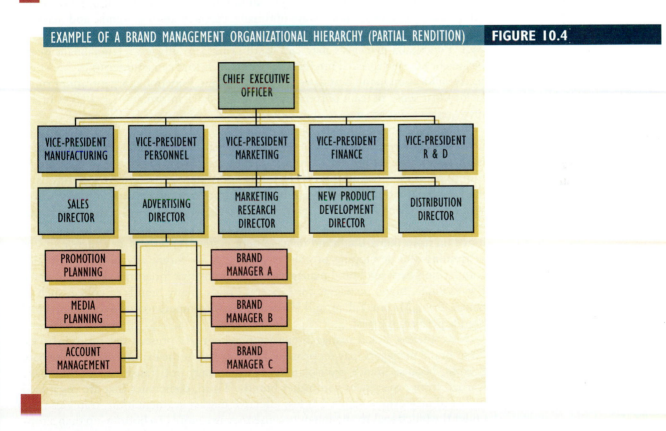

EXAMPLE OF A BRAND MANAGEMENT ORGANIZATIONAL HIERARCHY (PARTIAL RENDITION) FIGURE 10.4

brand managers report to the advertising director, although they sometimes are responsible to product managers, group product managers, or (at firms such as Procter & Gamble) category managers (e.g., the brand manager for Tide reports to the category manager for laundry products). Note that separate brand managers take charge of each brand. Moreover, brand managers (sometimes also called product managers or marketing managers) coordinate and administer the entire marketing program for their brands. They develop marketing strategies, plans, and forecasts; work with advertising agencies to develop ads; interact with coworkers responsible for designing, making, selling, and distributing the product; participate in pricing decisions; design promotions; gather and interpret information on how well the product is doing after launch; initiate improvements; and generally manage the product and its marketing throughout the life cycle.[10]

Which organizational type works better? No one can say definitively. Firms selling in the same general product category succeed with both approaches. Many consumer goods firms employ a brand management arrangement. General Foods, for instance, uses the brand management organization in its cereal and coffee product groups, among other places. Thus, General Foods hires separate brand managers for nutritional cereals, family cereals, and children's cereals, as well as for regular, instant caffeinated, and instant decaffeinated coffees. Procter & Gamble also uses a brand management system. On the other hand, PepsiCo employs a functional organization.[11]

Although firm guidelines are not possible to state, we might speculate on possible pros and cons of the functional and brand management organizations. Functional arrangements are simple and promote cross-fertilization among brands, because one or more individuals are directly involved with multiple brands and can apply their learning and experiences to all brands. But in functional organizations, effort and resources are not always optimally allocated among brands, and marketing subfunctions, such as distribution, will compete for attention and resources as well. Functional managers may lack valid criteria to efficiently coordinate many brands or may have vested interests or pet projects that run counter to the most effective allocation for all brands under their purview. Functional organizations often lack a clear sense of team purpose and may not share information as well as brand management systems do.

Indeed, the strength of the brand management arrangement lies in the assignment of overall responsibility to a single individual (or small number of individuals). Managers whose reputation is thus on the line are strongly motivated to pay attention to all of their brands and to efficiently coordinate manufacturing, design, and marketing activities related to the brand. Moreover, brand managers tend to respond faster than functional area managers to changes in the market and environment. Because many young professionals start out as assistant brand managers and move up from there, the brand management system represents an effective means of training and developing promising managers for future advancement. Finally, competition between brand managers can be a positive force within the company. For example, brand managers for General Foods' many brands of coffee, such as Sanka, Brim, Maxim, Yuban, and Maxwell House, compete to make their individual brands perform the best.

Nevertheless, brand management arrangements do present several drawbacks. First, brand managers may emphasize the short run at the expense of the long run. Second, because brands are isolated, managers may not transfer what they have learned from experiences with other brands. Third, companies that are organized by brand may exhibit somewhat less effective market segmentation strategies than under the functional arrangement because they use more of a bottom-up than a top-down process for initiating and making many marketing decisions. The functional arrangement results in better organization and coordination of market selection and segmentation. Finally, brand competition can become dysfunctional if conflicts emerge within the firm and/or excessive cannibalization of sales across brands occurs. The use of category managers represents a compromise between a pure brand management and functional management organization.

Every firm handles its communication needs differently. Until recently, many firms conducted advertising research, planned media, created copy, produced ads, and purchased media time as in-house functions. The Coors Brewing Company did so up until the late 1970s, and Quaker Oats, General Electric, and Scott Paper still do some of their own advertising.

However, as the tasks associated with advertising proliferate and become more complex, difficult, and expensive to execute, most firms have hired advertising agencies to handle their communication needs. Of course, nearly all firms employ internal people to coordinate communication and contacts with ad agencies. Some companies retain certain advertising tasks in-house and farm out others. Lipton, for example, often plans and buys media, but hires outside agencies to design and produce its ads. Whatever the arrangements, most modern organizations' communication programs rely on advertising agencies.

The Advertising Agency

Advertising agencies plan, create, execute, and place advertisements in media for clients (i.e., for advertisers). Figure 10.5 presents a typical organizational structure for a medium-sized ad agency. Note the four major components: administration, creative services, marketing services, and account services.

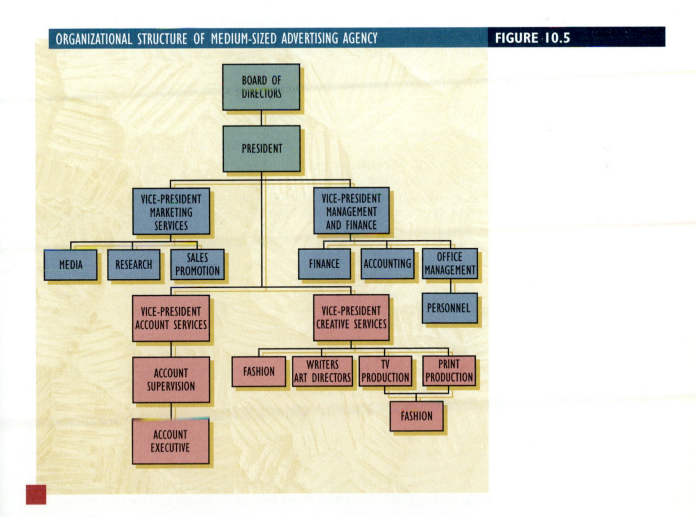

ORGANIZATIONAL STRUCTURE OF MEDIUM-SIZED ADVERTISING AGENCY **FIGURE 10.5**

Administration, headed by the vice president of management and finance, sees to the everyday management of financial, accounting, and personnel matters for the agency as a business.

An agency's *creative services* staff designs, develops, and produces the actual ads. Such staff includes artists, copywriters, photographers, television producers, designers, and other creative specialists who take the goals and plans formulated by advertisers and account people and translate them into real ads. Obviously, this is a highly subjective and nonlinear activity, as the name "creative services" implies.

Marketing services departments consist of technical support who emphasize marketing research, media planning, and sales promotion. Typically, marketing researchers have backgrounds in behavioral science and statistics; media planners have training in optimization and operations research; and sales promotion people come from a variety of backgrounds, such as liberal arts and business.

The center of any advertising agency is the *account services* group. Most agencies use a counterpart of a brand management arrangement; that is, each separate client brand will generally be handled by an account manager. Account managers interact with client firms and manage and coordinate all the activities needed to deliver an ad. For example, account managers work with clients to formulate advertising strategies by considering goals with respect to the psychological stages through which consumers pass (e.g., awareness, interest, desire, intention formation), broad themes to stress in advertising copy, product attributes to emphasize, definition of the target market(s), and so on. Account managers also administer the advertising program within the advertising agency by coordinating marketing research, media planning, message design, production, and other agency functions.

Clients compensate advertising agencies in a variety of ways.[12] Usually, the advertiser pays the media to run its ad, and for its services, the advertising agency receives a percentage (usually 15 percent) of the amount billed to the advertiser.[13] For example, an ad agency might produce a television ad for Anheuser-Busch to run during the Super Bowl. The media billing of $1 million would result in compensation of $150,000 to the agency, and the agency would receive that $150,000 commission each time the ad is shown.

Occasionally, advertising agencies are paid through a fee system. That is, at the outset, the client agrees to pay the agency's specific fee for services rendered. Still another source of compensation is a markup on materials used or actual payment of prespecified costs. Some advertisers pay flat commissions plus bonuses tied to performance.[14] Overall, most advertiser-agency relationships involve some negotiation and combination of compensation schemes. Incentive-based sliding scales, in which the commission percentage is pegged to the performance of the agency, are becoming more popular.[15]

The Media

The media are channels of communication that carry messages from an advertiser to a target audience; most commonly, the media include radio, television, newspapers, magazines, outdoor ads (posters, billboards, painted bulletins), direct mail, and miscellaneous vehicles (e.g., the Yellow Pages or specialty items such as calendars and pens). In the United States and most nontotalitarian societies, the media are independent institutions, although they are frequently subject to some regulation by governments.

To get a picture of the relative use of the media and how this has changed over time, look at Table 10.5, which shows total expenditures allocated to various media for a 40-year period. Note that the relative proportion of money spent on newspapers, magazines, business publications, radio, and outdoor ads has declined significantly over the period, whereas advertising expenditures on television, direct mail, and miscellaneous media have increased or remained the same as a proportion of total expenditures. Observe further that advertisers' use of local television and local radio has increased dramatically, perhaps reflecting the need to reach specific market segments with custom-tailored ads. Finally, note that newspaper advertising represents the single largest expenditure, although its percentage of the total has declined from about 36.3 percent in 1950 to 26.1 percent in 1989. Television advertising is the second largest category, and direct mail, which has been growing fastest in recent years, comes in third.

Which media are the most effective and efficient? It depends, because experts measure effectiveness and efficiency based on various criteria. Table 10.6 presents four frequently used media—television, radio, magazines, and newspapers—and evaluates them based on 35 criteria. The comparisons in Table 10.6 present the following generalizations: television ads reach the most people; radio costs the least on a per 1,000 people reached basis; magazines score high on sensory stimulation; humor is best executed on television; newspapers facilitate selective ad positioning, whereas television does not; television is best for brand name registration, whereas magazines and newspapers are worst; and radio is the most consistently monitored medium across seasons, whereas television is the poorest.

Table 10.6 Comparison of Four Media on 35 Criteria

Criterion	Television	Radio	Magazines	Newspapers
Total population reach (adults and children)	Very Strong	Good	Fair	Good
Selective upscale adult reach	Fair	Good	Very Strong	Good
Upscale adult selectivity (per ad exposure)	Poor	Fair	Very Strong	Good
Young adult selectivity (per ad exposure)	Fair	Very Strong	Very Strong	Fair
Cost per 1,000 ratios	Fair–Good	Very Strong	Strong	Good
National media availabilities and uniform coverage	Very Strong	Poor	Good	Poor
Local market selectivity	Good	Good	Poor	Very Strong
Ability to control frequency	Fair	Good	Good	Very Strong
Ability to pile frequency upon reach base	Very Strong	Very Strong	Good	Fair
Ability to exploit time-of-day factors (in scheduling)	Fair	Very Strong	Poor	Poor
Ability to exploit day-of-week factors (in scheduling)	Fair	Very Strong	Poor	Very Strong
Seasonal audience stability	Poor	Very Strong	Good	Good
Predictability of audience levels	Fair–Poor	Good	Good	Very Good
Depth of demographics in audience surveys	Poor	Poor	Very Strong	Fair–Good
Reliability and consistency of audience surveys	Fair–Good	Good	Fair–Good	Good
Ability to monitor schedules	Good	Poor	Very Strong	Very Strong
Ability to negotiate rates	Good	Fair	Poor	Poor
Fast closing and air dates	Fair	Good	Poor	Very Strong
Opportunity to exploit editorial "compatibility"	Poor	Fair	Very Strong	Good
Selective ad positioning	Poor	Fair	Good	Very Strong
Advertising exposure	Good	Good	Good	Good
Advertising intrusiveness	Very Strong	Good	Fair	Poor
Audience concern over ad "clutter"	Very High	High	Almost None	Almost None
Emotional stimulation	Very Strong	Fair	Fair	Poor
Sensory stimulation	Fair–Good	Fair	Very Strong	Fair
Brand name registration	Very Strong	Good	Fair	Fair
Product or efficacy demonstrations	Very Strong	Poor	Fair	Fair
Ability to exploit attention-getting devices	Very Strong	Poor	Very Strong	Good
Ability to use humor	Very Strong	Good	Poor	Poor
Ability to use slice-of-life approach	Very Strong	Good	Poor	Poor
Ability to convey detail and information	Fair	Fair	Very Strong	Very Strong
Ability to stimulate imagination	Fair–Good	Very Strong	Fair	Poor
Package identification	Good	Poor	Very Strong	Good
Prestige and respectability of the medium	Fair	Fair	Very Strong	Strong
Ability to talk person-to-person with audience	Fair–Good	Very Strong	Poor	Poor

Source: The Media Book *(New York: Min-Mid Publishing, 1978), pp. 433, 436.*

BEHAVIORAL DIMENSIONS OF ADVERTISING

Advertising agencies draw heavily upon principles from the behavioral sciences as they design ads. Much of this is done subjectively and is an outgrowth of the culture and philosophy of the advertising agency. Particular agencies' styles run throughout their ads. At the same time, agencies also employ objective findings from marketing and the behavioral sciences and from their own research as they design ads. In this section, we show how art (creative styles) and science (behavioral and marketing research) come together in effective advertisements.

Ad Agency Creative Styles

An advertising agency, like any company, has a personality that emerges in both its business approach and its products.[16] Often, the personality of an agency is closely tied to its leadership, particularly the influence of its current leaders and the charisma and creativity of its founders. We consider here four relatively distinct ad agencies, each of which owes its style to the inspiration of one or more people: the Leo Burnett agency (Leo Burnett), the Doyle Dane Bernbach agency (William Bernbach), the Ogilvy & Mather agency (David Ogilvy), and the Ted Bates and Company agency (Rosser Reeves). Perhaps no other area of marketing success is so dependent on intangible, subjective inputs as is the design and production of advertisements.

Leo Burnett

Leo Burnett created advertisements for a long list of products, including Kellogg's cereals, 7-Up, Nestlé, Phillip Morris, Procter & Gamble, United Airlines, Maytag, Pillsbury, and Allstate Insurance. You probably recognize at least some of the following slogans or "salespeople," all created by the Burnett agency: "Me and my RC," "Fly the Friendly Skies of United," the Jolly Green Giant, the elves of Keebler Cookies fame, the lonely Maytag repairman, Charlie the Tuna, "You're in good hands with Allstate," Morris the Cat, and the Pillsbury Dough Boy.

Burnett's ads for these companies and products feature common elements: many of the ads emphasize emotions and/or humor. At the same time, they typically focus on genuine product attributes in a realistic or functional way. As a consequence, Leo Burnett's ads are often described as "warm and believable." They create pleasant feelings yet do so without excessive embellishment and without making false claims. A good example is provided in the "Fly the Friendly Skies of United" ads. Burnett's agency added music to a catchy phrase, and the ads exuded a human quality

The Pillsbury Dough Boy: Who wouldn't love this warm and squishy guy who represents comfort food?

Mr. Clean, with his updated image, conveys efficiency and absolute cleanliness.

highlighting pleasant airline personnel and pleased customers of all ages and backgrounds. The United Airlines ads also demonstrate another of Leo Burnett's agency trademarks: ads frequently center on ordinary, everyday people. They show individuals with whom the viewers can readily identify. This aspect of Leo Burnett has been called "the common touch" and creates a wholesome image. Many of Burnett's ads for Procter & Gamble demonstrate this quality (for example, ads for Cheer laundry detergent).

Occasionally, Leo Burnett employs animation, with characters such as Charlie the Tuna, the Keebler Cookie elves, the Jolly Green Giant, Tony the Tiger, Mr. Clean, and the Pillsbury Dough Boy, supplying an element of fantasy that entertains and delivers the message in a nonthreatening way. Such characters may also enhance consumers' ability to remember brand names and product attributes over time because animated images are memorable. And animated characters are ideally suited for communicating warmth and humor. Finally, Leo Burnett uses animation dramatically to convey a story. In a typical application, one cartoon character will inform another (a foil) of a particular brand's benefits. Rather than lecturing the audience directly, the ad indirectly educates the consumer. This "foil" tactic is a common one in literature and drama, and is discussed in chapter 9. Such stories reduce consumers' skepticism and defenses that arise when people try to directly persuade us to do something, and, in general, the tactic is consistent with theories of observational learning.[17] Closely related to their use of foils, Leo Burnett's agency also frequently attempts to portray the "inherent drama" in a product:

> Of course we . . . stress this so-called inherent drama of things because there is usually something there. . . . If you can find the thing about that product that keeps it in the market-place . . . something about it that makes people continue to buy it . . . capturing that, and then taking that thing . . . and making the thing itself arresting.[18]

Thus, although we might not empathize with the lonely Maytag repairman, we get the point that the manufacturer's products are of a very high quality and are made to last. Each ad reenacts the repairman's search for someone who needs his services, which will give him a purpose in life.

One of Leo Burnett's most successful campaigns was for Marlboro cigarettes. Up to about 1954, Marlboro was primarily purchased by and for women. Its sales were minuscule compared to market leaders such as Camel and Lucky Strike, and Marlboro was not even distributed nationally. The cigarette could be bought with either an ivory tip or a red "beauty" tip, which were designed to hide "embarrassing" lipstick stains. Studies showed that men viewed Marlboro as a "feminine" or "sissy" cigarette. Then Philip Morris asked Leo Burnett to handle the advertising. Using research that showed heavy smokers to be young to middle-aged men and blue-collar workers, they decided to go after this market. No brands were directed exclusively toward these men, who expressed a desire for "full, honest flavor" in their cigarettes.

Thus, Burnett developed Marlboro ads in the mid to late 1950s that used the theme "delivers the goods on flavor." Ads stressed a strong-tasting cigarette, and masculine themes were introduced, especially in print media. For example, fisherman, tennis players, and other sportsmen were featured. Often the ads highlighted a tattoo on the back of the hand or arm to symbolically convey a "macho" image. Burnett also tried cowboy themes, and by the early 1960s, the theme became "You get a lot to like with a Marlboro—filter, flavor, flip-top box." Burnett used the cowboy image almost exclusively throughout the 1960s, and in 1972 the theme was changed again to "come to Marlboro country," which is still used today. The ads create a strong aura of masculinity by showing rugged cowboys, spectacular scenery, cattle and horses, brown tones, and so on.

Leo Burnett was so successful that Marlboro soon became the sales-leading cigarette in the United States. Since 1980, Marlboro has regularly captured more than 20 percent of the market, with Winston a distant second.

Most of Leo Burnett's ads employ a "soft sell" approach to advertising. Their goal is not to be too offensive, pushy, or intrusive. They impact the marketplace subtly through positive affect and realism. Among all ad agencies, Leo Burnett seems to employ the most equal balance in its emphasis between message content and structure, as well as a certain amount of repetition.

Doyle Dane Bernbach

Doyle Dane Bernbach (DDB) concentrates more heavily on message structure than content, or, in the words of William Bernbach: "Execution can become content; it can be just as important as what you say."[19] Many of DDB's ads seem to follow a philosophy of "how it is said is more important than what is said"—the medium is the message.[20] Yet, as we describe in a moment, humor and refutational arguments have been central to DDB's ads as well.

Let us look at some of the more successful DDB ads. Although you might not have heard of DDB, you are certain to recognize some of its ads. Doyle Dane Bernbach was the first agency to advertise Volkswagen in the United States. They handle advertising for American Airlines, G.T.E., Polaroid, Stroh's beer, and some of Procter & Gamble's products. You may remember the Avis "We're number two, we try harder" campaign. Or the Jack-in-the-Box warning, "Watch out, McDonald's!" DDB also developed the recent series of ads on Mobil 1 Oil. Doyle Dane Bernbach has done ads for American Tourister luggage and Alka Seltzer, too. What common tactics, themes, or formats can you identify in many of the foregoing ad executions?

One common thread is the use of humor. DDB employs humor because it attracts and holds consumers' attention, and it rewards the audience. In a sense, if consumers see an ad that pleases or entertains them, they will be more inclined to look forward to the ad again and perhaps develop a positive attitude toward the brand. This sequence of

> viewing → reward → enhanced probability of viewing again and developing positive affect

contains elements of operant conditioning. Humorous ads also tend to stimulate involvement, and hence deeper information processing.

Similarly, many DDB ads use refutational arguments. They acknowledge a drawback or shortcoming of a brand and then turn it into an asset or selling point. For example, DDB took clients who were not market leaders and positioned the brands relative to the leaders in order to increase their visibilities and enhance their images. Avis, for example, was successfully positioned in relation to Hertz, the number one company in rental cars. DDB hoped that people would perceive Avis as a more accommodating firm in its drive to overtake Hertz. (However, experts believe that the Avis campaign did little damage to Hertz. Instead, the campaign increased primary demand and took sales away from firms lower in market share.[21])

Another DDB refutational approach picks one or more attributes of a brand that seem to be a problem and then turns them into an advantage for the seller using clever themes and hilarious executions. For instance, the Volkswagen "bug" appeared to compare unfavorably to Detroit's lineup of fancy medium and full-sized cars. But DDB was able to use the bug's seemingly ugly appearance and small size to advantage by stressing its low cost, economical performance, and homely attractiveness. Indeed, VW bug owners are almost religiously loyal.

Still another DDB tactic employs a storyline that contains an unusual turn of events. For example, one classic ad for VW opens with a shot of boots worn by a person walking through heavy snow in the early morning. He enters his garage, starts the car, and drives to another garage. Up to this point no words are spoken, and nothing is said about what the ad is about or who its sponsor is. At the second garage, the man climbs into a large snowplow and drives away. The following query ended the ad: "Have you ever wondered how the man who drives a snowplow drives to the snowplow? This one drives a Volkswagen. So you can stop wondering." Building an ad around an unusual turn of events injects an element of mystery or suspense into the ad. The audience becomes curious, riveting its attention on the ad. Suspense also involves viewers with the ad psychologically and increases the chance that they will recognize the brand, remember it later, and perhaps evaluate it positively.

Doyle Dane Bernbach will sometimes put its clients' brands through tough tests of the product. Subjecting a brand (and also occasionally its competitors) to a difficult test may forcefully convey the focal brand's superior functionality or durability. For example, one DDB ad for American Tourister luggage showed a huge gorilla savagely banging a suitcase against concrete and steel bars. Of course, the suitcase survived intact, implying that it will satisfy even the most demanding customers—and survive even the most harsh luggage handling.

DDB ads follow a number of other principles.[22] DDB tries not to appear condescending, but rather to treat the audience with respect. Copy is factual and avoids puffery. DDB places less emphasis on repetition than does Leo Burnett. Rather than overplaying the same ad or always using the same theme, DDB produces new executions continually. They attempt to develop unique personalities for their brands. The philosophy of DDB can be summed up through the following words of William Bernbach:

> The most important thing as far as I am concerned is to be fresh, to be original. . . . Because you can have all the right things in an ad, and if nobody is made to stop and listen to you, you have wasted it.[23]

In a word, *creativity* is the guiding principle of DDB.

Ogilvy & Mather

David Ogilvy, like Leo Burnett and William Bernbach, has had a major impact on how advertising is conducted. Among his most central directives are the following:

What you say is more important than how you say it.

Give the facts.

Be well-mannered, but don't clown.

If you are lucky enough to write a good advertisement, repeat it until it stops pulling.

Every advertisement should be thought of as a contribution to the complex symbol which is the brand image.

It is the total personality of a brand rather than any trivial product difference which decides its ultimate position in the market.[24]

Thus two watchwords of Ogilvy's approach are *rationality* and *imagery*. Ads are designed to appeal to the intellect—the thinking side of human nature. Emotional appeals using humor are downplayed, in marked contrast to ads by Leo Burnett or Doyle Dane Bernbach. This rationality and imagery can be found almost universally throughout Ogilvy & Mather's ads for its clients: American Express, Hershey Chocolate, Sears Roebuck, Schaeffer beer, General Foods (e.g., Maxim coffee), and Unilever. Even its ads for Dove soap are more cognitive than are ads for Dove's competitors such as Camay, which emphasize traditional "femininity." That is, Ogilvy & Mather's ads stress functional product benefits.

Second, Ogilvy & Mather's ads emphasize brand image, which, as discussed in chapter 8 on product life cycles, has become increasingly important for marketing everyday products as competition increases:

> The greater the similarity between brands, the less part reason plays in brand selection. There isn't any significant difference between the various brands of whiskey, or cigarettes, or beer. They are all about the same. And so are the cake mixes and the detergents, and the margarines. The manufacturer who dedicates his advertising to building the most sharply defined personality for his brand will get the largest share of the market at the highest profit.[25]

Thus Ogilvy & Mather's ads focus relatively less on product attributes and instead attempt to create brand images. To create an image, their ads contain many thought-provoking themes and frequently highlight famous personalities. Helena Rubinstein appeared in ads for cosmetics, and Ted Williams and Johnny Miller in ads for Sears, for example. Brand image creation has also been a central focus in Ogilvy & Mather's ads for luxury or exclusive products. For instance, themes of prestige or status have been used to sell Rolls-Royce cars ("At 60 miles an hour, the loudest noise in this Rolls-Royce comes from the electric clock"), travel, and Schweppes drinks. A more recent successful image campaign by Ogilvy & Mather is the Pepperidge Farm bread truck driven by a wizened New England baker.

Many Ogilvy & Mather ads have excelled with effective and creative copy. You may recall seeing its "Come to Shell for Answers" campaign, which distributed an eight-page booklet on driving techniques, proper care of automobiles, and other tips as an educational promotion for consumers. This program not only increased customer awareness about Shell and built positive attitudes, it also generated general public acclaim and recognition by government officials for its excellence.[26]

Four final points to note with respect to Ogilvy & Mather concern repetition, comparative advertising, research, and recent strategy changes. The agency tends to repeat the same ads a lot, similar to the practice of Leo Burnett but unlike DDB. Second, Ogilvy & Mather avoids comparative ads. As Philip Levine, Senior Vice-President and Executive Director of Research at Ogilvy & Mather, has stated:

> Our study of television commercials that name names suggests that there is little to be gained from this type of advertising for the advertising industry, the advertiser, or the consumer. The only one who may benefit is the competitor who is named in the advertising.[27]

This illustrates a third dimension of Ogilvy & Mather—the agency places a high value on consumer research. Leo Burnett also conducts relatively high amounts of research, but DDB takes a more intuitive approach and places less emphasis on research. David Ogilvy softened his opposition to the use of humor recently and also no longer advocates celebrity ads, as they "are far below average in their power to sell."[28]

Ted Bates

Rosser Reeves helped make Ted Bates and Company one of the leading advertising agencies. Its accounts through the years have included Bufferin, Palmolive soap, Colgate toothpaste, Viceroy and Kool cigarettes, Prudential Insurance, M&M candy, Coors beer, and Maybelline. You might remember some of their slogans: "It writes the first time, every time" (Bic pens), "They melt in your mouth, not in your hand" (M&M candy), "Colgate cleans your breath as it cleans your teeth," and "How do you spell relief? R-O-L-A-I-D-S." Recent clients include Delta Airlines, Electrolux, Optus, National Australian Bank, and many others.

Ads from the Ted Bates agency have typically followed Rosser Reeves's philosophy, which emphasizes a "hard sell" approach as more effective than the soft sell.[29] The Ted Bates agency believes that factual, forceful ads have more impact per ad than do humorous or so-called creative ads, which may simply entertain or detract from the message. Bates's ads use fear- or anxiety-provoking copy or somewhat irritating or offensive executions to make their points forcefully. Their impact is augmented through repetition—and lots of it. One classic Reeves ad was for Anacin: A hammer banged on an anvil as a person winced with seemingly excruciating headache pain; the copy promised "Fast, Fast, Fast Relief." Many people might not realize that this one ad for Anacin ran for more than 10 years without a change, and although it cost only $8,200 to produce, it is reputed to have earned more money for the manufacturer than the film *Gone with the Wind* generated.[30]

The Ted Bates agency produces generally more factual and cognitive ads than even Ogilvy & Mather. The objective of such a largely rational (as opposed to a lighter or emotional) perspective is nicely put in Rosser Reeves's "unique selling proposition" (USP):

> Each advertisement must make a proposition to the consumer, not just words, not just product puffery, not just show window advertising. Each advertisement must say to each reader: "Buy this product, and you will get this specific benefit." The proposition must be one that the competitor either cannot, or does not, offer. It must be unique—either a uniqueness of the brand or a claim not otherwise made in that particular field of advertising.[31]

The USP chosen for a brand is often given a scientific character in an ad. Thus, Certs contains "a magic drop of Retsyn," Colgate has "MFP fluoride," and "only Viceroy gives you 20,000 filter traps in every filter tip." By focusing on a specific product benefit (hopefully a unique one), the agency feels that consumers' self interest will be stimulated and serve as the primary motivator of sales. Many of Bate's ads use very concrete, human elements in their USPs. For example, recent USP's include: "Fresh, made to order fast food" (Wendy's, U.S.A.), "Evergood Coffee, a triumph of taste over tradition" (Norway), "Safeway is the place to shop for families with young children" (Safeway, U.K.), and "The bank that understands your bigger picture" (National Australian Bank), all award-winning executions.

Despite its emphasis on a factual, hard-sell pitch, however, the most effective ads for the Ted Bates agency seem to be those that combine a USP with fear-arousing stimuli. These might be ones stressing physical consequences (e.g., cavities) or social embarrassment (e.g., bad breath).

Comments on Ad Agencies

In retrospect, the four advertising agencies presented show quite different styles. Which is the most effective? This is impossible to say with certainty. As Table 10.3 reveals, each agency is doing quite well, so there may be multiple routes to success. Creating and producing effective ads is a complex endeavor that combines creativity, research skills, managerial know-how, and luck. Each agency must begin with its own skills and resources and then allow its ads to evolve. Because every agency begins with different inputs and because such a creative, serendipitous process is unpredictable, diverse approaches to similar problems emerge. Of all marketing processes, advertising agencies are perhaps most subject to organizational culture and the social construction of reality.

Many other agencies could also have been chosen to illustrate the art and diversity of advertising. For example, Young and Rubicam's approach revolves around the following tenets: "It [i.e., the creative approach] must have the right strategy, be believable, have drama, make the product a hero, make a friend and build on and be consistent with the basic personality of the product."[32]

You probably have seen Young and Rubicam's ads for Kentucky Fried Chicken, Pabst beer, Jell-O (with Bill Cosby), Dr. Pepper, and Oil of Olay. NW Ayer, another leading advertiser, attempts to portray "human contact" in its ads. Thus, its ads for AT&T have successfully stimulated people to "reach out and touch someone" through long-distance phone calling, and its ads for Bud Light beer have stressed emotional situations where athletes overcome adversity to perform splendidly. Still another ad agency, D'Arcy-MacManus & Masius, often uses celebrities "to cut through media clutter and accomplish long-term goals"[33] for establishing a competitive edge, memorability, continuity, and a unique image. Nowhere is this more evident than in its ads for Florists' Transworld Delivery (FTD) where Merlin Olsen, a former all-pro football player (now commentator), is the spokesperson. Notice that this celebrity focus in ads directly contradicts David Ogilvy's views. The vastly different styles and strategies in the advertising business illustrate how important subjective, creative input can be in managerial decisions. Before we turn to the managerial side of advertising, we consider how contemporary advertising reflects some findings from the behavioral sciences.

Behavioral Science Principles in Advertising

Repetition and Wearout

There is a wealth of literature on ad repetition and wearout.[34] Ads must be repeated for a number of reasons. At the *microlevel* of individual consumers' psychological reactions, repetition attracts their attention. Many ads and other stimuli compete for the consumer's scarce time. Moreover, people tend to tune out ads and they have "low involvement" with most ad-carrying media; repetition is needed to "break through" perceptual barriers. Consumers also forget information in ads and must be reminded periodically of their content. Finally, repetition reaches deeper and deeper into consumers' minds: Persuasion sometimes requires more repetition than simple awareness.

FIGURE 10.6 ADVERTISING WEAROUT

Note: Wearout occurs with respect to awareness, interest, believability, attitude, and sales.

At the *macrolevel* of aggregates of consumers, repetition reaches greater and greater percentages of the market who are unaware of the product, brand, or key selling points. Further, repetition is needed to "move" higher and higher percentages of the target audience through the stages of information processing and decision making; that is, from awareness to interest to desire to action. Eventually, repetition reaches a saturation point, and greater efforts to reach people lead to diminishing returns as audiences tune out overly familiar material. Indeed, the relationship between repetition and aggregate responses such as awareness, recall, attitude change, and sales appear to be S-shaped (see Fig. 10.6). Let us take a deeper look at the effects of repetition at both the micro- and macrolevels.

Microlevel Processes

Herbert E. Krugman, a leading practitioner at General Electric, asserts that consumers need only three exposures to an ad to achieve the desired effects of advertising.[35] His argument is the following. The first exposure to an ad by individual consumers attracts their attention. Each consumer reacts with a "What is it?" response. Later, a second exposure has two effects, according to Krugman: an evaluative "What of it?" reaction, and the recognition response of "Aha, I've seen this before!" Krugman believes that subsequent exposures do not lead to deeper information processing. The third and each succeeding exposure act as reminders, and consumers call up from memory that which is already known and has been learned. Krugman maintains that more than three exposures not only wastes resources but also leads to audience disengagement—in essence ads become only so much "noise" to consumers. Ads work powerfully "only when the . . . consumer . . . is interested."[36] A final point Krugman makes: People really forget very little in the sense that, although they may not recall ads very well, their ability to recognize previously seen ads is very strong.[37]

Even though most of Krugman's hypotheses have not been tested directly, other research tends to support them. For example, most ads contain relatively simple messages, so it seems probable that one or two exposures will attract consumers' attention and lead to an evaluative (e.g., good or bad) reaction to the message, advertised brand, or overall ad execution. And all of us at one time or another have found ourselves tuning out ads after hearing or seeing the same ad on multiple occasions.

From a psychological standpoint, how might repetition affect a consumer? Aside from the obvious effects of increasing the depth of our learning, providing reinforcement, and maintaining top-of-the-mind awareness, repetition has subtle and not always positive impacts. A common outcome is that consumers' attitudes toward a brand can level off and even decline after repeated exposure to an ad or similar ads, because they either become bored with an ad and ignore its message, counterargue against the message, or become irritated with the ad and downgrade the advertiser. The observed decline in awareness or attitude is termed *wearout*.

Psychologists offer varied interpretations of the effects of repetition. They seem to agree on the common effects of repetition on learning. Repeated exposure helps consumers transfer information (e.g., the brand name or a key product attribute) from short-term memory to long-term memory. Through rehearsal (mentally repeating information), chunking (grouping of bits of information in sets), or the use of mnemonics (conscious word or picture associations with the information), advertisers can enhance the probability that consumers will store the information. Repetition in the early stages of exposure can maintain "top-of-the-mind" awareness, as well as aid in the retrieval of information from long-term memory.

All of these outcomes occur in addition to classical conditioning or mere exposure effects.[38] Classical conditioning suggests that repeated exposures of an arousing ad along with a brand name may lead to the development of positive feelings, depending on the strength of the arousing stimulus, the number of repetitions, and other factors. The mere exposure effect may also result in positive feelings through repeated exposures of a neutral stimulus (e.g., a brand name), but the exact psychological mechanisms are little understood.

Social psychologists also suggest that repetition may lead to certain "cognitive responses."[39] Repeated exposure may stimulate counterarguments, supporting arguments, source derogations, or application of particular schema (i.e., more-or-less automatic application of mental categories used to interpret ads; for example, "experts' statements can be trusted"). Although these responses can occur after a single exposure, multiple exposures seem to reinforce these cognitive effects. For example, repeated messages may habituate consumers to the ad such that their reactions become less marked. In a sense, people may react with "I've heard that before," and lose interest. Or consumers may generate message-related thoughts detrimental to the brand, such as "maybe brands Y and Z are just as good as the advertised brand." Alternatively, some consumers might respond to such repetition by generating nonmessage-related thoughts. After repeated television ads, for example, receivers may find their minds drifting into thoughts unrelated to the message, brand, or ad execution. They may thus become receptive to competitors' appeals or parallel competing activities, or they may simply disengage from the focal brand.

A final point to note is that affective responses might be generated along with or independent of cognitive responses. Thus, the thought processes discussed above might be accompanied by emotional responses. Or emotional responses might be the primary reaction consumers have to some ads. Further, any response can be related to the message, the sponsor, the spokesperson, the overall ad execution, or acts or things entirely unrelated to those objects. Marketers use each of these to produce desired effects.

Macrolevel Processes

Although empirical evidence confirms that ads do wear out at the aggregate level, most managerial models had not recognized this phenomenon until recently.[40]

Simon's ADPULS model accounts for wearout and predicts different responses in the marketplace, depending on whether advertising is increased or decreased. His model also provides guidelines for advertising about whether ads should be repeated constantly or "pulsed"—that is, spaced intermittently. The mathematical models for macroeffects of repetition are too involved to present here, and the reader is referred to the literature for more details.

Solutions to Wearout

What can an advertiser do to forestall or overcome wearout? The easiest and perhaps most frequently used tactic is simply to change how the same message is delivered. For instance, if humor is a focal message tactic, when wearout occurs, ads could rely on other humorous executions to emphasize the same selling points. Or one spokesperson could be substituted for another. Because consumers often "see through" this approach and again become indifferent to ads, such a tactic is often a short-run alternative at best.

Advertisers get somewhat better results when they change from one message mode to another. For example, a humorous campaign that has begun to wear out might be changed to one with celebrity testimonials or slice-of-life executions (i.e., where two "real" people argue about the merits of a brand). Or advertisers might introduce additional information or subtly distracting affects in an ad with the hope that people will be motivated to concentrate more closely to catch the new update. Advertisers may speed up commercials electronically, add background music, or introduce other slightly distracting sights or sounds. Finally, one might try new media, switching from television executions to print media campaigns that pick up on salient attributes or themes. This should be particularly effective for compensating for wearout at the macro level, where different segments of people patronize the media differently.

Ad designers can make the above changes without necessarily changing the central content of the message. Nevertheless, if message content is more important than message structure, advertisers may lose out when they fail to emphasize functional appeals or unique features. Such advertisers might reduce wearout by introducing new brand attributes, benefits, or selling appeals. Mobil Oil first advertised Mobil 1's fuel savings and increased operating efficiencies at very hot or cold temperatures. As this message began to wear out, Mobil added an emphasis on long oil drain time (25,000 miles, or 40,000 kilometers). Adding this new product attribute took place late in the campaign only after Mobil had tried various humorous executions that featured the original two product benefits. Thus wearout often ultimately hinges on making actual changes in a product, not merely changing execution styles or media.

Affect, Cognitions, and Consumer Involvement

Chapter 9 explored how the communication mix generally operates through two fundamental psychological states: affect (emotions) and cognitions (rational thoughts). Here we discuss a planning model that combines these ideas and is actually used by one advertising agency. Before we describe the model, however, we must briefly introduce another concept: involvement. For purposes of discussion, we define three types of consumer involvement: product involvement, media involvement, and message involvement.[41] *Product involvement* is the degree to which consumers are motivated to purchase and/or use a product. Advertisers assess the degree of involvement based on how much consumers need the product or desire it. Perceived risk may also be a factor. For most people, the purchase of an automobile, stereo set, or insurance constitutes a high-involvement product acquisition because of the financial, social, or

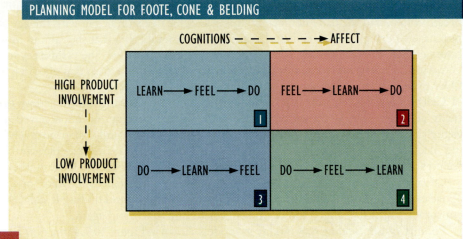

psychological risk involved. In contrast, the purchase of coffee, toothpaste, a hamburger, or a novel is a relatively low-involvement buying act, for most people.

Media involvement refers to the degree of attention consumers allocate to a particular mode of communication. Face-to-face interactions are generally high involvement, whereas television is a low-involvement medium. Magazines are somewhere in between these two, at least with respect to processing of ads. *Message involvement* measures how important or relevant the audience considers the focal issue in an ad to be. Typically, consumers are more involved with messages that address their reasons for buying a particular brand (e.g., due to its attributes or benefits). Consumers may also become more or less involved with a spokesperson, such as an attractive commentator or celebrity, or even with brand image that satisfies an ego need.

Foote, Cone & Belding, a leading national advertiser, employs a conceptual model in its planning activities to better manage its clients' accounts.[42] Shown in Figure 10.7, this model combines product involvement, affective and cognitive effects, and hierarchy-of-effects sequences into a fourfold classification.

Cell 1 of Figure 10.7 applies to consumers purchasing products with which they are highly involved and that place high cognitive demands on the consumer. An example would be a first-time buyer of a personal computer. Such consumers are probably highly involved because the product is expensive and risky. Consumers must also process a lot of cognitive material because computer attributes are complex, and their use is complicated. These first-time buyers must first devote a considerable amount of time and mental effort to learn about computers, different brands, and applications (e.g., office and home management software, recreational games, educational programs). After a learning period, potential buyers develop preferences for features and brands and other feelings (e.g., "I like Mac systems better than Windows software"). They then *act* on the feelings they have developed through shopping behaviors and purchase (the "do" stage in Fig. 10.7, cell 1).

Cell 2 of Figure 10.7 presents consumer decisions such as the purchase of clothing. Consumers are highly involved, but their affective reactions rather than cognitive processing initiate (and perhaps dominate) the decision process. Hence, feelings develop first ("I love that coat"), then thinking states ("Can I afford it?" "Will it go with my suit?"), and finally action ("I will go to another store to compare quality and prices").

Supermarket coffee purchases might fit cell 3. Imagine that Susan has used the last of the instant coffee on Wednesday morning. On her return home from work later that evening, she goes into a convenience store and "mindlessly" picks up milk, bread, coffee, and the daily newspaper. Susan's coffee decision began with the act of purchase—perhaps out of habit and as a result of remembering that she ran out nine hours earlier. Every morning when Susan makes instant coffee, she reinforces her decision and learns more about future decisions ("Boy, this is a great cup of coffee"). Over time, this should enhance Susan's feelings for the coffee.

Cell 4 resembles cell 3 but represents situations in which feelings follow actions directly and then lead to thoughts. For example, at midmorning, an unperceived or vaguely perceived hunger pang might stimulate purchase of a candy bar from a vending machine. While biting into the bar, the consumer might experience pleasurable feelings and then think "how good a buy the candy is" and "I think I will have another."

Of course, we could have as easily chosen negative sequences for each of the above examples. For instance, after biting into the candy bar and finding it stale, the consumer might feel angry and decide "never to buy this brand again."

Foote, Cone & Belding may modify its models shown in Figure 10.7. First, note that the dimensions represent end points on a continuum rather than mutually exclusive categories. While cognition represents believed rational facts or perceived means-ends connections, and affect represents pure emotion, most consumers' mental states are mixtures of cognitions and affect. For instance, most evaluations (e.g., good or bad judgments) contain thinking and feeling elements.

Second, as time passes and consumers gain experience, some purchase events move from cell 1 to cells 2, 3, or 4, depending on the circumstances. Although first-time coffee purchasers might be relatively involved in the purchase because of their lack of knowledge about the many brands available, their later purchases will most certainly occur almost automatically, perhaps even habitually. This illustrates movement from cell 1 to cell 3. Similarly, women buying cosmetics exemplify movement from cell 2 to cell 4. Purchases based primarily on cognitive decisions sometimes also change over time and become more affective as consumers become more loyal to a product. Figure 10.7 shows the most common temporal shifts as dashed arrows. Sometimes, however, changes may occur upward and to the left instead of this typical downward and to the right pattern. For instance, an affectively based purchase of a fine wine, novel, or classical music recording might evolve into both deeper cognitive appreciation and more highly involved decisions over time. And an impulse or habitual purchase might trigger greater involvement over time.

Applying Foote, Cone & Belding's Model. Foote, Cone & Belding uses the planning model in at least three ways.[43] First, as a rough guide early in the planning process, a client's product is categorized into one of the four cells. If the product falls in cells 1 or 3, for example, then advertising copy should stress primarily rational appeals. If, on the other hand, the product falls into cells 2 or 4, emotional content will probably be more important and memorable to consumers. More specifically, Foote, Cone & Belding believes the following creative approaches best fit the respective cells:

- cell 1: demonstration of product use and benefits; considerable copy to convey detailed information
- cell 2: emotional appeals to involve audience; use of ego or self-esteem appeals
- cell 3: induce trial (e.g., through point-of-purchase displays, samples, coupons); reminder ad executions
- cell 4: gain attention so as to arouse personal tastes; emphasize social connections

Second, Foote, Cone, & Belding uses the model to select media. Cell 1 products require more involving media, such as magazines or direct mail, with larger ads to attract attention. Cell 2 products also require involving media, but also can reach consumers through strong television executions because their appeal is largely emotional. Products in cell 3 can be effectively advertised on radio, short TV spots, small print or poster ads, and point-of-purchase displays. Finally, cell 4 products demand media with greater attention-getting emotional appeals: billboards, newspaper ads, and point-of-purchase displays. Of course, managers use these generalizations only as loose guidelines, because any particular application may deviate from the norm and require fine-tuning.

Third, Foote, Cone, & Belding uses the planning model shown in Figure 10.7 to test ad copy. As we discuss later in this chapter, rational and emotional ads and high- and low-involvement products dictate different ad-effectiveness measurement procedures. Whereas recall measures might be adequate for cell 1 products, and actual purchase histories or aggregate sales might be sufficient for cell 3 and 4 products, those in cell 2 generally require deeper emotional processing—either more visual (e.g., recognition) or deeper (e.g., arousal, attitude) indicators.

MEASURING THE EFFECTIVENESS OF ADVERTISING

Does it really pay to advertise? Organizations certainly believe so, or they would not pay so much money to do it. But does advertising really help organizations reach their goals?

Most executives maintain that the ultimate objective of advertising is to influence sales, either immediately or in the long run. We do not know very much about how advertising affects sales. Some research shows a positive relationship between advertising and sales, but very little is known about whether the relationship shows cause-and-effect or merely correlation.[44] Sales are very complex phenomena influenced by a variety of factors, which each vary from situation to situation and from time period to time period. For example, sales are influenced by competing products' prices, the prices of complements, and the price of the firm's own brand. Then, too, sales are affected by product quality, packaging, distribution practices, promotions and deals, changing consumer tastes, and economic and social conditions. Advertising probably determines sales to a certain extent as well, but to disentangle the relative impact of each force is nearly an impossible task—or at least researchers have met with little success to date. Nevertheless, companies' monetary commitment to advertising each year suggests that it plays a very large role.

Managers must decide how much to spend on advertising, which media to use, what messages to transmit, how to present the messages, and so forth as part of the overall promotion mix. Although managers may not be able to directly link these controllable factors to actual market sales responses, they can examine the influence of particular ads on consumer psychological reactions and behavior to see how effective the ads will be. Such research takes place in the laboratory, through focus groups, in surveys, and in panels, as discussed in chapters 5 and 7 on market research and new product development. In effect, managers judge ad efficacy by measuring ad impact on intervening variables (consumer psychological responses) between seeing or hearing ads and finally buying the product. These methods trade off some realism in exchange for better control of extraneous factors and manageability of the research process.

Most often, advertisers measure ad influence through people's brand-name awareness, knowledge, recall, recognition, beliefs about product attributes, interests, attitudes, or intentions as a function of exposure to ads. Most tests of ad effectiveness are performed on television ads, although magazine and radio ads undergo considerable testing as well. Typically, sponsors hire independent research services to conduct such tests. Next we describe some research companies and their approaches. The term *copy testing* describes most tests that measure how effectively particular ads influence consumers' psychological and choice responses.

Recall and recognition tests are the most commonly applied procedures in ad effectiveness testing. Recall and recognition, however, entail somewhat different mental processes. In recall tests, respondents are given minimal cues and asked to generate the target information from memory. In recognition tests, respondents are presented with the target ad and asked whether they have seen it before. Recall is thus more difficult than recognition; indeed, the scores for ads are generally much higher for recognition than for recall. Both measure aspects of memory, but researchers do not know whether they measure unique or overlapping mental states.[45] Recognition scores may also carry considerable amounts of measurement error, which researchers remedy by deriving "proven recognition" scores: differences in recognition scores between respondents previously exposed to an ad and those not exposed.

Masked recognition procedures can sometimes produce more accurate scores. Researchers cover or remove the name of the brand from an ad and ask readers to identify the brand in the ad they have seen before. Notice that this task lies between the recall and pure recognition tasks described above.

Television Ad Copy Testing

Burke Marketing Research, Inc.

Burke uses the most common method for measuring ad effectiveness: the "day-after recall" test. Other firms (e.g., Gallup & Robinson, Inc.) also use this method with minor variations. Day-after recall testing consists of the following.

The day after an ad appears on commercial television, firms call households by randomly drawing telephone numbers in a target viewing area. Researchers ask respondents if they watched the test program on the previous day. If viewers answer yes, they are considered "program viewers." Next, researchers ask the program viewers (usually a sample of 200) if they were awake and in the room during the entire program and did not change channels. If viewers respond positively, they are classified as a "commercial audience" (typically numbering about 140). This commercial audience is then asked further questions to determine any effect the target ads produced. Researchers focus on three ad effectiveness measures: claimed recall, related recall, and actual ad content. In claimed recall tests, pollsters mention (depending on the sponsor's desires) either the product category or both the brand and product category to respondents and ask them if they recall the ad. In related recall tests, respondents must also provide correct details from the ad (e.g., any audio or video content that 'proves' the person saw the ad). Researchers formulate simple percentages, called "Burke scores," for claimed or related recall. Finally, researchers may record instances of actual content recalled by each respondent. For example, they may note which key selling points respondents recall or specific descriptions of the ad, spokesperson, and so forth. Depending on the client's needs, Burke and other firms monitor day-after recall in any one or more of 33 cities in the United States.

A "good" Burke score depends on the audience (e.g., men or women, demographic profile) and the product category. Burke has formulated norms reflecting averages for product classes; a Burke score of 24 percent is considered the norm across a wide variety of product classes such as soft drinks, detergents, and dog food. If a sponsor ad scores above 24 percent, the ad is generally considered "effective." Although Burke does not claim that its measures show persuasiveness or propensity to buy, the tests imply that recall scores represent a necessary indicator of ad effectiveness in reaching into the stages of information processing through which consumers pass (i.e., attention, interest, evaluation, decision making, and choice). That is, because recall is probably a necessary state for consumers to progress through the hierarchy of effects, these tests provide indirect measures or proxies for the impact of an ad on consumer behavior.

Common wisdom suggests that Burke scores are directly proportional to the length of an ad; the frequency that a brand name is mentioned and/or shown; the earlier the brand is mentioned or shown in the ad; the use of animation (i.e., animation increases recall); the more that an ad ties into past ads (e.g., through use of the same spokesperson over time); the importance of product attributes to an audience; the number of linkages made to the brand name and its benefits; and more generally the cognitive information in an ad.

Such day-after recall measures work well in that they are naturalistic (i.e., ads are tested "on-air"), relatively inexpensive, fast, and easily understood. In addition, these data are often broken down for sponsors based on audience type and allow Burke to ask other questions (at additional cost). The method seems to work best for new brands or products with at least a few clear attributes—that is, functional products—as opposed to those with intangible benefits.

A major drawback with recall tests is that they tend to give superficial results that may not correlate very highly with consumer attitudes or intentions toward a brand. Moreover, they seem to overemphasize cognitive content and overlook emotional responses. Finally, managers may not be able to get Burke scores much above the norm, and may not have a clear indication how much above the norm their scores must be to achieve their various goals.

Day-after recall tests are postexposure measures of advertising effectiveness because the target ad has already been produced and shown to the public. Burke also measures advertising effectiveness prior to exposing the ad to the public, via the "Clucas Diagnostic Advertising Research Technique." Television ads in either rough or finished form are shown at a test location to viewers who are asked to write down any thoughts that come to mind *as they watch the commercial*. This procedure more accurately determines the time in consumers' minds that ads are effective and provides information useful in the design phase of advertising. It trades "on-air" realism for a more diagnostic approach and may save advertisers the expense of placing an ad prior to testing. Recently, advertisers seem to have adopted such preexposure test procedures in favor of day-after recall and other postexposure methods. Nevertheless, day-after recall remains the most popular method at this time.

Bruzzone Research Company

Rather than using telephone interviews to collect consumer responses to ads, Bruzzone employs mail surveys to measure the effects of television ads. They take a random sample of 1,000 households and ask respondents to comment on 8 to 15 different commercials. Each commercial is presented as a storyboard (a pictorial summary of the ad) with the brand name removed. Typically, about 500 people return the questionnaire.

Researchers obtain at least six measures from these surveys: (1) how well respondents recall the ad; (2) how well respondents recognize the brand name from a list of three choices; (3) how interested respondents are in the message; (4) how well potential consumers like the ad; (5) what reactions are to the brand (e.g., attitudes); and (6) a checklist of commercial characteristics (e.g., was the ad believable, clever, silly).

On the positive side, the Bruzzone method is somewhat cheaper than many other services, tests many ads, and yields large representative samples, rather than sampling only specific cities. On the negative side, some nonresponse biases are possible, the presentation is somewhat artificial, and some of the drawbacks of the Burke approach also apply to the Bruzzone method.

AdTel, Inc.

AdTel measures ad effectiveness naturalistically and employs dependent variables that approximate advertisers' ultimate goal of final sales. At testing sites at one or more of three cities across a geographical target area, potential consumers see commercials on a dual cable-television system. Some people may see test ads with one particular copy strategy; others see ads of another strategy or see no test ads and thus act as a control group. Respondents fill out questionnaires that provide attitudinal measures and related responses, and they record actual purchases in panel diaries. The sample for each cable split numbers 1,000.

AdTel's methods allow them to monitor effects over a long period of time. Their methods involve naturalistic viewing in the sense that people view test ads embedded in regular programming. They control extraneous factors such as distributional differences in products across geographical areas or the weather because the location is the same for test and control samples. In addition, they obtain measures of actual purchases and large samples. On the other hand, AdTel's methods may produce erroneous purchase histories because people may forget to record their purchases or misrepresent them. Also, those people participating might not be representative of the country as a whole or desired target markets.

Communicus, Inc.

Communicus uses two different methods to test television ads. First, they visit homes or conduct on-the-spot public solicitations and ask respondents to watch ads on a portable 8-mm film projector-viewer. Second, the researchers conduct group video-tape viewings on television. Typically, Communicus recruits respondents in public places such as shopping malls or busy pedestrian areas. Unlike Burke or AdTel, however, Communicus asks people to watch commercials in an unusual way. Participants observe segments of an ad. For example, a 30-second ad might be divided into three segments that represent distinct ideas or themes. At the end of each segment, the researcher stops the commercial and asks viewers about segment content, their comprehension of the selling points, and their views of how important the information was. Next, respondents are shown the entire uninterrupted ad, and researchers question each person's understanding of the ad and their intent to try the brand.

Although Communicus's method provides quality, in-depth information that can serve useful diagnostic purposes, the small sample sizes may not be representative of target markets. Another drawback is that viewings are conducted under artificial conditions. Finally, error can result in the analysis of the open-ended, subjective responses.

ASI Market Research, Inc.

Los Angeles–based Audience Studies, Inc. uses a still different technique for measuring the effectiveness of television ads. It recruits respondents to view "television previews" in a theater setting, using about 400 people at a time. At the outset, respondents fill out questionnaires that solicit background information and brand preferences for the product categories to be tested (usually four) and for control categories. Then the respondents watch a sequence of television pilot shows and ads, fill out a questionnaire, and participate in group discussion. This sequence may be repeated. ASI measures interest and involvement in the ad via a hand dial controlled by viewers throughout the viewing. Brand recall, recall of ad content, preference change, and diagnostic feedback are determined from the group discussions.

ASI's method poses several advantages, such as large samples, the ability to test a number of ads, and tests that provide cognitive, affective, preference, and qualitative information. On the downside, ASI's viewings are not representative of in-home viewing, their samples may not be representative, and their measures may not relate to intentions or actual purchasing behavior.

Print Ad Copy Testing

Recall and recognition measures are the two most frequently applied indicators of print ad effectiveness. On occasion, researchers also measure reader interest, like or dislike for an ad or brand, or other tailored criteria. We briefly describe the recognition and recall procedures next.

Recall of Print Ads

Audience Studies employs test procedures typical for the industry. The day after exposure to a test magazine, readers are contacted and asked, "Do you recall seeing any advertisements in this issue of (magazine) for (product category)?" Those who answer yes are asked to identify the brand. If they identify the brand correctly, researchers ask them to describe the ad. To be counted as positive recalls, respondents must mention a general piece of information contained in the ad. ASI measures recall based on simple percentages as well as other responses such as product interest and ad-generated ideas and impressions.

Gallup & Robinson use a slightly different procedure to measure recall, which they term "proved name registration." Readers are first asked to recall and describe ads from a target magazine. The only cue they receive is the sponsor of the ad. To be counted as a recall, readers must identify some content of the ad. Gallup & Robinson also measure how well readers remember key selling points in an "idea playback profile" as well as readers' attitudes in a "favorable buying attitude" score.

Recognition of Print Ads

Starch Inra Hooper measures recognition of print ads. First, it identifies readers of the focal magazine. Next, through a page-by-page search guided by the researcher, respondents are asked if they saw or read the ad(s) on each page. Readers who answer yes are asked to describe what they saw or read. Researchers obtain three measures. First, they note the percentage of readers who claim to have seen an ad before (designated as "noted"). Second, they record the percentage of readers claiming to have seen or read particular parts of the ad indicating the brand or advertiser ("associated"). Third, they measure the percentage of readers who claim to have read 50 percent of the ad copy or more ("read most").

As with television ad recall and/or recognition procedures, print ad testing also focuses on cognitive rather than affective ad impact. Recall or recognition tests may imperfectly predict consumer attitudes, intentions, and actual behaviors.

Copy Testing in Other Media

Firms also test copy for ads in other advertising media such as radio or billboards. For purposes of brevity, we do not describe the procedures here. However, most of the techniques aim to measure recall, recognition, or, on occasion, consumer attitudes (e.g., like or dislike). Radio ad copy testing is similar to television ad copy testing, and billboard ad copy testing is similar to print ad copy testing.

Final Comments on Copy Testing

Copy testing procedure accuracy is widely debated in both practitioner and academic circles.[46] Many authors believe that day-after recall and similar measures overemphasize the cognitive side of consumer behavior at the expense of the emotional. Foote, Cone & Belding has tested both television and print ads using recall and masked recognition measures. It found that recall does tend to underrate "emotional" ads, whereas masked recognition appears suitable for both "rational" and "emotional" ads.[47] Probably neither procedure adequately monitors the depth and breadth of cognitive or affective processes. Furthermore, the industry still needs testing procedures that can accurately predict intentions, trial, and repeat purchase behaviors.

ADVERTISING MANAGEMENT

A Framework

We have touched upon many facets of advertising and considered many of the advertising decisions that managers must make (e.g., copy design and testing, organizational structure). Chapter 9 introduced many of the options facing the advertising manager as well (e.g., message content and message structure, media choices, spokesperson effects, and audience characteristics). Advertising decision elements are numerous and complex, to say the least, and advertising is only one of many issues that a marketing program must resolve. Managers face myriad challenges and difficulties. In this section of the chapter, we briefly outline a model that shows how managers plan and control advertising efforts.

Figure 10.8 presents Stanford Professor Michael Ray's communication planning model, portrayed from the point of view of an organization confronted with advertising decisions.[48] Note that the process begins with managers' *situation analysis*. Top managers evaluate company strengths and weaknesses along with broader organization goals and the competition. Next, managers must assess their *marketing objectives*. These objectives constrain the *communication budget*. Indeed, budget decisions limit the overall communication effort and the personal selling, promotional, advertising, and public relations mix. Once top managers set goals and determine a budget, marketing managers allocate, design, monitor, and manage the communication effort. *Implementation* and *control and evaluation* constitute central elements of the communication decision process. We now consider some of the decision processes sketched in Figure 10.8.

Advertising Goals and Budgeting

Managers set broad advertising goals to encourage consumers to try their products, to switch brands, to develop brand loyalty, and to increase per capita consumption. At the same time, managers formulate intermediate and operational goals, such as producing specific levels of consumer awareness, determining recall and recognition rates, encouraging consumers' knowledge of product attributes, and meeting consumers interests, liking, intentions, and so forth in particular markets. Some firms use formal models such as DAGMAR (defining advertising goals, measuring

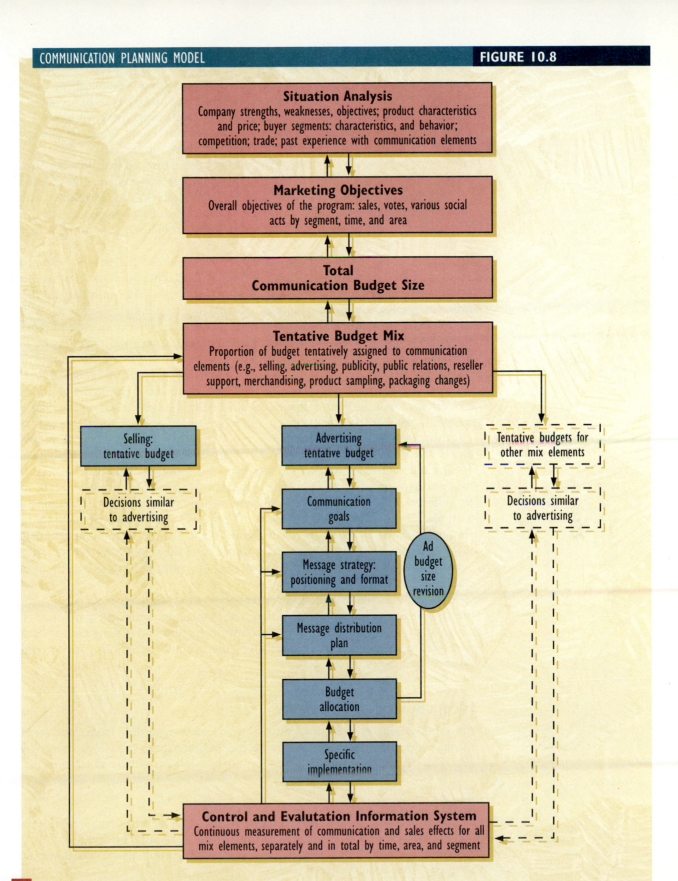

Source: Michael L. Ray, "A Decision Sequence Analysis of Developments in Marketing Communications," Journal of Marketing 37
(January 1973): 31. Reprinted wtih the permission of the publisher.

advertising results) to help them plan advertising programs, but discussion of the details is beyond the scope of this text.[49]

To achieve their goals, managers must have resources—financial, personnel, technological. Firms set budgets for various projects in many ways. On occasion, executives or groups of executives set budgets based on their *subjective judgments*. More commonly, firms use *percentage of sales* figures as rules of thumb. They use some percentage of previous years' sales or this year's expected sales (e.g., 2 percent) to set advertising budgets for the current year. It has been estimated that between 50 and 70 percent of all firms set their advertising expenditures as a percentage of sales.[50] Still other times ad budgets are based on *competitors' expenditures*. Firms may match the competition (in total dollars or as a percentage of sales), set an amount above the competition to out-promote them, or set their budget below competitors' so as not to threaten them.

Managers have found that setting budgets by subjective judgments, percentage of sales, or competitor levels is a hit-and-miss affair. They wish to set advertising budgets at levels appropriate to stimulate sales. Advertising is a controllable variable influencing sales, so a method more closely tied to the intended effects of ads will in the long run better achieve organization goals. The *objective-and-task-approach* helps managers set budgets so that advertising meets organization goals more closely. The organization first defines a specific goal (e.g., "60 percent awareness of our new product by consumers within four months"), and then advertising agencies, in conjunction with the firm, design tasks (number of ads to show, the media to use, and so forth) to reach the goal. Firms thus set necessary budgets based on the tasks required. Usually, marketing managers will weigh multiple goals, multiple tasks, and a number of alternative scenarios. Advertisers typically work closely with ad agencies to arrive at a viable budget and advertising campaign.

The task-and-objective method attempts to discover specific relationships between ad expenditures and consumer responses. Marketers may *experiment*, by trying different ads and varying the number and scheduling of ads in selected cities, for example, to see differential responses.[51] They may ascertain consumer response through *statistical modeling*, by relating sales to advertising expenditures.[52] Finally, some firms use a *normative approach* for discovering the relationship wherein managerial judgments are quantitatively used (e.g., in optimization models) to predict responses in a simulation.[53]

Whatever method managers use to set budgets, they must consider costs, such as message design and media costs. As they make budgetary decisions, firms must take a long-run perspective, continuously monitoring results and making changes when necessary to ensure that their advertising budgets and programs fit with corporate goals and strategies.

Media Selection

Marketing managers must make three basic decisions regarding media: the general medium (e.g., magazines) or media to use; the specific vehicles (e.g., *Time* versus *Sports Illustrated*) to employ within media; and how to schedule ads within and across media.[54]

Media Choices

What media work best for advertising? Primary options include television, radio, magazines, newspapers, billboards, direct mail, the World Wide Web, and/or the Yellow Pages. Among other criteria, decision makers must balance communication characteristics, audience reach, and cost.

First, communication characteristics describe each medium's ability to convey information and influence the consumer. Some media are better than others for attracting attention, stimulating emotions, demonstrating product attributes or benefits, and instilling conviction and intent to try the product. Table 10.6 compares four leading media on these and other characteristics. For example, magazines strongly convey sensory stimulation, whereas radio does only a fair job at doing so. Magazines convey humor poorly (with a few notable exceptions), but television does so especially well. Marketing managers must match media ability to message content and structure aimed at the target consumer. They need research about viewers' reactions to one medium or another, likely consumer characteristics, and how both of these match the product context. Decision makers often use the kind of demographic and psychographic profiles of audiences and target markets discussed in earlier chapters.

Second, audience reach, or the number of people exposed to particular media, also varies by media type. Some media, such as newspapers or television, reach wide segments of the population. About 80 percent of U.S. adults read newspapers one or more times a week,[55] and nearly 60 percent of all U.S. households watch television between 7 P.M. and 11 P.M. Indeed, the average household watches 6 hours and 26 minutes of television a day.[56] With 98 percent of all homes equipped with a television, we can readily appreciate the power of television to reach the U.S. public. On the other hand, some media are quite selective, reaching narrowly defined audiences. For instance, ads placed in *Car and Driver, Successful Farming,* or *Factory* reach automobile buffs, farmers, and plant managers, respectively. Again, managers must consider consumers' characteristics (e.g., personality, motivation, self-image, income) and their reading and viewing habits, along with the distribution of media, when they choose a communication channel.

Finally, managers must consider the cost of each media choice. Table 10.7 presents some comparisons as a rough guide. Managers must balance the desired audience

TABLE 10.7 INDICATION OF COMPARATIVE COSTS OF SELECTIVE MEDIA

Medium	Costs
Television	Spot TV ad for 30 seconds varies between about $4,000 (daytime) to $13,000 (prime time)
	National market = $1,000,000 or more for a 30-second ad, depending on program
	Average prime-time 30-second ad costs about $120,000
Radio	For network radio, the average cost per 1,000 people reached is about $2.85
	For spot radio, it is about $4.50
Magazines	The average cost per 1,000 people reached for 10 selected consumer magazines is about $12.00
Newspapers	Daily inch rate for black and white ad varies between $8,000 and $25,000, depending on size of market
Billboard	$1,000 to $30,000 per month, depending on location
Direct Mail	About $500 to $700 per 1,000 pieces
Yellow Pages	$500 to $1,500 for a 2-inch column
Transit	$51,000 monthly on 400 New York City buses

Note: Costs show considerable variability across vehicles and number of people reached and are only estimates.

reach against the cost as they choose a medium. Media costs per sale vary as well. Direct mail costs more than magazines when considered on the basis of per 1,000 people reached, but is less expensive on a per order basis.

Vehicles Choices

Once advertisers choose appropriate media for advertising, they must then select specific entities within those media. Again, managers must evaluate each vehicle's communication characteristics, audience reach, and costs. Although these choices seem complex and numerous, a number of paid research services provide data to help decision makers. For instance, Arbitron, A.C. Nielsen, Leading National Advertisers, the Simmons Marketing Research Bureau, Media Records, Publishers Information Bureau, and Mediamark Research supply vehicle exposure data for television, radio, magazines, and/or newspapers.

Mediamark Research provides typical data consisting of a sample of about 20,000 adults covering more than 40 product categories, broken down by 18 demographic, 20 psychographic, and a number of usage segments. Such services may provide managers with answers to such questions as: What magazine most efficiently reaches male fisherman 18 to 35 years old? Which newspaper in city A reaches the most older adult women with incomes over $40,000 per year? What percentage of homes will watch *60 Minutes* on a Sunday evening?

Media Schedules

The choice of media and vehicles answers the question of where to advertise. But managers must also decide when and how often to repeat the message. We touched upon this scheduling issue when we discussed repetition and wearout. Decision makers must decide how many exposures per person are optimal, what proportion of the target audience the ad should reach at this repetition level, and when to place ads (e.g., time of day, days of the week, months in the year).

Basically, managers may follow any one of four generic strategies. First, they may simply maintain even ad expenditures (or sizes of ads) over time. This strategy is most appropriate if consumers purchase uniformly over time (i.e., the product is not generally subject to cyclical or seasonal buying). It is also a viable strategy if the brand is very well known and/or if competitors also advertise uniformly and managers do not want to risk open rivalry that might escalate into an expensive "ad war." However, the maintenance or level strategy is a passive one, its attempt to stimulate sales and match competitors is neither very aggressive nor tied well to consumer or market forces.

Second, managers may start a campaign with high advertising levels and then decrease advertising (or ad size) over time to some maintenance level. This strategy is common for new-product introductions, where managers try to build awareness early. Sometimes firms repeat this approach periodically such that they create a general rise and fall strategy over time.

Third, managers may use an intermittent (pulse) strategy over time. For example, they might place ads on the radio only on Mondays. Or alternatively, they may employ heavy media usage for 10 days, followed by no advertising for a week, then resumption, then no advertising, and so on. Of course, companies may combine strategies so that they employ heavy-light-heavy-light sequences with minimal advertising (e.g., once per week) at all times. Managers often use this intermittent strategy to optimize consumer learning or reinforcement. They may also use it to "stretch budgets" or to coincide with particular consumption patterns. For example, snack ads on the television seldom appear during the dinner hour, but appear at increasing frequencies during the later evening hours. Similarly, ads for greeting cards appear just before Christmas, Valentine's Day, and Mother's Day, but are less frequent at other times of the year.

Finally, managers may change ad exposure scheduling, depending on the conditions. Changes in competitor moves, income, buyer preferences, or other factors typically dictate a fine-tuning in scheduling over time.

Media Models

Managers' media, vehicles, and scheduling choices are probably based more on art than science. They learn from trial and error, and media planners also play a strong role. Nevertheless, management scientists have developed models to aid in the decision-making process. The reader is specifically referred to the original presentations of two of them: MEDIAC and ADMOD.[57]

Concluding Comments on Advertising Management

In addition to setting goals, formulating budgets, and planning media strategies, managers must make many other advertising decisions. As Figure 10.8 showed, and as we mentioned earlier in this and the preceding chapters, managers must also decide on advertising copy. They address numerous message content, structure, and spokesperson choices. Integrating all of these decisions into a coherent advertising program and into an overall marketing effort is no easy task. Organizations have found it necessary to hire and develop specialists in a wide variety of functional areas and to rely on outside providers of expertise to more effectively plan and execute their marketing communication efforts.

SOCIAL AND LEGAL ASPECTS OF ADVERTISING

Advertising and Society

Advertising has a pervasive and powerful influence on individual consumers, economic conditions, and society as a whole.

Effects of Ads on Individuals

Many social commentators question whether advertising manipulates the public. Over the years, advertisers have been accused of playing on the subconscious motives of people[58] and even of using techniques such as subliminal advertising.[59]

Do ads manipulate us? Are we induced to buy things that we neither want nor need? Exactly how do ads affect us?

Most research to date has examined only people's opinions and attitudes toward advertising. Tables 10.8 and 10.9 summarize two such studies. People appear to be generally either positive or indifferent toward advertising, but a sizable minority appears to be negatively predisposed. What are their complaints?

One study found that respondents categorize 23 percent of ads as annoying (i.e., irritating) and 5 percent as offensive (i.e., vulgar, morally bad, or dishonest).[60] The

TABLE 10.8 ATTITUDES TOWARD ADVERTISING: THE BAUER AND GREYSER FINDINGS

Attitude	Percentages	
	1964	1967
Favorable	41	49
Mixed	34	31
Indifferent	8	3
Unfavorable	14	15
Unclassifiable	3	2

Source: R. A. Bauer and S. A. Greyser, Advertising in America: The Consumer View (Boston: Division of Research, Graduate School of Business Administration, Harvard University, 1968), p. 393. Reprinted with the permission of the publisher.

rest (72 percent) were either informative or enjoyable. People found ads for soaps, detergents, dental supplies, mouthwashes, depilatories, and deodorants most annoying, and ads for liquor, cigarettes, and beer most offensive. Another study found ads for feminine hygiene products, women's undergarments, and hemorrhoid products most irritating.[61] Thus, certain ads appear to arouse strong negative reactions in at least some people.

But do the effects of ads go deeper than this? Do ads shape values, influence lifestyles, and actually stimulate people to take actions that they would not normally take? Most research to date suggests that even though subliminal messages may arouse people, such ads do not necessarily produce behavior changes.[62] Moreover, experts have argued that most consumers typically react to ads with reasoned judgments, healthy skepticism, critical appraisal, counterargumentation, and—on occasion—outright rejection.[63] Even children, who generally have been believed to be especially vulnerable to the influence of advertising, display such reactions.[64]

On the other hand, through classical conditioning, cognitive learning, or the mere exposure effect, ads may influence our emotions in the short run and shape our values and beliefs in the long run.[65] However, advertising's role as a socializing agent is little studied and even less understood. Some evidence exists showing that stereotyping occurs with respect to the portrayal of African Americans[66] and women[67] in ads. But we know little about exactly how and to what degree ads in-

TABLE 10.9 ATTITUDES TOWARD ADVERTISING: THE BARTOS AND DUNN FINDINGS

Attitude	Percentage
Fans	23
Skeptical Enthusiasts	22
Moderates	26
Aesthetic Critics	17
Rejectors	12

Source: R. Bartos and T. Dunn, Advertising and Consumers (New York: American Association of Advertising Agencies, 1976), pp. 68–69. Reprinted with the permission of the publisher.

fluence people over long periods of time. In the broadest sense, advertising represents a kind of chicken-and-egg story in that it both reflects and influences individual consumer's needs.

Although we may not know much about the long-run psychological effects of ads in a scientific sense, legal developments have clarified many issues.

The Effects of Ads on the Economy

In contrast to our relative ignorance of how ads influence us in a long-run psychological sense, we know much more about the role of advertising in the economy.[68] We can make both pro and con arguments about whether these effects are positive or negative.

On the positive side, advertising provides financial support to the mass media, which encourages economic growth, informs consumers about new products, and, in general, serves as a necessary tool for organizations to respond to and influence demand. In addition, economists maintain that advertising lowers prices[69] and enhances competition.[70]

On the negative side, economists sometimes charge that advertising creates false product differentiation or produces barriers to market entry because of its high cost, which in turn increases industry concentration and monopoly power and profits.[71] Indeed, research seems to suggest that advertising permits some manufacturers to charge a premium for their goods.[72]

In short, advertising apparently has both positive and negative consequences for the economy and consumers. Some of the detrimental effects are counteracted by competition in the marketplace and by actions taken by the judicial and executive branches of government. Other negative consequences, such as excessive or false product differentiation, are difficult to define or prove.

A delicate balance must be maintained between the needs of special interest groups and the freedom of individuals and firms. Most societies attempt some healthy balance between social equity and innovation and risk taking. It is difficult to say where the line should be drawn. We can only ensure that imbalances will be addressed by encouraging and institutionalizing debate and political conflict among the players. This is exactly what has evolved in many modern economies, where consumer groups, companies, government bodies, and other groups interact to work out their needs for the common good.

The Effects of Ads on Society

Advertisements do affect society, but their impact is complex and reciprocal. Consider the issue of materialism. Has advertising made people more materialistic? Certainly over the past century, members of nearly all societies have come to use more and more material goods and services. Did advertising produce materialism or did advertising develop to help people better meet their materialistic needs? The answer is probably a little of both. At times, advertising arouses needs in us; at other times, our needs already exist and advertising is one of a number of facilitators leading to fulfillment of those needs. The questions of which needs are "genuine" and which are "artificial" probably cannot be answered objectively or scientifically, but rather fall within the realm of ethics and the law.

A qualitative study by a leading psychologist points to the difficult problem of studying the social effects of advertising and how many issues must be considered in a study about the effects of advertising on the smoking behavior of women.[73] Prior to about 1920, very few women in the United States smoked. Then advertisers began showing women in ads for cigarettes—not merely as incidental or decorative copy, as in previous ads, but actually smoking—on billboards and in many print ads. Also, advertisers used various promotional tactics. For instance, they hired attractive women to "light up" in public places, such as New York's Waldorf-Astoria Hotel. Opinion leaders were given free cigarettes and encouraged to smoke "for the liberation of women." Even debutantes in parades appeared as promotional tools by advertisers. By 1935, about 18 percent of women smoked, and this increased to a peak of around 33 percent in the mid-1970s, after which smoking declined somewhat.

Advertisers employed a variety of techniques to persuade women to smoke throughout this period. They used celebrities as spokespersons and made sexual and health claims freely (e.g., smoking soothes sore throats). Firms created promotions based on classical conditioning principles, psychoanalytic psychology, and communication theory, subtly and not so subtly.

Can we say that advertising caused women to smoke? Certainly, ads stimulated some women to try smoking for the first time, which served as a reinforcement for others to continue smoking once they began. Yet, did these women do so because of the ads or because they chose to do so? Did they have a need to smoke or did advertising "make" them do it? Was the need a desire for pleasure, an addictive habit, or something else? Would women have eventually smoked anyway, even without advertising?

Perhaps the social setting in these decades provides a partial answer. Women may have started smoking out of peer pressure so as to fit in with a group or create a particular self and social image. In addition to advertising and promotion effects, we must consider word-of-mouth communication and social pressures to smoke. Perhaps the growth in smoking was just as much a function of everyday social processes as it was due to the influence of advertisements. Socialization through exposure to paid advertisements, movies, novels, role modeling by respected public figures, peer pressure and so on surely played a supportive part.

In any event, large numbers of women did not begin smoking overnight. If advertising played a role, its effects appear to have taken a long time to take hold—perhaps decades. Although each single ad might arouse us emotionally or stimulate thoughts, the effects are generally short-lived and/or of a low magnitude. Ads must be repeated over a long period of time for more permanent or deep-seated effects to arise. At the same time, psychological, cultural, social, and legal forces interact with advertising. It is no wonder that the social effects of advertising are so difficult to discover and that so few have tried.

Nevertheless, marketers in general and advertisers in particular must consider the effects of their actions carefully. They must rely on personal morals and standards of conduct, as well as more formal codes of ethics prescribed by professional associations and organizations. Thoughtful and fair legal and regulatory governmental bodies must consider the needs of all parties. It may not be possible to ascertain the hidden or long-run effects of advertising, but everyone involved—advertisers, ad agencies, government, and consumers—must at least attempt to do so to reduce the number of negative implications. No one can say positively that advertising made women smoke and thus indirectly contributed to the increased incidence of lung cancer in women. Yet each individual involved with advertising bears the responsibility to face such questions to maintain self-respect and protect the interests of society.

Advertising and the Government

The Federal Trade Commission, an agency of the federal government created by Congress in 1914, regulates U.S. advertising,[74] and similar bodies exist in many other countries. Since its creation, the powers and responsibilities of the FTC have been revised and in most cases expanded through the passage of key acts (e.g., the Wheeler-Lea Act of 1938 and the Magnuson-Moss Act of 1975) and the enforcement of laws in key court cases. The FTC has taken some important actions to directly protect consumers and ensure fair competition.[75] We take up these unfair practices in chapter 12 on pricing.

Deceptive Advertising

The FTC's primary responsibility is to detect and provide remedies for deceptive ads.[76] One definition of "deceptive advertising" might be any advertisement that is factually false or misleading. However, this definition is too vague, and the ultimate test of what is deceptive must often be determined through the courts. Since 1938, legislation and court decisions have used one or more of the following criteria to determine deception:

- untruthful aspects of ads
- failure to reveal facts, especially those potentially harmful
- consumers' net general impression of the ad, irrespective of its factual content
- vague or ambiguous assertions that can be interpreted in multiple ways, where one or more interpretations involves a deceptive claim in one or more of the three senses listed above

To prevent deceptive ads, the FTC requires that advertisers provide documentation (e.g., laboratory reports or survey studies) showing that all claims the firm makes in ads are true and that the ad agency used research evidence to prepare the ads. Further, the FTC encourages the use of comparative advertising of two or more brands. This form of advertising has become popular in recent years.

In addition to demanding that false advertising campaigns be dropped or changed, the FTC can impose fines and require the advertiser to perform corrective advertising. A well-known example of corrective advertising was the FTC-mandated $10.2 million campaign ($50 million in current terms) by Warner-Lambert correcting earlier assertions that Listerine mouthwash prevented colds and sore throats.

Other FTC Actions

The FTC regulates celebrity endorsements or other testimonials sponsored by advertisers. Endorsers who claim to use the brand in an ad must actually do so. Also, average consumers must be able to expect similar performance or benefits from use of the brand as the endorser claims to obtain.

Bait-and-switch advertising—in which a firm advertises a brand at an unusually low price, the consumer discovers subsequently that the item is not available, and sales personnel attempt to sell another item at a higher price in its place—is also regulated by the FTC. Indeed, any advertising practice injuring consumers in some way involves the FTC.

PROMOTION AND PUBLICITY

Promotion

Firms create promotions or incentives to encourage purchase or selling.[77] Table 10.10 presents an estimate of the relative use of various modes of promotion in the United States. Promotions are sponsored by sellers and are typically directed at consumers, dealers, or the sales force.

TABLE 10.10 RELATIVE PERCENTAGE USE OF PROMOTIONS BY METHOD

Promotion Method	Relative Percentage
Premiums, incentives, specialties	25
Business meetings, conventions	19
Direct mail	15
Trade shows, exhibits	15
Point-of-sale displays	11
Printing, production, audiovisual, fees, etc.	10
Promotion, advertising space	5
Total	100

Source: Derived from R.A. Strang, "Sales Promotion—Fast Growth, Faulty Management," Harvard Business Review (July–August 1976), p. 118.

Consumer Promotions

Whereas most advertising aims to induce psychological responses (e.g., awareness, interest, desire, preference, or intention) and only indirectly to stimulate behavior, consumer promotions aim at producing an action response. To do this, marketers may employ one or more of a variety of stimuli.

Firms give *coupons* to consumers with the promise of a price reduction or a mailed rebate. Coupons may be printed in magazines or newspapers, put on or within packages, stacked in free-standing inserts, or mailed directly to consumers. Some supermarkets now have video display terminals that show available coupons and print out and dispense them on command. An estimated 310 billion coupons are distributed each year in the United States, and nearly 95 percent of all households use them.[78] Coupons are popular in many countries, including Belgium, Canada, Italy, Spain, and the United Kingdom. Thus, coupons appear to be a popular incentive for consumers. On the other hand, coupon redemption rates can vary widely, depending on product category, brand, and media used to communicate to consumers; and coupons may not induce brand loyalty. Furthermore, retailers find coupons a nuisance to handle, and manufacturers sometimes pay large sums of money to fraudulent redeemers. Despite these shortcomings, couponing is used extensively.

Another popular consumer promotion involves *free samples*. Firms mail free samples, hand them out on the street, deliver them door to door, offer them in a store display or demonstration, or attach them to related products. Sampling is an expensive way to promote, but it effectively encourages trial. Often, free samples are produced in smaller or single-use sizes to reduce costs. However, to build consumer liking or preference, a new brand must be used repeatedly, so small sampling may not always be enough to accomplish the firm's goals.

Still another frequently used consumer promotion is the *premium*. A premium is a free or low-priced "gift" given to consumers when they purchase a brand at regular price or send in a boxtop, brand identification mark, or UPC code from a previous purchase. The use of premiums is believed to cost the sponsor somewhat less than other promotions. Because the consumer must first make a purchase, a larger number of total sales typically result. In a sense, premiums are a reward following trial or regular usage and act as operant conditioning or instrumental learning reinforcements. That is, behavior occurs first (purchase and usage), followed by a reinforcement (the premium), which in turn increases the probability that the consumer will purchase the brand again. Trading stamps are another form of premiums sometimes used in different parts of the world.

Other forms of consumer promotions include *bonus packs, contests, games, prizes, refunds,* and *cents-off deals* (e.g., price reductions announced on the package label or near the packages on display in a store). In a more subtle type of promotion, firms give consumers free gifts, termed *specialty advertising,* such as pens, calendars, coffee mugs, playing cards, or other items. The items usually display the seller's name, brand, and even address or telephone number displayed conspicuously so that the consumer is reminded of the seller. Specialty advertising is also used as a dealer promotion tool.

One major drawback with consumer promotions is that they sometimes do not build brand preference or encourage repeat sales. Rather they serve merely as a free gift or price reduction. Their effect may also be short-lived. In the aggregate, if enough new purchasers try the product because of the promotion, it may generate more revenue than the costs. Managers must experiment with various promotions to determine their value. Consumer premiums may lower the quality image of the brand. The consumer might think, "If the brand is so good, why do they have to give me something else to try it?" Nevertheless, because consumers are not very involved with certain products and thus may buy competing brands without much thought, consumer promotions may be the only way firms can overcome consumer resistance or habit and induce trial or switching.

Dealer Promotions

Dealers, too, typically need incentives to carry and push a sponsor's brands. As firms become more competitive and brands proliferate, overlapping in features and benefits, a firm may need to provide additional value to break through the competition. This is especially true for low-involvement products and those characteristic of media clutter. Thus, firms target dealers (e.g., retailers, wholesalers) for special promotional efforts.

Perhaps the most important dealer promotion, at least in the retail trade, is the *point-of-purchase (POP) display.*[79] Actually, these displays act as both consumer and dealer promotions. A POP promotion consists of a sign, poster, or other attention-getting device that dealers place next to merchandise or present conspicuously with related merchandise away from competitors' brands and other products. For example, supermarkets, drugstores, and liquor stores will position special displays of toothpaste, soaps, wines, canned goods, or other items at the ends of aisles or on colorful cardboard stands in the aisles. Manufacturers typically provide such displays free of charge to the retailer. Expenses may be shared for more complex and expensive displays. POP displays aim to place communication stimuli as close as possible to the actual act of purchase. Because people may be indifferent to some purchases, have not fully made up their minds before shopping, or have not considered certain products or brands, sellers can utilize such displays to stimulate purchase, as a last-minute aid to consumers' decision-making processes.

A second commonly used dealer promotion is the *allowance.* Here a manufacturer will give a wholesaler or retailer free merchandise, actual cash awards, money for advertising, or discounts in exchange for dealers' first-time purchases, volume purchases, or special selling efforts.

Still other dealer promotions consist of special *gifts, bonuses, contests, prizes, free training* or *business advice, free vacations,* and *specialty advertising items.* The value of such seemingly unimportant or gimmicky appeals is that they are novel, even exciting, and provide rewards and recognition in addition to normal compensation. The *trade show* and *convention* are two additional forms of dealer promotions.

Sales Force Promotion

Firms often use incentives to motivate their own sales forces. These incentives add to salespeople's salaries, bonuses, or commissions and include *contests, prizes, free trips, gifts,* and other forms of reward. Some companies even provide catalogs of gifts and send them to the spouses of salespeople in the hope that family pressures will motivate sales. Chapter 11 on personal selling covers such motivators further.

Final Comments on Promotion

In order for promotions to work, managers must recognize that they interact with other marketing mix stimuli, and especially with advertising. Indeed, many promotions reach the consumer only through advertising. Advertising and promotion themes can mutually reinforce each other. One study showed that sales of coffee were 0.6 purchases per 100 shoppers when no advertising or POP displays were used, 2.5 purchases per 100 when only displays were used, 1.9 purchases per 100 when only ads were used, but 8.1 purchases per 100 when both ads and displays were used.[80] The use of both tactics seems to have increased their impact. This type of "interaction effect" has been found for snack foods, paper products, soft drinks, and many other everyday items.

The issue facing marketing managers is not so much a choice of whether to advertise *or* to promote. Rather, most marketing efforts require both advertising and promotion. The question managers must answer is what proportion of each method to employ. In practice, firms use a wide range of advertising-to-promotion budget ratios, even within the same industry. A common ratio is 70:30 for everyday consumer goods. That is, of the total communication budget, 70 percent is spent on advertising and 30 percent on promotions. Other ratios are possible, of course, and in fact are used, depending on the circumstances. Many firms allocate portions of their budgets (typically small amounts) to publicity as well.

Many factors enter the decision process on which ratio to use. One consideration, for example, is buyer behavior. How do consumers make decisions? Ready-to-eat cereals are an example. Many consumers make lists of groceries to buy before they embark on their weekly shopping trips. This would seem to indicate that advertising is crucial, as people have preferred brand(s) in mind before entering the store. Other consumers do not decide on a brand until they pass the shelves in the store. This tends to suggest the importance of in-store point-of-purchase displays, cents-off deals, and other promotion techniques. However, even those who make up their minds before shopping may be influenced by coupons or free samples sent by mail. Likewise, those who have not decided on a brand before shopping may be influenced by information seen in ads that ultimately yield high "top-of-the-mind awareness" while they pass a display of breakfast cereal. Hence, for cereal at least, firms invest a lot in both advertising and promotion. A reasonable advertising-to-promotion ratio might be 70:30 or 65:35, for example, depending on how new or popular the cereal is and how much competition exists.

On the other hand, managers for headache or cold remedies must set the ratio of advertising to promotion higher, perhaps 90:10. Here, consumers purchase in urgent contexts or when they are about to run out of their medication. From a seller's viewpoint, consumers must be made aware of a brand and have the brand's image repeatedly reinforced through advertising. Few consumers decide on such purchases because of POP displays or other promotions. Yet, because sellers want consumers to try new brands or switch from a competitor's brand, they need some promotion, such as free sampling or couponing. Therefore, a high advertising-to-promotion ratio is dictated.

Another consideration managers weigh as they set the advertising-to-promotion ratios is, of course, the degree and nature of competition. Imagine that you are the brand manager for Hires root beer, a soft drink with a small market share. What advertising-to-promotion budget would you set? If Coca-Cola, PepsiCo, 7-Up, and the other leading companies use an 80:20 ratio, should you follow suit? Probably not. Although the same ratio would in some sense meet the competition, the other firms have such larger budgets overall that Hires would be "outshouted" in the marketplace, and you would realize no competitive advantage. A better strategy might be to use a 30:70 ratio, say, placing more emphasis on consumer and dealer promotions. Hires' problem is twofold: (1) to get people to try its brand and switch brands (therefore suggesting couponing and POP displays) and (2) to get stores and restaurants to stock it (suggesting allowances and free goods).

In addition to buyer behavior and competitive factors, a firm must consider the products' life-cycle stage as they consider the advertising and promotion budget. Introduction and growth stages suggest advertising and promotion campaigns that will increase consumer awareness and retailer deals to gain acceptance in the store. Mature products require small changes and fine-tuning of tactics. The decline stage often suggests withdrawal of advertising and promotion supports.

Direct Marketing

Direct marketing is another marketing tactic that closely resembles promotion, although there are key differences. *Direct marketing* tactics allow firms to communicate directly to potential customers (usually through multiple media). Consumers, in turn, buy directly from the firm. No intermediaries such as wholesalers or retailers are used. The most widely used means of direct marketing communication is through mail catalogs. However, direct marketing by telephone and television companies are also common. Typical examples of direct marketing include catalogue companies (e.g., Eddie Bauer, L.L. Bean, JCPenney), publishing houses, and book and record clubs. Financial service organizations such as credit card divisions now increasingly use direct marketing as well. Direct marketing works especially well with consumers who do not have the time, ability, or inclination to travel to stores. Of course, so many companies use it that it may have lost its edge.

Publicity

Publicity[81] is "any form of nonpaid commercially significant news or editorial comment about ideas, products, or institutions."[82] Newspapers, television or radio stations, or magazines usually convey such information. Although firms do not pay for publicity, their products or services benefit from the coverage, and the firm typically provides most of the information through news releases or other documents. Indeed, firms spend considerable time and money to place stories in the news media. The major advantage of publicity, other than its free aspect, is that the public generally perceives the information more positively than if the firm were to advertise it. People perceive the media as impartial and may even see publicity as an endorsement, whereas they typically perceive advertisers as self-serving.

Organizations attempt to coordinate their advertising and promotion campaigns with publicity. Sometimes publicity will lead advertising, introducing the product to the public. Some advertisers will, of course, quote favorable publicity in their ads. But publicity is a double-edged sword. Firms have no real control over what is said and how it is said, and negative publicity can be disastrous. For example, sales of the rotary engine Mazda were allegedly hurt by the Environmental Protection Agency's publication of its very low gas mileage. Magazines such as *Consumer Reports* can influence sales as well, yet firms have no input to their evaluations or publications.

Public relations is targeted not only at the community at large. Firms publicize to segments in trade or special-interest magazines. Lobbying might also be regarded as one form of public relations, as are rumors. At one time or another, Burger King, McDonald's, and Wendy's were rumored (falsely) to use red worms instead of beef in their hamburgers. Any firm should have formal procedures to quickly counteract any rumors once they arise.[83]

SUMMARY

Marketing communication is a complex yet essential function for any organization. It literally serves as the means to respond to or influence demand and other environmental forces. The four major communication tools include

- advertising
- promotion
- publicity
- personal selling

In the broadest sense, we might view the objectives of communication as increased sales through focus upon

- new users who have never tried the product class
- former users of the product class who no longer purchase it
- users of the competitors' brands
- switchers who are loyal to no brand
- current users who might consume more.

Advertising is perhaps the most far-reaching, and on a per capita basis the least expensive, communication tool. At the same time, its impact is not as strong or compelling as more direct modes of influence such as personal selling. Yet, advertising remains an essential managerial tool. Indeed, for everyday consumer products, it is perhaps the most important means of communication. For other products and services, it shares center stage with promotion, publicity, or personal selling.

We saw that the key actors in any advertising effort consist of the advertiser, the advertising agency, and the media. These independent institutions cooperate among themselves to transmit messages to the public at large or special target markets. Of course, it should be remembered that considerable competition exists among advertisers in the communication media, too. Effective marketing requires an unusual degree of coordination between firm and advertising agency. Special roles within each institution facilitate this. Figures 10.3 and 10.4 sketch two typical organizational structures used for management from the firm's side, and Figure 10.5 shows the structure of a typical ad agency. The brand manager of the firm and the advertising account executive in the agency perform the facilitating exchanges between organizations.

The *behavioral science* dimensions of advertising are of utmost importance. Advertising agencies exhibit unique approaches, which we termed *creative styles*. For example, the Leo Burnett agency typically uses humor or emotions. Their ads might be described as "warm and believable," and they sometimes use everyday people in the ads to convey a wholesome image and "the common touch." On occasion, animated characters are used to communicate a story (e.g., light drama), enhance remembrance, and in a nonthreatening way indirectly educate the consumer. The firm of Doyle Dane Bernbach relies relatively more on message structure and execution. Its ads also generally employ large amounts of humor to attract and hold consumers' attention. Sometimes they use refutational arguments, or at other times a story line will present "an unusual turn of events." In still other DDB ads, the product will be put through an unusual test to dramatically show its utility. Ogilvy & Mather tends to emphasize the rational side of consumption. Special effort is given to the creation of a unique brand image as well. The Ted Bates agency, in contrast, is known for its hard sell. It typically emphasizes facts, a unique selling proposition, and on occasion fear appeals. Most other ad agencies express their own unique personalities through their ads.

Over time, a decline in advertising effectiveness commonly occurs due to *repetition and wearout*. At the microlevel, this happens because people become bored with repeated messages and ignore it, or they may become irritated and counterargue against it or downgrade it. At the macrolevel, markets become saturated, and a proportion of previously reached audiences either tune out, counterargue, or switch allegiances to competitors.

Wearout might be ameliorated through a variety of means. Ad structure might be changed. For example, a switch from factual to humorous executions might be attempted. Alternatively, ad copy might be altered. For instance, new product attributes could be communicated. Finally, new advertising media can be tried. A switch from television to radio might be in order.

The Foote, Cone & Belding planning model (see Fig. 10.7) categorizes in terms of *product involvement* (either high or low), the primary type of processing (cognitive or affective), and the order of processing (e.g., learn → feel → do or feel → learn → do). The model can be used as an aid in the design of copy, selection of media, and copy testing. The discussion of affect, cognitions, and consumer involvement integrates many of the principles discussed in this and the preceding chapter. *Media involvement* is also a factor in advertising and promotion.

The measurement of *advertising effectiveness* uses a number of techniques, most of which rely on measuring psychological responses such as recall, recognition, attitudes, or intentions as dependent variables. The advantages of these procedures lie in the ease of data collection and presentation of findings. Moreover, the variables measured represent necessary changes in consumer responses that are, in turn, intermediate between exposure to an ad and actual purchase. At least, the responses are associated with processing of ads and serve as rough predictors of the likelihood of purchase. On the other hand, measurement techniques can be inaccurate. Further, some procedures (e.g., recall) possibly overestimate cognitive responses and underestimate emotional aspects of ads. One must therefore have a clear idea of what response is desired and select a method accordingly. Even with the best of procedures, however, the question of validity must be faced, as psychological responses are often too far removed from the ultimate behavioral responses desired.

In regard to *advertising management*, Figure 10.8 presents an overall framework for managing the communication function in general and advertising in particular. An important activity in this regard concerns *goal setting and budgeting*. Goals are set broadly in terms of ultimate organization ends and gross communication objectives (e.g., desired product trial). More specific goals with respect to awareness, recall, recognition, or intentions are also formulated.

Budgets are financial plans designed to aid goal attainment. They are set on the basis of a variety of criteria.

- Subjective judgments of managers are sometimes used. Such methods should be based on real skills of decision makers who take into account the ability of advertising to produce sales.
- A rule of thumb, such as a fixed percentage of sales, or budgets set to meet or overtake the competition (e.g., 120 percent of a competitors' budget) are also used.
- The objective-and-task method is perhaps the most justified and valid procedure. Here the firm defines a specific goal and then sets a budget necessary to carry out the activities designed to accomplish the goal.
- Some organizations use experimentation, statistical modeling, or normative mathematical modeling to estimate budgets.

Media selection involves various decisions.

- The type of media to use.
- The primary options include television, radio, magazines, newspapers, billboards, direct mail, the World Wide Web, and/or Yellow Pages.
- The choice of a medium is influenced by the number of people in the audience, their attributes, the cost of advertising there, and the ability of the medium for accomplishing desired goals such as product demonstration, conveying facts, or stimulating emotions.
- The specific vehicle to use within each medium or media chosen. For instance, if magazines are chosen, a technical advertiser might select a professional magazine, whereas a mass marketer might opt for *Time*.
- The schedule of media advertising. This is a timing issue of when and how often to advertise: a constant level, a high level followed by decline, pulsing, and responsive tactics.

The social and legal aspects of advertising involve the effects of ads on people as individuals. These effects range from short-lived emotional or thinking stimulation to long-term accumulations of beliefs, values, and socialization.

- On the negative side, ads can have annoying and offensive qualities or involve manipulation and subliminal messages. They may even cause higher prices, false product differentiation, the creation of barriers to entry, and promotion of market concentration and monopoly power.
- On the positive side, advertising can have effects on the economy. Advertising is thought to serve an informative function for consumers in economic decision making, to financially support the mass media, to encourage economic growth, and to provide an essential linkage to consumers for strategy implementation by firms.

Advertising also affects society at large. It has the potential for creating or contributing to social problems. And as with all of life's actions, it raises moral and ethical issues for individuals, institutions, and society. The choices are not unique to advertising, but they take on added importance given the power and visibility that advertising has.

Self-regulation and especially the activities of the FTC have a strong influence on advertising practices. This is especially true with regard to deceptive advertising and the use of bait-and-switch tactics. Thus, the government has an impact on what is said in ads.

Promotions are designed to provide an incentive to the respective audience. Examples include consumer promotions (e.g., couponing, sampling, the use of premiums), dealer promotions (e.g., point-of-purchase displays, allowances), and sales force promotions (e.g., contests). Moreover, the incentive is more directly action oriented than typical advertising appeals. However, many promotions are communicated through advertising. Also, the use of both promotions and advertising can achieve significantly more sales than the use of either one alone. The ratio of advertising to promotion is a strategic choice that must be based upon how consumers make decisions, what the resources of the firm are, what the competition is doing and is likely to do in the future, the stage in the product life cycle, and other factors.

Publicity, too, is a useful communication mode. The trick is to influence in a positive way any information communicated by a firm or its products and picked-up by the media.

QUESTIONS FOR DISCUSSION

1. Broadly speaking, the ultimate goal of advertising is to increase sales. Name five senses in which sales might increase in response to advertising.

2. Firms typically organize their marketing tasks by functions or brands. Briefly describe and contrast these alternative forms of organization design.

3. Describe the structure and functions of modern advertising agencies. Upon whose shoulders does the advertiser-agency relationship rest?

4. Advertising agencies differ considerably in their underlying philosophies and creative styles. What implications does this have for advertisers in the selection of an agency and the management of everyday relations?

5. What is the phenomenon of advertising wearout and how can advertisers combat it?

6. Describe the advertising planning model of Foote, Cone & Belding. How might it be used in practice?

7. Discuss the issues surrounding the measurement of advertising effectiveness.

8. The heart of Ray's communication planning model (see Fig. 10.8) is the budgeting process. Describe how budgets are set in practice. What budgeting process would you recommend, and why?

9. What are the key decisions that must be made in media selection and on what bases are they made?

10. Contrast the effects of ads on individuals, the economy, and society at large. Given the pros and cons, do you think advertising should be controlled more or less than it is now? What should the role of advertising be?

11. What is the purpose of promotions? Discuss the forms of promotions.

12. On what basis should the ratio of advertising to promotion budget be set?

NOTES FOR FURTHER READING

1. Steuart Henderson Britt, Stephen C. Adams, and Allan S. Miller, "How Many Advertising Exposures per Day?" *Journal of Advertising Research* (December 1972): 3–9.

2. James F. Engel, Martin R. Warshaw, and Thomas C. Kinnear, *Promotional Strategy: Managing the Marketing Communication Process* (Homewood, Ill.: Irwin, 1991), p. 484. The $10.84 amount is based on computations from Simmons' data.

3. Robert J. Coen, "Vast U.S. and Worldwide Ad Expenditures Expected," *Advertising Age*, November 13, 1980. In 1960, the United States accounted for about two-thirds of world expenditures on advertising, but is expected to constitute only about 40 percent by the year 2000.

4. Robert S. Trebus, "The Socialist Countries," in S. Watson Dunn and E. S. Lorimor, *International Advertising and*

Marketing (Columbus, Ohio: Grid Publishing, 1979), pp. 349–360. See also Philip Hanson, *Advertising and Socialism* (White Plains, N.Y.: International Arts & Science Press, 1974).

5. *Standard Directory of Advertisers* (Skokie, Ill.: National Register Publishing Company, 1978).

6. *Advertising Age*, September 29, 1993, p. 1.

7. *The Works of Samuel Johnson*, LL.D, IV (Oxford: Talboys and Wheeler, 1825), p. 269.

8. David A. Aaker, Rajeev Batra, and John G. Myers, *Advertising Management*, 4th ed. (Upper Saddle River, N.J.: Prentice-Hall, 1992), p. 7.

9. Two other arrangements are organization by geographical territory and organization by end user. For purposes of brevity, these will not be discussed here. Also, it should be noted that combinations of the four types of organizations are sometimes employed. For instance, the brand management system is often embedded in a functional hierarchy.

10. For a discussion of the role of a brand manager in modern organizations, see Richard M. Clewett and Stanley F. Stasch, "Shifting Role of the Product Manager," *Harvard Business Review*, January–February 1975, pp. 65–73; and Ann M. Morrison, "The General Mills Brand Manager," *Fortune*, (December) 1981, pp. 99–107.

11. "The Brand Manager: No Longer King," *Business Week*, June 9, 1973.

12. See *Agency Compensation: A Guidebook* (New York: Association of National Advertisers, Inc., 1989).

13. Fifteen percent is the most common commission, but it can vary according to the medium or country advertised. For example, outdoor ads typically have a 16.67 percent commission.

14. Marcy Magiera, "Carnation Links Pay, Research," *Advertising Age*, March, 6, 1989, p. 1.

15. Judann Dagnoli, "Campbell 'Incentive' Pares Agency Pay," *Advertising Age*, April 30, 1990, p. 53.

16. Portions of the following discussion on advertising agency styles are drawn from David A. Aaker and John G. Myers, *Advertising Management*, 2nd ed. (Upper Saddle River, N.J.: Prentice-Hall, 1982) and Michael L. Ray, *Advertising and Communication Management* (Upper Saddle River, N.J.: Prentice-Hall, 1982). The author also wishes to thank Professors Brian Sternthal and Richard Yalch for ideas used herein.

17. Albert Bandura, *Social Learning Theory* (Upper Saddle River, N.J.: Prentice-Hall, 1977).

18. Denis Higgens, *The Art of Writing Advertising* (Chicago: Advertising Publications, 1965), p. 44.

19. Quoted in Martin Mayer, *Madison Avenue, U.S.A.* (New York: Pocket Books, 1958), p. 64.

20. Marshall McLuhan, *The Medium Is the Message* (New York: Random House, 1967).

21. Jerry Della Femina, with Charles Spokin, ed., *From Those Wonderful Folks Who Gave You Pearl Harbor* (New York: Simon and Schuster, 1970), pp. 38–39.

22. Aaker and Myers, *Advertising Management*, pp. 349–350.

23. Ibid.

24. David Ogilvy, *Confessions of an Advertising Man* (New York: Atheneum Publishers, 1963), pp. 99–103.

25. Ibid., p. 102.

26. "Come to Shell for Answers: Summary Report," Ogilvy & Mather, New York, September 4, 1978.

27. Philip Levine, "Commercials That Name Competing Brands," *Journal of Advertising Research* (December 1976): 14.

28. Thomas Watterson, "Top Ad Exec's Lament—TV Commercials 'Silly,' " *San Francisco Examiner*, November 13, 1983, D1–D3.

29. Rosser Reeves, *Reality in Advertising* (New York: Alfred A. Knopf, 1961).

30. Higgens, *The Art of Writing Advertising*, p. 124.

31. Reeves, *Reality in Advertising*, p. 47. See also Michael Bungey, "USP's Benefit Still Stands Tall in Noisy 1990s," *Advertising Age*, March 3, 1997, p. 18.

32. "Ayer, Y & R Share Agency of the Year Honors," *Advertising Age*, March 14, 1979, 1ff.

33. "Research Suggests Using Celebrity Spokesman as Focal Point for Floral Group's Consumer, Trade Ads," *Marketing News*, November 11, 1983.

34. Herman Simon, "ADPULS: An Advertising Model with Wearout and Pulsation," *Journal of Marketing Research* 19 (August 1982): 352–363; Bobby Calder and Brian Sternthal, "Television Commercial Wearout: An Information Processing View," *Journal of Marketing Research* 16 (May 1980): 173–186; George E. Belch, "The Effects of Television Commercial Repetition on Cognitive Response and Message Acceptance," *Journal of Consumer Research* 9 (June 1982): 56–65; C. Samuel Craig, Brian Sternthal, and Clark Leavitt, "Advertising Wearout: An Experimental Analysis," *Journal of Marketing Research* 13 (November 1976): 365–372; Michael L. Ray and Alan G. Sawyer, "A Laboratory Technique for Estimating the Repetition Function for Advertising Media Models," *Journal of Marketing Research* 8 (February 1971): 20–29; Alan G. Sawyer, "Repetition and Affect: Recent Empirical and Theoretical Developments," in A. G. Woodside, J. N. Sheth, and P. D. Bennett, eds., *Foundations of Consumer and Industrial Buying Behavior* (New York: American Elsevier, 1977), pp. 229–242; Alan G. Sawyer and Scott Ward, "Carry-over Effects in Advertising Communication," in J. N. Sheth, ed., *Research in Marketing*, vol. 2 (Greenwich, Conn.: JAI Press, 1979), pp. 259–314; Alan G. Sawyer, "Repetition, Cognitive Responses, and Persuasion," in R. E. Petty, T. M. Ostrom, and T. C. Brock, eds., *Cognitive Responses in Persuasion* (Hillsdale, N.J.: Erlbaum, 1981), pp. 237–261; John T. Cacioppo and Richard E. Petty, "Effects on Message Repetition and Position on Cognitive Response, Recall, and Persuasion," *Journal of Personality and Social Psychology* 37 (January 1979): 97–109; Margaret

Henderson Blair, "An Empirical Investigation of Advertising Wearin and Wearout," *Journal of Advertising Research* (December 1987/January 1988): 45–50.

35. Herbert E. Krugman, "Processes Underlying Exposure to Advertising," *American Psychologist* 23 (April 1968): 245–253; Herbert E. Krugman, "Memory without Recall, Exposure without Perception," *Journal of Advertising Research* 17 (August 1977): 7–12; Herbert E. Krugman, "Why Three Exposures May Be Enough," *Journal of Advertising Research* 12 (December 1972): 11–14; Herbert E. Krugman, "What Makes Advertising Effective?" *Harvard Business Review*, March–April 1975, pp. 96–103.

36. Krugman, "Why Three Exposures May Be Enough," p. 13.

37. Recent research supports this latter assertion. See Richard P. Bagozzi and Alvin J. Silk, "Recall, Recognition, and the Measurement of Memory for Print Advertisements," *Marketing Science* 2 (Spring 1983): 95–134. Although people as individuals tend to have stronger powers to recognize an ad than to recall it, aggregate measures across consumers and ads generally show that recognition and recall measures are both highly correlated and stable over at least short periods of time, such as three weeks.

38. R. B. Zajonc, H. Markus, and W. R. Wilson, "Exposure Effects and Associative Learning," *Journal of Experimental Social Psychology* 10 (1974): 248–263.

39. See the discussion on the cognitive response model in chapter 9. See also Peter Wright, "Cognitive Responses to Mass Media Advocacy," in R. E. Petty, T. M. Ostrom, and T. C. Brock, eds., *Cognitive Responses to Persuasion* (Hillsdale, N.J.: Erlbaum, 1981); Sawyer, "Repetition, Cognitive Responses, and Persuasion"; Cacioppo and Petty, "Effects of Message Repetition"; Belch, "Effects of Television Commercial Repetition"; and Calder and Sternthal, "Television Commercial Wearout."

40. Russell I. Haley, "Sales Effects of Media Weight," *Journal of Advertising Research* 18 (June 1978): 9–18; John D. C. Little, "Aggregate Advertising Models: The State of Art," *Operations Research* 27 (July–August 1979): 629–667; Simon, "ADPULS."

41. The notion of media involvement was first described in H. E. Krugman, "The Impact of Television Advertising: Learning without Involvement," *Public Opinion Quarterly* 29 (Fall 1965): 349–356. See also H. E. Krugman, "Memory without Recall." See, in addition, Rajeev Batra and Michael L. Ray, "Operationalizing Involvement as Depth and Quality of Cognitive Response," in R. P. Bagozzi and A. M. Tybout, eds., *Advances in Consumer Research*, vol. 10 (Ann Arbor, Mich.: Association for Consumer Research, 1983); B. T. Johnson and A. H. Eagly, "Involvement and Persuasion: Types, Tradition, and the Evidence," *Psychological Bulletin* 107 (1990): 375–384; and R. E. Petty and J. T. Cacioppo, "Involvement and Persuasion: Tradition versus Integration," *Psychological Bulletin* 107 (1990): 367–374.

42. David Berger, "The Consumer Mind: How to Tailor Ad Strategies," *Advertising Age*, June 9, 1980; "A Retrospective: FCB Recall Study," *Advertising Age*, October 26, 1981; Richard Vaughn, "How Advertising Works: A Planning Model," *Journal of Advertising Research* 20 (October 1980): 27–33; Brian T. Ratchford, "New Insights about the FCB Grid," *Journal of Advertising Research* (August/September 1987): 24–38.

43. Vaughn, "How Advertising Works."

44. D. G. Clarke, "Econometric Measurement of the Duration of Advertising Effects of Sales," *Journal of Marketing Research* 13 (November 1976): 345–357; R. Ackoff and J. R. Ernshoff, "Advertising Research at Anheuser-Busch Inc. (1963–1968)," *Sloan Management Review* 16 (Spring 1975): 1–15.

45. Bagozzi and Silk, "Recall, Recognition, and the Measurement of Memory."

46. H. A. Zielske, "Does Day-After Recall Penalize 'Feeling Ads'?" *Journal of Advertising Research* 22 (February–March 1982): 19–22; Bagozzi and Silk, "Recall, Recognition, and the Measurement of Memory"; Krugman, "Why Three Exposures May Be Enough"; Krugman, "Memory without Recall, Exposure without Perception."

47. Zielske, "Does Day-After Recall Penalize 'Feeling Ads'?"

48. Michael L. Ray, "A Decision Sequence Analysis of Developments in Marketing Communications," *Journal of Marketing* 37 (January 1973): 29–38.

49. R. Colley, *Defining Advertising Goals for Measured Advertising Results* (New York: Association of National Advertisers, 1961); D.C. Marschner, "DAGMAR Revisited—Eight Years Later," *Journal of Advertising Research* 2 (April 1971): 27–33. See also G. L. Lilien, A. J. Silk, J. J. Choffray, and M. Rao, "Industrial Advertising Effects and Budgeting Practices," *Journal of Marketing* 40 (January 1976): 16–24.

50. A. J. San Augustine and W. F. Foley, "How Large Advertisers Set Budgets," *Journal of Advertising Research* 15 (October 1975): 11–16; C. Gilligan, "How British Advertisers Set Budgets," *Journal of Advertising Research* 17 (February 1977): 47–49. See also N. K. Dhalla, "How to Set Advertising Budgets," *Journal of Advertising Research* 17 (October 1977): 11–17.

51. J. C. Becknell Jr. and R. W. McIssac, "Test Marketing Cookware Coated with 'Teflon'," *Journal of Advertising Research* 3 (September 1963): 4–5. See also G. J. Eskin, "A Case for Test Market Experiments," *Journal of Advertising Research* 15 (April 1975): 27–33.

52. L. J. Parsons and F. M. Bass, "Optimal Advertising-Expenditure Implications of a Simultaneous-Equation Regression Analysis," *Operations Research* 19 (May–June 1971): 822–831.

53. J. D. C. Little, "A Model of Adaptive Control of Promotional Spending," *Operations Research* 14 (November–December 1966): 175–197; B. M. Enis, "Bayesian Approach to Ad Budgets," *Journal of Advertising Research* 12 (February 1972): 13–19.

54. H. Assael and H. Cannon, "Do Demographics Help in Media Selection?" *Journal of Advertising Research* 12 (December 1972): 7–11; J. D. McConnell, "Do Media Vary in Effectiveness?" *Journal of Advertising Research* 10 (October 1970): 19–22; J. Z. Sissors, "Matching Media with Markets," *Journal of Advertising Research* 11 (October 1971): 39–43; D. Gensch, *Advertising Planning* (New York: American Elsevier, 1978).

55. *Facts about 1980 Newspapers* (Washington, D.C.: American Newspaper Publishers Association, 1980).

56. *Nielsen Report on Television 1980* (Northbrook, Ill.: A. C. Nielsen Company, 1980).

57. J. D. C. Little and L. M. Lodish, "A Media Selection Model and Its Optimization by Dynamic Programming," *Industrial Management Review* 8 (Fall 1966): 15–23; J. D. C. Little and L. M. Lodish, "A Media Planning Calculus," *Operations Research* 17 (January–February 1969): 1–35; D. A. Aaker, "ADMOD: An Advertising Decision Model," *Journal of Marketing Research* 13 (February 1975): 31–45. See also V. Srinivasan, "Decomposition of a Multiperiod Media Scheduling Model in Terms of Single Period Events," *Management Science* 23 (December 1976): 349–360; Roland Rust, *Advertising Media Models: A Practical Guide* (Lexington, Mass.: Lexington Books, 1986).

58. V. Packard, *The Hidden Persuaders* (New York: Pocket Books, 1957).

59. W. B. Key, *Subliminal Seduction* (Upper Saddle River, N.J.: Prentice-Hall, 1973); W. B. Key, *Media Sexploitation* (Upper Saddle River, N.J.: Prentice-Hall, 1976); and W. B. Key, *The Clamplate Orgy* (Upper Saddle River, N.J.: Prentice-Hall, 1980).

60. R. A. Bauer and S. A. Greyser, *Advertising in America: The Consumer View* (Boston: Division of Research, Graduate School of Business Administration, Harvard University, 1968), p. 183.

61. D. A. Aaker and D. Bruzzone, "Audience Reactions to Television Commercials," *Journal of Advertising Research* 21 (October 1981): 15–23.

62. T. E. Moore, "Subliminal Advertising: What You See Is What You Get," *Journal of Marketing* 46 (Spring 1982): 38–47; J. Saegert, "Another Look at Subliminal Perception," *Journal of Advertising Research* 19 (February 1979), 55–57.

63. F. M. Nicosia, *Advertising Management and Society* (New York: McGraw-Hill, 1974); Bauer and Greyser, *Advertising in America*.

64. S. Ward, "Children's Reactions to Commercials," *Journal of Advertising Research* 12 (April 1972): 37–45.

65. R. B. Zajonc, "Feeling and Thinking: Preferences Need No Inferences," *American Psychologist* 35 (February 1980): 151–175; Bandura, *Social Learning Theory*.

66. H. H. Kassarjian, "The Negro and American Advertising, 1946–65," *Journal of Marketing Research* 6 (February 1969): 29–39.

67. A. E. Courtney and S. W. Lockeretz, "A Woman's Place: An Analysis of the Roles Portrayed by Women in Magazine Advertisements," *Journal of Marketing Research* 8 (February 1971): 92–95; C. Scheibe, "Sex Roles in TV Commercials," *Journal of Advertising Research* 19 (February 1979): 23–27. See also A. E. Courtney and T. W. Whipple, *Sex Stereotyping in Advertising: An Annotated Bibliography*, (Cambridge, Mass.: Marketing Science Institute, 1980); and M. Butler and W. Paisley, *Women and the Mass Media* (New York: Human Science Press, 1980).

68. J. L. Simon, *Issues in the Economics of Advertising* (Urbana: University of Illinois Press, 1970); M. Pearce, S. M. Cunningham, and A. Miller, *Appraising the Economic and Social Effects of Advertising* (Cambridge, Mass.: Marketing Science Institute, 1971); J.-J. Lambin, "What Is the Real Impact of Advertising?" *Harvard Business Review*, May–June 1975, pp. 139–147; J. M. Ferguson, *Advertising and Competition: Theory, Measurement, Fact* (Cambridge, Mass.: Ballinger, 1974); D. G. Tuerck, ed., *Issues in Advertising: The Economics of Persuasion* (Washington, D.C.: American Enterprise Institute, 1978); P. W. Farris and M. S. Albion, "The Impact of Advertising on the Price of Consumer Products," *Journal of Marketing* 44 (Summer 1980): 17–35; R. Schmalense, *The Economics of Advertising* (Amsterdam: Elsevier/North-Holland, 1972); P.N. Bloom, *Advertising, Competition, and Public Policy* (Cambridge, Mass.: Ballinger, 1976); Y. Brozen, ed., *Advertising and Society* (New York: New York University Press, 1974).

69. L. Benham, "The Effect of Advertising on the Price of Eyeglasses," *Journal of Law and Economics* 15 (October 1972): 337–351; R. L. Steiner, "Does Advertising Lower Consumer Prices?" *Journal of Marketing* 37 (October 1973): 19–26.

70. J. Backman, *Advertising and Competition* (New York: New York University Press, 1967).

71. See, for example, Ferguson, *Advertising and Competition*.

72. Farris and Albion, "Impact of Advertising."

73. S. Winokur, "Freud and Fashion: Tobacco Firm's Seduction of Women," *San Francisco Examiner and Chronicle*, August 21, 1983, pp. A6–A7; S. Cunningham, "Not Such a Long Way, Baby: Women and Cigarette Ads," *Monitor* (American Psychological Association), November 1983, p. 15.

74. S. E. Cohen, "Advertising Regulation: Changing, Growing Area," *Advertising Age*, April 30, 1980; D. Cohen, "The FTC's Advertising Substantiation Program," *Journal of Marketing* 44 (Winter 1980): 26–35; R. F. Wilkes and J. B. Wilcox, "Recent FTC Actions: Implication for the Advertising Strategist," *Journal of Marketing* 38 (January 1974): 55–61; J. L. Welch, *Marketing Law* (Tulsa, Okla.: Petroleum Publishing Co., 1980); B. J. Katz et al., eds., *Advertising and Government Regulation* (Cambridge, Mass.: Marketing Science Institute, 1979); Brozen, *Advertising and Society*.

75. A considerable amount of self-regulation occurs within the advertising industry, too. For example, the Council of Better Business Bureaus has a body of members (the National Advertising Division), which hears complaints. Unsatisfactory compliance with the National Advertising Division's mandates will lead to review by the National Advertising Review Board, a group of 50 people (40 advertising professionals and 10 public members). Failure to comply with this latter body's recommendations will result in referral to a government body such as the FTC. Still another self-regulatory mechanism is the Code Authority of the National Association of Broadcasters, which handles radio and television ads. Members agree to abide by this code, which supplies guidelines for areas such as children's ads, ads for alcoholic beverages, and ads for personal care products. The American Association of Advertising Agencies and the Association of National Advertisers also have codes of conduct. Finally, individual state governments also regulate aspects of advertising, such as bait-and-switch practices.

76. D. M. Gardner, "Deception in Advertising: A Conceptual Approach," *Journal of Marketing* 39 (January 1975): 40–46. M. T. Brandt and J. L. Preston, "The Federal Trade Commission's Use of Evidence to Determine Deception," *Journal of Marketing* 41 (January 1977): 54–62.

77. S. J. Levy, *Promotional Behavior* (Glenview, Ill.: Scott Foresman, 1971); M. Chevalier and R. Curhan, *Sales Promotion* (Cambridge, Mass.: Marketing Science Institute, 1975); O. Riso, ed., *Sales Promotion Handbook*, 7th ed. (Chicago: The Dartnell Corporation, 1979); R. A. Strang, *The Promotional Planning Process* (New York: Praeger, 1980); G. R. Smith, *Display and Promotion*, 2nd ed. (New York: McGraw-Hill, 1978); J. F. Engel, M. R. Warshaw, and T. C. Kinnear, *Promotional Strategy*, 4th ed. (Homewood, Ill.: Irwin, 1979). R. M. Prentice, *Consumer Franchise Building* (Chicago: Commerce Communications, 1984).

78. Garrie Goerne, "Clutter Anyone?" *Adweek's Marketing Week* (April 8, 1991): 22–24; Ira Teinowitz, "Coupons Gain Favor with U.S. Shoppers," *Advertising Age* (November 14, 1988): 64; B. Spethmann, "Countries Crave Coupons," *Advertising Age* (July 15, 1991): 26.

79. M. Chevalier, "Substitution Patterns as a Result of Display in the Product Category," *Journal of Retailing* (Winter 1975–76): 65–72; J. P. Kelly and E. D. Robinson, "Sales Effects of Point-of-Purchase In-Store Signing," *Journal of Retailing* (Summer 1981): 49–63.

80. Statement by the Point-of-Purchase Advertising Institute (1978), quoted in D. I. Hawkins, R. J. Best, and K. A. Coney, *Consumer Behavior: Implications For Marketing Strategy* (Plano, Tex.: Business Publications, 1983), p. 563.

81. H. F. Moore and B. R. Canfield, *Public Relations: Principles, Cases, and Problems*, 8th ed. (Homewood, Ill.: Irwin, 1981). Jordan Goldman, *Public Relations in the Marketing Mix* (Lincolnwood, Ill.: NTC Business Books, 1984).

82. *Marketing Definitions* (Chicago: American Marketing Association, 1960).

83. Fredrick Koenig, *Rumor in the Marketplace* (Rover, Mass.: Auburn House Publishing 1985).

CHAPTER 11

SALES AND SALES MANAGEMENT

CHAPTER OBJECTIVES

When you are done with this chapter you should have achieved the following:

- An understanding of the sales function and its strategic role within the marketing organization
- A basic understanding of the fundamental roles and tasks involved in selling and the different approaches that salespeople can use to make their efforts more effective
- An understanding of the tasks sales managers face, including issues of salesforce design, building, and management
- A basic understanding of the intricacies of salesforce motivation through intervention, structure, and compensation programs

CHAPTER OUTLINE

Selling Typewriters in the Age of Personal Computers

Dobbsie Witherow is a marketing representative at the Wm. Dierickx Company in Bellevue, Washington. Dierickx is a large-volume office equipment supplier. Among its many product lines, Dierickx sells electronic typewriters from manufacturers such as Panasonic and Lexmark International.

In the current environment, many people respond to the idea of selling typewriters with skepticism. In an age of personal computers on every desk, most people assume that businesses no longer need typewriters. Skepticism is certainly a common reaction when Witherow first approaches customers with the idea of buying a typewriter. She knows, however, that typewriters remain an important tool in most business offices and that new typewriters with digital features can be very beneficial.

Even the most modern and virtual offices still need typewriters occasionally and Dobbsie Witherow is ready to oblige.

Witherow has found, for example, that typewriters outperform personal computers for typing multiple-copy forms such as courier labels, packing slips, insurance documents, and bank signature cards. Typewriters are also easier to use for typing short informal memoranda and are an absolute necessity when computer systems break down, even if for just a few hours. Witherow's research reveals that most companies, from corporate giants to small businesses, keep at least one typewriter at every office site, and it is used at least once per day, but often multiple times per day.

Dierickx trains its salesforce to take a problem-solving approach to sales, and Witherow is no exception. Her response to skeptical customers is to show them proof that their company actually uses typewriters. Most often she uses customer's past typewriter and typewriter supply purchase records, which are available from Dierickx company files. In addition, Witherow often identifies where customers might use or need typewriters and verifies their existence before making a sales pitch.

After overcoming customers' initial skepticism by showing them that they still need typewriters, Witherow moves quickly into listing the tasks for which typewriters are being used and how replacing older models will benefit companies. Witherow has a base of more than 20,000 currently in-use typewriters in her sales territory, most of which are old IBM Selectric typewriters with relatively high repair costs. Witherow uses her knowledge of currently used typewriters to highlight the features of her new product and to give the customer precise cost savings and enhanced efficiency projections for the new typewriter being considered. Such estimates are important because they simplify the customers' decision processes and expedite purchase approval.

In her approach to selling typewriters, Witherow does not fit common sales stereotypes, such as being pushy and selling unneeded products. Instead, Witherow and other Dierickx salespeople act as consultants who find solutions to customer problems, and their sales success suggests they are doing it right.

Source: Francy Blackwood, "Mastering the Mastodon Sell," *Selling*, May 1994, pp. 18–20. This copyrighted material is used with permission from *Selling* magazine, a publication of *Institutional Investor,* 488 Madison Avenue, New York, NY 10022.

THE SALES PROFESSION: TODAY AND INTO THE TWENTY-FIRST CENTURY

The Strategic Importance of the Sales Function to Organizations

In marketing, the sales function is most typically considered part of promotion. It is one of the ways in which information about products and services is presented to customers, and it plays an important role in promoting practically all products. For complex and expensive products, the importance of personal sales is obvious, because such sales require persuasive and informative promotional efforts that can only be delivered personally. But even in marketing consumer packaged goods, such as paper towels and cookies, the sales function is important to secure retailer cooperation. Convincing a retailer to allocate shelf space to new consumer products, or to not take away shelf space from existing products in favor of a competitor's new products, often requires the same persuasive and informative promotional effort as selling new computers. It seems clear, therefore, that sales can seldom be overlooked in a company's overall marketing strategy.

Many consumers tend to think of personal sales only in terms of aggressively trying to convince customers to buy the company's products or services, without any regard for customer welfare. That view of personal sales may have been justifiable in the days of door-to-door aluminum-siding salespeople, or in the legends of street vendors who sold magic lamps and flying carpets. Salespeople who will sell anything to anyone without regard for customer needs, however, are not really as common as our cultural myths make them appear. In fact, they are quite rare in an age in which customers have many choices and competition is at an all-time high.

For many companies, salespeople represent the most complete embodiment of the marketing orientation: people committed to understanding and serving customers as thoroughly as possible while safeguarding their company's profitability and good reputation. A well-trained and motivated salesforce can be the focal point where all aspects of a company's marketing strategy come together—the means by which that strategy is communicated to customers. At the same time, salespeople can contribute substantially to develop and enhance the company's overall marketing efforts. Research suggests, in fact, a mutual influence between a company's marketing orientation and its salespeople's behavior.[1] Companies that show a marketing orientation through other aspects of their marketing mix (e.g., products, advertising, pricing, distribution) hire better performing salespeople, which in turn advances the company's reputation and marketing effectiveness. For many companies, the salesforce is the primary point of contact with customers and the market environment. In these companies, salespeople are strategically valued and respected.

We can see this marketing orientation in the Witherow example. At Dierickx, Witherow represents the company's complete product line, and most of her customers depend on Dierickx for the bulk of their office supplies. Witherow has formed long-term relationships with many customers and is responsible for selling all of the company's products. Because customers seldom buy all the different types of office supplies in a single purchase, a key aspect of Witherow's job is to maintain a relationship that allows repeated and frequent contact and encourages customers to think of Dierickx whenever needs arise.

Another facet of Witherow's job is to negotiate transaction details, such as delivery schedules, pricing, and credit terms. This is particularly important on expensive products such as typewriters and fax machines, which because of their cost are important purchases for many companies. When buying expensive products, customers expect and demand some flexibility on the seller's part on items such as credit terms and quantity discounts, which Witherow must negotiate. Witherow has to be aware of her company's policies and her customers' needs, and be ready to negotiate in good faith without jeopardizing her company's profits.

Witherow must track customer orders once they are received by Dierickx, and respond to any customer questions after she has delivered the products. With some products, Witherow also gets involved in training customers directly or making sure that customers get training. Witherow must meet customer needs both before and after the sale, and her responsiveness with each individual order helps preserve the relationship and the potential for future business.

In addition to being responsive to customer needs, salespeople must also respond to requests from other areas of their own organizations. For example, management may ask sales representatives to provide new product ideas or to evaluate proposed advertising, sales promotions, and service enhancements. Salesperson input is important because local markets can vary substantially from national trends, and what sells in Seattle might not go over in Peoria. Salespeople also identify opportunities for new business for other areas of their company, and coordinate their activities with other marketing efforts, such as sales promotions and advertising.

Salespeople demonstrate a marketing orientation via their close association with the company's image. For many customers, the salesperson "is" the company, and buyers equate continuity in the salesforce with supplier continuity in all other areas. This often translates into customers wanting to deal with the same person on a repeated basis. Although salespeople can sometimes transfer an account relationship to other personnel, over time they can expect to accumulate a number of personal customer relationships that they must maintain.

Overall, it is easy to see that salespeople such as Witherow do not fit the sales stereotypes of yesterday. Although their primary responsibilities are to respond to the demands of customers and prospects, and to present their companies' products in the best possible light, salespeople such as Witherow contribute significantly to their company's strategic marketing efforts. Their jobs often require understanding and coordinating virtually all areas of the business, and their efforts influence many other aspects of the marketing mix.

Providing Market Intelligence and Influencing the Marketing Mix

Witherow performs many of the functions and tasks that salespeople may take on, which appear in Table 11.1. This list was developed using interviews, focus groups, and a questionnaire administered to almost 1,400 salespeople from 51 companies. The diversity of this list further supports the claim that salespeople are more than promoters of products to unsuspecting customers. Some experts argue, in fact, that the sales function bridges the gap between consumers and producers, and that it significantly influences all areas of the business. Table 11.1 lists important areas for both buyers and sellers, touching on all four areas of the marketing mix: product, price, promotion, and distribution.

Sales as a Shared Function

Thus far, we have discussed various aspects of selling in the context of professional salespeople and their responsibilities. Limiting the application of selling principles or participation in sales efforts only to sales personnel, however, can be a serious mistake for many companies. Although companies need sales professionals to promote products

TABLE 11.1 FUNCTIONS AND RELATED TASKS PERFORMED BY SALESPEOPLE	
Functions and Tasks	**Affected Areas of the Marketing Mix**
Selling Function	Promotion, Pricing
Plan	
Develop leads	
Identify decision makers	
Make sales calls	
Respond to current accounts	
Negotiate	
Working with Others	Product, Distribution
Expedite orders	
Handle shipping arrangements	
Assist service personnel	
Servicing the Product	Product, Distribution
Learn and test equipment	
Supervise installation	
Train customers	
Supervise and perform repairs	
Managing Information	Product, Promotion
Provide technical information to customers	
Manage customer feedback	
Summarize information on customer needs	
Perform competitive assessments	

and services, contact between buying and selling organizations occurs at many other functional levels, and every encounter brings with it the potential for enhancing the business relationship. For example, complex installations such as specialized manufacturing machinery and large-scale computer systems often require substantial customization to meet customer needs, and extensive training of customer personnel. In these situations, the sales process involves technicians, trainers, and sales professionals who must act as a team in their commitment to customer satisfaction and to sustaining a marketing orientation.[2] Many companies, such as DuPont and General Electric, have formalized team selling and instituted sales team management systems. As discussed in chapter 6, complex products sometimes also lead to partner relationships between buyers and sellers, in which case team efforts are even more vital. Partner relationships and their influence on sales are discussed in the next section.

Even when selling standardized products that do not require formal teams and relationships, however, other organization members also have contact with customers and can influence the customer's overall satisfaction level. Contact between Microsoft and Dierickx, for example, is not limited to Witherow and a professional buyer. Dierickx's delivery and installation technicians, service representatives, and accounting personnel also work with Microsoft and should see themselves as potential salespeople. A service representative, for example, may find that Microsoft is

TABLE 11.1 FUNCTIONS AND RELATED TASKS PERFORMED BY SALESPEOPLE—CONTINUED

Functions and Tasks	Affected Areas of the Marketing Mix
Servicing Accounts	Promotion, Distribution
Set up displays and shelves	
Take inventory for customers	
Handle local advertising	
Attending Meetings	Distribution, Promotion
Attend sales conferences and meetings	
Attend client and customer conferences	
Attend product exhibitions	
Training and Recruiting	Promotion, Distribution
Train and recruit new sales representatives	
Train and recruit new distributors	
Distribution	Distribution, Pricing
Maintain relations with distributors	
Sell to distributors	
Handle terms of repayment and credit	
Entertaining	Promotion, Distribution
Entertain clients (e.g., dinners, lunches)	
Host parties for clients	
Traveling	

Source: Summarized from William C. Moncrief III, "Selling Activity and Sales Position Taxonomies for Industrial Salesforces," Journal of Marketing Research 23 (August 1986): 261–270 (with minor text modifications).

having problems with a typewriter because Microsoft is using a lower quality ribbon than what the manufacturer recommends. The service representative can inform Witherow of the problem, or can take customers through a needs assessment and convince them to adopt a better quality ribbon. Even if other Dierickx employees are not formal members of the salesforce, they can sustain a team spirit that contributes to company sales while enhancing customer service.

Even if companies are not in highly competitive situations, it is important that employees other than sales personnel see themselves as potential salespeople, as illustrated by Marketing Anecdote 11.1. Employees should see that at different times they can fulfill different sales roles, and that encounters with their customers can often involve tasks such as needs assessments, presentations, and closings. Another example in which employees across several areas are involved in sales is that of BriskHeat Corporation. BriskHeat produces low-tech heating products for manufacturing, such as heating blankets and jackets that wrap around pipes to prevent content condensation. Although its products are low-tech, the production facilities of the customers who buy BriskHeat products are not. BriskHeat engineers are often in contact with customers in conjunction with the BriskHeat salespeople, and these engineers are recognized as an integral part of the overall sales effort.[3]

In 1993, Kiwi International was a small, employee-owned airline in an intensely competitive industry. It owned only eight jets, flew a limited 26 flight-per-day schedule, and had little name recognition. But it had more than 600 committed and highly effective salespeople that worked for little or zero compensation and made personal calls on travel agents. Even more dramatic, these salespeople commanded instant credibility with their customers because they both owned and supported Kiwi's air operations. Kiwi's salesforce was its employee-owners.

Kiwi was created by a group of airline professionals who lost their jobs when their previous employers went out of business. Pilots, mechanics, and flight attendants from defunct airlines, such as Eastern, Midway, and Pan Am, pooled their funds and started an airline that would let them return to the skies and offer service superior to that of their competitors. They succeeded, with flights that offered more leg room, good-quality meals, and unrestricted rates at half the price. Their most challenging task, however, was to gain awareness and support from travel agents in their primary markets.

At the time, travel agents wrote about 80 percent of all airline tickets nationwide and were an important element in any carrier's marketing strategy. Most airlines gained travel agent support by offering them special bonuses for recommending their flights to passengers. Most agents had no personal contact with airline personnel, relying on airline reservation systems for schedule and fee change informa-tion. A small airline such as Kiwi could not take these usual approaches because Kiwi's rate structure and profit margins did not allow for special bonuses and the airline had limited funds for advertising to final consumers. Instead, Kiwi adopted a direct-sales approach, asking employee-owners to make direct sales calls on travel agents in their primary markets.

Kiwi employees developed their own prospect lists of eight to ten travel agents near their homes. They also received training on how to make an effective sales call, including getting the travel agents' attention, creating interest in Kiwi, expressing conviction about Kiwi's product, creating a desire for Kiwi's product, and asking for the business. Kiwi salespeople found that these personal calls effectively got travel agents' attention. In addition, they found that making calls in uniform added an element of credibility that made it easier to tell Kiwi's story and generate interest.

Overall, Kiwi's sales approach was a success. Given the tight financial constraints at its inception, Kiwi survived on the strength of its pilots and flight attendants personally generating interest with travel agents. Direct sales calls resulted in sales increases as high as 1,000 percent with some travel agencies in 1993.

Source: Joe Brancatelli, "On a Wing and a Sale," *Selling,* November 1993, pp. 43–49. This copyrighted material is used with permission from *Selling* magazine, a publication of Institutional Investor, 488 Madison Avenue, New York, NY 10022.

The Changing Face of Sales in the Global Village

Three factors contribute to the changing nature of the sales function in modern corporations:

- Increasing diversity in both the salesforce and the customer base
- The growing importance of relationship marketing

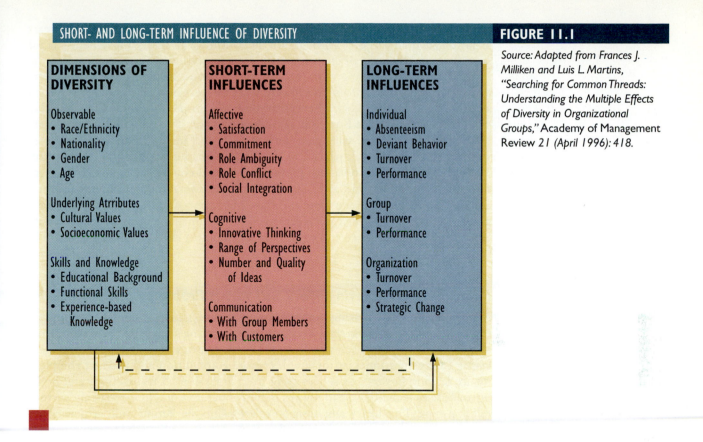

FIGURE 11.1

DIMENSIONS OF DIVERSITY

Observable
• Race/Ethnicity
• Nationality
• Gender
• Age

Underlying Attributes
• Cultural Values
• Socioeconomic Values

Skills and Knowledge
• Educational Background
• Functional Skills
• Experience-based
   Knowledge

SHORT-TERM INFLUENCES

Affective
• Satisfaction
• Commitment
• Role Ambiguity
• Role Conflict
• Social Integration

Cognitive
• Innovative Thinking
• Range of Perspectives
• Number and Quality
   of Ideas

Communication
• With Group Members
• With Customers

LONG-TERM INFLUENCES

Individual
• Absenteeism
• Deviant Behavior
• Turnover
• Performance

Group
• Turnover
• Performance

Organization
• Turnover
• Performance
• Strategic Change

Source: Adapted from Frances J. Milliken and Luis L. Martins, "Searching for Common Threads: Understanding the Multiple Effects of Diversity in Organizational Groups," Academy of Management Review 21 (April 1996): 418.

• Telecommunications and information technology, which allows virtual links across large distances

Global Diversity

Diversity implies more than differences in observable characteristics, such as gender, race, ethnicity, nationality, or age. Figure 11.1 lists some of the dimensions that underlie these outward differences and some of the factors that diversity is likely to influence. Many studies have found substantial differences in cultural and socioeconomic values behind outward characteristics. Such differences can have a substantial effect on how well people understand one another and work together.[4]

These differences arise in many ways, such as how we shake hands or greet other people, how we negotiate with others, or how we approach problem-solving tasks.[5] Because diversity is rising in both the salesforce and the customer base, its effect on how people interrelate will undoubtedly have increasingly significant implications for sales activities. Salespeople need to anticipate diverse mindsets, values, abilities, and perspectives and adjust their behavior so as to preserve an open channel for communications and persuasion. These differences in mindsets, values, and perspectives also affect salespeople's overall attitudes and performance, as shown in surveys of job satisfaction, organizational commitment, role ambiguity, and role conflict. Sales managers, who must diversify their salesforces to suit their markets, also need to adjust their management approach to keep their salespeople motivated and committed.

Salesforce and customer base diversity represent a global challenge to marketing managers. The proportion of women, African Americans, and Latinos employed in sales in the United States, for example, has been increasing for more than 20 years at all managerial levels.[6] Throughout the world, civil rights movements, labor shortages, and the ease of cross-national labor migrations have also increased the representation of diverse groups in sales organizations. In the Middle East, shortages of trained professionals have drawn Asian workers into oil-rich countries such as Kuwait and Saudi Arabia, whereas diversity in Europe is generated by the influx of workers from Eastern European nations and Africa. The unified European market will further require sales managers to deal with many different nationalities within a single salesforce, which can also be said for the fast-growing Pacific Rim mega-market. Asian cultures can present substantial challenges to marketers from the United States, Europe, and Latin America, because of the fundamental cultural and value differences among these areas (see Marketing Anecdote 11.2). Around the globe, salespeople and their managers need to recognize the changes that diversity creates in the marketplace and within organizations, if they are to be successful in the twenty-first century.

Relationship Marketing: Hard Sell versus Problem Solving

A second factor contributing to the changing nature of sales is the growing importance of *relationship marketing*. Relationship marketing's influence on a company's overall marketing approach was discussed in chapter 6, where we emphasized marketing to organizational customers. Increased competition and product complexity are leading buyers and sellers away from arm's-length transactions and high-pressure sales techniques, and toward more cooperative and longer-lasting partner relationships. This heavy emphasis on relationship marketing and partnering has significant implications for the sales function.

Salespeople are typically a company's primary contact with its customer base, as well as an important conduit through which partner relationships must be built. Although partner relationships demand close interaction at multiple levels of the buying and selling organizations and the sharing of large amounts of technical and financial information, the salesperson often makes the initial contact and serves as a coordinator of the relationship-building efforts. A similar relationship-building and coordination role is performed for the buying company by the purchasing professional.

Three environmental factors that involve salespeople serve to make partner relationships a better way for doing business for many companies. One is product complexity and accelerated upgrade schedules, which require salespeople to continually educate customers. In the information management services industry, for example, salespeople are often the first ones to receive a call from customers who have questions. Information services companies such as Electronic Data Systems (EDS) and Andersen Consulting have technical assistance departments, and some customers with highly technical questions can be referred to those specialists. Maintaining relationships, however, requires that salespeople remain responsive and helpful and able to provide accurate answers to simple questions. Fulfilling part of the consultative role helps maintain high levels of customer satisfaction and paves the way for sales of future product upgrades or new products.

Second, buyers and sellers commonly develop products and processes jointly. Many products sold to organizations are highly versatile and can be adapted to fit many customers' specific needs. Such customization requires that buyers and sellers work together to set product performance parameters. Information management services companies such as Electronic Data Systems, for example, customize their products, but they also require customers to change their procedures to

Business practices in Japan and the United States differ substantially in practically all functional areas, and sales is no exception. The Japanese emphasize continuous improvement, protocol, relationships, and long-term planning, which are prominent in sales activities as well as in manufacturing and product development. Emphasis on these factors makes the Japanese approach to selling an almost perfect opposite to the most frequently used U.S. approach. The Japanese are a great example of ethnic and cultural diversity reflected in different communication styles.

The speed with which a company name and the product being sold are mentioned is a good example. In the United States, salespeople are trained to introduce themselves and their company affiliation almost immediately, and to move quickly past pleasant conversation to the purpose of their visit. Salespeople in the United States firmly believe the idiom "Nothing happens until someone sells something." In Japan, however, practically everything happens before the sale is closed.

In Japan it is not uncommon for salespeople to spend months or even years developing a relationship before even mentioning the company name or the product brand they represent. The purpose of the repeated contacts might be understood early and clearly, but it is not mentioned until a relationship has been firmly established, and it is clear that the seller has a firm understanding of the buyer's business and concerns. Even introductions are different in Japan, where initial contact between companies often takes place at very high management levels and the salespeople must wait to be introduced to prospective customers by their managers. In the United States, many salespeople are encouraged to prospect and make unannounced calls on potential customers, and they are the only point of personal contact between the selling and buying companies.

In Japan, after introductions are made, the relationship building starts, with gifts and entertainment being expected and playing an important part in the communication process. Luxurious and expensive gifts are the norm in Japan, and a breach of etiquette in this area can sour the relationship and close the door on a potential sale before business is ever discussed. Gift giving in the United States is perceived as bribery, and actually prohibited by many companies concerned that their buyers will make decisions on the basis of personal interest instead of the company's welfare.

Many Japanese companies have learned the diverse sales approaches practiced in the United States and other countries, and they adopt them in their foreign business transactions. They expect the same deference to diversity from foreign companies seeking to do business in Japan. Although sensitivity to diversity is practiced by buyers and sellers alike, it is advisable for foreign salespeople doing business in Japan and other countries to learn the practices of the country and comply with them whenever possible.

Source: Based on Paula Champa, "How to Sell in Japan," *Selling,* December 1993, pp. 39–47. This copyrighted material is used with permission from *Selling* magazine, a publication of Institutional Investor, 488 Madison Avenue, New York, NY 10022.

accommodate remote data processing and other practices. Salespeople play an important role in managing the joint development of the final product.

Last, markets are increasingly competitive and the hard-sell techniques that U.S. companies traditionally have used no longer work well. One of the best ways to retain customers is to establish close and beneficial partner relationships, making it costly for buyers to switch vendors.[7] A salesperson's understanding of the buyer's culture and the best ways to achieve objectives within the buyer's organization are some of the hard-to-replace benefits buyers get from partner relationships. In protecting marketing relationships against competitive forces, therefore, salespeople play a major role.

Although to a lesser extent than in organizational marketing, relationship marketing is also important in selling consumer products, particularly consumer durable goods such as automobiles, personal computers, and electronic home entertainment equipment. Whenever a marketer is dealing with complex and fast-changing products and stiff competition, salespeople find it advantageous to act as consultants to the customers.

Marketers have also recognized the cost advantage to relationship marketing, if it keeps the customers loyal enough to rely on the vendor for future business. It is easier and less costly to get repeat business from existing customers than to create new business from noncustomers. Two factors contribute here: the number of sales calls it takes to make a sale and the actual cost of sales encounters. Studies indicate that it takes an average of seven sales encounters to make a sale to new organizational customers, compared to only three encounters with existing customers.[8] Depending on a company's per-sales-call costs, this difference can have a significant influence on profits. In the fabricated metals industry, for example, the average cost of a sales call by a senior salesperson is $194.35.[9] This translates into an almost $800 cost difference between selling to a new customer and an established customer. Of course, costs escalate dramatically when sales calls involve multiple representatives from the sales organization, as is often the case in industrial sales. It makes good financial sense, therefore, for salespeople to establish good relationships with customers and preserve long-term repeat business.[10]

Information Technology

A third factor changing the nature of sales is the growth in information technology as a means to reach customers more efficiently and conveniently. Many companies have turned to telemarketing to enhance contact with customers while making more efficient use of sales personnel.

Some telemarketers use communications technology to sell products to final consumers, as in the case of the dinnertime telephone calls offering lawn-care services and credit cards. Many firms also use telemarketing to maintain personal contact with existing or potential customers who are already well informed and perhaps ready to place orders. In sales to both individual consumers and organizational customers, telemarketing can surmount geographic, physical, and time boundaries, and give customers greater convenience while reducing costs to sellers.

Many mail-order companies use telemarketing to facilitate contact between customers and salespeople. Retailing giants such as Lands' End, L.L. Bean, and Eddie Bauer have built their empires on the strength of telemarketing sales, and their reach is truly international. Many companies also use telemarketing to reach organizational customers. Extensive telemarketing is used to reach small accounts by marketers ranging in size from the Union Pacific Railroad to Massachusetts Envelope Company.[11] The main advantage of telemarketing to most users is lower sales call costs. Because person-to-person sales contacts are costly and small accounts generate low sales volumes, personal sales calls can absorb the profits. Telemarketing sales calls are substantially cheaper and can make even small transactions profitable. At the same time, telemarketing provides small accounts with benefits such as convenient access, extended hours, and immediate response to customer demands. Depending on the type of product being sold, the lower costs and faster response of telemarketing may make it the preferred sales method for practically all the sales contacts of some businesses.

Telemarketing can also work for high-dollar-value transactions. As part of its sales reorganization, IBM established IBM Direct, a telemarketing center in Atlanta, Georgia. IBM Direct employs 180 telemarketing representatives who sell everything from computer supplies to mainframes, all from their high-technology offices in Atlanta. Sales transactions may often exceed $100,000 at IBM Direct, with most sales directed at existing IBM customers who seek upgrades to existing systems or ancillary products and services. IBM Direct works closely with the IBM field sales organization. Because the sales organizations do not compete for commissions, they exchange leads in both directions regularly. IBM Direct is open five days a week for 12 hours per day and sells more than $1 billion per year. It has brought IBM the typical advantages of telemarketing, such as lower cost per sales contact and more efficient use of sales personnel. The most important benefit, however, has been faster response time to customer needs, which IBM believes will contribute to higher overall customer satisfaction.[12]

Technological breakthroughs in digital switching and fiber-optics transmission, competition in the telecommunications industry, and the global linking of countries and markets via microwave, satellite, and other land-and-space–based communication systems have lowered the costs and increased the speed and quality of telemarketing sales contacts dramatically, making them highly desirable alternatives to person-to-person encounters for some products. Some of these same factors have also given rise to the commercial development of the World Wide Web, as illustrated by Marketing Anecdote 11.3. Although the World Wide Web has grown dramatically in the past several years, it continues to evolve in its marketing applications and scope. The web is unlikely to replace all other forms of telemarketing in the near future, nor will it ever replace one-on-one sales contacts across all industries. It has already changed the way in which some sales efforts are conducted, however, and is likely to generate more changes to sales practices in the future. It is important, therefore, for salespeople and their managers to stay abreast of developments in the area of computer-mediated exchange, and to adjust their strategies and tactics in order to remain competitive.

SALES ROLES

The term "salesperson" covers a large variety of jobs that differ in the activities involved. A sales clerk at a convenience store, for example, primarily takes orders and delivers products or services in response to customer requests. In this situation the customer has already decided to purchase, what to purchase, and how much. A cemetery plot salesperson, in contrast, tries to sell customers something they don't even want to think about, much less purchase. The second role is clearly more difficult than the first, which probably explains at least in part why people who actively "sell" products are often paid more than people who just "take orders."

"Order taker" and "seller" are two of five currently relevant roles that salespeople play.[13] Others appear in Table 11.2 on page 430, which presents one of several sales role classifications advanced in marketing.[14] Although some sales jobs involve only a

The World Wide Web, an integrated network of computers that spans the globe, has in the last few years become accessible to consumers via their personal home computers. The World Wide Web has permanently altered the way business is transacted around the world. Since 1994, commercial use of the web has grown exponentially. Up-to-date information on web use and capabilities changes so quickly and dramatically, in fact, that published statistics from various sources disagree substantially and are often out of date within days. Many marketing managers and researchers, however, seek to understand how the web influences all marketing functions, convinced that the widespread use of the web will have a significant and hard-to-predict impact for the conduct of marketing.

The World Wide Web has significant implications for the sales function in both industrial and consumer markets. The World Wide Web allows buyers and sellers to exchange more information at higher speeds and lower costs than ever before. It also allows communications across cultural, social, linguistic, and geographic boundaries in ways never before experienced. Sellers use the web to conduct market surveys and keep track of consumer shopping behavior unobtrusively on a global basis. Buyers compare and contrast complete product offerings of manufacturers on the web, and use "smart agents" (programmed search utilities) to sift through many sellers' databases. Smart agents access vendor web sites and extract information as instructed by the customer. A smart agent programmed to seek out the best deals in personal computers, for example, can access the web sites from companies such as IBM, Compaq, Dell, and Micron, and retrieve product feature and price information that fits with performance and cost parameters specified by the customer.

The end result of high-speed, low-cost information exchange in both directions is an enhancement, or in some cases replacement, of salespeople in the roles of disseminating and gathering infor-

single role, most professional sales positions play different roles at different times. This is illustrated by the variety of roles involved in the daily activities of a business development officer at a bank, as seen in Figure 11.2 on page 431.[15]

The variety in roles seen in Figure 11.2 is found in most sales positions. A sales clerk working for a mass merchandiser or department store, for example, acts most often as an order taker, but may also serve as a missionary when customers ask questions about products they have already purchased, or as a seller of ancillary products or services offered by the store. The extended warranties sold by retailers of major appliances and electronic equipment are examples of such ancillary services. Sales clerks offer these warranties because of their high profit margins and commissions. Automobile salespeople normally act as sellers, but sometimes act as missionaries at auto shows, or as trade servicers when helping the service department deal with a dissatisfied customer. In fact, car buyers' increasing sophistication has changed car sales personnel into conveyors of knowledge rather than aggressive sellers.[16] GM's Saturn division, for example, has built its success in part via a sales approach that trains salespeople to answer questions and offer the customer the opportunity to experience the product, but not to pressure customers to buy.[17]

Salespeople must determine the role they will play based on the type of product or service being sold. If they sell industrial installations (e.g., machine tool equipment, conveyor systems), for which the investment is large and the lead times long, salespeople often act initially as missionaries, transition to the institutional seller's

mation. High-speed, low-cost information exchange, however, has also caused an increase in the amount of information received by consumers, sometimes leaving them unable to make decisions as quickly as they did before having access to the web. Salespeople for companies using the World Wide Web are redirecting their energies. Rather than providing information about products, they now want to help customers make sense of the large amounts of information available. The consulting role remains very applicable for salespeople, but their emphasis is on solving problems through a search and evaluation process. Because the web is primarily used by sophisticated, educated, and well-to-do customers, the medium cannot be ignored and salespeople in more and more marketing companies need to adjust their sales approach to fit the new marketing realities.

The World Wide Web, and perhaps other computer-mediated environments, have become a permanent and influential part of the marketing landscape. For salespeople and their managers, the challenge is to learn its strengths and limitations quickly, and to adjust their operational modes and customer approaches accordingly. The principles of exchange remain the same over the web as they are in person-to-person contacts, telemarketing, or any other means of selling, and sales remain an important marketing function.

Sources: Katie Haffner and Matthew Lyon, *When Wizards Stay Up Late: The Origins of the Internet* (New York: Simon Schuster, 1996).

Donna L. Hoffman and Thomas P. Novak, "Marketing in Hypermedia Computer-Mediated Environments: Conceptual Foundations," *Journal of Marketing* 60 (July 1996): 50–68.

Donna L. Hoffman and Thomas P. Novak have been researching the implications for marketing theory and practice of the World Wide Web since 1993. Their web site is continually updated in terms of published research and access to other research sites. It can be reached at http://www2000.ogsm.vanderbilt.edu.

role during the decision process, and complete the process as order takers. The sale of products to resellers, on the other hand, requires the seller role early, as salespeople first try to get an audience with buyers and then try to secure at least a trial order for their products at the meeting. This was the case with Dan Gallo, a salesperson for Sanford Corporation.[18]

In the early 1980s, Gallo sold office stationery and supplies for Sanford Corporation to small- and medium-sized independent stores and acted as a trade servicer for businesses who did not know the best ways to set up writing instrument displays. During the mid-1980s, however, he started approaching retail giants such as Wal-Mart and Target because he saw that that these stores sold an increasing share of all writing instruments. Gaining access to professional buyers at large retailers was not easy, but through careful planning and persistence Gallo was able to convince retailers to carry the Sanford line, and in the process gave his company a substantial boost in business volume.

Retail salespeople who see themselves primarily as order takers may miss additional sales opportunities. Retail customers are increasingly sophisticated and resist high-pressure sales, but they are also affluent and predisposed to impulse purchases if the product "seems right." Customers predisposed to buy on impulse are good candidates for a sales approach that promotes complementary products. A man buying a business suit, for example, is a good candidate for a second suit, an extra pair of slacks, dress shirts, and other accessories. The salesperson should also be prepared to assume a missionary role in advising the customer on color combinations, the construction of the suit, or the alteration services offered by the retailer.

TABLE 11.2 SALES ROLES

Missionary: This role focuses on building goodwill with the customer toward the products or services being represented. The missionary role provides current and potential customers with information about products and services, and with additional assistance as required. Missionaries seldom take orders or try to close a deal. Some sales positions are primarily missionary in scope, such as medical detailers who represent pharmaceutical companies in their contacts with physicians. In consumer sales, an example of a missionary is someone handing out samples at a grocery store and encouraging customers to try the brand.

Trade Servicer: This role is primarily responsible for increasing business from current customers by providing them with merchandising and promotional assistance. Large consumer goods companies, such as General Foods, have salespeople who call on retailers and help them set up shelf displays to maximize the sales of their products. There is no equivalent role in sales to consumers.

Sellers: This role focuses on generating additional purchases from current and potential customers by communicating how the product or service meets their needs and persuading customers to make a purchase. Most people associate the sales role with sales positions. The role can vary in the balance between logical and emotional approaches used to persuade the customer and in how much pressure is placed on the customer. There are many examples of sellers in both organizational and consumer markets, ranging from the sale of office supplies by traveling salespeople to the Mary Kay consultant.

Order Taker: This role performs routine order writing and account maintenance activities in response to customer requests. A typical order taker is a retail salesclerk who responds to customer requests but takes no active role in informing or persuading the customer. Order takers are also used by direct mail marketers that offer toll-free telephone service for customers to place orders. Toll-free telephone service for order placement is also offered by some companies that sell to organizational buyers.

Institutional Seller: This role is responsible for informing and persuading the many persons normally involved in purchase decisions at large businesses and institutions. Although this role is concerned with getting customers to place an order, it is often more concerned with promoting a common understanding among the multiple decision makers of their company's needs and how the product or service being offered meets those needs. An equivalent role in sales to consumers occurs when a family is making a large purchase and the salesperson helps to resolve differences and make sure that all members of the deciding group are informed and persuaded.

Source: Summarized from William C. Moncrief III, "Selling Activity and Sales Position Taxonomies for Industrial Salesforces," Journal of Marketing Research *23 (August 1986): 266–268 (modified and expanded to include retail sales positions).*

Having established the importance of the sales function and the breadth of activities involved, we now focus on the selling process and other factors that salespeople should consider. Salespeople are better able to manage their varied activities and the numerous demands on them when they understand the common stages associated with all sales encounters.

THE SALES PROCESS

Every sales encounter can be subdivided into three general stages, which in turn are further divided into steps. The three stages—the preliminary stage, the face-to-face selling stage, and the follow-up stage—are illustrated in Figure 11.3.

Source: Personal interviews and observations of business development representatives at a large bank. Part of a larger study on bank marketing practices.

TIME	ACTIVITIES
6:30 to 7:30 a.m.	Exercise group. Follow up on yesterday's conversation with Dr. Colón on 401(k) plans for his office. He is also looking to open a second office in South County and will need financing. [Chance to cross-sell products]
8:00 to 8:30 a.m.	Meeting of the Investment Committee [waste of time]
8:30 to 9:15 a.m.	Mrs. Carlisle and Daniel Rush—Daniel's office. Mrs. Carlisle wants to fund revocable trust for Misty (daughter). [Should be a good meeting]
9:30 to 11:30 a.m.	Presentation to Crawford family on the benefits of a living trust for their disabled son, using proceeds from $5 million settlement. Their attorney, Joe Franklin, will be present and opposes the trust idea. Mary Thomas (CPA) will also be present and supports the trust. [Tough meeting]
11:30 a.m. to 12:00 noon	Drive to South County branch office re: Mr. Peters. Branch says he is having second thoughts about the investment account he opened. [Needs assurance.] Check voice mail from car.
12:00 to 12:45 p.m.	Meet with Emma Lewis (branch manager) to get details on Mr. Peters and plan the meeting. Emma is concerned with losing Mr. Peter's commercial accounts. [Will have to sell Emma on our services also.]
1:00 to 2:00 p.m.	Mr. Peters.
2:30 to 3:00 p.m.	Call on Dr. Waters. Discuss the information on employee benefit plan administration mailed last week and get approval for formal analysis and proposal. [Going well]
3:30 to 6:30 p.m.	Meeting with pension management committee for the city government on the pension management services. Union representatives, the city comptroller, and a financial consultant have been invited. [Fifth meeting this month.]

This framework applies equally to industrial and consumer sales, to the different sales roles discussed earlier, and to all types of products and services. The approach may vary, but the stages and steps still appear in some form. This framework, therefore, illustrates the continuity of the sales function across different situations.

The Preliminary Stage

As the label implies, salespeople lay the groundwork well in advance of sales encounters, and these preliminary activities contribute to their effectiveness. In *The Art of War*, the great strategist Sun Tzu observed:

> The general who wins a battle makes many calculations in his temple before the battle is fought. The general who loses a battle makes but few calculations beforehand.[19]

FIGURE 11.3 STAGES AND STEPS IN THE SALES PROCESS

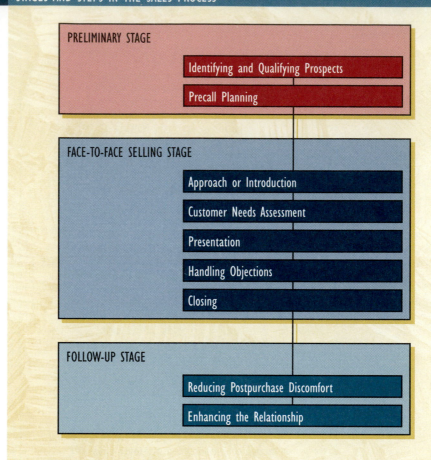

Sun Tzu's point is simple: advanced preparation is critical in any endeavor where forces oppose us. In most sales situations the salesperson must overcome three major factors: customers' resistance to change, customers' unwillingness to be influenced by others, and competition from other producers and products. Advanced preparation is critical for overcoming opposing forces and achieving success.

Identifying and Qualifying Prospects

Time spent identifying prospects for products or services is well spent. Although many people believe that good sales leads are difficult to find, it is even more difficult to sort through the leads to find those that fit with the company's objectives and merit the investment of sales resources. This sorting and selection process is called *qualifying prospects*. A sales call involves a commitment of time and resources considerably greater than those involved in actual meetings, with the average cost of a sales call exceeding $200.[20] At this price, making sales calls indiscriminately can be a substantial drain on company profits. Salespeople must, therefore, spend time studying their potential customers carefully.

A good place to start is with current customer files, looking for opportunities to increase sales to people and companies who already have a positive attitude toward the seller. Salespeople should make it a habit to periodically review their current customer base, particularly when product offerings or business climates change. Qualifying current customers for new products is also easier because information about current customers is typically available from the company's management and marketing information systems.

Beyond current accounts, prospect names and addresses can be gleaned from many sources, ranging from industry and regional business directories, such as Dunn & Bradstreet directories or Standard & Poor's *Register of Corporations*, to the local Yellow Pages. For companies using the World Wide Web to promote their products, information gathered from visitors to a web site can also identify prospects.

Financial information useful in qualifying prospects is often available from credit bureaus, which have become easily and economically accessible. In addition to financial information, salespeople can learn about the prospect's current and future plans, and translate that knowledge into projected needs for the company's products and services. For this kind of research, salespeople use a variety of sources. Friends and acquaintances, business publications, the prospect's competitors and customers, contacts through civic organizations such as Kiwanis, and many other sources are available and need to be checked frequently. In gathering the names and addresses of prospects, and information about their current and future plans, however, salespeople should be careful to remain within the generally accepted ethical bounds for the handling of confidential information. The line between aggressive information gathering and invading customers' privacy can sometimes be a thin one.

Precall Planning

Once salespeople have qualified prospects, they plan and rehearse their presentation before approaching potential customers. Having sufficient information about the target company or person is often the difference between a productive or nonproductive sales presentation.[21] A list of possible questions to investigate beforehand is listed in Table 11.3. Obviously, the topics to investigate should be tailored to the product being sold and the customer being solicited.

As part of advanced planning, salespeople should also consider the distribution of power in their relationship with the customer. As discussed in chapter 6, the balance of power in buyer-seller relationships has significant implications for a company's marketing strategy. Given that salespeople are the primary points of contact with customers, they may be more affected by power imbalances and may need to be more aware of power in the relationship than any other member of the marketing team. Organizational researchers John French and Bertram Raven provide a useful classification for power.[22] They have proposed five different bases of power: reward power, coercive power, legitimate power, expert power, and referent power. Detailed explanations and examples of these bases of power are illustrated in Table 11.4 on page 435.

A crucial but often ignored step in precall planning is setting realistic objectives for the meeting. Getting the prospective customer to make a purchase may not always be the wisest objective, because it may be unattainable. A salesperson with unrealistic expectations, in fact, runs the risk of coming across as excessively demanding and alienating the customer. Sometimes the buying process is slow and salespeople may be well served to adopt more incremental and highly specific objectives, such as gaining access to the key decision maker or setting the date and time for a more formal analysis of customer needs. The more specific the objectives, the better the salesperson can measure progress and make efficient use of sales meetings.

One last element in precall planning and preparation is to rehearse approaching the customer. Salespeople working together practice via role plays, in which one acts as the prospect and the other as a salesperson. The value of practicing the approach

TABLE 11.3 POSSIBLE PRECALL QUESTIONS

1. What is the business of the company or customer?
2. What are its products and markets?
3. Who is the actual decision maker in buying the product or service I sell?
4. Who handles the actual process of the purchase?
5. Who else influences the buying decision?
6. How often does this company or customer buy my product or service?
7. Who is the company's competition? Does my company do business with that competitor? If so, how much?
8. What plans does the company have that could affect its future need for my product or service?
9. How well is the company satisfied with its current supplier?
10. Can this company give us enough business to make this call worthwhile?
11. Is the company's staff technically well informed? Can we help them develop greater expertise?
12. Do we (or can we) use their products or services in our company?
13. Do any of our top executives know any of their executives personally?

Source: Adapted from "So You Want to Be a Salesperson," training materials from Burnett Temporary Personnel, Houston, Texas, June 21, 1983.

is to increase the salesperson's familiarity with the material, which makes the initial contact smoother and more involving to the customer. One obvious danger in this is that delivery becomes automatic and insensitive to the customer's response. A second danger is that the salesperson's precall assumptions about the customer are incorrect, and the smooth and seamless but misinformed delivery may actually offend the prospect. Salespeople need to proceed carefully and test the validity of their assumptions in the initial stages of the actual sales encounter, suggesting that practicing should not lead to thoughtless presentations.

Qualifying and Precall Planning for Retail Sales

Qualifying prospects and precall planning also apply to retail sales, even when specific information about customers is not available until they walk through the door. Qualifying and planning in retail sales can be done in terms of *ideal prospect profiles:* prototypical combinations of characteristics (attire, language, demeanor) that can be associated with some level of propensity to buy. Automobile salespeople, for example, make an initial assessment of people's likelihood to buy based on the vehicle they drive into the lot, their gender, and the clothes they wear.[23] A well-dressed person driving a two-to-three-year-old compact model, for example, is a more likely candidate for a mid-sized luxury model than someone driving a ten-to-twelve-year-old model and dressed poorly. The second person is more likely to be shopping for an inexpensive model or a used car.

Retail salespeople can also practice their approach with other colleagues, with one person adopting the role most representative of some ideal prospect profile while the others practice. Automobile dealers place considerable emphasis on advanced preparation by salespeople and invest in their training.[24] Other retailers that also emphasize salesforce preparation are upscale department stores, such as Nordstrom, and home improvement centers, such as Home Depot and Lowe's.

TABLE 11.4 THE FIVE BASES OF POWER

Reward Power:	Comes from the ability to offer something of value to the other party. Examples of reward power in salespeople are the ability to offer quantity discounts or special considerations. Buyers have power when they can offer large volume purchases.
Coercive Power:	Comes from the ability to inflict punishment on the other party with minimal cost to self. An example of coercive power in salespeople is the ability to withhold product with minimal loss of sales (in times of shortages). Buyers have coercive power when they can reject a sales offer and there are no other buyers available.
Legitimate Power:	Comes from formal position or authority. Sellers or buyers have legitimate power when contractual obligations exist that benefit one at the expense of the other.
Expert Power:	Comes from having knowledge or information the other party needs. An example of expert power in salespeople is technical knowledge necessary to improve the productivity of existing assets. Buyers have expert power when they have information on distribution sources the seller needs.
Referent Power:	Comes from having an image or reputation the other party finds attractive. Sellers have power when they represent a brand with which the buyer wants to be associated. Buyers have referent power when they offer an outlet the seller finds attractive for image reasons.

Source: John R. P. French and Bertram Raven, "The Bases of Social Power," in Dorwin Cartwright, ed., Studies in Social Power (Ann Arbor: University of Michigan Press, 1959), p. 150–167.

The Face-to-Face Selling Stage

Having prepared thoroughly, salespeople turn their attention to the sales encounter. A sales encounter can be divided into five steps, illustrated in Figure 11.4. The figure also illustrates that these steps are seldom reached in linear fashion. Although the call starts with an introduction, moves through all the steps, and ends with a closing, the process can actually cycle through the steps several times. The salesperson tries to advance the encounter from needs assessment to presentation and ultimately to closing while handling customer objections that interrupt the process. At any step beyond the approach, customers may raise objections, and the salesperson may handle those objections within the same step or by going back to a previous step. Ideally, each iteration results in the customer being more reassured and moving closer to a successful closing.

Approach

The approach step aims to establish rapport with the customer and reduce any tension caused by being interrupted or by meeting someone for the first time. If possible, such meetings should be set up ahead of time, so the buyer expects the salesperson. Customers may nevertheless consider meetings as interruptions and be on the defensive against "being sold." A smooth and noninvasive introduction is very important. In an industrial sales situation, where personal contact will probably be extensive, sales professionals should hand buyers business cards as they state their names and that of their companies, so that buyers have contact information clearly

FIGURE 11.4 STAGE AND CYCLES IN FACE-TO-FACE SELLING

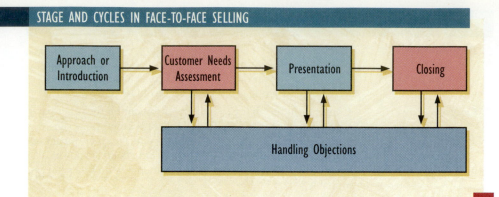

summarized from the start. How business cards are presented varies between cultures (e.g., in Japan business cards are presented with both hands) and it is important for salespeople to study the expectations of the customer in this regard.

Effective sales meetings in the United States and other Western countries seem to contain relatively little nonbusiness conversation, and salespeople state their purpose early. Buyers are interested in what salespeople have to say about improving the business and appreciate salespeople who show respect for their time. As discussed in Marketing Anecdote 11.2, however, this "get to the point" preference is not true in some Pacific Rim countries, where it is important to be very well acquainted personally before business transactions take place. The approach must also be tailored to buyer expectations. It should also be rehearsed, and salespeople should have several approach routines with which they are comfortable. This helps the salesperson make last-minute adjustments if on arrival the situation does not match expectations.

In retail sales, the approach must often be more direct and merchandise oriented than in commercial sales. Buyers do not expect a personal relationship to develop with the salesperson, particularly when buying consumer goods with relatively low value. A good approach, therefore, is to point out a feature of the product that may be of interest to the customer. A salesperson in an apparel store, for example, might notice that the customer is examining an overcoat, and open with a statement such as, "it also comes in dark gray and navy, and in 100 percent wool or a wool blend." This type of approach works much better than the typical "May I help you?" because it focuses attention on the product and away from the customer's indecisiveness. Successful retail salespeople also develop different approach routines and rehearse them.

Customer Needs Assessment

Salespeople start to assess customer needs in the preliminary stage, but in most sales situations they must gather additional information during the initial meeting. Just as generals scout the battlefield to verify their intelligence reports, salespeople need to verify or disconfirm their preconceived ideas and make adjustments to their planned presentation. Having asked for permission to proceed, good salespeople pose questions that lead customers to speak in detail about their needs, feelings, and concerns. Both close-ended questions (requiring yes and no answers) and open-ended questions (requiring elaborate answers) should be used to give customers ample opportunity to express their thoughts.

It is also important for salespeople to periodically review the information already gathered, typically by summarizing the major points the customer has made and asking for confirmation and clarification as required. These reviews are called *checking questions*, and serve three purposes. First, they reduce the possibility of misunderstandings. Second, they signal to the customer that the salesperson is listening. Third, they move customers toward a more positive disposition by having them express agreement with the seller. This last point is subtle but very important. When people go public with an attitude or intention, they become less likely to change it because of a psychological mechanism called *behavioral commitment*.[25] Asking customers to agree with you publicly is a good way of reinforcing a positive disposition toward you and your ideas.

Our discussion thus far suggests that needs assessment can be done in a single meeting. Although this is often true when selling to many U.S. companies, in some domestic and many foreign companies we cannot assume that the next step—presentation—will proceed quickly. As discussed earlier, needs assessment can be deliberately slow in some companies and many foreign cultures, to give the customer sufficient time to evaluate the salesperson and the company, or to get permission from other members of the organization to reveal more about the company's needs to an outsider. At times, salespeople must be prepared to back off from the needs assessment stage into another round of getting acquainted or to postpone further needs assessment until a future meeting. Ultimately, however, the needs assessment step leads to the presentation.

In many buyer-seller relationships, customers may also demand information about the seller's cost structure, quality management practices, stability, and technical resources. As partner relationships with suppliers have become more common among large- and medium-sized companies, business customers looking for partner relationships with suppliers want to understand the seller as much as the salesperson wants to understand the customer. They may offer to trade information about their company in exchange for information about the seller, or to postpone further discussion of the seller's offer until they have had a chance to study the seller's operations. Customers looking for partner relationships are changing the way that the United States and other Western countries do business. The demands of these relationships have given rise to a set of widely shared principles for salespeople, such as those illustrated in Table 11.5.

Presentation

The presentation is the point at which the salesperson gets to explain why the product or service offered meets the needs of the customer better than other products they are using or considering. The salesperson should focus on the most important customer needs, highlight how the product or service meets those needs, and link the features of the product to the benefits it provides. If salespeople anticipate at least some of the customer's needs, ask sufficient questions, and listen well, they should have enough information to tailor their presentations and increase the customer's interest in what is being offered. Salespeople often need to rely on memorized facts and figures, but they must know those facts and figures well enough to tailor the order of presentation and emphasis to the particular customer.

At the end of the presentation, customers should have a good understanding of how the product or service meets their most important needs. They should also be convinced that the salesperson has their best interests at heart. This does not mean that customers are ready to buy, because they may still need to address other concerns (e.g., price, service contracts), but how the product meets important needs should be clear in the customers' minds. A salesperson may conclude the presentation by reinforcing

TABLE 11.5 DO'S AND DON'TS IN SELLING TO CUSTOMERS SEEKING PARTNER RELATIONSHIPS

Do's

- Know your product and competition better than the buyer.
- Be a tough, but open, negotiator.
- Have the backing of your company to establish partner relationships.
- Understand the customer's future plans and offer ideas about how your company can help further them.
- Be willing to change your processes and products.
- Offer something unique—a technological change, a new way of delivering, or a large price concession.
- Get to know all the people interested in the products, from purchasing managers to engineers.
- Make sure to keep on top of potential product problems.
- Be able to explain how your company plans to improve the quality and reliability of its products.

Don'ts

- Use industry buzzwords without knowing what you're are talking about.
- Portray your company as quality-conscious if it is not.
- Focus exclusively on short term sales goals.
- Talk about strategic alliances or partnerships without having the support of your company.
- Say "We want your business, and we'll make it up later."
- Try to persuade purchasers to buy something that does not meet their needs.
- Simply talk pricing.
- Give canned presentations.
- Come without ideas.
- Knock the competition.
- Fly by the seat of your pants.
- Offer product today that you are not likely to have tomorrow.
- Roll over dead in negotiations.

Source: Linda Corman, "The World's Toughest Customers," Selling, September 1993, pp. 49–55. This copyrighted material is reprinted with permission from Selling magazine, a publication of Institutional Investor, 488 Madison Avenue, New York, NY 10022.

the links between needs and benefits through questions such as, "Do you see how the product meets . . . ?" A typewriter salesperson may ask, for example, if the customer sees how buying an electronic typewriter enhances clerical productivity. A "yes" response is a good signal that the customer is ready to move toward closing.

Closing

When closing, the salesperson asks the customer to take action that achieves the sales-call objectives. As mentioned earlier, sales-call objectives may be a signed contract, an actual exchange of product for payment, or approval to proceed with a more formal proposal. Regardless of the objective, closing is most effective when the salesperson asks for specific and measurable action. For example, if the objective is approval to meet with an attorney to finalize a contract, a good closing sets a date, time, and venue for the meeting. A closing that leaves future behaviors unspecified is not as good because it does not move the process forward in specific ways.

Although most salespeople understand the importance of asking for action and committing the buyer to the next step, they often fail to close the sale properly for fear of being rejected. Quite often salespeople arrive at the point of closing after spending a lot of effort in preparation and the presentation. Naturally, they may fear that their proposal will still be rejected. At the same time, they may also hope that if the presentation went well, the customer will take the next step without being prompted. Salespeople must remember that customers see a good presentation as part of the selling job, and seldom feel obligated to buy based on a good presentation alone. They must be led.

Widely different closing styles work, and salespeople choose which to use based on the sales situation and personal preference. The most direct is to ask for action that finalizes the sale or achieves the objective directly. Closings such as, "I recommend we finalize the sales contract and get things moving," or "Let's set a date for meeting with the attorney," are *direct closings* that call for specific action. Another closing style is to present customers with options that tacitly assume they have agreed to the desired action. Asking, "Would you like to meet next Wednesday morning at 10:00, or would Thursday be better?" without asking directly if a future meeting is acceptable, is an *assumptive closing*. In retail sales, an assumptive closing would be "Will this be charge or cash?" without asking the customer if they want the product. Assumptive closings can help move a fearful or indecisive customer to action because they bypass the tough "yes" decision in favor of a less significant one. Customers who need to remain in control, however, may see assumptive closings as manipulative and thus respond negatively.

Handling Objections

Sales encounters seldom proceed as a sequential process from introduction to closing. They are best characterized as an iterative process, which, after the introduction, can go through needs assessment, presentation, and closing several times, with each cycle punctuated by the customer raising one or more objections. Objections are customer responses to salespeople's statements or suggestions. If objections are left unaddressed, they can keep salespeople from achieving their objectives.

Objections seldom indicate a serious mistake by the salesperson. In fact, they are a sign that the customer is interested enough to respond to the salesperson's comments. Objections are a natural by-product of a process designed to introduce change into the customer's life and of the difficulty all people have with perfect communication. For example, if customers misconstrue a salesperson's intentions in asking needs assessment questions, they will likely raise objections. They are also likely to raise objections if the presentation misrepresents their needs, makes claims that are not substantiated, or if the salesperson attempts to close before all concerns have been addressed. Given that objections are almost inevitable and can come up at any step in the process, the salesperson needs to know how to handle them. Handling objections involves listening, clarifying, and problem solving.

Once objections and problems are defined, salespeople look for solutions. In our example, the salesperson might review the training assistance included with the purchase of a fax machine, or offer to be present at the installation and train everyone who will use it. The salesperson wants to offer solutions to the real problems so that the sales process can continue. Every sales encounter is different, and objections come in as wide a variety as customers. The possible reasons for objections and the tools for uncovering them, however, are surprisingly consistent. The key is to see objections as part of the process and as indicators of customer interest, and to respond to them by listening, clarifying, and problem solving.

The Follow-up Stage

The follow-up stage does not occur in all sales encounters, because in some situations the act of purchase is a logical conclusion to the relationship. When we buy a small appliance from Wal-Mart, for example, the sales relationship ends at the moment of purchase, because service and warranty are handled by other areas of the retailer's organization or by the manufacturer. Customers seldom remember much about the salesperson who sold them a toaster, and they do not expect to deal with the same person every time they shop at that store. In other situations, however, follow-up is important.

Follow-up helps to reduce postpurchase discomfort and enhance the buyer-seller relationship. *Postpurchase discomfort* is common after most purchases, but it is particularly noticeable when the purchase is costly or when other members of the household or organization may disapprove. The purchase of a new pickup truck, for example, represents a large investment and is likely to produce some concerns about having made the right decision after the deal is finalized. The purchase of typewriters, computers, and other office equipment can also produce discomfort because of the large investment, or if the equipment must be used by people who might disapprove of its performance. Follow-up contact helps eliminate postpurchase discomfort by affirming the customer in his or her decision. Follow-up is similar to handling objections in that the salesperson should listen carefully to the customer, clarify what the customer has expressed, and offer solutions to problems. Beyond handling problems, the follow-up can revisit important benefits of the new product or service, and reassure the customer that the salesperson remains interested in the customer's needs.

Enhancing the relationship, a second objective of follow-up, is particularly important when the product or service is part of a broader product line, or when the customer is part of a large organization and the same needs exist in other areas. Effective follow-up capitalizes on goodwill accrued from meeting the customer's needs by asking for help to reach other areas of the business or to meet other needs of the company. Salespeople should not assume that the customer automatically sees all the possible areas in which the salesperson can help, or even that the solution for one area is easily applicable somewhere else. Part of follow-up is to help customers see these possibilities and enlist their support. In fact, follow-up can be an effective generator of sales leads that are less costly to develop because credibility and trust are already established. If a fax machine was sold to the accounting department, for example, it may be possible in follow-up to ask for the names of people in sales, manufacturing, and other departments who might also need fax machines.

It should be clear that the sales position in most companies is both important and complex. When managed effectively, it can be a powerful means of promoting products or services. We now turn our attention to the issues of effective salesforce management.

MANAGING THE SALESFORCE STRATEGICALLY

Early in this chapter, we made the case that salespeople embody a company's marketing orientation, and thus they are very important to the overall success of a company's marketing efforts. This being the case, it follows that sales managers are strategically important for most companies because they recruit, train, and deploy the salesforce. In addition, managing the salesforce is operationally important, because it differs from other marketing functions in one important facet. In contrast to staff functions such as product planning, market research, and advertising, sales is a line function with a direct effect on revenue and profitability in most companies. Sales managers, therefore, are concerned on a day-to-day basis with the company's well-being and with how the people under them are contributing toward it, in addition to being concerned about strategic issues. Sales management is important at both strategic and operational levels.

The breadth of sales managers' responsibilities can be separated into three broad areas, illustrated by Figure 11.5. First of all, sales managers design the salesforce. They decide how to integrate it into the rest of the organization, including the choice between having an internal salesforce or using external salespeople such as manufacturer's representatives. Salesforce design also includes decisions on the level of supervisory control, territorial deployment, and salesforce size. Second, sales managers build the salesforce by selecting, recruiting, training, and managing what is often one of the company's largest investments. Finally, sales managers must continually evaluate and adjust the salesforce in response to ever-changing environments.

Designing the Salesforce

As sales managers decide issues affecting salesforce integration, goals, structure, and size, they must consider the company's strategy and overall position in the market. Sales managers typically make major changes in these areas in three-to-five-year strategic periods, in response to current status and future expectations. In between these upheavals, sales managers regularly monitor and adjust salesforce deployment.

Salesforce Integration: Internal versus External Salespeople

Some companies rely on intermediaries to reach final customers; these intermediaries are, in effect, external salesforces. If companies use their own employees as well as intermediaries to reach customers, they must manage both internal and external salesforces. Many salesforce management issues, such as size and compensation, are the same for internal and external ones, so these managerial task areas are not significantly different between internal and external salesforces. Costs, however, differ significantly between internal and external salesforces, as do the levels of control that managers can exercise. These differences must be considered when structuring the salesforce.

An internal salesforce is often more expensive than an external salesforce for several reasons. External sales personnel, such as manufacturers' representatives, normally sell many products for different noncompeting producers and can sell multiple products for several companies in one sales call. This makes the sales call more efficient and lowers each product's cost per call. These lower costs are frequently reflected in lower commission rates. Table 11.6 on page 443 illustrates some historically typical commission levels for different industries.

Internal salespeople, in contrast, represent only one company's products. Even if the total time involved in the actual sales call is less for one company's products than for those of several companies, the time involved in travel, preparation, and waiting is higher as a percentage of total available time, resulting in a higher cost per call by product. One additional cost advantage of an external salesforce is that it can be terminated

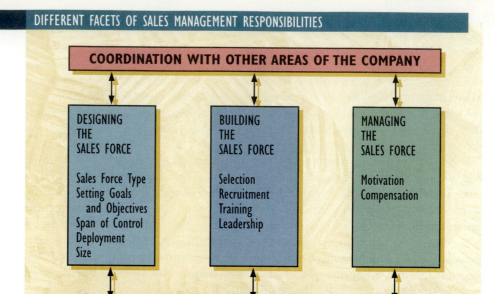

more quickly and with less expense than an internal salesforce. This can be an important advantage when salesforce size is set under high uncertainty conditions.

Internal salesforces also cost more because of the distribution of fixed and variable costs. External salesforces are typically compensated through commissions based on the dollar value of products or services sold. Commission rates historically vary by industry, as illustrated by Table 11.6, but are always tied to sales volume.[26] When sales are high, compensation costs are high, but when sales are low, compensation costs drop. Internal salesforces, in contrast, normally involve some fixed expenses (e.g., medical and worker's compensation insurance) even when take-home pay is solely commission-based, and are even higher when compensation has salary elements as well. Fixed expenses remain even when sales volumes are down, and thus reduce the company's financial flexibility. Fixed and variable costs and compensation approaches are further discussed later in this chapter.

Although internal salesforces are more expensive than external ones, they are much more under the sales manager's control and can be more responsive to the strategic needs of the company. An internal salesforce dedicates itself only to the company's products and can put more effort into meeting customer needs. Being focused only on the products of one company also enhances salespeople's ability to respond to market or company changes. External salespeople, in contrast, can be distracted by their many products and pulled in different directions by the companies they represent. Finally, internal salesforces can perform nonsales functions, such as servicing accounts, collecting information, and serving on product and promotional strategy planning groups. External salespeople are seldom willing to donate nonpaid time to perform such duties.

Two factors influence sales managers' decisions to use internal or external salespeople. First, sales managers need to consider the company's overall strategy and the nature of its products. Companies striving for strong relationships with customers, high levels of service, and high customer satisfaction may need more from their

TABLE 11.6 AVERAGE MANUFACTURER'S AGENTS' COMMISSION RATES

Product or Service	Average Commission Rate (percent)
Advertising products or services	16
Building materials and supplies	8
Computers	10
Electronic consumer products	6
Food products and services	15
Marine products and services	10
Paper products	11
Plastics (industrial)	6
Sporting goods and supplies	8

Source: Adapted from "Survey of Selling Costs: Special Issue," Sales and Marketing Management *(February 16, 1987): 59 (with minor formatting modifications).*

salesforce than external salespeople normally provide. Highly complex products or services that require installation and postpurchase support, for example, are difficult to sell through external salespeople unless the salespeople are compensated for repeated contacts. The same can be said for products that depend on repeat business to be profitable. Dierickx, for example, makes its profits from both the complex equipment (e.g., typewriters and facsimile machines) and supplies for that equipment (e.g., ribbons and ink cartridges) that it sells, which helps explain why it supports an internal salesforce and rewards its salespeople for building relationships. Even if external salespeople are compensated for multiple contacts, their attention to customer needs is likely to be lower than that of internal salespeople because they must also service other companies' product lines.

On the other hand, managers must consider their companies' finances, and working capital needs in particular. Supporting an internal salesforce requires working capital to cover costs when sales are low or payments are delayed. A company that needs all available cash for capital investment in other areas (e.g., production, materials acquisition) may be able to reduce working capital demands by adopting an external salesforce and treating all sales expenses as variable costs. The sales manager, working with other company managers, must consider these issues when designing the salesforce.

Setting Goals and Objectives

Setting goals and objectives is a multilevel process, because they must be set for the salesforce as a whole, and for each individual salesperson. Goals refer to long-term and broad-level aspirations, such as a 20 percent increase in new accounts for the coming year. Objectives refers to more immediate aspirations, such as 10 fax machines sold this month. In setting goals and objectives, sales managers need to consider both company and environmental factors, and need to look beyond immediate tactical concerns to more long-term strategic issues. Goals and objectives can be set in terms of desired outcomes or desired behaviors, and be focused on sales volume, profitability, number of customers, or other criteria. Table 11.7 presents a partial list of criteria that managers use to establish goals and objectives and evaluate performance.

Effective sales managers consider two related factors when basing goals and objectives: the company's overall market position and the market's current growth rate. Companies with superior products in high-growth markets, such as Intel and

TABLE 11.7 BASES FOR GOAL SETTING AND PERFORMANCE ASSESSMENTS

Outcome Goals

Dollar value of sales volume

Number of new accounts

Dollar value of new accounts

Percentage of quota achieved

Dollar value of sales per account

Dollar value of sales per order

Percentage of territory potential achieved

Improvement over past year's performance

Self-rating of performance

Supervisor overall rating

Peer overall rating

Rank among peer salespeople in terms of some standard

Number of old accounts lost

Gross margin on sales volume

Profitability on sales volume

Behavior Goals

Number of total calls in a set time period

Number of calls per order

Organizational citizenship (e.g., sportsmanship, conscientiousness)

Time management efficiency

Adherence to norms and sales plans

Knowledge of product, company, market, and/or competitors

Customer satisfaction (measured objectively by surveys and other means)

Motorola in the computer microprocessor market, can set goals in terms of the number of new customers. A good measure of salesperson performance in such situations is an increase in the total number of adopters of the product in the specific market.

If the market is not growing or if the company is at a disadvantage relative to competitors, a better basis for goals may be the number of customers that switch over from competitors. Such has been the situation in the more mundane dynamic random access memory (DRAM) market, even as the computer microprocessor market experienced substantial growth. In this situation, a more suitable performance objective may be customers new to the brand or company but not to the product category. Sometimes it is even necessary to set goals and objectives in terms of protecting existing business, and in such situations performance may best be measured in terms of the least number of sales and account relationships lost to competitors.

Tied closely to a company's position in the market is its profitability and return on investment. Sales volume does not always provide the best performance measure for companies or for product lines within companies. A product line with stable to declining demand, which is being used to fund development in other areas (i.e., referred to as a cash cow in chapter 2), should have salesforce goals set to preserve cash flow and reduce expenses. Overall profitability or gross margin per account are good bases for goals and objectives in such situations. Companies whose product lines are protected by patents or other market barriers, however, may be better off using return on investment as a performance standard, and setting goals to maximize sales or profitability.

Thus far we have discussed outcome-oriented goals and objectives. As managers set goals and objectives, they should also consider the different roles and tasks they expect salespeople to fulfill, and set behavioral as well as outcome-oriented goals and objectives. For example, business development representatives, as illustrated in Figure 11.2, help maintain existing relationships as well as develop new ones, which involves taking on missionary, order taker, trade servicer, and seller roles all in the same day. Not all such roles generate measurable outcomes, but all are important to companies' marketing efforts. Thus, it is reasonable to expect that salespeople's goals and objectives will include not only outcomes, but also behaviors that are strategically important.

Not only must managers set outcome and behavioral goals and objectives, they need to make such performance criteria specific. It is not enough to tell salespeople that they are expected to bring in new business or to service accounts. The number of new accounts, the level of customer service, the timing and focus of customer contacts, and other tasks should be spelled out in quantifiable terms. Be they outcome standards (e.g., dollar sales, number of new accounts), or behavioral ones (e.g., time spent with existing customers), specific goals and objectives lead to more effective management.

Structure of the Salesforce

Salesforce structure concerns sales managers because of its effect on reporting and accountability. In most organizations, accountability and coordination follow the chain of command implicit in the organizational chart, and digressions from that chain can result in mishandling of customer needs. At the same time that organizational structure facilitates coordination, however, it can also stymie responsiveness by increasing the time required to make decisions. The structuring of the salesforce therefore can have serious implications for the company's achievement of sales goals and strategic objectives. A structure that is incompatible with the company's marketing strategy can render all other aspects of the sales program ineffective. As they design salesforce structures, sales managers need to decide on the level of supervision most compatible with salesforce responsibilities, taking into account the complexity and diversity of the company's products and customers.

Level of Supervision. In terms of level of supervision, a sales manager needs to decide what span of control is best for the salesforce. *Span of control* refers to the number of people reporting to a supervisor, and it can be wide (many people reporting to one supervisor) or narrow (few people reporting to one supervisor). Companies that adopt a wide span of control for the sales organization have a "flatter" organizational structure with fewer layers of management. Companies adopting a narrow span of control have "taller" organizational structures with more layers of management.

Most people believe that modern sales organizations should be flat, assuming that such organizations are more responsive to customers and the environment all the way to the top. In the computer industry, for example, a wide span of control has allowed companies such as Hewlett-Packard to be more responsive, whereas traditionally tall

FIGURE 11.6 | SALES ORGANIZATION WITH SPAN OF CONTROL AT 10

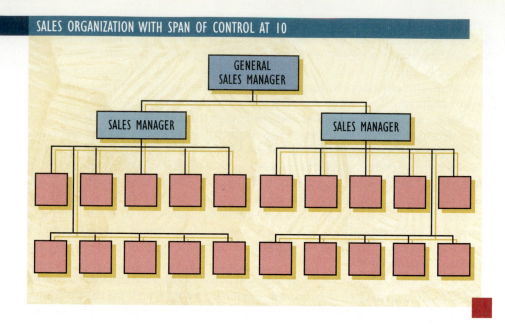

organizations such as IBM and Digital Equipment found themselves responding slowly and were forced to redesign their salesforce.[27] A wide span of control is not the right choice for all companies, however, and sales managers must base span of control on what makes sense for the company, and not on the latest prescription for organizational design.

Some companies' structures allow sales managers to supervise many salespeople. For example, a company with a relatively simple product line and homogeneous customer base may have 20 to 30 salespeople under a single manager, with salespeople operating effectively with little supervision. A salesforce organization with 20 salespeople and a span of control of 10 is illustrated in Figure 11.6. For companies with complex product lines or customer relationships, it may be impractical for a sales manager to have more than five or six salespeople to supervise, and as the total number of salespeople needed to serve the market increases, so does the number of managers required to maintain the same span of control. Figure 11.7 illustrates a company that also has 20 salespeople, but with a span of control of 5. Notice that the narrower span of control adds a layer of management.

Complexity and Diversity of the Customer Base and Product Line. Sales managers must consider the complexity and diversity of the company's customers and products when structuring salesforces. Sales managers can deploy salespeople on the basis of geography, product, account size, or combinations of these variables in order to better respond to market conditions.

Geographic structure is one of the most commonly used and easiest to administer methods for deploying the salesforce. In a typical design, managers divide the company's total market (state, multistate, national, or global) into regions and subregions with roughly equal sales potential. Each region is a single salesperson's exclusive responsibility and is designed to provide adequate challenge and compensation. Because markets differ in the physical proximity between prospects, regions can vary substantially in terms of the geographic area they cover. An Eli Lilly sales territory in New York City, for example, may cover only 20 square blocks, whereas the same sales potential in South Dakota may be spread out over 200 square miles.

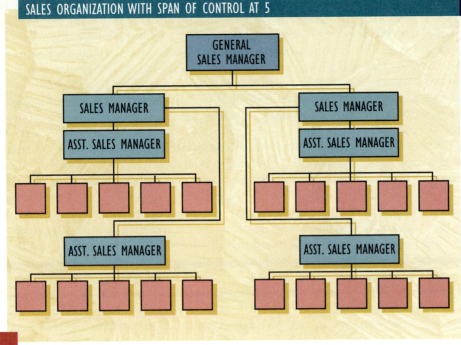

Geographic structures hold several advantages. Salespeople have well-defined territories over which they can take ownership, which in turn often motivates salespeople toward greater commitment to their customers and to closer relationships. When rewards are linked directly to performance, geographic territories also enhance the salespeople's sense of accomplishment and control. In addition, geographically based sales territories make travel expenses easier to manage.

Managers may choose geographic districts based on their market potential vis-à-vis whatever criteria make the most strategic sense for goal setting and performance evaluation (e.g., sales volume, profitability, number of potential accounts). Districts may also vary in terms of sales challenge or customer sophistication, and in this way managers can use them to differentiate salespeople. Inexperienced salespeople are often assigned less challenging districts with lower sales potentials, and later promoted to more challenging and rewarding districts.

A geographic structure also poses some disadvantages. First, as a company's product line expands, individual salespeople with exclusive regions may not be able to sell all products effectively because they lack skills or knowledge. Second, if customers within a territory differ significantly in terms of sophistication or needs, a single salesperson may not be able to service all of them adequately. This can result in territorial inequity—some salespeople have to work very hard to meet customer needs, whereas other salespeople have less demanding customers.

Balancing the need for equity in the workload and reward potential in different geographic territories can be a difficult task. Fortunately, it is one to which computing power can be applied. A number of linear programming techniques have been developed, focusing on different parameters and with varying levels of complexity.[28] Sales managers often use such tools to develop tentative territorial deployment schemes, which they can later adjust based on other factors.

Given the challenges involved in selling a diverse or complex product line, some companies organize their salesforces by *product category* or even by models within the category. Many companies in high-technology industries, such as IBM and General Electric, use such a structure. Product-based structures are also attractive to companies that sell durable consumer products, such as automobiles and appliances, where dealers that sell products from multiple manufacturers sometimes assign primary selling responsibility to different salespeople. Such structures may also work in the nondurable consumer products area, where differences in how products are marketed to final consumers result in salesforce specialization by product category (e.g., women's nylons are sold differently from canned soup and require a different salesforce structure).

A shortcoming of the product structure approach is that companies will sometimes have several salespeople visit the same customer, with each one selling something different. This can result in higher travel expense and duplication of effort. Multiple sales calls can also dilute the seller's bargaining power. Dilution of bargaining power has been a serious concern to consumer products firms, as large retailers with centralized purchasing dominate the retail market. Borden Corporation, for example, found itself with eight different sales organizations in the snack foods industry, because of several acquisitions, at the same time that its customer base shrank due to consolidations in the food retail business. As many as 28 different Borden salespeople were calling on a single customer, causing a serious erosion of the company's influence with retailers. Borden responded by reorganizing its salesforce and distribution system into a single organization to deal with big customers.[29]

Account size provides another basis for structuring the salesforce, with customer size normally measured in terms of sales volume or the diversity of the products purchased. Relationships with customers who buy large quantities or large assortments of products often require special handling. Large customers may have unique product specifications, materials management demands, or special pricing requirements. Some even require special promotional programs from producers to help achieve their own marketing objectives. A large retailer, for example, may demand concurrent special pricing and promotions from several producers in order to have a seasonal sales event, such as a President's Day or Fourth of July promotional sale. Large customers may also be more sophisticated and demanding than smaller customers in how they manage their inventory. However, they often require less personal servicing from the salesforce.

Differences among customers' demands can be substantial and make it impractical to have the same salesforce call on customers of different sizes within the same territory. This has led some firms to organize their salesforces by account size, where some salespeople specialize on a few large accounts and others service many smaller accounts. Commercial banks, such as First Chicago, use size as a means of deploying their salesforce, with some salespeople calling on national-level accounts such as Quaker Oats, whereas others call on what are commonly called middle-market accounts. One advantage of organizing by account size is that it allows sellers to be more responsive to both large and small customers' demands. One disadvantage is the expense of having multiple salespeople cover the same geographic area. Another disadvantage is that difficulties can arise when customers grow, for example, and are no longer within the size category assigned to their current salesperson. Sales relationships often depend on specific individuals as primary sales contacts, and marketers can jeopardize customer relationships by switching sales representatives because of size constraints. This can also result in feelings of inequity among salespeople who lose large accounts after cultivating the relationships and contributing to their customers' growth.

Many firms sell such a wide assortment of products and services to such a large variety of customers that a combination of geographic, product, and account size,

FIGURE 11.8

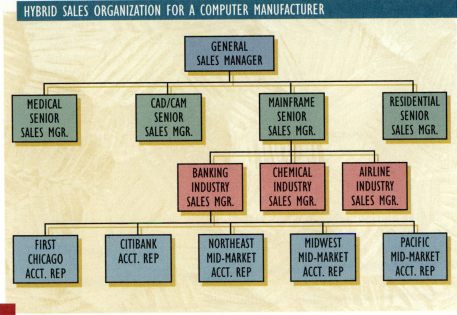

HYBRID SALES ORGANIZATION FOR A COMPUTER MANUFACTURER

known as a *hybrid structure*, may be required. Such an organization is illustrated in Figure 11.8. In this example, a manufacturer of computer equipment has a product-structured top-level sales management team (i.e., medical diagnosis equipment, computer-aided design and manufacturing workstations, mainframes, and home personal computers). Subsequent levels of the sales organization, however, are structured first by industry type (e.g., banking, chemical) and then by the size of the customer. Under the banking industry, large customers such as Citibank may get dedicated salespeople, whereas smaller banks may be serviced by one salesperson covering their geographic area, such as the Pacific Northwest region of the United States.

The obvious advantage of a hybrid sales structure is its responsiveness to customer types. The disadvantage is the difficulty of managing programs and people across such a wide spectrum. Companies that adopt hybrid sales structures must consider the additional managerial challenges and costs involved and weigh the positives and negatives of such an approach. Hybrid structures that combine geographic and account size dimensions, for example, present sales managers with a wider array of motivation and control challenges than single-dimensional structures. Companies must also design other areas of the sales management function to meet the challenges that these structures represent.

Size of the Salesforce

How many salespeople to hire is another area of concern for sales managers, because of the dangers in having a salesforce that is too big or too small. On the one hand, an undersized salesforce can result in substandard account service and failure to capitalize on the market's potential. On the other hand, an oversized salesforce represents higher costs, and can produce detrimental competition between salespeople for rewards and promotions.

To determine the correct size for the salesforce, sales managers must consider how frequent and intense they wish customer contact to be, and the percentage of time actually available to salespeople for sales activities. In the snack foods industry, for example, salespeople responsible for arranging product on the shelf need to visit customers at least once per week. In contrast, life insurance salespeople need to contact existing customers only every three to five years in order to review their needs, and they spend most of their time cultivating new customer relationships.

Desired intensity of contact refers to the level of involvement salespeople should have with their customers, and it is dictated primarily by the complexity of the product being sold. The sale of customized computer services, for example, requires intimate knowledge of the customer's business operations to properly diagnose needs and solutions. In contrast, the sale of personal computers and off-the-shelf software does not require much more than a superficial understanding of the customer's needs. Another consideration, the percentage of time available for selling, requires sales managers to keep in mind the other demands placed on salespeople and estimate how much productive sales time salespeople actually have. As discussed earlier, salespeople often need to assume multiple roles in a day's work, and not all roles are conducive to immediate sales productivity. Figure 11.2, for example, shows that the business development representative made only three sales calls, accounting for only 25 percent of the day, and it has been estimated that average salespeople spend only 49 percent of their time selling.[30] Sales managers must staff for productive sales time, and allow for time spent on other duties.

Sales managers must also decide if salesforce size will be determined on the basis of existing sales, potential sales, or some combination of the two. For a company just starting or entering a new area, it makes sense to base salesforce size on realistic estimates of the company's sales potential. Companies in slow or zero-growth markets are better off setting salesforce size on the number of existing customer relationships and looking for ways to improve the efficiency of current sales efforts. By using estimates or actual calculations of the factors mentioned above, a sales manager can calculate ideal salesforce size for the company, as illustrated by Marketing Anecdote 11.4.

Salesforce size calculations can be complex because of the number of parameters involved, but computer programs assist sales managers with these calculations. The bigger challenge is in estimating all the parameters required for the calculations. Determining that the average sales call for a machine tool customer will take two hours and that salespeople will spend an hour preparing and reporting for every hour in actual sales contact can be determined only through careful observation and experience in the particular industry, and this knowledge does not frequently transfer across industries or product categories. This helps explain why experienced sales managers are valuable and command high salaries. The wrong decision in terms of salesforce size can cost a company dearly in terms of lost sales or excessive costs.

Building the Salesforce

Once they design their salesforces, sales managers build the salesforce by selecting suitable candidates, recruiting them into the salesforce, and training them to sell effectively. Whereas managers address salesforce design issues only every three to five years, salesforce building activities are ongoing and occupy a large portion of the sales manager's time. Sales managers must remain aware of their companies' cultures and marketing strategies, and build salesforces that are compatible with their strategic goals.

Selection

The most accurate way of checking if someone will be a successful salesperson may be to let them do the job and to evaluate the results, and indeed that is how some companies do it. This is a very expensive method, however, when we con-

ACME Tool is a fictitious manufacturer of machine tool equipment. It has operated profitably in New England for 75 years, but because of competitive pressures in its home market, ACME has decided to expand into the Great Lakes region of the United States (Ohio, Michigan, Indiana, Illinois, Wisconsin, and Minnesota). Alex Glover is the sales manager for ACME Tool. Based on his experiences in New England and data from Dunn & Bradstreet's *Million Dollar Directory*, Glover has determined that there are 5,000 users of machine tool equipment in the Great Lakes region, of which 700 are of a size and type that ACME Tool can service. Glover has also determined it will take an average of six visits per customer over a 12-month period to achieve a sale, and that the average sales call will last about two hours. For every hour of actual sales contact, salespeople will spend approximately the same amount of time preparing and reporting on the outcome, which means actual selling time will be only 50 percent of total time available. The calculation for the salesforce is as follows:

Required number of hours
= 700 accounts × 6 visits per account × 2 hours per visit = 8,400 hours

Actual hours available per salesperson
= 50 hours per week × 50 weeks per year × 50% = 1,250 hours

Salesforce size = 8,400/1,250
= 6.7, which rounds to 7 full-time salespeople

If ACME Tool wanted to accelerate the development of the market to 6 months instead of 12 months, it would need twice as many salespeople to make the necessary contacts because the 8,400 hour requirement will remain the same but there will be only 500 hours per salesperson available. Increasing the number of accounts contacted initially to 1,400, because of inefficiencies in the screening process, would also result in increased demands for salespeople. In that case, however, initial sales contacts would be shorter and result in a shorter average sales call, although the number of accounts contacted would be higher. ACME Tool also needs to consider possible reductions in efficiency as the sales effort progresses and only the more difficult customers remain.

Estimating of salesforce size can be complex, and many factors can render initial estimates faulty. Experience often improves the initial salesforce estimates, but even the most experienced sales managers can make mistakes. For this reason, many companies combine external and internal salespeople when developing a new market, and eliminate the external salespeople as the company's knowledge of the market increases and the customer base stabilizes.

sider the training time and lost sales that it takes to discover someone is in the wrong job. Some advance planning and screening, therefore, can go a long way toward improving the chances that new hires will be productive and successful salespeople.[31]

Sales managers can learn much about successful salesperson characteristics from their own salesforces and from their competitors' employees. Sales managers can begin by identifying specific behaviors and traits that contribute to sales success in the context of particular customers or sales situations. The objective is to be as exhaustive as possible in terms of the factors contributing to making the sale. Some tactics for assembling this list are observing successful salespeople within the company, doing self-assessments, and observing the efforts of salespeople outside the organization whenever possible.

As they observe sales efforts, managers should combine the specific traits and behaviors noted into more general characteristics that can be measured in some form. One approach is to combine observed traits and behaviors of several experienced salespeople into general characteristics and compare the results. Once characteristics are established, sales managers need to go back to the sales context and rank them in order of importance. This is a critical step because it is unlikely that all candidates will be high in all characteristics, and in some instances characteristics may be partially contradictory, so that high levels of one are associated with low levels of another. Sales managers need to determine which characteristics are most important to their companies and be ready to give up on less important traits.

One example of a desirable characteristic is having a learning orientation, typically manifested by the salesperson being intrinsically interested in the job and in improving oneself. A learning orientation is desirable in fast-changing environments in which the sales approach needs to be changed frequently, and it has been linked to working both harder and smarter.[32] Another characteristic is self-efficacy, which is manifested in salespeople's high levels of confidence about specific aspects of the sales job. High self-efficacy is important in highly competitive sales environments because it has been linked to salespeople dealing successfully with setbacks, high uncertainty in outcomes, and high manager expectations.[33] It is possible, however, for salespeople high in self-efficacy to be overconfident and thus not have a high learning orientation. In such situations, there are two desirable characteristics at odds with one another, and sales managers may need to decide which characteristic is more appropriate to emphasize in the selection process.

Something for sales managers to keep in mind is that some characteristics can be engendered in salespeople through training, whereas others are more effectively acquired with the sales candidate. Sales managers need to balance the cost of effective in-house training against the higher salaries paid to more skilled salespeople. The sales manager needs to take careful inventory of the company's training resources, as well as the urgency behind having a productive salesforce. If the company does not have resources to develop characteristics in-house, it may opt for hiring salespeople that already have the desired characteristics, even if they come at premium salaries. In the 1980s, Wilkinson Sword switched from an external to an internal salesforce and established a sophisticated sales effort in less than a year. The company hired experienced salespeople from competitors in the health and beauty aids industry and gave them only minimal training on Wilkinson's policies and procedures.[34] Other companies, such as Motorola, are known for relying on internal training and for being unwilling to pay a premium for sales talent developed elsewhere.

Sales managers must also find ways of measuring the desired characteristics in sales candidates—a task for which sophisticated tools have been developed. Research suggests that the results of psychological tests and detailed biographical information are some of the best predictors of overall success.[35] A by-product of setting selection criteria is that the remaining list of characteristics (those characteristics that the company will develop internally) is a good start toward designing the training program.

Some sales managers rely primarily on interview evaluations and letters of reference as a way of measuring the desired characteristics in sales candidates. A serious problem with interviews and letters of reference, however, is that they are highly susceptible to biases caused by the candidate's attractiveness and citizenship behaviors (e.g., courtesy)—attributes that may have little bearing on the candidate's suitability for a sales position.[36] Because of the problems with these techniques, many companies also use psychological tests and biographical information to evaluate candidates on desired characteristics.[37] Tests and biographical information are used either to complement or to replace some of the more subjective measures discussed earlier. Some companies even suggest using techniques outside the psychological mainstream, such as handwriting analysis, as a way of reducing the risk of making a poor choice of candidates.[38] The advantage of objective measurement techniques is the availability of data from external sources with which to calibrate the scale to the company's needs.

One danger arises in using objective measurement techniques. Some of these techniques may systematically discriminate against some racial or ethnic groups because of the way they ask questions, causing candidates from those groups to have lower scores and be overlooked for positions for which they are otherwise qualified. It is possible, for example, that the situational questions asked by an empathy measure make Latino men come across as low on empathy simply because they cannot relate to the situations, and not because they are really low in empathy. If low-scoring Latino men are systematically excluded from consideration because of a faulty measure, the company could be liable to charges of discrimination.

Such discriminatory behavior can put companies in violation of Equal Employment Opportunity (EEO) regulations, even if the company is unaware that it is discriminating. The Equal Employment Opportunity Commission (EEOC), in existence since 1964, manages a body of regulation addressing the representation of ethnic and gender groups who have been discriminated against by past hiring practices. Although the EEOC does not have direct police powers, it has used the court system effectively to take action against violators of EEO standards. A company using measurement techniques in good faith might nevertheless be found guilty of discrimination if its measurement practices are found to be systematically biased against certain groups and the company cannot present other evidence to defend its candidate choices. It is in a sales manager's best interest to examine and validate measurement techniques used for screening sales candidates, and to use multiple measures if there is cause to think some measures are biased.

Regardless of EEO concerns, sales managers must establish some way to measure if their selection criteria really help predict success. One possible method is to give the same tests to the current salesforce and identify those criteria that are most closely correlated to successful track records. One drawback of this method is its reliance on historical information, which can be misleading if current environmental factors are affecting salesforce success. Thus managers must periodically review the standards and methods used to insure they are sensitive to the company's needs and the environment.

Recruiting

In competitive job markets, setting standards is seldom enough to insure an effective salesforce. Quite often, companies in the same industry set similar standards for their salesforces and end up competing for the same sales candidates. Sales managers must develop a profile for selecting candidates and a recruiting program that attracts the right ones in the right numbers.

Recruiting targets in terms of numbers and composition should consider the company's historical rate of attrition and its sales strategy. Turnover in sales organizations can be quite high. In addition to the common causes of attrition (e.g., retirements, spouse relocation, career changes), successful sales organizations are susceptible to raids by competitors who are unwilling or unable to develop their salespeople internally and are looking for ready access to new markets. Firms also lose salespeople because of poor fit with the job or the company.

Sales managers should anticipate changes in the company's strategy or market conditions that can affect salesforce size and composition. Market expansion, changes in the number of territories, and salesforce reorganization should all be considered in recruitment planning. A significant source of change in recruiting practices during the 1990s has been corporate downsizing. Part of IBM's reorganization in the early 1990s, for example, involved reducing the size of the salesforce by 50 percent, and at the same time redirecting salespeople into consultative roles. IBM sales managers had to adjust their external recruiting, initially to reduce the size of the salesforce, and later to recruit functional experts (e.g., manufacturing engineers) into specialized sales teams.[39]

Once recruiting targets are set, sales managers must turn their attention to actually recruiting salespeople, a process that is somewhat similar to selling. Given keen competition for better candidates, the sales manager needs to identify sources of candidates and design a strategy to reach them. The most promising sources of candidates depend on the company's selection standards. For companies looking for experienced salespeople, the most likely sources are the employment roles of leading industry competitors. In contrast, companies that rely on internal training look for trainable candidates who are willing to work their way up the ladder. Typically, internally trained positions appeal more to people used to the classroom environment and able to accept slower career development, making college campuses good sources of candidates. Other possible sources of candidates are employment agencies, recruiting specialists, and the armed forces.

Training

Training is an essential activity that takes place not only when salespeople first enter companies, but throughout their careers. Depending on the complexity of the sales task and company goals, sales managers must decide on formalized or on-the-job training. If formal training is done, the manager must also decide whether it will be developed internally or externally. Table 11.8 illustrates the key decisions involved in designing and managing a sales training program, and categorizes them as general objectives, specific goals, and operational decisions.

Leadership

Clearly, building a salesforce is an ongoing endeavor. Sales managers contribute to the health of their salesforce on a daily basis, and through more of their actions than those that are officially linked to building it. One of the most effective means available to sales managers for building a good salesforce is their leadership.[40]

Much more has been written about leadership in the sales and sales management literature than can be covered in this book, but most of it affirms some fundamental points. First, effective leadership is often done by example. Sales managers who show enthusiasm for their company's objectives will be an inspiration to most salespeople. Second, leadership also means being sensitive to the needs of salespeople and being willing to help them overcome hurdles and improve themselves in the process. This means providing assistance when required, answering questions or giving feedback, and being a keen observer and evaluator of both good points and items needing improvement. Third, evidence shows that effective leadership in sales organizations involves activities in several areas, such as providing structure, fitting assignments to personalities, managing conflict, and coaching.

TABLE 11.8 SUMMARY OF DECISION AREAS IN SALES TRAINING PROGRAMS

General Objectives	Specific Goals	Operational Decisions
To convey knowledge.	Educate the person about the company rules and procedures, the industry, customer behavior, the product, aspects of the marketing mix, and similar matters.	*When:* Before or after observation of experienced salespeople or cold calling? Once initial training is completed, how frequently in subsequent years?
To develop selling and managerial skills.	Train the person in the methods of selling.	*How:* Lectures, books, cases, tapes, demonstrations, role playing, group discussions, tutorials, or combinations of these?
To more broadly increase sales effectiveness and reduce selling and personal costs.	Instill positive attitudes, high motivation, personal pride, and organizational commitment.	*Who:* Outside consultants and training companies? In house director of training and staff development? Successful salespeople? District managers?
		Where: On the job, central office, decentralized district offices, special conference centers, or other locations?

Providing Structure. Providing structure for the salesforce reduces uncertainty and provides guidelines for carrying out the company's objectives. Sales managers provide structure by setting objectives such as sales quotas, cost parameters, profitability standards, or any other specific goals they set for salespeople. They also provide structure by clarifying the rewards for good performance and the sanctions for poor performance, and by being consistent in their application. Sales managers can provide further structure by establishing reasonable reporting requirements and by following up on reports of problems or opportunities on a timely basis. Timely follow-up is critical to preserving both the integrity of other structural elements and the credibility of the reporting system.

Fitting Assignments to Personalities. Good salespeople are qualified to handle the accounts or territories they have been assigned. Good leaders achieve this by knowing their people well and by adopting a participatory style in planning salespeople's approaches to their jobs. There are many variations on the idea of having salespeople manage themselves, but the principles are fundamentally the same. Letting salespeople help define personal objectives and set priorities gives them a greater sense of ownership and contributes to salespeople feeling that the job is meaningful. Very few people will feel the job they helped design is unimportant. Participation also makes the goals and objectives a more integral part of the salesperson's daily thinking. Good leadership involves knowing how much to delegate and how much to control in this area.

Managing Conflict. Conflict is an ever-present aspect of sales management. It arises between salespeople and customers, between customers and the company, among salespeople, between salespeople and management, and between the salesforce and other areas of the organization. Leaders should not automatically assume that conflict is dysfunctional, just like good salespeople do not automatically assume objections are negative. Conflict can be a signal of a potential problem, but leaders can see it as an invitation to explore other alternatives. A small amount of conflict over how to approach a problem or to set priorities can produce even better solutions than those proposed originally. Good leadership, therefore, suggests that conflict is an opportunity to clarify issues and improve performance. In being good leaders, sales managers should also respond to conflict calmly, and seek to understand all sides of an issue. Some conflict must be resolved via the manager's authority, but other conflict can be resolved through negotiation and in ways that promote ownership of the decision. What a sales manager cannot do is ignore conflict and hope it will go away. Sales managers who are aware of conflict within the salesforce can take action to avert its detrimental effects and lead the salesforce to the opportunities it offers.

Coaching. Coaching involves critically observing salespeople's performance, giving them ideas on how to improve, and providing them opportunities to practice newly acquired skills. Coaching is part of the training function, except that it is informal and constant. Sales managers need to observe salespeople's behavior and respond with sensitivity to the areas in which they need help. They also need to preserve salespeople's dignity and personal commitment, which sometimes entails letting the person fail for a while before offering assistance. For any kind of help to be successful, the recipient must be willing to accept it, and salespeople are not always ready to receive direction or admonition at the first sign of trouble. The effects of coaching on reducing uncertainty and low self-confidence are obvious. Even if the salesperson refuses to ask for help immediately, knowing that the sales manager is available to give direction is reassuring.

Coaching can also involve helping salespeople deal with challenges in their personal lives. Although we often hear the admonition that "personal problems should not be brought into the workplace," this is empty advice for professionals whose self-concepts are intimately connected to their jobs. Salespeople are no exception. The demands and personal trauma that some salespeople face as part of their jobs are almost certain to invade their private lives, and the opposite effect is also likely. Thus, sales managers often are required to coach salespeople through personal problems.[41] Problems that affect the performance of one salesperson quite often have secondary effects on other members of the organization. Good leadership requires that sales managers help address some thorny issues for the benefit of the salesforce and the company.

Managing the Salesforce

Two aspects of salesforce management have high strategic importance: motivation and compensation. Their strategic importance stems from several reasons. First, they are highly interrelated and must be managed in tandem. Second, they are closely linked to the company's overall performance in terms of sales volume and profitability. Compensation is a good motivator of salespeople, but it is also a drain on company profits. Managing motivation through compensation and other means, therefore, is important in order to have both a satisfied salesforce and healthy company profits. The ideal is to have salespeople who are motivated to make profitable sales. Third, the interface between salesforce motivation and job satisfaction through compensation and other means is far from clear. Sales managers, therefore, need to supplement their technical knowledge with intuition in order to manage their salesforces successfully. Not surprisingly, management issues around motivation and compensation occupy a large part of sales managers' time.

Motivation, Satisfaction, and Supervision

The day-to-day motivation of a salesforce is by far the most demanding aspect of being a sales manager. Although all management positions can be difficult, keeping the salesforce motivated is made challenging by the nature of the sales job. Salespeople usually have substantial responsibilities and are left to work on their own. They are less accessible to the manager than other employees and tend to develop a strong sense of independence and self-reliance. At the same time they are also vulnerable to market vagaries, competitors' actions, and customer rejection on a daily basis, and function without the benefit of a support group. Somehow, management must provide direction and encouragement to salespeople at a distance and in an ambiguous and sometimes hostile climate.

The challenge of motivating a salesforce has not gone unnoticed by marketing scholars and practitioners. From their research, we have learned much about the relationship between satisfaction and motivation, what factors affect satisfaction and motivation, and techniques available to sales managers for improving satisfaction and motivation. Before discussing some of these topics, however, we need to distinguish between motivation as a relatively stable dispositional trait and as a psychological state that is affected by the environment. We use the terms *trait motivation* and *state motivation* to distinguish between the two types of motivation.

Trait motivation can be thought of as a baseline level of self-drive, which is largely determined by experiences early in life. Some people have a stronger need to succeed than others, for example, and are consequently more motivated. People vary substantially in their trait motivation levels. One way for a sales manager to make sure that the desired motivation levels are present in the salesforce is to hire people with already high trait motivation levels. Sales managers often try to assess this characteristic in sales candidates during the selection process.

State motivation is a temporary force affecting behavior that is at least partially controlled by the immediate environment. When the market is slow, for example, salespeople may be motivated to work harder in order to maintain their current compensation levels. State motivation can complement or counteract dispositional motivation. Thus, highly motivated people can become demotivated by the environment, and vice versa. The motivation to succeed in any sales assignment is a combination of both trait and state motivation, but the tools available to the manager are primarily directed at state motivation.

Distinguishing Satisfaction and Motivation. Another distinction that sales managers must make is between satisfaction and the motivation to achieve.[42] Salespeople are satisfied when they have an overall positive feeling about their current positions, and they are motivated when they have a strong drive to do the job and do it well. When salespeople are highly motivated by the rewards they are offered and have a strong sense of being able to achieve their objectives, they are usually satisfied with their jobs and perform well. They are also more likely to remain loyal to their current employers.[43] However, salespeople may be satisfied for reasons other than fulfilling their motivation to achieve. In those circumstances, satisfaction is not necessarily associated with high performance, although it can still be associated with high loyalty. Some people, for example, are naturally complacent and easily satisfied, and may be loyal to a company and unlikely to quit, but also unlikely to strive for high performance levels. Salesperson satisfaction can also result when sales managers use resources poorly, such as allowing salespeople to do little work while still receiving a good salary.

Salespeople may also be motivated without being satisfied. A common source of this type of motivation is fear of losing a job or other types of punishment. When salespeople are motivated by fear, they are often looking for a way out, which suggests that they may be looking for another position at the same time they are working hard to achieve their sales goals. Sales managers need to be attentive to salespeople's satisfaction and motivation, and try to maximize the satisfaction associated with fulfilling a high motivation to achieve. The ideal situation is having a salesforce focused on achieving their sales objectives and being highly satisfied with the challenge and opportunities those objectives represent.

Factors Affecting Satisfaction and Motivation. As mentioned earlier, satisfaction and motivation are affected by many factors, some dispositional and others environmental. Sales managers can control only environmental factors, and those only partially, so their overall ability to manage salesforce satisfaction and motivation is limited. Nevertheless, the tools available to sales managers have been found to be effective if used properly, and to make a measurable difference in the performance of the salesforce. Sales managers can affect both satisfaction and motivation by how they treat their people and structure their jobs. They can also affect motivation and satisfaction through a variety of rewards.

Research has shown that a key factor affecting salespeople's motivation and satisfaction is seeing their work as meaningful. Salespeople who understand how their efforts contribute to the company's success, who believe the products and services they offer are beneficial to the customer, and who see themselves as important members of their organizations tend to be more satisfied and more motivated than salespeople who do not feel the same way.[44] In addition, research has also shown that the amount of effort expended by salespeople has a direct influence on their job satisfaction separate from job performance, suggesting that when salespeople are nurtured into giving their best, they feel better about their jobs even when things don't go well.[45] The type of feedback, in terms of it being positive or negative, has also been shown to influence performance and job satisfaction.[46] Positive feedback increases both performance and satisfaction, whereas negative feedback increases salesperson knowledge but is not motivational.

At a deeper level than that of verbal affirmations, however, salespeople's sense of worth in their jobs depends in part on how well their roles are defined and how much irresolvable conflict they experience. The absence of well-defined roles is called *role ambiguity*, and the presence of irresolvable conflict is called *role conflict*. Role ambiguity and role conflict are some of the most extensively researched variables in sales management; they influence motivation, satisfaction, and performance.[47]

Both role ambiguity and role conflict involve matters of degree, and it is almost impossible to avoid some of each in a sales position. Any job that asks people to meet with strangers in unfamiliar places and make sense of their business and offer solutions under time pressure has a high potential for job ambiguity: How much should I push? When do I ask for action? Is this a demand-creation or an order-taking role? These are examples of the many questions that can cross a salesperson's mind and produce a sense of ambiguity. Conflicting demands are also usually present in sales encounters. Salespeople need to reconcile customer demands for good product performance at the lowest possible cost with their companies' demands for selling at profitable prices. In many circumstances salespeople must also reconcile demands from other parts of the organization (logistics, manufacturing, accounts receivable) and sometimes even different demands within the customer's organization. High levels of role ambiguity and role conflict have been shown to affect salesforce performance adversely, and sales managers need to be sensitive to these factors and take action to keep them under control and offset their negative effects.

Role ambiguity and role conflict have different effects on satisfaction and motivation.[48] Excessive levels of role ambiguity and role conflict affect satisfaction negatively, but only excessive levels of role ambiguity affect motivation negatively. It appears that salespeople who face considerable role conflict but maintain a good sense of what needs to be done are more motivated to resolve the conflict and get the job done. Salespeople who face high role conflict and do not know what they can or cannot do, or even if they do not face conflict but are uncertain as to what they should be doing, lose motivation.

Sales managers can affect the level of role ambiguity and role conflict faced by salespeople through judicious personal intervention and by carefully defining procedures and policies.[49] Personal intervention refers to one-on-one contact with the salesperson. Defining procedures and policies refers to establishing rules and methods for doing things that provide external constraints for the salesperson. Both personal intervention and more clearly defining procedures and policies reduce role ambiguity and conflict. Sales managers, for example, can give salespeople specific directions as to what needs to be achieved in specific sales calls and then ask for a written report as a way of reinforcing the verbal instructions. Both of these actions can reduce role ambiguity by providing an external definition of the task. Sales managers can reduce role conflict by clarifying their companies' positions on pricing and delivery, for example, or by reconciling sales objectives that make conflicting demands (e.g., 10 percent increases in annual sales *and* profits).

Sales managers need to be careful, however, not to go too far in terms of external controls and interventions. Although salespeople benefit from these actions, they may also see such actions as encroaching on their autonomy or as questioning their abilities. Salespeople tend to work autonomously and typically enjoy their independence. Too much external control by a sales manager can make them feel threatened and result in lower satisfaction. Sales managers must be careful about how much they intervene, and become personally comfortable with letting their people experience some role ambiguity and conflict in their work.

Administering Rewards

An obvious way to affect motivation and satisfaction is by administering rewards. The motivation to achieve is a function of the rewards promised and the salesperson's belief that the rewards can be attained. By choosing rewards and performance standards carefully, sales managers have a direct impact on the motivation of salespeople. Table 11.9 lists the results of a survey on the types of rewards salespeople

Reward	Attractiveness (percent)	Usage (percent)
Cash	95	53
Special Training	87	NA
Stock Options	85	(included in "Other" below)
Trip with Companion	77	29
Recognition and Praise	76	NA
Merchandise	63	51
Pat-on-the-back	63	NA
Plaques	46	34
Parking Space Privileges	35	(included in "Other" below)
Lunch with CEO	25	(included in "Other" below)
Honorary Titles	NA	5
Other (includes company dinners, entertainment, time-off, shares of stock, etc.)	NA	34

Note: NA = not applicable.

Source: Adapted from Christina Lovid-George, "What Motivates Best," Sales & Marketing Management (April 1992): 113–114 (with minor modifications).

find most motivating and the types of rewards used most commonly by companies. As we would expect, monetary rewards are the most highly rated and used. We discuss these forms of compensation later in this chapter. For nonmonetary rewards, it appears companies are responsive to many of the desires of salespeople. Merchandise, travel, plaques, and stock options are examples of rewards that salespeople find motivating, and are being used by at least some companies. The survey also reveals some interesting differences.

First, note that salespeople consider special training very motivating, yet it is not listed as something that companies use regularly. Many salespeople, probably those who have high learning orientations, are interested in opportunities to improve their skills and will work harder for those opportunities. For sales managers, salespeople's interest in training is a double bonus because using special training as an incentive can result in motivated and productive salespeople. The second difference is between the value that salespeople place on recognition and a pat-on-the-back and the frequency with which their companies use these rewards. Perhaps the respondents to this survey simply don't remember how often they are praised; if this is the case, sales managers need to find ways of making those instances more memorable. On the other hand, if salespeople are correct in perceiving their companies as deficient in administering praise and recognition, sales managers are overlooking an inexpensive and effective motivator.

External salesforces appear to respond to different types of rewards as effective motivators. External salespeople (e.g., sales agents, manufacturer's representatives) tend to place a higher value on special training, travel, and merchandise than do internal salespeople. They place a lower value, however, on recognition and praise, plaques, and dinners with the CEO or other senior executives.[50] It makes intuitive sense that external salespeople find more motivation from rewards that improve their immediate welfare and less from rewards that reassure them of being appreciated as an integral part of the organization, because they have no official ties to the company.

Compensation and Incentives

Companies use many different methods to compensate salespeople, but most can be classified into fixed compensation, commission compensation, and hybrid programs. Table 11.10 illustrates the percentage of firms in different size categories that use each approach, based on a survey conducted by the Dartnell Corporation that included more than 850 companies and 90,000 salespeople.

Across the size categories, most companies use hybrid programs that combine fixed and commission compensation in varying amounts. This is primarily in response to the complexity of the sales function and the multiple objectives that compensation programs try to achieve. In addition to motivating aggressive selling and high levels of performance, compensation programs must also encourage salespeople to pursue objectives that further their companies' strategic goals. Consider, for example, a small firm that is short on working capital and depends on the steady influx of cash to meet its obligations. Such a company may need to adopt a straight commission system that pays salespeople when payment is received for goods sold, in order to remain solvent. Another example may be a company seeking new accounts, such as BriskHeat Corporation in Columbus, Ohio. In order to promote fast growth, BriskHeat has a tiered compensation program in which the commission rate is set at 5 percent for the first 12 months of a new account relationship, and drops to 2 percent thereafter.[51] In contrast, if a company were facing temporary production constraints because of a shortage of raw materials, it would not want a compensation system that encourages new accounts. Instead, it would probably redirect its salesforce to maintaining current account relationships through higher levels of service, and would alter its compensation system to reflect the new strategic objectives.

Beyond reconciling compensation programs with company marketing strategy, sales managers need to be concerned with how the compensation plan affects the individual performance of salespeople. Sales managers need to understand the different approaches to compensation and some of their advantages and disadvantages.

Fixed Compensation Programs. Fixed compensation programs are those in which a fixed salary is paid each period regardless of the salesperson's performance. Fixed programs often are used when it is difficult to ascertain the salesperson's contribution to the sale or when factors such as advertising and promotions are the primary causes of demand. Salespeople who are predominantly order takers, such as telemarketing representatives for IBM Direct, are often paid a straight salary. Straight salary is also used when sales are primarily a team effort and salespeople act more as consultants or coordinators than demand creators. Fixed compensation programs are easy to administer, and because compensation is a fixed cost, they also make capital budgeting and planning easier. One additional benefit is that fixed compensation programs reduce the incidence of jealousy and dysfunctional intraorganizational competition because of large salary differences.

The primary disadvantage of fixed compensation programs is that they weaken the connection between performance and compensation. This weaker connection tends to reduce the motivating effect of compensation, and may undermine sales managers' ability to channel sales effort into necessary but perhaps more challenging or threatening assignments. This was a problem that Digital Equipment

TABLE 11.10 USE OF COMPENSATION PLANS BY SIZE OF FIRM

Company Size	Percentage of Surveyed Firms of this Size	Percentage of Companies Using		
		Fixed	Commission	Hybrid
Less than $5 million	26.0	19.5	15.6	64.9
$5 to $25 million	33.7	18.3	10.3	71.4
$25 to $100 million	18.9	14.7	10.8	74.6
$100 to $250 million	6.8	14.0	2.6	83.3
More than $250 million	14.6	14.2	1.9	84.0

Source: Adapted from Dartnell's 29th Sales Force Compensation Survey, 1996-1997 (Chicago: The Dartnell Corporation, 1996).

Corporation was trying to address when it redesigned its sales compensation program, as discussed in Marketing Anecdote 11.5.[52]

Commission Compensation. Under commission compensation programs, salespeople are paid a percentage of sales, gross margin, or net profit on each sale, depending on what measure of performance the sales manager chooses. Commissions can range widely, as seen in Table 11.6, and they are usually higher for products that are difficult to sell. Commission compensation has historically been used by companies facing capital constraints and trying to minimize fixed costs, or by companies whose products demand minimal account servicing and require primarily a strongly motivated salesforce. Insurance, automobiles, and securities are products sold often on commission. Contemporary trends toward relationship marketing across industries, however, suggest that the proportion of companies using pure commission compensation programs may decrease.[53] The primary advantage of commission compensation is the direct link between performance and reward, which makes compensation highly motivating, focuses the salesforce, and gives the sales manager more control over salesperson behavior. High motivation and task focus of commission compensation have led companies in the financial services market in Canada, such as the Bank of Montreal and CIBC Mortgage Company, to adopt this form of compensation.[54]

Commission compensation programs, however, reduce the manager's ability to control other salesforce behaviors. For example, salespeople on straight commission seldom take time to talk with people from other departments, or to help address the concerns of existing customers. Another disadvantage is that many salespeople find the erratic and unpredictable compensation stream unnerving, and leave jobs with straight commission compensation programs when given a chance to have a more stable income. This creates high rates of turnover and increases the amount of time spent by the sales manager in selection, recruiting, and training. High turnover is particularly costly for companies with sophisticated training programs. One other disadvantage is that commission-only programs often promote rivalries among salespeople and can lead to detrimental competition for customers instead of cooperation. Rivalries among salespeople have been a problem for several financial service providers in Canada. These disadvantages may well account for the relative low popularity of commission compensation programs.

Hybrid Compensation. Hybrid compensation combines fixed and commission compensation into a single package. As Table 11.10 shows, these are by far the most frequently used programs, and the most popular hybrid variation is

In 1988, Digital Equipment Corporation (DEC) had sales of $1.3 billion, making it the number two U.S. computer producer behind IBM. Markets change quickly in the computer industry, however, and by 1992 the company faced declining sales of its mainstay products and a market that was not interested in its new processor and other products. DEC had built its reputation and market power throughout the 1980s on the excellence of its minicomputers. By 1992, however, minicomputers as a product category were losing market share to the increasingly powerful workstations produced by Sun Microsystems and to the personal computers and servers sold by companies such as Compaq, Apple, IBM, and Hewlett-Packard.

Facing weak demand for its products, DEC made several changes to its salesforce as part of its new marketing strategy. One of its first moves was to adopt a hybrid sales compensation plan, in which 30 percent of the average salesperson's compensation came from straight sales commissions. Concurrent with changes to the compensation plan, sales and marketing efforts were refocused on key product lines, such as hardware and software for networking large numbers of personal computers, and high-end workstations based on DEC's advanced Alpha chip. Budget plans, compensation, and incentive plans were adjusted to fit with the company's new strategic objectives, and the overall size of the salesforce was reduced substantially. DEC also reduced the size of the sales management staff and increased its span of control, although the company had to back away from some of its initial plans due to organizational resistance. By 1994, the market remained difficult for DEC, and its salesforce was reduced by an additional 33 percent, as it also reduced the number of customers it approached directly.

The refocused and smaller salesforce was successful in convincing many existing customers to upgrade their systems, thus stemming DEC's fast decline in market share.

In the area of personal computers, however, DEC took a different approach by reducing the number of customers reached directly to almost zero, and adopting an external salesforce. DEC forged distribution partnerships with several large resellers at both the consumer and industrial levels. Even with its highly motivated salesforce, DEC found that margins on personal computers were too low to support an internal salesforce. Resellers had lower operating costs on a per unit basis and could sell the units profitably. DEC focused its internal salesforce on higher-margin products such as video and network servers. Although DEC remains in a very competitive market and is working hard to regain some of its past successes, its redesigned salesforce has contributed positively to its efforts.

Sources: Melinda Carol Ballou, "37,000 Depart in DEC Retirement Plan," *Computerworld*, September 6, 1992, p. 109.

Mary Brandol, "Digital Overhaul Receives Mixed Reviews," *Computerworld*, July 18, 1994, p. 1.

David Churbuck, "Rebuilding DEC," Forbes, August 15, 1994, pp. 44–45.

Gary McWilliams, "Desperate Hours at DEC," *Business Week*, May 9, 1994, pp. 2–29.

Gary McWilliams, "DEC's Comeback Is Still a Work in Progress," *Business Week*, January 18, 1993, pp. 75–76.

Gary McWilliams, "Punching in a Whole New Set of Commands at DEC," *Business Week*, October 12, 1992, p. 160.

Gary McWilliams and Peter Burrows, "It Looks Like a PC Maker, Walks Like a PC Maker," *Business Week*, December 12, 1994, pp. 106–107.

Craig Stedman, "Digital Veers from Vertical Structure," *Computerworld*, January 31, 1994, p. 4.

straight salary plus a bonus. Bonuses are usually based on amounts sold over some quota or on the amount of new business generated. Hybrid compensation programs share in some of the advantages and disadvantages of both fixed and commission compensation. The motivational influence of hybrid plans is greater than that of fixed compensation, but at the same time the amount of control the sales manager has is lower. The management challenge is to blend the different parts of the program in a way that maximizes the motivational advantages while reducing the loss-of-control disadvantages. For example, Digital Equipment Corporation was trying to increase sales motivation without losing control in the early 1990s when it eliminated the fixed salary plan that the company has used since its inception and replaced it with a hybrid plan in which up to 30 percent of compensation for salespeople was commission based. Some of the changes made by DEC to its sales management practices are summarized in Marketing Anecdote 11.5. The DEC story also reveals that making radical changes to compensation programs is difficult when these changes go against established company practices and culture.

In designing the final compensation program, the sales manager should consider some additional factors. First, program rules must be easy to understand. Second, salespeople must perceive the goals of the program to be both fair and achievable. Third, compensation programs must be easy to administer. Lastly, the program should be designed to compensate attractively but not excessively, particularly as it compares to compensation programs in other areas of the firm. Salespeople need to be rewarded for the additional stress of being vulnerable and alone, but the pay must be perceived as fair by others in the company.

Incentives. Earlier in this chapter we briefly discussed that noncash rewards or incentives are good motivators. Incentives are most often used to supplement compensation programs; instead of being tied to overall performance, incentives are used to signal the achievement of prespecified goals or levels. Exceeding quota by 10 percent or achieving $1 million in sales may be achievement levels associated with specific incentives such as paid vacations in Hawaii or golf club sets. Incentives are often used in special contests designed to focus sales attention on specific products or services. Other companies use incentives, such as company cars and parking privileges, to reward milestones in a salesperson's career. One unique aspect of incentives is that they are usually awarded with great fanfare and have value to the salesperson as a form of recognition in addition to their intrinsic benefits.

In managing incentives, as in everything else, the manager needs to make them compatible with organizational values and the practices of other departments. Incentives that create a sense of inequity or tarnish the reputation of the salesforce can reduce the salesforce's ability to work with other departments.

Managing Sales Managers

Although we discussed sales managers' responsibilities from selection to compensation as if sequential, most sales managers deal with issues pertaining to all these major areas on a daily basis. It is easy to see, therefore, that sales management can be both an exciting and challenging position. It is certainly not a position for which everyone is well suited. General marketing managers who oversee a sales function need to choose carefully the people they appoint as sales managers, and not fall into the trap of promoting their best salespeople into management positions for which they are not suited.[55] Sales managers, like the salesforce, must be managed with an eye to both strategic and operational considerations.

SUMMARY

The sales function exists in practically all commercial enterprises, and for many businesses it is their most complete embodiment of their marketing orientation. Salespeople are often the employees most directly responsible for serving customers and keeping them satisfied while preserving the company's reputation and profitability. At the same time, salespeople can also be an important source of market intelligence. Salespeople can have substantial influence on their company's marketing mix, products, pricing, distribution, and promotion.

The composition and execution of the sales function is changing in response to market and environmental forces. Three major factors influencing the sales function are:

- global diversity, as cultural and national boundaries are subordinate to economic and commercial interests
- the emphasis on relationship marketing, which often asks salespeople to be problem solvers instead of aggressive promoters
- the development of powerful and diverse information technologies, which makes it possible to sustain contact with the customer almost continuously and without regard to geographic distance

Salespeople fulfill a number of roles, depending on the situation and the tasks they are called on to perform. Some tasks are in response to customer demands, such as order taking and trade servicing. Other tasks are proactive, such as selling and missionary work. In a single day, a salesperson is often called on to fulfill every task, and within a relationship the tasks may vary substantially between encounters.

The sales process is divided into three major stages, with each stage involving several substages or tasks:

- The preliminary stage is the preparation for the sales encounter. It involves identifying and qualifying prospects and precall planning.
- The face-to-face selling stage is the actual sales encounter. It typically involves iterative movement between introduction, customer needs assessment, presentation, and closing, with each iteration punctuated by a customer objection that must be handled.
- The follow-up stage is contact subsequent to the sale to ensure customer satisfaction and enhance the relationship.

Managing the salesforce is a strategically sensitive position, given the importance of the sales function. It can be divided into three sets of responsibilities: designing the salesforce, building the salesforce, and managing the salesforce.

- Designing the salesforce involves decisions on the use of internal salespeople (employees) or external salespeople, such as manufacturers' representatives. This decision must take into account the company's products and marketing strategic objectives, as well as its financial constraints. Designing the salesforce also involves:
- setting goals and objectives for the salesforce that are consistent with the company's strategic goals
- setting the size of the salesforce so these goals can be achieved
- deploying the salesforce in terms of geographic, product, account size, or other strategically sensible factors or combination of factors

- Building the salesforce involves selecting the best people in terms of the company's needs and the candidate's interests and abilities. Selection must also be sensitive to the changing nature of the market environment. Once candidates are identified, they must be recruited and trained. Training involves teaching the candidates about the company and its products, as well as about the techniques to use in the many different tasks and roles that salespeople fulfill. Because of the dynamic nature of the market and most companies, training is an ongoing process for salespeople and their managers.

- Managing the salesforce refers to the day-to-day motivation and leadership of the salesforce. Sales managers need to provide the level of guidance and assistance that keeps their salespeople motivated and satisfied with their positions. Too much guidance is demotivating because it impinges on salesperson autonomy. Not enough guidance is also problematic because it can cause high levels of role ambiguity and conflict. To manage motivation, sales managers also control compensation and incentive plans. Compensation is managed so as to be motivating while allowing the sales manager some control over the efforts of the salesforce.

QUESTIONS FOR DISCUSSION

1. Describe the strategic importance of the sales function and why salespeople can be the most complete embodiment of the marketing orientation of some companies. Give examples of some companies for which this may be true and explain.

2. Describe the three major factors that are changing the face of selling around the world and explain how these factors are influencing the sales function.

3. Assume you work for Wm. Dierickx Company in a sales position similar to that of Dobbsie Witherow. In what ways are the factors changing the face of selling likely to be manifest in your day-to-day activities? How would any of them affect how you sell typewriters?

4. Describe the major roles fulfilled by salespeople and give examples of each of these roles.

5. Consider the situation at Kiwi International and explain which roles may be fulfilled by the Kiwi personnel calling on travel agents. Tell how those roles would be different when calling on travel agents that have never sold a Kiwi ticket versus calling on a regular Kiwi user.

6. Describe the World Wide Web and its implications for selling.

7. The sales approach of Kiwi International is one in which personal contact is used instead of the electronic contact typically used by the major airlines. Are there any potential changes to the effectiveness of Kiwi's approach relative to the major airlines if the majors make more extensive use of the World Wide Web than they have in the past?

8. Assume you are the business development officer illustrated in Figure 11.2, and you are transferred to the San Francisco sales office and given the task of developing a relationship with several Japanese executives. How would you expect the amount of time you spend on different sales tasks to change? How would the entries in your daily planner change in terms of venue, the people contacted, and amount of time allocated to the sales calls?

9. Describe the three major stages of the sales process and the substages or tasks under each. Why is the face-to-face sales stage called an iterative process?

10. What are the major advantages and disadvantages of relying on an external salesforce? What would Dierickx gain by using an external salesforce? What would it lose? Would it make sense for Dierickx to adopt an external salesforce?

11. Assume that ACME Tool wants to expand into the Asian market and you are the sales manager. Your research shows there are 15,000 potential customers in Asian markets of Hong Kong, Taiwan, and China, of which 7,000 are of a size and type that ACME can service. You have also determined it will take an average of 15 visits per customer over an 18-month period to achieve a sale, and that the average sales contact will last about two hours. For every hour of actual sales contact, your salespeople will spend approximately the same amount of time preparing, which means actual selling time will be only 50 percent of total time available. Calculate the salesforce size required to enter all three markets simultaneously.

12. If, as ACME's sales manager, you deployed your salesforce between Taiwan, Hong Kong, and China, what would be the basis for your territorial structure? If you had additional information that of the 7,000 potential customers only 20 represent 30 percent of the potential business, would you preserve the same structure? If you would change the structure, how would you change it and why?

13. Explain why it is important to combine objective and subjective means for evaluating candidates for a salesforce. What are the advantages and disadvantages of each type of measurement technique?

14. If, as ACME's sales manager, you were building a salesforce in Asia, what would be your major concerns in terms of selecting and training a salesforce? Could you apply the same techniques in the selection process? If not, what would you change? What would be the primary operational concerns (who, how, when, and where) of your training program if you were hiring nationals to call on accounts in their own countries? How would your operational concerns differ if you were hiring U.S. experts in temperature control technologies to call on Asian customers?

15. Distinguish between motivation and job satisfaction. Can salespeople have one without the other? Would either state be more beneficial than having salespeople that are both motivated and satisfied?

16. What are the various tools and techniques available to the sales manager to ensure adequate levels of job satisfaction and motivation? Would the importance of these tools and techniques be different for a sales manager at Dierickx than for a sales manager at IBM? Explain your answer.

17. Describe several situations in which a straight salary compensation plan would be appropriate and explain what would need to be different for straight commission or hybrid compensation plans to be more appropriate.

NOTES FOR FURTHER READING

1. For more information about the interplay of market orientation and salesforce behavior, see Judy A. Siguaw, Gene Brown, and Robert E. Widing II, "The Influence of the Market Orientation of the Firm on Salesforce Behaviors and Attitudes," *Journal of Marketing Research* 31 (February 1994): 106–116.

2. Cathy Hyatt Hills, "Making the Team," *Sales and Marketing Management* (February 1992): 54–57.

3. Geoffrey Brewer, "To the Max," *Sales and Marketing Management* (March 1996): 49–55.

4. For a comprehensive review of the literature and synthesis of the issues surrounding diversity in organizations, see Frances J. Milliken and Luis L. Martins, "Searching for Common Threads: Understanding the Multiple Effects of Diversity in Organizational Groups, *Academy of Management Review* 21 (April 1996): 402–433.

5. S. E. Jackson, K. E. May, and K. Whitney, "Understanding the Dynamics of Diversity in Decision Making Teams," in R. A. Guzzo and E. Salas, eds., *Team Effectiveness and Decision Making in Organizations* (San Francisco: Jossey-Bass 1995), pp. 204–261.

6. William E. Lissy, "Currents in Compensation and Benefits," *Compensation & Benefit Review* (September-October 1994): 11.

7. For more discussion on how the cost of switching vendors is influenced by relationship marketing, see T. Paul, "Relationship Marketing for Health Care Providers," *Journal of Health Care Marketing* 8 (September 1988): 20–25; and L. A. Crosty and N. Stephens, "Effects of Relationship Marketing of Satisfaction, Retention, and Prices in the Life Insurance Industry," *Journal of Marketing Research* 24 (November 1987): 404–411.

8. Based on figures from Marianne Matthews, "If Your Ads Aren't Pulling Top Sales Talent," *Sales & Marketing Management* (February 1990): 75–79. For more information on the range of costs associated with sales calls and the number of calls required to make a sale, see *Dartnell's 27th Salesforce Compensation Survey* (Chicago: The Dartnell Corporation 1992), pp. 1–6.

9. *Dartnell's 27th Salesforce Compensation Survey*, p. 5.

10. For more extensive recommendations for salespeople involved in building partner relationships, see Barry J. Farber and Joyce Wycoff, "Relationships: Six Steps to Success," *Sales and Marketing Management* (April 1992): 50–58.

11. For the story on Union Pacific, see Patricia Sellers, "How to Remake Your Salesforce," *Fortune*, May 4, 1992, pp. 98–103. For the story on Massachusetts Envelope Company, see Howard Scott, "How to Handle Smaller Accounts," *Nation's Business*, (September 1994): 48R.

12. Based on "Managing Phone Sales: There Is a Difference," *Sales and Marketing Management* (June 1995): 39–40.

13. Based on William C. Moncrief III, "Selling Activity and Sales Position Taxonomies for Industrial Salesforces," *Journal of Marketing Research* 23 (August 1986): 261–270; modified and expanded to include retail sales positions.

14. Other classifications, in chronological order, are Robert N. McMurry, "The Mystique of Super-Salesmanship," *Harvard Business Review*, March–April 1961, p. 114; Derek A. Newton, *Sales Performance and Turnovers*, (Cambridge, Mass.: Marketing Science Institute, 1977); and Alan J. Dubinsky and P. J. O'Connor, "A Multidimensional Analysis of Preferences for Sales Positions," *Journal of Personal Selling and Sales Management* (November 1983): 31–41.

15. This example is based on interviews and observation of a business development representative at a large bank. The names have been disguised.

16. For more information about the changes taking place in automobile sales in the United States, see Keith Naughton, "Revolution in the Showroom," *Business Week*, February 19, 1996, pp. 70–76.

17. For more examples of the Saturn sales approach being copied, see "Rethinking the Salesforce: Are Commission-only Structures a Thing of the Past?" *Chemical and Engineering News*, July 31, 1995, pp. 11–14; Kathleen Kerwin and David Woodruff, "Can Olds Hitch its Wagon to Saturn's Star," *Business Week*, November 22, 1992, p. 76; and James Bennet, "Buying Without Haggling as Cars Get Fixed Prices," *New York Times*, February 1, 1994.

18. For more information, see Leslie Whitaker, "Rewriting the Script," *Selling*, March 1994, pp. 24–26.

19. Sun Tzu, *The Art of War* (New York: Dell Publishing, 1983), p. 11 (translated by James Clavell).

20. Matthews, "If Your Ads Aren't Pulling Top Sales Talent." The numbers have been adjusted for inflation.

21. One of six important factors identified as contributing to salesperson failure is not planning sales presentations carefully. Other factors are (1) poor listening, (2) failure to concentrate on top priorities, (3) lack of effort, (4) inability to determine customer needs, and (5) inadequate product knowledge. For more information on these factors, see Thomas N. Ingram, Charles H. Schwepker Jr., and Don Hutson, "Why Salespeople Fail," *Industrial Marketing Management* (22 August 1992): 225–230.

22. John R. P. French and Bertram Raven, "The Bases of Social Power," in Dorwin Cartright, ed., *Studies in Social Power* (Ann Arbor: University of Michigan Press, 1959), pp. 150–167.

23. For more information on the cues used by automobile salespeople, see Michael Etgar, Arun K. Jain, and Maroj K. Agarwal, "Salesmen-Customer Interaction: An Experimental Approach," *Journal of the Academy of Marketing Science* 6, 2 (1978): 1–11.

24. For more information about the sales training of automobile salespeople, see James Bennet, "Buyer Beware: A Charm School for Car Salespeople," *New York Times*, March 29, 1995.

25. For a discussion of the psychological mechanism, see Charles A. Kiesler, *The Psychology of Commitment* (New York: Academic Press, 1971). For a discussion of commitment in business organizations, see Gerald R. Salancik, "Commitment and the Control of Organizational Behavior and Belief," in B. M. Staw and G. R. Salancik, eds., *New Directions in Organizational Behavior* (Chicago: St. Clair Press, 1977), pp. 1–54.

26. "Survey of Selling Costs: Special Issue," *Sales and Marketing Management* (February 16, 1987): 59.

27. See, for example, John Verity, "Deconstructing the Computer Industry," *Business Week*, November 23, 1992, pp. 90–100; Ira Seger, "The Few, the True, the Blue," *Business Week*, May 30, 1994, pp. 124–126; and Mark Maremont, "Digital's Turnaround: Time for Phase Two," *Business Week*, June 19, 1995, pp. 130–135.

28. For more information, see Andris A. Zoltners and Prabhakant Sinha, "Sales Territory Alignment: A Review and Model," *Management Science* (November 1983):

1237–1256; Leonard M. Lodish, "Sales Territory Alignment to Maximize Profits," *Journal of Marketing Research* (February 1975): 30–36, Probha Sinha and Andres Zoltners, "Matching Manpower and Markets," *Business Marketing* (September 1988): 95–98; and R. S. Howick and M. Pidd, "Salesforce Deployment Models," *European Journal of Operations Research* (October 1990): 295–310.

29. For more information, see Zachary Schiller, Wendy Zellner, Rod Stodghill, and Mark Marement, "Clout! More and More Retail Giants Rule the Market Place," *Business Week*, December 21, 1992, pp. 66–73.

30. For more information, see William A. O'Connel and William Keenan Jr., "The Shape of Things to Come," *Sales & Marketing Management* (January 1990): 36–41.

31. For a more academic perspective on selection, see E. J. Randall and C. H. Randall, "Review of Salesperson Selection Techniques and Criteria: A Managerial Approach," *International Journal of Research In Marketing* 7 (December 1990): 81–96.

32. Harish Sujan, Barton A. Weitz, and Nirmalya Kumar, "Learning Orientation, Working Smart, and Effective Selling," *Journal of Marketing* 58 (July 1994): 39–52.

33. Jhinuk Chowdhury, "The Motivational Impact of Sales Quotas on Effort," *Journal of Marketing Research* 30 (February 1993): 28–41.

34. Rayna Skolnik, "The Birth of a Sales Force," *Sales & Marketing Management* (March 1986): 42–44.

35. For more information on different basis for predicting job performance, see John E. Hunter and R. F. Hunter, "Validity and Utility of Alternative Predictors of Job Performance," *Psychological Bulletin* 96 (1984): 72–98.

36. Although no research has been conducted on the influence of attractiveness and citizenship behavior on candidate selection, it has been conducted on the influence of these factors on sales manager evaluations of sales personnel, and found to bias their assessments. For more information see Thomas E. DeCarlo and Thomas W. Leigh, "Impact of Salesperson Attraction on Sales Managers' Attributions and Feedback," *Journal of Marketing* 60 (April 1996): 47–66; and Scott B. Mackenzie, Philip M. Podsakoff, and Richard Fetter, "The Impact of Organizational Citizenship Behavior on Evaluations of Salesperson Performance," *Journal of Marketing* 54 (January 1993): 70–80.

37. For more information on the use of different techniques for salesperson selection, see Alan J. Dubinsky and Thomas E. Barry, "A Survey of Sales Management Practices," *Industrial Marketing Management* 11 (1982): 136.

38. For more information, see William Keenan Jr., "Handwriting Analysis—What Can It Tell You?" *Sales & Marketing Management* (April 1990): 44–48.

39. For more details on the IBM sales reorganization, see Seger, "The Few, the True, the Blue."

40. For more information on how leadership affects the behavior of salespeople see: Pradeep K. Tyagi, "Relative Importance of Key Job Dimensions and Leadership Behaviors in Motivating Salesperson Work Performance," *Journal of Marketing* 49 (Summer 1985): 76–86.

41. The AIDS epidemic throughout the world has been a significant challenge for many companies, and sales organizations are no exception. For an excellent treatment of the effect of AIDS on a sales organization, see Ron Stodghill II, "Managing AIDS: How One Boss Struggled to Cope," *Business Week*, February 1, 1993, pp. 48–52; and Ron Stodghill II, Russell Mitchell, Karen Thurston, and Christina Del Valle, "Why AIDS Policy Must be a Social Policy," *Business Week*, February 1, 1993, pp. 53–54.

42. There are many discussions of satisfaction and motivation in the literature. For a more in-depth look at this topic, some possible readings are Richard P. Bagozzi, "Salesforce Performance and Satisfaction as a Function of Individual Differences, Interpersonal, and Situational Factors," *Journal of Marketing Research* 15 (August 1978): 517–531; Richard P. Bagozzi, "Performance and Satisfaction in an Industrial Salesforce: An Examination of Their Antecedents and Simultaneity," *Journal of Marketing* 44 (Spring 1980): 65–77; R. C. Becherer, Fred W. Morgan, and Lawrence M. Richard, "The Job Characteristics of Industrial Salespersons: Relationship to Motivation and Satisfaction," *Journal of Marketing* 46 (Fall 1982): 125–135; Douglas N. Behrman and William D. Perreault, "A Role Stress Model of the Performance and Satisfaction of Industrial Salespersons," *Journal of Marketing* 48 (Fall 1984): 9–21; and Steven P. Brown and Robert A. Peterson, "Antecedents and Consequences of Salesperson Job Satisfaction: Meta-Analysis and Assessment of Causal Effects," *Journal of Marketing Research* 30 (February 1993): 63–77.

43. Brown and Peterson, "Antecedents and Consequences of Salesperson Job Satisfaction."

44. For a more in-depth treatment of this topic, see Becherer, Morgan, and Richard, "The Job Characteristics of Industrial Salespersons."

45. Steven P. Brown and Robert A. Peterson, "The Effects of Effort on Sales Performance and Job Satisfaction," *Journal of Marketing* 58 (April 1994): 70–80.

46. Bernard J. Jaworski and Ajay K. Kohli, "Supervisory Feedback: Alternative Types and Their Impact on Salespeople's Performance and Satisfaction," *Journal of Marketing Research* 28 (May 1991): 190–201.

47. An in-depth discussion of role ambiguity and role conflict and their influence on salespeople is beyond the scope of this book. For more information on the multidimensional nature of role ambiguity, see Jagdip Singh and Gary K. Rhoads, "Boundary Role Ambiguity in Marketing-Oriented Positions: A Multidimensional, Multifaceted Operationalization," *Journal of Marketing Research* 28 (August 1991): 328–338; and Jagdip Singh, "Boundary Role Ambiguity: Facets, Determinants, and Impacts," *Journal of Marketing* 57 (April 1993): 11–21. For discussions of the link between role ambiguity and conflict and

job performance and satisfaction, see Gilbert A. Churchill Jr., Neil M. Ford, Steven W. Hartley, and Orville C. Walker, "The Determinants of Salesperson Performance: A Meta-Analysis," *Journal of Marketing Research* 22 (May 1985): 103–118; and Brown and Peterson, "Antecedents and Consequences of Salesperson Job Satisfaction."

48. For more detail on the varied influence of role ambiguity and conflict on satisfaction and motivation, see Behrman and Perreault, "A Role Stress Model"; and Louis W. Fry, Charles M. Futrell, A. Parasuraman, and Margaret A. Chmielewsky, "An Analysis of Alternative Causal Models of Salesperson Role Perception and Work-Related Attitudes," *Journal of Marketing Research* 23 (May 1986): 153–163.

49. Many of the articles referenced in this section address the effect of sales manager behavior on salespeople. For additional information, see R. Kenneth Teas, "Supervisory Behavior, Role Stress, and the Job Satisfaction of Industrial Salespeople," *Journal of Marketing Research* 20 (February 1983): 84–91; and Pradeep K. Tyagi, "Perceived Organizational Climate and the Process of Salesperson Motivation," *Journal of Marketing Research* 19 (May 1982): 240–254.

50. Edwin Bobrow, "Reps and Recognition: Understanding What Motivates," *Sales & Marketing Management* (September 1991): 82–86.

51. Geoffrey Brewer, "To the Max," *Sales and Marketing Management* (March 1, 1996): 49–55.

52. For more information, see Gary McWilliams, "Punching in a Whole New Set of Commands at DEC," *Business Week*, October 12, 1992, p. 160.

53. For more detailed information, see "Rethinking the Salesforce."

54. For more information, see Richard Wright, "Paid for Performance," *Canadian Banker*, November 1, 1995, pp. 17–22.

55. For more on the difficulties often faced by salespeople promoted to management positions, see Bill Kelley, "From Salesperson to Manager: Transition and Travail," *Sales and Marketing Management* (February 1992): 32–36.

CHAPTER 12

PRICING: MACRO, BEHAVIORAL, AND MANAGERIAL DECISIONS

CHAPTER OBJECTIVES

When you are done with this chapter, you should have achieved the following:

- An appreciation for how market forces and social and legal constraints affect pricing at the macrolevel
- An understanding of how pricing is based on consumer behavior
- A basic understanding of the strategies and tactics of price setting
- An insight into the future directions in pricing

CHAPTER OUTLINE

Price setting is a topic shrouded in mystery and misconceptions. In premodern times, sellers frequently did not know what prices to charge and buyers were often equally ignorant of what sellers were likely to charge. Typically, prices were determined as outcomes of negotiation between buyers and sellers. A seller might set a price, but buyers knew that, unless the seller had a monopoly, the price could invariably be bid down. Price setting via negotiation occurs less frequently today but can be found in bazaars, housing markets, and auto dealerships in many parts of the world. Even in the most industrialized countries, prices for such goods as televisions, stereo systems, and other electronic equipment are subject to some negotiation in certain dealerships, although many customers may be unaware that they need not pay the "list price." Likewise, prices paid by organizations for machinery, services, and supplies are often open to negotiation.

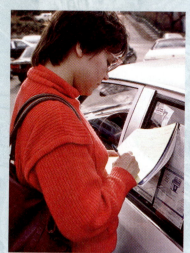

Auto manufacturers have their pricing practices down to a science.

Nevertheless, today managers set prices for most consumer goods and services and many industrial goods before the customer and company ever meet. How do they do this? Textbooks often present price setting as a strictly rational activity where managers take into account costs, demand, and competition before deciding upon the optimal (usually the "profit maximizing") price. Although there is a kernel of truth to this portrayal, price setting in practice is more complex than classic textbooks would lead us to believe.

Sometimes managers are unable to obtain valid information on costs, demand, and competitor behavior, and therefore price setting is a hit or miss activity, often relying on convention or rule of thumb. Likewise, in many parts of the world, managers set prices in openly collusive ways. They meet with their competitors directly or through trade or professional associations and collectively decide on prices acceptable to all. Such practices are legal in most countries; only in the United States, United Kingdom, and a few other countries do laws forbid such collusion. Even in the United States, collusion in price setting still occurs, despite the law. A good example is the cellular telephone industry, where two researchers* recently claimed that sellers collude and prices are significantly above competitive levels.

*Philip M. Parker and Lars-Hendrik Röller, "Collusive Conduct in Duopolies: Multimarket Contact and Cross-Ownership in the Mobile Telephone Industry," INSEAD Working Paper Series, Fontainebleau, France, 1996.

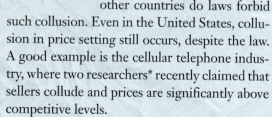

In this chapter, we look at the meaning of price from the viewpoint of society (i.e., economic, legal, and ethical issues), consumers, and managers. Whatever form prices take—bribes, dues, duties, fares, interest, premiums, rates, rents, or tolls, to name a few—it is important to think of price as that which consumers give up to obtain a product or service. Besides money, consumers forgo time and undergo psychological and social costs to acquire goods and services. From one point of view, price is also the outcome of an implicit negotiation and power struggle among governments, firms, and consumers. Each party not only takes into account its own needs and responsibilities and the constraints and opportunities it faces, but tries to influence how prices are set.

PRICE AT THE MACROLEVEL

Figure 12.1 presents a framework for looking at the macro aspects of prices. Notice the three broad *outcomes* that prices influence: societal, organizational, and individual consumer outcomes. These outcomes are, of course, shaped by many other forces, but prices play an important role. At the societal level, prices can be seen to regulate the allocation and use of scarce resources and to insure that goods are produced at more or less reasonable levels of efficiency. Prices also indirectly affect the level of employment and interact with inflationary and other economic forces. Although the relationship is not well understood, prices are also connected to the distribution of income, producing or thwarting social equity depending on their ebb and flow. At the organizational level, the prices that a firm sets and the prices set by other firms often influence the profitability and market share and growth of these firms. Finally, prices have an obviously important impact on the well-being of consumers. The prices consumers pay ultimately shape their level of satisfaction and overall standard of living.

All of these outcomes—societal, organizational, and personal—are shown in Figure 12.1 to be affected by *pricing behavior*. We say more about the nature of pricing behavior at the psychological and managerial levels later in this chapter. For now, we note that firms devote considerable time and money to determine what level of prices to set for their products. The levels they set can often be interpreted in relation to competitors (e.g., price leadership or following) and consumers (e.g., price discrimination, skimming, penetration).

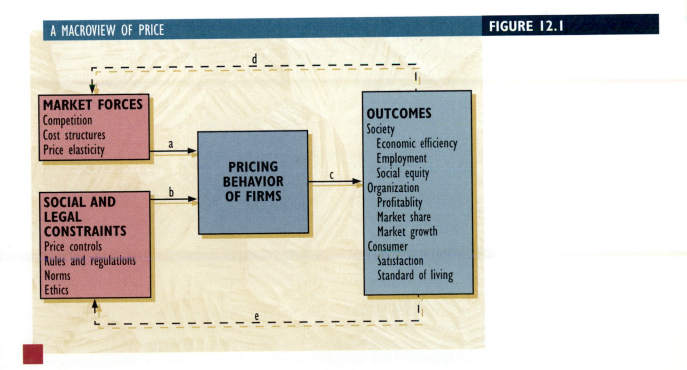

A MACROVIEW OF PRICE   **FIGURE 12.1**

In general, at the macrolevel, we can explain pricing behavior as a function of two factors: *market forces* and *social and legal constraints*. If prices were set entirely on the basis of market forces (arrow a in Fig. 12.1), we would have the ideal market economy. For example, under pure competition the firm has little freedom to set the level of its price, whereas under oligopolistic conditions, the firm has more leeway. If prices were set entirely on the basis of social and legal forces, in contrast, we would have the ideal planned economy (arrow b in Fig. 12.1). In reality, no society in the world today is either a perfect market economy or a perfect planned economy. All systems involve a mixture of market forces and social and legal constraints in the determination of price (and output). The United States tends to emphasize a market system, but laws and regulations govern pricing behavior in important instances. Similarly, China is largely a centrally planned system, yet managers sometimes have freedom to set prices in response to market forces. Thus, it is important to consider both paths a and b in Figure 12.1 if we are to comprehend price at a macrolevel.[1] We begin with an analysis of market forces and social and legal constraints as they apply to price.

Market Forces

From an economic standpoint, we know that price plays a fundamental role. At the microlevel, consumers are presumed to maximize utility and firms are assumed to maximize profits. Both do this subject to their budget constraints: that is, their income and the prices of desired goods and services. When we aggregate up to the level of groups of consumers (e.g., a market) or groups of firms (e.g., an industry), we can see that consumers and producers respond to prices set as a consequence of supply and demand forces in the marketplace. Moreover, the prices that both set—consumers for their labor and firms for their goods—are dependent on market forces. Three of the more important market forces are competition, cost structures, and price elasticity.

Competition

Typically (to take the viewpoint of the seller), we may identify three structural conditions under which organizations function: competition, oligopoly, and monopoly (see Table 12.1).

Under pure competition, the number of sellers of the same product is large, and firms have little freedom to determine what prices to set for their products. Firms therefore choose a price equal to the market price for all sellers. (A somewhat different case is monopolistic competition, in which many sellers market differentiated products or services.)

Under an oligopoly, a few sellers of the same product (the homogeneous oligopoly) or similar products (the differentiated oligopoly) exist, and each has some freedom to set its price at a level different from the others. Nevertheless, firms in an oligopoly usually discover that their freedom is limited by demand, costs, and the actions of their rivals.

Finally, under a monopoly, a single seller has considerable freedom to set its price. Yet, even here, demand and cost factors constrain that freedom somewhat.

In sum, then, the proposition is that at least a part of pricing behavior, such as the price level, is determined by competitive market forces embodied in structures of pure competition, oligopoly, or monopoly faced by the seller. To simplify our discussion of these forces, we consider here only the case of relatively homogeneous products. The more important, but also more complicated, case of product differentiation is de-

TABLE 12.1 THREE BASIC ECONOMIC STRUCTURES FACED BY A SELLER

Structure Type	Description
Pure competition	Many sellers market essentially the same product or service.
Monopolistic competition	Many sellers market somewhat differentiated products or services.
Homogeneous oligopoly	A small number of firms market basically the same product or service.
Differentiated oligopoly	A small number of firms market somewhat differentiated products or services.
Monopoly	A single seller exists with no close substitutes.

scribed later in the chapter under the context of managerial views of price. The topics of monopolistic competition and differentiated oligopoly are considered also.

Pure Competition. To see the influence of pure competition on prices, let us look at Figure 12.2. We begin with the market before equilibrium (case A in Fig. 12.2) where the numerous firms in the industry face a short-run supply, S_1. The interaction of industry supply and market demand (D_1) yields a (short-run) equilibrium price of $P_{1,I}$ (r in the figure). This is the price taken as a given, at least temporarily, by the firm represented at the left of case A. With this price ($P_{1,F}$), the firm is motivated to produce $q_{1,F}$, because this will maximize profits. That is, when marginal cost (MC) equals $P_{1,F}$, the profit will equal $x - y$ (as calculated from average total cost (ATC), quantity, and price considerations). The presence of profits, however, will motivate new firms to enter the market, and we will eventually experience a corresponding shift in industry supply to S_2, (see case B in Fig. 12.2). This, in turn, will reduce the price toward an equilibrium value, $P_{2,I}$ (see path $r \rightarrow s$). The firm will thus face a new price, and pressures will force the output of a new quantity, $q_{2,F}$, where $ATC = MC = P_{2,F}$. Here, no profits are realized and only total costs are recovered (see path $x \rightarrow z$ in Fig. 12.2).

In short, firms competing under pure competition are forced to operate efficiently in the sense that the average costs per unit are at a minimum. Consumers benefit by paying a lower price than they would under other structures. Firms presumably make just enough (a "nominal" profit) to motivate them to remain in the market (indeed, they can sell all they produce at a satisfactory price) but perhaps not enough to innovate in the long run. In any event, pure competition determines the long-run price for the market ($P_{2,I} = P_{2,F}$). Although no flawless examples of perfect competition exist, agricultural crops approximate this situation. But even here, government actions in the form of price supports or outright purchases change the situation somewhat. One can readily understand why farmers, who continually face pressures to sell at a relatively low price and not make a profit, lobby for government intervention to subsidize higher prices. Conflict between farmers and government is particularly acute in Europe and Japan, where the change to a more market-driven system for agricultural goods has been slow.

In sum, under pure competition, firms cannot really control their pricing but must accept the going rate. They face little or no strategic choices with respect to pricing. The firm's demand curve is horizontal.

Monopoly. Before we discuss the more common case of an oligopoly, let us consider the rather rare case of a monopoly (see Fig. 12.3, p. 477). Notice first that

FIGURE 12.2   PRICING UNDER PURE COMPETITION

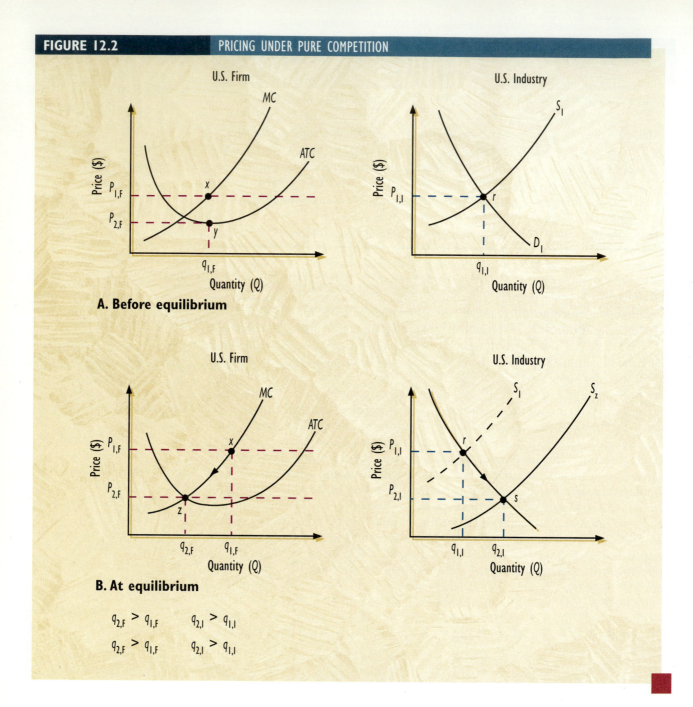

A. Before equilibrium

B. At equilibrium

$$q_{2,F} > q_{1,F} \qquad q_{2,I} > q_{1,I}$$
$$q_{2,F} > q_{1,F} \qquad q_{2,I} > q_{1,I}$$

monopolies (and oligopolies) face downward-sloping demand curves. Different quantities of the firm's product will be demanded at different prices. The monopolist therefore is able to make strategic choices with respect to the pricing decision.

A downward sloping demand curve has two important implications. First, a firm facing such a demand function knows that the quantity sold will be a function of the price it sets, and, therefore, care must be taken to determine the price best meeting the firm's goals. We call the movement along a particular demand curve arising from a change in price the *price elasticity of demand*. The important aspects of this are discussed in the next section of this chapter. For now, note that price elasticity of de-

FIGURE 12.3

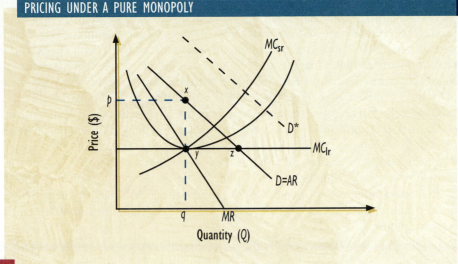

mand refers to the buyer's sensitivity to changes in the price of a product. It does not change the demand curve but rather exploits its properties.

The second implication of a downward-sloping demand curve is the concept of *demand shifts*. An example is shown in Figure 12.3, where the existing demand curve, D, is shown parallel to a potential new demand function D^* (shown as dashed lines). Demand actually increases from D to D^* to produce more units sold at a given price. Of course, the demand curve might shift to the left (i.e., decrease). A shift in demand might occur as a consequence of an increase or decrease in the purchasing power of consumers or a change in the price of a substitute for the product in question. It is important to recognize the distinction between price elasticity and shifts of demand. The phenomena have different causes and different implications for society, management, and the consumer, as developed below.

To return to pricing under a monopoly, we can see in Figure 12.3 that when MC equals MR, the firm will charge p and sell q. Notice that p is greater than MC here, whereas $p = MC$ under pure competition. First, unlike the profitless pure competitor, the monopolist usually achieves a profit: profit = $(x - y)q$. Indeed, its freedom to set a price within at least a narrow to moderate range almost assures this outcome. Second, whereas the pure competitor produces efficiently (i.e., at the minimum total cost per unit of output), the monopolist need not necessarily do so. However, it is possible for a monopolist to produce efficiently and/or fail to make a profit; nothing within economic theory prevents this from happening. On the other hand, given economic theory, pure competition must ultimately result in no profit and efficiency of production. These implications of the theories should be kept in mind, for they show that, in the sense of profits and productive efficiency of a firm, pure competition and monopoly need not differ, although they often do in practice. About the only differentiating point we can definitely make is that the price for a pure competitor will always equal marginal costs, whereas the price of a monopolist must be greater than marginal cost. Without demonstrating this here, one can show that the price a monopolist sets restricts output and results in less total consumer satisfaction in the market than had the firm set $p = MC$. Thus, in this sense, the price set by a monopolist is detrimental to social welfare.

The concept of a monopoly as a solitary seller does not exist in most countries except perhaps for relatively small firms in isolated geographical areas or for new products for a short time in their introductory stages. Some examples of large firms in the United States approaching a monopoly include Campbell, with about 85 percent of the canned soup market, and (up until deregulation) Western Electric, with about 85 percent of the telephone equipment market. But in recent years, even these firms have been losing market share as new competitors enter the market.

Oligopoly. An oligopoly occurs when there are a few sellers, and each has some effect on market price and possibly on the pricing practices of others in the industry. But how many sellers is "a few"? One author suggests that an oligopoly occurs when the leading four firms in an industry control at least 40 percent of the market.[2] By this rule of thumb, it is estimated that more than half of the firms in the United States operate in oligopolistic markets. Leading examples are the producers of beer, automobiles, ready-to-eat cereals, gasoline, refrigerators, computers, and copy machines.

Let us examine a typical oligopoly. Figure 12.4 displays the conditions faced by a two-firm oligopoly (i.e., a duopoly). For simplicity, we assume that the two firms have the same MR function and face demand D. However, firm A has higher marginal costs than does firm B (i.e., $MC_A > MC_B$). Under these conditions, firm A will prefer to set its price at P_A, whereas firm B will desire to set its price at P_B. Although not shown in the figure, one can easily see that the respective prices resulting from equating $MR = MC$ for firms A and B are optimum for each; and if one firm were forced to accept the price set by the other, profits would be lower. Therefore, the firms face a dilemma of what price to set. They must each take into account the potential pricing behavior of the other since the market will not support two different prices in the long run.

We know that the price each sets will most likely be somewhere between P_A and P_B, inclusive. But how will the firms decide on their own price levels? One way might involve direct contact and a negotiated price between P_A and P_B. However, one or both firms may prefer not to do this, to maintain a perceived competitive edge. Also it may violate a law against collusive agreements. A second manner of resolution might entail a decision process wherein each firm takes into account its best

| FIGURE 12.4 | PRICING UNDER A TWO-FIRM OLIGOPOLY |

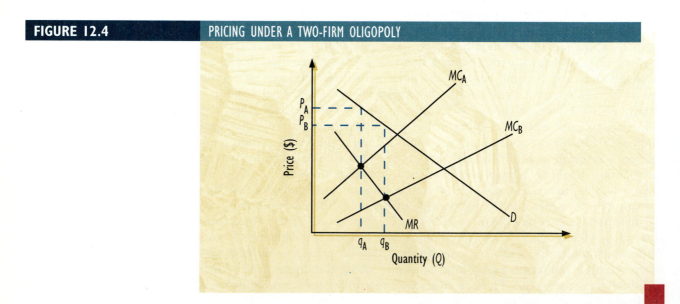

guess as to the action or reaction of the other firm before setting its own price. For example, firm B might decide, because it is in the better cost position, to take the lead and set a price slightly above P_B. In this way, it attains profits close to its optimum, but at the same time does not threaten firm A as much as if P_B were set. Thus, the likelihood for a pricing war is reduced. Nevertheless, this is not a very well defined rationale to tell us exactly what price will be set.

Economists have developed theories for predicting price in oligopolistic situations. These include explanations based on game theory, the theory of kinked demand functions, and other frameworks.[3] We limit our discussion here to kinked demand curves, for simplicity.[4] Figure 12.5 illustrates a typical case. Consider the kinked (i.e., bent) demand curve CKB faced by firms in an oligopolistic industry. This curve reflects the believed situation arising from decisions performed by rivals in the industry. Based on their judgments, the firms decide to price at p. Their logic is something like the following. For prices greater than p, the quantity sold will decrease rapidly because of the relatively flat portion of the demand curve CK. Therefore, no firm will be motivated to raise prices, as its profitability will be reduced (assuming other firms retain the lower price). This rationale rests on the assumption that, should one or two firms, say, raise their prices, then other firms can increase production and meet the excess demand, yet remain at their old price p. For prices less than p, in contrast, the quantity sold increases less rapidly than it might under nonkinked conditions. Thus, firms are not motivated to lower prices, as this too results in less profitability.

The kinked demand curve CKB can be derived from two demand curves implicitly faced by a decision maker. Demand curve AKB in Figure 12.5 represents the situation wherein the decision maker assumes that rivals will act so as to match any move of the decision maker. Demand curve CKD represents the situation wherein the decision maker assumes that rivals will hold their price constant at p no matter what the decision maker does. In the kinked demand theory, it is presumed that a decision maker anticipates that a rival will opt for the least favorable option in response to a price change. That is, if a decision maker decides to raise the price, it is assumed that rivals will stand pat. Similarly, if a decision maker decides to lower the price, it is presumed that rivals will follow suit. The combination of these strategies yields the kinked demand curve shown in Figure 12.5.

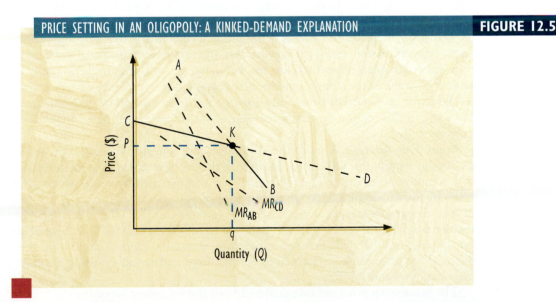

PRICE SETTING IN AN OLIGOPOLY: A KINKED-DEMAND EXPLANATION **FIGURE 12.5**

The important aspects of oligopolistic pricing are the following. First, firms have some leeway in setting prices. Second, nevertheless, they are interdependent with other firms, and this interdependence, in addition to restrictions resulting from cost and demand factors, constrains their actions. Third, based on kinked demand theory, firms tend to reject price cutting as a viable strategy. Fourth, firms also face pressures to hold prices constant, even in the face of moderate cost increases and shifts in the demand function.

Nevertheless, two limitations of kinked demand theory deserve mention.[5] First, empirical data have not always corresponded to the theory. Second, the theory does not accurately specify what exact level p will be achieved.

A final dimension of oligopolistic pricing is that the theory applies best for homogeneous products. Product differentiation tends to lessen the need for firms to take each other's actions into account, although it does not eliminate interdependencies among rivals for a share of the market.

Critique of Economic Theories of Price. Although economic theories represent useful frameworks for viewing price, they pose some drawbacks. Perhaps the most significant shortcoming concerns the assumptions upon which most models are based. Consumers are assumed to have perfect knowledge (e.g., to be aware of all brands and prices) and to maximize utility. To the extent that they are ignorant of alternative brands and use decision rules other than utility maximization, the theory will be in error. At the same time, economic theories presume that managers have knowledge of costs and demand, but considerable error can exist here as well. Further, economic theories have not as yet fully integrated other decision requisites with the pricing decision. In fact, most economic theories assume that product, communication, and distribution decisions have already been made or do not interact with the pricing decisions. Finally, the economic theories omit determinants of price, such as power and conflict within the firm over goals and resources, and social and political constraints.

Cost Structures

Pricing behavior is obviously influenced by costs. But the nature and extent of the effects are not well understood. In the long run, costs provide a lower bound on what prices a firm sets. However, everyday price setting is guided more by short-run considerations, with costs only suggesting rough guidelines. We might think of the pricing behavior of firms as being influenced by many forces: competition, costs, demand, social and legal constraints, and strategic managerial considerations related to goals of profitability, market share, growth, and marketing mix interactions. Each of these forces might, on occasion, have a separate effect on pricing behavior, and at other times only one or a few forces might be determinative. We focus in this section on cost forces, but it should be remembered that cost is only one input.

Break-even Analysis. One of the most basic cost concepts is break-even analysis. To understand this idea, let us begin with the problem faced by a small retailer of automotive accessories. The retailer has been approached by a salesperson who is selling car ice scrapers. The wholesale price offer to the retailer is $1.50 for this deluxe, all-purpose scraper. This, then, is the variable cost (VC) to the retailer. The retailer estimates that sales of ice scrapers will entail a fixed cost (FC) of about $600 for the year, and that, based on past experience, about 400 can be sold to local residents. What price must be charged to recover fixed and variable costs at this estimated sales volume (q_E)?

The break-even price can be calculated from the following formula:

$$P = \frac{FC + VC \times q_E}{q_E}$$

$$= \frac{\$600 + \$1.50 \times 400}{400}$$

$$= \$3.00$$

This is the price under which sales volume exactly covers fixed plus variable costs. A price greater than $3.00 would produce a profit.

Actually, the retailer's problem could have been reformulated in slightly different terms. That is, given VC and estimated FC, the retailer might have felt that the price that had to be charged (as a result of market forces) was "about $3.00." The problem is then to determine what quantity would have to be sold to break even. The break-even quantity can be calculated from the above formula, rearranged as follows:

$$q_{BE} = \frac{FC}{P - VC}$$

Substitution into this equation yields $q_{BE} = 400$. Figure 12.6 presents a graphic representation of the concepts in break-even analysis.

Break-even analysis is often a useful tool for making decisions. It formally introduces cost constraints into the decision-making process. However, it has a fundamental limitation. To calculate a break-even price, one must estimate demand. Conversely, to calculate a break-even quantity, one must estimate a viable price. Hence, the value of the approach is limited by the means and accuracy of demand or price estimation procedures. Perhaps more disconcerting, whichever way one applies the formula—either to determine price or to determine demand—one must assume that either demand or price is given. In other words, the theory assumes that, if we use the formula to compute price, we have no influence over demand (and vice versa). In reality, depending on the market structure, price influences demand, and demand influences price. So in this sense, the theory is based on a false assumption.

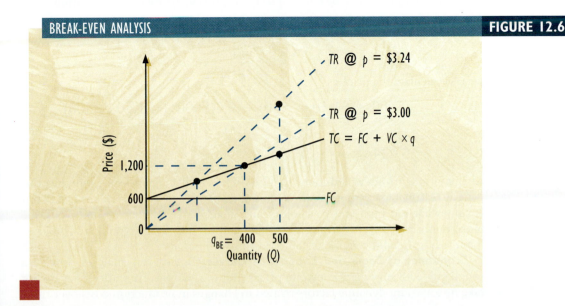

BREAK-EVEN ANALYSIS   **FIGURE 12.6**

Marketing Anecdote 12.1

Break-Even Analysis in the Airline Industry

Lufthansa Airlines reported operating losses of $315 million in 1991. To stem the losses and return to profitability, Chairman Juergen Weber used a break-even analysis to guide his corrective actions, which focused primarily on drastic cuts in fixed and variable costs. Weber froze wages, reduced entry-level salaries, increased hours worked by pilots and crews, downsized the workforce by about 6,000 people, reduced capital spending, removed 26 aircraft from regular service, and combined some European and North Atlantic routes. The measures worked. Lufthansa broke even by the second quarter of 1993 and today is again profitable.

Source: Adapted from Anthony L. Velocci Jr., "Lufthansa Managers Buoyed by Second-Quarter Results," *Aviation Week & Space Technology*, July 12, 1993, p. 30.

Moreover, the theory assumes that costs can be validly divided into fixed and variable components. Although this is true in the short run, it is definitely not true in the long run because most costs are effectively variable. Another problematic assumption is linearity in costs—nonlinearities may be the rule.

Nevertheless, in practice, managers have found that break-even analyses provide useful guidelines and occasionally are accurate (see Marketing Anecdote 12.1). Sometimes, because of information limitations, break-even analyses are the only procedures that can be applied. A final point to note is that break-even analyses have been used also to estimate the price needed to yield a *target rate of return.* To see this usage, let us return to Figure 12.6. Suppose the retailer of ice scrapers again estimates $FC = \$600$ and $VC = \$1.50$, and further suppose that the salesperson, as an incentive, offers to pay for an advertisement in the local newspaper for each of the first four weeks in late fall. The retailer might predict that with the free advertising 500 scrapers could be sold.

Assuming that the retailer normally aspires to make a 20 percent profit above total costs, what price must be charged to realize this goal? By using the formula

$$P = \frac{FC + VC \times q_E}{q_E}$$

we can calculate the price as

$$P = \frac{(\$600 + \$1.50 \times 500) + 0.2(\$600 + \$1.50 \times 500)}{500}$$

$$= \$3.24$$

At this price, profits will amount to $270. The retailer must decide whether this price is reasonable to stimulate the required demand. The retailer might feel that it is somewhat too high and psychologically unattractive. Perhaps $3.19 would be more unobtrusive. With an estimated demand of 500, $3.19 would still be profitable, as the break-even price is $2.70 at this volume.

Economies of Scale and Experience Curves. Break-even analyses provide a rough guide for how costs constrain prices. But the analyses are static. They do not take into account dynamic factors related to changes in production costs over time, size of an organization, its technology and production functions, and other factors. Two important cost-related forces shaping price are *economies of scale* and *experience curve effects*. Economies of scale refer to decreases in the costs of producing a product per unit as the volume of production increases over time. This results from more efficiently using inputs and spreading fixed costs over a greater volume. Actually, it is possible to achieve economies of scale in nearly every phase of an organization's operations, from manufacturing, to purchasing, marketing, and research and development, for example. Economies of scale are important market forces allowing firms producing at high volumes to set relatively lower prices than smaller firms.

Experience curves refer to the phenomenon of declines in unit costs as a firm accrues experience over time in the production of a product.[6] In general, costs decline by a constant amount each time the *cumulative* output doubles. ("Cumulative" here means that past output is added to present output at each point in time to yield a new total, termed cumulative output. The idea is that past experience should result in some learning and that a measure of this can be gained by adding past output to present output at each point in time.) Figure 12.7 illustrates the principle of the experience curve: as cumulative output increases, costs decline by a constant amount, given by the slope of the line.

Why should costs decline? Presumably, the firm "learns" over time to better coordinate production, increase the productivity of machinery and equipment, and so on. Presumably, workers also better learn how to perform their tasks over time. Thus, costs decline over time.

Notice that the experience curve phenomenon is different from the cost savings resulting from economies of scale. Economies of scale depend on the size of the firm and can be achieved even in the short run. Learning from experience requires time and occurs to a certain extent for all firms, even smaller ones. The phenomena described by experience curves and economies of scale arise from different determinants of costs.

As with economies of scale, when experience accrues and costs decline, a basis exists for setting a relatively lower price. Figure 12.8 shows how this happened for the Ford Model T automobile in the first quarter of this century. Notice that the price dropped from nearly $4,000 in 1909 to about $1,000 in 1923. Much of this drop was due to both experience effects and economies of scale.

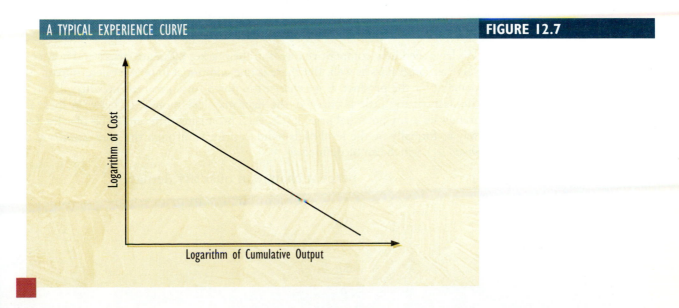

A TYPICAL EXPERIENCE CURVE　　　　　　　　　　　　　**FIGURE 12.7**

Logarithm of Cost

Logarithm of Cumulative Output

Source: William J. Abernathy and Kenneth Wayne, "Limits of the Learning Curve," Harvard Business Review 52 (September–October 1974), p. 111.

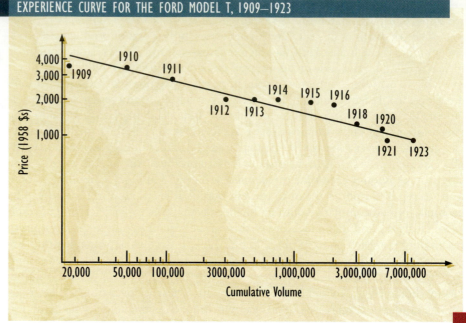

Finally, we should realize that it is not time, per se, that drives costs downward. Rather it is the particular learning in time that is crucial. By enhancing the conditions for learning, the slope of the experience curve can be made steeper.

Other Cost Considerations. Costs depend on many factors, but because of space limitations, we can do little more than list them here. One factor depends on the bargaining power of the firm, which, in turn, will be a function of the availability of substitute goods, the number and size of suppliers, the size of the focal firm and its purchase amount, and other factors. Similarly, the nature of the firm's accounting and costing procedures will affect computed costs and, hence, prices. Finally, a whole host of economic and technical forces within and outside the firm will also shape costs.

Price Elasticity

We have seen how competitive forces in the market influence prices and how costs serve as constraints as well. But there is one additional important determinant: the demand for the product. If we charge too much for a product, no one will buy it. Similarly, if too little is charged, the firm may lose money. In between these extremes lie many potential price levels, each promising different levels of sales. One way to formally tie the level of demand to price is through the *price elasticity of demand* (e_p), which can be defined as

$$e_p = \frac{\text{percent change in quantity demanded}}{\text{percent change in price}}$$

$$= \frac{\dfrac{\Delta q}{q}}{\dfrac{\Delta p}{p}}$$

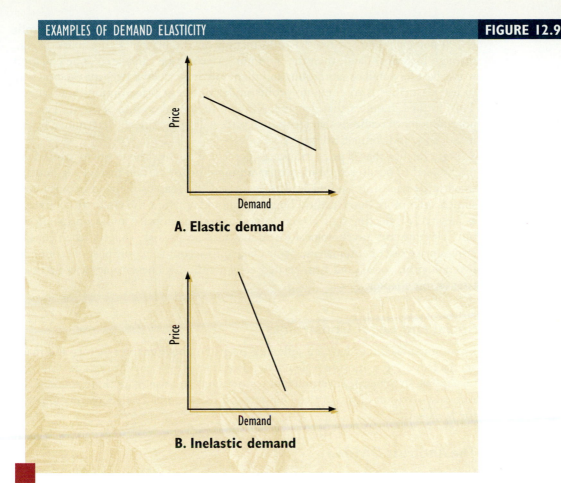

A. Elastic demand

B. Inelastic demand

This equation shows how much of a change in sales we can expect if we change price by a particular amount. Three possible values for e_p deserve mention. First, consider $e_p < -1$. Here the percentage change in quantity demanded is greater than the percentage change in price. For example, if price decreases from \$5 to \$4 and sales go from 2,000 to 3,000 units, then $e_p = -2.5$. It can be shown that total revenue will increase if $e_p < -1$. We say that demand is therefore elastic (see Fig. 12.9A). If $e_p = -1$, then the percentage change in demand equals the percentage change in price. Here no change in revenues will result from a price change. This is called unity elasticity. Finally, if $0 > e_p > -1$, then the percentage change in quantity demanded will be less than the percentage change in price. Total revenues will decrease with a price cut. We say that demand is thus inelastic (see Fig. 12.9B). Generally, for the vast majority of products, e_p will be negative.

The concept of elasticity is useful as a tool for showing how revenues will change if we change prices. By doing a sensitivity analysis, one can determine the range of prices producing a corresponding range in revenues. Of course, managers are often more concerned with the effect of price on profits. Consequently, one needs to take into account costs as well as revenue when considering elasticity effects. From economic theory considerations,[7] it can be shown that profits will be maximized when

$$\text{Percent of markup} = \frac{-1}{1 + e_p} \times 100\%$$

For example, for $e_p = -2$, the percent of markup on costs needed to maximize profit is 100 percent. Thus, if one has information on the elasticity of a market (e.g., through historical data), then the optimum price can be calculated. The equation works best for retail organizations and then only imperfectly. Perhaps the best way to use elasticities is to compute profits under different price options and ranges. This, in turn, requires that demand, VC, and FC be taken into account. The important point to realize is that an optimal price will be complexly determined by demand, cost, and competitive forces.

Note further that if price influences perceived quality, the elasticity coefficient might need to be altered. Within certain ranges or for certain market segments, a small price rise (drop) might lead to increased (decreased) demand because consumers infer more (less) quality. Thus, one should not view the elasticity coefficient as inevitably reflecting only classic economic notions of price and quantity effects, but that consumer psychological forces may also be at work. Indeed, when considering a price rise or cut, managers must take into account a whole host of economic, psychological, social, and firm-related considerations. These topics are discussed later in this chapter.

Social and Legal Constraints

Environmental forces have an influence over and above market factors and managerial leeway. The most prevalent and powerful forces occur through governmental actions. In general, governmental restrictions can arise from three sources: the Antitrust Division of the Justice Department, the Federal Trade Commission, and the president.[8]

The Antitrust Division

In the United States, the Antitrust Division of the Justice Department has responsibility for enforcing antitrust laws. It shares this responsibility with the Federal Trade Commission. The Antitrust Division's activities are divided between the investigation of violations of laws and the initiation of court action against alleged violators. Court action occurs in cases adjudicated before one of the federal district courts. Although both the FTC and Antitrust Division can initiate civil actions against violators of antitrust laws, only the latter can engage in criminal complaints. Table 12.2 summarizes the more important antitrust legislation since its inception with the Sherman Act of 1890. With respect to pricing, the most important aspects of legislation apply to price fixing, price discrimination, and deceptive pricing.

Price Fixing. Price fixing is any agreement among firms to set prices at levels in concert with each other. Such a practice is illegal in the United States but is allowed in many parts of the world in one form or another. The rationale for the U.S. legislation is basically that price fixing is a restraint of trade and lessens competition. The Justice Division generally seeks criminal prosecution of price fixers under Section 1 of the Sherman Act. The penalties for conviction now may include personal fines of $100,000 and corporate fines of $1 million per count and/or prison sentences up to three years. The Justice Division can, of course, institute civil suits that may result in court injunctions to cease and desist from the illegal practices. Further, the Clayton Act permits persons injured by antitrust violators to sue for three times the amount of damages (commonly called "treble damages"). To give a picture of the extent of legal action, by the early 1980s corporate fines often totaled $11 million yearly, as many as 30 people per year were sentenced to an average of 100 days in prison, and private antitrust suits per year often totaled more than 1,500.

TABLE 12.2 SUMMARY OF SOME IMPORTANT LEGAL DEVELOPMENTS AFFECTING PRICING BEHAVIOR IN THE UNITED STATES

Date	Development	Description
1890	Sherman Act	Section 1: "Every contract, combination in the form of trust or otherwise, or conspiracy, in restraint of trade . . . is . . . illegal."
		Section 2: "Every person who shall monopolize, or attempt to monopolize . . . any part of trade . . . shall be deemed guilty . . ." and penalized by imprisonment and/or fine.
		Section 4: Attorney General empowered to initiate suits.
		Section 7: Injured private persons can sue for recovery of three times the amount of damage.
1903	Antitrust Division of Justice Department	Created to enforce Sherman Act
1914	Clayton Act	Section 2: ". . . it shall be unlawful . . . to discriminate in price between different purchasers . . . when the effect of such discrimination may be to substantially lessen competition or tend to create a monopoly. . . . Provided that nothing . . . shall prevent discrimination in price . . . on account of differences in the grade, quality or quantity of the commodity sold, or . . . for differences in the cost of selling or transportation, or . . . to meet competition . . ."
1914	Federal Trade Commission Act	Section 5: Outlawed "unfair methods of competition." Set up an agency to enforce Clayton Act, investigate business practices, perform research, and conduct conferences.
1936	Robinson-Patman Act	Section 2a: ". . . it is unlawful . . . to discriminate in price between different purchasers for commodities of like grade and quality . . . where the effect . . . may be substantially to lessen competition or tend to create a monopoly . . ." But discrimination may be permitted to dispose of perishable, obsolescent, or seasonal goods; to make due allowances for differences in "the cost of manufacture, sale, or delivery"; or "in good faith to meet an equally low price of a competitor."
1938	Wheeler-Lea Amendment to FTC Act	Broadened FTC's jurisdiction to include practices that injure the public broadly and not merely those that directly injure a competitor. For example: deceptive advertising.
1974	Federal Antitrust Statute	Makes it a felony to violate federal antitrust laws; increases fines for individuals up to $100,000, for corporations up to $1,000,000 per count; and for violation of the Sherman Act, extends upper limit of prison sentences to three years.
1983	*Fall City Industries, Inc.,* v. *Vanco Beverage, Inc.* (51 LW 4275)	Clarifies and amplifies the "marketing competition" defense of Robinson-Patman Act by permitting seller to offer price differentials when a competitor has lower prices in a general area of selling.

This tends to understate the impact of the law, as the threat of legal action often results in out-of-court settlements. The law also serves as a deterrent, forcing firms to carefully weigh their actions.

Price Discrimination. Price discrimination occurs whenever there are unjustified price differences for the same product sold by a single seller. The Clayton Act directly forbids it (as does its amendment, the Robinson-Patman Act). However, discrimination is permitted (1) if cost differences exist in manufacture, selling, or delivery; (2) if the price is needed to meet lawful competition; or (3) if the price reflects different uses for the product, distribution in different markets, or sales at different points in time. (Other conditions apply, but are too numerous to mention here.)

The rationale for legislation against price discrimination rests with the belief that price discrimination restrains trade and lessens competition. Indeed, some economists feel that price discrimination additionally influences the distribution of income and allocative efficiency in detrimental ways. The interpretation of the law has sometimes been so difficult that some firms have refrained from using price as a stimulus but rather have resorted to nonprice competition out of fear of possible infringement. Whether this has enhanced or thwarted overall competition is difficult to judge. Moreover, although the original logic behind legislation was to protect small businesses, the vast majority of enforcement procedures has occurred against small businesses rather than their larger rivals. Nevertheless, since the early 1960s, when the number of price discrimination complaints was about 74 per year, activity has subsided considerably to an average of less than 6 per year in the last decade or so.

Deceptive Pricing. Deceptive pricing is an umbrella term used to capture a variety of practices. One form of deceptive pricing concerns false claims as to the amount of discount offered the public. For example, some furniture retailers have been known to claim a huge discount on a new piece of furniture where the undiscounted price has been inflated considerably. Another form of price deception occurs when the seller overcharges on numerous options associated with a base product. The automobile industry has been an alleged perpetrator of this practice, although the 1958 Automobile Information Disclosure Act makes this somewhat more difficult to do. Still another form of deceptive pricing is the presence of hidden charges or other costs. In the area of consumer credit services, for example, the 1969 Truth in Lending Law requires up-front disclosure of all finance charges and the actual interest rate charged on an annual basis. Unfortunately, there are so many ways to deceptively present prices in the marketplace that one cannot hope to rely on a law for each. Although the Federal Trade Commission is active through prosecution and the setting of guidelines for sellers, one must, in the end, rely perhaps more on a combination of trust in the seller and vigilance on the part of the buyer.

The Federal Trade Commission

The Federal Trade Commission is a federal agency charged with performing both investigatory and adjudicative functions related to business practices. It is responsible for enforcing compliance to the same legislation as under the charge of the Antitrust Division of the Justice Department. It does this through the issue of decrees (a direct communication to a violator) or formal complaints issued in court. In addition, the FTC (1) holds trade practices conferences where industries participate in reviews of their practices with the FTC; (2) conducts research on economic, marketing, or financial matters related to unfair competition or deceptive practices; and (3) investigates complaints initiated by others. An important aspect of the FTC is the investigation and adjudication of deceptive practices such as false or misleading advertising, as well as the pricing irregularities noted above. Much of its powers and responsibilities stem from the 1914 FTC Act and the 1938 Wheeler-Lea Amendment to the FTC Act (see Tab. 12.2).

The President

The final environmental constraints we consider are directives originating from the president and other officials in the Executive Branch of the federal government. Although usually reserved for grave emergencies such as wartime, the president has occasionally issued controls in "normal times." In 1971, for example, President Nixon instituted a three-month wage and price freeze. Further controls were instituted in 1972 and 1973, but were eliminated in 1974 after numerous problems arose with shortages of products such as fertilizers, steel, petroleum, and food. The reason the shortages came about can perhaps be best seen in the case of the petroleum industry. The president froze heating oil prices at the level of August 1971, a low point for the year. In normal times, manufacturers begin in late summer to produce heating oil in anticipation of the coming winter. However, the low price set during the 1971 price freeze discouraged this, so they switched to the production of more gasoline, which was fixed at a very high price because of the time of year. The net result was a shortage of heating oil in the winter. The problem was compounded further by a simultaneous high worldwide demand for petroleum (precipitated by economic boom times nearly everywhere) and price increases by the Organization of Petroleum Exporting Countries (OPEC).

Because of the impossibility of achieving adequate and equitable controls, the president obviously prefers not to contemplate their application. As an alternative, "jawboning" or "moral suasion" is often employed. Presidents since Kennedy have resorted to persuasive attempts to induce sellers to voluntarily restrain wage and price increases. Predictably, this has resulted in mixed success at best. It is a very difficult task for government to control prices, and both market and planned economies have found that attempts to do so often backfire.

BEHAVIORAL FOUNDATIONS OF PRICING

Economic models and common sense suggest that consumers take into account the prices of products and services in their consumption decisions. But exactly how and to what extent do they do so?

Figure 12.10 presents an outline of consumers' psychological processes between the time they first become aware of the price of a product and the time they integrate the price and its meaning for them with other decision criteria, prior to deciding whether to purchase.[9] Consider first on-line processes in the center of the figure, which occur in short-term memory. The input to on-line processes arises from two sources. First, consumers retrieve information concerning prices from memory (path a in Fig. 12.10). This might entail the recall of the price paid in the past or witnessed previously in the media, or it may involve the mental construction of an expected price. Consumer reference prices are crude measures of such expectations.[10] Second, consumers learn about prices through presentation of such stimuli as advertising, salespersons' pitches, point-of-purchase displays, or word of mouth communication (path b).

Figure 12.10 shows that the perception of prices leads either to automatic processes (path c) or deliberate processes (path d). Automatic processes are appraisals or action tendencies, which directly influence an intention to purchase (path e). This happens for frequently purchased products when consumers act out of habit and select needed products if prices are in acceptable, familiar ranges. It also occurs for impulse items when prices are perceived as enticingly low. Still another instance of automatic activation of intentions as a function of price happens when consumers decide at time 1 to purchase goods at time 2, on the contingency that the price must drop below some predetermined level.

Deliberative processes begin with cognitive elaboration of perceived price information. Sometimes the information is stored in long-term memory to be used later in decision making (path f). At other times, the information is evaluated immediately for its meaning by consumers (path g). Evaluative processes are either simple, such as manifest in the application of rules (e.g., simple go–no go decisions based on

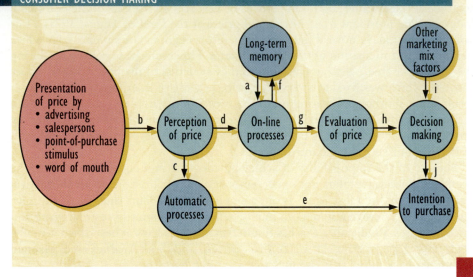

ongoing standards), or complex, such as involved in the assessment of multiple consequences of purchase and integration of the assessments into a summary representation (e.g., expectancy-value attitudes).

Evaluative processes influence decision making directly (path h) and become coordinated with information obtained from other marketing mix stimuli (path i). We return to the components of decision making later in this section of the chapter. The influence of price ends with the intention to purchase (path j).

Each of the steps shown in Figure 12.10 is subject to distortion or breakdown, thus making the effects of prices on decision making problematic. Research is only now beginning to address the processes shown in Figure 12.10.

One area in which insights have been gained is the study of the encoding of price information. In one study, researchers surveyed consumers in supermarkets immediately after items were placed in shopping carts.[11] Consumers were asked to recall the price of the item. Surprisingly, only 47.1 percent of shoppers could recall the price of the item selected, and only 58.9 percent of shoppers claimed to have checked the price before selecting the item. Given that knowledge of prices is a necessary condition for decision making, as implied by economic theories,[12] it thus appears that consumers use price information in decision making, if at all, in complex ways.

How do consumers take into account prices of goods and services? Some research suggests that consumers react not so much to objective price levels and compare these to internal standards or reference prices, but rather they respond subjectively to cues that, whether valid or not, hint at low prices (e.g., point-of-purchase claims of specials).[13] At least, this has been documented in a number of studies. Nevertheless, other research indicates that consumers do, on occasion, compare low price claims to prices stored in memory.[14]

Researchers are now focusing upon the conditions that lead consumers to respond either thoughtlessly or thoughtfully to price information. For example, one study found that as income of consumers increases, accuracy of price recall actually decreases.[15] Likewise, it was found that a brand's promotion status serves as a cue that prompts consumers to process price-related information in greater depth and therefore subsequently recall price more accurately.

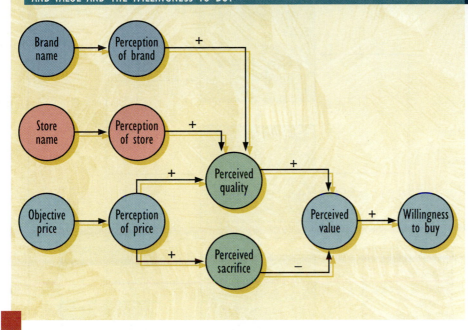

FIGURE 12.11

EFFECTS OF PRICE, BRAND NAME, AND STORE NAME ON PERCEIVED QUALITY, SACRIFICE, AND VALUE AND THE WILLINGNESS TO BUY

Source: William B. Dodds, Kent B. Monroe, and Dhruv Grewal, "Effects of Price, Brand, and Store Information on Buyers' Product Evaluations," Journal of Marketing Research *(August 1991): 308.*

The integrative model in Figure 12.11 presents an overview of how price information is processed and coordinated with information on brand name and store name.[16] Perceived value directly determines the willingness of consumers to buy. It is a judgment made by consumers through the cognitive integration of two competing appraisals: perception of product or service quality (see chapter 7) and perception of the sacrifice a buyer must endure to purchase the product or service. As quality increases, value increases; conversely, as the sacrifice increases, value decreases. Sacrifice is basically governed by the price the consumer must pay to acquire a product or purchase a service. It includes the sales price plus other costs incurred, where the latter might encompass transportation, storage, opportunity, and psychological costs.

Perceived quality is a function of the processing of three cues: perception of the brand (see chapter 8), price, and store, if applicable. Although it is possible for brand, store, and price to have independent effects on perceived quality, some research suggests interactive effects: brand name and store name cues enhance the effect of price on perceptions of quality.[17] The model in Figure 12.11 is supported in a study of the purchase of calculators and stereo headset players.[18]

PRICE SETTING IN PRACTICE: STRATEGIES AND TACTICS

Behavioral theories of consumer reactions to price rest on a stimulus → organism → response conceptualization. That is, price as a stimulus is acted upon psychologically by consumers, and the particular reaction is determined by the nature of the psychological processes involved. Managers must take into account how consumers process pricing information if they are to make effective decisions. The approaches managers use to set prices take into account consumer behavior to different degrees, ranging from little or no consideration of consumer behavior to more informed points of view.

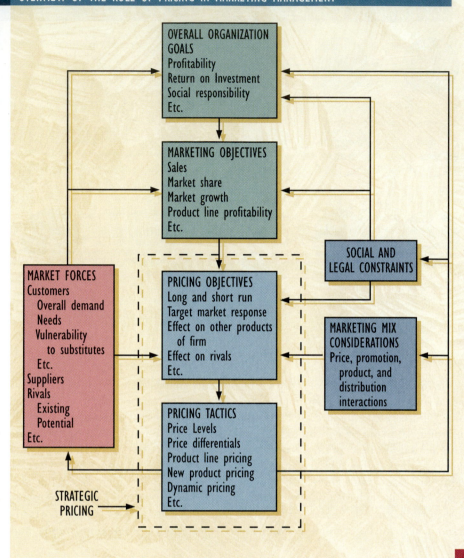

Figure 12.12 summarizes the central components in price setting. Notice first that a pricing program begins with *overall organization goals*. These are the ultimate ends and objectives necessary for the survival of the firm and the effective implementation of its mission. The goals are typically formulated as targets related to profitability, return on investment, meeting customer needs, being socially responsible in terms of employment and the environment, and so on. These central goals influence and constrain the means required to meet the goals. Broadly speaking, the means encompass production, personnel, marketing, research and development, financial, accounting, and other programs. Each of these, in turn, has its own subgoals, termed "objectives." Only *marketing objectives* are displayed in Figure 12.12, but the objectives of the other programs interact with these. Marketing objectives reflect goals for sales, market share, market growth, product-line profitability, brand image, and so on. Although the line between marketing objectives and the goals of the firm is often a fine one, the former are derived from the latter and are more spe-

cific and/or serve as intermediate steps in the pursuit of the latter. Similarly, *pricing objectives* are even more specific and focused than marketing objectives. They typically serve as substeps needed to achieve the marketing objectives.

The most important pricing objective is the desired target market and its response: that is, what is the target market, how does it behave, and what response do we desire from it with what price strategy? The objective might be to attract a particular segment, to penetrate a market, to generate as much revenue as possible in the short run, or to smooth out seasonal fluctuations in demand, for example. Similarly, specific goals for trial and repeat buying in particular markets or segments may be specified.

Somewhat less important, but nevertheless essential, are goals related to other products in the firm and to competitive rivals. For instance, the firm might have a policy that the price set for a new product should enhance the quality image of the company, should not compete or conflict with the prices of other products, and should not cannibalize their sales, as well. Similarly, with respect to rivals, the policy might be to meet competition, to act as a price leader, or to undercut the largest market shareholder, among other possibilities. There are other pricing objectives, but the aforementioned are the most fundamental. A key analysis to perform is quality functional deployment (see chapter 8), where firm constraints are balanced against competitive and customer criteria.

Note in Figure 12.12 that pricing objectives are not merely derivatives of marketing objectives and organizational goals. In fact, pricing objectives are also strongly influenced by market forces, social and legal constraints, and marketing mix considerations. Consider first the role of market forces. Pricing objectives depend on the size and nature of the potential market. The psychology of consumers is a factor, as is the availability of substitute sources of satisfaction through completely different products. Managers must gain an understanding of how consumers will respond to different price levels and how a focal product relates to consumers' total market basket. Suppliers play a role largely through their bargaining relationship with the focal firm and the effect this has on the latter's costs. And when setting pricing objectives, the firm must consider not only the reactions of existing rivals but the potential for new entrants. A low price, for example, risks retaliation from an old rival, whereas a high price invites the entry of a new rival. Next, social and legal constraints provide direct guidelines that need to be taken into account in any pricing program. We discussed these earlier in this chapter.

Finally, marketing mix considerations constitute perhaps the most complex interactions. Indeed, any response of a market will depend upon the pattern of pricing, promotion, product, and distribution stimuli. Each of the marketing mix stimuli has the potential to complement or interfere with the others, depending on the circumstances. Hence, the firm must thoughtfully coordinate its marketing tactics if it is to obtain the desired response.

After a firm has set sound pricing objectives, it is in a position to implement them through pricing tactics (see Figure 12.12). *Pricing tactics* refer to the specific actions the firm takes, as reflected in the price levels it sets, price differentials, product line pricing, new product pricing, dynamic pricing (i.e., pricing over time), and other actions. These actions, in turn, feed back upon marketing forces, the marketing mix, social and legal constraints, marketing objectives, and goals of the firm. Pricing tactics for the Internet, for example, are discussed in Marketing Anecdote 12.2.

Traditional Managerial Approaches to Pricing

Although most firms perform break-even analyses of one form or another, only a minority go much beyond this to take into account such criteria as noted in Figure 12.12. Even for these latter firms, activities are often limited to a specification of one

The price to charge for a product or service is a complex decision that involves appraisals of customer needs, costs, and competitor behavior. Often it takes time and adjustments in tactics to get things right.

Consider the case of pricing services on the Internet. In early 1996, AT&T's WorldNet Service was the first Internet company to offer unlimited monthly services at a flat rate of $19.95 per month. This was perceived as a bargain by consumers, and soon CompuServe, Netcom On-line Communication Services, Sprint, MCI Communications, and America Online,

Although the Internet provides access to products and information unimaginable even ten years ago, Internet providers still have to decide how to price their services to users and to advertisers.

among others, followed suit. To compound matters, many small competitors with little corporate or brand name recognition entered the market, only to confuse consumers further.

But by early 1997, many firms began to have second thoughts. The main problem was that the $19.95 fee did not cover costs, let alone provide for a profit. In addition to advertising and promotional costs, the primary costs to Internet providers include infrastructure costs and customer support costs. One industry expert estimated that the break-even point for flat-rate use is 8 to 10 hours

objective and its relation to a single tactic. For example, some firms set the prices for their products based on the criterion of short-run profit maximization. It will prove informative to briefly examine a few of the more frequently applied approaches in order to discover their assets and shortcomings and point the way to needed developments.

Commonsense or "Seat of the Pants" Pricing

Managers, who for one reason or another know little about the psychology of consumers but who nevertheless have acquired considerable wisdom over the years, use a number of rules of thumb to set prices. We consider a few of these below.

Customary Pricing

Customary pricing is the practice of using a single, well-known price for an extended period of time. Thus, for as long as possible, newspaper publishers have tried to maintain the price of a daily paper at 75 cents, theaters have attempted to keep

of usage per month. With many users calling the help lines and many partaking in 20 or more hours of use per month, providers have had to reassess their pricing policies.

Firms such as Netcom On-Line and CompuServe have abandoned flat-rate fees and returned to hourly charges. Other firms have narrowed the services provided under flat rates and charge extra for such services as customer support and high-speed connectivity. Still others have instituted tiered pricing schemes for the amount and type of services demanded. In early 1997, Prodigy Internet offered a two-tiered scheme: unlimited monthly services for $19.95; 10 hours per month for $9.95. It is likely that soon firms offering tiered-pricing will need a third level for usage greater than 20 hours per month.

America Online, currently the largest provider, with more than 7 million customers, instituted its flat-rate pricing in December 1996, and may be one of the few providers able to sustain the $19.95 pricing scheme. Its infrastructure costs are estimated at only $0.25 per hour, whereas competitors' infrastructure costs are between $0.80 and $1.30 per hour per user.

Providers are facing many problems. It is difficult to estimate demand. In addition to an unknown total market potential, high variability of usage is common, and the need for on-line help is equally unpredictable. Costs are difficult to anticipate, too, and vary considerably by firm. Part of the constraints are economies of scale. A number of firms operate with only 500,000 customers, whereas others supply millions. Then, too, many competitors exist, services are numerous and complex, and advertising is perceived inadequate, confusing, and gimmicky. These factors, coupled with uncertainty on the part of consumers as to why and how much they might use the Internet, explain why consumers feel confused.

In the short run, consumers need simplified pricing schemes until they learn better about the Internet and their personal needs. In the long run, we are likely to see a shake-out and consolidation as firms discover whether Internet access is a viable business for them.

Source: Jared Sandberg and Thomas E. Weber, "Why the $19.95 Internet Fees May Not Last," *Wall Street Journal*, December 24, 1996, p. B6.

the price of movie tickets at about $7, and taverns have fought to hold the price of a beer below $2. Presumably, the logic of customary pricing is that consumers get used to paying a certain amount over time and, especially for frequently purchased products, might come to resent a price change. Customary prices and frequent purchases lead consumers to take the costs of consumption for granted. But price changes serve as shocks, making the cost of the product salient. Moreover, from the retailer's perspective, the maintenance of prices tends to reduce administrative work associated with changing price tags, updating records, and other tasks. Because the costs to the seller frequently rise, however, some adjustments eventually must be made. Typically, to maintain profits, and at the same time retain the customary price, the seller must reduce the size of the product or alter its ingredients in the face of cost increases. This has its own dangers, however, and can be done only infrequently. For example, although candy bar producers are able to periodically shave an ounce or two off the "standard" size, they can do this only once or twice without reaching a point where people will no longer perceive the bar to be worth the price or to satisfy their cravings for a snack. In periods of rapid inflation with rising costs for raw materials and labor, manufacturers are often forced to make numerous adjustments in product size and quality. Indeed, the pressures are such as to ultimately require a price change, and a new customary price must be set, with the cycle beginning anew.

Charm Pricing

Sellers often set prices on the basis of the presumed psychological meaning of the numbers used to express the prices—a method called charm pricing. In what might be termed the tactic of *conspicuous consumption pricing*, a high price is set with the hope that buyers will perceive the product to be unique, consist of special ingredients, or reflect exemplary workmanship. The thinking is also that people buy things not only for what the product is in a physical sense but also for what it means in broader psychological or social senses. A high price might even be sought by some potential purchasers as part of their need to express a particular lifestyle or communicate their wealth and taste in a public way. Rather than reflecting the material costs of the products, per se, prices of goods and services in boutiques, specialty shops, and exclusive restaurants often stem from a conspicuous consumption pricing policy.

Another form of charm pricing is called *odd-or-even pricing*. A common belief among some retailers is that a price should end only in an odd number (usually a 5, 7, or 9) *or* only in an even number (typically an 8). Furthermore, whenever possible, it is recommended that the odd or even number be part of an overall price set just below a round number. For example, the strategy is based on the premise that $1.98 will be perceived to be more than 2 cents less than $2.00 or that 49 cents will be taken to be greater than a penny below 50 cents. When should one use an odd or an even price? No research exists and the logic is unclear, but it may be that an even price has the advantage of being both aesthetically pleasing and unobtrusive, whereas an odd price is more dissonant and eye-catching. Hence, the choice of one tactic over the other involves trade-offs and is largely a matter of opinion or trial and error.

Still another variant of charm pricing is what one might call *representational pricing*. Here the seller selects a price for a product on the basis of the symbolic meaning of the number as reflected in another object, event, or behavior associated with that number. For instance, pieces of furniture will sometimes be priced at $1,776, souvenirs will be offered at $7 or $11, and drinks in a nightclub at special times such as "the happy hour" will be sold at 69 cents. Can you guess what these numbers might mean *and* why they are used in these specific cases? Overall, practitioners of representational pricing hope that the affect or feelings connected with a number will transfer to their products and perhaps be remembered more readily.

Price Lining

Price lining is the tactic of offering a number of variations of a type of product with each variation priced at a different level. Generally, three different versions of a product will be displayed at three different prices. The three product versions are known as a "price line." The practice is nearly universal in the retail trade: fast-food chains such as A & W offer three sizes of hamburgers (papa, mama, and teen burgers); appliance stores sell inexpensive, medium-priced, and high-priced brands of radios and televisions; and supermarkets provide inexpensive dealer brands and moderate- and high-priced national brands of the same products.

The goal of price lining is multifaceted and intimately related to the overall strategy of market segmentation. Because consumers differ considerably in both their tastes and financial resources, a wide variety in the quality of the same product type is demanded by the public. In an attempt to appeal to as broad a spectrum as possible, sellers provide a wide range of products to conform to the diverse tastes and incomes of their clienteles. In addition, the ability to offer a price line gives merchants considerable leverage to entice buyers to seek products just above their normal price and quality level. This practice is termed *trading up* and is, of course, notoriously practiced by the automobile industry, among other sellers. Car salespeople constantly attempt to persuade customers who show an initial preference for a compact car with few options, say, to purchase an intermediate-sized car with more luxurious accessories. The seller is motivated to persuade customers to trade up because the higher-priced versions of a brand are generally more profitable. The buyer is tempted to "move up" because the product is usually perceptibly of higher quality or offers additional advantages, and at the same time the increase in price is deceptively low when compared to the overall price that one would have to pay for the low-priced model. For example, a recent ad for men's suits in a discount store offered three options: "good" ($99), "better" ($139), and "best" ($199). A person finding the $99 suit attractive, for instance, might well change his mind after seeing what "only $40 more" could buy. In fact, marketers will sometimes offer more than three "quality" lines to reduce the price gap between levels. Furthermore, for each product version at each price level, accessories are sometimes offered in a way that increases the total price above the one for the next highest level. This, in turn, may lead consumers to reevaluate their needs and resources and jump to the next level.

One danger with price lining is that it may be confusing and make consumers' tasks more difficult. Too many alternatives and options may be costly to produce, stock, and maintain, as well. Then, too, if some consumers originally willing to pay a higher price find that the lower priced model is "satisfactory," sellers may even experience less revenue.

Price Reductions

Consumers will sometimes refrain from making a purchase because they perceive the price to be "just a little too much" for the quality of the product offered and/or for what they think they can afford. This common resistance to buying can be overcome sometimes through the judicious use of two price changing tactics: (1) the use of "sales" or "specials" and (2) discount pricing. The major appeal of a *sale* (i.e., a temporary decrease in price) is that consumers believe they are getting a product that is worth more than its price and/or are better able to afford the product and will be able to purchase more of other goods with the savings. The use of a sale allows the seller not only to dispose of slow-moving goods to make way for new styles or products, but also, in the process, to win a class of purchasers that might not have ever entered the market in the absence of a sale.

Another alleged advantage to the retailer is that sales of certain items draw people into the store and the consumers then either trade up and/or purchase other goods that capture their attention. Supermarkets, for example, will advertise milk, bread, or other staples at very low prices, hoping that once customers are in the store they will buy numerous more profitable items. The low-priced goods, which might even be sold below cost, are called "loss leaders." Periodic sales sometimes create excitement among consumers, who look forward to sales and comb the newspapers, travel from store to store on "bargain hunts," and generally anticipate and plan to take advantage of the "steals." In this way, the sales-conscious consumer has taken over some of the functions normally performed by the seller: namely, communicating one's wares and getting them to the consumer. Finally, the whole notion of a sale for some buyers is an opportunity to express one's astuteness or self-image. Certain individuals even find the search for and apparent inconvenience of a sale as a challenge or adventure. For others, however, sales are strictly utilitarian.

Sales have drawbacks, of course. Aside from the increased expense of signs and advertising, a sale can cease to be a novelty. Although difficult to estimate, firms may experience lost revenues to the extent that customers refrain from buying unless or until an anticipated future sale occurs. At the same time, all sellers risk cheapening the image of their brands and alienating previous buyers who paid full price by placing goods on sale.

Discounts function in a way similar to sales: the buyer is believed to interpret the reduction as a means of getting more for less. Typically, discounts are more or less constant price reductions offered to the public and sold in an establishment (i.e., a "discount store") identified as dealing in reduced-price merchandise.

For consumer goods, the use of sales and discounts varies from country to country. In Germany, for example, one seldom sees a discount store, and sales generally occur only in February. Sales occur more frequently in Italy, but not nearly as often as in the United States.

For industrial buying, discounts are offered as a matter of course. Typically, discounts are given for three reasons. One is to serve as inducements for purchase, much the same as in consumer buying during sales. A second is to meet the competition. The third is that buyers expect the discount and failure to meet this expectation risks inducing an imbalance in the quid pro quo inherent in such exchanges. In general, there are three types of discounts offered in the industrial trade: cash, functional, and quantity discounts. Each is briefly described below.

Cash Discounts. A cash discount is a price reduction offered the buyer under the condition that the discounted price be paid within a certain period of time; otherwise, the full price must be paid. The most common terms are 2/10, net 30. This means that a 2 percent discount is provided if the bill is paid within 10 days, but if the option is not taken, then the full price is due within 30 days. For example, assume that a buyer agreed on a purchase price of $6,000 and was offered 2/10, net 30. Then, if the bill were paid within 10 days, $5,880 would be due; otherwise, the full $6,000 would be payable within 30 days. Other cash discounts are, of course, offered, such as 3/10, net 30, for instance.

From a buyer's standpoint, cash discounts represent a cost savings and in this way function as incentives. From the seller's viewpoint, cash discounts are believed to encourage prompt payment and to build goodwill. However, cash discounts incur risks for both parties in that sellers and buyers still must weigh the opportunity costs of engaging in the exchange. As with all of the forms of discounts discussed herein, virtually no research exists as to their true effects.

Functional Trade Discounts. Functional discounts are allowances a seller offers to a buyer for services rendered. Although this might entail outright payments, more often it consists of reductions in the purchase price of goods. Generally, the amount of discount varies, depending on the type of buyer and functions performed. For example, a manufacturer of soap selling to a full-service wholesaler might offer a 25 percent discount to cover services performed by buyers in the general category of distributors, plus an additional 10 percent discount for conducting specific promotions. The same seller, assuming no laws are violated, might offer a grocery store only a 15 percent discount for the services it performs plus a 5 percent promotion allowance. The grocery store presumably gets less of a discount than the distributor because it performs fewer services. The schedule of discounts might even be more complex such as "25, 10, 5, and 2/10, net 30." What this means is that for a quantity of goods selling at a list price of $2,000, say, the buyer can deduct 25 percent of $2,000 for a category discount, yielding an effective price of $1,500. Then,

10 percent of this total is subject to a discount for a particular service rendered (e.g., advertising), leaving $1,350. And for a second specific service (e.g., providing credit), $67.50 is allowed (i.e., 5 percent of $1,350), leaving $1,282.50. If payment is made within 10 days, only $1,256.85 is due (a 2 percent discount); otherwise, $1,282.50 must be paid within 30 days.

From the seller's perspective, the functional discount is the price one must pay to obtain the services of marketing intermediaries. As discussed in the chapter on channels of distribution, intermediaries can assume much of the marketing burden including that related to storage, shipping, promotion, extending credit, and other functions. Functional discounts are also a means to stimulate sales from otherwise reluctant buyers.

Quantity Discounts.   Price reductions based on how much a buyer purchases are termed quantity discounts. Two types exist. A *cumulative quantity discount* is based on the total amount purchased over a period of time. A *noncumulative quantity discount* is based on the amount purchased at a single point in time. A quantity discount might be set on the criterion of units bought (e.g., $2.00 per unit for 1 to 99 units, $1.95 per unit for 100 to 499 units, and $1.90 per unit for 500 or more units) or the dollar value of the purchase (e.g., a 5 percent discount for orders from $3,000 up to and including $10,000, and an 8 percent discount for orders of more than $10,000). Because of legal constraints (e.g., the Robinson-Patman Act), quantity discounts must reflect cost savings due, for example, to a savings in billing or shipping.

What are the effects of quantity discounts? Aside from the obvious financial motivations on the part of buyers and demand stimulation motives on the part of sellers, there is the possibility that quantity purchases could alter the balance of power between buyer and seller. To the extent that quantity discounts induce large purchases and result in buyers concentrating their orders from one or a few sellers, the vulnerability of either party can be affected, depending on the importance and magnitude of the sale for the parties and the alternatives available to each. Switching costs will be incurred as a function of the substitutability of one seller to another for the buyer, the critical nature of the resources to both buyer and seller, and the level of the resources exchanged.

Profit Maximization

Many firms state that profit maximization is their goal and follow formal procedures for working toward this end. One approach is to rely on the normative implications of economic theory. To see how economic theory might be used as a price-setting tool, let us consider the recent experiences of a husband and wife company making two-piece jogging suits. The company is called Stayfit (a fictitious name). The daughter of the owners has completed a marketing course, and, being eager to both apply her knowledge and help her parents, has prepared an economic analysis designed to maximize short-run profitability of the firm. Her reasoning and calculations follow.

First, based on two years' experience in the Atlantic Seaboard states, Stayfit's costs were estimated as $20,000 fixed and $20 per suit variable. Thus, a cost equation could be written as

$$TC = 20,000 + 20q$$

where TC = total cost and q = quantity. The next problem was to determine an equation for predicting demand as a function of price. The owners of Stayfit saw a market niche for moderately priced jogging suits in New England, because at that time only inexpensive (less than $40) or expensive (more than $100) suits sold there at retail. Through years of tinkering in the garage, one of the owners had developed an innovative and inexpensive machine for sewing fabric, and the other owner had designed a simple, but functional, outfit. In addition, over time, the owners had astutely made purchases of odd-lot quantities of a high-quality synthetic fabric at very low prices. Indeed, Stayfit's suits had the look and feel of suits costing $100 or more. Hence, the owners believed that they had the ability to make the suits as well as a differential advantage over the competition.

Their estimate of demand as a function of price was pieced together through data from a trade publication, their own sales experience with similar products in other areas of the country, and conversations with a friend of the family who worked for the purchasing department of a large clothing chain. From this information they forecast that the New England market could absorb about 8,000 jogging suits at a retail price of approximately $40 and only about 1,300 at a retail price of close to $100. Somewhere between these limits was an optimum price for them to charge to maximize their profits. The daughter of the owners used a simple straight-line estimate of demand as a function of price by connecting the points provided in the above forecast. The demand curve in Figure 12.13A shows wholesale prices (about 50 percent of retail). The equation for this curve is

$$q = 12,480 - 224p$$

where p = price. This seemed like a good guess, as marketing texts almost universally illustrate profit maximization with a linear demand function. Notice that, as our intuition tells us, market demand falls as prices increase.

The final step in the analysis was to compute a price that maximizes profit. We can do this by first computing total revenue (TR):

$$TR = pq = 12,480p - 224p^2$$

Then, profit (P) equals $TR - TC$:

$$
\begin{aligned}
P &= 12,480p - 224p^2 - 20,000 - 20q \\
&= 12,480p - 224p^2 - 20,000 - 20(12,480 - 224p) \\
&= -224p^2 + 16,960p - 249,600
\end{aligned}
$$

This profit equation can be solved graphically, by trial and error, or with the calculus, to show that $p = \$38$ yields the greatest profit. At $p = \$38$, $P = \$71,424$ and $q = 3,968$ suits. Overall, a wholesale price of $38 would seem to allow the retailer the opportunity to charge about $80, and the projected profit for Stayfit is impressive. Everyone was, in fact, enthusiastic about the prospects.

Before proceeding, however, the principals decided to get the opinion of a neutral party, a marketing professor. The professor was impressed with most phases of the analysis, but felt that the demand curve was unrealistic. Although the end points used to estimate it seemed valid, given the information provided, the linear shape appeared to misrepresent consumer reactions. Consumers are often more resistant to price increases for certain ranges of prices than the linear function reveals, and they are less receptive to price decreases for some price ranges as well. Moreover, the professor felt the absolute level of predicted quantity demanded appeared somewhat too high at most price levels. As a consequence, he recommended the price-quantity demand function shown in Figure 12.13B. The equation for this function is

$$q = 3.2(10^6)\, p^{-2}$$

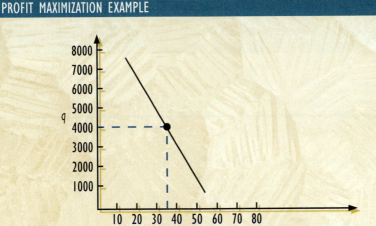

A. A linear demand function

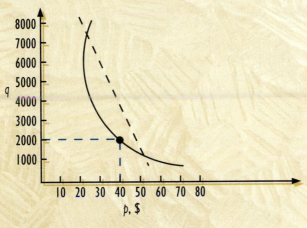

B. A nonlinear demand function

The quantity sold again decreases as price increases, but the rate and level better match intuition. Following the procedure outlined above, one can see that the optimal price for profit maximization is $p = \$40$ with a predicted profit of $P = \$20,000$ at a quantity demanded of $q = 2,000$. Although the computed price is not too far from that arising from the linear analysis, notice how much lower profits and sales are.

Assuming that the nonlinear curve is closer to reality, let us briefly look at the implications of the analyses. A first point to note is that had Stayfit followed the linear analysis and chosen to sell the jogging suits at $38, it would have sold about 2,217. Unfortunately, it would have produced 3,968 suits. With only $84,246 in revenues and total costs of $99,360, it would have operated at a loss. Perhaps Stayfit could have sold the 1,751 remaining suits later at a lower price to offset the losses, but clearly the forecast profit of $71,424 was way out of line.

A second issue to examine concerns what action to take based on the more realistic nonlinear analysis. Table 12.3 presents a sensitivity analysis showing the effects

TABLE 12.3 SENSITIVITY ANALYSIS OF PROFITS AND QUANTITY DEMANDED TO CHANGES IN PRICE FOR THE PROFIT MAXIMIZATION EXAMPLE

Price p	20	23.43	25	30	40	50	60
Quantity q	8,000	5,829	5,120	3,556	2,000	1,280	8,899
Profits P	−20,000	0	5,600	15,556	20,000	18,400	15,556

of choosing different price levels on expected profits and quantity demanded. Notice that the break-even price is $23.43 with a break-even quantity of 5,829. Notice further that profits do not vary much from about a price of $30 all the way up to about $50 or more. On the other hand, once the price falls below $30, profits drop off dramatically. Given their desire to fill the intermediate price niche of the market between $40 and $100 suits, Stayfit felt that the retailers might accept a price of no higher than $30 to $35 so that they could, in turn, sell the suits in the $60 to $70 range. This tactic, however, gives Stayfit a sure profit of only $15,556. Because they had another business opportunity promising a profit of $50,000, Stayfit decided not to produce the suits and enter the New England market. Had they followed the linear analysis implications, they would have entered the market. The outcome? Well, five months after making their decision, the bottom fell out of the jogging suit market, and retailers who had been selling suits at around $100 were forced to put them on sale for $50 or less to get rid of their stock. Stayfit would not have fared well. In contrast, the venture that they did enter, children's formal suits, was relatively profitable, yielding about $40,000 above costs in the first year.

Before we discuss other pricing strategies, let us mention some shortcomings of the profit maximization approach. (1) The biggest hang-up is that its accuracy rests on how well one can estimate costs and demand.[19] Demand is very difficult to estimate, and cost estimates usually contain considerable errors in measurement as well. (2) The goal of profit maximization tends to obscure the value of other goals. Perhaps the firm would be willing to accept less than maximum profits if it needed to do so to gain a foothold in a market, for example. (3) Profit maximization as described above does not explicitly take into account the reactions of rivals. (4) Profit maximization ignores the influence of social and legal forces. (5) Profit maximization is short-run oriented and fails to take into account long-run objectives and changing contingencies. (6) Profit maximization fails to incorporate the role of other marketing mix decisions. For these reasons, firms often pursue approaches other than profit maximization when setting prices.

Some Frequently Applied Alternatives

Six of the more common strategic alternatives to profit maximization include revenue maximization, cost minimization, market share leadership, market skimming, market penetration, and market differentiation.

Revenue Maximization

Some firms use sales maximization as their criterion in setting prices. The motivation is simple. Often not enough cost data are available to compute a profit maximization price, and profit maximization's numerous other flaws make it problematic. On the other hand, the most visible and direct measure of the success of a firm is its sales. Measures of sales are easily obtained, and, indeed, management tends to use sales as a barometer of the health of the business, as a criterion for promotion and bonuses, and as a guide for planning in production and other areas of operations. Given further that sales are correlated with profits, one can see that this goal has many attractions. However, one still must be able to estimate demand as a function of price. Although one avoids the problems with making accurate cost estimates, the need for good demand estimates has the same problems as does the profit maximization procedure. Also, because the correlation of sales with profits is usually less than perfect, the tactic frequently results in suboptimum performance. For example, with $TR = 12,480p - 224p^2$ for the linear analysis of Stayfit, one can calculate the revenue maximization price as $p = \$27.86$. This price, however, yields $P = \$49,042$ for the linear analysis and $P = \$12,405$ for the nonlinear analysis. Both numbers are significantly under the maximum levels.

Cost Minimization

Another frequently practiced strategy is to strive to keep costs at a minimum. Porter terms this the strategy of "overall cost leadership" and notes that its successful implementation requires aggressive construction of efficient-scale facilities, vigorous pursuit of cost reductions from experience curve effects, tight cost and overhead control, avoidance of marginal customer accounts, and cost minimization in areas such as R & D, service, salesforce, advertising, and so on.[20] The motivation for a cost minimization approach might stem from a number of sources. First, the firm might have accurate estimates of costs only and at the same time feel it is impossible to specify a demand function. Second, a cost minimization strategy usually permits the firm to set a low price and thereby gain a competitive advantage over rivals. Finally, the cost minimization strategy is a deterrent to new entries in the market because potential rivals know that they face an uphill battle requiring large losses in the beginning and continued stiff competition throughout the product life cycle. For a firm to employ a cost minimization strategy successfully, it is believed that it must have a relatively high market share, bargaining power over suppliers, or other advantages.[21]

One might think that all firms strive to keep costs down and that such a strategy does not differentiate one firm from another. However, this is not necessarily the case, as other goals often take priority. Some firms, for example, aim for the quality-conscious segment of the market. This forces them to pay relatively more for product ingredients, workmanship, and/or advertising. Hence, for some firms, a lexicographic rule is followed such that costs have a lower priority than product quality. Hewlett-Packard consistently followed this pattern for many years by pricing its small computers at the top of the line. Nevertheless, many firms such as Texas Instruments, Black & Decker, and Beaird Poulon (maker of chain saws) practice a cost minimization strategy to advantage. This allows them to set relatively low prices. Other firms, such as DuPont, watch costs closely yet price somewhat above market average as part of their pricing strategies.

Price setting under the larger goal of overall cost leadership operates primarily on a cost-plus basis. That is, a final price is set as a particular increase above costs. The increase may be set as a function of historical practice, industry norms, or to achieve a certain goal such as sales or profitability. Notice that price setting can, and in fact often does, entail employing combinations of objectives.

General Motors, for example, sets its prices as cost per unit plus an additional amount needed to achieve a return on capital of about 15 percent (after taxes). The cost per unit and total revenue, of course, are based on estimates of demand, and if these are in error so will be the anticipated return. In addition to costs and desired return, General Motors and other firms using such an approach may adjust the final price on the basis of consumer price sensitivity, competition, and other considerations. Price setting for General Motors and other automotive companies has become more fickle in the 1990s because of the use of rebates, low-cost financing, extended warranties, automobile leasing, and changes in the overall product offerings, such as bundling of features under a single price. Also the overall prices of automobiles are so high and automobiles are so much more durable and reliable than in the past that consumers are holding onto their automobiles for longer periods of time. All this makes estimation of demand and price setting more difficult for manufacturers. Thus, it can be seen that price setting is a complex process that is part art and part science.

Market Share Leadership

Still another popular approach for some firms is to work for market share leadership. The belief is that this not only is required for survival but also that it leads directly to higher profits.[22] Price, of course, plays a very important role. Sometimes this means setting a price as low as possible to win the most sales. At other times, conditions are such that one must set a relatively higher price to create an image of product superiority and recoup high promotion and other costs. In either case, the company fine-tunes its price—either up or down—to achieve a particular market share. Pricing to achieve a market share is done even by firms below the market leader. These firms attempt to adjust their tactics to maintain their market position or perhaps move up a slot or two. Because of company goals or other constraints, however, they may not ever be able to achieve the top spot and they price accordingly. A firm that sets prices in order to maintain or achieve a particular market share must, of course, have a marketing information system attuned to the marketplace if it is to be successful. This means placing special emphasis on data gathering, statistical modeling, and simulations.

Market Skimming

An old approach to pricing new products is known as market skimming.[23] Here the firm sets its price at a high level with the aim of either leaving the market at a later predetermined point in time or lowering its price systematically over time. The strategy is based on the premise that potential customers will be relatively insensitive to price and eagerly purchase the product at a relatively high level. This will be possible to the extent that the product satisfies a genuine need and no substitutes exist in the market. Also, from the firm's standpoint, a high price tends to generate greater profits when it most needs them, and it keeps demand down to a manageable level until it can increase productive capacity. Many producers of toys and novelty items use this approach to pricing when they introduce new products before the Christmas holidays. After the holidays and throughout the following year, they gradually lower the price to draw in the more price-sensitive patrons.

One drawback to the skimming policies in general is that it tends to entice other producers into the market, as these firms view the high-price conditions as an opportunity for growth and profitability. Another point against the approach is that, depending on the product and public's reaction, skimming may be viewed as an exploitive ploy. Further, some people may withhold purchases from a firm because they know that they can wait and "the price will eventually fall." A few years ago, a large group of consumers anticipated that hand calculator prices would drop, and therefore waited a year until they fell from $150 to $29.95 in one case. Thus, firms that regularly apply a skimming policy may find that it backfires because people are "onto their game."

DuPont and Polaroid practice pricing policies akin to skimming. For example, Polaroid priced its Model 100 instant camera at about $165 initially, and then over a 15-year period, systematically changed the design and eliminated certain features so that it could price its Shooter camera at about $25.

Market Penetration

The opposite of market skimming is market penetration pricing, where a low price is set for a new product with the hope that it will quickly lead to high sales and gain a foothold in the market. It is a demand stimulation tactic based on the assumption that consumers are price sensitive. Its major disadvantages are that it often takes longer to make a profit than with a higher pricing policy and it is difficult to later raise prices, should conditions call for it. On the other hand, penetration pricing tends to discourage new entrants because they know that they will have to price low and fight it out with the existing competitors.

A good example of penetration pricing is the case of Mercedes-Benz.[24] In 1967, the average of price of a Mercedes in the United States was approximately $4,000, about $1,500 above the average price of all cars. Although prices of all cars rose slowly year by year, Mercedes-Benz maintained this differential for three or four years. Then, beginning in the early 1970s, Mercedes-Benz increased its prices at a rate greater than the average rate of all cars. By the early 1980s, the average price of Mercedes cars was approximately $28,000, or about $18,000 above the average car price. Thus, over about a 15-year period, the price of Mercedes cars increased sevenfold, whereas the average price of all cars increased only fourfold. Mercedes-Benz followed a penetration pricing strategy and achieved a stronger foothold in the market. By the mid-1990s, however, it has become increasingly difficult to accelerate price increases and Mercedes-Benz has introduced production into the United States and undergone strong cost-cutting measures, among other practices.

Overall, we know very little about what exact price to set for new products, and market skimming and penetration guidelines are very rough rules of thumb at best. For this reason, firms are increasingly turning to simulation, experimentation, and other more formal procedures as aids in decision making.

Market Differentiation

The strategy of market differentiation attempts to create an offering that is perceived to be unique by a target market. This is done in one or both of two ways. First, uniqueness is achieved through the entire offering bundle. That is, one achieves a unique offering by varying the characteristics of the product, its package, its price, its promotional image, its distribution, or combinations of these. Notice that this dimension is broader than the usual concept of product differentiation, which is limited to changes in the physical product. We can attain uniqueness through an orchestration of the entire marketing mix. Second, uniqueness is achieved through the selection of a target market. That is, who one markets to and where they are located define a second dimension of uniqueness. Table 12.4 presents a categorization of the kinds of differentiation arising from the crossing of market offering with target market. For simplicity, we have used product as the market

TABLE 12.4 TAXONOMY FOR MARKET DIFFERENTIATION CASES

Target Market	Market Offering (e.g., Product)	
	ONE HOMOGENEOUS OFFERING	**HETEROGENEOUS OFFERINGS**
One specific market	I Quasi differentiation	III Concentrated differentiation
A few specific markets	II Focused differentiation	IV Multi- differention
No specific market (i.e., everyone)	V Undifferentiated marketing	

offering dimension, even though the concept of market offering is broader, including other marketing mix elements.

Undifferentiated marketing occurs when the marketer attempts to sell to everyone rather than people in a well-defined target market (case V in Tab. 12.4). If, at the other extreme, the marketer has a single homogeneous offering (e.g., one version or model of can opener) and sells this to one specific customer (e.g., a nationwide retailer), this is quasi differentiation (case I). It is quasi in the sense that the seller most likely achieved the differentiation by default. Focused differentiation, case II, occurs when one homogeneous offering is marketed in a few specific markets. For example, some small farmers in the South grow only oranges but market a portion of their crop to small retailers, a portion to schools, and a portion directly to the public in roadside fruit stands. Another instance of differentiation (concentrated differentiation) occurs when a producer has heterogeneous offerings and sells these to one specific market (case III). This occurs, for instance, in the real estate business. Some real estate agencies market only to the very wealthy but offer them a product line consisting of luxury homes and condominiums, investment properties, vacation villas, or time-sharing arrangements. Finally, multidifferentiation (case IV) happens when heterogeneous offerings are sold to a few specific markets. Some large retailers fit this category in that they sell a wide product line but sometimes have ongoing bargain basements along with their main stores. Cases II and IV, of course, apply to situations in which there are more than "a few" specific target markets.

The major advantage of a differentiation strategy is that it permits firms greater price flexibility and the potential for higher profits. At the same time, it strengthens firms' positions vis-à-vis rivals. One disadvantage is that, in the course of achieving differentiation, the opportunity to achieve large volumes of sales or a high market share is sometimes traded off. Differentiation tends to produce an increase in market share within some target groups, but can result in overall decreases in sales among an entire market or the subset formed by all of the focal targets. So we often see a redistribution of sales after a differentiation strategy is employed. Typically, it is hoped that an increase in profitability will compensate for the overall decrease in sales if it occurs. Of course, if the firm is highly successful in the new markets, net sales may not decrease and could conceivably even rise. Another disadvantage of differentiation is that costs often rise disproportionately because it is expensive to achieve differentiation due to research, product development, material costs, labor, and promotional expenditures.

We have spoken of differentiation in a broad sense as if it were achieved through target market specification and marketing mix orchestrations. Differentiation can also be achieved through pricing (in combination with target markets). This is known as price discrimination, which not only has legal sanctions against it, but can be morally undesirable as well. Nevertheless, economists have identified three prerequisites for which price discrimination works profitably. First, the seller must have at least a moderate amount of control over the price. This means that market forces and social and legal restrictions play a relatively minor role. Thus, price discrimination is performed more frequently in oligopolistic than in competitive industries. Second, the price discriminator must be able to choose target markets such that each has different price elasticities. Third, the opportunity for buyers to resell in another market must be negligible or limited.

A final issue concerning market differentiation is product line pricing. Every firm with two or more products to sell faces this problem. The problem occurs especially when offerings in the product line are related to each other. That is, pricing becomes difficult when the price of one good influences the demand for another and vice versa. This happens in two ways. First, products might be substitutes. Retailers of tires, for example, face a pricing problem because each car owner can be sold only different grades of the same size tire and because often only a few different sizes of tires will fit on the same car. Moreover, the retailer might sell two or three different brands of tires. Under these conditions, the sales of all tires are highly interrelated in that a customer will usually purchase only one option while excluding the others. Thus, from the retailer's perspective, a price increase in one brand, grade, or size of tire will result in an increase in demand for another. For a somewhat analogous issue, see the discussion on bundling in Marketing Anecdote 12.3.

Similarly, when products are complements, pricing is complicated. An interesting example occurs in the muffler installation trade. Mufflers, tail pipes, and exhaust pipes typically wear out at about the same time. Retailers competing for the repair business advertise lifetime guarantees on the mufflers even though few, if any, will actually last that long. The catch is that the muffler is priced very low, at about $30 to $40, but tail and exhaust pipes, which are not guaranteed, are priced very high. Thus, the retailer still makes a hefty profit on later sales of pipes despite having to provide worn-out mufflers "free." In this example, the prices of the muffler and pipes are highly interrelated complements, and a decrease in the price of the former (i.e., it is free) results in an increase in the sale of the latter for the retailer offering the deal.

A somewhat analogous strategy is used by sellers of men's electric shavers, where the shaver is priced relatively low, but replacement cutters and screens are priced higher than their costs would seem to warrant. Thus a new shaver might sell for $70 but replacement cutters and screens might go for $25, despite representing a smaller fraction of the original purchase price.

The task facing a firm with a product line is to set prices for the entire line so as to maximize the achievement of the goals of the firm. One procedure for determining an optimal price is to examine the industry and cross-elasticities for the offerings in a product line to ascertain the range of sales for changes in price. This can be done in a simulation.[25] Next, one can observe changes in costs as prices and revenue change. The ultimate goal is to compute the effects on profits so that an optimum strategy can be found.

For the 1996–1997 National Hockey League season, the Detroit Red Wings sold special ticket packages that offered groups of games together. One version included a Detroit Red Wing and Colorado Avalanche game bundled with two other NHL games with Detroit and other opponents and two games between college hockey teams. All games were played at the Joe Louis Arena in downtown Detroit. This tactic bolstered demand for the relatively less popular college hockey games by offering fans a chance to see an NHL game between Detroit and the previous year's Stanley Cup champions, Colorado.

Bundling is defined as the strategy of selling two or more products or services as a "package" at a special price. Common examples include assortments of nuts, fruits, and cookies sold at Christmas and other holiday times; season tickets for sporting and artistic events; vacation packages for transportation and lodging; cable and satellite television services; and computer hardware and software combinations.

A recent study investigated three strategies for pricing entertainment events: (1) each performance priced and offered separately; (2) season tickets only (i.e., all performances priced and offered as a single bundle); and (3) mixed bundling (i.e., the combination of (1) and (2)). The findings showed that profits were greatest for mixed bundling and least for season tickets only.

Source: R. Venkatesh and Vijay Mahajan, "A Probabilistic Approach to Pricing a Bundle of Products or Services," *Journal of Marketing Research* (November 1993): 494–508.

Managing Prices

Price setting involves balancing constraints against objectives. Figure 12.14 shows the most important factors in this regard. Notice first that the manager's final decision involves the determination of at least four things:

1. the level of the price to set
2. the optimum time to reveal the price and contingencies for making changes in the future
3. the means for operationalizing the price
4. the manner of communicating the price

The price might be set at a high, low, or moderate level. It might be revealed early or late in an introductory ad campaign. It will need to be integrated with the product life cycle and anticipated competitive responses over time, as well. A price can be actualized entirely as a monetary cost to the customer, or it might be expressed through a combination of deals, credits, trade-ins, or other complex arrangements. Finally, it can be communicated in a variety of ways: in the media, on the product, on the wall or a display, verbally, by letter, and so on. Each of these decision outcomes depends on the managers' decision processes whereby firms' constraints and goals are balanced. This, in turn, may be guided by organization policies, past practices, and formal models and simulations designed to arrive at quantitative goals.

Notice in Figure 12.14 that many constraints need to be considered. These reside in economic, legal, government, social, and firm restrictions. Notice also in Figure 12.14 that many goals will enter the decision process (e.g., return on investment, market share).

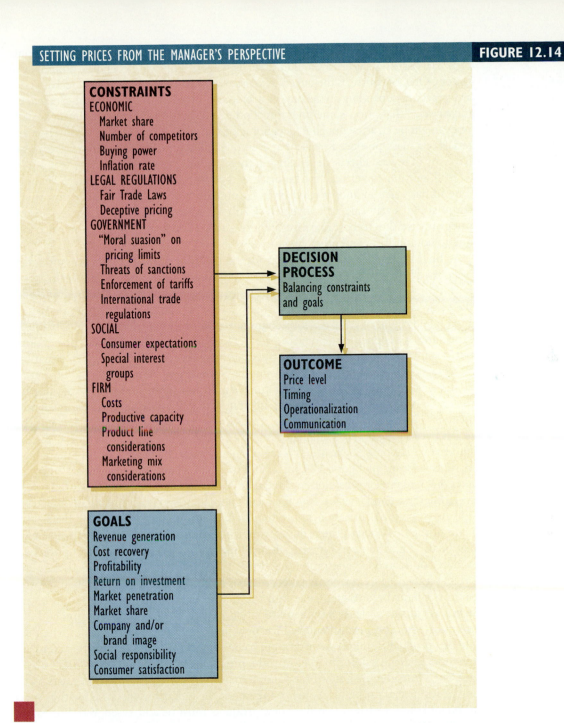

CONSTRAINTS
ECONOMIC
  Market share
  Number of competitors
  Buying power
  Inflation rate
LEGAL REGULATIONS
  Fair Trade Laws
  Deceptive pricing
GOVERNMENT
  "Moral suasion" on
    pricing limits
  Threats of sanctions
  Enforcement of tariffs
  International trade
    regulations
SOCIAL
  Consumer expectations
  Special interest
    groups
FIRM
  Costs
  Productive capacity
  Product line
    considerations
  Marketing mix
    considerations

DECISION
PROCESS
Balancing constraints
and goals

OUTCOME
Price level
Timing
Operationalization
Communication

GOALS
Revenue generation
Cost recovery
Profitability
Return on investment
Market penetration
Market share
Company and/or
  brand image
Social responsibility
Consumer satisfaction

Let us turn now to some of the considerations taken into account when balancing constraints and goals. For purposes of discussion, we divide the decision-making task into pricing new products and pricing throughout the remainder of the product life cycle.

Pricing New Products

New-product pricing varies, depending upon the degree of "newness." Different issues arise for products entirely new to the market as compared to the introduction of a new brand in a market already containing more or less similar offerings.

For entirely new products, the objective is to entice people to buy the product, if only on a trial basis. What price should the manager set? This will depend on a number of factors. One, of course, is the buyer. The price one sets may be perceived as a barrier or an attraction, depending on the buyer's resources and tastes. At the same time, managers must realize that prices sometimes signal other things to buyers, such as quality. A low price might be an attraction, but, depending on the product, might suggest inferior materials or a mass-produced article that everyone will eventually own. High prices might have any of several effects, depending on their meaning to customers.

Still another buyer reaction to price is the anticipation of future price changes. The initial price in and of itself or in combination with other information might stimulate an early sale or conversely lead to postponement. Some buyers expect prices to rise due to cost increases, whereas others anticipate systematic price cuts due to competition and other pressures.

A final buyer-related issue to consider is the role of incentives. The monetary price may be only part of the actual cost to a buyer. Coupons, credit, deals, transportation, storage, service, and guarantees constitute factors either interacting with the price or actually raising or lowering it. Life-cycle costs, such as the price of gas and oil and replacement parts for a chain saw, also need to be factored in. Obviously, expectations depend on the type of product (e.g., its complexity, patent protection), but it is important for managers to consider buyer reactions in any given situation.

At least two approaches for forecasting buyer reactions to prices should be considered. Conjoint analysis provides a quantitative indication of buyer reactions to price and the trade-offs among other product attributes. Another methodology is qualitative analysis. Through in-depth interviews, focus groups, or other techniques, it is possible to discover subtle and often counterintuitive reactions of potential buyers. U.S. consumers take shopping by mail and correspondence via word processing for granted, but many Europeans find personal contact and writing by hand more personal.[26] This affects the purchase of pens, clothing, and many other goods. Qualitative research reveals such differences and is a useful complement to conjoint and other quantitative analyses.

The pricing of entirely new products will be influenced also by the firm's estimate of the life cycle of the product, the likely entrance of competitors, and financial goals (e.g., the need for cash, desired return on investment). Two options are usually contrasted: a penetration (i.e., low-price) strategy or a skimming (i.e., high-price) strategy. The former is taken when a long product life is anticipated, competitors might be attracted later into the market by profit attractions, and/or the firm has considerable cash on hand to pay for the intense communication and distribution efforts typically required for new products. The latter is taken when the life of a product is unknown or thought to be short, competitors are expected to enter soon, and/or cash for market introduction is in short supply.

When introducing a new brand into a market in which competition exists, pricing poses special problems. Some of the same considerations discussed with respect to buyer reactions toward entirely new products must be addressed, too. For example, the ability of people to afford the product, along with their perceptions of quality and their willingness to trade price for product attributes, must be assessed. In addition, however, management must evaluate the buyer's reaction to price in the light of prices of likely competitors. Because a new entrant to an ongoing market hopes to attract both nonusers of the product class and buyers of rival brands, it must set a price that, in combination with other features of its brand, gives it a differential advantage. This, in turn, means that brand positioning and marketing research will be essential (see Marketing Anecdote 12.4).

Generally, if the firm strives for mass market appeal, it will set its price to meet the competition or score somewhat below it. On the other hand, if it goes after mar-

Snapple introduced ready-to-drink iced tea to the market in 1988. It packaged the tea in 16-ounce bottles priced at $1. The price was based on Snapple's analysis of buyer behavior, forecast product life cycle, the threat of later entrants, and financial goals. With 75 percent of all households in the United States drinking iced tea, the venture seemed like a good bet, and indeed, by 1992 Snapple had a 33 percent market share.

Recognizing the opportunity, PepsiCo joined with Unilever and Coca-Cola with Nestle to introduce their own brands of ready-to-drink iced teas. The problem was how to compete effectively with the market leader, Snapple. The solution was to target supermarkets, bundle the iced teas in packs of multiple bottles or cans, and, importantly, set lower prices per drink.

One industry analyst, Joshua Levine, credits Pepsi's and Coke's success to its recognition of perceived value as a key strategic issue: "A sluggish world economy since 1990 has made consumers everywhere rabid about value, which doesn't necessarily mean the lowest price but does mean the best deal for the precise mix of features the buyer wants."

Snapple made a new product out of an old concept—and competitors soon followed suit.

Sources: Rahul Jacob, "Meet the New Consumer," *Fortune,* Autumn/Winter, 1993, p. 6.

Joshua Levine, "Watch Out, Snapple!" *Forbes,* May 10, 1993, pp. 142–146.

---

ket niches, it may price high, especially if it has a strongly differentiated product. How high or how low must be within the bounds of buyer acceptability. The firm's degree of departure from the norm will additionally be governed by product life cycle and internal constraints. Thus, a price above or below the norm or the competition might be set in response to a declining or growing market or the return on investment or other financial needs of the firm.

Pricing over the Product Life Cycle

Price setting does not end with the introduction of a new product or brand. As time passes, managers must continually evaluate the necessity to revise prices either upward or downward. Again, the characteristics of buyers are central concerns. In addition to tracking buyer tastes, firms must devote efforts to analyses of special classes of buyers. For example, firms should regularly analyze current buyers, former buyers who no longer purchase the product, former buyers who purchase from the competition, buyers loyal to rivals, switchers, and nonbuyers. This is necessary so that firms can retain their present clientele, bring back old friends, entice buyers from the competitors, and induce trial from nonusers. Indeed, an understanding of buyer behavior might even lead to increased consumption from regular customers. In any case, it is important to analyze the differential effects of the current price and potential changes on various classes of buyers.

At the same time, price alterations might be necessitated by changes in product design, distribution, and communication tactics. For instance, the manufacturer of brand X raisin bran cereal might add more raisins per box, switch from the use of wholesalers to direct delivery in its own trucks, or decrease its advertising and promotion budgets. Each of these changes would have an effect on sales that must be coordinated with price in an overall program.

Then, too, as the prices of supplies, labor, and raw materials change, so, too, do the costs of production. This might require a price change to bring revenue and other financial goals into line.

Finally, even if buyer behavior, marketing mix, and costs were to remain constant, the firm might have to change prices simply in response to competitive pressures. This implies that the firm must monitor competitive moves and have a model for estimating the effects of any price changes on its own sales. Indeed, management must consider competitive conditions along all dimensions of the marketing mix, not merely price. We discuss this aspect later in the chapter. Again, fast, accurate marketing information systems are needed.

The product life cycle for personal computers has made pricing decisions for sellers especially difficult in recent years. Prior to 1990, it took about four years to come out with new computers. In the early 1990s, this time was reduced to two years, and today about one year is all it takes. The compressed life cycle has had a number of effects. For sellers, prices have to be lowered periodically to meet the competition. A rough rule of thumb is that prices decline by nearly half only six months after introduction. For buyers, the temptation is to wait for prices to drop. But by waiting they not only forgo the advantages of the new computer in the interim, they are likely to be faced later with the choice of the lower-priced computer versus a brand new one with better features but a much higher price. The frequent price changes and ongoing introduction of better machines makes for a confusing market.

Value pricing is an important strategic tool that has especially worked in industrial markets. Marketing Anecdote 12.5 details this approach.

NEW DEVELOPMENTS AND FUTURE DIRECTIONS IN PRICING

Price Response Analysis

An important consideration in the determination of what price to set is the timing and magnitude of the response of sales to a change in price.[27] The so-called "law of demand" asserts that as price rises demand falls. But it does not specify the exact path that the inverse relation takes.

Figure 12.15 summarizes four possibilities in a *static* sense. Each shows that, as price increases, sales tend to decrease but at different rates. We have already seen the linear and multiplicative models in an earlier example. The curves represented in Figures 12.15A and 12.15B can be written in mathematical form, respectively, as $q = a - bp$ and $q = ap^b$, where a and b are parameters and are different in each equation. Notice that in the linear relation, as price changes by a fixed amount, quantity demanded will also change by a fixed amount at all points on the curve. A price increase (decrease) of one unit will result in a decrease (increase) of b units in demand at all levels of price. For the multiplicative relation, in contrast, the amount of increase or decrease in demand will depend on price level. For instance, at p_1 in Figure 12.15B, a small increase in price will result in a greater drop in demand than a com-

Price and quality govern value, but people differ on their priorities or trade-offs given to price versus quality. The differences are not limited to variation across consumers within a market or country—they can also be seen across countries. U.S. consumers place highest priority on price and seemingly are willing to sacrifice quality to pay a lower price. Europeans, by contrast, tend to demand higher quality and are willing to pay more for it. Nevertheless, no matter where consumers draw the line on price and quality, they are sensitive to value appeals: getting more for less.

A nice illustration of this for consumer products can be seen in the success of the Taco Bell fast-food restaurants in the 1990s. Beginning with the idea that consumers are highly price sensitive when choosing a fast-food restaurant, Taco Bell revised its pricing strategy to price most items on its menu below $1. To accomplish this goal and its objective to increase sales, new items were developed, food preparation was streamlined, advertising was increased, and floor space was reallocated to increase the area for customer seating. The changes proved to be profitable, and indeed other fast-food chains were forced to revise their pricing and product lines in response.

As the eating habits of U.S. consumers have matured, growth in full-service, sit-down chains has mushroomed. It is estimated that sales for this category amount to $100 billion a year, nearly as much as the traditional combination take-out/sit-down establishments. No wonder Americans eat out of the home more than 200 times a year!

Consumer Reports recently surveyed 82,000 consumers of 62 full-service, sit-down chains. Value, defined by *Consumer Reports* as consumers' subjective judgment that "the chain offered excellent value for the money," was a key criterion used by consumers in their evaluation of the restaurants (food taste, atmosphere, and service were additional attributes). The winners, based on overall scores: Cracker Barrel for family restaurants, Luby's for cafeterias, Ryan's for budget steakhouses, and Houston's for dinner houses. Close seconds in each of the above categories were Bob Evans, Piccadilly, Golden Corral, and Romano's Macaroni Grill, respectively.

Value pricing is more complicated for industrial goods and services, where buyers often undergo detailed decision making. Industrial buyers are concerned with the total or life-cycle costs of the purchases they make. Typically total costs include the purchase price plus start-up costs and expenses for maintenance, operations, and replacement parts. The difference between the total price a customer would be willing to pay and the start-up, maintenance, operations, and replacement costs is known as the *economic value to a customer* (EVC). Sellers try to price their goods at a point between their own costs and the EVC. Indeed sellers obtain a premium for their products to the extent that they can show customers that savings are to be had by purchasing the sellers' product instead of competitors'. Savings are demonstrated by comparing various components of life-cycle costs for the sellers' and competitors' offerings. James C. Anderson et al. consider nine methods used by businesses to assess customer value for industrial goods in their 1993 article.

Sources: James C. Anderson, Dipak C. Jain, and Pradeep K. Chintagunta, "Customer Value Assessment in Business Markets: A State-of-Practice Study," *Journal of Business-to-Business Marketing* 1, 1 (1993): 3–29.

John L. Forbis and Nitin T. Mehta, "Economic Value to the Customer," *McKinsey Staff Paper* (Chicago: McKinsey & Co., Inc., February 1979): 1–10.

"Looking for a Good Meal?" *Consumer Reports*, September 1996, pp. 10–17.

Joseph White, " 'Value Pricing' Is Hot as Shrewd Consumers Seek Low-Cost Quality," *Wall Street Journal*, March 12, 1991, p. A1.

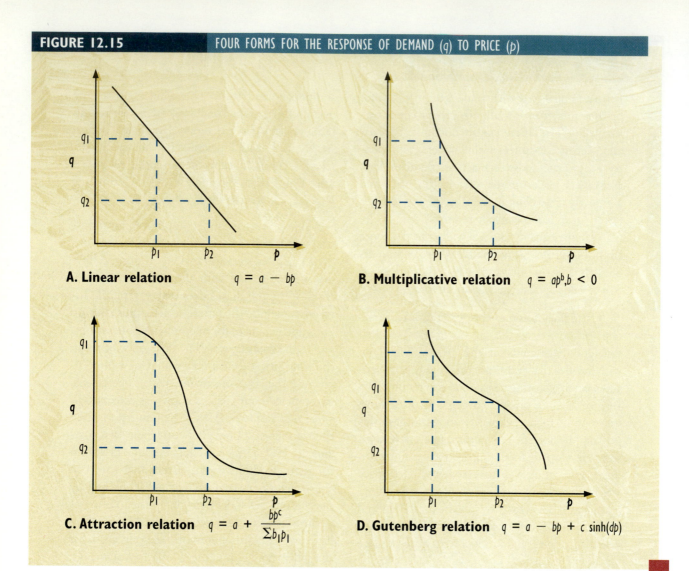

A. Linear relation $q = a - bp$

B. Multiplicative relation $q = ap^b, b < 0$

C. Attraction relation $q = a + \dfrac{bp^c}{\Sigma b_i p_i}$

D. Gutenberg relation $q = a - bp + c\, \sinh(dp)$

parable increase at p_2. Moreover, a small increase in price at p_1 will result in more of a decrease in demand than had the curve been a linear one.

The attraction relation shown in Figure 12.15C allows other possibilities to happen. For example, at p_1, a small increase in price will result in a decrease in demand at a rate less than the decrease in either the multiplicative or linear cases. At p_2, small changes produce effects similar to those found in the multiplicative case. The Gutenberg relation (Fig. 12.15D), in contrast, shows somewhat similar reactions to price changes at p_1 as does the multiplicative case, but at p_2, a small increase in price will produce more of a drop in demand than a comparable change under the multiplicative or linear models. In sum, the four response curves shown in Figure 12.15 permit the manager to make a wide range of predictions for changes in price. The task for the manager is to perform simulations and/or historical analyses to discover which curve best reflects the organization's situation. To focus on only the linear curve so often used in decision making is most likely an invalid practice in a majority of situations.[28] Indeed, as shown in Figure 12.15, the predictions made by the other curves are often at variance with the linear function.

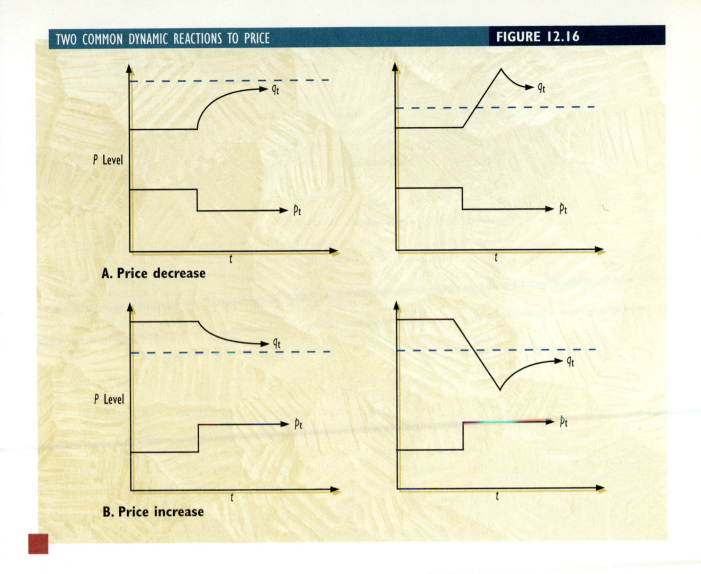

A. Price decrease

B. Price increase

Another way to take into account the effects of price changes on demand is through *dynamic* modeling. The relations shown in Figure 12.15 apply only if the price-to-quantity relationship remains constant over time. If the relation is known to change over time, then an approach that represents these changes should be applied. Consider the relations shown in Figure 12.16. Here we represent quantity demanded and price as functions of time and show them together to indicate their parallel changes. On the left side of Figure 12.16A, a price decrease results in an increase in demand, with a rise at a decreasing rate to a saturation level. The right side of Figure 12.16A, in contrast, shows an increase in demand followed by a decrease to the saturation level. Figure 12.16B illustrates the parallel effects of a price increase. In addition to the time paths shown in Figure 12.16, we might envision situations in which the path to saturation first rises (declines) at an increasing (decreasing) rate and then at a decreasing (increasing) rate. Other paths are possible, too. The points to stress are that price changes have different ultimate effects, proceed there at different rates, and take diverse paths, depending on the circumstances. Management scientists are only now beginning to study these effects.

The final time-related response issue concerns the product life cycle. Generally, it has been assumed that price elasticity increases during the introduction and growth stages, reaches a maximum during maturity, and thereafter begins to fall during the downturn in sales. Hermann Simon, a management consultant in Europe, argues, however, that price elasticity is maximum at the introduction and decline stages and minimum during maturity.[29] Thus, two completely opposite views exist. We really do not know the true relationship of these opposites because the topic has not been researched much to date. The issue is important, however, because the change in price elasticity over time has implications for the levels of sales and profits that the firm can expect.

Marketing Mix Considerations

Marketers have long recognized that there are close relationships among the elements of the marketing mix. This is perhaps most evident when we casually observe the association between price and advertising of consumer goods in the marketplace. Firms that charge a premium price for their products generally spend more on advertising than do lower-priced rivals. Heinz, for example, regularly sells its ketchup at wholesale from 10 to 20 percent above the competition and also spends more money on advertising. As the president of Heinz, Richard B. Patton, describes the situation:

> Our goal is to blend advertising and pricing to produce optimum market share and profit margins. Our feeling is that consistency in advertising and pricing strategies is important to the success of any consumer product.[30]

Consistency typically means setting advertising and prices in relation to one another. Those firms that set higher prices generally spend relatively more on advertising. Other forms of promotion, such as couponing, are important as well (see Marketing Anecdote 12.6).

The rationale for a correlation between pricing and advertising is a multifaceted one that has numerous and sometimes conflicting interpretations.[31] One idea is that once a firm has gained a foothold in the market through differentiation, it can charge higher prices than newer or less successfully differentiated brands. To maintain its lead, however, it must continue to outspend the competition in advertising. Lesser rivals, in turn, rely relatively more on pricing to gain a share of the market and thus set a lower price and spend relatively less on advertising. Still another explanation is that advertising makes consumers more price sensitive. For example, advertising might first stimulate the consumer's awareness of the advertised brands. Then, when shopping, the consumer compares these brands on price, ignoring the unadvertised brands, which presumably set lower prices. Because the advertised brands have higher costs and aim for higher profits, we see a positive correlation between price and advertising across all products in a class. A final explanation is really a "nonexplanation": some researchers maintain that it is so difficult to measure price and advertising that any relation can be found. Prices and costs vary across rival brands and across wholesalers and retailers, complicating the determination of price effects. Similarly, omitted variables such as product quality or systematic consumer differences confound things further. In addition, high advertising expenditures are sometimes associated with high costs (and high prices), but occasionally they indirectly lower costs through economies of scale and other effects resulting from increased demand. So, for these and other reasons, the price relation is difficult to foretell.

Couponing in the United States is big business. Each year, distributed coupons are valued at more than $300 billion, of which consumers actually redeem $6–8 billion, and a $7 billion industry has arisen that produces, distributes, and processes coupons. Coupons contribute to the purchase of an estimated $100 billion or more of goods each year. Ready-to-eat cereals have historically been the greatest category for coupon redemptions. About 30 percent of all consumers redeem coupons, a pervasive habit that marketers cannot ignore.

Sellers use coupons for at least three reasons. First, coupons provide incentives to first-time buyers, and the hope is that many of these consumers will become regular users. Second, coupons entice some consumers to switch from competitors' brands. Finally, couponing gives sellers a certain amount of control over the prices retailers charge to consumers. Whereas retailers sometimes pocket trade discounted prices (i.e., cash, functional, or quantity discounts) rather than passing the savings on to the consumers, they are obligated to redeem coupons, thereby providing a direct incentive to consumers.

Research reveals that three factors govern the decisions of consumers to use coupons. First, consumers must have a certain degree of self-efficacy in the sense that they have confidence in their ability to obtain, organize, store, and effectively execute the use of coupons. Second, consumers must have favorable instrumental beliefs; that is, they must believe that the actions needed for coupon use will lead to attainment of their goals concerning coupon usage. Last, consumers must view coupon usage and the activities leading up to it as enjoyable and challenging. A recent study demonstrated that all three factors—self-efficacy, instrumental beliefs, and positive affect—had to be present for effective, continued coupon use by consumers.

Manufacturers have a love-hate relationship with couponing. On the one hand, they know that consumers expect them to provide coupons and that sales do increase when coupons are used. On the other hand, the processing and handling of coupons is a nuisance, the redemption rate goes up and down unpredictably, and many consumers buy the product only when coupons are offered. Also, some brand-loyal buyers use coupons, thereby defeating one of its purposes.

Sellers periodically toy with the idea of abandoning coupons. In 1996, for example, Procter & Gamble stopped using coupons in three New York markets and reduced couponing across the country. The risk in stopping coupon usage is twofold. First, some first-time purchasers and potential brand switchers may not try one's brand if coupons are not available. Second, as firms see their competitors abandoning coupons, they may view this as an opportunity for them to use coupons to advantage. One way that Post cereals, a division of Kraft Foods, more effectively used coupons beginning in 1996 was to offer generic coupons that could be used on any of its 22 brands; at the same time, they cut prices by 20 percent.

It is unlikely that manufacturers will give up using coupons any time soon. Couponing, like other promotion tactics, works because consumers expect and are rewarded by them, and marketers recognize that, employed skillfully, they give firms leverage over competitors.

Sources: Richard P. Bagozzi, Hans Baumgartner, and Youjae Yi, "Appraisal Processes in the Enactment of Intentions to Use Coupons," *Psychology & Marketing* 9 (1992): 469–486.

Robert C. Blattberg and Scott A. Neslin, *Sales Promotion* (Upper Saddle River, N.J.: Prentice-Hall, 1990).

Martha M. Hamilton, "Clip Those Coupons While You Can," *The Washington Post National Weekly Edition*, May 20–26, 1996, pp. 19–20.

Nevertheless, Professors Farris and Reibstein have reported a strong positive relationship between relative advertising and average relative price for a sample of 227 consumer goods businesses[32]: the greater the advertising expenditures, the higher the price. In their survey, these authors measured relative advertising and then asked each business to compare its advertising budget as a percentage of sales with the budgets of its leading competitors. The responses were categorized as spending "much less," "somewhat less," "about the same," "somewhat more," or "much more." Similarly, relative price was measured by asking firms to compare their average factory selling price with those of their leading competitors. This question was answered with a quantitative response in percentages (e.g., +4 percent higher than competitors, −2 percent lower, and so forth). Farris and Reibstein also found that the positive relationship between advertising and pricing held for variations in product quality, whether one was in the maturity or decline stages of the product life cycle (but not the introduction stage), whether the product was inexpensive (less than $10) or expensive (greater than $10), or whether the market was stable in terms of changes in competitors' sales. The relationship held to a greater extent for high market (as opposed to low market) share businesses, however. Finally, firms that were more consistent in their pricing and advertising policies tended to have greater return on investments. It should be noted that, in a larger study on the same data where more variables were statistically controlled, relative price and relative advertising were positively related for industrial goods firms but *not* for consumer businesses.[33] Therefore, the nature of the relationship between advertising and pricing should be regarded as tentative until more research is done.

What about other marketing mix interactions with price? Unfortunately, we know very little about how pricing varies with product quality, distribution, or nonadvertising promotions. What is needed, further, is not only research establishing the presence of such relations but a rationale and guidelines for managers on how to set prices optimally in the face of such interactions.

SUMMARY

This chapter considered pricing from macro (i.e., economic, legal, and social), micro (i.e., customer behavior), and managerial perspectives. With respect to economic aspects of pricing, little leeway is afforded in setting prices in purely competitive industries, and even monopolies have less flexibility than one might imagine. Oligopolies, the more common market conditions, have more flexibility. Although economic theory predicts prices fairly well under the ideal forms of competition (i.e., when products are undifferentiated), it has less to say for the cases where product differentiation exists. These cases are more interesting and realistic, and they pose special strategic issues for firms, especially concerning price setting.

In *break-even analysis*, the relationship between quantity (q) and price (p) is

$$q = \frac{FC}{p - VC}$$

where FC = fixed costs and VC = variable costs. Thus, given the price, one can estimate demand; or, alternatively, given an estimate of demand, one can compute the price to break even.

- Break-even analysis is an intuitive, easy-to-apply concept. It is useful when one has no knowledge of the specific responses of consumers. However, it has the following shortcomings:

- its effectiveness depends on how well one can estimate demand or on what the market will bear in pricing
- it assumes that costs can be broken down into fixed and variable components, an assumption that flies in the face of the tendency of most costs to become variable in the long run
- costs are assumed linear, when in fact this is seldom so
- it puts one in the position of taking demand as a given.

Yet, successful marketing is predicated on a belief that management can, in effect, influence demand through strategic pricing. Nevertheless, break-even analysis does properly remind one that costs ultimately need to be considered when pricing. Two factors affecting costs, and therefore pricing, are *economies of scale* and the *experience curve effect*.

- Economies of scale refers to the phenomenon whereby the costs of producing and marketing a product typically decline per unit as the *actual volume* goes up. Economies of scale occur primarily in the purchasing of materials, use of labor, shipping, and advertising.
- The experience curve effect describes the observation that, as *cumulative volume* increases, costs decline by a constant amount. Experience curve effects are reflected in the learning of skills and managerial know-how.

Price elasticity is defined as

$$e_p = \frac{\text{percentage change in quantity demanded}}{\text{percentage change in price}}$$

- Price elasticity shows how much of a change in sales one can expect if the price is changed by a specific amount. Although useful in forecasting and planning up to a point, it has the following shortcomings:
- it applies when everything else is held constant (a notion difficult to implement)
- it neglects some potentially counteracting elements such as those embodied in price/quality effects; that is, it is a coarse-grained tool overlooking many consumer psychology and competitive forces occurring at a finer-grained level.

The social and legal constraints on pricing involve the Antitrust Division of the Justice Department, the Federal Trade Commission, and the president. Some pricing practices under their purview include price fixing, price discrimination, and deceptive pricing.

The *behavioral foundations of pricing* examines the steps consumers go through as they process pricing information, as illustrated in Figure 12.10. Processing is either automatic (e.g., external information on pricing initiates habitual rule-following behavior) or on-line (e.g., external price information or internal stored prices are retrieved from memory and cognitively elaborated upon and influence evaluations, then decision making). Price and other information (e.g., brand and store name) are used in decision making to arrive at judgments of perceived value (see Figure 12.11).

Managerial issues in pricing involve setting prices to *maximize profits, maximize revenue, minimize cost*, or to capture *market share leadership*.

- Maximizing profits requires knowledge of cost and demand equations. Because these are difficult to estimate and contain error, pricing by profit maximization is infrequently done in practice. Also, this approach fails to take into account competitive, long-run, and other factors.

- Given the practical and theoretical problems with profit maximization, some firms strive to maximize revenue. This still requires accurate estimates of demand, however. Moreover, even with good demand estimates, the price determined by using the method will generally not be the profit maximizing price. Still, the approach has its place in certain contexts.

- To minimize costs, one does not need accurate estimates of demand, but reasonable data on costs are essential. To the extent that such data are lacking, however, the approach is problematic. Nevertheless, many firms use a modification such as cost-plus pricing or overall cost leadership.

- Market share leadership pricing is also done on occasion. Here the hope is that a chosen price will attract a large share of consumers relative to competitors. The premise is that market share leads to profitability, a controversial proposition.

- Other pricing policies exist as well. When a firm employs different prices for different customers, we term the tactic market differentiation pricing. Such an approach is generally illegal except under certain conditions. Value pricing (see Marketing Anecdote 12.2), customary pricing, and charm pricing are other methods.

For *new products*, either *market skimming* or *market penetration* are the most common options.

- In market skimming, the firm sets its price at a high level with the aim of either leaving the market at a later time or lowering its price systematically over time.

- In market penetration, a low price is set with the hope that it will quickly lead to increased sales and gain a foothold in the market.

- In *product-line pricing*, the firm sets prices of its related products or brands in order to achieve goals such as maximum total profits, maximum revenues, or the minimization of cannibalization. The firm must consider the effects of the prices of individual brands on the sales of its complements and substitutes.

For pricing from the individual decision maker's perspective, four outputs must be determined:

- the level of price to set
- the optimal time to reveal the price and determination of price contingencies over time
- the means for operationalizing the price
- the manner of communicating the price

For pricing new products, a key factor is the need to size up the buyer. This means researching customers' rational and subjective reactions to the price as well as their judgments about where the price will be in the future. Similarly, the buyers' likely reactions to incentives must be assessed because these closely interact with price effects. New product pricing also must include product life cycle, potential competition, and financial considerations.

Price revisions constitute another activity essential for successful marketing. Here the firm must estimate the effects of prices on its current buyers, nonbuyers of the product class, brand switchers, people loyal to competitors' brands, and previous buyers of the firm's brand who now buy other brands. At the same time, price alterations must be evaluated in the light of changes in costs, product design, distribution, and marketing communication programs.

New developments and future directions in pricing include *price response analysis*, which focuses on the relationship between price and demand, as well as quantitative relations in both static and dynamic senses, and the relationship between pricing and other marketing mix variables.

QUESTIONS FOR DISCUSSION

1. According to economic theory, how are prices set under conditions of pure competition? Monopolistic competition? Monopolistic conditions? Oligopolistic conditions?
2. What are the main problems with economic theories of price setting?
3. What role does break-even analysis play in the setting of prices?
4. What effects do economies of scale and experience have on price setting?
5. What is price elasticity and what implications does it have for management?
6. What role do the following play in pricing: the Antitrust Division of the federal government, the Federal Trade Commission, the president?
7. Discuss how consumers process information on price. What is the relationship of price to perceived value?
8. What is customary pricing? Charm pricing? Price lining? Why are they practiced?
9. Discuss the profit maximization approach to price setting and consider its pros and cons.
10. Revenue maximization, cost minimization, and market share leadership are three other approaches to setting prices. Briefly discuss these and note their assets and liabilities.
11. What are market skimming and market penetration strategies, when are they used, and what benefits and liabilities do they offer?
12. Discuss the practice of value pricing. What is the concept of economic value to the customer?
13. In any price-setting program, four broad decisions must be made. Name these and discuss their relationship to marketing and organization goals and constraints.
14. What are some of the key factors to consider when pricing new products? Discuss the issues surrounding the pricing of products over the product life cycle.
15. What is price response analysis, and how can it help the manager?
16. What is the relationship of price with other decisions in the marketing mix?

NOTES FOR FURTHER READING

1. We omit discussion of feedback effects from outcomes to market forces and to social and legal constraints (paths d and e, respectively), for simplicity. The study of how the economy coordinates production activities with society's demand for goods and services can be found in the economic subfield of industrial organization. For relevant treatments of this subject matter, see, for example, F. M. Scherer and David Ross, *Industrial Market Structure and Economic Performance*, 3rd ed. (Boston, Mass.: Houghton Mifflin, 1990).

2. See, for example, ibid.
3. For a discussion of some of the frameworks, see Jack Hirschleifer, *Price Theory* (Upper Saddle River, N.J.: Prentice-Hall, 1976); and Thomas Nagle, *The Strategy and Tactics of Pricing* (Upper Saddle River, N.J.: Prentice-Hall, 1986).
4. Interesting treatments of kinked demand curves can be found in Walter J. Primeaux Jr. and Mark R. Bomball, "A Reexamination of the Kinky Oligopoly Demand Curve," *Journal of Political Economy* 82 (July–August 1974): 851–862;

Walter J. Primeaux Jr. and Mickey C. Smith, "Pricing Patterns and the Kinky Demand Curve," *Journal of Law and Economics* 19 (April 1976): 189–199; and Julian L. Simon, "A Further Test of the Kinky Oligopoly Demand Curve," *American Economic Review* 59 (December 1969): 971–975. See also Nagle, *Strategy and Tactics of Pricing*. A phenomenon not considered at this point is price leadership. This occurs when one firm in the industry initiates price changes and others follow suit. The price leader often is the market leader in terms of sales, technology, or other factors. In addition to the constraints provided by supply and demand, a market leader must typically look out for the interests of all in the industry as well as its own. Thus, price setting even in this case is partly determined from outside pressures.

5. See Hirschleifer, *Price Theory*; Primeaux and Smith, "Pricing Patterns and the Kinky Demand Curve"; and Nagle, *Strategy and Tactics of Pricing*.

6. Useful references include Bruce D. Henderson, *Perspectives on Experience* (Boston: Boston Consulting Group, 1970); William J. Abernathy and Kenneth Wayne, "Limits of the Learning Curve," *Harvard Business Review*, September–October 1974, pp. 109–119; C. Carl Pegels, "Startup of Learning Curves—Some New Approaches," *Decision Sciences* 7 (October 1976): 700–713; B.D. Henderson, *Henderson on Corporate Strategy* (Cambridge, Mass.: Abt Books, 1979); and William W. Alberts, "The Experience Curve Doctrine Reconsidered," *Journal of Marketing* (July 1989): 36–49.

7. See George Stigler, *The Theory of Price*, rev. ed. (New York: Macmillan, 1952), p. 38.

8. Local and state or provincial laws can be factors, too, but will not be discussed here.

9. Aspects of this model have been discussed by Jacob Jacoby and Jerry C. Olson, "Consumer Response to Price: An Attitudinal, Information Processing Perspective," in Y. Wind and B. Greenberg, eds., *Moving Ahead in Attitude Research* (Chicago: American Marketing Association, 1977); Valerie A. Zeithaml, "Issues in Conceptualizing and Measuring Consumer Response to Price," in T.C. Kinnear, ed., *Advances in Consumer Research*, vol. 11 (Provo, Utah: Association for Consumer Research, 1984), pp. 612–616; and Peter R. Dickson and Alan G. Sawyer, "The Price Knowledge and Search of Supermarket Shoppers," *Journal of Marketing* (July 1990): 42–53.

10. Russell S. Winer, "A Reference Price Model of Brand Choice for Frequently Purchased Products," *Journal of Consumer Research* 13 (September 1986): 250–256. See also James G. Helgeson and Sharon E. Beatty, "Price Expectation and Price Recall Error: An Empirical Study," *Journal of Consumer Research* (December 1987): 379–386; and Manohar Kalwani and Chi Kin Yim, "Consumer Price and Promotion Expectations: An Experimental Study," *Journal of Marketing Research* (February 1992): 90–100.

11. Dickson and Sawyer, "The Price of Knowledge and Search of Supermarket Shoppers." See also John Le Boutillier,
Susanna Shore Le Boutillier, and Scott A. Neslin, "A Replication and Extension of the Dickson and Sawyer Price-Awareness Study," *Marketing Letters* 1 (1994): 31–42.

12. George J. Stigler, "The Economics of Information," *Journal of Political Economy* (June 1961): 213–225; Richard Thaler, "Mental Accounting and Consumer Choice," *Marketing Science* (Summer 1985): 199–214.

13. Peter M. Guadagni and John D. C. Little, "A Logit Model of Brand Choice Calibrated on Scanner Data," *Marketing Science* (Summer 1983): 203–238; J. Jeffrey Inman, Leigh McAlister, and Wayne D. Hoyer, "Promotion Signal: Proxy for a Price Cut?" *Journal of Consumer Research* (June 1990): 74–81.

14. Donald R. Lichtenstein, Richard G. Netemeyer, and Scot Burton, "Distinguished Coupon Proneness from Value Consciousness: An Acquisition–Transaction Utility Theory Perspective," *Journal of Marketing* (July 1990): 54–67; Tridib Mazumdar and Kent B. Monroe, "Effects of Inter-Store and In-Store Price Comparisons on Price Recall Accuracy and Confidence," *Journal of Retailing* (Spring 1992): 66–89.

15. Kirk L. Wakefied and J. Jeffrey Inman, "Who Are the Price Vigilantes? An Investigation of Differentiating Characteristics Influencing Price Information Processing," *Journal of Retailing* (Summer 1993): 216–233.

16. William B. Dodds, Kent B. Monroe, and Dhruv Grewal, "Effects of Price, Brand, and Store Information on Buyers' Product Evaluations," *Journal of Marketing Research* (August 1991): 307–319.

17. Kent B. Monroe and R. Krishnan, "The Effect of Price on Subjective Product Evaluations," in Jacob Jacoby and Jerry C. Olson, eds., *Perceived Quality: How Consumers View Stores and Merchandise* (Lexington, Mass.: Lexington Books, 1985): 209–232.

18. Dodds, Monroe, and Grewal, "Effects of Price, Brand, and Store Information."

19. For a good discussion of cost estimation issues, see Nagle, *Strategy and Tactics of Pricing*; and Kent B. Monroe, *Pricing: Making Profitable Decisions* (New York: McGraw-Hill, 1979).

20. Michael E. Porter, *Competitive Strategy: Techniques for Analyzing Industries and Competitors* (New York: Free Press, 1980), p. 35.

21. Ibid., p. 36.

22. Robert D. Buzzell, Bradley T. Gale, and Ralph G. M. Sultan, "Market Share—A Key to Profitability," *Harvard Business Review*, January–February 1975, pp. 97–106.

23. For an early discussion of market skimming, see Joel Dean, "Pricing Policies for New Products," *Harvard Business Review*, November–December 1950, pp. 28–36. For an update, see Joel Dean, "Pricing Policies for New Products," *Harvard Business Review*, November–December 1976, pp. 141–153. A recent treatment can be found in David Besanko and Wayne Winston, "Optimal Price Skimming by

a Monopolist Facing Rational Consumers," *Management Science* (May 1990): 555–567.

24. Hermann Simon, "Pricing Opportunities and How to Exploit Them," *Sloan Management Review* (Winter 1992): 55–65.

25. See David B. Montgomery and Glen L. Urban, *Management Science in Marketing* (Upper Saddle River, N.J.: Prentice-Hall, 1969); Glen L. Urban, "A Mathematical Modeling Approach to Product Line Decisions," *Journal of Marketing Research* 6 (February 1969): 40–47.

26. Douglas Lavin, "European Consumers Decide High Tech Is a Low Priority," *Wall Street Journal*, December 27, 1996, pp. A1, A8.

27. Some of the material presented in this section was stimulated by discussions the author had with Hermann Simon, a management consultant and professor in Germany, and in a seminar held at Bielefeld University with his research fellows.

28. For a presentation of many common functional forms, see Philippe A. Naert and Peter S. H. Leeflang, *Building Implementable Marketing Models* (Boston: Martinus Nijhoff, 1978), ch. 5.

29. Personal communication with Hermann Simon.

30. Quoted in Paul W. Farris and David J. Reibstein, "How Prices, Ad Expenditures, and Profits Are Linked," *Harvard Business Review*, November–December 1979, pp. 173–184.

31. See Farris and Reibstein, "How Prices, Ad Expenditures, and Profits Are Linked"; Robert L. Steiner, "Does Advertising Lower Consumer Prices?" *Journal of Marketing* 37 (October 1973); Robert L. Steiner, "Marketing Productivity in Consumer Goods Industries—A Vertical Perspective," *Journal of Marketing* 42 (January 1978): 60–70; Dick R. Wittink, "Advertising Increases Sensitivity to Price," *Journal of Advertising Research* 17 (April 1977): 39–42; John F. Cady, "An Estimate of the Price Effects of Restriction on Drug Price Advertising," *Economic Inquiry* 14 (December 1976): 493–510.

32. Farris and Reibstein, "How Prices, Ad Expenditures, and Profits Are Linked."

33. See Paul W. Farris and Robert D. Buzzell, "Why Advertising and Promotional Costs Vary: Some Cross-Sectional Analyses," *Journal of Marketing* 43 (Fall 1979): 112–122.

CHAPTER 13

DISTRIBUTION SYSTEMS FROM A PRODUCER'S PERSPECTIVE

CHAPTER OBJECTIVES

When you finish this chapter, you should have achieved the following:

- A basic understanding of how the United States and global economies depend on distribution systems, and how those systems evolved to their current state
- A familiarity with the fundamental components of distribution systems
- An understanding of the criteria by which marketing managers design and evaluate distribution systems
- A familiarity with the basic factors involved in managing ongoing distribution relationships.

CHAPTER OUTLINE

At Inland Steel Industries, Distribution Is Both a Business and a Marketing Tool

Inland Steel has been in the metal manufacturing business since 1902. Throughout the years it produced the steel used in many of the products and infrastructure we take for granted, ranging from the sheet metal used in automobiles to the massive beams used for the construction of buildings and bridges. In the current environment, Inland has to pay as much attention to the movement of steel as to its manufacturing, and it has built a profitable business in the process. In an industry segment that is growing (steel distribution), Inland has created the nation's largest service center network. Inland positioned itself as one of the most versatile and responsive steel distributors in the world through acquisitions and careful investments in plant and equipment. It is an industry leader, with revenue and profits from the distribution side of the business that match those of the steel manufacturing side.

Inland Steel thrived in the 1980s in part because of their innovative distribution practices.

Having an extensive steel distribution system provides several advantages for Inland. One advantage is that it can move its own product into different markets efficiently. Because of its extensive network, Inland responds quickly and effectively to large- and medium-sized customers' special demands while maintaining economies of scale in the manufacturing side. In contrast to other steel manufacturers, which use their distribution centers as a dumping ground for output, Inland allows its service centers to operate with considerable autonomy. Inland's service centers respond to customer requests more quickly than

can the mills, and take advantage of opportunities that would otherwise be lost. Inland's distribution centers, for example, can respond to rush orders for standard support steel from construction companies within 24 hours versus the several days or even weeks required by a traditional steel mill.

A second advantage is that the distribution system allows Inland to be more responsive to customer demands for advanced processing of steel prior to delivery. Manufacturers of automobiles and large appliances, for example, are moving away from in-house metal cutting and bending operations, and they are looking for sources of partially or fully processed components. Inland's service centers have the capacity and flexibility necessary to meet varied customer demands profitably, even when the volumes are relatively low. They are also quicker in responding to market changes. Inland's capacity and flexibility have allowed the company to meet customer demands for just-in-time delivery of steel panels for the automotive industry.

A negative aspect of being involved in both steel manufacturing and distribution activities, however, is that the two different aspects of the business require different marketing and management styles. Steel manufacturing focuses on long production runs, and consequently looks for long-term contracts and stable demand. In contrast, distribution is fundamentally a service business in which quick response and delivery are as important as the technical or performance features of the product. Inland has resolved these differences by allowing its distribution subsidiaries to function autonomously in their dealings with suppliers and customers, to the extent that they may purchase stock from competing steel producers and sometimes even bid on jobs against the parent company. For Inland's senior management, however, it is a small price to pay for the advantages gained. Inland's distribution operations give its steel manufacturing side a competitive advantage, as well as being a legitimate and profitable business venture on their own.

Sources: Robert Levy, "Hanging Tough: It's not Always Easy Getting to Be 95, Even If You're a Company. Here's how Three Did It," *Business Month*, July–August 1988, pp. 92–96.

Robert Preston (1991), *American Steel: Hot Metal Men and the Resurrection of the Rust Belt*, New York: Prentice Hall.

Charles Silver, "Want It Painted? We'll Paint It," *Forbes*, November 16, 1987, pp. 142–144.

The Inland situation illustrates many of the points about distribution or channel systems that are discussed in this chapter. Inland's network of service centers gives the company greater control of the flow of goods from the mill (the manufacturing site) to the final customer. It also allows it to stabilize production schedules, which in turn contributes to efficient operations and better employee relations. There are other ways of stabilizing demand in steel manufacturing, but they normally involve deep price cuts in periods of slow demand. Inland avoids price and profit fluctuations by regulating the inventory levels at the service centers.

The benefits to Inland of having an extensive distribution center do not stop with operating efficiencies. By allowing service centers to individually process and sell product according to market demands, Inland can be much more responsive to customer needs while preserving the company's goals of profitability and long-term growth in a competitive market. Not all buyers of steel products are of the same size or have the same demands. For every large, steady customer such as Chrysler, for example, there are probably hundreds of small- and medium-sized customers whose needs are less consistent and predictable, but who can nevertheless be profitable with the right distribution system. Recently, large customers have moved toward long-term contracts in exchange for lower prices. Profit margins on these contracts are usually thin and can be seriously affected by inefficient production, so Inland must focus on long-term relationships and steady demand. Small- and medium-sized customers, in contrast, are more likely to be spot buyers and will pay higher margins for quick turn around. It is unlikely, however, that mills can respond to this variety of customer demands because of the lead times required for efficient operation. Spot orders would still take three to four weeks between order and delivery, which is not acceptable to most customers. Even if acceptable, these short runs would adversely affect efficiency, quality, and manufacturing costs. Inland's distribution centers are equipped to handle spot demand and serve to buffer the mills from these customers. Both long-term contract and spot buyers are satisfied at margins that more than cover the costs of inventory and equipment at the service centers. This system has greatly improved Inland's image in the steel industry.

Another interesting aspect of the distribution system illustrated by the Inland case is that members of distribution systems are marketing entities in their own right and share many of the same marketing challenges faced by producers. In the

TABLE 13.1 MARKETING-MIX CONCERNS OF DISTRIBUTION-FOCUSED COMPANIES

Company	Industry	Product	Price	Promotion	Distribution
Inland	Steel distribution	Grades of steel in stock; custom services	Standard pricing for services; repeat business discounts	Direct sales; order-taking function	Location of distribution centers; relationships with transportation providers
Kroger	Food retailer	Product assortment; national and private labels	Pricing for profitability by line; promotional discounting	Advertising	Location of stores based on population and shopping habits
McKesson	Drug wholesale	Product assortment and depth	Quantity discounts	Direct sales; order-taking function	Warehouse location; relationships with transportation providers

Inland situation, the distribution centers are involved in marketing their services to many customers that would not be approached by the manufacturing divisions, as well as to some shared customers. Inland's distribution centers are concerned with what services to offer, how to price those services, what type of salesforce to hire, and where to locate service facilities to reduce transportation costs—the same marketing mix elements (product, price, promotion, and distribution) that concern producers of steel and other products. Examples of how marketing mix elements are manifest in the case of the Inland distribution centers and other distribution-focused companies are illustrated in Table 13.1.

As Inland achieves its goal of having the distribution system contribute as much to the company's revenue and profits as its manufacturing operations, the marketing concerns of the service centers will become increasingly important. In fact, the distribution side can become more important to success than the manufacturing side, particularly in the marketing of commodity products for which availability influences purchasers' decisions. Many steel products are difficult to differentiate as to manufacturer and are sold as commodities. This means that products are interchangeable between manufacturers and when one manufacturer does not have the product, customers will contact other manufacturers until they find the desired product. By having a variety of products available at a distribution center, Inland meets a greater proportion of customer requests than other manufacturers. In fact, carrying a wide assortment of products is a key factor in the success of large wholesalers such as McKesson Corporation and retailers such as Kroger. The marketing concerns of retailers and wholesalers are discussed in chapter 14.

INTEGRATING DISTRIBUTION SYSTEMS WITH MARKETING STRATEGY

A *distribution system* can be defined as the set of people, organizations, and equipment involved in the satisfactory flow of goods or services from the producer to the customer, and it is designed to help achieve the manufacturer's goals and objectives. The design of the distribution system and how it affects customer satisfaction and the achievement of company goals and objectives depend on several factors.

One of those factors is the product or service being marketed. For some types of products, the distribution system has little relation to what the customer receives. In the case of computer diskettes, for example, the distribution outlet has no effect on how diskettes perform, and because diskettes are relatively inexpensive, the distribution outlet has little effect on demand as well. For this reason, consumers can purchase most major brands of diskettes through a variety of outlets ranging from computer stores to mail-order outlets. In some circumstances, a customer might pay a slightly higher price for convenient access (e.g., the lobby store of a hotel late at night), or an extraordinarily low price (e.g., at going-out-of-business sales), but for the most part diskette prices stay within a narrow range, and the distribution system is not very relevant to the marketing strategy.

For personal computers, in contrast, the distribution system can have a significant impact on the computer system's performance because it affects the availability of the service and technical assistance that many customers consider an integral part of a computer package. The choice of a distribution system for personal computers, therefore, needs to be an integral part of the overall marketing strategy. During the 1980s, the use of mail-order distribution and technical assistance via telephone allowed companies such as Dell Computer and Gateway 2000 to sell computers at substantially lower prices than traditional computer retailers, and to take market share away from brands sold primarily through retailers, such as IBM and Compaq. In the 1990s, Compaq, IBM, and other manufacturers responded with their own direct-marketing programs, as well as with special models sold only through mass discounters and at prices comparable to mail-order packages. In other words, IBM and Compaq switched to a different distribution system to regain market share.

Another factor affecting the design of distribution systems is the company's brand objectives. Some companies seek widespread recognition for their products and want them to be available wherever and whenever the customer needs it. If many retail establishments are available, the company may use a distribution approach that maximizes the number of stores that carry the brand and use mass advertising to create recognition. Such is the case with the chocolate candy products of Mars. Another company selling similar products, however, such as Godiva Chocolatiers, may prefer a more exclusive image and limit distribution to only the high-income segment of the population. We also see contrasting distribution strategies in the case of coffee. General Foods wants high volume for its Maxwell House brand, and distributes it to most grocery outlets in the United States. Gevalia Kaffe, in contrast, is targeted at upscale coffee drinkers and distributed only through direct mail.

These examples illustrate the importance of distribution system decisions and how they must be integrated into a company's marketing strategy. In fact, a company's distribution system can affect all other areas of the marketing mix. We saw in the case of Dell and Gateway, for example, that the distribution system gave them a pricing advantage over their competition. The companies' promotional plans, including factors such as type and frequency of advertising and the media used, can also be affected by the distribution system. Maxwell House uses mass media advertising to encourage brand recognition and preference in the grocery store, whereas Gevalia relies on high-quality direct mail appeals and expensive premiums (e.g., coffee makers) to encourage trials. Distribution systems can even affect the design of the product or the level of service being offered. For example, Inland can offer more predelivery processing of steel products than other steel producers offer because of its independent service centers.

One last way in which distribution systems can influence the overall marketing efforts of a company is through their longevity and resistance to change. The complexity and substantial investments required by distribution systems make them long-term commitments that are difficult to change.[1] Whereas advertising can be changed with just a few weeks of production lead time, and pricing with the stroke of a pen or keyboard, changes to distribution systems often require personnel movement, new facilities, and new systems development. Distribution systems, therefore, tend to remain stable far longer than other elements of the marketing mix. In any fast-changing environment, existing distribution systems can represent constraints that must be taken into account in the development and execution of marketing strategies. Because of their effect on practically all other aspects of the marketing mix, distribution systems can be valuable assets or serious liabilities. They must be managed by looking at both their long- and short-term implications for all areas of the business.

THE BENEFITS OF DISTRIBUTION SYSTEMS

Distribution systems are a great benefit to producers. But they also generate utility far beyond the profit and loss considerations of individual companies, touching the lives of consumers in many different ways, and often influencing the overall health of economic systems. We begin by describing the contribution that distribution systems make to society at an aggregate level.

Broad Economic Value

The main contribution that distribution systems make to society is to allocate resources more efficiently. To better understand this, imagine what it would be like if only producers and consumers existed and no intermediaries of any kind could be found. Under these conditions, you as a consumer would have to contact the producers of all the products you need or want directly, or you would need to wait until the producer contacted you; in all cases, one of the parties to the transaction would have to physically transport the goods to or away from the other. In such a world, you could not go to the supermarket to purchase eggs, fish, produce, or coffee. Instead you would have to contact the dairy farmer, fisherman, fruit and vegetable grower, and coffee producer individually. In addition, you may need to contact more than one of each type of producer to find the best value, or you may not be able to find the product at all if the product was out of season, unless a producer had storage facilities. The end result of this world without intermediaries is that it would take considerably more effort to purchase eggs, fish, produce, coffee, and all other products. When we consider the vast array of products we purchase from retailers and other intermediaries, we see that consumers' lives would be very difficult without intermediaries.

Life would also be more difficult for producers. Consider egg farmers, who, without a distribution system, would need to sell door-to-door or spend valuable time in high-traffic areas in the hope that consumers would pass by and purchase their products. Both of these alternatives are almost certain to result in lower sales than what an intermediary arrangement would produce. In addition, because time spent selling takes away from producers maintaining and improving manufacturing systems, it seems reasonable to expect that the overall cost of eggs to consumers would be higher with a system without intermediaries, and reduce the probability of a sale even more because the price would be out of reach for some customers. Given higher prices and lower volumes, the end result of not having intermediaries is a lower living standard for consumers as well as producers.

A more general representation of the economic value intermediaries create is illustrated in Figure 13.1. In panel A, we see an economic system with six producers

FIGURE 13.1   COMPARISON OF DIRECT-CONTACT AND MEDIATED MARKETING SYSTEMS

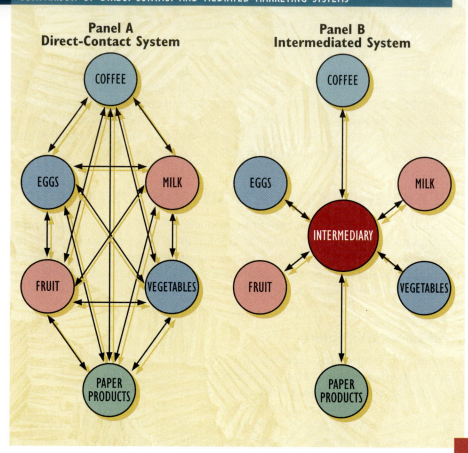

who are also consumers, and no intermediaries. Let us assume each producer-consumer has a limited amount of energy (time) to allocate to either producing or trading, and that the sum of all producer-consumer energies becomes the resources of the economy. Further assume that production yields resources, but trading does not, because trading uses up a small amount of energy and simply redistributes remaining resources. This means that when people are producing, they create new resources and the economy is better off, but when they are trading they simply move resources around, and the economy's wealth is reduced by the amount of energy consumed. In panel A each producer must interact with five other producers to have access to each product category, resulting in a system total of 15 transactions that consume energy. If instead you have one intermediary, as in panel B, only six transactions are required. Producers sell their surplus and purchase the goods produced by others in one transaction. Because each producer enacts only one transaction instead of six, the amount of energy used in trading is reduced. Even when single transactions involve multiple goods or services and the intermediary does not produce (and consequently does not contribute wealth directly to the economy), trade still creates an economy-wide savings of resources, which can be redeployed into production. Our egg farmer, for example, will have many more hours per week to improve production. Thus, the intermediary creates economic savings for the system and the savings become more dramatic as the number of producer-consumers increases.

Roles of Intermediaries

Two forces underlie the need for intermediaries: the discrepancy of quantity and the discrepancy of assortment.

Discrepancy of quantity is the difference between the quantity typically demanded by customers and the quantities that can be produced economically by manufacturers. To function efficiently, most manufacturers must produce in large quantities. In most circumstances, however, the average customer buys only a fraction of the seller's output, and the timing of supply and demand differ. For some products, such as steel, to be cost effective, manufacturers must produce large quantities at a time (e.g., have long production runs), although buyers purchase the product in smaller quantities and unpredictably over the entire year. For other products, such as air conditioners, economy demands that manufacturers stretch out production over the whole year, although customers buy in very large quantities during relatively short periods (e.g., summer months). Both of these situations demand that products be warehoused and transported to market only as buyers' and sellers' needs become evident.

Wholesalers, retailers, and other intermediaries help reconcile discrepancies of quantity. Many small producers, such as family farms or artisans, do not have the time or resources to sell their products directly. Instead they sell to intermediaries who often also buy the output of similar suppliers, thus assuming an *accumulation* role. By accumulating the output of many small producers, intermediaries can create trading economies of scale that are not available to the producers, and sell their products for a better price and in a more time-efficient manner. *Trading economies of scale* are savings generated by intermediaries through large quantity buying and/or selling, and this allows more efficient transfers of resources in the market.

A related second role performed by intermediaries is that of *breaking bulk*. In many industries, companies produce and package in quantities that exceed any single buyer's potential demands. Rather than dividing the product themselves, however, these companies sell to intermediaries who can subdivide the large quantities into smaller ones. Food processors such as Kraft, for example, produce in truckload quantities, which they sell to food wholesalers such as Supervalu. These intermediaries break down the bulky output of producer into quantities that match customer demands. Thus, part of the role of Inland's distribution centers is taking large shipments of steel from the mills and breaking them down into smaller lots.

Discrepancy of assortment, the second force that underlies the need for intermediaries, is the difference between the variety of products typically demanded by customers and the variety that can be produced economically by manufacturers. Most producers make only one or a limited range of products, whereas customers demand a broad range of products and services. Because consumers cannot meet all their needs by going to individual producers, someone must bring the required range of goods together in one or a few places accessible to buyers. The discrepancy of assortment is reconciled by intermediaries performing two roles: sorting and assorting.

In *sorting*, intermediaries divide producers' output into different grades or qualities to reach target groups with different needs. A coffee wholesaler, for example, might purchase coffee beans in very large quantities from Colombia and Kenya and separate the finer grades for sale to Gevalia and Maxwell House, selling lower grades to institutional buyers such as vending machine operators. In this situation the intermediary sorts the product.

In *assorting*, intermediaries accumulate a wide selection of products for time-conscious consumers. When buying computers, for example, consumers need processors, monitors, paper, diskettes, and many other supplies and equipment involved in operating a personal computer system. Most manufacturers, however, are good at producing only one or two of these products. Iomega, for instance, produces high-capacity storage systems, but it does not produce motherboards or printer ribbon. Instead of forcing customers to contact Iomega directly for cartridges and tape drives, and other producers for other components, the computer store stocks the complete assortment of products that computer customers want and meets all the customers' needs at one time.

Functions of Intermediaries

It is clear that intermediaries help satisfy producer and consumer needs by making the marketing of goods more efficient, thus contributing to their economic welfare. At a general level, therefore, it can be said that intermediaries help generate some of the utility that is typically associated with marketing, as discussed in chapter 1, with *utility* defined as the ability to satisfy human need. In practice, intermediaries perform many functions that generate utility, and it is at this level that marketing managers need to be knowledgeable and involved.

Among the many types of utility that economists classify, the marketing of goods and services is usually associated with four: form, possession, time, and place (see chapter 1). Of these four, distribution systems primarily provide *time utility* and *place utility*, as seen in most of our examples thus far. Intermediaries provide time utility by making the product or service available *when* the customer wants or needs it, and they provide place utility by making the product or service available *where* the customer wants or needs it. Intermediaries can also provide form and possession utilities in some circumstances, primarily in the marketing of expensive products with high levels of social meaning, for which the purchasing experience is as important as the product itself. One example of intermediaries that provide utility in all forms are Land Rover dealers, as described in Marketing Anecdote 13.1.

Intermediaries may perform many functions to provide utility. Not all intermediaries perform all functions, and often the needs of customers and producers are met by groups of intermediaries working together. Table 13.2 lists general functions served by intermediaries, with the functions separated into those that serve consumers, producers, or both consumers and producers. Note that these are very broad categories, and that many more specific services and benefits rendered by intermediaries can fall into each class. Also note that this classification is strictly from a producer's perspective, so it is deliberately oversimplified. In reality, some intermediaries provide utility for other intermediaries in the distribution channel, performing functions that benefit neither producers nor consumers directly. For example, drug wholesalers often extend credit to independent drugstores. In such situations, the credit is not provided to either the producer or the consumer directly, but it helps the drugstore offer a better assortment and lower prices, which benefits both consumers and producers indirectly.

Functions Benefiting Consumers

Intermediaries provide a key benefit to consumers by offering variety. Intermediaries stock product lines in a choice of grades, colors, sizes, and other distinguishing attributes. They make it possible for consumers to compare and choose products or services that best meet their needs. This function is a direct response to discrepancies in quantity and assortment. In the United States and other economies that permit market competition, consumers take variety for granted and seldom recognize it as a benefit. This is not true, however, in many

The Land Rover brand has been recognized and admired around the world for many years. It is most commonly associated with rugged off-road utility vehicles that are most at home on safari in Africa and racing across the underdeveloped plains of Asia. In recent years, however, sport-utility vehicles have become very popular with urban and suburban drivers who are seeking to communicate their practicality, individuality, and strength through the

A Land Rover isn't just a vehicle—it's an experience! These upscale SUVs come with a whole range of complementary products.

cars they drive. Many companies have entered the sport-utility vehicle market to capitalize on this market shift, and often with products that are less costly than the Land Rover's $38,000 price tag. Few of them, however, can provide as much of the complete image that sport-utility vehicles are meant to communicate as what Land Rover can achieve through its Land Rover Centers.

Land Rover dealers across the United States, working with the parent company, have moved away from the more traditional approach of selling cars and trucks on the strength of their features, adopting instead an approach that sells the complete promise of adventure and fun and the means to achieve it. Along with the complete line of Land Rover products, Land Rover stores feature a wide assortment of Land Rover gear, such as clothing, gloves, boots, fishing gear, and even hunting equipment In addition, they also have a test track on-site, on which the interested buyer and family can experience some of the Land Rover's off-road potential and fantasize about trips in the wild. Land Rover buyers can walk away from the dealership with first-hand knowledge of their vehicle's abilities and performance, and with accessories linked to the Land Rover name that allow them to communicate their desired image even after leaving their Land Rover in the parking lot. In this sense, Land Rover stores provide more than time and place utility; they also provide form utility through the gear and test track that might very well enhance the consumption experience. When coupled with the possession utility of on-the-spot financing, Land Rover stores are a good example of a distribution system providing marketing utility of all types.

Source: Personal interviews conducted with Land Rover representatives at the 1996 Chicago Auto Show. For additional information, see Keith Naughton, "The Ralph Lauren of Car Dealers," *Business Week*, November 20, 1995, pp. 151–155.

parts of China, for example, where distribution systems are inadequate or nonexistent and customers have few choices in most product categories. Most rural Chinese consumers find only one type of bath soap at the store, when they can find it at all; such consumers are often willing to wait in line and pay high prices for soap imported from Western countries. For these consumers, the notion that "soap is soap" is not true at all.

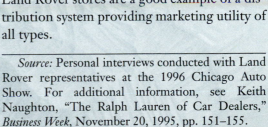

TABLE 13.2 FUNCTIONS PERFORMED BY THE DISTRIBUTION SYSTEM FOR CONSUMERS AND PRODUCERS

Functions for Consumers	Functions for Producers	Functions for Consumers and Producers
Variety	Storage	Risk
Value	Financing	Personal contact and education
Atmosphere	Gathering information	Transportation
Location		Promotion

Related to variety is the function of value. The choices that intermediaries provide for consumers not only meet consumers' distinctive demands, but also match consumers' economic resources with their preferred use of those resources. Consumers assign particular products or services different degrees of importance, and thus differ in how much they are willing to pay. Intermediaries give consumers a choice about how much of their economic resources to give up for a product or service. As they purchase automobiles, for example, some consumers see their vehicles as extensions of themselves and will spend substantial amounts of money to buy the "right" car. For other, more utilitarian consumers, automobiles are simply a means of transportation, and they will spend considerably less. Automobile dealers acting as intermediaries allow consumers with different tastes in automobiles to find what they want by offering new and used cars ranging from economy to luxury models.

Another important distribution system function is location. Not only do intermediaries make goods available to consumers, they also provide a variety of locations, so consumers can satisfy their needs for economy, status, *and* convenience as they shop. Intermediaries make products available in establishments that vary in terms of many attributes, and can accommodate a wide variety of tastes and preferences for relatively little cost. For example, milk can be available at warehouse outlets for economy-minded shoppers, at grocery stores for consumers doing household shopping, and at convenience stores for people hurrying home from work.

Atmosphere relates to location and can be provided by intermediaries as well. Consumers sometimes seek store image and ambiance as an end in itself, and although it is typically a part of the buying process that has little to do with the actual product, in some circumstances ambiance can be an integral and important part of the consumption experience. Ambiance is certainly an important part of what Land Rover Centers provide, because it helps customers develop adventure fantasies that will hopefully enrich their ownership experience. In some situations, ambiance may even be more important than the products purchased, such as when people go shopping at the "right" store, with the full intention of returning all the goods at a later time. The thrill is in the act of buying, not the product itself. The "right" store, however, can vary between Neiman Marcus, Urban Outfitters, or Kmart, depending on the individual consumer.

Functions Benefiting Producers

Two functions that distribution systems perform for producers focus on economic concerns, and are illustrated in the Inland Steel case at the beginning of this chapter. Inland's distribution centers provide an important storing function for Inland steel mills. Distribution centers purchase all steel output from the mills that is not already committed to customers, store it, and later sell it on the spot market. The mills benefit because they can schedule long and more efficient production runs.

Steel mills also benefit from the related cash flow financing function. By taking title to the goods, Inland distribution centers release cash that Inland steel mills can use for reinvestment and operating expenses—cash that the mills may otherwise have had to borrow. The cash flow financing function is important to all business, but especially to small- and medium-sized producers, who are often strapped for working capital.

Intermediaries also provide producers with assistance in gathering information. As discussed in chapter 5, market research takes many different forms, and the most effective research is often done by people actively selling products in the field. In chapter 11, we discussed that some companies rely on their salespeople for this function. Many producers, however, also rely on intermediaries as a sources of market information. The benefit of information, of course, is that producers can respond more appropriately to consumer demands.

Functions Benefiting both Consumers and Producers. Some intermediary functions, such as the reduction of risk, benefit both consumers and producers. Intermediaries reduce producers' risk in several ways. First, they absorb small variations in demand by providing a buffer for production output. By adjusting their inventory levels, intermediaries can allow producers to maintain steady production schedules and capture production economies of scale by using resources more efficiently. Steady production schedules may also reduce labor tensions caused by frequent changes in job assignments and the pace of work as well as extend the life of manufacturing equipment. This function is very important, for example, to automobile producers. Dealers often absorb small downturns in demand by increasing their inventories, which allows the plant to continue producing at a steady rate.

Producers' risk also decreases to the extent that intermediaries assume title to the goods and absorb losses from damaged or stolen goods. Some large intermediaries can spread the risk of losses in a product category over a large enough base that it becomes bearable, whereas the same loss would be devastating to an individual producer. One hypothetical example is a producer of beach toys selling to Wal-Mart. Many beach-toy producers are small injection molding operations, and they typically produce and sell their products to retailers during the winter months, well ahead of the typically hot summer weather that motivates consumer purchases of plastic buckets and shovels. When they purchase early, retailers such as Wal-Mart assume the risk that the upcoming summer will be cold and rainy and the demand for beach toys will thus be low. If manufacturers had to assume the risk directly, a poor year might put many such firms out of business, whereas poor beach toy sales in a single year will merely inconvenience Wal-Mart.

Distribution systems also reduce risks for consumers. Intermediaries provide continuity of service, more local access, and at least some screening of products and services for safety and reliability. Risk assumption, in fact, has become a characteristic that some intermediaries use to attract customers. The upscale retailer Nordstrom, for example, has a "money back, no questions asked" return policy that customers value highly, and this helps Nordstrom maintain its image as a premier retailer. Risk reduction is also offered by charge and credit cards companies such as American Express and MasterCard, who protect customers against product failure and accidental damage for a limited time when products are purchased with their cards.

Personal contact is another function performed by intermediaries that benefits both producers and consumers. Personal contact offered to consumers needs little elaboration—intermediaries often provide sales personnel who explain products and services to customers and help them in making decisions. For some products, such as cosmetics, personal contact can be a critical factor; some customers become so attached to a particular salesperson that they switch brands if the salesperson changes employers. The same can be said for financial and stock brokerage services, where account representatives often take many of their customer relationships with them when they change employers.

The personal contact function performed by intermediaries for producers is different. Many producers have technical and manufacturing talent, but lack sufficient resources for sales and intelligence gathering. For some of these companies, an in-house salesforce may not be feasible, but they can gain regional or national representation through intermediaries. Sometimes the intermediary can provide direct contact with the consumer, as in the case of Quick Candy, which sold gourmet lollipops directly to Kmart, and in this way had access to lollipop consumers on a national basis.[2] Other times intermediaries provide access to other intermediaries, as in the case of Time-Warner, which sells some of its products to major book distributors for resale to bookstores across the nation.

Another important function provided by intermediaries is transportation. Producers as well as consumers benefit greatly from the availability of intermediaries, who transport goods expediently and economically. This has been true from ancient times, when people who owned means of transport, such as camels, mules, or boats, would contract with merchants to move goods from points of supply to points of demand. Throughout history, improvements in transportation technology have been closely linked with rising living standards, and this remains true today. Producers benefit from transportation advances in two ways. First, the availability of transportation through intermediaries reduces the capital investment required to get goods to market and releases funds for reinvestment or profit. Second, producers can ship goods in the quantities demanded by customers more economically due to economies of scale when transportation intermediaries combine shipments from more than one producer going to the same location.

This ability to ship goods economically in just the right quantities also helps consumers by making products affordable. Even more important to consumers is availability. Advances in transportation make it possible to have a greater variety of goods available in a greater variety of places and times, and this in turn makes consumers' lives safer and more comfortable. It is easy to appreciate how transportation has changed the quality of life over the last 200 years, as we have progressed from mule-drawn carts to airplanes. But even in the last 20 years, transportation advances have changed lifestyles as well. For example, expedited parcel delivery by companies such as United Parcel Service (UPS) has contributed to increased mail-order shopping. UPS and other parcel deliverers make it possible to order a package from a retailer such as L.L. Bean in Maine for delivery to Iowa in two to three working days at a cost not much higher than the bulk transport cost incurred by local retailers. Transportation intermediaries have been an important factor in the growth of mail-order retailing in the U.S. market.

Mail order, of course, makes life more convenient for today's busy consumers. It also makes life safer. People living in high crime areas, or elderly consumers, for example, do not have to go out shopping in the evening hours if they use mail-order services. Expedited delivery even makes it possible for some retailers to have substantial sales volume in overseas markets. Japanese consumers, for example, use toll-free numbers, fax machines, and expedited parcel delivery to purchase apparel items from retailers such as Lands' End and Eddie Bauer in the United States, and make their purchases more conveniently and economically than from local Japanese retailers.[3]

The promotion function is not typically associated with intermediaries, but many provide some form of promotion that can greatly benefit both producers and consumers. We have already discussed how intermediaries provide personal contact, and such face-to-face selling is one type of promotion. Intermediaries also participate in other forms of promotion, ranging from cooperative advertising to administering contests and special events. For example, wholesale distributors often administer producer-sponsored advertising and sales promotion programs in their local market. The producer benefits because information is distributed and promotional efforts are managed by local personalities and are often associated with the name of a respected local business. From the consumer's standpoint, information and promotional premiums from local sources are often more credible and trustworthy than those gathered from 30-second commercials and remote sources.

The functions discussed thus far are only a few examples of what intermediaries do, and there is some overlap between the categories used here. The list of functions performed by intermediaries in modern markets continually changes in response to economic and environmental factors. Earlier we described how Inland's distribution centers changed in response to just-in-time demands from customers, and how the distribution of computer diskettes has changed as personal computers have come into widespread use. In both of these cases, the functions of intermediaries changed as markets changed.

The different functions of intermediaries are related as well, because intermediaries can be concurrently involved in any and all aspects of production, exchange, and consumption of goods and services. The interrelatedness of the functions discussed here in many ways exemplifies the richness of intermediaries' contributions to marketing. For many products and services, intermediaries make the difference between success and failure.

THE EVOLUTION OF DISTRIBUTION SYSTEMS

The broad economic value of distribution systems discussed earlier has been a reality since ancient times. Central to most of the advanced early civilizations such as Babylon and Egypt were waterways, by which transportation of bulk products was possible, and the marketplace, where merchants came to exchange foreign goods for local products. Merchant ships and caravans made different parts of the world known to one another and helped spread innovation and culture, and sometimes oppression and destruction as well. In the Roman Empire, for example, commercial intermediaries were as important as infantry legions in bringing the cultures of the Mediterranean basin under Rome's control. Intermediaries moved with the Roman armies and made foreign markets available to local producers in areas under Rome's military control. These new trading arrangements made local landowners dependent on Roman markets and made it unprofitable to break away from Rome. One example is the market for olive oil. Roman policies of repatriation and the suppression of local customs often encouraged the consumption of olive oil in geographic areas where olives could not be cultivated, which dramatically increased demand for olive oil in producing areas. As a result, growers and merchants in olive-producing areas became wealthy and increasingly influential in their communities, and because they depended on the Roman infrastructure to keep merchant routes open, these influential citizens helped to keep any rebellion against Roman policies at bay.

In addition to benefiting the Roman Empire, distribution systems also benefited the local economies and the lives of the common people. Trade throughout the empire created higher demand for locally produced goods and services and improved the living standards of most local producers. In most instances, producers earned more profits from what they sold through intermediaries than the profits earned by the intermediaries themselves, and they reinvested these profits in larger and more efficient means of production.

In contrast, the decline in living standards throughout most of Europe during the Middle Ages was due at least in part to the decline of the Roman distribution infrastructure. It is interesting that at the same time that Europe was mired in poverty and disease, civilizations such as China, India, and Islam prospered, concurrent with the growth in reach and sophistication of their distribution systems. As Western Europe emerged into the age of discovery, intermediaries were again highly influential. Much of the exploration and settlement of the American and Asian continents by European powers was funded by intermediaries looking for new product sources and trading opportunities, and it was the transportation and distribution of agricultural products such as sugar, tobacco, and coffee, more than that of gold and silver, that sustained their economic might for several centuries. Even after the Industrial Revolution gave prominence to manufacturing over agriculture as a source of wealth, intermediaries were still instrumental in moving goods into the hands of consumers, which spurred the industrial system to greater output.

A vivid example of the important role of intermediaries in economic development is the historical domination of the Japanese economy by the *keiretsu*, or trading companies. When Japan began establishing an industrial base in the early 1900s, the initial investments for machinery and equipment came from intermediaries who traded Japanese products around the world and could serve many of the functions that intermediaries serve today. Through ownership, economic dependencies, and cooperative agreements, the *keiretsu* gained substantial control over Japanese industry—control they largely maintain to this day by serving the same intermediary functions, as well as through more subtle methods, such as interlocking directorates, low-interest financing through affiliated banks, and the placement of people supportive of their interests in policy-setting government posts.

In Europe, Asia, and the Americas, the influence of intermediaries is discernible in the geographic positioning of major cities. With very few exceptions, major global cities (e.g., New York, Montreal, Buenos Aires, Tokyo, Hong Kong, London, Rio de Janeiro) began as settlements on the coast or along major navigable rivers. These cities prospered in part, because access to water transportation made available a greater variety of products and services at lower costs than could be found in other areas, making them attractive places in which to live and do business. A second generation of major cities, such as Denver and Phoenix in the United States and Calgary in Canada, owe their rapid and sustainable development to the railroads and roadways that gave them access to distribution systems.

Theories of Distribution System Development

In addition to the historical perspective just described, theorists have attempted to explain the life cycle of distribution systems in more abstract and all-encompassing ways. The most popular of these attempts is the *wheel of retailing*.[4] This model suggests that new retail institutions emerge as limited-service, low-price, and low-margin operations, giving them an advantage over established retailers who have expanded their services and must therefore charge higher margins to cover their overhead costs. The new low-cost retailers gain a foothold in the market at the expense of established retailers and might even drive some established retailers out of business. Over time, however, the new retailers expand their services and organizations, and their costs rise as well, which in turn provides opportunities for new retailers at the low end of the market, and the cycle repeats. Some aspects of the retail development cycle are evident in the story of Sears and some of its competitors (see Marketing Anecdote 13.2), although it is clear that the Sears story is much more complex than the theory suggests. The wheel of retailing, for example, does not explain how Sears was able to reposition itself and meet the emerging needs of middle-income women shoppers; nor does it support the emergence of convenience stores and vending machines, which have been high-margin operations from their inception.

The concept of a life cycle for intermediary types is useful, however, in understanding why distribution systems cannot remain static. The notion of a life cycle originates in biology and suggests that life forms prosper as long as their environments are conducive to growth, and that environmental changes that make survival more difficult will weaken and eventually extinguish the life form. This model transfers by analogy to the domain of intermediaries. As we look at the history of intermediary forms, we see that certain types seemed to prosper for a while, only to be replaced by other types following changes in the environment.

In the retailing area, convenience stores grew rapidly in the 1960s, but today their sales are either flat or declining because of environmental changes. Some convenience stores are located in areas in which the incidence of crime has increased, and they are frequent targets for thieves. Consumers afraid of being caught in a store robbery or of being assaulted in the parking lots of convenience stores are abandoning them for other retailers. Other convenience stores are in areas where the population has aged and people no longer live the hectic lifestyles that make convenience stores attractive. Video rental stores may undergo similar changes as their market becomes saturated and entertainment tastes change. On-demand access to movies via pay-per-view channels and other cable-based sources of entertainment may also adversely affect the demand for rented videos.

In the transportation services area, the express delivery business provides another example of a distribution system life cycle. Federal Express was one of the most successful companies of the 1970s as it capitalized on the need for express delivery of sensitive documents and state-of-the-art logistics technology. More efficient competitors, such as UPS, and low-cost facsimile machines, however, have caused a drop in the demand for some Federal Express services in the 1990s, and forced it to reposition itself.[5] The environment that nurtured overnight document delivery as a business has now endangered that business's viability, while at the same time giving rise to new opportunities.

As producers design and manage their distribution systems, they need to consider the environment and its effects on the life cycle of intermediaries. A bedding manufacturer such as Serta or Simmons, for example, would do well to consider the future of traditional furniture stores and department stores in the face of new types of retailers, such as single-line discounters (e.g., Heilig-Meyers) and wholesale clubs (e.g., Sam's). Other competing producers may already be capitalizing on the new types of intermediaries and hence be better positioned for future growth.

The Role of Psychological and Political Processes

Because distribution systems are composed of people, psychological and political processes play important roles as distribution systems develop. These processes are evident, for example, whenever people get accustomed to certain ways of doing business and resist change (psychological), or whenever outside organizations seek to influence the conduct of exchange in different ways (political).

Psychological and political processes are involved in the development of distribution systems at the same time as the economic and competitive forces discussed in chapter 3, but they are not always in harmony with those forces. It took almost

For most of this century, Sears was a great example of a retailer adapting successfully to its environment. It all began in 1886, when Richard W. Sears started selling watches by mail order. In the late nineteenth century the dominant form of retailing in the United States was the general store, and only large cities such as New York and Chicago boasted department stores. Enterprising retailers, however, began issuing catalogs and allowed rural shoppers to extend their purchasing power beyond local merchants. Richard Sears was following the lead of pioneers such as Aaron Montgomery Ward, who published his first catalog in 1872.

By 1910, Sears had expanded its offerings to thousands of items. Families could order just about anything from the Sears, Roebuck and Co. catalog. Apparel, soft goods, small appliances, and tools were standard features in many catalogs, but few had a selection as wide as Sears. In addition, Sears overcame the natural resistance of consumers to buying products they have not experienced by establishing mail-order houses throughout the rural United States, where the products could be seen and touched before being ordered. At one time or another Sears offered through its catalog and mail-order houses items such as plows, harvesters, covered wagons, motorcycles, automobiles, water pumps, violins, toilet paper, iceboxes, refrigerators, washers, dryers, stoves, fruit trees, grapevines, home remedies, books, furniture, bedding, and even kits for building a house on your own lot. Sears brought the products of the world to the mailboxes of rural America.

In the 1920s, Sears began adding retail stores to its catalog operations and mail-order houses, locating them close to its primary small-town markets. Capitalizing on its reputation and product depth, Sears offered prices below those of local stores and captured market share quickly. It opened stores in small- and medium-sized cities nationwide, and achieved almost immediate success. By the late 1930s, Sears was the world's largest retailer.

Sears' greatest growth came between the end of World War II and the 1960s. As automobile ownership grew in the United States, stores no longer had to be located near public transportation routes or in downtown areas. Sears recognized this trend early and invested in shopping-center and mall-based stores. But, as predicted by the wheel of retailing, the company had also become slow in responding to market changes, and its high overhead eroded its price advantage. Mass discounters, such as Woolworth, Kmart, and later Wal-Mart, arrived in the late 1950s, and they made substantial inroads into traditional Sears markets by offering lower prices on a more limited selection of products. During the 1970s and 1980s Sears suffered large declines in market share. The company was slow to adjust its strategies, fell behind in the adoption of new ideas, and became distracted by diversification into nonretail ventures, such as real estate (Coldwell Banker) and financial services (Dean Witter and the Discover credit card).

One way in which Sears lagged competitors was its venerable mail-order service. The 1980s saw explosive growth in mail-order retailing as millions of women entered the workforce and no longer had time for traditional shopping. It should have been a bonanza for Sears, given its long history in catalog retailing. Unlike its

10 years, for example, for laws deregulating the transportation industry to be instituted by Congress, even though such laws were economically and competitively justifiable in the early 1970s. Much of the resistance came from transportation providers who were afraid of change or felt threatened by the prospect of more efficient competitors. These companies formed a powerful political lobby that delayed

competitors, however, which offered 24-hour toll-free order service, accepted all major credit cards, and offered expedited delivery, Sears did not use 1-800 numbers, operated only during limited hours, would not accept credit cards other than Sears and Discover, and used arcane transportation providers.

Sears' decline continued throughout the 1980s and early 1990s, and culminated in the 1993 closing of its $3.3 billion money-losing catalog operations. Following the closing of its catalog business, Sears embarked on a repositioning strategy that targets its mainstream retail business, and is based on Sears' core competencies and reputation. Important to Sears' strategy was selling most of its nonretail investments, such as Dean Witter, Coldwell Banker, Discover, and the Allstate Insurance Company, and closing more than a hundred nonperforming stores in small towns. Also important was meeting more of the needs of its primary customer base—middle-income women between the ages of 25 and 54. To this end, Sears embarked on a $4 billion dollar renovation and expansion program, and has sought to expand its appeal to these core customers by improving its offerings in women's apparel and cosmetics.

Some examples of Sears' tactical moves are in its cosmetics and merchandising areas. True to its history of creating brands, such as Kenmore and Craftsman, Sears launched its Circle of Beauty line of cosmetics in 1995. It is positioned to compete in quality with department store brands such as Estee Lauder and Chanel, but is priced for its core customers. The line also caters to the overrepresentation of African American and Latina women in its customer base by including color selections for darker complexions. Sears has also changed its merchandising strategy by moving away from national programs toward those targeted by region. Although it maintains large stores in many locations, for example, Sears has also started opening small, single-line stores, such as Sears hardware stores and Homelife furniture stores, and operates the Western Auto chain of auto parts stores and the National Tire and Battery chain of light auto repair centers. The objective is to meet the needs of customers with limited time to shop and who want to stay away from the mall.

In its current strategy, Sears is responding to increasingly diverse markets and demands for value and customer service that characterize the 1990s. Sears' rebound strategy has been widely discussed by the business community, and it works. It is made possible by consumers who are once again making Sears the place "where America shops."

Sources: Susan Chandler, "Drill Bits, Paint Thinner, Eyeliner," *Business Week*, September 25, 1995, pp. 83–84.

Susan Chandler, "Where Sears Wants America to Shop Now," *Business Week*, June 12, 1995, p. 39.

Kevin Kelly, "The Big Store May Be on a Big Roll," *Business Week*, August 30, 1993, pp. 82–85.

Cyndee Miller, "It Was the Worst of Times," *Marketing News*, March 15, 1993, pp. 1ff.

Cyndee Miller, "Redux Deluxe: Sears Comeback an Event Most Marketers Would Kill For," *Marketing News*, July 15, 1996, pp. 1ff.

"Shaking Up Sears," *Chain Store Age Executive*, January 1993, p. 70.

"Tough Love Leaves $3.3B Up for Grabs," *Chain Store Age Executive*, March 1993, pp. 28–30.

deregulation efforts. Here we see psychological and political forces being combined to resist change, even though the changes were ultimately beneficial for the economy and the transportation industry.

Established distribution systems, like most other organizations, become comfortable and seek to protect and enhance their positions. Sometimes these efforts persist even when the current arrangements no longer make economic sense. This happens because people's jobs are threatened, because of the rights of companies and individuals within a political system, or simply because of the inevitable conflicts of interests between individuals and organizations. Regardless of the reasons, the end result is that at any point in time the existence and success of intermediaries are functions of economic factors, greater efficiency, psychological forces, and political clout. Not all types of intermediaries today are as effective as they could be, and not all government supports or restrictions are optimally beneficial. As the transportation industry illustrates, however, economic efficiency considerations are very strong and will eventually prevail in the design of distribution systems. Intermediaries will continue to prosper only as long as they benefit consumers and producers. Producers designing distribution systems must be sensitive to the forces affecting intermediaries, and seek ways of balancing their often conflicting trends. They must be careful not to become too dependent on distribution systems that exist for noneconomic reasons alone.

Legal and Ethical Implications of Distribution Systems

The importance of healthy intermediaries has not been lost on governments. Many countries take legislative and fiscal action to encourage the development of intermediaries. This is particularly noticeable in the nations of Eastern Europe, where most countries have production capabilities but lack the distribution systems that can close the geographic and demand-timing gaps between producers and consumers. Russia, Poland, Bulgaria, and other newly created free-trade economies have begun to invest in local and global distribution systems that will open their markets to other countries and position their goods and services in foreign markets.

Other examples of government actions that support intermediaries are the provisions for easier trade among countries in the European Union and among Canada, Mexico, and the United States as encouraged by the North American Free Trade Agreement (NAFTA). Although international free-trade agreements do not provide funds for intermediaries, they greatly reduce the costs involved in trade between member countries, making international distribution more profitable. Both Kmart and Wal-Mart, for example, invested aggressively in new stores in Mexico and Canada after NAFTA was ratified, because the agreement lowered import tariffs in both markets and allowed these companies to be price competitive with local retailers.[6]

The role of intermediaries is becoming even more important as we advance toward a global economy. Intermediaries working in industries such as textiles, energy, mining, and food production have made products available to customers in some of the fastest growing economies in Latin America, Africa, and Asia. One example is the role that intermediaries such as import-export companies, brokers, and transportation companies have played in the development of Taiwan's industries, which in turn have made that small country an important player in the global economy. The acceleration of information dissemination discussed in chapter 3 has been accompanied by an acceleration of distribution, and both have contributed to quicker and broader diffusion of advances throughout the world. Whereas it took more than 30 years between the invention of the refrigerator and its worldwide availability, for example, it took less than 10 years for minicomputers and less than three years for personal computers to gain global acceptance.

Distribution systems also have a dark side. Although they bring improved living standards to many people, sophisticated distribution systems also make it easy for the strong to exploit the weak. In the times of the Roman Empire and European colonizers, for example, distribution systems facilitated the slave trade, and although slavery has for the most part been eradicated in the twentieth century, the potential for exploitation remains.

Countries vary, however, in terms of what is considered acceptable and nonacceptable arrangements between producers and their intermediaries, and this must be taken into account by marketing managers involved in international distribution. Take, for example, the issue of parallel distribution or gray markets, which refer to the selling of trademarked products through distribution channels that are not authorized by the trademark holder. If automobiles were sold in Puerto Rico both by authorized dealers and by importers who buy them from U.S.-based dealers and ship them to the island, it would be considered a gray market. In the United States, there are laws against gray market activities, and authorized dealers can take legal action against unauthorized parallel importers. Not all countries, however, consider gray markets illegal or detrimental, and U.S.-based distributors trying to protect their authorized distributor status in other countries may find their court systems uncooperative.[7] It can be argued, in fact, that gray markets are economically beneficial to consumers because they lower prices. Such is the case in countries where there are no laws against monopolistic control of manufacturing or distribution, because they permit many people who cannot afford the monopolists' prices to still own products and enjoy their benefits. It is possible, therefore, that the legal position most beneficial in the United States is economically and socially unjustifiable in other countries. Marketing managers are well advised, therefore, to consider the legal and ethical implications of their distribution systems, but to always take into account the cultural and social contexts in which they are operating.

COMPONENTS OF MODERN DISTRIBUTION SYSTEMS

Marketing distribution systems can be classified along separate but related dimensions. The two most common are the relationship that various distribution system members enjoy and the number of levels in the distribution channel. *Distribution channel* is another term for distribution system: the set of people, organizations, and equipment involved in the satisfactory flow of goods or services from the producer to the consumer.

Although we discuss these classification dimensions separately, it is important to realize that they are interrelated, and that different types of relationships may exist within the same level-types of channel arrangements. Single-level distribution arrangements, for example, can be corporate, contractual, or conventional. It must also be noted that these classification schemes are useful for learning about distribution systems and their functions, but that real-life systems seldom fit nicely within any single category. In most industries, distribution systems evolve to meet the demands of the environment, and a wide variety of arrangements are possible.

Relationship Types in Distribution Systems

In terms of relationships, distribution systems may be categorized as corporate, contractual, or conventional. *Corporate distribution systems* are those in which a single company owns all levels of the distribution channel between producer and consumer. One common example involves banks that operate branch systems. In most such systems all branches, regardless of their location relative to bank headquarters, are fully owned and operated by the bank. Other common examples of corporate distribution systems are Sherwin-Williams paint stores, in which stores and manufacturing facilities are owned by the same parent company.

Contractual distribution systems are those in which the relationship between the producer and other distribution system members is intimate and relatively long term, but ownership remains separate. Examples of contractual distribution systems are those that exist between automobile manufacturers and their dealers. Automobile dealers operate as independent businesses who contract with manufacturers for a supply of new vehicles, parts, and other goods and services in exchange for representing the manufacturer in a given market. Relationships between auto manufacturers and their dealers are very close, as exemplified by their mutual involvement in each other's managerial decisions, and these relationships can last for many years.[8] In terms of ownership, however, dealers and auto manufacturers are separate legal entities in most cases.

Conventional distribution systems are those in which the relationship between producer and distribution channel members is at arm's length, must be reestablished for each new transaction, and can change from one transaction to the next. This has historically been the most common type of distribution system relationship, and it remains in widespread use today across many industries. Most universities, for example, purchase office furniture from multiple companies. In most cases, there is no official long-term agreement between any single office furniture producer and the university. Every time the need emerges for office equipment, the university goes to several office furniture producers for bids, and negotiates the terms of purchase for that transaction with the producer that best meets the university's needs at that time. The producers that get the business can differ from one purchase instance to the next, and the official channel relationship must be reestablished every time.

Conventional distribution systems can vary in terms of how much influence one distribution channel member can exert over others, and sometimes the larger, more influential members exercise substantial management control over other members of the system. One example is the arrangement between the large retailer Kmart and the small producer Quick Candy, in which Kmart has considerable input to Quick Candy's production and distribution decisions on a daily basis. Similar arrangements also exist between large manufacturers of durable goods (appliances, autos, machinery) and their suppliers, and are called *administered distribution systems*. The term *channel captain* is often used in reference to the channel's most influential member.

Different Levels in the Channel of Distribution

In terms of levels in a channel of distribution, there is technically no limit to their possible number, but there are practical limits as to how many transaction levels between producers and consumers can be managed effectively. Consequently, producers in the United States seldom work with more than three levels in a channel, and often try to work with fewer levels if possible. Thus, the most common level category distinctions for distribution channels are zero-level, single-level, and multilevel systems, as illustrated in Figure 13.2. In other countries, such as Japan, more than three levels in a distribution system are quite common.

Zero-Level Systems

A zero-level, or direct distribution, system involves a producer selling directly to final customers, and is illustrated by the leftmost flow column in Figure 13.2. In zero-level systems, the producer either initiates the contact, as in door-to-door sales and home-party programs, or waits for customers to initiate contact, as in company-owned retail stores. Door-to-door selling has been used effectively to sell products ranging from magazines to refrigerators, and remains popular with products sold as fund raisers (e.g.,

FIGURE 13.2

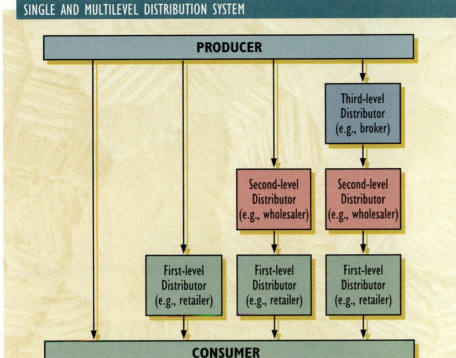

SINGLE AND MULTILEVEL DISTRIBUTION SYSTEM

cookies, magazine subscriptions). Home parties are also used extensively by consumer-goods producers. They are used to sell cosmetics (Avon), kitchenware (Tupperware and Cutco Knives), intimate apparel (UndercoverWear) and many other products.

Another form of direct distribution is *automated distribution*, such as vending machines or automated teller machines (ATMs). In these systems, producers use technology to provide reliable, versatile, and convenient distribution to consumers. Automated distribution systems are not necessarily a low-cost approach (vending machines and ATMs are notoriously expensive to maintain), but their convenient access generates transactions that might not otherwise take place. In some countries, in fact, the need for convenience has pushed the use of automated vending far beyond the typical sale of candy, beverages, and cigarettes, as illustrated in Marketing Anecdote 13.3. Advances in computer technology are making automated distribution systems even more popular, with airline and railroad tickets now being sold through interactive systems.[9] Some experts suggest that as many as 25 percent of all airline ticketing will be done through electronic ticket outlets by 2000. Automated vending is one area in which different types of relationships are possible, with some producers (e.g., Coca-Cola) owning their own machines (corporate), whereas others have long-term leases on space in vending machines owned by others (contractual), or move their products in and out of vending machines owned by others in response to market conditions (conventional).

Direct mail is another form of direct distribution used by producers, most often used to sell highly specialized products to small commercial market segments. Customized office management software for institutions (e.g., churches) and professionals (e.g., medical, legal) is frequently sold via direct mail. Direct mail also

Mention Tokyo, and most people think of streets congested with millions of people, small houses, and shops with limited storage space, and a hectic pace of life matched by few if any other cities in the world. In Tokyo, both space and time are at a premium, and convenience shopping has been refined to a fine art, clearly evident in their use of automatic vending machines.

Tokyo vending machines distribute consumer products at all levels, ranging from $100 Armani ties and stuffed animals to $30 bottles of whiskey to $5 glasses of beer—in some cases replacing all live sales personnel. Vending machines in Tokyo are also much more numerous and located much more conveniently than vending machines in the United States. There are almost as many vending machines in Japan—a country roughly the size of Montana—as there are in all of the United States. Quite often, machines for very expensive products are located on street corners or parks next to Coke machines, and are designed to be aesthetically compatible with the landscape. They are also designed to be ergonomically compatible with their target audience, varying in height and access based on the product category.

There are several factors that contribute to the widespread use of vending machines in Japan. First is the almost total absence of vandalism and petty theft, making it possible to leave expensive inventory (e.g., $100 ties) in unattended machines. Second is the limited amount of storage available in the average Japanese home, where the refrigerator is seldom larger than five cubic feet (compared to the typical U.S. refrigerator size of 20 cubic feet). Third is the congestion in the streets and sidewalks, which makes transporting the large number of items typical of a U.S. shopping trip a serious challenge. Tokyo shoppers buy much of what they need as they need it, and vending machines make it very convenient and safe to do so. As long as urban and social conditions in Tokyo remain as they are, its use of vending machines is likely to increase in terms of number and the variety of products for which they are used; and as congestion, disposable income, and consumer demands continue to escalate in other metropolitan markets around the world, they are likely to emulate the Tokyo example.

Source: Mary Jordan, "Coin-Operated Japan: An On-the-go Lifestyle Helps Make Tokyo the Vending Machine Capital of the World," *Washington Post,* National Weekly Edition, March 25–30, 1996, p. 13. © 1996 *The Washington Post.* Reprinted with permission.

allows producers to reach individual consumers. Microsoft, for example, used direct mail when it introduced the Windows 95 operating environment in 1995; and achieved move than 60 percent adoption by previous Windows 3.0 and DOS users in less than a year.

When intermediaries are introduced, the distribution system becomes a *vertical distribution arrangement.* Any distribution system with one or more intermediaries at different functional levels (e.g., wholesale, retail) is a vertical distribution system, as opposed to *horizontal distribution arrangements* in which two or more organizations at the *same* functional level form a cooperative arrangement. Vertical distribution systems are commonplace, such as when Procter & Gamble uses Safeway to distribute disposable diapers. Horizontal distribution systems are not as common. An example of a horizontal arrangement would be a U.S. producer of beverages using a local producer's network to distribute its product in Europe. Such was the case with Gatorade, which had a horizontal agreement in the early 1980s with a producer of olive oil to use the same distribution network in the Spanish market. In this instance, two producers use the same distribution system for their mutual benefit. Gatorade has since abandoned the horizontal agreement and uses its own vertical distribution system throughout much of the European market.

Single-Level Systems

Single-level systems, which have one intermediary between producer and customer, come in different forms. In this section we discuss three general types used by producers: those that use an external salesforce, those that sell directly to retailers, and those that franchise. Figure 13.2 illustrates only one of these types: producers who sell directly to retailers.

External Salesforce. Chapter 11 discusses the choice between an internal and an external salesforce as a decision made by companies, but in that chapter we view the decision from a sales manager's perspective. From a distribution perspective, the decision can be seen as a choice between a single-level or zero-level system. Companies with limited operating capital often use an external salesforce, taking advantage of the financing and personal contact functions that intermediaries offer. This approach releases funds to improve other areas of the business, but companies must also give up some control over the customer relationships. External sales personnel are seldom as committed to protecting producers' interests as a company's own employees, and they often shift loyalties as profit margins change. An external salesforce is not a good choice for manufacturers whose products require extensive explanation or service, or for strategies focused on long-term relationships with final customers. It is more suitable for products that are differentiated on the basis of their technological capabilities, such as complex machinery, proprietary software, and patented mechanical devices. Many industrial products are sold through an external salesforce. External salesforces can be used under contractual arrangements, such as manufacturer's representatives who commit to represent the producer for a specified period of time. They can also be used under conventional arrangements, such as brokers who renegotiate terms with producers every time there is a change to the product or the market.

External salesforces are also sometimes used to sell goods and services to consumers. Independent insurance agents, for example, represent different insurance companies concurrently but are not employed by any one company, and real estate agents can represent various developers but remain as independent salespeople. In similar fashion, some financial planners sell investment products for several mutual fund companies, but they are not employed by the fund managers. The relationships that real estate agents, independent insurance agents, and financial planners have with their suppliers are best characterized as contractual arrangements.

External salesforce arrangements can vary in terms of the salesforce taking or not taking ownership of the products. Independent insurance agents, real estate agents, and financial planners are all examples of external salesforces that do not take ownership. Distribution arrangements in which an intermediary's marketing system is contracted by a producer, but the marketing intermediary never takes ownership of the products being offered, are sometimes called *brokered arrangements*. Publisher's Clearing House, for example, manages direct marketing programs for magazine publishers such as Time-Life and McGraw-Hill, but never takes title or handles the publications they sell. Brokered arrangements are common in the distribution of industrial commodities, such as farm produce, minerals, and processed metals.

Producers of these types of products hire brokers to find buyers and make all distribution-related arrangements (e.g., transportation, letters of credit, import-export permits), but retain title to the goods until they are shipped to the final buyer.

Selling Directly to Retailers. In another single-level distribution arrangement, producers sell directly to retailers, as in the case of Quick Candy selling its lollipops to Kmart. Personal computer giants such as Packard Bell, Compaq, and IBM also use direct sales to retailers as part of their overall strategy, primarily targeting electronic discounters such as Circuit City. All of these companies have product lines designed specifically for distribution through discount retailers, supplemented by other lines aimed at commercial and professional office customers.[10]

Direct sales to retailers has a long history, as illustrated by the case of Sears. Since the 1930s, Sears has bought products directly from producers; in some cases becoming the producer's sole customer. Throughout much of its history, however, Sears exercised such arrangements only with small producers. More recently, selling directly to retailers has become an increasingly common initiative among consumer products giants such as Procter & Gamble and Unilever, and large apparel manufacturers such as VF Corp. and Levi Strauss. Large retailers such as Sears, JCPenney, and Wal-Mart, who want to eliminate levels of intermediaries in search of lower prices, have in many cases demanded such arrangements. Large companies go along with these arrangements because it gives their products visibility on the shelves of the world's largest retailers, and because it gives them access to the consumer purchase information that these stores collect at the point of sale. In some situations, in fact, meeting the distribution demands of large retailers can produce a significant competitive advantage, as illustrated in Marketing Anecdote 13.4.

Selling directly to retailers often requires large investments in computer equipment and software, bar-coding hardware, and materials-handling and packaging equipment. These investments often add up to millions of dollars, putting them out of reach for most small- and medium-sized producers of consumer goods. For those companies, the primary channel arrangements are multilevel systems involving wholesalers, retailers, and other intermediaries, generally called *facilitators*. These arrangements are discussed in the sections on multilevel distribution systems.

Most direct-to-retailer distribution arrangements are contractual and require a high level of integration between producer and intermediary. Both producers and retailers are hesitant to enter into such arrangements unless there is some assurance of a long-term stream of business coming from the relationship. Having a contractual arrangement, however, does not always mean there is equity between the parties, as discussed in the section on ethical concerns of single-level distribution systems.

Franchising. Another contractual single-level marketing arrangement used frequently for consumer and industrial products is franchising.[11] Although not all franchising involves a single-level system, many products and service marketers use this approach because it gives producers more control over the final sale than the more conventional multilevel arrangements. In franchise arrangements, the *franchiser* (e.g., producer) provides the *franchisee* (e.g., retailer) with support services and exclusive rights to market its products. In return, the franchisee agrees to pay franchise fees and follow franchise-specific procedures, which can be quite extensive. Quite often franchisees are restricted from selling directly competing products or services, and must observe strict sales and operational practices. Franchise arrangements are roughly categorized as trade-name franchising or business franchising, depending on the restrictions placed on the franchisee.

The jeans market in the United States has long been large and competitive, with brands such as Lee, Levi's, and Wrangler fighting for shelf space with designer brands such as Girbaud, and private label brands such as Britannia; and as long as shelf space remains at a premium and controlled by large companies like JCPenney and Wal-Mart, the competitive fervor is not likely to subside.

Two of the biggest players in this market are VF Corporation, manufacturer of Lee and Wrangler jeans, and Levi Strauss, producer of Levi's Original jeans and variations such as the highly successful 501/505 line. Each company markets a complete line of products, considered by some consumers to be highly substitutable. In their distribution systems, however, their strategies are far apart.

In order to control retail shelf space and gain the cooperation of large retailers, VF has invested heavily since the early 1990s in electronic data interchange hardware and software, which allows the company to monitor individual retailer sales and inventory levels, and restock within an average of 48 hours from the time of sale. On a daily basis, for example, VF receives sales information from Wal-Mart's point-of-sale systems, processes it, and issues instructions to its warehousing or manufacturing facilities for restocking by size and style as needed. The product leaves the VF facilities prelabeled to Wal-Mart specifications and ready to go on the shelf on arrival. Such fast turnaround is a big improvement over the long-term industry average of two to three months. This level of service has made VF popular with retailers ranging from mass discounters to department stores, and has helped it gain market share at the expense of Levi Strauss and other competitors.

Levi Strauss, facing the same competitive environment, has opted for a more mixed strategy. It has been building its electronic data interchange capabilities at a slower pace than VF, following the lead of retail giants such as JCPenney and Wal-Mart instead of taking the initiative. At the same time, however, it has also been building its company-owned stores, and experimenting with unique offerings, such as custom-fit jeans. Levi Strauss has applied computer technology to improving communications with its manufacturing sites and accelerating their response times dramatically, and has been able to attain 10- to 12-day delivery of custom-fit jeans for only a $10 premium over regular jeans. In effect, Levi Strauss is building a corporate single-level distribution system to supplement its existing systems, and trying to reduce its dependence on increasingly powerful retailers who are less likely than company-owned stores to build the Levi's brand image.

It is unlikely that either of these distribution strategies will conclusively prove to be better than the other, because their success is affected by all other aspects of the companies' marketing strategies. The obvious winners in this competition are consumers, who have more product and outlet choices at highly competitive prices.

Sources: Alice Z. Cuneo, "Levi Strauss Sizes the Retail Scene," *Advertising Age*, January 23, 1995, p. 4.

Mark Hendricks and Susan Hasty, "L. S. & Co. Tries on Custom-Fit Jeans," *Apparel Industry Magazine*, January 1995, pp. 32–34.

Faye Rice, "One Writer's Hunt for the Perfect Jeans," *Fortune*, April 17, 1995, p. 30.

Joseph Weber, "Just Get it to the Stores on Time," *Business Week*, March 6, 1995, pp. 66–67.

Trade-name franchising gives the franchisee exclusive rights to market the franchiser's products, provided that the franchisee complies with stipulations such as using special displays, participating in promotional events, and promising to not use the products as loss leaders (discussed in chapter 10). In most trade-name franchising arrangements, franchisers do not control store layout, location, or the noncompeting inventory carried by the retailer. Black & Decker, for example, has no control over the operations of its hardware store dealers.

Some trade-name franchise arrangements, however, are more restrictive. U.S. automobile distribution, for example, has historically been done by trade-name franchisees. Dealers are given the right to sell a brand such as Ford, Toyota, or Dodge in an exclusive geographic area, provided they have an adequate sales and service facility, maintain a specified parts inventory, and participate in at least some manufacturer-sponsored promotional programs. Some auto distribution arrangements also restrict the other brands of automobiles that dealers can sell and require that they not sell directly competing lines. Car dealerships are classified as trade-name franchises in spite of these restrictions because the producer does not impose a specific method of doing business on the franchisee; dealerships are free to choose their own marketing style.

Business franchising, on the other hand, does regulate franchisee marketing methods. Business franchising is one of the fastest growing forms of retailing in the United States, and is also becoming popular in other parts of the world. This growth has been fueled largely by the shift toward a service economy and the popular desire to be self employed. In a typical business franchise, the franchisee makes a substantial up-front payment to the franchiser and agrees to comply with procedural rules that touch on most aspects of the business. Quite often, franchisees must build specialized facilities or invest in equipment built to the franchiser's specifications. In exchange for these investments, franchisees receive extensive marketing support. Product and/or service design is tightly controlled by the franchiser, who is also responsible for all marketing research. Franchisers also promote the product (other than direct sales), price the product line, and choose locations.

McDonald's is a familiar example of a business franchise system; it has existed for more than 40 years and continues to be highly successful. A McDonald's franchisee's investment can be as high as $1,000,000, primarily to cover initial fees and build a facility to McDonald's specifications. Franchisees must also pay ongoing fees of approximately 12 percent of their gross sales. Franchisees must adhere to strict cleanliness standards, follow rigorous procedures in food preparation and material handling, buy raw materials and supplies only from specified sources, and attend company-sponsored training at their own expense. Despite these requirements, hundreds of people are willing to do what it takes to become McDonald's franchisees every year because they will be joining one of the most consistently successful prepared-food enterprises in the world. Other fast-food chains, such as Burger King and Wendy's, make similar demands from their franchisees, and offer them a similar potential for success.

Business franchising is used in industries other than fast food, and some of its applications are very creative. H & R Block, for example, franchises a nationally recognized tax and accounting services program and continues to look for innovative ways to serve taxpayers. In recent years, H & R Block franchisees have started offering electronic tax return filing and loans secured by tax refunds to differentiate themselves from other tax preparation services. Quick oil change and lubrication services have also become a profitable franchise area throughout the United States and Canada. Shops such as Jiffy Lube offer oil and filter change, lubrication, and servicing of other systems in as little as 15 minutes for a price not much higher than the retail cost of materials. They are a welcome retail service alternative to busy consumers who cannot service their own vehicles or wait for hours at a traditional service station.

Legal and Ethical Concerns Associated with Single-level Distribution Systems. As mentioned earlier, distribution systems can give considerable power to intermediaries, and whenever there is a large concentration of power, the potential for illegal and/or unethical behavior also arises; successful single-level arrangements are no exception.

One current concern is the effect that mass discounters who buy directly from producers have on small retailers and wholesalers. Mass discounters' primary motivation is to buy at lower cost so they can offer prices below those of competitors and still make a profit. At an aggregate level it is a practice that benefits consumers, because lower prices improve consumers' purchasing power and standards of living. But at an individual business level, powerful mass discounters create serious problems for more traditional intermediaries. Wholesalers, for example, have experienced substantial drops in sales, and retailers that do not have the same buying power as mass discounters are being forced out of business. At the level of the local economy, these dislocations often eliminate jobs and give the mass discounter a virtual retail monopoly. The impact on small retailers of aggressive mass discounter expansion has been so severe that in some cases small retailers have petitioned the FTC to investigate mass discounters' distribution and pricing practices, claiming some of the practices violate antitrust regulations. Others have filed law suits in local courts for unfair pricing practices and have won favorable settlements.[12] This is an issue likely to remain at the forefront on retail industry watchers.

Another concern is the practice by powerful channel members of forcing smaller and less powerful members to make specialized investments in plant and equipment, only to drop them from the channel when lower-cost options become available or markets change. Take the hypothetical example of a small U.S.-based lamp manufacturer having to invest in die-casting machinery in order to win a lamp contract from Kmart or Sears. Die-casting machinery is expensive and requires four to five years of use to recover the investment. If Sears or Kmart require the lamp manufacturer to invest in such equipment, and then cancel the contract a year later, the U.S.-based producer would experience great hardship and may even go out of business. Investments in special computer equipment and software for electronic data interchange are also common requirements of large channel members, and can have the same effect when contracts are terminated early. Calls have been issued by small producers and some consumer groups for government investigation of such practices among large retailers.[13]

A third area of concern is franchising. In this area, the inherent structure of the franchiser–franchisee relationship lends itself to abuse because in most situations large and powerful franchisers have great control over much smaller and weaker franchisees. While franchiser arrangements provide opportunities for many people to operate their own businesses, unscrupulous franchisers can take advantage of less sophisticated and financially strapped individuals. Recent years have seen increasing franchise complaints filed with the Federal Trade Commission, as well as numerous calls for franchise regulation.[14] Franchisers, of course, object to FTC intervention, claiming it disrupts their operations and causes franchisees to lose business.

In most situations, problems between channel members are not resolved through legal intervention but through cooperative problem solving and smart marketing strategy.[15] The second most common way to resolve problems is through third-party arbitration, used most commonly in high-investment stakes situations, when the issues are complex, or when the resolution is likely to have long-term policy implications.

In cases in which small channel members are at risk because of required specialized investments, it has been suggested that they offset the transaction-specific investments with other investments that give them control over other aspects of the distribution arrangements.[16] The lamp manufacturer, for example, might invest in patenting a unique switch system that consumers find attractive and no other competitor can offer. This would restrict the retailers' options and protect the lamp supplier. In cases where intermediaries are required to make investments to better service the producers' customers, the offsetting investments can be to expand the relationship with the customers and win their loyalty, thus undermining the producer's control.

The abuse of power by some channel members also poses ethical dilemmas for managers of distribution systems.[17] Although forcefully manipulating channel arrangements can generate short-term gains, it can also produce substantial social costs that will not be evident until much later. Slavery, for instance, produced great wealth to sugar and cotton producers in North America and the Caribbean, but also incalculable social losses in the eighteenth and nineteenth centuries. In like manner, the loss of viable economic sectors such as wholesaling or small retailers can have serious economic consequences that will not arise until 10 or 15 years later. Marketing managers need to consider the ethical implications of their distribution system decisions, both short-term and long-term, rather than waiting for social costs to become unbearable. Producers such as General Electric and Whirlpool, who protect small retailers against electronics and appliance discounters by giving them their own product lines and technical support services, seem to lead the way in farsighted programs.[18]

Multilevel Distribution Systems

Multilevel systems are illustrated by the two rightmost columns in Figure 13.2. Multilevel systems feature more than one intermediary between the producer and the consumer. In the United States the most common multilevel system is the two-level arrangement in which producers sell to wholesalers who sell to retailers who sell to consumers. These arrangements typically feature independent intermediaries and arm's-length transactions, making them conventional arrangements.

Consider, for example, the case of A. T. Cross, a manufacturer of writing instruments.[19] Cross's multilevel system is similar to the one highlighted in Figure 13.2. The company produces a broad range of writing instruments that vary in their use of precious metals and writing technology (e.g., ball-point, pencil, soft-tip) and range in price from less than $10.00 to more than $100.00. Their objective is to cater to the demands of consumers at different income levels for beautiful and practical writing instruments. Although some Cross products are sold directly to companies for use as promotional gifts (as discussed in chapter 9), most are sold to individual consumers. The millions of potential Cross customers in the United States alone shop at thousands of retail establishments, and the number and variety of establishments makes it too costly for Cross to use direct distribution to all retailers. Instead, the company sells directly only to retail and corporate accounts who are willing to make a large investment in inventory, and uses wholesalers serving different sectors of the retailing industry (e.g., jewelry stores, bookstores, department stores) for most of its other accounts.

Multilevel systems have some advantages and disadvantages. They typically include wholesalers, retailers, and common carriers. Common carriers (not shown in

Fig. 13.2) provide transportation services (air, truck, rail) and carry goods for any shipper, using standard rates and routes. An important characteristic of multilevel arrangements is that title or ownership moves with the product; first to the wholesaler, then to the retailer, and finally to the consumer. Title brings with it both risks and control. As the product moves through the channel, wholesalers and retailers in turn assume the risks of damage, loss, and sudden shifts in demand for as long as they hold title to the product. This is a benefit to the producer, who can then focus on other factors, such as product design and manufacturing, and not worry about pricing or merchandising. Another benefit of multilevel systems to producers is that they receive payment from the wholesaler when goods are shipped rather than when they are sold to consumers, which accelerates the producer's cash flow.

The benefits of reduced risk and faster cash flow, however, come at the cost of giving up control over the product line and its final sale to consumers. Although Cross tries to create demand for its products through advertising, final consumers encounter many competing brands (e.g., Parker, Mont Blanc) at the point of sale and can easily be swayed by another product's styling or by the retailers' suggestion of another brand. Cross also has no control over how the product is presented at the store in terms of shelf position, visibility, and other merchandising concerns. Merchandising can vary in importance by product, but it is very important for luxury products such as expensive writing instruments.

Cross's arrangement with its wholesalers is a conventional distribution arrangement because the producer, wholesaler, and retailer are all independent entities, and they relate to each other primarily at arm's length. It is also possible to have corporate or contractual multilevel distribution systems. These are multilevel systems in which intermediaries are owned or contractually controlled by other intermediaries or by the producers. For example, True Value, Sentry, and Pro hardware stores are retailer cooperatives that own their wholesale distributors, and thus can be classified as corporate distribution systems. Wholesaler-sponsored distribution systems are also possible, such as the Independent Grocers Association (I.G.A.). I.G.A. grocers are affiliated but not owned by wholesalers, however, and the arrangement must be classified as a contractual distribution system.

Producer cooperatives are a third distinct example of a multilevel system in which the intermediary is owned by another channel member. Producer cooperatives are most frequently found in the agricultural sector and are owned by their farmer members. Their primary function is to facilitate the movement of goods and services both to and from the farm; they are, in effect, large, privately owned distribution systems. Growmark, for example, serves farmers in Illinois, Iowa, and parts of Missouri and Indiana. It functions as an intermediary for farmers in the purchase of commodities such as fertilizer, seed, feed, and fuel; it is also involved in the sale and transportation of farm produce to domestic and foreign markets. Some producer cooperatives have even developed their own consumer brands, such as Sun Maid raisins and Diamond walnuts.

Note that the classification of distribution systems is somewhat arbitrary. True Value and I.G.A. are clearly multilevel systems in terms of product movement, but from an organizational perspective they are not true multilevel systems because producers sell to a single organization that controls both wholesale and retail activities. From the producer's perspective there is only one transaction; these are single-level arrangements even though the physical movement of the product involves more than one level. This reinforces our earlier point about classification schemes being useful for learning, but oversimplifying the rich variety of systems that exist in the marketplace.

Managing multilevel channel arrangements can be challenging and complex. It requires that marketing managers reconcile the type of arrangement (e.g., producer cooperative, wholesale voluntary, conventional) with the decision-making processes and structures (e.g., bureaucratic, participative, negotiated), and this combination of factors has implications for different competitive tactical areas (e.g., services offered, use of promotions).[20] Not all channel arrangements can be managed the same way, and some producers, such as Cross, may need to adopt slightly different procedures with its individual channels. Although this increases the cost and complexity of distribution management, it is a small price to pay for the flexibility and large-scale market penetration that multilevel distribution can provide.

Multiple-Channel Arrangements

Multiple-channel arrangements exist when producers manage different level-type and relationship arrangements concurrently, in order to maximize distribution. The manufacturing arm of Inland, for example, sells directly to automobile manufacturers through long-term contractual arrangements, to its distribution centers through a corporate arrangement, and occasionally in the spot market or through brokers in conventional arrangements. In a year's time, Inland sells steel through each of the distribution arrangements represented in Figure 13.2 and probably through other variations. Inland is willing to accept the varying distribution arrangements and levels of control over the final sale as a cost of doing business.

Multiple-channel arrangements have become more popular in recent years, as a result of changes in the retailing environment. The growth in do-it-yourself home improvement and auto repairs by consumers, for example, has motivated mass discounters to expand their product lines, and made it economically feasible for producers to sell directly to discounters while also maintaining their more traditional distribution channels. In chapter 6 we saw that the Delphi–Energy Management Systems Division of General Motors sells air filters and spark plugs directly to major discounters such as Western Auto, to other divisions of General Motors and their dealers, and to wholesalers who cater to small auto parts stores and auto repair shops.

Another manufacturer that has responded to the increase in do-it-yourself practices by consumers is American Standard, which sells standard-grade plumbing products to wholesalers and discount-grade products to home-improvement discounters such as Home Depot and Lowe's. This practice of offering different grades of products through various channels is also used by other producers. A recent study, for example, found 62 variations on the same size of television from the same manufacturer being sold by different discount retailers in a single metropolitan area.[21] Other examples of products with large numbers of brand variants were 35 mm cameras, with 37 variants, and sleeping bags, with 40. In some cases the feature and performance differences between branded variants from the same producer are minimal, but in other cases they can be substantial, because manufacturers must sometimes alter the quality and features of a product in order to meet mass discounters' demands for lower prices. Consumers must be careful in their purchases and not assume that all products carrying the same brand are of similar quality.

One last retailing development that facilitates multiple-channel arrangements are manufacturers' outlet malls. These retail centers feature single-producer outlets for Reebok, Levi's, and Pfaltzgraff, among many others and have become very popular with price-conscious consumers. The stores are owned and operated by producers who maintain distribution arrangements with other retailers also. Producers find outlet malls an attractive supplement to their traditional distribution systems because at least a portion of outlet-mall customers would not purchase the same products in traditional retail stores. Sales to these customers represent incremental business for the producer. Other outlet-mall customers, however, purchase items that they would have otherwise bought at other retail stores. Some retailers have thus come to see manufacturer's outlets as direct competition from the producer, and have dropped a manufacturer's products when an outlet opens nearby. In order to maintain their multiple-channel systems, some producers have responded to retailer concerns by agreeing to locate outlets no closer than 30 to 35 miles from traditional retailers offering the same products.

DESIGNING AND EVALUATING DISTRIBUTION SYSTEMS

Managers address two goals in the design and evaluation of distribution systems: meeting target market demands and supporting the producer's long-term strategic objectives. Ideally, these goals are compatible, but differences in both the internal and external environments produce a myriad of possible tactical approaches to their achievement. It is important, therefore, that marketing managers design and evaluate their distribution systems after careful consideration of both their internal capabilities and market conditions. Of critical importance is gaining the cooperation of intermediaries in maintaining a long-term orientation at all levels of the distribution channel.

Achieving a Long-Term Orientation

Intermediary demands are generally stated in terms of performance "here and now." Retailers and other intermediaries who take title to goods and put their own resources at risk do not tolerate producer mistakes, nor products that fail to live up to consumer expectations. Even in long-term contractual arrangements between producers and intermediaries, including the increasingly popular partnership arrangements discussed in chapter 6, the focus of most transactions is meeting immediate needs in ways that profit all parties. Failure to meet those goals puts all the good intentions for a long-lasting relationship in jeopardy. Kmart and Delphi–Energy Management Systems, for example, may have a long-term contract, but every time Kmart buys oil filters it tailors the order to current demands and will be dissatisfied if there are discrepancies between what is ordered and what is received, or if the product fails. Given these pressures, it is easy for channel members to develop a short-term orientation when designing and evaluating distribution systems.

Distribution system decisions, however, cannot take just a "here and now" perspective. Regardless of the type of system (corporate, contractual, or conventional) and the number of levels involved, it takes time and money to train people, print order forms, establish reporting systems, and work out the myriad details that ensure a smooth and secure flow of goods. All channel members make large investments that require long-term stability to realize positive returns. In addition, as we have already discussed, distribution systems have a social impact both in the way they affect consumers and in their effect on the many people these systems employ. When designing distribution systems, producers and intermediaries need to consider the long-term implications of their systems in terms of customer satisfaction and social responsibility, as well as the shorter-term concerns of profitability and success.

The two most important determinants of a long-term orientation in channel relationships are the levels of trust and interdependence existing between producer and intermediaries.[22] Trust has a similar effect on both producers and intermediaries, with higher levels of trust being associated with more long-term orientation. Interdependence, however, has different effects. When intermediaries are more dependent on producers than producers are on them, they are more likely to have a long-term orientation. If the producer, however, is the more dependent party in the relationship, intermediaries are less likely to have a long-term orientation. To engender a long-term orientation throughout the distribution system, marketing managers must build trust through their words and actions. It is important as well for producers to provide reasons for intermediaries to be dependent on them, such as exceptional products, healthy profit margins, or services that no other producers offer, and to reduce their own dependence on intermediaries whenever possible.

Internal Capabilities and Constraints

Internal capabilities and constraints that marketing managers should consider are relatively easy to identify because they are no different from those considered for any other marketing decision. First, companies need to consider their *internal company resources* and make sure the distribution system will not tax the company beyond its capabilities. A proposed distribution system that doubles production output and employment demands in a matter of weeks or months, for example, probably cannot be absorbed by most companies, and thus should not be adopted. Companies need to consider the condition of their capital assets (plants, equipment, office space), their information systems' capabilities and ease of change, and their human capital. A new distribution system can have implications for all of these areas if it results in large shifts or increases in demand within a short period after implementation. Overtaxing any one of these areas can cut short the gains from redesigning the distribution system and put the company into a precarious market position. The distribution system should build on company strengths and offset its weaknesses, as illustrated by the different strategies of Levi Strauss and VF Corporation in Marketing Anecdote 13.4.

Companies also need to consider both the level and nature of their *cost structures* in designing their distribution systems, because distribution arrangements vary in terms of the costs and the financial constraints they impose on the company. Companies with large capital reserves and low production costs, for example, may consider establishing capital-intensive corporate distribution systems, particularly if the firm has high growth potential and needs to control its distribution from manufacturing to consumer. That seems to be the case for Levi Strauss, as it pursues its company store and custom-fit jeans strategy. Levi Strauss is a large company and can afford the multibillion dollar investment its strategy requires. Companies with high fixed cost, that face high capital demands from other areas, or that need flexibility, however, are probably better off with less binding contractual or conventional systems, even if the choice means lower per unit profits and less control and integration. Although VF is also a large company, it sees flexibility as strategically desirable, and chooses to sustain contractual distribution rather than corporate distribution arrangements.

External Factors

Beyond structural and cost concerns, companies also need to consider their external environment. In particular, they must examine *competitor's strategies* and how they affect the company's potential markets. Competitors with established distribution relationships are difficult to displace, and new companies may find more success with distribution strategies that bypass existing systems instead of challenging the status quo directly. By placing company-owned stores in select locations Levi Strauss seeks to bypass existing competitive arrangements.

Producers also need to consider *available intermediaries* and how they fit with a company's plans and abilities. Not all intermediary arrangements are equally compatible with a company's culture and managerial practices, and incompatible distribution arrangements can disrupt company operations. When IBM first started selling personal computers in the early 1980s, its traditional salesforce could not handle the product adequately and this forced the company into new distribution arrangements. Traditional IBM salespeople were used to selling large capital investments (e.g., mainframes, minicomputers, and peripherals), which involved high levels of customization using IBM-controlled hardware and software. They had a difficult time selling what the market saw as standardized appliances, for which all customization was done by the user and most software and peripherals were not IBM controlled. In a break with past practices, therefore, IBM distributed its personal computers through independent dealers, a move often considered a key factor in the IBM PC's early success.

Finally, companies need to consider *general market demands*. The performance criteria used by customers differ by industry and geographic location, and these differences can have a significant impact on the distribution system design. In general, current consumer and industrial markets emphasize three areas: expediency in distribution, intensity of market coverage, and adaptability to meet market changes.

Expediency

Expedient distribution has long been a concern in industries that deal with perishable products. The food industry is a classic example of a sector for which timely delivery is critical. Large companies such as Keebler, Nabisco, and Frito-Lay have multilevel corporate systems that control the movement of products all the way to the grocery store shelf, whereas other companies, such as Stokeley–Van Camp and Del Monte, control distribution through contracts with warehousing and transportation specialists.

A factor adding to the importance of expediency is the growing popularity of inventory management based on the *just-in-time* philosophy. This philosophy focuses on minimizing the amount of material held in inventory, so that manufacturing deviations surface quickly and can be corrected with a minimum of scrap output.[23] It is closely related to the philosophy of continuous improvement practiced by many Japanese companies, and helps explain why Japan leads the world in technologies that support the just-in-time approach. In Japan, just-in-time methods have been adopted in virtually every industry (see Marketing Anecdote 13.5). Today these practices are being applied by companies throughout the world.

As mentioned in chapter 6, the automotive industry has made just-in-time practices an indispensable criterion for evaluating suppliers. To sell components to the U.S. auto industry, suppliers must have competitive products, promotion, and pricing, as well as the capacity for expedient delivery. Just-in-time practices have helped improve the quality of autos produced in the United States, and are being adopted by other assembly-intensive industries such as appliances and computer hardware. Even some retailers (e.g., Wal-Mart, Sears), are adopting such systems, and service industries will likely adopt some variations of just-in-time methods in the future.

Marketing managers considering just-in-time practices as an integral part of their distribution system, however, should keep in mind the high costs involved in developing such a system, as well as the lead times involved. Just-in-time systems require cross-functional and interorganizational integration, with people from engineering, purchasing, materials management, marketing, and accounting all working together, sharing information, and helping one another solve problems.[24] It takes

In Japan, 7-Eleven convenience stores are part of the Ito-Yokado franchise system, one of Japan's largest retailers. As in the United States, the Ito-Yokado 7-Eleven stores are owned and operated by independent franchisees—but the similarities stop there. One difference, size, has the Ito-Yokado 7-Eleven stores averaging only 1,100 square feet instead of the more traditional U.S. size of 2,000 square feet; this difference reflects the scarcity of real estate in Japan. Another important difference is the frequency with which stores change items in stock. Although they offer roughly half the number of items as their U.S. counterparts, Japanese franchisees replace between one half and two thirds of their stock items annually, compared with 20 to 25 percent in the United States. Overburdened inventories, resulting in lower turnover and poorer on-time performance, is a problem these Japanese stores are trying to overcome. Ito-Yokado's objective is to sell only the products and quantities franchisees need. As a result, excess and obsolete inventory decreases substantially, whereas cost efficiency and on-time performance increases dramatically.

To achieve these objectives, Ito-Yokado has implemented a point-of-sale data collection system that tracks product sales by date and time. Computerization is a key to inventory efficiency. The computer collects minute-to-minute data on the type and amounts of products being purchased, as well as the gender and approximate age of customers. Ito-Yokado marketers analyze this information and develop hourly sales profiles for each store. Store owners are given summary reports on the type of customers to expect at different hours of the day and the products they will purchase. This information is used to control inventory while helping to schedule staffing levels and maintenance activities.

With these data, Ito-Yokado has expanded its line of high-margin prepared foods, which are kept fresh without heavy use of preservatives. One example is rice balls, which are distributed fresh to each store three times a day, just ahead of peak selling periods. Deli products and baked goods also are delivered in the same manner. The average 7-Eleven store receives up to 12 daily shipments from temperature controlled trucks. Just-in-time delivery is the ability to deliver goods within a specified window of time, therefore greatly reducing inventory and the need for warehousing space on the side of the retailer. For example, perishable food losses in fresh tuna have been reduced or eliminated, resulting in greater availability, improved quality, and customer satisfaction, along with overall savings for the store. Finally, expedient delivery of the right amount at the right time reduces working capital requirements and persistent in-store space problems.

On the flip side, just-in-time practices are not a panacea. In many cases, cycle times and lead times are still too long and inventory is still too high. A 1995 U.S. survey found that 57 percent of buyers were holding inventories too high relative to sales. But the trend is shifting. Forty-three percent said they would begin to cut stock by the end of the year. However, in Japan, adopting just-in-time methods has given the Ito-Yokado stores a competitive edge.

Sources: John K. Courtis, "JIT's Impact on a Firm's Financial Statements," *International Journal of Purchasing & Materials Management*, 31, 1 (1995): 46–50.

"Ito-Yokado Rolls a 7-Eleven," *Chain Store Age Executive*, January 1992, p. 33–48.

Allison Lucas, "Through Thick and Thin, But Just in Time," *Sales & Marketing Management*, 147, 12 (1995): 70.

Patrick C. Scanlon, "Time as the Key to Inventory Management," *Production & Inventory Management Journal*, 36, 2 (1995): 39–44.

considerable time and effort to institute such systems, and intermediaries who promise what amount to turnkey just-in-time systems will probably be very disappointing.[25]

Marketers should also be mindful of the drawbacks of just-in-time practices. Just-in-time distribution systems are highly susceptible to interruptions in the flow of products caused by natural disasters and other environmental factors outside the producers' control, and they can place companies at higher risks than companies with large inventory holdings. On January 17, 1995, for example, a devastating earthquake struck the Kansai area of South Hyougo Island in Japan, with the epicenter near the city of Kobe. The earthquake disrupted transportation and manufacturing operations throughout much of southern Japan, and within hours caused shutdowns of factories far from the quake site, but which were dependent on just-in-time suppliers from the quake area. Another example is the susceptibility of companies such as Ford and General Motors to strikes at their just-in-time component-manufacturing facilities. In some cases, a shutdown at a component-manufacturing facility can cause assembly plants stoppages within hours.

Producers designing distribution systems need to consider the current and potential future demands for expediency in their industries, as well as the positive and negative aspects of different distribution approaches to improve expediency. As mentioned earlier, distribution systems are difficult and expensive to change, and it is better to design expediency into the system than to try to incorporate it later.

Intensity

Marketing managers must also decide how many outlets to locate in a geographic area. They have three basic distribution strategy options, illustrated in Table 13.3: intensive, selective, and exclusive distribution. As with other classification schemes used in this chapter, intensive, selective, and exclusive are relative terms for which operational definitions vary depending on the product type and how it is purchased by consumers. A retailer of car and home electronics, such as Best Buy, may think of 10 to 15 outlets in a major metropolitan area such as Chicago or New York as intensive distribution. For Coca-Cola or PepsiCo, however, intensive distribution in Chicago or New York means thousands of outlets ranging from vending machines to convenience stores to restaurants of all types.

Producers who use *intensive distribution* want to have the product available in as many outlets as possible within a specified market area. Such a system is especially appropriate for low-price goods purchased in small quantities, such as candy, toothpaste, or beverages. It is also appropriate for relatively undifferentiated products or services that consumers purchase habitually or on impulse. For example, fast-food marketers such as McDonald's and Taco Bell try to differentiate their products by culinary themes (American versus Mexican), and position their outlets as exclusive, since the outlets cannot sell the competitors' products (e.g., Taco Bell cannot sell Big Macs). At a more aggregate level, however, these are intensive distribution systems. McDonald's, Taco Bell, and other fast-food producers recognize that consumers will not go too far out of their way to pick up a quick meal, because many consumers of fast foods are more concerned with convenience than cuisine style. It is unlikely, for example, for most consumers to drive long distances past many other fast-food outlets to eat a Big Mac. Fast-food retailers position their stores in high-traffic locations, and design them to serve a relatively small geographic area. In other words, they rely on intensive distribution to reach their markets. In contrast, more upscale restaurant chains, such as Mountain Jack's and Chi-Chi's, rely on selective distribution. They offer products and atmosphere distinctive enough for

TABLE 13.3 INTENSIVE, SELECTIVE, AND EXCLUSIVE DISTRIBUTION STRATEGIES

	Coverage	Major Strengths	Major Weaknesses	Appropriate Products
Intensive	Maximum	Maximizes exposure to the brand	Danger of overexposure and consumer wearout Receives less attention from intermediaries	Low-priced goods purchased in small quantities: candy toothpaste beer and soda
Selective	Limited	Choose intermediaries most compatible with the product and image More control over merchandising practices Better relations with intermediaries	Lost sales due to intermediary placement or sales execution Can be difficult to implement for multiproduct companies if not all products use a selective approach	Branded products with distinctive characteristics or that require training or extended contact between consumer and intermediary: appliances automobiles sports equipment
Exclusive	Single point	Maximizes strong brand image advantages Highest level of control over merchandising practices	More susceptible to imperfect substitutes sold by other intermediaries Limited exposure to consumers	Products with very high brand loyalty or unique along multiple attributes: Harley-Davidson motorcycles Rolls Royce automobiles Gucci jewelry

customers to sacrifice driving time as well as price. Consequently, a major metropolitan area such as Chicago may have more than 100 McDonald's outlets, but only six or seven Mountain Jack's.

Intensive distribution systems also work well with some types of industrial products, such as electrical or plumbing supplies. Items such as wall switches, wall plugs, and copper fittings are produced to industry standards and very difficult to differentiate. Thus, producers of these goods want as many distributors as possible in any given geographic area. We can find standard grade Leviton-brand electrical supplies, for example, at hardware stores, home improvement stores, mass discounters, and electrical supply outlets.

Intensive distribution is advantageous to the extent that more people are exposed to the brand, making initial and repeat purchases more likely. One disadvantage is that such overexposure may wipe out any sense of differentiation between products in the same category, if they become perceptual fixtures at the store. A second disadvantage is that intermediaries may not devote much time to selling a product that every other intermediary also carries.

Companies that opt for *selective distribution* choose a limited number of outlets, positioned either to reach the target population or to protect the interests of the intermediaries in exchange for their greater involvement in selling the product. Selective distribution is most suitable for products or services that have distinctive characteristics and for which customers are willing to do some comparison shopping. Consumer goods brands such as Hewlett-Packard in computers, Yamaha in stereo equipment, and Amana in home appliances appear only at select establishments in a geographic area. These producers have invested heavily in developing a product and brand image differentiated from those of competitors, and they use a select distribution system to accentuate those differences. Because these products are typically more complex than those that benefit from intensive distribution, salespeople must explain features and answer consumers' questions. By protecting their intermediaries' ability to sell the products profitably, producers using selective distribution encourage greater sales emphasis on their products. Selective distribution also applies to industrial products that can be differentiated and require some sales effort by intermediaries. Hyster-Yale has adopted a selective distribution approach for its line of forklift trucks and materials-handling equipment, relying on intermediaries to present the product favorably.

Selective distribution systems present several advantages. First, producers can be more discriminating and choose only those intermediaries who are financially sound and respectable, and who know the products and the customers. Second, selective distribution permits greater control over pricing, selling, and other marketing functions than intensive distribution through greater cooperation and integration with intermediaries. Finally, selective distribution often results in shorter channel arrangements, which are less susceptible to conflict and more responsive to market changes. Selective distribution arrangements may work against producers, however, when sales are missed because of disagreements between the customer and the intermediary, or because the intermediary is not conveniently located. Selective arrangements also offer slightly less control over merchandising factors than exclusive distribution.

Exclusive distribution is adequate for products that are highly specialized and differentiated from competing ones, or for products that require careful control all the way from producer to final consumer. As the name implies, exclusive arrangements grant only one intermediary in any market the right to offer a brand or product. In exchange, these exclusive intermediaries agree not to sell competing brands, or products, and to meet certain performance requirements. Exclusive arrangements are usually only for products that enjoy very high brand loyalty, and for which customers are willing to make great sacrifices. Some examples of consumer products sold under exclusive distribution arrangements are Rolls-Royce automobiles and Harley-Davidson motorcycles.

A relatively small percentage of consumer products are sold through exclusive arrangements. Industrial products with exclusive distribution arrangements are more common, however, because many of them are highly complex and easy to differentiate. It happens often that industrial customers with a specific need must choose between only two or three alternative products, and each of these products is sold by exclusive representatives in their geographic area. One example is Allen-Bradley, a manufacturer of plant control systems, which normally has only one authorized representative for its products in any major market.

Exclusive distribution systems maximize strong brand image effects that benefit intermediaries, while minimizing competition from other intermediaries. Both of these factors contribute to higher profit margins and consequently motivate greater sales efforts by intermediaries. Such arrangements also give producers more leverage with intermediaries, by which to exercise more control over pricing, selling, and other practices. The disadvantages of exclusive distribution systems include their relatively weak market coverage and primordial reliance on brand image to attract customers. Unless a brand is very strong and highly recognized, exclusive distribution results in limited exposure for the product and lower market penetration.

When deciding how intense their distribution system should be, producers need to consider several factors. First they should define the type of product they sell and how well it can be differentiated from competing products. They must also take brand image and loyalty into account, both to protect the brand and to take advantage of customer preferences. Finally, producers need to consider how much they need to control product positioning, particularly when other elements of the marketing mix are highly integrated. As the need for control rises, selective and exclusive arrangements become better choices. In the case of Harley-Davidson motorcycles, product, price, advertising, ancillary merchandise (jackets, shirts, hats, and so on), and product service are all highly integrated and must be merchandised carefully. Thus, it makes sense for Harley to adopt exclusive arrangements that allow it to work closely with its dealers.

Adaptability

Companies that can adapt, be they producers or intermediaries, are better able to address unforeseen changes in the market and have a significant competitive advantage in volatile markets. As discussed in chapter 3, today's fast-changing environments demand quick marketing mix adjustments, including the distribution system. Given that the structural and investment characteristics of distribution systems make them difficult to change, adaptability must be built into the system. The Inland distribution centers are one example of how companies build adaptability into their distribution arrangements. The demand for steel in the United States has become less predictable in recent years, because customers have reduced their stockpiles at the same time that low-priced one-time spot sales by foreign producers have become more common. Consequently, customers are more likely than in the past to enter the market with diverse demands and expect a quick response. Inland's service centers help the company adapt as quickly as the market demands to remain competitive, while buffering its steel mills from erratic demand fluctuations.

The way companies build adaptability into their distribution systems varies by the type of product and market conditions. Inland uses company-owned service centers. IBM and Compaq build adaptability by using different retailer types concurrently (e.g., specialty computer stores, mass discounters, and mail order sales) and adapting their product lines to meet the demands of the different target customers these retailers serve. Many companies build adaptability by accelerating the flow of information between themselves and their intermediaries, and using that fast-flowing information to drive their production schedules.

Of course, such adaptability comes at a cost. Complex information management systems, multiple product lines, and large-scale service centers represent expenses to the company. In addition, adaptability demands a certain amount of slack in the producer's operational systems; slack that can reduce efficiency and profitability. The slack may take the form of excess information processing capacity, one or two extra people, or uncommitted funds, but in every case these resources can be deployed quickly in response to environmental jolts. It is difficult, if not impossible, to establish highly adaptable systems that are also optimally efficient. In fast-changing environments, however, no efficient system will be profitable if it is not responsive to customer needs. Slack, therefore, is something that marketing managers should add to their distributions systems and defend against the demands of other areas of the company.

From our discussion of expediency, intensity, and adaptability, it is clear that designing a distribution system can be a complicated process. Producers must assign values to each of these critical dimensions, and evaluate alternative distribution system designs and required compromises with those values in mind. Above all, distribution systems must be designed to fit each company's strategic objectives and its existing marketing and financial capabilities. Marketing managers must consider not only ideal systems, but also what they can realistically implement. They also need to consider the ethical and legal implications of their decisions (see Marketing Anecdote 13.6).

MANAGING DISTRIBUTION SYSTEMS

Even after producers establish their channels of distribution, it takes considerable effort from all parties involved to keep them running smoothly. Although it may seem that the shared interests in meeting customer needs and profitability that characterize distribution systems would be enough to keep them operating well, these ideal expectations are seldom realized. Intermediaries in all types of arrangements have a common interest in customer satisfaction and profits, but they have to address the needs of many constituencies and are often limited in their managerial and operational practices. Like most other organizations, intermediaries allocate resources to the most salient problems and manage by focusing on significant variations from normal operations. In addition, conflicts over policies, procedures, and rights and responsibilities often produce serious differences between producers and intermediaries. Many producers have responded to the challenges of managing distribution systems by developing partner relationships with intermediaries through trust and interdependence, and by focusing attention on motivation and control of channel members, conflict management, and communications.[26] These are very similar concerns to those of partner relationships between buyers and sellers, as discussed in chapter 6.

Relationships

Partner *relationships* exist between producers and intermediaries when each is genuinely interested and committed to the other's success. The idea of partner relationships has been around since the early 1960s, and such arrangements have become increasingly popular as customers demand tighter and longer-term relationships with fewer producers and intermediaries.[27] In some industries, such as automobile manufacturing, competitive pressures and volatile markets have increased the mutual dependence between producers and intermediaries. But even relatively stable and prosperous industries have moved toward partner relationships and increased cooperation among members of the distribution system.

Some of the most popular examples of partner relationships come from Japanese industry. In the Ito-Yokado 7-Eleven case of Marketing Anecdote 13.5, the producers of rice balls have formed a partner relationship with the intermediary. These producers schedule their production cycles according to information from 7-Eleven stores, and make adjustments in volume and product composition in response to store demands. Producers trust the 7-Eleven stores to make them more efficient, and in effect allow the intermediary to control how they run their business.

Although partner arrangements are becoming increasingly common throughout the world, not all partner relationships are as close as that between the rice ball producers and the 7-Eleven stores. It has been argued that partner relationships can vary substantially in how much managerial influence they exert on one another, depending on how the channel is governed.[28] Bilateral governance systems, in which each partner exercises equal influence in channel decisions, are characterized by negotiated changes and problem solutions. One example of a distribution arrangement that is moving toward more bilateral governance is that of Chrysler with many of its suppliers, as illustrated in Marketing Anecdote 6.1 in chapter 6.[29] Unilateral governance

Governments and societies have worked to establish competitive fairness in distribution systems for centuries. A concern in the United States and other countries, to varying degrees, has been the restriction of competition in ways that exploit consumers. Distribution arrangements that restrict competition or artificially control supply or demand in order to manipulate prices are often suspect and closely monitored. For example, any distribution arrangement that requires customers to purchase goods and services in quantities other than what they need, or from sources other that the ones they want to use is illegal in the United States, if it is found to give sellers monopolistic power. Such arrangements are called *tying agreements*, and have recently been a concern to government agencies overseeing franchising practices.

Equally suspicious are arrangements between producers and intermediaries that require *reciprocity*. Reciprocity occurs when a producer agrees to use an intermediary only if the intermediary purchases from the producer or performs other functions that benefit the producer. Some of the most infamous reciprocity arrangements were those developed by railroad and steel companies in the late nineteenth century. In exchange for long-term commitments to ship large volumes of raw materials and finished goods via specific railroads, some steel companies sought to influence railroad freight rates to other steel companies, and thus gain a price advantage. This practice hurt small producers, who complained to the government, and this led to the Interstate Commerce Commission's strict regulation and policing of freight rates and routes in all transportation modes.

When it comes to global distribution, however, tying agreements and reciprocity demands can be touchy issues. The use of both tying agreements and reciprocity demands in distribution systems, and the standards that distinguish acceptable and unacceptable behavior along these lines, emerge from underlying social standards that can vary substantially among countries. Reciprocity demands that are widely acceptable in Pacific Rim countries, for example, have been found excessive in some European countries and in the United States. If members of a distribution system come from different countries and have different standards of behavior, conflict can occur in the channel because compliance with one set of standards is almost certain to offend members with other standards. Usually, companies in more restrictive countries, such as the United States, accuse competitors operating in more lenient countries of collusion and predatory practices, when in fact the accused companies are operating well within the parameters of acceptable behavior in their own countries. The cooperative arrangements that characterize the Japanese systems, such as what the Ito-Yokado 7-Eleven stores have with rice ball producers, have a discernible channel captain. Unilateral governance systems give rise to faster-acting distribution systems, but also tend to be shorter lived than bilaterally governed systems. Another difference is that information is shared more freely between producers and intermediaries in bilaterally governed systems, and both parties feel more comfortable making suggestions on how the other should run operations than in unilaterally governed systems, where information and suggestions tend to flow from the channel captain to other channel members. Regardless of the governance style adopted, partner relationships involve much more cooperation, information sharing, and mutually beneficial objectives than market governed systems, in which all parties are primarily focused on only their own immediate gains.

keiretsu, for example, are often seen by U.S. competitors as unfair competition, and have led to high-level diplomatic discussions and misunderstandings between the United States and Japan. Similar accusations have also been leveled against large Korean companies, such as Hyundai and Samsung.

Companies involved in global distribution need to know the laws and customs of the countries in which they do business. If the companies are headquartered in the United States, they also need to be aware of the restrictions placed on them by the Foreign Corrupt Practices Act, because some distribution arrangements that are acceptable elsewhere could be illegal in the United States. In the United States, courts determine the legality of a distribution arrangement, using several major pieces of legislation enacted in the last 100 years as a framework. They are the Sherman Act of 1890, the Clayton Act of 1914, the Federal Trade Commission Act of 1914, the Robinson-Patman Act of 1936, and the Antimerger Act of 1950.

From roughly 1930 to 1970, the overall climate in the United States did not favor large companies and dealt harshly with distribution arrangements that gave them any advantage. During the 1980s and 1990s, the regulatory and legislative environment shifted toward a more pro-business attitude and reversed some of the previously implemented restrictions. In a series of landmark decisions, the Supreme Court expanded the definition of permissible vertical and horizontal distribution arrangements, and allowed large companies to cooperate more freely. In addition, Congress repealed many transportation regulations when that industry was deregulated in 1980. One outcome of these acts was unprecedented consolidation in the transportation industry, which in turn has contributed to consolidation in the wholesale and retail sectors.

This does not mean, however, that distribution systems can be designed without concern for legality. Governments and societies remain firmly set against exploitative behavior and will punish companies that seek to take advantage of consumers. One current concern is with distribution systems that can be seen as violating the civil rights of specific groups, such as ethnic and racial minorities, for example, when grocery chains close down small geographically dispersed urban and suburban stores and rely primarily on suburban megastores accessible only by car. Such practices can be seen as excluding inner-city populations—made up primarily of African Americans and Latinos—with limited transportation options. Given that the overall position of the legal system is that all people should have equal access to goods and services within reasonable geographic parameters, distribution systems that discriminate may not be acceptable.

In highly competitive and fast-changing markets, companies can achieve strategic advantages by adopting partner relationships with at least some intermediaries. Many companies find it impossible to collect sufficient market intelligence to keep pace with changes or to know their customer base as well as intermediaries do, because the intermediaries have direct contact with customers. Particularly for small- and medium-sized companies, and for large producers of diverse product lines dealing with a dispersed customer base, intermediary contact may be one of their only sources of customer information. Many food industry producers, for example, have come to rely on intermediaries to drive their product allocations by store because intermediaries have much more accurate knowledge of consumption patterns.

Economic and competitive trends suggest that partner relationships between producers and intermediaries are likely to persist and increase.[30] In fact, intermediary influence on customer decisions is likely to increase as well. Thus, producers should embrace the idea of partner relationships with at least some intermediaries and strive to build trust and cooperation in the relationship. Responsiveness to intermediary suggestions, a willingness to share operational information, and a genuine interest in intermediaries' welfare will preserve and strengthen these relationships, and will make both parties better able to compete.

Motivation

Motivation means the stimulation of enthusiastic and aggressive marketing on the part of intermediaries. In the same way that companies try to motivate employees to render their best efforts in support of company's objectives, producers must work hard at getting intermediaries to commit enthusiastically to their common goals, and to protect the image and interests of the company. Producers motivate intermediaries in a number of ways. Designing an attractive product and creating a unique brand image are necessary parts of the process, because intermediaries are more enthusiastic about products and brands with differential advantages. This is rarely enough, however, because other producers with adequate products can improve their images or add incentives and services that make up for product deficiencies. What producers need to bear in mind is that intermediaries are managed by people, and that many of the same things that motivate employees are also likely to motivate intermediaries, even if administering these benefits may be somewhat different.

Tangible Incentives

We have already discussed close working relationships and a genuine interest in helping intermediaries. In addition, producers can motivate intermediaries by giving them rewards. Rewards can take many different forms, a subset of which is listed in Table 13.4.

High margins and trade discounts are some of the more frequently used motivators in distribution system management. *Margin* is the difference between the selling price an intermediary uses and the price it pays for the goods. Higher gross margins typically mean higher profits for intermediaries, all other things being equal, and higher profits frequently lead to stronger interest on the part of the intermediary to carry and promote the producers' products.[31] Producers must balance the motivating effects of higher margins with the adverse effects that higher margins may have on consumer demand. They also need to keep in mind that an intermediary's profitability is a function of both margin and volume. High margins will not motivate if they lead to reduced sales volumes and profits due to customers resisting high prices. Producers need to assess consumers' price sensitivity, the pricing of competing products, and the preferences of intermediaries in order to set margins that are motivating.

Producers also use other motivating incentives and rewards. *Promotional allowances* frequently encourage intermediary cooperation. These are reductions in the price of goods sold to an intermediary and/or direct payments made to intermediaries in exchange for local advertisement by the intermediary, additional or more favorable shelf space, priority in sales presentations, or enhancing the producer's marketing effort in other ways. Promotional allowances have become institutionalized in some consumer product categories, such as breakfast cereals and beverages, and intermediaries sometimes absorb them without making the expected additional efforts to sell the brand. Promotional allowances tend to work only for short periods of time because they are easily matched by competitors.

TABLE 13.4 WAYS OF MOTIVATING INTERMEDIARIES

Tangible rewards
  High margins
  Promotional allowances
  Incentives to employees (e.g., contests, gifts, training, travel, merchandise)

Tangible services
  In-store demonstrations
  Financing
  Business consulting advice
  Generous return policies
  Support services (e.g., promotion planning assistance, access to WWW information)

Intangible incentives
  Leadership
  Respect
  Consideration
  Cooperation

In addition to promotional allowances, producers sometimes use one-time awards tied to contests or promotional gifts to motivate intermediaries. These rewards often work well to influence behavior of individual members of the intermediary's organization. The employees of intermediaries often act as sales agents for a producer, particularly in the distribution of industrial goods that receive little mass promotion. Research has shown that these "external salespeople" tend to place value on special training, travel, and merchandise, and that contests and programs offering these types of rewards can be effective motivators.[32] Such incentives can have the additional advantage of being harder for competitors to duplicate because they are typically tailored to the intermediaries' needs, and at the same time they are compatible with the producers' image and strategies. Thus, such incentives may remain effective for longer periods of time.

Still another incentive is the *provision of services* to the intermediary. This can include supplying personnel for in-store demonstrations, financing inventories, providing advice on inventory management and merchandising practices, training sales personnel, and offering generous return policies. Food producers, for example, often place their staff in grocery stores to offer samples of their products and answer questions, thereby reducing the burden on the retailer's employees. Another example is the flight schedule and reservation systems that airlines make available to travel agents free of charge, which reduces the burden on travel agents and hopefully leads to more tickets being sold for the sponsoring airlines' flights.

Intangible Incentives

Less tangible practices can also have a significant effect on motivation. Among these are leadership and everyday support. Respect, friendly advice, concern for the intermediary's welfare, participative goal setting, a positive attitude, setting a good example, fairness, and sincere well-deserved praise can all effectively motivate intermediaries. Such behaviors are absolutely necessary in partner relationships, but can also motivate members of more traditional contractual and conventional distribution systems. Other intangible motivators include giving responsibility to intermediaries and treating them as equals. These actions suggest that producers listen to intermediaries' suggestions and even actively seek their input when contemplating changes. In recent years, for example, the historically antagonistic and sometimes acrimonious relationships between car dealers and manufacturers have slowly given way to more conciliatory and respectful relations, which have been credited with improving consumers' quality perceptions.

Control

Control is closely related to motivation. It involves monitoring intermediaries' performance and correcting any improper actions or practices. In contrast to motivation, which involves guiding channel members toward desired goals by inspiring specific behaviors, control involves the surveillance and correction of behaviors that intermediaries have already undertaken. Control involves multiple functional areas in producer organizations, such as sales, accounting, shipping, and manufacturing. Depending on the closeness of the relationship between producer and intermediary, control practices can also affect multiple intermediary functions. Producers exercise control through both economic and organizational means; the best control is achieved when both means are implemented.[33]

Producers must closely coordinate control and motivation initiatives because their methods frequently overlap. For example, some companies that use promotional allowances as motivators also enact control procedures for monitoring the frequency and quality of intermediary-sponsored advertising, and provide feedback to intermediaries. Companies that use control procedures must be careful not to exert excessive pressure on intermediaries and thereby lose their support. Properly administered control procedures can have a positive effect on motivation by reducing intermediaries' uncertainty about producer expectations.

Control is one management area in which marketing information systems (discussed in chapter 5) can be used advantageously. Effective control requires frequent data collection about costs, sales, special problems, and other information, and producers must then apply sound qualitative and quantitative methods to perform analyses and interpret results. Such research allows for more accurate budgets and performance standards, and for better evaluation of different motivational, compensation, and promotional programs. Continual monitoring also helps producers detect problems early and take corrective action. The point-of-purchase information collected by the Ito-Yokado 7-Eleven stores and its use in controlling and improving producer performance is a good example of how management information systems can help producers exercise more judicious control.

Even if they have sophisticated management information systems in place, however, companies must not ignore informal control mechanisms. Some of the most effective monitoring and correction can be done through informal dialogue, because it focuses attention on common goals instead of on violations. The point to remember is that distribution systems are based on human relationships between intermediaries and producers, and that these relationships represent substantial investments. Producers must protect distribution relationships just as they protect other important personal relationships, and the means of doing so are surprisingly similar.

Conflict Management

Inevitably, conflicts arise among intermediaries and between manufacturers and channel members. Most often, divergent interests, competitive pressures, and mismanaged relationships cause problems. All of these types of conflicts can be relatively easy to resolve, but can lead to very destructive outcomes if left unattended.

Divergent interests and differences of opinion are probably the most common type of intrachannel conflict. They may be rooted in incompatible priorities over objectives, strategies, or tactics, as in the case of a producer who wants to keep prices high to preserve an image of quality whereas the intermediary wants to lower prices to stimulate demand. Conflicts of interest can also occur because an intermediary cannot devote as much attention to a brand as the producer wants, or an intermediary believes that the producer's expectations are unreasonable. Sometimes divergent priorities give rise to feelings of neglect and unfulfilled promises; in these situations the problems can be more serious, resulting in resentment and retaliation.

Saturn Corporation, for example, works hard to reinforce its marketing philosophy and to reassure its dealers in order to eliminate conflicts over the company's fixed-price and no-pressure sales approach. Initially, Saturn's departure from long-established pricing and selling techniques caused conflicts with dealers, who felt that Saturn was protecting its reputation at their expense. Saturn's responsiveness to other dealer matters, however, reduced the dealers' concerns and, because the fixed-price, no-pressure sales approach has proven very popular with car buyers, it turned many Saturn dealers into some of the most loyal auto dealers among automobile producers.

Competitive pressures among intermediaries, and even between producers and intermediaries can also give rise to conflicts. These are often manifest in disagreements over how to divide profits between manufacturer and intermediary or how account support and other resources are allocated among intermediaries in a channel. The perception that a producer favors one intermediary at another's expense often causes particularly troublesome conflict, and can often be based on nothing more than differences in how the producer's representative gets along with intermediary personnel. Perceptions of favoritism and unfairness can result in resentment, suboptimal performance, sabotage, and even the dissolution of the relationships. One last possible source of conflicts are glitches in personal relationships between representatives from each party, where language, gestures, and even personalities can distort the message and lead to serious differences.

Before we discuss ways in which conflict can be resolved, we should acknowledge that conflict is not necessarily undesirable. Some amount of conflict in a channel can be beneficial when it prevents the parties from taking things for granted or when it clears the air.[34] Some types of conflict—if they do not get out of control—may even be necessary to create the proper motivational climate. In addition, conflict between organizations can lead to greater cohesion and cooperation among groups within a company, and to the restructuring of tasks and formal relationships.

In general, conflict can be managed by using one of the approaches to handling conflict illustrated in Table 13.5.[35] These approaches can be useful in distribution systems because they assume both parties are mature enough to understand their own interests and those of the other party. No single style works best in all situations; all have strengths and limitations and are subject to situational constraints.

The primary strength of *integrating* is its long-lasting impact, because it deals with underlying causes of conflict. Its primary weakness is that it is very time consuming. One mechanism suitable for integrating is to develop superordinate goals that capture producer and intermediary interests. Superordinate goals—objectives beneficial to all parties—such as "to defend U.S. jobs against Japanese competition," have united producers and intermediaries in such industries as steel, machine tools, and semiconductors. Another possible mechanism is to exchange personnel in key positions, so that each side gains first-hand experience in the business concerns of

TABLE 13.5 APPROACHES TO MANAGING CONFLICT

Integrating (Problem Solving):	Interested parties confront issues and cooperatively identify problems, generate and weigh alternative solutions, and select solutions. This style is appropriate for complex issues plagued by misunderstanding. It is inappropriate for resolving conflicts rooted in opposing value systems.
Obliging (Smoothing):	This style involves playing down differences while emphasizing commonalties. It focuses on encouraging cooperation. It is appropriate when it is possible to eventually get something in return. It is inappropriate for complex and worsening problems.
Domination (Forcing):	This style relies on formal authority to force compliance of one party to the demands of another. It is appropriate when an unpopular solution must be implemented. It is inappropriate in an open and participative climate.
Avoiding:	This tactic involves either passive withdrawal from the problem or active suppression of the issue. The style is appropriate for trivial issues or when the costs of confrontation outweigh the benefits of resolution. It is inappropriate for difficult and worsening problems.
Compromising:	This is a give-and-take approach involving moderate concern for both self and other. It usually demands that both parties give up something of value. This style is appropriate when the parties have opposite goals or possess roughly equal power. It is inappropriate when its overuse would lead to inconclusive action.

Source: Table summarized from M. Afzalur Rahim, "A Strategy for Managing Conflict in Complex Organizations," Human Relations, January 1985, p. 84 (with minor modifications).

the other. High levels of integration between intermediary and producer operations have been a hallmark of the single-level distribution arrangements discussed earlier, particularly between large retailers such as Wal-Mart and companies such as Philip Morris and VF Corporation.[36]

Obliging, an expedient way of encouraging cooperation, provides only a temporary fix and seldom addresses the fundamental problem. Conflicts that are resolved by obliging have a tendency to reemerge. One mechanism suitable for this style is *channel diplomacy,* in which producers or intermediaries take the initiative for resolution and voluntarily give way to the other. One example is the early 1990s move by some distributors of recorded music to lower prices and support the concurrent sale of used and new compact discs by retailers at a time when other distributors were taking punitive action, as discussed in chapter 6. Another good mechanism for obliging is cooptation, in which the parties form a task force involving representatives of producers and intermediaries to emphasize common interests and reduce differences.

Although *domination* may provide an expedient, short-term solution, its primary weakness is that it often breeds resentment and might give rise to other conflicts. Its main advantage, other than expediency, is that the required action is usually very clear and unambiguous. Domination via the administration of coercive or legal power is possible only when the producer or intermediary has power over the other party, which is most often achieved through the control of resources of critical importance to the other party. The use of coercion, however, often hinders efforts to find long-term solutions to conflict, and companies that have power may be better off using noncoercive influence strategies, because the combination of unused power and noncoercive influence strategies elicits more cooperation from other channel members.[37] Some useful insights into the use of power in distributions systems are discussed in Marketing Anecdote 13.7. This discussion barely scratches the

Different conceptual treatments of power and its antecedents have been applied to distribution systems. A commonly used typology of the bases of power is that suggested by marketing researchers Kasulis and Speckman.

Reward–Providing financial incentives, support services, or other benefits

Coercive–Withholding support or threatening termination of the relationship

Legitimate–Exercising contractual requirements for specific behaviors

Expert–Using unique expertise and trust to win compliance

Referent–Offering to share image or reputation in exchange for compliance

Informational–Persuading others as to the merits of one's position with data

There is a great similarity between this framework and the one proposed by psychologists John French and Bertram Raven and discussed in chapter 11. French and Raven developed their model to explain interpersonal relationships; Kasulis and Speckman extended it by attributing individual-level characteristics to organizations. We must be careful, however, in how far we push the analogy between individuals and organizations. For example, how should we classify the power that a channel member gains by indirectly influencing the availability of credit to other members through its deposit relationships with the lender? In this situation the power source is difficult to classify under one of the six bases listed above because there is no direct contact or explicit appeal to any one source.

An alternative perspective on power has been proposed by organizational researchers Jeffrey Pfeffer and Gerald Salancik, who see organizations as interdependent with other elements in their environment, and believe that organizations that control critical resources can exercise power over other organizations that are dependent on these resources. This applies directly to distribution systems in which channel members are organizations; whatever channel member controls the most important resource (information, shelf space, financial resources) has power over other members who need that resource. In a way, resource-dependence theory incorporates the Kasulis and Speckman framework in that each of the six bases of power can be seen as the control of a different resource.

Other perspectives on power and influence in distribution systems use even more distinct views of organizations (e.g., organizations as political entities or economic players), and each one has strengths and weaknesses. No conceptual model of power is perfect. Managers responsible for distribution systems should be aware of different frameworks with which they can make sense of any situation and make a habit of looking at the issues from more than one angle to make sure no critical factors or opportunities are being overlooked.

Sources: John R. P. French and Bertram Raven, "The Bases of Social Power," in Dorwin Cartwright, ed., *Studies in Social Power* (Ann Arbor: University of Michigan Press, 1959).

Jack J. Kasulis and Robert E. Speckman, "A Framework for the Use of Power," *European Journal of Marketing* 14 (1980): 183.

Jeffrey Pfeffer and Gerald Salancik, *The External Control of Organizations: A Resource Dependence Perspective* (New York: Harper & Row, 1978).

surface of power—an important element in all intermediary relationships, which has been the subject of substantial research.[38]

The primary strength of *avoiding* is that it is a natural human reaction and consequently it is easy to implement. Its weakness is that it sidesteps the root problems and provides only temporary relief at best. Some of the mechanisms suggested for other styles can also facilitate avoiding, such as channel diplomacy focused on inane issues and exchanges of irrelevant personnel. In all situations, the real conflict issues are ignored, and the semblance of activity and cooperation are maintained. Joint memberships in trade associations and unnecessary system reorganizations are other ways of avoiding real issues.

The primary strength of *compromising* is that it should not generate resentment. Its primary weakness is that sometimes the give-and-take focuses on irrelevant issues in order to give the appearance of progress, while leaving real problems unresolved. Mediation, arbitration, and channel diplomacy provide the best mechanisms for implementing compromise. Channel diplomacy is preferred because it avoids using a third party and the potential for corrupting the mediator.

Communication

Communication in a distribution system flows in both directions, as illustrated in Figure 13.3. In highly volatile and fast-changing environments, successful marketing depends on timely and accurate information, and communication is equally important for both producers and intermediaries. Consequently, maintaining and enhancing the communications system is critical. As Figure 13.3 illustrates, the types of communications that flow between producers and intermediaries differ, although communication functions remain the same: information, research, and influence.

Information Function

Everyday operations can work only when players distribute timely and accurate information. Policies must be conveyed, points of clarification made, problems solved, and the like. Such routine communication occurs through personal visits and tele-

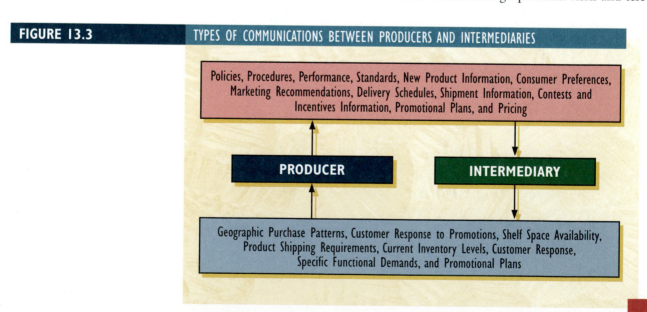

FIGURE 13.3 TYPES OF COMMUNICATIONS BETWEEN PRODUCERS AND INTERMEDIARIES

Policies, Procedures, Performance, Standards, New Product Information, Consumer Preferences, Marketing Recommendations, Delivery Schedules, Shipment Information, Contests and Incentives Information, Promotional Plans, and Pricing

PRODUCER   **INTERMEDIARY**

Geographic Purchase Patterns, Customer Response to Promotions, Shelf Space Availability, Product Shipping Requirements, Current Inventory Levels, Customer Response, Specific Functional Demands, and Promotional Plans

phone conversations with the salesforce, through seminars and special presentations, and through memoranda and other written communications. Some also occurs informally through unplanned contacts at professional or trade association meetings, social gatherings, and other occasions. Because there are many and diverse opportunities to share information, error and confusion can creep into the distribution system. Consequently, all system members must give special consideration to clarity and timeliness as they exchange information. They must pay special attention to the patterns and flow rates of information so that the information is transferred accurately, quickly, and in sufficient detail to run the business efficiently.

In addition, both producers and intermediaries must foster communication skills internally. This includes salespeople and purchasing agents, in addition to accounting, shipping, and receiving personnel. They must employ appropriate means to transmit, receive, and decipher information, and must update procedures frequently to remain competitive. Finally, some structural aspects of the communication system deserve special attention. In an era of global distribution by using electronic data interchange, for example, companies must secure their information flows against loss of data caused by interference as well as by deliberate electronic eavesdropping. Parties must also build translation facilities into their systems to handle language and format differences, such as the different use of commas and periods in accounting information, or nonuniform use of vocabulary. Systems designed to overcome language and format barriers greatly enhance information flow and channel effectiveness.

Research

Communication also functions for the gathering, analysis, and interpretation of market information. This includes data on customer needs and demands as well as other distribution system members' needs and preferences. Producers must establish data gathering systems and keep the flow of market intelligence open if they wish to remain responsive to the market. Their efforts must include formal data collection through surveys, reports, and point-of-sale systems, as well as informal sources such as industry observers and informants, trade publications, and even the internal communications of intermediaries and competitors when available.

Several factors enter into the collection of market information. Companies should not promote unethical behavior in their research efforts, nor should they ignore information that gives them a competitive advantage. Producers and intermediaries also need to be concerned with the political implications of channel data flow. Controlling market data can be a significant source of power, which must be used judiciously. Companies need marketing information systems that monitor and evaluate channel operations. They should also give attention to how information is disseminated internally and to channel members. Careful communication enables companies to access many sources of market intelligence adequately.

Influence

In addition to collecting and distributing information, communication may also trigger action. As discussed in other sections of this chapter, managing a distribution system involves getting intermediaries to do specific things at specific times to position the product favorably. This requires persuasion, motivation, and sometimes forceful intervention, all of which require communication. A well-managed communication system can coordinate complementary messages to different levels of the channel, or reinforce the importance of a desired action. The communication system, for example, can deliver research reports recommending a pricing strategy for women's suits to a retailer's purchasing manager, followed by a letter from the general sales manager and a phone call from the salesperson to the buyer responsible for women's suits. Multiple communications at different levels of the retailer's organization will reinforce the message. This type of influence strategy, however, requires careful coordination and timely feedback from the producer's salesforce, and it must take into account the channel's climate and power structure. Communication tactics need to be matched to channel conditions in order to optimize channel outcomes.[39]

SUMMARY

Distribution systems are important to all areas of the marketing mix, and can be important in a company's marketing strategy. Distribution systems must be integrated into other marketing initiatives and be compatible with the company's objectives. Their design must also consider the types of products or services being marketed, along with other relevant aspects of the marketing mix.

Distribution systems provide benefits to producers and consumers, such as:

- making the exchange of goods and services more efficient
- overcoming differences in the quantity produced and the quantity demanded
- overcoming discrepancies of assortment produced and assortment demanded
- providing time and place utility for consumers

To provide these benefits, distribution systems perform functions for consumers and producers, such as:

- offering variety and value to consumers
- storing and gathering information for producers
- reducing risk for consumers and producers
- providing personal contact
- transporting and promoting products
- providing credit

Distribution systems have been important since ancient times. They were instrumental in the rise of the Roman Empire, and are very important to the industrialized economies of North America, Europe, and the Pacific Rim as well as the merging economies of Africa and Central and South America. The development of distribution systems has been described using models such as the wheel of retailing and life cycles. These models, however, ignore psychological and political factors that also influence the permanence of distribution systems. They also downplay ethical and legal factors. Governments in many countries are investing heavily in distribution systems, and such intervention can be expected to change global trade patterns. Government action is also threatening elements of current distribution systems, such as large mass discounters and convenience stores. Marketers need to consider these factors when planning distribution systems.

Distribution systems can involve different types of relationships, multiple levels, and different types of intermediaries within those levels. Intermediaries are most generally classified as wholesalers, retailers, and facilitators. Distribution system relationships can include corporate, contractual, and conventional arrangements. Distribution systems can be zero-level, single-level, or multilevel systems. Single-level systems can include using an external salesforce, direct sales to retailers, and franchising. In all circumstances, distribution systems should be compatible with the product, the organization, and the company's resource base, and should be sensitive to current technology and available information.

When designing and evaluating distribution systems, marketers must consider factors such as expediency, intensity of market coverage, and adaptability as important performance areas. Expediency has become increasingly important in recent years, and has led to widespread adoption of just-in-time inventory management. Intensity of geographic market coverage is affected by the type of product in the following ways:

- Intense distribution has many outlets and is best for inexpensive, low image products.
- Selective distribution has limited outlets and is best for branded, midpriced products.
- Exclusive distribution has only one outlet in an area, and is best for image-laden products.

Managing distribution systems often involves partner relationships and requires careful management of motivation and control of intermediaries. Marketers must also manage conflict effectively, using techniques such as integrating, obliging, domination, avoiding, and compromising. Communication between producers and intermediaries has three dimensions: information flow, research, and influence. All three must be considered to improve system effectiveness.

QUESTIONS FOR DISCUSSION

1. Which of the benefits that Inland Steel gets from its in-house distribution system would also be available to a chemical manufacturer such as DuPont? What benefits gained by Inland would not be available? Are there benefits to DuPont not available to Inland?

2. How much does the distribution system affect what customers receive when they purchase photographic equipment? living-room furniture? a ball-point pen? intimate apparel? computer games?

3. Retail banking services are usually distributed through a network of branches and automated teller machines within a specific geographic area. This distribution system is very capital intensive and difficult to change. Consequently, it is reasonable to expect that other elements of the marketing mix must adapt to it. What aspects of a bank's product, pricing, and promotion strategies would you expect to be most affected by the distribution system? How would they change if banking were done through interactive TV systems?

4. What roles might a wholesale food distributor serve for a small manufacturer of Korean foods? for Denny's Restaurants? for the U.S. armed forces?

5. In what ways do consumers of candy products benefit from 7-Eleven stores? from Winn-Dixie stores? from Sam's Wholesale Clubs?

6. In what ways do producers of candy products benefit from 7-Eleven stores? from Winn-Dixie stores? from Sam's Wholesale Clubs?

7. The wheel of retailing explains the development of retail establishments. How do convenience stores violate the predictions of the model? Can you think of other retail establishments that also violate the model?

8. The life cycle model suggests that decline of any distribution system is inevitable. Do you agree with this model? Develop a long-term strategy for home-shopping services (a new distribution system) based on your answer.

9. Intermediaries offering transportation services have been accused of helping the illegal drug trade by transporting bulk packages in which drugs are hidden. Transportation companies have argued they are innocent because they are merely transporting sealed freight and cannot be held responsible for its content. Do transportation companies have an obligation beyond efficient and timely transportation?

10. L.L. Bean is a retailer of sporting goods and apparel. It sells by direct mail as well as at a retail store in Freeport, Maine, which is open 24 hours per day, seven days per week, year around. Is this a zero-level, single-level, or multilevel system? Is it a single-channel or multichannel system? Explain your answers.

11. Assume you are in charge of the distribution system for a brand of Russian beer being imported into the United States. In Russia, this is a very popular brand and is sold in all stores that sell beer. What type of distribution intensity is the Russian system? What type of distribution intensity would you recommend for the U.S. market? Why?

12. Now assume you are having a conflict with one of your U.S. intermediaries. The intermediary is pricing the beer high and sales are dropping. This is threatening your position in the market and has your superiors in Russia upset. What are your options for managing the conflict? Which would you adopt to preserve the relationship with the intermediary and improve the sales volume concurrently? What will you have to do with your superiors in Russia?

NOTES FOR FURTHER READING

1. The relatively fixed nature of the distribution system is an axiom of most scholarly work on marketing channels. For the transaction economics–based foundations of this perspective, see Oliver E. Williamson, *The Economic Institution of Capitalism: Firms, Markets, Relational Contracting* (New York: The Free Press, 1985).

2. For more information, see Wendy Zellner and Marti Benedetti, "The Meek Who Make Good with the Mighty," *Business Week*, December 21, 1992, p. 73.

3. For more information, see Edith Hill Updike and Mary Kuntz, "Japan is Dialing 1-800 BuyAmerica," *Business Week*, June 12, 1995, pp. 61–64.

4. Stanley C. Hollander, "The Wheel of Retailing," *Journal of Marketing* 24 (July 1960): 37–42.

5. For more information about competition in the express delivery business, see David Greising, "Watch Out for Flying Packages," *Business Week*, November 14, 1994, p. 40.

6. For more information about the activities of U.S. discount retailers in Mexico and Canada after NAFTA, see William C. Symonds, Geri Smith, and Stephen Baker, "Border Crossings: NAFTA Would Fulfill the Promise of a Continental Market," *Business Week*, November 22, 1993, pp. 40–42; and Geri Smith, "NAFTA: A Green Light for Red Tape," *Business Week*, July 25, 1994, p. 48.

7. For more on the economic facilitators of gray markets and their legal status, see Dale F. Duhan and Mary Jane Sheffer, "Gray Markets and the Legal Status of Parallel Importation," *Journal of Marketing* 52 (July 1988): 75–83.

8. For an example of auto dealer–manufacturer cooperation, see Bill Vlasic, "Who's that Guy in Chrysler's Front Seat?" *Business Week*, October 30, 1995, p. 40.

9. For more information, see Kevin Alexander and Andrea Rothman, "Will Travel Agents Get Bumped by These Gizmos?" *Business Week*, June 28, 1993, p. 72.

10. For more detailed information, see Peter Burrows, "Where Compaq's Kingdom is Weak," *Business Week*, May 8, 1995, pp. 98–102; and Larry Armstrong, "More Red Meat Please," *Business Week*, May 22, 1995, pp. 132–134.

11. This section takes a contractual perspective on franchising. For an organizational economics perspective on franchising, see James A. Brickley and Frederick H. Dark, "The Choice of Organizational Form: The Case of Franchising," *Journal of Financial Economics* 18 (1987): 401–420.

12. Wal-Mart has been a common target of such complaints due to its size. Not all such complaints receive public attention, but some examples of legal action against Wal-Mart can be found in Wendy Zellner, "Not Everybody Loves Wal-Mart's Low Prices," *Business Week*,

October 12, 1992, p. 36, and "An Unkind Cut from Wal-Mart," *Business Week*, October 25, 1993.

13. For additional examples, see Zachary Schiller, Wendy Zellner, Rod Stodghill, and Mark Marement, "Clout!," *Business Week*, December 21, 1992, pp. 66–73.

14. A number of examples covering a 10-year period were documented in Michele Galen, Laural Touby, Lori Bongiourno, and Wendy Zellner, "Franchise Fracas," *Business Week*, March 22, 1993, pp. 68–73. Although this issue received less public notice as franchise expansion slowed in the 1990s, the potential for regulatory action remains.

15. Rajiv P. Dant and Patrick L. Schul, "Conflict Resolution Processes in Contractual Channels of Distribution," *Journal of Marketing* 56 (January 1992): 38–54.

16. For a more detailed discussion of dependence-balancing practices, see Jan B. Heide and George John, "The Role of Dependence-Balancing in Safeguarding Transaction-Specific Assets in Conventional Channels," *Journal of Marketing* 52 (January 1988): 20–35.

17. For a more extensive discussion of the role that power and conflict play in distribution systems, and the benefits and costs they can generate, see John F. Gaski, "The Theory of Power and Conflict in Channels of Distribution, *Journal of Marketing* 48 (Summer 1987): 9–29.

18. Information based on interviews with Whirlpool and General Electric marketing executives

19. Information based on conversations with A. T. Cross sales personnel.

20. For a detailed discussion on reconciling these factors from a transaction economics perspective, see F. Robert Dwyer and Sejo Oh, "A Transaction Cost Perspective on Vertical Contractual Structures and Interchannel Competitive Strategies," *Journal of Marketing* 52 (April 1988): 21–34.

21. For more information on branded variants, see Mark Bergen, Shantanu Duta, and Steven M. Shugan, "Branded Variants: A Retail Perspective," *Journal of Marketing Research* 33 (February 1996): 9–19. This study focuses on how a large number of branded variants spread among retail competitors increases the complexity of purchasing and reduces the likelihood that consumers will engage in comparison shopping across stores. It documents substantial numbers of branded variants across 14 product categories.

22. Shankar Ganesan, "Determinants of Long-Term Orientation in Buyer-Seller Relationships," *Journal of Marketing* 58 (April 1994): 1–19.

23. For a more detailed discussion of the just-in-time philosophy, see Shigeo Shingo, *Revolution in Manufacturing, SMED* (Cambridge, Mass.: Productivity Press, 1985). A common misconception is that just-in-time systems are intended to reduce in-stock inventory. Although just-in-time practices often result in reduced inventory carrying costs, this is not their primary objective. Just-in-time programs deployed as a means of reducing inventory levels are easily compromised whenever quality problems emerge in order to maintain the same rate of production output. Just-in-time programs designed to reduce waste and quickly bring manufacturing deviations to the surface, however, allow the production process to stop until quality is restored; they produce their savings in lower warranty costs and higher customer satisfaction.

24. Gary L. Frazier, Robert E. Spekman, and Charles R. O'Neal, "Just-In-Time Exchange Relationships in Industrial Markets," *Journal of Marketing* 52 (October 1988): 52–67.

25. "Are Distributors Selling JIT or Just-the-Sizzle," *Purchasing*, May 22, 1986, pp. 73–80.

26. For more detailed and theoretical discussions of the manner in which these and other factors contribute to relationships, see James C. Anderson and James A. Narus, "A Model of Distributor Firm and Manufacturing Firm Working Partnerships," *Journal of Marketing* 54 (January 1990): 42–58.

27. Partner relationships with key suppliers and intermediaries are among the practices recommended by Richard M. Cyert and James G. March, *A Behavior Theory of the Firm* (Upper Saddle River, N.J.: Prentice-Hall, 1963). Such suggestions have been echoed many times in recent years by academicians and consultants, such as Arthur Andersen & Co., *Facing the Forces of Change: Beyond Future Trends in Wholesale Distribution* (Washington D.C.: Distribution Research Education Foundation, 1987).

28. Jan B. Heide, "Interorganizational Governance in Marketing Channels," *Journal of Marketing* 58 (January 1994): 71–85.

29. James B. Treece, "Improving the Soul of an Old Machine," *Business Week*, October 25, 1993, pp. 134–136.

30. For a more in-depth discussion of the determinants of relationships, see Christine Oliver, "Determinants of Interorganizational Relationships: Integration and Future Directions," *Academy of Management Review* 15 (April 1990): 241–265.

31. For an analytical investigation of key factors involved in intermediary motivation, see Vithala R. Rao and Edward W. McLaughlin, "Modeling the Decision to Add New Products by Channel Intermediaries," *Journal of Marketing* 53 (January 1989): 80–88.

32. Edwin Bobrow, "Reps and Recognition: Understanding What Motivates," *Sales & Marketing Management* (September 1991): 82–86.

33. Kathleen M. Eisenhardt, "Control: Organizational and Economic Approaches," *Management Science* 31 (February 1985): 134–149.

34. The potential benefits that can accrue from well-managed conflict are discussed by Anderson and Narus "A Model of Distributor Firm and Manufacturer Firm Working Partnerships"; and by Kenneth G. Hardy and Allan J. Magrath, *Marketing Channel Management: Strategic Planning*

and Tactics (Glenview, Ill.: Scott, Foresman, and Co., 1988). At the more general level of buyer-seller relationships, potential benefits have been discussed by F. Robert Dwyer, Paul H. Schurr, and Sejo Oh, "Developing Buyer-Seller Relationships," *Journal of Marketing* 51 (April 1987): 11–27.

35. This discussion is based on M. Afzalur Rahim, "A Strategy for Managing Conflict in Complex Organizations," *Human Relations*, January 1985, p. 84; and Louis W. Stern and Adel I. El-Ansary, *Marketing Channels*, 3rd ed. (Upper Saddle River, N.J.: Prentice-Hall, 1988).

36. For examples of how producers change their operations to achieve more integration with retailers, see Greg Burns, "Will So Many Ingredients Work Together?" *Business Week*, March 27, 1995, pp. 188–191.

37. Gary L. Frazier and Raymond C. Rody, "The Use of Influence Strategies in Interfirm Relationships in Industrial Product Channels," *Journal of Marketing* 55 (February 1991): 57–69.

38. For additional information on power and its effect on organizations, see Jack J. Kasulis and Robert E. Spekman, "A Framework for the Use of Power," *European Journal of Marketing* 14 (1980): 183; Jeffrey Pfeffer and Gerald Salancik, *The External Control of Organizations: A Resource Dependence Perspective* (New York: Harper & Row, 1978); Jeffrey Pfeffer, *Organizations and Organizational Theory* (Cambridge, Mass.: Ballinger Publishing Company, 1982), pp. 192–207; Gary L. Frazier, "On the Measurement of Interfirm Power," *Journal of Marketing Research* 20 (May 1983): 158–166; John F. Gaski, "The Theory of Power and Conflict in Channels of Distribution," *Journal of Marketing* 48 (Summer 1984): 9–29; and John F. Gaski and John R. Nevin, "The Differential Effects of Exercised and Unexercised Power Sources in a Marketing Channel," *Journal of Marketing Research* 22 (May 1985): 130–142.

39. Jacki Mohr and John R. Nevin, "Communication Strategies in Marketing Channels: A Theoretical Perspective," *Journal of Marketing* 54 (October 1990): 36–51.

CHAPTER 14

MARKETING CONCERNS OF WHOLESALE, RETAIL, AND PHYSICAL DISTRIBUTION INTERMEDIARIES

CHAPTER OBJECTIVES

When you are done with this chapter, you should have achieved the following:

- An understanding of the roles played in marketing distribution by wholesalers, retailers, and physical distribution companies
- An insight into how marketing principles are applied in the management of wholesalers, retailers, and physical distribution companies
- A basic understanding of current trends in wholesaling, retailing, and distribution, and how these industries are likely to change in the future

CHAPTER OUTLINE

Supervalu, the nation's largest wholesale food distributor, serves stores through a network of distribution centers, from which products move in its own trucks and in those of major trucking companies. Supervalu also owns retail stores in many major U.S. markets. By participating in the wholesale, retail, and physical distribution aspects of the grocery industry, Supervalu achieves greater levels of integration between its various businesses, which in turn results in both better customer service and higher profitability.

Wholesale operations represent the largest segment of Supervalu's business, and its physical distribution operations (warehousing and transportation) serve the company's wholesaling interests. Supervalu organizes its operations into four logistical and seven marketing regions to cover 48 states. Logistical regions are designed to reduce in-transit times from producer to warehouse to retailer by taking advantage of existing U.S. truck and rail transportation networks. Warehouses and truck fleets aim to provide fast and efficient delivery throughout the system. Supervalu bases its marketing regions on existing concentrations of Supervalu customers and on growth potential of geographic areas such as the Southeastern United States. Within these logistical and marketing regions, Supervalu services hundreds of independent grocery stores and small grocery chains with a wide array of products as well as services such

Supervalu represents one of the new fully integrated wholesale-to-retail supermarket businesses.

as retail development, retail accounting, real estate planning, advertising management, and merchandising support. By offering such services, Supervalu helps its customers compete against such national giants as Kroger and A&P Stores, and regional giants such as Winn-Dixie in the Southeast and Jewel in the Midwest.

But focusing on wholesale operations has not been enough for Supervalu in some high-growth markets. It operates retail stores in 31 states, including the highly successful Cub Foods chain of grocery stores. Headquartered in Stillwater, Minnesota, Cub Foods has stores in populous states such as Washington, Ohio, Illinois, and Colorado, and has been expanding aggressively in high-growth areas such as Atlanta, Georgia. Cub Foods' growth strategies include prime locations, a wide assortment of high-quality products, and competitive pricing. Cub Foods also targets convenience, in which it is an industry leader. In select stores, Cub Foods operates in-store minimarts—separate and highly accessible areas stocked with high-volume convenience items (like milk and bread) and designed for quick in-and-out service. One innovative aspect of the Cub Foods minimarts is that some of the construction and shelf management costs are underwritten by companies with which Cub Foods has established comarketing programs. Participating manufacturers such as Philip Morris and Mars help pay for minimart construction in exchange for dedicated point-of-purchase displays that give their brands preferential locations, especially for habitual purchase items.

By operating its own retail stores, Supervalu competes with its own customers and is sometimes forced to make strategic marketing trade-offs between its operating businesses. In the highly competitive Atlanta market, for example, Cub Foods' expansion has not been as aggressive as some industry experts predicted. Atlanta is a highly fragmented grocery market in which large chains such as Publix and Kroger compete, but where no single chain dominates and many independent chains are very successful.

Supervalu's involvement in all areas of the grocery business make it a major player in the grocery industry. The wholesale industry looks to Supervalu for leadership, and producers treat it with respect. In all areas (wholesale, retail, and physical distribution), Supervalu exemplifies good marketing practices.

Sources: "Convenience at Cubs," *Progressive Grocer,* August 1995, p. 13.

Michael Garry and Glenn Snyder, "Turning Partnering into Reality," *Progressive Grocer,* September 1993, pp. 44–46.

Hoover's MasterList Database (Austin, Tex.: The Reference Press, 1996).

"Mike Wright Has Service in the Bag," *Fortune,* June 4, 1990, p. 62.

Steve Weinstein, "Georgia on Their Minds," *Progressive Grocer,* October 1994, pp. 99–100.

Pam Welsz, "Philip Morris, Mars et al., Go CO-with In-Supermarket C-Stores," *Brandweek,* March 20, 1995, p. 16.

To most consumers in the United States, the name Supervalu does not mean much, other than perhaps as a name across the side of tractor-trailers on the highway. To producers such as Philip Morris, Kraft, and Procter & Gamble, however, Supervalu is one of the largest and most powerful grocery wholesale and retail companies in the U.S. market, and an important part of their distribution systems. In the grocery industry, large wholesale operations such as Supervalu, Fleming Companies, and Rykoff-Sexton, as well as retail companies such as A&P and Safeway, act as intermediaries. They control much of the shelf space in U.S. grocery stores, and can influence greatly the success or failure of practically all consumer packaged goods that they sell. Intermediaries also permeate other consumer products industries, such as apparel, television, personal computers, appliances, and automobiles, and practically all industrial products markets. Intermediaries often control display space and customer access in many markets, and can influence final purchase decisions substantially. No marketing strategy, therefore, is complete without careful attention to intermediaries.

Supervalu and other intermediaries contend with marketing concerns of their own, and they need to be market oriented. Supervalu's decision to slow down its Cub Foods expansion in Atlanta was an important strategic marketing decision. At roughly the same time Supervalu was scaling back in Atlanta, it was pursuing aggressive expansion in Indianapolis against Kroger, even though it cost the company some independent accounts in that market. In both situations, the company was trying to enhance services to final consumers profitably, and Supervalu had to work out compromises in some areas of the business.

Supervalu and its counterparts in other product markets also make tactical marketing decisions in areas such as product assortment, wholesale and retail pricing, advertising, salesforce management, types of promotion, and the location of stores and warehouse locations. The specific details of intermediaries' marketing concerns may differ in some aspects from those of producers, because they do not have to address product design questions. In general, however, intermediaries face many of the same marketing challenges as producers, and they need to be concerned with the application of marketing management techniques. This chapter focuses on the marketing concerns of wholesalers, retailers, and physical distribution providers as independent businesses. We cover the following topics for each intermediary type:

- An overview of the industry sector and its most important constituencies.
- The functions served by companies in this sector.
- The different types of companies in the sector and their primary functions.
- The historical development and current trends in the sector.
- The marketing decisions that companies in this sector face.

WHOLESALING

Wholesaling refers to the marketing activities required to sell goods or services to companies who resell them or use them to run their own businesses. In its wholesale operations, Supervalu mostly sells consumer packaged goods to independent grocers and Cub Foods for resale. It also sells services, such as real estate planning and merchandising management, to help independent grocery stores run their businesses more efficiently and competitively. Another example of a wholesaler is McKesson, a drug wholesaler with international operations and sales in excess of $13 billion. In the United States, McKesson sells ethical and over-the-counter drugs to thousands of independent and small chain drug stores. In addition, it sells products and services used by drug stores to provide better service to consumers, such as specialized packaging and computer services for tracking prescription information. Even after selling its highly profitable PCS Health Systems division to Eli Lilly & Company, McKesson has remained a highly influential wholesaler of drugs and related services.[1] Although most consumers have never heard of McKesson, they are nevertheless affected by the company. Illustrating the economic significance of the wholesale sector, Table 14.1 lists the top 15 U.S. wholesalers by sales revenue. In 1995, 56 of the top 1,000 U.S. firms were involved in wholesaling, with sales of more than $200 billion and employment of more than 438,000 people.[2] But the impact of the wholesale sector extends beyond its financial and economic impact. Throughout the world there are hundreds of regional or specialty wholesale companies that are strategically important regardless of their size.

One such wholesaler is Bearing Distributors (see Marketing Anecdote 14.1). Bearing Distributors and similar companies are normally called industrial distributors. Though they differ from wholesale merchants such as Supervalu and McKesson in that their operations are more complex and their customers are larger, Bearing Distributors and many other wholesalers share some of the same marketing concerns.

Because wholesaling is defined by the activities and functions performed, companies are often active in both wholesaling and retailing simultaneously. Supervalu is such a company, although its wholesale and retail areas are operationally and managerially separate. Wholesaling and retailing functions can also coexist within the same organization. Consider, for example, a home improvement center that sells kitchen cabinets and fixtures, such as Lowes or Home Depot. A kitchen sink and faucet purchased from such a store by a homeowner who is remodeling the kitchen is a retail transaction. But if the same sink and faucet were sold to a contractor do-

TABLE 14.1 FIFTEEN LARGEST WHOLESALERS IN THE UNITED STATES IN 1995

Name	Sales Revenue (in millions of dollars)	Profits (in millions of dollars)	Employees
Fleming Companies	17,502	42	44,000
Supervalu	16,564	43	43,500
McKesson	13,326	405	12,200
SYSCO	12,118	252	28,100
Alco Standard	9,892	203	36,500
Bergen-Brunswig	8,448	64	4,770
Cardinal Health	7,806	85	4,000
Arrow Electronics	5,919	203	7,200
Merisel	5,802	(9)	3,250
Genuine Parts	5,262	309	22,500
Foxmeyer Health	5,177	42	2,823
Bindley Western	4,672	16	894
Amerisource Health	4,669	10	2,600
Avnet	4,300	140	9,000
Intelligent Electronics	3,475	(19)	3,500

Source: "Fortune 1000 by Industries," Fortune, April 29, 1996, pp. F63–F64.

ing the remodeling, it becomes a wholesale transaction because the contractor will resell the products to the consumer as part of the job.

Most companies deal primarily in either retail or wholesale transactions, and consequently we can make broad distinctions between them, but we must keep in mind that overlap does exist. In the following sections, we focus our attention on companies involved primarily in wholesale activities.

The Importance of Wholesaling

Wholesalers serve two important constituencies: customers and producers. Wholesalers' customers are typically companies that buy products for resale or to support their business operations, and the relationship between wholesalers and their customers is not much different from the relationship between producers who use a direct sales approach and their customers. Wholesalers' customers have needs that must be met. If wholesalers are paying attention to customer needs and tailoring their marketing mix accordingly, they typically succeed. If they do not meet customer needs, customers look for alternative sources. Relationships with customers must be managed as carefully by wholesalers as by any other marketer.

Producers come to wholesalers for assistance in distributing their products and often depend on the wholesalers' presence and reputation to get their products in front of retailers and final customers. A small bearing manufacturer in central Ohio, for example, may not be able to get its limited product line in front of a General Electric buyer, so it turns to Bearing Distributors for assistance.

At the same time, wholesalers depend on a steady influx of quality products from producers to meet their customers' demands, making the wholesaler-producer relationship important to both parties. Wholesalers do not think of producers as

Bearing Distributors is a Cleveland-based medium-size distributor of bearing, power distribution equipment, and conveyor belting. A company with a long history of excellent service in the United States, it counts among its customers Fortune 500 companies such as Ford, Procter & Gamble, and General Electric, and many small and mid-sized companies. In its latest expansion efforts, however, Bearing Distributors has ventured into global markets, starting with operations in Hungary and expanding to serve other Eastern European markets.

An interesting aspect of Bearing Distributors' expansion into Europe is that it was initiated at the request of one of its major U.S. customers, General Electric's Lighting Business Group. As Eastern European countries shifted from centrally controlled to open markets in the late 1980s and early 1990s, most major U.S. companies saw the potential for trade with these companies. General Electric was one of the first companies to move into Eastern Europe, through the acquisition of Tungsram, a previously state-owned lighting equipment manufacturer in Hungary. Tungsram had been operating in Hungary for many years and had a well-trained workforce. Its manufacturing methods and capabilities were antiquated and inefficient, however, reflecting the typical communist governments' preference for full employment over efficient and profitable operations. General Electric saw Tungsram as an opportunity to improve efficiency and output while lowering costs, making it possible for the company not only to service the needs of the Hungarian market, but also to export lighting equipment to other Eastern and Western European markets.

Upon taking control of Tungsram, however, General Electric found that part of the company's inefficiencies arose from a lack of standardization in the component parts used to maintain manufacturing equipment, and the inability of existing industrial distributors to secure standardized components on a timely basis. General Electric turned to Bearing Distributors to manage industrial procurement at its Tungsram operation. The business was attractive to Bearing Distributors for two reasons: it enhanced relations with General Electric, and it helped the company enter a new market with at least one secure large customer. The risks came from doing business in a country with antiquated telecommunication systems and distribution facilities, where most managers and workers had never functioned in a competitive market.

Bearing Distributors stepped up to the challenge, assigning top-level executives to develop partnering relationships with European and U.S.-based suppliers, negotiate contracts with truck and rail operators throughout Europe, and tap into the nascent cellular telephone industry in Hungary for some of its telecommunication needs. The company has met all of General Electric's demands for component standardization. In addition, it has used its newly acquired expertise to serve the needs of companies such as ALCOA and Ford, as they expand in Hungary, and thus further strengthen its presence in Eastern European markets.

Sources: "The Emerging Role of International Distribution: Entering the Arena," *Industrial Distribution Supplement*, September 1995, pp. S16–S23.

Jane Perlez, "GE Finds Tough Going in Hungary," *New York Times*, July 25, 1994, pp. D1ff.

Gail-E. Schares, Zachary Schiller, and Patrick Oster, "GE Gropes for the On-Switch in Hungary," *Business Week*, April 26, 1993, pp. 102–103.

Michel Syrett and Klari Kingston, "GE's Hungarian Light Switch," *Management Today*, April 1995, pp. 52–53.

customers, because producers sell to wholesalers instead of buying from them, but wholesalers must recognize their need for healthy producers and to nurture those relationships as much as they nurture relationships with customers.

The Functions of Wholesalers

Wholesalers serve producers and customers by performing different functions, illustrated in Table 14.2, which we noted in chapter 13. In this chapter, we view the functions from the intermediary's point of the view rather than the producer's, which gives the discussion a different flavor. Wholesalers performing these functions, for example, see them as elements of their marketing mix, to be managed in the same ways that manufacturers manage different aspects of their operations in order to be more marketing oriented.

Not all wholesalers perform all of the functions listed on Table 14.2, and some of the functions are more important than others, depending on the industry in which the wholesaler works and the relative size of its customers and suppliers. Promotion, for example, is more important to producers dealing with Supervalu than to producers dealing with Bearing Distributors, given the greater importance of brand image in consumer products marketing compared to industrial products marketing. Wholesalers need to consider the demands for different functions by their customers and producers, and deploy resources to best meet market needs.

Different Types of Wholesalers

Wholesalers differ in the functions they assume and the industry in which they operate. We sometimes apply similar labels to significantly different wholesale operations in different industries, and some industries use different labels for the same package of functions. In the steel industry, for example, a wholesaler that stocks maintenance tools and supplies is called a mill supply house, whereas a wholesaler assuming the same functions for the food processing industry is called an industrial distributor.

Yet a number of broad categories of wholesalers generalize across multiple industries (see Table 14.3, page 587). They are distinguished on the basis of the types of products they handle, the functions they serve, the responsibilities they assume (e.g., taking or not taking title to the goods), and by how their compensation is determined. Different industries may have other bases for segmenting wholesaler types because the importance of the categorization parameters will vary.

Two broad categories of wholesalers are (1) merchant wholesalers and (2) brokers and agents. *Merchant wholesalers* are independent businesses that take title to the product they distribute. In the United States, they are the single largest group of wholesalers, responsible for more than 50 percent of all wholesale activity. *Brokers and agents* are also independent businesses, but they do not take title to the products. These two wholesaler types differ in other ways as well. One major way is the number of functions they serve. As can be seen in Table 14.3, merchant wholesalers serve more functions on average than brokers and agents. Merchant wholesalers assume title to goods and see themselves as suppliers to customers. Thus, they have more control over transactions with customers. Brokers and agents, in contrast, see themselves as facilitators and allow buyers and sellers more latitude.

In general, we can represent the variety of wholesaler-types by positioning them in terms of how much responsibility they take for the goods they offer and the spectrum

TABLE 14.2 FUNCTIONS PERFORMED BY WHOLESALERS

Functions	Description	Examples from Supervalu
FUNCTIONS FOR CUSTOMERS		
Variety	Providing products and/or services that meet a variety of customer needs with the right attributes and in the right quantities	Supplies independent grocery stores with thousands of dry goods and fresh produce on a daily basis
FUNCTIONS FOR PRODUCERS		
Storage	Holding product safely and ready for distribution in response to market demands	Stores frozen products in refrigerated warehouse facilities
Financing	Monetary arrangements that meet working capital needs	Takes title to some goods and releases producer capital
Gathering information	Gathering and compiling customer and market data useful to producers in production scheduling and market planning	Gives on-line and real-time customer database access to producers via Internet connections
FUNCTIONS FOR PRODUCERS AND CUSTOMERS		
Risk	Reducing exposure to theft, damage, and other market and natural factors that can cause losses	Secures and insures warehouse and transportation facilities
Personal contact and education	Having personnel available to represent producer and/or customer interests on a one-on-one basis	Has sales representatives who contact grocery stores and handle customer questions and demands
Transportation	Moving product between different locations safely and on time	Provides transportation through internal fleet and contract services
Promotion	Highlighting new products and services from manufacturers, educating customers, and managing promotional programs aimed at internal salesforce	Participates in promotional campaigns that encourage customer adoption of new products and services

of their services, as illustrated in Figure 14.1 on page 589. This diagram shows that wholesale intermediaries can be important and highly involved members of distribution systems even if they don't assume title to the goods. Manufacturers agents, for example, maintain personal contact, assure variety, gather information, and promote goods, and they have considerable responsibility for the success of a product line without ever assuming title to the goods. The same can be said for purchasing agents, who can virtually shape the product array offered by retailers but do not take ownership or provide financing. Figure 14.1, although not an absolute classification scheme, illustrates how wholesaler roles and relationships are multidimensional. Wholesalers' compensation depends largely on the degree of responsibility they take in transactions.

Marketers responsible for their companies' distribution systems must understand what wholesalers do in their industries and categorize the alternative types of wholesalers in terms of the most important dimensions. Intermediaries have considerable latitude in the functions they choose to serve, so their functions vary even among the same wholesaler types. Of course, marketers need to remember that wholesalers are businesses with their own marketing concerns.

TABLE 14.3 TYPES OF WHOLESALERS

	Typical Products Handled	Functions Served	Responsibilities	Compensation
BROKERS AND AGENTS				
Brokers	Commercial real estate and insurance	Personal contact	Bring buyers and sellers together and facilitate exchange; no title to products	Commission set on value of the transaction
Commission merchants	Commodities (e.g., farm products, raw minerals)	Personal contact and transportation	Responsible for product in transit; no title to products	Commission set on value of the transaction
Manufacturers' agents	Complementary products in different industries (e.g., sports equipment, plumbing supplies, furniture)	Personal contact, variety, information gathering, promotion	Long-term contracts, exclusive and professional representation in exchange for protected territories; no title to products	Commission based on the price of the product; bonuses based on special promotions
Selling agents	Bulk manufactured products (e.g., chemicals, textiles)	Personal contact, variety, pricing, promotion, negotiation, information gathering	Short-term arrangements with substantial marketing latitude awarded to agent; no title to products	Commissions based on transaction value
Purchasing agents	Products in fragmented industries (e.g., apparel)	Personal contact, variety, information gathering, and negotiations on behalf of retailers	Identify suitable products and suppliers, represent small retailers in negotiations with vendors; no title to products	Various methods, such as commissions or percent of retail profits
MERCHANT WHOLESALERS: LIMITED SERVICE				
Cash and carry wholesalers	Limited lines of fast moving items (e.g., produce, perishables)	Personal contact, information gathering, negotiation	Find buyers for perishable products, negotiate quick transactions; no title	Profit margins
Drop shippers	Bulk raw materials (e.g., lumber, coal)	Personal contact, negotiation	Assume title and financial responsibility for in transit goods; does not handle the product directly	Profit margin
Mail-order wholesaler	Low volume products (e.g., office supplies)	Variety, information gathering, storage, transportation, financing, risk, promotion	All tasks involved with marketing of goods to other businesses; assumes title to goods	Profit margin and bonuses from producers
Rack jobbers	Consumer packaged goods (e.g., snacks, beverages, paper goods)	Personal contact, merchandising, risk, transportation, financing, information gathering	Sell and deliver goods to small retailers, pricing, set up displays, stock shelves; assumes title to goods	Profit margin and bonuses from producers

TABLE 14.3 TYPES OF WHOLESALERS—CONTINUED

	Typical Products Handled	Functions Served	Responsibilities	Compensation
MERCHANT WHOLESALERS: LIMITED SERVICE				
Truck wholesalers	Perishable consumer goods (e.g., bakery goods, dairy products)	Personal contact, risk, transportation, information gathering	Sell and deliver goods to small retailers daily; assumes title to goods	Profit margin
MERCHANT WHOLESALERS: FULL SERVICE				
Industrial distributors	Maintenance and repair supplies, equipment components, and tools used by manufacturers	Personal contact, risk, information gathering, transportation, storage, financing, promotion, variety	All tasks involved with marketing of goods to other businesses; assumes title to goods	Profit margin and bonuses from producers
Wholesale merchants	Wide variety of consumer goods sold by retailers (e.g., apparel, drugs, groceries, books, hardware, appliances)	Personal contact, risk, information gathering, transportation, storage, financing, promotion, variety	All tasks involved with marketing of goods to other businesses; assumes title to goods	Profit margin and bonuses from producers

Developing Trends in Wholesaling

The growth and overall health of the wholesaling sector has historically been linked to developments in transportation and the concentration of population in urban centers. Historically, we find evidence that as cities grew and became more accessible to different modes of transport, some merchants evolved from selling to final consumers (e.g., from being retailers) to supplying the needs of other merchants. These "wholesale" merchants were often wealthy and powerful, buying in large quantities at favorable prices for resale at a profit, and controlling transportation in and out of their markets. Such wholesalers also had contacts in many markets and

Jobbers provide important coordination between wholesalers and retailers to get products to their final markets.

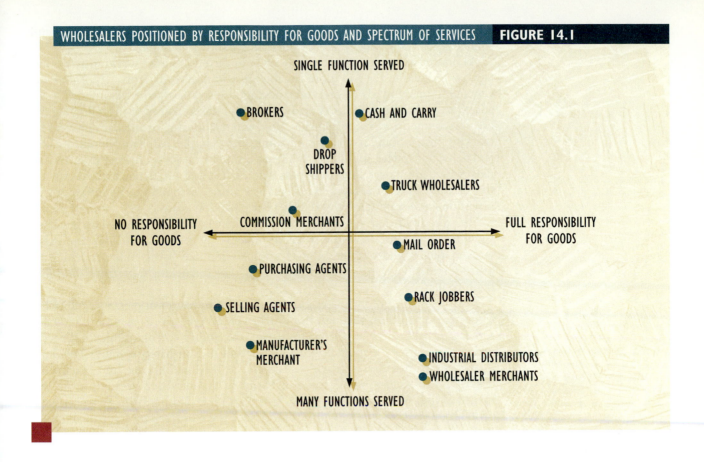

SINGLE FUNCTION SERVED

●BROKERS   ● CASH AND CARRY

●
DROP
SHIPPERS

●TRUCK WHOLESALERS

NO RESPONSIBILITY   COMMISSION MERCHANTS ●   FULL RESPONSIBILITY
FOR GOODS   FOR GOODS

●MAIL ORDER

●PURCHASING AGENTS

●SELLING AGENTS   ●RACK JOBBERS

●MANUFACTURER'S
MERCHANT   ●INDUSTRIAL DISTRIBUTORS
●WHOLESALER MERCHANTS

MANY FUNCTIONS SERVED

remained abreast of developments in a wider sphere of influence than smaller retailers, allowing wholesalers to anticipate demand and supply fluctuations and insure a relatively steady flow of goods. In U.S. colonial times, for example, wholesalers would observe fashion developments in Paris and London, and make
purchases of raw textiles in advance of the arrival of such fashions in U.S. markets.

In the 1990s, many wholesalers around the world still function in this manner.
Trading companies across many Asian countries, for example, control transportation and wholesale distribution of products, and profitably anticipate the arrival of
new products and fashions into their markets. In the United States and other industrialized countries, however, traditional roles of wholesalers have changed drastically in the past 10 years. Some developments threaten the overall viability of
wholesalers, or at least limit their ability to perform certain functions profitably,
whereas others create new opportunities for wholesaler growth and expansion, and
new ways of doing business. Wholesalers in the 1990s face significant and exciting
marketing challenges and opportunities.

Factors Currently Threatening Wholesalers

Three related developments threaten wholesalers:

- increased efficiency and availability of truck transportation
- increased availability and access to electronic data interchange via the World
  Wide Web
- growth of large retailers.

These factors are already putting pressure on U.S. and Canadian wholesalers, and similar pressures will likely affect wholesaling in other countries.

As limited access highways have been built throughout the world, truck delivery has become faster and more reliable, in addition to its native flexibility advantage in many markets, and the trucking industry has grown dramatically. In addition, global truck industry regulation has relaxed considerably, allowing increased competition, route consolidation, and the offering of ancillary services by trucking firms. Some trucking companies, for example, offer multipoint pickup and delivery services, and break-bulk and limited storage services at their terminals, which allows retailers to bypass wholesalers and order truck-sized quantities directly from producers. Such services allow customers to negotiate lower prices on large shipments and reduce transportation costs as well, both of which weaken the hold that wholesalers have on their markets. Wholesalers have responded to pressure from the trucking industry by bringing transportation services in-house, and by integrating transportation and break-bulk services with other services (e.g., information gathering), which trucking companies find difficult to match.

Also pressuring the wholesale industry is an explosion in electronic data interchange capabilities through the World Wide Web, gives producers and customers, whether very small or very large, the ability to communicate directly with one another.[3] Using applications written in Sun Microsystem's Java language, companies with computers as diverse as IBM mainframes and Macintosh desktops can exchange information easily in standardized formats over the World Wide Web. Such companies can thus coordinate customer needs with production schedules in real time, and render the wholesalers' traditional coordination and inventory buffering functions superfluous. The World Wide Web eliminates some of the computer system gaps that separate companies, and which wholesalers used to bridge. Wholesalers are responding to this threat by establishing their own presence on the World Wide Web, by assisting small companies to establish web sites and access in exchange for continuing patronage, and by educating customers about web pitfalls, such as security breaches and potential fraud by disreputable firms. Although the web eliminates some wholesaler competitive advantages, it is a confusing and complex medium, and many producers and customers need guidance to work with these new tools. For wholesalers who are able to add web expertise to the functions they serve through personal contact, therefore, the web represents additional marketing opportunities.

A third factor threatening some wholesalers is the substantial growth of retail giants such as Wal-Mart and Sears at the expense of independent retailers. As discussed in chapter 13, large retail chains have become increasingly powerful as consumers direct more and more shopping dollars toward them. Most of these retail giants purchased from wholesalers in their early years, but now far surpass even the largest wholesaler in terms of purchasing power.

Large retailers threaten wholesalers in two ways. First, they deal directly with manufacturers and force them to adjust their sales practices to match large retailers' preferences. Fleming, for example, had to change some of its pricing strategies and suffered some financial setbacks in response to Procter & Gamble's cuts in trade promotions, a move strongly influenced by demands from Wal-Mart and other large retail chains.[4] Second, large retailers are systematically putting many independent retailers out of business. In some markets, large retail chains have been steadily undermining the traditional wholesaler domain for several years, putting one or more wholesale companies out of business entirely. Surviving wholesalers have consolidated their own operations into larger companies with even more purchasing power, and expanded their services to protect their remaining independent retail customers.

Factors Creating Opportunities for Wholesalers

Two environmental factors generate opportunities for wholesalers: the growth in information-technology capabilities and accessibility, and the opening up of international markets. These factors will shape the wholesale sector well into the twenty-first century.

Although the World Wide Web threatens some wholesaler-provided functions, the explosion in information-technology capabilities and availability also creates substantial opportunities for wholesalers around the world. The 1980s and 1990s have seen more progress in information processing power and availability than the preceding 40 years, and harnessing these capabilities allows wholesalers to offer an array of services wider than ever before. Information-processing advances have allowed more extensive gathering and management of market information. Recent years have seen an exponential increase in the amount of consumer and business data available from sources such as the U.S. Census Bureau, industry and trade associations, and major news agencies around the world, and most of this information can be accessed and integrated with relative ease using a personal computer. Wholesalers who use available data wisely can provide customers and producers with detailed and up-to-date information about their target markets. Although these data are available to customers and producers also, many of them do not have the industry knowledge necessary to glean as much from the data as is possible, making wholesalers valuable as consultants who interpret the data.

The storage function also benefits from information technology. Radio-frequency data terminals, high-speed scanners, and powerful personal computers and servers allow wholesalers to construct and operate warehouse facilities where customer orders are received directly into multiorder picking schedules and filled within minutes of arrival. Producer shipments can then be processed immediately and made available for order filling.[5] Warehouse facilities with these capabilities cost roughly the same as more conventional warehouses, and can make wholesalers an integral part of just-in-time operations for small- and medium-sized suppliers and customers. In effect, information technology allows wholesalers to channel and expand their industry knowledge in new ways, and to service their customers while continuing to expand their advantage-giving market expertise. Wholesalers need to see information technology and data access as golden opportunities to grow and expand in the twenty-first century.

The opening of international markets represents perhaps the most dramatic set of current opportunities for wholesalers based in industrialized countries. Fueled by factors such as the opening of previously controlled economies in Eastern Europe, lower trade barriers in Asia, trade partnerships such as the North American Free Trade Agreement, and continuing progress toward the European Union, international trade has increased dramatically since the 1970s and has become a vital element for most successful wholesalers' marketing plans. U.S.- and Canada-based wholesalers, who have the world's most advanced distribution systems, can carry their expertise into practically all parts of the world. The partnership between Bearing Distributors and General Electric's Tungsram venture in Hungary is just one example of how wholesalers can take their expertise into other countries.

Another example is Varlen Corporation's pursuit of opportunities in the Russian market. Varlen is a medium-sized manufacturing and distribution company serving several industries. One of their more successful business units sells components to railroad car manufacturers, and has established a working relationship with the largest manufacturer of railroad cars in Russia. Russia has the world's largest and perhaps most modern rail system, but its railcar stock is seriously outdated and dilapidated. Russia's rail system is managed differently from that of the United States and most Western countries, and poses some unique safety and maintenance problems. The way that railcars are coupled and decoupled in Russian railyards, for example, places substantial strain on the railcars' braking systems and can cause considerable damage to cars that use Western-style brake couplings. Varlen has adapted its brake coupling technology and distribution practices to cater to the Russian railcar market better than other Western rail component producers, and stands poised to grow dramatically as the Russian government improves its rail system.

Experts have suggested that distribution know-how and systems are among some of the most exportable products that Western distributors can offer.[6] The U.S. Department of Commerce has identified ten emerging markets: the Chinese Economic Area (China, Taiwan, Hong Kong); India; Indonesia; South Korea; South Africa; Poland; Turkey; Mexico; Brazil; and Argentina. In practically all of these markets, foreign wholesalers lag behind U.S., Canadian, and Japanese firms in terms of systems integration, information technology, industry knowledge across multiple product categories, and logistics management. Whereas companies such as Supervalu and Fleming provide their customers with up-to-the-minute information on warehoused and in-transit inventories, wholesalers in many of the emerging markets rely on paper systems to track inventory levels and orders, if they have systems at all. Fleming has capitalized on its expertise in these areas, for example, to expand its wholesale and retail operations in Mexico.[7] To compete in world markets, producers and customers in emerging markets must move products in and out of their facilities quickly and maintain low inventories whenever possible. Wholesalers in the United States and other industrialized countries excel at these very tasks, providing excellent opportunities to enter such developing markets and accelerate the market's rate of development while establishing relationships with dynamic companies, and can establish a presence in some of the fastest-growing economies and industries in the world.

Responding to Threats and Opportunities

Wholesaler response to threats and opportunities can vary substantially, depending on environmental factors and company resources. Studies of wholesaler-distributors have revealed a number of strategies that wholesalers pursue to offset environmentally caused threats or improve their competitive position. Table 14.4[8] lists 10 such strategies roughly according to the size of investment required for their implementation. Some strategies are exemplified by K. J. Electric in Marketing Anecdote 14.2, a company that has successfully implemented strategic moves such as asset redeployment, value-added services, systems selling, and niche marketing.

Marketing Decisions of Wholesalers

Earlier in this chapter we mentioned that wholesalers are business entities that face the same challenges that producers do. Therefore, it should come as no surprise that the marketing concerns of wholesalers have the same general categories that we used for producers. Wholesalers face target market decisions, product and service assortment decisions, promotion decisions, distribution or place decisions, and pricing decisions.

TABLE 14.4 WHOLESALER STRATEGIC OPTIONS

Strategic Option	Description	Industry Example
Expansion into international markets	Expanding wholesale or related activities into foreign markets	Bearing Distributors expands into Hungary and other Eastern European markets.
Forward and backward integration	Moving into retailing or manufacturing	Supervalu acquires and expands Cub Foods.
Mergers and acquisitions	Making investments in smaller companies or combining with companies of similar size to gain economies of scale and access to other markets	Fleming acquires Scrivner, another grocery products wholesaler.
Corporate diversification	Investing in nonrelated businesses to reduce cyclical exposure	McKesson ventures into managing pharmaceutical costs for large health-care sponsors (e.g., companies).
New technologies	Applying computer and communications technology to improve responsiveness and service level	Supervalu implements inventory management, store location models, and floor planning programs.
Asset redeployment	Selling off marginal business and using the proceeds to invest in more promising areas of the business	McKesson later sells its pharmaceutical cost management operation to Eli Lilly and Company.
Proprietary brands	Selling in-house brands at higher margins	Inmac, a computer accessories distributor, sells products under the Inmac brand, which it designs and manufactures under contract.
Value-added services	Adding services such as preprocessing of materials, expedited delivery, just-in-time delivery, electronic data interchange, and other differentiating features	A. M. Castle, a metals distributor, preprocesses steel sheets for automobile manufacturers.
Systems selling	Offering complete merchandising programs to retailers	Handleman, an electronics components distributor, offers complete home entertainment merchandising programs.
Niche marketing	Specializing in product categories to become the dominant supplier	Richardson Electronics focuses on distribution of technically obsolete electronic technology products, such as electron tubes and power semiconductors.

Source: Summarized from Robert F. Lusch, Deborah S. Coykendall, and James M. Kenderdine, Wholesaling in Transition: An Executive Chart Book (Norman: University of Oklahoma, Distribution Research Program, College of Business, 1989). University of Oklahoma and multiple industry sources used for examples.

Target Market Decisions

In an increasingly complex and dynamic market, wholesalers can no longer count on traditional market definitions, or try to please everyone. Instead they must choose their target markets carefully, based on criteria that make business sense. Some of the criteria that wholesalers can use are size (e.g., servicing only small and medium retailers), needs for specific services (e.g., customers that need only financing and break-bulk services), specific industries (e.g., railcar manufacturing), and types of customers (e.g., independent drugstores, machine shops). Wholesalers need to choose market segmenting criteria that best match their strengths and abilities, and allow them to operate profitably. Once they choose target customers, wholesalers

K.J. Electric, an industrial distributor of power transmission systems headquartered in Syracuse, New York, serves much of upstate New York. In recent years sales have grown in excess of 35 percent in a geographic market in which population has declined by approximately 18 percent. K.J. Electric's success secret is really not a secret at all—the company has achieved high current customer loyalty and gained new customers by adding services that increase the customers' dependence on it.

One of K.J. Electric's primary focus areas has been on educating both their employees and customers. In employee training, K.J. Electric holds weekly product training sessions in which technicians, salespeople, and office personnel learn the latest technologies in power transmission, and learn about innovative applications of products distributed by the company. Suppliers present some lessons, and they typically appreciate the chance to speak to K.J. Electric's enthusiastic staff. K.J. Electric's in-house engineers present other programs about product solutions the company has developed for specific customers to encourage application with other customer accounts. All K.J. presentations are videotaped and remain available for review by all personnel.

In training of customers, K.J. Electric has adopted a philosophy of "show the customer, don't just tell them." The traditional business approach in the power distribution industry is for customers to provide specifications to distributors, who respond with written proposals. Customers spell out system performance characteristics in detail and sometimes use computer simulations to generate projections, but they seldom test proposed distribution systems before installation begins. To differentiate itself, K.J. Electric has set up a demonstration room in which engineers build prototypes of proposed power transmission systems and show customers how systems actually go together and perform. This approach serves two purposes. First, it gives customers and engineers opportunities to identify and correct problems with the proposed design before the installation takes place. Second, it gives K.J. Electric a chance to showcase innovations that may improve on initial customer specifications, but that may be rejected if presented in other ways.

K.J. Electric also recognizes that ongoing relationships with existing customers are much more cost-effective than developing new accounts, and they have instituted a marketing communications program that links customers

need to build strong relationships and create dependencies with their customers without exploitation. In addition, they must not hesitate to terminate relationships that are no longer profitable, or with companies no longer in their target group.

Product and Service Assortment Decisions

It may seem odd to speak of product decisions when discussing wholesalers because they do not "produce" anything. They do provide product assortments to customers that might otherwise not be available, however, and in that sense they have products. Wholesalers must choose their product assortments carefully, both to protect their profitability and to meet their most important customers' needs. As done by K.J. Electric (Marketing Anecdote 14.2), many wholesalers categorize products in terms of market attractiveness and eliminate marginal lines in favor of greater depth within lines

to the company at multiple levels. Instead of funneling all account contact through sales staff, K.J. Electric personnel in accounting, engineering, maintenance, and purchasing all develop intimate knowledge of different accounts and are encouraged to befriend counterparts at customer firms. The more K.J. distributed knowledge about customers, the more responsive it can be to problems and opportunities across all functional areas. K.J. Electric's responsiveness has made it the supplier of choice in its geographic market for tough and urgent jobs. The company has also expanded its contact base among customers that use decentralized purchasing for equipment. In organizations with multiple manufacturing sites, different factories may use different suppliers of power distribution systems, because decisions in the different plants are most often made by production managers. But these same large companies often have centralized engineering or accounting staffs who are aware of company purchases from alternative suppliers. By having frequent contact with customers across functional areas, K.J. Electric has a richer information flow than companies relying only on their salesforces, and K.J. can respond to opportunities even when their salespeople are not initially involved.

Last, K.J. Electric has extended its integrated systems design services. This takes two directions. First, the company offers complete systems solutions to its customers, which makes installation and maintenance easier because it involves only one supplier. Second, K.J. Electric has extended its product array to include turnkey systems, engineered to satisfy the needs of a broad range of customers with minor adjustments by sacrificing some performance. Turnkey systems are quicker to install and priced lower than custom installations, because components are standardized and purchased in larger quantities. The use of turnkey systems allows K.J. Electric to compete for rush jobs at the low end of the price spectrum, while also being able to provide custom installations to customers that demand them. By expanding its services and integrating their functional operations, K.J. Electric has differentiated itself from other suppliers and achieved significant marketing success.

Sources: George M. Fodor, "Training Breeds Customer Loyalty," *Industrial Distribution*, May 1989, pp. 94–99.

"K.J. Electric Earns $1.1 Million Motor Contract," *Industrial Distribution*. September 1994, pp. 21–22.

that can be integrated into complete systems. Many wholesalers have also recognized that they cannot meet all customer demands and have opted for meeting some needs better than anyone else. This also applies to services, where the demands are never-ending and profitability drains substantial. Wholesalers must choose to offer only those services that give them a competitive advantage. Varlen Corporation, for example, gave its Russian customers free advice about how to do business with U.S. companies in addition to selling them railcar components, because as Russian trade improves in other areas, the demand for railcars, components, and other Varlen products in Russia will also improve. Wholesalers can also identify some ancillary services for which customers will be willing to pay a premium, and offer those services as extra-cost options.

Promotion Decisions

In the wholesale sector, most promotional activities take place through the salesforce. As discussed in chapter 11, a well trained and managed salesforce can be a valuable asset. Wholesalers need to move away from traditional views of selling, however, and embrace current trends, such as team selling, telemarketing, and the World Wide Web sites.

The current environment suggests that wholesalers can consider using other promotional activities as image-building techniques. Sponsoring select educational events or political lobbying that protects consumers, for example, can give wholesalers considerable visibility and favor with customers. For instance, a regional drug wholesaler sponsored seminars that help independent drug stores compete with mass discounters, and generated considerable goodwill and customer loyalty. Although discounters may react negatively to such a move, most discounters do not buy from wholesalers anyway.

Distribution or Place Decisions

Although current transportation and communication technologies make location irrelevant for many wholesalers, other aspects of the distribution system have become increasingly important. Historically, wholesalers have underinvested in material handling and electronic data interchange technology, and have lagged behind large retailer and producer advances. But as pressures have mounted and responsive information and delivery systems have been demanded by small, medium, and large companies, wholesalers have had to respond accordingly. Wholesalers who want to remain competitive need to treat electronic data interchange, automated material handling, and other applications of information technology as standard fare, and no longer as optional enhancements.

Pricing

The biggest concern in the pricing area is the constant downward pressure on wholesaler margins at the same time that demands for services continue to escalate. Wholesalers need to improve their data-gathering systems to remain abreast of cost and price information in the product categories they carry, and set prices in ways that reflect shifts in producer policies and price sensitivity. The days of time-honored mark-up levels and promotional allowances across all product lines seem to be gone as global competition has increased across practically all industrial sectors. The average customer today receives much more product and price information than they did 20 years ago, so wholesalers must get and remain price competitive. Wholesalers also need to charge for costly services like breaking bulk, warehousing, and consulting.

RETAILING

Retailing involves selling goods and services to final consumers for their personal use. Retailers range in size and scope from giants, such as Marui Company in Japan, Wal-Mart in the United States, and the Edouard Leclerc group in France, to local gas stations and street vendors outside a baseball stadium. Most people around the world encounter retailers. In the United States alone, as illustrated in Table 14.5, the top 10 food and drug retailers account for approximately $118 billion in sales, and the top 10 general merchandisers for more than $249 billion in sales. Thirty-four drug and food retailers and 22 general merchandisers are among the largest 1,000 U.S. companies, including three (Wal-Mart, Sears, and Kmart) in the top 20. All the firms involved in retailing among the largest 1,000 companies in the United States account for more than $616 billion in sales and employ almost 4.8 million

TABLE 14.5 TEN LARGEST FOOD AND DRUG RETAILERS AND GENERAL MERCHANDISERS IN THE UNITED STATES IN 1995

Name	Sales Revenue (in millions of dollars)	Profits (in millions of dollars)	Employees
FOOD AND DRUG RETAILERS			
Kroger	23,938	303	200,000
American Stores	18,309	317	121,000
Safeway	16,398	326	113,000
Albertson's	12,585	465	80,000
Winn-Dixie	11,788	232	123,000
Walgreens	10,395	321	68,800
Publix Super Markets	9,471	242	95,000
Vons	5,071	68	29,600
Eckerd	4,997	93	46,437
Thrifty Payless Holdings	4,659	(35)	31,200
GENERAL MERCHANDISERS (MASS MERCHANDISERS AND DISCOUNTERS)			
Wal-Mart Stores	93,627	2,740	675,000
Sears Roebuck	35,181	1,801	275,000
Kmart	34,654	(571)	250,000
Dayton-Hudson	23,516	311	214,000
JCPenney	21,419	838	205,000
Federated Department Stores	15,049	75	119,000
May Department Stores	12, 167	752	130,000
Dillard Department Stores	6,097	167	40,312
Nordstrom	4,114	165	34,700
Fred Meyer	3,429	30	27,000

Source: "Fortune 1000 by Industries," Fortune, April 29, 1996, pp. F51–F53.

people. These numbers exclude the thousands of small retailers that dot the countryside, selling everything from food to fortune telling, and employing more than 25 million people. Retailing is a major industry worldwide and an integral part of modern economic systems.

The Functions of Retailers

The functions of retailers are listed in Table 14.6. Retailers have three major exchange constituencies: producers, wholesalers, and consumers. These three groups need retailers to complete the exchange cycle. Retailers' primary focus is on consumers, and most of the functions they perform are aimed at meeting consumer needs. In the fashion and apparel sector, for example, retailers interpret and shape consumer needs and wants, and provide guidance to textile and apparel manufacturers around the world. Retailers' increasing influence and economic importance demands that marketers understand their roles in the current environment.

TABLE 14.6 FUNCTIONS PERFORMED BY RETAILERS

Functions	Description	Examples from Sears
FUNCTIONS FOR CUSTOMERS		
Variety	Providing products and/or services that meet a variety of customer needs with the right attributes and in the right quantities	Has more than 875,000 items in apparel, automotive, home and garden, appliances, electronics, and other areas
FUNCTIONS FOR PRODUCERS AND WHOLESALERS		
Storage	Holding product safely and ready for distribution in response to consumer market demands	Manages regional warehouse facilities to which many small and medium suppliers ship their products
Gathering information	Gathering and compiling customer and market data useful to producers in product and market planning and production scheduling	Gives on-line database access to producers via Internet connections
FUNCTIONS FOR CONSUMERS AND PRODUCERS/WHOLESALERS		
Financing	Monetary arrangements that meet working capital and individual consumer budgeting needs	Offers consumer credit in various forms (proprietary credit card, major cards); takes title to some goods and releases producer capital
Risk	Reducing exposure to theft, damage, product failure, and other market and natural factors that can cause losses to consumers and producers	Offers liberal return policies and operates customer service centers; secures and insures warehouse and transportation facilities
Personal contact and education	Having trained personnel to represent producer interests and respond to consumer needs on a one-on-one basis	Has well-trained sales personnel on the retail floor; has professional buyers responsible for supplier accounts
Transportation	Moving product between different locations safely and on time	Provides home delivery of some products through internal fleet and contract services and transportation from warehouse to stores
Promotion	Highlighting new products and services, educating customers, advertising, managing promotional programs aimed at internal salesforce	Spends millions of dollars in advertising and in-store promotions of private and national brands; offers informative promotional materials for product lines (e.g., tools); administers sales contests

Function Differences among Retailers

Of course not all retailers serve all of the functions listed in Table 14.6 nor do all retailers serve them to the same level of sophistication. But retailers have been giving more attention to functions as a source of differentiation and competitive advantage. Long-standing retailing tradition, as embodied by the general store, was to provide some level of service in each function area and leave in-depth specialization by function to producers and wholesalers. This is no longer the case. To better serve customers, many retailers have expanded their functional abilities or have extended their abilities to serve certain functions while ignoring others. In the process, retailers have invaded the traditional realms of both producers and wholesalers. In addition, and perhaps of greater importance, functional specialization has created many more retailer types.

Types of Retailers

Retailers are of many types, and more continue to emerge as market conditions change. We could classify retailers according to many different schemes, but for our purposes, we focus on product variety, pricing, and some unique differentiating characteristics to categorize retailer types, and discuss their outlooks, as summarized in Table 14.7.

Department Stores

Department stores in the late 1990s are recovering from one of the toughest periods in their history. During the 1970s, 1980s, and early 1990s, the department store sector went through serious upheaval, punctuated by a stream of companies in financial trouble, friendly and hostile consolidations, and market share losses. Venerable department store names such as Bergner's and Marshall Fields were in danger, and some experts were pessimistic about the industry as a whole. The industry has bounced back since that time, however, and holds optimistic expectations for the next several years. One example is that of Carson Pirie Scott & Company, illustrated in Marketing Anecdote 14.3 on page 603. In 1993, Carson emerged from bankruptcy into an era of positive growth and profitability in its Midwest markets, by using some of the same marketing strategies that made Nordstrom successful and introducing a few innovations of its own.

Discount Stores and Mass Merchandisers

The same period that saw department stores in trouble was also difficult for traditional mass merchandisers, such as Sears, JCPenney, and Montgomery Ward. These stores were troubled by some of the same problems as department stores: being out of touch with customer needs, poor customer service, lagging technology, and poorly defined strategies. As exemplified by Sears, mass merchandisers consolidated and downsized their operations throughout the 1980s and early 1990s, and only recently started posting gains in market share and profitability once again.[9]

Catalog Showrooms and Broad Line Catalog Retailers

Catalog showrooms expect moderate and selective growth throughout the rest of the 1990s, as do broad-line catalog retailers such as Spiegel—retailer types that compete in many product categories with discounters. The battle for consumer dollars during the early 1990s between established retailers and new retailer types caught some companies in these sectors by surprise and has forced some retrenchment.

These sectors had done relatively well during the 1990s, and early projections are for relatively steady growth throughout the next decade.

Supermarkets

Supermarkets have also changed in response to competitive forays, particularly by superstores, hypermarkets, and warehouse clubs. Supermarkets still enjoy a location advantage over many of their competitors, and they are capitalizing on this advantage by expanding their stores and services, offering private label brands, and providing limited one-stop shopping. Profitable ancillary services, such as pharmacy, video rental, bakeries, and floral shops have appeared in many supermarkets. Supermarkets are also embracing high technology, implementing sophisticated shelf management programs and fully automated cashiering systems,

TABLE 14.7 TYPES OF RETAILERS

Types of Retailers	Product Types	Pricing Strategy	Differentiating Characteristics	Examples
BROAD ASSORTMENT RETAILERS				
Department stores	Wide selection of top-quality national and private brands: primarily apparel, furniture, appliances, household comfort, and electronic equipment	Full retail price with occasional promotions such as seasonal sales and limited national brand sales	High levels of customer service (e.g., gift wrapping, delivery); liberal return policies	Macy's, Eaton's, Marshall Fields, Bloomingdale's
Mass merchandisers	Very wide selection of medium-quality products and services: apparel, furniture, appliances, household comfort and electronic equipment, automobile parts, optical centers, and photographic studios	Full retail price with regularly rotating promotions by product category; seasonal price promotions	Very wide array of products and services with basic customer services either free or at a nominal fee	Sears, JCPenney, Montgomery Ward
Discount stores	Limited selection in high-volume categories, wide variance in quality levels: apparel, furniture, appliances, household comfort and electronic equipment, automobile parts	Price discounts across all product categories, with rotating deep discounts by product area; heavy seasonal price promotions	Low everyday prices and periodic deep discounts	Wal-Mart, Kmart, Target, Venture
Supermarkets	Food, household cleaning goods, health and beauty aids; some delicatessen and bakery operations	Typical margins on food less than 1 percent; higher margins on household and other products	Focus on food; small size (12,000–15,000 items); urban, small town, and neighborhood locations	Safeway, Jewel, IGA Stores (associated with Independent Grocers Association)
Superstores	Same as supermarkets plus other products and services of medium quality: greeting cards, books, magazines, casual apparel, shoe repair, video rentals	Price discounts across all product categories, with rotating deep discounts by product area; margins on food less than 1 percent; seasonal price promotions	Range in size from 35,000 to 60,000 square feet; focus on enhanced convenience and customer service, one-stop shopping	Schnuck's, Kmart Superstores
Hypermarkets	Same as superstores plus other products and services: stock furniture, home improvement products, auto parts	Price discounts across all product categories, with rotating deep discounts by product area; margins on food less than 1 percent; seasonal price promotions.	Range in size from 60,000 to more than 200,000 square feet; focus on enhanced convenience and customer service, one-stop shopping	Leedmark, Meijers, Fred Meyer

TABLE 14.7 TYPES OF RETAILERS—CONTINUED

Types of Retailers	Product Types	Pricing Strategy	Differentiating Characteristics	Examples
BROAD ASSORTMENT RETAILERS				
Off-price retailers	Limited and varying selection in categories, wide variance in quality levels: apparel, small appliances, auto parts, household comfort and electronic equipment	Deep discounts on all product categories; price promotions vary randomly based on availability of discounted goods	Purchase overstocked goods, discontinued models, and irregulars at discounted prices; low-service stores, often located in low-rent shopping districts	Big Lots, Value City
Catalog showrooms	Limited selection in medium-quality consumer durable categories: sports equipment, electronic goods, jewelry, small appliances, toys	Price discounts across all product categories, with rotating deep discounts by product area; seasonal price promotions	Offer low prices by cutting down on staffing and floor space, stock is kept in low-overhead, attached warehouse space	Service Merchandise, Best Products
Warehouse clubs	Same as hypermarkets in product array but very limited selection in product categories	Deep discounts offered, part of discount achieved by use of economy-sized packages only	Warehouse-like ambiance (e.g., bare walls); charge membership fees; offer very limited services	Sam's Warehouse, Costco
LIMITED ASSORTMENT RETAILERS				
Specialty stores	Deep assortment in a narrow product line: shoes, apparel, computer equipment, jewelry, etc.	Full retail price with occasional promotions such as seasonal sales and limited-time name-brand sales.	High levels of customer service (e.g., gift wrap) and assistance with purchase decision, liberal return policies	Athlete's Foot, The Limited, B. Dalton, Florsheim
Factory outlets	Deep assortment in the product lines of a single manufacturer, typically in related categories: athletic footwear, apparel, housewares	Discounts between 10 percent and 25 percent from full retail, discontinued goods and irregulars as much as 50 percent off	Most often found in factory outlet malls, away from urban areas and traditional retail establishments for same brands	Van Heusen, Levi's, Pfaltzgraff, Nike
Convenience stores	Limited selection of quick-turnover grocery and emergency items	Higher margins than supermarkets on grocery items, full retail price on nongrocery items; few promotions	Often associated with gasoline retailers; offer prepared foods and beverages for immediate consumption	7-Eleven, Super Pantry, Big Foot, Starvin Marvin, Stop and Go
Category killers	Deep assortment in a narrow set of related product lines: sports equipment, electronics, appliances, toys	Price discounts on all product categories, rotating deep discounts by product area; seasonal price promotions	Deep selection of products in related lines; typical store size 25,000 to 35,000 square feet; located in suburban strip malls	Circuit City, Toys "Я" Us, Home Depot

TABLE 14.7 TYPES OF RETAILERS—CONTINUED

Types of Retailers	Product Types	Pricing Strategy	Differentiating Characteristics	Examples
NONSTORE RETAILERS				
Broad-line catalog retailers	Wide array of medium-quality products: apparel, small appliances, household comfort and electronic equipment	Full or slightly reduced prices on name-brand merchandise, lower prices on private labels; some seasonal and off-season promotions	Convenience of home shopping, toll-free 24-hour order service	Spiegel
Single- or narrow-line catalog retailers	Deep assortment of high-quality goods in a narrow set of related product lines	Full or slightly reduced prices on name-brand goods, lower prices on private labels; some seasonal and off-season promotions	Convenience of home shopping, toll-free 24-hour order service	L.L. Bean, Lands' End, Eddie Bauer, other specialized retailers with national coverage and targeted consumer groups
Home-shopping service	Wide and shallow array: primarily consumer durables, apparel, jewelry, luxury goods	Full retail price plus handling charges	Convenience of home shopping, products displayed on television, toll-free order numbers, credit cards accepted	QVC, Home Shopping Network
Vending machines	Wide variety of products globally: candy, soft drinks, emergency products (e.g., stamps, wrapped gifts); also used to sell services: banking, airline tickets	Full retail price or higher, depending on location	Accessible at all times in high-traffic areas	All major beverage brands, hard goods from department stores (in Japan), ATMs for many banks, Airline Computerized Ticketing machines
World Wide Web retailers	Deep assortment of high-quality goods in a narrow set of related product lines	Full or slightly reduced prices on name-brand goods	Convenience of computer shopping and complete control of pace of transaction; access anywhere computer is available	Firefly, Wal-Mart On Line, Peapod Virtual Supermarket, new entries almost daily

at which customers use scanner panels and debit cards to handle their own check-outs.[10] Technology has also allowed supermarkets to tailor their product offerings to tastes in their specific regions.

Superstores, Hypermarkets, and Warehouse Clubs

As recent entries into the retailing field, superstores, hypermarkets, and warehouse clubs all aim to provide one-stop shopping for food and regularly purchased hard goods at discounted prices. All three retailer types have experienced substantial growth in the 1990s. Tight economic conditions and consumers' convenience concerns influenced these retailers' initial success. As demands for customer service and value have gained importance among consumers, however, their growth has slowed. For example, many customers find the low level of service at warehouse clubs and some hypermarkets unacceptable, and have returned

Carson Pirie Scott & Company is the corporate name for the former P. A. Bergner chain of department stores, a chain that includes Gimbel's, Boston Stores, Bergner's, and Carson Pirie Scott stores throughout Indiana, Illinois, Minnesota, and Wisconsin. Carson filed for bankruptcy in 1991, after a series of acquisitions left the company unfocused and in deep financial trouble. Carson's management did not give up on the fundamental strength of its company, however, or on department stores as a viable retailer type. Management recognized that they had forgotten marketing fundamentals such as segmenting the market, meeting customer needs, and having good relationships with suppliers, and they moved to address these weaknesses.

While Carson was still under bankruptcy supervision, it made substantial changes in its product strategy. One change was to focus on career-minded customers (professional men and women with distinct and relatively stable apparel needs). Carson's management committed to offering a product array that would keep those customers coming back for both their professional and casual apparel, and altered its merchandising practices to implement this strategy. One tactical move was to expand the career apparel sections in its stores by eliminating some salesfloor storage areas and downsizing or eliminating furniture sections.

Another change was to react quickly to fashion shifts instead of trying to anticipate them. Carson benefitted by reducing losses from products that never caught on and had to be marked down several times before being sold. The challenge lay in being able to move quickly enough to take advantage of typically short-lived fashion trends. To achieve this objective, Carson established relationships with purchasing agents, through which it made most of its fashion apparel purchases. Although their product costs have risen, the purchasing agents' expertise has greatly improved Carson's market responsiveness. The company has reduced the number of clearance racks on the sales floor, and the few products that do not sell as expected are moved out very aggressively, improving the flow of salesfloor operations, reducing clutter, and enhancing the company's reputation for selling quality fashion items.

Carson has also installed powerful point-of-sale terminals in many of its stores. Because of its bankruptcy troubles, Carson had allowed its stores to run down and fall behind the technology curve, and customer service had deteriorated. Checkout lines were often slow, and checkout personnel had to get manager approval for many transactions for which the system was ill-equipped. The targeted career-minded customers, typically busy shoppers, did not appreciate waiting in line at checkout desks and would often buy less or go to other department stores.

The new point-of-sale system has improved checkout operation efficiency to the point that even when high-volume sales events are held, checkout lines are practically nonexistent. It has also allowed the company to reduce substantially training hours for new salespeople, and to devote most of that time to customer service training, instead of company policy training. The new system displays company policy information as needed on the register displays. Coupled with store renovations in its key markets, the new point-of-sale system has greatly improved Carson's image.

Sources: Robert Berner and Jonathan Auerbach, "Retailers Post Strong Results for Quarter," *Wall Street Journal*, August 16, 1996, p. A2.

"Carson Pirie Scott, AAFES Cited for Systems Innovation Excellence," *Chain Store Age*, January 1996, pp. 93–94.

"Carson Pirie Stock Offering," *New York Times*, November 1, 1993, p. D4.

"Carson's Quantum POS Leap," *Chain Store Age Executive*, January 1994, pp. 98ff.

Susan Reda, "P. A. Bergner's 'Little Black Dress' Theory," *Stores*, July 1993, pp. 58–60.

Gary Samuels, "No Dinosaur," *Forbes*, April 10, 1995, p. 66.

Snyder Drug Stores

Snyder Drug Stores holds its own against retail giants such as Wal-Mart and Walgreen's by staying firmly focused on its core drugstore products and offering an unparalleled level of customer service. The company operates more than 64 stores throughout the Midwest and is the market share leader in its Minneapolis home market.

Snyder management recognizes that customer service will not necessarily bring in new customers, but that it will keep existing customers loyal, and they strive for superior customer satisfaction in all areas of the business. Their approach contrasts sharply with the low service level characteristic of most large chains, which use pharmacies as traffic builders but not a core aspect of the business. At Snyder, the commitment to customer service is reflected in the staff training and store design. Drug counters are low, to encourage interaction between consumers and the pharmacist, aisles are wide for easy maneuvering and product access, and a secluded waiting area with comfortable chairs

and complementary coffee and tea make waiting for prescriptions more pleasant.

Snyder also caters to busy consumers by offering 24-hour pharmacies and a toll-free pharmacy hot line, both of which are featured in Snyder's award-winning advertising. In addition, Snyder has installed Express kiosks in some stores. The 800 square foot kiosks feature facsimile transmissions, copiers, postage machines, Western Union service, packaging and shipping, film processing, and other services in a central area. Snyder has also invested in state-of-the-art technology, which allows it to keep track of prescription information and respond to patient emergencies quickly. The emphasis on responsive and caring service has been well received by consumers, who not only remain loyal, but tell others about the Snyder Drug Stores' approach to drug retailing.

Eagle Hardware and Garden Centers

Eagle Hardware and Garden, less than a decade old, operates stores primarily in the Pacific Northwest and Hawaii. It is credited with revolutionizing the home improvement industry

to more traditional supermarkets, specialty stores, and department stores for most of their purchases. Growth is likely to remain modest for these retailer types into the next century.

Specialty Stores, Factory Outlets, and Category Killers

Specialty stores, factory outlets, and category killers share a similar narrow product line focus, and are consequently affected by market trends in similar ways. Increased consumer emphasis on value and service, for example, is often reflected in a desire by consumers to have enough choices to allow very discriminating purchases, even if it means paying a slightly higher price. This desire among consumers gives retailers with deep offerings in a narrow set of product categories a competitive advantage over companies with limited offerings in more categories; thus specialty stores, factory outlets, and category killers have an advantage over discounters, mass merchandisers, and other broader-line retailers.

For specialty stores, the outlook is mixed. Retailers that offer value, convenience, and service should continue to do relatively well into the next century, because many consumers still seek these core benefits. Retailers that misjudge their markets or are unresponsive will continue to lose market share as department stores, discounters,

with its unique combination of warehouse-style home improvement retailing and high-service home decor areas. Most Eagle Hardware and Garden stores are designed as concentric circles. The outer circle uses the warehouse format commonly found in home improvement centers: metal shelves packed floor to ceiling, self-service access, and thousands of different items. The inner circle takes on a different ambiance, however, with carpeted floors, model displays of the latest home improvement ideas, and informative showcasing of new products for all areas of the home (e.g., kitchen, bathroom, recreation room, patio). Eagle's home decor and improvement centers are designed as a system responsive to consumer needs for information, coordination, planning, and financing. Eagle Hardware also recognizes that consumers vary in terms of how much assistance they need, and has designed its stores to facilitate customers finding their preferred level of service.

One of the main ways in which Eagle responds to consumers is its well-trained retail salesforce. Eagle employees must have 60 hours of product and customer service training per year, and each store has an in-house trainer to ensure that new personnel are trained quickly. Training covers product areas such as plumbing, electrical, and kitchen fixtures, and skills such as sales presentation and interpersonal communications. Competitors such as Home Depot and Builders Square may copy some of its approaches, but Eagle Hardware and Garden remains the dominant home-improvement retailer in its markets, and a good example of responsive marketing.

Sources: Faye Brookman, "Nuts & Bolts & Ideas," *Stores,* March 1994, pp. 38–39.

Debra Chanil, "Fly Like an Eagle," *Discount Merchandiser,* April 1993, pp. 30ff.

Irene Clepper, "Snyder's Commercials Keep Them Laughing—and Coming," *Drug Topics,* February 8, 1993, pp. 114–116.

Robert La-Franco, "Comeuppance?" *Forbes,* December 4, 1995, pp. 74–76.

Marianne Wilson, "Snyder's Drug, a Twin Cities' Staple: Midwest Chain Holds Tight with Extensive Commitment to Service," *Chain Store Age Executive,* January 1993, pp. 77–78.

and other retailer types go after many of the same customers. Two examples of successful specialty stores that have followed the value, convenience, and service recipe are Snyder's Drug Stores and Eagle Hardware and Garden, as illustrated in Marketing Anecdote 14.4.

Off-Price Retailers and Convenience Stores

Off-price retailers and convenience stores can expect declining market share over the near term, despite their focus on providing important consumer benefits (low price and convenience). In the case of off-price retailers, flat or declining sales volumes are caused primarily by consumers' higher emphasis on value. Many modern consumers are careful about what they purchase and will pay a little more for products they expect to last longer. Because off-price retailers stock primarily irregular and discontinued items, many of their goods are perceived as poor values by these consumers. Another factor contributing to off-price retailer declines is the establishment by other retailer types of in-store outlets that sell irregulars and discontinued products—outlets that compete directly with off-price retailers but offer a more pleasant store environment.

Many convenience stores also face declining sales because of shifting consumer preferences, but in their case it is a preference for safety. Many convenience stores are located in urban and high-traffic suburban areas, where crime generally has been increasing.

Convenience stores combined with gasoline retail, however, have done well and are expected to grow as the number of commuters continues to increase. Standard Oil, Mobil Oil, Royal Dutch Shell, and other gasoline retailers are spending millions of dollars in the United States and Canada to convert many of their gasoline retail stores to combination fuel and food stores. A related trend is the combination of fuel retailing with fast-food chains such as Subway, Taco Bell, and McDonald's.[11] Capitalizing on the fast-paced lives of many commuters, fast-food producers have been expanding their presence at gas stations nationwide.

Vending Machines

Although vending machines are hardly new, technology advances have expanded the array of products and services they can dispense, and improved their security and design. Vending machines continue to proliferate throughout much of the world, and are used to distribute a wide array of goods and services. Financial service providers adopted this technology early, as banks used to them to extend their branch networks into malls, airports, and other high-traffic areas. More recently, vending machines update airline reservations and distribute airline tickets.[12]

Narrow-line Catalog Retailers, Home-Shopping Services, and World Wide Web Retailing

Nonstore retailer types all use information technology to provide greater convenience to consumers, and have experienced substantial growth globally. Narrow-line catalogs, for example, have proliferated on the strength of desktop publishing, database management software, toll-free phone lines, and expedited delivery services to the point where affluent families in the United States, Canada, Japan, and other countries receive hundreds of catalogs annually, offering tens of thousands of products. Narrow-line catalog retailing has been adopted by traditional retailers such as Sears; has created retailing giants such as L.L. Bean, Lands' End, Eddie Bauer, and J. Crew; and has opened retailing opportunities for unusual institutions such as the Metropolitan Museum of Art in New York City. Narrow-line catalog retailing also cuts across national borders, such as when Japanese consumers order products from U.S. retailers using toll-free numbers and expedited delivery services.[13] Narrow-line catalog retailing should continue to grow, although at a slower pace, over the next several years, given the wide availability and low cost of the technologies that make it possible.

Home-shopping retailers, such as QVC and the Home Shopping Network, have also grown in their global appeal. Satellite TV technology makes it possible to span national borders with home-shopping services in much the same way as narrow-line catalogs. Home-shopping retailers appeal to a segment often not reached by other retailer types—home-bound shoppers who are uncomfortable with printed catalogs for various reasons, but who cannot get out to traditional retail stores. The outlook for home-shopping services is for continued moderate growth, given their unique way of presenting products. The outlook has moderated somewhat from the early 1990s, when the advent of interactive TV was believed to be imminent.[14] The technology to support interactive television broadcasting has proved elusive and far more expensive than originally envisioned, leading to a scaling back of development plans in this medium. Taking its place with some consumers, however, has been retailing through the World Wide Web.

The World Wide Web has been discussed in several chapters thus far, given its far-reaching implications for many areas of marketing.[15] In retailing, the web makes it possible for consumers to access the product offerings of any retailer who establishes a web site, from anywhere a link to the web can be established, and at virtually any time. Encryption technology has increased the safety of financial transactions on the web to the point that shopping with credit or debit cards is as safe on the web as it is at most retail stores. Technology also allows retailers to segregate markets and tailor their web presentations based on consumers' shopping histories.

The future of web-based retailing looks very promising, although it reaches a select and relatively small market segment—affluent and highly educated people who are highly computer literate. The global purchasing power of this market segment is substantial, but it represents a relatively small percentage of the total population. For web-based retailing to really succeed, retailers must find ways of making the technology available to consumers who are not heavy users of personal computers and sophisticated information technology. Web appliances, such as those marketed by Oracle, are aimed at such consumers.

Developing Trends in Retailing

The evolution of retailing types in industrialized and developing economies is linked to developments in consumer lifestyles, and has been for more than a hundred years. By looking at retail development in the United States since the 1800s, as illustrated in Figure 14.2, we find a connection between consumer lifestyle and retailer development that extends over the decades and gives us insights into current retailing trends.

During the early nineteenth century, the United States had primarily an agrarian economy with little disposable income. Consumers bought only what they needed, and general stores with a wide array of utilitarian products were sufficient for much of the country. In large cities, specialty stores developed around craftsmen, with limited success. Department stores emerged after the Civil War, as the industrial might of the country turned from war products to consumer products, and they were followed

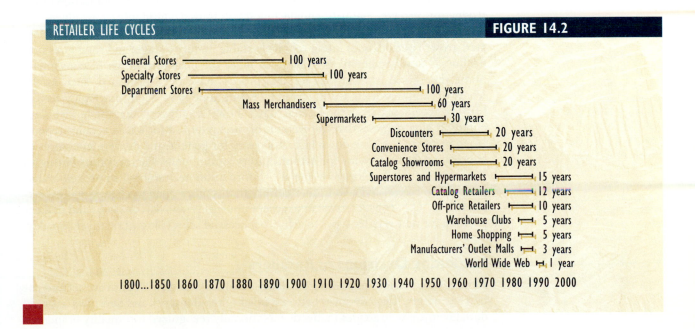

RETAILER LIFE CYCLES — FIGURE 14.2

General Stores ———————————— 100 years
Specialty Stores ———————————— 100 years
Department Stores ⊢————————————— 100 years
Mass Merchandisers ⊢——————— 60 years
Supermarkets ⊢————— 30 years
Discounters ⊢———— 20 years
Convenience Stores ⊢——— 20 years
Catalog Showrooms ⊢——— 20 years
Superstores and Hypermarkets ⊢—— 15 years
Catalog Retailers ⊢—— 12 years
Off-price Retailers ⊢—— 10 years
Warehouse Clubs ⊢— 5 years
Home Shopping ⊢— 5 years
Manufacturers' Outlet Malls ⊢ 3 years
World Wide Web ⊢ 1 year

1800...1850 1860 1870 1880 1890 1900 1910 1920 1930 1940 1950 1960 1970 1980 1990 2000

quickly by mass merchandisers who used the then-modern rail system to reach rural and small-town consumers with mass-produced affordable goods. Department stores and mass merchandisers met the consumers' needs for variety, and grew early in the twentieth century as general population levels and prosperity increased.

After 1945, an increase in the affluence of the average consumer took place to which retailers once again responded. Between 1945 and 1970, supermarkets proliferated across the country and mass merchandisers expanded into suburban shopping malls, in response to greater consumer mobility. Discounters also enjoyed great success, focusing on selling high-volume items at low prices. Discounters succeeded in part because consumers started demanding value in their purchases, and refused to pay high prices for goods they purchased often.

Demands for variety, value, and convenience continued to shape the U.S. retail landscape as it entered the economic instability of the 1970s, 1980s, and 1990s. Variety remains very important to consumers, and has motivated recent growth in specialty stores and narrow-line catalog retailers. At the same time, increasing demands for lower prices and higher value have made warehouse clubs and manufacturers' outlet stores successful, and convenience has contributed to the growth of catalog retailers, home-shopping services, and web-based retailing. Thus, consumer lifestyle changes have shaped the retailer types found in the United States for more than a hundred years, and are likely to be the key determinants of any future changes.

The pattern of retail development evident in the United States can also be found in other countries, provided that adjustments are made for timing and cultural factors. In Europe, for example, hypermarkets had an earlier start and a more prolonged growth stage than in the United States because of differences in the level to which Europeans rely on automobile transportation and their more recent embracing of the fully mobile lifestyle. Japan—which is more congested than the United States and where small retailers have a powerful political lobby—does not have as much development of mass merchandisers and discounters, but upscale department stores and independently owned convenience stores are very popular, and the same emphasis on value, variety, and convenience exists as in the United States.

Figure 14.2 illustrates another important aspect of retailer development; that retailer-type life cycles seem to be shrinking. The idea of a life cycle composed of introduction, growth, maturity, and decline stages is used commonly for products and has also been applied to retailer types.[16] A retailer type emerges, enjoys an accelerated growth period, goes into a relatively stable maturity stage, and then goes into decline as new retailer types emerge to meet the changing needs of consumers. Some theoretical explanations for this process have been proposed, such as the wheel of retailing discussed in chapter 13, but none have been thoroughly tested. Historical evidence from the United States, however, suggests that the model is accurate. It also suggests that the amount of time required for a new retailer type to reach maturity has gone down from 100 years for general and department stores to approximately three years for manufacturers' outlet malls. Factors contributing to this accelerated development include information technology, improved transportation services, and a consumer culture that is more open to change and experimentation. U.S. consumers seem to accept unusual retail sources easily, and make it possible for new retailer types to achieve successful sales volumes relatively quickly.

Marketing Decisions of Retailers

Retailers face serious marketing challenges and look for new ways to attract and retain customers. The crossover between existing retailer types and new ones has rendered many past strategies ineffective. Nationally recognized top-quality brands no longer appear in only one type of store, and many services are offered by many retailers. Companies that wish to differentiate themselves from competitors need to be sophisticated marketers and pay attention to all elements of the marketing mix.

Target Market Decisions

It is no longer enough to differentiate between market segments based on economic or social level classifications, because of the increased social diversity, as discussed in chapter 3, and the fact that many retailers already draw customers from across the standard segments. Astute retailers must also look at consumer lifestyles and other more unique characteristics to define attractive target markets that they can defend against competitors.

One example of successful target marketing is Tianguis, a small southern California supermarket chain.[17] Tianguis supermarkets appeal to the large Latino or Hispanic population of the area, both in their food products (e.g., handmade tortillas and jalapeño peppers) and in their ambiance and services. Live mariachi bands appear on a regular basis, and the prerecorded music is decidedly south-of-the-border. Meat cutters are trained to package cuts favored in Mexico and Latin America, and shelves are stocked with familiar home-country brands. Tianguis stores even have Western Union booths available so immigrant workers can send money to their families in other countries. In the late 1980s, Tianguis spent millions of dollars in research and store refurbishing, and realized weekly sales increases of more than $1.7 million. Remaining independent, it expanded its regional customer base substantially via its targeting strategy. Its success attracted grocery giant Vons, which acquired the chain in 1992 after finding it impossible to copy Tianguis' success.

Product and Service Assortment

In terms of products, retailers must decide on the breadth and depth of their product array, because these offerings determine to a large degree how consumers will view them. If Tianguis were to offer a large array of foods, but only from one or two provincial states in Mexico, it would have a deep and narrow product offering that might not be acceptable to all its customers. Tianguis needs to ensure that its product mix is wide enough to meet the southern California Latino population's diversity, and deep enough to be credible as a purveyor of foods to the Latino market.

Differentiation based on ambiance works beyond grocery stores like Tianguis. Such atmosphere also works for retailers outside the grocery business. American Eagle Outfitters, for example, uses a "jungle safari" decor to promote a sense of adventure that complements its products—a motif also used by Land Rover dealerships, as seen in chapter 13. Fashion retailer GAP uses music and lights to simulate an entertainment club environment. The key to successful retailer differentiation, be it through merchandise, atmosphere, or other tangible means, is to do it in a way that attracts customer attention and elicits positive attitudes toward the store.

Retailers must also decide on what services to offer customers. The general trend for the last 30 years toward reduced service for the sake of lower prices has resulted in retailer types, such as warehouse clubs and self-serve home-improvement centers, where service is almost nonexistent. More recently, however, consumers have developed a counterreaction to low service, and some retailers are finding it advantageous to use service as a differentiation strategy. Nordstrom department stores and Eagle Hardware and Garden Centers are examples.

In choosing their service offerings, retailers need to trade off between effectiveness and cost. Some services, such as free alterations and liberal return policies, can be very costly and subject to customer abuse. But other popular services can be implemented at relatively low marginal costs; some supermarkets, superstores, and drugstores, for example, have adopted around-the-clock operations.

Promotion Decisions

Promotional activities vary among retailer types. Some retailers choose to emphasize the personal sales aspects of promotion, and make sure they have well-trained staff in sufficient numbers to meet customer demands. Fashion apparel retailers rely on personal service. Although companies that sell complex and high-priced products such as automobiles, computers, and home entertainment systems must also develop a sophisticated salesforce, other retailers place more emphasis on mass media advertising and sales promotions.

Department stores, discounters, catalog showrooms, and mass merchandisers commonly use print media to make customers aware of special sales and their seasonal products' selection.

In terms of sales promotions, methods vary by type of retailer as well. Many supermarkets double the value of manufacturer's discount coupons up to some maximum value or publish their own discount coupons, a practice also common among discounters. In addition, discounters frequently use seasonal sales promotions (e.g., Dollar Days), during which they advertise reduced prices on many items throughout the store.

Pricing Decisions

Prices constitute an important positioning and differentiation factor when used to signal value and exclusivity. Some retailers set prices deliberately high to limit their clientele, and offset the high prices by offering many services and generous return policies. Fine department stores such as Bloomingdale's in the United States and Marui in Japan and exclusive specialty shops in high-income areas, such as Rodeo Drive in Beverly Hills, set their prices this way. Other retailers, especially mass merchandisers and discounters, offer low prices on all their merchandise, and look to efficient operations and high volume to produce sufficient profits.

A third strategy is to use low prices on select items to attract customers into the store, hoping that, once in the store, the customers will be motivated to purchase other products at regular prices. These low-priced products are sometimes called loss leaders, and vary depending on the type of store. Convenience stores, for example, often sell milk at cost to attract customer traffic. Mass merchandisers seasonally advertise low-priced, low-quality merchandise, fully expecting customers to trade up once they see that the low-priced goods are not likely to be durable. Strategies like this can backfire, however, if customers come to associate low-quality products with the store's image. It can also backfire for producers, if their products are used as loss leaders and customers come to think of the brand as low quality. Stores might use loss leader pricing tactics only once or twice a year, and many producers try to prevent the use of their products as loss leaders altogether.

Distribution or Place Decisions

Retailers' location decisions can have significant implications for their success, for customers, and for the welfare of the community at large. In choosing a site, retailers need to consider how the location fits their product and image strategy, and they need to project the implications of their decisions over a long period of time because most real estate arrangements involve the multiyear leases. Product, promotional, and pricing decisions can be adjusted more quickly. Retailers also need to tailor distribution intensity to the image they wish to project. Some factors that retailers need to take into account are:

- the number of potential customers in the vicinity
- the number of customers actually passing by the store
- the type of clientele that frequents the area relative to the target market
- future plans for commercial development in the area
- future plans for roads that will alter traffic patterns

Wal-Mart initially avoided major metropolitan areas and centrally located shopping centers. In its early years, Wal-Mart deliberately placed stores in small towns that were overlooked by other discounters, and usually built stores on the outskirts of the town in relatively inexpensive land. This allowed Wal-Mart to offer low prices and attract customers despite their less convenient locations. Even now, Wal-Mart seldom locates stores in already established commercial strips, looking instead for slightly less accessible but attractively priced land. In contrast, Kohl's department stores looks for locations in already established commercial areas close to shopping malls anchored by large department stores. Its strategy is to draw customers on their way to or from the mall, and gain their patronage by offering nationally recognized brands at lower prices.

For some retailers, location is critical, and they will pay whatever rent is necessary to be centrally accessible to consumers. Fashion apparel retailers depend on impulse buying for their sales. For fashion apparel and other highly discretionary products, price is not as much of a factor in the purchase decision as availability at the moment of decision, and retailers who are not in the right place at the right time will miss customers. These retailers often charge relatively high prices for their products and use services and atmosphere to encourage consumers to purchase impulse products. Location is also critical for staple products that are widely distributed and for which customers are unlikely to do extensive shopping. Thus gasoline retailers and convenience stores often appear at major intersections.

In the 1980s, the trend has been the creation of megamalls that include extensive recreational and entertainment facilities in addition to retail stores. The Edmonton Mall in Edmonton, Canada, and the Mall of America in Bloomington, Minnesota, are large regional centers that draw customers from more than a 100-mile radius; they offer entertainment such as Broadway reviews and complete amusement parks inside the facility. In the 1990s, the emerging trend has been toward highly accessible smaller malls designed to allow consumers a choice between in-mall shopping and targeted access to stores direct from the parking lot.

PHYSICAL DISTRIBUTION

Physical distribution can be separated into two broad sectors: transportation and warehousing. Transportation involves the movement of goods between producers, intermediaries, and final consumers, and it provides place and time utility. Storage or warehousing involves holding goods until demand catches up with supply, which suggests it also produces time utility. In the United States, Europe, and the Pacific Rim, both transportation and storage had developed into large economic sectors with thousands of employees and a vital role in the commercial enterprise. Marketing managers should understand these industries, both as important components of distribution systems and as marketers in their own right. Historically, physical distribution providers have made some of the most significant contributions to the marketing function, and they continue to be influential and important today.

Modes of Transportation

Five recognized transportation modes dominate this sector: water, railroad, truck, pipeline, and air. Each mode has advantages and disadvantages and faces interesting challenges and opportunities in the near future. Each transportation mode's relative performance on six important dimensions appears in Table 14.8.

Water Transportation

Water transportation is the oldest mode in consistent use and also the slowest. It is still the most economic means to transport bulky products such as grain and metal ore, and is likely to remain the primary means for intercontinental transportation of commodity products. Water transportation is also the primary means of shipping oil and coal to industrialized countries such as Japan, Taiwan, and the United States. It is also an important intracontinental transportation mode in all major continents that have navigable inland waterways. Rivers such as the Amazon and Rio Plata in South America, the Nile in Africa, the Ganges in Asia, the Danube and Rhine in Europe, and the Mississippi and St. Lawrence in North America are important conduits of raw materials and manufactured products from all over the world to the countries that border them.

In spite of its importance, water transportation faces serious challenges in the years ahead. One of the most important is the need for more speed. In fast-moving economies and markets, getting products to market quickly can be the difference between success and failure. This applies to products ranging from commodity farm products (e.g., corn, wheat, soy beans) to custom-built machinery. Practically all other modes of transportation are faster than water, and have been continually undermining water transportation's hold on even its most traditional markets. Although technological development, such as ocean-going jet freighters, can help offset some of the speed disadvantage of water transportation, this mode also suffers in that the loading and unloading of products and product handling through docking facilities can also slow the process considerably.[18]

Another threat to water transportation comes from the demanding environmental controls and regulations that water carriers must meet in many countries. Water pollution and environmental imbalances have become a major concern around the world, and many countries severely restrict the types of vessels used in their territorial waters. In the United States and Europe, for example, double-hulled tankers are required for petroleum transportation, and all water vessels are restricted in their disposal of lubricants and engine waste. Restrictions are also imposed on the

TABLE 14.8 RELATIVE PERFORMANCE OF TRANSPORTATION MODES

Mode	Cost per Mile	Delivery Speed	Shipment Frequency	Stability in Schedules	Flexibility in Goods Handled	Number of Locations
Water	5	1	1	2	5	3
Rail	3	4	3	4	5	4
Truck	2	4	5	4	3	5
Pipeline	3	2	5	5	1	1
Air	1	5	3	3	2	2

Scale: 1 = *very poor performance*
2 = *poor performance*
3 = *medium performance*
4 = *good performance*
5 = *very good performance*

dumping of ballast tanks that may transport species, such as the zebra mollusk, into new ecological environments.

Environmental and safety restrictions increase the cost of water transportation at a time when it is already experiencing losses to other modes. If companies involved in water transportation are to remain competitive, they need to improve their efficiency and responsiveness to market forces while integrating technologies that meet social and national demands. The pursuit of efficiency and lower operating costs, however, suggests fewer jobs and possibly lower wages for the industry as a whole, and puts the high-cost commercial marine fleets in the United States and some European countries at the risk of becoming obsolete quickly.

Railroads

Railroads provide a cheap means of intracontinental transportation, and the added advantage of access to locations wherever tracks can be laid. Throughout the world, railroads move more freight than any other mode, in large part due to its high share of total freight movement in Canada, China, Russia, and the United States. In all of Eastern Europe, for example, the railroad system is a key factor in trade expansion, and countries are working to make their railroads compatible with other commonly used transportation modes. Like ships, railroads are used to transport bulky nonperishable and semiperishable products such as grains, metal ore and minerals, and manufactured products. In general, railroads are a growing and profitable industry around the world.

One successful innovation allowed by deregulation has been single commodity trains at negotiated rates. These trains carry a single commodity from a producer's facility to a limited number of delivery sites. Railcar handling is greatly reduced, allowing these trains to move quickly and at a cost to producers lower than any other mode. Technological advances allow computerized track and trains control, which has also increased railroad operational efficiency and speed of delivery. Current systems allow individual railcar tracking at all stages between point of shipment and destination, anywhere in the continental United States and Canada. This makes it easier to move cars in and out of in-transit trains, which in turn shortens delivery time. More recently, advances in information technology have allowed several rail companies, such as CSX railroad, to give customers access to their rail-tracking systems, allowing shippers to also track their shipments on-line. Computerized track control has also reduced maintenance costs for railroads by eliminating the need for two track systems along many routes, which in turn has lowered shipping rates.

The railroad industry around the world also faces demands for speedier cargo movement. Many railroad beds in the United States and other countries can support trains moving between 85 and 90 miles per hour, but not the 200-mile-per-hour and greater speeds required to compete in the delivery of some products. Another challenge facing the industry is the need for intermodal transfers of freight to reduce handling time. In some manufacturing industries, intermodal shipment is already the standard, as containers are moved from ocean-going vessels to railcars, and later to truck trailers without the cargo ever being handled directly. Similar efficiencies are being demanded by a growing number of industries and matched by other transportation modes. Although railroad companies have set the pace for intermodal development, they need to continue innovating if they are to sustain their competitive advantage.

Truck Transportation

Trucks have always been more flexible than other modes of transport, because they can deliver wherever there are roads and require relatively inexpensive loading facilities. Prior to the development of limited-access highways, the primary drawback of trucks was their slowness and unreliable delivery performance because of the unevenly maintained road system over which they moved. This is still the case in countries such as Russia and China, where road development has been practically nonexistent since the 1950s.[19]

In the United States, long-distance truck transportation grew most with the advent of the interstate highway system. Before interstates, trucks were used primarily for short-haul movement, but now they work for long-distance transportation at costs sometimes below that of rail transportation, and with the increased flexibility of door-to-door delivery. In Western Europe and Japan, trucks represent the primary means of freight transportation, because their railroad systems are mostly geared to lightweight passenger transportation. Truck transportation's popularity has been recently enhanced by the adoption of just-in-time materials management systems in the United States, Canada, and Europe, because such systems require the frequent and timely delivery most amenable to trucks.

In the 1980s, the U.S. government deregulated the truck transportation, and aggressive price competition ensued. Pricing became so aggressive and profit margins so narrow in the industry that some trucking companies resorted to unnecessary risks in their driving and to neglecting safety maintenance on their equipment. Although other transportation modes also have safety and environmental responsibilities, the trucking industry puts a larger number of people at risk on a regular basis and in a greater variety of ways, and consequently needs to exercise even more stringent self-control or run the risk of regulations and external controls that will limit its competitive options.

Truck traffic may also accelerate road decay in some countries and lead to inordinate amounts of air pollution and environmental damage. Restrictions have been proposed for truck emissions, trailer weight and length, and hours of on-the-road operation in many communities in response to these problems, with varying degrees of success. Regulations and restrictions in any one of these areas will adversely affect truck transportation efficiency and competitiveness.

Pipelines

Pipelines have transported water for many centuries; some built by the Roman Empire are still standing today. Today, pipelines primarily transport petroleum from oil fields to refineries, and commodities such as gasoline, diesel, and other forms of refined petroleum products to major distribution terminals. They also transport natural gas from gas fields right into the consumer's home or place of business, and coal slurry to some electricity-generating plants.

Pipelines provide a steady supply of product to the destination site and they are relatively dependable in all weather conditions. But pipelines are expensive to build and do not lend themselves well to irregularly demanded products. Pipeline usage is unlikely to grow dramatically in the near future, especially because the environmental impact concerns and maintenance costs will likely curtail their development.

Air Transportation

Air transportation has been the fastest growing transportation mode in the last two decades. Although it still handles less than 1 percent of all freight as measured in ton-miles, it has become a significant provider in some areas. Air transportation has made the most dramatic gains in the movement of high-value, low-weight products such as the integrated circuits used in computers and other electronic products.

Many of these integrated circuit boards are assembled in the Pacific Rim countries of Singapore, Taiwan, and Korea. Normally, goods from these countries move to the United States, Canada, Europe and other markets by water transportation, taking between five and seven weeks to arrive at their destination. Given their light weight and high value, however, air freight is more economical, both because of just-in-time delivery possibilities and because this quicker freight allows quicker financial settlements. In the computer and electronics industries, therefore, most products are transported by air.

Air transportation also works for larger and bulkier products, provided they have high value added. General Motors uses air freight from Europe to transport antilock brake components installed in some of its more expensive models. It also used specially modified airplanes to transport complete body assemblies for the Cadillac Allante while the car was in production. The Allante was assembled in Detroit, but the bodies were hand-crafted by Pininfarina in Italy and flown to Detroit, and the Allante's status as a luxury item allowed GM to bear the cost of doing so. Some high-fashion apparel producers also use air freight both to protect their merchandise and to expedite the products' introductions once they are manufactured.

One last use of air transportation that has grown dramatically is expedited delivery offered by companies such as Airborne, Federal Express, and UPS. These companies have found the expedited delivery of small packages and letters very profitable, and have made substantial investments in air fleets to better control package movement. The pioneer in the air transportation of small packages was Federal Express, who started the service in the mid 1970s and dominated the industry in the early years. Other companies have since copied and improved on Federal Express's services, making the industry highly competitive.[20]

The biggest threat to air transportation is the health of airlines in general. Except for very large shipments in specialized cargo planes and express carriers' dedicated fleets, most air freight moves by commercial airlines that also carry passengers and have been plagued by performance and financial problems since the early 1980s. Many airlines have seen their service levels decline as they cut back personnel and try to become more efficient, and this has affected the predictability of air freight transportation. Unpredictable performance will hurt the air transportation industry as other transportation modes strive to improve their reliability and service levels.

Warehousing

In an age of mass production and geographically dispersed markets, manufacturers need storage services as much as ever. Historically, warehouses would receive large shipments of goods and hold them until the title holder requested the goods be shipped to another destination. This was an important service, given that shipments were infrequent and sometimes seasonal, and merchants were forced to buy far greater quantities than they needed or could store. Merchants needed safe and accessible storage, and warehouses met that need. Products were sometimes stored for several months before they were transported to the final customer. Warehousing companies seldom took title to the goods, but they were responsible for their safety while in the warehouse facility.

These services are still required in many industries, and primarily those in which procedures are numerous and fragmented. Grain elevators, for example, store farm commodities such as corn and soybeans from hundreds of farm operations, waiting either for demand to materialize or for prices to rise above limits set by the product's owners. Other examples of fragmented industries are book publishing, video games, and computer software. In such industries, large warehousing and distribution companies such as Ingram Industries and The Andersons give producers a unified point of contact with customers. In seasonal industries, such as air conditioners and ski equipment, warehouses also store products that are manufactured at relatively steady rates during the year, but sold for only a limited time. *Public warehouses* are independently operated and hold products for many different producers and intermediaries under one roof. *Private warehouses* are controlled by a single company for its own use.

Modern warehousing reaches well beyond the simple product storage, and in some industries has become an integral part of manufacturing operations. One of the primary extensions to warehousing in recent years has been breaking down large loads for reshipment in smaller quantities in response to just-in-time demands. Although many manufacturers find just-in-time practices beneficial, their suppliers often resist just-in-time, because it pushes manufacturing inefficiencies out of the customer's facilities and into the supplier's shop floor. This has certainly been true in the automotive industry, where major manufacturers have asked suppliers to alter production schedules and adopt considerably less efficient production runs to meet just-in-time inventory levels.

Some suppliers have responded by shipping to warehouses in efficient quantities and letting warehouse operators break down their shipments into lot sizes that meet assembly plant demands. One of the first examples of this type of arrangement was the Flow-Thru-Terminal, owned by UNIT Corporation and supplying the Buick City assembly plant in Flint, Michigan, during the 1980s. The Flow-Thru-Terminal and similar operations receive shipments from hundreds of suppliers on a daily basis and break them down into just-in-time-sized lots demanded by the plants they service. In the case of Buick City, the lot sizes were the amount of inventory required for four hours worth of production.

Warehouses such as the UNIT terminal are sometimes called *distribution centers;* they differ from traditional warehouses in the sophistication of their freight handling and the level of bulk breaking they perform. Modern distribution centers use computerized inventory tracking and computer-controlled storage and retrieval equipment. In addition, instead of holding product for weeks or months, most hold products for only several days or even just a few hours. Their role has shifted away from holding the product until demand materializes to redistribute product into quantities that are more manageable at the point of sale or use.

The number of traditional public warehouses has gone down in recent years. Declining need for warehousing services has been caused by wholesaler- and retailer-owned storage facilities, by transportation companies that have adapted their terminals for short-term storage, and by joint ventures between producers and storage providers like the Flow-Thru-Terminal. Warehouse industry emphasis will likely continue to shift from storage to freight handling and bulk-breaking services for different industries. Just-in-time practices and pressures for more efficient operations will keep demands for new services growing.

Marketing Decisions of Physical Distribution Providers

Transportation and warehousing companies are service providers, and in this sense no different from other companies that market their services to producers. They are an integral part of distribution systems, and as such they can be important to producers' overall marketing strategies. They face decisions in the areas of target market, products and services, pricing, promotion, and distribution or location.

Target Market Selection

Decisions on which customers to target have become increasingly important in the physical distribution industry since it was deregulated in the early 1980s. Starting in 1980, restrictions on locations and routes started to be removed, and competition for major markets became more intense. Transportation companies must now analyze market potential against their strengths and weaknesses, and be as selective in their marketing strategies as any other marketer.

Some transportation companies have targeted specific industries and have adapted their systems and procedures to best serve those specific customers' needs. CSX railroad is a major user of intermodal technology, provides services to industries that want to reduce load handling (e.g., Asian electronic product manufacturers). Other transportation providers have limited their marketing to certain geographic areas where they might already have a competitive advantage, or to areas that have been ignored by other competitors. This last strategy works only when distribution or transportation companies have a sustainable advantage over competitors. Industry overcapacity and the ease of entry make it highly unlikely that competitors will ignore any lucrative markets for very long. This suggests that physical distribution companies also need to pay close attention to their competitive environments and try to avoid direct confrontation with other companies unless they have sufficient resources to outlast the competition.

Product and Service Decisions

Transportation and warehousing providers have become more diverse in the products and services they offer and in the types of relationships they maintain with customers. As illustrated by the UNIT Flow-Thru-Terminal, many physical distribution providers are much more involved in the operational decisions of their customers, and have adjusted their own operations to better integrate with customer demands. In addition to just-in-time materials management capabilities, some customers demand greater availability of freight status information and more scheduling flexibility. Some customers have gone as far as integrating the warehouse or carrier information systems into their own information systems in order to have up-to-the-minute data on all inbound and outbound freight as well as the goods stored in all warehouse locations. Demands for system responsiveness also require that all carriers use bar code technology and electronic tracking of freight services. The ultimate objective is to make all elements of the physical distribution system dynamic and flexible enough to accommodate market fluctuations.

The push for flexibility is largely motivated by demands for just-in-time materials management, as discussed in chapter 6. Differences exist between global markets, however, in how companies balance flexibility and responsiveness with efficiency. In Japan, for example, just-in-time systems are disarmingly simple, relying on the physical exchange of paper cards to control material flow. The system works because suppliers are in close proximity to manufacturing or retailing sites. In the United States, Canada, China, and other large countries, distances can be much greater and weather or other potential disruptions to timely delivery can be much more pronounced. Electronic data interchange and global positioning systems can bridge the gap by giving producers and other customers more accurate knowledge of the location and status of material in transit, even if it is hundreds of miles away. Physical distribution facilities located close to primary customers will probably need less electronic sophistication than more distant ones.

The biggest challenge facing transportation and warehouse operators is differentiating their products and services enough to develop and maintain customer loyalty. For many years, industry regulation stymied development of innovative applications and restricted provider diversity. Currently, many state regulations still set limits on the size of transportation vessels, the routes that can be used, and even on the localities that transportation companies can service. Not all airlines can fly to the same airports, nor can all ocean-going vessels enter the same ports. The transportation and warehousing industries are playing catch-up, both in terms of marketing expertise and in establishing product-development functions that can come up with innovative solutions to customer problems. Only companies willing to make these investments will be able to sustain competitive differentiation and succeed on a basis other than low price.

Pricing Decisions

Price decisions follow directly from carriers' and warehouse operators' abilities to differentiate themselves from competitors. Those companies that can tailor services to customer needs will be able to charge premium prices. Companies offering the standard fare of products and services will have to compete based on price and will either price at very narrow margins or not get any business.

Pricing decisions in the physical distribution sector, particularly for transportation companies in the United States, are a relatively new challenge. Since deregulation, these companies have had to learn not only the financial aspects of competitive pricing, but also the psychological aspects of image pricing and customer sensitivity to price thresholds, as discussed in chapter 12. Some companies have done well and operate profitably. Other companies have made serious pricing mistakes and have gone out of business. The continuing adjustment of pricing practices and mind-sets in response to changing market conditions will likely remain a significant challenge to the sector for the foreseeable future.

Promotion Decisions

Promotion decisions are nothing new to physical distribution providers, but it is an area in which they are also making changes. The historical mainstay of promotion programs in the physical distribution area has been sales, and it remains the primary promotional approach used by most companies. Physical distribution arrangements are frequently complex and risky, and are best developed and maintained through face-to-face contact with customers. The topics of conversation in sales presentations and the level of knowledge expected from competent salespeople are changing though. In the regulated era, all salespeople had basically the same products and prices to offer, and sales presentations were more focused on establishing personal friendships that would reduce the chances of customers going to competitors. Promotional gifts and sponsored parties were used by carriers and warehouse operators to win customer loyalty, and salespeople were often selected based on looks and charm.

The current environment has shifted the focus from personal appeal to technical competence and a deep understanding of the customer's business. Today's sales presentations focus on solutions to unique transportation and storage problems and on ways of making customers more competitive and efficient. The requirements for a successful salesperson have changed as well. Many companies hire logistics experts and people with technical backgrounds in their target customer's industry. They have also established training programs and empowered their salespeople to work more closely with customer representatives in developing new products and services. Some carriers and warehouse operators, such as Federal Express, UPS, and UNIT, have gone so far as to develop account management teams with responsibility for a limited number of accounts in the same industry sector.

Promotional activities are likely to grow in importance as these companies look for ways of communicating more effectively their advances, and of protecting established relationships from competitors. Some large companies already use mass media, and this will likely increase its penetration. The primary promotional tool and the one needing most attention, however, will continue to be personal sales. With the current trends in products and pricing, it is unlikely that personal relationships will become less important anytime soon.

Distribution or Location Decisions

Achieving *kanban*-style operations often involves a trade-off between sophisticated computer system integration and facility location close to customer operations. As customers demand more responsiveness, some warehousing and transportation companies find it advantageous to establish small dedicated facilities close to their major customers, and to make these facilities physical extensions of the customer's operations. Some have gone as far as giving the customer permanent access to their facility, and the customers have reciprocated by making transportation company representatives permanent members of committees and work groups.

On the other hand, telecommunications advances and flexible transportation have made physical proximity less of an issue for many companies and have allowed them to locate in low-cost areas. Some trucking companies, for example, now control their fleet movement from large facilities in rural areas close to major interstate highways, and some railroads, such as CSX and Illinois Central, have moved their operation centers away from major commercial hubs because they no longer need a physical presence to control railcar movement. The primary concern in location decisions is whether physical proximity is important to the customer relationship. Where it is important, carriers and warehouse operators respond with custom facilities and highly integrated operations. Where it is not important, companies use their newly gained flexibility in communications to reduce operating costs.

SUMMARY

The three major areas of the distribution system—wholesaling, retailing, and physical distribution—are all critically important to producers. They are also recognized as industries of great economic importance in their own right, and as facing significant marketing challenges of their own. Companies in each of these areas face marketing challenges in the areas of:

- target market selection
- products and services
- pricing
- promotional activities
- distribution

For some of these companies, the problems are very complex, and the implications of their decisions can have a significant impact on producers as well.

It is important for marketing managers to realize that members of the distribution system can be marketers also, and to understand how they operate and the nature of their marketing concerns. This will enable marketing managers to communicate better with channel members and to understand their decisions. It will also help the marketing manager to better control the motivation and behaviors of other channel members, and to manage a more effective distribution system.

1. Compare and contrast the complexity and difficulty of marketing management facing Bearing Distributors and Supervalu in the following areas:

   a. definitions of the marketing problems

   b. marketing strategy definition

   c. integration of functional areas into cohesive marketing tactics

2. Assume that General Electric's Tungsram subsidiary decides to bring some functions currently provided by Bearing Distributors. Which functions would a producer such as Tungsram find easiest to bring in-house and which would be better left with the wholesaler?

3. Based on the examples of other wholesalers described throughout the chapter, what defensive tactics can Bearing Distributors make to protect its investment if Tungsram threatens to bring wholesaler functions in-house?

4. Strategic Distribution is an industrial distributor that operates in-plant stores for many of its customers. What are the differences between Strategic Distribution and a retailer? and a traditional industrial distributor?

5. What are some of the hindrances that wholesalers seeking international expansion are likely to encounter and how are such hindrances best overcome? Is it possible and strategically viable for international subsidiaries to serve functions different from the parent company?

6. List in bullet format the marketing decisions that K. J. Electric seems to have made in the following areas:

   a. target market

   b. product and service assortment

   c. promotion

   d. distribution

   e. pricing

   Does K. J. Electric seem to have a well-integrated marketing strategy? Explain.

7. If you compare the economic and employment impacts of wholesalers and retailers in the United States from Tables 14.1 and 14.5, it seems clear that retailers have a larger economic impact. One hundred years ago the economic impact levels were reversed. Does this mean that wholesaling will cease to exist? Explain.

8. Based on the functions served by retailers, compare and contrast Wal-Mart and Sears. Which functions seem to be most important to their individual strategies? What environmental changes could cause a reversal in their position on Table 14.4?

9. The distinctions between retailers and the projections by sector in the chapter focus on convenience, value, variety, and service as factors important to consumers? Are there other factors of equal importance to consumers? How can these additional factors affect the development of existing retailer types or the emergence of new ones?

10. Figure 14.2 illustrates the time from inception to maturity for different retailer types. What happens to retailer types once they reach maturity? Is it possible to still find examples of all retailer types listed in Figure 14.2? Why?

11. List in bullet format the marketing decisions that Carson Pirie Scott & Company seem to have made in the following areas:

a. target market

b. product and service assortment

c. promotion

d. distribution

e. pricing

Does Carson seem to have a well-integrated marketing strategy? Explain.

12. Assume you are the marketing manager for Lowe's (the second largest home improvement retailer in the United States after Home Depot). You are responsible for developing a strategy for new stores Lowe's is introducing in markets dominated by Eagle Hardware and Garden Centers. What functions would you use to differentiate yourself?

13. Still assuming you are the marketing manager for Lowe's, develop a defensive strategy for stores in markets that you dominate but into which Eagle Hardware and Garden is planning to enter.

14. In China, practically all major modes of transportation are either antiquated or nonexistent. If you were the marketing manager for Coca-Cola, trying to establish a presence throughout all of China quickly, what transportation mode would you choose? Would you expect your initial choice to be the only transportation mode you use as the Chinese market for beverages grows and matures over the next 20 years? Explain.

NOTES FOR FURTHER READING

1. Sharon L. Oswald and William R. Boulton, "Obtaining Industry Control: The Case of the Pharmaceutical Distribution Industry," *California Management Review* 38 (Fall 1995): 138–162. Joan Harrison, "Going Upstream in Drug Marketing," *Mergers & Acquisitions*. vol. 29, Sept./Oct. 1994, p. 43.

2. For more information, see "Fortune 1000 by Industries," *Fortune*, April 29, 1996, pp. F63–F64.

3. For more information, see John W. Verity, "Invoice? What's an Invoice?" *Business Week*, June 10, 1996, pp. 110–112; and R. Lee Sullivan, "Powerhouse," *Forbes*, March 13, 1995, p. 134.

4. For more information, see Wendy Zellner, "A Warehouse Full of Woes at Fleming," *Business Week*, September 23, 1996, pp. 98–102.

5. For more information, see Kathryn C. Boggs, "A New Balance to Warehousing and Distribution," *IIE Solutions*, August 1995, pp. 24–28.

6. For more information, see "The Long View," *Industrial Distribution Supplement*, September 1995, p. S28.

7. For more information, see Zellner, "A Warehouse Full of Woes at Fleming."

8. Summarized from Robert F. Lusch, Deborah S. Coykendall, and James M. Kenderdine, *Wholesaling in Transition: An Executive Chart Book* (Norman: University of Oklahoma, Distribution Research Program, College of Business, 1989).

9. For more information, see Susan Chandler, "An Endangered Species Makes a Comeback," *Business Week*, November 27, 1995, p. 96; and Suzanne Woolley, "In the Bargain Basement of Retail Stocks," *Business Week*, November 27, 1995, p. 89.

10. Scott LaFee, "Your Next Job: Checkout Clerk," *Business Week*, October 9, 1995, p. 8.

11. For more detailed information on McDonald's strategy in this area, see Greg Burns, "French Fries with that Quart of Oil?" *Business Week*, November 27, 1995, pp. 86–87.

12. For more information, see Keith Alexander and Andrea Rothman, "Will Travel Agents Get Bumped by These Gizmos?" *Business Week*, June 28, 1993, p. 72.

13. Edith Hill Updike and Mary Kuntz, "Japan Is Dialing 1-800 BuyAmerica," *Business Week*, June 12, 1995, pp. 61–64.

14. For more information, see "High Performers Led by Rebounder," *Chain Store Age Executive*, November 1991, p. 33.

15. Donna L. Hoffman and Thomas P. Novak, "Marketing in Hypermedia Computer-Mediated Environments: Conceptual Foundations," *Journal of Marketing* 60 (July 1996), pp. 50–68.

16. William R. Davidson, Albert D. Bates, and Stephen J. Bass, "Retail Life Cycle," *Harvard Business Review*, November–December 1976, pp. 89–96.

17. For more information, see Jack Feuer, "Tianguis: The Future Beckons," *Adweek's Marketing Week*, February 2,

1987, p. 12; Michael Garry, "A Common Enthusiasm," *Progressive Grocer*, April 1992, pp. 60–61; and Steve Einstein, "This Company Is Not Broken," *Progressive Grocer*, July 1994, pp. 30–32.

18. For more information, see Joseph Weber, Ariane Sains, and Edith Hill, "Warp Speed on the High Seas," *Business Week*, September 18, 1995, pp. 155–160.

19. For more information on distribution in China, see Stephen R. Frewen, "Cracking the System," *China Business Review*, September–October 1995, pp. 12–18.

20. For more detailed information on industry competitiveness, see Chuck Hawkins and Patrick Oster, "After a U-Turn, UPS Really Delivers," *Business Week*, May 31, 1993, pp. 92–93; and David Greising, "Watch Out for Flying Packages," *Business Week*, November 14, 1994, p. 40.

CHAPTER 15

INTERNATIONAL MARKETING STRATEGIES: ISSUES IN DESIGN AND IMPLEMENTATION

CHAPTER OBJECTIVES

When you are done with this chapter, you should have achieved the following:

- An ability to discuss globalization and culture, and identify the opportunities and challenges that international marketers face

- An understanding of the major issues in making international market selection, market entry, and marketing program decisions

- An insight into how organizational structures and processes evolve as their level of international market participation increases.

CHAPTER OUTLINE

THE EMERGENCE OF GLOBAL MARKETS
Economic Integration
Global Competition
Universal Consumers
Strategic Process
The International Marketing Challenge

THE PERVASIVENESS OF CULTURE
Self-Reference Criterion and Ethnocentric Decisions
Cultural Relativism
Culture is Multilevel, Multidimensional, and Dynamic

MARKETING INTERNATIONALLY: MOTIVATIONS AND OPPORTUNITIES
Enhanced Competitiveness and Competence
Learning
Diversified Sales
Market Leadership

MARKET SELECTION
Marketing Objectives and Market Selection
The International Market Selection Process
The Role of International Market Research
Measurement Problems in International Marketing Research
Grouping International Markets: Definition and Segmentation

PATTERNS OF ENTRY
The Internationalization Process
Market Expansion Paths
Modes of Entry

MARKETING PROGRAM ISSUES
Standardization "Versus" Adaptation?
Standardization or Adaptation Revisited: A Framework for Managers

(continued)

Whirlpool Spins Into European Markets

Whirlpool Corporation, the Benton Harbor, Michigan-based appliance manufacturer, faced a mature major-appliance market in the United States in the late 1980s. With key competitors—General Electric, Maytag, and White Consolidated—fighting for market share, and profit margins in its home market shrinking, Whirlpool began to redefine its market. Traditionally, the appliance industry had limited its definition of the market to U.S. buyers, but in 1989, Whirlpool spent $1 billion to buy a 47 percent stake in N.V. Philips' appliance business from the Dutch consumer electronics giant. This acquisition, completed in 1991, was the first step in Whirlpool's strategy to become a worldwide leader in the appliance industry, and catapulted the company into the number one position.

Whirlpool has come a long way from the uncoordinated patchwork it acquired from Philips. At the time, the European appliance industry presented a daunting picture of independent national companies, each manufacturing unique

The familiar washing machine, microwave, and refrigerator take on a different look in other countries.

models for their own national markets. Although the Philips brand was recognized throughout Europe, its use of 11 different national advertising agencies resulted in an equal number of brand images, many of which were in conflict with each other. As its managers assembled the building blocks of a profitable and competitive global appliance business, Whirlpool leveraged its core strengths in the appliance business to exploit the cost advantages of common manufacturing processes and core products. This strategy allowed Whirlpool to sell products with standardized interiors and market-customized exteriors, thereby capitalizing on economies in purchasing and production while ensuring customer satisfaction.

Whirlpool built brand awareness through their initial strategy of dual branding—"Philips by Whirlpool"—complemented by a $135 million pan-European advertising campaign. By 1994, they had done away with the Philips name and plethora of ad agencies. By 1996, Whirlpool had launched 11 redesigned product lines and manufactured 85 percent of their European major appliances on common platforms. Even though competitors question Whirlpool's view of Europe as a uniform market, Whirlpool's CEO, David Whitwam, dismisses skeptics, asserting that national differences are exaggerated.

Whirlpool has also transferred many aspects of its European strategy, including dual branding and concentrated manufacturing, to the Chinese and Indian markets: It has entered into manufacturing joint ventures across the People's Republic of China (PRC) and bought a majority share in two Indian companies. Its ventures in the PRC are strategically located in different geographic areas; Whirlpool thereby learns about the provincial markets of the PRC. Beijing Whirlpool Snowflake Electric Appliance Company manufactures refrigerators just south of Beijing, Shanghai Whirlpool Narcissus Company manufactures washing machines in an export processing zone in Shanghai, and Whirlpool SMC Microwave Company manufactures microwave ovens in Shunde in Guangdong province in the south. Similarly, a purchase from Kelvinator, the second-largest refrigerator manufacturer in India, will manufacture air conditioners and microwave ovens. A second venture in India, with the TVS group, will manufacture dishwashers, clothes dryers and washing machines. Billboards and print advertisements in the big cities promote the global expertise and quality that Whirlpool brings to India. They also reflect its dual branding approach to developing brand awareness among local consumers. It is clear that Whirlpool's marketing strategy in Asia is consistent with Whitwam's philosophy that appliance markets worldwide have more similarities than differences as well as his strategy of global leadership. Today, Whirlpool markets its products in more than 120 countries and has manufacturing locations in the United States, Europe, Latin America and Asia.

Sources: Based on the author's involvement with Whirlpool's Greater China operations in 1995 and the following:

"Call it Worldpool," *Business Week*, November 28, 1994, pp. 98–99.

Regina Fazio Maruca, "The Right Way to Go Global: An interview with Whirlpool CEO David Whitwam," *Harvard Business Review*, March–April, 1994, pp. 135–145.

"Shotgun Wedding," *Business India*, July 18–31, 1994, pp. 70–72.

THE EMERGENCE OF GLOBAL MARKETS

I am a citizen, not of Athens or Greece, but of the world.

–Socrates (469(?)–399 B.C.)

Many individuals and corporations have recently had to transform their local and domestic market views to address global concerns. For some, this global outlook is a frame of mind; for most, it is a reality in which they are immersed. People everywhere are barraged with instantaneous images of events, products, ideas, and lifestyles from other parts of the world creating a global village.[1] Products, services, and entire business formats that originate in one part of the world are not only available but often sought and eagerly consumed elsewhere. Many international marketers are "denationalized":[2] products and corporate identities transcend their countries of origin and become familiar names around the globe. Examples include Japanese companies such as the electronics giant Sony and the supermarket chain Yaohan, German automobile manufacturer Mercedes-Benz,

Italian clothing retailer Benetton, British cosmetics retailer The Body Shop, and the Swedish furniture retailer IKEA. U.S. companies include toy retailing giant Toys "Я" Us, jeans manufacturer Levi Strauss, fast-food restaurant McDonald's, and soft drink marketer Coca-Cola.

Since the 1970s, companies have seen traditional market boundaries become increasingly blurred. Management writers and practitioners use the term "globalization of markets"[3] in a variety of ways.

Economic Integration

First, at a macroeconomic level, markets are becoming more economically integrated, as reflected in the faster growth of world exports compared to world economic output. According to the World Trade Organization, this trend has accelerated in the 1990s as countries liberalize their trade regimes, that is, reduce the tariff and nontariff barriers to trade.

Global Competition

Second, at the industry level, global competitors continue to emerge. As industrial productivity and production scales increase, and as companies in various industries face competitors who design and implement their own strategies globally, competition becomes global. Advertisements and articles in *The Economist*, *Business Week*, and *The Wall Street Journal* in the last three years provide one indicator of this trend. Companies use terms such as "global reach" and "global partnership" and advertising tag lines presenting global capability credentials. Predictably, many firms that advertise such global capabilities are in the airline, telecommunications, banking, and investment industries. But nations also promote themselves in these terms (such as the United Kingdom promoting itself as the call center for Europe) as they compete for the foreign direct investments of multinational corporations (MNCs), as do advertisers in a variety of product categories, such as beer and automobiles.

Universal Consumers

Third, the term "globalization" refers to consumers' increasing universality of tastes, preferences, and behaviors worldwide. The biggest impediment to the emergence of a universal consumer are cultural differences, as the following quote from a general manager at Procter & Gamble's European headquarters illustrates:

> There is no such thing as a Eurocustomer so it makes no sense to talk about Eurobrands. We have an English housewife whose needs are different from a German hausfrau. If we move to a system that allows us to blur our thinking we will have big problems.
>
> Product standardization sets up pressures to try to meet everybody's needs (in which case, you build a Rolls-Royce that nobody can afford) and countervailing pressures to find the lowest-common denominator product (in which case, you make a product that satisfies nobody and which cannot compete in any market). These pressures probably result in the foul middle compromise that is so often the outcome of a committee decision.[4]

Strategic Process

Finally, globalization describes the strategic approach—including marketing strategies—and worldwide organizational control systems that global corporations use as they attempt to compete with competitors in global markets. As competitive pressures force companies to manage their operations on a worldwide basis, top executives push to standardize marketing programs, centralize marketing decisions, and coordinate implementation of marketing decisions worldwide. The real dilemma marketing managers face is this: how to balance the competitive and corporate-level strategic push for standardization and centralization with the pull for adaptation from heterogeneous customer needs, preferences, and behaviors across markets.

Global markets are emerging for many reasons. American historian Daniel Boorstin eloquently suggests that we live in an age driven by "the Republic of Technology [whose] supreme law . . . is convergence, the tendency for everything to become like everything else."[5] On the consumer side, globalization occurs as:

- Electronic media and international travel shape consumer preferences.
- Regional economic entities, such as the European Union (EU), Asian Free Trade Area (AFTA), and North American Free Trade Agreement (NAFTA) area develop and expand.
- Formerly closed, state-controlled economies transition to open, market-driven economies.

On the supply-side, firms compete to

- overcome the limitations of small or maturing domestic markets
- take advantage of economies of scale and scope
- cater to increasingly large global market segments

Table 15.1 describes some of the differences between local and global markets.

The International Marketing Challenge

We may be tempted to conclude that because a brand is available worldwide, the company that markets it has a globally standardized marketing strategy or that consumer tastes are becoming more similar.[6] But such may not entirely be the case—a

TABLE 15.1 GLOBAL AND LOCAL MARKETS: A COMPARISON

	Local or National Markets	Global Markets
Markets	Defined by country borders	Transcend country borders
	Individual markets isolated	Markets are interconnected
Customers	Local and national segments	Cross-national segments
Competition	Primarily among domestic firms	Regional or global competition
	MNCs compete country by country	Few, large competitors world-wide
Company strategies	Local; few benefits from coordination across markets	Regional/global; coordination has significant benefits

Source: Based on Kamran Kashani, Managing Global Marketing: Cases and Text *(PWS-Kent, Boston: 1992), and Theodore Levitt, "The Globalization of Markets,"* Harvard Business Review, *May–June 1983, p. 92-102.*

global *brand* strategy does not even imply a global *product* strategy, and certainly not global distribution. For example, let us look beneath the thin veneer of commonality—the enormous popularity of the Coca-Cola brand in many countries. (see Marketing Anecdote 15.1). Coca-Cola has developed brand recognition for Coke and attempts to build a global image through its standardized advertising, but it has had to vary the sweetness of its product concentrate to cater to different consumer preferences. Coke has also adapted its distribution in various markets, such as by aggressively finding its way into Japanese vending machines and identifying influential partners such as the Swire-Pacific group, one of the three most powerful *hongs*, or conglomerates in Hong Kong, and its bottler, to facilitate its expansion in the PRC. In a similar vein, Coke has been able to expedite various government approvals more recently by bringing on board Robert Kuok, an influential Chinese businessman from Malaysia with excellent *guanxi*, or connections, throughout the region.[7]

Similarly, firms such as IKEA have become successful by identifying and targeting global market segments and using a standardized marketing approach, as highlighted in Table 15.2. However, even IKEA had to change its marketing mix significantly in order to turn a profit in the United States. They had to redesign products, such as larger beds measured in inches rather than European metric measures and larger plates for pizza and larger glasses to accommodate the U.S. passion for ice. IKEA adjusted their sourcing mix to manage unfavorable exchange rates between the dollar and kroner and to avoid frequent stock-outs. Local production now accounts for more than 45 percent of its U.S. furniture sales, compared to 15 percent in 1990. Also, because Americans dislike standing in line at stores, IKEA added more cash registers and modified their store layouts.

Consumer preferences for many product categories vary across and within countries. In addition, countries vary significantly in their marketing infrastructure (e.g., roads and highways, communications facilities, payment services, credit institutions, advertising media, distribution channels). Therefore, the fundamental issue confronting marketers is not *whether* to standardize international marketing strategy, but rather *when*, *how*, and *to what extent* various elements of marketing strategy and mix should be adapted. Further, as markets globalize, companies with multimarket presence such as Whirlpool Corporation in our opening vignette find that organizing operations across markets—through centralizing and coordinating marketing decisions, and coordinating marketing strategies with other elements of the firm's strategy such as sourcing, manufacturing, and R&D—is crucial to ensure consistency in product quality and image across markets.

In the postwar years, as Coca-Cola strove mightily to consolidate its territorial gains, its efforts were received with mixed feelings. When limited production for civilians got under way in the Philippines, armed guards had to be assigned to the trucks carting Coke from bottlers to dealers, to frustrate thirsty outlaws bent on hijacking. In the Fiji islands, on the other hand, Coca-Cola itself was outlawed, at the instigation of soft-drink purveyors whose businesses had been ruined by the Coke imported for the solace of the GIs during the war. Most of the opposition to the beverage's tidal sweep, however, was centered in Europe, being provoked by the beer and wine interests, or by anti-American political interests, or by a powerful blend of enology and ideology. Today, brewers in England, Spain, and Germany are themselves bottling Coke on the if-you-can't-lick-'em-join-'em principle. . . . In Western Europe, Coca-Cola *has had to fight a whole series of battles—varying according to the terrain*—not all of which have yet been won, although victory seems to be in sight. Before Coca-Cola got rolling in West Germany, for instance, it had to go to court to halt the nagging operations of something called the Coordination Office for German Beverages, which was churning out defamatory pamphlets with titles such as "Coca-Cola, Karl Marx, and the Imbecility of the Masses" and the more succinct "Coca-Cola? No!" In Denmark, lobbyists for the brewers chivied the Parliament into taxing cola-containing beverages so heavily that it would have been economically absurd to try to market Coke there. . . . At last word, however, the Danes were about to relent. But in Belgium the caps on bottles of Coke, including bottles sold at the Brussels Fair, have had to carry, in letters bigger than those used for "Coca-Cola," the forbidding legend "Contient de la cafeine."

Source: E. J. Kahn Jr., *The Big Drink* (New York: Random House, 1959), as quoted in the *Harvard Business Review*, May–June 1986, p. 68. Italics added.

THE PERVASIVENESS OF CULTURE

My shoes are Japanese, my trousers English, the hat on my head Russian, but my heart is Indian.

–Translated from a Hindi film song

Some academics have challenged the notion of globalization in the sense of the homogenization of needs and wants,[8] calling it the "myth of globalization."[9] Little systematic empirical evidence supports the emergence of a "world consumer." On the contrary, a substantial amount of anecdotal, case, and research evidence suggests that cultural variables provide strong resistance to such convergence. Cultural differences, far from being a vestige of the past, present corporations with tremendous challenges as they design and implement their international marketing programs (see Marketing Anecdote 15.2). "Global" products and services may be available worldwide but the reasons people in various markets consume them generally differ. Further, these products and services have different meanings for people of different cultures. For example, whereas many Americans are attracted to fast-food restaurants for the convenience of efficient service, Poles and Russians may patronize McDonald's because they feel they are buying into an American or Western lifestyle or because eating there is a status symbol.

TABLE 15.2 IKEA's SUCCESSFUL GLOBAL MARKETING APPROACH

Market definition and target segment	Global niche of young, upwardly mobile, urban couples. Preference for casual, contemporary styles and one-stop shopping.
Product	Large assortment of more than 10,000 products. Functional, easy to assemble, knocked down and packed flat, standardized furniture.
Distribution and retail environment	Complete shopping destination. Large showroom with warehouse centers, located for easy access by automobile. Self- and full-service items. Room displays, kids' playroom, and in-store Scandinavian cafe.
Communication	Annual catalogue covering all products and guaranteeing prices, projecting store image. Position as unique retailing concept, with products sourced globally, and furniture subjected to highest "Swedish" quality control.
International and global presence	More than 70 company-owned stores in the Americas, Europe, and Asia.
Sourcing	Network of 2,300 suppliers in 67 countries. Suppliers get long-term contracts, design and technical advice, and leased equipment. IKEA gets low prices and exclusive dealing.
Price positioning	Value-priced. Scale economies and designed-in cost savings translate into prices 30 percent below competitors.

Source: Based on Ingvar Kamprad and IKEA, Harvard Business School case 9-390-132, 1990; and "Furnishing the World," The Economist, November 19, 1994, pp. 79–80.

The meaning of the word "culture" derives from its Latin roots: it is often used to refer to art, education, literature, and music. Social and cultural anthropologists use the term "culture" in a broader sense as the set of symbols, heroes, meanings, rituals, and values shared by a society—"the collective programming of the mind which distinguishes the members of one group or category of people from another."[10] In this sense, culture is all-encompassing: it includes acceptable norms of dressing, communicating, and eating; organization of social (and business) institutions; relationships among people; relationships between humans and nature; and the meaning of time in a given society.

Culture presents a challenge to marketers for three broad reasons, described next.

Self-Reference Criterion and Ethnocentric Decisions

The first challenge to marketers is that cultural norms are not innate, but learned, and much of the learning takes place in early childhood. Consequently, people use the self-reference criterion (SRC)—an "unconscious reference to one's own cultural values"—in interactions with people of other cultures. Managers may be susceptible to the SRC when making marketing decisions,[11] resulting in ethnocentric decisions. Such decisions assume that the domestic frame of reference is equally appropriate for international markets, and so differences in international markets are not recognized, and the marketing program is not adapted appropriately. Mary Kay Cosmetics, a Texas-based multilevel marketing company, has a range of products and a selling formula that works in the United States, but until the early 1990s it had not been very successful internationally. In part, corporate managers unconsciously assumed that women in other markets would follow a skin-care regimen similar to their U.S. counterparts. Their conclusion that Mary Kay's products were universal resulted in a product line with insufficient depth and adaptation relative to Avon, their major competitor. This proved to be a substantial hurdle as the company considered expanding into the PRC, where,

Campbell Soup's CEO, David Johnson, sees global growth as salvation. Unlike its competitor, CPC International, which derives a majority of its revenues from outside North America, Campbell had historically been insular, and had never developed a global plan. In growing market share abroad, Campbell has managed to overcome many cultural obstacles—its brands are not simply transplanted. Prepared food is neither as easily sold nor as universal as soap or cigarettes. Canned soup may be a tough product to sell overseas because of the differences in local and regional tastes. Campbell competes with mother's homemade soup in Poland, where it has introduced eight varieties of condensed *zupa*, including the staple chicken noodle, and plans to introduce a local peppery tripe soup, *flaki*. In the PRC's Guangdong province, Swanson brand watercress and duck-gizzard soup is popular. Campbell has developed other products for the attractive Chinese market, where per capita soup consumption is the highest in the world: scallop broth, radish and carrot soup, and pork, fig, and date soup. Argentines dislike chicken noodle, and the Mexicans line up for the spicy Creama de Chile Poblano soup. Campbell tests its adaptation to cultural preferences in regional taste kitchens where representative target groups provide insight into recipes and help refine flavors. Catering to local tastes is fine up to a point, but Campbell draws the line on such Asian favorites as dog soup and shark fin soup!

Source: Based on "Campbell: Now It's M-M-Global," *Business Week, March* 15, 1994, pp. 52–54; and "Hmm. Could Use a Little More Snake," *Business Week,* March 15, 1994, p. 53.

compared with the United States, women had very few choices in quality skin-care products and were willing to pay a premium for imported brands. Mary Kay's managers were simultaneously faced with a very different Japanese cosmetics market where, in contrast to their U.S. counterparts, women had a seven-step skin-care regimen and therefore needed a greater variety of products adapted for each step.[12]

Cultural Relativism

The second problem that international marketers face is cultural relativism. No absolute criteria exist for judging cultures other than one's own. Cultures are not inherently better or worse than one another, just different. It is important to appreciate this fact in all aspects of marketing, but it is vital in communications, advertising, and interpersonal interactions such as personal selling and negotiations.

Communication Orientation and Time Orientation

We now consider two aspects of culture[13]—communication orientations and time orientations—in the context of intercultural negotiations. Cultures vary in how explicit message content is. In low-context (LC) cultures, messages are explicit, verbal, and contained in the words. High-context (HC) cultures, on the other hand, depend on implicit, nonverbal cues and a complete understanding of the context for their communications. Figure 15.1 illustrates various countries' contextual orientations.

People also vary in the extent to which they are time bound. Monochronic (M-time) cultures treat time as a tangible commodity that they value, save,

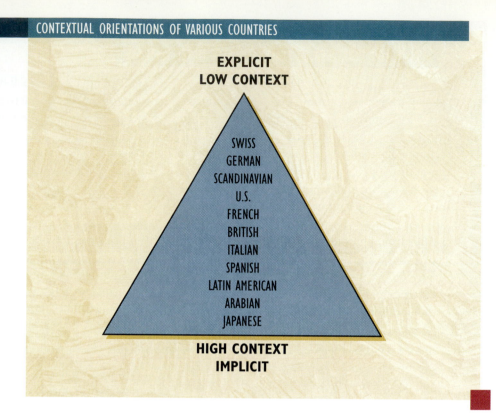

spend, lose, or waste. With their linear concept of time, M-time cultures do one thing at a time, and tend to keep strict schedules and agendas. Polychronic (P-time) cultures are characterized by simultaneity and a greater involvement with people than with schedules. Most LC cultures operate on M-time, whereas HC cultures operate on P-time. The dominant U.S. culture is M-time and LC; thus Americans generally enter meetings and negotiations promptly, focus singularly on the tasks at hand (which the negotiation partner might find pointed and rude), communicate quite directly, and expect to complete discussions within a stipulated period. P-time and HC Middle Easterners or Latin Americans, less concerned about punctuality, comfortably handle multiple tasks (which American negotiators might find disruptive) while in negotiations, speak more indirectly, and exhibit less concern with achieving closure at a particular time. Imagine the possible perceptual errors, attributions, and judgments that each party may make about the other.[14]

Culture is Multilevel, Multidimensional, and Dynamic

The third challenge marketers face is that culture has a variety of focal points: familial, organizational, subnational (e.g., regional, urban and rural, tribal, social class), and national. Because individual consumers belong to multiple groups, marketers may not be able to predict which culture will influence consumers' behavior, making it more difficult to pinpoint the cultural differences that are most meaningful for the marketers' decisions. This problem is exacerbated by the fact that particular individuals may not fit their nation's cultural profile. Despite these difficulties, managers may use five cultural dimensions for broad strategy-planning purposes. These national cultural dimensions reflect approaches for dealing with the basic problems that all human societies face. Table 15.3 provides a summary of these national cultural dimensions and their possible marketing implications.[15]

TABLE 15.3 DIMENSIONS OF NATIONAL CULTURE

Fundamental Human Issue	National Cultural Dimension	Meaning of Dimension	Example of Countries	Possible Implications for Marketing
Relation to authority	Power distance (PD)	The degree of inequality; reflects interdependence and hierarchical relationships	Low PD countries (e.g., Austria, Scandinavia, United States of America have more consultative decision-making styles than high PD countries (e.g., Malaysia, Central and Latin America, Arab countries, Indonesia).	In negotiations, relationships will be more hierarchical in relatively high PD countries. *Example:* Vertical relationships, with sellers depending on buyer goodwill (*amae*) in Japanese negotiations). In the United States (low PD relative to Japan), buyer/seller relationships are horizontal.
Conception of self: relation to group	Individualism-collectivism	The degree to which persons in a country view themselves as separate and individual, or as part of a group	More collectivist countries (e.g., Central America, Southeast Asia, Japan) value the stability of in-group relationships over the personal achievement valued in more individualist countries (e.g., United States of America, Great Britain).	In collectivist countries, reciprocity is important; and collective goals, harmony and consensus of group are valued. *Example:* Japanese supply and distribution *keiretsu* are difficult for outsiders to break into because they might disturb the harmony between members in the existing *keiretsu*).
Conception of self: gender issues	Femininity-masculinity	The extent to which persons value nurturing and caring roles, as opposed to assertiveness, earning, and material possessions	More feminine countries (e.g., Scandinavia, Thailand) value nurturing of relationships more and materialism less than masculine countries (e.g., Japan, Italy).	*Example:* Customer service concepts may be easier to drive home in feminine cultures.
Ways of dealing with uncertainty and conflicts, including control of aggression and expression of feelings	Uncertainty avoidance (UA)	The extent to which people in a country are threatened by ill-defined, ambiguous and risky situations, and exhibit a preference for continuity and stability	People in countries high in UA (e.g., Greece, Portugal, Japan) resist innovation, and prefer security, stability, precision and rules, whereas people in countries low in UA (e.g., Singapore, Sweden, Hong Kong) are comfortable with risks and innovation.	*Example:* Changes in retailing have been much more rapid in Northern Europe (Great Britain, France, Germany) than in Southern Europe (Greece, Portugal, Spain), where countries have higher UA scores.

TABLE 15.3 DIMENSIONS OF NATIONAL CULTURE–CONTINUED

Fundamental Human Issue	National Cultural Dimension	Meaning of Dimension	Example of Countries	Possible Implications for Marketing
Ways of dealing with time	Life orientation—long term (LTO) or short term (STO)	The extent to which people are oriented toward the future (LTO) versus the present and past (STO)	People in LTO countries (e.g., China, Hong Kong, Taiwan, Japan, South Korea) value status ordering, thrift, perseverance, and a sense of shame more; those in STO countries (e.g., Pakistan, Nigeria, Philippines, Canada, United States of America) place higher value on tradition, stability, protecting face, and reciprocation.	*Example:* Credit-card companies may have a bigger challenge increasing card usage in LTO countries, where savings are valued highly.

In addition to the multiple focal points at which culture operates, its many aspects are interrelated. Thus language, religion, the dimensions of national culture, time, and communications orientations cannot easily be separated, so managers face a complex and multifaceted task as they strive to truly understand a particular culture. Finally, cultures are constantly evolving, as people borrow and assimilate the artifacts, language, and ideas of other cultures. At the surface, cultures may seem to be changing and becoming more similar; however, this apparent pace of change may not reflect the true pace of cultural change, which could be a lot slower.[16] Thus, people may adopt the symbols of a foreign culture, but hold closely to more basic aspects—such as religion—of their own culture. In addition, in the face of a perceived cultural onslaught from overseas, people and governments may attempt to protect their own cultures by limiting exposure to foreign cultures through a variety of travel, media content, import, and foreign direct investment restrictions (see Marketing Anecdote 15.3). For marketers, the challenge lies in understanding culture, predicting the pace and direction of cultural change, and, if possible, leading such change.

MARKETING INTERNATIONALLY: MOTIVATIONS AND OPPORTUNITIES

Foreign customers made us better in every way. That's the real benefit to going international.
–John McConnell,[17] CEO, Labconco Corporation

Companies may be motivated by the various opportunities international marketing provides, such as enhanced competitiveness and competence, learning, diversified sales, and market leadership.[18]

Enhanced Competitiveness and Competence

When firms compete internationally, their products, processes, and services may be designed to meet the standards of the "toughest" customers they serve. Resulting quality improvements may provide positive spillover effects for all customers. In

Viva la French

The French have always been passionate about their language. The state has long attempted to protect the French language, beginning with the royal decree of 1539, which required the use of French in all legal and official documents. The language has come to symbolize French national identity, and is even a nostalgic reminder of past cultural and imperial glory. Contemporary French conversations are littered with words and phrases that reflect their Anglo-American roots: *le meeting, le brainstorming, le blue jean, le fast food, le off-shore joint venture,* and *le one-man show.* Several past attempts to protect the "language of the Republic" from the onslaught by foreign invaders include a 1975 law banning the use of foreign words in advertisements, official documents, and television broadcasts if a suitable French word exists, and the publication of a "Dictionary of Official Terms" with 3,500 French neologisms to replace foreign words. On June 30, 1994, a new law was passed in another such attempt: in addition to requiring that foreign words be replaced by those in the dictionary in most advertisements, broadcasts, and documents, the law requires that international conferences organized by French nationals in France allow participants to speak in French and provide written French summaries of all foreign-language speeches and documents.

Singapore: Asian Values, Not Western Liberalism

The Advertising Standards Authority of Singapore (ASAS), an industry watchdog group with representatives from the advertising industry and the Ministry of Information and the Arts (MITA), has actively discouraged agencies from running Western-influenced advertisements that are detrimental to Asian family values. ASAS now examines the core values being promoted by the advertisement, in addition to penalizing advertisers who mislead, misrepresent, or overclaim. Since Prime Minister Goh Chok Tong's National Day Rally speech on August 21, 1994, several advertisements in the *Straits Times* and on radio have been withdrawn or modified. These advertisements include a print ad for Bristol Myers–Squibb's Sustagen created by Leo Burnett–Kuala Lumpur, in which a son speaks rudely to his father, and a radio spot for Qantas that the authorities claimed encouraged spending "in a big way." The Sustagen ad was conceived by creative Asians at the agency and had been running without consumer complaint in both Malaysia and Singapore since 1993. Although the changes have been "voluntarily" made by advertisers, it is worth noting that the government has substantial influence over Singapore Broadcast Corporation. A MITA spokesman said, "we should discourage advertisements which show Singaporean men, women and children behaving as if they were Westerners."

The Many Europes

An apparent paradox has emerged in Europe: as pan-European institutions based in Brussels grab more power, and technology and business erase borders between countries, many Europeans are holding on to their heritage as fiercely as they can. "People like to have an identity. People in Europe sometimes like to have more than one. Catalans in Barcelona will tell you they are Catalans first, Europeans second and Spaniards third. Scots in Glasgow may even forget to add that they are Britons third. The rallying cry of many European regional separatist movements is 'Independence within Europe.' There seems to be room for lots of loyalty. Many of the Belgians who stood up for 'Ode to Joy' the other night count themselves as Walloons or Flemings, proud of their French or Dutch mother tongues, yet prepared to show genuine grief over the death of King Baudouin last year (and undying support for the Red Devils, the Belgian World Cup soccer entrant), all the while being among the fiercest believers in a federal Europe. The British, loyal to Her Majesty the Queen, home milk delivery and the meatless sausage—all of which from time to time seem under threat from the EU (European Union), according to British tabloids—nonetheless enthusiastically enact European legislation designed to take advantage of wider European markets.

And what is the lesson in all this? Europe will change, but don't expect Europeans to get fanatical about it. 'Today, between Madrid and Stockholm you find eight different languages and five different ways to cook steak,' says Javier Alvarez Vara, a Spanish businessman. 'In 10 years, you'll find eight different languages and maybe four ways to cook steak.' "

Euro TV

For several years, European culture ministers have been struggling with the issue of appropriate foreign-content restrictions on television and the multimedia industry, such as on-line services and video-on-demand. Quotas (50 percent) for non-European programming were first introduced in the European Union's 1989 "Television without Frontiers" legislation, but have not been enforced because of a loophole that requires broadcasters to devote a majority of time to Euro programming "where practicable." Proponents hope to raise European content on television to the 80 percent level that U.S. programming currently has, despite the fact that competition seems more effective than quotas at promoting production. France, which has rigid quotas and limits the number of channels, has the weakest program production sector; it has, however, been the strongest advocate of tougher broadcasting rules. Germany, which has no quotas and many channels, has a vibrant production sector. In addition to helping Europe's struggling movie industry, those who advocate stricter quotas argue that they would serve the additional purpose of promoting European culture.

Sources: Viva la French is based on Comedie Francaise, *The Economist*, July 9, 1994, p. 54. Singapore anecdote is based on Singapore Reworks Ad Code, *Advertising Age International*, October 17, 1994, pp. I–8. The Many Europes is excerpted from Philip Revzin, All Deliberate Speed, *Wall Street Journal*, September 30, 1994, p. R24. Euro TV is based on EU Proposal May Limit TV Spots, *Advertising Age*, January 9, 1995; Rights to Buy, *The Economist*, April 22, 1994, p. 64; and European Companies Lobby to Defeat Proposed Controls on Media Industry, *Wall Street Journal*, February 12, 1996.

addition, selling to larger markets provides companies with economies of scale in design, production, sourcing and marketing, as the Whirlpool case at the beginning of this chapter illustrates. Reduced costs may in turn translate into greater value to customers in the form of lower prices.

Japanese buyers are known for the detailed suggestions they provide on product and process improvements.[19] Lestra Design, a French manufacturer of expensive duvets, in attempting to sell to Japan, encountered several rounds of product testing from their buyers: the Japanese importer folded duvets, held them in the light of a window, and slapped them vigorously. The importer made suggestions for improving duvet quality in order to eliminate the cloud of down dust that emerged from the duvets during such testing, and provided Lestra Design managers with the opportunity to observe a state-of-art manufacturing plant that produced duvets of a quality acceptable in Japan.[20]

Learning

Companies learn to be flexible by doing business in multiple countries, economies, and cultures. In addition, the process of marketing internationally—such as participation in trade shows and contact with international distributors and advertising agencies—can provide significant information on customer requirements, advertising campaigns, and competitors' actions.

As Sun Microsystems worked to develop a global brand image, they received feedback from the off-shore affiliates of their advertising agency, J. Walter Thompson (JWT) about their proposed "Network the Dog" campaign. Sun chose the dog, a greater Swiss mountain dog, because they thought it had universal appeal as a trustworthy, likable, hard-working, and powerful companion. JWT's international offices noted that although "Network the Dog" was appropriate for most Western European markets, dogs were not suitable advertising symbols in Muslim countries (e.g., United Arab Emirates, Malaysia) where they were likely to be perceived as unclean. Sun and JWT learned that their symbol was not "universal" and had to reconsider the direct transferability of the campaign.[21]

Diversified Sales

International marketing may help companies expand market coverage and extend product life cycles, and thus allow them to enjoy economies of scale. This is especially important for companies in countries where the domestic market is small, such as Japan, Switzerland, and Italy, or where domestic markets are mature, revenue growth slow, and pressures on profit margins high, such as in many developed country markets. Thus, geography may partly explain why Anglo-Dutch Unilever, Dutch Philips, Swiss Nestlé, and Swiss-Swede ABB seem to appear everywhere, and why Japanese and South Korean companies have aggressively pursued internationalization: relatively small domestic markets force companies to look for international opportunities. On the other hand, many U.S. companies' relatively recent internationalization drives, such as those by AT&T, Campbell, and Whirlpool, result from late maturing of the U.S. market for their products and services.

Ford's European revenues helped it weather the storm created by Japanese competition in the U.S. automobile markets in the early 1980s. By plowing profits from Europe into its U.S. operations, Ford made a comeback in its home market. Ford's diversified market base helped it recover much faster than General Motors, which, although twice Ford's size, was essentially a one-country company and floundered much longer.[22]

Al-Kabeer International, an India-based meat company and the market leader in the Arab market for fresh-frozen meat (mutton, beef), faced a total ban on their products in the late 1980s in Saudi Arabia, their largest market. Largely because the reasons for the ban were unclear and its duration unknown, Al-Kabeer's management decided to expand with a limited product line to the United Kingdom to reduce their exposure in the Middle East, as well as to secure a foothold in the European Union.[23]

Market Leadership

Many writers have compared international competition to a global chess game, where firms must "strike" competitors in markets where they are most vulnerable in order to protect and build their own domestic and global leadership positions. Presence in a number of markets provides companies with the ability to cross-subsidize their operations in various markets by using profits earned in one part of the world to build a presence in another.

In the early 1970s, Michelin used its profits from Europe to attack Goodyear's home market. In response to Michelin's attack on the U.S. tire market, Goodyear could have responded by reducing prices, increasing advertising, and offering dealers better margins. By doing so, Goodyear stood to lose much more than Michelin, for whom the U.S. market accounted for only a small share of its worldwide revenues. Instead, Goodyear counterattacked Michelin by aggressive tire marketing in Europe, where Michelin had more to lose. By turning Michelin's attention toward protecting its home market, Goodyear managed to check the pace at which Michelin could take a share of the U.S. market.[24]

MARKET SELECTION

If the profits are great, the risks are great.

–Chinese proverb

Marketing Objectives and Market Selection

As noted in chapter 2, marketing managers must make decisions that fit well with company strategy: decisions on international marketing objectives should precede selection of particular markets. Does the company want to preempt competitors by entering the international market early? Is the company willing to invest in building markets? Early entry into international markets has many advantages—a head start in developing brand-name recognition, consumer preferences, and distribution channels—but it is also risky. Early entrants may face the daunting tasks of building primary demand in the product category and creating marketing infrastructures. Consequently, their investment can be substantial and payback periods long. In many countries that are transitioning to market economies, trade, foreign direct investment, and foreign exchange restrictions provide preferential treatment for domestic companies, reduce foreign companies' ability to repatriate earnings, and add costs to doing business in those countries.

McDonald's may have been able to justify its early opening of a store in Russia based on revenue generation potential alone, but its primary purpose was to establish itself before other Western fast-food outlets. McDonald's of Canada began negotiations with the Soviets in the late 1970s, but it took more than a decade of perseverance before they finally obtained permission to set up their first Moscow store which opened in 1992.

AT&T's tardy entry into the Chinese telecommunications market illustrates the potential losses associated with being a late entrant. In the electronic switching equipment market, AT&T followed many of its competitors—Ericsson, Northern Telecom, Siemens, and NEC—into the PRC. The Chinese government had earlier approached AT&T for assistance in building the country's telecommunications infrastructure, and AT&T turned them down because of the riskiness of investing in China. Subsequently, its competitors were able to negotiate with the Ministry of Post and Telecommunications to select standards that matched their switches, making it more difficult for AT&T to eventually compete in China.

Many companies, including Honeywell and Procter & Gamble, entered the Japanese market with long-term market-share objectives, recognizing that it takes years to build relationships with Japanese customers and penetrate Japanese distribution systems. When the entrepreneurial Indian meat company, Al-Kabeer, entered the Gulf markets in the late 1970s, their vision to be a leader in these markets was reflected in their company name, which means "the great." To do this, they had to build a distribution infrastructure because the "cold chain" that ensures meat quality in developed markets from wholesale freezer storage to refrigerated trucking and retail freezer capacity was not well developed. This was a challenge in these markets, where a motorable road system was itself only beginning to develop. Today, Al-Kabeer's distribution channels are the envy of many larger multinational corporations.[25]

The International Market Selection Process

Once a company has decided on its overall international marketing objectives, managers must decide on which individual markets to enter. Firms often select initial international markets based on a heuristic—their similarity to home markets. Market similarity may be measured using statistics on aggregate production and transportation, personal consumption, trade, and health and education levels. Or market similarity may simply be captured by geographic or psychic proximity to the home market, reflecting a desire to minimize risks. Thus U.S. firms will often enter markets in Canada, Australia, and the United Kingdom (not coincidentally all English-speaking markets) before they enter the less similar markets of Spain, South Korea, or India.[26]

Market similarity can work well if the company also pays explicit attention to buyer behavior and institutional variations in each market, rather than attempting to duplicate a successful formula. Colgate-Palmolive chose to expand into Canada with Cleopatra, a perfumed soap that sold very well in France, based on their perception that Quebec resembled France. Not only was the soap market in Canada already mature, but the Quebecois French preferences and buying habits were very different from their European counterparts.[27] Al-Kabeer International established itself in Dubai in the United Arab Emirates (UAE), and then sequentially began

FIGURE 15.2 | APPROACH FOR MARKET SELECTION

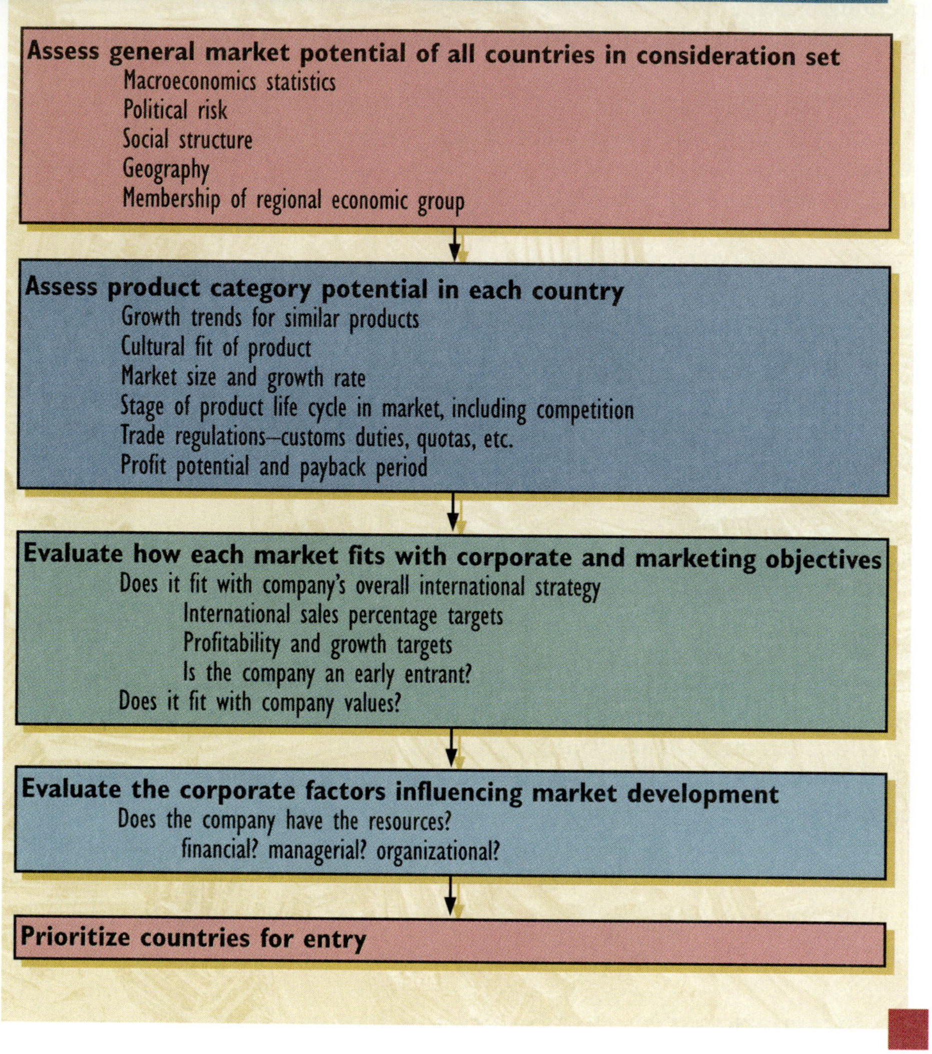

Assess general market potential of all countries in consideration set
Macroeconomics statistics
Political risk
Social structure
Geography
Membership of regional economic group

Assess product category potential in each country
Growth trends for similar products
Cultural fit of product
Market size and growth rate
Stage of product life cycle in market, including competition
Trade regulations—customs duties, quotas, etc.
Profit potential and payback period

Evaluate how each market fits with corporate and marketing objectives
Does it fit with company's overall international strategy
International sales percentage targets
Profitability and growth targets
Is the company an early entrant?
Does it fit with company values?

Evaluate the corporate factors influencing market development
Does the company have the resources?
financial? managerial? organizational?

Prioritize countries for entry

distributing its products to other Gulf countries proximal to the UAE, including Saudi Arabia, Bahrain, Oman, Qatar, and Kuwait. Al-Kabeer managers, however, also looked at these countries' markets to assess the extent to which each had the market characteristics that had helped them define their original marketing approach in the UAE, including the presence of a large South Asian expatriate population looking for value-priced, quality meat.[28]

The market selection process for a particular company may be simple—where a heuristic such as market similarity is used to evaluate a single market—or comprehensive—using a multistage screening process such as the one illustrated in Figure 15.2 to evaluate several markets and prioritize them for entry.

The Role of International Market Research

International market research—research to help managers make decisions in more than one country[29]—can help overcome psychic distance, and can provide useful information for every major international marketing decision, including market se-

TABLE 15.4 THE ROLE OF INTERNATIONAL MARKET RESEARCH

Marketing Decision	Focus of Research
Internationalization	Demand estimation
	Competition assessment
	domestic
	international
	global
Market selection	Ranking world markets
	market potential: size and growth
	country political risk
	strategic importance
	competitive intensity
	business and regulatory environment
Market segmentation	Attitude and lifestyle research
Marketing budget	Competitor spending
	Research and media costs
	Media effectiveness
	Sales and distribution costs
Mode of entry	Market size and growth potential
	Market infrastructure
	Government policies
	trade
	foreign direct investment
	currency
	Political risk
	Competitor strategies
	Partner availability
Marketing program	Income distribution
Target segments	Income elasticity
Positioning	Usage occasions, habits
Product policy	Cultural traits
Communications	Language, literacy
Pricing	Media coverage
Personal selling	Channel structure
Distribution	

lection, as summarized in Table 15.4. Market research[30] helps the international marketing effort in two important ways. First, it provides information so that marketing program and product design decisions more accurately reflect the commonalties and differences of individual markets. Second, it can help win local management support in implementing marketing programs by communicating that headquarters' managers are concerned with developing a fact-based understanding of the local market context. Results of concept testing, test marketing, attitude research, advertising pretesting, research on shopping behavior, and media research may be used to persuade local managers that a particular marketing program will work in their market. They may also be used by headquarters to judge the merits of local requests for adaptations to uniform strategies.[31] In addition, local managers' participation in the research process improves the likelihood they will actively support and implement the marketing program.

Measurement Problems in International Marketing Research

Experienced international research firms make up a $5 billion industry, with the largest firms concentrated in the United States, Western Europe, and Japan. Nielsen, Information Resources and the Gallup Organization are U.S. research firms that have a growing share of their revenues generated overseas. London-based MRB Group and Research International also offer substantial international research experience.[32] Choosing a research provider is difficult because the international research industry is fragmented, international research issues are complex, and many firms lack experience with the major issues involved in such research. The infrastructure for international market research in terms of organizational capabilities of the client or research agency has not developed as rapidly as the need for such research. Multimarket product and advertising campaign launches are becoming more frequent, requiring simultaneous research in several markets. Yet, the harmonized data and research techniques companies need to make cross-border comparisons on consumer response to branding, positioning, and communications strategies are not easily available. To ameliorate these problems, many multinational advertising agencies are gradually establishing relationships with local agencies in many countries, such as J. Walter Thompson's relationship with MARG, India's largest research company.

Despite the availability of specialized research agencies, it is important that international marketers be able to lead such research and focus it on their requirements, which calls for familiarity with the major international research issues.[33] For international research to support international program design decisions and encourage local management to implement such programs, the research must be multicountry in scope, representative of the company's major markets, and uniform in method. In addition, it must explicitly address data availability, equivalence, and bias issues.

Data Availability

First, current and accurate data, which we often take for granted in the United States, cannot so easily be guaranteed in other national contexts where data may not even be available. The United States is one of the most sophisticated markets in terms of the availability of secondary data sources. Therefore, international research is often a process of gathering data first-hand through field trips, electronic surveys, and a network of business partners such as advertising, market research, and consulting firms. Where possible, international researchers need to use a variety of approaches and sources to cross-validate data and ensure that the data are comparable across markets. For example, when using aggregate trade data to evaluate market potential, international data sources are often preferable to local sources such as the trade statistics maintained by most countries. Countries seldom compile data uniformly, and the underlying differences in definitions, measurement, accounting, and reporting principles will lead to incomparable data.

Secondary data from a variety of sources often provide an inexpensive starting point for international research. These data sources include:

- United Nations, International Monetary Fund, and World Bank trade data, including the *United Nations Statistical and Demographic Yearbook*, the *UNESCO Statistical Yearbook*, and the World Bank's annual *World Development Report*.
- Data from the Department of Commerce, Small Business Administration, country trade missions, and various state export promotion agencies, in the United States.
- Data complied by trade promotion offices of most countries and regional trading groups.
- Reports from private organizations, such as The Economist Intelligence Unit's *Country Reports*, *Market Studies*, and *World Outlook*, Dun and Bradstreet's *International Market Guides*, the various Business International publications, Worldcasts and Predicasts worldwide data on various regions, and the newsletters and published studies of major international advertising and consulting firms.

Equivalence Issues

Second, it is difficult to establish equivalence in international market research because such research takes place in multicultural and multilinguistic environments, and companies face time pressures in getting products and campaigns launched throughout a particular region or across the globe. Of course, comparability, or equivalence, is a concern when companies use either primary or secondary data, but primary market research faces additional challenges. These include high data collection costs; language, literacy, and cultural issues; attitudes toward marketing and market research; and the obstacles posed by poorly developed communications infrastructures. For example, people in many formerly state-controlled economies are unfamiliar with commercial market research and may therefore be wary of researchers.

Researchers need to consider many categories of cross-cultural equivalence to ensure that research results are comparable. The four major categories are construct equivalence, measure equivalence, sample equivalence, and instrument administration equivalence.

Construct Equivalence. *Construct equivalence* establishes that a concept has the same content and meaning in different research contexts. Many seemingly "universal" marketing concepts in fact have culture-specific connotations. For example, consumer dissatisfaction has various meanings, depending on the context. Dutch and U.S. people differ in the extent to which they express dissatisfaction with a product or service. Dutch consumers experience more inconvenience and unpleasantness when complaining than do U.S. consumers; but they are also less likely to feel any social obligation to complain.[34] In developing countries, company-specific instances of poor service may be attributed to the poor overall quality of institutions in the country, confounding the concept of dissatisfaction. Complaining behavior may mean something completely different in countries where close personal relationships between buyers and sellers develop. Attitudes toward waiting (for customer service) may be dramatically different in M-time cultures ("I wasted my time") compared to others. Similarly, people's conceptualizations of themselves may vary across individualist and collectivist cultures: In more individualist cultures, the self is seen as distinct from and separate from others, whereas in collectivist cultures, this boundary distinction is somewhat blurred. Partly as a consequence of this, the opinions of significant others are critical in collectivist cultures, so that Japanese experience greater levels of social anxiety than do Americans.[35] Also, many concepts have no direct equivalent in other cultures and are therefore unsuitable for cross-national use. For example, the Dutch *gezelligheid* or Dane *hyggelig*, which associate certain products with "togetherness" have no equivalents in English.

Measure Equivalence. *Measure equivalence* suggests that the research instrument (questionnaire, personal interview, telephone interview, focus group, and so forth) is perceived and used consistently across cultures. People of different cultures differ in their perceptions of whether telephone interviews are appropriate, which in turn will influence their responses. People of different cultures also understand language and use response scales differently. For example, northern Europeans prefer a four-point scale to a five-point forced choice scale. Latin Americans are more likely to use extreme points of a scale to express their individualism, whereas Indians, for similarly intense opinions, may use only the center of the scale. Translation is a big concern of international market researchers. For example, Koreans use the same word for "ethnic" and "foreign": Koreans all belong to one ethnic group, and anyone belonging to another ethnic group is "foreign." Thus a questionnaire designed for use in India that attempts to discover ethnic differences across the various states will, if used in Korea, reveal only differences between Koreans and non-Koreans.

Sample Equivalence. *Sample equivalence* suggests that samples should be drawn from similar sample frames, and use comparable selection techniques so the sample composition and responses are comparable across countries. This is tricky because of definitional differences and because researchers wish to simultaneously ensure representative country samples. Thus, a sample of equal numbers of men and women to investigate household food-shopping behavior may not represent decision makers in countries where men usually buy the food.

Instrument Administration Equivalence. *Instrument administration equivalence* refers to comparable data-collection methods, data currency, and contextual background of the data collection. Data collected over the period of a month in countries with normal or low inflation does not compare accurately with data collected in countries with hyperinflation, where data age rapidly and the exact hour and date at which data are collected matters. Similarly, researchers will find it difficult to establish equivalence when they are studying products and concepts that are taboo in certain cultures (e.g., birth control products, feminine hygiene products).

Researcher and Respondent Biases

Third, international research is prone to both observer and respondent bias. Observer bias stems from the SRC: problem definition and research design are based on what the researcher thinks is important rather than the actual issues of importance in each international market. Market research must explicitly distinguish between etic and emic approaches. *Etic* international research uses concepts that apply universally across cultures, whereas *emic* research uses culture-specific concepts. Systematic research across countries can attempt to develop pancultural concepts by comparing, combining, and modifying concepts that are specific to each of the cultures studied. In doing so, market researchers must make explicit assumptions about whether they are looking at cross-national differences (in which case countries are implicitly being used as proxies for cultures) or cross-cultural differences (in which case they need to specify what aspect(s) of culture are of interest).[36]

Respondent biases include socially desirable responses, biases that stem from different cultural disclosure norms, varying levels of experience with responding to market research, and ethnic biases. For example, market researchers in China may encounter responses that reflect "ideals" rather than existing realities. Further, interviews and focus group discussions in much of Asia may be biased by a tendency for younger respondents to respect and defer to opinions of their elders. Respondents from different nations may have different responses based on their attitudes toward the country of origin of the product or concept being tested as well as toward the researcher.[37]

Overcoming Research Problems

Companies use several methods to establish data and concept equivalence and improve the reliability and validity of their research. They may extensively test concepts and research instruments in each of the contexts being studied, use "local" market research partners, or obtain feedback from informants on the cultural relevance and adequacy of the study. Researchers use methods such as interviews and focus groups to elicit feedback, back-translations to ensure that cultural and not merely lexical translations are made, and statistical analysis to determine validity of concepts and reliabilities of all measures used within and across country and cultural groups.

Formal "Western-style" market research may often be preceded or replaced by more "hands-on" approaches.[38] There are cross-national differences in the definition and focus of research, the amount of research conducted, and the adoption of research results. For example, Japanese companies place credence on soft data from "walking around" and observing new channels in which they are interested or that already carry their products, making detailed notes on the behavior of channel members and customers. Thus, it is not unusual to see groups of Japanese executives in the marketplace taking note of how business is conducted. This "context-specific" knowledge is supplemented with hard data on actual sales, deliveries, and so on. Canon, Matsushita, and Kao are just a few Japanese companies that base market entry and distribution strategies on a combination of the direct, observational research conducted by their middle and senior managers, and data on product flows through various channels. Compared to their U.S. counterparts, Japanese companies conduct more channels and sales research.[39]

In addition, Japanese managers draw a distinction between *honne*, the true desires of the individual, and *tatemae*, the outward manifestation or explicit statement of that desire. Further, they believe that *honne* must not be revealed, so *tatemae* will not accurately reflect *honne*, and therefore quantitative analyses are unlikely to reveal *honne*, especially for new products. Therefore, deep interactions and observations of lead users and current customers are the best approach to determining the answer to the question about which Japanese marketers care most: What kind of product and service do the customers need? Honda adopts the *sangen*, or three actuals, approach in its research—actual product, actual person, actual situation—which is largely observational.[40] Similarly, engineers at Toshiba's medical systems division began research on new ultrasound scanners by identifying a leading surgeon whose work they observed every Friday for a year in 1970. They continued to work with the surgeon throughout the development of their ultrasound scanning equipment.[41]

Grouping International Markets: Definition and Segmentation

International marketers may define and segment target markets to select new markets or to extend successful marketing approaches to new, similar international segments. As discussed in chapter 5, market segmentation identifies meaningful segments for designing marketing programs. In fact, international marketing success depends to a large extent on a firm's ability to segment its world markets so that managers may develop marketing programs for homogeneous groups of customers. Researchers usually take one of two broad segmentation approaches: (1) cluster countries or areas to form larger markets, based on the premise that the countries are internally homogeneous and also similar to each other; and (2) cross-national segments, based on the premise that there are many dissimilar intracountry groups that have corollaries in other countries.[42]

Traditional International Market Segmentation

Traditionally, the country approach has dominated. Firms have segmented international markets by country classification, grouping countries into homogenous clusters, based on one or more macrovariables. Relevant classification variables or bases of segmentation and examples of each include:

- economic (per capita gross national product)
- demographic (urban population percentage)
- technological (durable goods ownership)
- institutional (number of wholesalers)
- geographic (climatic conditions)
- legal or political (currency convertibility restrictions)

For example, the World Bank uses per capita gross national product (GNP) to group countries into five categories—low-income economies, middle-income economies, high-income oil exporters, industrial market economies, and nonreporting nonmember economies. Business International, a U.S. provider of international business statistics, uses multiple indicators—population; television, telephone, and automobile ownership; steel, cement, and electricity production—to compute measures of market attractiveness. It measures market attractiveness by using market size (total potential), intensity (concentration of purchasing power), and growth (historical five-year rate of increase in market size). These indices allow managers to compare country opportunities quickly, as well as to group countries into markets that are large, but growing slowly (United States, Japan); small, but growing rapidly (India, Turkey, South Korea, Taiwan); small, but intense (West Germany, Italy, France); and so on.[43]

Firms use another aggregate approach to cluster international markets: geographic or regional economic groupings. For example, some management thinkers such as Kenichi Ohmae, formerly of the management consulting firm McKinsey & Company, have suggested that the "triad" markets of North America, Western Europe, and Japan are critical, homogenous markets in which large companies must create a substantial presence.[44] Many companies implicitly segment world markets geographically by organizing their companies to cater at the broadest level to "home market" and "rest of the world," or "domestic" and "international markets." Alternately, markets in North America, Europe, Central and South America, Asia, Australia, and the Middle East may be treated as separate from an organizational standpoint, and therefore implicitly as market segments. Examples of regional economic groups as market segments include the three major groups—EU, NAFTA, and AFTA—and smaller groupings, such as the European Free Trade Association (EFTA) and Mercosur in South America. Countries within these regional groups join forces to create large markets that allow free trade among members of the group.

Although such aggregate geopolitical and demographic approaches to clustering international markets may provide useful "first-cuts" at market definition, market potential assessment, and market grouping, they have two broad limitations. First, such approaches assume intracountry homogeneity, so they focus heavily on differences across country groups and underestimate potential similarities. Yet, the affluent youth in Bombay or Lagos are likely to be more similar to their counterparts in New York, London, and Brussels than to youths in rural India or rural Nigeria. Likewise, consumers in the south of France may resemble those in parts of Spain and Italy more than those in the north of France, so marketing approaches developed for France as an aggregate market may not be effective across that country.

Second, these approaches are not based on actual consumer values, lifestyles, and behaviors, but on geographic and economic proxies for such behavior. Thus, traditional international segmentation approaches may not yield managerially useful market segments. That is, an attempt to gain economies by using a uniform marketing approach for the resulting segments would be futile. As an example, consider the much-awaited European "single market." Andrew Hilton, writing for the *Harvard Business Review*, dubs it the "Euro-myth," and points out that even in sectors where integration should have been fairly straightforward, Europe is and will remain a "mosaic of markets." In addition to regulatory and institutional differences, consumer preferences and behavior create this mosaic.[45] Thus, although some bankers might be tempted to look at Europe as a single financial services market, the reality is that some products, such as bank loans, are very much local business.

Intermarket Segmentation

Marketing managers will find much more useful those segmentation schemes that address particular marketing applications and product categories and are based on actual consumer attitudes and behaviors. One recent international segmentation approach, based on actual consumer behavior, groups countries according to similarities in the patterns of new product diffusion, using historical sales to estimate diffusion patterns. This approach could potentially provide firms with better sales growth rate estimates for particular product categories than do traditionally derived segments.[46]

Other approaches to international segmentation recognize cross-country or intermarket segments[47] and use psychographic data—personality, cultures, attitudes and lifestyles—to arrive at segments. Global Scan, created by international advertising agency Backer Spielvogel Bates Worldwide (BSB).[48] provides a segmentation scheme based on comprehensive annual surveys of consumer activities, interests, opinions, values and product usage collected from 15,000 consumers in North and South America, Asia, and Western Europe. The segmentation scheme relies on 250 measures, half of which relate to global values and the other half to local market characteristics. BSB identifies five segments that stretch across most countries:

- *Strivers* (24 percent of sample). Young people, busy trying to succeed, with demanding, fast-paced lives, and additional pressures from starting families.
- *Achievers* (20 percent of sample). Baby boomers, who have achieved what the strivers are struggling to achieve; these are opinion leaders, who care about health, fitness, and style.
- *Traditional* (19 percent of sample). Conservative people, unwilling to accept change, who subscribe to traditional values.
- *Adapters* (19 percent of sample). Older consumers who are comfortable with change, while keeping their traditional views.
- *Pressured* (16 percent of sample). Predominantly women of every age group, with pressures of work, family, aging, economic, and so on; convenience products often fit their lives.

When they use an international segmentation approach based on actual consumer behavior, marketing managers will have a better appreciation of which marketing programs to transfer across markets and what adaptations will be necessary. Companies such as IKEA, Revlon, Reebok, IBM, and Tetra-Werke use uniform marketing programs to address the needs of cross-national segments they derive from consumer demographic and psychographic data.

PATTERNS OF ENTRY

Supreme excellence consists in breaking the enemy's resistance without fighting.
–Sun Tzu, *The Art of War*

Those who do not know the lay of the land cannot maneuver their forces. Those who do not use local guides cannot take advantage of the ground.
–Sun Tzu, *The Art of War*

Companies face a variety of decisions once they select markets of interest:

- market expansion, or the number of markets to be entered and the pace and order of entry into various markets
- mode of entry, or the institutional arrangement to be used to sell and support their products and services in a market
- marketing mix or program, including product line and branding decisions, positioning, pricing, promotion, and distribution

The Internationalization Process

Many companies enter into international markets opportunistically in response to inquiries from interested potential customers, or when their own customers move into new markets.[49] As some of our examples illustrate, other companies enter international markets strategically: they consider the pros and cons of international market participation, decide on target shares of revenue from international markets, and recognize that—despite the long payback period—international market development has substantial long-term profit potential.

Firms—especially small- and medium-size ones—typically move through a series of stages in the internationalization process, as illustrated in Figure 15.3. With the "gradual acquisition, integration and use of knowledge about foreign markets and operations," successive stages reflect greater levels of commitment to international markets,[50] associated with which are greater levels of risk, but also greater levels of control over operations:[51]

1. ad hoc exports, based on inquiries from international buyers
2. indirect exports through agents and distributors who manage export logistics
3. direct exports, in which the company itself manages export logistics
4. licensing, in which the company transfers manufacturing rights to a partner in return for a royalty
5. equity investment in a joint venture or fully owned subsidiary to manufacture in the international market

Managers' experience of international markets and international marketing helps them to overcome the psychic distance arising from language, culture, education, business practice, and legislative differences. Companies' abilities to in-

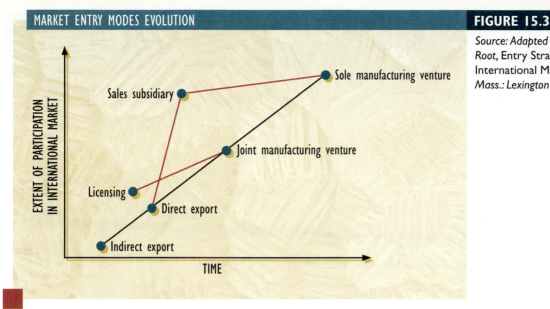

Source: Adapted from Franklin R. Root, Entry Strategies for International Markets *(Lexington, Mass.: Lexington Books, 1994).*

crease their commitment to particular international markets, as well as to progressively take their products and companies into new and different markets, grows as they accumulate experience. This progression is reflected in Whirlpool's Asian market development approach. Beginning in 1988, they used independent distributors, but have since opened three regional offices to serve Southeast Asia, greater China, and Japan; opened a design and product development center in Singapore to serve the entire region; and entered into several manufacturing joint ventures and fully-owned ventures in China and India.[52] Whirlpool eventually wants to develop a company-owned distribution system, replacing some or all of their distributors. As a firm's level of international participation increases, and it progresses from being primarily a domestic firm with an export strategy to a multidomestic firm, and on to a global firm, so do its managerial orientations, as described in Table 15.5.[53]

Market Expansion Paths

Companies must make two major market expansion decisions: the first relates to their overall market expansion approach—the number of markets to enter and the rate at which to enter the markets—and the second to their market entry sequence.

Market Concentration or Diversification?

A *market concentration* strategy involves sequential, gradual rate of growth in the number of markets served, committing greater resources to developing each individual market. *Market diversification* involves simultaneous, rapid penetration of a large number of markets, spreading resources somewhat thinly across markets. Firms may select a market diversification strategy over a concentration strategy when their target markets have the following characteristics:

- Marketing efforts produce rapidly diminishing returns, sales growth is low, and sales in individual markets are unstable. Individual markets are likely to contribute a small and unsteady share of overall revenue, so multimarket presence

TABLE 15.5 INTERNATIONAL ORIENTATIONS AND INTERNATIONAL MARKETING CONCEPTS

Marketing Concept	International Orientation	Description
Domestic market extension	Ethnocentric	Look for export markets where domestic product can be sold without any modifications; marketing strategy is the similar to domestic strategy.
Multidomestic markets	Polycentric	Individual markets viewed as vastly different; products developed locally; little coordination of marketing program across markets.
Global markets	Regiocentric or geocentric	International markets viewed as regional or global with significant similarities; substantial coordination of marketing activities across markets.

Source: Based on Philip R. Cateora, International Marketing, *(Homewood, Ill.: Irwin, 1996).*

is important. Single-country markets in Europe and the Middle East are not large enough for many companies, so these companies may choose to enter several countries simultaneously.

- Being first or early to market is important. Competitors are easily able to block entry by tying up distribution channels, or are able to easily imitate strategy in other markets, so preempting them is important. Alternately, if consumers are likely to be extremely brand loyal, or purchase infrequently such as for consumer durables, building brand awareness and preference early is important. Finally, for industrial products with long selling cycles, the successful distribution of which includes sales and revenues of spare parts and service contracts, marketers who secure early entry have advantages because buyers are locked in to the use of their machines, and their channel partners have an established stream of revenue from sales of maintenance contracts, replacement parts and service.

- Markets are interdependent. Media spillovers generate demand for the company's products in other countries where potential customers are exposed to its advertising.

A market diversification strategy allows a company to reap benefits from economies of scale in designing and implementing their marketing approach. Thus, diversification is appropriate when few adaptations are required in product, distribution, and communications, and when the company has sufficient resources to devote to rapid multimarket entry.[54]

Tatra, a Czech heavy-truck manufacturer attempting to revitalize its markets in the aftermath of declining demand at home and in Russia, stands at the crossroad of new market development. Its initial attempts at selling to several markets in different parts of the world—a market diversification approach—have not met with much success. Its trucks, historically built for Siberian conditions, need substantial adaptation for most other markets where conditions are not as severe as in Siberia. Tatra will also need to invest in developing channels for its trucks and spare parts and service areas. Tatra managers might more appropriately concentrate their efforts on identifying and developing one market at a time.[55]

Citibank launched its credit card in all the major markets of Southeast Asia using a market diversification approach. Within a period of 18 months in 1989 and 1990, the company launched the premium-positioned and premium-priced product in Indonesia, Singapore, Taiwan, Thailand, Australia, India, and Malaysia with the slogans, "Not Just Visa, Citibank Visa," and "Not Just MasterCard, Citibank MasterCard." A market concentration strategy was not feasible, because none of the individual markets offered sufficient potential for Citibank to break even, nor a large enough population in the targeted segments, given the effective customer conversion rate of their marketing vehicles.[56]

Market Entry Sequence

Decisions on market entry sequence—in what order to enter mature developed-country markets, or developing-country markets with high growth potential—often reflect a company's overall strategy. Companies interested in short-term revenue and profit generation will prefer large, high-growth markets. Contrast this approach with that of many Japanese companies whose overall objective is long-term market share dominance. Consider the historical evidence on the expansion paths of Japanese companies, "the quintessential global marketers."[57] Japanese firms took one of three global expansion routes. In some industries (steel, autos, cameras, watches), Japanese firms moved from developing their protected domestic markets to developing-country markets. These markets were attractive because they presented minimal competition, and the Japanese could quickly benefit from scale economies. Only then did the Japanese move into other, developed-country markets, focusing within these markets on segments that competitors had ignored, and gradually adapting products to cater to new markets. Japanese brands now dominate the U.S. and European markets in many categories, including motorcycles, cameras, and watches.

A second expansion path that the Japanese firms typically employed with high-technology products such as computers, for which developing-country markets were too small, was from their domestic markets directly into developed-country markets. Markets that were similar to the United States but were not as highly competitive, including Australia, provided relatively low-risk "test markets." When the companies eventually entered the United States and Europe, they were initially unable to compete based on new or unique technology. Consequently, they built market share by pricing aggressively and distributing through local distributors, who branded the products with their own names. They approached developing countries next using similar strategies, in time to ride the growth wave in these markets.

Their third expansion path, evident in the color television and sewing machine markets, began with new product development targeted at the United States and other developed-country markets. When demand for these categories in Japan grew, the Japanese firms took their products to their home market, and then to developing-country markets.

All three of the above market entry sequences share four market entry strategy elements. Volume was critical for the Japanese companies—the objective was to move down the experience curve quickly in order to bring costs down rapidly. Second, they entered international markets at penetration prices—facilitated in the first two cases by profits from protected domestic markets—which also helped build volume. Third, Japanese companies avoided head-on confrontations with competitors, making quiet inroads[58] into each of the markets they entered, through local distributors and private label branding. Finally, their approach of working with local "partners" was part of a strategy for learning about the markets—a strategy that many Korean companies adopted later.[59] The main "lesson" from this historical pattern is that clear strategic international marketing objectives with all the elements of international marketing strategy and programs working synergistically toward achieving those objectives are critical for success.

Modes of Entry

A naive decision rule for selecting modes of entry for international markets would be to use the same entry mode regardless of market characteristics. Mary Kay Cosmetics' and Amway's historical uses of multilevel "pyramid" marketing in all their markets reflect such standardized modes of entry. Such an approach might succeed if the entry mode happens to be appropriate for the market. An alternative approach would be to select appropriate entry modes based on a cost-benefit analysis of all options—exporting, brand or process licensing to a local manufacturer, or investing in production facilities in the local market—given the company's international marketing objectives. See Figure 15.3 for a listing of modes of entry.[60]

Exporting

Exporters face a broad choice between indirect and direct exports, depending on whether they themselves take on the task of managing the export process. They may use domestic or international intermediaries, such as export management companies, trading companies, brokers, importers, local wholesalers and retailers, or piggybacking arrangements with companies that have complementary products to export indirectly. To export directly, companies can use their own salesforce from their home countries and/or overseas sales offices. As the Japanese experience shows, many firms benefit from using intermediaries in the early stages of international market development. Despite the advantages of using intermediaries, direct or company-managed exports offer advantages in the following situations:[61]

- Export volume is high, so companies may be able to capture economies of scale (larger volumes) and scope (combining many product lines) by exporting directly.

- Sales patterns are uncertain, so it is more difficult to evaluate the performance of independent export intermediaries than your own salesforce.

- Investment and time required for training salespeople are high and customer knowledge requirements are substantial. Companies who train their own employees are better able to educate and support customers through their dedicated salesforce than intermediaries, who often carry multiple, competing product lines.

Thus, Al-Kabeer International's initial foray into the Gulf markets involved exporting small consignments of frozen meat from Bombay. When increasing order size and frequency revealed large market potential, the owners opened a sales office in Dubai because they felt that using intermediaries limited their ability to assess and exploit market opportunities. Another contributing factor to their "going direct" was that the Gulf markets needed substantial development. Customers who were used to fresh meat needed to be educated about the benefits of fresh-frozen meat before they were willing to try it. In addition, retailers needed to be motivated to install freezers and dedicate space to the meat products. Managers felt that their own sales force could tackle both tasks effectively to ensure sales growth.

Managers face three additional considerations in deciding whether to use direct or indirect export strategies: distribution infrastructure, company market power, and long-term market strategy. In markets that have poorly developed or nonexistent distribution infrastructures—such as emerging markets in Central and Eastern Europe and in China—a company may have no choice but to develop the channels for the product themselves. In order to get around the problems of poorly developed retailing, and to ensure that their jeans were sold in an environment consistent with their image, Levi's Polska opened their own Original Levi's stores in Poland. Firms face similar circumstances when existing channels are "blocked" to new entrants who have relatively little market power, such as in the highly concentrated European food distribution industry. The largest wholesale buying groups account for a much greater percentage of total food turnover in France, Germany and the United Kingdom than in the United States. Add to this increasing retail concentration, with a few large, powerful supermarket chains with coordinated cross-border purchasing, and the emergence of store brands, and it becomes clear why newcomers to European markets find it difficult to get a foot in the door. Finally, when firms' objectives include long-term market development, such as Procter & Gamble in Japan, they may consider establishing their own presence in order to learn about the market and to maintain greater control over product marketing.

When firms use direct salesforces or sales subsidiaries, combined with local distributors in target markets, they need to understand the legal environment as well as the structure and management of distribution channels in the international market. Careful distributor selection is of paramount importance because legal systems in most countries make it extremely difficult to terminate distributor relationships. Distribution channel structure, functions performed by various channel members, and the basis for motivating intermediaries vary substantially across markets:[62]

- Channels in developed economies are typically shorter and more vertically integrated than those in developing countries.[63]

- The functions performed by intermediaries vary in different countries. Firms may have to provide distributors with territorial exclusivity, which in turn makes it more difficult for later entrants to find exclusive distributors. In some countries, channel members play key roles in defining product quality.[64]

- Building close personal relationships with channel partners is a necessary prerequisite for penetrating many markets, and is often an important means of motivating intermediaries.[65]

A look at the Japanese distribution system, often described as a nontariff barrier to trade, illustrates these points. Japan features a complex, multilayered distribution system, unlike many of its Western counterparts. This system supports a large number of intermediaries per capita, *tonya* arrangements in which wholesalers sell to each other, and highly fragmented retailing. Because retailers are small and shelf space is limited (very similar to the "mom and pop" shops in the United States), wholesalers carry inventory, deliver in small lots, and provide financing to subwholesalers and retailers. Manufacturers, in turn, must ensure that they deliver sufficient variety to their channel members, and constantly introduce new products. The entire system functions as a web of tight, close, personal relationships among manufacturers, wholesalers, and retailers. The U.S. stereo manufacturer, Bose Corporation, made attempts to develop channel relationships *nihonshiki* (Japanese style) in order to sell its high-end audio speakers in Japan.

Licensing

International licensing includes a variety of contractual arrangements by which companies make intangible assets available to licensees for royalties and other payments. These include know-how, trademarks, and brand and company names, and are often accompanied by technical, managerial, and marketing assistance. Firms may adopt a licensing strategy, despite lower control over local marketing operations than direct investment, because licensing arrangements allow them to penetrate international markets rapidly. Further, licensing allows firms to establish local manufacturing presence—which helps establish credibility with customers and helps reduce parallel imports—while circumventing foreign ownership restrictions, reducing exposure to risks of host government appropriation, transferring local adaptation costs to the licensee, and lowering resource commitments relative to direct investments. The single biggest risk associated with international licensing is that firms may lose intellectual property rights and may unwittingly create competitors. One approach to minimize this risk is to build territorial restriction clauses into licensing agreements. Competition among licensees in neighboring territories limits any potential damage from licensees that do not actively develop markets for the firm's brands.

Two widespread and highly visible forms of international licensing for market development are trademark licensing and franchising. Disney products sold around the world are just one example of the potential of trademark licensing. International franchising has witnessed explosive growth (with U.S. companies in the forefront) because it requires lower capital and managerial involvement in each international market than do direct investments.[66] In addition to licensing their names, franchisers such as Avis, The Body Shop, and Hilton Hotels usually license entire business formats. Franchisers benefit from continuous revenue streams, usually a percentage of sales. To gather direct information about market potential, as well as to indirectly monitor their franchisees, companies may maintain one or more company-owned outlets in each market. International franchising appears to provide growth opportunities at lower risk than direct investment; however, franchisers must provide continued and active support to their franchisees to ensure success, and to protect quality and brand image.

Legally, though, licensing is a double-edged sword. First, all countries do not automatically register trademarks: use is necessary to establish ownership in common-law countries, whereas code-law countries require registration. To register trademarks in the United States (a common-law country), companies must demonstrate the actual and continued use of the trademark (that is, sales of trademarked products). Thus U.S. companies may assume that trademark use constitutes sufficient proof of ownership. In code-law countries, however, the first party to register a trademark is considered its owner. In some countries, registration must be followed by use within a reasonable period. McDonald's had to fight an expensive legal battle in Japan to buy back its trademark, which had been registered by a Japanese firm. Therefore, firms should register their trademarks in all potential target markets to avoid having to buy back their own trademarks.

Trademark infringement—the illegal use of trademarks to make counterfeit and fake products—presents a second major threat that can cause companies to lose revenues to counterfeiters. Even worse, poor-quality imitations can damage product and company reputations. Trademark licensers have to be proactive in defending their trademarks, revenues, and reputations. Swatch, the Swiss watch company, has an aggressive policy for reducing the threat from counterfeits: its product design makes imitation difficult, advertising raises consumer awareness, and the company actively monitors channel members to ensure that they do not carry fakes.

Local Production

Companies may choose to invest directly in local production, either in joint ventures or in wholly owned facilities. Such investments bring high risk, but also provide companies with greater control over country operations, as illustrated in Figure 15.3. Companies may be motivated to invest by the local market potential or by nearby markets. Or they may be trying to capture low-cost manufacturing possibilities or circumvent trade barriers. For many companies, exporting to China is not feasible. Restrictions such as import bans and high customs duties have been instituted by the Chinese government to protect national industries and encourage their development. Companies that want to sell to the huge Chinese market must therefore consider investing in Chinese manufacturing plants.

The most significant marketing gains from direct investment accrue from firms being close to the market, being able to gain credibility with customers and governments, and having greater control over international marketing operations. Thus, Pepsi-Cola enjoyed a critical advantage by being the "local" carbonated beverage in the U.S.S.R., where it was the earliest Western company to establish bottling facilities. With perestroika, this type of insider advantage no longer works, and is actually working against Pepsi. The Russian consumer has turned to imported Coke, the consumption of which brings greater status. Honda—notably *American Honda Company*—and Toyota capitalize on their U.S. production by positioning their cars as U.S.-made, thereby attempting to overcome U.S. consumers' anti-Japan sentiments and sell to customers who want to "buy American."

For many companies, control over marketing operations dominates their mode of entry decisions. Despite the associated risks, these companies choose to invest in local production over other entry options because direct investment allows them to maintain control, especially when the company wants to protect its manufacturing technology. For this reason, many companies prefer direct investment in sole or wholly owned corporations to investment in joint ventures. For example, Coca-Cola left India in the 1970s when the government placed restrictions on maximum foreign ownership of corporations. As Indian policy makers remove these restrictions to compete for foreign direct investment, interest in India from corporations worldwide has resurged. This includes Coca-Cola, which has acquired Parle Exports for an estimated $40 million, together with India's four most popular soft drink brands—Thums Up, Limca, Gold Spot, and Maaza—and a network of 54 bottling plants nationwide. Coca-Cola's objective is to be the leader in the Indian soft-drink market, and with this acquisition Coca-Cola–owned brands have eclipsed PepsiCo with a market share of 58 percent. PepsiCo, which entered India before Coca-Cola's reentry, is saddled with a variety of ownership-related restrictions.[67]

MARKETING PROGRAM ISSUES

The prospects for American car manufacturers in Europe would appear to be good if they will meet the conditions and requirements of these various countries but to attempt to do so on the lines on which business is done in America would make it a fruitless task.

–James Couzens, Ford Motor Company, 1907

Over a quarter century ago, Harvard Business School's Robert D. Buzzell raised the standardization issue in his "Can You Standardize Multinational Marketing?"[68] At the time, prevailing wisdom dictated that marketing was very

IN CASABLANCA, A SLIVER OF BONE REVEALED A CHUNK OF HISTORY when Dr. Jean-Jacques Hublin unearthed a few fossilized skull fragments. Then Hublin and a team of IBM scientists fed this shattered 3-D jigsaw puzzle into a unique program called Visualization Data Explorer." The tiny pieces helped form an electronic reconstruction of our early ancestor, the first Homo sapiens. This new IBM technology has turned time back 100,000 years, uncovering clues to the origins of mankind. What can visualization technology reveal to you? Call 1-800-IBM-3333, ext. G101, and see.

Solutions for a small planet®   IBM.

much a local problem, best left to local management in each country. Indeed, relative to other business functions, marketing must be more responsive to customer requirements and market contexts, therefore making marketing programs the most difficult to standardize. Fifteen years later, Harvard Business School's Theodore Levitt pointed out that standardization is inevitable.[69] One of the primary challenges international marketers face is to balance standardization and adaptation in order to address both market-driven consumer needs and efficiency-driven corporate needs.

Standardization "versus" Adaptation?

Standardization strategies mandate that firms offer a common product or use a common marketing approach regionally or globally. *Adaptation* strategies, on the other hand, call for customizing product and marketing for individual markets. The very act of transferring a successful product to new markets suggests some amount of standardization in the product and the way it is taken to market. Such standardization arises naturally as exporters attempt to capitalize on proprietary processes and scale economies. In addition, many products that were previously adapted for international markets are becoming increasingly standardized as global competition increases.

For example, the Fiesta, Ford Motor Company's 1972 attempt to create a standardized car for Western Europe based on input from all its European subsidiaries, came at a time when car manufacturers were more sensitive to the differences in drivers' preferences in different European countries. More recently, in another attempt to reduce new product development costs, Ford CEO Alex Trotman launched the Ford 2000 program to eliminate duplication and reduce the number of models sold worldwide. Teams of Ford employees from different parts of the world collaborate at five "vehicle centers," each of which designs a different type of vehicle for worldwide markets. Ford's prototype of a "world car"—branded Mondeo in Europe, where it was launched in 1993, and Contour and Mercury Mystique in the United

States, where it was launched in 1994—is a forerunner of this trend toward product standardization.[70]

Practically speaking, companies must identify both the benefits of and obstacles to standardization, as well as which elements of the marketing program are best standardized. The benefits and obstacles are common to all elements of the marketing program; as we discuss them, we provide examples of standardization or adaptation of the various marketing program elements.

Benefits of Standardization

Consistency with Customers. With media spillovers and customer travel across markets, common marketing approaches build consistent brand images across markets and reinforce brand identity. In the 1960s, Nestlé adopted a unified advertising approach across Europe, and indeed across the world, with its common "fresh-ground aroma" theme for its instant coffee Nescafé.

Chevron Corporation is considering a global branding campaign because managers recently realized that key government decision makers do not sufficiently recognize Chevron as a force in the oil extraction and refining business. This poor company recognition stems from a lack of consistency: a plethora of names are used in Chevron's exploration ventures, such as Aramco in the Middle East and Tenghiz-Chevroil in Kazakhstan. Chevron's lack of brand equity in these business markets parallels poor corporate brand recognition in consumer markets for value-added products such as lubricants, where use of the brand Caltex in several large markets disassociates the products from the company.[71]

Customer Preferences. For many types of companies, such as those with multi-national operations and international retailers who source worldwide, customer needs are becoming globally more uniform. Further, recent research suggests that some segment- and product-specific consumer behaviors do not vary across cultures or countries.[72] Universal customer preferences and behaviors would justify standardized marketing.

In the mid-1980s, Saatchi & Saatchi positioned itself as the only advertising agency that could cater to advertisers' needs for uniform advertising worldwide. Ogilvy and Mather currently uses its international organizational capabilities for providing IBM—a global company with similar advertising needs in many markets—with seamless advertising support worldwide as IBM begins to manage its brand globally.

Exploiting Good Ideas. Because good ideas are difficult to find, success in one market prompts wholesale transfer to other markets. Particularly in creative areas such as communications, experts suggest that universal campaigns can be effective anywhere.[73]

To transition from local brands to the Whirlpool brand, Whirlpool Corporation found success with dual branding in Europe. It linked its name with established ones, and facilitated the transfer of brand equity to the Whirlpool name. Whirlpool has since used the same dual-branding approach in other markets.

Cost Savings. Clearly, firms can accrue substantial savings, especially as they design and produce more efficiently, if they are able to sell the same basic product across international markets. Common advertising approaches can also yield savings, both in production and media planning.

In what has become a classic example of standardized marketing, Italian washing machine manufacturers were able to gain market share and make profits in all major European markets despite prevailing differentiation among competing brands, largely because their lower production and marketing costs translated into lower prices and volume sales.[74] Nearly 30 years later in the same industry, Whirlpool faced a dilemma when it bought Philips Electronics' appliance division. Whirlpool had to convert a barely profitable "amalgam of independent national companies" in which "washing machines built in Italy and in Germany did not share a single screw."[75] As illustrated in the opening example of this chapter, Whirlpool's strategy to standardize many aspects of its production and marketing program has enabled the company to cut costs.

Citibank's advertising outlays for their multicountry credit card launch in the Asia-Pacific were substantial, raising their break-even volume. Despite the pressures associated with a rapid regional rollout and the common positioning platform, Citibank chose to create expensive, tailored, country-specific television advertisements, thereby forgoing the savings that standardized regional advertisements would have brought.

Improved Coordination and Control. Companies with standardized marketing programs can more efficiently coordinate their activities across borders. For example, price harmonization—standardizing prices across markets after allowing for differences in exchange rates—is necessary if companies want to avoid "gray markets," that is unauthorized product transshipments across country borders.[76] Similarly, companies using uniform distribution approaches reduce the likelihood of "gray market" activity.

Nonstandard distribution and pricing may heighten consumer perceptions of inequity, such as in European automobile retailing, where prices of the same model vary significantly across countries. Whirlpool's decision to standardize its advertising approach—both advertising content and a single agency—across Europe was motivated by an attempt to better control not only its brand image, but also agency relationships and advertising implementation.

Obstacles to Standardization

Despite the benefits of standardization, several obstacles stand in the way of standardizing marketing programs. Marketers need to adapt their mix to address differences in market characteristics, industry conditions, legal environments, and marketing infrastructures (distribution channels, advertising agencies, and media). We have already discussed the most ubiquitous of these—cultural differences. The major obstacles to standardization are summarized in Table 15.6, illustrated in the following example, and discussed in the following sections.

Obstacles to Standardization: An Illustration

The infant formula controversy sparked in the early 1970s illustrates many of the obstacles to standardization and provides a vivid example of how a standardized approach can have serious, long-term consequences for marketing organizations. Nestlé and other infant formula companies marketed their brands of infant formula to mothers in developing countries by replicating their successful marketing approach from developed countries. Thus, they promoted products through physicians and hospitals, and distributed free samples and promotional materials to mothers through salespeople dressed in nurses' uniforms. As a result, mothers in many developing countries mistakenly believed that infant formula was better for their infants than breast milk. Many mothers were willing to pay the high prices charged for infant formula because it offered them the convenience of time away from their infants, thereby allowing them to work. Although they paid the high price, mothers often tried to stretch the product, flagrantly violating usage instructions and giving their infants excessively diluted formula. Usage conditions—squalor and caretakers who were themselves children—did not permit sanitary preparation of the formula and exacerbated the violations. Almost every element of the marketing program turned out to be inappropriate for the developing-country context, resulting in infant mortalities, worldwide negative publicity, a seven-year boycott of all Nestlé's products, a World Health Organization code on marketing breast milk substitutes, and industry- and world-wide revamping of formula marketing.[77]

The infant formula manufacturers' failure to adapt their marketing approach to developing-country markets raises an additional issue for international marketers—that of ethical or moral considerations in marketing. Differences in product safety, advertising, and packaging standards, as well as attitudes toward business practices such as bribery, constantly present ethical challenges for the international businessperson. In the infant formula case, Senator Edward Kennedy (D–MA) advised marketers to improve their postsales surveillance to better understand the conditions under which their products are used and to adjust their marketing practices accordingly. A Swiss court judge similarly suggested that Nestlé should reconsider the use of advertising practices that had transformed a life-saving product into a life-threatening product.

In fact, a Nestlé manager who was involved in the process and was present at the signing of the joint declaration with the International Olympic Boycott Committee that ended the seven-year boycott stated:

> The Nestlé boycott teaches two lessons. The first, which is ignored only at great peril, is that issues that can arise to threaten a company are as likely to be sociopolitical as financial, and that no company, especially a large visible company, is exempt from the possibility of some political crisis arising. Therefore, executives owe it to themselves and their firms to become as competent at managing political issues as they are at managing profit-and-loss issues. In today's world, public policy and profits are equally important to a company's survival."[78]

TABLE 15.6 OBSTACLES TO STANDARDIZATION IN INTERNATIONAL MARKETING

Factors Limiting Standardization	Possible Implications for Marketing Program Elements			
	Product	Price	Distribution	Advertising/Promotion
MARKET FACTORS				
e.g., Lower per capita incomes in developing markets	Offer smaller package sizes	Lower base price	Accept and offer channel members lower margins	Focus on value
STAGE OF PRODUCT LIFE CYCLE				
e.g., Lower competition in the introductory stages in developing markets	Simpler products; less product differentiation Shorter product lines	Less price competition	Channels may have to be developed	Build awareness
REGULATORY ENVIRONMENT				
e.g., Lower intellectual property protection in some markets	Build-in antipiracy protection (e.g., film, software)	Set higher prices to meet desired profit objectives	Develop greater control over distribution to minimize unauthorized channels	Create awareness on counterfeits; offer incentives to prevent consumers from buying pirated products
INSTITUTIONAL ENVIRONMENT				
e.g., Distribution and communications infrastructure poor in emerging markets	Modify product form (e.g., shelf-stable milk where refrigeration is not developed) Improve packaging (protects products from in-store damage)	Control over prices and gray markets may be more difficult	Channels may need to be developed, resellers trained, and company-owned distribution set up	Quality of advertising may vary. Media schedules difficult to monitor. Sampling frames for direct mail promotions not easily available
ORGANIZATIONAL ENVIRONMENT				
e.g., Multinational structure with substantial decision autonomy to country managers	Product form, brand names, brand identities will vary across markets	Prices vary across markets depending on local objectives and competitive situation	Channels used in various markets differ; price and margin variations result in transshipments and loss of control	No central advertising agency is used. Message content varies. Media spillovers likely. Inefficient use of marketing resources

Variations in Regulations and Standards

When market regulations or standards are not all equivalent, marketers may adjust their products and programs to the lowest common denominator. This issue provides a moral dilemma for marketers of many product types, especially those with health and safety ramifications. Senator Gaylord Nelson summarized the issue well in 1967 U.S. Senate Subcommittee Hearings on the marketing of the drug Chloromycetin. Clinical use had established that this drug was effective in the treatment of a wide variety of bacterial and viral infections. Nelson expressed concern about the absence of warnings in Parke Davis's international advertising. Parke Davis's director of quality control responded that corporate advertisements met the standards required in each country. Nelson countered that he assumed that at minimum such requirements would be met, but that Parke Davis should also consider the "serious moral question involved that ought to be brought up," which was the fact that "in countries where the people do not know any better, where the country is not protected by laws . . . [Parke Davis] would have no compunction about running an ad that will fool a doctor." Drug companies were not marketing to the standard of safety or the "proper standard," and, he said, should therefore be indicted on "moral grounds."[79]

Bribery

The Foreign Corrupt Practices Act (FCPA) of 1977 followed in the wake of the Watergate affair when the U.S. attorney general's office revealed payments by large U.S. companies to foreign politicians. Using a very broad definition of bribery, the FCPA, the only legislation of its kind in the world, makes it illegal for U.S. companies to make payments to individuals or political groups abroad, and requires companies to institute internal controls. It excludes small facilitating payments and tips to civil servants to expedite administrative formalities. Because bribery practices and ethical attitudes toward bribery in international business transactions are not uniform in all countries, and not even in all developed countries, some researchers have argued that the FCPA is detrimental to U.S. firms abroad.[80] Others argue, however, that the FCPA has not had a negative impact on U.S. businesses abroad.[81]

The Organization for Economic Cooperation and Development (OECD), recognizing that differences in bribery-related legislation is an international businessperson's dilemma, has recently developed a code for international conduct. Managers must recognize, however, that norms for appropriate behavior vis-à-vis bribery are largely culture-specific and implicit. In addition to the long hand of the U.S. law, corporations may standardize practices by developing codes on the types of international payments and gift-giving that are acceptable.

Organizational and Human Issues

The "not invented here" syndrome—internal resistance in company subsidiaries and affiliates to ideas and programs originating elsewhere—hampers an organization's ability to standardize marketing programs and processes. Marketing managers in many countries may be accustomed to autonomy in decision making and resist the introduction of product and communications ideas from other markets into their own. In its attempt to launch a global brand campaign in mid-1995, Sun Corporation found that its subsidiary in the United Kingdom was reluctant to adopt the campaign. U.K. corporate communications managers preferred to continue with the campaign they were already using, developed recently in association with their local advertising agency. These managers felt that the advertising they had developed locally reflected a positioning platform that was more appropriate for the U.K. market. In addition, they were satisfied with their relationship with their ad agency, and were reluctant to switch to a headquarters-mandated agency.[82]

Standardization or Adaptation Revisited: A Framework for Managers

Figure 15.4 suggests that marketing is generally the least standardized of all business functions. Managers may find it useful to think of the nature of a marketing decision as either strategic (what to do, or program design) or tactical (how to do it, or program implementation). More benefits accrue to standardizing strategic decisions—those that affect the performance of the company as a whole—than implementation decisions. In fact, providing local managers with autonomy in implementation may be one way of ensuring that marketing programs are flexible enough to respond to emerging local needs.

Lego, the Danish children's toy company that attempts to standardize their marketing approach worldwide on the premise that kids are alike everywhere, struggled in the U.S. market in the face of look-alike, lower-priced competitors such as Tyco. Its U.S. managers requested permission to package their toys in buckets, which parents seemingly preferred because toys could be put away easily after each use. Managers at Lego headquarters in Billund, Denmark, rejected this request, however, on the grounds that the bucket would cheapen Lego's reputation, give it a "me-too" appearance, and was a deviation from Lego's standardized approach. Two years later, when Lego managers recognized that strategy implementation needed to be flexible to meet local market challenges, Lego was finally able to grow market share in the United States. The bucket idea proved so successful in the United States that it was subsequently adopted worldwide—also with great success—during the Christmas season in 1988.[83]

Figure 15.4 also suggests that some elements of the marketing program, such as product design, may be better standardized than others, such as sales promotion. Lego found that their U.S.-style promotional giveaways, such as bonus packs and gifts, were viewed by Japanese mothers as unappealing, expensive, and wasteful. Similar reactions were found in several other toy markets. Marketers

FIGURE 15.4	GLOBAL MARKETING PLANNING MATRIX

Adapted from John A. Quelch and Edward J. Hoff, "Customizing Global Marketing," Harvard Business Review, *May–June 1986.*

Increasing Adaptation   **Increasing Standardization**

←——————————————————————→

BUSINESS FUNCTIONS

Marketing   Purchasing   Finance & Accounting   Research & Development   Manufacturing

ELEMENTS OF MARKETING MIX

Nature of Marketing Decision

Implementation   Strategic

Marketing Element

Customer Service   Distribution   Packaging   Product Positioning   Product Design

Sales Promotion   Advertising Copy   Advertising Themes   Branding

MARKET SEGMENTS

Unique (e.g., high cultural grounding)   Very Similar (e.g., low cultural grounding)

often find benefits in unifying their image by centralizing their corporate image, branding, and positioning. Thus, Gillette uses an umbrella positioning statement worldwide—"Gillette: The Best a Man Can Buy." Similarly, British Airways has used "The World's Favorite Airline" to unify all its advertising worldwide since 1983 when it first adopted a single, global-concept campaign to improve its corporate image. British Airways' local managers were responsible for decisions on the media weights, frequency, and exposure of the four-concept campaign executions, and for the content of local, tactical advertising, thereby giving them some decision-making autonomy and encouraging support for the global, corporate image campaign.

Finally, certain types of market segments or product categories are more culture-bound and thus need more adaptation than others. Products whose purchase and consumption have deep cultural associations, such as food and drink, are much more culture-bound than, for example, computers.[84]

As they decide which marketing elements are best standardized, managers need to consider three issues: (1) the basis for customer decisions, (2) marketing's role in the firm's overall strategy, and (3) the possibility of mass customization. In addition, they need to identify whether the decisions pertain to marketing programs (i.e., product, communications, pricing, and distribution issues) or marketing processes (decisions on various aspects of marketing strategy). Decisions on marketing program standardization or adaptation may be compared to the somewhat similar decisions on marketing process centralization or decentralization. We discuss the former in this section; decisions on marketing processes are discussed in the next section on organizing for international marketing.

Customer Decision Making

As pointed out earlier in this chapter, international segmentation helps firms identify homogeneous groups of customers for whom they can design and implement uniform marketing approaches. To ensure that they properly adapt marketing programs, marketers should clearly understand, in consumer behavior terms, why they define their markets as they do. In other words, they need to know what factors influence customer decision making, and which of these factors are most critical in determining similarities and differences between customers.

Even after they have determined segments and designed standardized programs for similar segments, idiosyncratic aspects of customer behavior in particular segments might require a certain amount of adaptation either in elements of the marketing program or in program implementation. For example:

- An advertising campaign designed for worldwide use might have to be translated into many local languages or need to be modified to avoid embarrassments. Parker Pen Company, in taking its "Avoid Embarrassment—Use Parker Pens" slogan into Latin America, discovered that one connotation of embarrassment in Spanish was pregnancy, and that they were unwittingly promoting their pens as contraceptives.

- Product names may have to be changed so that consumers understand what they are buying. McDonald's renamed the Quarter Pounder as Royal Cheese in Europe, where the metric system is used.

- Global companies such as IKEA and The Body Shop have to quote prices in local currencies, which requires adaptations, albeit minor, to promotional materials.

- Smaller and simpler packaging might have to be used in developing countries, where income levels do not permit large purchases. Procter & Gamble sells smaller shampoo packages in China, including single-use packages that would be sold as samples in the United States.

- Usage instructions might have to be communicated pictorially, or by using personal media such as itinerant missionary salespeople where literacy levels are low. In many countries, Ciba-Geigy, a pharmaceutical company, uses pictures to explain how its antimalarial drug should be taken.

- International marketers might have to modify their distribution strategies because of established relationships among existing channel members and between these channels and customers. Manufacturers of a variety of consumer products may find that the only way to enter Japanese distribution systems is to gradually build relationships with channels.

- Advertisements designed for the Japanese markets always include reference to the company name in addition to the brand advertised. Because Japanese customers do business with a company, it is important to reinforce the company name even in mass communications.

Product-country Images. One aspect of customer decision making that influences marketers' decisions to adapt their approaches is the way in which customers use product-country images.[85] Product-country images include country-of-origin cues such as "Made in" labels, origins embedded in brand or company names (Kentucky Fried Chicken, Singapore Airlines), brand names that indirectly convey origins (Toyota, Lamborghini), and historical associations such as French perfume, Chinese silk, or English tea.

When customers from particular markets use such images as signals of product quality, marketers may benefit from creating and promoting product-country images in their logos, advertising, branding, and packaging. Examples include use of positive stereotypes in Canadian beer advertising "Lowenbrau: Tastefully Engineered in Germany," which capitalizes on customer perceptions that German-engineered products are superior, and Credit Suisse's "Incredibly Swiss, Incredibly International" slogan, which capitalizes on the Swiss banking industry's stellar reputation.

Negative product-company images among consumers create a challenge for companies as they enter international markets. Kia, the Korean automobile manufacturer, found in U.S. focus groups that Korean cars were perceived as low quality. Its entry strategy included humorous comparative advertising that deliberately associated the Kia with Honda (a Kia follows a Honda around on a long drive through varied and tough terrain), in order to capitalize on the high-quality image of the "Japanese" car. Kia's objective in using the direct visual comparison and product testing was to turn attention away from the negative image of Korean products and to eventually change this image.

In a world where products are becoming increasingly global, with components and labor inputs from around the world, marketers must understand how individuals use information on product-country images. Some experts, including Kenichi Ohmae, argue that product-country images are increasingly unimportant: "At the cash register, you don't care about country-of-origin or country-of-residence. . . . You don't worry about where the product was made. . . . All you care about is the product quality, price, design, value, and appeal to you as a consumer."[86] However, the reality is that, although many consumers may buy for the reasons Ohmae states, it is not because they are unaware of product-country images. In fact, consumers and industrial buyers use product-country images as they create, reinforce, and change their product perceptions, even though the cues they use may not always accurately reflect the product's origins. Thus, in addition to functioning as signals of quality, product-country images may enhance user status. For example, Chongqing Automotive Engine Plant (CQAEP), a licensee of Cummins Engine in the United States, refers to the products it manufactures in China's Schezwan province as "Cummins engines." Buyers therefore associate CQAEP products with the Cummins reputation of "American high quality."[87] In countries with histories of import restrictions, customers are often willing to pay huge premiums for imported products because they are perceived as high quality or because they enhance their buyers' status.

Marketers incorporate regionalization and globalization in building their product-country images: regional and global cues also convey a panregional base of expertise or a "world" origin (e.g., Eurocar, United Colors of Benetton). Because increasingly products are built from components from multiple parts of the world, and may even be assembled in multiple locations, it is quite complicated to concisely describe a product's origins. Marketers may turn such complexity to their advantage by emphasizing the particular product-country image that particular customer segments value most. Automobile manufacturers use different slogans to reflect this. Volkswagen's Jetta is "German-engineered," and Honda and Toyota play up the "Americanness" of their brands in advertisements specifying where the automobiles are made and U.S.-made components.

Marketing's Role in the Firm

The marketing function can facilitate economies in other functional areas,[88] such as design and production, in three ways:

- *Providing information:* Market research can provide information that some companies may use for designing universal products or creating products made of standardized modules, which may be assembled differently and efficiently to cater to the needs of different markets.

- *Demand creation:* Marketing can go a step further, and actually create demand for universal products through advertising.

- *Segmentation:* Taking advantage of homogenization across countries, and segments within countries, marketing may position identical products differently or use customer service to differentiate products in different markets, so that "upstream" processes such as design, purchasing, and manufacturing can become more standardized and cost efficient.

Mass Customization

Technological advances allow manufacturers to tailor products and advertisements for various market segments without incurring huge additional costs. Mass customization[89] possibilities might eventually narrow the savings gap that standardization strategies have over adaptation strategies.

Finally, standardization or adaptation decisions should not be static, but should evolve with a company's markets and strategies. Thus, in the early stages of developing their operations in Japan, Kentucky Fried Chicken's (KFC) Japanese joint venture had almost complete autonomy (decentralized marketing process, which we discuss below), and was able to make the adaptations to their stores, menu, recipes, customer service, and business protocols necessary for success in Japan. As KFC's international operations—particularly their stores in Asia—grew, however, the corporation had to reevaluate the appropriateness of the adaptations, what they meant for KFC's global image, and how differences across markets would be addressed.

ORGANIZING FOR INTERNATIONAL MARKETING

In strategy, it is important to see distant things as if they were close and to take a distanced view of close things.

–Miyamoto Musashi, *The Book of Five Rings*

Globalization is not about standardization but about a quantum increase in complexity. Turning the organization inside out ... the periphery has to come to the center.

–Gruppo GFT, Harvard Business Review 1991

Organizing and planning for international marketing[90] is crucial for success. Companies use three main organizational approaches—export departments, international divisions, and global organizations—to serve international markets, reflecting greater levels of international market participation. Of course, these three forms of international organization often coexist in large international companies.

Export Department

In the early stages of internationalization, companies create export departments, sometimes under the leadership of a sales manager, organized mainly as a support function to handle the paperwork associated with international financing, shipping, and payment collections that normally accompanies exports. At this stage, marketing decisions are generally made at the company headquarters, perhaps with some inputs from overseas agents, distributors, and customers.

International Division

As international sales volume grows, companies may justify creating national sales or manufacturing subsidiaries and international divisions to oversee the company's international activities. At this stage, marketing decisions are likely to be decentralized, with individual subsidiaries operating autonomously. Many U.S. and European multinational companies—such as Procter & Gamble, Unilever, and Nestlé—have historically been organized as "flag planters,"[91] or "decentralized federations"[92] of fairly independent national subsidiaries.

At headquarters, the international division is generally staffed by personnel in planning, product research and design, manufacturing, marketing, human resources, and finance, who provide support services to the various international organizations. These international organizations may themselves be organized so that the primary lines of responsibility are drawn by geography or by product or product group. Alternatively, firms may use a matrix organization—a combination of geographic and product grouping with dual lines of responsibility—that attempts to be sensitive to both global product and local adaptation needs. Companies with geographic organizations typically have regional vice-presidents who oversee the countries' operations in their regions, and have several country managers reporting to them. The regional vice-presidents report to the head of the international division. Product organizations may have vice-presidents responsible for the worldwide sales of each product or product group.

Geographic organizations may suffer from excessive decentralization and insufficient coordination of product strategy across countries and regions. On the other hand, product organizations, while championing product policy across the world and developing centralized product expertise, may underrepresent the viewpoints of individual international markets. Worse, they may lack customer or account management capabilities, which can be a serious limitation for business marketers. Large international customers are forced to deal with several product groups, rather than having a single point of contact with the company.

Citibank's corporate business group struggled with these issues in the 1980s. Many of Citibank's large corporate customers had multicountry organizations and global financial services needs. Yet, Citibank's organizational structure and processes did little to encourage its country managers to pay attention to markets other than their own, or to the international product needs of their clients. Often, one group at the bank had no knowledge of what the other was doing for a particular customer. Citibank's solution was one that many companies have attempted, a matrix organization, as described earlier. Citibank created the World Corporation Group to serve the needs of its largest international customers, and developed a global account management system to measure the profitability of global accounts. This organizational structure, the accompanying reporting system, and associated incentives, such as highly visible dinners with Citibank's chairman and bonuses for global account profitability, encouraged country managers to think in terms of the best way the bank could serve their global clients.

Global Organization

As a company's operations become global, managers must ensure that autonomous, local operations are successfully coordinated with each other and integrated with overall corporate and marketing strategy. The key issues at this stage involve how much autonomy subsidiaries should have; how much influence product, country, regional, and headquarters managers should have over various marketing decisions; and how coordination should be achieved. At one extreme, companies with a *global strategy* treat the world as a single market and standardize their marketing approach; this strategy is particularly useful in industries that are capital intensive and have homogeneous demand, such as consumer electronics. At the other extreme, companies using a *nationally responsive* or *multinational strategy* need to provide sufficient local autonomy to deal with local standards and preferences. Finally, companies with a *"glocal"* strategy standardize core strategy elements while adapting others.

Thus, for global companies, the management of marketing processes is critical, especially decisions on the configuration and coordination of marketing activities worldwide.[93]

Configuration and Coordination of Marketing Activities

The key configuration issues managers face include:

- To what extent marketing decisions should be geographically concentrated or dispersed, that is, centralized or decentralized.
- If centralized, where to centralize the decision—corporate or regional headquarters.
- If centralized, how to ensure sensitivity to local environments in their marketing negotiations, and in the design and implementation of marketing programs.

Companies such as Nestlé and Allergan use central branding, advertising, and packaging directives, as well as global brand books and center-sponsored local and cross-national research to centralize key elements of their international strategy. They provide product and local managers with guidelines on the overall positioning and "look and feel" of the marketing campaign. Headquarters may increase sensitivity to local environments by inviting local managers into headquarters to involve them in the process of creating these materials, as well as using a multiregion, lead country approach for implementing various central initiatives.

When marketing decisions are decentralized, the key coordination issues marketing managers face are:

- Should the company coordinate marketing across markets, or let each market be autonomous?

- How can the company balance bottom-up approaches that benefit from local marketing information with the coordination across markets necessary for efficient operation?

- What organizational structures and processes are best suited to transferring marketing programs to new markets?

- How can the firm integrate international marketing activities with the other functional areas of the company?

Marketing managers must coordinate their decisions and programs to avoid a plethora of brands and inconsistent brand identities. At the same time, the firm needs to maintain creativity at the local level so that national subsidiaries develop new product and communications ideas. Coordination can be a Herculean challenge because local managers, especially in large markets, are likely to fight to protect their turf. Further, faulty implementation of any aspect of global strategy can lead to a "not-invented-here" syndrome and rejection of central directives. Market research, broad vision, flexible implementation, and systematic follow-up are therefore essential for successful worldwide program implementation.

Companies who wish to coordinate their operations worldwide while maintaining sensitivity to local markets might look to the experience of successful global corporations such as Matsushita, Philips, Whirlpool, Unilever, and Ericsson. These companies use a variety of approaches to achieve these dual objectives:

- designing-in subsidiary involvement in management processes
- explicitly linking product development to market needs
- people-integrating mechanisms such as transfers, temporary assignments, and teams such as multicountry and multiregion brand teams to launch new brands
- creating interdependence among various units
- creating strong corporate identification

For example, Whirlpool developed a series of real-world projects called "One-Company Challenges" using cross-cultural teams who were empowered to create processes for global product-strategy reviews and product-creation. The company used these challenges to encourage employees at various levels and locations to think globally.[94]

In sum, "the adoption of a global perspective should not [therefore] be viewed as synonymous with a strategy of global products and global brands. . . . *In essence*, a global perspective implies planning strategy relative to markets world-wide."[95] Further, "the *processes* underlying the way international marketing decisions are conceptualized, refined, internally communicated, and, finally, implemented in the company's international network have a great deal to do with their performance."[96]

SUMMARY

International marketers are challenged by the simultaneous emergence of global markets and the pervasiveness of cultural variables. As markets become global, there is a push for standardizing marketing programs and centralizing marketing decision making. Marketing managers must understand the various aspects of culture, including the self-reference criterion, and the vastly different cultures of people in different markets.

There are many benefits to be reaped from international marketing, including enhanced competitiveness, learning, diversified sales, and market leadership. These benefits are also key motivators for entering international markets. In selecting which markets to enter, managers must make sure that target markets are consistent with their international marketing objectives. Market selection decisions may be guided by heuristics or a formal, hierarchical screening process.

Research plays a key role in market selection decisions, marketing program decisions, and in creating buy-in for these programs in various markets, that is in marketing process. To be useful, international research needs to address a variety of measurement issues including data availability, equivalence, and biases. In addition, it needs to be multisite and, to ensure comparability across countries, uniform in method.

Segmentation allows marketers to group markets logically to gain benefits of using a uniform approach for each market segment, as well as understanding when it is appropriate to transfer an approach that is successful in one market to another.

- Traditional international market segmentation is based on country differences
- Intermarket segmentation attempts to discover segments that transcend country borders, using attitudinal, lifestyle, and behavioral consumer data.

The internationalization process is usually characterized by incremental steps, with each step representing greater commitment to international markets into increasingly dissimilar markets. By internationalizing gradually, managers reduce the risks of international marketing while gaining familiarity with international marketing processes. The pattern of international market entry includes decisions on:

- the number of markets to enter
- the pace of entry
- the sequence in which to enter large, mature, or small growing markets
- the mode of entry into individual markets.

These managerial decisions are affected by the objectives of the firm, structure of competition in the target markets, and increasing levels of risk, control and commitment.

Once a market is selected, decisions must be made on the marketing mix that will be used. For the international firm, there are many benefits of standardizing the marketing mix, in particular, consistency with customers, similarity in customer preferences, cost savings, getting extra mileage out of good ideas, and enhanced control. However, market characteristics, industry conditions, legal restrictions, and the existence of marketing institutions all limit the feasibility of standardizing product, pricing, distribution, salesforce management, and promotions. Marketing managers must also be sensitive to the moral and ethical issues implicit in their marketing-mix decisions, especially because customer and competitor behavior in different international markets is governed by their own cultures and legal systems.

Customer decision making, including the use of country-of-origin cues, marketing's role in the firm, and the technological possibility of mass customization, offer marketers direction in the extent of standardization desirable and feasible in their marketing programs. Managers may also improve flexibility, control, and responsiveness to local markets by:

- standardizing strategic elements while localizing implementation
- standardizing core marketing mix elements while localizing less important elements of the mix
- standardizing marketing for product categories that require global integration while permitting greater flexibility in others where tastes are more culture-bound and national responsiveness is therefore important

The marketing organization and processes must evolve to reflect companies' international market participation. A firm may have an export department, international division, or move to a global organization in which international marketing is integrated into the firm's operations rather than managed separately. For global organizations, key managerial process issues include the configuration and coordination of various marketing elements to ensure that the firm balances its standardization and control needs with local market responsiveness needs so that creativity and participation of managers worldwide are encouraged.

QUESTIONS FOR DISCUSSION

1. Some argue that the globalization of markets is resulting in a convergence of preferences, and that therefore companies should use standardized marketing approaches worldwide. Identify the merits and pitfalls of such an argument.

2. As marketing manager of a small company selling a range of organic algae-based nutritional supplements (vitamins), you are tasked with identifying new markets. When you suggest expanding overseas, the CEO disagrees vehemently, pointing out that the company is small and resource constrained, and the risks of international marketing are too great. Defend your viewpoint, and present a systematic international market entry approach that quells the CEO's concerns about risk.

3. The German headquarters of an international company faces strong resistance from its country managers in Thailand, its regional headquarters for the Asia-Pacific, on the launch of a new corporate-image advertising campaign. Thai managers feel that their current advertising emphasizes product benefits sought by local customers and is effective. Why is securing Thai support advisable? How might Germany secure Thai support?

4. What factors would you consider in selecting the mode of entry for an international market? In your view, what are the key issues involved?

5. A major multinational corporation plans to launch a new product in its three most important markets simultaneously. To save time, they request the regional vice-presidents of each market to conduct market research on the potential for the product. As a strategic marketing consultant brought on board to oversee the launch, what advice do you have for the company? In particular, what guidelines might you issue to the regional vice-presidents?

6. What are the pros and cons of a global branding strategy? When might such a strategy be most effective?

7. Nestlé failed to conduct market research on the developing-country markets before launching its infant formula in these markets. What can other companies learn from Nestlé's experience?

8. In the 1980s, there was a dramatic increase in the number of U.S. consumers who wanted to "Buy American." How might international marketers who were exporting their products to the United States compete with their U.S. counterparts?

9. In what ways do buyers use product-country images? What is the implication for marketers?

10. Why do marketers need to coordinate their marketing decisions across international markets? What are the benefits? challenges?

NOTES FOR FURTHER READING

1. The notion that technology determines the structure of society, transforms the environment, redefines industries and markets is found in Marshall McLuhan, *Understanding Media: The Extensions of Man* (New York: McGraw-Hill, 1964); Rosabeth Moss Kanter, "Thinking across Boundaries," *Harvard Business Review*, November–December 1990, pp. 9–10; and Theodore Levitt, "The Globalization of Markets," *Harvard Business Review*, May–June 1983.

2. Kenichi Ohmae, "Managing in a Borderless World," *Harvard Business Review,* May–June 1989.

3. This term is attributable to Levitt, "The Globalization of Markets." Much of this section is based on Jean-Claude Usunier, *International Marketing: A Cultural Approach* (Hertfordshire, London: Prentice-Hall International [UK] Ltd., 1993).

4. Procter & Gamble general manager Vizir Launch, quoted in Harvard Business School case 9-384-139, 1983.

5. Daniel J. Boorstin, quoted in Levitt, "The Globalization of Markets."

6. For the debate, see Levitt, "The Globalization of Markets"; and Michael E. Porter, "The Strategic Role of International Marketing," *Journal of Consumer Marketing* 3, 2 (Spring 1986). See also Ohmae, "Managing in a Borderless World," on the crucial role of adaptation—what he calls "insiderization"—for success in individual markets.

7. "Coke Pours into Asia," *Business Week*, October 28, 1996, pp. 72–76.

8. J.J. Boddewyn, Robin Soehl, and Jacques Picard, "Standardization in International Marketing: Is Ted Levitt in Fact Right?" *Business Horizons*, November/December 1986, pp. 69–75.

9. Susan P. Douglas and Yoram Wind, "The Myth of Globalization," *Columbia Journal of World Business* (Winter 1987): 19–29.

10. Geert Hofstede, *Cultures and Organizations: Software of the Mind* (London: McGraw-Hill, 1991).

11. James E. Lee, "Cultural Analysis in Overseas Operations," *Harvard Business Review*, March–April 1966, pp. 106–114.

12. *Mary Kay Cosmetics: Asian Market Entry*, Harvard Business School case 594-023, 1993.

13. Edward T. Hall, *Beyond Culture* (New York: Bantam Books, 1981).

14. John L. Graham and Roy A. Herberger Jr., "Negotiators Abroad—Don't Shoot from the Hip," *Harvard Business Review*, July–August 1983, pp. 160–168.

15. Hofstede, *Cultures and Organizations*.

16. Richard Mead, "Where Is the Culture of Thailand?" *International Journal of Research in Marketing* 11 (1994): 401–404.

17. Quoted in "The G Factor," *Inc.*, January 1992, p. 68.

18. The following discussions are based in part on "The G Factor," pp. 68–73.

19. "The Japanese Are Tough Customers," *New York Times*, January 29, 1978.

20. Based on a case by Jean Claude Usunier, *Lestra Design in International Marketing: A Cultural Approach*, (Hertfordshire, London: Prentice-Hall International [UK] Ltd., 1993 pp. 233–242).

21. Based on the author's study of international concept research and correspondence between the lead agency—J. Walter Thompson, San Francisco—and the Dubai and Kuala Lumpur offices, 1995.

22. Peter F. Drucker, "The Transitional Economy," *Wall Street Journal*, August 25, 1987, p. 26.

23. Based on "Al-Kabeer International Expansion," a case based on field research by the author.

24. Gary Hamel and C. K. Prahalad, "Do You Really Have a Global Strategy?" *Harvard Business Review*, July–August 1985, pp. 139–148.

25. Based on "Al-Kabeer International Expansion," a case based on field research by the author.

26. William H. Davidson, "Market Similarity and Market Selection: Implications for International Market Strategy," *Journal of Business Research*, 11 (1983): 446.

27. Based on Colgate-Palmolive: Cleopatra, IMD Case, Laussane, Switzerland, 1988-89.

28. Based on "Al-Kabeer International Expansion," a case based on field research by the author.

29. Susan P. Douglas and C. Samuel Craig, *International Marketing Research* (Upper Saddle River, N.J.: Prentice-Hall, 1983).

30. For details on types of research for various marketing program decisions, see ibid.

31. Kamran Kashani, "Beware the Pitfalls of Global Marketing," *Harvard Business Review*, September–October 1989.

32. Based on "The Advertising Fact Book," *Advertising Age*, January 2, 1995.

33. The discussion on cross-national research issues is based on Douglas and Craig, *International Marketing Research*; Marieke de Mooij, *Advertising Worldwide*, 2nd ed. (Hertfordshire, London: Prentice-Hall International [UK] Ltd., 1994), chapter 10; Philip M. Rosenzweig, "When Can Management Science Be Generalized Internationally?" *Management Science* 40, 1 (1994): 28–39; and Usunier, *International Marketing*, chapter 5.

34. M. Richins and B. Verhage, "Cross-Cultural Differences in Consumer Attitudes and Their Implications for Complaining Behavior," *International Journal of Research in Marketing* 2 (1985): 197–205.

35. Shuzo Abe, Richard P. Bagozzi, and Pradip Sadarangani, "An Investigation of Construct Validity and Generalizablity of the Self-concept: Self-consciousness in Japan and the United States," *Journal of International Consumer Marketing*, vol. 8 (1996): 97–123.

36. Saeed Samiee and Insik Jeong, "Cross-Cultural Research in Advertising: An Assessment of Methodologies," *Journal of the Academy of Marketing Science* 22, 3 (1994): 205–217.

37. Ravi Parameswaran and Attila Yaprak, "A Cross-National Comparison of Consumer Research Measures," *Journal of International Business Studies* (Spring 1987): 35–49.

38. J. Johansson and Ikujiro Nonaka, "Market Research the Japanese Way," *Harvard Business Review*, May–June 1987, pp. 16–22.

39. Earl Naumann, Donald W. Jackson Jr., and William G. Wolfe, "Examining the Practices of United States and Japanese Market Research Firms," *California Management Review*, Summer 1994, pp. 49–69.

40. J. Johansson and Ikujiro Nonaka, *Relentless: The Japanese Way of Marketing* (New York: Harper Business, 1996).

41. Jean-Philippe Deschamps and P. Ranganath Nayak, *Product Juggernauts* (Cambridge, Mass.: Harvard Business School Press, 1995), chapter 5.

42. S. P. Sethi, "Comparative Cluster Analysis for World Markets," *Journal of Marketing Research* 8 (August 1971): 348–354.

43. Another study in the same vein uses demographic data to arrive at five groups of countries. See T. Cavusgil, "A Market-Oriented Clustering of Countries," in Hans Thorelli and S. Tamer Cavusgil, eds., *International Marketing Strategy*, 3rd ed. (Oxford: Pergamon, 1990), pp. 201–211.

44. Kenichi Ohmae, *Triad Power* (New York: Free Press, 1985).

45. Andrew Hilton, "Mythology, Myths, and the Emerging Europe," *Harvard Business Review*, November–December 1992, pp. 50–54.

46. Jedidi Helsen and Wayne DeSarbo, "A New Approach to Country Segmentation Utilizing Multinational Diffusion Patterns," *Journal of Marketing* (October 1993): 60–71.

47. Much of this section is based on Salah S. Hassan and Roger D. Blackwell, eds., *Global Marketing: Perspectives and Cases* (Orlando, Fla.: Dryden, 1994), pp. 53–75 (Salah S. Hassan and Roger D. Blackwell, "Competitive Global Market Segmentation"), and pp. 76–100 (Salah S. Hassan and A. Cosku Samli, "The New Frontiers of Intermarket Segmentation").

48. Hassan and Blackwell, *Global Marketing: Perspectives and Cases*.

49. Consider the growth of multinational banks, advertising agencies, and law firms, many of whom followed their customers into new markets.

50. This theory was developed based on the experience of Swedish firms; see J. Johanson and J. E. Vahlne, "The Internationalization Process of the Firm—A Model of Knowledge Development and Increasing Foreign Commitments," *Journal of International Business Studies* 8, 1 (1977): 23–32; and J. Johanson and F. Wiedersheim-Paul, "The Internationalization of the Firm: Four Swedish Case Studies," *Journal of Management Studies* (October 1975): 305–322. Despite increasing homogeneity and the decreasing explanatory importance of psychic distance, the model has been supported in other contexts; see T. S. Cavusgil, W. J. Bilkey, and G. Tesar, "A Note on the Export Behavior of Firms: Exporter Profiles," *Journal of International Business Studies* 10, 1 (1979): 91–97; T. S. Cavusgil, "On the Internationalization Process of Firms," *European Research* 8 (November 1980): 273–281.

51. Franklin R. Root, *Entry Strategies for International Markets* (Lexington, Mass.: Lexington Books, 1994).

52. From Regina Fazio Maruca, "The Right Way to Go Global: An Interview with Whirlpool CEO David Whitwam," *Harvard Business Review*, March–April 1994, pp. 135–145.

53. Philip R. Cateora, *International Marketing* (Homewood, Ill.: Irwin, 1996); Yoram Wind, Susan P. Douglas, and Howard V. Perlmutter, "Guidelines for Developing International Marketing Strategy," *Journal of Marketing* (April 1973): 14–23.

54. This discussion is based on Igal Ayal and Jehiel Zif, "Market Expansion Strategies in Multinational Marketing," *Journal of Marketing Research* 43, 2 (Spring 1979).

55. Aneel Karnani and Jacob de Smit, "Tatra Koprivnice: Think Off-Road, Think Tatra," University of Michigan Case, 1993.

56. "Citibank: Launching the Credit Card in Asia Pacific (A)," Harvard Business School case 595-026, 1995.

57. See Gary E. Willard and Arun M. Savara, "Patterns of Entry: Pathways to New Markets," *California Management Review* 30 (Winter 1988): 57–76, for fascinating descriptive accounts; and Somkid Jatusripitak, Liam Fahey, and Philip Kotler, "Strategic Global Marketing: Lessons from the Japanese," *Columbia Journal of World Business* 20, 1 (Spring 1985): 47–53.

58. This approach to international market entry has been dubbed the "silent war" by Ira Magaziner and Mark Patinkin, *The Silent War* (New York: Vintage Books, 1990). Willard and Savara, "Patterns of Entry," also discuss it, quoting from Miyamoto Musashi, *A Book of Five Rings:* "It is beneficial to strike at the corners of the enemy's force. If the corners are overthrown, the spirit of the whole body will be overthrown. To defeat the enemy, you must follow-up the attack where the corners have fallen." The Japanese companies view underserved market segments as the "corners" that provide them with their windows of market opportunity. This strategy has the added advantage that incumbents might mistakenly dismiss the entrants as temporary solutions to short-term market conditions. For example, U.S. auto manufacturers may have been slow to react to the threat from small Japanese cars because they believed that small car demand would be short-lived like the fuel crisis of the early 1970s.

59. See Magaziner and Patinkin, *The Silent War,* on Samsung.

60. Much of our discussion on modes of entry is based on Root, *Entry Strategies for International Markets.*

61. See Erin Anderson and Anne T. Coughlan "International Market Entry and Expansion via Independent or Integrated Channels of Distribution," *Journal of Marketing* (January 1987), p. 7; Saul Klein, Gary L. Frazier, and Victor J. Roth, "A Transaction Cost Analysis Model of Channel Integration in International Markets," *Journal of Marketing* (May 1990), pp. 196–208.

62. Our discussion on the indirect or direct export decision also applies to the decision to use a company-owned channel or an independent distributor within the target country.

63. Janeen E. Olsen and Kent L. Granzin, "Vertical Integration and Economic Development: An Empirical Investigation of Channel Integration," *Journal of Global Marketing* 7, 3 (1994): 7–39.

64. Usunier, Lestra Design in International Marketing.

65. Bert Rosenbloom, "Motivating Your International Channel Partners," *Business Horizons,* March–April 1990, pp. 53–57.

66. For descriptions of the spread of U.S. franchising systems worldwide, see Donald W. Hackett, "The International Expansion of U.S. Franchise Systems: Status and Strategies," *Journal of International Business Studies* (Spring 1976); and Bruce Walker and Michael J. Etzel, "The Internationalization of U.S. Franchise Systems: Progress and Procedures," *Journal of Marketing* (April 1973).

67. "Coke Pours into Asia," *Business India,* November 8–21, 1993, p. 21.

68. Much of this section is based on Robert D. Buzzell, "Can You Standardize Multinational Marketing?" *Harvard Business Review,* November–December 1968.

69. Levitt, "The Globalization of Markets."

70. "Ford: Alex Trotman's Daring Global Strategy," *Business Week,* April 3, 1995, pp. 94–104.

71. From discussions with the Chevron account manager and director at Chevron's corporate advertising agency, J. Walter Thompson, in San Francisco, August 1995.

72. Niraj Dawar and Philip Parker, "Marketing Universals: Consumers' Use of Brand Name, Price, Physical Appearance, and Retailer Reputation as Signals of Product Quality," *Journal of Marketing* 58 (April 1994): 81–95. This study examines the use of brand name, price, product appearance, and retailer reputation as signals of quality; the authors suggest that the existence or nonexistence of marketing universals have implications for standardizing or adapting both marketing program and resource allocations across cultures.

73. Arthur C. Fatt, "The Danger of 'Local' International Advertising," *Journal of Marketing* (January 1967), quoted in Buzzell, "Can You Standardize Multinational Marketing?"

74. Levitt, "The Globalization of Markets."

75. "Call it Worldpool," *Business Week,* November 28, 1994, pp. 98–99.

76. Frank V. Cespedes, E. Raymond Corey, and V. Kasturi Rangan, "Gray Markets: Causes and Cures," *Harvard Business Review,* July–August 1988.

77. "Nestlé Alimentana S.A. Abridged," Harvard Business School case 9-590-070, 1990.

78. Rafael D. Pagan Jr., "The Nestlé Boycott: Implications for Strategic Business Planning," *Journal of Business Strategy* 6, 4 (Spring 1986): 13.

79. See "Competitive Problems in the Drug Industry, 1967: Hearings Before the Subcommittee on the Monopoly of the Select Committee on Small Business," 90th Congress, 1st Session, 2178–2179, 2222–2223 (1968). In Deborah L. Rhodes and David Luban, *Legal Ethics* (Westbury, N.Y.: Foundation Press, 1992), pp. 369–373.

80. J. G. Kaikati and W. A. Label, "American Bribery Legislation: An Obstacle to International Marketing," *Journal of Marketing* 44 (Fall 1980): 38–43.

81. Kate Gillespie, "Middle East Response to the US Foreign Corrupt Practices Act," *California Management Review* 29, 4 (1987): 9–30; and John L. Graham, "Foreign Corrupt Practices Act: A Manager's Guide," *Columbia Journal of World Business* 18, 3 (1983).

82. Based on the author's observation of information exchange and negotiations among the members of the various organizations concerned, 1995.

83. Kamran Kashani, "Beware the Pitfalls of Global Marketing," *Harvard Business Review,* September–October 1989.

84. John A. Quelch and Edward J. Hoff, "Customizing Global Marketing," *Harvard Business Review,* May–June 1986.

85. Parts of this section are based on Nicolas Papadopoulos and Louise A. Heslop, eds., *Product-Country Images: Impact and Role in International Marketing* (New York: International Business Press, 1993).

86. Kenichi Ohmae, "The Global Logic of Strategic Alliances," *Harvard Business Review,* March–April 1989, pp. 143–154.

87. Based on the author's involvement with CQAEP during 1995.

88. Parts of this section are based on Michael E. Porter, "The Strategic Role of International Marketing," *Journal of Consumer Marketing* 3, 2 (Spring 1986).

89. Roy Westbrook and Peter Williamson, "Mass Customization," *European Management Journal* 11, 1 (March 1993): 38–45.

90. This section is largely based on Quelch and Hoff, "Customizing Global Marketing"; and Christopher A. Bartlett and Sumantra Ghoshal, "Organizing for Worldwide Effectiveness: The Transnational Solution," *California Management Review* 31, 1 (1988).

91. From Fazio Maruca, "The Right Way to Go Global."

92. Bartlett and Ghoshal, "Organizing for Worldwide Effectiveness."

93. Suggested in Porter, "The Strategic Role of International Marketing."

94. From Fazio Maruca, "The Right Way to Go Global."

95. Douglas and Wind, "The Myth of Globalization." Emphasis added.

96. Kashani, "Beware the Pitfalls of Global Marketing." Emphasis added.

CHAPTER 16

FORMULATING AND IMPLEMENTING THE MARKETING PLAN

CHAPTER OBJECTIVES

When you are done with this chapter, you should have achieved the following:

- An ability to present the elements of marketing planning
- An ability to compare and contrast the various ways in which firms organize their marketing functions
- An understanding of the issues associated with implementing marketing programs

CHAPTER OUTLINE

Xerox: Achieving Customer Satisfaction via Clear Goals and Excellent Implementation

In the 1970s, Xerox found itself losing market share to Japanese copier competition. Having entered at the low end of the market, Canon, Konica, Minolta, Mita, Ricoh, and Sharp now all threatened to take customers from Xerox in every segment, as they offered trade-ins to higher-end machines. Xerox needed a plan to staunch the bleeding and keep its leadership position.

In the early 1980s, the company began by stating that its overall objective was to become the industry leader in all aspects of customer satisfaction. Xerox strategy was implemented comprehensively throughout the organization. Top management provided sustained support and leadership, both in setting overall strategy—customer satisfaction was a higher-order objective than market share or financial goals—and in acting as exemplars in customer interactions. Xerox benchmarked its toughest competitors, as well as the reliability, cost, and service leaders in all industries. It set annual quality goals for each year from 1983 to 1987, and provided quality training to all employees.

Chairman and Chief Executive Officer of Xerox Corporation, David T. Kearns, shakes President Bush's hand after being announced the winner of the Malcolm Baldrige National Quality Award at a November 2 ceremony at the Department of Commerce. The award is given for production of quality goods and services in the United States.

Xerox viewed its product quality program as an integral component of its customer satisfaction program and vice versa—"Leadership Through Quality" principles were used throughout the organization, including marketing. It recognized that product quality could only partly contribute to customer satisfaction, and that every customer interaction was an opportunity to build satisfaction. Decision-making authority was therefore decentralized to the field: three marketing functions—business operations, sales, and service—began to operate as teams to reduce conflicting objectives and provide customers with continuity.

Performance measurement and market research were very important to the successful implementation of Xerox programs. It adapted its recruiting, measurement, and reward systems to shift from a product/internal focus to customer/external focus, and developed a customer satisfaction code of conduct. A tracking system flagged problems, which were promptly given attention. Market research explored and confirmed customer concerns and preferences, and provided the basis for introducing a 100 percent customer-defined performance guarantee.

Xerox's focused strategy and consistent, integrated implementation paid off. The company gained 1 to 1.5 share points each year since the "Leadership Through Quality" strategy was adopted in 1983. Product development cycles were shortened by 30 percent. According to Dataquest, a leading industry analyst, Xerox products in 1989 were the best in five of the six segments in which they competed. Also in 1989, Xerox Business Products and Systems won the Malcolm Baldrige National Quality Award.

Source: Based on "Xerox Corporation: The Customer Satisfaction Program," Harvard Business School case 9-591-055, 1993.

DEVELOPING AN EFFECTIVE MARKETING PLAN

The general who wins a battle makes many calculations in his temple before the battle is fought. The general who loses a battle makes but few calculations beforehand.

Sun Tzu, *The Art of War*

Marketing planning is concerned with setting objectives, designing programs, and specifying the tactics required to implement a chosen marketing strategy.[1] Like other approaches to problem solving, marketing planning begins with *intelligence*, or situation assessment, and moves on to *design* of alternatives, *selecting* the best alternative, and, finally, to *implementing* the selected alternative. In many small, entrepreneurial firms, it is difficult to distinguish between planning and implementation: plans are often "in the leader's head," and planning processes are rarely formal.

The sheer complexity of size in multiproduct, multimarket companies has led to internal segmentation, initially into divisional structures in the 1950s and 1960s, and subsequently into strategic business unit (SBU) structures. Managers in these firms needed *planning systems*—systematic ways to analyze the factors that affect their business, determine the impact of trends on the business, assess the opportunities and threats they face, evaluate their strengths and weaknesses relative to competition, and choose the marketing program they would use to meet their objectives, given their forecasts of future conditions. These systems became important not only as a means by which corporate strategy could be tied to SBU strategy, but also as the means by which senior managers could manage the whole as more than a sum of the parts.[2]

Elements of Marketing Planning: Content

The Scott Paper example (see Marketing Anecdote 16.1) illustrates the benefits of developing a marketing plan. A formal marketing plan document has many added benefits. First, companies may integrate marketing plans into their broader business plans. In doing so, senior managers are able to assess the consistency of efforts across strategic business units, as well as evaluate the performance of these units in relation to their stated objectives and performance goals. Thus, the plan provides the basis for uniform budget allocation, coordination, and control across the corporation. Second, managers can use the plan as an effective communication tool to ensure that everyone in marketing and across the organization understands marketing's objectives, the issues facing marketing, and how marketing plans to deal with them. Further, the marketing plan focuses attention in two ways: all participants in the planning process become knowledgeable about key issues; and it provides a means by which managers can keep sight of their objectives and priorities, despite the day-to-day troubleshooting. Finally, the marketing plan provides the basis for tracking and redefining efforts over the planning horizon.

At the most general level, every marketing plan must deal with three broad questions: Where are we now? Where do we want to go? How do we get there? Although plans can vary substantially in length and format, depending on the industry, type of company, and competitive situation, all plans must address these issues as delineated in the following outline:

I. Where are we now?

    A. Situation analysis: Descriptive statement of factors affecting the business

        1. Internal factors: Assess the firm's resources, capabilities, and skills.

        2. External factors: Assess broader environment, consumers, and competitors.

According to Al Dunlap, who is credited with the turnaround of Scott Paper:

> When you play a sport, you have a game plan. The same is true of winners in business. Call it a strategy, an operating plan, or even a recipe; regardless of the name, it's a roadmap for success based on knowing what you do best versus the competition, and recognizing customer needs. Scott [in April 1994, when Dunlap took over as CEO] had no strategy. Not on an individual brand basis, not on a collective brand basis, not on a global basis. Nicolosi's [senior vice-president of Scott's Worldwide Consumer Products Business] first job was to construct global strategies for the consumer business. Absent that, we might as well have locked the doors and walked away.

Scott completely revamped its marketing approach by introducing a marketing planning process. Marketing in the company was traditionally done by engineers. Employees kept track of the number of tons of paper sold, and attempted to sell at the best price. No one spoke or thought in terms of brands. A situation analysis revealed that these internal factors were a key stumbling block to progress. Further, several external factors were also constraining profitable growth. Scott had a hodgepodge of brand names worldwide—Scotties, Scot Towels, Cottonelle, and Andrex—including 27 in the United States. Worse, the same brand was often of vastly different quality in different parts of the country.

Scott's objective was to grow their branded consumer business profitably. To do this, their strategy, "Scott the World Over," was to build the Scott brand name globally, as well as to establish consistency in product quality and image. As part of this strategy, the company eliminated the 31 percent of their products and redundant stock-keeping units that either did not fit their line or drained their resources, and repackaged 107 products to position and sell better. Scott appointed global advertising and packaging-design houses *before* their strategy was finalized to benefit from simultaneity. Finally, Scott hired key personnel from leading consumer goods companies to create a change from being an industrial paper company to being a consumer-products marketer. They reorganized the marketing function by product category and gave a single person responsibility for performance—profit and loss, sales volume and value, share, margins, inventory, and so on—and for working with colleagues in the Asian and European operations to share learning.

Overall, Scott's coherent planning efforts brought them market share gains, a quality reputation, sales growth of about 25 percent, and tissue margins of 20 percent in under two years. Nineteen months after Dunlap took over the reigns, Scott Paper merged with Kimberly Clark in a stock swap that valued Scott at $9 billion to create the second largest consumer-products company in the United States.

Source: Adapted from Albert J. Dunlap, *Mean Business* (New York: Times Business, 1996), pp. 139–151; extract/quote from p. 141.

B. Opportunity and problem statement
  1. Summarize the situation analysis.
  2. Use judgment to prioritize opportunities in the context of firm's resources.
II. Where do we want to go?
  A. Statement of objectives

    1. Include quantitative objectives to facilitate implementation and performance monitoring.

    2. Include primary marketing and functional objectives.

III. How do we get there?

  A. Action plan

    1. Tactics and implementation: Lay out activities and responsibilities.

    2. Define timeline.

    3. Determine how problem areas will be addressed.

    4. Conduct sensitivity analyses: How will situational deviations affect actions and performance?

  B. Statement of expected results

    1. Assess resource requirements.

    2. Assess costs, revenues, and profitability.

    3. Develop pro forma financial statements.

The formal plan document may take on a variety of formats and lengths, but will usually begin with an executive summary and move on to discussing each of the three broad questions. An integral component of all plans must be detailed information on marketing tactics, timing, and performance measures.

Elements of Marketing Planning: Process

Managers must consider several broad issues when designing the marketing planning *process*, as delineated in the following outline:

I. Participation

  A. Who has overall responsibility for the planning process?

  B. How should the planning components be shared?

  C. Who should be involved, either as sources of information or to ensure that their viewpoints are considered?

II. Scheduling

  A. How often should planning be done?

  B. Should planning be done at predetermined intervals or as market developments demand?

III. Scope

  A. What should the planning horizon be?

  B. How detailed should the plans be?

IV. Approval and review

  A. Who is responsible for signing off?

V. Monitoring

  A. How should plan execution be ensured? measured?

The key objectives of the marketing planning process are to ensure that the plan reflects the viewpoints of key organizational constituents. This is especially so for those who will be implementing the plan, so that their buy-in is secured *during* the process. Implementers are less likely to feel that such plans are imposed on them by a top-down process. Further, such plans are less likely to be questioned on the grounds that they are based on unrealistic assumptions about an individual manager's area of operation.

Marketing planning may be conducted periodically in synchronization with strategic and financial planning. In addition, it may be useful to consider the nature of the company's business. For example, the appropriate marketing planning periods for firms in rapidly changing, turbulent environments such as Microsoft Corporation are likely to be much shorter than for those in relatively stable, mature environments such as Boeing.

Planning horizons, as well as the degree of detail in the plan, vary widely according to company and industry. Thus, in terms of the evolution of planning systems in the modern corporation, managers first had developed annual marketing plans because of the natural fit with annual budgeting and financial planning cycles. It was only a matter of time before firms recognized that they needed to think in longer terms for effective market planning, at minimum to fit with their capital budgeting and production planning cycles. Most companies now develop multiple plans, with annual and multiyear horizons. The meaning of "long term" can vary, however, from 3 to 5 years for many North American companies, to 10 or 20 years, or longer, for many Japanese companies. Typically, plans with a shorter horizon will have a greater level of detail, particularly on tactical and implementation issues, than those with a longer horizon. Further, because of the substantial uncertainty associated with the longer term, plans with a longer horizon will often incorporate scenario planning, laying out alternate scenarios and the proposed company programs for each scenario.

Top management involvement in planning is critical, not merely for approval, but during the planning process, to demonstrate the importance of planning, as well as to ensure that they are cognizant of the realities incorporated into the plan. And finally, for a plan to be an operational document and actually implemented, it must include specific action suggestions and performance measures.

Effective Marketing Planning

Strategies develop in two ways. First, strategies *emerge* from line, field, and operational managers' piecemeal reactions to various events, such as new competitors and changing technology. Eventually, these bottom-up changes accumulate to reveal a pattern change in strategy. The danger of relying exclusively on this approach is that it is reactive and lacks the capacity for major proactive change. Further, the pieces may not all fit together coherently. Second, strategies are the *deliberate* consequence of an analytical, often top-down, process of matching capabilities with opportunities. The advantage of this approach is coherence and speed: senior managers can rapidly translate their vision for the company into a plan. Both approaches are necessary for organizational survival. Emergent strategy is likened to bubbles with flexible, transparent boundaries that easily expand and join with other bubbles; deliberate strategy is likened to a box, with a hard-edged, rigid structure that gives rational meaning to strategy.

Managers may effectively combine the two approaches into an *adaptive planning* framework. The four distinguishing features of adaptive planning are:[3]

- Top management's guidance provides vision to motivate the planning process, and ensures that the selected strategy will be backed with adequate resources.
- Bottom-up analysis of key dimensions of customer behavior and preferences, channel behavior, and technological and competitive issues provides a grounded understanding of the opportunities and threats facing the business.
- Competitive advantage and customer satisfaction may each provide integrating themes to ensure that operational and corporate managers focus on similar issues rather than exclusively on tactical and global concerns, respectively.
- The planning process is flexible and adaptable to manage learning.

Western-style strategic planning proceeds in a lengthy, linear process from a broad statement of overall objectives to specific objectives to an action plan, and includes very specific time schedules and responsibility assignments. The Japanese approach to market planning, in stark contrast, is fuzzy. It is based on incremental, experiential learning. Typically, substantial initial observational information gathering in the field is followed by a decision to do something small to "test" the market and get feedback,, and then do something small again. Thus, in contrast to the detailed planning and product positioning research that preceded the 1964 launch of the Ford Mustang, Toyota and Honda both entered the U.S. market nose first in the early 1960s. Honda's launch vehicle was its large 250cc motorbike, whereas Toyota's was the Toyopet, the largest car it made in Japan. Both entries may have undoubtedly benefited from prior research. The Japanese, however, kept a close eye on the market, learned from their mistakes, and adjusted what they were doing.

The key to Japanese companies' repeated successes is that what they lack in a priori research, they more than make up in perseverance: constantly "doing," and keeping themselves updated firsthand about market developments. The advantage of *not* having a grand plan is that the Japanese are less constrained by one, and can therefore be nimble. The Japanese marketing planning cycle of observe–discuss–decide–observe allows them to reconfigure their actual implementation approach multiple times, while a Western company is still in the planning stage.

In terms of the elements of strategy formulation and implementation, more attention is paid to the latter. In fact, the Japanese add a third stage, execution. Formulation is "what to do" and implementation is "how to do it," but execution is actually "doing it." Execution allows the Japanese to *commit* themselves incrementally; *reverse* or change their approach as frequently as required; *learn* by trial and error about market response, competitors, and customers; *imitate* competitive actions to avoid uncertainty; and *churn* the market by creating new rules and leaving strategic market planners in the lurch!

Source: Based on Johnny K. Johansson and Ikujiro Nonaka, *Relentless: The Japanese Way of Marketing* (New York: Harper Business, 1996), pp. 36–78.

Marketing planning processes differ substantially across cultures. Marketing Anecdote 16.2 provides a description of some of the differences between Western and Japanese strategic market planning. The Japanese dive from broad strategic vision right into implementation—without the detailed analysis that is characteristic of Western companies' marketing planning processes—learning largely from a repeated trial and error approach in the market.

STRUCTURING MARKETING MANAGEMENT FUNCTIONS

Actually, marketing is so basic that it is not enough to have a strong salesforce and to entrust marketing to it. Marketing is not only much broader than selling, it is not a specialized activity at all. It is the whole business seen from the point of view of its final result, that is, from the customer's point of view.

Peter Drucker, *The Practice of Management*

The Marketing Organization–Environment Relationship

Strategy and implementation are a "cascade phenomenon" whereby goals and decisions flow down an organizational hierarchy "much like water does from pool to pool in a Japanese garden."[4] Consequently, organizational design and management are critical factors in successful strategy implementation. As organizations adjust their strategies to capitalize on new opportunities presented by the changing environment, there are pressures for organizational structure and processes to evolve to meet the needs of the new strategies.

In this context, managers may use two broad dimensions to understand how marketing organizations are structured: horizontal and vertical differentiation. Horizontal differentiation refers to the differences in tasks and orientations of units at the same horizontal level in the organization. Vertical differentiation refers to decentralization or centralization of decision making in the organization. Marketing organizations are usually differentiated or concentrated along four dimensions: product, market, geography, and function. Marketing functions are further distinguished according to whether they are internal (e.g., advertising, sales promotion, new product development, market research) or external (salesforce, customer services). These functions are further differentiated on the basis of market or product. Combining these bases of differentiation, there are three generic structures for marketing organizations.

First, a product-based organization differentiates both internal and external functions by product lines. Second, a market-based structure differentiates by geographic area and by industries served. Third, a hybrid, or matrix, combines a product-based structure for internal functions with a market-based structure for the salesforce and other external activities. Most observed marketing organizations are combinations of these three generic structures. These structures are illustrated schematically in Figure 16.1.

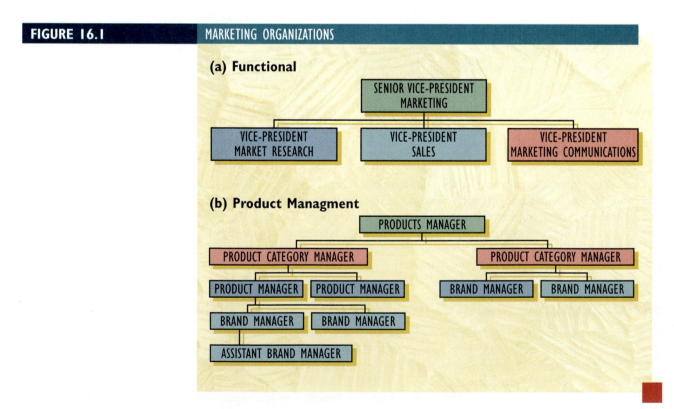

FIGURE 16.1 MARKETING ORGANIZATIONS

(a) Functional

SENIOR VICE-PRESIDENT MARKETING

- VICE-PRESIDENT MARKET RESEARCH
- VICE-PRESIDENT SALES
- VICE-PRESIDENT MARKETING COMMUNICATIONS

(b) Product Managment

PRODUCTS MANAGER

- PRODUCT CATEGORY MANAGER
  - PRODUCT MANAGER
  - PRODUCT MANAGER
    - BRAND MANAGER
    - BRAND MANAGER
      - ASSISTANT BRAND MANAGER
- PRODUCT CATEGORY MANAGER
  - BRAND MANAGER
  - BRAND MANAGER

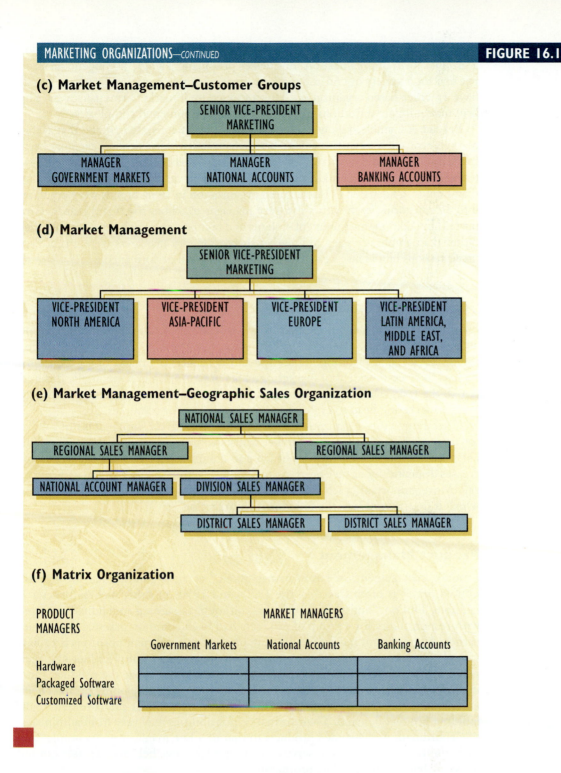

(c) Market Management–Customer Groups

SENIOR VICE-PRESIDENT MARKETING

MANAGER GOVERNMENT MARKETS

MANAGER NATIONAL ACCOUNTS

MANAGER BANKING ACCOUNTS

(d) Market Management

SENIOR VICE-PRESIDENT MARKETING

VICE-PRESIDENT NORTH AMERICA

VICE-PRESIDENT ASIA-PACIFIC

VICE-PRESIDENT EUROPE

VICE-PRESIDENT LATIN AMERICA, MIDDLE EAST, AND AFRICA

(e) Market Management–Geographic Sales Organization

NATIONAL SALES MANAGER

REGIONAL SALES MANAGER

REGIONAL SALES MANAGER

NATIONAL ACCOUNT MANAGER

DIVISION SALES MANAGER

DISTRICT SALES MANAGER

DISTRICT SALES MANAGER

(f) Matrix Organization

PRODUCT MANAGERS

MARKET MANAGERS

	Government Markets	National Accounts	Banking Accounts
Hardware			
Packaged Software			
Customized Software			

Marketing organizations tend to be more differentiated in more complex market environments, an idea that stems from contingency theory. This theory suggests that there is no single most effective way of organizing; rather the choice of organization form should consider the situation.[5] Thus, marketing organizations must evolve to reflect the changing realities of a firm's markets, and, simply, must be designed from the outside in. Multiproduct businesses producing for relatively homogeneous markets, such as consumer-goods businesses and pharmaceutical firms, usually adopt a product form of organization. Businesses producing a single homogeneous product line for a variety of end-use markets, such as equipment manufacturers, usually have a market-based organization. Multiproduct, multimarket firms usually have hybrid marketing organizations to cope with the environmental complexity.

Procter & Gamble, a pioneer of the brand management system, found that as their markets evolved, competition among brand managers within a product category began to create conflicts and inefficiencies. As their markets matured and power shifted down to their retailers, P&G shifted its focus to the management of product categories rather than brands. Under P&G's restructured organization in 1988, brands were organized into 39 categories, each with a category manager to whom the brand managers reported. In addition, measurement systems and compensation policies were modified: rather than emphasize sales and market share, category managers were given direct profit responsibilities and were responsible for financial performance.

Functional Organization

A common form of marketing organization is made up of functional marketing specialists, such as those in sales, marketing communications, market research, customer service, and planning. These specialists report to a marketing group head, such as the vice-president of marketing. This organization is horizontally differentiated: the tasks that each specialist group performs are distinct, making it difficult for the marketing head to evaluate competing claims for resources.

Even though this organizational form is administratively simple, it is not suitable for large multiproduct or multimarket firms. As firms diversify their product lines and markets, the administrative burden and complexity of each specialist's job increases dramatically, as they need to provided marketing support for the growing array. More important, each product category and/or market needs a champion, which it does not have in the functional organization.

Product Management

Product management, or brand management,[6] as an organizational form in the United States is often traced to the 1920s and 1930s in firms such as Procter & Gamble, DuPont, and General Motors, although assigning individual managers with responsibility for a group of products had been common practice since much earlier. An important motive for creating product management positions is to have a single person or a group or team in charge of a product line. Product managers perform the gamut of functions required to launch and manage the product, ranging from strategic to tactical: developing product strategy, developing product communications, conducting market research, initiating product improvements, and building product demand. Their formal responsibilities may vary from administrative coordination of assigned products to that of a line manager with complete responsibility for a product's or service's marketing success, held accountable not just for sales, but also for product profitability.

The number of product managers and the number of layers in the product/brand management hierarchy are functions of the number of different products in the marketer's mix, how the product lines are related to each other, and the size of individual product markets. Thus, brand managers, responsible for individual brands, may report to product managers who are responsible for a particular group of brands or a product line and in turn report to product category managers.

A product/brand management approach offers the key benefit of ensuring that brands and products—key company marketing assets—receive sufficient marketing attention. In addition, because product managers at all levels are given profit responsibility, they have incentives to select the most effective marketing programs. Finally, product/brand management positions require managers to work with all marketing subfunctions as well as other functional areas of the firm, making their role the "hub of the wheel."[7] Therefore, from a company's human resources point of view, a product/brand management position provides incumbents with excellent training for general management positions. Product managers typically do not have line authority over the many other functional areas whose contributions are necessary for product-market performance. Consequently, their effectiveness is largely a function of their ability to wield influence to persuade others to work together to optimize the attention paid to their products.

Product management career paths are marked by rapid promotions to larger portfolios of brands and "more important" product categories, encouraging managers to focus on the short-term performance of their brands, often to the detriment of long-term brand and category performance. Another challenge associated with using a product/brand management approach is keeping sight of the reality that the product is just one means of meeting the needs and wants of customers. An integral part of the product/brand manager's job is to work with various marketing specialists and others to ensure that their product is marketed effectively. From the customer's perspective, though, value may lie in the availability of product packages and cross-purchasing economies. Product managers must therefore have incentives to look beyond the needs of their product, and to provide solutions for the customer. This suggests that choosing an organizational structure is not enough—managers need to design appropriate marketing *processes* to encourage customer orientation.

Market Management and Geographic Organizations

There are two forms of market organizations, depending on whether the company defines its markets by industry or customer group served, or by geography. Companies selling to broad geographic markets usually organize their salesforces geographically. Thus, salespeople in a particular territory might report to district sales managers, several of whom, in turn, report to regional sales managers. The regional sales managers report to a national sales manager. National sales managers of several countries might then report to a sales manager for that area of the world.

Historically, many companies have used this approach to organize their salesforces because of small spans of control and on the premise that sales is a local activity requiring local region-specific skills and information. The other marketing functions may also be organized to parallel the salesforce organization. This approach makes particular sense when a firm's geographic markets are all distinct, and the marketing approach appropriate for each market is different; that is, when geography is an appropriate basis for segmenting markets.

When firms segment their markets on the basis of their customers' buying behaviors, the appropriate form of organization for the firm's marketing is market management. Here, the marketing responsibilities are organized around the customer groups served rather than around geography. The biggest strength of a market organization is that marketing activities are designed for particular user segments. Thus, the market management organization ensures that customer needs are understood and marketing programs developed to cater to those needs—the ultimate objective of all marketing.

Matrix Organization

Companies use a matrix organizational structure to address the complexities of marketing in a multiproduct, multimarket environment, where many products are sold to many markets. The objective of a matrix organization is to simultaneously optimize both product and market potential. This is achieved by encouraging market managers to develop the marketing picture for a number of products and product managers to think about the possibilities for expanding product usage. Thus, market managers reflect the needs of the customer segments, and product groups may compete—or even cooperate—with each other to serve those needs.

Matrix marketing organizations raise a variety of issues: Should market research be product or market focused? How should the salesforce be organized? And, how should the reporting and incentive systems be structured? Thus, the best way to organize related marketing activities is not always clear. In looking for answers to these issues, the general rule that customer-oriented firms adopt is to carefully examine the implications of their organizational structure and processes to ensure that the selected configuration effectively meets customer needs.

Creating a Market-Driven Organization: The Role of Organization

Market driven organizations[8] must meet two requirements. First, they must adopt marketing as a philosophy and commit themselves to customer orientation. Second, they must deliver better customer value than their competitors. The key question

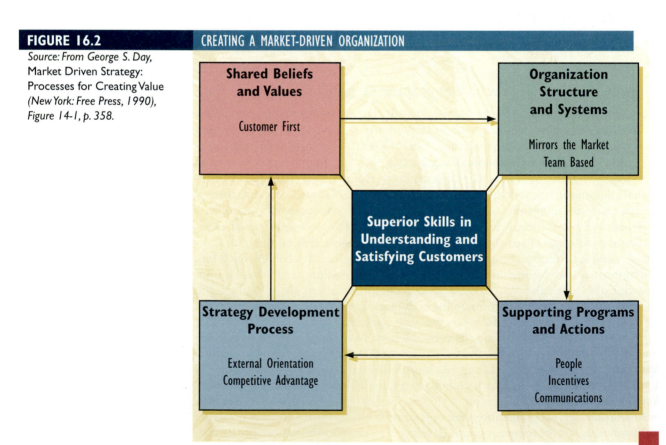

FIGURE 16.2

Source: From George S. Day, Market Driven Strategy: Processes for Creating Value (New York: Free Press, 1990), Figure 14-1, p. 358.

CREATING A MARKET-DRIVEN ORGANIZATION

Shared Beliefs and Values

Customer First

Organization Structure and Systems

Mirrors the Market
Team Based

Superior Skills in Understanding and Satisfying Customers

Strategy Development Process

External Orientation
Competitive Advantage

Supporting Programs and Actions

People
Incentives
Communications

is: How can firms achieve and sustain a market-driven orientation? Figure 16.2 provides a concise analysis of the four interdependent means by which firms can do this.

In order to ensure that every activity performed in the marketing organization is focused on customer-defined service requirements, market-driven organizations explicitly recognize that the purpose of organizational structure and processes is to support market-driven behavior across all business functions. Consequently, it is important that people near the customer—generally field sales and customer service personnel—have the authority to perform their jobs effectively, through sufficient autonomy in tactical and implementation issues, and through providing inputs into the design of products and marketing programs.

The marketing organization must mirror the market in order to focus all functional activities around market opportunities. McGraw-Hill shifted from a product-focused organization (in which books, magazines, and statistical services were each separate groups) to a market-focused organization in 1986. The 19 multimedia market groups each developed databases focusing on the needs of a specific industry. This organization, better suited to customer-need–driven product innovation, stimulated new communications vehicles such as on-line services.

A complete organizational restructuring is not always necessary. Managers may achieve the same ends by organizing their processes through product and project teams that invite the participation of all concerned groups in the organization. Thus, the focus shifts from a linear, over-the-wall one in which communication is sequential, to concurrent, open discussion.

IMPLEMENTING THE MARKETING PLAN

If the Japanese lack foreign knowledge, then how do they succeed so often? The short answer is: by applying themselves diligently.

–J. Johansson and Ikujiro Nonaka, *Relentless: The Japanese Way of Marketing*

Managers must recognize that formulating an excellent marketing plan is akin to winning less than half the battle. Further, selecting the appropriate marketing organization, although necessary, is not sufficient to ensure that the marketing plan and associated programs will be successful. Developing the right processes to translate the plan into action is critical for success.

Thus far, we have spoken largely about the various elements of marketing strategy and marketing programs, namely the *what to do* of marketing. We now turn to the issue of implementation—*how to* accomplish the marketing strategy, *who* should carry out the required activities, and *when* and *where* they should be done. Thus, marketing implementation refers to the processes by which marketing plans are translated into action.[9]

For every element of strategy, there must be a corresponding implementation element that describes how the strategy will be executed. The relationship between strategy and implementation is a close one, and lines of distinction between the two are often blurred. As Figure 16.3 indicates, it is always advisable to scrutinize marketing practices before making judgments about the merits of a strategy or attempting to modify strategy. Good implementation may be responsible for translating an excellent strategy into a runaway success, or mitigating the damage from a poor strategy. For example, companies such as Frito-Lay and United Parcel Service expect that their line managers will exercise good judgment when translating corporate, strategic marketing directives into local reality.

Conversely, poor implementation may sink the best strategy, often masking the reality that the strategy was excellent but suffered only from poor execution.

FIGURE 16.3

RELATIONSHIP BETWEEN STRATEGY AND IMPLEMENTATION

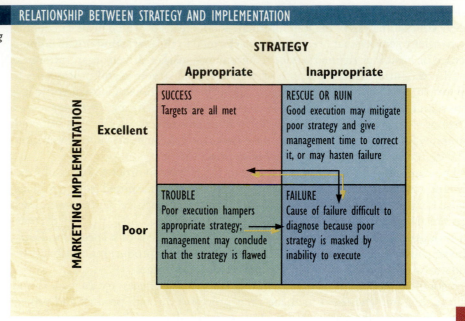

Source: Thomas v. Bonoma, "Making Your Marketing Strategy Work," Harvard Business Review, March–April 1984, pp. 69–76.

Consider, for example, the statistic that one third to half of all new industrial products fail to meet the launching firm's objectives. Further, the key reason identified for the failure of new products is poor management of the product launch, and, in particular, of the handoff from product groups to sales and service groups—that is, poor implementation.[10] Managers may fail to recognize, for example, that existing salespeople have poor incentives to invest in learning about the new products, educating customers about them, and selling and supporting them. They may therefore fail to design appropriate implementation incentives. Consequently, sales of a good product may never "take off." Of course, failure is inevitable when both strategy and implementation are poor.

Challenges to Appropriate Marketing Implementation

Structural issues—the way marketing functions, programs, and systems are managed, and the nature of marketing leadership or policies—present a challenge to appropriate implementation. Human skills—in particular, the execution skills and informal marketing practices that exist within the organization—provide an antidote.

Functions

Senior corporate and marketing managers may have difficulty performing the basic marketing functions well for a variety of reasons. First, they may engage in the various functional activities somewhat mechanistically, without a strong belief in the principles underlying their marketing efforts. As a result, they may spend a particular amount on advertising because "everyone in this industry is doing it" or because "we have always done it," and not because they believe that advertising will increase awareness, build image, or improve sales.

Second, marketing managers at headquarters may be distanced from the realities in the field, whether they be sales operations, regional divisions, or international subsidiaries. They may, wrongly, assume that the functions are being implemented elsewhere. In reality, salespeople, regional managers, and country managers may adapt headquarters' strategic functional imperatives in order to cater to the realities of the local market. For example, managers in the United Kingdom, Unilever's lead market for a household cleaner branded Domestos, insisted that it be positioned as a "lavatory germ killer" in all future markets. In West Germany and Australia, the only two markets outside the United Kingdom where Domestos was successful, the success was due to managers deviating from the central guidelines to meet local realities, positioning the brand as an "all-purpose sanitary cleaner" and a "bathroom plaque remover," respectively.[11]

This faulty assumption that functions are being implemented elsewhere often has bearing in the area of salesforce management. Thus, central pricing directives such as no-discounting will be modified in practice by good salespeople in selling situations where bargaining is of intrinsic value to buyers,[12] or where buyers' rewards are directly tied to their negotiated discounts.

Third, any strategic functional decisions that are made without a careful consideration of internal factors, such as the firm's financial and human resources, are likely to suffer, either because it is not feasible to implement them or because implementation is poorly supported. Sensitivity analyses are necessary to assess whether the firm has sufficient resources to support the strategy even in the worst-case scenario when sales projections are lower than estimated, or competitive reactions are more aggressive than anticipated. All new strategy initiatives require behavior modification from employees, and usually additional effort; managers must ensure that they critically examine whether the strategy fits with organizational capabilities, and whether they have the incentive systems required to engender employee support in place.

Analyzing the firm's strengths and weaknesses also allows managers to focus their efforts on developing functional areas of implementation excellence, rather than diffusing their efforts across all functions. For example, British retailer Marks & Spencer has developed a 100-year reputation for managing the relationships in its domestic supply chain. In some cases, companies may be able to leverage this process capability to secure a competitive advantage in a wide variety of markets. In 1967, Newell, a small drapery hardware manufacturer, developed exceptional strengths in distribution: focused control systems, computerized links with mass merchandisers to facilitate paperless invoicing and automatic inventory restocking, and "good–better–best" merchandising of basic products in which retailers usually carry a single brand with a variety of quality and price levels. These strengths have driven Newell's 15 percent annual earnings growth and allowed it to achieve leading market positions in a number of low-priced, infrequently purchased product categories, including drapery hardware, cookware, glassware, paintbrushes, and office products.[13]

Programs

Marketing programs—combinations of marketing and nonmarketing functions for particular products or markets—also present implementation challenges. The two main problems here are lack of direction from senior management and programs that are outside the firm's mission. Companies with a surfeit of good marketing strategies may face this dilemma—how should they be prioritized for implementation? Similarly, support for implementing marketing programs that are inconsistent with the firm's overall mission may be more difficult to garner. Recall the example of Lego's toy bucket introduction in chapter 15. Adopting this idea from a competitor was inconsistent with the firm's overall strategic positioning as an innovator and quality leader; management's fear that a "me-too" reputation might mar the firm's image delayed for two years implementation of a strategy that eventually proved to be highly successful.

Systems

Corporate systems often present key stumbling blocks during implementation: they often fail to provide managers with useful data and are a huge source of inertia and politicization. Brand managers need actionable data dissaggregated by segment, by channel, and so on to provide them with profitability analyses; however, their systems may provide only aggregate data. Few companies have good systems for tracking the results of their marketing programs—such as their advertising and direct mail campaigns.

Investments in technology may encourage inertia: they may be used as defense for continued use of outmoded processes, even when the changing environment calls for a change in practice. Finally, personnel at various levels of the organization may window-dress reports they submit to their managers, to ensure that the reports look like the ideal they were expected to achieve. In large, diversified salesforces, performance monitoring of individual salespeople is virtually impossible. Salespeople may have incentives to modify their call reports to "meet" their quotas, rather than accurately report their daily activities. Thus, the organizational information purpose of such reporting systems may yield under political pressures.

Policies

Good implementation follows a clear articulation of "marketing identity," or *who we are* and "marketing direction," or *what we are about.* These two intangibles provide line managers with a sense of mission and an understanding of what is important, within which they can operate, prioritize tactical decisions, exercise autonomy, and recognize the limits of their flexibility. Firms whose leaders are unable to provide this overarching framework may find their programs floundering from poor implementation.

The Implementation Mix

Excellence in marketing practice is a result of the orchestrated efforts of all concerned. Managers must adhere to the principles underlying good implementation and remember that it is people throughout the organization, guided by well-conceived performance metrics, and in partnerships with others within and across the concerned organizations, that make good marketing practice.

Principles

The principles underlying the development of good implementation approaches are that they should be responsive and flexible, and consistently followed up and monitored. In the mid-1980s, Polaroid Europe repositioned its instant photography from a "party camera" platform to a serious, utilitarian platform. Managers were interested in adopting the successful Swiss advertising approach. In order to be responsive to each country's needs, Polaroid assembled a pan-European task force to test the concept's applicability and potential for the various markets. The highly successful "Learn to Speak Polaroid" campaign was a result of this two-year implementation effort. It was a bottom-up and highly flexible approach: local implementation could incorporate preferred illustrations from a variety developed by their advertising agency, and subsidiaries could modify the slogan where the translation did not accurately convey the message.[14]

Follow-up is required to ensure continued commitment to program implementation, and monitoring provides data on how well the implementation efforts are meeting objectives. In addition, such efforts on the part of top management serve to infuse the organization with a mission to ensure marketing initiatives are executed, as this chapter's lead story on Xerox illustrates.

People

Often, the execution skills that individuals at all levels bring to the organization improve the quality of implementation by creating an informal organization that parallels the formal and compensates for many of its deficiencies. In particular, individuals may use their *allocating skills* to create informal time and monetary budgets. They may complement this effort by using their *organizing skills* to informally transfer best practices within the organization and their *interacting skills* to recruit the best efforts of others in the organization and in partner companies. Finally, *monitoring skills* may be used to make sense of poorly designed formal information systems, and to develop parallel control systems.

As discussed in chapter 2, organizations use internal marketing to capitalize on the potential of their people and communicate important objectives and values, as well as to let employees know their roles, how much autonomy they have, and how they should act to ensure that organizational objectives are met. Marketing Anecdote 16.3 discusses how Nordstrom has successfully leveraged its employees to become the number one customer service company in the United States.

Performance

All good marketing implementation is characterized by systematic follow-up and performance measurement. As we discuss in chapter 17, performance measures should be part of an overall control system that not only measures performance, but also directs employee and channel partner efforts, rewards good performance, flags deviations that require managerial attention, and provides information on appropriate corrective actions.

Marketing programs are often launched with much fanfare and publicity, including top management presentations and press conferences. Much of the communication during such events deals with what the program is intended to achieve, and the objective, in addition to gaining publicity, is to motivate all concerned to adopt and execute the program. To sustain the momentum built by the prelaunch and launch activities, and indeed to ensure effective implementation and program survival and success, managers must take adequate steps to follow up with appropriate postlaunch activities.

Digital Equipment Corporation's experience with launching a standardized sales management program in Europe is instructive. In an effort to improve salesforce productivity and customer service, DEC introduced uniform systems for the 2,500 salespeople in its 17 regional subsidiaries. Country sales managers were reluctant to implement the program because it infringed on their valued autonomy. Regional headquarters held regular information and coordination sessions that provided a forum for sharing successes and developing troubleshooting solutions. This continuous management support for more than two years after the program launch not only signaled managerial commitment, but succeeded in recruiting the full support of the European sales managers.[15]

J. Willard Marriott Jr. and David Glass, heads of Marriott International and Wal-Mart Stores, respectively, state that "Nordstrom" and "outstanding customer service" are synonymous. Further, Nordstrom is a national model and the customer service benchmark toward which everyone strives. How has this Seattle-based chain of department stores achieved this enviable reputation? According to Leonard Lauder, president and CEO of Estée Lauder Companies, Nordstrom is a family business that treats its customers as extended family. Donna Karan, the famous fashion designer, points to Nordstrom's one-to-one customer communication approach, and Howard Schultz, chairman and CEO of Starbucks Coffee Company, points to the direct link between "empowering your employees and creating a long-term sustainable relationship" with customers.

Indeed every aspect of Nordstrom's organization, culture, and processes is geared toward

Nordstrom's has built a retailing empire by pampering their customers, emphasizing old-fashioned and sometimes cutting edge service.

achieving superior customer service. It is *informally* organized as an inverted pyramid with customers on the top, followed in descending order by sales and support people; department managers; store managers, buyers, merchandise managers, regional managers, and general managers; and, at the bottom, the board of directors. The company did not even have a formal organization chart at the time it went public. On the premise that the interface between the person on the floor and the customer is crucial, all tiers work to support sales.

Nordstrom goes a step further. Employees everywhere in the inverted pyramid are empowered to make decisions they feel are in the best interests of their customers. For example, from making special deliveries, to offering "an unconditional, money-back guarantee," to giving free replacements of merchandise, to drop-

Partnerships

Partnerships are the final element in the implementation mix. Managers must recognize the interdependencies among groups in the organization, and with marketing partners. Chapter 2 discussed the evolution of marketing from function to philosophy permeating the organization. Consistent with this view, the implementation effort must be coordinated in three ways. First, the various marketing functions, such as advertising, selling, distribution, marketing research, and product management, must be coordinated with each other. Second, marketing must be coordinated with other functional areas of the firm. And finally, the firm's marketing functions and programs must be coordinated with the efforts of its marketing partners.

For example, managers implementing a new product launch need to coordinate salesforce training, product placement, direct mail, advertising, and other promo-

ping prices to match a competitor's salespeople, not rulebooks, decide what should be done. Buyers and vendor partners are encouraged to spend time on the floor interacting with customers. This gives buyers first-hand knowledge of customer concerns and preferences, which they can leverage in their product selection decisions. Couple this with decentralized buying for individual stores or a few stores under the guidance of experienced, lead buyers, and buyers can afford to take risks by ordering an unusual item that might have local demand without jeopardizing the corporate bottom line.

Responsibility is not the only motivator in Nordstrom's entrepreneurial atmosphere. In contrast to competing retailers, Nordstrom puts a larger percentage of its promotional money into selling costs—wages, commissions, benefits—compared to advertising. The company, a pioneer among apparel retailers in commission selling, sets aggressive goals for its employees, offers high sales commissions, free thank-you notes and postcards, and access to in-store word-processing departments for salespeople to customize correspondence with their clients. Finally, Nordstrom treats its salespeople like competitive athletes, regularly providing them with training opportunities: videotapes on the best salespeople, frequent staff meetings used as workshops to develop selling techniques, recognition in the form of Customer Service All-Stars or Pacesetter status, events and outings, special business cards, and a 33 percent discount card—13 percent more than regular employees. Nordstrom's employee profit-sharing retirement plan also encourages loyalty. Finally, and essential to sustaining its culture, are Nordstrom "heroics," a growing, publicized dossier of true stories of incredible customer service.

And does all this work? Certainly its unambiguous position as the customer service leader in the retailing industry would suggest that "The Nordstrom Way"—fetching higher sales volume through extraordinary customer service inspired through a multitude of means—is very successful. And in terms of a concrete performance metric—sales per square foot of selling space—Nordstrom's average of $400 far exceeds the Macy Department Stores' $150.

Source: Based on Robert Spector and Patrick D. McCarthy, *The Nordstrom Way*, (New York: Wiley, 1995).

tional efforts. They also need to ensure that production schedules are coordinated with the purchasing department to confirm material availability, and that marketing is aware of production constraints. Finally, managers must make sure that the efforts of packaging design firms, advertising agencies, direct-mail companies, and distributors all add up to a coherent whole.

The trend toward hybrid marketing systems—using multiple distribution and communications channels to expand market coverage—increases the importance of partnering in marketing implementation to ensure that marketing tasks are performed effectively. For many years, IBM sold through a single source, a company-owned salesforce. As the market for small, low-cost computers grew, IBM recognized the limitations of a single channel. It began expanding into new channels, ranging from dealers and value-added resellers to direct mail, telemarketing, and catalog selling, not only doubling its own salesforce, but also adding 18 new channels in less than 10 years. Inevitably, such hybrid marketing systems present huge implementation hurdles, especially stemming from conflict between marketing units over who has the right to sell to particular market segments, and loss of control to indirect channels. Thus, implementation of hybrid systems and of successive changes to the system requires a coordination of efforts of all channel partners: drawing boundaries that the various marketing channels, company-owned as well as independent, respect; providing incentives to respect these boundaries and put additional effort into new activities; ensuring that all relevant customer and sales information is handed off from one marketing unit to the next; and measuring the productivity and performance of each unit.[16]

Forging partnerships among all concerned ensures that the marketing program is administered smoothly from the customer's point of view. Paul Allaire, chairman and CEO of Xerox, succinctly points to the importance of such an orchestrated effort: "Unless each function has a different customer—and in our business, they don't—you have to link together activities that were always run separately. They're not going to integrate themselves; they haven't for a hundred years."[17]

Technology is providing an increasingly powerful means of facilitating marketing implementation, in particular, intra- and interdepartmental coordination and interorganizational coordination. Robert Herres, head of insurance company United Services Automobile Association (USAA), provides an example of technology's role. For a seemingly simple customer-service matter—recording address changes across all lines of business—USAA customers found that they had to call each business separately. It took about 18 months to put the necessary systems and processes in place so that a single customer call would be sufficient. "Technology also forced us to think about how and where our processes intersect. Alignment across businesses is critical for us to exploit efficiencies of centralized information management while we decentralize service delivery."[18]

Integrating Marketing Functions

Traditionally, marketing roles and responsibilities, and indeed organizational processes overall, have been arranged sequentially. Marketing was at the end of the organizational value chain executing corporate strategy. Within marketing, sales and service groups executed product strategy. As a result of their distinct roles in the customer management process, each of these marketing functions had different priorities, paid attention to different information, used different performance measures, and had varied information requirements. These differences in turn led to narrow departmental vision, communications fracas, and suboptimization of overall customer service delivery. Table 16.1 summarizes these differences.

There are two broad and compelling reasons for moving from the sequential and distinct approach to integrated marketing functions.[19] First, the functions are interdependent: each is responsible for a subset of all the marketing tasks that need to be performed. Figure 16.4 illustrates these interdependencies. The potential problems are pointed out by Frank Cespedes: "Sales and product see the world differently: a customer might be interested in a package of products, yet each product unit is primarily interested in its product line and resistant to altering price or terms and conditions for the sale of the package. But industrial customers are looking for productivity improvements and a vendor provides those improvements with a system, not individual products."[20]

The systems integration business in the computer industry provides just one example: the seller provides customers with a package solution—planning, design, implementation, and ongoing management of integrated systems. Sellers' organizations, as a result, have to seamlessly bridge gaps between various hardware and

TABLE 16.1 TYPICAL DIFFERENCES AMONG MARKETING GROUPS AT INDUSTRIAL FIRMS

	Product Management	Field Sales	Customer Service
HIERARCHY OF ATTENTION			
	Operate across geographies, with specific product responsibilities.	Operate within geographical territories, with specific account responsibilities.	Operate within geographies, with multiple product and account responsibilities.
Time Horizons Driven by:	Product development and introduction cycles. Internal budgeting processes.	Selling cycles at multiple accounts. External buying processes.	Product installation/ maintenance cycles. Field service processes.
MEASUREMENT SYSTEMS			
	Performance measures based on profit-and-loss and market-share metrics.	Performance measures based primarily on annual, quarterly, or monthly sales volume.	Measures vary, but typically "customer satisfaction" and cost efficiencies.
INFORMATION FLOWS			
Data Priorities:	Aggregate data about products and markets (defined in terms of segments).	Disaggregate data about geographical markets, specific accounts, and pertinent resellers.	Disaggregate data about product usage at accounts.
Key Data Uses:	Role of data makes compatibility with seller's planning and budgeting categories a criterion of useful information.	Role of data makes compatibility with buyers' categories a criterion of useful information; "timely" data as a function of varied selling cycles at assigned accounts.	Role of data makes compatibility with relevant technical vocabularies a criterion of useful information.

Source: Frank V. Cespedes, "Industrial Marketing: Managing New Requirements," Sloan Management Review *(Spring 1994), pp. 45–60.*

software product groups and training and support groups within their own and sub-contracting organizations. These interdependencies exist, however, not only in industrial firms, but in all companies at all steps in the vertical channel. Many apparel retailers (e.g., Banana Republic and Benetton) have carved out a competitive edge based on their ability to merchandise and sell precoordinated clothing selections. These selections are not just packages in terms of fashion coordination, but also in terms of price and the customer value they offer. Such sales depend on these firms' abilities to coordinate their design and sourcing functions, as well as distribution and merchandising. Similarly, upstream in the consumer-goods business, large multibrand manufacturers such as Sara Lee and Procter & Gamble have set up automated links with their major retailers. The resulting automatic inventory replenishment, customized ordering and delivery schedules, and associated in-store merchandising services and profitability analyses provide benefits to both buyers and sellers—and the ultimate consumer. They also increase the interdependencies between brand and account management, as well as other groups such as manufacturing, logistics, and information systems.

The marketing environment has changed dramatically—products are a combination of tangible product and intangible service elements. As shown in our examples, the proportionate value to the customer of intangible service elements is growing. Further, growth in product variety makes it difficult to coordinate the customer

FIGURE 16.4

MARKETING FUNCTION INTERDEPENDENCIES

Source: Adapted from Frank V. Cespedes, Managing Marketing Linkages: Text, Cases, and Readings, (Upper Saddle River, N. J.: Prentice-Hall, 1996), table 2, p. 20.

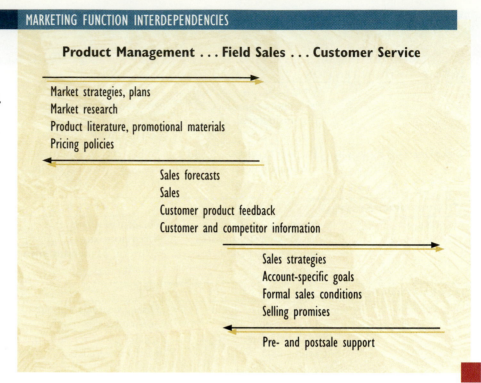

Product Management . . . Field Sales . . . Customer Service

Market strategies, plans
Market research
Product literature, promotional materials
Pricing policies

Sales forecasts
Sales
Customer product feedback
Customer and competitor information

Sales strategies
Account-specific goals
Formal sales conditions
Selling promises

Pre- and postsale support

interface, or to learn about the needs of various customer groups from field personnel. In addition, buyers' objectives have changed from minimizing acquisition costs (the traditional "three quotes, lowest bid" approach to purchasing) to managing total costs in use, including additional possession and usage costs (the contemporary supply-chain management approach). Finally, accelerated product life cycles reduce the time available for performing marketing tasks sequentially and for redeveloping flawed implementation approaches.

Four broad and interdependent approaches for dealing with these issues and achieving marketing function integration are:

- Structural linkages, such as formal headquarters liaison units. These units facilitate interfunctional interactions at all stages of product and market planning as well as implementation.

- Field systems, such as multifunctional account teams. Such teams coordinate interactions across groups at key accounts.

- Management processes, such as career paths and training programs that cross over functions. The primary objective of such training is to develop managers with an empathic understanding of the issues that other departments face.

- Information systems, such as market research that addresses the needs of all groups and not merely product/brand management; and joint databases for product, sales, and service, to facilitate coordination.

Finally, the purpose of all integration is not to make everyone responsible for everything, nor to eradicate the specialization that stems from the distinctive vantage point each function has in the customer value delivery process. It is to explicitly recognize that interfunctional interdependencies can be efficiently and effectively linked to create additional value for the customer.

For most firms, marketing planning is the formal means by which they analyze their situation, identify objectives, and identify action plans. There are two aspects of marketing planning: content and process.

- The content of a plan addresses the broad issues of the firm's current situation, where they would like to get, and their proposed approach for getting there. Of great importance, for a marketing plan to be meaningful, it must address implementation issues, including performance measures and a schedule. The formal plan document is itself of value as an informational, communications and coordination tool.

- The process of marketing planning varies across firms. Explicitly or implicitly the planning process must deal with issues of participation, scheduling, scope, approval and performance monitoring. To be effective, the process must be adaptive, combining the benefits of a top-down approach with those of a bottom-up approach. Such planning processes are unified by top management's participation and a common theme—the overall marketing mission of the firm—grounded in market realities, and flexible enough to deal with emerging issues.

The role of the marketing organization is to support market planning and execution of marketing programs. Consequently, there is no single best way of organizing the marketing function. There are a variety of marketing organizations based on function, product, or market, and observed marketing structures are variations and combinations of these. Each form has its advantages and disadvantages. In general, however, the "best" marketing organization is one that mirrors the marketing environment facing the firm. Thus, the marketing organization needs to evolve and adapt to changing market realities. Often, though, managers may avoid restructuring by using cross-functional product and project teams.

Implementation is a necessary leg of successful strategy. It is closely linked to strategy, with the result that it is easy for managers to confuse the two. Marketing leadership and the way marketing functions, programs, and systems are operated present implementation hurdles. In particular, managers may fail to provide overall direction, consistent support, and a belief in their programs; they may be blinded by strategy and assume that implementation will be carried out elsewhere; and they may be constrained by prior investments in technology.

Successful implementation stems from an underlying recognition that it should be flexible and monitored. Consistent top management support and regular performance measurement are both required. Further, managers need to motivate the people involved to bring their best efforts to bear on the program. Finally, increased interdependence of business processes is making it necessary for managers to forge partnerships both within the firm and with its marketing partners.

In addition to interdependence, there is a second reason why partnerships and integrating marketing functions have become crucial for implementation. The marketing environment has changed in a variety of ways, making the traditional sequential approach to marketing function interactions irrelevant and ineffective. Firms may adopt a number of approaches—from formal headquarters coordination approaches, information systems, and cross-functional careers to field-based coordination approaches such as multifunctional teams—to integrate their marketing functions. These integration efforts are geared toward linking interdependencies effectively to create additional customer value.

1. You work for a small entrepreneurial company that has recently experienced explosive growth in several markets. The company CEO has always done the marketing planning for the company on the back of an envelope, so to speak. Identify the potential problems of such an approach. Develop a proposal to justify adopting a planning system.

2. After spending many years in a variety of product management positions in Europe, you have recently accepted a similar job at a major Japanese automobile company. You are increasingly frustrated by the seeming lack of marketing planning. How might you attempt to introduce elements of Western planning into the Japanese company? What do you see as the pitfalls of the Japanese approach?

3. Your company—a large consumer packaged goods marketer—has a national salesforce organization with many layers of local and regional sales management. As part of the marketing intelligence and research group, you have witnessed a dramatic increase in the extent of centralized purchasing by your major grocery and wholesale club customers. What do you see as major pressures on your firm's marketing organization? What recommendations do you have for the company? What additional information might you want?

4. Why might a global bank such as Citibank need to adopt a matrix organization? What are the associated challenges?

5. You work in the field sales operations of a major industrial equipment supplier. Once you have made a sale, you hand over the order (and the customer) to the customer service group. There have been an increasing number of complaints in the recent past from customers on a variety of order-processing, quality, and delivery issues, although the firm has been an industry quality leader for the past five years. As part of a corporate customer satisfaction initiative, you are asked to identify possible causes and solutions. What might you discover? What do you recommend?

6. As an investment banker, you have developed a new product, and the marketing group has developed an excellent plan for its launch. Your colleagues, who will have to "sell" the new product, are all very successful and busy with their current portfolio of customers and products. The plan, however, pays inadequate attention to this issue. How might the bank motivate all of you to implement the plan?

1. This section is based largely on George S. Day, *Market Driven Strategy: Processes for Creating Value* (New York: Free Press, 1990), pp. 45–85; Robert J. Dolan and Alvin J. Silk, "Marketing Planning and Organization," Harvard Business School note 9-585-106, 1993; and Donald R. Lehmann and Russell S. Winer, *Analysis for Marketing Planning* (Homewood, Ill.: Irwin, 1988).

2. Derek F. Abell, *Managing with Dual Strategies: Mastering the Present, Preempting the Future* (New York: Free Press, 1993).

3. Day, *Market Driven Strategy*, pp. 56–57.

4. Thomas V. Bonoma, *The Marketing Edge* (New York: Free Press, 1985), p. 9.

5. Jay R. Galbraith and Daniel A. Nathanson, *Strategy Implementation: The Role of Structure and Process* (St. Paul, Minn.: West Publishing, 1978).

6. The terms "product management" and "brand management" are often used interchangeably. Product management is the term more commonly used in industrial companies, and reflects a greater role emphasis on product development, sales, and distribution relative to consumer goods companies. In the latter, there has traditionally been a greater emphasis on the media and advertising aspects of a brand manager's role.

7. See Frank V. Cespedes, *Concurrent Marketing: Integrating Product, Sales and Service* (Cambridge, Mass.: Harvard Business School Press, 1995) for an excellent discussion of the role of product managers, field sales managers, and customer service.

8. This section is based on Day, *Market Driven Strategy*, pp. 356–375; and Cespedes, *Concurrent Marketing*, pp. 89–216.

9. Thomas V. Bonoma, "Making Your Marketing Strategy Work," *Harvard Business Review*, March–April 1984, pp. 69–76. This section is partly based on this article.

10. Frank V. Cespedes, *Managing Marketing Linkages: Text, Cases, and Readings* (Upper Saddle River, N.J.: Prentice-Hall, 1996).

11. Kamran Kashani, "Beware the Pitfalls of Global Marketing," *Harvard Business Review*, September–October 1989.

12. Jean-Claude Usunier, *International Marketing: A Cultural Approach* (New York: Prentice-Hall International (UK) Ltd., 1993), pp. 283–288.

13. David J. Collis and Cynthia A. Montgomery, "Competing on Resources: Strategy in the 1990s," *Harvard Business Review*, July–August, 1995, pp. 118–128.

14. Kashani, "Beware of the Pitfalls of Global Marketing."

15. Ibid.

16. Rowland T. Moriarty and Ursula Moran, "Managing Hybrid Marketing Systems," *Harvard Business Review*, November–December 1990, pp. 146–155.

17. Quoted in David A. Garvin, "Leveraging Processes for Strategic Advantage," *Harvard Business Review*, September–October 1995, pp. 76–90.

18. Ibid.

19. This section draws heavily from Cespedes, *Concurrent Marketing*; and Cespedes, *Managing Marketing Linkages*. The reader is encouraged to read these excellent books for more information on integrated marketing functions.

20. Cespedes, *Managing Marketing Linkages*, p. 23.

CHAPTER

17

EVALUATING AND CONTROLLING THE MARKETING EFFORT

CHAPTER OBJECTIVES

When you are done with this chapter, you should have achieved the following:

- An understanding of the motivational role of marketing controls
- An ability to discuss the importance of performance measurement and specific performance measures
- A basic understanding of how marketing activities are controlled

CHAPTER OUTLINE

The Myth and Reality of Measuring Marketing Performance

Myth 167: If the market program works, we'll know it. If it doesn't, we'll know that too. Tracking research is a waste of money.

Truth: The research should do more than track. It should tell you not only what you're doing, but *what to do.*

Performance measurement is essential to avoid the untimely death of good marketing programs that were suffering only from poor implementation. Many organizations, however, do not budget for tracking research: managers may not understand or believe that the research can improve marketing, or they may simply view it as a waste of money.

Even not-for-profit organizations need to measure how effectively their direct-mail campaigns reach their audiences and produce results.

A major credit-card company launching a new premium card in 1993, targeted it at affluent Americans with over $75,000 annual incomes. The card would be accepted worldwide, would provide entry into private clubs around the world, a credit line of $30,000 and valet services, all for an annual charge of $500. The financial analysis suggested that a 5% customer conversion rate translated into breaking-even in the first-year. The results of their concept test suggested that they would actually make money that year: 15% of prospects would convert into customers. The product was launched at a total cost of $20 million.

Less than six months later, it was clear that the effort had failed: less than half a percent of prospects signed up. Managers initially concluded that poor market research had grossly overstated potential. There was little that could be done about that except to treat the expenses as sunk and abandon the effort.

However, a tracking study management commissioned led to the conclusion that poor marketing—a program that had failed to generate awareness and comprehension—dealt the final blow. What performance measures did this post-mortem research track? All input–output relationships: the number of brochures mailed, the proportion of people who received the direct mailing (60%); of those, the number that had read it (less than 50%); of those the number who were aware of the new service (71%); of those, the number who understood it (25%); of those, the number that signed up or were about to (16%).

Consistent with the field tracking results, content analysis of the direct-mail brochure revealed that it failed to effectively communicate the relative benefits of the new product. In contrast to the artificial, forced-exposure setting of the concept test in which each ratio was 100%, the drop-off rate at each stage was high in the real world, yielding only a 0.5% effective prospect conversion rate.

Questions that tracking research can help answer include: Are we achieving our goals?

Are we spending the right amount of money on the various components of our marketing mix? How are our promotional efforts performing compared to competitors'? Which media vehicles are working best? Are we changing buyer perceptions and attitudes? How can we do better? In the card launch example, had a renewed effort been desirable, the research suggested that assumptions on marketing response needed to be more realistic, the mailing procedure reconsidered, and the message clearer and more persuasive. Thus, such research provides both a *scorecard* and a *blueprint*. The first reveals how well the company is doing in relation to its goals and the competition. The second suggests areas and ways in which the program can be changed to improve performance.

Source: Excerpted from Kevin J. Clancy and Robert S. Shulman, *Marketing Myths that Are Killing Business* (New York: McGraw-Hill, 1994), pp. 275–277.

REWARDING RESULTS: MOTIVATING MARKETING EFFORTS

"Motivation refers to those actions taken by the manufacturer to foster strong [channel] member cooperation in implementing the manufacturer's objectives. . . ." Current approaches to motivating [channel] members are often inadequate, consisting of "hastily improvised trade deals, uninspired distributor contests, and unexamined discount structures."

–Bert Rosenbloom, 1991[1]

There is a whole world of rewards and penalties that take social rather than monetary forms.

–Kenneth J. Arrow, 1985[2]

The main tasks in marketing strategy are to *formulate* strategy (decide what to do) and *implement* it (achieve results).[3] Marketing managers therefore need systems not just for planning (as discussed in chapter 16), but also for control of marketing activities. These control systems typically consist of objective setting (which is a part of the planning system and connects the planning and control systems), performance measurement, evaluation, correction, feedback, and reward. As the quotes at the beginning of this chapter suggest, organizations must develop control systems not only for their own employees, but also for their marketing partners. Much of the marketing effort of taking a product or service to market is shared by a firm and its channel partners; here we discuss the key issues involved in designing control systems for these two entities, largely with reference to employee control systems. The principles we discuss also apply to control systems for channel partners and may be extended to other marketing partners.

Managers need to consider three fundamental issues in designing marketing control systems. First, what are the dimensions of good performance, how should they be measured, what should the performance standards be, and how should they be established? Second, what corrective actions should be taken when performance standards are not met? The control system should not only flag deviations (from desired performance) that require managerial attention, but also provide information on appropriate corrective actions. Third, what rewards should be used and how should they be tied to performance? The control system should not only measure performance, but also motivate employee and channel partner efforts—with monetary and nonmonetary rewards—by directing their efforts as well as providing incentives for and rewarding performance.

Why Motivating Marketing Effort Is Important

Although managers recognize the measurement and change aspects of the control system, they often are not as clear about the motivational aspects, which are equally important. There are several reasons why marketing control systems should aim to motivate desired marketing efforts.[4] First, line marketing people (or marketing partners) know their markets better than senior managers. Top marketing management often does not have the specialized knowledge of operational responsibilities that is necessary for defining appropriate marketing behavior. Second, even if they were able to directly monitor all marketing efforts continuously—a time- and resource-intensive task because line managers and marketing partners are dispersed and value their autonomy—they may not be able to assess the adequacy or inadequacy of such efforts. Finally, the control system must direct line managers' attention to the long-term goals of the organization, to overcome their natural tendency to focus on short-term concerns.

How Marketing Efforts Are Motivated

Managers use a variety of means to motivate marketing performance. These means may be formal, encoded in the control system, or informal, as evident in the actual implementation patterns that are supported and rewarded by senior managers or in the organizational culture. In the late 1980s, management imbued the Xerox Corporation organization with the belief that customer satisfaction was the route to marketing performance (e.g., sales, share) and financial performance (e.g., return on investment, shareholder value). This organizational culture provided the overarching framework within which Xerox developed formal programs and systems for delivering customer value, and which reinforced and supported these systems.

The key content elements of a formal control system are its performance *measures* and *standards*, and the manner in which rewards are linked to performance. Performance measures should express or be strongly correlated with the firm's marketing objectives. They should also be at an appropriate level of aggregation (or disaggregation) to reflect results that are controllable by the marketing personnel concerned. For each performance measure, performance standards must be selected to reflect minimum, acceptable, and outstanding performance.

The control system should also describe what rewards (and penalties) are linked to performance evaluations and how they are linked to results. Performance-contingent compensation is accounting for a greater proportion of total compensation as managers recognize that excellent results can be achieved by creating incentives for performance by their best marketing personnel. Because the performance-reward links direct employee efforts, they should reflect the company's priorities, including the desired trade-offs between short-term and long-term performance. Table 17.1 illustrates a few of the forms each of these elements can take.

Issues in Selecting Elements of Control Systems

Managers designing control systems[5] must, to ensure the appropriate motivational elements are built in, understand the relationship between marketing efforts and results. Often, however, this means-ends relationship is unclear, so that the market

TABLE 17.1 ELEMENTS OF MOTIVATIONAL MARKETING CONTROL SYSTEMS

Performance Measures	Sales volume
	Sales value
	Sales growth
	Market share
	Customer satisfaction
Performance Standards	Previous year's level
	Previous year plus additional target
	Competitive levels
	Budget, based on situation analysis (ambitious, average, easy)
	What it takes for industry leadership position
Rewards	Salary increases
	Commissions
	Bonuses
	Greater autonomy
	Recognition
	Promotions
	Stock options

response curve has a huge stochastic element. First, achieved results are the consequence not only of marketing efforts, but also of several exogenous, uncontrollable, and often unpredictable factors. For example, sales increases may stem from increased selling efforts of the salesforce, or a variety of other factors such as a sudden spurt in demand or decrease in competitors' marketing efforts. Second, for certain types of marketing efforts, such as industrial products with long selling cycles, it is difficult to estimate the market response curve a priori. Third, even in cases where managers can predict the market response curve, they may not be as knowledgeable as the employees or channel partners involved in the marketing effort. This asymmetric information is partly the result of employees and channel partners being more intimately involved with the marketing tasks and partly because they are closer to the market. For channel partners, it is also increasingly a consequence of excellent proprietary and wholesaler- or retailer-sponsored information and decision support systems to support their own decision making. Further, actual observation of efforts is an expensive proposition, and may not be feasible for the best employees and powerful channel partners.

The most common performance measures used in most corporations are *results*, but the objective is to motivate employee and channel partner *efforts* to achieve those results, so this lack of knowledge on the part of managers presents a dilemma for those designing motivational elements into control systems. First, rewards that are linked to results over which employees have little control unnecessarily places them at risk. This means that the firm bears the higher costs of compensating their employees for assuming this risk, for example in the form of higher base salaries and commission rates. Worse, the reward system may have little motivational impact because employees have no control over results, or even a negative impact (e.g., frustration) when employees believe that their compensation is not consistent with their efforts, results, risks, or alternate employment opportunities.

An alternative to linking rewards to results is linking them to employee efforts. This approach has the advantages of directly motivating behaviors that management deems desirable, as well as making it risk-free for the employees to engage in those behaviors. Therefore, managers may find it attractive in situations where outcomes are unpredictable, as well as to direct employee attention to behaviors that are linked to longer-term objectives that may be less directly linked with short-term market performance.

Examples include customer education and customer service activities. In order to do this, however, managers must be able to specify desirable behaviors, observe or monitor actual efforts, and assess whether such efforts are the best for achieving desired market performance. As we have discussed, this is often difficult to do because of limited information.

To summarize, when selecting from the vast array of available performance measures, managers must remember that their choices will *communicate* important trade-offs to employees, *direct* employee efforts, and *influence* achieved performance. Managers also need to balance their own and organizational informational and control needs with the need to motivate marketing personnel.

An Example: Salesforce Control Systems

Academic researchers have examined the relevance of these ideas in the context of salesforce compensation. Their general findings suggest that managers may structure a salesperson's compensation (a dominant part of any salesforce control system) to motivate sales performance. Consistent with our discussion of the issues affecting control system design, the proportion of salary (noncontingent compensation) in the salesperson's total compensation is directly related to:[6]

- amount of time the salesperson spends on nonselling (versus selling) activities
- high uncertainty, including uncertainty in the sales–response curve
- ease of evaluating salesperson performance
- lack of resources for monitoring salespeople
- difficulty of replacing salesperson
- salesperson's risk aversion

On the other hand, when the sales effort–sales response relationship is unambiguous, the proportion of performance-contingent compensation or commission is higher. Because many of these factors vary with selling-, product-, and application-specific experience and the nature of the sales territory, managers may consider offering a menu of compensation plans to ensure that individual salespeople are motivated by plans designed with their own situations in mind. More generally, managers designing control systems must recognize that external uncertainty and the nature of the sales–response curve vary across the organization and across product markets. Therefore, performance measures, standards, and rewards need to be broad and flexible enough to accommodate these differences.

Managers may also find it useful to create an organization-wide marketing culture—such as a customer-service orientation—within which all activities are performed. This culture serves a particularly useful motivational purpose in difficult situations where it is not easy to specify all desired activities nor to measure all results.

These design principles can be useful in a variety of contexts in the marketing organization, including manufacturer–distributor relationships, vendor relationships, advertiser–agency relationships, and the internal marketing organization (manager-subordinate relationships). Essentially, these situations all share the characteristic that principals (such as national sales managers, marketing communications managers, and other senior marketing managers and headquarters marketing staff), who are somewhat removed from the market, are attempting to motivate agents (such as salespeople, trade partners, agency executives, and field marketing personnel with account or customer service responsibilities), who are actually performing the tasks.

MEASURING PERFORMANCE

Effective marketing is serious business. Before the organization invests a single dollar in the annual marketing program, it should challenge the marketing manager to demonstrate the profit-directed thinking that went into each critical decision in the plan. It should demand to see the anticipated return on the organization's investment in the plan as a whole.

–Kevin J. Clancy and Robert S. Shulman, 1994[7]

The first step in performance measurement is understanding why it is important and what purposes it is to serve. Next, managers must decide on the dimensions of performance and how they should be measured. Finally, managers need to agree on a process for establishing performance standards and on the standards themselves.

The Importance of Performance Measurement

In addition to motivation, marketing control systems are used for a variety of nonmotivational purposes, including developing accountability for marketing performance, monitoring it, obtaining feedback, and taking corrective actions. One of the biggest challenges companies face is developing accountability for marketing performance. This is partly because the marketing function may not be sufficiently important in the organization and partly because of dominance of the product management system in which promotions are earned for good short-term performance.

There are many factors that increase the likelihood that a company's marketing performance measurement will be successful and its managers accountable for the programs they adopt:[8]

- A formal marketing planning process exists, and the emphasis is not only on strategy but also on implementation.
- Senior managers know the right questions to ask about each program's performance.
- Every marketing program has realistic, specific, and measurable objectives, as illustrated in Table 17.2.
- Marketing program objectives are tied to profitability.
- Managers use automated intelligence and decision-support systems to develop and evaluate their plans.
- Managers measure many aspects of performance, including performance relative to competitors and relative to their investments.
- Managers recognize and believe that the relative effectiveness of alternative programs can be assessed.

TABLE 17.2 MEANINGFUL MARKETING OBJECTIVES

Market	Poor Objective (not precise or measurable)	Meaningful Objective (precise, measurable, actionable)
Packaged good	Increase share	10 percent average dollar market share for first year
Savings bank	Increase number of customers	20 percent increase in number of customers who open a new savings account with more than $10,000 by end of year two
Bank credit card division	Grow card business by cross-selling banking customers	50 percent of all current banking customers to be converted to credit card customers in one year
Medical imaging equipment company	Improve access to all members of buying group at major health-maintenance organizations	Increase call frequency and coverage to meet at least three major purchasing decision makers at each of the top 10 accounts by the end of the first quarter

- Managers pay attention to both short-term and long-term marketing performance.
- Managers recognize that marketing performance will improve with monitoring.
- Marketing managers remain accountable for the market and financial performance of the programs they launch, rather than getting promoted out.
- Managers believe that marketing performance can be audited like financial performance is, and actually conduct an independent audit of the marketing function.

As discussed in chapter 16, regular performance measurement is critical for successful implementation of marketing plans and programs. The starting point for performance measurement is the marketing planning process during which the various programs are defined, and performance measures and standards are selected. Performance measurement has many benefits. It is a means of tracking how much progress has been made with marketing programs and developing accountability for performance.

Managers must weigh the benefits of tracking single measures of performance against those of tracking a number of measures. No single performance measure can capture the well-being of the marketing organization. Further, every marketing program has multiple objectives, so multiple measures of performance are required to assess how well program objectives are being met. Multiple measures provide a more complete picture of marketing performance by attempting to capture its many dimensions. For example, advertising campaign performance may be measured in relation to a variety of specific objectives developed with respect to brand and advertising awareness, familiarity, attitudes, purchase considerations, preferences, and sales.

Managers must also understand the trade-offs between tracking short-term and long-term measures. Whereas the former may describe the results of past marketing efforts and some current marketing efforts (such as promotions intended to boost short-term sales), the latter reflect where the firm is headed. It is not possible to measure the full performance impact of many marketing programs—such as product quality and customer satisfaction initiatives, awareness and image advertising, and distribution channel changes—in the short run.

What Performance Measures Are Most Appropriate?

The relevant performance measures vary for different aspects of the marketing program and at different levels of the marketing organization. The appropriate measures at each organizational level are those that reward personnel at that level for their areas of responsibility, and results that are largely controllable by them. In addition, multiple aspects of each performance measure must be examined: current period measure, comparison with previous period(s), comparison with targeted performance or the performance standard, and comparison with competitors and/or industry leaders.

Sales Performance

At all levels of the business—aggregate business, product category, product line, and brand—and for all market groups—market segment, customer account, geographic territory and channel—measures of sales performance include sales volume, sales value, sales growth, and market share. Both unit and dollar (or relevant currency) sales at each level are important, because price and volume are interrelated. Thus, depending on the price elasticity of demand, large unit sales may be achieved at low prices, or a price increase may cause a disproportionate volume decline, which will be revealed only by tracking both figures. Analysis of sales by market group provides an understanding of the composition of aggregate sales performance, including the segments that are large and growing, stable, or declining.

Measuring market share at each level provides the firm with information on whether it is growing or shrinking relative to major competitors. A firm could witness an upward trend in sales as a result of an expanding market, but its competitive performance in terms of share could actually be deteriorating. Conversely, declining sales in a shrinking market may not be as bad if a firm can hold or grow its market share.

Market share is the ratio of a company's sales (volume or value) to market sales, so a clear market definition is essential to a meaningful market share measure. In computing market share for its Coke brand, Coca-Cola may define its market as all colas, all carbonated beverages, or all soft drinks, depending on how it views its market and its competition. It will also have to decide on whether it will consider all markets, including those in which it has no presence (because these markets represent potential), or only its served markets. A company's share of its served markets is always greater than its share of the aggregate market. By examining the combined market share of the top few competitors, a company can determine how concentrated or fragmented competition is.

Financial Performance

Financial performance measures include gross contribution and profit, net contribution and profit, profitability of sales, return on assets, and return on investment. As illustrated in Figure 17.1, the Strategic Profit Model provides a firm with a useful framework within which to conduct its overall financial analysis, as well as diagnose the sources of its profitability problems.

Many firms use return on assets to track their profitability because it reflects two key financial ratios: profit margins (net profits/net sales) and asset turnover (net

FIGURE 17.1

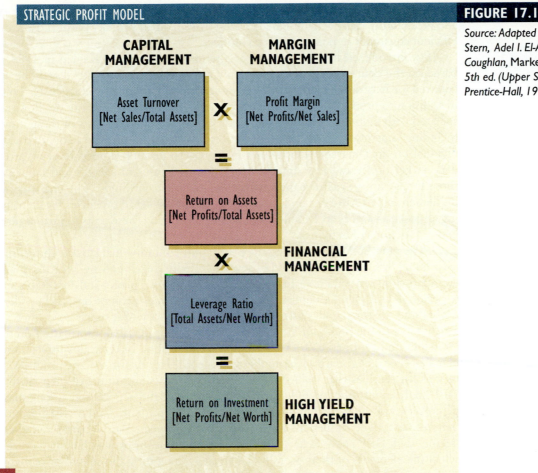

Source: Adapted from Louis W. Stern, Adel I. El-Ansary, and Anne T. Coughlan, Marketing Channels, *5th ed. (Upper Saddle River, N.J.: Prentice-Hall, 1996), p. 452.*

sales/total assets). Firms may increase their profit margins by increasing prices and/or reducing costs, or their asset turnover by increasing sales and/or improving asset efficiency. The tremendous success of Price/Costco and others in the wholesale club industry stems from effectively containing costs and increasing sales to boost their profit margins. These companies are able to manage costs through coherent, systemwide efforts, such as effective purchasing, including negotiating package, volume and delivery deals with their suppliers; a no-sale, no-discount, no-coupon policy; locations in less expensive real estate; and a merchandise mix that emphasizes high-volume, quick-turnover items. They also carefully manage their assets to maximize sales per square foot of warehouse space, minimize inventories and accounts receivable by negotiating delivery terms with suppliers and instituting a no-credit sales policy.

These quantitative measures are all related to short-term financial performance. It is useful to track these measures over time, as well as in relation to competitors, overall industry standards, and industry leaders. The Profit Impact of Market Strategies (PIMS) database provides subscribing companies with the opportunity to make such comparisons. Managed by the Strategic Planning Institute, the PIMS database now covers more than 4,000 SBUs across Europe and North America.[9]

In addition to aggregate financial analyses, managers should conduct marketing profitability analyses by product, segment, channel, and so forth to assess the relative profit contribution of each. Increasingly, such profitability analyses strive to identify and improve the contributions of each marketing activity and entity to overall costs and profitability using activity-based costing (ABC), direct product profit (DPP), and efficient consumer response (ECR) techniques.[10]

ABC, introduced by management accountants Cooper and Kaplan in 1988, is based on the concept that all costs directly attributable to a product should be accounted for in order to gain a complete understanding of total product costs. Thus, in addition to production costs, ABC encourages managers to identify the flows associated with taking the product to market and to allocate the costs of these flows, including logistics, distribution, information, customer service, and so on, to the individual product-market. This allows managers to develop a microlevel or product–market profit and loss statement, to identify causes of success and failure at these levels, and to redirect their marketing efforts accordingly. The challenge in implementing an ABC system is to develop a common set of processes for identifying all costs, as well as acceptable principles for allocating these costs to various marketing functions or activities.

DPP is a method for examining the profitability of individual stockkeeping units (SKUs) at the wholesale and retail levels. Initially developed by McKinsey and Company for General Foods in the 1960s, DPP creates a profit-and-loss statement for each SKU. By including data on trade and consumer promotions, and by identifying and measuring all costs—labor, space, inventory, transportation—directly attributable to the SKU, DPP gives channel members detailed information on the contribution of individual SKUs to their overall profits. In turn, this information may be used to negotiate with suppliers on the sales terms for specific products, as well as for services that reduce channel member costs and improve their profits. DPP analyses not only provide the basis for much of the negotiation among manufacturers and their channel members, but also help identify high-cost products that are most likely to benefit from cooperation between manufacturer and channel member. DPP analyses have become important means by which manufacturers select the elements of their overall sales strategy, including the role of price-based tactics (i.e., deals) and non–price-based tactics (e.g., reduction in number of SKUs to improve category profitability, better packaging and delivery, provision of stocking and merchandising personnel, less-than-case-load shipping).

ECR includes a number of practices geared at matching point-of-purchase stock availability at every stage of the marketing process as closely as possible with demand at that stage. ECR has its origins in just-in-time manufacturing systems, and is based on the premise that timely demand-based product flows through the system improve efficiency and minimize total marketing costs. Its focus is on the logistics aspects of marketing, including delivery, stocking, and inventory replenishment systems, and its success is based on excellent, integrated information systems.

Expense Analyses

A third category of performance measures that is meaningful across every level of the organization is expense, or efficiency, analyses. Aggregate marketing expense-to-sales ratios reflect the cost of marketing and its subfunctions to the firm. Advertising-to-sales, salesforce-to-sales, and sales promotion–to-sales ratios may be used to develop an understanding of the firm's marketing approach relative to competitors' approaches (for example, "we are advertising intensive, while competitors seem to be spending more on promotions").

This aggregate expense analysis may be combined with profitability analyses to reveal areas to which marketing needs to turn its attention. Managers must then ask if it is possible to improve the efficiency of each of its marketing efforts. For each marketing function, there is a hierarchy of measures that may be used to measure efficiency, each related to a higher-order marketing objective.

Advertising efficiency may be tracked by measuring:

1. advertising costs per media vehicle
2. achieved reach (for target markets) of each vehicle
3. achieved awareness per dollar spent
4. achieved positive attitude per dollar spent
5. achieved purchase intention
6. achieved inquiries (may be measured by including a direct response element such as a toll-free number, web address, or local retailer in the address)
7. achieved sales attributable to the advertising
8. cost per additional sales dollar

These measures may be used to evaluate the relative performance of alternate media, as well as alternate advertisements.[11]

It is easier to assess the impact and efficiency of *sales promotions* and direct mail programs because their objectives are more specific—to stimulate trial and sales. Such measures include:

1. awareness generated by the promotion
2. inquiries generated as a result of the promotion
3. sales attributable to the promotion
4. percentage of sales resulting from the promotional effort
5. percentage of coupons redeemed
6. costs per type of sales promotion

Alternate promotional vehicles such as end-of-aisle displays, point-of-purchase displays, price featuring, couponing, give-aways, and so forth can be compared using these measures.

Distribution efficiency, including *salesforce efficiency* may be assessed using ABC and DPP techniques and by tracking measures such as:

1. number of sales calls per dollar spent
2. percentage market coverage achieved per dollar spent
3. number of inquiries generated per dollar spent
4. number, size, or value of orders per sales call
5. number of new customers per dollar spent
6. average sales revenue per dollar of selling or distribution expense

Salesforce efficiency measures may be used to compare the efficiency of alternate territory and time allocation models for salespeople, whereas distribution efficiency measures may be used to compare the performance of alternate channels.

Functional Performance Measures: An Example

Because the relevant performance measures for each marketing subfunction vary according to overall marketing objectives and specific program objectives, marketing managers' choices of performance measure must be guided by these

TABLE 17.3 DISTRIBUTION PERFORMANCE: ASSESSING RESELLER PERFORMANCE

SALES PERFORMANCE

1. Over the past year, the dealer has been successful in generating high revenues for us, given the level of competition and economic growth in the dealer's market area.

2. Compared to competing dealers in the territory, this dealer has achieved a high level of market penetration for us.

FINANCIAL PERFORMANCE

1. Our cost of servicing the dealer is reasonable, given the amount of business that the dealer generates for us.

2. We made inadequate profits from this dealer over the past year because of the amount of time, effort, and energy we devoted to assisting this dealer.

RESELLER COMPETENCE

1. The dealer has the required business skills necessary to run a successful business.

2. The dealer demonstrates a great deal of knowledge about the features and attributes of our products and services.

RESELLER COMPLIANCE

1. In the past we have often had trouble getting the dealer to participate in our programs.

2. The dealer almost always conforms to our procedures.

RESELLER ADAPTATION

1. The dealer senses long-term trends in the market area and frequently adjusts marketing practices.

2. The dealer makes an effort to meet competitive changes in the sales territory.

RESELLER GROWTH

1. The dealer will either continue to be or will soon become a major source of revenue for us.

2. Over the next year, we expect the revenue generated from this dealer to grow faster than that from other competing dealers in the same territory.

CUSTOMER SATISFACTION

1. We have frequently received complaints from customers regarding this dealer.

2. The dealer provides customers with good assistance in the solution of any problems involving our products and services.

Source: Adapted from Nirmalya Kumar, Louis W. Stern, and Ravi S. Achrol, "Assessing Reseller Performance from the Perspective of the Supplier," Journal of Marketing Research 29 (May 1992): 251–252.

objectives. Table 17.3 provides a list of performance measures that manufacturers may use to assess reseller performance. From this table it is obvious that there are numerous facets to reseller performance. Therefore, manufacturers interested in increasing market share may focus on sales performance, whereas those predominantly concerned with profitable growth may use the financial and growth measures.

Customer Satisfaction

Firms are increasingly paying attention to customer satisfaction, not only as the ultimate marketing objective, but also as a guiding philosophy for all marketing efforts, as well as an overall measure of their marketing performance. Firms may complement and cross-validate their own surveys of customer satisfaction with information from related organizations such as trade partners, as well as independent rating organizations.

Customer satisfaction measures should be based on customer perceptions of the firm's total offering, including its service and mode of delivery. In addition, firms may track a variety of related performance measures, including some objective measures such as product quality, sales, and service efficiency.

Ford Motor Company, as part of its Ford 2000 program, has developed a critical focus on all processes for achieving customer satisfaction.[12] This includes adoption of a brand management system, based on the recognition that automobile buyers have a proliferation of choices and that quality and performance standards across competing products have converged, thereby making product-based competitive advantage short lived. Ford has set customer satisfaction and owner loyalty standards which include detailed standards on a variety of dealer activities that Ford thinks are closely associated with customer satisfaction perceptions. These include such microactivities as time to greet a service customer, time to write up the service order, time to provide an estimate for the work, and so forth. Marketing Anecdote 17.1 further discusses the importance of customer satisfaction measurement in the automobile and other industries.

Establishing Performance Standards

Performance standards are often based on the previous year's standards, and can either be the same as, or a certain percentage higher or lower than, the previous year's standards. The current year's standards may be based on an assessment of whether the standards were met in the past, and how realistic they are, given changes in the marketing situation. This approach is simple and allows for continuity. Alternatively, the standards may be set based on competitors' standards. This heuristic is also simple, but ignores many important factors influencing achievability.

Performance standards should be the result of a systematic analysis of market conditions, including the inputs of field marketing personnel, and set as a part of the marketing planning process. Managers must also decide how challenging they want the standards to be, remembering that standards should always be realistic and achievable. As described in Marketing Anecdote 17.2, Nordstrom successfully uses goal setting and contests as a way of setting challenging targets for its employees in many performance areas ranging from sales to customer service.

CONTROLLING MARKETING ACTIVITIES

Finally, when the control system reveals that performance standards have not been met, managers need to decide on corrective actions. As the opening example for this chapter suggests, a well-designed control system will suggest areas requiring improvement as well as the actions required.

The standards selected influence *when* managers need to step in to manage performance deviations. In many organizations, there is a tendency to set standards that are highly achievable.[13] This practice improves the predictability of all planning, the frequency with which targets are met, and the rewards earned by responsible managers, including how "good" they look, and the feeling that they are "winners." It also reduces the costs of control and improvement, because managers who manage by objective or by exception need not intervene when the cycle of goal-setting and achievement is satisfactorily completed, or at least when there are no negative variances. These benefits need to be weighed against the substantial costs of underachieving relative to actual market potential.

The simple question, "Are you happy?" has transformed the automobile industry, and threatens to do the same to airlines, hotels, credit cards, and others. J. D. Power III's initial foray into the customer satisfaction tracking business was from his kitchen in 1968, conducting market research for Toyota, his first customer, on what problems customers were having with their cars. His Agoura Hills, California–based J. D. Power and Associates is now a $40.3 million revenue business with operations in six countries— U.S., Canada, U.K., Japan, Korea and Brazil.

The company is in the business of tracking a key performance indicator—*customer satisfaction*—for companies in different industries. In the automobile industry, the studies are based on mail surveys of car owners from vehicle registration rolls. Power statistically analyzes people's perceptions of everything from the look and feel of their cars to how often they needed to be repaired, to arrive at a number of performance indices. The surveys are sent out to tens of thousands of people who have, depending on the survey, bought their cars in the last 90 days, or within one to five years.

The J.D. Power Award for customer satisfaction speaks volumes to potential buyers.

J. D. Power and Associates reports that subscribers buy detailed information on not only their own customers' satisfaction but also that of their competitors' customers. They are not only a performance review but also a prescription for what to do. Their five most famous primary automotive studies are: the Sales Satisfaction Index (on the sales experience); the Initial Quality Study on new cars; APEAL or Automotive Performance, Execution and Layout conducted after 90 days; the Customer Satisfaction Index based on a survey one year after purchase; and Vehicle Dependability, conducted after five years.

Nowhere has Power had as much of an impact as in the automobile industry, which it has been tracking since the late 1980s; Power has more credibility than any other independent evaluation, including *Consumer Reports*. Since Power endorsements echo consumer sentiment, they have great influence on buyer decision making, perhaps more than advertising, regular trade reviews, and dealer advice. Naturally, companies are willing to pay Power as much as $250,000 for the privilege of including the prestigious "#1 in Customer Satisfaction: J. D. Power and Associates" in

SUMMARY

Marketing control systems have three major aspects:

- monitoring, or performance measurement
- corrective action
- motivating appropriate marketing efforts

their advertising. Arguably, Power has led product quality in this industry, with manufacturers competing for the top positions in his quality and satisfaction studies.

But why does customer satisfaction as a performance measure mean so much? For a variety of reasons. First, product quality levels are at an all-time high, and people are increasingly influenced by other factors, including seemingly unlikely ones such as the shape and size of cupholders in their cars. Thus, technical quality is taken for granted, and perceptions of the sales and service experience, as well as of a variety of frills, are driving factors in consumer happiness and decision making. So Power is expanding his performance measures to include a list of dealers nationwide with the most satisfied customers. Further, satisfied customers are more loyal, so creating a satisfied customer increases customer retention and increases the efficiency of marketing expenses. Further, better product quality reduces warrantee and service expenses, and customer aggravation, increasing the overall effectiveness of marketing efforts.

More important, as the following quotes suggest, senior executives across a broad spectrum of industries recognize that customer satisfaction is part of a cycle, related to many other performance indicators, and an important route to understanding their long-term sales growth prospects.

It's no longer a matter of customer satisfaction. At 1-800-FLOWERS we strive for "Customer Jubilation." Every one of our employees is challenged to give the customer something to brag about. That creates word-of-mouth (WOM) and it's good old WOM that makes us more profitable, able to attract great talent, and assures us a corporate culture that is prideful and motivated. It's a great cycle.

—Jim F. McCann, President, 1-800 Flowers

Customer satisfaction is THE most critical factor in any business enterprise. Without it, one cannot achieve the benefits of customer loyalty—repeat business, referrals and reduced marketing costs.

—Frank A. Olson, chairman & CEO, Hertz Corporation

"Customer Satisfaction" is: the superordinate objective of any well run business. It must be the focus of a never ending pursuit that includes excellence in quality, cycle time and product and service leadership. The result of this relentless focus will be greater growth, greater market share, and improved profitability.

—George M. C. Fisher, president, chairman & CEO, Eastman Kodak Company

Source: Based on "Mr. Satisfaction," *Los Angeles Times Magazine,* October 13, 1996; and Armen J. Kabodian, *The Customer Is Always Right* (New York: McGraw-Hill, 1996).

Managers often underestimate the importance of the marketing control system's motivational goal. Motivating marketing effort is important because senior and staff marketing personnel are removed from line marketing activities and therefore not entirely able to assess what behaviors are appropriate. Further, high costs and resource constraints may reduce their ability to continuously monitor these activities. In designing marketing controls as motivational tools, managers need to make decisions on performance measures and standards, recognizing that they will be able to motivate employees only if they set concrete, challenging, yet realistic goals, and reward employees for results that they are able to control. Rewarding employees and marketing partners for their efforts helps direct these efforts toward activities that, although important to the achievement of long-term marketing objectives, may not have an immediate impact on results.

Aggressive goal setting ties the entire Nordstrom organization together, as sales associates, managers, and buyers all try to meet their personal daily, monthly, and annual goals, as well as those of their departments, stores, and regions. If a department fails to meet a day's target, the manager raises it the next day. Managers use the public address system to announce stories of large sales. Store managers have bonuses tied to sales increases and expense-to-sales percent targets, and are driven to make sure that all associates meet their goals.

A typical annual sales goal meeting has the atmosphere of a classroom before an examination, with all buyers and store managers doing feverish calculations as each of their peers announce their targets. A description of the 1979 sales meeting is revealing. A regional manager recorded each person's targets beside their name on a large chart. At the end of this process, the regional manager uncovered his own target for each manager. The excitement levels were high as each individual was booed (if their own targets were lower than the regional manager's target for them) or cheered (when their targets were higher)!

In addition, the company loves to "manage by contest," using intercompany competition as a motivational tool. As a way of improving performance in any area, Nordstrom holds a contest. Good suggestions, and excellent sales-per-hour or sales-per-month are rewarded with cash prizes, trips, awards, and public praise. One example of how Nordstrom implements these contests is the $250,000 Super Service Challenge held for 18 weeks from September 1 to December 24, 1993. It was Nordstrom's biggest customer service contest, with cash awards for outstanding customer service in many individual areas, such as timeliness of approach to customers as well as team areas such as store cleanliness. Momentum and excitement were kept high by giving out five $2,500 individual prizes every two weeks. In addition to setting new achievement standards, the contest revealed individuals' potential and boosted Nordstrom's sales and earnings substantially.

Source: Based on Robert Spector and Patrick D. McCarthy, *The Nordstrom Way* (New York: Wiley, 1995).

Good performance measurement begins with a recognition of its importance. Usually multiple measures will be selected to reflect sales performance, financial performance, and expense and efficiency performance. Selected measures vary with the overall objectives of the marketing program, as well as specific objectives relating to individual subfunctions. Increasingly, firms are using a single overarching objective such as customer satisfaction to guide their choice of other performance measures.

The main issue in selecting performance standards is managerial judgment on how challenging the standards should be. Inputs from field marketing personnel incorporated into a systematic planning process usually will assure that employees will subscribe to the standards and strive to achieve them.

Often, managers select achievable standards over challenging standards, because, in addition to the psychological benefits of achievement, these standards reduce the need for intervention to control and improve the marketing activity. One danger in this approach is that marketing will underachieve relative to potential performance. A good control system will not only flag problems that need managerial attention, but also suggest what needs to be done.

QUESTIONS FOR DISCUSSION

1. As a newly appointed assistant brand manager, you are informed that your overall compensation package will include two bonus elements tied to customer satisfaction and brand equity. Further, your prospects for promotion are also tied to these two performance areas. How might you feel? Why?

2. You have been selling sophisticated medical imaging equipment in the United States for more than 10 years. You know your products, competing offerings, and the buying patterns and procedures of major hospitals and laboratories. You have earned your autonomy, and a large percentage of your substantial paycheck is from commissions on sales. The company has recently revamped its salesforce management system and sent you a proposal with detailed guidelines on calling patterns, sales reporting requirements, and market coverage. It includes a new compensation package with a greater salary and reduced commissions. What is your likely reaction? How successful will the company be in implementing this plan if your profile represents the typical salesperson in the company? What about the likelihood of success with a new, inexperienced salesforce?

3. As an advertising manager for a new campaign, you are evaluating the brand manager's proposal. Its stated objectives are to increase brand awareness and improve corporate image. What questions do you have for the brand manager to help you refine these objectives to ensure that the new ad campaign is implemented successfully? Why?

4. After five years as head of the marketing team at a leading company in the retailing industry, you have just accepted a job at a company that is a market follower. Your mandate is to improve marketing performance. You face a culture in which sales goals are designed to be easily achieved, employee aspirations are not very high, and follow-up of marketing initiatives is sporadic. What aspects of the marketing control system might you change? How?

NOTES FOR FURTHER READING

1. Bert Rosenbloom, *Marketing Channels: A Management View*, 4th ed. (Chicago: Dryden, 1991).

2. Kenneth J. Arrow, "The Economics of Agency," in J. W. Pratt and R. J. Zeckhauser, eds., *Principals and Agents: The Structure of Business* (Boston, Mass.: Harvard Business School Press, 1985), pp. 37–51.

3. Much of this discussion is based on Kenneth A. Merchant, *Rewarding Results: Motivating Profit Center Managers* (Boston, Mass.: Harvard Business School Press, 1989).

4. Mark Bergen, Shantanu Dutta, and Orville C. Walker Jr., "Agency Relationships in Marketing: A Review of the Implications and Applications of Agency and Related Theories," *Journal of Marketing* 56 (July 1992): 1–24.

5. This section and the next are based on Erin Anderson and Richard L. Oliver, "Perspectives on Behavior-based versus Outcome-based Salesforce Control Systems," *Journal of Marketing* 51 (October 1987): 76–88; Kirti Sawhney Celly and Gary L. Frazier, "Outcome-based and Behavior-based Coordination Efforts in Channel Relationships," *Journal of Marketing Research* 33 (May

1996): 200–210; Frank V. Cespedes, "Control versus Resources in Channel Design: Distribution Differences in One Industry," *Industrial Marketing Management* 17 (1988): 215–227; Frank V. Cespedes, "A Preface to Payment: Designing a Sales Compensation Plan," *Sloan Management Review* 31 (Fall 1990): 59–69; Bernard J. Jaworski, "Toward a Theory of Marketing Control: Environmental Context, Control Types, and Consequences," *Journal of Marketing* 52 (July 1988): 23–39; Bernard J. Jaworski and Deborah J. MacInnis, "Marketing Jobs and Management Controls: Toward a Framework," *Journal of Marketing Research* 26 (November 1989): 406–419; and Richard L. Oliver and Barton A. Weitz, "The Effects of Risk Preference, Uncertainty, and Incentive Compensation on Salesperson Motivation," *MSI Report No. 91-104*, February 1991.

6. George John and Barton A. Weitz, "Salesforce Compensation: An Empirical Investigation of Factors Related to Use of Salary Versus Incentive Compensation," *Journal of Marketing Research* 26 (February 1989): 1–14.

7. Kevin J. Clancy and Robert S. Shulman, *Marketing Myths that Are Killing Business* (New York: McGraw-Hill, 1994), pp. 275–277.

8. Ibid.

9. For additional information, see Robert D. Buzzell and Bradley T. Gale, *The PIMS Principles: Linking Strategy to Performance* (New York: Free Press, 1987).

10. This discussion is based on Louis W. Stern, Adel I. El-Ansary, and Anne T. Coughlan, *Marketing Channels*, 5th ed. (Upper Saddle River, N.J.: Prentice-Hall, 1996).

11. For additional information, see Kevin J. Clancy and Robert S. Shulman, *The Marketing Revolution* (New York: Harper Business, 1991); and Stanley Rapp and Thomas L. Collins, *The New MaxiMarketing* (New York: McGraw-Hill, 1996).

12. From a talk by Mr. Ben Lever, executive director of marketing research, Ford Motor Company, at the Marketing Science Institute's Conference, Use and Usability: Business Focused Market Research, September 12–13, 1996, Boston; and interviews conducted by the author with leading Ford dealers in southern California.

13. Merchant, *Rewarding Results*.

CREDITS

Chapter 1
Page 2: Frank Siteman/PhotoEdit.
Page 20: SuperStock, Inc.
Page 26: Teri Stratford.

Chapter 2
Page 48: Property of AT&T Archives. Reprinted with permission of AT&T.

Chapter 3
Page 88: Joseph Sohm/Stock Boston.
Page 116: SuperStock, Inc.
Page 121: Courtesy Mazda.

Chapter 4
Page 136: © Teri Stratford. All rights reserved.
Page 138: Cindy Charles/PhotoEdit.
Page 140: David Young-Wolff/PhotoEdit.
Page 143: Tony Freeman/PhotoEdit.

Chapter 5
Page 172: Partnership for a Drug-Free America.
Page 181: AP/Wide World Photos.
Page 181: Stock Boston.

Chapter 6
Page 212: Copyright 1997 GM Corporation. Used with permission GM Media Archive.
Page 238: NASA Headquarters.
Page 241: Focus on Sports, Inc.

Chapter 7
Page 266: Kathy Willens/AP/World Wide Photos.
Page 270: Lands' End, Inc.
Page 289: Uniphoto Picture Agency.

Chapter 8
Page 304: Courtesy Ricoh Corporation.
Page 324: Byron Cohen/Castle Rock Entertainment.

Chapter 9
Page 329: © Teri Stratford. All rights reserved.
Page 354: M. Siluk/The Image Works.

Chapter 10
Page 364: Mary Kate Denny/PhotoEdit.
Page 377: Pillsbury Company.
Page 378: Procter & Gamble.

Chapter 11
Page 417: Teri Stratford.
Page 457: Dan Bosler/Tony Stone Images.

Chapter 12
Page 472: Fay Torresyap/Stock Boston.
Page 494: L.L. Bean.
Page 494: L.L. Bean.
Page 511: © Teri Stratford. All rights reserved.

Chapter 13
Page 525: Inland Steel Industries.

Page 533: Porter Gilford/Gamma-Liaison, Inc.

Chapter 14
Page 580: SuperValu.
Page 580: SuperValu.
Page 580: Kurt Foss/SuperValu.
Page 588: Bill Wessman/The Stock Market.

Chapter 15
Page 624: Courtesy Whirlpool.
Page 624: Courtesy Whirlpool.
Page 624: Courtesy Whirlpool.
Page 626: R. Ian Lloyd/The Stock Market.
Page 637: Courtesy Ford Motor Company.
Page 656: Courtesy of International Business Machines Corporation. Unauthorized use not permitted.
Page 657: Sun Microsystems, Inc./JavaSoft.

Chapter 16
Page 676: Photo supplied by Xerox corporation. Photo courtesy AP/Wide World Photos.
Page 692: Greg Smith/SABA Press Photos, Inc.

Chapter 17
Page 701: Teri Stratford.
Page 714: Copyright 1997 GM Corporation. Used with permission GM Media Archive and J.D. Power and Associates.

INDEX